THE ROUTLEDGE
ENCYCLOPEDIA OF
AFRICAN LITERATURE

THE ROUTLEDGE ENCYCLOPEDIA OF AFRICAN LITERATURE

Edited by Simon Gikandi

Routledge
Taylor & Francis Group

LONDON AND NEW YORK

First published 2003 by Routledge as *Encyclopedia of African Literature*
First published in paperback 2009 as *The Routledge Encyclopedia of African Literature*
by Routledge

2 Park Square, Milton Park, Abingdon, Oxon OX14 4RN

Simultaneously published in the USA and Canada
by Routledge

270 Madison Avenue, New York, NY 10016

Routledge is an imprint of the Taylor & Francis Group, an informa business

© 2003, 2009 Routledge

Typeset in Baskerville by Taylor & Francis Books Ltd
Printed and bound in Great Britain by
CPI Antony Rowe, Chippenham, Wiltshire

British Library Cataloguing in Publication Data
A catalogue record for this book is available from the British Library

Library of Congress Cataloging in Publication Data
Encyclopedia of African literature / edited by Simon Gikandi.
p. cm.
Includes bibliographical references and index.
1. African literature–Encyclopedias. I. Gikandi, Simon.
PL8010 .E63 2002
809'.896'03–dc21

2002072757

ISBN 10 0-415-23019-5 (hbk)
ISBN 10 0-415-54962-0 (pbk)
ISBN 10 0-203-36126-1 (ebk)

ISBN 13 978-0-415-23019-3 (hbk)
ISBN 13 978-0-415-54962-2 (pbk)
ISBN 13 978-0-203-36126-9 (ebk)

Contents

Editorial team

General editor

Simon Gikandi
University of Michigan, USA

Associate editors

Aida Bamia
University of Florida, USA

Kenneth Harrow
Michigan State University, USA

Isabel Hofmeyr
University of the Witwatersrand, South Africa

Eileen Julien
Indiana University, USA

Ntongela Masilela
Pitzer College, USA

List of contributors

Hédi Abdel-Jaouad
Skidmore College, USA

Adélékè Adéèkó
University of Colorado at Boulder, USA

Peter F. Alexander
University of New South Wales, Australia

Roger Allen
University of Pennsylvannia, USA

Apollo O. Amoko
University of Florida, USA

Susan Z. Andrade
University of Pittsburgh, USA

David Attwell
Universiy of Natal, South Africa

Ousmane Ba
University of Gabon, Libreville, Gabon

F. Odun Balogun
Delaware State University, USA

Aida A. Bamia
University of Florida, USA

Carole M. Beckett
University of Natal, South Africa

Sid Ahmed Benraouane
University of Minnesota, USA

Ann Biersteker
Yale University, USA

Stephen Bishop
University of New Mexico, USA

Debra S. Boyd-Buggs
Winston-Salem State University, USA

Emmanuel Chiwome
University of Zimbabwe, Zimbabwe

Magali Compan
University of Michigan, USA

John Conteh-Morgan
Ohio State University, USA

Brenda Cooper
University of Cape Town, South Africa

Eleni Coundouriotis
University of Connecticut, USA

Gaurav Desai
Tulane University, USA

Samba Diop
Harvard University, USA

André Djiffack
University of Oregon, USA

Neil Doshi
University of Michigan, USA

Kandioura Drame
University of Virginia, USA

Dorothy Driver
University of Cape Town, South Africa

Maureen N. Eke
Central Michigan University, USA

Frieda Ekotto
University of Michigan, USA

Ernest Emenyonu
University of Michigan, USA

Rasheed El-Enany
University of Exeter, UK

Roger Field
University of Western Cape, South Africa

Graham Furniss
SOAS, University of London, UK

Rachel Gabara
Princeton University, USA

Carmela Garritano
Michigan State University, USA

Harry Garuba
University of Cape Town, South Africa

Olakunle George
Brown University, USA

Ferial J. Ghazoul
American University in Cairo, Egypt

Simon Gikandi
University of Michigan, USA

Susan Gorman
University of Michigan, USA

Seth Graebner
Washington University, USA

William Granara
Harvard University, USA

Kwaku A. Gyasi
University of Alabama, USA

Malcolm Hacksley
National English Literary Museum, South Africa

Waïl S. Hassan
Illinois State University, USA

Jarrod Hayes
University of Michigan, USA

Huma Ibrahim
Long Island University, USA

Ena Jansen
University of the Witwatersrand, South Africa

Cilas Kemedjio
University of Rochester, USA

Sue Kossew
University of New South Wales, Australia

N.P. Maake
University of Pretoria, South Africa

Beverly B. Mack
University of Kansas, USA

Lisa McNee
Queen's University, Canada

Véronique Maisier
Southern Illinois University, USA

Meredith Martin
University of Michigan, USA

Danielle Marx-Scouras
Ohio State University, USA

Ntongela Masilela
Pitzer College, USA

Khaled Al Masri
University of Michigan, USA

Joseph Mbele
St Olaf College, USA

Mona N. Mikhail
New York University, USA

Jabulani Mkhize
University of Durban-Westville, South Africa

Rosemary Moeketsi
University of South Africa, South Africa

Reidulf Molvaer
Frogner, Oslo, Norway

Jenny Mosdell
Rhodes University, South Africa

Zodwa Motsa
University of South Africa, South Africa

Lydie Moudileno
University of Pennsylvania, USA

Phaswane Mpe
University of the Witwatersrand, South Africa

Lupenga Mphande
Ohio State University, USA

Mpalive-Hangson Msiska
Birkbeck College, University of London, UK

David Murphy
University of Stirling, UK

Stephanie Newell
Trinity College, Ireland

M'bare Ngom
Morgan State University, USA

Thengani H. Ngwenya
University of Durban Westville, South Africa

Raymond Ntalindwa
UK

André Ntonfo
University of Yaoundé, Cameroon

Wangar wa Nyatetū-Waigwa
Weber State University, USA

Anthère Nzabatsinda
Vanderbilt University, USA

Vincent O. Odamtten
Hamilton College, USA

James Ogude
University of the Witwatersrand, South Africa

Dan Odhiambo Ojwang
University of the Witwatersrand, South Africa

Charles Okumu
Vista University, South Africa

Martin Orwin
SOAS, University of London, UK

Osayimwense Osa
Clark Atlanta University, USA

Kwadwo Osei-Nyame, Jnr
SOAS, University of London, UK

Jean Ouédraogo
SUNY-Plattsburgh, USA

George Odera Outa
University of the Witwatersrand, South Africa

Kofi Owusu
Carleton College, USA

B. Akin Oyètádé
SOAS, University of London, UK

Grant Parker
Duke University, USA

Elaine M. Pearson
National English Literary Museum, South Africa

Phyllis Peres
University of Maryland, USA

Bhekizizwe Peterson
University of the Witwatersand, South Africa

Katarzyna Pieprzak
University of Michigan, USA

Nasrin Qader
Northwestern University, USA

Timothy J. Reiss
New York University, USA

Phillip Rothwell
Rutgers University, USA

Zahia Smail Salhi
University of Leeds, UK

Meg Samuelson
University of Cape Town, South Africa

Mineke Schipper
University of Leiden, The Netherlands

Riham Sheble
American University in Cairo, Egypt

Janice Spleth
West Virginia University, USA

Deborah A. Starr
Cornell University, USA

Anissa Talahite-Moodley
University of Toronto, Canada

Alexie Tcheuyap
University of Calgary, Canada

Emmanuel Tené
University of Minnesota, USA

Michel Tinguiri
Burkino Faso

Sarra Tlili
University of Pennsylvania, USA

Farouk Topan
SOAS, University of London, UK

Marie L. Umeh
CUNY, USA

M. Vambe
University of Zimbabwe, Zimbabwe

Jean-Marie Volet
University of Western Australia, Australia

Adebayo Williams
Savannah College of Art and Design, USA

Nana Wilson-Tagoe
University of London, UK

Christopher Wise
Western Washington University, USA

Clarisse Zimra
Southern Illinois University at Carbondale, USA

Introduction

Overview

African literature has been defined by several dominant threads and accompanying paradoxes. In both its oral and written forms it has a long history rooted in the continent's famous storytelling and performance traditions, and its classical civilizations are as old as that of any other geographic region of the world. The linguistic traditions of Africa are ancient, dating back to the Egypt of the pharaohs, the Carthage of the Romans, the Sudanese empires, the Eastern Christian traditions of Ethiopia, the kingdoms of the Lakes region and southern Africa, and the Islamic heritage of West and Eastern Africa. Yet it is only in twentieth century, especially its last half, that African literature became an institutionalized subject of study and debate in the institutions of education and interpretation. Thus, African literature has the sense of being simultaneously old, almost timeless in its themes and forms, and new, the latest addition to global literary culture. Written and oral literature in Africa is now associated with the continent's drive for freedom from foreign domination and the search for a common identity. Yet the most powerful and compelling literary texts are associated with some of the most catastrophic events in the history of the continent, most notably slavery and colonialism. The first African writers in the European languages in the eighteenth century were slaves, or former slaves, who turned to writing to assert their own humanity, reclaim the memories lost in the process of enslavement, or affirm their new identities in the enslaving cultures. At the same time, the foundations of a modern African literature were laid by the process of colonization. In fact, it was the institutions of colonialism, most notably Christianity, the school, and later the university, which enabled the production of what are now the dominant forms of African literature.

It is, of course, true that forms of creative expression developed in Africa outside the orbit of colonialism and that the continent's living heritage of oral literature bears witness to this autonomous tradition; it is also true that literatures in ancient African languages such as Arabic and Geez emerged outside the tutelage of colonialism. However, it was during the high colonial period in the nineteenth and twentieth centuries that written literature spread across the continent and became an important ingredient of its cultural geography. The major periods of African literary history have been associated with the colonial encounter and its aftermath. Still, this association between colonialism and the production of African literature calls attention to an irony that has to be considered one of the key features of the continent's literary history: while the majority of African writers were the products of colonial institutions, they turned to writing to oppose colonialism, especially its political, cultural, and social programs and practices, or to question the central claims in its doctrine of rule and conquest. It is not accidental that the most significant period in the history of African literature, the first half of the twentieth century, was also the great age of African nationalism in both the continent and its diaspora. African literature seemed to reach its high point with the two decades of decolonization, the 1950s and 1960s, when the majority of African countries became independent of their European colonizers. Literature celebrated the coming into being of the new African nation and the assertion of a new culture and identity.

By the late 1960s, it was apparent that the narrative of independence was not the utopian moment many writers and intellectuals had anticipated and celebrated. Contrary to expectations, decolonization did not represent a radical break with the colonial past; rather, the institutions of colonialism seemed to persist and thrive and to become Africanized. Intellectuals and writers unhappy with the continued domination of African countries by Western political and economical interests conceived literature to represent the crisis of decolonization and to imagine ways out of it. In effect, amidst what later came to be known, in the 1980s and 1990s, as the crisis of postcoloniality, creative writing and other forms of cultural expression continued to bear witness to the changing nature of African societies and cultures in the age of globalization. If literature has become important to the study of Africa's history and culture in a variety of disciplines ranging from anthropology to natural science, it is because it constitutes an indelible record of the continent's long past, its complicated present, and its future possibilities.

In calling attention to the dominant threads and paradoxes of African literature, there is always the danger that the diversity of the continent and its complicated history will be subsumed by the desire for a larger narrative of culture and society. It is perhaps the case that one of the lasting legacies of the association between literature and cultural self-assertion is the emergence and consolidation of a master narrative of African literature. But beneath this larger story, the cultural geography of African literature is defined by multiple traditions and contexts. The fact is that while it is easier to talk about a unified literature, creativity on the continent takes place in hundreds of languages, draws on thousands of diverse ethnic, national, and regional traditions; Africa is a continent of many countries, religions, polities, and styles. The *Encyclopedia of African Literature* is intended to capture these diverse traditions while at the same time recognizing the things they share in common.

Purpose and structure of the encyclopedia

The *Encyclopedia of African Literature* is a large-scale work of over 350,000 words covering important aspects of African literature produced in all the major languages. It contains almost 700 entries on the major historical and cultural issues concerning the study of African literature, the theoretical and critical issues that have affected its interpretation, and the movements and institutions that have governed its development as a field of scholarship. Because the work is intended to be the most comprehensive reference work on African literature to date, it focuses as much on established writers and their texts as on newer and lesser-known writers. The purpose of the encyclopedia is to provide a comprehensive body of knowledge on African literature from the earliest times to the present. The intention is to produce a work that will be both an essential resource for teaching and an invaluable companion to independent study, a reliable source of facts and features on African literature, and a solid guide for further study.

African literature has become a major ingredient of scholarship and teaching on Africa across the disciplines. It is regularly used in courses in non-literary disciplines such as history, anthropology, sociology, and even environmental studies and the health sciences. The encyclopedia will hence be an important reference work for students of African literature and non-specialists in other disciplines. This point was kept in mind in the writing of the general and individual entries. While there have been numerous reference works on African literature in the last thirty years, the goal of the encyclopedia is to produce an accurate and up-to-date compendium of knowledge on literary culture on the continent. The information contained in the entries is hence the latest on authors, texts, and contexts. While the information presented in the entries is based on established facts, it is also presented with an awareness of changing practices in literary and cultural scholarship, of theoretical developments in African literature, and of the significance of local traditions, contexts, writers, and movements on global literary studies. It is the aim of the encyclopedia to provide local knowledge about African literature but within the context of regional and global knowledge.

The greatest period of literary production in Africa has been in the twentieth century and, for this reason, the majority of entries in the encyclopedia will be from this phase. Nevertheless, the encyclopedia aims to reach back in time to account for the significance of earlier periods of writing and oral literature, eras that constitute an important background to modern African literature. Wherever possible, overview entries are intended to establish vital connections between traditions of literary production in Africa across time and space. In addition to specific topics, writers, and histories, the encyclopedia includes entries on major literary movements such as negritude and pan-Africanism, key regional literary traditions, literatures in major African languages, and institutions of literary production such as newspapers and publishing houses. The encyclopedia is being published at a time when there is a rethinking or re-evaluation of knowledge about Africa and in the context of dramatic changes in the nature of the disciplines, institutions, and technologies of representation that have shaped the study of the continent in the past. For this reason, entries on general themes and major authors have striven to be sensitive to the historical context in which African literature has been produced, of changing debates about its interpretation, and its relation to international intellectual movements such as Marxism and feminism, structuralism and poststructuralism, postmodernism and postcolonialism. The encyclopedia contains extensive biographical references to African writers with information about their professional lives, wherever available, and brief descriptions of their major works and primary themes and the significance of their contribution to African literature. Entries, which range in length from a few lines to around 3,000 words, have been organized alphabetically for general ease of access. The entries are self-contained but they have been extensively cross-referenced. Suggestions for further reading are included at the end of most entries.

Readership

The encyclopedia is intended to be a starting point for the wider exploration of African literature and not an end in itself. For this reason, it has been targeted at readers who are either discovering African literature for the first time or who are seeking facts on topics, writers, and movements.

The encyclopedia has been conceived as an aid to the study of African literature, the source of highly differentiated contextual information through which a variety of users can supplement or initiate work in African literature. The structure and organization of the encyclopedia and the suggestions for further reading which follow most entries are designed to be of optimum use to potential users, including students in other disciplines who are seeking a new way of thinking about African questions, or teachers of African studies who are increasingly required to teach outside their own areas of specialization. The encyclopedia is also directed at general readers who may have an interest in African studies and those who see African literature as an important point of entry into the complex histories of the continent.

Criteria for selection

From its conception, one of the challenges facing the editor of this encyclopedia was the range of criteria to be used in the selection of entries, given the extensive cultural geography of Africa and its complex literary and linguistic traditions. Faced with the difficulties of containing African literature in one volume, previous editors of reference works have tended either to limit themselves to one linguistic tradition (Arabic, English, and French) or to divide the continent into North and sub-Saharan Africa. Each of these choices has tended to create a false sense of African literary history and cultural geography, ignoring the fact that, in spite of real geographic and linguistic divisions, writers have been in conversation with one another across boundaries and traditions. For this reason, this encyclopedia has sought to encompass many literary traditions in one volume. Since Routledge has already published a two-volume *Encyclopedia of Arabic Literature*, one with an obvious focus on the ancient and classical traditions, the editor decided to concentrate on Arabic literature in the modern period. Readers seeking information on older literary genres are advised to refer to the *Encyclopedia of Arabic Literature*.

In the end, not all the goals and ambitions of this project were fulfilled. While it was our goal to include biographical entries on almost all writers on the continent, African literature is such an extensive and continuously expanding field that some writers may have fallen through the cracks. In addition, Africa produces new writers every year and our efforts to keep up with new developments have not always been successful. While we have striven to include the most accurate details about writers' lives and careers, information was not always available or accessible as the project went to press. Sometimes there were significant transformations even as the project went to press. Some significant writers such as Léopold Sédar Senghor, Francis Bebey, and Mongo Beti died just as the project was about to go to press, and we could not trace the death dates of a few writers who, judging from their birth dates, are obviously dead. One of the most significant achievements of this project was the attention paid to writers in African languages who have often been neglected in previous reference works. We have included entries on major African language literatures and authors, but we are also aware that some linguistic traditions are not represented here. This omission has nothing to do with lack of space or any sense of canonicity or significance; it simply reflects our inability to find specialists working in those traditions.

Acknowledgements

A project of this size and magnitude is impossible without the editorial, intellectual, and practical help of a large number of people and I would like to take this opportunity to thank the following for their invaluable help. First, there is the editorial team at Routledge in London: Fiona Cairns came up with the idea for this project and was responsible for its conception and commission; as the managing editor of the project, Stephanie Rogers guided me at every stage of the project, maintaining an extensive database and communicating with contributors, in sometimes difficult circumstances, with professionalism and care; Alfred Symons shepherded the project through production; and, as copy-editor, Liz Jones turned what appeared to be a mass of fragments in cyberspace into a coherent whole. The associate editors of this project provided invaluable advice regarding their areas of expertise: without the help of Aida Bamia I would have been lost in the field of Arabic literature; Eileen Julien and Ken Harrow helped me avoid errors of fact and omission in the fields of Francophone literature; Isabel Hofmeyr and Ntongela Masilela were superb guides in expanding the range and knowledge of the different literatures of Southern Africa. In addition, Ntongela took on the task of writing several crucial entries late in the project. At the beginning of this project I set out to use the most diverse range of contributors, convinced that the best perspective of the continent's culture could best be provided by scholars spread out across the various continents in which African literature is read and taught. I would like to thank our contributors, especially those who live and work in Africa, for bringing their range of scholarship and reference to this work. I would also like to thank former and current graduate students at the University of Michigan who eagerly undertook the task of writing entries, sometimes at short notice: Apollo Amoko, Magali Compan, Neil Doshi, Rachel Gabara, Susan Gorman, Meredith Martin, Khaled Al Masri, Katarzyna (Kashia) Pieprzak, and Deborah Starr. Susan Gorman also helped with the translation of some entries from French to English. As usual, Meredith Martin provided me with exemplary research assistance. Funding in the form of a sabbatical and research funds was provided by the University of Michigan through the College of Literature Art and Sciences (LSA), the Rackham School of Graduate Studies, the Robert Hayden Collegiate Professorship, the Department of English and the Program in Comparative Literature. Finally, while individual contributors are responsible for their entries, I am solely responsible for any errors and omissions in the overall project.

Aba, Noureddine

b. 1921, Sétif, Algeria; d. 1996, Paris,
France

playwright and poet

The Algerian-born Noureddine Aba has written
numerous plays and poems on a variety of
political topics: post-independence corruption
and political repression, the Algerian revolution,
the plight of Palestinians and the Middle East
conflict, Nazi Germany (inspired by his presence
as a journalist at the Nuremberg trials), and
French colonial rule. In addition, he has frequently examined the fate and experience of
individual relationships in the midst of political
upheaval. In *Gazelle après minuit* (Gazelle after
Midnight) (1979) and *Gazelle au petit matin* (Gazelle
in the Early Morning) (1978), for example, the *fait
divers* of a young couple discovered dead at the
moment of independence serves as the inspiration
for sequences of love poems. In his plays, he often
makes use of political farce, and his poems
frequently draw on thickly layered references to
history. His short stories, however, draw on the
tradition of Arabic tales such as those found in the
Arabian Nights. Using figures such as a sultan to
represent arbitrary post-independence rule, they
are therefore more allegorical in their relation to
politics. Two of these short stories were adapted
from his children's books.

Further reading

Aba, N. (1979) *Gazelle après minuit* (Gazelle after
Midnight), Paris: Minuit.

JARROD HAYES

Abbas, Ferhat

b. 1899, Taher, Algeria; d. 1985, Algiers,
Algeria

politician and essayist

Ferhat Abbas's political activities began before
World War II. His *Manifesto of the Algerian People* was
the basis of several nationalist organizations. At the
beginning of the revolution, Abbas favored an
Algerian republic within a French federation that
would give Algerians equal rights as citizens, but
once it become clear that such a solution was
unworkable, he joined the National Liberation
Front (FLN), for which he frequently presented a
diplomatic face abroad. He served as president of
the provisional government and was the first
president of the National Assembly. Abbas's essays,
not strictly history yet much more than autobiography, draw on his experiences to analyze the
various stages of Algeria's political evolution in the
twentieth century. His first books analyze the
inequities and hypocrisy of French colonial rule,
and subsequent books take on the revolution itself
and the subsequent betrayal of its ideals. Though
he was treated as an assimilationist or sell-out by
more radical nationalists, by the end of the
twentieth century some had begun to re-evaluate

his early condemnations of the FLN's fratricidal tendencies and of the dangers of a one-party state.

Further reading

Stora, Benjamin and Daoud, Zakya (1995) *Ferhat Abbas: une utopie algérienne* (Ferhat Abbas: An Algerian Utopia), Paris: Denoël.

JARROD HAYES

Abbé Gubennya (Abe Gubañña/Gubagna)

b. 1933/4, Ethiopia; d. 1980, Ethiopia

poet, novelist, and short story writer

Abbé Gubennya was one of Ethiopia's most popular authors. He attended church school and then government schools for twelve years. He worked as a journalist and in the Ministry of Health before turning to writing full time. In his works, he expressed sympathy for the underdog and fought oppression and backwardness, prescribing simple remedies. His works were particularly attractive to young readers. He could use fanciful methods, as in *Aliwwelledim* (I Refuse to be Born) (1962/3), told by a fetus that does not want to enter a corrupt society. For this and later books he was imprisoned. He published more than twenty books in Amharic and two in English. He also wrote essays, poems, short stories, and novels, particularly including *And lennatu* (His Mother's Only Son) (1968/9), about Emperor Téwodros II. But he was perhaps best known as a writer of short stories, many of them collected in *Yereggefu abeboch* (Fallen Flowers) (1971/2), and poems. He met much adversity under Hayle-Sillasé, and welcomed the Marxist revolution of 1974 but was soon disillusioned.

Further reading

Molvaer, R.K. (1997) *Black Lions*, Lawrenceville, New Jersey: Red Sea Press.

REIDULF MOLVAER

ʿAbd al-Majīd, Ibrahīm

b. 1946, Alexandria, Egypt

novelist

Born in Alexandria, the Egyptian novelist and short story writer Ibrahīm ʿAbd al-Majīd has published nine novels and four collections of short stories. He studied philosophy at Alexandria University, then in 1974 moved to Cairo, where he currently lives. His fiction ranges from the stylistically direct and carefully plotted to the lyrical and incoherently structured. *Lailat al-ʿIshq wa al-Dam* (The Night of Love and Blood) (1983), a novella, illustrates the attempts of a female character, Wardah, to enjoy a fulfilling life by highlighting her sexual emancipation in a masculine society. *The Other Place* (1996) (*al-Baldah al-Ukhrā*) (1991) portrays the struggles of nationally and religiously diverse workers in Saudi Arabia in the 1970s, and criticizes the materialistic and socially corrupt generation that emerged after the discovery of oil. His most popular novel, *No One Sleeps in Alexandria* (1999) (*Lā Ahad Yanām fī al-Iskandariyah*, 1996), explores the rapidly changing social, cultural, and political conditions in Alexandria during World War II. Among other aspects, the novel traces the gradual loss of the cosmopolitan character of the city, and records Muslim and Coptic joint resistance to German and Italian military attacks. In *Tuyūr al-ʿAnbar* (The Birds of Ambergris) (2000), ʿAbd al-Majīd presents a panoramic image of Alexandria after the 1952 revolution, focusing on the grim fate of Egyptian intellectuals under Nasser's regime.

Further reading

Al-Rāʿi, ʿAlī (2000) *al-Riwāyah fī Nihayat Qarn* (The Novel at the End of a Century), Cairo: Dār al-Mustaqbal al-ʿArabī.

KHALED AL MASRI

Abega, Séverin-Cécile

b. 1955, Cameroon; d. 2008, Yaounde, Cameroon

writer

The Cameroonian Francophone short story writer Séverin-Cécile Abega is best known as a writer of **children's literature** in Africa, mixing moral lessons with humor and perceptive social commentary. His writing often attacks intellectual and material pretension, especially that based on European standards, and extols hard work, cleverness, and village life. His most widely read collection, *Les Bimanes* (The People Who Work with Their Hands) (1982), contains seven short stories that exemplify this attitude. It contains tales that criticize those who employ fancy clothing, advanced degrees, and money as symbols of a superior social status and individual worth, while praising those who remain true to and unashamed of their origins and undistinguished social status. His work is not, however, staunchly anti-European or anti-modernity (see **modernity and modernism**); rather it illustrates the abuses that result from blind devotion to such markers of "civilization" and reactionary disdain for their absence. In this sense, it can be compared to the satirical short stories and plays of Guillaume **Oyônô-Mbia**. Abega is also a professor at the University of Yaoundé I and has an extensive number of scientific (anthropological) publications, often dealing with religion, marriage, and women's roles in society.

Further reading

Abega, Séverin-Cécile (1982) *Les Bimanes* (The People Who Work with Their Hands), Abidjan: Nouvelles Éditions Africaines.

STEPHEN BISHOP

Abel, Antoine

b. 1934, Seychelles

writer and poet

The Seychelles short story writer and poet Antoine Abel is legitimately called "the father of Seychelles literature" due to his pioneering writing of both **short stories** and poetry (see **poetry and poetics**) that were both linguistically and culturally centered on his native islands. He was, in fact, the first Seychelles writer to bring his country's unique Creole culture and language to the world stage with his *White-Tailed Tropicbird (Paille-en-queue)* (1969), and then with a series of collections of short stories and poetry, most of which were published internationally in 1977. The majority of Abel's short stories feature a trickster figure named Soungoula, who alternately plays hero and villain but who always emerges triumphant. The stories are quite short and are representative of an oral tradition (see **oral literature and performance**). The majority of his poems are also short and display a preoccupation with pastoral themes and nature. He has written, however, several strongly political and intensely emotional poems that belie a tendency towards simplicity and rusticity elsewhere. Although the Seychelles is officially bilingual (English–French), Abel writes exclusively in French and Creole. The Festival Kreol des Seychelles yearly awards the Prix Antoine Abel in his honor.

Further reading

Abel, Antoine (1977) *Contes et poèmes des Seychelles* (Tales and Poems of the Seychelles), Paris: P.-J. Oswald.

STEPHEN BISHOP

Abraham, Elie-Charles

b. 1919, Madagascar; d. 1989

poet and essayist

Elie-Charles Abraham is a poet and essayist who wrote prolifically between 1950 and 1970. His poetry, written in the wake of Madagascar's failed revolution in 1947 and up through its peaceful transition to independence in 1960, reflects a period of relative political calm. Relying on well-established French literary standards, Abraham's poetry exalts the beauties of Madagascar and depicts the island as a bucolic place free from political, economic, and social difficulties. His traditionally structured poems are melancholic in tone and draw upon elements of history and ethnography specific to Madagascar. Although he mainly wrote in French, Abraham also published poems in his native language of Malagasy. He also contributed non-fiction essays to a variety of literary magazines and from 1945 to 1947 he was the director of the literary and political bilingual magazine *Anivon' ny riaka – l'île australe* (The Austral Island) which he founded with Régis Rajemisa-Raolison.

Further reading

Abraham, E.C. (1949) *Flux et reflux* (Flux and Reflux), Antananarivo: Imprimerie de la Société Malgache d'Édition.

MAGALI COMPAN

Abrahams, Lionel

b. 1926, Johannesburg, South Africa;
   d. 2004, Johannesburg, South Africa

poet, essayist and publisher

The South African poet, essayist and publisher Lionel Abrahams started writing early in his life, but unlike many writers of his generation he was not published until much later. His first book was published when he was 50. As a student of H.C. **Bosman**, Abrahams' earliest works were attempts to secure his mentor's reputation and to promote the works of young writers, most notably Oswald **Mtshali** and Wally **Serote**, through small magazines and literary clubs. Unlike many writers of his generation whose works were driven by the politics of apartheid (see **apartheid and post-apartheid**) and racial discrimination in South Africa, Abrahams shunned politics and protest literature, believing that art was more effective as a vehicle of personal interaction. Although he protested the banning of writers under the apartheid government's censorship act of 1966, he remained consistent in his belief that the value of art lay in

its aesthetic rather than its political value. Abrahams' poetry, collected in *Thresholds of Tolerance* (1973), *Journal of a New Man* (1984), *The Writer in the Sand* (1988), and *A Dead Tree Full of Live Birds* (1995), is often introspective, concerned with the troubled state of the inner life, mortality, and fading memories. His only novel, *The Celibacy of Felix Greenspan* (1977), is the story of a disabled man's struggle to use his mind to overcome what others consider to be his deformed body. This work, based partly on Abrahams' own life, is one of the most powerful treatments of disability in African literature.

Further reading

Cullinan, Patrick (ed.) (1988) *Lionel Abrahams Reader* Johannesburg: Ad. Donker.

SIMON GIKANDI

Abrahams, Peter

b. 1919, Vrededorp, Johannesburg, South Africa

novelist, poet, and short story writer

The South African poet, short story writer, novelist, essayist, and journalist was born to an Ethiopian father and a colored mother in Vrededorp, a colored slum in Johannesburg. He spent his early years with relatives in the countryside before returning to Vrededorp at age 11, when he began his formal education. Work as an office boy at the Bantu Men's Social Center, an institution frequented by Johannesburg's small African middle class, exposed him to figures associated with the Harlem Renaissance. He completed his education at St Peter's Secondary School. Es'kia **Mphahlele** was among his contemporaries. According to his autobiography, while at St Peter's, Abrahams made his first social and political contact with left-wing whites.

Abrahams' earliest published work was poetry, which appeared in the newspaper *The Bantu World*, followed by an anthology, *A Black Man Speaks of Freedom!* (1940). After a brief period in Cape Town, where he made contact with several figures involved in left-wing politics, he traveled to

Durban. From there he left South Africa, working his passage on a freighter, and settled two years later in England.

In London he was employed by the Communist Party of Great Britain's book distribution agency and its paper the *Daily Worker*. With *Dark Testament* (1942), an anthology of short stories written in South Africa between 1930 and 1938, and his first novel *Song of the City* (1945), Abrahams broke with the Communist Party in part because he refused to submit his texts for party clearance. During the early to mid 1940s he was associated with African intellectuals and students such as Nkrumah and **Kenyatta** and was active in the politics of pan-Africanism (see **diaspora and pan-Africanism**). He was, indeed, one of the organizers of the 1945 Pan-Africanist Conference in Manchester.

From the start his work had a self-consciously autobiographical dimension. He presented *Dark Testament* (1942: London) to his readers as "stories taken from the everyday lives of some of the people I have known ... They are spread over eight years, which are also the number of years of my odyssey from darkness to light."

In *Song of the City* (1945) Abrahams expresses his reservations about liberal political solutions to the "native question," which at that time took the form of segregation, and his personal objections to Marxism. Both this novel and *Mine Boy* (1946) deal with the impact of urbanization on Africans and the political awakening that often accompanied this transition from rural to urban settings. His next novel *The Path of Thunder* (1948) deals with the impact on a rural community comprising coloreds and white Afrikaners of Lanny Swartz, a colored school teacher. Swartz returns in order to educate and uplift his community. This and his relationship with an Afrikaans woman – within the genre of interracial relationships an unusual role reversal for the time – has tragic consequences for both of them.

Wild Conquest (1950) challenges the pioneer myth of the Great Trek, but was regarded as clichéd and derivative of Sol **Plaatje**'s *Mhudi*. By this time some of the main themes of Abrahams' work had emerged: that social and political conflict occurred through racial and national struggles; that the aims of an enlightened leadership could only be judged against the stage of development of the people; that

history was a process of becoming civilized; that conflict would lead to material progress and the formation of a liberal and egalitarian community. The documentary *Return to Goli* (1953) and the **autobiography** of his South African years *Tell Freedom* (1954) followed. The former was based on his impressions of a return visit to South Africa which the London *Observer* had commissioned him to write. Through this piece and a BBC talk delivered in 1952, he confirmed his commitment to liberalism. His autobiography has novelistic qualities; it expresses his need to define himself and to establish the links between the experiences that enabled him to leave South Africa. The work also questions uncritical support for the benefits of traditional African society.

Abrahams moved to Jamaica in 1957, where he became editor of the *West Indian Economist*. Initially his *A Wreath for Udomo* (1956) was regarded as a reactionary and pessimistic account of postcolonial African politics, but it is now seen as a prophetic work on postcolonial Ghana and Kwame Nkrumah. *A Night of Their Own* (1965) was set in South Africa during the early 1960s after the African National Congress and Pan-African Congress had been banned. Its main character, a black South African artist, has returned to South Africa by submarine with funds for the underground movement which must then facilitate his departure. The plot contains many improbable elements, and there is a strong sense of distance between the main characters and the ordinary people who inhabit the novel.

Abrahams' shift from themes associated with Africa and the liberation struggle is evident in *The Quiet Voice* (1966), published under the pseudonym Peter Graham, and *This Island Now* (1966). In the former, unlike *A Wreath for Udomo*, he argues that Western culture and education sanction white power and privilege. Set in the Caribbean and concerned with the problems of postcolonial rule and racial consciousness, the latter novel is a more considered and structured work than its predecessor. *The View from Coyaba* (1985) shifts between Jamaica, the south of the USA, Liberia, and Uganda. It reviews the history of the relationship between whites and blacks in the old and new worlds. This was followed by *The Coyaba Chronicles*. Both an autobiography and a reflection on racial hatred, it concludes with the observation that race and color are "mindless foolishnesses with which man destroyed and side-tracked his brother man" (2000: Jamaica). In 2001, Abrahams published *The Black Experience in the 20th Century*, an autobiographical account of his post South African years, an exploration of his journey in the political landscape of pan-Africanism, and a meditation of life in the black diaspora.

Further reading

Abrahams, P. (1942) *Dark Testament*, London: Allen and Unwin.

——(2000) *The Coyaba Chronicles*, Jamaica: Ian Randle Publishers.

Chiwengo, N. (1999) "Exile, Knowledge, and Self: Home in Peter Abrahams's Work," *South Atlantic Quarterly* 98, 1: 163–75.

Ensor, R. (1992) *The Novels of Peter Abrahams and the Rise of Nationalism in Africa*, Essen: Verlag Die Blaue Eule.

Gray, S. "The Long Eye of History: Four Autobiographical Texts by Peter Abrahams," *Pretexts: Studies in Writing and Culture* 2, 2: 99–115.

Wade, M. (1972) *Peter Abrahams*, London: Evans Brothers.

ROGER FIELD

Abruquah, Joseph Wilfred

b. 1921, Gold Coast (now Ghana)

novelist

Educated at the Gold Coast Methodist institution of Mfantsipim School, and at London's King's and Westminster Colleges, Joseph Wilfred Abruquah's *The Catechist* (1965) and *The Torrent* (1968) are semi-autobiographical portraits of Africans undergoing Western education. Covering the period of World War II, *The Catechist* charts the vicissitudes of Catechist Afram as he is forcibly moved from one missionary station to another. Afram and his children's transition from adolescence into adulthood is also a political allegory about homecoming and the role of the Western-educated class within nation-building. Like *The Catechist*, *The Torrent*

makes emphatic statements on Fante/Nzema/Ghanaian culture – often projected simply as an "African" way of doing things. In *The Torrent*, Josiah Afful's colonial education, his encounters with his adversaries, his romances and his exertions through life are shown to be shaped as much by his idiosyncrasies as by the sociocultural and historical forces that regulate the lives of his schoolmates. Neither novel, however, makes a clear preference for a choice between either the modernity of "the West" or an adherence to older African ways. Instead, Abruquah presents the difficulty of negotiating the precarious path into the fast-changing world over which his protagonists endeavor to establish some control.

KWADWO OSEI-NYAME, JNR

Abu Zayd, Layla

b. 1950, El Ksiba, Morocco

novelist and short story writer

The Moroccan writer Layla Abu Zayd has written novels and short stories in Arabic, many of which have been translated into English. Her work is centered primarily on the struggle of Moroccan women for emancipation against the background of the movement against colonialism (see **colonialism, neocolonialism, and postcolonialism**). Her first novel, *Year of the Elephant: A Moroccan Woman's Journey Toward Independence, and Other Stories* (1990) was the first novel by a Moroccan woman written in Arabic to be translated into English. Through its depiction of the plight of a divorced woman in asserting her voice in a male-dominated society during the years leading to the country's independence from French rule, this first novel sets the pattern for Abu Zayd's subsequent works, which explore the intersection between personal relationships and larger historical events. The autobiographical or semi-autobiographical perspective in her novels, and the use of multiple female voices modeled around the oral tradition of storytelling, are characteristic features of her work. The presence of independent heroines who interrogate traditional gender roles places Abu Zayd's fiction within the tradition of North African feminist writing established by authors such as Nawal **el-Saadawi** and Fatima Mernissi.

Further reading

Abu Zayd, L. (1989) *Year of the Elephant: A Moroccan Woman's Journey Toward Independence, and Other Stories*, trans. Barbara Parmenter, Texas: University of Texas Press (Modern Middle East Literature in Translation Series).

ANISSA TALAHITE-MOODLEY

Achebe, Chinua

b. 1930, Ogidi, Nigeria

novelist

The publication of Chinua Achebe's first novel, *Things Fall Apart*, in 1958, is now considered to be one of the seminal moments in the history of African literature in the English language. Although there were several important writers in the English language before Achebe, including such major figures as Amos **Tutuola**, Peter **Abrahams**, Sol **Plaatje**, and Cyprian **Ekwensi**, Achebe's novel has become the starting point for many discussions of the African novel. *Things Fall Apart* is certainly the most widely read and known work of African literature both inside and outside the continent and an important reference point for many novels written in the last decade of formal colonialism in Africa and the first decade of independence (see **colonialism, neocolonialism, and postcolonialism**). Achebe's other novels, *No Longer at Ease* (1960), *Arrow of God* (1964), *A Man of the People* (1967), and *Anthills of the Savanna* (1987), spanning a significant period of postcolonial Africa, have equally been influential in mapping out the nature of African culture and the institutions of literary interpretation.

Because these works occupy such a crucial place in the teaching of African literature, there is a sense in which Achebe has become the nexus for the history and criticism of this tradition of letters. And while there is no general consensus on why Achebe's novels came to occupy such an important place in the history of African literature, there is no doubt that part of his appeal has been due to the fact that from the moment he started writing in the early 1950s, he has produced novels whose form and content have been driven by the desire to imaginatively capture the key moments of African history from the beginning of colonialism to what has come to be known as postcoloniality. In both their subject and their aesthetic concerns, Achebe's major novels are located at the point of contact between European and African cultures and are concerned with the political and linguistic consequences of this encounter.

Indeed, Achebe's novels can be divided into two categories: First, there are those works that are concerned with recovering and representing an African precolonial culture struggling to retain its integrity against the onslaught of colonialism. *Things Fall Apart* and *Arrow of God* belong to this category: they are narrative attempts to imagine what precolonial society could have looked like before the European incursion and the factors that were responsible for the failure of Igbo or African cultures in the face of colonialism. These novels are themselves cast in a dual structure, with the first part seeking to present a meticulous portrait of Igbo society before colonialism, and the second part narrating the traumatic process in which this culture loses its autonomy in the face of the colonial encounter. Unlike some of his contemporaries, however, Achebe does not seek to recover the logic of a precolonial African culture in order to romanticize it, but to counter the colonial mythology that Africans did not have a culture before colonialism. As he noted in an influential essay called "The Role of the Writer in a New Nation" (1964; 1973: London) Achebe's works were concerned with what he considers to be a fundamental theme – "that African people did not hear of culture for the first time from Europeans; that their societies were not mindless but frequently had a philosophy of great depth and value and beauty." At the same time, however, these narratives are often attempts to explore the fissures of precolonial culture itself in order to show why it was vulnerable to European colonialism.

In his second set of novels, *No Longer at Ease*, *A Man of the People*, and *Anthills of the Savannah*, Achebe turns his attention away from the past to diagnose and narrate the crisis of decolonization. While the novels dealing with the past have been influential for showing that Africans had a culture with its own internal logic and set of contradictions, and hence derive their authority from their capacity to imagine an African past derided or negated in the colonial text, the second set of novels have been popular because of their keen sense of the crisis of postcoloniality and, in some cases, a prophetic sense of African history, the attendant promise of decolonization and its failure or sense of discontent.

From another perspective, Achebe's novels have been influential because of their acute capacity to map out the cultural fault in which African cultures and traditions have encountered the institutions of modern European colonial society. In fact, it could be said that Achebe's early novels were the first to popularize the tradition/modernity paradigm that, though constantly questioned in many theoretical works, continues to haunt the study of African literature and culture. But as has been the case for most of his writing career, Achebe has been able to produce novels that both set up paradigms and deconstruct them. While *Things Fall Apart* derives most of its power from the ability to position precolonial Igbo society in opposition to an encroaching colonial culture, it is also memorable for the way it problematizes the nature of Igbo society and deprives it of any claims to cultural purity. In this novel, it is those who seek to protect the purity of culture, most notably Okonkwo, the hero of the novel, whose lives end up in ignominy. In *No Longer at Ease*, the subjects who had subscribed to the logic of colonial modernity are increasingly haunted by the choices they make, wondering where they stand in the new dispensation. And in *Arrow of God*, clearly one of the major novels on the colonial situation, attempts to subscribe to the idiom of tradition are shown to be as lacking as the logic of colonization itself.

Although Achebe is now considered to be the premier novelist on the discourse of African identity, nationalism (see **nationalism and post-nationalism**), and decolonization, his main focus, as he has insisted in many of the interviews he has given throughout his career, has been on sites of cultural ambiguity and contestation. If there is one phrase that sums up Achebe's philosophy of culture or language, it is the Igbo proverb: "Where

one thing falls, another stands in its place." The complexity of novels such as *Things Fall Apart* and *Arrow of God* depends on Achebe's ability to bring competing cultural systems and their languages on to the same level of representation, dialogue, and contestation. In *Arrow of God*, for example, the central conflict is not merely a racial one between white Europeans and black Africans, or even an epistemological encounter between an Igbo culture and a colonial polity, but also a struggle between idioms and linguistic registers. Although the novel is written in English, as are all of Achebe's works, it contains one of the most strenuous attempts to translate an African idiom in the language of the other. Although we read the world of the Igbo in English, Achebe goes out of his way to use figures of speech, most notably proverbs and sayings, to give readers a sense of how this culture might have represented itself to counter the highly regimented and stereotyped language of the colonizer.

Ultimately, however, the authority of Achebe's works has depended on their role as cultural texts. This does not mean that they are not imaginative works, or that their formal features are not compelling, or that they are valuable primarily as ethnographic documents; rather, Achebe's novels have become important features of the African literary landscape because they have come to be read and taught as important sources of knowledge about Africa. For scholars in numerous disciplines, such as history and anthropology, *Things Fall Apart* and *Arrow of God* are read as exemplary representations of African traditional cultures at the moment of the colonial encounter. And although *No Longer at Ease* has not had the same cultural effect as these other novels, it is clearly indispensable in the mapping out of the space of transition from colonialism to postcolonialism. For students trying to understand the violent politics of postcolonial Nigeria, especially the period of corruption and military coups in the mid 1960s, there is perhaps no better reference than *A Man of the People*.

The parallel between Achebe's works and their historical and social referents is so close that it is difficult not to read his major novels as major documents of the African experience. For this reason, Achebe's novels are notable for their sense of realism (see **realism and magical realism**). Indeed, while a novel like *Anthills of the Savannah* is unusual in its bringing together of techniques drawn from realism, modernism (see **modernity and modernism**), and what has come to be known as magic realism, rarely does Achebe's work reflect an interest in formal experimentation for its own sake. The use of a multiplicity of forms in this novel can be connected to the author's desire to account for a postcolonial crisis that cannot be contained within one feature of novelistic discourse. It is perhaps because of his commitment to realism that Achebe's novels have tended to be out of fashion in institutions of interpretation dominated by theories of **structuralism and poststructuralism**.

At the same time, however, Achebe's sense of realism, as a technique and mode of discourse, is not that of the nineteenth-century European novel with its concern with verisimilitude, the experiences of a unique bourgeois subject undergoing the process of education, and a language that seeks to make communities knowable, although Achebe's novels do seek to make African communities knowable. As he himself has noted in an early essay called "The Novelist as a Teacher" (1965; 1973: London), he started his career envisioning the role of writing as essentially pedagogical – "to help my society regain belief in itself and put away the complexes of the years of denigration and self-abasement." Achebe is attracted to realism because it enables him to imagine African cultures, especially postcolonial cultures, possible and knowable.

However, Achebe's novels operate under the shadow of modernism and modernity for two closely related reasons: First, his early novels were written in response to a set of modern texts, most notably Conrad's *Heart of Darkness*, in which African "barbarism" was represented as the opposite of the logic of modern civilization. Since he was educated within the tradition of European modernism, Achebe's goal was to use realism to make African cultures visible while using the ideology and techniques of modernism to counter the colonial novel in its own terrain. Second, modernity was an inevitable effect of colonization in Africa. As Achebe was to dramatize so powerfully in *Things Fall Apart* and *Arrow of God*, the disruption of the African polity was made in the name of colonial modernity; it was also in the name of being

modern that some African subjects would defect from their own cultures and identify with the new colonial order. Indeed, Achebe's "postcolonial" novels are concerned with the consequences of colonial modernity. The sense of instability that characterizes the process of decolonization in *No Longer at Ease* arises as much from doubts about the future of the imagined community of the Nigerian nation as the main character's entrapment between the culture of colonialism, represented by the shaky idiom of Englishness, and the continuing power of what were once considered to be outdated customs such as caste. Similarly, behind the comic mode of *A Man of the People* is a serious questioning of the nature of power once it has been translated into a nationalist narrative that is unclear about its idiom and moral authority.

Ultimately, the continuing influence of Achebe's works, and their now classical status, goes beyond their topicality and their role as sources of knowledge about Africa. Achebe's novels are cultural texts to the extent that they have an imaginative relationship to the African experience and hence cannot be properly interpreted outside the realities and dreams of an African political configuration. This concern with the meaning of the past in the pressure of the moment of writing is pronounced in Achebe's short stories (*Girls at War and Other Stories*) (1972) and two collections of poems (*Beware Soul Brother and Other Poems*, also published as *Christmas in Biafra and Other Poems*) (1972/3), many provoked by the Nigerian civil war. In all these works and four collections of essays, Achebe has been responsible for making the African experience, in a historical and cultural perspective, the center of an African literature. He has been persistent in his claim that the main concerns of an African literature arise from a fundamental engagement with what he would consider to be the stream of African history and consciousness. In formal terms, Achebe's novels, like his own life, reflect the variety of influences that have gone into the making of African literature, ranging through the folk traditions of the Igbo people of Eastern Nigeria, the idiom of the Bible and the culture of the Christian missions (see **Christianity and Christian missions**), colonial education (see **education and schools**), the university and the institutions of English literature.

Further reading

Achebe, Chinua (1973) "The Novelist as a Teacher" and "The Role of the Writer in the New Nation," in G.D. Killam (ed.) *African Writers on African Writing*, London: Heinemann.

Gikandi, Simon (1991) *Reading Chinua Achebe: Language and Ideology in Fiction*, London: James Currey.

Innes, Lynn (1990) *Chinua Achebe*, Cambridge: Cambridge University Press.

SIMON GIKANDI

Adamou, Ide

b. 1951, Niger

poet and novelist

The Nigerien writer Ide Adamou has produced two volumes of poetry and two novels since he started writing in the late 1980s. His first volume of poetry, containing forty-four poems, was published in 1984 and was entitled *Cri inachevé* (Unfinished Cry). Most significantly, although most of Adamou's work is in French, his first collection of poetry contains ten poems written in the Zarma language. This collection highlights the importance of literary production in national languages in Africa and provides a model and method for the production of this kind of literature. His novel *La Camisole de paille* (The Straw Camisole) was published in 1987. The work describes the difficulties of the confrontation of traditional and modern values, and uses its female main character to embody and symbolize the values of independent Niger. His latest volume of poetry, *Sur les terres de silence* (On the Lands of Silence), continues to treat the same themes of suffering and independence as his first volume, while the novel *Talibo, un enfant du quartier* (Talibo, a Child of the Neighborhood), which was published in 1996, is concerned with the conflict between Islamic and French educational systems.

SUSAN GORMAN

Adiaffi, Anne-Marie

b. 1951, Abengouro, Côte d'Ivoire; d. 1995, Abidjan, Côte d'Ivoire

novelist

Anne-Marie Adiaffi was born in 1951 in the Côte d'Ivoire city of Abengouro. After attending primary and secondary school in the Côte d'Ivoire, she continued her education in Marseilles. She then went to Dakar, where she earned a bilingual secretarial diploma. Thereafter, she returned to the Côte d'Ivoire and worked as a secretary in a bank. Though she began writing in the early 1980s, her literary career began in earnest in 1983 when she started working at the Nouvelles Éditions Africaines publishing house in Abidjan. In the following years, she published two novels with Nouvelles Éditions Africaines. The first, *Une Vie hypotéqué* (A Mortgaged Life) (1983), is a smart, satiric novel chronicling the turmoil of a young girl who runs away after living under the threatening shadow of an elderly "benefactor" to whom she has been betrothed since before her birth. In 1989, Adiaffi published her second novel, *La Ligne brisée* (The Broken Line), which follows the fortunes and misfortunes of a man named Sonanfe after his village banishes him because of his chronic bad luck. Adiaffi worked for Nouvelles Éditions Africaines until just before her death, in 1995 in Abidjan.

MEREDITH MARTIN

Adiaffi, Jean-Marie

b. 1941, Bettié, Côte d'Ivoire; d. 1999, Abidjan

writer

The Ivorian writer Jean-Marie Adiaffi claims to be the product of two literary traditions: the postmodern West and the African oral tradition (see **oral literature and performance**). He considers compatriot Bernard **Dadié** an important literary forebear. His best-known novel, *The Identity Card* (*La Carte d'identité*) (1980), is the first part of an ambitious project entitled *Assanou Atin* (The Path of

Liberation), a double trilogy comprising three novels and three works of poetry and spanning the periods of slavery, colonialism (see **colonialism, neocolonialism, and postcolonialism**), and independence in the African historical experience. Cultural identity and its relationship to the healing of social ills on the African continent constitute important preoccupations in Adiaffi's writing. Adiaffi says his dream is to learn from other traditions without relinquishing his own heritage in order to achieve two comfortable syntheses: between the heritages that have contributed to his literary consciousness, and also between his deep political commitment and his equally profound concern for style. His complex creative work in many ways reflects this vision. Adiaffi has also authored a critical work, *Lire Henri Konan Bédié: le rêve de la graine* (Reading Henri Konan Bédié: A Dream of Rebirth) (1996), a leftist reading of Bédié's *Paroles* (Words).

WANGAR WA NYATETŨ-WAIGWA

Adotevi, Stanislas

b. 1934, Lomé, Benin

academic and philosopher

The Benin philosophy professor Stanislas Adotevi has been a staunch critic of the **negritude** movement throughout his career as an essayist, educator, and philosopher. He was one of the first French-speaking African intellectuals to join the English-speaking intellectual chorus, led by Wole **Soyinka**, that was already decrying negritude's philosophy. He has written a large number of articles, but his most famous work remains *Negritude and Negrologists* (*Négritude et Négrologues*) (1972). In this work, as in his articles, Adotevi attacks negritude as a form of "mysticism" that prevents Africans from achieving true independence and progress. He sees it as an empty idealization of the past rather than an effective solution for the future, often singling out Léopold **Senghor**'s poetic vision of negritude as a particularly tragic example of Africans accepting a colonial image of Africa. Instead of such "cults of the past," Adotevi advocates the

modernization and development of African governments, economies, education, and other social institutions. To achieve this goal, he advocates active revolution, in the Marxist tradition (which he distinguishes from 1960s African socialism), rather than the neocolonialism and underdevelopment he sees negritude's self-satisfied pride as permitting.

Further reading

Adotevi, Stanislas (1972) *Négritude et Négrologues* (Negritude and Negrologists), Paris: Union Générale d'Éditions.

STEPHEN BISHOP

Afewerq Gebre-Iyesus (Afä-Wärq Gäbrä-Iyäsus)

b. 1868, Ethiopia; d. 1947

novelist

Afewerq Gebre-Iyesus was Ethiopia's first novelist. He attended church schools and was sent to Italy to study painting. Back home, he annoyed the empress and went abroad again, spending 1894–1922 in Italy and Eritrea. He taught Amharic to Italians, and wrote an Amharic grammar, a conversation guide, a story of Emperor Minilik, and, upon the request of Italian colleagues, a novel, *Tobbiya*, which was published in Rome in 1908. Although the novel tells the story of a girl, Tobbiya, it indirectly presents Ethiopia, of which she is a symbol, as the light of the world. Much later, *Tobbiya* was reprinted in Ethiopia and used in schools briefly before the 1974 revolution, after which it was again neglected. It has thus had little influence on other Ethiopian authors.

Upon returning to Ethiopia in 1922, Afewerq Gebre-Iyesus held government positions in commerce and also worked as a judge, but when Italy invaded Ethiopia in 1935 he joined the enemy. After liberation in 1941, he was arrested and vanished. He probably died in 1947.

Further reading

Rouaud, A. (1991) *Afä-Wärq*, Paris: Centre National de la Recherché Scientifique.

REIDULF MOLVAER

Afrikaans literature

Afrikaans literature is a highly contested site in which the ideologies of colonialism, language, culture, race, and gender identity formations come into play (see **colonialism, neocolonialism, and postcolonialism**; **gender and sexuality**). The tip of Africa irrevocably became a contact zone when Khoisan people were faced with Dutch settlers in 1652, followed by Malay-speaking Indonesian slaves, French Huguenot refugees in 1688, German immigrants, and British colonizers around 1800. In this melting pot, negotiation, barter, miscegenation, religious teaching of Islam and Christianity, war, and migration all contributed to the blending of languages. So-called "kitchen Dutch" developed, initially spoken mainly by Dutch women, children, and slaves. Reacting to the harsh anglicization policies of the British who ruled the Cape as from 1806, a group of white Cape-Dutch male intellectuals rallied around this hybrid language, claiming that "Afrikaners" should read and write in the language they spoke. On 14 August 1875 the Genootskap voor Regte Afrikaners (Society of True Afrikaners) was formed. *Die Afrikaanse Patriot* (The Afrikaans Patriot) and *Ons Klijntjie* (Our Little One) published some of the first efforts at Afrikaans literature. At the same time, codification and standardization gave the newly imagined Afrikaner community a language with which they differentiated themselves not only from speakers of Dutch and English, but also from mixed race and black speakers of other varieties of Afrikaans. These were considered inferior to the standard which by 1925 was recognized as the official language, together with English, by the South African parliament. In 1933 *Die Bybel* appeared in Afrikaans translation. The white cultural margins which were invented for Afrikaans and Afrikaans literature suited an emerging political order, especially after the National Party came to power in 1948. But after the 1994 democratic elections, Afrikaans became just one of eleven official languages of South Africa, leading to a huge decline in status and subsidy benefits, and forcing gatekeepers of standard Afrikaans to embrace all sectors of the larger alienated Afrikaans language community.

The colonial phase of Afrikaans literature consists of diaries and travel reports in Dutch, e.g. Jan van Riebeeck's *Daghregister* (1651–62), reports by Van Meerhoff, Wikar, Adam Tas, D.G. van Reenen, and fragments from the humorous diary of Johanna Duminy (1757–1807). Diaries kept by migrants into the interior, so-called "Voortrekkers" such as Louis Tregardt, and Susanna and Erasmus Smit who left the Eastern Cape about 1838, were forerunners of the decolonization phase which was formally announced by the above-mentioned "patriot" authors, e.g. S.J. du Toit, Jan Louis Cachet, Pulvermacher, and F.W. Reitz. Besides these literary efforts, often appropriations of European forms, the first Afrikaans grammar and spelling books were published. The stage was set for the emancipation of Afrikaans literature. This coincided with strong anti-imperialist feelings resulting from the South African War (1899–1902).

Cultural leaders, e.g. J.H.H. de Waal, author of the historical novel *Johannes van Wyk* (1904/6), J.H. Hofmeyr, G.S. Preller, and D.F. Malan, led the ideological struggle, while poetry by Jan F.E. Celliers, C. Louis **Leipoldt**, Totius (J.D. du Toit), and Eugène N. Marais (most notably "Winternag" (Winter Night) in 1905) quickly elevated the young literature to mature heights. During the 1930s and 1940s realistic and romantic novels were written, often idealizing pastoral life, e.g. C.M. van den Heever's *Somer* (Summer) and *Laat vrugte* (Late Fruit). "Farm novels" continue to be written to this day in often postmodern style, e.g. by Anna M. Louw and Etienne van Heerden. Dutch-born Jochem van Bruggen (the *Ampie* trilogy) and Jan van Melle (the 1936 classic *Bart Nel*), and South Africans C.J. Langenhoven and M.E.R. (renowned for her autobiography *My beskeie deel*, 1972) are the best remembered.

In the 1930s, poets W.E.G. and N.P. **van Wyk Louw**, Elisabeth **Eybers**, and Uys Krige brought radical renewal, while D.J. **Opperman**, Ernst van Heerden, S.J. Pretorius, S.V. Petersen, G.A. Watermeyer, Barend Toerien, Merwe Scholtz, P.J.

Philander, Adam Small (in the Cape variant), George Weideman, and T.T. Cloete have diverse poetic voices. The enigmatic Italian-born Peter Blum dazzled readers with his Afrikaans collections *Steenbok tot poolsee* (From Capricorn to the Arctic Ocean) (1955) and *Enklaves van die lig* (Enclaves of the Light) (1958), while Paris-based Breyten **Breytenbach** made his amazing debut in 1964. Besides Eybers there are many important women poets, e.g. Ina Rousseau, Sheila Cussons, Ingrid Jonker – whose poem "Die kind" (The Child) was read by Nelson Mandela in parliament – Antjie **Krog**, and Wilma **Stockenström**.

A further breakthrough in Afrikaans literature was represented by novelists and dramatists who, strongly influenced by French philosophy, were contributing to the avant-garde magazine *Sestiger* (Sixty), breaking with the dominant tradition of realism (see **realism and magical realism**) and rallying against government censorship. Jan Rabie set the experimental stage with his 1956 short stories *Een-en-twintig* (Twenty-One) and his political *Bolandia* novels. Most important were Etienne Leroux (famous for his Jung-inspired *Silberstein* trilogy and *Magersfontein, O Magersfontein!*) and André P. **Brink**. Bartho Smit (*Moeder Hanna*) (Mother Hanna), *Putsonderwater* (Well Without Water), *Christine*, and P.G. du Plessis (*Siener in die Suburbs*) were later followed by dramatists Deon Opperman and Reza de Wet.

Since the "Sestigers" Afrikaans prose has become ever more diverse. Elsa **Joubert**, Karel **Schoeman**, and Etienne van Heerden all engage very differently with the theme which J.M. **Coetzee** describes as Schoeman's quest: "What is the meaning of Africa and how can it be known?" John Miles, Chris Barnard, Jeanne Goosen, Marlene **van Niekerk**, Lettie Viljoen/Ingrid Winterbach, and Christoffel Coetzee construct, often in historiographic metafiction, personal and collective pasts. Hennie Aucamp, Koos Prinsloo, Johann de Lange, and Joan Hambidge have brought gay and lesbian issues center stage, while Kwêla publishes a vast array of previously stifled and marginalized black Afrikaans voices. A.H.M. Scholtz's *Vatmaar* (1995) has had huge success.

Afrikaans literature plays an important seismological role in the ever volatile South African society, while Afrikaans historiography (notably J.C. Kannemeyer) and literary scholarship traces developments, including the acknowledgement of forgotten women and emerging black Afrikaans authors. Efforts are made to break down the historiographic divide between literatures written in Afrikaans, English, and African languages in combined university departments of comparative South African literature, both locally and abroad.

Further reading

Coetzee, J.M. (1988) *White Writing: On the Culture of Letters in South Africa*, New Haven and London: Yale University Press.

Kriger, Robert and Kriger, Ethel (eds) (1996) *Afrikaans Literature: Recollection, Redefinition, Restitution*, Amsterdam and Atlanta, Georgia: Rodopi.

Van Coller, H.P. (ed.) (1999, 2000) *Perspektief en profiel: 'n Afrikaanse literatuurgeskiedenis* (Perspective in Profile), 2 vols, Pretoria: J.L. van Schaik.

ENA JANSEN

Agualusa, José Eduardo

b. 1960, Huambo, Angola

writer

As with most postcolonial writers elsewhere in Africa, the works of the Angolan writer José Eduardo Agualusa, who lives in Lisbon, have been written against the experience of decolonization and the failure of the dream of national independence, and as a counterpoint to those writers such as **Pepetela** and Luandino **Vieira** who used their fiction to champion nationalism (see **nationalism and post-nationalism**). At the same time, however, Agualusa has been concerned with both the colonial and postcolonial versions of Angolan history (see **colonialism, neocolonialism, and postcolonialism**) and one of the things his novels have in common is their concern with the role of narrative in the discovery or repression of truth. In *A Conjura* (The Conjurer) (1989), Agualusa turns to the Angolan past to question colonial Portuguese perspectives on Angola's history, while in *Nação Crioula* (Creole Nation) (1997) he rewrites Eça de

Queiroz's 1900 travel narrative, *A Correspondência de Fradique Mendes* (Following Fradique Mendes), to recover the absent Angolan subject in the colonial text. Although Agualusa's works reflect his interest in historical events and figures and an intertextual relation with old texts, they are at the same time indirect commentaries on the politics and culture of the Angolan state. This critique is most manifested in *Estação das Chuvas* (1996), a fictional novel, written mostly in epistolary form, on the life of the Angolan poet, Lídia do Carmo Ferreira, who was involved in the nationalist movement in Angola but disappeared in mysterious circumstances after independence.

Further reading

Guterres, Maria (2000) "History and Fiction in José Eduardo Agualusa's Novels," in Charles M. Kelley (ed.) *Fiction in the Portuguese-Speaking World*, Cardiff: University of Wales Press, pp. 117–38.

SIMON GIKANDI

Aidoo, Ama Ata

b. 1940, Abeadzi Kyiakor, Ghana

dramatist, poet, novelist and short story writer

The Ghanaian dramatist, poet, novelist, and short story writer Ama Ata Aidoo was born at Abeadzi Kyiakor in the central region of Ghana. Aidoo's career as a writer began while she was still an undergraduate at the University of Ghana with the 1964 performance of *The Dilemma of a Ghost* (1965). Her work, with its consistent regard for gender issues, effectively uses elements of Ghanaian and African oral traditions and styles to place these concerns in the larger context of Ghana's and Africa's struggles against colonialism, neocolonialism and other forms of oppression and exploitation (see **gender and sexuality**; **oral literature and performance**; **colonialism, neocolonialism, and postcolonialism**). Aidoo's second work, the play *Anowa* (1970), is set in the late nineteenth century, and is an adaptation of an old Ghanaian legend. In her collection of short stories,

No Sweetness Here (1970), Aidoo turns her critical yet compassionate attention to the postcolonial period of Ghana's history. This collection demonstrates Aidoo's abilities as a storyteller and witty social critic. *Our Sister Killjoy* (1979) is an innovative novel that examines, through the interplay of prose and poetry, the maturation of a young Ghanaian woman, Sissie, who travels to Germany and England before returning to Ghana. Her second novel, *Changes: A Love Story* (1991), which won the 1992 Africa section of the Commonwealth Writers' Prize, recounts the trials and tribulations in the life and loves of Esi Sekyi, a young educated career woman. Aidoo's sensitive depiction of her major character's second marriage to a polygamous man affords her the opportunity to explore the uses of Africa's past in an era when women and men are attempting to create more meaningful personal and public lives. Aidoo's other works include her two volumes of poetry, *Someone Talking to Sometime* (1985) and *An Angry Letter in January* (1991) which address many of the themes found in her other works; a collection of short stories, *The Eagle and the Chicken and Other Stories* (1987), and *Birds and Other Poems* (1987), both inspired by oral tradition, belong to the tradition of **children's literature** in Africa. Her second collection of short stories, *The Girl Who Can and Other Stories* (1997), while dealing primarily with conditions in late twentieth-century Ghana, directed her readers' attention to the position of children in such a world. Aidoo's importance as one of Africa's leading writers is confirmed by the increasing number of critical studies devoted to her and her work.

Aidoo began writing seriously while attending the University of Ghana at Legon, where the production of her first drama, *The Dilemma of a Ghost*, in 1964 was quickly recognized as exceptional by Ghanaian musicologist J.H. Nketia and writer and educator Efua T. **Sutherland**. After graduating, Aidoo was given a junior research fellowship at the Institute of African Studies where she worked in the field of drama and under the direction of Sutherland, Joe **De Graft** and others. *The Dilemma of a Ghost* is both structurally and thematically related to the traditional dilemma tale. By focusing on the questions and problems of appropriate moral behavior, the dilemma tale invites the audience to adjudicate between conflicting possibilities of action. The drama centers on the problems of childbearing, infertility, and exogamy that arise when Ato Yawson, the protagonist, returns to Ghana with an African-American wife, Eulalie Rush. The consequences of this unannounced marriage symbolize both the private and the public dilemmas of the postcolonial subject and her or his society. The protagonist, as the representative of the Ghanaian petit-bourgeois intellectual, is confronted in perhaps the most immediate and intimate of circumstances – marriage and family – with the problem of what Chinua **Achebe** has characterized as the "clash of cultures." Ato's family, represented by his mother Esi Kom, are naturally surprised, suspicious, and antagonistic toward their new daughter-in-law and all she represents as an African-American, "a tree without roots" and a reminder of the transatlantic slave trade. The ideological and stereotypical assumptions of both Eulalie and her new in-laws give rise to the seemingly irreconcilable encounter between the West (the United States) and Africa (Ghana).

Between 1966 and 1970, under a number of sponsorships, Ama Ata Aidoo continued writing, traveled, and taught at various institutions around the world. Her second play *Anowa* (1970) and her first collection of short stories, *No Sweetness Here* (1970), confirmed Aidoo's abilities as a writer of multiple talents. Upon returning to Ghana, she accepted a lectureship at the University of Cape Coast where she taught through the 1970s. Aidoo's second drama is an examination of the interaction and consequences of the personal, public, and economic forces that, in part, explain the post-independent situation in Ghana. The play is loosely based on a famous traditional Ghanaian legend; but by focusing on the lives of the protagonist, Anowa, and her husband, Kofi Ako, against the background of rising British colonial ambitions in Fanteland, Aidoo achieves a greater sense of historical validity than the background of the play might suggest. The drama clearly shows the connection between sexual oppression and colonial domination. In this play, Ama Ata Aidoo succeeds in delineating the particular confluence of forces, both internal and external, which accelerated the marginalization of women in precolonial and colonial African (Ghanaian) societies. What

becomes clear in the drama is that the issue of gender oppression, no less than other oppressions, is materially based. The conflict that emerges between husband and wife over the growth of their trading business and the purchase of slaves leads to the (ir)resolution characteristic of the dilemma tale. Aidoo's use of the techniques gleaned from the Akan oral tradition is not confined to the deployment of the dilemma tale convention.

In her collection of short stories, *No Sweetness Here*, we find the eleven stories infused with both structural and thematic elements whose origins are in the oral tradition. The stories which make up the collection may be read as distinct tales but, like many traditional storytelling events or performances, they are best appreciated as elements of an integrated dramatic performance. Individually and collectively the stories examine, in greater variety and detail, the problems of late twentieth-century Ghanaian society. Whether Aidoo uses a male or female voice, an urban middle-class or peasant character to narrate the stories, they all have an underlying concern with the discord caused by the multiple oppressions of class, gender, and national origin. This discord has become attenuated during the post-independence era. Stylistically, all the stories emphasize the dramatic orality of narrative performances, even though the printed word seems dominant.

In 1979, Aidoo published what was then her most ambitious work, *Our Sister Killjoy: Or, Reflections from a Black-Eyed Squint*. It was a mélange of prose and poetry in which the protagonist, Sissie, embarks on a four-part journey to maturity. It can be read as a more intense reversal of Conrad's journey into the Heart of Darkness, because Sissie travels into a more horrifying "heart of whiteness." By the end of her perilous journey, Sissie not only finds her own voice, through which to articulate her fears and hopes, but she is able to unequivocally express a commitment to the betterment of Africa.

After serving briefly as Ghana's education minister from 1982 to 1983, Aidoo moved to Harare, Zimbabwe, to live and work. Ama Ata Aidoo had always written poetry, and the lyrical quality of her first novel is a testament to her abilities as a poet. So it was not surprising when her long-awaited first volume of poetry, *Someone Talking to Sometime* (1985), was published soon after she settled in Harare. The poems in this collection span the first two decades of her career as a writer. The volume embodies her concerns as a woman, an African, a university teacher, and a Third World writer. In addition, the final section of *Someone Talking to Sometime*, "Tomorrow's Song," looks towards an uncertain future that affirms the possibility of meaningful change without romantic evasions. Through her lucid and evocative language, Aidoo insists that her audience, as participants in their own postcolonial nightmare, must wake up. Her words are like an alarm sounding a dire warning before it is too late to do anything but atrophy.

While in Zimbabwe, Ama Ata Aidoo published her two works for children, *The Eagle and the Chicken and Other Stories* (1987) and *Birds and Other Poems* (1987), as well as finishing her second novel, *Changes: A Love Story* (1991). This work, very unlike her first novel, reflects a style evocative of her short stories. The novel is divided into three parts, each of which recounts the trials and tribulations in the life and loves of Esi Sekyi, a young educated career woman caught at another kind of crossroad from that which confronted her male precursor, Ato Yawson, in *The Dilemma of a Ghost*. Esi is an ambitious civil servant in the Department of Urban Statistics who, after ending her first marriage on the grounds of marital rape, falls in love with the polygamous Au Kondey, a northerner for whom things seem to have changed. The structure and style of the novel clearly show that Aidoo has refined her use of the oral tradition. The second part of the novel begins with a dialogue between two women, Aba and Ama, which stylistically echoes Aidoo's earlier works; just like the conversation of the two women, "your neighbors," in *The Dilemma of a Ghost*, this overheard exchange creates the inter- and contextual frame in which the issues of a woman's place and her relationship to another man or men are emphasized by placing them within the web of a historicized neocolonialism. Ultimately, the consequences of trying to create a workable modern-day polygamous marriage are disastrous for Esi, Ali, and those with whom they interact.

Aidoo's second volume of poetry, *An Angry Letter in January* (1992) focuses on Africa and the African diaspora during the closing decade of the twentieth century. Like her first collection, this second volume is divided into two sections. The poems are introduced by a poetic statement of refusal, a genuine testimony "Of Love and Commitment," the articulation of the desire not to betray one's principles, one's self or selves. Part One, "Images of Africa at Century's End," consists of poems that explore the past and present in relation to the idea and reality of home and exile, self and other on the continent and in the diaspora. Part Two, while a natural extension of the first section, shifts our perspective to one that allows us to more clearly appreciate "Women's Conferences and Other Wonders." The poems in this part, while focusing our attention on motherhood and womanhood, the process of teaching and learning, ultimately document a (w)rite of passage.

After the publication of her second volume of poetry, Aidoo returned to Ghana to begin a number of ventures, including a publishing concern and an NGO for young women writers. In the midst of these activities, Aidoo published her second volume of short stories, *The Girl Who Can and Other Stories* (1997), in Ghana. This volume includes a few works that had been previously published; however, the majority was specially assembled for the collection. Although the dramatic intensity of her first collection of stories is less evident, there is the characteristic storytelling quality to the narratives. Thematically, the stories focus more on the condition of children and suggest the potential of the next generation to overcome the problems that have bedeviled their parents' struggles. As exemplified in all her work, Aidoo clearly demonstrates her superior skill in the utilization of the oral traditions; in the diversity of genres in which she works; and in her control over the content and style that characterize her major literary products. Her work is marked by a cutting wit and profound insights into human nature. Her dedication to her art and audience, and her concerns as a woman, writer, and teacher, motivate her to continually examine and explore the complexities of the issues of gender, race, and class in an exemplary fashion.

Further reading

Azodo, Ada Uzoamaka and Wilentz, Gay (eds) (1998) *Emerging Perspectives on Ama Ata Aidoo*, Trenton, New Jersey: Africa World Press.

Odamtten, Vincent O. (1994) *The Art of Ama Ata Aidoo: Polylectics and Reading Against Neocolonialism*, Gainesville, Florida: University of Florida Press.

VINCENT O. ODAMTTEN

Aïssa, Salim (pseudonym of Boukella)

b. Algeria

novelist

Salim Aïssa is the pseudonym of Boukella, an Algerian novelist known for his detective stories set in contemporary post-independence Algeria. The author's originality emerges from his ability to combine the detective story genre and a humorous critique of postcolonial society (see **colonialism, neocolonialism, and postcolonialism**). *Mimouna* (Mimouna) (1987), his first novel, is the story of a 26-year-old man who comes out of prison and finds himself involved in a burglary even though he has tried to lead a life free of crime. The novel is characterized by much digression which plunges the reader into the day-to-day experiences of ordinary Algerians. Other innovative aspects of the novel include the use of a language that challenges social clichés and conventions. In his second detective novel, *Adel S'emmêle* (Adel Gets Involved), published in 1988, Salim Aïssa continues to portray the underworld of criminals and the police as a way of exploring contemporary Algerian society and its complexities. Both novels, which were first published in Algeria, are dominated by the use of humor in portraying the daily struggle for survival in a society where the colonial past, the experience of socialism, and the dynamics of post-independence form the main background. The author also works as a journalist for *Algérie-Actualité*.

Further reading

Aïssa, S. (1987) *Mimouna*, Algiers: Laphomic.

ANISSA TALAHITE-MOODLEY

Akare, Thomas

b. 1950, Kenya

novelist

The Kenyan novelist Thomas Akare ranks alongside Meja **Mwangi** and Charles **Mang'ua** as one of the most notable narrators of the urban experience in modern Kenya, a theme which began to gain prominence in the 1970s. His first novel, *The Slums* (1981), tells of the life of a destitute young man who survives by washing cars and who, towards the end of the novel, decides to commit a robbery in the hope that life in prison will be much better than the precariousness of life on the street. *Twilight Woman* (1988) is a gloomy portrait of a woman who comes to the city to join her husband, a migrant worker, but soon resorts to prostitution. Akare's fiction captures the unhappy mood, prevalent in Kenyan **popular literature**, in which the pleasures of modernity (see **modernity and modernism**) are always depicted as being haunted by the sense of alienation and social disintegration that come with rapid changes in society. Rendered in a documentary and journalistic style sometimes named "mechanistic realism," Akare's novels have played a crucial – although largely unacknowledged – role in the development of the kind of Kenyan popular fiction that depicts life as a series of absurdities, and in the debates about the consequences of modernity.

DAN ODHIAMBO OJWANG

Alapini, Julien

b. 1906, Dahomey (now Benin); d. 1970, Benin

ethnographer, linguist, and playwright

Julien Alapini is best known for his 1941 collection

of folk tales *Contes dahoméens* (Dahomean Tales) as well as several ethnographic studies, including *Les Initiés* (The Initiates), of the traditional religious customs of his native Dahomey (now Benin) published in the 1950s. Trained as a teacher, Alapini taught in primary schools all over Dahomey while pursuing his own research and writing. Not just an ethnographer but also a linguist and playwright, he went on to publish an important grammar and dictionary of the Fon language and a collection of plays entitled *Acteurs noirs* (Black Actors), both in the last decade of his life. A Catholic and a great admirer of French culture, Alapini sought to follow in the footsteps of earlier colonial ethnographers. He condemned the ancestral beliefs he studied as "fetishistic" and "pagan," as not religion but superstition, and hoped that his work would function to demystify them and lead Africans to Christianity and "modern science."

Further reading

Alapini, Julien (1953) *Les Initiés* (The Initiates), Avignon: Éditions Aubanel.

RACHEL GABARA

Aliyu, Akilu

b. 1918, Jega, Nigeria; d. 1998, Nigeria

poet

The Nigerian writer Akilu Aliyu was perhaps the greatest Hausa poet of his generation (see **literature in Hausa**). Immersed in the tradition of Hausa poetry written in the Arabic script (*ajami*), Aliyu was a consummate wordsmith whose facility and erudition in the nuances of the Hausa language drew recognition within the Hausa-speaking world, for example through an honorary doctorate from a Northern Nigerian university. His chanted recitation of poetry was heard on radio and in public gatherings – particularly, during periods of civilian rule, in support of the main northern opposition political party, the Northern Elements Progressive Union (NEPU) and its leader, Malam Aminu Kano. Born in Jega, in the northwest of Nigeria, Aliju's early Koranic education led

on to periods studying under a number of leading scholars of Islam in the Tijaniyya brotherhood in Kano and then, for twenty-three years until 1959, in Borno in northeastern Nigeria. His subsequent return to Kano marked his most productive years as a poet, with an oeuvre of lengthy poems running into the hundreds.

Further reading

Furniss, Graham (1996) *Poetry, Prose and Popular Culture in Hausa*, Washington: Smithsonian Institution Press.

GRAHAM FURNISS

Alloula, Malek

b. 1937, Oran, Algeria

poet and critic

The Algerian poet and critic Malek Alloula has published several collections of poems as well as a critical study of colonial photography. A key member of the post-independence generation of Algerian poets, Alloula has explored themes dealing with his country's past and questions of memory in the context of the challenges of building a new independent nation. In his collection of poems entitled *Villes et autres lieux* (Cities and Other Places) (1979), the city is represented as the site of historical roots, but also the source of alienation and fragmentation. Another important aspect of Alloula's work is his analysis of the representation of women in the colonial context. One of his most famous books, *The Colonial Harem* (1986), is a critical study of the image of Algerian women as represented in colonial photography. The writer uses theories of representation of "otherness" to provide an insight into the intersection between the political and the sexual in the context of colonialism. Until 1975, Malek Alloula was known for his work as a journalist and contributor to the Algerian newspaper *Algérie-Actualité*. He now lives in Paris and is the president of an organization that keeps alive the memory of his brother, Abdelkader Alloula, a key figure in Algerian theater, who was assassinated in Algeria in 1994.

Further reading

Alloula, M. (1986) *The Colonial Harem*, trans. Myrna Godzich and Wlad Godzich, Minneapolis: University of Minnesota Press.

ANISSA TALAHITE-MOODLEY

Aluko, Timothy

b. 1918, Nigeria

engineer and novelist

The Nigerian engineer and novelist Timothy Aluko is not considered to be a major figure in African fiction, but he is clearly an important one because of both the themes of his works and their place in Nigerian writing in English. He started writing in the 1950s, a period that is now considered to be the golden age of modern African writing, and although he was trained as an engineer, his novels were based on many of the themes of **popular literature** and experience that he observed as a government public works officer in Western Nigeria. His earliest novels, *One Man, One Machete* (1965), *Kinsman and Foreman* (1967), and *One Man, One Wife* (1966), belong to what has come to be known as the "conflict of cultures genre," but Aluko treats themes such as the clash between Christians and non-Christians, husbands and wives, and workers and their bosses, with irreverence and humor. In his later novels, Aluko turned to the subject of politics, poking fun at the practices and beliefs of the new African ruling class in *Chief the Honourable Minister* (1970), *His Worshipful Majesty* (1973), and *Conduct Unbecoming* (1993). While Aluko's novels cover the whole range of subjects that have dominated African literature in the modern period, they have often been considered as entertainment and have perhaps not gained him the recognition he deserves as a humorist and satirist.

Further reading

Griswold, Wendy (2000) *Bearing Witness: Readers,* *Writers, and the Novel in Nigeria*, Princeton, New Jersey: Princeton University Press.

SIMON GIKANDI

Amadi, Elechi

b. 1934, Aluu, near Port Harcourt, Nigeria

engineer, army officer, and novelist

The Nigerian engineer, army officer, and novelist Elechi Amadi came to writing through an unusual path. He had studied physics and mathematics at University College, Ibadan, one of the cradles of Nigerian education and literature, and after a brief period of teaching he was commissioned into the Nigerian army where he achieved the rank of captain. Amadi's first novel, *The Concubine* (1966), was a powerful rendering of a woman struggling with the forces of nature and traditional beliefs and it has been one of the most popular novels in schools and universities in Anglophone Africa. Concerned with questions of fate and the supernatural, Amadi was one of the few writers of his generation who could write novels in which the issue of colonialism was conspicuous by its absence (see **colonialism, neocolonialism, and postcolonialism**). In *The Concubine*, as in *The Great Pond* (1968) and *The Slave* (1978), Amadi's focus was on local, precolonial, communities which he sought to represent according to their own rules, beliefs, and mythologies. During the Nigerian civil war in the 1960s, Amadi was one of a few Eastern Nigerian writers and intellectuals who continued to serve the federal government and he was twice arrested by the Biafran authorities. He represents his experiences and perspectives of the civil war in *Sunset in Biafra* (1973), a memoir, and *Estrangement* (1986), a novel on the destructive effects of the war on personal and social relationships.

Further reading

Palmer, Eustace (1972) *An Introduction to the African Novel*, London: Heinemann.

SIMON GIKANDI

Amadou, Ousmane

b. 1948, Niger

poet, novelist, lawyer, and journalist

The Nigerien writer Ousmane Amadou came to literature through an interest in both law and journalism, and his writing is thus intrinsically involved with the judicial and political systems of his native country. Amadou's oeuvre, which ranges from poetry to screenplays, novels, and political tracts, demonstrates his versatility; however, it is in his novels that he has made the most distinct impression on Niger's literary scene. After the 1974 seizure of power by Seyni Kountche, Amadou served as the press attaché for the presidency for a period of four years. It was during this period that he wrote his first novel, *Quinze ans, ça suffit!* (Fifteen Years, That's Enough!) (1977), a work that attacks the injustices and abuses that were to be found in the political system of Hamani Diori, the president of Niger immediately following independence. His *Chronique judiciaire* (Judiciary Chronicle) (1987) is a loosely fictionalized account of Nigerien court cases, which the author uses in order to illustrate how the system worked and was abused. Amadou has also written a book entitled *L'Itinéraire* (Itinerary), on Kountche and Ibrahim Bare Mainassara, the man who staged a military *coup d'état* in 1996. In the 1990s, Amadou published two novels, *L'Honneur perdu* (Lost Honor) and *Le Témoin gênant* (The Embarrassing Witness), focusing upon the democratization process and the difficulties encountered by political movements committed to social change.

SUSAN GORMAN

Amali, Samson

b. 1947, Nigeria

linguist, poet and playwright

Although he has been writing plays and poems since he was a student at University College, Ibadan, the Nigerian linguist, poet, and playwright Samson Amali is not well known outside his native Nigeria. This is largely because most of his works have been published privately in Nigeria and have hence not entered the international networks that promote writers and their works. In addition, Amali's work has not gained much critical attention. Yet he is a prolific writer with several collections of poetry and plays based mostly on his research in Idioma oral culture and ritual drama (see **oral literature and performance**). During a career as a researcher at the Institute of African Studies at the University of Ibadan, Amali has published a collection of Idioma and Tiv oral texts and he has been working on an oral history of the Nigerian civil war.

Further reading

Amali, Samson (1971) *Poems: A Conversation*, Ibadan: University Bookshop of Nigeria.
——(1968) *Selected Poems*, Ibadan: University Bookshop of Nigeria.

SIMON GIKANDI

Amon d'Aby, Jean-François

b. 1913, Côte d'Ivoire

playwright

This too-little-sung pioneer is one of the key names in the genesis of Ivorian modern theater. In 1938 he co-founded, with Germain Coffi Gadeau, Le Théâtre Indigène de la Côte d'Ivoire (TICI), a cultural association involved in the promotion of local drama. In 1953 he teamed up with Gadeau and Bernard **Dadié** to form the Cercle Culturel et Folklorique de la Côte d'Ivoire (CCFCI), a culture and folklore club. At the same time, Amon d'Aby was a member of the Jeunesse Ouvrière Chrétienne (JOC), the Young Christian Workers' Association. He wrote plays for all three organizations: seven for the JOC, three for the TICI, and four for the CCFCI. His plays present cultural themes, lessons in Christian virtue, attacks on what he considers to be fetishists and charlatans, and a criticism of various precolonial or traditional social customs. In the course of his writing career, Amon d'Aby's secular theater evolved from writing plays based on indigenous oral storytelling and performance (see oral literature and performance) to more modernized forms based on techniques borrowed from European theater. Besides these dramatic works, he has also authored three ethno-sociological studies and several collections of folk tales and legends.

Further reading

Bonneau, Richard (1973) "Jean-François Amon d'Aby, dramaturge ivoirien" (Jean-François Amon d'Aby, Ivorean Dramatist), *L'Afrique Littéraire* 27: 10–20.

WANGAR WA NYATETŨ-WAIGWA

Amrani, Djamal

b. 1935, Sour el-Ghozlane, Algeria

playwright and journalist

The Algerian writer Djamal Amrani belongs to the postcolonial generation of North African writers in French (see **North African literature in French**), a generation for whom the struggle for national liberation from colonialism has played a key role in the shaping of art and literature (see **colonialism, neocolonialism, and postcolonialism**). Djamal's key involvement in the Algerian liberation struggle gave him inspiration and provided the key themes in his writing. One of Amrani's key works is *Le Témoin* (The Witness), an autobiographical account of his experiences in the Algerian nationalist movement, which was published in 1960. The book gives a detailed account of the author's arrest and imprisonment in 1957 after taking part in the 1956 students' strikes. The narrative is based on real-life events which afflicted the writer and his family during the war. It is also a powerful account of repression and a denunciation of the torture perpetrated by the French army in Algeria. After independence, Amrani continued his career as a writer by publishing numerous collections of poems and short stories, most of which were published in Algeria. The memory of the war continued to be a central concern for the writer, although the debates of postcolonial society are also present in his later writings. Djamel Amrani is

today considered a key figure of Algerian poetry in French. He has also made significant contributions in the fields of theater, journalism, and radio.

Further reading

Amrani, D. (1960) *Le Témoin* (The Witness), Paris: Édition de Minuit.

ANISSA TALAHITE-MOODLEY

Amrouche, Jean

b. 1906, Ighil Ali, Algeria; d. 1962, Paris, France

poet

Born a Kabyle in conquered Algeria, baptized a Catholic by converted parents, raised in Tunisian exile, trained in French universities, celebrated as a major poet for two lyrical collections emblazoned with the thematics of loss, Jean-El Mouhoub Amrouche stood at the conflux of worlds he could not reconcile. So did others in his family. His mother, Fadhma Aïth Mansour, started her autobiography, *My Life's Story* (*Histoire de ma vie*) in 1945 at his urging. Published after his death and hers, it remains a superb document at the intersection of literature and ethnography. His sister, Taos **Amrouche**, a novelist, became the world-famous performer of her mother's ancestral song-poems. Brother and sister had transcribed them, and Jean published them as *Chants berbères de Kabylie* (Berber Songs from Kabylia) in 1939. During the Algerian war of independence (1954–62), his nephew Marcel ran a radio series on the ancient Maghrebian past, a proud move when colonizers still preferred to view North Africa as the cradle of irreducible savagery. French citizens through an accident of history, the Amrouches remained rooted in their culture, its language, and, above all, its poetry. Subjects of empire caught in the process of decolonization, they were, in Derek Walcott's famous phrase, "divided to the vein."

The poet therefore came by his calling as a birthright. The mystical yet austere verses of *Cendres* (Ashes) (1934) and *Etoile secrète* (Secret Star) (1937), steeped in the spirituality of ancient Greece and the

New Testament, turn to Berber lore to "mourn an entire people, now defunct, stirring inside its shroud" (*Cendres*). The central part of *Etoile secrète*, "La Parole de l'absent" (The Word/s, or Voice, and Absence), sets up a Christic self who yearns for the vanished power of the Word. The voice is grave, sober, elliptical; drama is achieved in the high-wire tension between restrained neo-classical forms and the effulgent, barely controlled, near-pagan images of a loss that Christian faith cannot soothe.

By 1945, Amrouche had become a contributor to prominent newspapers, penning in 1946 his most famous essay on the transcultural self, *L'Éternel Jugurtha* (Eternal Jugurtha), a thinly veiled self-assessment. The Maghrebian prince who, raised in Rome, united fractious Berber tribes against Rome before dying a war captive, proved an irresistible emblem for themes already developed in his poetry: exile, betrayal, and the haunting longing for the vanished land of origins. A full ten years before Albert **Memmi**'s own *The Colonizer and the Colonized* (*Portrait du colonisé*), Amrouche dissected the uneasy love–hatred entanglement of the colonial subject. As the colonial war worsened, Amrouche, like Albert Camus, whom he resembled in intensity and lyricism, was pitilessly criticized. Less opaque than Camus's own, however, Amrouche's collected essays *Un Algérien s'adresse aux Français* (An Algerian Addresses the French People) document his wrenching estrangement. Turning to radio, he sought solace in a series of probing literary exchanges, started in 1954 with the grand old man of French letters, André Gide. With great acumen, a 1956 interview featured one promising youngster, **Kateb** Yacine, who had just published *Nedjma*, the foundational text of modern Maghrebian letters.

Teacher, poet, journalist, and essayist, whom Mohammed **Dib** hails as Promethean "fire-snatcher" in the 1985 symposium dedicated to *L'Éternel Jugurtha*, Amrouche left a small but powerful oeuvre that deserves to take its rightful place on the world's literary stage.

Further reading

Yacine, Tassadit (ed.) (1994) *Jean-El Mouhoub Amrouche: un Algérien s'adresse aux Français: ou* *l'histoire d'Algérie par les textes (1943–61)* (Jean-Il Mouhoub Amrouche: An Algerian Addresses the French People: or The History of Algeria through Writings (1943–61)), Paris: L'Harmattan.

CLARISSE ZIMRA

Amrouche, Taos

b. 1913, Tunis, Tunisia; d. 1976, Saint-Michel-l'Observatoire, France

novelist and ethno-musicologist

The author of four richly poetic novels, Taos Amrouche was better known in the last decade of her life as an ethno-musicologist, the world-famous performer of her mother's ancestral song-poems. Descended from a long line of Kabyle "sooth-singers," this only daughter of a richly artistic Berber family – Jean **Amrouche** was her brother – was baptized Marie-Louise Taos.

As Taos, she published a first novel, the coming-of-age story of a young Maghrebian girl, *Jacinthe noire* (Black Hyacinth), in 1947. With the sequel, *Rue des tambourins* (Tambourine Street) (1960), she defiantly switched to her mother's Christian name, Marguerite, a name the mother had been forbidden in colonial Christian schools because, although a convert, she had not been properly baptized. The novel featured a fearsome Berber matriarch ruling over an extended family in the throes of cultural and religious dislocation. She reverted to Taos for two more works, *L'Amant imaginaire* (The Imaginary Lover), whose narrator in her thirties, is a writer and ethno-musicologist, and *Solitudes ma mère* (Solitude, My Mother), whose narrator is in her forties and a performer.

This nominal slippage was but one symptom of the conflicted quest that would mark both her life and her art, her often expressed conviction, whether in interviews or in her writings, that she felt at home nowhere, could find solace with no one: "whether among Moslems or French, I am always the only one of my kind" (*Tambourins*, 1960: Paris). She had public as well as private reasons for her searing self-doubts. Her works were published long after completion: eight years for the first, ten for the second; a full twenty years for each of the next two. Critics have impugned male readers taken aback by female narrators who unflinchingly explore the yearnings of a woman's body along with those of her soul: narrators who can be as cruelly lucid about their own shortcomings as they are generous about the shortcomings of others; narrators who find neither peace nor self-acceptance. In a 1988 public lecture, her compatriot Assia **Djebar** expressed her conviction that, as a power-player in the tightly knit Parisian editing world, Jean Amrouche may have discouraged others from looking at Taos's work, whose searing honesty offended his Maghrebian sense of (male) honor.

Given the hermetic, highly private quality of Jean's own oeuvre, it may well be that he found Taos's deliberate unveiling too close to the bone. Uprooted from the tightly knit Berber clan for which she yearns – whether painted as nurturing in *Jacinthe* or as suffocating in *Tambourins* – each of her characters discovers that she can never "go home again." Her thematics centers on the existential quest for a spiritual absolute that must be mediated by human love to transcend its own selfishness, yet is doomed by human imperfection. As her fictional structures become increasingly complex, her models run the modernist gamut from Gide to Milosz, whose poetry yields the title to her last and posthumous memoir, "Solitude, my mother, tell me my life once more." One cannot help but wonder whether the difference was not that Jean, born in the ancestral village and living his early years there, was more grounded, whereas for Taos, born in a first exile (Tunisia), to live in a second (France) and a third (Spain), there was no "home" to go back to.

Yet she eventually found a way to reintegrate the group: performing took her "home." Her mother, Fadhma Aïth Mansour, was a *clair-chantant*, schooled in the oral forms – reserved exclusively to women – of a culture that honored these soothsaying performers yet half-feared and half-revered their androgynous powers. The siblings had recorded and translated their mother's traditional poems in the 1930s, although they appeared under Jean's lone signature as *Chants berbères de Kabylie* (Berber Songs from Kabylia). In 1960, Taos reissued and expanded the gathering in *Le Grain magique* (The Magic Grain). Thereafter, she was to "come home again" in one magnificent performance after another throughout the world.

Select bibliography

Amrouche, Taos (1960) *Rue des Tambourins*, Paris: La Table Ronde.

Further reading

Brahimi, Denise (1996) *Taos Amrouche. Romancière* (Taos Amrouche. Novelist), Paris: Joelle Losfeld.

CLARISSE ZIMRA

Angira, Jared

b. 1947, Kenya

poet

The Kenyan poet Jared Angira studied commerce at the University of Nairobi where he was also the editor of the journal *Busara*. He has spent much of his working life in the Kenyan civil service, and published seven volumes of poetry, which include *Juices* (1970), *Silent Voices* (1972), *Soft Corals* (1973), *Cascades* (1979), *The Years Go By* (1980), and *Tides of Time: Selected Poems* (1996). In 1999, his moving eulogy to the late Julius Nyerere appeared in *The Sunday Nation*. Hailed by Wole **Soyinka** and lauded by Ezenwa-Ohaeto as "one of the most exciting poets in Africa," he has not received the critical acclaim many think he deserves. Deeply meditative, Angira's work is deceptively simple and his choice of words may occasionally seem at odds with the gravity of his subject. As a Marxist poet – he once proclaimed: "Karl Marx is my teacher; Pablo Neruda my class prefect (when I am in the classroom) and my captain (when I am on the battlefield)" – his poetry evinces a critical concern with social injustice in post-independence society.

Further reading

Ezenwa-Ohaeto (1996) "Conscious Craft: Verbal

Irony in the Poetry of Jared Angira," *African Literature Today* 20: 87–101.

DAN ODHIAMBO OJWANG

Aniebo, I.N.C.

b. 1939, Nigeria

novelist

The Nigerian military officer, writer, and educator I.N.C. Aniebo is unusual among his country's writers in that he did not start his career at the university but in the Nigerian military, where he trained as an artillery officer and started writing stories under a pseudonym to avoid censorship. Aniebo fought on the side of Biafra during the Nigerian civil war, and his first novel, *The Anonymity of Sacrifice* (1974), was one of the first fictional accounts of this traumatic event. What makes the novel compelling is both Aniebo's first-hand account of the horrors of war and his sense of the personal conflicts that emerge in the context of the conflict, often pitting people ostensibly on the same cause against one another. This concern with the interior conflicts between individuals, plotted against a rapidly changing cultural and political background, is also the central theme in Aniebo's second novel, *The Journey Within* (1978). In this work Aniebo focuses with the domestic conflicts between a married couple struggling to find peace and comfort in their private lives against the backdrop provided by a harsh urban postcolonial environment (see **colonialism, neocolonialism, and postcolonialism**). A collection of his early army stories and new ones dealing with the civil war was published in *Of Wives, Talismans, and the Dead* (1983). After completing his higher education at the University of California, Los Angeles, Aniebo returned to Nigeria to teach at the University of Port Harcourt.

SIMON GIKANDI

Anyidoho, Kofi

b. 1947, Ghana

poet and educator

The Ghanaian poet and educator Kofi Anyidoho comes from a family of Ewe poets and oral artists (see **oral literature and performance**), who include his own mother Abla Adidid Anyidoho, and the poet and novelist Kofi **Awoonor**. He was educated at the University of Ghana and in several universities in the United States. He is the author of several collections of poetry: *Elegy for Revolution* (1978), *A Harvest of Dreams* (1985), *Earth Child* (1985), *The Fate of Vultures* (1989), and *Ancestral Logic and Caribbean Blues* (1993). Anyidoho's poetry has won many awards in Africa and abroad including the Langston Hughes Prize and the BBC Arts for Africa Award. He is also the author of *Akpokplo*, a play in Ewe. Like the poetry of Awoonor, Anyidoho's verse draws heavily on the Ewe elegiac tradition, using an ancient idiom of mourning and cantation to reflect on the postcolonial moment in Africa and its diaspora. Anyidoho has been a major figure in the promotion of the arts and culture in Africa and abroad, having served as the president of the African Writers' Association (the United States) and director of the African Studies Institute at the University of Ghana.

SIMON GIKANDI

Aouchal, Leïla

b. 1936, Caen, France

autobiographer

Born to a French middle-class family in the city of Caen, France, Leïla Aouchal married an Algerian immigrant worker at the age of 19, and moved to Algeria in 1956 to become an Algerian citizen upon independence in 1962. Her work *Une Autre Vie* (Another Life) (1970) is a chronicle of her experiences as she tries to integrate into her new life and new identity in the midst of the turmoil of the Algerian war of independence. Her purpose for writing this book is to explain the process of this transformation from the French woman that she was to the Algerian woman that she became.

NASRIN QADER

apartheid and post-apartheid

If, as Bertrand Russell said, war banishes ambiguity, then presumably demobilization restores it. This deduction is generally borne out in South African literature which, like its parent culture and South African society at large, is rediscovering ambiguity with a vengeance after the legal demise of apartheid. The prospects for South African literature after apartheid were the subject of heated speculation in the early 1990s. Comparisons were made with Soviet literature after *glasnost*: if apartheid was the main theme of South African literature, what was it going to do when apartheid was gone? There were predictions of an impasse and the end of careers built on the diagnosis of apartheid's ills or the celebration of resistance to it.

While there has been a sea-change, however, there has been no impasse. Some of the paradigmatic shifts can be fairly easily schematized. Under apartheid, there was pressure to subordinate aesthetic self-consciousness to political necessity, which resulted in a privileging of documentary realism. To challenge this dispensation meant being associated with the forces of reaction. Post-apartheid culture, however, is more receptive to irony, play, and aesthetic detachment. Similarly, under apartheid writers were expected to address the great historical issues, whereas now there has been a resurgence of the personal. Finally, under apartheid, particularly in the intense 1980s, anxiety about the future was endemic; now, writers are concerned predominantly with the past, in keeping with the drive towards reconciliation in the public sphere, a process typified by the Truth and Reconciliation Commission.

It would be a mistake, however, to assume that these changes have been abrupt. The end of apartheid has not brought an epistemological crisis, partly because issues of aesthetic representation and its relation to history and political life were visibly contested throughout the 1980s. One area of focus was the work of Njabulo **Ndebele**, the essayist and writer of short fiction, who called for a refined attention to the unheroic side of everyday life under apartheid. A second was the work of J.M. **Coetzee**, whose oblique, allegorical, and avowedly fictive writing opened spaces for the post-apartheid imagination to flourish, even during apartheid's worst years. Finally, on the eve of the unbanning of the liberation movement and the start of negotiations, there was a volatile and widely publicized intervention in the arts by Albie Sachs, a constitutional lawyer and cultural commentator in the ANC, who told "cultural workers" that there should be a five-year ban on the slogan "culture is a weapon of the struggle" in order to allow the movement's art to acquire greater depth and complexity. Sachs made no reference to his own literary precursors, but the debate was productive.

With the point of reference swinging from the future to the past, it is the elusive present that escapes attention. This would serve as one explanation for the celebrated and controversial status of J.M. Coetzee's *Disgrace* (1999), winner of the Booker Prize. Coetzee's protagonist, a literary humanist in a corporatized university whose particular failing is aestheticized lust, undergoes criminal torture at the hands of black assailants, who also gang-rape his daughter. Products of an irredeemable past are thus subjected to victimization fueled by a culture of reparation, this being the most obvious implication of the title. As in previous novels, however, Coetzee's skepticism about prevailing historical relationships is eased by muted utopian gestures, promptings of an ethical consciousness which emerges partly from the writing itself. Nadine Gordimer also tackles the present, in *The House Gun* (1998), about a white middle-class professional couple who endure their son's conviction on a murder charge, a situation reflecting the legacy of endemic violence.

The new emphases in the culture are apparent in a burgeoning confessional and autobiographical literature, which extends well beyond the literary (see **autobiography**). Nelson Mandela's *Long Walk to Freedom* (1994) is surrounded by the autobiographies of other luminaries in the struggle, and on the other extreme the assassin Eugene de

Kock has published from prison a confessional account of his life as a servant of apartheid. In fiction, semi-autobiographical writing with a confessional impulse is common in both English and Afrikaans. Mark Behr's *The Smell of Apples* (1996), Jo-Anne Richards's *The Innocence of Roast Chicken*, Jann Turner's *Heartland*, André P. **Brink**'s *Rights of Desire* (2000), and in Afrikaans, Marlene **van Niekerk**'s *Triomf* (1994), are representative examples.

One strain of post-apartheid writing entails an ethical meditation on the relationship between past and present, and the desire not to relinquish the past to the amnesia necessitated by nation-building and reconstruction. Jeremy **Cronin**, a public figure in the Communist Party and now ANC member of parliament, whose literary reputation was established under apartheid with *Inside* (1983), a volume of prison poems, offers a sustained meditation on the dangers of forgetfulness in *Even the Dead* (1997). Sindiwe **Magona**, who established herself with autobiographical writing on childhood under apartheid, has produced *Mother to Mother* (1998). A work of contemporary historical fiction, it responds to the incident in which Amy Biehl, a Fulbright student and volunteer fieldworker in voter education, was murdered in a Cape Town township on the eve of the first democratic election of 1994 by youth affiliated to the Pan-Africanist Congress. Magona's narrative is in the voice of the mother of the perpetrator, addressing the mother of the victim, in an appeal for understanding based on an appreciation of the past. Mandla **Langa**, former ANC exile and now senior policy-maker in broadcasting, has produced *Memory of Stones* (2000), a novel developed from material first explored in the title story of a collection of short fiction, *The Naked Song* (1998), about amnesia and betrayal within the liberation movement.

Another strain of post-apartheid narrative deals with the recovery of identities which had been marginal under the apartheid-era obsession with the obviously bipolar dynamics of race. In film, such as *The Man Who Drove with Mandela*, and in short fiction, such as Shaun de Waal's *These Things Happen* (1996), a new visibility is given to inscriptions of gayness. Zoe **Wicomb**'s *David's Story* (2001), which follows the success of her short fiction cycle *You Can't Get Lost in Cape Town* (1987),

deals with colored identity through a metafictional, historiographic narrative recalling the history of Khoi and Griqua communities in the eighteenth and nineteenth centuries.

It is still unclear whether a consensus will develop involving criticism of South Africa's post-apartheid leadership, the direction followed by postcolonial writing in countries throughout sub-Saharan Africa, but there are signs of disenchantment. In younger black poets like Lesego Rampolokeng, Kgafela oa Magogodi, Sandile Dikeni, and a group of performance poets known as the Botsotso Jesters, there is much disappointment and some unmitigated anger directed at the new government's apparent failure to deliver social and economic justice. Formally, such writing carries some of the declamatory energy of the Soweto poets of a generation earlier, but it is no less influenced by global styles like rap and hip-hop. Zolani Mkiva is more closely associated with the traditional role of the *mbongi* or praise poet, having performed on state occasions such as Mandela's inauguration, but even his work exploits the license of the traditional poet to criticize.

The most ambitious and successful work of fiction by a black writer to appear on the post-apartheid scene to date is Zakes **Mda**'s *The Heart of Redness* (2000). Like the younger poets, Mda is not afraid to criticize nepotism and corruption, but his energy is focused more expansively on reinventing inherited fictional strategies and revisiting history. Mda first became known as a dramatist, and an interest in ritual and symbolization informs his prose. Prior to *The Heart of Redness*, he had produced the acclaimed *Ways of Dying* (1997), which has been transposed to the theater as both play and opera. It deals with the relationship between a self-invented professional mourner, Toloki, and Noria, a prostitute-turned-childcare-activist, and the affirming existence they manage to eke out of the scorched earth of the apartheid township. *The Heart of Redness* offers two parallel narratives, one situated in the 1850s during the "cattle-killing movement," the event which ended Xhosa resistance to British occupation after protracted warfare, and the other situated in the contemporary village of Qolorha where the cattle-killing began in the prophecies of Nonqawuse. The protagonists of each narrative are twinned, suggesting an ancestral return. The apartheid era has already begun to fade in Mda's detached treatment of "the Middle Generations"; instead, the emphasis falls on conflict between traditionalists and modernizers within the parallel communities (see **modernity and modernism**). In this novel, the decisive historical cusp is not the end of apartheid, but the moment of modernity's nineteenth-century incursion which, as in Achebe, reconfigures indigenous patterns of affiliation and allegiance, leaving a lasting legacy through to the present. Arguably, the historiographic sweep of Mda's narrative is made possible by post-apartheid conditions.

Mda's fiction enables us to revisit an unfortunate division in South African literature between white writers who respond to international currents in modernism and postmodernism, and black writers whose attention has been directed at the more dire project of opposing apartheid, and whose representational range has accordingly, though with some exceptions, been restricted to documentary realism (see **realism and magical realism**). *Ways of Dying* and *The Heart of Redness* are the most noteworthy texts to disrupt this opposition, given their historiographic and metafictional qualities.

In conclusion, a few remarks are called for concerning South African literary history after apartheid. Before the transition, major statements by literary historians called for a common, multilingual, and properly national literary history, in opposition to the balkanization of the various racial and linguistic traditions which had previously characterized literary-historical writing, a situation which embarrassingly repeated the dominant political culture. One would expect that the advent of democracy would bring about conditions more favorable to the project of establishing a common history. The most impressive recent attempt at redrawing the literary map is Michael Chapman's *Southern African Literatures* (1996), which attempts no less than a comprehensive history of all the literatures in all the major languages of the region, including those of South Africa's neighbors. And yet, Chapman's reception was controversial because, like any act of integrative cultural nationalism, it was vulnerable to charges of under-representing minority traditions. The difficulties inherent in the task are elaborated in

contributions to a collection of essays, *Rethinking South African Literary History* (1996). Among the objections to a composite history is the observation that while there has been some cross-pollination of traditions in the context of the mission school, writers in different languages have rarely listened to one another in anything like a lively sense of tradition. In other words, comparatism is bound to be superficial. Other contributors feel that a national literary history is premature when the histories of the literatures in the various African languages, and women's writing, have not yet been adequately documented. There is also a sense of ennui around the project in a critical environment in which canonicity and nationhood are increasingly in question. The irony here is that while post-apartheid historical conditions have made the prospect of a national literary history seem more real, the deeper linguistic and cultural constraints have yet to be overcome.

DAVID ATTWELL

al-A'raj, Wasini

b. 1954, Tlemcen, Algeria

novelist and short story writer

Author of at least fifteen novels, short story collections, and literary studies, all in Arabic, Wasini al-A'raj was born in Tlemcen, Algeria. He earned a PhD in Arabic literature in Damascus, Syria, writing a thesis on the Algerian novel. He has taught Arabic literature at the University of Algiers. Al-A'raj's fiction centers around the repercussions of the prolonged war of independence on Algerian society and the disappointments of the post-independence period, while emphasizing Algerian national identity. The style of his early fiction reflects the influence of classical Arabic literature, but since the late 1980s he has used a language close to the speech patterns of Algerians, mixing colloquialisms and French words with Arabic. Nevertheless, his writings continue to draw on the Arabic literary heritage in his reworking of the maqama genre and stories from the Koran and *The Thousand and One Nights*.

Further reading

Bamia, Aida (1999) "Al-A'raj, Wasini," in Steven Serafin (ed.) *Encyclopedia of World Literature in the 20th Century*, 3rd edn, Farmington Hills, Michigan: James Press.

WAÏL S. HASSAN

Armah, Ayi Kwei

b. 1939, Sekondi-Takoradi, Ghana

novelist, short story writer and essayist

The Ghanaian novelist, short story writer and essayist Ayi Kwei Armah is a pre-eminent prose stylist among his generation of postcolonial writers. A pan-African vision propels themes like self-help and regeneration in his fictional work, while his non-fiction writing is centrally concerned with the politics of interpretation and with the sociopolitical realities that impinge upon, and are in turn reflected in, literary texts.

Armah was born in 1939 at Sekondi-Takoradi. He entered Harvard in 1960 after pre-college education at Achimota and Groton. The Harvard undergraduate years yielded noteworthy developments: first, Armah's interest in what he would later describe as "the social realities buried under . . . words, images and symbols" made him change his area of study from literature to the social sciences; and, second, the interest in social studies went hand in hand with the desire to create his own works of art. Armah found himself increasingly drawn to the sociopolitical conditions that shape creativity, and he subsequently abandoned his study at Harvard in his senior year to travel to Africa and work with individuals and movements committed to creating "better social realities" in place of exploitative ones. The months out of school provided Armah with a crash course in disillusionment and hardships. He was seriously ill by the beginning of 1964, and was hospitalized initially in Algiers and later in Boston.

In his essay, "One Writer's Education," Armah recalls his hospitalization, impending return to Ghana from the US, and his resolve to "revert to writing, not indeed as the most desired creative option, but as the least parasitic option open to me." In the next three years, 1964–7, Armah would write *The Beautyful Ones Are Not Yet Born* (1968) and begin both *Fragments* (1970) and *Why Are We So Blest?* (1972) while in Ghana. In September 1967, he left Ghana to take up a job in Paris with the journal *Jeune Afrique* for a year, before going to the US to undertake graduate study at Columbia University. By the time Armah was ready to leave the US for Kenya in June 1970, he had completed his study for the Columbia MFA degree, finished writing his second novel, *Fragments*, and taught briefly at the University of Massachusetts. If the 1960s were years of shifting interests and inevitable decision-making, of idealism and disillusionment, of illness and healing, and of departures from and returns to Africa, they were also years of productivity for the scholar–writer. In addition to his first novel, Armah published several short stories ("Contact," "Yaw Manu's Charm," "An African Fable," and "The Offal Kind") and essays ("African Socialism: Utopian or Scientific," "A Mystification: African Independence Revalued," and "Fanon: The Awakener") in prominent journals such as *New African*, *The Atlantic Monthly*, *Présence Africaine*, *Harper's Magazine*, *Pan-African Journal*, and *Negro Digest*.

In August 1970 Armah moved to Tanzania, where in addition to teaching at the College of National Education he learnt Swahili (see **Swahili literature**) and completed two novels, *Two Thousand Seasons* (1973) and *The Healers* (1978). After leaving Tanzania in 1976 he taught at the universities of Lesotho and Wisconsin, and published essays occasionally in *Asemka* and *Présence Africaine* and mainly in *West Africa* on topics as diverse as the criticism of fiction, Marxism, **translation**, the Caliban complex, the **language question** in African literature, the teaching of creative writing, Ancient Egyptian hieroglyphic writing, and the so-called "Third World." In 1995 Armah's sixth novel, *Osiris Rising*, was published by Per Ankh, an African printing and publishing company based in Popenguine, Senegal, where Armah now lives.

Armah's reputation ultimately rests on his novels, which have been central in the shaping of the canon of African literature. The opening pages of *The Beautyful Ones Are Not Yet Born* introduce readers to an author who exercises the kind of control over language, imagery, and narrative pace that is breathtakingly impressive. Descriptive passages – as detailed and evocative as the ones focusing on a bus coming to a stop at dawn, the protagonist going to "the downstairs lavatory," and the escape of a corrupt politician after a coup – complement one's initial impressions and speak to the novelist's sustained brilliance; but it is also hard to miss the observation that Armah's imagery and language, like the graphic intensity of his descriptive passages, belong to a world that is putrid to the core. The "marvelous" rendering of "rottenness" is inscribed in the scene in which the bus conductor inhales the cedi's "marvelous rottenness" with "satisfying pleasure." The author derives little pleasure from using the colonizer's language to present the postcolonial viewpoint for, no matter how effectively he is using that language, it still remains a rotten choice. Armah's ambivalence is reflected in the "painful kind of understanding" that makes Teacher, one of the characters in the novel, use "words that mix ... beauty with ... ugliness, words making the darkness twin with the light." Mixing up the received connotations of words and the assumed meanings of symbols is Armah's way of naming, interrogating, and subverting familiar tropes of, and the worldview traditionally sponsored by, the language he is using. Language, then, is a function of the pervading putrescence in Armah's first novel. The hope is that "a new flowering" will emerge "out of the decay," and the novel's title suggests that this "new flowering" will correspond to the birth of the unusually "beautyful," rather than the conventionally "beautiful," ones.

Baako, the artist-protagonist in *Fragments* (1970: Boston), knows he does not want to "do the usual kind of writing," but deciding what "kind of writing" to commit himself to is anything but easy. The kind of writing Armah explores in his second novel owes its genesis to what he describes in his essay "Larsony" (*Asemka*, 1976) as "a conversation with my elder brother concerning the quality of life at home." The novel that comes out of this conversation is meticulously structured; its storyline is made to fold back on itself to reflect the inevitability of a return after departure, and narrative framing augments that important theme. The novel begins and ends with "Naana," an affectionate Akan word for an old woman, and the intervening chapters also bear Akan headings. Knowledgeable readers can also discern the cadence of the Akan mother tongue in the Naana sections, particularly in the nuanced rhetoric that accompanies the pouring of libation. It is significant to note that while the main narrative suggests that "the quality of life at home" continues to deteriorate, its frame subscribes to a different philosophy ("the larger meaning which lent sense to every small thing ... years and years ago") and points to a different way of looking at the world ("the circular way" which allows for the return of departed ones and guarantees an unbroken circle of life). Those who have lost their way because of the "great haste to consume things [they] have taken no care nor trouble to produce," face a dead end; for others, like Naana, who have not lost their way, "the whole world and the whole of life" are open to them.

Armah takes up the dead-end issue in a different but related context in *Why Are We So Blest?* and turns his full attention to the way – lost and found – in the next three novels. The phrase "why are we so blest?" is taken from an essay commemorating Thanksgiving in the USA read aloud by Mike, one of the characters in the novel, who observes that the author of the piece "didn't set out to write about the underprivileged ... It's the story as told from our point of view" (1972: New York). Stories about the underprivileged told from their point of view need to be written, but neither Modin nor Solo, the other characters in the novel, are in a position to do so. Solo's words are "impotent," and Modin finds himself in a situation that leads him to a dead end; both participate in a ritual predicated on self-annihilation. We only need to recall the Lusophone, Francophone, Anglophone and Euro-American strands in this novel to place "dead end" in its broader context. Solo has been trained in Lisbon and speaks Portuguese, among other languages; the America-educated Modin also speaks other languages, but English is his forte; and the latter's companion, Aimée, is a European-American. The three meet in nominally French-speaking Laccryville, where freedom fighters from the Portuguese colony of Congheria have opened a bureau. The meeting and its aftermath yield nothing constructive because the setting (for the meeting and for the novel) is barren, Aimée is a parasite, and Solo, like Modin, has "become a ghost" even "before [his] death." The unenviable fate of Solo and Modin could be read as replicating that of an increasing number of Africans in "great haste to consume things [they] have taken no care nor trouble to produce," but it is clearer in this case than before that production and consumption are not divorceable from arts and letters: the dead end Solo and Modin have been led to seems to have implications for "African" literatures that participate in the ritualized celebration of European traditions in European languages.

Armah invites readers of his fourth novel, *Two Thousand Seasons*, to imagine a continent with people of great promise reduced to giving up their natural, human, and intellectual resources for the enrichment of others season after season after season. He then presents an alternative vision: what if, over the seasons, a few people initially, and more people eventually, decide to take a different path toward self-recovery, toward harnessing those natural, human, and intellectual resources for the common good? In its fictional context, the question "what if?" like the invitation to imagine, calls for suspension of disbelief and opens doors to potentially limitless possibilities in the novel's reconstruction of the past. The scope of the reconstructed past that stretches back to "origins" is epical; the language that serves the purpose of epic reconstruction ebbs and flows like the "unending stream of ... remembrance" it lets loose. In *Two Thousand Seasons*, and later in *Osiris Rising*, Armah sketches on his own narrative canvas the import of Langston Hughes' pregnant declarations: "I have known rivers ancient as the world ... /I looked upon the Nile and raised the pyramids above it."

Classical Akan storytelling tradition provides the template for Armah's account of the fall of Kumasi to British forces led by Garnet Wolseley in *The Healers*. In consonance with the template, the Akan mother tongue that appears briefly in *Fragments* is reformulated and pulled to the narrative core of the historical novel as the "tongue of the storyteller, descendant of masters in the arts of eloquence." Significantly, the motif of departures and returns that has been central to Armah's work since the second novel is echoed at the end of *The Healers* when the healer-woman observes that the whites who "wish to drive us apart" are in fact "bring[ing] our people together again." Ast's return to her ancestral home in *Osiris Rising* continues and revises this trend. In preparing herself adequately for her journey, Ast gets much more active support from her grandmother Nwt than Naana could offer Baako in *Fragments*. Ast still has to deal with formidable obstacles in her journey, but it turns out to be a propitious journey that bridges old and new ways in the never-ending quest to create life-affirming worlds and realities. By drawing both thematic material and narrative structure from the Isis–Osiris myth for his sixth novel, Armah adds depth as well as contemporary resonance to the word "old" in "old and new ways." In the process he challenges his readers to re-examine terms like "exile," "home," "influence," the "oral" and the "written" in the context of old and new African literatures; he insists that the "language problem" demands immediate and continuing attention from writers, translators, and policy-makers; and he believes that African writers and their work deserve informed criticism of lasting value. His novels, short stories, and essays make him as important a writer as any to the past, present, and future of African literatures.

Select bibliography

Armah, A.K. (1970) *Fragments*, Boston: Houghton Mifflin.
——(1972) *Why Are We So Blest?*, New York: Doubleday.
——(1976) "Larsony or Fiction as Criticism of Fiction," *Asemka: A Bilingual Literary Journal of the University of the Cape Coast*, 4: 1–14.
——(1995) *Osiris Rising*, Popenguine, Senegal: Per Ankh.

KOFI OWUSU

Arriz Tamza, Maya

b. 1957, Berber region, Algeria

storyteller, novelist and playwright

Maya Arriz Tamza (pseudonym of Saoud Bousselmania) was born in the Berber region of Algeria. For Arriz, the contradiction of an identity that is at once Berber (the people seen as autochthonous to North Africa) and Algerian manifests itself in his chosen pseudonym, which refers to the Tamza (Berber) region of northwest Algeria. Inveterate storyteller, novelist, and playwright, Arriz is known equally for his literary production as he is for his work at the 7 Candles Theater (of which he is the co-founder) in Maubourget, France. Among the diverse works of his oeuvre is *Le Soupir du Maure* (The Moor's Sigh) (2001), a play that is memorable for its depiction of the fall of the last Moorish kingdom in Europe or, as Arriz explains in the prefatory note, the last kingdom to unite the Orient and the Occident. Coinciding with the discovery of America in 1492, the demise of the kingdom marks, for Arriz, the end of peaceful coexistence between Arab, Jewish, Berber, and Christian peoples.

NEIL DOSHI

art

From ancient rock paintings and Nok sculptures to contemporary political paintings, the visual arts have exercised an important influence on African modes of self-representation and on how the peoples of the continent have been perceived by outsiders. Art is considered to be an important component of both the unity and the distinctiveness of African cultures, touching as much on how individuals relate to aesthetic questions and ideas such as beauty and sensibility, and on how nations and communities are identified as collective entities. In African social history, works of art have been the most powerful signifiers of collective cultural, or "tribal" affiliation, and different African groups have come to be associated with their most prominent forms of visual art. Thus, it is hard to think of the Asante without the images of their delicate gold figures or the Fang and Senufo without their evocative mask figures. Representation of artistic forms such as masks in writing are often used to explore African mentalities, cosmologies, and essential identities or to frame debates on the value of culture. For writers such as Wole

Soyinka, or filmmakers like Ousmane **Sembene**, visual art has been the basis of a rethinking of the black aesthetic and the politics of representation.

Some of the central ideas in artistic movements such as **negritude** were derived from the visual arts, and this influence is apparent in the poetry and poetics of the major writers in this tradition, most notably Léopold Sédar **Senghor**. Discussions about the nature of African art were also crucial in the formulation of the idea of the New Negro in the Harlem Renaissance. But the influence of African art has been perhaps most remarkable in the constitution of the African diaspora where art forms brought across the Atlantic by slaves have survived, albeit in modified forms, as insignias and organizing principles of black life in the new world. From the early modern period to the present, African art has been an important mediator between the continent, the African diaspora, and the global community, and artistic treasures from Africa, many of them looted through the process of colonial conquest, adorn major European museums. Afro-Portuguese ivory figures from the early modern period, for example, are some of the most remarkable examples of the artistic exchange between Africans and their European invaders; the discovery of African masks by modern painters such as Picasso was to change the nature of art; more recently, African art has been crucial in the transformation of notions of globalization and connoisseurship. In Africa itself, both ancient and popular art has come to function as a register of debates about history, memory, and selfhood.

Further reading

Fabian, J. (1996) *Remembering the Present: Painting and Popular History in Zaire*, Berkeley, California: University of California Press.

Roberts, M.N. and Roberts, A.F. (eds) (1996) *Memory: Luba Art and the Making of History*, New York: Museum for African Art.

Thompson, R.B. (1984) *Flash of the Spirit: African and Afro-American Art and Philosophy*, New York: Vintage.

SIMON GIKANDI

Aseffa Gebre-Mariyam Tesemma (Assefa G.M.T.)

b. 1935, Ethiopia

poet

Aseffa Gebre-Mariyam Tesemma is best known as the author of Ethiopia's national anthem. He attended church, mission, and government schools, and joined the Ministry of Education, where he became associated with radical reformers. After teaching in Ethiopia, he was sent to the Soviet Union, teaching Amharic at Leningrad University, where he also studied Russian. Meanwhile he wrote many poems, which were published only after the 1974 revolution. At Addis Ababa University he obtained a BA in 1970, and for a short time he studied in Edinburgh. In 1975, he translated Gogol's *The Inspector General*, which was produced at the National Theater, and wrote the new Ethiopian national anthem. Noteworthy was his work for the Academy of Ethiopian Languages, which published poetry in Ethiopic, language dictionaries, etc. In 1979, he published a collection of poems called *Yemeskerem Chorra* (Rays of September), and the year after a collection of poems in English, *The Voice*. These and other poems have had wide appeal. Around the turn of the twenty-first century, he migrated to the United States.

Further reading

Molvaer, R.K. (1997) *Black Lions*, Lawrenceville, New Jersey: Red Sea Press.

REIDULF MOLVAER

'Ashour, Radwa

b. 1946, Cairo, Egypt

short story writer and academic

A rising star amongst the growing numbers of women writers in the Arab world and North Africa, Radwa 'Ashour was born in Cairo, Egypt in 1946 to a middle-class family. After graduating from Cairo University with a BA in English literature (1967), she proceeded to obtain her doctorate in Afro-American literature from the University of Massachusetts in 1975. She was then appointed as a faculty member in the Department of English Literature at Ain Shams University, in Cairo. She proceeded to have a successful academic career while experimenting with fiction writing. She is also a respected critic of Arabic literature, with an emphasis on Palestinian literature, an understandable interest in light of her marriage to the Palestinian poet Mu'en Barghouti. She has also introduced the Arab reader to writings from West Africa. Radwa 'Ashour's earliest novel *al-Rihla*, published in 1983, was an account/memoir of her graduate student experience in the United States; it is a welcome addition to the growing library of memoir writings. This budding author proceeded systematically to add to her repertoire, balancing her academic career with her life as an author of stature. Her 1985 novel *Hajjar Dafi* (A Warm Stone) was followed in 1989 by *Khadija war-Sawsan* (Khadija and Sawsan).

In 1992 she produced *Siraj*. But it is her trilogy *Gharnata* (Granada) (1994) which has won her great acclaim. *Mariama war-Raheel* (Mariama and the Departure) (1995) won her the best literary prize during the first Arab Women's Book Fair, held in Cairo in 1995. The trilogy is a historical work which spans over a century (1492–1609) in al-Bayazin in Granada during the Arab presence in Andalusia. This monumental work traces the lives of members of the family of a bookbinder, Abu Jaafar, over four generations. Through the lives of these generations, the author painstakingly documents the traumatic uprooting of the Arab presence in Andalusia. The shock to the Arab psyche and ethos is meticulously and perceptively narrated. The poignant last days of the glorious Arab presence are seen not so much through famous rulers but rather through the lives of simple people as custodians of the Arab identity and dreams.

As a literary critic, Radwa 'Ashour is well aware of the narrative techniques which she cleverly deploys in her work. She succeeds in exploiting the linguistic potentialities of the language and at times moves us into poetic spaces. Her novels also revisit history from a philosophical perspective. The well-respected Egyptian critic Ali al Ra'i acclaimed the trilogy as a work that succeeded "in bringing historic truth in a vibrant reality." She has indeed succeeded in creating vivid personas in Abu Ja'ffar, Saad, and Salima, among many others.

In an important interview in *al-Ahram Weekly* (23–9 November 1995) the author introduces us to the workings of her inner mind and perhaps to those of several writers of her generation; Radwa 'Ashour states,

> The exceptional alertness to time and place and the need to record are characteristics common to all writers of my generation. The major formative influence of 1967 has often been pointed out. The events which preceded the June [1967] defeat of the Arabs as well as the subsequent failures made us particularly conscious that history was not only out there in books and records of the past, but is a living experience of everyday life. Great wars, great expectations, heavy losses, defeats, traumatic changes, fractures and dislocations and the constant insecurity of a human will negated and of subjects acted upon rather than acting ... [are events that shaped our generation]. Of my four published novels, two are set in the past. But I do not consider the two set in present-day Cairo less historical. Whether the locale is early sixteenth-century Granada or an imaginary island off the African coast or present-day Cairo, history is always there – a pervading presence hovering like a silent shadow through the text, on its margins or behind it.

Some of her work has appeared in English translation in *My Grandmother's Cactus* (1993), notably "Safsafa," "The General," and "I Saw the Date Palms." In 1999 she wrote *Aflyāf* (Phantasm), which was highly acclaimed by the critics.

Further reading

Ghazoul, Ferial J. and Harlow, Barbara (eds) (1994) *The View from Within: Writers and Critics on Contemporary Arabic Literature*, Cairo: American University in Cairo Press.

MONA N. MIKHAIL

Aşlān, Ibrāhīm

b. 1939, Tanta, Egypt

novelist

Ibrāhīm Aşlān, an Egyptian novelist and short story writer, was born in Tanta, and then moved to Cairo at the age of 8. He published his first short stories in *al-Majallah* and *Ḥiwār*, literary journals of the early 1960s. In lucid language, Aşlān's fiction explores the psychological impact of everyday life, emphasizing the passage of time on the ordinary people, while foregrounding the intellectual's estrangement in Egypt. His first collection of short stories, *Buḥayrat al-Masā'* (The Pond of Evening) (1967), captivated critics with its painstaking structure and subtle nuances. His first novel, *Mālik al-Ḥazīn* (The Heron) (1983), brought him indelible literary fame. It is a complex and condensed work in which he scrutinizes the lives of numerous characters inhabiting a relatively secluded poor neighborhood. The novel illuminates the shifting economic and political conditions from Nasser's reign to that of Sādāt. In an extraordinarily detailed description, *Wardiyyat Lail* (The Graveyard Shift) (1992) characterizes the constant movement of telegram employees from the post office to the streets at night. People's anxiety and loneliness grow as they see intimacies of the past diminish. *ʿAṣāfīr al-Nīl* (The Sparrows of the Nile) (1999) philosophically contemplates the meaning of death.

Further reading

Al-ʿĀlim, Maḥmud Amīn (1994) *al-Bunyah wa al-Dalālah fī al-qiṣṣah wa al-Riwāyah al-ʿArabiyyah al-Muʿāṣirah* (Structure and Meaning in the Contemporary Arabic Short Story and Novel), Cairo: Dār al-Mustaqbal al-ʿArabī.

KHALED AL MASRI

Aslan, Mahmoud

b. 1898, Tunis, Tunisia; d. in the 1970s

novelist

The Tunisian writer Mahmoud Aslan, like his

compatriot Tahar **Essafi**, was an active participant in literary life during the French Protectorate
of Tunisia (1881–1956) producing novels, short
stories, and plays, founding the journal *Tunis
littéraire et artistique* and the weekly newspaper
devoted to Franco-Muslim understanding *Le Petit
Tunisois*, and playing a key role in the Society of
North African Writers and its journal *La Kahéna*.
Sympathetic to French culture and civilization, his
work primarily tackles the idea of a union between
East and West and argues for the possibility of a
Franco-Muslim identity. The play *Entre deux mondes*
(Between Two Worlds) (1932) and the novel *Les
Yeux noirs de Leila* (The Black Eyes of Leila) (1940)
both address issues of identity in French Protecto-
rate Tunisia through the possibilities and problems
of Tunisian–French marriages. His other works,
such as the short stories *Scènes de la vie du Bled*
(Scenes from Life in the Bled) (1932) and *Contes du
vendredi* (Tales from Friday) (1954), are concerned
with the description of local life and customs in
Tunisia from the author's childhood and are often
full of ethnographic details.

Further reading

Aslan, Mahmoud (1932) *Entre deux mondes* (Between
    Two Worlds), Tunis: La Kahéna.

KATARZYNA PIEPRZAK

Assaad, Fawzia

b. 1929, Cairo, Egypt

novelist

A Francophone Egyptian writer, Assaad was born
in Cairo. She was educated in French schools and
went to Paris for further studies, where she
obtained a doctorate in philosophy, and wrote a
book on Kierkegaard in Arabic and a study in
French on Nietzsche in Egypt. She taught for
several years in Egyptian universities before moving to Switzerland. She became well known in
literary circles with the publication, in 1975, of her
largely autobiographical novel, *L'Égyptienne* (The
Egyptian), which depicts the impact of the 1952
Egyptian revolution and the subsequent wars with

Israel on the life of an Egyptian Coptic woman. In
the process of narrating the woman's story, the
author delves into family relations among the
Coptic Christians of Egypt and their rites of
passage, including birth, marriage, and death. In
her novel *L'Égyptienne*, Assaad expresses an Egyptian nationalist point of view and finds the
liberation from British hegemony one of the
significant features of the revolution. The presentation of events in the novel is free from an explicit
ideological stance and the narration unfolds in a
conventional way. The mixing of strands from the
author's personal life with imaginative characters
often based on real political and social figures,
commonly known as "autofiction," is popular in
Egypt and particularly among women writers.
Other novels by Assaad, *Des enfants et des chats*
(Children and Cats) (1987) and *La Grand Maison de
Louxor* (The Great House of Luxor) (1992), are
informed by ancient Egyptian history and mythology.

Further reading

Assaad, Fawzia (1975) *L'Égyptienne* (The Egyptian),
    Paris: Mercure de France.

FERIAL J. GHAZOUL

At-Tawfīq, Ahmād

b. 1943, Marigha, Morocco

historian and novelist

A historian by formation, at-Tawfīq is also a
novelist. He was born in Marigha, a village in the
High Atlas mountains, near Marrakesh. He taught
history at the University of Rabat till 1976 and in
1989 he was appointed director of the Institute of
African Studies. In 1995 he became the director of
the public library in Rabat.

His first three novels, *Jārāt Abī Mūsā* (Abi Musa's
Neighbors) (1997), *Shujayrat Hinnā' wa Qamar*
(Henna Shrubs and a Moon) (1998), and *As-Sayl*
(The Flood) (1998), provide a panoramic view of
Moroccan country life. Though primarily con-
cerned with a message of coexistence between
Arabs and Berbers, at-Tawfīq fills his novels with

the traditions of his Berber culture, manipulating them in significant metaphors, as observed in *Shujayrat Hinnā' wa Qamar.* There, the moon and the henna tree represent the diversity of the Moroccan society. His female characters are strong women who rescue men and other victims of society's customs and traditions. This positive portrayal reveals the author's respect for Moroccan women, and familiarity with their circles, a knowledge derived from a childhood spent in the company of the family women. With *Gharībat al-Husayn* (The Stranger of al-Husayn) (2000), at-Tawfīq directs his attention to the period of national struggle for independence from France, parallel to a love story between a Moroccan man and a French woman. The title of the novel refers to an Andalusian musical form.

At-Tawfīq's attachment to his country's traditional culture is reflected in the abundance of folk poems quoted in his novels. Moreover, his books provide a valuable insight into the world of Moroccan magic and Sufi practices.

Further reading

Bamia, Aida A. (2001) "Arabic Literature," *Book of the Year, Encyclopedia Britannica*, Chicago: Encyclopedia Britannica.

AIDA A. BAMIA

autobiography

Introduction

Autobiography is one of the most important and controversial genres in the history of African literature. Even before the emergence of modern writing on the continent, autobiography or related forms of life histories and narratives were crucial to different African cultures. Arabic literature, for example, has a long history of autobiography, usually accounts of the careers of mystics and religious leaders, dating to the medieval period. Many Arabic medieval autobiographies started as oral performances (see **oral literature and performance**), which were later transcribed into written texts. Often, these texts would be an amalgam of accounts of the lives of distinguished persons, religious commentaries, and accounts of travel, but, unlike later autobiographies in the Arabic tradition, they were not concerned with the inner or private lives of their subjects. Early African writers in the European languages were also concerned with the production of narratives in which they could turn their own experiences into a commentary on the status of the African in the period of enslavement and colonialism (see **colonialism, neocolonialism, and postcolonialism**). Slave narratives were perhaps some of the first autobiographical narratives by Africans in the modern period. In this category belong classic works such as Olaudah Equiano's *The Interesting Narrative of the Life of Olaudah Equiano or Gustavus Vassa the African* (1789).

For many years it was assumed that there were no autobiographical narratives in the many oral cultures of the continent, but recent research has called attention to the existence of indigenous traditions of life narratives, including the *taasu* form among the Wolof of Senegal and the *oriki* tradition among the Yoruba. These forms are both integral to oral cultures and central to representing forms of identity, and it is surprising that it has taken a long time for scholars to recognize the autobiographical dimension of modes of representation that don't seem to conform to autobiography as it has traditionally been defined in the European tradition.

The focus on the autobiographical factor in oral narratives and performances has extended our understanding of the genre itself. This is an important development because one of the reasons why autobiography has been a controversial genre on the continent is that, in spite of its popularity among writers, scholars, and politicians, it has tended to be defined in relation to the genre as it has emerged and developed in relation to European literature. The most dominant theoretical studies of autobiography have often called attention to the development of the genre at a certain period in Western culture, expressing the peculiar concerns of European culture and structured by a concern with individuals often at odds with their communities. Very little attention has been paid to the role of autobiography as one of the forms in which individuals seek to identify with communities from which they have been alienated by their education or experience, which has often been the case in Africa.

Since the publication of the major studies on African autobiography in the 1970s, most notably James Olney's *Tell Me Africa* (1973), critics have made the assumption that the uniqueness of African autobiography is predicated on its attempt to reconcile a structure that privileges the individual subject with collective identities. At the end of the twentieth century, however, especially under the influence of poststructuralist theories of cultural production and narrative, the dichotomy between individual and collective identity, and indeed between European and African modes of representing selfhood, has been questioned. In addition, instead of presenting African autobiographical writings as part of a unified genre, critics and literary historians have turned their attention to specific traditions, such as women's life narratives, which question some of the established notions about autobiography on the continent. This new thread is reflected in critical works on African autobiography published in the 1990s, most notably the essays collected in special issues of *Itinéraires et contacts de cultures* (1991) and *Research in African Literatures* (1997), and Lisa McNee's pioneering study, *Selfish Gifts: Senegalese Women's Autobiographical Discourses* (2000).

The uses of autobiography

In spite of the surrounding debates and disputes, autobiographical discourses have been central in the making of an African literary tradition and constitute one of the major bridges between creative writing and other modes of cultural production on the continent. Indeed, many African writers of fiction such as Bernard **Dadié**, Wole **Soyinka**, and Es'kia **Mphahlele** have turned to autobiography in order either to respond to specific moments of crisis in their lives or to reflect on the process by which they came to writing. Often, novelists have seen autobiography as the ideal form for linking very personal experiences to the collective stories of Africans in both the colonial and the postcolonial period. While the most prominent autobiographies from Africa are the works of popular literary or political figures writing in the second half of the twentieth century, the

genre has had a long history in the life of cultural production on the continent. During the period of slavery and early colonialism in the eighteenth and nineteenth centuries, African writers turned to autobiographical writing as a medium for affirming their identities as human beings. One of the arguments used to justify the enslavement of black Africans, for example, was that they were incapable of rational thought; the ostensible lack of a written literature was presented as evidence of this failure. In response, former African slaves started writing to affirm their rational subjectivity and to provide testimonies about the cultures from which they had been torn by enslavement.

In the face of the processes of radical social change engendered by colonialism, especially in the nineteenth century, African writers turned to autobiography as a way of mediating their location and dislocation between precolonial and colonial cultures and as a way of making sense of the forces of change. At the turn of the nineteenth century and for most of the early twentieth century, autobiography and related genres such as memoirs and testimonies were important vehicles in the struggle against colonialism and the promotion of pan-Africanism and other discourse of black identity. Autobiography has also been connected to other issues central to African literature and culture in the modern period. For example, narratives about the self have often charted the process by which Africans were inducted into colonial culture and there are countless testimonies on the alienation that was generated by colonial education and modernity (see **education and schools**; **modernity and modernism**). In situations of racial or political oppression, such as apartheid in South Africa (see **apartheid and post-apartheid**) or postcolonial dictatorship in many countries on the continent, many writers, especially imprisoned ones, would turn to their own experiences to speak against the culture of oppression and silence.

While colonialism provided the most prominent context and subject for African autobiography, the genre was also affected by the struggle against colonialism; indeed, some of the most prominent autobiographies on the continent were written by leading nationalists who sought to use examples drawn from their own lives and experiences to indict colonialism itself. After decolonization, autobiography continued to be an important aspect of bearing witness to the crisis of decolonization in Africa. Given the number of autobiographies produced on the continent in the last hundred years, it is difficult to list or categorize even the major texts in this tradition. A more accessible way of thinking about the hundreds of autobiographical texts that have been produced on the continent in over two centuries of writing is to think about the key themes in this tradition and some representative texts.

Autobiography and cultural nationalism

Perhaps one of the most enduring aspects of African autobiography in the modern period has been its preoccupations with questions of cultural nationalism (see **nationalism and post-nationalism**) – the evocation of the values of a precolonial African world as a counter to the alienating forces of colonial modernity. There is a strong tradition of autobiography, especially in the period after World War II, when African writers believed that their own personal experiences could be transformed into collective testimony. Writing in this tradition falls into two broad categories: what Olney has called ethnographic autobiography and the political memoir. In the former category, which includes such famous works as Jomo Kenyatta's *Facing Mount Kenya* (1938) and Benjamin Akiga's *Akiga's Story* (1939), the authors are not concerned with the development of their own personalities; in fact, many of them try to sublimate their own individual stories in order to celebrate their cultures, which they see as collective and organic units. While they are valued as autobiographies, texts such as *Facing Mount Kenya* and *Akiga's Story* can be read as autobiographies of cultural groups, the Gikuyu (see **Gikuyu literature**) and the Tiv respectively.

The emphasis on the unified collective experience in these works is, however, part of a larger ethnographic and political design: the authors seek to use ethnography, a discipline associated with colonialism, to counter the image of Africa as uncultured and uncivilized in colonial discourse and to question specific cultural and political policies of the colonial government. In Kenyatta's

work, for example, the author sets out to show that the Gikuyu had a powerful and viable precolonial culture, one governed by specific rules and practices. Against the claim by colonial officials and missionaries that customs such as female "circumcision" are barbaric, Kenyatta tries to argue that they are an integral part of the history and culture of his people, that they are driven by a well-thought-out logic, and are hence not irrational practices. An important aspect of works like these is their insistence on the value and integrity of a precolonial polity and the insistence on its rationality, almost its equivalence to Western culture itself. Often relativist in tone, ethnographical autobiographies are at once assertions of African cultural pride and a plea to the colonizers not to impose their own standards on the African world.

In spite of their preoccupation with precolonial society, however, ethnographic autobiographies were written against the background of colonial rule in Africa and thus function under what we may call the anxiety of the institutions of colonialism, including colonial education and Christianity (see **Christianity and Christian missions**). This anxiety, which is evident in works such as Damien d'Almeida's *Le Jumeau; ou mon enfance à Agoué* (The Twin; or My Childhood in Agoué) (1966) or Bonnu Ojike's *My Africa* (1946), emerges from the authors' consciousness of their location between two worlds – what they consider to be a vanishing precolonial culture and the more powerful universe dominated by colonial institutions. While these works set out to provide ethnographic details about a specific African culture, they derive their power from their authors' narration of their own encounters with both the vanishing precolonial world and colonial modernity, which they conceive as representative of their generation. And while these works adopt a rhetoric strategy demanding of empathy and understanding – they are pleas to Western readers to understand the cultural dislocation of the new African – they are also powerful testimonies on the process of change that has brought about this state of cultural alienation.

In many instances, ethnographic autobiographies are written as specific interventions into colonial debates on some of the prominent issues of the day. Written at a time when African nationalists and the colonial government were involved in a heated battle of words over policies of land tenure, Kenyatta's *Facing Mount Kenya* foregrounds the question of land which it simultaneously represents as the material foundation of Gikuyu culture and the source of the crisis that has generated nationalism. What makes these ethnographic narratives autobiographical is their authors' insistence that they are witnesses to powerful cultural processes, that what makes their knowledge authoritative when compared to the works of European ethnographers is that it is based on their inside knowledge and experience of the culture being represented.

A second form of political autobiography is one that emerged in Africa in the last years of colonial rule when triumphant nationalists produced stories of their own lives as one way of charting the journey that had culminated, or was about to culminate, in independence. The list of works in this category is too long to enumerate here, but it is safe to say that almost all the so-called founding fathers of African nations produced autobiographies in the last years of colonialism or after their countries became independent. Some of the most prominent works in this category include Obafemi Awolowo's *Awo: The Autobiography of Chief Obafemi Awolowo* (1960), Nnamdi Azikiwe's *My Odyssey: An Autobiography* (1970), Kenneth Kaunda's *Zambia Shall Be Free: An Autobiography* (1962), and Kwame Nkrumah's *Ghana: The Autobiography of Kwame Nkrumah* (1957). Like many other works in this tradition, these autobiographies or memoirs were written by subjects who had chosen to play a public role in the theater of colonialism looking back on what they considered to be their own constitution in relation to the nations that they were (in their minds) destined to lead. Unlike ethnographic narratives, the political memoirs were not concerned with detailed representations of a particular culture or ethnic group; rather they were focused on the making of the politician who was cast as the figure of an awakening nationalism.

One of the paradoxes of these works is that they celebrate the life of an individual, such as Kwame Nkrumah, who is in turn transformed into the representative figure of the new nation. And since the new nation does not exist as an ethnographic entity, its traditions are invented through the narration of the nationalist's life. In a sense, this kind of autobiography, like other narratives designed to imagine the nation, becomes what Benedict Anderson calls, in *Imagined Communities* (1991), a simultaneous act of remembering and forgetting: specific experiences under colonialism are powerfully evoked but ethnicities are repressed so that the new nation can be exhibited as the product of the author's drive to harmonize a diverse set of interests into a unified national body. Thus Nkrumah's autobiography provides few details of his Ani culture, but it is a memorable testimonial on the constitutive power of the colonial school and its institutions, cultural nationalism, and ideologies of pan-Africanism. Nkrumah represents himself as the figure that brings these forces together to forge a modern national consciousness.

The moment of decolonization in Africa thus leads to the production of a certain kind of political memoir which, in both its structure and its ideological claims, seeks to affirm the role of the unique nationalist, the representative man, and, in the process, to overcome the distinction between the private and the public by affirming the life experiences of the nationalist subject as symmetrical to that of the nation. In calling his autobiography *Ghana*, Kwame Nkrumah was not in doubt that his life, from his colonial childhood at Cape Coast and his education at the mission school at Achimota to Lincoln University, the University of Pennsylvania, and his subsequent entry into politics, paralleled the modern history of the country he founded. An interesting dialectic, then, comes to characterize the emplotment of the writing self, and, by implication, the nationalist narrative: the nation provides the framework within which the story of the private self is plotted; the private self in turn provides the empathy that endows the narrative of nationalism with its moral authority. When Kenneth Kaunda called his memoir, *Zambia Shall Be Free*, he was taking it for granted that what might otherwise be considered a unique and unusual life was really a typological representation of the nation he was to lead to independence.

Apartheid, imprisonment, and autobiography

Some of the most powerful forms of autobiography in Africa have emerged out of adverse political and social conditions, especially the ones in which authors were imprisoned or silenced by banning orders. In South Africa, for example, the policies of racial segregation practiced by the colonial government, which were to culminate in the establishment of the apartheid state in 1948, generated a literature of resistance that assumed an autobiographical form. One of the earliest works in this tradition was Sol **Plaatje**'s *Native Life in South Africa* (1916), a first-hand account of the social dislocation and economic hardships triggered by the Native Lands Act of 1911, which effectively deprived blacks of most of their land. Influenced by W.E.B. DuBois' *The Souls of Black Folks*, Plaatje's book was both a detailed account of scenes of black poverty and abjection and also an allegory on the unmooring of Africans from their ancestral landscapes.

Once apartheid and racial separation had become an official policy of the state, black South Africans turned to autobiography as one of the forms they could use to bear witness to their personal and collective humiliation and their determination to create alternative centers of culture and selfhood. One of the great ironies of literary history in Africa is that some of the most powerful autobiographies were written to resist official doctrines that sought to represent blacks as second-class citizens. Autobiography became popular in South Africa precisely because it foregrounds those areas of the self and culture that the state sought to contain or repress. One of the earliest uses of autobiography as part of a cultural strategy against racism in South Africa was Peter **Abrahams**' *Tell Freedom* (1954), a work that was to spell out, in its overt thematic concerns and its form, the strategic connection between the writing of the self and the politics of protest.

Although Abrahams' book was written after he had left South Africa, it foregrounded three of the areas in which autobiography would become central to the cultural politics of southern Africa. First, in telling the complicated story of his racial origins and his struggle to find a place in South Africa as one who had been defined as a colored,

Abrahams was presenting a prima-facie case against the rigid racial doctrines that had become a marked feature of politics in his country. His autobiography called attention to the racial and cultural hybridity which was, contrary to emerging policy, a feature of South African society. Second, Abrahams pegged his mapping of identity on the acquisition of education and in so doing he sought to transcend the limits placed on him as a colored. It was through the education of the self, especially a literary education, that he sought to break out of the confines of class, race, and caste. Third, Abrahams' autobiography was primarily the story of how he became a writer and he posited the mastery of writing, and literary culture in general, as one of the means in which he had discovered his true identity and expanded his horizons.

These issues were to be repeated in other famous autobiographies from South Africa, including Es'kia Mphahlele's *Down Second Avenue* (1959) and Bloke **Modisane**'s *Blame Me On History* (1963). Written inside South Africa at one of the most repressive moments in the country's history, a period characterized by the imposition of the Bantu Education Act and the wholesale destruction of multiracial communities such as Sophiatown, these works no longer had the lyrical or optimistic tone of Abrahams' pioneering work. They were still invested in the mapping of identity, the process of education, and the making of writers, but they expressed rage and despair at a system that responded with banning orders and enforced exile. Autobiography in South Africa was to be supplanted by other genres in the 1970s, but well into the last years of apartheid, new works, most notably Ellen **Kuzwayo**'s *Call Me Woman* (1985) and Don Mattera's *Sophiatown: Coming of Age in South Africa* (1987), were providing compelling retrospective narratives of how different subjects and communities had responded to the tragedy of apartheid. A surprising legacy of the autobiographies of apartheid was the impact they were to have in postcolonial African societies, especially among imprisoned writers who saw them as models of how to resist the culture of silence. This influence is most palpable in the prison memoirs of Wole Soyinka (*The Man Died*) (1972) and Ngugi wa Thiong'o (*Detained*) (1981), and perhaps less obviously in

Nawal el-Saadawi's *Memoirs from the Women's Prison* (*Mudhakkirati fi sijn alnisa*) (1982).

Autobiography, education, and literary culture

One of the reasons why autobiography has been such a prominent feature of African literature is because of its engagement with questions of education and literacy, which have been crucial in the making of modern culture on the continent. Many of the traditions of autobiography discussed above were concerned with the question of education from three perspectives. First, the autobiographies of cultural nationalism were written by people whose claim to be the representatives and representers of their culture depended not simply on their knowledge of ethnographic practices, but also their education in the Western tradition. Nationalist autobiographers posited themselves as native informants; in this role, their authority was predicated on their education in colonial institutions. Second, especially in regard to the autobiographies produced to resist apartheid, education was one of the major battlegrounds on which the politics of race and identity were contested and, at the same time, one of the key ingredients in the subject's struggle to assert their identity and to break out of the prisonhouse of racial discrimination. Third, autobiography would come to function, as it does in Wole Soyinka's *Ake: The Years of Childhood* (1981), as an indirect celebration of the process of education and the cultivation of a literary sensibility. In all these cases, autobiographers assumed they had come to their true identity, even when this was a troubled identity, through the process of education.

The education of the self as the condition of the possibility of writing is apparent in many canonical works of modern African literature, which have a strong autobiographical content. Indeed, some of the most prominent works in this tradition, Camara **Laye**'s *Dark Child* (*L'Enfant noir*) (1953), Assia **Djebar**'s *Fantasia, an Algerian Cavalcade* (*L'Amour, la fantasia*) (1985), and Mariama **Bâ**'s epistolary novel *So Long a Letter* (*Une si longue lettre*) (1979), often blur the line between autobiography and fiction. Critics have often noted that it is sometimes difficult to draw the line between the fictional and the autobiographical in these works, and it is perhaps in this sense that African autobiographical texts have transformed the genre of life writing.

Finally, a major transformation of the genre and the institution of literary culture that it has enabled is apparent in the emergence of women's autobiographies, especially in the 1980s and 1990s. If African autobiographies are dominated by the site of the school as the place where the self is either torn away from traditional culture or is liberated from its strictures, it is in the women's autobiographies that flowered in the last two decades of the twentieth century that the ambiguity of education and literacy – and indeed the genre of autobiography itself – have been explored at their fullest. During this period, the publication of autobiographies by leading women writers, including Nafissatou **Diallo**, Ken **Bugul**, and Kesso **Barry**, have challenged the connection between public events and private experiences that had defined African autobiography for almost fifty years. Confronted by these new works, critics have been forced to question the relations between the private and the public in autobiographical narratives and to pay greater attention to both resist and redefine the conventions of the genre.

Further reading

Anderson, Benedict (1991) *Imagined Communities: Reflections on the Origin and Spread of Nationalism*, London: Verso.

Geesey, Patricia (1997) *Autobiography and African Literature*, special issue of *Research in African Literatures* 28, 2.

Kilpatrick, H. (1991) "Autobiography and Classical Arabic Literature," *Journal of Arabic Literature* 22: 1–20.

McNee, Lisa (2000) *Selfish Gifts: Senegalese Women's Autobiographical Discourses*, Albany, New York: State University of New York Press.

Mouralis, Bernard (ed.) (1991) *Autobiographies et récits de vie en Afrique* (Autobiographies and Life Accounts in Africa), special issue of *Itinéraires et contacts de cultures*, 13, 1.

Olney, James (1973) *Tell Me Africa: An Approach to African Literature*, Princeton: Princeton University Press.

SIMON GIKANDI

Avila Laurel, Juan-Tomás

b. 1966, Equatorial Guinea

novelist and editor

Juan-Tomás Avila Laurel is a member of the "new" Equatorial-Guinean literature movement, a generation of young authors whose first texts began to appear in the 1990s. Avila Laurel has explored different genres such as poetry, short story, and novel. He is considered one of the leading representatives of what has been called "New Guinean lyricism." *Poemas* (Poems) (1994), his first book, is an anthology of poetry in which he reflects on the immediate postcolonial reality in Equatorial Guinea. He has also published a collection of short stories, *Rusia se va a Asamse* (Rusia is Going to Asamse) (1999), a novel, *La carga* (The Burden), published in Valencia, Spain (2000), and a historical essay on the situation of colonialism, *El derecho de pernada* (The Right of Pernada) (2000). Avila Laurel is the editor of *El Patio*, a cultural journal published by Centro Hispano-Guineano in Malabo, Equatorial Guinea, where he resides.

Further reading

Avila Laurel, Juan-Tomás (1994), *Poemas* (Poems), Malabo: Ediciones del Centro Cultural Hispano Guineano.

——(1999) *La carga* (The Burden), Valencia: Palmart Editorial.

——(2000) *El derecho de pernada* (The Right of Pernada), Malabo: Ediciones Pángola.

M'BARE NGOM

Awoonor, Kofi

b. 1935, Wheta, Ghana

poet and novelist

Previously published as George Awoonor-Williams, the Ghanaian poet and novelist Kofi Awoonor was born in a Ewe family in Wheta and was educated at Achimota School and the University of Ghana. He also studied at University College London and later in the United States. As the editor of *Okyeame* he was involved in the discovery of new poets in Ghana in the early 1960s and he was also an influential figure in the government of Kwame Nkrumah, serving at one time as the director of the Ghanaian Film Corporation. Awoonor has also been a researcher into vernacular Ghanaian poetry and many of his early poems, collected in *Rediscovery and Other Poems* (1964) and *Night of My Blood* (1971) and major anthologies of African poetry such as Gerald Moore and Ulli Beier's *Modern Poetry from Africa* (1963) and Wole Soyinka's *Poems of Black Africa* (1965), are renowned for their application of the imagery and rhythms of Ewe oral forms, especially the dirge, to contemporary concerns. Awoonor's first novel, *This Earth My Brother* (1971), reflects the thematic and formal concerns associated with the novel of disenchantment in Africa and uses techniques borrowed from modernism, especially the interior monologue, to represent the negative education of an African intellectual who returns home hoping to help build a new nation only to be confronted with a world of corruption and decay, which leads to an eventual mental breakdown. Imprisoned and exiled twice (first in 1966 for his association with Kwame Nkrumah and later in 1975 for allegedly being involved in a "Ewe" coup plot), Awoonor reflected on his experiences of exile in the poems collected in *The House by the Sea* (1978). His period of exile, and a later stint as Ghana's ambassador to Brazil, got Awoonor interested in the lives of blacks in the diaspora (see **diaspora and pan-Africanism**), the result of which was *Comes the Voyager at Last* (1992), the story of an African-American's journey to Ghana to escape racism in the United States and his defiant search for a place he can call home.

SIMON GIKANDI

Axélos, Céline

b. 1903, Alexandria, Egypt; d. 1994

poet and short story writer

A Francophone Egyptian writer, Axélos was born Céline Tasso in Alexandria in a family of Lebanese origin. She studied in French schools and frequented the literary salons of Alexandria. She kept a diary of her impressions strictly for herself, and it was only late in her life that she was convinced to publish her work. She published two collections of poetry, *Les Deux Chapelles* (The Two Chapels) in 1943, followed by *Les Marches d'ivoire* (The Steps of Ivory) in 1952. She also wrote short stories for children. Her poetry is classified as romantic, and is touched by mysticism. She meditates in her verse on imprisonment and deliverance, waiting and fulfillment. She also has an unpublished collection entitled "Les Amphores" (The Amphoras).

Further reading

Axélos, Céline (1943, 1952) *Marches d'ivoire* (The Steps of Ivory), Alexandria: Edition Cosmopolis.

FERIAL J. GHAZOUL

B

Bâ, Amadou Hampâté

b. 1901, Bandiagara, Mali; d. 1991,
Abidjan, Côte d'Ivoire

novelist, poet, ethnologist, traditionalist,
and historian

The Malian novelist, poet, ethnologist, traditionalist, and historian, Amadou Hampâté Bâ is perhaps
best remembered for the saying "An old man that
dies is a library that burns." Promulgated to the
level of a proverb and often cited, sometimes out of
context, this saying has come to epitomize what
Hampâté Bâ stood for: the defense and illustration
of African traditional values. Born at the dawn of
the twentieth century in Bandiagara in Mali,
Hampâté Bâ constituted himself, well before his
old age, into a "living library" for everything that
touched on the source of African precolonial
culture and history. Having lost his father at the
age of 2, he was adopted by a provincial chief and
at age 12 was sent to the French colonial school.
Even as a student at the French school he
continued his Koranic studies under the direction
of his spiritual master, Tierno Bokar, and therefore
stayed attached to the traditions of Islam and his
ancestors.

During the period of French colonialism in West
Africa (see **colonialism, neocolonialism, and
postcolonialism**), Hampâté Bâ occupied several
positions as an assistant and interpreter to the
colonial administration before he was sent to
Dakar in 1942, where, at IFAN (Institut Fonda-
mental d'Afrique Noire) he undertook ethnological
and religious research in the former French African
territories. In 1951, a scholarship from UNESCO
enabled him to travel in France where he worked
with other Africanists at the Musée de l'Homme.
In 1958 he founded the Social Science Institute in
Bamako and became its director. From 1962 to
1970 he was a member of the Executive Council of
UNESCO. In this organization, as well as through
his other works, he became famous for his untiring
struggle in the service of oral cultures (see **oral
literature and performance**) and for his
incessant call for dialogue among nations and
peoples. Appointed Ambassador of Mali to the
Côte d'Ivoire following independence, Hampâté
Bâ never ceased to carry out, in addition to his
administrative duties, a series of historical, religious, anthropological, and literary works that have
made him today one of the most illustrious
champions of the defense of African oral tradition.

Although his writings generally deal with
traditional African stories and history, they can be
grouped under certain specific headings. Among
his initiatory stories are *Koumen, textes initiatiques de
pasteurs peuls* (Koumen, Initiatory Texts by Peul
Shepherds) (1961), *Kaïdïra* (1964), *L'Eclat de la grande
étoile* (The Brightness of the Great Star) (1974), and
Njeddo Dewal, mère de la calamité (Njeddo Dewal,
Mother of Calamity) (1985). In these initiatory
stories, Hampâté Bâ continued the work that had
been carried out for generations by griots and other
traditional storytellers, the people he considered to
be the keepers of African oral tradition. For him,
the griots – composed of musicians, singers, and
oral historians – were important in African cultures
because they were the vehicles through which
history was recalled, sung, and celebrated. He

considered the oral transmission of tradition to be a sacred duty, and he consistently argued that African traditional society recognized the right and freedom of master storytellers to adorn their stories in the description of scenery and characters and to eventually include didactic digressions in their narratives. He insisted that one of the distinguishing characteristics of the oral style of narration was its poetic character; adornment was acceptable as long as the storyteller respected the unchanging framework of the story and the events that formed its structure. It is this traditional way of storytelling that Hampâté Bâ sought to capture in his initiatory texts.

Aside from griots and storytellers, the prominent Malian Koranic teacher Tierno Bokar played an important role in Hampâté Bâ's perception of himself, his society, and the world. It is therefore not surprising that, as an essayist, Hampâté Bâ devoted important works, *Tierno Bokar, le sage de Bandiagara* (Tierno Bokar, the Sage of Bandiagara) (1957) and *Vie et enseignement de Tierno Bokar, le sage de Bandiagara* (The Life and Teachings of Tierno Bokar, the Sage of Bandiagara) (1980), to this great spiritual leader. In these essays, Hampâté Bâ demonstrates his debt to Tierno Bokar, who inculcated in him the twin principles of tolerance and love.

As a traditionalist, Hampâté Bâ was a great historian who believed strongly in the power of Africa's history to shape events on the continent. He believed that one of the major effects of World War I was to provoke the first big rupture in the oral transmission of traditional knowledge and history. In his opinion, this break-up in the oral transmission of Africa's cultural heritage unleashed several social factors that have since made the African situation worse in the history of the world. His historical works, *The Living Tradition: General History of Africa* (1981) and *L'Empire peul du Macina: 1818–1853* (The Peul Empire of Macina: 1818–1853) (1984), can be read as attempts to reconstruct and restore significant aspects of the lost history of Africa.

Hampâté Bâ was also a novelist. His most important work in this regard was *L'Étrange Destin de Wangrin* (The Strange Destiny of Wangrin) (1973), a novel that is supposed to be the true story of the picaresque and rather immoral life of an old

interpreter called Wangrin. Wangrin recounted his stories to Hampâté Bâ, who then transcribed and translated them into French. But this unique novel was much more than the transcription of the stories of an adventurer; on the contrary, it provided African readers with probably the richest literary account of colonialism. Colonialism was, of course, an important theme in all of Hampâté Bâ's works. His memoirs, *Amkoullel, l'enfant peul* (Amkoullel: A Peul Childhood) (1991) and *Oui, mon commandant* (Yes, My Commander) (1997), paint a ruthless but noble picture of an African life at the beginning of the century. It is the life of a young colonized boy, an intellectual through his French education (see **education and schools**) but well versed in African traditional ways, who decides to turn the relationship between master and servant to his advantage. In writing his memoirs, Hampâté Bâ's profound desire was to be a witness not only to his own life but also, through it, to the African society and the men and women of his time. He wanted others to see the African world in which he had lived and which he carried within himself.

During his long life, Hampâté Bâ demonstrated the possibility of bringing together or synthesizing a living African tradition, built on spirituality, and what he considered to be the positive elements of modernity (see **modernity and modernism**). True to his dictum that "An old man that dies is a library that burns," he sought, through his writing, to rescue African traditional values from the depths of time. In a word, he was the exemplar of a living African culture.

KWAKU A. GYASI

Bâ, Amadou Oumar

b. 1917

poet

This Mauritanian poet has authored many volumes with regional and international resonance. Among his most noteworthy publications are *Dialogue d'une rive à l'autre* (Dialogue from One Side of the River to the Other) (1966), *Poèmes peuls modernes* (Modern Fulani Poetry) (1965), *Presque griffonnages ou la francophonie* (Almost Scribbling or Francophonie)

(1966), *Témoin à charge et à décharge* (Witness for the Prosecution and the Defense) (1977), *Paroles plaisantes au coeur et à l'oreille* (Soothing Words to the Heart and the Ear) (1978), *Odes saheliennes* (Sahelian Odes) (1960), *Les Mystères du Bani* (The Mysteries of the Bani) (1977), *Le Foûta Tôro au carrefour des cultures: les Peuls de la Mauritanie et du Sénégal* (The Fouta Toro at the Crossroad of Cultures: The Fulani of Mauritania and Senegal) *Mon Meilleur chef de canton* (1966). Bâ is a renowned scholar of the Fouta Toro, and his poetry is a monument to the culture, history, and anthropology of the Fulani living on both sides of the Senegal River. As a witness to brisk social changes, Bâ provides an interesting perspective on his people, his country, and the challenges facing the whole African continent in the wake of independence, nationalism (see **nationalism and post-nationalism**), and nationhood. Central to the author's work is the theme of identity as a quest or re-conquest. His writings decry the human misery of exile and showcase the religion, customs, and stories of his people. Interpreters, chiefs, opportunistic intellectuals, the army, and corruption are often the subjects of attack in Bâ's poetry. He has frequently tackled issues regarding women, the law, and politics, while often embedding them in the language of jesting, or *dendiraogu*. He was one of the first West African writers to raise the **language question** in African literature, challenging the adoption and suitability of French as the unquestioned language of African writing. As a scribe for his society, Bâ has skillfully managed to transcribe the oral history and folklore of the Fulani of the Fouta Toro, thus preserving it from loss through oblivion or extinction. He is also notable for translating the Koran into Fulani.

JEAN OUÉDRAOGO

Bâ, Mariama

b. 1929, Dakar, Senegal; d. 1981, Dakar, Senegal

novelist

In addition to belonging to the first generation of Western-educated women in her country, the Senegalese novelist Mariama Bâ also occupied a prominent place among Francophone African women writers. The major influences on her life were the traditional milieu of her childhood and youth, defined by Islam and African cultural beliefs, and her French formal education. These influences are evident in her major works and her social concerns, especially in regard to the condition of women in Africa. Despite having written only two novels before her premature death, Bâ is considered by many critics to be one of the most important figures in Francophone African writing in general, and Francophone African women's writing in particular. Her first novel, *So Long a Letter* (*Une si longue lettre*) (1979), which won the 1980 Noma Award for Publishing in Africa, has been described by Abiola Irele as "the most deeply felt presentation of the female condition in African fiction." Mbaye Cham describes this condition, which is pronounced in both *Letter* and *Scarlet Song* (*Un Chant écarlate*) (1981), Bâ's second novel, as one of "abandonment ... both physical and psychological" (1987: Trenton).

What distinguished Bâ's writing was not so much the originality of its dominant theme but the thoroughness with which she treated the condition of women in Senegal, a treatment that transformed Bâ's writing into a critique not just of the representation of gender in African writing (see **gender and sexuality**), but of society as a whole and, most particularly, postcolonial Senegalese society. At the same time, Bâ manipulated the epistolary genre to create a form very different from the traditional (European) epistolary novel. Indeed, the very title of Bâ's first novel, *So Long a Letter*, announces an epistolary novel in a familiar European tradition; however, her appropriation of this genre is much more innovative than might first appear to be the case, for unlike the continuous exchange of letters between two or more parties in the traditional epistolary novel, Ramatoulaye's long letter, which lies at the center of Bâ's novel, is never sent. For this reason, then, *Letter* functions like a journal. On another level, however, the use of a specific interlocutor makes the novel appear, to its readers, like an open letter.

Finally, much of the form and substance of her novels was drawn from the Wolof and Islamic traditions of her country (see **Wolof literature**; **Islam in African literature**). In *Letter*, for example, she appropriates both the rite of passage and *mirasse*, what Cham describes as "an Islamic principle [defining] ... the nature of inheritance in the Islamic family" (1987: Trenton). Within the context of this tradition, Ramatoulaye becomes the heir to a social legacy against her wishes, but she also takes up a traditional social structure and a religious precept and uses them to critique the social and religious status quo of her society. Likewise, notes Cham, "the cultural concept embodied in the Wolof proverb, '*Kou wathie sa toundeu, toundeu boo feke mou tasse* (When one abandons one's own hillock, any hillock that one climbs thereafter will crumble)' informs the form and substance of *Scarlet Song*."

In both her novels, Bâ depicted the female condition in Senegal through the competing lenses of caste/class, sex/gender, culture, and race. In *Letter*, the protagonist, Ramatoulaye, writes about the lives of individual women (including her own and that of her bosom friend, Aissatou) who have, in some way, been abandoned by their husbands. She demonstrates how caste, sex/gender, and culture contribute to the destruction of these women's marriages. Aissatou's mother-in-law, a woman of noble birth unable to accept her son's marriage to a blacksmith's daughter, deliberately sets out to have Aissatou supplanted by a more acceptable wife. At the same time, the men take advantage of Islam's tolerance of plural marriages to justify their actions, while the women lack the means to protest against such acts, since submissiveness is seen as a cultural dictate. Culture, likewise, prescribes the submission of offspring to parents. In obedience to the mother, young Binetou marries Modou (hence destroying Ramatoulaye's marriage), and Modou marries his cousin, hence alienating his first wife, Aissatou.

Scarlet Song complicates the issue of the female condition even further, with the addition of the race dimension. This allows Bâ to show that the oppression or repression of women is not culture-bound. The French female protagonist's mother, Mathilde, has no freedom to think for herself or act independently of her husband, even in her relationship with their daughter, Mireille. The novel's tragic ending is shown to be the result of a multiplicity of social problems, including the subjugation of women which, combined with racism and the cultural expectations of the African mother-in-law, affects both the French and Senegalese families involved in this domestic narrative.

Thematically, Bâ's novels went beyond merely depicting the female condition. She was interested in exploring and illustrating how women colluded with the very institutions that oppressed them, the insidious nature of racist mental programming, and the abuse of religious and social practices that rationalize the oppressive and self-interested behavior of individuals within the group. This behavior affects not only women in the hands of men and other women, but also children, especially in cases where parents are eager to use their offspring in attempts to raise their own social status. Bâ considered herself a feminist, but some Western feminists would contest that claim under the pretext that she depicts a heroine who accepts a plural marriage. However, in an interview with Alioune Touré Dia, Bâ powerfully argued that although every woman has at some moment dreamt of having a husband to herself, social exigencies do sometimes force women to resign themselves to polygyny.

Further reading

Cham, Mbaye B. (1987) "Contemporary Society and the Female Imagination: A Study of the Novels of Mariama Bâ," in E.D. Jones, E. Palmer, and M. Jones (eds) *Women in African Literature Today* Vol. 15, Trenton, New Jersey: African World View.

D'Almeida, Irene (1994) *Francophone African Women Writers: Destroying the Emptiness of Silence*, Gainesville, Florida: University Press of Florida.

WANGAR WA NYATETŨ-WAIGWA

Baccouche, Hachemi

b. 1917, Tunisia

novelist

The Tunisian writer Hachemi Baccouche lived through both the French Protectorate of Tunisia (1881–1956) and its aftermath, and his work is a reflection of the historical realities he witnessed. His first novel, *Ma foi demeure* (My Faith Remains)

(1958), is the story of a Tunisian–French interracial marriage during the final years of the protectorate and the first years of Tunisian independence. The main character is attached to the values of both civilizations and struggles between the two, despised by Tunisians and Frenchmen alike. *La Dame de Carthage* (The Lady of Carthage) (1960) is set in sixteenth-century Carthage, but once again addresses questions of mixed identity and cultural allegiance through the amorous unions of a Frenchman and a Christian slave, and a Spanish soldier and a Muslim noblewoman. Like his compatriots Tahar **Essafi** and Mahmoud **Aslan**, Baccouche advocates the possibility of a pacific union between Europe and North Africa. In his essay, *Décolonisation* (Decolonization) (1962), Baccouche explores the complex issues decolonizing countries face, including the abuses of nationalism, justice, and power, and questions what lessons should be taken from the colonial experience.

Further reading

Baccouche, Hachemi (1958) *Ma foi demeure* (My Faith Remains), Paris: Nouvelles Éditions.

KATARZYNA PIEPRZAK

Badian, Seydou Kouyaté

b. 1928, Bamako, Mali

playwright

Born in Bamako on 10 April 1928, Seydou Badian completed his secondary schooling in France before completing a doctorate in medicine at the Université de Montpellier in 1955. He was to assume important governmental positions under the socialist government of Modibo Keita, serving as minister of rural economy and later as minister of planning before resigning in 1966 to return to the medical profession. Following the fall of the Keita regime in 1968, Badian was jailed by the new military rulers of Mali for seven years. Since his release in 1975, he has lived in exile in Dakar, Senegal.

Although he is a proven talent in various literary genres, Seydou Badian's 1963 *Caught in the Storm* (*Sous l'orage – Kany*) remains to date the most

popular and recognizable novel from Mali. He authored other important novels such as *Le Sang des masques* (The Blood of Masks) (1976), *Noces sacrées: les dieux du Kouroulamini* (Sacred Nuptials: The Gods of Kouroulamini) (1977), and plays of a historical nature such as *The Death of Chaka* (*La Mort de Chaka*) (1961), a loosely adapted drama from the South African epic, *Congo: terre généreuse, forêt féconde* (Congo: Generous Land, Fertile Forest) (1983), and a political pamphlet, *Les Dirigeants d'Afrique noire face à leur peuple* (The Leaders of Black Africa and Their People) (1964). Through his novels Seydou Badian exposes the pains of an old and growing Africa troubled by the conflict of generations, shifting social values, and the need for good governance. Although he has functioned as a theoretician of African politics, Badian is first and foremost a student of both oral and written history, concerned with the effect of the past on the nature of present and future society. In *The Death of Chaka*, Badian represented the emblematic Zulu king as a source of pride for all black Africans fighting for independence; there were important lessons that the present generation of African leaders could learn from Chaka's life, victories, and death. This play, which was written before the 1960s, speaks to the pan-African vision of history and is intended as a plea for political commitment. In his didactic novel, *Caught in the Storm*, the author launched an attack on various aspects of African traditions, including arranged marriages, polygamy, and superstition. In the novel, a transition to modernity is begun by the female protagonist who wins over her parents to the just cause of her marriage – vehemently opposed by her father and the old guard at first – with a suitor she freely chooses. The emancipation of women finds a natural ally in Western education or the European school.

Badian's later novels deal with the dangers facing the continent in its dealings with the outside world. In these works, the disappearance of forms of African **art**, such as the giant N'Tomo mask, is cause for grave concern as it signals the severance of the black African soul from its sacred past and ancestral beliefs, the memory-knowledge and acknowledgement of which are essential for the writer. Badian's work is a praise song of African social life and customs, when they are not dehumanizing, as well as a warning of the threats the continent faces from the "sick dreams" of Westernization. For Badian, the eternal Africa lives in the sacred vestiges of its past, and his solution to the identity crisis sweeping across the continent in the aftermath of colonialism (see **colonialism, neocolonialism, and postcolonialism**) and decolonization is to suggest that black Africans ought to be critical of certain aspects of their traditional cultures, while resisting the urge to relinquish their sacred link to the soil, soul, and history. Badian is critical of the sacrifice of sacred African art forms, such as the masks, on the altar of foreign museums. In *Caught in the Storm*, as in his other works, Badian recommends humility and a tempered approach to the new generation of African intellectuals who, in his view, must play the game of conciliatory diplomacy in their dealings with their traditionalist forefathers if they are not to be perceived by the former as "a legion of termites attacking the sacred tree." In his works, Badian insists that the strength to be derived from ancient wisdom can be garnered to guide Africans through the turbulent zones of modernity (see **modernity and modernism**); without the guidance of ancient knowledge, the African is bound to confront modern life in its most extreme forms and to be unable to deal with the ups and downs of the historical voyage into the third millennium. For this reason, Badian's work remains for the most part moralizing, as well as illustrative of the **negritude** ideal in its suggestion that the best of African customs can be grafted to Western education to produce the ideal African.

JEAN OUÉDRAOGO

Bakhaï, Fatima

b. 1949, Oran, Algeria

novelist and lawyer

Born in Oran, Algeria, Fatima Bakhaï spent the greater part of her childhood in France. She later returned to post-independence Algeria to complete a degree in law, and from 1975 to 1981 served as magistrate at the Oran court. She has since pursued dual careers as a novelist and as a lawyer. Among her novels, *Dounia* (1995) and *La Scalera*

(1993) are striking for the ways in which major historical events are woven into the narratives of the texts. For instance, the protagonist of *Dounia*, a young girl for whom the novel is named, matures during the French occupation of Oran in 1830. As the reverberations of the invasion impact Dounia's family, the young woman herself takes up arms against the colonizer. Narrating a "local" history of Algerian invasion – as perceived through the eyes of the colonized – the novel bears testament to the oft-neglected role of women in the resistance to colonial enterprise.

NEIL DOSHI

Bakr, Salwa

b. 1949, Cairo, Egypt

novelist, short story writer, and journalist

An Egyptian novelist and short story writer as well as editorialist in major Egyptian and Arab newspapers and magazines, Salwa Bakr has in the last two decades made a name for herself as a leading feminist to be contended with. Many of her works have been translated into French and German, and to a lesser degree into English. At the beginning of the twenty-first century she hit the headlines through the publishing of a two-part novel *al-Bashmouri* (1998), a historical narrative which caused quite some controversy in literary circles. She situates the action of the novel in the Abbasid era, that golden age for Islam which not only witnessed a vast empire that ruled in what is today the Middle East and North Africa, but also enjoyed great prosperity and, more importantly, the flourishing of the arts and literature. Bakr was, however, more interested in recording the so-called Bashmouri revolt during which Egyptian Christians (Copts) fought their Abbasid (Iraqi) rulers, mainly protesting the destitute conditions under which they lived. Salwa Bakr focuses on a relatively obscure medieval historical revolt, basing her research on eye-witness narratives of contemporary historians. That historical narrative enables our writer to delve into social, cultural, and artistic domains surrounding this revolt, which was ultimately crushed and its leaders deported into exile to Iraq. The second part of this historical novel has been harshly assessed on several counts. Mahmoud al-Wardani, the well-known writer, admits that Salwa Bakr has written a first part which is "tightly constructed," allowing the novelist to exploit "the full ironies" of her sources, but feels that the second part is in many ways redundant. Several other critics feel that many points she raises in that second volume are unjustified from a literary point of view, most notably her naïve stance *vis-à-vis* religion: namely, that regardless of the dictates of any religion, people could and should seek to live in a tolerant and just society. Critics almost all agreed that presenting this historical novel set in the ninth century AD was too reductionist in its approach. The novel's protagonist, a Coptic deacon, is part of a complex array of characters who tackle the sensitive question of the role of Christian minorities within a larger Muslim society, in this case the Abbasid empire.

Salwa Bakr's short stories deal with many gender-related issues, as do her numerous editorials. She is outspoken and forceful and never shies from getting into literary arguments. She is undoubtedly one of the growing number of women writers to walk in the footsteps of Nawal **el-Saadawi**, the militant activist and feminist.

MONA N. MIKHAIL

Balboa Boneke, Juan

b. 1938, Equatorial Guinea

writer

As with many writers of "La generación perdida" ("The lost generation") of Equatorial-Guinean writers, Juan Balboa Boneke began his writing career during his first exile in Spain, where he spent more than fifteen years. He is one of the most prolific authors of Equatorial Guinea. He has explored different literary genres, including mostly poetry, essays, and the novel. His poetry, as he acknowledges, is profoundly influenced by Spanish poet Leon Felipe. His publications include essays, *Dónde estas Guinea?* (Where are You, Guinea?) (1978), *La transición politica de la República de Guinea Ecuatorial, historia de un fracaso* (Political Transition of

Equatorial Guinea, History of a Failure) (2000); poetry, *O'Boriba* (*El exiliado*, The Exile) (1982), *Susurros y Pensamientos comentados: desde mi vidriera* (Commented Whispers and Thoughts from My Window) (1983), *Sueños en mi selva* (Dreams from the Jungle) (1987), and *Requiebros* (Compliments) (1994); and a novel, *El reencuentro. El retorno del exiliado* (Meeting Again. The Return of the Exiled) (1985). Exile plays a central role in Balboa Boneke's literary production and his works examine, from diverse perspectives, the experience of what he calls *"La orfandad de tierra* (homeland orphanhood)." Balboa Boneke is a member of the Agrupación Hispana de Escritores (the Hispanic Writers' Association) and has received two major literary awards: the Premio Extraordinario del Concurso Literario de Primavera (1982) from the Agrupación Hispana de Escritores, and the Premio Literario del Concurso Literario "12 de octubre." After the fall of the regime of dictator Francisco Macías Nguema in 1979, Juan Balboa Boneke ended his exile and returned to Equatorial Guinea, but in the 1990s he was forced to leave the country again and he has since lived in exile in Spain.

Further reading

Balboa Boneke, Juan (1985) *El reencuentro. El retorno del exiliado* (Meeting Again. The Return of the Exiled), Madrid: Ediciones Guinea.

——(1987) *Dónde estás Guinea?* (Where are You, Guinea?), Palma de Mallorca: Imprenta Politecnica.

——(1987) *Sueños en mi selva* (Dreams from the Jungle), Malabo: Ediciones del Centro Cultural Hispano Guineano.

M'BARE NGOM

Bamboté, Pierre Makombo

b. 1932, Ouadda, Republic of Central Africa

novelist and poet

Born in Ouadda, Republic of Central Africa, Pierre Makombo Bamboté is one of the premier writers of his country. His collection of short stories

Nouvelles de Bangui (Bangui Stories), published in 1980 but written between 1963 and 1964, offers a vivid and nostalgic depiction of the land of his childhood. *Princesse Mandapu* (Princess Mandapu) (1972) is, however, Bamboté's most acclaimed fiction. Drawing from a mysterious conflict opposing two powerful men in a small Central African town, Bamboté has built an entangled plot allowing him to scrutinize, with unexpected detachment for these times, both the realities and drama of a postcolonial society. While the novel is ostensibly set in the 1930s, it is preoccupied with the events that are often associated with the period of independence in Africa, especially in the early 1960s. Avoiding a direct criticism of colonialism and neocolonialism or postcolonialism in this twirling novel (see **colonialism, neocolonialism, and postcolonialism**), Bamboté seeks to institute a counter-discourse against both paradigms, and for this he has won praise for his originality and his innovative style. His other publications include a book for children, *Les Randonnées de Daba* (Daba's Journey) (1965), and a collection of poetry, *La Poésie est dans l'histoire* (When History is Poetic) (1960).

Further reading

Ngate, Jonathan (1988) *Francophone African Fiction: Reading a Literary Tradition*, Trenton, New Jersey: Africa World Press.

EMMANUEL TENÉ

Bandele-Thomas, 'Biyi

b. 1967, Kafanchan, Nigeria

short story writer

Since his publication of *The Sympathetic Undertaker and Other Dreams* in 1991, Bandele-Thomas has come to be recognized as one of the most promising of a new generation of African writers who have drawn on their hybrid cultural and linguistic experiences to transform the nature of African literature in European languages. While earlier generations of African writers in English

were interested in either affirming or questioning the nature of African realities and using forms of either realism or modernism (see **realism and magical realism**; **modernity and modernism**), Bandele-Thomas's works combine both modes of representation to great effect. His short stories are concerned with the harsh political and social reality of life in Africa and the process of education through which young Africans apprehend this world (see **education and schools**). At the same time, however, his characters often function at a supra-natural level, one of dreams and madness, which functions as a counterpoint to a daily life that rarely makes sense. For this reason, his works can be read as postmodern. In his other major work of fiction, *The Man Who Came In from the Back of Beyond* (1992), Bandele-Thomas is concerned with characters whose lives read like books, and presents experiences in which life is so much embedded in fiction and where truth is sometimes blurred by the illusions that surround it. Bandele-Thomas has lived and worked in Britain since the late 1980s and he has been active on the London stage, where his plays *Resurrection* (1994) and *Two Horsemen Return* (1994) were first produced.

SIMON GIKANDI

Barry, Kesso

b. 1948, Mamou Province, Guinea

autobiographer

When the Senegalese writer Kesso Barry published her autobiographical work, *Kesso, princesse peule* (Kesso, Peul Princess) (1988), many critics were still insisting that African **autobiography** was an appendage of the Western tradition of life-writing. While the sheer abundance of autobiographical works from Africa has dispelled that myth, there is still no clear articulation or definition of an African autobiographical aesthetics. *Kesso* represents an interesting case because it subverts the autobiographical genre and the ostensible meaning of the narrative. Kesso subverts her tale most explicitly by dedicating the book to her daughter, who has no knowledge of Africa, then rejecting her experiences abroad and her French husband and mixed-race daughter, claiming "si c'était à refaire, je ne le referais pas (if I had to do it over again, I wouldn't do it again)" (*Kesso*, 1988: Paris, p. 233). Kesso suffers from the ambiguity of life as a culturally hybrid product of colonialism (see **colonialism, neocolonialism, and postcolonialism**). Implicitly, she subverts the text's autobiographical character by eliding facts, claiming that she cannot remember details, or that dates are unimportant to Africans. Ultimately, the text's truthfulness is at stake, for Kesso blandishes the reader, just as she did her father and her husband in the text.

Further reading

Barry, Kesso (1988) *Kesso*, Paris: Seghers.
D'Alméïda, Irène (1997) "Kesso Barry's *Kesso*, or Autobiography as a Subverted Tale," *Research in African Literatures* 28, 2: 67–82.

LISA McNEE

Bassek, Philomène

b. 1957, Dschang, Cameroon

novelist

The Cameroonian Francophone novelist Philomène Bassek has written one novel, *The Stain of Blood* (*La Tache de sang*) (1990). The novel is a search for a female voice in a masculine society, played out in the relationship between a 55-year-old mother of ten, Mama Ida, and her eldest daughter, Patricia. Mama Ida has recently discovered that she is again pregnant and that the pregnancy will almost certainly kill her. Patricia, a "modern" woman who seeks to balance a successful career with family, counsels her to abort. The resultant conflicting generational views of a woman's responsibilities and place in a masculine society offer the reader a choice as to the degree to which to side with one or other woman's philosophy, while making clear that the ultimate struggle is to gain the respect and status men acquire and possess so casually. In this respect, it is somewhat reminiscent of aspects of Mariama **Bâ**'s *So Long a Letter* (*Une Si Longue Letter*) (1979) in its balanced presentation of different solutions for different women. Bassek is also a teacher of philosophy at the renowned Lycée Leclerc in Yaoundé.

Further reading

Bassek, Philomène (1990) *La Tache de sang* (The Stain of Blood), Paris: L'Harmattan.

STEPHEN BISHOP

Bazié, Jacques Prosper

b. 1955, Ouagadougou, Burkina Faso

poet, novelist, and journalist

Born in Ouagadougou (Kadiogo) in Burkina Faso, Jacques Prosper Bazié studied journalism and occupied various important positions within the Ministry of Communication in his country. In 1999, he was appointed as the cultural advisor at the Embassy of Burkina Faso in Canada. Jacques Prosper Bazié is one of the most prominent playwrights in Burkina Faso and his work has often been compared to that of Wole **Soyinka** in its structure and style. He has also written poems, short stories, plays, and novels. Some of his important works include three collections of poems, *Orphelin des collines ancestrales* (Orphan from the Ancestral Hills) (1983), *Césarienne* (Cesarean) (1984), and *La Saga des immortels* (The Saga of the Immortals) (1987); two novels, *La Dérive des Bozos* (The Drift of the Bozos) (1988) and *L'Épave d'Absouya* (The Wreck of Absouya) (1986); a play, *Amoro* (1988); and a collection of stories, *Cantiques des Soukalas* (The Canticle of the Soukalas) (1987). In all these works Jacques Prosper Bazié, who has won several literary contests in Burkina Faso, draws on his own experiences of social life in his country and tries to fuse his writing with his vision of life, seeking to simultaneously entertain and educate his readers.

MICHEL TINGUIRI

Be'alu Girma

b. 1938/9, Supé, Ethiopia; d. 1984, Addis
Ababa, Ethiopia

journalist and novelist

Be'alu Girma became socially involved in Ethiopian society and worked mainly as a journalist and
novelist. He did well in school and universities,
both in Ethiopia and in the United States, where
he obtained an MA in journalism. His investiga-
tive journalism revolutionized the daily and weekly
newspapers he edited, but it also created powerful
enemies. Early in his writing career, he wrote two
popular novels, *Kadmas bashager* (Beyond the
Horizon) (1969/70) and *Yehillina dewel* (The Bell
of Conscience) (1974), later rewritten as *Haddis*.
His strong social views seemed to fit the socialist
rather than the imperial government after the
revolution of 1974. *Yeqey kokeb tirri* (The Call of the
Red Star) (1979/80) was revolutionary, but in
Oromay (Now or Never) (1983) he criticized the
socialist leaders, and the government arrested him
in 1984; no more was heard of him and he has
been presumed dead ever since. Although the
government sought to confiscate *Oromay*, copies of
the book survived and were photocopied, and this
ensured the steady increase in Be'alu Girma's
fame. He is now considered to be one of Ethiopia's
greatest writers.

Further reading

Molvaer, R.K. (1997) *Black Lions*, Lawrenceville,
New Jersey, Red Sea Press.

REIDULF MOLVAER

Bebey, Francis

b. 1929, Douala, Cameroon; d. 2001,
Paris, France

musician, novelist, and playwright

An accomplished musician, novelist, and playwright, Francis Bebey was an influential but
fiercely independent voice in African **art**s. Born
in Cameroon and educated in Douala, Paris, and

the US, he began his career as a journalist in the
1950s. In the late 1950s and early 1960s he spent
some time in Ghana and other African countries
working with the Société de radiodiffusion de la
France d'outre-mer, the French radio network, as a
journalist. In 1968, he took up the position of
director of the music section with UNESCO in
Paris. After resigning his position in 1974, he
returned to his lifelong passion for live African
music and gave innumerable concerts until his
death in 2001.

Francis Bebey's love for music went back to his
childhood, as did his interest in African instruments
such as the sanza, which remained a central part of
his performance and compositions throughout his
career. His study, *African Music: A People's Art*
(*Musique de l'Afrique*) (1969), provides an interesting
insight into African musical arts, which he argues
have been dominated by music since time immemorial. Many of Bebey's songs, which explore
the human condition with wit and humor, have
become well known. These include "Agatha," "La
Condition masculine" (The Masculine Condition),
"Mwana," and "Ponda." True to himself, Bebey
remained independent of musical trends throughout his career and managed to engage in musical
activities, mainly on his own terms and for his own
enjoyment.

Like his music, Bebey's literary career spans the
whole of his diverse childhood and adult experiences and includes many novels, tales, short stories,
and poetry. His first novel, *Agatha Moudio's Son* (*Le
Fils d'Agatha Moudio*) (1967), was awarded the
Grand Prix de l'Afrique Noire in 1968 and
remains his best-known work. However, such texts
as *Three Little Shoeshine Boys* (*Trois petits cireurs*) (1972),
which was reissued four times between 1984 and
1996, *The Ashanti Doll* (*La Poupée ashanti*) (1973) and
King Albert (*Le Roi Albert d'Effidi*) (1977) are already
classics of both Cameroonian and African literature. His last two novels, *The Minister and the Griot* (*Le
Ministre et le griot*) (1992) and *The Child of Rain*
(*L'Enfant pluie*) (1994) which was awarded the Prize
Saint Exupéry, are further testimony to Bebey's
philosophy, humanity, and love of African tradition,
and to the subtle irony in his reading of
contemporary history. Bebey was the author of a
book of tales drawn from the African oral tradition

(see **oral literature and performance**) and several collections of poetry.

Further reading

Bebey, F. (1963) *La Radiodiffusion en Afrique noire* (Broadcasting in Black Africa), Paris: Éditions St Paul.

Hoyet, D. and Bebey, F. (1979) *Francis Bebey: écrivain et musicien camerounais* (Francis Bebey: Cameroonian Writer and Musician), Paris: F. Nathan.

Ndachi Tagne, D. (1993) *Francis Bebey*, Paris: L'Harmattan.

JEAN-MARIE VOLET

Begag, Azouz

b. 1957, Villeurbanne, France

social scientist and novelist

The son of Algerian immigrants, Azouz Begag was born in the Lyonnais suburb of Villeurbanne, France. He completed his doctorate in economics at the University of Lyons 2, and since 1980 he has served as a researcher at the National Center for Scientific Research (CNRS) in Paris. Social scientist, novelist, and author of **children's literature**, Begag's multiple careers intersect in his powerful depictions of Beur (French of Maghreb origin) culture, which permeate his texts (see **Beur literature in France**). Begag's works center upon the crisis of the young Beur who, struggling against poverty, unemployment, and racism, is caught between two cultures and, indeed, between tradition and modernity. Begag's first novel, *Le Gone du Chaâba* (The Kid from the Township) (1986) won both the Prix Sorcières and the Prix Bobigneries. Drawing upon the circumstances of the author's own childhood, the text thematizes the deep rift between Western scholarship and "traditional" education as it is transmitted through the family unit. Among Begag's more prominent critical works is *Écarts d'Identité* (*Spaces of Identity*) (1990). Co-written with Chaouite Abdellatif, this study seeks to disrupt the generic

stereotypes of Beurs and to explore their marginal status in French society.

Further reading

Begag, Azouz (1986) *Le Gone du Chaâba* (The Kid from the Township), Paris: Éditions du Seuil.

NEIL DOSHI

Békri, Tahar

b. 1951, Kasserine, Tunisia

poet and essayist

Tunisian poet and essayist Tahar Békri was born in Kasserine, but he is a longtime resident of Paris where he teaches Arabic literature and civilization at the University of Paris XIII. Békri has emerged as one of the most prolific and original French-language poets in the last decade. His early poetry, collected in *Le Laboureur du soleil* (The Sun's Ploughman) (1983), *Le Chant du roi errant* (The Song of the Errant King) (1985), and *Le Coeur rompu aux océans* (The Oceanworthy Heart) (1988), is marked by the painful experience of exile from the homeland. Settling in Paris to escape political harassment in his native Tunisia, Békri developed a keen sense of the transient and the ephemeral rendered in a language that is at once profoundly personal but also elegantly ornate if not mundane. The many trials that he describes as a result of his own personal experience of exile are fused and transcended later, especially in *La Sève des jours* (The Sap of Days) (1991) and *Les Chapelets d'attache* (The Rosary of Anchorage) (1993), to become a metaphor for the condition of the writer condemned to live, as he is, between languages, cultures, and countries. Self-willed exile and nomadism have become positive, even felicitous, experiences and the hallmark of his more recent poetic oeuvre, notably in *Les Songes impatients* (Impatient Dreams) (1997). It is also important to note that Békri writes with equal mastery both in French and in Arabic. His transnational poetic scope is clearly visible in his Arabic-language volumes *Poems to Selma* (1989) and *Diaries of Ice and Fire* (1997).

Further reading

Békri, Tahar (1992) "On French-Language Tunisian Literature," *Research in African Literatures* 23, 2: 177–82.

HÉDI ABDEL-JAOUAD

Belamri, Rabah

b. 1946, Algeria; d. 1995, Paris, France

poet, short story writer, and critic

Of Kabyle origin, the Algerian writer Rabah Belamri has left behind a significant oeuvre consisting of both prose and poetry as well as criticism. Oscillating between the real and the fantastic, Belamri's fiction draws significantly from the author's own life. For instance, his coming of age during the Algerian war for independence and his concurrent loss of vision are mirrored in the events that transpire in the life of the protagonist of *Shattered Vision* (*Le Regard blessé*) (1995). In the novel, the protagonist's personal trauma becomes a metaphor for the dire state of Algeria; the character's inability to see mirrors the "blindness" of a fractured, war-ridden nation. A versatile writer working across genres, Belamri remains equally appreciated for his short stories, poetry, and collections of proverbs. He deserves credit for recuperating and valorizing both oral narrative techniques and local lore that are parts of the collective and popular imagination. He is additionally remembered for his important study of the Algerian poet, Jean **Sénac**.

Further reading

Belamri, Rabah (1995) *Shattered Vision*, trans. Hugh A. Harter, New York: Holmes and Meier.

NEIL DOSHI

Bemba, Sylvain (Sylvain N'Tari-Bemba)

b. 1934, Sibiti, Congo; d. 1995, Paris, France

playwright, novelist, short story writer, and essayist

The Congolese playwright, novelist, short story writer, and essayist Sylvain Bemba belonged to the first generation of Congolese writers including **Tchicaya UTam'Si**, Guy **Menga**, and Théophile Obenga. He worked as a journalist, musician, and librarian; he was also involved in local politics. His literary work mostly analyzed the Congolese experience under colonialism and the country's postcolonial trauma (see **colonialism, neocolonialism, and postcolonialism**). Sylvain Bemba contributed to the colonial journal *Liaison* (Link) and the current affairs publication *La Semaine africaine* (African Weekly), a Catholic newspaper. Extremely reserved, he used many pseudonyms such as Congo Kerr, Rufus, Yves Botto, Michel Belvain, and Martial Malinda, and only his cultural chronicles were signed with his real name. Frustrated by his short political career and very sensitive to the role of intellectual friendship, he mentored Congolese writers of the new generation such as **Sony Labou Tansi**. His creative material ranged from African history to popular imaginary, from African oral resources to classic mythology (see **oral literature and performance**).

Further reading

Djiffack, André (1996) *Sylvain Bemba: récits entre folie et pouvoir* (Sylvain Bemba: Accounts between Madness and Power), Paris: L'Harmattan.

ANDRÉ DJIFFACK

Ben, Myriam

b. 1928, Algiers, Algeria

poet, novelist, short story writer

The granddaughter of a musician of Andalusian Arabic music, on her mother's side, and the daughter of a fervent anti-colonialist father, the Algerian poet, novelist, short story writer, and painter Myriam Ben figures among the militant combatants in the Algerian war of independence. She began her artistic career in 1967 and has published multiple collections of poetry, a novel entitled *Sabrina, ils t'ont volé la vie* (Sabrina, They Have Stolen Your Life) (1986) and a collection of short stories, *Ainsi naquit un homme* (Thus a Man was Born) (1982). A member of both l'Union des Écrivains Algériens (the Union of Algerian Writers), and l'Organisation Nationale des Anciens Moudjahidines (the National Organization of Former Fighters for Liberation), her work, like her life, has been a marriage of the political and the social with the poetic. While her prose as well as her poetry finds its voice from within the national experiences of Algeria, her work surpasses these boundaries and opens towards a global concern for liberation.

Further reading

Achour, Christiane (1989) *Myriam Ben*, Paris: L'Harmattan.

NASRIN QADER

Ben Hadouga, 'Abdelhamid

b. 1928, al Mansura, Algeria; d. 1996, Algiers, Algeria

novelist and short story writer

An Algerian novelist and short story writer, Ben Hadouga was born in al Mansura, Algeria, and was initially educated at home by his father before attending school in Tunisia, where he subsequently earned a degree in Arabic literature from al-Zaytuna University. Ben Hadouga and Taher **Wattar** are the two most important Algerian novelists writing in Arabic. Ben Hadouga has published more than fifteen Arabic novels, short story collections, and plays (in spoken Algerian Arabic) for radio and television. His 1971 *Rih al-janub* (Southern Wind) was the first Algerian novel in Arabic. His fiction portrays the effects of the protracted war of independence on Algerian

society, the trials of the post-independence era, and social and political corruption, which he often links with urban, as opposed to rural, life. Ben Hadouga also championed women's rights, portrayed strong female characters both in urban and in rural settings, and criticized outworn customs related to marriage and gender roles.

Further reading

Bamia, Aida (1996) "Ben Hadouga, Abdelhamid," in Reeva Simon, Philip Mattar, and Richard Bulliet (eds) *Encyclopedia of the Modern Middle East*, New York: Macmillan.

WAÏL S. HASSAN

Ben Jelloun, Tahar

b. 1944, Fez, Morocco

novelist

Novelist, poet, and short story writer, Tahar Ben Jelloun is the most well-known and critically acclaimed Moroccan writer of the twentieth century. In 1987, he was the first North African writer to be awarded the prestigious French literary prize, the Prix Goncourt, for his scandalous novel *The Sacred Night* (*La Nuit Sacrée*). His prolific opus, composed entirely in French and including over ten novels, six volumes of poetry and five works of non-fiction, is overwhelmingly concerned with violently marginalized identities. While the majority of his fiction explores a distinctly Moroccan universe of ancestral legends, religious rites, mystical experiences, and popular myths, Ben Jelloun's non-fiction is primarily engaged with the social and political problems of immigration.

The literary production of Tahar Ben Jelloun tackles many of the questions addressed in post-colonial theory: marginalization, ambiguity, plurality of voice, language and identity, subalternity, images of the "other," the manipulation of myth, the legacy of colonialism, immigration and gender (see **colonialism, neocolonialism, and post-colonialism**; **gender and sexuality**). Ben Jelloun's novels delve deep into Moroccan culture in order to exhume the marginal worlds of characters such as prostitutes, madmen, street-children, and abused women, worlds and voices that have been silenced by dominant powers and official discourse. In so doing, he explores the power of the unseen and the secret, partly revealing and partly concealing a mystical and sensual universe that is simultaneously beautiful and extremely violent.

This universe has been of great interest to literary critics who have published numerous interpretations of Ben Jelloun's work, ranging from linguistic analysis to questions of city and space in his novels. However, while Ben Jelloun's work has been widely celebrated, certain scholars, especially from the Arab world, have criticized his novels for pandering to Western desires for an exotic Orient and fueling preconceived ideas of Islam through his depictions of Sufi mysticism. Likewise, feminist scholars have been greatly disturbed by the sexual violence towards women that Ben Jelloun reenacts in the majority of his work.

Ben Jelloun as poet of the body: his early work

Tahar Ben Jelloun began his literary career as a poet, a genre that he maintains is still dearest to his heart and a genre that has allowed him to push the limits of the novel into new and experimental directions. In the 1960s and 1970s, Ben Jelloun published his poetry extensively in the Moroccan cultural journals *Souffles* (Breaths) and *Integral*, and was actively involved with a group of socially engaged Moroccan writers, intellectuals, and artists that included the novelist Abdelkebir **Khatibi** and the poet Abdellatif **Laâbi**. Ben Jelloun's poetic work from this period primarily addresses social inequalities and political injustices as they present themselves in postcolonial Morocco and as they are faced by North African immigrants in France. This criticism is loosely veiled in a landscape of the sexual body. In one poem, "Asilah se maquille" (Asilah Puts on Make-Up), Ben Jelloun critiques the gentrification of the small fishing village of Asilah by a corrupt Moroccan bourgeoisie and a wealthy European tourist class, comparing the village to a prostitute. Yet another piece, entitled "Hommes sous linceul de silence" (Men Under a Shroud of Silence), describes the immigration experience through the rape and emasculation of the Arab immigrant. In his poetry, the body becomes the primary canvas of expression upon which Ben Jelloun inscribes stories of violence, corruption, and abuse.

When in 1973 Ben Jelloun published his first novel *Harrouda*, it shocked readers not only for its structurally chaotic hallucination between poetry and prose, but also for its graphic sexual violence. The book begins with a musing on female genitalia, embarking on a spiral course to describe the sexual purity and degeneracy of two Moroccan women through the eyes of a young boy. Both the prostitute Harrouda and the boy's mother incarnate the violence and shame of sexuality in the boy's imagination, and Ben Jelloun explores the young boy's relationship to both women through scenes, fantasies, desires, and memories of erotic violence. In his early poetry, Ben Jelloun shows an engagement in the relationship between sexual bodies and cityscapes; in *Harrouda* this is amplified as he inserts three cities into the narrative that function symbolically as characters in their own right: Fez, the most traditional and repressive of Moroccan cities, Tangier the vice-ridden, and finally an imaginary and liberating city of the future.

The poetic hallucinations of *Harrouda* presage both the experimental narrative structure and thematic preoccupations of two of Ben Jelloun's other early works: the 1978 and 1981 novels *Moha le fou, Moha le sage* (Moha the Mad, Moha the Wise) and *La Prière de l'absent* (The Prayer of the Absent). In the former, Ben Jelloun explores the idea of a plural voice. The title character Moha not only speaks for himself but also permits other voices and narrators to speak through him. Through the marginalized character of a madman, Ben Jelloun is able to deconstruct the unified and censorial voice of official discourse. This plurality of voice, coupled with the ambiguous physical geography of the novel identified simultaneously as towns in Morocco, Tunisia, and Algeria, allows Ben Jelloun to destabilize and deterritorialize the idea of a unified subject and a unified identity. In *La Prière de l'absent*, Ben Jelloun continues to play with the idea of madness and plurality, using the body of Yamna to channel mysterious voices of "the ancestors" that send her and her companions on a mission to search for memory. The three principal characters,

Yamna, an old prostitute who exists as an image of her former self, Sindibad, a beggar with amnesia, and Boby, a man with dreams of becoming a dog, wander together throughout Morocco, from Fez to the distant south, on an unknown mystically ordained mission to educate a voiceless child from a secret world. While structurally this novel is less experimental than those that precede it, the play on memory, body, voice, and absence explores the limits of Moroccan culture, delving deeply into secret and mystical realms.

The explosion of gender in *The Sand Child* and *The Sacred Night*

In the 1985 work *The Sand Child* (*L'Enfant de sable*), Ben Jelloun takes the Western form of a novel into a distinctly Arabic tradition: the *halqa*, the circle of storytellers. Different narrators compete with each other to take up, modify, and add to the story of Ahmed né Zahra, a young woman who is raised by her father to be a man. The chaotic relationship of the storytellers, who all claim to be witnesses to the life of the man/woman, is only surpassed by the chaotic life of simulation in which Ahmed is engaged. After producing seven girls, Ahmed's father is horrified when his eighth child is also born a female and swears to raise this last child as a male. Through great effort and deception, including a faked circumcision and a marriage, Ahmed is able to pass all the societal tests of gender, becoming his father's inheritor of wealth and social power. Through the novel, Ben Jelloun takes apart the question of gender and its construction in Morocco, exploring the liberating and constraining entry of a woman into the world of male power. Through gender, he addresses the problem of image and plural identities.

The award-winning 1987 novel *The Sacred Night* is a continuation of the story of Ahmed/Zahra. When the novel opens, the circle of narrators as well as the narrative itself has dissolved into argument and contention. As the story falls apart, Ahmed/Zahra appears among the narrators to tell of her own life; however, in Ben Jelloun's hands this by no means results in a cohesive and uncomplicated account. On his deathbed, the father reveals to Ahmed what he has done and frees him from the simulation of manhood. From this moment Zahra

is reborn as a woman and must deal with the exploration of her new sexuality and gender. Through a narrative that mixes events with dream sequences and hallucinations, Zahra recounts her sexual awakening as a journey through violence, rape, perversion, and murder. While in *The Sand Child*, Ben Jelloun questions the construction of gender in Moroccan society, in *The Sacred Night* he takes one step further into the problematic realm of gender and sexuality, drawing out physical and mental violence in an almost unbearable intensity.

Exile, loneliness and racism: social commitment and Ben Jelloun's non-fiction

While the majority of Ben Jelloun's fictional work is concerned with giving voice to Moroccan taboos and exploring the margins of the country's culture, Ben Jelloun's non-fiction is primarily engaged in the exploration of another form of marginalization, that of the Moroccan immigrant in France. In 1973, he published a poetic novel entitled *Solitaire* (*La Reclusion solitaire*) that addresses the loneliness of a Moroccan immigrant in France who is separated from his family and home. The economy of words in the text conveys the poverty of immigration and the crushing and indescribable nostalgia of an imagined homeland brought on by exile. In the 1984 non-fiction book *French Hospitality* (*Hospitalité française*), Ben Jelloun breaks through the veils of poetry to produce a politically engaged analysis of French xenophobia and racism. Drawing from his own experiences as a North African immigrant in France, Ben Jelloun discusses how the problems of French hospitality are indicative of larger issues such as the legal and social status of minorities in Europe at the end of the twentieth century, and the strained relationships between former colonizer and formerly colonized people, and Islam and the Judeo-Christian West. Ultimately, however, Ben Jelloun returns to individual experience, arguing that immigration is inherently a violent transformation of the self and a silencing of the past. What is needed at the end of the journey from one country to another is an acceptance, an extended hospitality towards new hybrid subjects and states of existence. In his illustrations of the French case, Ben Jelloun chronicles the damaging effects of French racism on both first- and second-generation immigrants, focusing especially on young children.

When his own daughter turned 10 and began questioning how she was seen and treated in French society, Ben Jelloun felt the need to write a book specifically for children on the many questions of racism. In 1999, he published *Racism Explained to My Daughter* (*Le Racisme expliqué à ma fille*) which was almost immediately translated into fifteen languages, with prefaces from international celebrities such as Bill Cosby. The book is structured through a set of questions that might be posed by a child, such as "Has racism always existed?" and "Why do Africans have black skin and Europeans white skin?" These questions invite responses and further questions, and thus create a dialogue around racism. Ben Jelloun writes that he composed the book through conversations with his own daughter and her friends, in the hope that it would not only create an awareness of the problems facing children in contemporary France, but also battle the silence and resignation with which both immigrants to France and the French themselves treat the subject. Ben Jelloun's personal commitment to break the silence surrounding social issues of the day is also evidenced by his frequent contributions to newspapers such as *Le Monde* in Paris, and his radio show on the French station Medi 1.

Tahar Ben Jelloun's works are widely translated into English and are invaluable to students of the postcolonial Islamic and African world.

Further reading

Aresu, Bernard (1998) *Tahar Ben Jelloun*, New Orleans: CELFAN/Tulane University.

Ben Jelloun, Tahar (1987) *The Sand Child*, trans. Alan Sheridan, San Diego: Harcourt Brace Jovanovich.

——(1989) *The Sacred Night*, trans. Alan Sheridan, San Diego: Harcourt Brace Jovanovich.

——(1996) *Poésie complète: 1966–1995* (Complete Poems, 1966–1995), Paris: Éditions du Seuil.

Bousta, Rachida Saigh (1999) *Lecture des récits de Tahar Ben Jelloun: Écriture, mémoire et imaginaire*

(Reading the Narratives of Tahar Ben Jelloun), Casablanca: Afrique Orient.

KATARZYNA PIEPRZAK

Ben Salah, Rafik

b. 1948, Tunisia

novelist

Although born and raised in Tunisia, the novelist Rafik Ben Salah has spent most of his adult life in Switzerland. These circumstances have allowed him to fuse together the literary traditions of his birthplace and adopted homeland into a vibrant narrative voice that explores both the nostalgia and cultural discovery of exile. His first novel *Retour d'exil* (Return from Exile) (1987) was awarded the Prix Génération 2001 for the best Franco-North African literary work. In *Lettres scellées au President* (Sealed Letters to the President) (1991), Ben Salah narrates the intertwined stories of the son who has left for Europe and the mother left behind. Exploring themes of liberty, abandonment, and betrayal, the novel reflects the cruel realities of life in late twentieth-century Tunisia and France. Cruelty and rumor dominate the critically acclaimed short stories *Le Harem en péril* (The Harem in Peril) (1999). In the first story a young woman with an abdominal tumor is believed by the villagers to be pregnant. Mixing oral and written narrative styles, Ben Salah leads his characters down a fine line between curiosity and conscience.

Further reading

Ben Salah, Rafik (1999) *Le Harem en péril* (The Harem in Peril), Lausanne: Éditions l'Age d'Homme.

KATARZYNA PIEPRZAK

Bénady, Claude

b. 1922, Tunis, Tunisia

poet

Tunisian poet Claude Bénady started his literary

career during the French Protectorate of Tunisia (1881–1956) writing for *La Kahéna*, the famous Tunisian literary journal and publishing house. His first collection of poems, *Chansons du voile* (Songs of the Veil), was published by *La Kahéna* in 1940. Six books of verse appeared in the following fifteen years, and in 1976 Bénady was awarded the Prix de l'Afrique Méditerranée for the entire opus of his work. In 1952, he founded the French literary journal *Périples* (Voyages) that later became his publishing house. Written in French, the major themes of his poems are memory and creation. In *Le Dégel des sources* (The Thaw of the Springs) (1954), he explores the poetic act and its sources of inspiration through naturalistic imagery. Moving between France and Tunisia throughout his life, Bénady also addresses questions of nostalgia and exile in his poems. In *Un Été qui vient de la mer* (A Summer that Comes from the Sea) (1972), he looks out into the Mediterranean Sea and questions the myths of origins, roots, and material identifiers of nationality.

Further reading

Bénady, Claude (1972) *Un Été qui vient de la mer* (A Summer that Comes from the Sea), Paris: Périples.

KATARZYNA PIEPRZAK

Benslimane, Jacqueline

b. Algeria

poet

Jacqueline Benslimane is the author of a collection of poetry entitled *Poèmes* (Poems) (1963) in which she brings together ten thematic poems, most singing of Algeria: its landscapes, its traditions, its turmoils, and its liberation. However, no matter what the theme, the central focus of Benslimane's poetry remains the Algerian woman.

NASRIN QADER

Bensmaia, Réda

b. 1944, Algeria

novelist and academic

The Algerian writer Réda Bensmaia is primarily known as a novelist and literary critic. His novel *Year of Passages* (1995) describes the return of the narrator to his native city of Algiers after years of exile in the US. In this novel, Mrad, the protagonist, returns to Algiers, like the author himself, with a changed vision and perspective on his society. More significantly, in its subject and style the novel is an attempt to combine a social critique of contemporary Algerian society and to experiment with literary form through the insertion of fragments of texts and the mixing of dialogues and quotations in French, English, and Arabic. These are some of the features that place the novel within the postmodern and postcolonial tradition of writing defined by fragmented realities and hybrid narratives (see **colonialism, neocolonialism, and postcolonialism**). In order for the significance of this novel to be appreciated, it needs to be read in the context of Bensmaia's critical writings and his contribution to poststructuralist theories, reflected especially in his work on the French critic Roland Barthes and in his collaboration with the French critic and philosopher Gilles Deleuze. Bensmaia is currently a professor of French and comparative literatures at Brown University, USA, where he is pursuing his writing in critical theory and literary fiction.

Further reading

Bensmaia, R. (1995) *Year of Passages*, trans. Tom Coley, Minneapolis: University of Minnesota Press.

ANISSA TALAHITE-MOODLEY

Bensoussan, Albert

b. 1935, Algiers, Algeria

novelist, academic, and translator

Born in Algiers of Jewish Sephardic parents, Albert

Bensoussan lived in Algeria until 1963 when he moved to France. He taught Spanish at the Sorbonne University, then moved to Rennes, in Brittany, in 1966. He worked at the University of Rennes as a professor, translator, and writer. His departure from Algeria constitutes the main theme of his work, and is seen by the writer as a triple exile: from his childhood, from his Jewish culture, and from his native land.

A prolific writer, Bensoussan wrote seventeen books between 1965 and 1998. His fictional writings consist of short stories and novels, all of which contain strong autobiographical material and show a deep attachment to his years spent in Algeria. In his novels Albert Bensoussan deals primarily with the pain of leaving his native country, with the nostalgia for his childhood years, and with the grief of losing his grandparents and his father. Inspired by the writer's memories of a happy childhood in northern Africa, a semi-autobiographical narrator present in most of his works describes in short narratives the life of a Jewish family in Algiers and in Algerian villages, elaborating on the children's games, on the Jewish rituals, on his grandmother's gift of healing in *L'Oeil de la sultane* (The Eye of the Sultana) (1996), or on his grandfather's encounters with the local rabbi in *L'Échelle de Mesrod* (Mesrod's World) (1984). Moreover, Bensoussan's frequent ironical references to France as Frime, which allude both to the coldness of the country, *frimas*, and to the French attitude of arrogance, *frime*, show a distrust of French politics prevailing in his writings since his first novel, *Les Bagnoulis* (The Bagnoulis), in 1965. His depiction of Algerian villages, his recollections of the entente prevailing between the Jewish and the Arabic communities in Algeria before the French colonization, and his usage of Arabic words and expressions in his narratives express the writer's nostalgia for a vanished world.

Another source of the writer's inspiration is his life in France and his status of Sephardic Jew living in diaspora. His adjustment to life in Brittany, called Breiz or *La Bréhaigne* (1974), the title of one of his major works, constitutes the subject of several introspective narratives, such as *Mirage à 3* (Mirage of 3) (1989), in which the narrator, estranged from a wife with whom he shares only memories of the native land, attempts to reconcile himself with his exile. Constantly torn between a vision of an idyllic Algeria, transformed in the writer's memory into a mythical lost paradise, and the gray skies of Rennes and the hostility of the French, the author expresses feelings of anguish and despair.

His non-fictional writings can be divided into two different areas: his translation of Hispanic works, and his theoretical writings on Francophone Jewish literature. Albert Bensoussan finds in translation an opportunity to play with words and phrases which constitutes one of his favorite occupations, as is immediately apparent in the prose poems of his fictional works as well. Bensoussan has a degree in Spanish literature, and since 1970 he has translated more than forty works by writers from Spain and from South America, showing a special interest in the works of Mario Vargas Llosa. In 1985 he received the Cultura Latina Prize for his translation work.

By staying close to his Jewish Sephardic ancestry, Bensoussan has demonstrated a keen interest in the Francophone Sephardic literature produced since the 1950s, and is the author of numerous articles on the subject. In his book *L'Échelle séfarade* (The Sephardic World) (1993), Bensoussan collects a few of these articles, further discusses the role of Jewish literature and analyzes the works of writers such as Albert Cohen, Elissa Rhais, Albert **Memmi**, and Edmond **Jabès**.

Further reading

Bensoussan, Albert (1974) *La Bréhaigne* (Brittany), Paris: Denoël.

——(1976) *Frimaldjézar*, Paris: Calmann-Lévy.

——(1978) *Au nadir* (At the Nadir), Paris: Flammarion.

——(1984) *L'Échelle de Mesrod* (Mesrod's World), Paris: L'Harmattan.

——(1988) *Le Dernier Devoir* (The Last Duty), Paris: L'Harmattan.

——(1998) *Le Chant silencieux des chouettes* (The Silent Song of Owls), Paris: L'Harmattan.

Schousboe, Elisabeth (1991) *Albert Bensoussan*, Paris: L'Harmattan.

VÉRONIQUE MAISIER

Berezak, Fatiha

b. 1947, Beni Saf, Algeria

poet and performer

Born in Beni Saf, Algeria, Fatiha Berezak is both a writer and a performer. Her first collection of poetry, *Le Regard aquarel I* (Watercolor Glance I) (1985), first performed in Paris, was a mix of poetry, dance, mime, and music. This work was followed by *Le Regard aquarel II* (1990) and *Le Regard aquarel III* (1992). In 1993 she published her first prose text, *Homsiq*.

Fatiha Berezak's work, prose as well as poetry, characterizes itself with a ceaseless effort to break down boundaries: between writing and performance, between prose and poetry, between fiction and social commentary. In her poetry, the boundaries of French language are challenged through neologisms and insertions of English words and phrases while, at the same time, her glance remains turned towards the political and the social conditions of women, immigrants, etc. Similarly, in her prose she breaks down the decisive boundaries between fiction, poetry, and political commentary, allowing us to enter a space where dream and reality are no longer distinguishable.

NASRIN QADER

Berrada, Mohammed

b. 1938, Rabat, Morocco

essayist and novelist

The essayist and novelist Mohammed Berrada has spent much of his life between Fez and Rabat, Morocco, cities ever present in his work. He began his career with a collection of short stories, *Salkh al-jild: wa-qisas ukhra* (Flaying the Skin and Other Stories) (1979), and two essays in literary criticism. Since then he has published several novels, including *Fugitive Light* (*Al-Daw' al-hāib*; *Lumière fuyante*) (1998), and *Mithla sayf lan yatakarrar* (As If Summer Will Not Return) (1999), concerning ancient Egypt. In these works, Berrada's clear style conveys a fragmented narration, bringing a new sensibility to the Arabic novel. His most important and accessible work, however, is his 1987 memoir,

The Game of Forgetting (*Lu\`bat al-nisyān*). It stages a self-conscious narrator, sometimes in conflict with the author, trying to make sense of a disparate and discordant stock of memories of childhood in Fez and Rabat. The text moves between narrators and time periods to create an intimate picture of family and cultural life in Morocco since the 1940s.

Further reading

Berrada, Mohammed (1996) *The Game of Forgetting*, Austin: University of Texas, Center for Middle Eastern Studies.

SETH GRAEBNER

Besong, Bate

b. 1954, Cameroon; d. 2007, Buea, Cameroon

poet

A PhD in English and literary studies from the University of Calabar (Nigeria), the Cameroonian writer Bate Besong is primarily known as a poet. He has published several collections of poetry, including *Polyphemus Detainee and Other Skulls* (1980), *The Banquet* (1994), *The Grain of Bobe Ngom Jua* (1985), and *Just Above Cameroon* (1998). He has also published important plays including *The Most Cruel Death of the Talkative Zombie* (1987), and *Beasts of No Nation* (1990). Concerned with the state of culture and society in postcolonial Africa in general and Cameroon in particular (see **colonialism, neo-colonialism, and postcolonialism**), Besong's works focus on specific social problems of the period after independence, such as injustice, corruption, social, political, and economic instability, as well as the sharp inequalities plaguing Africa and the resulting human suffering. His works appear to be a platform geared toward the denunciation of oppression inflicted by one group on another and the resulting tensions, including violence, and lack of social, economic, and political stability. In addition to teaching drama at the University of Buea in Cameroon, Besong is also an important critic whose essays have appeared in various international professional journals.

Further reading

Besong, Bate (1991) *Obasinjom Warrior with Poems after Detention*, Limbe: Nooremac Press.
——(1991) *Requiem for the Last Kaiser*, Calabar: Centaur Publishers.

M'BARE NGOM

Bessora

b. 1968, Brussels, Belgium

novelist

Born in Belgium (her father is Gabonese and her mother is Swiss), Bessora divided her childhood between Africa, Europe, and the USA. She eventually settled in France, where she studied for a PhD in anthropology. With the publication of two novels, *53cm* (1999) and *Taches d'encre* (Ink Stains) (2000) by Serpent à Plumes in Paris, she has established herself as part of the new generation of African writers, and like many of her contemporaries, especially those living and writing in Europe, Bessora writes about immigration and all the complexities of identity that arise in a world where the status of legal immigrant is not available to most people of color. Bessora's novel *Taches d'encre* is a humorous, exuberant work of fiction in which characters of different races make and try to break their relationships yet continue running into each other, thus forming an ever-closer circle. Bessora shows how, in the face of great anxieties, blacks and whites can have a life together. More importantly, it is because of her original style of writing that Bessora has been recognized as a significant voice in the new tradition of women writing in Africa.

FRIEDA EKOTTO

Beti, Mongo

b. 1932, Akométan, Cameroon; d. 2001, Douala, Cameroon

writer and publisher

The Cameroonian Francophone novelist, essayist, and publisher Mongo Beti (pseudonym of Alex-andre Biyidi) has been one of the most influential African writers of both the pre- and post-independence period. While he became famous detailing and criticizing the effects of colonialism through fictional novels (see **colonialism, neoco-lonialism, and postcolonialism**), he diversified the targets of his criticism as well as his critical media as his career progressed. He has gone on to attack political and social corruption of a diverse nature in fiction and non-fiction novels, essays, lectures, and articles, and through his founding and direction of both *Peuples noirs/peuples africains* (*Black Peoples/African Peoples*), a bimonthly periodical of political and cultural articles that criticizes neoco-lonialism, and La Librairie des Peuples Noirs (the Bookstore of Black Peoples), a bookstore that brings a wide variety of African literature and commentary to the public, especially literature that is critical of Cameroonian society. Until his death in 2001, Beti remained an important and active intellectual voice, continuously criticizing the state of African society and culture, and especially Cameroonian politics, even as he pursued a literary career.

Beti's career can be divided into four stages. The first is often referred to as his introductory or anti-colonial period. It represents the moment when he burst on to the international literary scene to great success and praise. These first works describe the problems and confusion brought about by coloni-alism in Africa, causing both suffering and alienation but also important divisions as African society becomes torn between ancestral tradition and European practices, Catholicism and indigen-ous religions, and other cultural conflicts. Although he is known primarily as a novelist, Beti's first published works were a short story, *Sans haine et sans amour* (Without Hate and Without Love), and an article/fiction, *Problèmes de l'étudiant noir* (Black Student Problems), in a 1953 issue of the periodical *Présence Africaine*. Written under the pseudonym Eza Boto, the article/fiction is an unusual combination of a study of the possibilities of the African novel and the beginnings of a fictional novel detailing the experiences of a young African student newly arrived in France. The work is especially prescient of Beti's later work, since he soon embarked on a career that saw him leading the development of the African novel as well as producing myriad articles and analyses of literary and social topics. Equally prophetic was his short story, which, through a retelling of a Kenyan's participation in the 1950s Mau Mau resistance, touches on the theme of guerilla resistance to oppressive state control that will serve as the backdrop for the novels that constitute his third stage.

Still writing as Eza Boto, Beti then produced his first novel, *Ville Cruelle* (Cruel City) (1954), a denunciation of the social and political hierarchy and resultant abuses of power under colonial rule. It describes the unfortunate events that befall a cacao farmer who comes to the city to sell his produce only to be cheated and abused repeatedly at the hands of people in positions of power. Interestingly, the novel does not simply concentrate on criticizing the colonial administration and administrators, as did most anti-colonial novels of the period, but focuses as well on those Africans who profit from the colonial presence at the expense of their fellow Africans. More successful than these first attempts at writing were his two subsequent novels, *The Poor Christ of Bomba* (*Le Pauvre Christ de Bomba*) (1956) and *Mission to Kala* (*Mission terminée*) (1957), both of which earned him international recognition and acclaim, including the Prix Sainte-Beuve of 1958 for *Mission to Kala*. *The Poor Christ of Bomba* is a savage satire concentrating on the conflict engendered by the introduction of Catholicism to indigenous religion. It details the travels of a misguided French priest as he attempts to install Catholicism in his mission territory in the 1930s, as told through the journal of his African cook. The cook is both respectful of his employer and intensely naïve concerning his activities. The satirical attack on the missionary is thus similar to that found in Ferdinand **Oyono**'s *Houseboy* (1956), in that the generally positive attitude and observations of the narrator function as ironic commentary that depends on the reader's complicity, willing or not, in the condemnation of missionary activity. For this reason, the novel elicited strong reactions, positive and negative, in Europe and Africa.

Mission to Kala also deals with cultural intermixing and conflict, although in a more general way. On the surface, the novel, narrated by the protagonist Jean-Marie, recounts his adventure as a young student who, upon returning to his village, was charged with retrieving a woman who had fled. The story is entirely secondary, however, to the presentation of how Jean-Marie reacts to village life and how the villagers react to him. This cultural conflict of mutual misunderstanding and incomprehension is based largely on divisions of tradition and modernity, and yet it is clear that neither society is without flaws. In this sense, the novel can be seen in part as a response to Camara **Laye**'s *The Dark Child* (1954), of whose idyllic representation of village life Beti was virulently critical. In the end, the conflict reaches a violent climax when Jean-Marie has a disagreement with his father and leaves to lead a life of perpetual vagabondage. Beti followed these two novels with *King Lazarus* (*Le Roi miraculé*) (1958), a novel that concerns itself with traditional political power and the destabilizing effect that colonial intrusion has on it. As already seen in *The Poor Christ of Bomba*, the primary representative of colonialism is a Catholic priest. When he and the converted aunt of the titular king successfully pressure the dying king to renounce his pagan ways and rid himself of his many wives, the resultant political uproar over broken family ties and alliances is calmed only when he is "de-converted" and allowed to re-establish his former ruling practices. The novel is often seen as a bridge between Beti's earlier novels of cultural conflict and the novels of his third stage that concentrate on independence from colonial control and influence.

Beti then began a long period of silence, often labeled the second "stage" of his career, even though it is characterized more by absence than production. Although active politically against both colonialism and the despotic regimes of post-independence Africa, he published nothing for fourteen years. While speculation as to the reasons for this extended hiatus range from practical concerns of work and education to political censure and threats, the exact reason for this silent stage has never been confirmed by Beti himself. Beti then burst back on to the literary scene with a non-fiction book, *Main basse sur le Cameroun* (Rape of Cameroon) (1972), which has been alternately described as a novel, an essay, and a political pamphlet. Regardless of its genre, the book was undeniably a literary bombshell. Detailing the 1970 political arrests of Ernest Ouandié and Monsignor Ndongmo in Cameroon and the eventual execution of the former, the book is, in fact, a dense collection of Cameroonian colonial history and of French newspaper articles covering the Ouandié and Ndongmo affairs. Beti thus notes not only the political motivations of the Cameroonian government, but the long-standing French attitude towards and involvement in Cameroonian politics. It was instantly banned, not only in Cameroon but France as well, confirming some of the arguments he was making. After a successful lawsuit against the French government in 1976, the book was re-edited and reissued in 1977 and then again in 1984.

Beti continued to write after this dramatic return to public view, producing a series of three novels denouncing the practices of neocolonialism and corrupt government that denied the promise of post-independence liberty and prosperity. The novels, *Remember Ruben* (in French also called *Remember Ruben*) (1974), *Perpetua and the Habit of Unhappiness* (*Perpétue et l'habitude du malheur*) (1974), and *Lament for an African Pol* (*La Ruine presque cocasse d'un polichinelle*) (1979), are often referred to as "the trilogy." In fact, the third novel (subtitled *Remember Ruben 2*) is a direct sequel to the first. The two novels, although decidedly fiction, are firmly rooted in the union organizing, political protests, and guerilla resistance of pre- and postwar Cameroon. Taking their inspiration (and titles) from the Cameroonian political and resistance figure Ruben Um Nyobé, these two novels detail the resistance, both successful and unsuccessful, against oppressive governmental regimes. While they are largely set in the colonial past, the critique of contemporary neocolonial abuses is evident. The second novel is less obviously a part of this trilogy as it follows the search by Essola into the details of his sister Perpetua's death. The connection is there, however, both generally, as Essola increasingly discovers that her years of suffering and eventual death are linked to a continuing neocolonial oppressive regime, and specifically, as frequent links are made between Perpetua and Ruben Um Nyobé's deaths.

In 1978, Beti launched *Peuples noirs/peuples africains* with the goal of establishing a forum for writers who wished to discuss political and cultural issues relevant to Africa. While the periodical features discussions on a wide variety of subjects –

literature, politics, cinema, activists, current events, and art, among many others – it has a strong unifying focus of exposing, criticizing, and eliminating neocolonialist practices and institutions in Africa. Beti remained director, often contributing articles himself, until 1991. It was during this time that he started what is often called the third stage of his literary career, writing a series of novels and articles criticizing the authoritarian, anti-democratic governments and leaders of Africa. This critique appears in *Les Deux Mères de Guillaume Ismaël Dzewatama* (Guillaume Ismaël Dzewatama's Two Mothers) (1983) and *La Revanche de Guillaume Ismaël Dzewatama* (Guillaume Ismaël Dzewatama's Revenge) (1984), which detail a family's involvement in an attempted coup against a corrupt authoritarian African president and the resultant hard times when the attempt fails. The novels are also noted for their treatment of the question of interracial marriage. *L'Histoire du fou* (The Fool's Story) (1994) also treats problematic issues in neocolonial Africa.

In 1992, Beti retired from his job as a teacher at a Rouen (France) high school and returned to Cameroon, beginning what could be labeled his fourth stage. Far from slowing down, however, Beti opened La Librairie des Peuples Noirs in Yaoundé and continued both his writing career and his political activity. Although not exclusively devoted to political and activist material, his bookstore was one of the only places in the country where one could find a wide selection of new books and periodicals that are critical of African, and especially Cameroonian, politics, culture, law, and other social issues. Beti also routinely spoke out in the press, in articles, and by means of protests and speeches concerning human rights, corruption, and sustainable economic development, among other topics.

At the beginning of the twenty-first century, Beti continued to be an active intellectual voice in literary studies, publishing, and African politics. He spoke and wrote with some regularity against the concept of a Francophone culture, arguing that it was a cultural aporia and artificial community that stunted the development of African literature and culture. His last novels were *Trop de soleil tue l'amour* (Too Much Sun Kills Love) (1999) and *Branle-bas en noir et blanc* (Pandemonium in Black and White) (2000), both of which continued the theme of criticizing African dictators, but with a wholly different approach as they constituted a kind of detective "thriller" series with recurring characters. Beti, along with Elizabeth Darnel, also has a collection of translated Caribbean and African stories, *The Story of the Madman* (2001). Despite his tremendous success, diverse interests and activities, and long-standing fame and notoriety, Beti scrupulously avoided participating in the production of a biography of his life, and therefore no such work yet exists.

Further reading

Arnold, Stephen H. (ed.) (1998) *Critical Perspectives on Mongo Beti*, Boulder, Colorado: Lynne Rienner.

Bjornson, Richard (1991) *The African Quest for Freedom and Identity: Cameroonian Writing and the National Experience*, Bloomington: Indiana University Press.

STEPHEN BISHOP

Beur literature in France

While immigration has existed as a field of study in French history since the mid twentieth century, it gained a new political momentum only in the 1980s. Before then the theme of immigration was discussed primarily in terms of economics and was used to refer to the role of the state in controlling the migratory flow of labor between France and its former colonies. After the 1980s, however, political discussion on immigration witnessed a new dynamic. The topic of immigration was elevated beyond economic relations to the realm of high politics, involving the discussion of issues related to cultural pluralism, national identity, multiculturalism, and nation-building. In these discussions the identity of Beurs (people of North African descent born in France) emerged as a central concept in the understanding of the debate surrounding ethnic minorities in a society that has traditionally considered ethnicity as a threat to social cohesion and national identity.

It is generally accepted that the birth of the Beur identity can be traced to the 1980s. Starting with the year 1981, a variety of artistic works originating from authors whose political and social status was then considered marginal to the French political establishment proliferated in the world of art and literature. In local radio, television shows, newspapers, theater, cinema, and literature, the concept of Beur emerged to refer to the second generation of North African immigrants to France. While the main issues raised in these artistic productions were related to racism, discrimination, and unemployment, their underlying theme was a struggle for the recognition of an emerging ethnic minority – one with different linguistics, religious and cultural practices – in France itself. At stake was the struggle for the redefinition of the classical conception of the French identity to include the full integration of the children of Arab and Muslim immigrants.

General overview

The birth of North African immigration in France today finds its origin in three large migratory movements from North African countries to France. The first movement was the one between 1918 and 1950. During this period, around 750,000 North African immigrants, mainly Algerians, were brought to France either as workers or as soldiers in order to replenish the population deficit created by the two European world wars. What facilitated this migratory flow, in the case of Algeria, was the legal status of Algerian workers who were not subjected to the usual legal requirements imposed by the French immigration legislation on its immigrants.

The second stage of immigration took place between 1950 and 1970. During this period, the rate of immigration from North Africa accelerated, with new migrants being attracted by the postwar economic prosperity in France. The decolonization movement that took place in the African continent in the 1960s was another factor that contributed to the acceleration of immigration between France and its former colonies during this period. In the case of Algeria, the 1962 Evian Agreement that regulated the transition between Algeria and France maintained the principle of free circulation between the two countries. An estimated 111,000 Algerians entered France between 1962 and 1965.

The third stage in the history of North African immigration in France came after 1970. Two aspects characterize this period. The first aspect was a change in the patterns of immigration. While in the first and the second stages immigration to France was primarily fueled by the need for labor, in this last stage North African immigration became one of settlement, in the sense that it brought to France workers whose intention was not to work and send money to the families they had left behind in the country of origin, but to seek the means to settle in France.

The second aspect that characterized the third stage of the movement of North Africans to France was the emergence of immigration as a political issue. Once it became apparent that new migrants were going to France to settle, immigration became an issue that defined political programs and the electoral campaigns of political candidates from the left and the right. By the end of the 1970s, immigration began to be perceived as a threat to the economic prosperity and the social cohesion of French society. Public perception quickly identified the term "immigrant" with that of Muslim Arab North African immigrants, thus rendering the word "immigrant" the object of political discussion on a range of social issues, including unemployment, violence, xenophobia, and racism. It is under these circumstances that the concept of Beur emerged in an attempt to circumvent the stigma associated with the term "immigrant," but, most importantly, to offer a new language for the new social reality that had been taking place in France.

Who are the Beur?

From a linguistics point of view, it is important to underscore the ambiguity of the word "Beur" and the difficulty in explaining its etymology, even to those who have an adequate grasp of the French language. The term "Beur," which means "Arab," comes from a French slang – the Verlan – that reverses words in order to read them beginning with their last syllable. There does not seem to be an intellectual consensus regarding the origin of this word, but authors generally agree on its meaning and its denotation. Regarding the ambiguous nature of the term, some authors argue that it is a reflection of the ambivalent status of the Beur

in French culture. As the writer Mehdi Charef has noted (1983: Paris), finding themselves "lost between two cultures, two histories, two languages and two colors," the Beur have chosen an ambiguous term as an expression of the identity malaise in which second-generation immigrants have found themselves.

For others, the word "Beur" is not an ambiguous term, but rather functions as an intentionally chosen form of linguistic camouflage that allows Arab North Africans to bypass the clichés associated with the word "Arab." It also allows them to transgress the social and political order that attempts to confine them to the immigrant status of their parents even when they were born in France. From this perspective, the use of the word "Beur" becomes a political strategy that employs a linguistic tool to re-appropriate the meaning of the word "Arab," a word that has been so damaged by the stereotypes of an ethnocentric approach to cultural diversity. While these interpretations are only epistemological, in reality the concept of Beur has helped elaborate an identity, and shape a debate about the rights of cultural minorities in a society that has been traditionally reluctant to recognize cultural difference, especially when it puts the cultural foundations of the dominant culture into question.

In France today, the term "Beur" has come to refer to a new generation of French citizens of North African origin and their cultural production. Sometimes called second generation, sometimes young immigrants, and sometimes Maghrebians, these are the children of first-generation North African immigrants. The term "Beur" encompasses different categories of North African immigrants who, although they share some cultural and social aspects with each other, do not have the same social and legal status and relationship to French society. Indeed, the concept of Beur refers to two distinct categories of North African immigrants. The first category refers to the children of North African labor immigrants. These children were born and raised in France as a result of the labor migration movement that took place between North African countries, mainly Algeria and France. What characterizes this category of Beur, besides its ethnic origin, is its socio-economic status. Labor immigrants in France during the glorious years of the French economy have been mostly assigned low-skilled jobs that required no education. This situation has not only limited their mobility inside French society, but it has also constrained them into a labor social status that has limited their access to the economic prosperity of French society.

The second category of North African immigrants refers to the Harkis, who are the children of Algerians who sided with the colonial administration against the Algerian revolution between 1954 and 1962. Born or raised in France, this category of Beur is in a much more complex situation than that of the children of labor immigrants. Because they bear the political scars of their own past and of the past of their parents, who were perceived to have made the wrong choice during the Algerian revolution, they are rejected by both French and Algerians alike, and thus their adjustment in France has been more difficult.

The problematic of the Beur identity

The problem that Beur identity poses to French society is intimately linked to the conception that the French have about the founding of their nation. Two perspectives have dominated the historical debate about the making of the French nation. The first perspective is often called Jacobean, but is also referred to as nationalist Catholic; political parties on the right and the extreme right advocate it using organic and biological criteria such as language, ethnicity, and religion to define the nation. In this perspective, it is argued that since the fifteenth century the French nation has assumed a form that corresponds to a big family unified by blood or religion. It is argued that the end product of this historical process of nation formation took place during the French revolution in 1789. Therefore, it is important to the Jacobean perspective that what came after this historical moment could not remake the foundations of the nation. Immigrants, welcomed mainly for economic reasons, were considered as guests and were expected eventually to return to their countries of origin. As a result this conception of nation does not recognize immigration as a process of nation-building, because it brings to the nation groups that do not fulfill the biological and organic criteria that this perspective considers important.

The second concept of the French nation is called republican. In this concept, the French nation is a nation of rights and responsibilities inspired by the philosophy of the Enlightenment. From this perspective, belonging to the nation is not defined by ethnic or biological criteria but by a desire, a social contract, and a political will that define the rights and responsibilities of individuals in their relationship to each other and to the nation. From this perceptive, immigrants are welcomed, but they are welcomed only as individuals and not as a group. Their assimilation and integration into the French nation is expected to take place through the institutions of the republic, such as educational institutions and language.

In both conceptions one can see that immigration, although it has played a major role in the process of nation-building, has not been fully recognized as a legitimate institution. In the first conception of nationhood, immigrants are clearly denied access to the French nation; in the second conception they are welcomed but have to comply with two conditions. The first condition is that they have to come as individuals and not as a social group. The second condition is that they are expected to assimilate and integrate into the nation. While this conception worked with early Catholic and other European immigrants who came to France from Italy and other parts of Europe during the nineteenth and twentieth centuries, it has posed a problem for the Beur specifically because they have resisted assimilation into the French republic. Most Beurs are Muslim, and because they come from a different religious background they are seen as maintaining a relationship of conflict with the idea of the French nation and its institutions; since all of them come from former colonies with prior social identities, the assimilation of the Beur community has come to be conceived as a problem.

Beur literature

The emergence of Beur literature in the 1980s

created a new space in which themes related to the affirmation of the difference, cultural hybridity, uprootedness, and displacement could be discussed for the first time in French literature by writers who had experienced displacement and uprootedness themselves. The stories and tales told by these writers have become part of a complex process of documentation that has made the Beurs' painful struggle for cultural pluralism an important part of the French cultural landscape.

In his autobiography Azouz **Begag**, a Beur writer, makes a clear reference to his Arabic identity through the use of Arabic names in titles and Arabic words in the body of a French text. In his first autobiography, *The Kid from the Township* (*Le Gone du Chaâba*) (1986), Begag chooses the word *chaâba* deliberately in reference to his social and ethnic belonging. Mehdi Charef, another Beur writer, represents the school not as a republican institution that provides the social and economic mobility that will help immigrants become integrated into the republic, but as a site of incarceration where the marginalization of immigrants is legitimized. Farida Belghoul, another Beur writer, in her account of her childhood describes the dilemma of North African women caught between an oppressive social origin and a colonizing host society. For Belghoul, the North African women's dilemma is that their promised emancipation ought to take place through the destruction of their ethnic and social identity.

Finally, it is important to look at the Beur literature as an act of enlightened rebellion in which Beur writers re-appropriate educational and literary institutions in order to reclaim ownership of an Arab Muslim identity.

Further reading

Charef, Mehdi (1983) *Le Thé au harem d'Archi Ahmed* (Tea in the Harem of Archi Ahmed), Paris: Mercure de France.

Hargreaves, Alec G. (1997) *Immigration and Identity in Beur Fiction: Voices from the North African Immigrant Community in France*, New York: Berg.

SID AHMED BENRAOUANE

Beyala, Calixthe

b. 1960, Douala, Cameroon

novelist

Calixthe Beyala is one of the most significant Cameroonian woman writers of the postcolonial period (see **colonialism, neocolonialism, and postcolonialism**) and she has won numerous literary prizes, including the Prix Goncourt in 1999, for her major novels, including *It is the Sun that Burned Me* (*C'est le soleil qui m'a brûlée*) (1987), *Your Name Shall Be Tanga* (*Tu t'appelleras Tanga*) (1988), and *Loukoum: The "Little Prince" of Belleville* (*Le Petit Prince de Belleville*) (1992). *C'est le soleil qui m'a brûlée* reflects many of the concerns in Beyala's novels: it is the story of Ateba, a 19-year-old woman living in the Quartier Général, the most miserable neighborhood in the town of Awu, located somewhere in Africa. Abandoned by her mother, a prostitute, and raised by a despotic aunt, she wonders why women accept the law, the yoke of the man, why they look for him obstinately, lending, selling, giving their bodies, their wombs, as if life could not be conceived of without a man at home. Ateba herself will be attracted to one of these men. She will "experience" a man. And in order to discover herself, she will discover and be scorched by the suns of desire, of custom, of traditions hardened in their most oppressive aspects, the suns that dry out the desert rather than give life. These experiences will make her aware that what she desires is gentleness, femininity, tenderness, and she will accomplish her entry into this new world by killing what la René Girard would call a "sacred" victim. For Ateba, it is necessary to embrace violence in order for love to emerge, to kill the man in order that a new female body may be born.

But in Beyala's novel the term "body" has more than a conventional sense: the body becomes a place of power, a site where language is articulated. Beyala's novels are concerned with the human body as a space in which other social and political signs are constructed. She is concerned with signs as they are produced in writing and on the body, scarifications carried by texts as well as flesh. Scarification is present in Beyala's writing in its division and spacing, and particularly in the ways in which the work is divided according to the distinction between oral and written narrative. Often in her novels, Beyala uses a narrator who is part of the community she describes but is also removed from it; the narrator's distance is marked by her "awareness" and also by her sense of being a cultural reminder – a recaller of important cultural information. In this sense, characters such as Ateba serve as a vatic source: an utterer, an exclusive font of knowledge for the community. In the struggle for the articulation of critical intervention, Beyala succeeds in using the European category of minority (which includes the marginal artist, the handicapped, the prostitute, etc.) as a smokescreen to distract those who would censor "subversive" messages in her writing and its controversial themes.

Further reading

Beyala, Calixthe (1995) *Loukoum: The "Little Prince" of Belville*, Oxford and Portsmouth, New Hampshire: Heinemann.

——(1996) *It is the Sun that Burned Me*, Oxford and Portsmouth, New Hampshire: Heinemann.

——(1996) *Your Name Shall Be Tanga*, Oxford and Portsmouth, New Hampshire: Heinemann.

FRIEDA EKOTTO

Bhêly-Quénum, Olympe

b. 1928, Ouidah, Benin

novelist and teacher

Born 20 September 1928 in Ouidah, Benin (formerly Dahomey), Olympe Bhêly-Quénum grew up in a large polygamous family. After completing his primary education in Benin, he traveled throughout his native country before moving to neighboring Nigeria, his maternal grandmother's country, evoked in his novel *The Call of Voodoo* (*Les Appels du vodou*) (1974), and then to Ghana (formerly Gold Coast), where he learned English at Accra's Achimota Grammar School. Back in Dahomey, he found employment as an assistant warehouseman with John Walkden, a

Unilever company, and used his savings to travel to France in 1948. Once there, he completed high school and his tertiary education, graduating from the Sorbonne in sociology and socio-anthropology, and from Caen (Normandy) in classical letters in 1955.

From 1955 to 1957, he taught French, Greek, and Latin at the Lycée of Coutances in Normandy. In 1958, he was transferred to the Lycée Paul Langevin in Suresnes, near Paris, and in 1959–60 he joined the Lycée Jacques Decour-annexe in Saint-Denis.

His first novel, *Snares Without End* (*Un Piège sans fin*) (1960), was published the year of Dahomey's independence. Between 1961 and 1963 he trained as a diplomat and graduated in diplomacy from the IHEOM (Institute of Higher Studies for Overseas Territories) but gave up diplomacy, choosing instead to embark on a career in journalism. He became the editor and director of *La Vie africaine* (African Life) and later the co-founder, with his wife, of the bilingual magazine *L'Afrique actuelle* (Africa Today). The novel *Le Chant du lac* (The Song of the Lake) (1965) and his collection of short stories, *Liaison d'un été* (A Summer Relationship) (1968), were published around that time.

In 1968, Bhêly-Quénum briefly joined UNESCO headquarters in Paris where he was employed as an African issues specialist.

Bhêly-Quénum's novel *L'Initié* (The Initiated) (1979) confirmed him as one of the most influential writers of Benin, very much inspired by his own experience and life in both France and Africa. His latter publications include a fascinating essay on Pouchkine (1999); a collection of short stories, entitled *La Naissance d'Abikou* (Abikou's Birth) (1998) that evokes important themes pertaining to African and Western perceptions of issues such as the value of a traditional upbringing, initiation, voodoo, racism, and freemasonry; and *Tigony* (*C'était à Tigony*) (2000), a novel that forcefully presents the social and political problems besetting postcolonial African society (see **colonialism, neocolonialism, and postcolonialism**). Olympe Bhêly-Quénum is a Chevalier de l'Ordre National du Bénin and the winner of the Literary Grand Prize of Africa for 1966.

Further reading

Bhêly-Quénum, O. (1999) "Pouchkine et le conte Africain" (Pouchkine and the African Tale) in D. Gnammankou (ed.) *Pouchkine et le Monde Noir* (Pouchkine and the Black World), Paris: Présence Africaine.

Bhêly-Quénum, O., Mercier, R. and Battestini, S. (eds) (1967) *Olympe Bhêly-Quénum, écrivain Dahoméen* (Olympe Bhêly-Quénum, Dahomian Writer), Paris: Fernand Nathan, Série Classiques du monde, Littérature africaine 4.

JEAN-MARIE VOLET

Bhiri, Slaheddine

b. 1947, Tunisia

novelist and poet

The Tunisian novelist and poet Slaheddine Bhiri is known for his literary explorations of exile and immigration. His semi-biographical novel *L'Espoir était pour demain: les tribulations d'un jeune immigré en France* (Hope was for Tomorrow: The Trials of a Young Immigrant in France) (1982) is the account of a young ambitious Arab student in Paris, based on Bhiri's own bifurcated life as a student of literature and a janitor, plumber, and physical laborer. Dedicated to those who live in oppression and who through their dignity want to break the bonds of subjection, the novel is an anguished and bitter indictment of French racism, its injustice, humiliation, and violence. Bhiri's main character, Dine, navigates the cruelty of Paris and the camaraderie of the immigrant class in order to find hope for himself and the future. In this work, Bhiri writes that suffering is beyond language and identity, passing straight through the soul; to have suffered greatly is to possess all knowledge. The theme of identity and exile is continued in Bhiri's 1993 collection of poems *De nulle part* (From Nowhere).

Further reading

Bhiri, Slaheddine (1982) *L'Espoir était pour demain: les*

tribulations d'un jeune immigré (Hope was for Tomorrow: The Trials of a Young Immigrant in France), Paris: Éditions Publisud.

KATARZYNA PIEPRZAK

Biko, Steve

b. 1946, King Williamstown, South Africa; d. 1977, South Africa

prose writer and political activist

Before he was arrested and killed by the South African secret police in 1977, Steve Biko was one of the most important and charismatic leaders in the struggle against apartheid (see **apartheid and post-apartheid**). Involved in student political activities in the Eastern Cape, Biko was expelled from one educational institution after another, including the medical school at the University of Natal, and constantly subjected to banning and restriction orders which limited his activities to his home town of King Williamstown and barred him from writing or speaking in public. He become a major force in South African politics when he helped found the Black People's Convention, one of the major organizations espousing the ideology of black consciousness. Biko's movement and its message had a powerful impact on the young generation of South African writers who emerged during and after the Soweto uprising of 1976. *I Will Write What I Like*, a collection of his powerful speeches, was posthumously published in 1979.

Further reading

Arnold, Millard (1978) *Black Consciousness in South Africa*, New York: Random House.

——(1978) *The Testimony of Steve Biko*, London: Maurice Temple Smith.

Biko, Steve (1979) *I Will Write What I Like*, ed. Aelred Stubbs, London: Heinemann.

SIMON GIKANDI

Birhanu Zerihun

b. 1933/4, Ethiopia; d. 1987, Ethiopia

novelist, short story writer, playwright,
   and journalist

Birhanu Zerihun, novelist, short story writer,
playwright, and journalist, renewed literary style
in Ethiopia with short clear sentences and
expressions at a time when an elaborate literary
style was in fashion. He was educated in church
and government schools, and then worked for the
government. He started writing in school, producing mostly poems, school plays, and newspaper
articles. In 1959/60 he became a full-time
journalist, and soon after he started writing
serious fiction. He often wrote about the subdued
position of women in Ethiopia in some of his
major novels, including *Ye'imba debdabbéwoch* (Tear-
ful Letters) (1959/60), *Yebedel fitsamé* (The Fulfillment of the Crime) (1964/5), *Amanuél derso mels* (In
and Out of the Madhouse) (1963/4), *Chereqa
sitweta* (When the Moon Comes Out) (1964), and
a collection of short stories, *Birr ambar sebberelliwo*
(He Pierced the Hymen) (1967/8). He also wrote
Dill kemot behwala (Victory after Death) (1962/3), a
novel based on the Sharpeville massacre in South
Africa. Later, he became more politically involved
and wrote a trilogy, *Ma'ibel* (Billow) (1974, 1980/1,
1981/2), about famine, exploitation of the peasantry, and social upheaval. He wrote two novels
about Emperor Téwodros II, *Ye'Téwodros imba*
(1965/6) (later turned into a play), and *Ye-Tangut
mistir* (1987). His major plays included *Tatennyaw
tewanay* (The Troubled Actor) (1982/3) and *Abba
Nefso* (1984/5), which were very popular with the
public.

Further reading

Molvaer, R.K. (1997) *Black Lions*, Lawrenceville,
   New Jersey: Red Sea Press

REIDULF MOLVAER

Biyaoula, Daniel

b. 1953, Poto Poto, Congo-Brazzaville

novelist

Born in Congo-Brazzaville, Daniel Biyaoula is the
author of two novels, *L'Impasse* (The Impasse)
(1996) and *Agonies* (Agonies) (1998), which have
contributed significantly to the foregrounding of
the theme of migration in the literatures of
Francophone black Africa. Biyaoula, who was
awarded the Grand Prix Littéraire d'Afrique Noir
in 1997, writes novels about characters who are in
confrontation with a society that they left years ago.
In *L'Impasse*, Biyaoula writes about characters who
return to their native country to discover that the
values they have acquired in foreign countries are
not always in agreement with African traditions.
Returning to the home country is hence considered
a test, but Biyaoula also uses his novels to represent
both the desperate social conditions on the African
continent and the individual's quest for recognition
by their community. In *Agonies*, Biyaoula continues
the exploration of the experiences of African
migrants in France introduced in *L'Impasse*, but
adds a complicated twist to the migration story in
the form of a tragic love story between African
migrants and French natives. Biyaoula's novels are
memorable for their use of a colloquial and
fragmented style and for their minute analysis of
the psychology of their characters.

Further reading

Biyaoula, Daniel (1996) *L'Impasse* (The Impasse),
   Paris: Présence Africaine.

FRIEDA EKOTTO

Blum, Robert

b. 1901, Tunis, Tunisia; d.

writer

A Francophone writer, Blum was born in Tunis
and in 1904 moved with his family to Egypt, where
his father was inspector of Jewish schools. He

worked as a journalist in Alexandria and Cairo. In 1929 he co-founded with Elian-Juda **Finbert** the Association of Francophone Writers of Egypt and also received a literary prize. He published novels, short stories, poetry, plays, and a literary anthology, *Anthologie des écrivains d'Égypte d'expression française* (Anthology of Francophone Writers of Egypt). His importance derives mainly from his role in founding journals and organizing literary activities. He co-founded the literary magazine *Flambeau* (Torch) and organized the first Francophone book fair in Cairo in 1931. He moved to Paris in 1956 and continued to write under the name of Robert Barret.

Further reading

Blum, Robert (1953) *Présence et autres comédies* (Presence and Other Comedies), Cairo: W. Axisa.

FERIAL J. GHAZOUL

Boateng, Yaw

b. 1950, Kumasi, Ghana

novelist, short story writer, and playwright

The Kumasi-born Yaw Boateng had his secondary and undergraduate education in Ghana before proceeding to Zurich to study for a master's degree in civil engineering. Boateng has written plays and short stories, but it is *The Return* (1977), his novel about the Asante empire, set in Kumasi of the 1800s, that best exemplifies his contribution to African literature. In the Asante capital, Akan and non-Akan, Muslims and non-Muslims, and warriors and civilians coexist in relative peace; immediate and potential threats to peace come from the trade in slaves and from European ships off the West African coast. The novel's main conflict between Seku and Jakpa, brothers from the Asante subject state of Gonja, localizes even as it illustrates the message that wars and conquests make enemies out of natural allies. The siblings' reconciliation at the end of the novel represents the triumph of individuals' resolve to right past wrongs. Unlike Ayi Kwei **Armah**'s *The Healers*, which focuses on the fall of the Asante empire, Boateng's story is about Asante at the height of its power. But in its concern within the history of Ghanaian and African literatures, Boateng's 1977 novel *The Return* anticipates and complements *The Healers*.

KOFI OWUSU

Boehmer, Elleke

b. 1961, South Africa

academic and novelist

Although she is primarily known as a critic of postcolonial literature in Britain (see **colonialism, neocolonialism, and postcolonialism**), South African-born Elleke Boehmer is also the author of three novels, *Screens Against the Sky* (1990), *An Immaculate Figure* (1993), and *Bloodlines* (2000), works in which she draws on her own experiences to explore what it meant to grow up in the white suburbs of apartheid South Africa, a country segregated by race, ethnicity, and class (see **apartheid and post-apartheid**). Boehmer's novels are often about heroines trapped within their privileged worlds and closed off from the larger political world around them. These novels are driven by a powerful rhetoric of failure and their characters struggle with the limits set by a world they find difficult to name or transcend, yet one that they cannot identify with. In her novels, as in her academic work in postcolonial literature, Boehmer constantly works to overcome the culture of guilt that has been associated with liberal white South African writers and to think through the possibility of making black consciousness itself part of white writing. While her novels are often about the enclosures of a privileged white culture, their characters strive to define themselves against the political movements associated with Steve **Biko** and the black consciousness movement of the 1970s.

SIMON GIKANDI

Bokoum, Saïdou

b. 1945, Dinguirayé, Guinea

novelist

Born in Dinguirayé, Guinea, Bokoum refers to himself as a Guineo-Malian. After his secondary education in Conakry (Guinea), Saïdou Bokoum entered the University of California at Berkeley in 1963 intending to pursue studies in medicine, but a year later he moved to Algiers before migrating to France to study law at the University of Paris, Nanterre, in 1965. He eventually graduated with a degree in the sociology of literature.

Since 1966 he has founded and headed several groups, most notably Kaloum Tam-Tam, Le Calao, and La Compagnie du Phénix. Since the early 1980s he has worked in the fields of both music and theatrical production in France and in the Côte d'Ivoire.

Bokoum is mostly known for his 1974 provocative novel *Chaîne* (Chain). Sexual violence, moral, social and physical disintegration are all part of the main protagonist's lot. The life of this African student-turned-immigrant in Paris is best summarized as a nightmarish-bordering-hellish existence. Autobiographical elements can be found in the novel as the personal and communal stories are woven to produce an inventory of horrors: solitude, profound sadness, wandering, exile, and "invisible" existence. Bokoum's apocalyptic novel provides a methodical exploration of the lives of black immigrants in France by juxtaposing racism, **homosexuality**, prostitution, and the making of a pariah society. In this novel Bokoum sees the experiences of his hero, Kanaan Niane, as the "living portrait of Africa in Paris." Presenting the question of immigration and displacement from within, Bokoum's novel rejects a linear construct and thus identifies with the tradition of the new novel; the author's use of "faulty" grammatical construction is often interpreted as a direct attack on the very concept of *Francophonie*, a signal of his refusal to be a black imitator only capable of repeating or copying from the European masters. One complaint against the novel, however, is that it focuses too narrowly on Kanaan Niane's story to the detriment of the other characters, who remain mere sketches, disappearing all too soon. From another perspective, however, this focus on the protagonist can be viewed as a measure of his social isolation. Similar concerns are echoed in *Dépossession* (Dispossession), which Bokoum wrote in 1976 while living in Avignon. In their content and formal concerns, Bokoum's writings reveal a striking affinity with the works of Yambo **Ouologuem**, most notably with his *Letter to Negro France* (1969) and *A Thousand and One Bibles of Sex* (1969).

JEAN OUÉDRAOGO

Bolamba, J'ongungu Lokolé

b. 1913, Congo; d. 1990, Zaire

poet

Referred to during his lifetime as Congo-Zaire's national poet, J'ongungu Lokolé Bolamba (also known as Antoine-Roger Bolamba) began his writing career as an editor for the short-lived review *Brousse* (Bush). After World War II, he was named editor of *La Voix du Congolais* (Voice of the Congolese), a review he directed until it ceased publication in 1959. After independence, he held several government offices. His literary production includes folk tales, poetry, essays, and a short story, but his most important work is a collection of fourteen poems, *Esanzo: chants pour mon pays* (Esanzo: Songs for My Country), published in 1955 by Présence Africaine with a preface by the **negritude** poet Léopold Sédar **Senghor**. This was the first work by a writer from the then Belgian Congo to be published in France. The collection includes two poems in the Mongo language with their French translations, and it is distinguished, in both form and content, from Bolamba's previous works by the fact that the poet strives to affirm what he considers to be a true African identity.

Further reading

Bolamba, Antoine-Roger (1977) *Esanzo: chants pour mon pays. Poèmes* (Esanzo: Songs for My Country), trans. Janis Pallister, Sherbrooke: Naaman.

JANICE SPLETH

Boni, Nazi

b. 1909, Bwan, Burkina Faso; d. 1969, Burkina Faso

novelist and essayist

Nazi Boni was born at Bwan (Mouhoun) in Burkina Faso and is considered to be one of the founders of the Burkinabé literature. In the first few years of independence in the 1960s, he played a major political and cultural role in his country, but he was soon forced into exile under the regime of Maurice Yaméogo due to his political views. Before he died in a tragic accident in 1969 he had already authored a well-known novel entitled *Le Crépuscule des temps anciens* (The Twilight of the Bygone Days) (1962) as well as an influential long essay called *Histoire synthétique de l'Afrique résistante* (Synthetic History of Africa under Resistance) (1971). As a member of the first generation of African intellectuals who fought for independence, Boni's fictional work was driven by a powerful political visions. In *Le Crépuscule des temps anciens*, he was interested in representing the rhythms of precolonial or traditional life among the Bwamu people and the interaction between the ancestors and different cosmic forces in this society. Like many authors of his generation, Boni believed that African people should undertake a close re-examination of their traditional values and see how these could be used in the establishment of a better social, cultural, and ethical basis for modernity and development (see **modernity and modernism**).

MICHEL TINGUIRI

Bopape, Heniel Diphete D.

b. 1957, Transvaal (now Limpopo Province), South Africa

novelist and playwright

The South African writer Diphete Bopape made a name for himself with the publication of *Makgale* (1978), a drama that deals with sons of a chief fighting over the chieftaincy. He subsequently broke new ground when he wrote and had published the novel *A Golden Vulture* (*Lenong la Gauta*) (1982), which introduced a sophisticated detective novel genre into Sepedi literature. His subsequent novels, *Dikeledi* (Tears) (1985) and *Rena Magomotša* (1987) did not, however, garner much attention, and *Dikeledi* is almost unknown to the general readership. *Bogobe bja Tswiitswii (Porridge of Tswiitswii)* (1985), his collection of short stories, provides humorous depictions of characters during rites of passage – for example, new experiences or discoveries that would alter the way they perceive life. Unlike the works of the prominent Sepedi writer, Oliver Kgadime **Matsepe**, the temporal setting of Bopape's fiction is contemporary, but he rarely deals directly with the national politics of South Africa. With regard to language and humor, Bopape's style is often simpler and more widely accessible to contemporary readership than is the case with Matsepe's works, and he has often proved to be popular with teachers and pupils alike. In the novels and the short stories, Bopape's language also bears explicit influences of English language structures and form.

PHASWANE MPE

Bosman, Herman Charles

b. 1905, Cape Town, South Africa; d. 1951, South Africa

poet and editor

The South African poet and editor H.C. Bosman's background as a writer was unusual. Born in an Afrikaner family in Cape Town, he came of age in the Transvaal Republic where he was employed as a teacher in the 1920s. Arrested for the murder of his stepbrother, he was condemned to death but received a reprieve. He spent four and a half years in prison and it was while he was serving his time that he started writing short stories based on his prison experiences. These stories were later collected in *Mafeking Road* (1947). After his release from prison, Bosman established a printing press and worked as a teacher and mentor for young writers, most notably Lionel **Abrahams**. After nine years spent in various European capitals, Bosman returned to South Africa at the outbreak of World War II where he worked as a journalist, editor, and translator. He died before he had completed the final editing of his novel *Willemsdrop*, and most of his short stories were published posthumously. An uncut version of *Willemsdrop* was published in 1998.

Further reading

Gray, Stephen (ed.) (1982) *The Collected Works of Herman Charles Bosman*, Cape Town: Human and Rousseau.

SIMON GIKANDI

Bouabaci, Aïcha

b. 1945, Saïda, Algeria

poet and short story writer

Born in Saïda, Algeria, and trained in law, Aïcha Bouabaci is both a poet and a short story writer. She began her literary career with a collection of poetry, *L'Aube est née sur nos lèvres* (Dawn is Born on Our Lips) (1985), followed by a collection of short stories entitled *Peau d'exil* (Skin of Exile) (1990).

Her poetry as well as her prose is writing that takes place on the border and is concerned with the border, in all its dynamics. In poetry, the relationship between silence and language and silence and poetry provides her with the axis around which her creativity evolves. In prose, the energy of the border becomes the exploration of the relationship between dream and reality, the possible and the impossible.

NASRIN QADER

Boudjedra, Rachid

b. 1941, Algeria

poet and playwright

A prolific poet, novelist, and playwright, Rachid Boudjedra is one of the most prominent contemporary Algerian literary figures. His work is extraordinarily diverse, perhaps finding its only unity in its rejection of traditional narrative forms and its manifest attempts to represent a modern

Algeria. Controversial and provocative, Boudjedra's first novel, *The Repudiation* (*La Répudiation*) (1969) consists of a series of recollections delivered by a narrator who describes the vices of so-called traditional Algerian society. Boudjedra published in French until 1982, at which point he began to publish in Arabic as part of a project to modernize the Arabic novel. However, his texts, often translated by the author himself, continue to be available in French. This shift in linguistic codes reflects the author's rejection of the colonizer's language, but it also reflects Boudjedra's vision of the underlying syncreticity of an Algerian identity comprised of both Arabic and French elements. Such a conception of a hybrid national identity has led Boudjedra to pose a vehement critique of the Algerian Islamic Salvation Front (FIS). In response to the 1992 publication of *Sons of Hatred* (*FIS de la haine* – a play on words in French), the FIS declared a series of *fatwas* on Boudjedra, obliging him to relocate to France.

Further reading

Boudjedra, Rachid (1995) *The Repudiation*, trans. Golda Lambrova, Colorado Springs, Colorado: Three Continents Press.

NEIL DOSHI

Bouraoui, Hédi

b. 1932, Sfax, Tunisia

poet and novelist

Hédi Bouraoui ranks with Albert **Memmi** and Abdelwahab **Meddeb** among the Tunisian literary figures best known outside his country. Poetry in French and English dominates his considerable output, which also includes several novels and a substantial body of literary criticism and theory. Born in Sfax in southern Tunisia, he was educated in France and the United States. Since then he has made his home in Canada, where he is Master of Stong College at York University, Toronto; he is also past president of the African Literature Association. His published works can be divided into two periods: his bibliography from 1966 to

1986 consists mostly of poetry while novels constitute most of his later output. Bouraoui's texts, however, break with notions of genre and boundaries. Titles like *L'Icônaison: romanpoème* (Iconaison: Novelpoem) (1985) or *Ignescent: prosèmes* (Ignescent: Proems) (1982) demonstrate the inapplicability of genre divisions to Bouraoui's work. Untranslatable neologisms, one of Bouraoui's favorite poetic devices, demonstrate his desire to combine genres and cross-cultural boundaries.

Much of Bouraoui's poetry explores the potentials of cross-cultural dialogue. Several of his collections, e.g. *Haituvois suivi de Antillades* (Haituvois, Followed by Antillades) (1980) and *Vers et l'envers* (Verse and Reverse) (1982), draw on his encounters with poets from other parts of the world – in these cases, Haiti and Bulgaria. Bouraoui proclaims his sympathetic familiarity with sub-Saharan Africa, Central America and the Caribbean, homes to cultures with which he feels a particular affinity as a Tunisian. His poems seem to call for complementary cultural productions across the formerly colonized world. This requires escaping the confinement of assigned identities; one of Bouraoui's poetic speakers says, "I dream ... Being a simple Mortal/ spending his life/ in all Motels/ of the World/ without identity" ("Crucified," in *Echosmos*, 1986: Oakville). Bouraoui's critical works have also reflected this overriding concern with cross- or intercultural identities, especially in the Canadian context.

In the mid 1990s, the poet turned to prose fiction. *Retour à Thyna* (Return to Thyna) (1997) combines the plot of a detective novel with echoes of Yacine **Kateb**'s *Nedjma*. Four young men gravitate around a symbolic and eroticized woman; they are investigating the death of an author, a character named Kateb. Bouraoui's novel is an encapsulated cultural history of Tunisia after independence, beginning with the elimination of a character whose voice stood in opposition to arbitrary government directives. Since *Retour à Thyna* Bouraoui has pursued his interest in cross-cultural poetics in *La Pharaone* (1998) and *Ainsi parle la Tour CN* (Thus Speaks the CN Tower) (1999). His career has demonstrated the versatility of North African literature in reaching for universal applicability, based on local inspirations.

Further reading

Bouraoui, Hédi (1986) *Echosmos: A Bilingual Collection*, Oakville, Ontario: Mosaic Press.

Michael, Colette V. (1989) "Création et alienation chez un poète contemporain," *Revue Francophone de Louisiane*, 4, 2: 91–8.

Sabiston, Elizabeth (2000) "Hédi Bouraoui's *Retour à Thyna*: A Female Epic?" *Dalhousie French Studies*, 53: 134–43.

SETH GRAEBNER

Bouraoui, Nina

b. 1967, Rennes, France

novelist

Born into a Franco-Algerian family in Rennes, France, Nina Bouraoui won early acclaim with her first novel, *Forbidden Vision* (*La Voyeuse interdite*) (1991). Published by Gallimard, it won the Prix Inter and set a French record for sales of a first novel. Since 1991, she has published five other novels: *Poing mort* (Dead Fist, an untranslatable homophone for "neutral gear") (1992), *Le Bal des murènes* (The Ball of the Morays) (1996), *L'Age blessé* (Wounded Age) (1998), *Le Jour du séisme* (The Day of the Earthquake) (1999), and *Garçon manqué* (Tomboy) (2000). Bouraoui's style and aesthetic concerns have meshed well with the preoccupations of critics on both sides of the Atlantic. Her fiction is marked by a fascination with violence, described with precise diction and an eye for detail. Bouraoui explores a wide range of trials and sufferings; she is particularly attentive to physical and cultural violence on women's bodies. Her protagonists inhabit constricted worlds of sexual repression, sickness, or animality, which they transcend solely through their own lucidity.

Further reading

Bouraoui, Nina (1995) *Forbidden Vision*, trans. K. Melissa Marcus, Barrytown, New York: Station Hill Press.

SETH GRAEBNER

Bouzaher, Hocine

b. 1935, Biskra, Algeria

poet, politician, and editor

Born near Biskra in southern Algeria, Bouzaher is known mainly for his political work with the FLN (National Liberation Front), the Algerian nationalist movement in France (1960–2), and for being on the editorial board of nationalist papers during the struggle against colonialism, namely the *Résistance algérienne* and *el-Moujahid* (1956–62) (see **colonialism, neocolonialism, and postcolonialism**).

His literary works include a collection of poems, a play, and a narrative. In 1960 he published *Voices in the Casbah* (*Des Voix dans la Casbah*). The first part of the book is a play, which is highly committed to the struggle for nationalism (see **nationalism and post-nationalism**) and is written as a contribution to the revolution that was taking place in Algeria in the 1950s. The second part of the book is comprised of poems, many of which are strong affirmations of the Algerian national character and identity. This work was followed in 1967 by *The Five Fingers of the Day* (*Les Cinq Doigts du jour*), a narrative dedicated to the Algerian revolution. In this narrative, the author presents an allegory of five brothers, representing the five political parties who merged to form the FLN on the eve of the revolution to serve Algeria, their figurative mother.

Further reading

Bouzaher, Hocine (1960) *Des Voix dans la Casbah* (Voices in the Casbah), Paris: Maspéro.
——(1967) *Les Cinq Doigts du jour* (The Five Fingers of the Day), Algiers: SNED.

ZAHIA SMAIL SALHI

Brew, Kwesi Osborne Henry

b. 1928, Ghana

diplomat, short story writer, and poet

A distinguished Ghanaian diplomat in the early 1960s, a short story writer and poet, Kwesi Brew's early work appeared in the University of Ghana's literary journal, *Okyeame*. In his first volume of poetry, *The Shadow of Laughter* (1968), he demonstrated his sensitivity to both his craft and his subject matter. Brew's poetry quietly and eloquently explores the complex history of Ghana and Africa from the horrors of the slave trade to the legacies inherited from colonialism and stewardship of the modern African political leadership (see **colonialism, neocolonialism, and postcolonialism**). His poetry has the authority of a traditional spokesperson, appealing across the generations with a mature vision and love of language. Whether in a poem from the 1960s, like "A Plea for Mercy," or one like "Dry Season," from *Return of No Return* (1995), Brew's work is particularly powerful and evocative.

Further reading

Awoonor, Kofi and Adali-Mortty, G. (eds) (1977) *Messages: Poems from Ghana*, London: Heinemann.
Moore, Gerald and Beier, Ulli (eds) (1984) *The Penguin Book of Modern African Poetry*, Harmondsworth, England: Penguin.

VINCENT O. ODAMTTEN

Breytenbach, Breyten

b. 1939, Bonnievale, the Boland, South Africa

poet and painter

There is an especial difficulty in trying to characterize the life and work of Breyten Breytenbach: this prolific South African-born writer has made much use of **autobiography** as a form, but the sophisticated ways in which he has done so defy any easy piecing together. Thus any account of Breytenbach falls prey to its subject's web of irony from the start. Born in Bonnievale, a small town in the hinterland of Cape Town known as the Boland, he spent his early years near there. He initially studied **art** at the University of Cape Town but left prematurely (1959), in order to travel in Europe. Indeed, Breytenbach's visual artistry remains a key to understanding his work, particularly his taste for the surreal. Though Breytenbach had written various works in Afrikaans (see **Afrikaans literature**), it was as a painter that he made a name for himself in the early 1960s while living in Paris.

In 1964 he received a major South African literary award, but was barred from accepting it in person when the government denied a visa to his wife, Hoang Lien or Yolande. Since she was Vietnamese-born, their marriage contravened the apartheid government's Immorality Act of 1957 (see **apartheid and post-apartheid**). This was a watershed in his evolving political consciousness, and ensured his status as a *cause célèbre* in the anti-apartheid movement. Years later the South African government relented under pressure, issuing both with visas. They visited South Africa in December 1972. Breytenbach was to recount the story of this journey in *A Season in Paradise* (1980). A second trip, in August 1975, was to take on a very different character: he entered South Africa under a false identity, apparently on a mission to establish an underground network of activists under the banner of a group called Okhela. As a strategic move this soon went awry, for the security forces trailed Breytenbach and eventually arrested him at Johannesburg airport as he tried to return to Paris. He was detained for two months, then tried and convicted on charges of terrorism. Despite a supposed plea bargain he received the maximum sentence of nine years, seven of which were spent in some of the country's highest security prisons in Pretoria and Cape Town, until he was released in December 1982. In *True Confessions of an Albino Terrorist* (1984) Breytenbach narrates his prison sojourn. Following his release he returned to Europe. A third autobiographical volume, *Return to Paradise* (1993), was devoted to a visit he made to South Africa in 1991, after the freeing of Nelson Mandela and the unbanning of the African National Congress. In keeping with his position as artist and social critic, Breytenbach openly criticized the ANC in the 1990s, despite having supported the organization earlier.

Though he has composed much poetry, in English and especially Afrikaans, the essay is perhaps Breytenbach's characteristic genre. *End Papers* (1986) and *Memory of Birds in Times of Revolution* (1996) contain selections of essays, including two open letters to Mandela written in

1991 and 1994. Even *A Season in Paradise* and *Return to Paradise*, works which consist of diary entries, read like thought-pieces inspired by the author's experiences and travels – "the account of a pilgrimage to where the navel-string lies buried – a memory of the heart, but also a region of the imagination" (*Memory of Birds*, 1986: New York, p. 106). Breytenbach, however, adapts the travel narrative to his own purposes; in fact, those works recount inner journeys as much as anything else. They are episodic in form and diaristic in style. In *Return to Paradise*, for example, his fascination with the seventeenth-century Dutch travel writer Olfert Dapper reflects his own position as a (South) African, a European, and an observer, and is linked to a creative tension in his writerly identity: that of the outsider who is also an insider, of one who is part of yet alienated from the Africa of his experience and imagination.

The reader is integral to Breytenbach's artistic economy. The prose works frequently begin with a direct address to the reader, and contain other addresses along the way. *True Confessions* starts with an address to the reader that conflates her with the police interrogator, as if the work is a response to questioning under duress. It is this uneasy relation between narrator and reader–interrogator, intimate but fraught, that energizes the work. Breytenbach's prose style ranges from lyrical simplicity to the impassioned density of anger. There is throughout a zest for playing with language, sometimes for its own sake in almost childish vein, but often as invective. Mordant wit abounds, for example, in his description of security police and prison personnel in *True Confessions*.

The surreal plays a prominent role in Breytenbach's writing. An example of this is *Mouroir: Mirrornotes of a Novel* (1984), which consists of prose vignettes. His artwork, too, involves hybrid animal–human creatures, bodily dismemberment, and other features that have evoked comparison with Hieronymus Bosch. In *Dog Heart* (1999) the central conceit is Breytenbach's conception of himself as a dog, using his sense of smell to find the grave of a long-deceased great-grandmother, whom he decides to "adopt." Again, death and memory are central. *All One Horse* (1989) and *Plakboek* (Scrapbook) (1994), in which paintings accompany individual essays and poems respectively, both typify the close embrace of image and word in his artistic vision. In both, surrealism is an abiding principle.

Breytenbach's playfulness with language, his surrealism and his obsession with memory underline the centrality of the imagination in his work. In many ways he was a postmodern figure before the term became popular: his playing with narrative frames, his valorization of hybridity, of the surreal, of the fragment, his itinerant lifestyle, his fascination with mirrors and with the contingency and multiplicity of identity, all point in this direction. Some aspects have their roots in his deep attachment to Buddhism. Indeed, the complexities of Breytenbach's identity and art have marked him, in the words of Walzer, as a "connected critic."

Further reading

Breytenbach, B. (1986) *Memory of Birds*, New York: Harcourt.

Coetzee, J.M. (1996) *Giving Offense: Essays on Censorship*, Chicago: University of Chicago Press.

Walzer, M. (1988) *The Company of Critics: Social Criticism, Political Commitment in the Twentieth Century*, New York: Basic Books.

GRANT PARKER

Brink, André Philippus

b. 1935, Vrede, Orange Free State, South Africa

novelist

André Brink is one of South Africa's most well-known writers of Afrikaans origin whose fourteen novels to date have been translated into thirty languages (see **Afrikaans literature**). A writer of novels, essays, and plays, academic, translator, and literary critic, Brink was born into a strictly Calvinist Afrikaans family who supported the ruling Nationalist Party. Brink was educated at Potchefstroom University from which he graduated in 1959 with an MA in both English and Afrikaans. He studied at the Sorbonne in the early 1960s and gained a doctorate from Rhodes University, Grahamstown, where he lectured for thirty years

before taking up a Chair in Literature at the University of Cape Town. Despite his extremely conservative background, Brink became a critic of apartheid from within Afrikaner ranks, a "betrayal" that led to the banning of the Afrikaans version of his 1973 novel, *Looking on Darkness* (*Kennis van die Aand*) (see **apartheid and post-apartheid**). This was the first Afrikaans novel to be banned by the Nationalist government and was the catalyst for Brink's decision to write in English as well as in Afrikaans, thus ensuring him a readership outside South Africa where such censorship did not apply. Since then, Brink has written all his novels in both English and Afrikaans, apart from *States of Emergency* (1988) which, for personal reasons, was written only in English. Brink was a founding member of the Afrikaans Writers' Guild, which pursued the right of freedom of speech for all South African writers.

Brink's literary reputation is strong both within South Africa and, even more so, internationally. He has been the recipient of many literary awards. In South Africa itself, his work has been awarded the CNA Award three times and international awards have included the Martin Luther King Memorial Prize, the Prix Médicis Étranger and a Légion d'Honneur in 1982. In 1987 he was made an Officier de l'Ordre des Artes et des Lettres. He has been shortlisted for the Booker Prize twice (for *An Instant in the Wind* and for *Rumours of Rain*).

Brink's own political "conscientization" began as a result of a period of study in Paris (1959–61) which coincided with the Sharpeville massacre. From the distance of Europe, he began to question the Afrikaner Nationalist values which he had previously unthinkingly accepted. The sense of guilt and shame at his own identification with Afrikanerdom engendered at this time is something that has haunted many of his literary works, and has contributed to his reputation as a "dissident" Afrikaner. Important, too, was the influence of the French existentialist writers on his work, particularly Sartre and Camus. In Europe, he became aware of contemporary trends in literature, and began experimenting with literary forms, particularly in reaction against the dominant realism of South African literature at that time (see **realism and magical realism**). In the mid 1960s, he was a founding member of the Sestigers, a group of

South African writers including Breyten **Breyten-bach** who had lived abroad and sought to revitalize South African literature with European experimental forms. They challenged the narrow taboos and repressions of traditional Afrikaner literature, particularly with regard to sex as a literary subject, as evidenced in Brink's early novels in Afrikaans such as *Lobola vir die Lewe* (A Bride Price for Life) (1962) and *Die Ambassadeur* (The Ambassador) (1963). In so doing, these writers became what Brink was to call "cultural schizo-phrene[s]," critiquing their own culture from within.

It was not until the 1970s, though, that Brink's own work was to take on an overtly political challenge to the apartheid system. His experience of the Paris student uprisings of 1968 on his return to France highlighted what for Brink was to become a central aspect of his work: the relation-ship between the individual and society and the sense of responsibility that a writer has in political struggle. This led him to return to South Africa to take up this responsibility in solidarity with other writers, English, Afrikaans, and African, in the struggle against apartheid. As Brink noted in *Reinventing a Continent* (1998: Cambridge, Massa-chusetts), on his return from France he was "possessed by the passionate need to define my roots and invent my subcontinent." Brink's 1983 collection of essays, *Mapmakers: Writing in a State of Siege*, provides a writer's credo regarding his perception of the role of a South African writer, emphasizing a highly political role for literature which he sees as a revolutionary act. The writer's responsibility in a situation such as that in South Africa after the Soweto uprising is to keep people informed "in a country dominated by official lies and distortions" and to "explore and expose the roots of the human condition" (1983: London, p. 152).

This sense of political commitment is clearly articulated in Brink's early novels. *Looking on Darkness* (1974; the English translation of the banned *Kennis van die Aand* of 1973) is an openly oppositional work, signaled immediately by its having a male "Cape colored" (mixed-race) narrator, Joseph Malan, whose first-person prison narrative chronicles the tortuous route by which he comes to be accused of the murder of his white lover, Jessica. Banned by the censors for being "pornographic, blasphemous, and Communistic," this novel is described by Brink as being "one of the first Afrikaans novels openly to confront the apartheid system." It deals with such issues as the struggle for identity of a "non-white" South African, love across the color-bar (which was, of course, both illegal and dangerous in apartheid South Africa) and the difficulty of direct political action in a repressive regime. *An Instant in the Wind* (1976) transposes the Australian Eliza Fraser story, that of a shipwrecked colonial woman who develops a relationship with an escaped convict, to eighteenth-century South Africa. By making the convict character, Adam Mantoor, a black slave and the female character, Elisabeth Larsson, a Dutch settler married to an explorer, Brink has her final betrayal of him take on both historical and contemporary significance. The sexual relationship between black man and white woman, the "great Thou-Shalt-Not," is explored here in a pre-apartheid context. A similar use of a historical event, a slave uprising in the Cape Colony in 1825, forms the starting point for *A Chain of Voices* (1982). Brink seeks in this novel to reinscribe the untold stories that the colonial record and history have "written out" or silenced in a narrative consisting of voices, black and white, male and female, alternately presenting personal testimonies in reply to the framing "Act of Accusation."

Two other novels dramatize the two sides of the Afrikaner – the one complicit with the apartheid regime; the other opposing it. *Rumours of Rain* (1978) is significantly set on the eve of the Soweto uprising. It chronicles the disintegration of the narrator, a wealthy Afrikaner businessman, Martin Mynhardt, whose carefully controlled world col-lapses with the conviction of his best friend, Bernard, for "terrorism," the revolt of his son, the loss of his mistress, and the selling-off of the family farm. Brink's ironic first-person account is used to illustrate the moral bankruptcy of the Afrikaner apologist. Despite his apparent self-examination, Mynhardt's narration is shown to be merely a "striptease of the soul" designed to expiate his guilt. Images of rain are used through-out to suggest the impending apocalypse and the inevitability of political change. In contrast to this representation of the "ugly Afrikaner," *A Dry White*

Season (1979) is narrated by a dissident Afrikaner, a writer of romantic fiction made to confront reality when his friend, Ben du Toit, involves him in his Kafka-esque battle for justice against the authorities by asking him to safeguard his papers. With Ben's "accidental" death, the narrator (along with the reader) is forced to journey from ignorance to enlightenment, increasingly implicated in the machinery of state control. Brink is said to have rewritten this novel in the aftermath of the death of Steve Biko.

A more metaphorical exploration of apartheid as a system is offered in Brink's 1984 novel, *The Wall of the Plague*. By cross-referencing other "plague literature," Brink explores the links between the responses of medieval Europe to the plague and the apartheid system itself. The act of writing is linked with the walls built in a futile attempt to keep out the plague, yet the novel implies that writing can ultimately be seen as a legitimate form of political action. Also concerned with the limitations and possibilities of writing as political action, *States of Emergency* (1988) uses metafictional devices to examine the intersections between the private and the political and the possibility of writing a love story in a political "state of emergency" in which the state controls all representations. This project is complicated by the deliberate inclusion in the text of actual incidents, people and events, and parallels between Brink's own life and work and the textual references within the novel.

An abiding theme of Brink's work has been that of history, and all his narrators are, as Brink points out in his essay *Reinventing a Continent*, in some way obsessed with reconstructing their history. Influenced particularly by Hayden White's notion of meta-history, Brink's later work highlights the narrative and fictive processes of history itself, as inventions and reinventions of selves and identity. *Imaginings of Sand* (1996), for example, uses the stories of Afrikaans women, most notably those of the grandmother of the story, to reinsert women's voices into the historical record while simultaneously emphasizing their invention and their fictiveness. The earlier novel, *On the Contrary* (1993), is similarly concerned with the processes linking storytelling and history as Brink uses narrative techniques close to magical realism to draw attention to the fictive and imagined nature of historical documents written by the real-life Estienne Barbier, Brink's narrator in the novel. Using Cervantes' *Don Quixote* and the historical figure of Joan of Arc as symbols of writerly and political rebellion (as signaled in the title), Brink explores the links between the lies, inventions, and unreliability of both history and fiction. A similar engagement with the interface between myth and history is evident in *The First Life of Adamastor* (1993) in which Brink rewrites a traditional myth about Africa – Camoens' first encounter with Africa that personifies the continent as the giant, Adamastor – linking this with tropes of sexual prowess and conquest.

One of Brink's projects in his later fiction has been to "re-imagine" the Afrikaner as belonging to Africa and sharing with Africans the need to oppose (British) colonization, illustrating "that sense of justice and liberty and that identification with Africa ... inspired by a history shared with black Africans" (*Mapmakers*, 1983: London, p. 22). Brink's epic novel, *An Act of Terror* (1991) epitomizes this in its representation of its protagonist, Thomas Landman, as a dissident in the true spirit (as Brink sees it) of Afrikanerdom. This redefinition of Afrikaners as themselves displaced and dispossessed enables Thomas to declare his kinship with other Afrikaner dissidents and to proclaim his identity as a "native of Africa."

Yet Brink is also aware of the rather precarious nature of Afrikaner identity in post-apartheid South Africa, acknowledging that the Afrikaans language is perhaps the last remaining way in which Afrikaners can define themselves, with the demise of the Nationalist Party and the reduction in influence of the Dutch Reformed Church. As Afrikaans is now only one of eleven official languages and is no longer privileged as it was by the ruling Nationalist Party, there is, Brink acknowledges, a growing sense of threat to the survival of the language. He continues, however, to write in both English and Afrikaans. His 2000 novel, *Rights of Desire*, deals with the sense of displacement of its narrator, Ruben Olivier, after losing his job in a library to an African replacement in the affirmative action process. In this novel and the earlier *Devil's Valley* (1998), as in his later essays, Brink does not resile from articulating the present-day problems of post-apartheid South Africa, such as violence, AIDS, and the abuse of power, despite his strong support for the African National Congress and for the project of reconciliation in a democratic South Africa.

Further reading

Brink, André (1983) *Mapmakers: Writing in a State of Siege*, London: Faber.
——(1998) *Reinventing a Continent*, Cambridge, Massachusetts: Zoland Books.
Jolly, Rosemary (1996) *Colonization, Violence, and Narration in White South African Writing: André Brink, Breyten Breytenbach, and J.M. Coetzee*, Athens, Ohio: Ohio University Press; and Johannesburg: Witwatersrand University Press.
Kossew, Sue (1996) *Pen and Power: A Post-Colonial Reading of J.M. Coetzee and André Brink*, Atlanta and Amsterdam: Rodopi.

SUE KOSSEW

Brutus, Dennis

b. 1924, Harare, Zimbabwe

poet

Of the poets who emerged in South Africa during the 1950s and 1960s, Dennis Brutus has been the one most associated with the literature of protest against apartheid (see **apartheid and post-apartheid**) and for many years he served as a model for the young writers who emerged in South Africa in the aftermath of the Soweto uprising of 1976 and the rise of the black consciousness movement of Steve **Biko**. Born in Rhodesia of South African "colored" parents, Brutus grew up in the Eastern Cape town of Port Elizabeth and was educated at the then black University of Fort Hare. In the late 1950s, Brutus developed an interest in politics and began the campaign against racial discrimination in sports. It was while he was traveling in Mozambique that he was kidnapped by the South African secret police and returned to Johannesburg. He was shot in the back while trying to escape from police custody and he was sentenced to eighteen months at the infamous

prison of Robben Island, where he joined such famous prisoners as Nelson Mandela, Govan Beki, and Walter Sisulu. Brutus had started writing poetry in the 1950s and his first collection of poetry, *Sirens Knuckles and Boots* (1963) was published while he was in prison. The poems in this collection reflected the works of the English poets (Donne, Tennyson, Browning, Hopkins, and Eliot) to whom Brutus had been introduced by his mother. The poems were characterized by the poet's attempts to balance classical poetic forms with the political themes that interested him, to mesh public issues such as the destruction of the landscape and his own deep sense of alienation with private reflections on feelings, including love and loss, which he considered to be an inevitable consequence of oppression. It was during his imprisonment that Brutus decided to shed what he considered the excess ornamentation of his earlier poetry, and determined to write poetry for ordinary people. The result was *Letters to Martha* (1968), perhaps Brutus' most influential collection of poetry. Because he had been banned from writing poetry after his release from prison, Brutus wrote the poems in *Letters to Martha* as letters to his sister-in-law, Martha. In addition to being direct and simple, the poems in this collection are haunting expressions and descriptions of prison life and the terror of confinement and political repression.

In 1965, Brutus and his family were allowed to leave South Africa on an "exit visa," which meant that they were barred from returning to the country. During this period, Brutus was active in anti-apartheid politics; as the founder and president of the South African Non-Racial Olympic Committee (SANROC), he was credited with South Africa's expulsion from the Olympic Games. Brutus's political activity took him to several countries in Europe, Africa, and Asia, and experiences from these travels were turned into poems or affected the nature of his verse. *Poems from Algiers* (1970) were reflections on what it meant to be an African and an artist, while *China Poems* (1975) represented a significant shift in Brutus's verse, from the simplicity of language and structure in the earlier poems to a tight haiku style influenced by the form of Chinese poetry that Brutus had discovered during a trip to Beijing. Brutus's haiku and post-haiku poetry has been described as eclectic, but it is more accurately a reflection of the way the previous forms he had experimented with in the 1960s and 1970s had been brought together in the poems he wrote in the 1980s. In the poems from this period, Brutus had expanded his range of political reference beyond South Africa to include other trouble-spots of the period, including Chile and Nicaragua. Other poems from this period were poetic praises of Brutus's political heroes such as Nelson Mandela and Oliver Tambo. Brutus's poetry has been published in at least eleven collections and during the struggle against apartheid it occupied a central place in the politics and poetics of southern Africa. In general, however, and especially after the end of apartheid, the critical reception of Brutus's poetry has been divided between those who read it within its political context, and hence value its immediate response to an evil system of oppression and discrimination, and those who are concerned with what are seen as its technical failures.

Further reading

Brutus, Dennis (1973) *A Simple Lust: Selected Poems*, London: Heinemann.
——(1991) *Stubborn Hope*, London: Heinemann.
Chipasula, Frank (1993) "A Terrible Trajectory: The Impact of Apartheid, Prison and Exile on Dennis Brutus's Poetry," in Abdulrazak Gurnah (ed.) *Essays on African Writing, 1: A Re-evaluation*, Oxford: Heinemann.

SIMON GIKANDI

Buabua wa Kayembe Mubadiate

b. 1950, Congo-Zaire

playwright

Buabua wa Kayembe's works are published mainly in Congo-Zaire where, as a leader in that nation's writers' union, he has actively promoted the development of a national literature. He appeared on the literary scene in 1977 with his first collection of poems, *Gazouillis* (Murmurings) and published a second collection of poetry, *Pour une poignée d'allusions* (For a Fistful of Allusions) in 1984. He is also

the editor of *Vociférations* (Shouts), an anthology of works by young poets, in which he describes his idea of what poetry should be. His literary reputation lies mainly in his dramatic works produced in Kinshasa, beginning with a melodrama based on mistaken identities entitled *L'Ironie de la vie* (Life's Irony). In *Les Flammes de Soweto* (The Flames of Soweto), he depicts the life and death of the South African activist Steve **Biko**. In *Le Délégué general, tragi-comédie en trois actes* (The Delegate General, a Tragicomedy in Three Acts), published in Paris by Silex, he denounces the fraud and corruption that had come to characterize Zaire by 1982. He has also produced fiction, including *Mais les pièges étaient de la fête* (But the Snares Were in the Celebration), a tale detailing the vicissitudes of life in Kinshasa in the 1980s.

JANICE SPLETH

Bugul, Ken

b. 1948, Ndoucoumane, Senegal

writer

Senegalese writer Ken Bugul, whose real name is Marietou Mbaye, is best known for her first novel, *The Abandoned Baobab* (*Le Baobab fou*), first published in 1983. To a certain extent, this autobiographical work takes its place beside such early African *Bildungsromanen* as Camara **Laye**'s *The Dark Child* (*L'Enfant noir*) and Hamidou **Kane**'s *Ambiguous Adventure* (*L'Aventure ambiguë*). As in these early works, Bugul draws on her own experiences and the tradition of **autobiography** in *The Abandoned Baobab*, to depict the predicament of coming of age at the intersection of cultures; in the process she also revisits some of the issues that preoccupied the authors of **negritude**, including the question of forging an authentic identity under the culture of colonialism (see **colonialism, neocolonialism, and postcolonialism**). In the novel, Ken, the protagonist, travels to Belgium in a futile quest for the Gauls, which, she has been taught, were her ancestors. She subsequently plunges into a crisis of identity. Initially, this crisis does not result from Ken's attempt to retrieve her African heritage, but rather from her desire to forge an identity that encompasses this heritage and European culture. The attempt at cultural retrieval occurs in the two sequels to *The Abandoned Baobab*, namely *Cendres et Braises* (Ashes and Embers) (1994) and *Riwan ou le chemin de sable* (Riwan or The Sand Track) (1999), in which the protagonist's return to her village seems definitive and also indicative of a quest for a better understanding of Ken's cultural and spiritual heritage in Senegal.

Unlike the earlier authors of *Bildungsromanen* in Francophone African literature, Bugul in her first two novels complicates issues of class, race, and cultural imperialism by adding the dimensions of sexuality, gender, and orphanhood to these established themes (see **gender and sexuality**). In Belgium and France, Ken (Marie in the second and third novels) is doubly objectified, first because, as one of her bosses in a nightclub tells her in *The Abandoned Baobab*, being female she can be nothing more than a consumer product. Second, being an African woman in the Europe of the 1960s and 1970s relegates her to the status of an exotic decorative object, and eventually to a slave of sorts. A significant aspect of Bugul's work is evident in her subversion of the glamorous image the West projects of itself *vis-à-vis* the colonized. Behind the West's artistic grandeur and economic progress, Bugul uncovers the moral degradation of artists and their patrons, as well as the ignorance, racism, and lack of imagination among the bourgeoisie. Finally, and most importantly, Bugul's novels are driven by the need – and courage – to speak the heretofore unspeakable, to represent the descent into prostitution, drug abuse, and madness of a protagonist from a devout Islamic background (see **Islam in African literature**).

After publishing three highly autobiographical novels, Bugul departs, in *La Folie et la mort* (Madness and Death) (2000), from the personal and historical to explore the collective state and fate of postcolonial Africa. In this novel she depicts a continent overcome with all sorts of problems, including poverty, war, dictatorship, and debt. With this novel Bugul takes her place among African writers of the latter half of the twentieth and the early twenty-first centuries who have increasingly moved from some of the questions of personal identity to focus on the collective destiny of a continent.

Further reading

Mudimbe-Boyi, Elisabeth (1993) "The Poetics of Exile and Errancy," *Yale French Studies* 82, 2: 196–212.

Watson, Julia (1997) "Exile in the Promised Land," in Gisela Brinker-Gabler and Sidonie Smith (eds) *Writing New Identities*, Minneapolis and London: University of Minnesota Press.

WANGAR WA NYATETŬ-WAIGWA

Bukenya, Austin S.

b. 1944, Masaka region, Uganda

playwright, novelist and essayist

Austin S. Bukenya was born in the Masaka region of Uganda and educated at Namugogo, Gayaza, Kisubi, and Namilyango. He was the first recipient of a BA degree (first class honors) at the University of Dar es Salaam in 1968, having studied literature, language, and linguistics. His earliest writings included two plays, *The Secret* (1968) and *The Bride* (1984), and an unpublished novel, "The Muhima Girl." For many years he lived and worked at Kenya's Kenyatta University and was associated with theater circles in Nairobi and with the Kenya Oral Literature Association (KOLA). Bukenya's most popular and controversial work is *The People's Bachelor* (1972), a satirical novel which puts the postcolonial African university "in the dock," with venom directed at the new elite that yodels in pleasure while the rest of the citizenry struggles to survive economic and social hardships. In addition to being a perceptive novelist and playwright, Bukenya has had a profound effect on the study of African oral literature (see **oral literature and performance**). His essay, "Oracy as a Tool and Skill in African Development," co-authored in the 1970s with the distinguished Ugandan academic Pio Zirimu, pioneered the study of oral literature in Africa.

GEORGE ODERA OUTA

Buruga, Joseph

b. 1942, West Nile, Uganda

poet

The Ugandan poet Joseph Buruga was born in West Nile and was educated at King's College, Budo, and Makerere University College, where he studied science. His prominence as a writer rests on one long poem, *The Abandoned Hut* (1969), a work in the "song" tradition initiated by **Okot p'Bitek**. When Buruga's poem was published, it had a mixed reception: some critics regarded it as a mere copy of Okot's *Song of Lawino*, with the only difference being that the main character was a man, not a woman; other critics, however, welcomed the poem as a significant addition to the "song school," taking up Okot's motifs and rhetorical strategies and placing them in a different context. However, Buruga's poem lacks the humor and wit that Okot uses effectively to give his poem the satirical bite which reduces Ocol and Clementine to the level they deserve, as mimics of a Western culture they do not fully understand and yet crave or desire. More importantly, Buruga's poem is rooted in the oral traditions of his Lugbara tradition and presents the dramatic encounter between the precolonial values that dominant family life and the modernity of the city (see **oral literature and performance**).

CHARLES OKUMU

Butake, Bole

b. 1947, Cameroon

playwright

The Cameroonian writer Bole Butake was educated in his own country and in Britain. In 1983 he was awarded a doctorat d'état èn lettres degree from the University of Yaoundé with a thesis on "Literature and the Nigerian Crisis, 1960–1970." He began his writing career with the publication of poems and short stories in *The Mould*, a journal of creative writing that he edited from 1976 to 1981. After the journal ceased publication, Butake started working in the field of drama where he has published titles such as *The Rape of Michelle* (1984), *Lake God* (1986), *The Survivors* (1989), *And Palm-Wine Will Flow* (1990), *Shoes and Four Men in Arms* (1990), and *Dance of the Vampires* (1999). Butake's major plays have been collected in *Lake God and Other Plays* (1999). In addition to writing and producing his own plays, he has directed the works of prominent playwrights such as Athol **Fugard**, Ola **Rotimi**, and Eugene O'Neil in Cameroon. In the 1990s he became heavily involved in theater for development, focusing on women's and children's rights, environmental protection, and the rights of minorities, especially the Baka of the equatorial forest. Butake has also been a professor of performing arts at the University of Yaoundé I.

OUSMANE BA

Butler, Guy

b. 1918, Karoo region, South Africa; d. 2001, Grahamstown, South Africa

poet

The South African poet Guy Butler was born in the mountainous Karoo region and was educated at Rhodes University, where he later went to teach, and Oxford University. After serving with British forces in North Africa and Italy during World War II, Butler returned to South Africa in the early 1950s and devoted most of his life to the promotion and preservation of the English language in the country. Influenced primarily by Shakespeare and the romantic poets, Butler's poetry struggled to reconcile his European sensibilities with the realities of Africa. As a liberal white writer, as he noted in his introduction to *A Book of South African Verse*, he had tried to belong to Africa but had found it uncooperative; he had then been forced to claim allegiance to a set of concepts, European ideals of culture and enlightenment, at odds with the landscape that both occupied and haunted his poetry. Many of his major poems, collected in *Selected Poems* (1975, 1989) reflect the tension between a poetic language that reflects powerful European influences struggling to manage a recalcitrant South African landscape. In his three volumes of **autobiography**, *Karoo Morning* (1977), *Bursting World* (1983), and *A Local Habitation* (1991), Butler strove to commemorate the Victorian world of his childhood and its long-disappeared sense of Englishness.

Further reading

Chapman, Michael (1996) *Southern African Literatures*, London and New York: Longman.

SIMON GIKANDI

C

Camara, Sory

b. Guinea

anthropologist and writer

A critic and scholar from Guinea, Sory Camara is known for his studies of Malinké oral tradition and performances (see **oral literature and performance**). His most prominent works in this regard include *Gens de la parole essais sur la condition et le rôle des griots dans la société Malinké* (The Keepers of Speech: Status and Function of the Griots in Malinke Society) (1976); his doctorate *Paroles de nuit* (Words of Night) (1978); and *Grain de vision: Afrique noire, drame et liturgie* (Speck of Vision: Black Africa, Drama and Liturgy) (1994).

Further reading

Camara. S. (1994) "Field of Life, Sowing of Speech, Harvest of Acts," *Oral Tradition* 9, 1: 23–59.

JEAN-MARIE VOLET

Campbell, Roy

b. 1901, Natal, South Africa; d. 1957, Portugal

poet and translator

The South African poet and translator Roy Campbell is perhaps the most controversial writer to have come from the region, often associated with extreme political views during his lifetime and out of place as much in the cultural establishment associated with English-speaking white South Africans as he was in the London of his exile, the Bloomsbury group, and its literary circles. Campbell left South Africa at the age of 17 and lived as a bohemian in London in the 1920s. He published his first major work, a long poem called *The Flaming Terrapin*, in 1924 at the age of 23. Returning to South Africa in 1924 Campbell tried to establish relationships with some of the major white writers in the region, most notably Alan **Paton** and William **Plomer**, but he soon fell out with many of his associates and returned to London. He was ostracized from English literary circles after the publication of *The Georgiad* (1931), a savage satire (in verse) on English literary culture. Campbell eventually moved to Spain and converted to Catholicism, becoming a strong supporter of General Francisco Franco and the Fascist forces during the Spanish civil war. Because of his extreme views on controversial social and racial issues, Campbell's politics has tended to overshadow some of his major literary contributions, including the powerful lyrical poems collected in *Adamastor* (1930), considered to be his best work. Campbell was strongly influenced by English poets, especially the Romantics, and his long poems reflect the influence of Dryden and Pope, but what made his best works memorable was his ability to use established forms of verse to represent the African landscapes of his youth and imagination. In spite of what have been considered by some to be his racist views, the main poems in *Adamastor* reflect Campbell's moving sense of the African landscape and his ability to fashion a language that would capture the rhythms of nature.

Further reading

Alexander, Peter (1982) *Roy Campbell: A Critical Biography*, London: Oxford

——(ed.) (1982) *The Selected Poems of Roy Campbell*, London: Oxford

SIMON GIKANDI

Capitein, Johannes

b. 1717, Ghana; d. 1747, Ghana

minister

Born on the West African coast of present-day Ghana in the era of the slave trade, Johannes Capitein was 7 years old when he was sold to Captain Arnold Steenhart, a Dutch slave merchant, who in turn gave him as a present to Jacobus van Goch, the chief trader at the Dutch fort of Elmina. Capitein was taken to the Netherlands in 1728 and lived with the Van Goch family in The Hague where he attended the Latin School. Capitein, who was baptized into the Dutch Reformed Church in 1735, also studied theology at the University of Leiden between 1737 and 1742; he was ordained as a minister in the Dutch Reformed Church in 1742 and appointed chaplain of the Elmina congregation in West Africa. Capitein's major work was a doctoral dissertation, *Dissertation politico-theological de servitude, libertati christianae non-contraria* (Politico-Theological Dissertation on Slavery), in which he argued that the institution of slavery did not necessarily contradict Christian teachings. In this dissertation, Capitein explored the writings of Western philosophers on the question of slavery and sought to contradict Aristotle's famous doctrine on natural slavery, the idea that some people were inherently born to be slaves. In Ghana, where he was to spend most of his life as a pastor and missionary, Capitein wrote the first Fanti–Dutch catechism, which was published in 1744 in Leiden.

Further reading

Debrunner, H.W. (1979) *Presence and Prestige: Africans in Europe*, Basel: Basler Afrika Bibliographien.

Prah, Kwesi Kwaa (1989) *Jacobus Eliza Johannes Capitein*, Braamfontein: Skotaville.

SIMON GIKANDI

Carlos, Jérôme

b. 1944, Porto-Novo, Benin

poet

Jérôme Carlos was born in Porto-Novo, Dahomey (now Benin), where he was later trained as a historian and journalist. He first appeared on the literary scene in 1973 with a book of poetry entitled *Cri de liberté* (A Cry for Freedom), inspired by the country's 1972 Marxist–Leninist revolution. Soon disillusioned with the reality of this revolution, however, he lived in exile in the Côte d'Ivoire from 1982 to 1994 before returning to Cotonou and taking up the position of director of the African Center for Positive Thinking. Carlos has worked in three major literary genres; since winning the Côte d'Ivoire's Grand Prize of Arts and Letters in 1988 for *Les Enfants de Mandela* (Mandela's Children), a book of short stories, he has published two novels. His 1990 novel, *Fleur du désert* (Desert Flower), satirizes a corrupt and repressive postcolonial African revolutionary regime. Also a scholar, Carlos has edited a textbook and written about the interrelationship of economy, technology, and culture in Africa.

Further reading

Carlos, Jérôme (1988) *Les Enfants de Mandela* (Mandela's Children), Abidjan: Éditions CEDA.

RACHEL GABARA

Casely Hayford, Adelaide Smith

b. 1868, Freetown, Sierra Leone; d. 1960, Ghana

short story writer and educator

The Sierra Leone short story writer and educator Adelaide Smith Casely Hayford was born in a Creole family in Freetown, but spent most of her early years in England where she received most of her education. She also studied music in Germany. Returning to Sierra Leone after an absence of twenty-five years, she was involved in numerous educational activities, including the establishment of the Girls' Vocational School in Freetown. During a second sojourn in England, she met and married Joseph Ephraim **Casely Hayford**, the distinguished Gold Coast lawyer and nationalist, and became active in several black nationalist and pan-African movements (see **diaspora and pan-Africanism**), including Marcus Garvey's Universal Negro Improvement Association (UNIA). She published her **autobiography** just before she died at the age of 91. Her short story "Mister Courifer" was published in *An African Treasury* (1961), the pioneering anthology of black writing edited by Langston Hughes.

Further reading

Cromwell, Adelaide M. (1982) *An African Victorian Feminist: The Life and Times of Adelaide Smith Casely Hayford*, Washington, DC: Howard University Press.

SIMON GIKANDI

Casely Hayford, Gladys May

b. 1901, Axim, Gold Coast (Ghana); d. 1950, Freetown, Sierra Leone

poet

The daughter of Adelaide Smith **Casely Hayford** and Joseph Ephraim **Casely Hayford**, Gladys May was born in Axim, Ghana, and was educated in local Gold Coast schools and in Wales. She developed an early interest in literature and started writing poetry and short stories at an early age; many of her works were published in both West African and American journals and newspapers. While her poetry reflected the tone and themes of what has come to be known as the Afro-Victorian mentality in Africa, reflecting the puritanism of her mission education and the values of a colonial middle class, Gladys May Casely Hayford also strove to represent the world around her with

sympathy and understanding. Her poetry does not feature prominently in many discussions of African literature, but it has been recognized as representative of a crucial moment in the emergence of writing on the continent and has been represented in major anthologies of African poetry.

Further reading

Hughes, Langston (1961) *An African Treasury*, New York: Pyramid.

——(1963) *Poems from Black Africa*, Bloomington: Indiana University Press.

SIMON GIKANDI

Casely Hayford, Joseph E.

b. 1866, Gold Coast (now Ghana); d. 1930, Gold Coast

politician, lawyer, journalist, educator and writer

Joseph Casely Hayford died before the Gold Coast colony in which he was born gained independence and was renamed Ghana. He was a nationalist leader who brought his activism to bear on his multiple roles as politician, lawyer, journalist, educator, and writer. His 1911 prose narrative, *Ethiopia Unbound*, has been a treasure-trove of ideas for succeeding generations of African writers. It has been the source of some of the central themes in African literature: the protagonist who studies abroad and returns home feeling no longer at ease, the affirmation of a people's "own language, customs and institutions" to forestall "national death," and the promotion of pan-Africanism come to mind (see **diaspora and pan-Africanism**). If Casely Hayford's main character, Kwamankra, appears to be too obvious a carrier of ideas like the ones noted above, it is partly because he is meant to serve the cause of "race emancipation." For an author who devoted much of his life to activist politics, the political cause had proven to be more important than narrative decorum. As co-founder of the National Congress of British West Africa, Casely Hayford reminds us that causes and ideas need not be mere rhetorical gestures. His contribution to the political and intellectual culture of Ghana and Africa remains to be fully appreciated.

KOFI OWUSU

Central African literatures in English

Writing in English in this region emerged much later than in other parts of the continent. It was not until the mid 1960s that a smattering of writing appeared. However, from the 1970s onwards there was a marked increase in output, spurred by the liberation struggle in Zimbabwe and by the anti-dictatorship fervor in Malawi, as well as by the political and intellectual cosmopolitanism in Zambia engendered by economic affluence and the cultural diversity arising out of a large refugee population from Zimbabwe, Mozambique, South Africa, Namibia, and Angola. Nevertheless, although Central African literature arrived on the scene later than its East and West African counterparts, its trajectory is not markedly different. There is the first phase of cultural affirmation and revalorization reminiscent of Chinua **Achebe**'s *Things Fall Apart* (1958), in which literature articulates a nationalist and decolonizing impulse, and then the second, when there is disenchantment with the postcolonial formation (see **colonialism, neocolonialism, and postcolonialism**). However, the way the issues of nationalism (see **nationalism and post-nationalism**) and of postcolonial disenchantment are dealt with varies from country to country, depending on the particular character of the colonial and postcolonial formation in each country. There is also a third stage where new concerns such as those of gender (see **gender and sexuality**) become an important part of the political agenda. Additionally, during this period there is also an attempt to move beyond the earlier forms of style, as dominant modes of writing such as realism themselves become objects of critique and transformation (see **realism and magical realism**).

Literature and anti-colonialism

Perhaps the first person to write creatively in English in the region is Malawi's David **Rubadiri**, whose poetry was anthologized in the early 1960s. His poem "An African Windstorm" (1965) is a celebration of Africa in a manner that would not be out of place in an anthology of **negritude** poetry, as here denigrated Africa is presented as source of pride and plenitude, thus undermining the conventional representation of the continent in colonial discourse. In Legson **Kayira**'s *The Looming Shadow* (1968) and especially in his *Jingala* (1969), the reason for revalorizing Africa is made more urgent as we see the erosion of tradition under the forces of Western modernity (see **modernity and modernism**). Modernity is also aligned with colonial hegemony, whose repression of African culture serves as a way of containing the African subject: removed from their indigenous symbolic system, they are concerned more with the question of cultural alienation than political rights. The first Malawian novel in English, *No Easy Task* (1966) by Aubrey **Kachingwe**, moves away from Rubadiri's pan-Africanism and examines the struggle for independence in Malawi, emphasizing how the process is accompanied by a profound change in the consciousness of the colonized. Education, which may have been intended as a tool of colonial ideological interpellation, becomes the very means of anti-colonial subversion (see **education and schools**). Although written much later, Edison Mpina's novel *Freedom Avenue* (1990) also addresses the same problem, especially the loss of land to white-owned tea plantations and the consequent creation of a Malawian regional labor diaspora in southern Africa.

The Unilateral Declaration of Independence (UDI) in 1966 by the white minority regime in Zimbabwe (Rhodesia) led by Ian Smith accelerated the struggle for freedom in Zimbabwe, a process in which literature formed an important part of the cultural resources of political conscientization and mobilization. The war of liberation and the question of colonialism are the main objects of concern in Zimbabwean literature from the 1960s to the 1980s. Solomon Mtswairo's *Feso*, originally published in Shona in 1956 (see **Shona and Ndebele literature**) and translated into English in 1974 occupies pride of place in the national canon of postcolonial Zimbabwe. Mtswairo's allegorization of colonialism in terms of African inter-ethnic warfare was not lost on the colonial government as the novel was banned. Even so, it provided a framework for subsequent literature in which the past was to offer an important setting for staging contemporary antagonisms. Mtswairo himself was to return to the theme in his *Chaminuka: Prophet of Zimbabwe* (1983), a political biography of the spirit-medium who lived between about 1808 and 1883. Stanlake Samkange's novel *My Trial for My Country* (1967), perhaps the first Zimbabwean novel in English, revisits the historical territory explored by Mtswairo and dramatizes the encounter between King Lobengula of the Ndebele and Cecil Rhodes, focusing on the tragic cultural misunderstanding which led to war and colonization. In *Year of Uprising* (1975) the writer studies the oppression accompanying the early years of colonial rule and the resistance mounted by the Ndebele and Shona nations against their oppressors between 1894 and 1897 – what is usually referred to as the First Chimurenga. In *The Mourned One*, published in the same year, the author pays tribute to some of the heroes of the struggle. In his *On My Trial for that UDI* (1986), he engages with the issues of colonial oppression and the struggle against the Rhodesian government as well with the difficulties of exile.

Similarly, the dominant theme in early Zambian literature is that of colonial oppression and the need for African cultural assertion. The best-known publication from Zambia is Kenneth **Kaunda**'s *Zambia Shall Be Free* (1962), which is an **autobiography** of the writer and the Zambian nation, tracing the history of nationalist resistance in the country and outlining the task of building a postcolonial nation. Anti-colonial resistance features highly in the first major Zambian novel in English, *The Tongue of the Dumb* (1971) by Dominic **Mulaisho**, which examines cultural conflict, showing how a precolonial African community resists religious conversion as well as the imposition of colonial authority. Equally attentive to issues of cultural and economic colonialism are Kapasa Makasa's *Bwana District Commissioner: White Colonial Master* (1989) and Binwell Sinyangwe's *A Cowrie of Hope* (2000). The theme is taken up again by other

Zambian writers, notably Andreya Masiye in *Before Dawn* (1970), which offers an almost anthropological study of the Nyanja people of Eastern Province, and Gideon Phiri's *Victims of Fate* (1972), in which tradition and modernity are shown to form a lethal disciplinary weapon, forcing a young man who has made his girlfriend pregnant to flee his home village and move to Lusaka where years later he unknowingly almost marries his own daughter.

These broad historical representations of resistance to colonial rule give way to greater formal complexity in the work of the younger generation of writers, especially those from Zimbabwe. Charles Mungoshi's *Waiting for the Rain* (1975) contrasts the Chimurenga war of the nineteenth century with the war of liberation in Rhodesia in the 1970s. His short story collection, *Coming of the Dry Season*, published three years earlier, addresses the profound emotional and psychological damage wrought on Africa by colonialism, showing how the African, as a subject, has been produced in terms of the hegemonic ideology of colonialism. The same kind of anguished concern with the spiritual and psychological condition of the colonized is discernible from Wilson **Katiyo**'s *Son of the Soil* (1976), a *Bildungsromanen* in which the protagonist's development from childhood and innocence is also accompanied by a steady and sometimes dramatic growth in awareness of his condition as a colonized subject.

Anti-colonial protest and cultural affirmation are dominant themes in the poetry of the region as well. Rubadiri's "When Mutesa Met Kabaka," which demonstrates how traditional African institutions were taken advantage of by the early agents of the colonial order, is one of the first poems from the region to combine a celebration of precolonial African culture with an understanding of its internal structural vulnerability. The only other poet from Malawi who examines the colonial theme intensely is Frank **Chipasula**, especially in *Whispers in the Wings* (1991), through his exploration of the racial formations of southern Africa and also his keen interest in the fate of subjects in the African diaspora (see **diaspora and pan-Africanism**).

There are several Zambian poets, such as Liebetraut Rothert-Sarvan in *Night Poems and Others* (1986), Johan Simons in *Agony of Heart* (1980),

Timothy Holms in *Double Element* (1985), Evaristo Ngalande in *I Cannot See* (1987), Akanshambatwa Mbikusita-Lewanika in *For the Seeds in Our Blood* (1981), and Parnwell Munatamba in *My Battery* (1982), who have touched on the theme of Africa and colonialism, but for a more in-depth study we must turn to Patu Simoko. Simoko's *Africa is Made of Clay* (1975), perhaps the first Zambian anthology of poetry in English, is a pan-Africanist elegy to the African past as well as a critical commentary on the negative excesses of postcolonial power. Similarly, L.C. Mambwe's *Africa is Mine and Yours* (1989) bemoans the loss of traditional values and, most significantly, the anthology combines cultural nationalism with a class analysis of postcolonial society, decrying the suffering of the masses and their exploitation by the new African elite. Mambwe's thematic concerns overlap with those of Lyamba wa Kabika, who in his *Swimming in Floods of Tears* (1983) uses a strong aphoristic voice to identify with the anti-imperialist fighters in Zimbabwe, Mozambique, and Namibia, as well as with the local poor.

It is in the poetry from Zimbabwe that we are offered a more sustained study of colonialism and its impact on traditional African culture. Mudereri Khadani, Charles **Mungoshi**, and Chenjerai **Hove** have all written on the subject, but the best example on this theme remains Musaemura Bonas **Zimunya**'s work. In *Zimbabwe Ruins* (1979), he locates Zimbabwean identity in the precolonial autochthonous space of the founding of the Great Zimbabwe, thereby reducing the colonial period to the status of the measurable and thus reversible historical temporality. In the poem "Jikinya," in *Kingfisher, Jikinya and Other Poems* (1983), he celebrates African womanhood as the embodiment of the African past in the present and the Zimbabwean nation.

Playwrights have also addressed themselves to the problematic of cultural colonialism. One remarkable approach to the question of the past has been the quarrying of oral tradition (see **oral literature and performance**), not only for themes but also for theatrical forms. The Malawian playwright Steve **Chimombo** shows particular interest in this use of oral material. In his play *The Rainmaker* (1975), we are taken back to the myths of the ancient Malawi kingdom for concepts of redemptive agency and also for a dramatic structure that is based on traditional rituals of ceremonial and religious performance. The celebration of past cultural and political formations sometimes takes the form of hero-worship, as in *Shaka Zulu*, a play by the Zambian playwright Fwanya Mulikita. The play is a complex examination of the life and times of the historical Zulu king, acknowledging the impact of the Zulu dispersal (*mfecane*) on the cultures of Central Africa, with large populations of people of Zulu or Nguni descent now settled in Zimbabwe, Zambia, and Malawi. The interest in history and precolonial Zambian kingdoms is also evident in Andreya Masiye's lyrical play, *The Lands of the Kazembe* (1973). K. Kasoma's *The Fools Marry* (1976) and Killian Mulaisho's *The Tragedy of Pride* (1988) demonstrate that the region's playwrights are interested not only in the larger issues but also in the everyday business of living, its comic as well as serious aspects. Indeed, in the work of Zimbabwean playwright Stephen Chifunyise, especially his *Medicine for Love and Other Plays* (1984), the past is explored in terms of its determining influence on the present, as the conflict between tradition and modernity is played out most intensely in the urban spaces.

War literature and postcolonialism

The literature of cultural affirmation and anti-colonial expression gives rise to what might be termed "war literature," a genre that predominates in Zimbabwe, where there was the most prolonged and bloody war of independence. Solomon Mtswairo's *Mapondera: Soldier of Zimbabwe* (1983) was one of the first novels in this genre, very much exhorting the nation to engage in war and offering the novel as the equivalent of the war songs of precolonial African society. If Mtswairo was only a cheerleader looking in at things from outside, after independence, former combatants offered an insider's perspective as they sought to register their experience of the war through literature. In *Death Throes: The Trial of Mbuya Nehanda* (1990), Charles Samupindi recasts the new Chimurenga in terms of the nineteenth-century struggle, presenting the earlier war as the spiritual and political uncon-scious of the present effort. Similarly, in Edmund Chipamaunga's *A Fighter for Freedom* (1983) and

Garika Mutasa's *The Contact* (1985) the war is viewed largely in heroic terms. However, in Samupindi's *Pawns* (1992) we are offered not only a more graphic picture of colonial brutality in Zimbabwe, but also a less than flattering representation of the liberation forces: young fighters are depicted as being at the mercy of sadistic nationalist commanders, implying that on occasion the white man's brutalization of the black man is transferred to the weaker of the same race. This is a point Tsitsi **Dangarembga** also makes in *Nervous Conditions* (1989) through the actions of Babamukuru. In *Harvest of Thorns* (1989), Shimmer **Chinodya** continues the interrogation of the purity of the war of liberation, exposing the brutality directed at women by fellow combatants. In the grim realism of the day-to-day experience of the guerilla fighter, we are given an antidote to the sometimes oversimplified and romanticized heroic narratives such as Mtswairo's.

There are also a number of works that shift the focus away from the combatants to how the war affected those who remained inside the country. In Shimmer Chinodya's *Dew in the Morning* (1982) and *Farai's Girls* (1984), the writer focuses on individuals who are so preoccupied with the business of living that they are almost detached from the world of war and change around them. In fact, the pursuit of personal interest in utter obliviousness to the larger issues echoes Samuel Chimsoro's *Nothing is Impossible* (1983), where we are presented with a hero whose main aim in life is to succeed personally and who, in the end, becomes so wealthy that even racist Rhodesia is forced to accept him into the exclusive Million Dollar Round Table Club. However, the most powerful evocation of the impact of the war on those who remained inside is Chenjerai Hove's *Bones* (1988: Harare). It alludes to the irrepressibility of anti-colonial resistance by its intertextual reference to the dying words of Mbuya Nehanda, that "you may kill me, but my bones will rise again," while also showing how this deep spiritual and historical dimension to the nationalist struggle is counterbalanced by internal differences among the African community. Clearly, some of this is attributable to the macrocosmic colonial oppressive public sphere, but a large part of it is engendered within the

autonomous sphere of African tradition and contemporary cultural practice.

The task of exposing the betrayal of nationalism and its ideals seems to have fallen mostly to Malawian writers. There is no similar depth of coverage of the theme in Zimbabwean or Zambian literature. In Zimbabwe there has been a prolonged national consensus since independence and there has been little criticism of the regime in literature. As for Zambia, Kenneth Kaunda's benevolent dictatorship, combined with his obvious commitment to pan-Africanism and the liberation of Rhodesia and South Africa, made him less vulnerable to the kind of criticism Malawian writers directed at Dr Hastings Kamuzu Banda. Nevertheless, while Robert Mugabe largely escapes criticism, Kaunda is not as lucky, since a character resembling him appears in Dominic Mulaisho's *The Smoke that Thunders* (1979), a text that confronts directly the problems of corruption in politics and business in postcolonial Zambia perpetrated by, among others, the leader of the country.

In Malawi, the notorious dictatorship of Hastings Banda fractured the nationalist alliance a few months after independence, sending a number of his cabinet colleagues into exile in neighboring countries. In *The Civil Servant* (1971) and *The Detainee* (1974), Legson Kayira began to engage with the relationship between subjectivity and the public sphere, concentrating on the way in which agents of the postcolonial state affect the lives of ordinary people. Ken Lipenga's *Waiting for a Turn* (1976) combines the real with the surreal in a refreshingly adventurous manner, and in the short story "Tiger" (published in *Waiting for a Turn*, 1976) Lipenga comments candidly on the political condition in the country, highlighting the master–slave relationship underlying political relations in Malawi. In Paul Tiyambe Zeleza's novel *Smouldering Charcoal* (1990) there is a much more overt political critique of the dictatorship, as well as an attempt to offer an alternative to the current political system in the form of socialism. Political oppression appears again in Felix Mnthali's *Yoranivyoto* (2000), in which the repression of the intellectual class by the dictatorship is seen as fueling resistance, forcing the emergence of strong women's agency. Obviously, Mnthali is better known as a poet. His *Sunset at Sapitwa* (1981) was one of the first collections of poetry from Malawi. It combines a philosophical and personal account of political repression in Malawi with a concern for a philosophical reflection on the issues of love, mortality, and history.

In Steve Chimombo's *Napolo* (1987) and *A Referendum of Forest Creatures* (1993), local myths and folk tales provide the material for poetic narrative structure and representation of political oppression. The most internationally acclaimed Malawian poet is Jack **Mapanje**, who in his *Of the Chameleon and the Gods* (1981) uses the conflict between tradition and modernity as a backcloth for investigating the uses and abuses of tradition and power in postcolonial Malawi. His *Chattering Wagtails of Mikuyu* (1993) revisits his prison experience, recording and reflecting on the human capacity for violence and brutality. In *Skipping without Ropes* (1997), the poet explores the aftermath of exile and the return to democracy. The earliest poetry anthology by a Malawian is perhaps *Visions and Reflections* (1972) by Frank Chipasula, who later went into exile from where he wrote *O Earth Wait for Me* (1984) and *Nightwatcher, Nightsong* (1986), and edited *When My Brothers Come Home: Poems from Central and Southern Africa* (1985). In his poetry, Chipasula laments the loss of freedom in his country and also agonizes over the fate of ordinary people. His concern for freedom extends to the suffering majority under apartheid and also in other parts of Africa and the Third World.

The disenchantment with nationalist discourse takes the form of existentialist detachment and even nihilism among some writers, especially Zimbabwean writers. It is the suspicion that the reversal of the colonial Manichean dichotomy in nationalist discourse elides fundamental and even more virulent internal differences that forces the hero of Stanley **Nyamufukudza**'s *The Non-Believer's Journey* (1980) into a kind of existentialist cynicism. Cynicism gives way to nihilism in Dambudzo Marechera's *The Black Insider* (1990), as the psychological and cultural alienation of exile evolves into a permanent state of anxiety, anger, and a heightened capacity for criticism and fault-finding. However, this form of dehumanization is traceable to the experience of colonialism back home as seen in the writer's novella *House of Hunger* (1978), which shows how urban social and

economic deprivation produced by the colonial order has an enduring and almost indelible effect on the formation of the subjectivity of the colonized. In its modernist thrust, Marechera's work also has a lot in common with that of his compatriot, Yvonne **Vera**, especially her *Butterfly Burning* (1998). However, Vera goes beyond modernism and existentialism, working with a form of transgressive aesthetics that echoes the concerns of magical realism.

Gender

Vera's work is much more focused politically than Marechera's in that it is committed to the revalorization of women's agency in Zimbabwe's history and contemporary society. Her historical novel *Nehanda* (1993) rewrites the narrative of Mbuya Nehanda in terms of a nationalist discourse in which women's agency is not merely spiritual, but also worked out in terms of forms of knowledge such as military tactics, traditionally a male preserve. The restoration of women's agency is elaborated in a poetics that is rich in instances of stylistic transgression, mixing the oracular with the mundane, prose and poetry, and a general disruption of the requirement for a clear relationship between cause and effect. In her *Without A Name* (1994), we are presented with a protagonist who wishes to reinvent herself in the city, her life having been destroyed by being raped by a soldier. However, her attempt to fashion a meaningful identity in the anonymity of the city does not succeed. In her disjointed recollection of her past and present, the protagonist lives out a split identity, caught between the desire for a plenitudinous future and the invisible weight of the past that constantly returns to frustrate any movement beyond the false identifications with the speculative "other" of her tortured life.

Similarly, Tsitsi Dangarembga in her novel *Nervous Conditions* (1988) presents women's psychical dissonance as a function of the interplay between colonialism and patriarchy. Nyasha, the anglicized daughter of a domineering Westernized father, feels an outsider when back in Zimbabwe, and she internalizes her cultural displacement, developing an eating disorder which threatens her life. However, Tambu, the protagonist, learns from the condition of her cousin not to denigrate the invaluable immersion in tradition she has had through the women around her: her grandmother and her mother, for example. Furthermore, through her mother's sister she is offered a model of strong womanhood anchored in the cultural values and lore of Shona society. In this *Bildungsromanen*, Tambu develops from a naïve village girl who worships everything Western, especially as represented by her uncle Bambamukuru, to a wary adolescent who is much more cautious of her uncle's position and what it signifies, realizing that, within the context of the racialized politics of Zimbabwe, he is merely an African overseer who is the black face of colonial authority. Through the rebellion of Maimuguru, the uncle's wife, she learns the difficulties in – but also the possibility of – combining tradition and modernity in producing new modes of gendered identity.

What Tambu learns through observation and education, the persona of Freedom Nyamubaya's poetry anthology, *On the Road Again* (1986: Harare), acquires painfully through the battlefields of the war of liberation. Nyamubaya, one of the few women military commanders of the nationalist forces, offers us a personal meditation on the experience of being on the front line. In her poem "A Fake Love," she explores the sensual relationship between the female combatant and her gun, a union that is conceived of as one between lovers. As in human affairs, the lover one day proves feckless, jamming and leaving the persona unprotected from the enemy. The poet also doubts whether independence has really brought about freedom. A particular target of her criticism is what she terms the "native intellectual," who aligns with the people during the struggle but after independence goes back to his corrupt ways. Clearly, she sees her writing as another form of warfare, saying,

> Now that I have put my gun down
> For almost obvious reasons
> the enemy is still here invisible
> my barrel has no definite target now
> Let my hands work –
> My mouth sing
> My pencil write
> About the same things my bullet aimed at.

In *The Storm is Brewing* (1984) Christina Rungano

offers a distant observer's view of the war, noting in the poem "The Comrades are Back" that the returning combatants may be surprised that the things they fought for are still a faraway dream. There is also an attempt to engage with the politics of gender subordination and elaborate a new form of identity. Another radical contestation of dominant gender ideology is to be found in a collection of short stories, *The Heart of Women* (1997), edited by Norah Mumba and Monde Sifuniso on behalf of the Zambia Women Writers' Association. The anthology explores the conflict between men and women and focuses on the violence involved in these relationships.

Popular literature

It must also be noted that the region has produced a sizable amount of popular literature, sometimes, as in the case of Aubrey Kalitera of Malawi, being aided and abetted by writers of similar ilk from other regions. The publication of Kalitera's *A Taste of Business* (1982) in Kenya seems to have been inspired and facilitated by the Kenyan writer David **Maillu** – a good instance of cultural cooperation among writers from different regions. Kalitera's writing includes *Fate* (1984), *To Felix, With Love* (1984), a collection of short stories, *She Died in My Bed* (1984), and a film, *To Ndirande, with Love* (1983). In *Why, Father, Why* (1983), he combines detection, mystery, and the traditional Malawian moral tale in order to produce a text that adapts the formulas of Western popular fiction to the cultural needs of Central Africa. Other Malawian writers have followed Kalitera's example, for instance Dede Kamkondo, who in his novel *The Truth Will Out* (1986) combines the detective motif with romance, bringing together two genres that are usually regarded as separate. The Zimbabwean writer Alexander Kanengoni, in his *Vicious Circle* (1988), also imaginatively adapts the protocols of Western popular literature to local circumstances. Zambia has not been left behind with regard to popular fiction. Grieve Sibale's *Murder in the Forest* (1998) is a gory narrative about the wiles of urban humanity. A rich businessman murders an immigrant tailor when he unwittingly meddles in the businessman's affairs. The novel also belongs to the genre in which newly arrived countryfolk are taken advantage of by seasoned city dwellers. Sibale's partner in crime, so to speak, is Alick Musonda, who in his three novels *Maliongo's Adventures: The Stolen Diary of a ZNS Recruit* (1995), *Solo* (1999), and *The Super Tomboys: Maliongo's Military Adventures* (2001) produces a raw but pleasurable cocktail of sex, violence, adventure, and mystery.

Clearly, the literature of the region offers a rich and diverse thematic and stylistic expression, with particular themes associated more strongly with some countries than others. It began with a strong interest in exploring the African past and tradition as a way of combating colonialism. Later, especially in Zimbabwe, literature registered and reflected on the war of liberation. With the objectives of nationalism not fully realized, some of the writers, especially those from Malawi and a few from Zambia, have used literature to document the abuse of power under the postcolonial leadership. There is also a vibrant popular fiction tradition which, though apolitical in the main, has contributed greatly to debates about tradition versus modernity. Moreover, the critique of the postcolonial formation has expanded into a concern with issues of gender as well of justice in general. The quest for a more equitable postcolonial society is also accompanied by a search for a new aesthetic of representation.

Further reading

Hove, Chenjerai (1988) *Bones*, Harare: Baobab Books.

Msiska, Mpalive-Hangson (1999) "Malawian Literature," in *Encyclopaedia of World Literature in the Twentieth Century*, Detroit: St James's Press.

Msiska, Mpalive-Hangson and Hyland, Paul (eds) (1997) *Writing and Africa*, London and New York: Longman.

Nyamubaya, Freedom (1986) *On the Road Again*, Harare: Zimbabwe Publishing House.

Roscoe, Adrian (1977) *Uhuru's Fire: African Literature East to South*, Cambridge: Cambridge University Press.

Zimunya, Musaemura (1982) *Those Years of Drought and Hunger: The Birth of African Fiction in English in Zimbabwe*, Gweru: Mambo Press.

MPALIVE-HANGSON MSISKA

Central African literatures in French

This entry discusses the literatures of the Central African Republic, Gabon, Republic of the Congo, Democratic Republic of the Congo, Republic of Burundi, and Republic of Rwanda.

Central African Republic

The Central African Republic has adopted Sangho, widely spoken, as its national language, but maintains French as its official language. This nation, rich in oral arts, has been slower than some of its neighbors to develop a written literature, although the colonial administrator René **Maran**, as early as 1921, immortalized the people and their culture in his classic novel, *Batouala*, which was awarded the Prix Goncourt. In 1972, Faustin-Albert Ipéko-Etomane collected and translated traditional legends in his anthology *Lac des sorciers* (Sorcerers' Lake). In the same year, the nation's most celebrated novelist, Pierre Makombo **Bamboté**, won critical acclaim for using an innovative narrative style in *Princesse Mandapu*. Published by Présence Africaine in Paris, the story details the activities of a dictatorial and abusive government official in an isolated village. The novels that have succeeded Bamboté's masterpiece have given voice to themes specific to national history. Pierre Sammy Mackfoy (also Pierre Sammy) draws on the period of colonization in *L'Odyssée de Mongou* (Mongou's Odyssey), and Cyriaque Robert **Yavoucko** offers variations on the theme of political and cultural resistance in his first novel *Crépuscule et défi* (Dusk and Defiance) (1979), a work that he subtitles in Sangho. Etienne **Goyémidé**, also a writer of plays and short stories, rehabilitates the pygmy culture of the southern forests in his novel *Le Silence de la forêt* (The Silence of the Forest) (1984), and returns to the slave trade for his subject matter in *Le Dernier Survivant de la caravane* (The Last Survivor of the Caravan) (1985), a narrative enriched by traditional proverbs, poetry, and songs. Gabriel Danzi satirizes the post-independence government in *Un Soleil au bout de la nuit* (A Sun at the End of Night) (1984). Much of the theater in this country has been performed but not published.

Ipéko-Etomane provides a valuable showcase for his own work and for that of other Central African poets in both French and Sangho in his 1983 *Anthologie de la poésie centrafricaine.*

Republic of Gabon

Gabon is one of the wealthiest countries in sub-Saharan Africa. French is the official language, a commonly shared means of communication in a country with a number of different ethnic groups, all speaking their own languages and dialects. As in many African countries, the first publications in French sought to preserve the traditional oral arts. André Raponda-Walker, the first Gabonese priest, published *Contes gabonais* (Gabonese Tales) in 1953. These were followed by similar efforts, the most noteworthy being the work by Philippe Tsira Ndong Ndoutoume on the *mvet*, an epic form introduced by the Fang. Gabon was represented at the first Festival of Black Arts in Dakar in 1968 by a play entitled *La Mort de Guykafi* (The Death of Guykafi) based on the exploits of a legendary warrior. The playwright, Vincent de Paul **Nyonda**, was a founding figure in Gabonese theater, and three of his plays were published in 1981 by L'Harmattan. Literary production in French gained momentum with the creation of a Ministry of Culture in 1973 whose mission was expressly to encourage the arts. As a result, the 1970s saw an upsurge in the publication of poetry by writers such as Georges Rawiri, Quentin Ben Mongaryas, and Maurice **Okoumba-Nkoghe** and in 1976, the Ministry of Education published the *Anthologie de la littérature gabonaise.* The novel in French developed later. Angèle Ntyugwetondo **Rawiri** has published three novels dealing with challenges faced by women in a changing society, beginning with *Elonga* in 1980. Okoumba-Nkoghe gained acclaim for *La Mouche et la glu* (The Fly and the Flypaper) in 1984, an elegantly written love story. Probably Gabon's most famous literary figure is Laurent **Owondo**, whose novel of identity and social change *Au bout du silence* (At the End of the Silence) was published in France by Hatier in 1985. Two plays by Josephine Kama Bongo, *Obali* (1974) and *Ayouma*, have both been turned into films. Justine Mintsa stands out among younger writers with her novel on the life of a woman student, *Un*

Seul tournant Makôsu (Makôsu, A Single Turning Point) (1994).

Republic of the Congo

During the colonial period, Brazzaville, the capital of the Republic of the Congo (formerly the People's Republic of the Congo), served as the administrative capital of French Equatorial Africa. Home of *Liaison,* a review founded in 1950 as a forum for Francophone Africa's creative minds, the country could nevertheless boast few published books during the colonial period. Among these were Jean Malonga's versions of traditional oral art, *Coeur d'aryenne* (Aryan Heart), published in 1954 and considered to be the first literary work from the Congo, followed shortly by *La Légende de M'Pfoumou Ma Mazono* (The Legend of M'Pfoumou Ma Mazono). The poetry of Martial Sinda, *Premier chant du départ* (First Song of Departure) won the Grand Prix de l'Afrique Équatoriale Française in 1955. By 1958, **Tchicaya UTam'Si** had already established himself as a major African poet with three collections of poems published in Paris. With independence in 1960, this nation, composed of over sixty ethnic groups, made French its official language and has in recent years produced an unusually large number of talented literary figures writing in that language, many of whom have demonstrated their genius in more than one genre.

By 1963, two theater troupes were active in Brazzaville. Sylvain **Bemba**, awarded the Grand Prix des Lettres by the president of the Congo for the totality of his literary work in 1977, had published *L'Enfer, c'est Orféo* (Hades, It's Orpheus) as early as 1969. Antoine Letembet-Ambily won the Grand Prix du Concours Théâtral Interafricain for *L'Europe inculpée* (Europe Indicted), a play published in Paris in 1970. **Sony Labou Tansi**, who founded the Rocado Zulu Theater in Brazzaville in 1970, also won awards for his work in the genre. Guy **Menga**, Tchicaya UTam'Si, and Maxime N'Debeka all produced important dramatic works.

But it is perhaps in the area of short story and novel that the Congo has made its greatest impact, and many of its writers have won international prizes for their prose fiction. The Grand Prix Littéraire d'Afrique Noire was awarded to, among others, Guy Menga for *La Palabre stérile* (The

Useless Palaver), Henri **Lopes** for *Tribaliks* (*Tribaliques*), Sony Labou Tansi for *L'Anté-peuple* (*The Antipeople*), and Jean Baptiste **Tati-Loutard** for *Récit de la mort* (Story of Death). Another figure whose fiction deserves mention is Emmanuel **Dongala**. Many of these writers have also produced poetry. In 1984 Léopold Pindy Mamonsono produced an anthology dedicated to the works of younger writers, *La Nouvelle Génération des poètes congolais* (The New Generation of Congolese Poets). Marie-Léontine **Tsibinda** has established herself as an important writer of both poetry and short stories and is only one of several women writers from the Congo to attract critical attention.

Democratic Republic of the Congo (formerly Zaire)

One of Africa's largest and most populous countries, with a rich precolonial history of empire among the Kongo, Teke, Luba, and Lunda peoples, the Congo Free State was "given" to King Leopold of Belgium by the Conference of Berlin. In 1908, the Belgian government assumed the administration of the territory until it gained independence in 1960. Official languages are French and the four major African languages: Luba, Swahili (see **Swahili literature**), Kongo, and Lingala. During the colonial era, education was primarily in the hands of missionaries who provided instruction in African languages; unlike the French, the Belgians did not undertake to produce a university-educated elite. These factors may have been instrumental in the somewhat later development of a literature in French. Among the first writers to publish in the language were Paul **Lomami-Tshibamba** whose narrative *Ngando* (Crocodile) received first prize in a literary competition sponsored by the Colonial Fair in Brussels in 1949. In 1955, *Esanzo, Chants pour mon pays* (Esanzo, Songs for My Country), a collection of poems by J'ongungu Lokolé **Bolamba**, was published by Présence Africaine in Paris. This was the first work by a writer from the Belgian Congo to be published in France.

The creation of national universities in Léopoldville (Kinshasa) and Elisabethville (Lubumbashi) in the decade prior to independence brought about the true flourishing of Congolese letters. The literary circle Pléiade du Congo and similar groups provided encouragement for many of the nation's future writers. Local publishers, including Saint-Paul Afrique, Mont Noir, and Okapi, provided a vehicle for a literature that had few European outlets. Poetry dominated the 1960s with the work of such writers as Clémentine **Nzuji**, who became one of the first African women poets to publish in French in 1967. The first major novel from Congo-Zaire to be published in France was V.Y. **Mudimbe**'s *Between Tides* (*Entre les eaux*) (1973), the story of an African priest who joins the resistance. The novel, which was published by Présence Africaine in 1973, was accorded the Prix Catholique. Other early novelists were Georges Ngal (see **Ngal Mbwil a Mpaang**) and Pius **Ngandu Nkashama**. All three of these authors, while continuing to publish, eventually chose to live outside the country, and many other writers who chronicled the Mobutu era now live abroad, including Thomas Mpoyi-Buatu, José Tshisungu wa Tshisungu, Bolya Baenga, Jules Emongo Lomamba, and Charles **Djungu-Simba Kamatenda**. Most of these writers have published at least some of their works with European presses. However, the most widely read novelist in Congo-Zaire, with over two dozen titles to his credit, was Batukezanga **Zamenga**, who was published exclusively in the country.

The Republics of Rwanda and Burundi

Rwanda and Burundi, both kingdoms founded in the seventeenth century when Tutsi warriors conquered the Hutu and Twa peoples of the region, were colonized first by Germany but were transferred to Belgium after World War I. As Ruanda-Urundi, these territories were governed by Belgium under a League of Nations mandate and then a United Nations trusteeship. These protectorates became independent in 1962 as two separate republics. The Belgian colonial policy originally fostered the use of African languages, and primary instruction since independence has taken place in Kinyarwanda and Kirundi, each being an official language along with French in its respective country. In Rwanda, English is also listed as an official language. Both countries have a rich oral and written corpus in their own languages and lack institutional support and publishing houses for the type of production in French that characterizes most former Francophone colonies. Theater in the national language is widely disseminated through radio broadcasts and contests. Oral forms and traditions thus play an important role in the creation of written texts in French. In Burundi, for example, Michel Kayoya published short texts in 1968 and 1970 depicting local customs and beliefs. In Rwanda, Alexis **Kagame** used French to make his literature and culture known to a Western audience in his 1951 volume *La Poésie dynastique du Rwanda* (The Dynastic Poetry of Rwanda) and other works. In 1978, Edouard Gasarabwe published a thesis on Rwandan thought, *Le Geste rwanda* (Rwanda Song), and followed it later with a collection of folk tales titled *Contes du Rwanda: soirées au pays des mille collines* (Tales from Rwanda: Evenings in the Country of the Thousand Hills). Other writing in French includes the work of Savério **Nayigiziki**, who won the Prix de Littérature Coloniale in 1949 for his novel of colonial society, *Escapade ruandaise* (Rwandese Escapades). Jean-Baptiste Mutabaruka is known for his poetry inspired by traditional Rwandan literary models. Among more recent writers in Burundi, Antoine Kaburahe, Frédéric Ngenzebuhoro, and Richard Ndayizigamiye have attracted critical attention for their work in various genres. In Rwanda, Cyprien **Rugamba** produced both poetry and theater before his death in 1994, and Pierre-Claver Katerpilari is known for his short stories. Ethnic conflict in both countries led to a period of political instability in the wake of independence that has done little to nurture the development of literature, although the survivors of genocide have often chosen to use French as the medium through which to bear witness to events, in works such as Yolande Mukagasana's autobiographical narratives about her experiences in Rwanda.

Further reading

Agence de Coopération Culturelle et Technique (ed.) (1995) *Littératures francophones d'Afrique Cen-trale: Anthologie* (Francophone Literatures of Central Africa: Anthology), Paris: Nathan.

JANICE SPLETH

Chakaipa, Patrick

b. 1932, Mhondoro, Zimbabwe

novelist

Patrick Chakaipa, the Zimbabwean writer and the head of the Catholic Church in the country, is one of the most widely read novelists in Shona (see **Shona and Ndebele literature**). He grew up in a powerful oral storytelling tradition in which his kinsfolk distinguished themselves as storytellers (see **oral literature and performance**). A member of the first generation of Africans who received missionary education, his works embody Christian values, as evident in *Rudo Ibofu* (Love is Blind) (1961). More importantly, in terms of form, he draws heavily from the storytelling tradition to produce captivating romances and vivid encounters of the Shona people with one another, with nature, and with colonialism (see **colonialism, neocolonialism, and postcolonialism**). Published between 1961 and 1967, his works comprise the classics of the colonial period. His two romances, *Karikoga Gumiremiseve* (Karikoga and His Ten Arrows) (1959), and *Pfumo Reropa* (The Spear of Blood) (1961), are household titles in the Shona literary world. His other novels, *The Village Alcoholic* (*Dzasukwa Mwana-asina-hembe*) (1967) and *Wait, I Shall Return* (*Garandichauya*) (1963), highlight the disruptive nature of colonial commerce on rural society, especially on the family institution. Chakaipa's works are distinguishable by their vivid and realistic delineation of detail. His works represent the peak form of Shona literature of the 1960s. He is a model of many writers of the 1970s.

Further reading

Kahari, G.P. (1972) *The Novels of Patrick Chakaipa*, Salisbury (Harare): Longman Rhodesia.

EMMANUEL CHIWOME

Chedid, Andrée

b. 1920, Cairo, Egypt

poet

An illustrious Francophone writer, Chedid was born Andrée Saab in Cairo of a family of Lebanese roots. She was educated in French schools and graduated from the American University in Cairo. Her first volume of poetry, *On the Trials of My Fancy* (1943) was in English, written shortly after her marriage to Louis Chedid. But since then she has been a prolific author in French, writing poetry, novels, short stories, and dramatic plays. She has been living in Paris since 1948 and has received scores of prizes and awards, and many of her works have been translated to English. One of them, *The Sixth Day* (*Le Sixième Jour*) (1960) is about the courage of a grandmother in a cholera-infested Cairo. It was made into a film by the Egyptian director Youssef Chahine in 1986.

In Chedid's poetry the inner world with its archetypal elements is explored. For her, writing is the site of rooting and uprooting simultaneously. Her novels are more specifically Egyptian than her poetry and deal with the human condition, as in her 1952 and 1962 collections, *From Sleep Unbound* (*Le Sommeil délivré*) and *L'Autre* (The Other). Two other collections of poems, *Néfertiti et le rêve d'Akhnatoun* (Nefertiti and the Dream of Aknatoun) and *Le Survivant* (The Survivor) were published in 1974 and 1982. Her plays include *Le Montreur* (The Demonstrator) and *Échec à la reine* (The Failure of the Queen), published in 1969 and 1984. She has also written short stories, including *L'Étroite Peau* (The Narrow Skin) published in 1965. Chedid's narrative style is lyrical, often marked by nostalgia for Egypt and Lebanon. She presents life in popular neighborhoods as well as among the elite, emphasizing the role of women without calling herself a feminist. The quest for human fraternity permeates her works and is manifested in the correspondence she sees between different generations, genders, nationalities, and religions.

Further reading

Chedid, Andrée (1987) *From Sleep Unbound*, trans. Sharon Spencer, London: Serpent's Tail.

—(1987) *The Sixth Day*, trans. Isobel Strachey, London: Serpent's Tail.

Linkton, Renée (1990) *The Prose and Poetry of Andrée Chedid: Selected Poems, Short Stories and Essays*, Birmingham, Alabama: Summa Publications.

FERIAL J. GHAZOUL

Cheney-Coker, Syl

b. 1947, Freetown, Sierra Leone

poet, journalist, and novelist

The Sierra Leonean poet, journalist, and professor Syl Cheney-Coker first came to the attention of critics and historians of African literature with the publication of his collection of poems, *The Graveyard Also Has Teeth* (1980), but he had been writing and publishing poetry since the early 1970s. Many of his early poems were heavily influenced by the movement of **negritude** and contain imagery drawn from one of the movement's major poets, Léopold Sédar **Senghor**. But in his first published group of poems, *Concerto for an Exile* (1973), Cheney-Coker was more concerned with his relation to the culture of Sierra Leone, especially his own location in a Creole culture rooted in the identity of former slaves and privileged within the culture of colonialism and the postcolonial landscape of the country (see **colonialism, neocolonialism, and postcolonialism**). In the title poem of this collection, "Concerto for an Exile," the poet wonders about his place as a subject and a poet in a situation in which the long history of conquest and enslavement continues to rise and haunt the present. In other poems from this period, he is interested in developing an idiom that might account for Sierra Leone's multiple, and sometimes conflictual, identities. If he locates his tormented self at the center of the poems collected in *Concerto for an Exile*, the new poems in *The Graveyard Also Has Teeth* are conceived as more public reflections, even conversations, with Sierra Leone. These poems are often concerned with the violent politics of postcolonialism, of unexpected coups and executions, of death and bloodshed, loss and exile. The themes of death and loss acquire a new urgency in Cheney-Coker's later poems, collected in *The Blood* *in the Desert's Eye* (1990), but now the poet seems to celebrate exile as the only way out of the truncated landscape of the postcolony. After twenty years of writing poetry, Cheney-Coker published his first novel, *The Last Harmattan of Alusine Dunbar* (1990), a panoramic and highly imaginative representation of the making of Sierra Leone and its communities who had returned from the slave ports of the New World to found a home in which they would live out their dreams of freedom. The novel, which won the Commonwealth Writers' Prize for the African region in 1991, was influenced by Latin-American boom literature of the 1960s and 1970s, and is now considered to be one of the earliest examples of magic realism in African fiction (see **realism and magical realism**).

Further reading

Fraser, Robert (1986) *West African Poetry: A Critical History,* Cambridge: Cambridge University Press.

SIMON GIKANDI

Chidyausiku, Paul

b. 1929, Zimbabwe

preacher and writer

Paul Chidyausiku, the Zimbabwean lay preacher, agricultural assistant, and later newspaper editor, is a widely read Shona writer (see **Shona and Ndebele literature**). He published the first Shona play, *Ndakambokuyambira* (I Warned You) (1968), which was for many years the only play available for study in schools. His novelette, *Disgrace is Worse than Death* (*Nyadzi Dzinokunda*) (1962) decries the corruption of values in urban African workers who are freed from precolonial, traditional African social structures by modernity and modernization (see **modernity and modernism**). In *Pfungwa Dzasekuru Mafusire* (The Thoughts of Uncle Mafusire) (1962), a collection of short stories and essays, Chidyausiku celebrates modernity over African traditional practices relating to healing, agriculture, marriage, and education (see **education and schools**). His vision typifies the enthusiasm with which the first generation of literate Africans

embraced modernization as a form of enlightenment. In *Marriage Rites* (*Nhoroondo Dzokuwanana*) (1958), he produced a tract intended to guide his readers in the ways of a modern marriage, seeking to blend the values and practices of traditional African marriages and Christianity (see **Christianity and Christian missions**). Chidyausiku's later publication, *Kupaiko Ikoko?* (What Kind of Generosity Is This?) (2000), is a collection of poems with a wide range of sociopolitical themes which reflect the mind of a critical patriot at work.

Further reading

Chiwome, E.M. (1996) *A Social History of the Shona Novel,* Zimbabwe: Juta.

EMMANUEL CHIWOME

Chidzero, Bernard

b. 1927, Zimbabwe

economist and writer

The distinguished Zimbabwean economist Bernard Chidzero is the author of *Mr Lazy-Bones* (*Nzvengamutsvairo*), the second Shona novel published by what was then the Rhodesia Literature Bureau, in 1957 (see **Shona and Ndebele literature**). His only work so far, the novel was one of the most widely read works in schools during the colonial period. In this short novel, based on stories of the historic encounter between Shona youths and colonial wage labor (see **colonialism, neocolonialism, and postcolonialism**), Chidzero captures the divergent ideas of the late colonial period, especially the possibility that a humane multiracial nation might emerge out of the political conditions offered by the Federation of Rhodesia and Nyasaland (1953–63). The novel was influential in its time because of its utopian vision, the belief that the contribution of African labor to the colonial enterprise could lead to racial harmony. This utopian vision was popular among whites and Africans educated in colonial schools in the 1950s, especially before the more pernicious government of Rhodesia supplanted the Federation, and Chidzero's novel was prescribed for study in schools at many levels throughout the colonial period. The writer uses devices from oral art to put across his vision (see **oral literature and performance**). Chidzero later became the first minister of finance in independent Zimbabwe.

Further reading

Kahari, G. (1986) *Aspects of the Shona Novel*, Gwelo: Mambo Press.

children's literature

Introduction

Although neglected for too long as a subject worthy of scholarly attention, children's literature in Africa has always been an important part of African literature. For generations, Africans have told stories in their multitudinous indigenous tongues to children and young people, and to adults as well, in their social, informal, or formal gatherings. For the majority of Africans, then, storytelling is not a new art, but one as old as the African continent itself. In the oral tradition, for example, African folk tales meant for education and entertainment abound on the continent (see **oral literature and performance**). Handed down principally by word of mouth from one generation to the next, these folk tales still function as tools for teaching the African cultural heritage. Today, communal or family gatherings for storytelling are a common feature in many rural areas on the continent, but this tradition is disappearing and being replaced by books in the cities, where people have to deal with various pressures of urban life.

African folk tales in print today are an insignificant proportion of the total body of traditional African folk tales. In storytelling sessions where these folk tales were shared in precolonial Africa before colonialism (see **colonialism, neocolonialism, and postcolonialism**), there were gifted traditional storytellers, such as griots, who relied heavily on their memory, imagination, charm, and verbal dexterity, to delight and mesmerize their audiences. In many African societies, these storytellers were held in high esteem

as sages and regarded as symbols of knowledge and wisdom. In fact, contemporary African-language and European-language writers for African children and young people learnt their art while sitting at the feet of these griots and storytellers. This is why quite a number of writers or folk tale collectors are honest and modest enough not to claim to be the actual composers of what they have transcribed or written down. For example, Birago **Diop** entitles his famous work, *Tales of Amadou Koumba* (*Les Contes d'Amadou Koumba*) first published in 1947, as an acknowledgement of his source. According to Diop, he only wrote down the stories told to him by the griot, Amadou Koumba. Similarly, Bob Leshoai's *Iso Le Nkhono* (South African Folk Tales for Children) (1983) is a collection of Sotho stories from southern Africa, and Cyprian **Ekwensi** has said that he first heard the stories published in *An African Night's Entertainment* (1962) from an old Hausa *mallam* (teacher).

It is significant to note that, in all these cases, the authors had rendered in English and in French stories that they heard, in all probability, told in indigenous African languages. But whether these stories are told by the griot, the professional storyteller, an illiterate lay narrator, or the writer trained in modern literary traditions, their major goal is to educate young children and to pass on the values and ideals of African culture. In addition, it is important to note that the traditional African literature has developed using different genres of storytelling including the folk tale, fiction, **autobiography**, and biography, plays, picture books, and illustrated books. In her book, *Children's Literature about Africa in English*, Nancy J. Schmidt notes that children's literature in Africa is an uncharted universe. At the same time, however, this literature is written in a variety of languages, including English, French, German, and Portuguese, as well as in major African languages such as Hausa, Swahili, Twi, Yoruba, and Arabic (see **literature in Hausa**; **Swahili literature**; **Yoruba literature**). Still, there is no bibliography which thoroughly covers children's literature about Africa in one European or African language, let alone in all the languages in which it has been written.

Colonialism, decolonization, and children's literature

Like other literary traditions on the continent, African children's literature did not escape the influence of colonialism. Indeed, the publication of fiction for African children began in the same early twentieth-century context as fiction for European and American children, except that what was produced for African children was out of touch with African reality. In its themes and functions, literature written for African children had a didactic thrust, very much like the one found in traditional African children's narratives, but its essentially foreign content did not seek to locate African children in their sociocultural environment. In this literature, African children were confronted by alien experiences such as winter, daffodils, Big Ben, and Trafalgar Square. While attempts to reach young Africans through simplified and abridged versions of European classics such as *Oliver Twist*, *Gulliver's Travels*, and *King Solomon's Mines* were laudable, they were not necessarily successful. Simplification and abridgment tended to drain the essential aspects of a work of art, nor did they Africanize the texts enough to overcome their alien character.

In the 1960s, when many African countries got their political independence, scholars were quick to note the dearth of books for children and young people dealing with authentic African experiences. In response to this lack, the African Universities Press was established in Nigeria in the early 1960s with the goal, as it proudly announced on the covers of its first publications, of providing "educational books chosen to answer the needs of Nigerian schools and colleges." The African Universities Press started its African Readers Library Series with the publication of its first title, *An African Night's Entertainment* (1962) by Ekwensi. The work was a contrast to the imported European literature for African children. Ekwensi's text renders in print in English a traditional African storytelling session intended for entertainment and education. Surrounded by an eager audience of "young men, old men, children, women" in the moonlit evening, the old storyteller announces that his story is "a long tale of vengeance, adventure and love." He unfolds the tragic story of Abu Baker with the goal of teaching a simple moral – that one should not take it upon oneself to wreak vengeance. In this respect, *An African Night* illustrates the function of most African folk tales, namely the instruction and entertainment of its audience.

What is interesting about *An African Night's Entertainment* is that a very similar work entitled *Jikin Magayi* had been published in Hausa twenty-eight years earlier, in 1934, by Mallam Tafida Zaria and Rupert East. A joint venture by an indigenous Hausa and a Briton, it was a successful attempt to put in print a traditional Hausa tale. But the print version of *Jikin Magayi* was accessible mainly to those who could read Hausa, and only became available to a wider African and global audience when Ekwensi published his own version. Accused of plagiarism by some critics, Ekwensi defended himself by saying that no one could own a folk tale, especially one that was commonly told in Northern Nigeria where he himself had grown up. It is not unusual for many writers of African children's literature, many of them educated in colonial schools, to adapt African oral literature and to publish it in European languages.

The postcolonial period

An important development in children's literature in the postcolonial period has been the proliferation of works intended to entertain young readers. In the 1970s, for example, Macmillan Publishers established the Pacesetters Series with a young adult readership in mind. According to Macmillan, all the novels in the Pacesetters Series deal with contemporary issues and problems "in a way that is particularly designed to interest young adults, although the stories are such that they will appeal to all ages." Today the novels in the series number about one hundred. While some are formulaic, dealing with adventure, romance, and mystery, a good number of them, like Buchi **Emecheta**'s *Naira Power* (1982), Agbo Areo's *Director!*, David **Maillu**'s *For Mbatha and Rabeka* (1980), and Jide Oguntoye's *Too Cold for Comfort* deal with young Africans in realistic African situations grappling with real social problems. For example, *Naira Power* and *Director!* describe the tragedy of two young African boys who rush into making money by stealing; the novels provide a subtle condemnation of a society that puts too much value on money and material possession. *For Mbatha and Rabeka* and *Too Cold for Comfort* are intended to illustrate another moral relevant to the lives of young adult readers – that love and marriage should not be trivialized.

Unlike many African writers for children, **Ngugi wa Thiong'o** chose to write his works for children, the Njamba Nene Series, in his indigenous tongue, Gikuyu (see **Gikuyu literature**), but they were later translated into English. Ngugi's goal was that Gikuyu readers could easily relate to the content of the series, but the series would reach an international audience in translation. The series depicts the activities of an ideal youth in Kenya during its bloody fight for independence from Britain in the 1950s. In his commitment to fighting for freedom and defending African traditional values, this idealized youth, Njamba Nene, is very different from Ngugi's passive youngster, Njoroge, who overcomes the harsh reality of the moment by dwelling on hope of better days to come in *Weep Not, Child* (1964). Perhaps in Njamba Nene Ngugi wants to present a perfect contrast to Njoroge – a young dedicated freedom fighter with arms – and not to celebrate children as gun masters. Ironically, however, the armed Njamba Nene recalls, despite his idealism, today's child armies, orphaned and kidnapped children in war-torn and crisis-ridden areas in Africa. Many writers of children's literature in Africa have argued that their works are connected to the ultimate goal of education in Africa – that is, the production of a well-rounded person who is sensitive, respectful, considerate, and loving. As a tool to realize this goal, children's literature in Africa is rarely geared toward notions of art for art's sake. On the contrary, this literary tradition is motivated by the belief that African children need exposure to a literature that addresses children and their fate in multifaceted situations. African writers for children, who derive inspiration from traditional African values in their desire to educate children and young people along an acceptable African way of life, produce works that are subtly or overtly didactic.

Further reading

Granqvist, R. and Martini, J. (ed.) (1997) *Preserving the Landscape of Imagination: Children's Literature in Africa*, Amsterdam and Atlanta: Rodopi.

Ikonne, C., Oko, E. and Onwundinjo, P. (eds) (1992) *Children and Literature in Africa*, Ibadan: Heinemann Educational.

Maddy, Y. and MacCann, D. (1996) *African Images in Juvenile Literature – Commentaries on Neocolonialist Fiction*, Jefferson, North Carolina: McFarland.

Osa, O. (1995) *African Children's and Youth Literature*, New York: Twayne.

Schmidt, N.J. (1981) *Children's Fiction about Africa in English*, New York: Conch Magazine.

OSAYIMWENSE OSA

Chimombo, Steve

b. 1945, Zomba, Malawi

poet, dramatist, playwright, novelist, short story writer, and literary critic

Born in Zomba, Steve Chimombo is probably Malawi's most accomplished poet, dramatist, playwright, novelist, short story writer, and literary critic. In *The Rainmaker* (1981) and *Python! Python! An Epic Poem* (1994) Chimombo delves into the Mbona and Napolo religious myths of his people, giving them a nationalist dimension. *Napolo Poems* (1987) contrasts the evasive behavior of the elites when confronted by social injustice with the courage that the ordinary people need to survive in a brutal postcolonial Malawian society (see **colonialism, neocolonialism, and postcolonialism**). *Napolo and the Python* (1994) and *The Wrath of Napolo* (2000) revisit the Napolo mythology, underlining how myth, as a system of signs, carries contradictory values reflecting conflicting social realities in Malawi. Myth enables Chimombo to restructure the experience of the poor, giving narrative form to their unstable lives. Steve Chimombo concedes that those experiences of the ordinary people are also contradictory: yearning for freedom and yet wanting to continue working with the values of the old system. In *The Basket Girl* (1990), Chimombo preaches love and patriotism and champions the humanism of the poor that has so often been ignored or trampled upon by the rich. For these towering literary achievements Steve Chimombo has won several awards, including the prestigious Noma Award for publishing in Africa (1988).

M. VAMBE

Chinodya, Shimmer

b. 1957, Rhodesia (now Zimbabwe)

poet, short story writer, novelist, and
    textbook writer

Shimmer Chinodya was born in Rhodesia, now Zimbabwe. He was educated in Gweru, the University of Zimbabwe, and in the US. Chinodya is a poet, short story writer, novelist, and textbook writer. Chinodya contributed some of his poems to T.O. McLoughlin's *New Writing in Rhodesia* (1976) and to Kizito Muchemwa's *Zimbabwean Poetry in English* (1978). *Dew in the Morning* (1982), Chinodya's first novel, was followed by *Farai's Girls* (1984), a novel that depicts the fence-sitting tendencies by some African elites during the liberation struggle. *Harvest of Thorns* (1989), Shimmer Chinodya's well-known novel, won the 1990 Commonwealth Writers' Prize for the Africa Region. The novel traces the cultural dislocation of the "ambi" generation of Africans of the 1960s. Against the background of poverty and potential cultural emasculation, Africans stand up to wage a protracted war of liberation. Benjamin, the main character of the novel, questions the political excesses of his commanders during the struggle against colonialism (see **colonialism, neocolonialism, and postcolonialism**), and after decolonization he bemoans the betrayal of independence by the nationalist leadership. In his collection of short stories entitled, *Can We Talk and Other Stories* (1998), Chinodya's primary theme is the need for dialogue between different sectors in postcolonial Zimbabwe as a prerequisite for solving the country's problems. In the 1990s, Chinodya was increasingly turning to film (see **cinema**) as a creative medium.

M. VAMBE

Chinweizu

b. Nigeria

poet, critic, and journalist

The Nigerian poet, critic, and journalist Chinweizu has been involved in some crucial debates in the criticism of African literature (see **literary criticism**). Educated in the United States in the volatile 1960s, Chinweizu was highly influenced by the black arts movement and its ideology of a black aesthetic. After teaching in the United States for a while, he returned to Nigeria where he set out to promote and popularize a pan-African consciousness (see **diaspora and pan-Africanism**) in his essays, poems, and anthologies. In *The West and the Rest of Us* (1980), his goal was to document the cultural and economic violence engendered by Western colonialism in Africa and the complicity of local elites in this process (see **colonialism, neocolonialism, and postcolonialism**). Chinweizu's major intervention in literary discussions was an essay, "The Decolonization of African Literature," co-written with Onuchukwa and Jemie, in which he attacked what he considered to be the elitism of African literature, especially poetry, and its concern with abstract themes and images at the expense of real experiences. The major target of attack in this essay, later expanded into a book titled *Toward the Decolonization of African Literature* (1980), was Wole **Soyinka**, who responded in a famous essays called "Neo-Tarzanism and African Literature." Chinweizu has worked for many years as a newspaper columnist in Nigeria, writing on literary, cultural, and political matters. He has published two collections of poetry and edited a major anthology of modern African verse.

Further reading

Chinweizu (ed.) (1988) *Voices of 20th Century African Literature*, London: Faber.

SIMON GIKANDI

Chipasula, Frank Mkalawile

b. 1949, Malawi

poet and critic

The Malawian poet and critic Frank Mkalawile Chipasula has spent much of his adult life in exile, first in Zambia and later in the United States, where he teaches English and literature. He has published the following anthologies of his own poetry: *Visions and Reflections* (1972), *O Earth, Wait for Me* (1984), *Nightwatcher, Nightsong* (1986), *Whispers in the Wings* (1991); and has edited *When My Brothers Come Home: Poems from Central and Southern Africa* (1985) as well as co-editing, with Stella Chipasula, *The Heinemann Book of African Women's Poetry* (1995). Chipasula's poetry is predominantly political, an anguished criticism of the dictatorship of Dr Kamuzu Banda in Malawi and similar regimes and formations such as the apartheid government in South Africa and the general exploitation of workers within international capitalism (see **apartheid and post-apartheid**). As is evident in those poems where Malawi is seen as a defiled or lost lover, he blends politics with the sensuousness of poets such as Pablo Neruda.

Further reading

Msiska, Mpalive-Hangson (1995) "Geopoetics: Subterraneanity and Subversion in Malawian Poetry," in Abdulrazak Gurnah (ed.) *Essays on African Writing 2*, Oxford: Heinemann.

Roscoe, Adrian and Msiska, Mpalive-Hangson (1992) *The Quiet Chameleon: Poetry from Central Africa*, London and New York: Hans Zell Publishers.

MPALIVE-HANGSON MSISKA

Choto, Raymond

b. 1962, Zimbabwe

journalist and novelist

A journalist with the *Zimbabwe Standard*, Raymond Choto first came to prominence in the field of Shona fiction (see **Shona and Ndebele litera-**

ture) with the publication of *Vavariro* (Determination) (1990), a satirical novel on war and independence, which marked a departure from the fictions of nationalism in postcolonial Zimbabwe and their celebration of the war of liberation (see **nationalism and post-nationalism**; **colonialism, neocolonialism, and postcolonialism**). In this novel, Choto traces the demise of the all-important wartime alliance of politicians, freedom fighters, and peasants, and decries the abandonment of the goals of the war in pursuance of the privileges of the erstwhile colonial masters. His second novel, *Tongoona* (1990), revisits the dialectic of tradition and modernity through experimentation with aspects of psychological realism that first enter the Shona literary scene through the works of Charles **Mungoshi** (see **modernity and modernism**; **realism and magical realism**). He highlights the disruptive nature of various Western subcultures on family unity especially as symbolized through African spirituality. Like Mungoshi, Choto highlights the neurosis that arises from cultural imperialism. Unlike Mungoshi, his novel ends in harmony, with the reunification of the African family. Choto has also published two novellas and a novel dealing with the themes of family, the conflict between traditional values and modern culture, and African spirituality.

Further reading

Kahari, G.P. (1990) *The Rise of the Shona Novel*, Gweru: Mambo Press.

EMMANUEL CHIWOME

Chraïbi, Driss

b. 1926, Morocco; d. 2007, d'Drome, France

academic and writer

Driss Chraïbi is the dean of Moroccan letters in French. A true cosmopolitan, Chraïbi can be said to be a writer marked by duality: he belongs to two worlds (Europe and Africa), two eras (of colonialism and postcolonialism), two cultures (Arab/Berber, Islamic and French) and two languages

(French and Arabic) (see **colonialism, neocolonialism, and postcolonialism**). This duality also extends to the choice of settings for his books, alternately oscillating between Morocco and the West, particularly France.

Chraïbi is a prolific writer. He has written sixteen novels, two collections of short stories, a number of radio plays, and countless essays and articles. While always cherishing his strong, almost mystical bond to his native Morocco, he has been, from the beginning of his writing career, an unwavering critic of its oppressive government and moribund institutions. But Chraïbi is not solely concerned with political and social mores; he is, above all, a writer, and one of the most gifted of Maghrebian storytellers at that.

Chraïbi's first novel, *Le Passé Simple* (The Simple Past) (1954), was so provocative that it was considered by some of his critics as sacrilegious. The protagonist Driss Ferdi castigates, with humor and irony, Chraïbi's favorite weapons, his own Arabic heritage and Islam, which he saw as a burden and an obstacle to his emancipation as an individual and an aspiring writer (see **Islam in African literature**). In his outrageous and iconoclastic denunciation of Moroccan patriarchal society, Chraïbi was in many respects a precursor of Salman Rushdie. His second novel, *Les Boucs* (The Butts) (1955), is no less vehement in its denunciation of racism. It is a novel about the precarious predicament of North African migrant workers in postwar France.

His subsequent novels, *L'Ane* (The Jackass) (1956) and *La Foule* (The Crowd) (1961), constitute a departure from the previous socially engaged novels. Both are parables of our human and universal civilization couched in archetypal and symbolic terms. With *Succession ouverte* (Heirs to the Past) (1962), Chraïbi returns to his Moroccan motifs and resurrects in the process his alter ego, Driss Ferdi, only to see him, this time, finally reconciled with his estranged father and his erstwhile downtrodden past. To counter patriarchal hegemony, Chraïbi espouses a vigorous pro-woman stance, which some of his feminist critics dismissed as a form of neo-patriarchy. This position is expounded in his novels *De tous les horizons* (From Every Horizon) (1968) and *Un Ami viendra vous voir* (A Friend Will Come to See You) (1967), and

particularly his incisively humorous *Mother Comes of Age!* (*La Civilisation, ma mère!*) (1972).

Clearly, the thematic of the feminine, particularly the mother, paved the way for his ulterior preoccupation with Mother Earth. At the center of this new topo-analytical space is Oum-er-Bia, the river that flows through Chraïbi's birthplace. This river symbolizes both his personal childhood and the collective memory of the Berber people. Chraïbi celebrates in *La Mère du printemps* (Mother Spring) (1982) and *Naissance à l'aube* (Birth at Dawn) (1986) his coming to terms with himself. Both can be read as hymns to Morocco and its people. Moreover, both novels exemplify Chraïbi's infatuation with magical realism. This is not to say that Chraïbi eschews politics for poetics. Indeed, Chraïbi still refers to himself as a nomadic writer, "a nomad with glasses," and an "insectuel" who continues to debunk bourgeois, regressive values. His sociological investigations are to be found at the heart of *Une Enquête au pays* (The Flutes of Death) (1981) and *L'Inspecteur Ali* (1991).

Not surprisingly, his bond to his native land and people led Chraïbi to the mystical. *L'Homme du livre* (The Man of the Book) (1994) is, in many respects, a foil to *The Simple Past*. Devoted to the life of the Prophet Muhammad, this fictionalized biography proves that, in spite of his earlier diatribes against Islamic formalism, Chraïbi is very attuned to the mystical – Sufi – experience of the Muslim faith. In turn, this biography spurned him to write his own autobiography, *Vu, lu, entendu* (Seen, Read, Heard) (1998), a masterful work that sheds new and interesting light on Chraïbi the writer and his time. In many respects, it is an "autobiographie au pluriel" where one learns a great deal about Chraïbi and his Morocco.

Further reading

Marx-Scouras, Danielle (1992) "A Literature of Departure: The Cross-Cultural Writing of Driss Chraïbi," *Research in African Literatures* 23, 2: 131–44.

Monego, Joan Phyllis (1984) *Maghrebian Literature in French*, Boston: Twayne.

HÉDI ABDEL-JAOUAD

Christianity and Christian missions

The influence of Christianity in African literature is so often taken for granted that in contrast to Islam, the other major religion in the continent (see **Islam in African literature**), or African traditional beliefs, it has attracted few serious and self-contained studies. One of the reasons why Christianity has drawn little attention as a subject of literary investigation is that its history in Africa is so closely aligned with colonialism and colonization that it is difficult to separate the two (see **colonialism, neocolonialism, and postcolonialism**). Christianity has appeared as a major theme in African writing in the works of such distinguished writers such as **Ngugi wa Thiong'o**, **Okot p'Bitek**, Ferdinand **Oyono**, and Mongo **Beti**. In the works of these writers, Christianity is represented, as in canonical African texts, as the cultural arm of imperial expansion and as the major agent in the alienation of Africans from their traditional cultures, the source of self-hate and mimicry, and one of the sources of the violence that separates families, communities, and nationalities. When Christianity is not represented as an agent of colonial domination and violence, it appears as the ambiguous force of civilization and Europeanization. Christianity appears as an ambiguous force of civilization in the works of those writers like Thomas **Mofolo** and Sol **Plaatje** in South Africa who identified with the colonial mission and its institutions while promoting work in African languages. But whether it is demonized as an instrument of domination or celebrated as the force of civilization and Europeanization, Christianity and Christian missions appear in African literature as nothing less than the source of the crisis of modernity and modernization (see **modernity and modernism**) that has haunted much of the continent as it has moved from colonialism to postcoloniality.

Early Christian missions

While the association of Christianity and colonialism has been one of the most powerful themes in African literature, it is just one dimension in a complex history. For one of the most important and yet often-forgotten aspects of African social history is that Christianity on the African continent precedes European colonization by several centuries. Ethiopia and parts of North Africa have been Christian since the fourth century and featured prominently in the geography of early Christianity. Even before the advent of Christianity in the Horn of Africa, there were extensive links and cultural exchanges between Ethiopia and the ancient Near East. Evidence of these links can be found in the numerous references to Ethiopia in the Bible and the prominence of Ethiopic figures, most notably the Queen of Sheba, in the Old Testament. Conversely, countless aspects of the culture of the country, many of which are reflected in the works of writers in Amharic and other Ethiopian languages, testify to the long and enduring influence of the Bible. In addition, until the rise of Islam as a major religious force in the ninth century, Christian communities scattered over North and northeast Africa constituted major centers of culture on the African continent.

Since they were an integral part of the early Christian community, the Egyptian and Ethiopian Coptic churches have a history and liturgical tradition whose links are to the Orthodox Christianity of the Near East rather than modern Europe. This tradition of Christianity emerged outside the circle of European colonialism and hence developed indigenous traditions with their own institutions, texts, and practices. Translations of the Bible in Geez, the language of ancient Ethiopia, have existed for several centuries although it is not clear when both the Old and New Testaments were translated into the language. Since the middle ages, numerous translations of biblical manuscripts have been preserved in libraries and monasteries.

Even when Christianity became a major factor in the African social landscape, it did not always come arm in arm with colonial expansion but in an ambivalent relation to it. In the age of European exploration and discovery, as the Portuguese made their way down the West African coast in search of a sea route to India they established forts and enclaves in which small Christian communities developed. A crucial moment in the history of Christianity during this era was the ascension to power of Nzinga Mbemba, a Christian since 1491, as the king of the massive kingdom of the Kongo. Nzinga Mbemba, otherwise known as Alfonso I, ruled the kingdom of the Kongo from 1506 to 1543. During this period Alfonso opened the country to Portuguese influence and supported the expansion of the Catholic Church, which was instituted as the state religion. Before it fell under the control of the Portuguese, the Catholic Church of the Kongo was headed by Alfonso's son, Henrique, as bishop.

Christianity in the era of colonialism

It was, however, during the age of European colonization in the nineteenth century that Christianity and Christian missions in African came to play a crucial part in the transformation of the culture of the continent, especially in those areas that were no longer under Islamic influence or within the spheres of influence of the old Christian communities. As the dominant European powers entered into the scramble for Africa, Christianity provided one of the most powerful ideological justifications for colonization and missionaries served as important agents in the partition of Africa into different zones of influence. The competition between agents of colonialism in places such as Uganda or Kenya essentially became also a struggle between different Christian denominations. It was soon taken for granted that Catholic missions and orders were preferred in the French or Belgian territories and that Protestant denominations were privileged in the British colonies. Catholic missions and orders could, of course, still operate in the British territories, just as Protestant denominations could set up churches and schools in the French and Belgian colonies, but the dominant mission in each sector reflected the official church in the colonizing or "mother" country. For most of the nineteenth century, different Christian groups were involved in massive competition for African converts, but, in retrospect, these missions had many beliefs and practices in common and these were directly connected to the nature of the colonial situation and the culture that it was to produce during this period.

Whether they were Catholic or Protestant, Christian missions were proud agents of empire and its ostensible civilizing mission. Christian missions may have occasionally questioned some of the violent practices of government agents, but they essentially supported the key goals of the European colonizers, namely the transformation of African societies into what was considered to be a modern polity, the recentering of morality in social life, and the production of new images and ideologies for the African subject. The main agents of nineteenth-century Christianity in Africa, people like David Livingstone, were usually represented as heroic figures ready to risk their lives in the name of their faith; but more than their religious zeal, these agents were most influential because of their ability to fuse their brand of evangelicalism with the culture of capitalism.

Much more than the task of converting souls, Christianity was to become important in Africa – and attractive to Africans – because of its association with the ideology of progress and modernity, both in terms of the material life of Christian converts, who were the first to be admitted into the institutions of capitalism and Westernization as diverse as trading stations and schools, and in terms of its promotion of a new code of conduct often based on Victorian values. As a consequence of this association of Christianity and a modern culture, some of the most influential Africans of the nineteenth and early twentieth centuries were converts to Christianity. One of the reasons why Christianity was to spread so quickly in many parts of the continent during this period was that both its material and its spiritual causes were championed and advanced by prominent African converts such as Tiyo Soga in the Eastern Cape and Ajayi Crowther in the Niger Delta. It is important to note that the influence of these figures in colonial Africa was due to their representation as models of proper Christian conduct, which seemed to be validated by the culture of capitalism with which their missions were associated. In addition, the mission, especially when headed by an African, was seen as a symbol of the possibilities of progress and civilization within the culture of colonialism.

While African literature contains many memorable examples of the adverse effects of Christianity on social structures, customs, and beliefs, there is clear evidence that, more than any other institution of colonialism in Africa, the Christian mission was admired as the site of a modern culture. Christianity thus came to be represented as an ambivalent force in African society. It was admired as one of the most important forces in the modernization of Africa. This was especially the case in the field of education and literacy (see **education and schools**). In most of the European colonies in Africa, education was left in the hands of missionaries. The kind of education provided to Africans often reflected the ideologies of the missions that sponsored the schools. But in spite of denominational or national differences, Christian missions assumed that there was an inextricable relation between Christianity, social upliftment, and what came to be known as the civilizing mission. Many Africans flocked to Christian missions because of the opportunities they provided within the economy of colonialism. At the same time, however, many Africans, including the product of Christian missions themselves, increasingly came to feel that Christianity was itself part of the mental colonization of Africa. There was disenchantment with one of the central tenets of Christianity: the association of social modernization and Christian conversion, the belief that one could only be admitted into the institutions of modern culture by giving up beliefs that had been held for centuries.

Still, one of the most important developments in the history of Christianity in Africa during this period was the development of independent African churches. These were often made up of groups that broke away from mainstream Christian churches over matters of doctrine or over disputes on the nature of African cultural practices within the church. Among the most important such movements were Simon Kimbangu's Church of Christ on Earth in the then Belgian Congo and John Chilembwe's Province Industrial Mission in Nyasaland. As in many other cases all over Africa, these independent churches and their leaders were either perceived as a threat to colonial authority or played an important role in the fight against colonialism. In 1915 Chilembwe led an uprising against the British colonial administration in Nyasaland, was arrested and executed. Simon Kimbangu, whose followers led the movement against taxation and forced labor in the Congo in the 1920s, was imprisoned in Elisabethville.

Not all independent churches were, of course, against established authority. Some were much more interested in developing an alternative theology or creating a space in which indigenous practices could be reconciled with Christian doctrines. Whether they were active agents against colonialism or acquiesced to established authority, these churches were actively involved in the translation and reinterpretation of Christianity to fit into what they considered to be the unique cultural condition of Africa. Significantly, most of the founders of independent churches were not the most educated or Westernized Africans, and there is little evidence of members of the African elite belonging to such churches. As nationalist movements developed in the continent, especially in the 1930s and 1940s, members of the African elite sought ways of separating the culture of modernity from colonialism and Christian doctrine. This is the main theme of key nationalist texts such as Jomo **Kenyatta**'s *Facing Mount Kenya* (1938), where the author makes a strong case for the modernization of Africa outside the European sphere of influence. In the period of decolonization in the 1950s and 1960s, when Christianity and colonialism were no longer closely associated, African intellectuals and clergy began to explore ways, and develop programs, for the indigenization of the Church. Between 1956 and 1962 the journal *Présence Africaine*, under the editorship of Alioune Diop, conducted a debate among Christian intellectuals and writers on the relationship between Catholicism and African culture.

Christianity and literature

What was the relationship between Christianity and literature in Africa? Except in areas of North Africa and the Muslim regions of the continent, African literature can be considered to have been a product of the Christian mission in two practical ways. First, the major writers in French, English, Portuguese, and even African languages came from a Christian background and were educated in Christian missions. It was in such schools that these writers first encountered the European tradition of literature, one which they considered important both in their self-fashioning as modern subjects and as an instrument for mediating their own complicated and ambivalent relationship to colonial culture. Second, Christian missions were the places in which African literature was first materially produced. The missions were the first to set up printing presses on the continent. These presses were primarily designed to print the Bible and other Christian literature, but they also produced materials to promote literature and in effect became key instruments in the production of a culture of reading on the continent. In addition, missions were central in other areas crucial to the production of literature. Missionaries were the first to alphabetize and standardize orthographies and to establish outlets for books in African languages.

As a consequence, not only were the most prominent writers in the major African languages products of missions, but also the foundational texts in this tradition were printed at mission presses, and sold and distributed by missionary bookshops. Xhosa literature had its genesis at the Lovedale mission; Sotho literature was first produced at the Paris Evangelical Missionary Society mission at Morija; it was at the Mariannhill Mission in Natal that B.W. Vilakazi, considered to be the most significant poet in the Zulu language, began his career in the 1920s. Except in the Islamic zones, it is difficult to conceive a history of African language literatures without the Christian missions. There was often tension between African language writers and their sponsoring missions, but the classic works produced at the missions reflected the influence of Christianity in their theme and structures. The influence of the Bible and Christian texts such as John Bunyan's *Pilgrim's Progress* is echoed in key texts in this tradition, such as Thomas Mofolo's *Chaka* and Chief **Fagunwa**'s *The Forest of a Thousand Demons: A Hunter's Saga* (*Ogboju ode ninu Igbo irunmale*) (1938).

In comparison to the role they played in the production and promotion of African language literature, the missions did not seem particularly interested in writing in the European languages. While the major African writers in the European languages were products of Christian missions, many did not begin writing until they had gone to universities which were, significantly, the only institutions of education not controlled by the missions. Still, even when it was published in Europe by major publishing houses, the work of the new breed of African writers who emerged in the period after World War II reflected the influence of Christianity and the Christian missions in both obvious and surreptitious ways.

For those writers concerned with colonialism as a theme, the institutions and doctrines of Christianity were often represented as the forces responsible for the disruption of African social life. In Chinua **Achebe**'s *Things Fall Apart* (1958) and *Arrow of God* (1964), for example, the passing of the old Igbo order becomes manifest when missionaries establish themselves in Eastern Nigeria, providing an alternative value system and political economy to those who had been marginalized in precolonial culture. In works such as **Ngugi wa Thiong'o**'s *The River Between* (1965), the Manichean world that emerges after the imposition of colonialism, the division of local society into two competing factions, is manifested in the struggle between the new Christian mission and adherents to traditional African religions or proponents of an independent Christian Church.

As a discourse of conversion, Christianity was often perceived as a form of mental colonization, one that led to the radical alienation of African subjects from their families and cultures without providing a space of identity in colonial culture. The relation between alienation and violence is the subject of Ferdinand Oyono's novel *Houseboy* (*Une Vie de boy*) (1956), presented in the form of a diary left behind by a young boy who dies in the hands of the colonizers he had adored enough to renounce his family. In their general critique of colonialism, some African writers were, however, concerned with what they perceived to be the hypocritical stance of missionaries, especially their identification with the colonial polity and obliviousness to the suffering of Africans. This is the subject of satirical works such as Mongo Beti's *The Poor Christ of Bomba* (*Le Pauvre Christ de Bomba*) (1956).

After decolonization, there was a significant change in the treatment of colonialism in African literature. The Church could no longer be represented as a direct agent of colonialism or neocolonialism, but the efficacy of the culture it had left behind could still be the subject of mockery and ridicule in works such as Okot p'Bitek's *Song of Lawino* (1969) and *Song of Ocol* (1979). In general, however, decolonization seems to have deprived

Christianity of its cultural edge. It was no longer the single most important force of cultural transformation on the continent; indeed, the new colonial state had taken over many of the functions of the missions in such crucial areas as education and publishing. Ironically, the diminished role of Christianity was a mark of its triumph, for the men and women who ran the new African state were often the products of the missions. After independence, Christianity could no longer be represented as a force extraneous to the African experience but a crucial part of the social and cultural fabric of postcolonial society. On the contrary, in postcolonial novels such as Tsitsi **Dangarembga**'s *Nervous Condition* (1989), the Church and its value systems had become one of the many strands that constituted the modernity of Africa with its problems and promises.

Further reading

Afigbo, A.E. (1985) "Religion in Africa during the Colonial Era," in Adu Boahen (ed.) *Unesco General History of Africa, VII. Africa under Colonial Domination 1880–1935*, London: Heinemann.

Mudimbe, V.Y. (1997) *Tales of Faith: Religion as Political Performance in Central Africa*, London: Athlone Press.

Oliver, Roland (1952) *The Missionary Factor in East Africa*, London: Longman.

Peterson, Bhekizizwe (2000) *Monarchs, Missionaries, and African Intellectuals*, Trenton, New Jersey: Africa World Press.

SIMON GIKANDI

cinema

African cinema is still developing, although Africa and Africans have played a major role in cinema history since its invention by the Lumière brothers in 1895. In their work *Arab and African Film Making* (1991: London), Lizbeth Malkmus and Roy Armes point out that "shows of the Lumière cinematograph were arranged in Egypt – in the backrooms of cafés in Cairo and Alexandria – as early as 1896." Similar shows were arranged in Algiers and Oran, Algeria, in the autumn of the same year and

in 1897. By the end of the 1920s, Arab filmmaking had begun in Tunisia and Egypt.

Unlike in North Africa, the first screening of cinema in sub-Saharan Africa was in Dakar, Senegal, the French colonial capital, in 1900. Anglophone Africa's first contact with cinema was in Lagos in 1903. Africa's presence in European and, later, Hollywood cinema before independence, however, was primarily as an exotic setting and backdrop for Western entertainment films. Generally, Africa and its people were objectified, often appearing as helpless or evil objects of Western gaze, and always located at the periphery of the story. In most of these films, Africans were cast as "adjuncts" to white heroes or central characters.

Cinema in the colonial period

In general, scholars of African film agree that cinema made its entry into Africa as entertainment for the primarily European population in African metropolises such as Alexandria and Cairo (Egypt), Tunis (Tunisia), Dakar (Senegal), and Lagos (Nigeria), and later through colonial educational documentaries from Europe aimed at Africans. According to Manthia Diawara (1992: Bloomington), through these films the colonial administrations reinforced the "systematic dismantling of indigenous African cultures and traditions." The British colonial administration's Bantu Educational Cinema Experiment, for instance, aimed to "educate adult Africans to understand and adapt to new conditions." Ironically, the films produced under the Cinema Experiment and its successor, the Colonial Film Unit (CFU), were made by Europeans for European audiences. But by 1949, the CFU had established a film school in Accra, Gold Coast, to train Africans to make films within the colonies for themselves. The film school, however, failed to train Africans as film directors or producers. Rather, Africans were trained to become "excellent assistants" to European filmmakers sent to West Africa. Also, after 1955, the CFU stopped financing African film production, leaving Africans to finance their own projects. Similar but unsuccessful attempts to establish African film schools were also made by the French in Algeria and the Belgians in the Congo.

Cinema in the postcolonial period

Serious film production by sub-Saharan Africans began only in the 1950s, pioneered by Paulin Soumanou Vieyra, who made the first short documentary, *Afrique sur Seine* (Africa on the Seine) in 1955. Mbye B. Cham (1996: London) describes African filmmaking as "a child of African political independence," born in "the era of heady nationalism and nationalist anti-colonial and anti-neocolonial struggle." African cinema's development as a postcolonial and post-independence phenomenon is also evidenced by the scanty scholarship on African film (see **colonialism, neocolonialism, and postcolonialism**). Indeed, much of the available serious scholarship on African cinema occurred in the last two decades of the twentieth century. These studies include: Imruh Bakari and Mbye Cham's *African Experiences of Cinema* (1996), Manthia Diawara's *African Cinema: Politics and Culture* (1992), Teshome Gabriel's *Third Cinema in the Third World: The Aesthetics of Liberation* (1982), Kenneth Harrow's *African Cinema* (1999), *Critical Arts*, 7, 1–2 (1993) and *Research in African Literatures* 27, 3 (1996), Lizbeth Malkmus and Roy Armes' *Arab and African Film Making* (1991), Françoise Pfaff's *Twenty-Five Black African Filmmakers* (1988), as well as Frank Ukadike's *Black African Cinema* (1994) and *Iris: Journal of Theory on Images and Sound: New Directions of African Cinema* (1995).

The "troubled" development of African film production and discipline can be attributed to a variety of factors, ranging from restrictive colonial administrative policies towards African-directed film production to unfavorable postcolonial national policies and failing economies, lack of financial resources and infrastructures, the dominance of Hollywood, and the absence of a viable African audience. Certainly, any discussion of African cinema must consider the impact of these factors. In fact, Ukadike (1998: London) notes, "the varied character of African films today reflects a convoluted historical pattern of development." And as Kenneth Harrow (1995: *Research in African Literatures*) observes, "it is hard to imagine any other aspect of culture so controlled by neo-colonial forces as is African film." Despite the lack of support from their national governments, which often perceive the films as critical of governmental

policies, independent filmmaking in Africa persists, often supported by external funding, as in the case of many Francophone filmmakers.

Today, filmmaking in Francophone Africa is more advanced than in the Anglophone countries, except Egypt and South Africa. In fact, critics contend that more than 80 percent of African films come from the Francophone regions. One reason for this disparity is the occasional support which Francophone filmmakers receive from their national governments, for example Senegal. Another is the support of foreign nations, such as Belgium and France, through funding and infrastructural resources such as film schools and editing studios. A blooming **video** industry, however, has emerged in Ghana and Nigeria as an alternative form of entertainment.

Also important for understanding African films are the nature and definition of African cinema. What is African cinema? Several studies, including those identified above, have addressed this issue. Perhaps it is no longer urgent to ponder a definition of African cinema. Although films by indigenous Africans continue to dominate the field, African cinema today is diverse and embraces films made by Africans and diasporic Africans (non-indigenous Africans) such as Isaac Julien, Sara Maldoror, Euzhan Palcy, and Raoul Peck, as well as collaborative teams of African and Western directors. Today, the diversity of film entries and screenings at FESPACO (Festival Panafricain du Cinéma de Ougadougou) is indicative of the growing heterogeneity of African cinema and its subjects. Any serious consideration of African cinema must, therefore, examine these shifts, the role of FESPACO, and the cinema's content and aesthetics, which have been described as oppositional to the dominant Hollywood escapist films and to European cinema.

At independence, Africans were still struggling to make their own films. However, as most critics of African cinema would agree, the emergence of independent African nations in the 1960s also marked the dawn of contemporary indigenous African cinema, signaled by Ousmane Sembene's first short *Borom Sarret* (1963), followed by his first feature, *La Noire de ...* (Black Girl) (1965). These films introduced Sembene to international audiences, garnering him acclaim as a pioneer of

African cinema. Other filmmakers, especially from Francophone Africa, followed Sembene's initial works. These filmmakers included Djibril Diop Mambety, whose avant-garde style deviated from the narrative style of earlier "return to the source" films such as Gaston Kabore's *Wend Kuuni* (God's Gift), which presented an idealized image of Africa.

Theories of African cinema

Undoubtedly, African cinema is still evolving, and this is evident in the varied and shifting thematic focus, narrative styles, and critical discourse of the films and their critics. Although African filmmaking at its infancy was aligned with the counterdominant filmmaking of "third cinema," perceived as oppositional to Western, particularly, Hollywood films, the nature of African films presently suggests a tradition still attempting to define itself. Manthia Diawara (1992: Bloomington) sees African cinema today as "a mélange of films made by Africans, people of African diasporic heritage and collaborative teams of African and Western directors." The critical discourse of African cinema also seems to struggle with the identity, nature, and classification of African films, as do various critics and filmmakers who have provided diverse paradigms and theoretical approaches for interpreting the films. For instance, Lizbeth Malkmus and Roy Armes (1991: London) suggest contextualizing African films within their informing historical, social, and cultural backgrounds. Other critics and filmmakers have adopted the ideological stance of the Argentinian scholars Fernando E. Solanas and Octavio Gettino and have defined African cinema also as "third cinema," emphasizing the "revolutionary" or resistant agenda and aesthetics of the cinema. One proposed classification aligns the films with "the theoretical positions" of their "auteurs" and the films' function as revealed by their effects on audiences. Thus, African films can be read as political or consciousness-raising, moral, cultural, commercial/entertainment-centered, and self-expressive.

For Teshome Gabriel (1989: London), however, African cinema's development mirrors Frantz Fanon's delineation of a postcolonial nation's evolution from domination to liberation. This evolution is represented by three phases. The first

is "the unqualified assimilation," marked by a close relationship with "Western Hollywood film industry" and its "aping," stylistically and thematically. The second phase, the "remembrance phase," when the "indigenisation and control of talents, production, exhibition and distribution" inform the thematic interests and language of the films, is, Gabriel contends, marked by "the movement for a social institution of cinema," examples of which are " 'cinema moudjahid' in Algeria" and " 'engaged' or 'committed cinema' in Senegal and Mozambique." During this phase, the filmmakers look to their indigenous cultures, folklore, and mythology, as well as histories for material and inspiration, addressing themes such as the clash of cultures and modernity versus tradition. This may be associated with the "return to the source" phase which some critics have noted in Ousmane Sembene's *Mandabi*, and Gaston Kabore's *Wend Kuuni*. Gabriel's third is the "combative phase," during which filmmaking becomes a "public service institution," an "ideological tool." This is the phase of liberation and emphasizes African agency and resistance; the film industries break the chains of Western control. Interestingly, Gabriel's theory simultaneously includes and excludes most African films, which thematically emphasize African agency and resistance although the films are produced with Western funds. While many filmmakers ideologically may belong to the combative phase, financially they are still struggling to reach Gabriel's second phase.

Unlike Gabriel, Manthia Diawara evaluates African films according to their thematic focus or content. Films can be described as dealing with "a return to the sources," "Africa without the presence of outsiders," and "the colonial question" in which the filmmaker addresses the historical confrontation between Africans and their colonizers. Diawara also suggests that some of these films, which he describes as "social realist narratives," deal with the tensions between modernity and tradition in African nations by linking some forms of modernity to neocolonialism and cultural imperialism, while at the same time refusing to romanticize African traditional societies.

While these diverse theories help to analyze rather than fix African films into rigid categories, such delineation is problematic and reductive, as many filmmakers begin to deviate from the "perceived" project of an oppositional or resistant "third cinema," to create hybrid films. This hybrid cinema Tomaselli *et al.* (1995: *African Cinema Research*) have described elsewhere as "a cinema of emancipation ... articulates the codes of essentially First World technology into indigenous aesthetics and mythologies." Indeed, while addressing postcolonial concerns, African filmmakers must compete effectively for a shrinking audience against an increasing presence of Hollywood and MTV's "action-oriented" and entertainment films in Africa. Furthermore, the hybridity of African cinema suggests the heteroglossic – that is, the multiple and complex nature of the voices and gazes of the filmmakers and the issues they address. African cinema is no longer dominated by male stories and voices or a preoccupation with redressing colonial ills, but now includes the voices of women filmmakers who employ documentary narratology to explore gender, history, and postcoloniality, as well as to tell personal and collective stories about women's experiences in particular African societies. Notable are films by Assia **Djebar**, Anne-Laure Folly, Salem Mekuria, Ngozi Onwurah, and Moufida Tlatl. These new voices and perspectives broaden the scope, nature, and gaze of African cinema, interrogating the often prescriptive ideological positions of earlier film directors and critics. Also, new male voices, especially of collaborative teams of Africans and Western directors, have contributed to the discussions of gendered and sexual identities in Africa.

The institutions of cinema

The emergence of post-apartheid South Africa (see **apartheid and post-apartheid**) and a number of southern African nations as important sites for film production, as well as the role of FESPACO, should be noted. Post-apartheid South Africa and several southern African nations, including Madagascar, Mozambique, and Zimbabwe, provide new locations for filming (Souleyman Cisse's epic film *Waati* was shot in Zimbabwe), as well as opportunities for inter-continental collaborations and the exploration of new subjects. FESPACO 2001 featured a South African delegation led by Winnie Mandela. FESPACO has also contributed to the development of African cinema. FESPACO, which meets every two years, was inaugurated in 1969 by FEPACI (Fédération Panafricaine des Cinéastes) in an attempt to attain cultural, political, and economic freedom for African films and filmmakers. FESPACO identified its primary goal as the liberation and promotion of African cinema by showcasing films made about Africans, for, and by them. The festival also aimed to contribute to the use of cinema as "a means of expression, education" and consciousness-raising. Since its inception, FESPACO has grown from a little-known festival that was attended by a few African and two European nations in 1969 to a recognized international festival, drawing several thousand attendees from various African and international nations. To further strengthen its role in the promotion of African cinema, in 1999 FESPACO established a fund to support the distribution of a film that wins its coveted highest prize, the Etalon de Yenenga.

Perhaps, like FESPACO, African cinema and filmmakers have come of age. Although African history and postcoloniality still dominate African films thematically, there are indications of shifting thematic foci. New themes include gender and sexual identities (see **gender and sexuality**), including **homosexuality** (gay/queer themes in *Woubi Cheri*, for instance), the changing social and economic positions of African women (*Faat Kine*), and the voice of a young hip-hop, MTV-bred youth culture. The future of African cinema will ultimately depend on its ability to negotiate new thematic, geographic, technological, and economic boundaries. Collaborations between African filmmakers and their Western counterparts have already begun, as have distribution efforts led by companies such as California Newsreel, Red Carnelian with South Africa's M-Net's New Directions, and Ousmane Sembene/Danny Glover's AmerAfric Films. Such collaborations may entail a revisiting of the definition and nature of African cinema. Perhaps, as Cameroonian filmmaker Jean Marie Teno suggests while commenting on the new video-film trend in Africa, "if we can embrace an alternative definition of [African] cinema ... we will certainly soon after see a dramatic increase in the number of films produced, and a diversification of subjects, styles, and voices" (2000: California).

Works cited

Bakari, Imruh and Cham, Mbye (eds) (1996) *African Experiences in Cinema*, London: British Film Institute.

Diawara, Manthia (1992) *African Cinema: Politics and Culture*, Bloomington: Indiana University Press.

Gabriel, Teshome (1989) "Towards a Critical Theory of Third World Films," in Jim Pines and Paul Willemen (eds) *Questions of Third Cinema*, London: British Film Institute.

Harrow, Kenneth (1995) "Introduction: Shooting Forward," *Research in African Literatures* 26, 3: 1–5.

Malkmus, Lizbeth and Armes, Roy (1991) *Arab and African Film Making*, London: Zed Press.

Teno, Jean Marie (2000) "Imagining Alternatives: African Cinema in the Year 2002," in California Newsreel (ed.) *Library of African Cinema 2000*, California: California Newsreel, p. 59.

Tomaselli, Keyan, Shepperson, Arnold and Eke, Maureen N. (1995) "Towards a Theory of Orality in African Cinema," *Research in African Literatures* 26, 3: 18–35.

Ukadike, N. Frank (1998) "African Cinema," in John Hill and Pamela Church Gibson (eds) *The Oxford Guide to Film Studies*, London: Oxford University Press.

MAUREEN N. EKE

Cissé, Ahmed Tidjani

b. 1942, Kangoléa, Guinea

playwright

Ahmed Tidjani Cissé was born in Kangoléa, Guinea and was imprisoned during the Sekou Touré regime. His experiences in prison have inspired most of Cissé's dramatic works and, in general, his interest in political theater. Although his plays comment on some of the most serious issues in Guinea, Cissé prefers to use a comic mode of dramatic expression, often using caricature and derision to represent the suffering of the people of Guinea under the postcolonial regime (see **colonialism, neocolonialism, and postcolonialism**). In his political theater, in works such as *Au Nom du peuple* (In the Name of the People) (1991), Cissé has sought to represent the suffering of the

people of Guinea in the contemporary period on stage. At the same time, in some of his plays, including *1789 in the Isle Saint Louis of Senegal* (1998) and *Tana de Soumangourou* (1988), he has sought to recover and represent key moments of African history in both their positive and negative elements.

OUSMANE BA

Clark-Bekederemo, John Pepper

b. 1935, Kiagbodo, Nigeria

poet, journalist, and playwright

Among the key members of the Ibadan generation that transformed the character of African literature in English in the 1950s, Clark-Bekederemo was perhaps one of the most influential, not only as the founder and editor of *The Horn*, the pioneering student journal that was to publish the first works of Wole **Soyinka** and Christopher **Okigbo** and other writers, but also as a major poet and playwright in his own right. Clark-Bekederemo's poetry and drama is clearly acknowledged as representative of the struggle, by this generation of African writers, to use the language of the colonizer – English in this case – to represent their own experiences and to encapsulate the sensibilities generated by local cultures and landscapes. Indeed, Clark-Bekederemo's early poetry is remarkable for its careful and methodical attempt to shape the conventions of English poetry, which Clark-Bekederemo had mastered as a student of literature at University College, Ibadan, to capture the rhythms and mythologies of his fishing cultures of the Ijo and Urhobo people of his native Niger Delta.

At Ibadan, Clark-Bekederemo had been educated in the best traditions of English poetry, from Shakespeare through the Romantics to the moderns, and his poetry reflected and continued to reflect these influences. At the same time, however, he was sensitive to the unique environment of the landscapes around him, from the university and market town of Ibadan to the rituals and myths of the fishing communities of the Niger Delta. Clark-Bekederemo's early poetry thus stands out as an example of one of the most important moments of transition in African, namely the shift from pure imitation of English prosody to an adaptation of inherited conventions to reflect the local conditions in which this poetry had been produced. As in the works of his fellow poets at Ibadan, most prominently Wole Soyinka and Christopher Okigbo, Clark-Bekederemo had turned to creative writing as one way of overcoming the alienation induced by the culture of colonialism and its system of education, which promoted European values at the expense of local experiences (see **colonialism, neocolonialism, and postcolonialism**; **education and schools**). It was through poetry and drama that the writer would rediscover the world the culture of colonialism had sought to repress. Ironically, one of the reasons why Clark-Bekederemo and his contemporaries could turn to the English language as their route to discovering the local landscape was their engagement with the idiom of modernism (see **modernity and modernism**). The teaching of modern poetry at Ibadan and other colonial universities was considered revolutionary for two closely related reasons. First, because the modernist poets were involved in a project whose goal was to break up the forms and conventions of language, they provided a model, especially in prosodic experimentation, that African poets like Clark-Bekederemo seized on in their attempts to reshape the English language and its forms to respond to African situations. A second and perhaps less obvious influence of modernism was its concern with themes derived from mythologies and rituals.

While the influence of English poets is most apparent in the early poems collected in *A Reed in the Tide* (1965), there is evidence that even at the beginning of his career Clark-Bekederemo was already involved in reformulating established conventions of English prosody to account for his own experiences of culture in the Niger Delta and other Nigerian regions. The poems in this collection are renowned for their simultaneous impressionist style and specific reference to famous places and events such as the city of Ibadan, tropical storms, and Fulani cattle. Clark-Bekederemo uses crisp and sharp images and measured verse to turn ordinary events into extraordinary linguistic experiences. Some of his most famous poems, such as "Ibadan," "Fulani Cattle," and "Dawn Rain,"

were written during this period. But perhaps Clark-Bekederemo's best poems were the ones he wrote in reaction to the Nigerian civil war (1966–70), later collected in *Casualties* (1970). Like many other Nigerian writers of the period, Clark-Bekederemo found himself torn from friends and associates, including members of the literary and cultural circles he had nurtured as a student at Ibadan and as a lecturer at the University of Lagos. He found his friends serving on both sides of the conflict. While he himself seemed ambiguous about the politics of the war, he continued to serve the federal government. And if he came to represent the war as a cataclysmic event, it was not simply because of the suffering it generated, although he was very much sensitive to this, but also because of the personal conflicts and moral dilemmas it had forced him to face. The war poems are hence much more than representations of the horrors of the conflict. They are certainly concerned with the loss of innocence and the collapse of youthful idealism, but they are most powerful in those occasions when they focus on the personal loss of friends and associations. In fact, some of the now famous poems in this collection are almost conversations with old friends like Okigbo and Chinua **Achebe**, who had found themselves on the Biafra side of the conflict.

Readers of the civil war poems cannot fail to notice the contrast between Clark-Bekederemo's spare, impressionistic, and moving diction and the horrors of the historical events they seem to want to narrate and transcend at the same time. In contrast, his later collections of poetry seem to be too ornamental, beautiful expressions without powerful referents. In the poems collected in *State of the Union* (1985), for example, he turns to an amalgam of subjects ranging from his observations of the social and political crisis in postwar Nigeria to representations of American life as observed during a tour in the 1960s. In *Mandela and Other Poems* (1988), he tries to find a majestic subject to match his gift of language by turning to heroes of pan-Africanism (see **diaspora and pan-Africanism**) such as Nelson Mandela and Oliver Tambo.

In addition to being an accomplished poet, Clark-Bekederemo has been a pioneer of African drama, and his plays, though not as well known outside Africa as those of his contemporary Soyinka, have been central in the shaping of theatrical expression on the continent. Clark-Bekederemo's most famous play was *Song of a Goat* (1961), one of the most powerful domestic tragedies in Anglophone Africa. While the play revolves around familiar questions of infertility, the author is able to endow the quotidian with an aura of majesty and tragedy by adopting collective rituals derived from the Niger Delta, including the slaying of a goat on stage. The tragic sense in the play also emerges from the author's conception of the Delta environment in which the tragedy takes place as hostile to human desires and aspirations.

One of the major criticisms leveled at Clark-Bekederemo's plays is that they are more successful as poems than as plays. Clearly, in those plays like *The Masquerade* (1964) and *The Raft* (1964), where the tragic moment and symbolism seem forced and the action melodramatic, the strength of the work lies in the author's masterful use of blank verse with a Shakespearean flavor. Whether his plays work well on stage or not, Clark-Bekederemo is attracted to tragedy because it allows him to account for what he considers to be the hostile landscape of the Niger Delta, a place in which ordinary people are pitted against the powerful elements of nature and the mythical forces that represent it. In 1966, Clark-Bekederemo published *Ozidi*, an epic based on an Ijaw saga, which he had recorded and transcribed during fieldwork in the Niger Delta. In this play, he tried to bring together all the great themes that he had been experimenting with in his poetry and early plays, including the heroic and often violent struggle between individuals holding opposing visions and the environment. Clark-Bekederemo's later plays continue the themes of his earlier works with a marked emphasis on the tension between individual desires and collective rituals. In addition to his poems and plays, he has also published *America, Their America* (1964), a travelogue based on his journey through the United States as a Fulbright Fellow in the early 1960s, and *The Example of Shakespeare* (1970), an influential collection of essays dealing with the problems and promises the English language and its literary tradition present to the African writer.

Further reading

Clark-Bekederemo, John Pepper (1991) *Collected Plays and Poems*, Washington, DC: Howard University Press.

Irele, F. Abiola (2001) *The African Imagination: Literature in Africa and the Black Diaspora*, New York: Oxford University Press.

SIMON GIKANDI

Coetzee, J.M. (John Maxwell)

b. 1940, Cape Town, South Africa

novelist

Generally regarded as South Africa's most acclaimed and internationally renowned novelist, J.M. Coetzee is one of only two writers to have been awarded the Booker Prize twice, first for *Life & Times of Michael K* in 1983 and then for *Disgrace* in 1999. Among his many other literary and academic awards, including a 1988 nomination for the Nobel Prize for Literature, this established his reputation as one of the most accomplished contemporary writers worldwide. He was awarded the Jerusalem Prize for Freedom in 1987 and, in the first words of his acceptance speech, articulated the paradox that "someone who … lives in so notably unfree a country … is honored with a prize for freedom." His work has been translated into many languages and is widely studied at universities and high schools around the world. In addition to being an academic (he holds the Chair of General Literature at the University of Cape Town), writer, and scholar, he is also an accomplished linguist, translator, cultural commentator, and one-time computer programmer. After graduating from the University of Cape Town with degrees in mathematics and English, he lived in England and the United States. He received his doctorate from the University of Texas at Austin in 1969, his doctoral thesis being a stylistic analysis of Samuel Beckett's fiction in English. This early academic interest in language and linguistics has informed all his writing, taking the form of an acute awareness of language as system and what Coetzee has called "the problems of language."

Coetzee's novels are generally seen as representing a break from the prevailing narrative forms of white South African writing – those of romance, pastoralism, and realism – to a self-conscious narrative form that enacts problems of authorship and authority, freedom and determination, and the colonizing nature of language itself. He has published eight novels, from his first novel *Dusklands* in 1974 to *Disgrace* in 1999. His non-fiction books include *White Writing: On the Culture of Letters in South Africa* (1988), a seminal study of South African literature; a collection of essays, *Giving Offense: Essays on Censorship* (1996), and *The Lives of Animals* (1999), a book which the publisher lists as non-fiction but which problematizes the boundaries between fiction and non-fiction. The collection of Coetzee's essays and his thoughts on their composition in the form of interviews with his co-editor, David Attwell, entitled *Doubling the Point: Essays and Interviews* (1992), is essential reading for any Coetzee scholar, charting his writing life. While Coetzee's *Boyhood: Scenes from Provincial Life* (1997) is categorized as a memoir and is clearly autobiographical (see **autobiography**), Coetzee writes in the third person, maintaining a characteristic sense of distance even in the process of writing about his own boyhood. Coetzee's childhood discomfort with his position as an outsider, a South African who is neither fully an Afrikaner nor English, a position he calls "social marginality," is clearly evoked in this text.

Coetzee's novels have, since *Dusklands*, been concerned with the ethics of reading and writing and have been informed by a strong theoretical frame of reference. This sets his work apart from other "white" South African novelists whose overt commitment to apartheid became a measure of their literary success. The self-referentiality and self-reflexivity of his novels is more postmodern than "political" and yet, in drawing attention to the very nature of authorship and authority, Coetzee is, of course, critiqueing and enacting the power relations inherent in textuality itself. Thus his novels can also be described as postcolonial in their emphasis on silencing, "othering," and the colonizing power of language. Yet a number of South African critics (many of them using Marxist critical practices) were disparaging about Coetzee's work, particularly his early novels in the apartheid years, suggesting that it avoided direct political

engagement and was thus irrelevant. Others, though, have pointed out the deeply political nature of Coetzee's work in its questioning of all extreme ideological positions with its focus on the nature of individual freedom. However, unlike other white South African writers with whose work his is often compared, such as Nadine **Gordimer**, André **Brink**, and Breyten **Breytenbach**, Coetzee rejects notions of writerly responsibility and what he calls the "structures of opposition, of Either–Or," which he takes as his "task to evade."

Four of his novels have specifically South African settings – *In the Heart of the Country* (1974), *Life & and Times of Michael K* (1983), *Age of Iron* (1990) and *Disgrace*. Each deals directly or indirectly with the ethics of living in an apartheid or post-apartheid state (see **apartheid and post-apartheid**), mainly through the anxious voices and silences of their protagonists. Magda, in *In the Heart of the Country*, seeks to overcome the mistress/servant relationship and to find a language that is not tied to a position of power over "non-white" others. Michael K's harelip, symbolic of his impeded access as a "colored" South African to discourses of power, seems to invite others to interpret him, but his own quiet escape to self-sufficiency eludes such performances of victimhood. Elizabeth Curren, in *Age of Iron*, who is dying of cancer, wishes to distance herself from the doll-like existence of other South African whites who, she suggests, are hollow within. The imagery of disease links Elizabeth's sick body with the infected body politic of the apartheid state, complicating her desire to remain untainted and drawing attention to issues of complicity and guilt. David Lurie, the academic protagonist of *Disgrace*, meditates on guilt and retribution, grace and disgrace, in a contemporary South Africa that is itself trying to come to terms with its disgraceful past, in the aftermath of what Coetzee has called the "audacious and well-planned crime against Africa" that was apartheid. Despite the seemingly obvious links with what many critics have labeled "the South African situation," Coetzee's novels function at an allegorical rather than an overtly political level.

Coetzee's other novels have varied settings but similarly morally anxious protagonists: *Waiting for the Barbarians* (1980), for example, uses an allegorical setting in an "outpost of Empire" at an unspecified time and place to examine the limitations of resistance by a "liberal" colonizer seeking "the side of justice" within a repressive imperial regime; *Dusklands* is set partly in America and Vietnam and partly in colonial South Africa, and links the two historical events of the Vietnam war and the Afrikaners' colonial incursions in South Africa to question versions of historical "truth"; *Foe* (1986), set partly on Defoe's famous island and partly in England, is presented as a pre-text to the canonical *Robinson Crusoe* and interrogates Defoe's ideological and literary assumptions, using postmodernist, postcolonial, and feminist theory; and *The Master of Petersburg* (1994), set in St Petersburg, is a complex narrative intertwining Dostoevsky's life and novels with a focus on the ethics of writing. In all four of these novels, the anxiety of authorship is an integral part of the text. Indeed, this self-reflexive obsession with narrative and the writing process itself is an important element in all Coetzee's novels.

Each of Coetzee's narrators and/or protagonists is carefully framed within the narrative so that irony and narrative distance always operate in the text to undermine any positions of certainty or moral rectitude. Always keenly aware of the need to foreground his narrators' often-problematic positionality and authority (or lack of it), Coetzee is also intensely conscious of the need to problematize all texts, including his own, admonishing those critics who would venture to find messages in his work, noting that novels should be read on their own terms, as works of fiction, not as political commentary. What he emphasizes is the importance of "taking nothing for granted" and the fact that, in his words, "everything is capable of being questioned." The link between authorship and authority is clearly drawn. In a remark to an interviewer who was trying to place his novels into the category of South African politics, he replied that his allegiance lay with the discourse of the novels and not with the discourse of politics. His insistence on the separation between novelistic and historical discourses is outlined in a lecture he gave in 1987 entitled "The Novel Today."

Despite Coetzee's refusal to provide a "master narrative" of his own work, his fiction invites, and has attracted, much critical commentary. Coetzee's reluctance to provide commentary on his own novels is a feature of written interviews with him which often take the form of Socratic dialogues, despite interviewers' attempts to elicit direct answers. The work itself, though, provides ample material for critical and academic analysis. The spareness of its prose, the intensity of its vision, and its complex layers of meaning and theoretical allusion draw the reader in, provoking interpretation and producing many different types of readings. There have been at least five full-length works of criticism on his work, two comparative studies, and a number of collections of critical essays on Coetzee and on individual works. *J.M. Coetzee: A Bibliography* was published in 1990. There are, in addition, hundreds of journal articles published internationally on his work. One area of critical attention is the intertextuality of Coetzee's novels, with its echoes of and reference to such literary precursors as Beckett, Kafka, Defoe, and Dostoevsky. Another is the theoretical framework of the novels, which have been variously described as Lacanian allegories, stories of South Africa, postmodernist and postcolonial.

His non-fiction is similarly concerned with ethical issues. *Lives of Animals* provides an intriguing debate, part fiction, part non-fiction, about the morality of human interaction with animals. The two sections of the text entitled "The Philosophers and the Animals" and "The Poets and the Animals" present the arguments of a fictional Australian feminist novelist, Elizabeth Costello, who has been invited to lecture on animal rights at Princeton University's Center for Human Values. Narrated by her son, a Princeton Physics professor, these lectures are framed, too, by non-fictional commentaries by well-known theorists, with an introduction by Amy Guttmann and "Reflections" by Marjorie Garber, Peter Singer, Wendy Doniger, and Barbara Smuts. Thus the text disrupts and complicates notions of fictionality and non-fiction. *Giving Offense: Essays on Censorship* (1996) is a more traditional collection of critical essays by Coetzee on the issue of censorship, ranging widely across issues of self-censorship, censorship by oppressive regimes such as that of apartheid South Africa, and contemporary feminist attitudes to pornography. *White Writing: On the Culture of Letters in South Africa* (1988) has become a standard critical work on South African literature, with its theoretically sophisticated analysis of the literature of "unsettled settlers," the whites of South Africa, and how such "white writing" imagined and imaged the African landscape and its indigenous inhabitants. The complex issue of the construction of a cultural identity of a people "no longer European, not yet African" is a central concern in the essays.

J.M. Coetzee is unique among South African novelists as an international figure whose work is not "just" about South Africa but has wider academic appeal in its allusive and multi-layered referencing of such theoretical issues as authorship and authority, intertextuality, the politics of representation, and the nature of discourse. His novels explore the infinite ways in which power operates – discursively, textually, politically, and personally. In Coetzee's own reflection on his novels, he identifies the "body with its pain" as "a counter to the endless trials of doubt." Each of his novels has been the subject of much critical attention and yet, as a number of commentators have found, the novels remain elusive and resistant to the reductiveness of some critical practices. This has led David Attwell to comment that any piece of writing about Coetzee can be seen as either, or both, "a tribute or a betrayal."

Further reading

Attwell, David (1993) *J.M. Coetzee: South Africa and the Politics of Writing*, California: University of California Press.

Head, Dominic (1997) *J.M. Coetzee*, Cambridge: Cambridge University Press.

Huggan, Graham and Watson, Stephen (eds) (1996) *Critical Perspectives on J.M. Coetzee*, London: Macmillan.

Kossew, Sue (ed.) (1998) *Critical Essays on J.M. Coetzee*, New York: G.K. Hall.

SUE KOSSEW

colonialism, neocolonialism, and postcolonialism

Colonialism has been one of the most persistent themes in African literature, and the colonial situation has affected the establishment and transformation of literary culture on the continent for several centuries. The most obvious reason for this influence is that most producers of what we now consider to be modern African literature were products of colonial institutions such as the Christian mission, the school, and university (see **Christianity and Christian missions**; **education and schools**), and that many of their models of what literature was were often derived from European examples. Another powerful manifestation of the colonial presence in African literature is that a large body of African literature was produced in European languages. The existence of a powerful body of oral literature and writing in African languages provides an important counterpoint to the assumed relationship between colonialism and African literature, but still it is hard to find an African literature that has completely escaped the colonial influence. This influence is more than literary in nature; on a deeper level, it reflects the trauma of the colonial encounter as a historical and sociological condition that was to affect the character of African literature for several centuries. For if African literature emerged as a discourse whose primary goal was to counter the Eurocentric idea that Africans did not have a culture and to will into being a decolonized African nation, as Chinua **Achebe** argued in 1965, then the identity of this literature was bound to be determined, both positively and negatively, by the colonial condition.

The culture of colonialism had a positive effect on the production of African literature because it introduced the mechanisms – the institutions of education, the printing press, and the readership – that made the modern idea of literature an important aspect of African life. Nevertheless, the negative effects of colonialism were numerous: it initiated a radical disorganization of traditional African societies, a denigration of African cultures and institutions, and a displacement of the norms and cosmologies that had shaped African identities. Both the positive and negative aspects of colonialism were taken up by several generations of African writers and they must hence figure prominently in discussions of African literary history. In addition, if the colonial problem continued to be a major theme in African literature even after decolonization, it was because the pressures of a new nationalism gave the colonial problem an inescapable immediacy (see **nationalism and post-nationalism**). It was difficult to have a literature of nationalism that did not have colonialism as its primary subject.

Historical overview

The European presence in Africa affected different parts and periods of the continent in a variety of ways, but we can identify at least four distinct periods in the history of colonialism in Africa. The first period, beginning with the arrival of European powers on the West African coast at the end of the fifteenth century and culminating with the major period of slavery in the seventeenth and eighteenth century, was characterized by attempts by formerly enslaved Africans to appropriate dominant literary conventions to counter the racist ideologies that had been used to justify slavery. In the eighteenth century, in particular, African writers such as Olaudah **Equiano** and Quobna Ottobah **Cuguano** used their writings to oppose slavery and to validate the humanity of the African; other writers, most notably Johannes **Capitein**, produced treatises arguing that slavery was not necessarily an affront to Christianity. In spite of their different approaches to the question of enslavement, early African writers in European languages were driven by the desire to prove that they could master writing as the mark of a human identity.

Although there is no record of much creative writing by Africans in the period after the abolition of slavery, this was the second important era in the colonial encounter, the time when colonialism spread across much of the continent and Christian missions were established, leading to the founding of the schools that were to educate the early generations of African writers and readers. From the establishment of the major missions in the 1820s up until the end of the nineteenth century, a distinct African literary culture, especially in African languages, became an important feature of the cultural landscape. The books printed at these missions were to lay the foundation for an African culture of letters. The setting up of a printing press at the Lovedale mission is a case in point: it was at this press that the first Xhosa grammar and translation of the Bible were first printed early in the nineteenth century; it was here that Tiyo Soga's famous translation of John Bunyan's *Pilgrim's Progress* was published in the 1860s.

The third period of the colonial encounter (1880–1935) has been considered remarkable by African historians not only because it was the era in which colonial rule was formally extended to most parts of the continent, but also because of the intensity and speed of the changes introduced by colonialism after the partition of the 1884–1885 conference in Berlin. During this period, the European powers sought to remake African societies in their own image, introducing new political systems and economies, and overthrowing ancient cosmologies and cultural systems. Significantly, it was during this time that the idea of literature and culture as a mode of resistance against the colonial system became crucial to the ideology of the African elite. From around 1900 to the end of the 1930s, a new generation of African writers and intellectuals turned their attention to both the problems and the opportunities provided by colonial modernity. In a series of manifestos issued in the first half of the twentieth century, black writers advocated the recognition of Africa as an important part of the modern world, and in the words of the organizers of the first Pan-African Congress in 1900, argued for the extension of "the largest and broadest opportunity for education and self-development" to "Negroes and other dark men." Culture in general and literature in particular were considered to be an important part of this process of recognition and the granting of modern opportunities. In addition to agitating for political and economic rights, the writers of these manifestos were concerned with the role of culture in the production of a modern African polity.

Literature was considered to be one of the most important instruments in the imagination of a modern African polity in the last phase of the colonial encounter, the high period of decolonization (1945–60). This phase was to witness the most extensive development of African writing; in their fictional and political writings, Africans vigorously challenged colonial notions about their continent, its culture, and history. In addition to providing a trenchant critique of colonialism, the works produced during this period sought to institute

African traditions as the basis of the imagined national community and to examine ways in which modernity could be secured outside the institutions of European culture. Thus, on the eve of independence, African writers became the most vocal champions of a traditional African past and a black aesthetic.

The role of colonial institutions

From as far back as the eighteenth century, colonial institutions have been some of the most visible vehicles through which the African literature was produced and disseminated. It was through institutions such as the colonial school and, later, the university, that African converts to Western modernity first began to explore the ways in which literary culture could be used to secure their own identities in relation to Europe. For many Africans, especially in the sub-Saharan region, the encounter with the institutions of colonial rule was often effected through Christian missions, which also acted as the vanguard of colonial expansion on the continent and as the custodians of European culture. As products of Christian missions, many African writers identified with the goals of the colonial mission, and when they wrote to oppose it, as was the case in the last two periods of colonial rule, they did so in a familiar Christian idiom.

The religious influence in African literature is to be found primarily in the use of the poetics of the Bible and in the concern with what has come to be known as the modernity/tradition conflict – the tension between African animism and Christianity (see **modernity and modernism**). Islam tended to complicate this opposition, especially in North and West Africa, where it had become established as the main religion, although more often African writers found it difficult to escape from the shadow of the missions that had produced them. But more than religious belief, it was the mission schools that were to prove indispensable in the emergence of an African literary tradition. For many Africans, the main attraction of these schools was their ability to confer the gift of literacy, often seen as the key to a modern life and identity. It was in such colonial schools as King's College, Budo (Uganda), Achimota (Ghana), Alliance High School (Kenya), the Lovedale Institute (South Africa), and the Lycée

William Ponty (Senegal) that the first generation of African writers were produced.

As writers and readers, the products of these missions considered literature to be important both as a weapon in the struggle against colonialism and as a vehicle of imagining a modern life. The expansion of colonial universities in the middle of the twentieth century was, however, a decisive factor in the emergence of a literature of resistance, for it was at these most privileged of colonial institutions that the most radical generation of African writers was produced. While many Africans arrived at colonial universities as devotees of Western culture, steeped in the major traditions of European literature and mores and often ignorant of their African ancestral traditions, they became, in the course of their education, discontented with colonialism. It was at colonial universities such as Ibadan and Makerere, both constituents of the University of London, that the literature of radical nationalism was first produced. The process of disenchantment with colonial culture was also reflected by those Africans who had gone to European countries, especially France, for their education.

The role of literature

Colonialism did not become the major and most persistent theme in African literature just because of the historical circumstances discussed above; it was also influential in the shaping of literary culture on the continent because of its inherent association with the ideas of modernity, culture, and the aesthetic. African literature was, of course, created in the crucible of colonial modernity and was thus concerned with the practices of modern life on the continent and the displacement and alienation engendered by modernization. Many African writers started writing to account for the ways in which colonial modernity had affected the life histories, experiences, and memories of pre-colonial societies or how it had produced subjects defined by their essential alienation. In the process of writing against colonial modernity, African writers accounted for their own location inside and outside the institutions of European rule. In addition, as scholars of postcolonial studies have argued, the idea of culture itself was so embedded in the colonizing process that it was often impossible for the colonizer and the colonized to invoke their identities without resorting to the language of cultural exclusiveness.

It is crucial to recognize the privileged position of literary culture in European modes of education in the African colonies. Often perceived as the standard of perfection and civilization, literary culture was considered to be so crucial in the colonization of the African that it occupied a pedestal in the education systems. It was not unusual for colonial headmasters to argue that Shakespeare (in the English colonies) and Molière (in the French territories) were more important than scientists and inventors. Consequently, many African writers considered such colonial edifices central to their literary projects; they believed that literature was central to the assertion of a new identity and the imagination of a national community.

Neocolonialism

A central issue in African culture and politics on the moment of independence was the continued influence of colonialism and its institutions in the newly independent states. Amidst the euphoria surrounding independence and the production of a literature that celebrated the coming into being of the new community of the nation, intellectuals and politicians alike were beginning to realize that, in structural and economic terms, decolonization had not led to the liberation of all spheres of political and especially economic life. Within the sphere of economics, relationships between the metropolitan European powers and the former colonies remained uneven and unequal, so much so that Kwame Nkrumah, who had heralded the independence of Ghana as the dawn of a new era, coined the term "neocolonialism" to refer to the political economy of the new nation. This is how Nkrumah explained the neocolonial relation in his book, *Neo-Colonialism: The Last Stage of Imperialism* (1965: New York): "The essence of neocolonialism is that the State which is subject to it is, in theory, independent and has all the outward trappings of international sovereignty. In reality its economic system and thus political policy is directed from outside." Nkrumah's view, developed during the

first few years of Ghanaian independence, was that the state was a victim of international capitalist relations and that political autonomy did not lead to the transformation of global forces such as commodity markets, which were still dominated by interests located in Europe and the United States. Political self-assertion appeared meaningless when confronted by economic paralysis.

But in his analysis of this situation, Nkrumah seemed to have missed the role played by African elites – including many in his own circle – in the enforcement of this situation, one that is dramatized vividly in the early novels of Ayi Kwei **Armah**, including *The Beautyful Ones Are Not Yet Born* (1968) and *Fragments* (1970). One of the most influential discourses on the political culture of neocolonialism, Frantz Fanon's *The Wretched of the Earth* (1963: New York), tended to represent the failure of national consciousness as much an effect of the continued dominance of colonial institutions and the nationalists' implication in the continuation of this relationship. In Fanon's discourse, neocolonialism was essentially the betrayal of the narrative of national liberation:

> National consciousness, instead of being the all-embracing crystallization of the innermost hopes of the whole people, instead of being the immediate and most obvious result of the mobilization of the people, will be an empty shell, a crude and fragile travesty of what it might have been.

Most of the literature produced in Africa in the late 1960s and 1970s took up the themes valorized by Nkrumah and Fanon from two directions. First, the language and structure of the novels of neocolonialism was predicated on one powerful motif – that nationalism was a narrative and experience caught between its promise and betrayal. This is evident in works such as Ngugi's *A Grain of Wheat* (1966), Ousmane **Sembene**'s *God's Bits of Wood* (*Les Bouts de bois de Dieu*) (1960), Ahmadou **Kourouma**'s *Suns of Independence* (*Les Soleils des indépendances*) (1968), and Ayi Kwei Armah's *The Beautyful Ones Are Not Yet Born*, to mention just a few. Second, the literature of neocolonialism was driven by the need to provide a critique of neocolonial economic relations, the persistence of imperialism in the fields of economics, and to imagine an alternative political economy based on the ideology of African socialism. This theme is dominant in works published in the 1970s and 1980s by radical writers, including Ngugi's *Petals of Blood* (1977), Sembene's *Xala* (1973) and *The Last of the Empire* (*Le Dernier de l'empire*) (1981), and Ama Ata **Aidoo**'s *Our Sister Killjoy* (1979).

Postcolonialism

By the late 1970s the discourse of neocolonialism was losing most of its steam, and by the 1980s it was no longer defining the field of African literature and its interpretation. There are no easy explanations for the dissipation of a term that had held so much sway in the period immediately following colonialism, but by the 1980s it had become increasingly apparent that the situation in Africa was much more complicated than the opposition between political sovereignty and economic dependence proposed by Nkrumah, a simple case of national betrayal, or even the failure of national consciousness as Fanon had proposed. Several reasons account for this rethinking of the nature of colonialism after independence. For one, in the 1980s many African states found themselves in perpetual political and economic crisis, one marked by the unexpected collapse of the modern institutions inherited from colonialism. With the collapse of the economic infrastructure and liberal political practices, it was hard to make the argument that the basic problem of African society was the existence of political freedom without economic power – none existed strongly enough to be contrasted. The postcolony was now posited as a state of crisis. At the same time, the paradigms on which the neocolonial argument had been built – the notion of progress, development, and ideology – were themselves being questioned by new poststructural theories (see **structuralism and poststructuralism**).

In these circumstances, as the term "neocolonial" appeared inadequate, a new term – "postcolonialism" – emerged as a possible alternative. Where neocolonialism had emphasized the continuity of colonial institutions and ideas after independence, postcolonial theorists were calling attention to the discontinuous and dialectical nature of this relation, arguing that while unequal economic relationships had perhaps survived decolonization, there were other spheres of social life, like culture, for example, where the culture of colonialism had been radically transformed. Indeed, postcolonial theory proposed a rethinking of colonialism itself. Instead of seeing colonialism as the imposition of cultural practices by the colonizer over the colonized, postcolonial theorists argued that the colonized had themselves been active agents in the making and remaking of the idea of culture itself. In effect, postcolonial theory posited the colonized and the subjects of the decolonized polity as active agents not simply in the constitution of the culture of the former colonies but also in the metropolitan world of the colonizers.

In the 1990s, postcolonial theories spread quickly in Europe and North America and became the basis of organizing the literature produced in the former colonies, including those in African. But in Africa itself there was strong resistance to many postcolonial theories, which were seen as essentially products of the European and American academy being imposed on local cultural practices. Part of this resistance emerged from what was seen as the transcendentalism implied by the notion of the "post" – the suggestion, as Ama Ata Aidoo complained loudly, that colonialism had been posted anywhere. There was a general feeling among African intellectual circles that postcolonial theory was premised on a critique of notions (history, nation, and consciousness) that were still central to subjects and citizens faced with the crisis engendered by the collapse of modern institutions. There was also a feeling that the issues privileged by postcolonial theory (difference, hybridity, and performativity) were not necessarily liberating in societies in which the invocation of these terms had been the basis of warfare, violence, and genocide. Postcolonial theory was, however, to become most influential in the works of the many African writers who live in the metropolitan centers, where it has opened up new ways of rethinking the geography of colonialism after empire and decolonization. This is evident in the works of a whole range of writers from Ben **Okri** in Britain to Leïla **Sebbar** in France.

Further reading

Boahen, A.A. (ed.) (1985) *Africa under Colonial Rule 1880–1935*, Berkeley: University of California Press.

Dirks, N. (ed.) (1992) *Colonialism and Culture*, Ann Arbor: University of Michigan Press.

Fanon, F. (1963) *The Wretched of the Earth*, New York: Grove Press.

Gikandi, S. (1996) *Maps of Englishness: Writing Identity in the Culture of Colonialism*, New York: Columbia University Press.

Nkrumah, K. (1965) *Neo-Colonialism: The Last Stage of Imperialism*, New York: International Publishers.

Young, Robert (2001), *Postcolonialism: An Historical Introduction*, Oxford: Blackwell.

SIMON GIKANDI

Condé, Maryse

b. 1937, Guadeloupe

novelist and essayist

One of the pre-eminent voices of Francophone literature, Condé is a prolific novelist and essayist. She was born in Guadeloupe and at 16 went to boarding school in France. She lived in Africa from 1960 to 1972 and then returned to Paris to complete her studies; she received her PhD from the Sorbonne in 1975 and has taught at various universities in Europe and the United States. She currently teaches French at Columbia University. Her fiction explores various aspects of the African diaspora and its multiple identities (see **diaspora and pan-Africanism**). Early in her career she wrote a number of plays, but since the publication of her first novel in 1976, *Heremakonon* (*Hérémaknonon*), she has produced a steady stream of fiction. *Heremakonon* is a first-person narrative by an educated young woman who has been driven out of her native Guadeloupe in shame over an inappropriate relationship, settles in Paris, and then travels to Africa as a way of recovering her identity. Like many of Condé's characters, Veronica tries to remain detached from politics, but her attempts to see Africa only as a cultural relic fail when she gets romantically involved with a man who is part of a dictatorship. Condé's second novel, *Season in Rihata* (*Une Saison à Rihata*) (1981) is also set in Africa, but her interest in Africa gains fuller scope in her historical novel *Segu* (*Segou, les murailles de terre*) (1984), which is her most widely read work. It is set in Mali and follows several families over four generations beginning at the end of the eighteenth century. This novel is Condé's effort to write an Afrocentric history of the nineteenth century where Europe and America appear at the margins of the characters' awareness. In the novel she creates a strong sense of the cultural diversity of West Africa. More recently, in *The Last of the African Kings* (*Les Derniers des rois mages*) (1992) she returns to the theme of African history and its lingering illegitimacy by creating a fictional narrative about the real-life descendants of Dahomey's King Behanzin, who was exiled by the French to the Caribbean after their conquest of Dahomey. Spero, a failed artist, tries to live beyond the legacy of his family which is viewed by most Antilleans as mythical and not historical. He marries an African-American, however, who sees him as a symbol of cultural authenticity. Spero refuses to meet his wife's expectations and struggles with his sense of cultural irrelevance and his exile.

Condé has written several novels that focus on her native Guadeloupe, the most important of which is *Crossing the Mangrove* (*Traversée de la mangrove*) (1989). *I, Tituba, Black Witch of Salem* (*Moi, Tituba ... noire de Salem*) (1986) is a historical romance about the Salem witch trials which focuses on the fate of a black slave from Barbados.

The 1990s were a particularly productive period for Condé. In addition to *The Last of the African Kings*, she published *La Colonie du nouveau monde* (New World Colony) (1993), *Windward Heights* (*La Migration des coeurs*) (1995), which is a rewriting of Emily Brontë's *Wuthering Heights* set in the Caribbean, and *Desirada* (*Desirada*) (1997).

Condé writes often on the subject of Creole identity and has published several studies of Antillean literature, the most important of which is *La Parole des femmes* (The Voice of Women) (1979). She has made periodic returns to drama, as in her 1988 play *Pension Les Alizés* (Hotel Les Alizés), and has become interested in **children's literature**.

Further reading

Pfaff, Françoise (1996) *Conversations with Maryse Condé*, Lincoln, Nebraska: University of Nebraska Press (includes extensive bibliography).

ELENI COUNDOURIOTIS

Conton, William

b. 1925

educator, historian, and novelist

A Gambian/Sierra Leonean educator, historian, and novelist, William Conton was educated at the University of Durham in the north of England and after graduation taught history at Fourah Bay College. He later served as principal of Accra High School in Ghana, before he returned to Sierra Leone where he was principal of two leading high schools and later the country's chief education officer. Conton's novel, *The African* (1960) was one of the first novels published in Heinemann's famous African Writers Series edited by Chinua **Achebe**. Written in the form of an **autobiography**, the novel revolves around the relationship between a black male student and a white South African girl, who meet in England and fall in love but discover that racial prejudice constantly comes between them. Conton used the romantic trope in the novel to introduce the problem of apartheid in South African and the politics of pan-Africanism into African literature (see **apartheid and post-apartheid**; **diaspora and pan-Africanism**). Behind its sometimes sentimental language, the novel was one of the first attempts to reflect on the violence engendered by racial discrimination in South Africa and political violence elsewhere on the continent, and to imagine the possibility of forgiveness and reconciliation as the precondition for the emergence of a United States of Africa. Literary critics did not have much patience for this kind of work in the 1960s and 1970s, and Conton's novel quickly disappeared into obscurity except for a harsh critique by Wole **Soyinka** in his discussion of ideology and social vision in African fiction. In retrospect, however, what appeared romantic and utopian in Conton's novel are now considered real

possibilities and realities, especially after the end of apartheid in South Africa in the early 1990s.

Further reading

Soyinka, Wole (1976) *Myth, Literature, and the African World*, Cambridge: Cambridge University Press.

SIMON GIKANDI

Cossery, Albert

b. 1913, Cairo, Egypt

poet

A Francophone writer, Cossery was born in Cairo in a well-to-do but not Francophone middle-class family. He was sent to French schools and became attracted to the poetry of Baudelaire. In 1931 he published his first work, *Morsures* (Bites), a collection of poems in imitation of Baudelaire's *Flowers of Evil* (*Fleurs du mal*). Cossery is, however, best known for his novels, which depict the life of marginalized characters in an urban setting, exuding the ambiance of Egyptian city life in popular quarters. Some of his novels have been adapted for the screen and have been turned into films in France and Egypt. Henry Miller, who came to know Cossery when the latter visited New York in the 1940s, has introduced Cossery's work in the US. Cossery has received several literary prizes, including the French Academy prize for Francophone literature. Cossery describes himself as an anarchist. He has been living in Paris, in the same hotel room, since 1945, and he says that he finds in his minimalist way of life – one without family, apartment, or car – a sense of liberation. Despite his long stay in France, his source of inspiration continues to be Egypt, even when the country is not named in his fiction.

Cossery depicts the misery of the poor and the marginalized, but sees in it the freedom of having nothing but the essential, the joy of living, and the absence of worries of the established social order. He finds in the indigenous city the warmth of crowds and the authenticity of freedom, which he often compares to the artificiality and the coldness of organized European cities. Third-world street life, with its cafés and conversations, with its chaotic and sensual registers, is depicted in Cossery's works; indeed, the only novel of his that is not situated in the city is *Les Fainéants dans la vallée fertile* (The Lazy Ones) (1964). The main characters in his short stories, as in *Men God Forgot* (1963) (*Hommes oubliés de Dieu*) (1941) are the little powerless people, spectators rather than men of action, who nevertheless are part of the human comedy. The characters of *Men God Forgot* are the wretched and the poor – the unemployed, the addicts, peddlers, and beggars – and yet the reader is drawn to sympathize with them. Brutal as the fictional underworld of Cossery seems, it retains nevertheless a measure of humanity and humor. Cossery's sarcasm and realism from below suggest the importance of capturing the simple pleasures of present moments despite the absurdity of situations and contexts. In *La Violence et la dérision* (Violence and Ridicule) (1964), Cossery undermines tyranny and pokes fun at rigged elections. His underprivileged protagonists do not lose their sense of humor despite their abuse, and are capable of occasional acts of tenderness towards each other. His novels, though written in French, adopt the vitality and rhythms of spoken Egyptian. His fiction revolves around men; when women are present they are mostly prostitutes.

Cossery received several prestigious prizes: the Grand Prix de la Francophonie (1990), the Grand Prix Audiberti (1995), and the Prix Méditerranée (2000).

Further reading

Cossery, Albert (1963) *Men God Forgot*, trans. Harold Edwards, San Francisco: City Lights Books.

FERIAL J. GHAZOUL

Couchoro, Félix

b. 1900, Ouidah, Dahomey (now Benin); d. 1968, Togo

novelist

Félix Couchoro has been claimed both as a Beninese and a Togolese author. Born in Ouidah, Dahomey (now Benin), to a Fon father and a Yoruba mother, both Catholics, Couchoro was educated in Catholic mission schools. He left Dahomey for Togo in 1939, where he spent most of the rest of his life, working as a teacher, a businessman, and later a journalist and newspaper editor. Couchoro's first work, *L'Esclave* (The Slave), which appeared in 1929, is considered to be not only the first Dahomean **novel** but among the first African novels. Set in a village in southwest Dahomey, the novel satirizes the Dahomean elite during the colonial period. Couchoro published most of his 22 novels in serial form in various newspapers and was thus able to reach a popular African audience. Although his first few novels were written in a standard metropolitan French and praised French culture and civilization, Couchoro soon adapted his French to the rhythm of Ewe and incorporated Ewe and Fon expressions and proverbs in his texts.

Further reading

Couchoro, Félix (1929, 1993) *L'Esclave* (The Slave), Lomé: Éditions Akpagnon, ACCT.

RACHEL GABARA

Couto, Mia (António Emílio Leite)

b. 1955, Beira, Mozambique

novelist and short story writer

Mozambique's foremost contemporary writer, Mia Couto rose to prominence with his first collection of short stories *Voices Made Night* (1990) (*Vozes Anoitecidas*) (1986). His manipulation of the Portuguese language, with which he constantly plays, has led to him being compared with James Joyce and José Luandino **Vieira**. His style is innovative, replete with neologisms and syntactical distortions. He has published a number of collections of short stories, poetry, and several novels, some of which are set against the backdrop of the Mozambican civil war that ended in 1992. The son of Portuguese parents, he is a white whose writing is often read to speak on behalf of the plight of an overwhelmingly black nation. For several years following the independence of Mozambique, he served as the head of the National News Agency.

Further reading

Couto, Mia (1990) *Voices Made Night*, trans. David Brookshaw, Oxford: Heinemann.
——(1994) *Every Man is a Race*, trans. David Brookshaw, Oxford: Heinemann.
——(2001)*Under the Frangipani*, trans. David Brookshaw, London: Serpent's Tail.

PHILLIP ROTHWELL

Craveirinha, José João

b. 1922, Maputo, Mozambique

poet

José Craveirinha is considered to be the most important Mozambican poet of the twentieth century. Born in Lourenço Marques (now Maputo), he is the son of a Portuguese settler and a Ronga mother. In the 1960s, he was imprisoned by the Portuguese colonial regime because of his sympathies for the liberation movement of Mozambique, FRELIMO. His earlier poetry is noted for its social concerns. It powerfully critiques colonial injustice and proposes a transatlantic **negritude**. He introduces Ronga words into his Portuguese text. His Ronga-titled *Karingana Ua Karingana* (Once Upon a Time) (1974) confirmed his status as Mozambique's foremost cultural inscriber. His later collection of poetry, *Maria* (1988), dedicated to the memory of his wife, was considerably more lyrical than his previous work, and revealed a sentimental side to the poet. He was the president of the Mozambican Writers' Association (AEMO), and in 1991 won the most prestigious award for writing in the Portuguese language, the Prémio Camões.

PHILLIP ROTHWELL

Cronin, Jeremy

b. 1949, Cape Town, South Africa

poet and politician

Jeremy Cronin was born in Cape Town. He describes his Catholic background as very formative morally and philosophically. At 18 he joined the South African Communist Party (SACP), attracted by its long tradition of non-racialism and its involvement in the struggle against apartheid (see **apartheid and post-apartheid**). He studied politics and philosophy at the University of Cape Town (UCT) and the Sorbonne before being appointed as a lecturer in philosophy and political science at UCT. In 1976 Cronin was sentenced to seven years in prison for printing and distributing SACP and African National Congress (ANC) publications. His first collection of poetry, *Inside*, was published shortly after his release in 1983. In this collection of poems, containing stark accounts of prison life, Cronin was able to fuse politics with his own innate sense of lyricism, which he had abandoned as self-indulgent while he was politically active. His literary style is influenced by black oral poetry (see **oral literature and performance**) and is infused with the African notion of *ubuntu*, the belief, expressed in the title of one of his early poems, that "A Person is a Person because of Other People." Between 1987 and 1990 Cronin lived in exile, mainly in Zambia. In 1995 he became deputy secretary-general of the SACP and in 1999 was appointed a member of parliament.

ELAINE M. PEARSON

Cuguano, Quobna Ottobah

b. 1757, Ghana; d. 1791

writer

Born in a Fante village on the coast of present-day Ghana, Ottobah Cuguano is one of a group of African writers who, in the age of European slavery and the Enlightenment, sought to use writing to refute the idea that blacks were not moral human beings worthy of freedom, and to deploy the gift of literacy in the cause of abolition. Sold into slavery when he was only 13, Cuguano worked in the slave plantations of the Caribbean for two years before he was freed and sent to England. Here, he worked as a house servant for the artists Richard and Maria Cosway, who introduced him to major English writers and abolitionists of the eighteenth century, most notably William Blake and Granville Sharpe. He was also to become active in the Afro-British abolitionist and literary circles, where he worked closely with Olaudah **Equiano**. Cuguano's *Thought and Sentiments on the Evil of Slavery* (1787) is now considered to be the most unequivocal and radical discourse produced by an African-born writer against the evils of slavery and the slave trade. In this work, Cuguano set out to systematically refute all the political and moral claims made against the character of the African, drawing on his own experiences to undermine the central tenets in pro-slavery arguments. Compared to the slave narrative of his contemporary, Equiano, Cuguano's treatise never acquired the status of a classical text and his skills as a writer were questioned for three centuries; questions were raised about his mastery of English, the authorship of his works, and the coherence of his arguments. Still, as the pioneer black writers of the eighteenth century began to be rediscovered in the last half of the twentieth century, Cuguano has come to be recognized as one of the founders of a literature of the African diaspora (see **diaspora and pan-Africanism**). There is no doubt that he had marshaled all the literary and religious sources at his disposal to attack the greatest evil of the modern period.

Further reading

Edwards, Paul and Walvin, James (1983) *Black Personalities in the Era of the Slave Trade*, London: Macmillan.

Gates, Henry Louis Jr (1988) *The Signifying Monkey: A Theory of African-American Literary Criticism*, New York: Oxford.

Sandiford, Keith (1988) *Measuring the Moment: Strategies of Protest in Eighteenth-Century Afro-English Writing*, London: Associated Universities Press.

SIMON GIKANDI

D

Dadié, Bernard

b. 1916, Abidjan, Côte d'Ivoire

writer

Bernard Dadié's literary production occupies an important place in African letters in general, but especially in the literature of the Côte d'Ivoire. Though his main work comes soon after that of the **negritude** movement, it nonetheless distinguishes itself from the literature of negritude by its confident rootedness in the author's African (Agni) heritage and its lack of nostalgia for a precolonial past. Like the negritude authors, Dadié is committed to the cultural rehabilitation of Africa; yet he writes not to retrieve a lost culture but to preserve one from which he has never been separated, having never – unlike a Camara **Laye** or a **Senghor** – been torn away from his country or made a French citizen. According to some critics, this explains the lack of nostalgia in his writing. However, even at a very young age as a student in French schools, Dadié possessed a mind that defied assimilation. His refusal to accept the inferior status to which Europeans insisted on relegating Africans and their cultures underlies Dadié's whole oeuvre. All of his writing in its vast diversity of genres (journals, newspaper articles, prison diary, poetry, folk tales, novels, plays, travel chronicles) grows out of and reflects his cultural and political commitment.

The years 1934–8 were a formative period for Dadié. During this time he kept a personal journal that contains many of the themes that were to dominate his later works. It was also during this period that he started writing plays. His unpublished play "Les Villes" (Cities), staged by students at Bingerville in 1934, was the first written play in Francophone sub-Saharan Africa. His second play, *Assémien Déhylé, roi du Sanwi* (Assemien Dehyle, King of Sanwi), was performed at the École William Ponty, one of the elite centers of education (see **education and schools**) in Senegal, in 1936 and at the Paris Exhibition of 1937. It was then published in a special issue of *Éducation Africaine*. In this play, based on a Baoule/Agni legend of beginnings dating back to the end of the eighteenth century, Dadié sought to provide a positive portrayal of African history to counter its distortions by colonial institutions, and to appeal to the Ivorians' sense of patriotism. To accompany the publication of *Assémien Déhylé*, Dadié wrote the article "Mon pays et son théâtre" (My Country and Its Theater), in which he highlighted differences between French and African theater, arguing that because storytelling in Africa was based on oral performance it was inherently theatrical in nature (see **oral literature and performance**). With these two pieces Dadié became the first African writer to propose a reformulation of the concept of theater in Francophone Africa. During the World War II years, Dadié, who was still based in Senegal, published several pieces in *Dakar-Jeunes* (Dakar-Youth) and, more importantly, he participated (with Alioune Diop, Guy Tyrolien, and Paul Niger) in the founding of *Présence Africaine*. It was during this period that he discovered, through a reading of a poem by Senegalese Issa Diop, a poetic form that would satisfy his search for a more supple vehicle for representing African cultural experiences.

Dadié's return to the Côte d'Ivoire in 1947 marked the beginning of an important period in his political and intellectual growth. From 1947 to 1953 Dadié worked as press reporter for the Democratic Party of the Ivory Coast and wrote many articles, some under pseudonyms. He considered the role of the press to be that of guide, advisor, and teacher of the people. The oratorical language of his newspaper articles was echoed in much of his other writing from this period. During his year of imprisonment for his political beliefs (February 1949 to March 1950), Dadié wrote his *Carnet de prison* (Prison Diary), documenting, in the words of Robert Smith (1992: Ivry-sur-Seine), the Ivorian people's "struggle for the progress, liberty and well-being of African populations; the heroic and active support of African women; the political prisoners and the subhuman living conditions in the prisons." The diary also gives insight into Dadié's personality, beliefs, and principles, as well as highlighting his literary talents. From his prison cell Dadié would use the diary form to denounce the West's colonization of Christianity for its own self-interest and challenge the West's claim to be the "model civilization" (see **Christianity and Christian missions**). For Dadié, a civilization based on dominance and not on human equality could not lay claim to true humanism. Dadié's literary career proper would, however, begin in the mid 1950s, with the publication of his first poetry collection, *Afrique debout!* (Up, Africa!) (1954). The publication of this first collection signaled the beginning of a literary career that would culminate in *Contes de Koutou-as-Samala* (Tales of Koutou-as-Samala) (1982).

Although there is much overlapping in the production of the various literary genres in Dadié's corpus, it is more useful to examine his work by genre than to attempt a chronological approach. Dadié's three collections of poetry – *Afrique debout!*, *La Ronde des jours* (Day In, Day Out) (1950), and *Hommes de tous les continents* (Men of All Continents) (1967) – parallel the Ivorian political scene thematically. Their liberty of form, language, and imagination (free from the classical constraints learned at Ponty), reflects Dadié's concept of human liberty. They also bespeak a cultural

consciousness that valorizes oral poetry and validates an African experience. For Dadié, both form and content must be freed from borrowed conventions. He believes that the role of the poet is to bear witness to a collective human experience, to represent quotidian life as well as spiritual reality. At the same time, the three collections of poems reflect the changing reality of the Ivorian and global scenes. In *Afrique debout!* Dadié indicts the colonial situation, which objectifies and dehumanizes people, and he criticizes certain elements in African culture that colluded with colonialism. The theme of human love (including Dadié's love for his people), coupled with the possibility of hope, dominates in *La Ronde des jours*. Dadié's notion of love is, however, complex: it is lucid but it acknowledges human failings; love exists in spite of human frailty. With the third collection of poems, *Hommes de tous les continents*, Dadié embraces the whole world and depicts the universality of the human struggle for liberty from oppression. Dadié's philosophy of freedom transcends color and geographical boundaries, and the examples he quotes in this collection span several continents.

Dadié considered folk tales and legends important for three main reasons. First, to be rooted in one's past ensures direction and stability, and for Africans this past is to be found in their folk tales and legends and their oral literary heritage in general, which fulfils the function of "museums, monuments, street signs, books." Second, tales help build community and cultural continuity as people gather around at the end of the day to pass on their heritage from generation to generation through storytelling. Third, by comparing national folklores, we discover that human beings the world over have much in common. Unlike the tales of many **negritude** writers, which function as nostalgic documents intended for the "other," Dadié's tales, intended for the initiated, proceed from the pen of a writer inhabited by his culture, celebrating that culture. In total, Dadié published sixteen legends in the collection *Légendes africaines* (African Legends) (1954), sixteen tales in *Le Pagne noir* (The Black Cloth) (1955), and nine tales for children in *Contes de Koutou-as-Samala* (Tales of Koutou-as-Samala) (1982), not to mention tales told within other genres, such as the tales in the novel *Climbié* (Climbié) (1956).

Dadié's fiction parallels his own life from his childhood to about 1950, when he was released from prison. Critics have therefore tended to classify the three texts that fall under this category as **autobiography**. Dadié, however, wants us to read *Climbié* in particular as the lived experience of a generation of young people – as history. From *Climbié* to *Les Jambes du fils de Dieu* (The Legs of God's Son) (1980) to *Commandant Taureault et ses nègres* (Commander Taureault and His Blacks) (1980), there is a historical and thematic progression. *Climbié* relates the development of a child into adulthood, and the development of the consciousness that will lead him to refuse assimilation and to become politically committed. The story of the child Climbié, though similar to that of Dadié himself, also represents the experiences of his whole generation, as already mentioned, and reflects the author's relationship to his history. The collection of short stories collected in *Les Jambes du fils de Dieu* follows a similar itinerary to *Climbié* and complements it. In both narratives we constantly see the opposition of the African and the colonial worlds. Dadié privileges the African world and its wisdom, suggesting that the African who has remained rooted in his culture has a more lucid understanding of the world than the Westerner or the culturally alienated African. The last of the fictional works, *Commandant Taureault*, depicts a specific period in Ivorian history – the struggle for freedom – and represents, therefore, a collective history.

In his adulthood, Dadié undertook travel to Europe and the United States, and out of his observations as a traveler he wrote three works commonly classified as chronicles: *An African in Paris* (*Un Nègre à Paris*) (1959), *One Way: Bernard Dadié Observes America* (*Patron de New York*) (1964), and *The City Where No One Dies* (*La Ville où nul ne meurt*) (1969). In these chronicles, the African, heretofore the West's object of study, becomes the observer and critiques the West through its own institutions, culture, and customs. The journey account hence serves to demystify the dominant discourse of the West about itself – the postcard image – from an African frame of reference. Again, in contrast to much African writing of the time, this is not the journey of the alienated African in search of his identity, nor the archetypal journey of initiation.

The traveler sets forth confident of his own identity, in a quest for the cure for social ills whose origin is the Western model of civilization that severs communication between the individual and the group. The chronicles pierce through the masks of Western civilization while demonstrating that alienated Africans also don the same masks.

After his early years of William Ponty theater, Dadié comes back to this genre in 1953, at first through what he terms "intermission theater," comprising sketches for the Cercle Culturel et Folklorique de la Côte d'Ivoire (Circle for Culture and Folklore of the Ivory Coast), which Dadié co-founded that same year. However, his discovery of Aimé Césaire's plays served as a catalyst for the birth of Dadié's major dramatic works, including *Monsieur Thôgô-Gnini* (1970), *Les Voix dans le vent* (Voices in the Wind) (1979), *Beatrice du Congo* (Beatrice of the Congo) (1970), and *Iles de tempête* (Tempest Islands) (1973). To a large extent Dadié used theater to reinforce the themes found in his other writing, but through a medium more directly accessible to the people. The first two plays portray protagonists who, through their contact with the West and Western institutions, have lost sight of the importance of the group and live only for themselves, the first pursuing material gain, the second going after tyrannical power. *Beatrice* and *Iles* showcase protagonists of the stature of Joan of Arc (Beatrice) and Napoleon (Toussaint). Dadié's political and cultural stance does not reject the West. Rather, he contends that Africa, too, has produced its heroes and heroines, and these should receive their share of the attention given to the study of cultures and civilizations. *Iles de tempête* illustrates this point well by depicting Toussaint and Napoleon side by side as heirs to the 1789 French revolution and as harbingers of new regimes.

Throughout his writing career, Dadié, who also served as a minister of culture in the Côte d'Ivoire, proved to be a true humanist, but not in the most Eurocentric sense, as one critic has argued, since he demonstrated that Europe (whatever its avowed intentions) was in practice centered on itself, not on humanity, and had therefore failed to measure up to the humanism it preached. Careful attention to Dadié's voice as it emerges in his work reveals a more radical stance than might appear on the surface, especially through its powerful critique of the doctrines of assimilation promoted by French colonialism and its showcasing of the value and dignity of African heritage.

Further reading

Smith, Robert Jr (1992) "Bernard Binlin Dadié: A Voice for All Seasons," in Edebiri Unionmwan (ed.) *Bernard Dadié; hommages et études*, Ivry-sur-Seine: Nouvelles du Sud.

Vincileoni, Nicole (1986) *Comprendre l'oeuvre de Bernard B. Dadié* (Understanding the Work of Bernard B. Dadié), Issy les Moulineaux: Éditions Saint-Paul.

WANGAR WA NYATETŬ-WAIGWA

Dakeyo, Paul

b. 1948, Bafoussam, Cameroon

poet

Born in Bafoussam (Cameroon), Paul Dakeyo is among the notable Francophone poets of the period following **negritude**. Dakeyo started his career by writing poems that were highly engaged in the defense of oppressed peoples. These poems were collected in *Le Cri pluriel* (The Plural Cry) (1975), *Chant d'accusation* (Song of Accusation) (1976), and *Soweto, Soleils fusillés* (Soweto, Suns Shot Down) (1977). In his later works, however, Dakeyo has turned towards themes that are more personal and intimate, and such works as *Les Ombres de la nuit* (Shadows of the Night) (1996) are characterized by absolute pessimism and disenchantment; less interested in ideology than his earlier works, Dakeyo's recent poetry falls back on lyricism to produce a poetry that is more universal in its dimensions. In these later works then, Dakeyo sees the act of writing as one of utter simplicity, a kind of degree zero, out of which an emotionally moving poetry emerges and orients itself.

Further reading

Dakeyo, Paul (1982) *Poèmes de demain: anthologie de la poésie camerounaise de langue française* (Poems of Tomorrow: Anthology of Cameroonian Poetry in French), Paris: Silex.

FRIEDA EKOTTO

Dangarembga, Tsitsi

b. 1959, Mutoko, Zimbabwe

novelist

When the Zimbabwean writer Tsitsi Dangarembga published her first and only novel, *Nervous Conditions* in 1989, she was immediately recognized as a major new force in African literature. Although born in Zimbabwe, Dangarembga spent her childhood in Britain and was educated in mission schools in Mutare, Cambridge University, and the University of Zimbabwe in Harare, where she studied psychology. It was at the University of Zimbabwe that she became involved in the theater and also started writing short plays and stories. *Nervous Conditions* reflects her background in two important senses. First, it is an autobiographical novel (see **autobiography**) that draws on her experiences as a black child from a middle-class family growing up in England and later having to struggle to reconcile her inherited Englishness with the traditional beliefs and practices of rural Zimbabwe. Second, the novel's probing attempt to understand the tormented lives of colonial subjects, especially women, reflects Dangarembga's interest and training in psychology. But the most important reason why the novel has quickly become a classic in the canon of African literature is its hybrid character, especially in relation to the history of the novel on the continent. Instead of breaking from the realism and modernism associated with her predecessors, Dangarembga's novel appropriates those formal practices and yet transforms them by focusing on questions of gender and the inner lives of African women (see **gender and sexuality**).

In terms of its subject, *Nervous Conditions* takes on the most familiar themes in African literature. It is concerned with questions of tradition and modernity (see **modernity and modernism**), the constitution and education of colonial subjects, the emergence of cultural nationalism, and the coming into power of a new African elite. At the same time, however, Dangarembga modified these themes in a subtle and gentle way, showing how, for example, the opposition between tradition and modernity which structured most African literature in the 1950s and 1960s was not as clear-cut as it initially seemed. Indeed, by placing women at the center of her novel she shows how they are neither the romantic embodiments of an African tradition nor active agents of modernity and modernization. The women in her novel are placed in a nervous condition in relation to both the traditions dominated by men and the modernity controlled by them. Whether at home or school, the two main characters in Dangarembga's novel, Tambu and Nyasha, like their mothers, exist at the edge of the world, denied entry into either the traditional or the modern domain. They are hence forced to create and re-create their own traditions and notions of the modern. Dangarembga's novel is told in realistic style (see **realism and magical realism**) that recalls the novels of Flora **Nwapa** and Buchi **Emecheta** rather than the magic realism of the women writers of her generation. But this use of realism enables her to focus simultaneously on the inner world of her characters, and their everyday experiences which take place against the background provided by Zimbabwe's journey out of colonialism.

SIMON GIKANDI

Dangor, Achmat

b. 1948, Johannesburg, South Africa

poet, playwright, short story writer, and novelist

The South African poet, playwright, short story writer, and novelist Achmat Dangor was born and raised in Johannesburg. A founding member of the cultural group Black Thoughts, he was banned for six years from 1973 under the censorship laws established by the apartheid state (see **apartheid and post-apartheid**). His two volumes of poetry and the novella *Waiting for Leila* (1981) explore the world of apartheid, especially its enforcement of racial segregation and the forced removals of communities. In his collection of poems, *The Bulldozer* (1983), Dangor constantly refers to the demolition of homes carried out by the state under the Group Areas Act, and *Waiting for Leila* has the infamous destruction of Cape Town's District Six as its backdrop. While it is firmly rooted in its social milieu, Dangor's poetry is nonetheless deeply personal and intimate, as evidenced by the title of his second collection of poems, *Private Voices* (1992). His later work, *Kafka's Curse* (1997), in particular, reveals a fascination with themes such as hybridity, sexual transgression, and metamorphosis, which mocks the apartheid state's insistence on purity while grappling with the question of colored identity. Hybridity is evident, too, on the formal level where realism, myth, fable, and canonical allusions blend to form a magical realist narrative (see **realism and magical realism**). Set in 1998, *Bitter Fruit* (2001) continues to probe these issues through realistic prose, with the preoccupations introduced by the Truth and Reconciliation Commission juxtaposed against the drama of a family trying to come to terms with their country's past and to make sense of its present.

MEG SAMUELSON

Dannyacchew Werqu (Daniachew Worku)

b. 1936, Ethiopia; d. 1994, Ethiopia

novelist

Dannyacchew Werqu is considered to be one of Ethiopia's more inaccessible authors due to his experimentation with the Amharic language and his philosophical outlook, which he may have acquired from his father, who had spent many years in France at a time when Ethiopia was still very isolated from the rest of the world. His mother was a good storyteller and set Dannyachew early on the path toward writing, first poems (some published in the collection *Imbwa belu* (Help Me!), (1974/6), then plays (*Sew alle biyyé* (I Thought These Were Real Men), 1957/8, *Tibelch*, staged 1967/8, and *Seqeqenish isat* (Fire Is Consuming Me Because I Have Not Got Your Love), staged 1959), finally novels (*Adefris*, 1969/70, and, unpublished at his death, "Shout It from the Mountain Top"), besides language books. He got his education in government schools and at the university at Addis Ababa before winning a scholarship to study creative writing at Iowa University. During his stay in the US, he wrote stories in English and a novel, *The Thirteenth Sun* (1973). His major work, however, is the novel *Adefris*, named after the main character, in which there is much discussion of Ethiopian culture and how Ethiopia ought to develop. In complicated language and abstract dialogues, it reflects ideas much debated at the time.

Further reading

Molvaer, R.K. (1997) *Black Lions*, Lawrenceville, New Jersey: Red Sea Press.

REIDULF MOLVAER

Danquah, J.B.

b. 1895, Bepong, Gold Coast (now Ghana); d. 1965, Nsawam, Ghana

scholar, lawyer, and politician

Modern Ghana owes its name to the recommendation of Joseph Boakye Danquah, the renowned scholar, lawyer, and politician who, ironically, died in jail as an enemy of the state under Kwame Nkrumah's regime. Danquah's scholarly work focused mainly on Akan society, culture, and laws. His foray into creative writing did not yield work comparable to his classic text on Akan theology, *The Akan Doctrine of God* (1944). The play *The Third Woman* (1943), for example, offers an uneven exploration of Akan folklore and the concept of God as creator. And so it is in the underappreciated role as reviewer that J.B. Danquah leaves his mark on the African literary scene. In his foreword to the first edition of R.E. Obeng's novel, *Eighteenpence* (1943: Ilfracombe, Devon), Danquah notes that Obeng's book

> is the first long novel in English ... published by a Gold Coast [present-day Ghana] man. Casely Hayford's *Ethiopia Unbound* which, in a way, was an imaginative story, was political in motive. *Eighteenpence* is a true novel in the sense of a

fictitious prose tale concerned with the more sensitive passions of the human heart.

These observations introduce his pioneering critical review of Obeng's work, one of the earliest novels in African literature in English..

Further reading

Obeng, R.E. (1972) *Eighteenpence*, 2nd edn, Tema: Ghana Publishing Corporation.

KOFI OWUSU

Danquah, Mabel (née Dove)

b. 1910, Ghana; d. 1984, Ghana

short story writer

The Ghanaian short story writer Mabel Danquah was educated locally and in England and lived for a while in the United States. She was a pioneering journalist and politician and the first woman elected to the Ghanaian Legislative Assembly in the early 1950s, in the years leading to independence. It was while she was working as a journalist for the *Accra Evening News* in the 1940s that Danquah started writing short stories. These dealt with the question of cultural conflict and the problems the new generation of Africans that came of age in the early half of the twentieth century faced as they tried to reconcile what were seen as disappearing cultural traditions and the culture of modernity. Her most popular short stories, "Anticipation," "Payment," and "The Torn Veil" have been collected in important anthologies of African literature, including Langston Hughes' *An African Treasury* (1960).

SIMON GIKANDI

De Graft, Joe Coleman

b. 1924, Ghana; d. 1978, Ghana

playwright, poet, novelist, and educator

Often referred to as "the elder statesman of Ghanaian letters," Joe De Graft was a playwright, poet, novelist, and educator. Between 1955 and 1960, De Graft developed the Mfantsipim Drama Laboratory, which utilized many Western formal traditions even as it sought to gradually meld a wholly Ghanaian and African content into a distinctly modern theater. De Graft's first published drama, *Sons and Daughters* (1964) showed both his potential and his shortcomings as a dramatist. However, during the 1960s De Graft's involvement with dramaturgy and Efua **Sutherland**'s productions at the Drama Studio was to help perfect his skills. De Graft was also a major contributor to the founding of the University of Ghana Legon drama and theater studies division in the early 1960s. In 1970, one of his best dramatic works, *Through a Film Darkly*, was published. For most of the 1970s he worked for UNESCO in Nairobi, Kenya. It was during this period that he published his critically acclaimed collection of poems, *Beneath the Jazz and Brass* (1975) and *Muntu: A Play* (1977).

Further reading

Fraser, Robert (1986) *West African Poetry: A Critical History*, Cambridge: Cambridge University Press.
Ogungbesan, Kolawole (ed.) (1989) *New West African Literature*, London: Heinemann.

VINCENT O. ODAMTTEN

Debeche, Djamila

b. 1926, Sétif, Algeria

writer

Djamila Debeche appeared on the already lively Algerian literary scene in 1947, when she founded a pioneering feminist magazine, *L'Action* (Action). Also that year, she published her first novel, the first by a North African woman writing in French, *Leila, jeune fille d'Algérie* (Leila, a Young Girl from Algeria). Debeche's work demonstrates that demands for women's rights in Algeria accompanied demands for an end to colonialism from the 1940s on. Debeche also published essays on the Algerian school system, including *L'Enseignement de la langue arabe en Algérie et le droit de vote aux femmes algériennes* (The Teaching of Arabic in Algeria and the Right

of Algerian Women to Vote) (1951), in which she linked Arabic literacy to political evolution. Her novel *Aziza* (1955) stages a French-educated woman who marries a fellow Algerian Muslim but finds she cannot live with his hidebound traditionalism. After divorcing, Aziza is shunned as a cultural traitor by both Europeans and Muslims. Nonetheless, she stays in Algiers, attempting to affirm an intercultural identity. The novel implicitly criticizes pro-independence leaders for ignoring those marginal to their movement, especially women.

Further reading

Debeche, Djamila (1955) *Aziza*, Algiers: Imbert.

SETH GRAEBNER

Dei-Anang, Michael Francis

b. 1909, Ghana; d. 1977, New York

poet and playwright

Michael Dei-Anang, the Ghanaian poet and playwright, was a major player in African and foreign affairs in Kwame Nkrumah's government. President Nkrumah wrote the foreword to *Ghana Glory* (1965), a collection of poems on Ghana and Ghanaian life Dei-Anang co-authored with Yaw Warren. Nkrumah's claim that Dei-Anang was his country's "foremost" poet at the time was not an exaggeration: Dei-Anang published five volumes of poetry from the mid 1940s to the mid 1960s. The poet's recurring themes, like "resurgent" Ghana, political and mental decolonization, the rehabilitated African personality, and reinterpreting Africa's past, work relatively well in the poetic compositions and give memorable expression to contemporaneous patriotic sentiments. Dei-Anang must have also been conscious of his audience abroad because the corrective function of a metaphor like "shaft of light" (which he naturally associates with Nkrumah, for example) is better appreciated in the context of the West's preoccupation with "dark Africa." In the play, *Okomfo Anokye's Golden Stool* (1960), Dei-Anang links the greatness of the Asante nation to that of Ghana (and Africa).

Here, as in much of his work, Dei-Anang suggests that Africa's past has had "golden" moments and those moments can be updated for modern times.

KOFI OWUSU

Deng, Francis

b. 1938, southern Sudan

diplomat, lawyer, and writer

The Sudanese diplomat, lawyer, and writer Francis Deng has held many senior positions at the United Nations since he started his association with the organization in 1992, working mostly with agencies dealing with human rights and displaced persons. Born in the southern Sudan among the Dinka people, he was educated in mission schools in the region before graduating with a degree in law from the University of Khartoum. Deng's major works have been in the areas of human rights, law, and conflict resolution, but he has also written works on Dinka oral traditions, songs, cosmological beliefs, and folk tales (see **oral literature and performance**). His literary output includes two novels, *Seed of Redemption* (1986) and *Cry of the Owl* (1989).

SIMON GIKANDI

Dhlomo, Herbert Isaac Ernest

b. 1903, Siyamu, Edendale, South Africa;
   d. 1956, Durban, South Africa

poet, novelist, essayist, and journalist

The posthumous publication of H.I.E. Dhlomo's *Collected Works* (1985) confirmed his stature as a pioneer in the development of black theater, poetry, journalism, and criticism in South Africa. Like his brother R.R.R. **Dhlomo**, H.I.E.'s pursuits were wide and varied and included spells as teacher, librarian, musician, and journalist on *Ilanga lase Natal* (Natal Sun) and *Bantu World* from 1926 until the mid 1950s. Dhlomo wrote over 20 plays, 140 poems and ten short stories, with many of these items either incomplete or possibly lost. His newspaper essays constitute some of the earliest sustained appreciation of African writing, culture, and social experience written by a black South African in the twentieth century.

Like many of his newly educated and urban contemporaries, Dhlomo embraced and championed the notion of "the New African" – a reworking of Alain Locke's "the new Negro" and W.E.B. Du Bois' "the talented tenth." "The New African" embraced Christian and liberal tenets, which were seen as marking a "progressive" and individualistic turn away from heathenism and tribalism. Yet despite all their "modernist" tendencies, "the New Africans" regarded precolonial African societies as powerful mnemonic sources of African independence and cultural integrity, especially in the face of the increasing segregation, discrimination and repression unleashed by the South African state after 1910.

In his essays on African drama and literature, Dhlomo advocated formal experimentation that included drawing on forms and ideas drawn from elsewhere, but he also constantly reiterated the immense riches of indigenous performance traditions and orature. These ideas are not always successfully realized, especially in his early play *The Girl Who Killed to Save* (Nongquase the Liberator) (1935). *The Girl Who Killed to Save* explores the cultural and political ambiguities surrounding the nineteenth-century cattle-killing episode amongst the Xhosa in the Eastern Cape. It was with the completion (between 1936 and 1939) of a quartet of plays based on the lives of "great Zulu chiefs," collectively called *The Black Bulls – Shaka* (presumably lost), *Dingane, Cetshwayo, Mfolozi* (presumably lost) – and *Moshoeshoe* and the publication of his well-known epic poem *Valley of a Thousand Hills* (1941), that Dhlomo's oeuvre started to articulate a pronounced nationalist aesthetic and ideology. The plays are exercises in memory work – reconstructing the past in its own right, devoid of colonial distortions and denigrations. Second, the dramas serve as complex allegorical critiques of the advance of colonialism, its appropriation of land and racist subjugation of Africans and their polities. Lastly, as celebrations of "great" African leaders they suggest the necessary qualities expected from modern-day leaders and caution against internal divisions and alliances with liberal whites. Dhlomo's writings presage much of the nationalist black writing produced in South Africa between 1960 and 1994 and their immense significance needs further scrutiny.

Further reading

Couzens, T. (1985) *The New African: A Study of the Life and Work of H.I.E. Dhlomo*, Johannesburg: Ravan Press.

Peterson, Bhekizizwe (2000) *Monarchs, Missionaries and African Intellectuals: African Theater and the Unmaking of Colonial Marginality*, New York: Africa World Press.

BHEKIZIZWE PETERSON

Dhlomo, Rolfes Robert Reginald

b. 1901, Siyamu, Edendale, South Africa; d. 1971, Siyamu, Edendale, South Africa

novelist and journalist

The elder brother of Herbert **Dhlomo**, R.R.R. Dhlomo was a pioneering writer and journalist in South Africa, and served as editor on important African newspapers such as *Ilanga lase Natal* (Natal Sun) and *Bantu World*. Dhlomo published *An African Tragedy* (1928), the first novel in English published by a black South African. *An African Tragedy* and *Indlela Yababi* (The Evil Way) (1946) lament the moral, physical, and political decay of city life while also criticizing certain traditional customs as being superstitious and retrogressive. Dhlomo also wrote a series of important and complex historical novels in Zulu that explore the lives and times of Zulu kings in the nineteenth century, *uDingane* (1936), *uShaka* (1937), *uMpande* (1938), *uCetshwayo* (1952), and *uDinuzulu* (1968). While ideologically still informed by key tenets of Christianity and relying on sources drawn from colonialism to varying degrees (see **Christianity and Christian missions**; **colonialism, neocolonialism, and postcolonialism**), the novels reconstituted the past as a vital period and example of independent African polity with a body of indigenous knowledge that was still pertinent in dealing with modern-day dilemmas. The novels were also subtle allegorical

critiques of the subjugation of the Zulu nation under segregation.

Further reading

Couzens, T. (1985) *The New African: A Study of the Life and Work of H.I.E. Dhlomo*, Johannesburg: Ravan Press.

BHEKIZIZWE PETERSON

Diabaté, Massa Makan

b. 1938, Mali; d. 1988, Mali

writer

Winner of several literary awards including the Grand Prix Littéraire de l'Afrique Noire (1971) and Grand Prix Léopold Sédar Senghor (1987), the Mali writer Massa Makan Diabaté was a talented playwright and novelist. He was also a literary scholar who published, singly and in collaboration with Jango Cisse, a number of important oral narratives from Malian griots (see **oral literature and performance**). On the whole, his oeuvre is framed by two important objectives: the needs to represent the vanishing manifestations of an expressive culture on stage and to document the process of transformation of Mande culture – centered in Kouta – as it evolved in the modern period.

Diabaté's major fictional work is the Kouta trilogy, which comprises *Le Lieutenant de Kouta* (The Lieutenant of Kouta) (1979), *Le Coiffeur de Kouta* (The Barber of Kouta) (1980), and *Le Boucher de Kouta* (The Butcher of Kouta) (1982). In these novels he captures successively the triumphant period of French colonialism, the rise of the nationalist movement for independence, and the postcolonial era up to the 1980s (see **colonialism, neocolonialism, and postcolonialism**; **nationalism and post-nationalism**). With colorful humor and a narrative style worthy of the griot, Diabaté meticulously depicts the transformations imposed by each period. He has successfully combined the virtues of the griot's oral art with the art of the novelist in these books, which met both remarkable popular success and critical praise.

KANDIOURA DRAME

Diakhate, Lamine

b. 1928, Saint-Louis, Senegal; d. 1987, Paris, France

poet and novelist

The Senegalese poet and novelist Lamine Diakhate was influenced by the poets of **negritude**, most notably by **Senghor**. This influence not only appears in the style of *Primordiale du sixième jour* (First Word on the Sixth Day) (1963) but also embraces the thematic range of his oeuvre, which focuses on Africa, Europe, and America. In his poetry one finds a celebration of the African past through the glorification of the achievements of its precolonial societies; the mournful denunciation of colonialism and its attendant abuses; and finally, the triumphant rebirth of Africa during the period of nationalism (see **colonialism, neocolonialism, and postcolonialism; nationalism and post-nationalism**). *Temps de mémoire* (Times Recalled) (1967) unites Africa and America through a celebration of black history and culture. *Nigerianes* (To the Women of Nigeria) (1974) is a tribute to Nigeria through its women. Diakhate extends this literary landscape into his prose fiction. *Prisonnier du regard* (Prisoner of the Gaze) (1975) deals with the past and the present in Senegal, while his novel *Chalys d'Harlem* (Chalys of Harlem) (1978) is the story of a Senegalese sailor who settles in Harlem after World War I. Chalys becomes a pan-African militant in the Garvey movement, achieves notoriety, and is elevated into the position of a respected elder of the black community.

KANDIOURA DRAME

Diallo, Koumanthio Zeinab

b. 1956, Labé, Guinea

poet and novelist

The Guinean writer Koumanthio Zeinab Diallo

began her literary career as a poet, continuing a family tradition, but her work mingles past and present traditions, poetry and narrative, and this accounts for its appeal to a diverse group of readers. Diallo's work expresses her pride and love for Fulani culture and traditions; although she is more interested in sentiment and art than politics or social criticism, she also expresses great concern for women's issues. Her first collection of poems, *Commes les pétales du crépuscule* (Like Petals at Dawn) (2000) was published in Togo, thus limiting its distribution, but her 1997 novel, *Les Épines de l'amour* (The Thorns of Love), published by L'Harmattan, the well-known French publisher, has reached an international audience. In this romance, Ramatoulaye Diallo falls in love with Alphadio Bah while she is visiting her grandmother's village. While social class does not pose a problem to the relationship, Ramatoulaye's father refuses to consider the match as the Bah and Diallo clans are enemies. After exhausting diplomatic means, Alphadio "kidnaps" his willing bride; but Ramatoulaye's father does not accept the marriage until he is on his deathbed. The novel defends the notion of romantic love and expresses the author's passionate belief that love can end hostility and unite warring groups in harmony.

LISA McNEE

Diallo, Nafissatou Niang

b. 1941, Dakar, Senegal; d. 1981, Senegal

writer

Although she rose to become a prominent writer of **autobiography**, **novel**s, and **children's literature**, the Senegalese writer Nafissatou Niang Diallo began her writing career as many fledgling writers do – that is, she shared her own experiences. However, her 1975 autobiography, *A Dakar Childhood*, reflects nothing of the awkwardness of early work. Rhetorically, it is a brilliant work of autobiography, if only because it succeeds in justifying the autobiographer's indiscretions for a society that values silence and associates discretion with nobility. Moreover, the text offers crucial information about women's lives during and after colonialism (see **colonialism, neocolonialism, and postcolonialism**). Although other African women such as Aoua Kéïta had already produced autobiographies, this work transformed the field of African autobiography by offering a strong female voice.

Senegalese women are considered vital to the functioning of society, and Diallo's ventures into fiction affirmed the importance of women in Senegalese history. *Le Fort maudit* (The Accursed Fort), published in 1980, is an historical romance set in the nineteenth century, when oppressive rulers and nobles waged war, pillaged, and virtually enslaved villagers. Thiane, the heroine of the novel, dies heroically after poisoning the evil warrior who has enslaved her people. *Fary, Princess of Tiali* (1987) is yet another historical romance about a heroine who sacrifices happiness to save her people. In this case, Fary is of the bardic caste. Bards were not allowed Muslim burial at the time, but Fary obtains this privilege for members of her caste by marrying the dwarf prince who is madly in love with her. The conviction that hard work and a strong will lead to success is also evident in Diallo's juvenile novel *Awa, la petite marchande* (Awa, the Little Vendor) (1981). Diallo is now considered to be one of the most important feminist writers in Africa. As an autobiographer, a novelist for adults and children, as well as in her roles as midwife, mother, and housewife, she gently urged those who came into contact with her and her works to reconsider women's roles in society. Her womanist ethic was rooted in a sincere belief that Senegalese women deserve more in life, but that harmonious relationships with men are vital to the well-being of women as well as children.

Further reading

McNee, Lisa (2000) *Selfish Gifts: Senegalese Women's Autobiographical Discourses*, Albany: State University of New York Press.

Stringer, Susan (1996) *The Senegalese Novel by Women: Through Their Own Eyes*, New York: Peter Lang.

LISA McNEE

diaspora and pan-Africanism

The emergence of an African diaspora

The emergence of an African diaspora, spread across the continents of Asia, Europe, and the Americas, was perhaps one of the most important events in the transformation of African literatures and cultures before, during, and after colonialism, although the mass movement of Africans to other parts of the world was often involuntary, carried out under conditions of enslavement, especially the transatlantic slave trade. As Franklin Knight has observed, it was through slavery that the distribution of Africans across the world became widespread across an unprecedented geographical area with extensive numbers of migrants and a historical duration unprecedented in its length. The "residual communities" this movement left in its wake, Knight observes, now form important constituents in several continents. The mass migration of Africans to the Americas, the Middle East, and Europe constitutes, in Knight's words (1989: Berkeley), "one of the major events of African and world history."

But even before the Atlantic slave trade, Africans had extensive relations with other parts of the world. In classical times, they had contacts with the Greeks and Romans and later both the Arabic and Jewish cultures of the Near East. In the circumstances, the exodus of African peoples into other parts of the world, whether voluntary or enforced, has become one of the constitutive elements of African literary and cultural history. One immediate impact of the emergence of the African diaspora in the ancient and modern worlds has been the marked presence of African subjects and traditions in many corners of the world, from classical Greece and the Ancient Near East to the black cultures of the new European Union who have produced literatures in different forms. Though often negated in the study of the foundational cultures of the Western or Eastern traditions, the African presence has been a visible mark in the construction of these traditions and their civilizations. There is perhaps no major aspect of the Western literary tradition that has not been touched by Africans, as objects of art, culture, and literature.

For over five hundred years, key elements of African culture have made their way into social practices of the Americas, so that it is not unusual to come across African-derived religions and cultures thriving in areas as diverse as rural Cuba and Haiti and the metropolitan centers of New York and Miami. During the same period, Africans have been ardent borrowers and consumers of other cultures, which they have remade in their own image. Indeed, while it is tempting to argue that the entry of European or American culture into modern Africa was supervised and enforced by colonialism (see **colonialism, neocolonialism, and postcolonialism**), it is imperative to remember that the spread of European and American culture, especially along the West African coast, was often initiated by Africans who had been repatriated from the West in the era of slavery. Some of the major agents of Westernization in Africa, scholars and preachers such as Johannes **Capitein** in the eighteenth century and Edward Blyden in the nineteenth century, had spent most of their early life in Europe or America. Journeys made by Africans across what has come to be known as the black Atlantic have been central in the configuration and reconfiguration of modernity (see **modernity and modernism**) and its attendant notions of nation, race, and culture.

Pan-Africanism and literature

To reflect on the idea of the African diaspora, then, is not only to rethink some of the foundational issues in African literary history, but also to recenter Africa in the making of the modern world. From a literary and cultural perspective the idea of African itself – the compulsive belief that there is a unified African culture that is the primary subject of an African literature – is itself a product of diaspora, for it was during the movements of African peoples in slavery and exile that they began to reconstitute their different regional and ethnic cultures as pan-African cultures. Not only were some of the earliest advocates of pan-Africanism black people born or brought up outside the continent itself, but in many cases native-born Africans acquired the pan-Africanist spirit that was to be one of the driving political and intellectual forces behind decolonization during their encoun-

ters with other black peoples in the diaspora. At one point or another, founders of the modern African nation (Jomo **Kenyatta**, Kwame Nkrumah, Namdi Azikwe, and Léopold Sédar **Senghor**), or an African literary tradition (Sol **Plaatje**, John **Dube**, Kobina **Sekyi**), had been part of a pan-African movement in Europe and America before they brought their ideas back to Africa.

The diaspora can be considered to be the crucible of African nationalism and by implication an African tradition of letters: it was in the diaspora that some of the most important literary movements in the history of African literature, including **negritude** and pan-Africanism, first emerged. Such movements were often the product of encounters between Africans from the continent and descendants of African slaves in the United States and the Caribbean, often meeting in European capitals. Such movements were indispensable in setting the terms for African literature and often created the political and social context for this literature. In addition, the writers and intellectuals from the African diaspora associated with these moments – Aimé Césaire, Leon Damas, and W.E.B. Dubois – can be considered the founders of African literature as much as the writers associated with this tradition.

The relationship between literary production and the ideologies of the African diaspora was symbiotic in form and character: the ideologies of blackness associated with political movements such as pan-Africanism became important themes in the literature produced by the powerful writers associated with these movements. At the same time, many writers came to occupy important positions as representatives of cultural nationalism because they seemed to embody a belief, dominant especially in the eighteenth and nineteenth centuries and the early twentieth century, that art was one of the key ingredients in the fight for human freedom and the construction of an autonomous African nation. Questions of culture and the role of literature in the social uplift of Africans were central in all pan-Africanist conferences from 1895 to 1958.

But if cultural and aesthetic practices associated with the African diaspora are as old as the dispersal of African peoples beginning in Asia Minor and the

Levantine Mediterranean before the Christian era, it is important to note that as a conceptual and descriptive category the idea of the African diaspora is fairly recent and its usage has been characterized by the debates and issues. According to some historians, it was not until the high nationalist period in the mid 1940s and early 1950s that the concept of the African diaspora became a uniform term for referring to the experiences of Africans in the global world. The term, whose descriptive and conceptual goal was nothing less than the production of a universal history of the African experience, was developed in reaction against a Eurocentric historiography which, even as late as the mid 1960s, was insisting that the African did not have a narrative of history. In the age of nationalism, scholars of Africa and Africans abroad began to invoke previous histories, often produced on the margins of Western discourses, which had sought to affirm the place of Africans in, and their contributions to, world history.

The idea of diaspora

But what generated the idea of the African diaspora in the first place? The most obvious reason is that from the mid nineteenth century onwards, Africans at home and abroad needed to counter the narratives developed by Europeans to justify colonialism and by Americans to rationalize slavery. In other words, the imagined nations of the pan-African imagination needed an affirmative version of the African experience, and this could be founded not simply in the heroic acts of Africans in the past, but also in the writings of those Africans or people of African descent who came forward to argue that Africa had not been a historical wasteland cut off from world history. "Africa is no vast island, separated by an immense ocean from other parts of the globe," noted Edward Blyden in an address he gave during his 1880 tour of the United States. It was not a continent "cut off through the ages from the men who have made and influenced the desires of mankind," but one closely connected "both as source and nourisher, with some of the most potent influences which have affected for good the history of the world" (Shepperson, 1993: College Station, Texas).

But developing an affirmative version of African

history, society, and culture had to confront a number of challenges. The first challenge attendant to the category of diaspora was already apparent in the very language of Blyden's address, the biblical language inherent in its title – "Ethiopia Stretching Her Hand" – and in its eschatological register. For Blyden, as for many of the pan-Africanists of the nineteenth century, the Bible was the ur-text of the discourse of the African world. As the historian George Shepperson has noted, for Africans in the diaspora, the Bible was "the major work through which the imagery and, by comparison, the idea of the concept of the African diaspora have developed" (1993: College Station, Texas). When the concept of diaspora became a central term of reference in the late nineteenth century, it could not escape the fact that the concept derived from the experiences of the Jewish people. But in order for the concept of diaspora to be applied to the experiences of the Africans in the New World, the term needed to be translated to apply to the African experience of exile and dispersal.

The question of diaspora had to deal with another challenge, what Elliott Skinner has described as the complex and dialectical contradiction that characterizes the relations between peoples in diasporas and their ancestral homelands: how to account for the painful forces that created the exile or dispersal in the first place, how to atone for the circumstances that led to the separation of self from home, and how to revert the discourse of exile and separation into one of identity and belonging.

A further challenge to the African appropriation of the idea of diaspora was methodological in nature: how to recover and reconstitute narratives of diaspora from their repressed or lost past and how to conceptualize and account for what appeared to be separate cultural survivals in new, syncretic worlds. This problem, which was the crux of a famous debate between Melville Herskovits and Franklin Frasier, two of the most prominent scholars of the African diaspora, has been one of the most contentious issues in the study of African cultures in the Americas. This was the context of this debate: in order to counter the thesis, prevalent in the 1920s, that the passage from the continent to American slavery had deracinated all the insignias of Africa in the culture of the slaves, Herskovits was keen to identify African elements in black cultures in the New World. By the same token, in order to claim American citizenship for black subjects, Frazier was keen to cast their relationship to Africa as no different from that of European migrants, such as the Pennsylvania Dutch, to their ancestral homes. If it now appears that both Herskovits and Frasier were right in their essential claims, it was not simply because the relationship between diasporas and homelands is inherently complex, but also because what the African diaspora is or is not depends on the periods and regions scholars choose to emphasize. African elements have been more pronounced in certain parts of the world than in others.

The final challenge facing scholars of the African diaspora is that the diasporic condition emerged from events that could not be explained simply in terms of what was happening in the homeland (Africa) or the diasporic space in Asia, Europe, or the Americas. On the contrary, the African diaspora was the product of the interaction between both places of origin and exile and thus demanded what Colin Palmer (1996: College Station, Texas) has called "explanations and justifications" that emerge from different periods of these encounters. For example, the idea of a unified pan-African culture was dominant in the nationalist period and tended to dissipate after decolonization. Until the 1960s, ideologies of pan-Africanism tended to have a greater appeal in the United States and the Caribbean than in South America and Europe. The increase in African migration to Europe in the 1980s and the emergence of African writers who work and live in European countries is increasingly changing the literary landscape. African literature thus comes to be located in a unique global moment: the continent's most important writers are as likely to be found in Europe and North America as they are in the continent itself. At the same time, African writers or their descendants have produced literatures that are increasingly being recognized as important to new homelands and diasporas in a variety of languages, traditions, and genres.

Further reading

Harris, Joseph E. (ed.) (1993) *Global Dimensions of the African Diaspora*, Washington, DC: Howard University Press.

Jalloh, A. and Maizlish, S.E. (eds) (1996) *The African Diaspora*, College Station, Texas: Texas A & M University Press.

Knight, F.W. (1989) "The African Diaspora," in J.F. Ade Ajayi (ed.) *General History of Africa*, vol. VI, Paris: UNESCO; Oxford: Heinemann; Berkeley: University of California Press, pp. 749–72.

Palmer, Colin (1996) "Rethinking American Slavery," in A. Jalloh and S.E. Maizlish (eds) *The African Diaspora*, College Station, Texas: Texas A&M University Press, pp.73–99.

Shepperson, G. (1993) "African Diaspora: Concept and Context," in Joseph E. Harris (ed.) *Global Dimensions of the African Diaspora*, College Station: Texas A & M University Press, pp. 46–53.

SIMON GIKANDI

Dib, Mohammed

b. 1920, Algeria

novelist

Mohammed Dib is one of Algeria's most prolific writers. In the 1950s his realist work dealt with the rise of nationalism (see **nationalism and postnationalism**), and in the 1960s he began to experiment with novelistic forms. His subsequent work never returned to conventional narrative forms. Both in his writings on independent Algeria in the late 1960s and early 1970s and in his later work on immigration and exile, extensive dialogue and interior monologue take precedence over plot. His novels, poems, and short stories treat a variety of themes: mad love, a fascination with insanity, an obsession with death, the discovery of a mysterious femininity, and the search for hidden meaning. In addition, he has analyzed **gender and sexuality** and explored the political dilemmas of Algerian society.

Dib's first three novels comprise the Algeria trilogy, which follows Omar from a childhood of urban poverty, to an agricultural workers' strike in the countryside (site of the colonial expropriation of peasants), to his apprenticeship as a weaver. In the 1962 novel, *Who Remembers the Sea?* (*Qui se souvient de la mer?*), the Algerian revolution is represented through dreamlike fantasy and science fiction. *Iriaces* and *spirovirs* (neologisms for colonial weapons) hover above, and Minotaurs (French soldiers) chase after moles (freedom fighters). In a postface, Dib compares this novel to Picasso's *Guernica*, which abandoned realism as inadequate to communicate the horrors of war. In Dib's novel, the confused narrator's wife is an urban terrorist over whom he loses control. The explosions in the colonial city also set fire to the conjugal bedroom as her fire burns him to the core of his masculinity. Water, maternity, and memory are associated through a set of poetic images discernible even in the title, which plays on the homophony between "mother" and "sea" in French. A number of his poems share this symbolism in addition to exploring erotic themes.

After the revolution, Dib wrote a number of novels in which characters with differing views engage in debates about Algeria's future. Dib never returned to Algeria, and his subsequent life abroad is reflected in his later novels and poems. Published in 1977, *Habel* is perhaps Dib's most provocative and least understood novel. The eponymous character (a biblical reference to Cain's brother) is an immigrant who frequently wanders about Paris. A writer, alternatively called the Old Man and the Lady of Mercy, introduces him to a secret life and practices he does not understand. This encounter with homosexuality challenges his notion of his own sexuality. During a gathering, he witnesses a performance of self-castration and is at once nauseated and enticed. He subsequently makes love with the Old Man, whom he then kills in revenge.

Further reading

Desplanques, François (1992) "The Long, Luminous Wake of Mohammed Dib," *Research in African Literatures* 23, 2: 71–88.

Dib, M. (1985) *Who Remembers the Sea?*, Washington, DC: Three Continents Press.

Hayes, Jarrod (2000) "Sex on Fire," in Jarrod Hayes, *Queer Nations: Marginal Sexualities in the Maghreb*, Chicago: University of Chicago Press.

JARROD HAYES

Dieng, Mame Younousse

b. 1940, Senegal

novelist

Mame Younousse Dieng is one of only a few Senegalese writers to publish in Wolof as well as in French (see **Wolof literature**). The policy of cultural assimilation that the French implemented in Africa during the period of colonialism retarded the development of literatures in African languages even further than is the case in Anglophone Africa (see **colonialism, neocolonialism, and post-colonialism**). Although the **language question** bedevils almost all African writers, Francophone Africa has yet to find a writer of **Ngugi wa Thiong'o**'s fame and stature who will support African-language literature. Indeed, most Francophone writers still publish in France. Writers such as Dieng or Cheikh Aliou **Ndao** deserve honor for publishing in their own language in Africa.

Authenticity as well as courage distinguishes Dieng's writing, for she writes about women's problems frankly. Her novels have a melodramatic touch; however, the skeptical reader must remember that women take great risks in Senegal when they choose to marry for love or fight for an education. Marriage brings suffering to Dieng's heroine Ndeela in her novel *Aawo bi* (The First Wife) (1992). Her only work in French, *L'Ombre en feu* (The Shadow on Fire) (1997), depicts a young woman's struggle to gain an education (see **education and schools**) and the right to choose her own husband. The novel ends tragically, but Kura, like Mame Younousse Dieng herself, is a memorable heroine.

Further reading

D'Alméïda, Irène (1994) *Francophone African Women Writers: Destroying the Emptiness of Silence*, Gainesville: University Presses of Florida.

Stringer, Susan (1996) *The Senegalese Novel by Women: Through Their Own Eyes*, New York: Peter Lang.

LISA McNEE

Diescho, Joseph

b. 1955, Namibia

novelist

Joseph Diescho was born and raised near the Roman Catholic mission of Andara in northern Namibia. Through the help and guidance of the Church he went to Rundu Secondary School and thereafter the University of Fort Hare, South Africa. After a brief period working for Consolidated Diamond Mines (CDM) in Oranjemund, he returned to Fort Hare to pursue higher studies. He later studied at Hamburg University in Germany and Columbia University in the United States of America.

In his first novel, *Born of the Sun: A Namibian Novel* (1988), Diescho tells the story of Namibia from colonialism to independence as it was experienced through a laboring man, following his life from childhood, through work in the mines, imprisonment, and later his involvement in the liberation struggle. His second novel, *Troubled Waters* (1993), is about transition. Set in the 1970s, the narrative focuses on two young people who are being shaken loose from their roots in family and culture by the winds of political change. Diescho, who is also a lay preacher in the Catholic Church in Namibia, has published two novels in Rukavango, his native language.

OUSMANE BA

Dike, (Roylini) Fatima

b. 1948, Langa, South Africa

playwright, actor, short story writer, and poet

The South African playwright, actor, short story writer, and poet Fatima Dike was born in Langa, near Cape Town. She received a good Catholic education (see **education and schools**) during which she developed a love of classics and history, and her English became as good as her mother tongue, Xhosa. Her choices for a career were, however, limited and at first she worked in steakhouses and a butchery. Then she was made

stage manager at the Space Theatre in Cape Town and encouraged to write her first play, *Sacrifice of Kreli* (1976), which was an instant success. Set in 1885, it tracks a defeated Xhosa king in exile, avoiding capture by the victorious British. In this, as in her other works, Dike considers the recovery and redeployment of stories from the period before apartheid vital to her understanding of the present (see **apartheid and post-apartheid**).

In 1979 Dike was invited to attend the International Writing Program at the University of Iowa. She remained in the USA for four years. Back in South Africa, she was a leading proponent of protest, black consciousness, and women's liberation in theater. Subsequent works record the drama of urban black life with an emphasis on the question of gender, especially the representation of strong, independent women in literature (see **gender and sexuality**). Dike considers that theater is a platform for liberation and that this notion has remained important in South Africa since the inception of democracy. She believes in a politics of humor, and especially the use of laughter as liberating.

ELAINE M. PEARSON

Diop, Birago

b. 1906, Dakar, Senegal; d. 1989, Dakar, Senegal

poet and storyteller

Birago Diop has left a profound imprint on African literature as perhaps the best author of folk tales. A member of the **negritude** movement, he first came to the attention of the public through his poem "Souffle" (Breath), published in *Anthology de la nouvelle poésie nègre et malgache* (Anthology of New Negro and Malagasy Poetry) edited by L.S. **Senghor** in 1948. With great economy, the poem captures the belief, common in African traditional societies, that the dead remain forever present among the living. But his greatest achievement has been the writing of folk tales inspired by the oral tradition of the griots and storytellers of the western Sahel, particularly Senegal and Mali (see **oral literature and performance**; **Sahelian** literatures in French). His celebrated books, *The Tales of Amadou Koumba* (*Les Contes d'Amadou Koumba*) (1947) and *Les Nouveaux Contes d'Amadou Koumba* (The New Tales of Amadou Koumba) (1958), have earned him a permanent place among the best of the pioneers of African literature. These stories seek to reveal an African culture from inside, thus allowing the reader to witness directly life in traditional, often rural settings, to laugh and to cry at the follies of humans through the example of animal characters who are endowed with a highly complex psychology. His **autobiography** provides an important insight into his own life and into a period and milieu hardly known today.

KANDIOURA DRAME

Diop, Boubacar Boris

b. 1946, Dakar, Senegal

novelist

Boubacar Boris Diop is one of the most talented postcolonial novelists from Senegal and his works are strongly characterized by a sustained meditation upon the postcolonial condition in Africa (see **colonialism, neocolonialism, and postcolonialism**). His four novels *Le Temps de Tamango* (The Time of the Tamango) (1981), *Les Tambours de la mémoire* (The Drums of Memory) (1990), *Les Traces de la meute* (The Tracks of the Pack) (1993), *Le Cavalier et son ombre* (The Horseman and His Shadow) (1997), *Murambi: le livre des ossements* (Murambi: The Book of the Stacks of Bones) (2000), and the play *Thiaroye, terre rouge* (Thiaroye Red Earth) (1981) all deal with the issue of memory. Two intertwined veins flow from his writings: an interrogation of the past through the present and an interrogation of the power of narrative to render the postcolonial condition intelligible. His engaging novels carry the reader off into an exciting adventure of mythology and history, legends and literature, individual and collective struggles for power. At the same time, the texts surreptitiously bring the reader to partake of the unsettling pleasures of writing as an adventure fraught with danger. In *Murambi*, a novel inspired by the Rwandan mass killings of 1994, Diop takes a turn

toward a deceptively simple transparent language and narrative mode, which he uses deftly to interrogate the naked bones of the dead. The novels of Boubacar Boris Diop have received many awards in Senegal and the Francophone world.

KANDIOURA DRAME

Diop, David Mandessi

b. 1927, Bordeaux, France; d. 1960, Dakar, Senegal

poet

Before he died in a plane crash, where his manuscripts were lost, David Mandessi Diop was considered to be one of the most promising black poets of his generation. And if few African writers have been mourned as much as Diop, it is because he was immensely popular among his readers and peers, largely because his poems, published in 1955 under the significant title of *Hammer Blows* (*Coups de pilon*), expressed so profoundly the spirit and mood of a large segment of black youth in Africa and the diaspora during the period of transition from colonialism (see **colonialism, neocolonialism, and postcolonialism**). Among **negritude** writers, his poetic language was more directly consonant with the sentiments of black youth coming to age during the watershed years of the struggle for independence. The son of a Cameroonian mother and a Senegalese father, Diop was born in Bordeaux and spent his childhood in France. But among his generation of writers, he was seen as the standard-bearer, in poetic terms, of the aspirations of a whole new generation of postcolonial writers, determined to act as agents of positive change and to initiate a black renaissance on the ashes of colonialism. Although his poetry is sometimes characterized as essentially militant, it covers, in fact, a greater range of tones and experiences and avoids exoticism and pedantic language. His poem "Rama Kam" remains one of the most vibrant love poems in African literature.

Further reading

Diop, David Mandessi (1973) *Hammer Blows and*

Other Writings, trans. Simon Mpondo and Frank Jones, Bloomington, Indiana: Indiana University Press.

KANDIOURA DRAME

Dipoko, Mbella Sonne

b. 1936, Cameroon

novelist, poet, and painter

The Cameroonian Anglophone novelist, poet, and painter Mbella Sonne Dipoko represents the first generation of Anglophone Cameroonian novelists and is still considered, along with Kenjo **Jumbam**, as one of the foremost writers of Anglophone Cameroonian literature. His novel *Because of Women* (1968) is one of the best-known Cameroonian novels written in English, and is certainly his signature work. The novel details the tribulations of a fisherman who has difficulty choosing between two potential wives, ultimately gaining neither in a series of tragic events borne of his inability to fathom his true desires and needs. The novel has been the subject of controversy, first when the British publishing house Heinemann initially balked at publishing a novel containing scenes of explicit sex in its famous African Writers Series, and then from accusations that the text was misogynist. His other novel, *A Few Nights and Days* (1966), is set in France and follows the lives of four students, including an interracial couple, and investigates African–European relations. Dipoko has also published a volume of poetry, *Black and White in Love* (1972). One of the poems, "Our Destiny," a 1963 poem in the **negritude** tradition, is frequently anthologized.

Further reading

Dipoko, Mbella Sonne (1968) *Because of Women*, London: Heinemann.

STEPHEN BISHOP

Djabali, Hawa

b. 1945, Créteil, France

novelist and playwright

Born in France, Hawa Djabali moved to Algeria after independence. Since 1989 she has been active in the Brussels theater milieu. Her novels and plays articulate analyses of gender relations in present and past Algeria with female characters who confront the many complex day-to-day forms of sexual harassment, discrimination, and oppression (see **gender and sexuality**). In the late 1990s, she examined the effect of fundamentalist movements on women's lives. Many of her characters are named only by personal pronouns, and her narrative voices often jump between first- and third-person pronouns. Djabali also frequently uses frank sexual language to articulate a harsh analysis of the institutionalization of sexuality in Algerian culture as well as the value of female desire. Her best-known work, the novel *Agave*, tells the story of Farida, who, like the plant named in its title, has lain dormant for dozens of years and then suddenly blossoms when she meets Aïcha, an eccentric storyteller and sculptor. In her works, nurturing relationships between women often provide a source for multiple forms of women's resistance as Djabali explores the possibility of a specifically Algerian feminism, often based on an alternative reading of "tradition."

Further reading

Djabali, H. (1983) *Agave*, Paris: Publisud.

JARROD HAYES

Djaout, Tahar

b. 1954, Hzeffoun, Algeria; d. 1993, Bainem, Algeria

journalist and writer

Born in Kabylia, the Francophone journalist and writer Tahar Djaout was an acerbic critic of bureaucratic absurdity and political repression in post-independence Algeria, as well as of the armed fundamentalist opposition which assassinated him in 1993. His early novel, short stories, and poetry explicitly treat questions of sexuality, and many of his early poems incorporate a violent writing style. In *Les Chercheurs d'os* (The Bone Searchers) (1984), the narrator digs up the remains of his brother, who died fighting in the revolution. These bones become a skeleton at the feast of the new elite's power, maintained by betraying the revolutionary ideals for which the brother fought. In *L'Invention du désert* (The Invention of the Desert) (1987), writing the history of an eleventh-century dynasty becomes an allegorical reflection on contemporary Algeria by revealing past examples of gaining power through religious policing and sexual repression. Subsequent novels deal with such political questions more explicitly. Perhaps no other Algerian writer has so dearly paid for his defense of liberty in the face of puritanism.

Further reading

Hayes, Jarrod (2000) "Skeletons in the Closet: Tahar Djaout's Betrayal of National Secrets," in Jarrod Hayes, *Queer Nations: Marginal Sexualities in the Maghreb*, Chicago: University of Chicago Press.

JARROD HAYES

Djebar, Assia

b. 1936, Cherchell, Algeria

novelist and filmmaker

Algerian-born, Muslim-raised, Paris-educated, Assia Djebar has been writing for close to half a century, accumulating a considerable body of works. She has tackled all genres: poetry, plays, short stories, novels, and essays. She has written, directed, and edited her own films, winning the Biennale Prize at the 1979 Venice Film Festival with her very first attempt, *La Nouba des femmes du mont Chenoua* (The "Nouba," or ritual festival, of the Women of Mount Chenoua). She has staged her own plays, as well as translated and directed the plays of others (Amiri Baraka's, for example). And in 2000 she authored an operatic libretto, "Filles

d'Ismaël dans le vent et la tempête" (Daughters of Ishmael, through Wind and Storm). Based on her 1991 narrative on the life of the Prophet, *Far from Madina*, this oratorio was performed to excellent reviews in Rome and at the Palermo Arts Festival. A second version, in classical Arabic this time, is commissioned for future performance in Holland.

She has been honored with multiple awards that recognize not only literary talent but moral courage as well; among these were the 1995 Maurice Maaeterlinck Prize in Brussels, the University of Oklahoma Neustadt Prize in 1996, the US-based Yourcenar Prize in 1997, the 1998 International Palmi Prize in Italy, and the Frankfurt Book Fair Peace Prize in 2000. No less symbolic was the 1997 Fonlon–Nichols Prize of the African Literature Association, for which her keynote speech rendered poignant homage to two predecessors, **Sony Labou Tansi** and Ken **Saro-Wiwa**, who had paid with their lives for their principles. As the 1994 president of Strasbourg's International Parliament of Writers, a European body committed to finding asylum for artists who have been threatened (the first president was Salman Rushdie), she was succeeded by Wole **Soyinka**. Such visibility has made her *persona non grata* back home, and it is not altogether certain that she is safe from reprisals in her self-imposed American exile.

A subject of empire, Djebar was born Fatma-Zohra Imalhayen on 30 June 1936 into an Arabo-Berber family. Her teacher father believed in the republican principles of 1789 and, shunning the veil, sent his daughters to French boarding school. Her mother, who insisted that they also receive Koranic training, revered the memory of a great-uncle beheaded for leading the nineteenth-century resistance against the French in the Chenoua mountains. His tribal last stand and the ensuing death by fire of men, women, children, and animals in the subterranean Dahra Caves figure prominently in the 1985 novel, *Fantasia: or an Algerian Cavalcade* (*L'Amour, la fantasia*), as does a piece on her father's fateful decision that would forever render her hostage to the colonizer's language. *Fantasia* is the first installment of an ambitious autobiographical tetralogy on which Djebar has been working for close to twenty years. Two more, *A Sister to Sheherazade* (*Ombre sultane*) and

So Vast a Prison (Vaste est la prison) have been completed. The fourth, *Les Larmes de Saint Augustin* (St Augustine's Tears), is in progress.

Djebar came of age as her country plunged into a brutal anti-colonial war that would last eight years (1954–62). By 1958, she was on the run and turned up in Tunis, where she finished a graduate degree under Louis Massignon, grand old man of Arabic studies in the West, while contributing to *el Moujahid*, the official mouthpiece of the revolution, under Frantz Fanon. Upon independence, she returned home to a teaching position at the University of Algiers. But further upheaval in her native land and increasingly difficult publishing conditions would result in a ten-year silence and a second exile to Paris in the 1980s. The civil war precipitated a third move to the United States in the 1990s, where she directed the Francophone Studies Center at the University of Louisiana–Baton Rouge. In 2001, she was appointed distinguished professor of French and Francophone literature at New York University.

She got her start barely out of her teens. In 1956, boycotting exams in solidarity with the Algerian war, she opted to pass the time writing. *The Mischief (La Soif)* came out the following summer to Parisian acclaim, in part because the author's tender age should have precluded such precocious diving into the lurid waters of adultery, abortion, and death among the acculturated Algerian upper class. To preserve propriety, she chose a pseudonym. Immediately translated in the US, *The Mischief* was favorably reviewed in the *New York Times* of 12 October 1958 and was soon followed by *Les Impatients* (The Impatient Ones), a novel in the same vein. Algerian nationalists were not amused. They condemned themes that did not serve the struggle, oblivious to the fact that her frank depictions of female eroticism heralded a revolution of a different order.

She turned to the realities of war with *Les Enfants du nouveau monde* (Children of the New World) (1962) and *Les Alouettes naïves* (Innocent Larks) (1967), stories centered on women's role in urban resistance as well as on the battlefield of a war where torture was practiced regardless of sex. Less sanguine than Fanon, who believed that their sacrifice would gain women the rights refused them under colonial oppression, Djebar was already hinting at their alienation. Her first collection of short stories, *Women of Algiers in Their Apartment (Femmes d'Alger dans leur appartement)* (1980) anticipated the systematic denial of their civil rights. Barely birthed, the new socialist paradise was returning to tired allegories of national purity that have yet to abate: Woman-as-Nation; Woman-as-Mother; Woman-as-Sacrifice; Woman-as-Islam. Conflating real human beings and political symbols, the official discourse blocked all female agency. By 1976, a new charter had re-established Islam as state religion.

Written in Algeria during her self-imposed silence but published in France in 1980, *Women of Algiers* prepared the ground for Djebar's monumental tetralogy, simultaneously born of her cinematic experimentation and her own research into familial history. In overlapping narratives, the collective oral memory transmitted by the ancestral grandmothers of the Chenoua mountains – some of whom appear in the film *La Nouba des femmes du mont Chenoua* – resists the official version of the conquerors, whose documents she quotes without editorial intervention, letting their unremitting brutality speak for itself. Djebar's tetralogy, which may well become her magnum opus, starts with the ruthless French invasion of the 1830s (*Fantasia*), uncovers the despair of modern women for whom independence has only brought further oppression (*Sheherazade*), and reaches all the way back to Numidia's defiance of Imperial Rome (*So Vast a Prison*). The last volume, *Augustine*, deals with the final days of St Augustine, the Maghrebian-born, Greek-taught, Roman-raised, Christian-convert bishop of what is now the Algerian sea-port of Annaba, and his dying meditation on the human cost of empire. The projected quartet embraces all of North Africa's hybrid past, uncovering its multiglossic, multicultural inheritance to challenge the West's too simple oppositional version of the relationship between colonial and postcolonial history.

· But the project also expands with a vengeance on thematics that have never left her: the silenced women of Islam. By the 1980s, as far as critics on either side of the Atlantic were concerned, Djebar had become the unchallenged feminist of North African letters, praised above all for "writing the body" ("écriture feminine"). The first two volumes of the tetralogy were translated in London within months of each other and her name was associated with that of Egyptian Nawal **el-Saadawi**, both celebrated as champions of women's eruption into modernity against an ever-repressive, ever-regressive tradition. In Djebar's case, the fact that unveiled women and Westernized intellectuals were the primary targets for assassination in her country's civil war only reinforced this stereotypical response. Djebar herself, however, in her many interviews has maintained a cautious distance from first-world feminism. Preferring liberation by reason of humanity and justice to liberation by reason of gender alone, she holds up a critical mirror to the West's patronizing gaze. For example, in *Ces Voix qui m'assiègent* (These Voices that Besiege/Obsess Me), a collection of essays presented for a doctoral degree at the Paul Valéry University of Montpellier (France) in 1999, she dissects the epistemological high-wire act of all postcolonial writers, male or female, who function in the colonizer's language. If she could once upon a time agree with Audre Lorde that the master's tools were lethal, she has since shed what she calls "this tunic of Nessus, the language of the Others in which I was enveloped from childhood" (*Fantasia*, 1985: London). Now, she confidently manipulates the language of the colonizer to decolonize the mind.

Thus she has interrupted her work on the quartet to take up political issues. Appalled at the fanaticism that bars women from public life, an eyewitness to the bloodbath in the streets of Algiers as fundamentalists battled government tanks, she responded in 1991 with *Far from Madina* (*Loin de Médine*). In this work, Djebar, a well-trained historian, stresses the active contribution of women to the embattled creed, a foundational role that subsequent leaders had erased altogether. A practicing Muslim, she accuses modern-day believers of distorting religion for political ends. As the number of victims from the political crisis in Algeria mounted in 1996, Djebar mourned the loss of her country's best and brightest in *Algerian White* (*Le Blanc de l'Algérie*), a dirge to colleagues, friends, and a murdered family member, that, for all its stunning beauty, did not eschew graphic details. Within the year, this was followed by a second collection of short stories, *Oran, langue morte* (Oran,

Dead Language), in which the author charged all sides in the Algerian conflict for shoring up a caricature of Islam in the dubious name of a singular Maghrebian authenticity.

Djebar's prodigious output continues. In the year 2000 alone, she was at work concurrently on the oratorio, which she wrote and staged, a series of lectures in Europe and the US, a novella, and the final volume of the tetralogy. Yet she has met with nothing but glacial silence or virulent *ad feminam* attacks in her homeland. For the tragedy that is Algeria today, mired like so many countries on the African continent in an imploding civil war that has killed over 110,000 civilians since 1990, a place enjoying neither peace nor prosperity forty-some years after the victorious 1962 liberation from the French, the writer indicts those who would force historical amnesia on the Maghreb. She loathes equally aging *apparachiks* eager to impose a monolingual Arab republic on a multi-ethnic, multiglossic reality, and fundamentalists determined to turn it into a medieval theocracy. A powerful ethical voice for Africa and for Islam, Assia Djebar has become the conscience of a nation.

Select bibliography

Djebar, Assia (1958) *The Mischief*, trans. Frances Frenaye, New York: Simon and Schuster.

——(1958) *Les Impatients* (The Impatient Ones), Paris: Julliard.

——(1962) *Les Enfants du nouveau monde* (Children of the New World), Paris: Julliard.

——(1967) *Les Alouettes naïves* (Innocent Larks), Paris: Julliard.

——(1969) *Poèmes pour l'Algérie heureuse* (Poems for Happy Algeria), Paris: Julliard.

——(1969) *Rouge l'aube* (Red Dawn), Algiers: SNED.

——(1979) *La Nouba des femmes du mont Chenoua* (The Nouba of the Women of Mount Chenoua), film, distributed in the US by Women Make Movies.

——(1980, 1992) *Women of Algiers in Their Apartment*, trans. Marjoljin de Jager, Charlottesville: University of Virginia Press.

——(1985) *Fantasia*, trans. Dorothy S. Blair, London: Quartet.

——(1987) *A Sister to Sheherazade*, trans. Dorothy S. Blair, London: Quartet.

——(1994) *Far from Madina*, trans. Dorothy S. Blair, London: Quartet.

——(1996) *Le Blanc de l'Algérie*, Paris: Albin Michel; English translation *Algerian White* (in progress), trans. David Kelley, New York: Seven Stories Press.

——(2000) *So Vast a Prison*, trans. Betsy Wing, New York: Seven Stories Press.

Further reading

Clerc, Marie-Jeanne (1997) *Assia Djebar: Écrire. Transgresser. Resister*, Paris: L'Harmattan.

Donadey, Anne (2001) *Recasting Postcolonialism: Women Writing Between Worlds*, Portsmouth, New Jersey: Heinemann Studies in African Literature.

Merini, Rafika (1999) *Two Major Francophone Women Writers: Assia Djebar and Leila Sebbar*, London: Peter Lang Series on Francophone Culture and Literature.

Mortimer, Mildred (1990) *Journeys through the African Novel*, Portsmouth, New Hampshire: Heinemann Educational.

Siebert, Renate (1997) *Andare ancora all cuore delle ferite: Renate Siebert intervista Assia Djebar* (Anchoring the Wounded Heart: Renate Siebert Interviews Assia Djebar), Milano: Tartaruga Edizioni.

CLARISSE ZIMRA

Djedidi, Hafedh

b. 1954, Tunisia

poet and novelist

Tunisian poet and novelist Hafedh Djedidi started his literary career as a cultural correspondent for the Tunisian newspaper *Le Temps*, a role that he still occasionally performs and enjoys. Although known primarily for his collections of poems, *Rien que le fruit pour toute bouche* (Nothing but Fruit for Every Mouth) (1986) and *Intempéries* (Inclemencies) (1988), his most celebrated work is the novel *Le Cimeterre ou le souffle du Vénérable* (The Cemetery or the Breath of the Venerated) (1990). In this novel, Djedidi plays with history, myth, and magic to spin the story of

his hero, Dhafer, who crosses through time and space, from the fall of the Arabs in Andalusia to the turn of the twentieth century. Inspired by the oral traditions of the *fdawi*, Tunisian public storytellers, Djedidi distributes the narrative of the novel between multiple characters. In so doing he claims to add his own pen to centuries of Tunisian stories. While the majority of his published work is written in French, Djedidi also writes in Arabic, exploring the interaction and interplay between the two languages.

Further reading

Djedidi, Hafedh (1990) *Le Cimeterre ou le souffle du Vénérable* (The Cemetery or the Breath of the Venerated), Paris: Présence Africaine.

KATARZYNA PIEPRZAK

Djinadou, Moudjib

b. 1965, Porto Novo, Benin

novelist

Born in Porto Novo, Dahomey (now Benin), Moudjib Djinadou attended the National University of Benin before studying law in France. After receiving his law degree in 1994 he worked for the United Nations High Commission for Refugees. Djinadou belongs to a new generation of Beninese writers; his literary career began in the late 1980s when he won third prize in the National Competition in Arts and Letters. He has since published four novels. He came to national attention when he won the first Beninese Competition in Arts and Letters for an unpublished first novel, and is best known for his 1991 *Mo Gbé, le cri de mauvaise augure* (Mo Gbé, the Ill-Fated Cry), one of the first African novels to deal with the subject of AIDS. "Mo Gbé," the name of the novel's protagonist, is a Yoruba expression which means "I'm done with," and AIDS is the last in a series of hardships (including drugs, rape, and prison) which befall Djinadou's ambitious hero.

Further reading

Djinadou, Moudjib (1991) *Mo Gbé, le cri de mauvaise augure* (Mo Gbé, the Ill-Fated Cry), Paris: L'Harmattan.

RACHEL GABARA

Djoleto, Amu

b. 1929, Ghana

novelist, poet, and educator

The opening lines of his poem, "A Passing Thought," describe Amu Djoleto, the Ghanaian novelist, poet, and educator: "What you do expect me sing, I will not, /What you do not expect me croak, I will." Some of Djoleto's own convictions emerge in the lesson Old Mensa learns in his first novel, *The Strange Man* (1967), that earthly posses-sions are poor substitutes for honor and health. Politicians who seem to be incapable of serving anybody but themselves bear the brunt of Djoleto's satire in *Money Galore* (1975). And in *Hurricane of Dust* (1987: Harlow), the novelist introduces readers to "Accra after four coups in ten years with a two-year interlude of elected government not to mention attempted coups." Djoleto has been an interested observer of the postcolonial Ghanaian sociopolitical landscape since the 1950s, and these observations inform novels such as *Money Galore* (see **colonialism, neocolonialism, and postcolo-nialism**). His writing suggests that the effect of a symbolic "hurricane" on the body politic, and the danger of the Ghanaian landscape itself being turned into mere "dust [and ashes]" by a metaphoric firestorm, have given him cause for concern; but he finds ways to remind his readers that there is good reason for having Old Mensa's house "guarded by a vigilant … dog, called Hope."

Further reading

Djoleto, Amu (1987) *Hurricane of Dust*, Harlow, UK: Longmans.

KOFI OWUSU

Djungu-Simba Kamatenda, Charles

b. 1953, Kamituga, Congo-Zaire

journalist, teacher, publisher, and writer

Charles Djungu-Simba Kamatenda began his prolific literary career with fables, stories, and comics for young people published by Éditions Saint-Paul in Kinshasa. In 1989, L'Harmattan published his political satire *Cité 15: roman zaïrois* (Slum 15: A Zairian Novel), dedicated to the homeless of the earth. While managing his own press, Éditions du Trottoir, with offices in Kinshasa and Brussels, Djungu-Simba published his next novel, *On a échoué* (We Have Failed) (1991), and a collection of poems, *Turbulences* (Turbulence) (1992). He also edited *Sandruma: On démon-cratise!* (San-druma: We democratize!) (1994), a collection of short stories inspired by political events in Congo-Zaire, thereby giving voice to authors whom Nadine Fettweis has termed *écrivains du silence*, "writers of silence," because of the absence of publishing outlets in countries with scarce material resources. Djungu-Simba has been a broadcaster and has also taught French at the National Pedagogical Institute in Kinshasa. In the post-Mobutu era, he published *En attendant Kabila* (Waiting for Kabila) (1997) before seeking refuge in Europe where he continues to write.

Further reading

Fettweis, Nadine (1995) "Les écrivains du silence. Présentation des écrivains zaïrois non exilés" (The Writers of Silence. Presentation of Non-Exiled Zairean Writers) *Matatu* 13–14: 93–105.

JANICE SPLETH

Dlamini, John Charles

b. 1916, Edendale, Pietermaritzburg, South Africa; d. 1997, South Africa

poet

Known as "Bulima Ngiyeke" (Foolishness Take Leave of Me), the South African poet John Charles

Dlamini was born in Edendale near Pietermaritz-burg. He was educated at St Thomas, Marianhill, Ntshanga, and St Francis College, before receiving his BA degree (1959) from the University of Natal. Dlamini taught in colleges including eShowe, eNtuzuma, and Oakford. His contribution to African literature is in Zulu poetry. Some of his works are *Inzululwane* (Dizziness) (1958), *Imfihlo Yokunyamala* (The Secret of the Disappearance) (1973), *Amavovo Ezinyembezi* (Dregs of Tears) (1981), *Isihluthulelo* (The Key) (1988), *Sadabuka Isizwe* (The Nation Mourns/is Torn) (1989), and *Kusindwe Ngobethole* (There is a Celebration) (1997). His special skill in word play always yields intricate rhyme and rich imagery in his poems. Dlamini is very sensitive to domination of one person by another, but his protest philosophy does not advocate hatred toward the white race, even in the works written during the apartheid period (see **apartheid and post-apartheid**); rather, it encourages self-respect and truthfulness for the African self. Bulima is one of the major poets who contributed to J.S.M. Matsebula's 1957 history-making Zulu anthology, *Iqoqo Lezinkondlo* (A Collection of Poems).

ZODWA MOTSA

Dongala, Emmanuel

b. 1941, Brazzaville, Congo

chemist, novelist, and poet

The Congolese writer Emmanuel Dongala was born to a Congolese father and a Central African mother and was educated in the United States and France, where he specialized in chemistry and physics. After serving as dean of science at the university in Brazzaville and the president of the Congolese chapter of PEN, the international writers' organization, Dongala was forced into exile during the Congolese civil war in the late 1990s. He came to international prominence with the publication and later translation of his third book, *Little Boys Come from the Stars* (*Les Petits Garçons naissent aussi des étoiles*) (1998), the story of an African boy who serves as the reader's satirical guide through key moments of Congolese history. The novel was awarded the Témoin du Monde Prize sponsored by Radio-France Intérnational. Dongala's earlier work, *The Fire of Origins* (*Le Feu des origines*) (1987) was praised for its weaving of social reality and myth and its subtle attempt to represent the history of Africa from the vantage point of postcolonial failure, and was awarded numerous awards including the Grand Prix d'Afrique Noire and the Grand Prix de la Foundation de France.

MEREDITH MARTIN

Doumbi-Fakoly

b. 1944, Kati-Coua, Mali

novelist

Doumbi-Fakoly was born in Kati-Coua, Mali, but grew up in Senegal and studied in France on a bank scholarship. After a brief return to Mali between 1978 and 1980, he returned to France where he currently lives. Doumbi-Fakoly writes primarily political, historical, popular, and young-adult novels. His 1983 book *Morts pour la France* (Deaths for France) is a historical novel based on the story of African troops who were deployed to fight for France during the Second World War. The poignant tale exposes the brutal methods of conscription by the colonial French, as well as the hostile reception the African soldiers received when they returned to their native countries. His second novel, *La Retraite anticipée du Guide Suprême* (The Expected Retreat of the Supreme Guide) (1984) is a denunciation of the dictators who ruled Africa during the first thirty years of independence. *Certificat de Contrôle Anti-Sida* (Anti-Sida Certificate of Control) (1988) tells the story of a young boy of mixed race whose African father is wrongly accused of having AIDS. In *La Révolte des Galsénésiennes* (The Revolt of the Galsene) (1991), African women go on strike against their traditional roles, culminating in a national conference.

MEREDITH MARTIN

Driver, C.J.

b. 1939, South Africa

novelist, poet, and biographer

Charles Jonathan (Jonty) Driver, South African novelist, poet, and biographer, son of an Anglican clergyman, was educated at the universities of Cape Town (BA Hons, BEd) and Oxford (BPhil). After headships at various schools in England and Hong Kong, he ended his teaching career as Master of Wellington College in England. Driver's writing is informed by his experiences as president of NUSAS (the anti-apartheid National Union of South African Students) which he headed in 1963–4, his detention on political grounds for his opposition to apartheid (see **apartheid and post-apartheid**), and the statelessness consequent upon the withdrawal of his passport by the South African government. The prevalent themes in his fiction are alienation, exile, and nostalgia for what is lost; loyalty and betrayal; and attempts to reconcile violent revolutionary activity with the demands of conscience in order to bring about a new social and moral order. His style is realistic – he claims: "I have no taste for the surreal and the fantastic." His novels: *Elegy for a Revolutionary* (1969), *Send War in Our Time, O Lord* (1970) – both of which were banned in South Africa – *Death of Fathers* (1972), and *A Messiah of the Last Days* (1974) are marked by vivid characterization, subtle depiction of intricate human relationships, an urbane tone, and great technical skill. He has published six slim volumes of lyrical, witty, and ironic poems: *Occasional Light* (1979), *I Live Here Now* (1979), *Hong Kong Portraits* (1986), *In the Water Margins* (1994), *Holiday Haiku* (1997), and *Requiem* (1997/8). His biography of the liberal political activist *Patrick Duncan: South African and Pan-African* (1980) was highly acclaimed. He is an occasional reviewer for British newspapers such as the *Guardian*.

MALCOLM HACKSLEY

du Plessis, Menán

b. 1952, Cape Town, South Africa

poet and novelist

The South African writer Menán du Plessis was born in Cape Town and studied linguistics at the University of Cape Town (where she later taught) while involved in trade union activity. She began writing poetry (see **poetry and poetics**) but found that she needed space to incorporate the ethical complexities of her involvement, as a white woman of Afrikaans descent, in the sociopolitical struggle against apartheid (see **apartheid and post-apartheid**). Her first novel was accepted for publication but she withdrew it, sensing that her voice was not yet sufficiently mature. In 1983 du Plessis published *State of Fear* and, in 1989, *Longlive!* Both novels were well received internationally and have been translated widely. When *State of Fear* won the premier South African Sanlam Literary Award in 1986, however, she used her acceptance speech to attack the corporation that sponsored the award and donated the prize money to the United Democratic Front (a front organization for the then-banned African National Congress). Du Plessis' novels draw on a strong tradition of realism in fiction (see **realism and magical realism**) and convey a strong sense of time and place, especially the city of Cape Town in the midst of violent police action and popular protest in the 1980s. Yet the gaze in her works is primarily inward, concerned with the inner questioning and quest of marginalized characters in response to sociopolitical circumstances.

ELAINE M. PEARSON

al-Dū'ājī, 'Alī

b. 1909, Tunis, Tunisia; d. 1949, Tunis, Tunisia

novelist, short story writer, journalist, and painter

A mostly self-instructed artist, the Tunisian author

'Alī al-Dū'ājī was a poet, short story writer, novelist, playwright, journalist, painter, and caricaturist. He was one of the founding members of the Taḥt al-Sūr group, an intellectual and artistic group that was established toward the end of the 1920s and that remained active throughout the 1930s in Tunis. Al-Dū'ājī was opposed to elitist attitudes in art and life, and called for a literature that could be appealing and accessible to "the people." The characters of his fictional works were often taken from the lower social class. He wrote in simple Arabic about everyday life issues. This trait in his work and the sense of humor that characterized his writings contributed greatly to his popularity. Despite the fact that al-Dū'ājī was a prolific writer, the major part of his work is either lost or inaccessible. His only published works are the short story collection *Sleepless Nights* (*Sahirtu minhu al-layālī*) (1991), *Jawla bayna ḥānāt al-baḥr al-abyaḍ al-mutawassiṭ* (Bar-hopping along the Mediterranean) (1973), and *Taḥt al-Sūr* (By the Wall) (1973). While the bohemian lifestyle which al-Dū'ājī led contributed significantly to the enrichment of his literary production, it also led to his premature death.

Further reading

al-Dū'ājī, 'Alī (1991) *Sleepless Nights*, trans. William Granara, Tunis: Beit al-Hikma.

SARRA TLILI

Dube, John Langalibalele

b. 1871, Natal, South Africa; d. 1946, Durban, South Africa

novelist

The recent historical consensus of South African intellectual history is that the publication in 1904 of the "The Regeneration of Africa" manifesto by Pixley ka Isaka Seme (1880–1951) launched the New African movement. The movement formulated its historical project as the construction of South African modernity (see **modernity and modernism**). What is not as yet widely recognized is that, together with this manifesto, the

essays of John Langalibalele Dube and Solomon T. **Plaatje**, respectively "Are Negroes Better Off in Africa? Conditions and Opportunities of Negroes in America and Africa Compared" (1904) and "Negro Question" (1904), established that for the successful construction of this modernity a unity between New Negro modernity and New African modernity was felt to be essential. The singular distinction of Dube is that modeling himself on Booker T. Washington, he founded two institutions, the Ohlange Institute in 1901 and the *Ilanga lase Natal* (Natal Sun) newspaper in 1903, both of which determined the shape of South African intellectual modernity across much of the twentieth century. A brilliant generation of South African intellectuals were educated at the Ohlange Institute and published their writings, at the forefront of South African literary modernism, in *Ilanga lase Natal*. Benedict Wallet Vilakazi (1906–47) wrote excellent essays in the 1930s in this intellectual forum, while H.I.E. **Dhlomo** (1903–56) published his great prose poems of 1947 in it. The contribution of John Dube by way of these two institutional forms of modernity to South African culture far surpasses his own literary efforts, such as the novella *An African Tragedy* (1929) and the historical romance *U-Jeqe: Insila ka Shaka* (Jeqe: Shaka's Servant) (1931).

NTONGELA MASILELA

Dunqul, Amal

b. 1940, Qina, Egypt; d. 1983, Cairo, Egypt

poet

This Egyptian poet has gained prominence as one of the most innovative Arab poets of the twentieth century. Born in the Upper Egypt village of Qina to an al-Azahar graduate who taught Arabic and composed poetry, Dunqul read the copious collections of classical Arabic poetry available on his father's bookshelves. After finishing high school, Dunqul moved to Cairo to study Arabic at Cairo University, but soon left without obtaining a degree. Starting his poetic career at the age of 18, Dunqul published six collections of poetry. The distinctiveness of his style is described as well structured, lucid, symbolic, and musical. His poetry, nationalistic in tone, gave voice to the angry revolutionists across the Arab world. *'Al-Bukā' Bayna Yaday Zarqā' al-Yamāma* (Weeping before Zarqa' al-Yamama) (1969), a commonly celebrated poem by critics and readers, laments the defeat of the Arab countries in the war of June 1967. His work employs Arab heritage to depict the bitterness and agony felt by Arabs after the defeat. Regarded as one of his most memorable poems, *Lā Tusāliḥ* (Do Not Make Peace) (1976), was an appeal to Sādāt not to wound the pride of Arabs by making peace with Israel, commonly viewed as a brutal betrayal. Dunqul died in 1983, after a long struggle with cancer.

Further reading

ᶜAblah, al-Rūwayni (ed.) (1999) *Sifr Amal Dunqul* (The Book of Amal Dunqul), Cairo: al-Hay'ah al-Misriyah al-ᶜĀmah Lil-Kitāb.

KHALED AL MASRI

E

Easmon, Raymond Sarif

b. 1913, Freetown, Sierra Leone; d. 1997

doctor, playwright, and novelist

The Sierra Leone doctor, playwright, and novelist R. Sarif Easmon was born into a distinguished family of physicians in Freetown. Easmon was an outstanding medical student at the University of Durham, England, winning major awards in biology and anatomy and qualifying as a doctor at the age of 23. After serving for two years as a medical officer in the colonial medical service, Easmon resigned in protest against the discriminatory character of the service and went into private practice. Easmon's play, *Dear Parent and Ogre* (1964), won the Encounter Magazine Prize, and was initially produced by Wole **Soyinka** in Lagos in 1961. Easmon's second play, *The New Patriots* (1965), was performed in several West African countries. Easmon's plays are semi-comical commentaries on politics and culture in a community undergoing the birth throes of independence and corruption in the institutions of government. Although he was better known as a playwright than a novelist, Easmon also published *The Burnt Out Marriage* (1967), concerned with the theme of cultural conflict and the opposition between the values of precolonial society and modernity (see **modernity and modernism**), and his short stories have been collected in *The Feud* (1981).

SIMON GIKANDI

East African literature in English

General introduction

What unites East African literatures, generally accepted as literatures coming from Uganda, Tanzania, and Kenya, is their shared experience of British colonialism (see **colonialism, neocolonialism, and postcolonialism**). These states came under British colonial rule under different circumstances and during different historical periods. They eventually came to be known as the British East Africa Protectorate and were all subjected to the same colonial design with little variation, leading to a profound impact on the culture and lives of the people of the region. This is particularly evident in the way in which literatures from the region set out to explore the effects of the structures of colonialism on the psyche, and the general social and political life of the people in the sub-continent. The colonial experience is easily the dominant subject in East African literature, and as a natural corollary, politics and its impact on the lives of the colonized subjects is the major motivating force behind these literatures. In a fundamental sense, East African literature is wedded to colonialism in both its simultaneous rejection and appropriation of those forms and literary archetypes that came with the colonial experience itself and in its vicious critique of colonialism as a social evil that alienates a people, wrenching it out of its being.

If colonial experience is the unifying factor in East African literature, it is also true that it separates the literatures of the three countries in a significant way. For example, unlike Kenya, Tanzania and Uganda were largely non-settler economies, and as a result they did not go through a protracted and traumatic liberation war to get back land, as Kenya did. Therefore there is no major anti-colonial war and corresponding myths, other than the Maji Maji rebellion in the case of Tanzania during a brief German rule before World War I, to which writers from these two countries, particularly Ugandan writers, can refer. If in Kenya Mau Mau provides the myth upon which the schismatic segments of the Kenyan society are brought to order and if in land remains a recurring metaphor for economic and political change. In Ugandan literature problems of colonialism and specifically of neocolonialism are figured more in terms of cultural imperialism brought about by mission education and the influence of Christianity (see **Christianity and Christian missions**; **education and schools**). In the 1970s and beyond, the "Idi Amin motif," the country's reign of terror under the former military dictator, dominates the literatures of Uganda. The significance of Amin's era in Uganda lies in the creative impulse it engendered among Ugandans and non-Ugandans alike, leading to almost unprecedented flowering of literature in East Africa, only comparable to Mau Mau literature in the region. Tanzania's literary scene was significantly influenced by Nyerere's Arusha Declaration of 1967, the official government policy that guided both the political and the cultural life of Tanzania and privileged the use of the Kiswahili language, leading to a burgeoning of **Swahili literature**. Nevertheless, compared to the other two East African countries, the production of literature in English in Tanzania has stagnated and remains less imaginative than in Uganda and Kenya.

The intellectual literary tradition

Much of East Africa's intellectual literary tradition, particularly in the 1950s and early 1960s, is rooted in what has come to be called the Makerere tradition. In this period, Makerere, a constituent college of the University of London, was the leading colonial institution of higher education in East Africa and the training ground for the pioneer East African writers. With its emphasis on English

language and English literature and culture, Makerere had a tremendous influence on the sub-continent's would-be writers. The establishment of a creative writing journal called *Penpoint* in the late 1950s provided a major growth point for a number of leading East African writers. Rajat Neogy's *Transition*, founded in 1961 and modeled after *Black Orpheus*, also opened up the desired space for creative expression in East Africa. But it was *Penpoint* that published the first writings of leading East African writers like **Ngugi wa Thiong'o** and Peter **Nazareth**, among others; indeed, the first anthology of East African writing edited by David Cook, *Origin East Africa: A Makerere Anthology* (1965), consisted of selections from the journal.

Makerere provided a fertile ground for the growth of East African literature by defining what constituted literature. The influence of the F.R. Leavis notion of the Great Tradition, which was the basis of literary education at Makerere, is quite evident in the early works of the pioneer writers from East Africa. It was from the English tradition that these writers first got their real literary models of what a poem, a novel, or a play was. The notion of the writer as a medium and of writing as an unconscious act of imagination that Ngugi writes about in his earlier essays in *Homecoming* (1972) has its roots in the Makerere tradition. The influence of the Great Tradition is most evident in the poetry from the region, which is dominated by modernist images, an obvious influence from T.S. Eliot, who had freed poetry from some of the conventions common in nineteenth-century poetic practice. The influence is also evident in the East African novel, which is heavily wedded to the European novel, particularly in those works rooted in the tradition of realism (see **realism and magical realism**). There was, however, a double consciousness that animated the pioneering works of these writers: while many of their works reflected the literary models inherited from colonial institutions, they were also influenced by those elements of oral African traditions they had been exposed to in their cultures and the use of popular myths, legends, and traditional modes of narrative and performance mark all the three major genres (see **oral literature and performance**). It is not uncommon to come across code switching and a hybrid of Kiswahili, indigenous languages, and English, particularly in drama. Indeed, much of the radical nationalism that one encounters in the early East African writings would not have been possible had the early literature from the region not been located in a cultural domain set outside colonial economy and statecraft (see **nationalism and post-nationalism**).

It was, however, not until the late 1960s and more specifically the early 1970s that a major shift took place in the intellectual and literary climate of East Africa. The actual shift was marked by **Okot p'Bitek**'s publication of *Song of Lawino* (1966) and, soon after, its sequel *Song of Ocol* (1969), works which signaled the emergence of a literary style that was pronounced by critics as African and revolutionary. Okot's poems or songs grew against the backdrop of a radical debate at Nairobi University about the kind of aesthetics that would liberate the emergent East African literature from the stranglehold of English writing and tradition. The call for the reconstruction of black aesthetics, Maughan-Brown writes, was very much in vogue in East African literary circles, long before it became an issue in South Africa under the banner of black consciousness. The culmination of these debates on the future of East African literature was a colloquium held at Nairobi University in June 1971 which led to the production of two sets of books: *Black Aesthetics in East Africa* edited by Pio Zirimu, and *Writers in East Africa* edited by Andrew Gurr and Angus Calder.

The basic question raised in these debates was about the kind of intervention the East African writers were prepared to make in shaping the new states that were beginning to change so rapidly. The consensus was for a liberating literature that would transform the very foundations on which cultures bequeathed to African nations by colonialism were built. The new direction in cultural revival was given further impetus by the emergence and consolidation of Nyerere's ideology of African socialism, which seemed to resonate with the new cultural spirit that the Nairobi University cultural activists had initiated. In the second decade after independence, Nairobi University and Dar es Salaam University would supplant Makerere in giving shape and direction to cultural creativity in East Africa. Amin's reign of terror had sent many

Ugandan writers into exile, a good number of whom joined the faculty at the University of Nairobi. The high point of this cultural period was the call, in 1968, by Taban Lo **Liyong**, Owuor Anyumba, and Ngugi wa Thiong'o for the abolition of the English department and the dislodging of the English tradition from its privileged position in independent Kenya.

Dar es Salaam itself had attracted some of the most radical Third World scholars, like Walter Rodney, whose theories on how Europe had underdeveloped Africa gained great currency in the intellectual circles. Coupled with the influence of the "dependency" school that was now popular in Latin America, and given the disillusionment that followed independence, East African writers found an attractive theme that gave credence to these new theoretical trends and the paralysis of the postcolonial moment. The influence of Fanon and Fanonism on a cohort of East African writers and scholars like Pio Zirimu, Peter Nazareth, Grant Kamenju, and Ngugi, who had met at Leeds where they had discovered Fanon's *The Wretched of the Earth* (1968), became evident. Fanon's prophetic study of the transition from colonialism to neocolonialism in Africa touched the imaginations of many writers and intellectuals, and in the next two decades (the 1970s and 1980s) the concerns of the writers would focus on the failure of independence to make a decisive break with colonialism, and the centrality of national culture in shaping the African revolution that was faltering. This radicalized vision of literature was to continue well into the 1990s.

Themes of East African literature in English

It is very difficult to provide a meaningful classification of themes in East African literature, given its significant growth over the last four decades of the twentieth century. However, a broad historical perspective gives a good indication of the major thematic trends that have come to define the sub-continent's literature. These include: cultural conflict and the restoration of community; political betrayal in the postcolonial state and the abuse of power leading to some of the most horrendous forms of violence and tyranny visited on ordinary people; and the representation of women and their place within the dramatic story of the new nation. Earlier on in the 1970s, an explosion of popular fiction modeled after the Western thriller and set mainly in the cities of East Africa had emerged. In thematic terms, this literature captures the nightmare of modernity and the decaying of values in the postcolonial state, which the rot and prostitution in the city has come to represent (see **modernity and modernism**). In the early 1990s, a growing body of literature emerged, largely from exiled minority writers of Indian descent, that seeks to contest the uniform narrative of the nation-state by showing its identities as shifting and fragmented.

The theme of restoration of community in East Africa started with the production of a critical mass of ethnographic and autobiographical writing, among the best known being a study of Kikuyu traditions by Jomo **Kenyatta**, *Facing Mount Kenya* (1938). The tension between modernity and tradition or precolonial society that Kenyatta captures was to become a major thematic strand running throughout much of East African literature. Most of the restorative narratives set out not only to reaffirm the African values in the same way the African ethnographers had done, but also to challenge and revise the biased image of Africa that they encountered in the colonial archives and the fictions of white narratives, most notably Karen Blixen and Elspeth Huxley, while at the same time appropriating those positive values and systems that modernity had bestowed on the continent. Indeed, one of the striking ironies of this literature, as is evident in Ngugi's *The River Between* (1965), is the fact that themes of political and cultural resistance to colonialism are complemented by themes of education, progress, and self-improvement.

From the late 1960s through to the 1970s and beyond, the theme of political betrayal that Ngugi had hinted at rather obliquely in *A Grain of Wheat* (1967), and was given eloquent expression in Okot p'Bitek's scathing critique of postcolonial culture in *Song of Lawino* (1966), became the concern of virtually every writer in the sub-continent. In Peter **Palangyo**'s *Dying in the Sun* (1969), the process of decolonization and independence was depicted as a journey into death rather than freedom. Robert **Serumaga**'s *Return to Shadows* (1969) also depicted the neocolonial condition in Uganda as a vicious cycle of darkness. The betrayal motif and an overwhelming mood of despair, which was also found in the poems of Richard **Ntiru** and the plays of Francis **Imbuga**, mark the literature of this period as casting a major cloud on the successes of independence.

Alongside the treatment of the theme of political betrayal was also a sustained exposure of corruption among the political elite. The betrayal of the ideals of independence and official corruption had led to a gross abuse of power and political violence in many parts of the region, especially in the 1970s and 1980s, and these two themes were captured vividly in Ugandan literature. The post-independence history of Uganda is without doubt more dramatic than that of Tanzania and Kenya. This is not to suggest that Uganda's neighboring states were less repressive, but rather to point to the disproportionate ways in which power was abused during and after Amin's reign of terror.

In the late 1970s and beyond the 1980s, Kenya's political scenario had also deteriorated quite markedly under the Kenyatta and Moi governments, leading to a drastic curtailment of freedom of expression among writers and intellectuals. The actual freezing of intellectual and cultural freedom was first directed at creative writers, with Ngugi as its first victim. Ngugi, like the Ugandan writers of the same decade, had predicted the Kenyan state's drive to create a culture of silence among its intellectuals in *Petals of Blood* (1977), a text that marked the beginning of a decidedly political novel in East Africa. It reconstitutes the nationalist struggles as the heroic narrative of workers and peasants and restores the voice to the ruled classes of Africa. The articulation of the working class and peasant interests in literature from the region only found similar echoes in Tanzania where the official policy had encouraged cultural activities committed to a socialist goal, which found expression in the prolific corpus of Kiswahili literature. The thematic focus on the emergence of individual and collective agency in the face of various forms of repression remained a major theme in the 1980s and beyond among radical writers.

A strictly historical approach to themes of East African literature creates the impression that these themes developed very much in a predictably linear fashion, but this was not the case. As early as the 1970s, a tradition of popular novels, fashioned after Western thrillers, was beginning to emerge, and these seemed to follow their own trajectory. This genre had its roots in urban life, which had created its own unique, yet dislocating, environment with a decidedly modernist values rooted in Western colonialism. The popular novels of writers such as Charles **Mang'ua** and David **Maillu** shifted the subject matter of fiction from politics and huge social issues to love, romance, prostitution, and sex. More recently, in the 1990s, a number of Ugandan writers, most notably Goretti Kyomuhendo and Regina Amollo, have turned to this genre to take up the issues surrounding the scourge of AIDS.

Although the representation of women has not been a major theme in East Africa, it certainly gained attention much earlier than popular prose or urban literature. In the early 1960s, Grace **Ogot** pioneered the writing of prose that was not only rooted in her Lwo (Luo) people's tradition of folklore, commonly associated with women, but also the development of a female literary model. Ogot's narratives are notable for their deviation from the characteristic conventions of male narrative. For example, Nyapol, the central protagonist in Ogot's major work, *The Promised Land* (1966), is a prototype of the strong female characters that came to dominate works of East African writers like Okot in the late 1960s and Ngugi in the late 1970s and beyond. These strong and resilient female characters, which Roger Kurtz has appropriately characterized as "Nyapol's daughters," have blossomed in both male and female writings from East Africa in the 1980s and 1990s.

Minority groups in East Africa, particularly the Asians largely living in exile, have produced the kind of literature that mimics in some ways some of the issues that East African writers had to deal with in the 1960s: namely, cultural identity in the face of an overwhelming Western modernity. Such writings tend to be of an autobiographical nature. The 1990s, in particular, witnessed the emergence of a special category of literature which sets out to explore what constitutes identity and creates community, while at the same time signaling how geographical, ethnic, political, and cultural makeup and differences serve as signifying aspects of the

complex issue of identity. This kind of fiction has come to be characterized as multicultural, largely because of the hybrid form that most of these writers have adopted to tell their stories and those of the minority groups to which they belong. The writing of cultural and racial locations has been one of the most important thematic aspects of this literature. Foremost of the writers is Moyez **Vassanji**, an East African Asian born in Kenya and raised in Tanzania, and currently living in Canada. The project of recovering and defining the self among minority writers closely associated with East Africa animates most works written by Asian and Arab writers like Abdulrazak **Gurnah**, and it is likely to continue beyond the so-called era of globalization.

Finally, the struggle against cultural imperialism that dominated literatures of writers like Okot p'Bitek and the imagination of many critics in the 1960s has become a major trope in East African literature, leading to a reassertion of the nationalist discourses that had been repressed in the immediate aftermath of independence. Since the 1980s there has been a major revival of the theme of "return to the source," which includes, among others, the call for the use of indigenous African languages in the writing of literature and the reconstruction of a national culture. Ngugi's essays, collected in *Decolonising the Mind: The Politics of Language in African Literature* (1986), were the defining moment of this new spirit. It was followed by a publication of his first novel ever to be written in Gikuyu (see **Gikuyu literature**), Ngugi's *Devil on the Cross*. His example found positive echoes and fertile ground in Tanzania, whose writers had been writing in Swahili for almost four decades. But even works written in English, such as Francis Imbuga's novel, *Shrine of Tears* (1993), took up the theme of national reconstruction and the restoration of the African cultures to their central place. The theme of cultural revival was best summarized in Ngugi's *Moving the Centre* (1992), a book whose thematic thread is tied to the flowering of what he calls "our plural cultures." It is by no coincidence that it is underpinned by this vision of cultural reconstruction, using the domination of Kenya's so-called national theater as its point of departure.

In conclusion, since 1965 when Taban Lo Liyong lamented the "literary barrenness" of East

Africa, arguing that East Africa had not produced any literature of substance as compared to West Africa or southern Africa, there has been a significant flowering of creative talent and creative works which reveal not only some depth of craft but also complex transformational processes under-pinning social meanings and values constitutive of East African society. The complexity referred to includes not simply the decisive break from colonialism as its central agenda, but also imagi-native experimentation with a variety of genres, the emergence of a radically new literature dealing with children's and women's issues hitherto ne-glected in the sub-continent.

Further reading

Killam, G.D. (ed.) (1984) *The Writing of East and Central Africa*, Nairobi: Heinemann.

Kurtz, Roger (1998) *Urban Obsessions, Urban Fears: The Postcolonial Kenyan Novel*, Trenton, New Jersey: African World Press.

Simatei, T.P. (2001) *The Novel and the Politics of Nation Building in East Africa*, Bayreuth: Bayreuth University Press.

Smith, A. (1989) *East African Writing in English*, London: Macmillan.

Viola, A., Bardolph, J. and Coussy, D. (1998) *New Fiction in English From Africa: East, West and South*, Amsterdam: Rodopi.

JAMES OGUDE

Echeruo, Michael J.C.

b. 1937, Okigwi, Nigeria

poet and literary critic

The Nigerian-born poet and literary critic Michael Echeruo was a member of the University College, Ibadan, generation that has produced some of the most important and influential writers in the English language in Africa. But unlike many of his contemporaries, his reputation rests on his work as a literary critic rather than a writer. He wrote some of the most penetrating criticism of British colonial writers in Africa, in particular Joseph Conrad and Joyce Carey, who were often seen as

representing the tradition against which the Ibadan writers wrote to revolt against. In addition to teaching at major universities in Nigeria and the United States, Echeruo also wrote poems, many of which were published by leading journals. *Mortality*, a collection of early poems, many of them reflecting the abstract imagery associated with Christopher **Okigbo**, Echeruo's contemporary at Ibadan, was published in 1968 just before the Nigerian civil war. Newer poems were published in a collection called *Distanced* (1975).

SIMON GIKANDI

Echewa, T. Obinkaram

b. 1938, Aba, Eastern Nigeria

novelist

The publication of Obinkaram Echewa's first novel, *The Land's Lord* in 1976 was an important event in the history of Nigerian literature after the civil war, affirming continuity with the country's major writers who had been caught in the traumatic events of the conflict and were still seeking new bearings and struggling to map out new directions for African fiction. Echewa's novel won the 1976 English Speaking Union Prize. His second novel, *The Crippled Dancer* (1986), was a finalist for the Commonwealth Fiction Prize for the African region. Echewa's work is unusual in the canon of African literature produced in the 1970s and 1980s in two senses. First, unlike the genera-tion of the 1970s, which was concerned primarily with the failure of decolonization and the dream of national independence, Echewa's works are con-cerned with the dynamics of African life in the precolonial period and, with the impact of the colonial on the African past, much like Achebe's early novels (see **colonialism, neocolonialism, and postcolonialism**). Second, although he has spent most of his adult life living and teaching in the United States, Echewa has not shown much interest in postcolonial and postmodern themes such as migration and exile; rather, his works are focused on African societies in Nigeria as he imagines them to have been before and during the moment of colonialism. In *I Saw the Sky Catch*

Fire (1992), for example, his interest is on the 1929 "Women's War" in Eastern Nigeria as it is related to a young Nigerian woman on the eve of her departure for the United States. It is through recalling the stories of the Igbo women's revolt that the main character is able to confront the uncertainties and the conflicting demands of being an African in America.

SIMON GIKANDI

education and schools

Systems and institutions of education have been central to the development of literature and culture in Africa for a variety of reasons. For one, it is hard to contemplate the institution of written literature on the continent outside the processes of education and the school. It was in colonial schools that many of the material and cultural conditions that made African literature possible, including the printing press and the bookshop, first evolved. In addition, the process of education and literacy triggered massive transformations in African culture and society and these were to impact the nature of literary expression on the continent. Through the education of a select number of Africans, the centers of African literary culture shifted from the oral tradition to a literary one (see **oral literature and performance**) and apart from leading to the growth of African literature in European languages, this process changed the terms of cultural discourse on the continent. Whereas before, literature, either oral or written in African languages, had concerned itself with sustaining conventions of writing that were primarily African in orientation, the colonial school shifted the focus toward the encounter between Africa and Europe.

With the shift of centers of intellectual activity from masters of the oral tradition to the newly educated elite, there was a radical change in the African cultural landscape and especially in the themes of literature itself. Literary culture was no longer about the authority of tradition or the continuity of history, but about the effects of colonialism on the African landscape, of the radical changes in cultural practices, of the consequences of colonial modernity, and of the alienating character of the process of education itself. Initially, the products of the schools, many of them set up by Christian missionaries, identified with colonial culture and what they saw as European civilization; many wrote works which exhorted the civilizing authority of Christianity and colonialism (see **Christianity and Christian missions; colonialism, neocolonialism, and postcolonialism**). This was especially the case in the literature produced in African languages under the tutelage of the Christian mission and affiliated organizations such as the literary bureau in Zimbabwe. But in the twentieth century, under the influence of cultural and political movements such pan-Africanism (see **diaspora and pan-Africanism**), **negritude**, and nationalism (see **nationalism and post-nationalism**), members of the African elite increasingly turned to writing to question the culture of the school and colonialism itself. Indeed, the classic African works such as **Achebe**'s *Things Fall Apart* (1958) and Ferdinand **Oyono**'s *Houseboy* (1956) were to become powerful testimonials against the cultural logic of colonialism. Given the significance of the school in the production of African literature and the close association between African writers and educational institutions, it is not surprising that education has been one of the major themes in modern African writing.

Forms of education

While literary culture is most visibly associated with the colonial school, this has by no means been the only form of educational institution in Africa, and it is important to recognize the variety of education centers on the continent, if only to understand the rich context in which African literature developed. There were, for example, African educational systems that predated the process of colonization itself, and to the extent that the new schools introduced on the continent by the European powers beginning in the nineteenth century catered primarily to a small elite, it could be said that the majority of Africans continued to be educated in precolonial systems, many of them based on oral traditions, everyday rituals, and life experiences. Agents of colonialism tended to discount the significance of such systems of education and to dismiss them as depositories of the kind of barbaric practices that a colonial education was supposed to overcome, but for African cultural nationalists, such as Jomo **Kenyatta** (*Facing Mount Kenya*) (1938), these traditional systems of education were the important centers of securing African values, ideals of community, history, and tradition.

More formalized centers of education were also to be found in precolonial Africa. These include the Koranic schools that are an indispensable part of Islam and Islamic culture in many parts of the continent (see **Islam in African literature**) and schools set up by the early Christian, mostly Coptic or Orthodox, churches in Egypt and Ethiopia. Both the Islamic and early Christian cultures considered the school to be an important institution for the dissemination of their values, for the preservation of their teachings, and for the production of teachers and interpreters of their central texts.

Colonialism and education

The colonial schools that emerged in Africa in the course of the nineteenth century were also closely associated with religious movements, but what made them different from the Koranic or Orthodox institutions was their close association with the agents of colonialism, including the administrative structures of the colonizing authority, and their investment in secular education. In other words, while the majority of colonial schools in Africa were sponsored by Christian missions, they were invested in the modernizing project of colonialism itself. The impact of Christian values was important to these institutions, but as Jean and John Comaroff have shown, the line between evangelization, the promotion of European values, and modernization was very thin. Indeed, by the beginning of the twentieth century, as the colonial governments began to take a keen interest in the education of their subjects, the evangelical nature of education tended to decline. From 1903 onwards, directives from Paris to French colonial officials insisted that the purpose of education was to spread French culture in the colonies, not to convert the African to Christianity.

In the circumstances, the impact of the colonial school was to be felt in three areas: first, in the development of an elite that was being educated into values and practices of Western culture, being incorporated into what Gail Paradise Kelly and others have described as a new linguistic and social environment, and in the process being marginalized within their own traditions. Second, educated Africans became symbols of modernity and modernization (see **modernity and modernism**), leading a lifestyle that marked them as different from their kith and kin, and one which, in theory at least, made their orientation toward Europe more important, rather than their own local identities. Third, these Africans who had gone to the colonial school became the interpreters and mediators between European culture and whatever remained of precolonial Africa.

Indeed, many of them turned to writing as a way of explaining African to Europeans and Europe to Africans. African literature is full of works that perform this interpretative role. At the same time, however, there is a general consensus that the process of colonial education in Africa was incomplete and the source of considerable disillusionment. The process of education was incomplete because it was creating a class of Africans whose educational orientation was toward Europe, yet ones who were not considered to be equal to Europeans. Even within the French colonial context, where the doctrine of assimilation reigned supreme, a closer examination of the curriculum shows that Africans were being taught to master French culture while at the same time being indoctrinated about their own difference and superiority of the whites over blacks. This is the dilemma narrated in Cheikh Hamidou **Kane**'s classic novel, *Ambiguous Adventure* (*L'Aventure ambiguë*) (1961).

In general, disillusionment often arose when educated Africans realized that the process of education that was intended to assimilate them into European culture had actually alienated them from their African roots. The literature of **negritude** is perhaps one of the most powerful expressions of this disillusionment with the idea of European superiority and an attempt to insist on the civilizational value of the negated cultures. In British colonies, on the other hand, Africans were often disillusioned by colonial education because it seemed to ask them to abandon their own traditions without providing any compensation, especially in regard to spiritual values. It was not unusual, as happened in central Kenya in the 1920s, for cultural nationalists to set up their own independent schools, in which they would try to reconcile traditional and modern values.

Education and literary culture

It is not an exaggeration to say that without the colonial school, modern African literature would not have taken the shape it did, especially in the twentieth century. As we have already seen, the colonial school created the men and women who were to become writers; it provided the means and process through which a literary culture could emerge both in European and African languages. In material terms, colonial schools were the first centers of book production and publishing in Africa, and the arrival of a printing press to a school, such as King's College, Budo, in Uganda, was considered to be a monumental event. At the same time, because the elite schools in Africa were fashioned after leading European centers of education, they tended to consider literary education to be central to the social upliftment of Africans. At King's College, Budo, the study of English and "the enjoyment of literature" was promoted by none other than Bishop Tucker, the Anglican primate of Uganda; at Alliance High School in Kenya the annual performance of a Shakespeare play was the highlight of the school year; at Mfantspim School in Ghana, dramatic societies were considered the centers of a proper culture. It was at such schools as the École William Ponty in Senegal and Government College, Ibadan, that important Africans encountered literary culture for the first time. While it is true that the majority of Africans were confined to vocational schools, the majority of African writers in the late colonial period were products of such schools. Bernard **Dadié** started writing plays at William Ponty, Wole **Soyinka** got involved in theater at Government College, Ibadan; **Ngugi wa Thiong'o** discovered literature at Alliance High School; David **Rubadiri** started writing poetry at King's College, Budo; Assia Djebar's literary journey began when she entered the French school in Algeria. The list could go on and on.

But the real impact of the institutions of education on African literature was to be felt at the university level, for it was here that a generation of Africans, in the period after World War II, turned to writing in order to question their own relationship to colonialism and ultimately to promote the cause of nationalism (see **nationalism and post-nationalism**). In order to understand the impact of the university on literary culture, however, it is important to understand the privileged role the university occupied in the African cultural landscape. We can start by noting that colonial governments did not, as a rule, encourage higher education for Africans. This was especially the case in the French colonies, where, up until World War II, the École William Ponty in Senegal was the only institution of higher education in French West Africa, and it served a very small group of *évolués*. In the British territories, the few institutions of higher education, often set up by missionaries or through private initiatives, were frequently the subject of dispute and the source of considerable anxiety.

This is evident in the debates surrounding the struggles by Fourah Bay College in Freetown to become a university. Although Fourah Bay was started in 1826 as a trade school, attempts by African nationalists to turn it into a fully fledged college often met stiff resistance from the colonial government, and it was not until 1876 that it became an affiliate of the University of Durham in Britain. In South Africa the Lovedale Institute was established in 1841, fashioned after Hampton and Tuskegee Colleges for blacks in the United States, but it was not until 1916 that it was to become the now historic University of Fort Hare. It is interesting to note that Fourah Bay College was the only university in West Africa until the opening of University College, Ibadan, in 1948, and that Fort Hare was to remain the only university for blacks in southern Africa until the late 1970s. There was no university in eastern Africa until the establishment of Makerere University College in 1949.

But it was precisely because they were so few that universities occupied such an important role both in the cultural life of the colonies – and later the postcolonies – and in the national imagination. In the nineteenth century, Africanus Horton, rushing to defend Fourah Bay against its detractors, declared the university "an instrument of restoring to Africans their lost glory." In his inaugural address to Liberia College, another great African nationalist, Wilmot Blyden, would tie the ideals of a university to the destiny of Africa, claiming that it was in liberal culture that a black intellectual empire would be constituted. Namdi Azikwe would later make an explicit connection between the university and the destiny of races and nations. As products of powerful nineteenth-century ideas about race, nation, and culture, these pan-Africanist (see **diaspora and pan-Africanism**) intellectuals believed that it was through culture that the ideals of a nation were expressed.

The university was important because it was, of course, the center of high culture. But most importantly, there was a tendency within this tradition of thought to equate high culture with literary culture; literary education was hence privileged in the new African universities. There was also the common belief that a connection between the university and the nation could be effected through literary culture. It is, of course, true that nationalist concerns were not at the center of literary education in the colonial universities, which by and large sought to promote European high culture and the central texts in the so-called Great Tradition. African writers and critics, most notably Ngugi wa Thiong'o, have indeed complained that their literary education only served to alienate them from their communities, traditions, and political contexts.

Still, something important was happening at the university in the 1950s, the last decade of colonial rule in most of Africa. Students were making the significant shift from being consumers of literature to becoming its producers. Through literary journals such as *The Horn*, edited by J.P. **Clark-Bekederemo** at Ibadan, and *Penpoint*, edited by Jonathan **Kariara** at Makerere, the first generation of African writers had started to produce a literature. Initially, their works would be imitations of European prosody and prose applied to the local cultural and natural environment. Increasingly, however, these works began to question dominant European forms or to transform them to account for the experiences that a colonial education had tried to exclude from its own narrow idea of culture. This is how African myths, traditions, and forms of speech started entering the works of literature.

Education in African literature

Education has not merely been the condition that has enabled African literature – it has also been one of its dominant themes. Given the preponderance of this theme in African writing, it is difficult to provide an overall account that will cover two centuries of writing in several languages. Still, it is important to make two generalizations about how education has functioned as a theme and structure in African writing. First, since African writers started writing fiction to account for their own (dis)location within colonial culture and to discover the African world foreclosed to them by colonialism, it was only natural that they would make their own experiences central to this meditation on the colonial situation. This accounts not only for the centrality of the tradition of **autobiography** in African writing, but also for that of autobiographical fiction. Some of the central novels in the African literary tradition from Camara **Laye**'s *Dark Child* (*L'Enfant noir*) (1953), al-Tayyib **Salih**'s *Season of Migration to the North* (1966), Assia **Djebar**'s *Fantasia* (1985) to Tsitsi **Dangarembga**'s *Nervous Conditions* (1989) are novels of education. They are premised on the crisis triggered in their subjects by the process of education, which functions both as an opportunity and as a loss. Education is an opportunity because it provides the characters with social mobility, material advancement, and the expansion of horizons. But it is also plotted as a loss because the more the characters move toward the horizons defined by colonial mobility, the more they are distanced from their natal spaces or at least from the mythology of a pristine culture. Many of the novels in this tradition are written from the perspective of this loss as their characters take stock of their situation and try to balance the relative privilege of their education with the loss it has engendered.

Another generalization to make is that the theme of education touches, directly or indirectly, on some of the other major concerns of African writing, including the nature of precolonial society, modernity and modernization, and even **gender**

and sexuality. As we have already seen, a concern with precolonial society becomes important to African writers seeking to deal with the personal crisis generated by colonial education. It is hence not accidental that the works that are most sensitive to the crisis of self triggered by a colonial education (Laye's *Dark Child*) are underwritten by a note of nostalgia, or that the fictions that are most skeptical about the process of education, for example Mongo **Beti**'s *Mission to Kala* (*Mission terminée*) (1957) or **Okot p'Bitek**'s *Song of Lawino* (1966) and *Song of Ocol* (1970), end by positing a pastoral world outside the orbit of colonialism. Since education is a major agent of social change, it features prominently in works concerned with modernity and its consequences on traditional rituals and beliefs. It is, indeed, one of the great ironies of African literature that the great defenders of such rituals and traditions as *osu* in Chinua Achebe's *No Longer at Ease* (1960) or ritual suicide in Soyinka's *Death and the King's Horseman* (1975) are highly educated Africans.

Education and postcolonial culture

With the end of colonialism in Africa, educational institutions have continued to occupy a central role in society. Indeed, it could be said that independence ensured the triumph of the colonial school in two senses. For one, while there was a massive expansion of institutions of education in postcolonial Africa, the older colonial schools tended to have a disproportionate influence in the government since they had produced the new elite that had come to power. In Kenya, to use just one example, at independence in 1963, Alliance High School, Kikuyu, founded in 1926, provided over a third of the cabinet of postcolonial government and its senior civil servants. Quite often the products of the old schools continued to champion the values they had learnt at school and to be attached to European high culture, which they sought to replicate in the postcolonial nation and its institutions. From another perspective, independence led to an attempt to rethink the nature of education itself, and in particular to marginalize the Eurocentrism of the curriculum

through processes of Africanization. In literature, for example, there was an attempt, beginning in the late 1960s, to place African literature at the center of literary education. In 1968, Ngugi wa Thiong'o, Henry Owour Anyumba, and Taban Lo **Liyong** initiated a project whose goal was nothing less than the abolition of the English department at the University of Nairobi. But this project was also premised on the centrality of literature in the cultural life of the nation, even when the significance of literary culture seemed marginal compared to the professional and vocational interests of many citizens. In this sense, too, it could be said that the idiom and ideology of the colonial school had triumphed in postcoloniality.

Further reading

Ade Ajayi, J.F., Lameck, L.K., Goma, K.H., and Ampah, Johnson (1996) *The African Experience with Higher Education*, London/Athens: James Currey/Ohio University Press.

Habte, Aklilu and Wagaw, Teshome (in collaboration with J. F. Ade Ajayi) (1993) "Education and Social Change," in Ali Mazrui (ed.) *General History of Africa: Africa since 1935*, Paris/Oxford: Unesco/Heinemann, pp. 678–704.

Kelly, Gaile Paradise (2000) *French Colonial Education: Essays on Vietnam and West Africa*, New York: AMS Press.

SIMON GIKANDI

Effa, Gaston-Paul

b. 1965, Cameroon

novelist

Born in Cameroon, Effa emigrated to France at age 16 and teaches philosophy in a high school in Lorraine. Among his major works are *The Cry that You Make Will Not Awake Anyone* (*Le Cri que tu pousses ne réveillera personne*) (2000), a powerful narrative about random killings in Africa. His earlier work, *Tout ce bleu* (All That Blue) (1996), is a lyrical long poem in which, after the fashion of Proust, the author recalls his Cameroonian childhood through the story of Duou, a fictional character. *Tout ce bleu* begins in Douala, Cameroon, where Duou is born and given away by his parents to Catholic nuns. Duou narrates his life as a lonely child lost in the midst of Catholic tradition. The second part of the book recounts his adult life in Paris, where he lives as an immigrant who has been integrated successfully into French culture. In this poem, Effa avoids the temptation to tell privilege stories with unique and intriguing plots; instead, he concentrates on the elaboration of a portrait of the hero, made of fragments from childhood memories. In the end, *Tout ce bleu* is a text generated by a particular nostalgia, and it recalls and represents a kind of lost paradise in which the author reconstitutes his childhood in a beautiful poetic language.

Further reading

Effa, Gaston-Paul (1998) *Mâ* (Mâ), Paris: B. Grasset.

FRIEDA EKOTTO

Efoui, Kossi

b. 1962, Anfoin, Togo

playwright

Born in Togo, Kossi Efoui is known primarily for his works as a playwright. His plays, including *Carrefour* (Intersection) (1990), *Récupérations* (Recuperations) (1992), *La malaventure* (The Misadventure) (1993), *Le Petit-frère du Rameur* (Rameur's Little Brother) (1995), and *Que la terre vous soit legère* (May the Earth Not Weigh upon You) (1996), have been performed principally in Europe. Efoui's plays are characterized by a mordant sense of humor and inimitable sense of linguistic invention, elements that are also evident in his novels, including *La Polka* (The Polka) (1998) and *La Fabrique de cérémonies* (The Construction of Ceremonies) (2001). Efoui's novels are set in places that are not clearly defined and they rarely bring Africa to mind. More than being a sign of alienation from

Africa, Efoui's ambiguous locales suggest that, in the context of the links between Europe and Africa in colonial history, Africa is in some sense everywhere.

Further reading

Efoui, Kossi (2001) *La Fabrique de cérémonies* (The Construction of Ceremonies), Paris: Éditions du Seuil.

FRIEDA EKOTTO

Egbuna, Obi

b. 1938, Eastern Nigeria

playwright and novelist

The Nigerian-born playwright and novelist Obi Egbuna went to study in England in 1961 and he has been living there ever since, working with various black artistic and cultural movements committed to the cause of Pan-Africanism movements (see **diaspora and pan-Africanism**). His writings have revolved largely around his experiences in England, as a student and political activist, or with imaginary reconstructions of African cultural issues such as polygamy. Egbuna's best-known work is perhaps his novel, *Wind Versus Polygamy* (1964), a satirical examination of the practice of polygamy against new regulations intended to "modernize" society. His play *The Anthill* (1965) concerns the experiences of African students in London, while the stories collected in *Daughters of the Sun and Other Stories* (1970) are often about the conflict between what has come to be known as traditional or precolonial society, as it confronts the process of modernity and modernization (see **modernity and modernism**). Egbuna has also written works on his imprisonment in London on a charge of plotting to kill police officers in London in 1970, and a pamphlet on the Nigerian civil war. In general, however, the critical reception of his works has been negative, with some critics assailing his fiction as unoriginal and his drama as sterile.

SIMON GIKANDI

Ekwensi, Cyprian

b. 1921, Minna, Nigeria

writer

Of the major Nigerian writers who came to prominence in the 1950s and 1960s, Cyprian Ekwensi was one of the most prolific and, after Amos **Tutuola**, the most controversial and enigmatic. Ekwensi was considered controversial because the subjects of his novels, short stories, and **children's literature** were experiences that were unusual in the then nascent African literature. His first novel, *People of the City* (1954), depicted the throbbing urban lives of the African working class and popular culture, and earned Ekwensi the title of Africa's Daniel Defoe. On its publication, the novel was welcomed by the reading public and it was to become one of the central texts in African **popular literature**. But the novel was also derided by critics and custodians of high culture, and was even censored in some circles and banned in Ireland! Ekwensi's second novel, *Jagua Nana* (1961), the remarkable story of an African Moll Flanders trying to make it in the city of Lagos, was attacked as pornographic and was the subject of heated debate in the Nigerian National Assembly. Even Ekwensi's first children's novel, *The Passport of Mallam Ilia* (1960), a work intended to provide Nigerian children with a literature with local characters and settings, was dismissed as un-Nigerian. If Ekwensi's writing career has been considered controversial and enigmatic, this is because of his interest in themes, such as sexuality, that were considered anathema in African writing in the 1950s. At the same time, it is clear that his critics were not exactly sure where to locate his works within the framework of literature as it had been developed by the institutions of criticism (see **literary criticism**).

In addition, Ekwensi's education was outside the norm as far as the making of a literary career was concerned. Like many young bright Nigerians of his generation, Ekwensi had studied at Government College, Ibadan, but unlike many of his contemporaries he had not proceeded to University College, Ibadan, for an education in the liberal arts and humanities; rather, he had gone on to study at a technical college and later at forestry

institutions. In fact, it was when he was working as a forestry officer that Ekwensi published his first work, *Ikolo and the Wrestler* (1947), a collection of Igbo folk tales (see **Igbo literature**). In the late 1940s, Ekwensi studied pharmacy in Lagos. It was during this period that he started writing short stories for the Nigerian Broadcasting Corporation. In 1951, Ekwensi went to England to continue his studies in pharmacy, and it was during his period overseas that he started writing his major novels and short stories. He returned to Nigeria in 1956, and as the country made its move from colonialism to independence (see **colonialism, neocolonialism, and postcolonialism**) he began to shift his interests from pharmacy and medicine to broadcasting. His influence in Nigerian broadcasting during the first few years of independence was evident in his appointment as the head of features in the Corporation, a position he was to occupy in the breakaway Republic of Biafra during the Nigerian civil war from 1966 to 1970.

In the literary history of African, Ekwensi has been hailed a pioneer but rarely recognized as one of the founders of the African novel, although his first work of fiction was published four years before Chinua **Achebe**'s *Things Fall Apart*. And yet, what appears to be Ekwensi's marginalization in the history of African literature is also recognition of the different path by which he came to writing, his charting of alternative themes for African literature, and especially his ability to overcome the division of high and popular literature within this tradition of writing. While major Nigerian writers of the 1950s located their writings solidly within the traditions of certain regions or ethnic groups, Ekwensi sought both to affirm his identity as an Igbo and also to celebrate the resources offered by the multicultural environment of the new Nigerian nation. While Ekwensi's parents were Igbos from Eastern Nigeria, he himself had grown up and come of age in northern Nigeria; he had been educated in the western region of the country. He was one of very few Nigerian writers who were fluent in Igbo, Hausa, and Yoruba, the three major languages of the country. Once he started writing, Ekwensi could draw on this background to produce some of the most cosmopolitan portraits of Nigerian society. Indeed, Ekwensi is primarily known for his urban novels. At a time when many

African novelists were looking back to history to try and recover a usable past, Ekwensi's concern in his first major works was to present as vividly as possible the lives of people in Lagos, the Nigerian capital, at a time of cultural and political transition.

People of the City can, in fact, be read as a collective portrait of new Africans trying to leave behind their rural homes and to remake themselves in the metropolis, which Ekwensi considered to be a microcosm of the new imagined community of the Nigerian nation. In his portrait of the city and the people who inhabit it, Ekwensi's novel registers the alienation his main characters have to experience as their dreams of a modern life are constantly frustrated by the harshness of an economy and culture based on money. Ultimately, what makes *People of the City* a classic of African writing is both its amalgam of themes and variety of characters and the author's acute sense of the fast-moving rhythms of the urban landscape. With the publication of *Jagua Nana* in the first years of Nigerian independence, Ekwensi established his reputation as the great novelist of the African city. In this novel, Ekwensi would return to the urban themes he had popularized in his first novel, but he had brought a new intensity to his portraits, and his sense of urban life and its multiple linguistic registers was outstanding. More importantly, Ekwensi represented the city from the perspective of a woman, Jagua Nana, and this was unusual in African writing of the time because questions of **gender and sexuality** were still considered either secondary to the concerns of the African writer or taboo. While the novel did not attract the attention of many critics, it was popular among its readers, many of whom could empathize with the main character's struggle with her own dilemmas and contradictions against the background of the world ushered by nationalism (see **nationalism and post-nationalism**) and postcolonialism.

The coming of Nigerian independence seemed to have given impetus to Ekwensi's writing especially because the throbbing life engendered by new political activities and configurations was felt mostly in the city. In *Beautiful Feather* (1963), he tried to weave his image of pan-Africanism (see **diaspora and pan-Africanism**) and his dream of a Nigerian nation with the changing life of a group of characters immersed in the postcolonial landscape. By the mid 1960s, as Nigeria slid into civil war and political turmoil, Ekwensi's political dream of a United Africa and Nigeria seemed remote and unrealistic. His pessimism is registered in *Iska* (1966), a work that predicted the chaos that was to haunt Ekwensi and his generation. Although he is now renowned for his urban novels, Ekwensi also produced other important works. Among these was *Burning Grass* (1962), a popular novel revolving around the lives of a Fulani cattle-herding family. His children's stories, most notably *The Passport of Mallam Ilia* and *Trouble in Form Six* (1966) have been some of the most widely read works in the field of children's literature in Africa. In addition, Ekwensi has published four books of folklore and two collections of short stories. Unfortunately, like his contemporary Tutuola, Ekwensi has tended to be marginalized both in postcolonial Nigerian society and the institutions of literary criticism in Africa.

Further reading

Emenyonu, Ernest (1974) *Cyprian Ekwensi*, London: Evans Brothers.

SIMON GIKANDI

Eltayeb, Tarek

b. 1959, Cairo, Egypt

novelist

Egyptian-born Sudanese novelist Eltayeb studied business administration in Cairo before earning a doctorate in social sciences and economics from the Wirtschaftsuniversität in Vienna, where he has resided since 1984. Eltayeb, who writes in Arabic, has published one novel, *Mudun bila nakhil* (Cities Without Palms) (1992), one play, *el-Asansayr* (The Elevator) (1992), and two collections of short stories, *al-Jamal la yaqif khalf ishara hamra'* (The Camel Does Not Stop at a Red Light) (1993) and *Udhkuru Mahasin* (Remember Mahasin) (1998). His latest work, a collection of poems and prose pieces entitled *Ein mit Tauben und Gurren gefüllter Koffer* (A Suitcase Full of Doves and Cooing) (1999) was published in a bilingual Arabic–German edition. Eltayeb's main themes have been the meeting of cultures, especially for individuals negotiating foreign surroundings, male–female relations within the Arab world and across cultures, and the drastic social change that has occurred in Egypt as a result of President Anwar Sadat's economic policies in the 1970s.

Further reading

Malina, Renate (1997) "An Interview with the Sudanese Author Tarek Eltayeb," *Research in African Literatures* 28, 3: 122–7.

WAÏL S. HASSAN

Emecheta, Buchi

b. 1944, Lagos, Nigeria

novelist

Today, the works of African women writers are assigned reading in university courses in women's studies, postcolonial literatures, and black women's writing. It was not until about two decades ago, however, that African women writers began to receive international recognition, although their male counterparts have enjoyed such privilege since Heinemann's publication of Chinua **Achebe**'s *Things Fall Apart* (1958). Among the writers whose works helped to transform the presence of African women writers in literature is Buchi Emecheta. Her depiction of the experiences of African, specifically Nigerian, women has challenged the stereotyped and idealized images of African women found in male texts. No discussion of African or black women's writing can be complete without her, for she is one of the best-known women writers in Africa today, sharing that position with others such as Ama Ata **Aidoo**, Mariama **Bâ**, Assia **Djebar**, Bessie **Head**, and Flora **Nwapa**.

Emecheta was born in 1944 in Lagos, Nigeria, of Igbo parents from Ibuza. Both Ibuza and Lagos provide settings in most of her works. She received her primary school education in Nigeria and was married before she was 16. In 1962, she emigrated to England to join her husband, who was already studying there. Emecheta has indicated that

England gave her "a cold welcome." She had two children before her eighteenth birthday. But, at 22, with five children, she left her abusive husband and found herself alone and poor in a society which considered her a second-class citizen. She has written extensively about this experience in her autobiographical novels *In the Ditch* (1972) and *Second-Class Citizen* (1974), published collectively as *Adah's Story* (1983), and in her **autobiography** *Head Above Water* (1986).

Barely surviving on welfare, she put herself through school and received a degree in sociology from the University of London. During this period, she also published stories about her personal experience of poverty, gender oppression, and racism in a column titled "Life in the Ditch" in the *New Statesman*. The collection of stories based on her observations of London, the British welfare system, the poor living conditions of the council flats, which she refers to as "Pussy Cat Mansions," and the oppression of women would provide the materials for *In the Ditch*. To date, Emecheta has published thirteen novels, one autobiography, two children's books, several stories and plays for children, and several essays and articles. She has also lectured in numerous institutions in Africa, Europe, and the United States. Her works have been translated into fourteen languages.

Although emerging more than a decade after many of the African male writers had gained international prominence, Emecheta has become one of Africa's rebellious women writers. She announced herself as an advocate for women's concerns with her first book *In the Ditch*. Her writing has attacked the predominantly male literary canon with its strident criticism of the second-class position accorded African women both by African traditional and patriarchal customs and by racism. According to Lauretta **Ngcobo** in her "Introduction" to *Let It Be Told: Black Women in Britain* (1987: London): "Buchi Emecheta understands the hidden feelings of African women and she voices them as perhaps no one has done before." Indeed, Emecheta is uncompromising in her representation of the disempowerment of women by a combination of unfavorable patriarchal and traditional structures both in Nigeria and in London. She has created female characters through whose voices and experiences she criticizes stereotyped one-dimensional and romanticized representations of women in male texts, whose constructions of women's identities are based exclusively on their biological and social functions as mothers, wives, and mistresses.

Generally, her works are populated with women who eventually challenge oppressive social or cultural restrictions. In *The Bride Price* (1976), Akunna rebels against tradition by choosing her own husband despite her family's objections. Although Emecheta acknowledges the importance of her character's struggle for self-determination, she explains later in *Head Above Water* that Akunna's death stems from her inability to "shake off all the tradition and taboos that had gone into making her the type of girl she was." Adah in *In the Ditch* and *Second-Class Citizen* as well as Kehinde in *Kehinde* (1994) defy cultural practices that bind them to emotionally abusive husbands and leave their marriages to embark on fictional journeys of self-discovery, as does Emecheta herself in her autobiography *Head Above Water*. In *Destination Biafra* (1982), Debbie Ogedemgbe is a Nigerian "Joan of Arc," who, despite opposition and the corrupt machinations of the political leaders, attempts to negotiate a peaceful resolution to the Nigerian civil war.

Emecheta's criticism of women's subordination includes a condemnation of women's complacency, hypocrisy, and unwitting complicity in their own subordination. Her criticism of patriarchy as a source of women's subjugation has also earned her the wrath of many male readers and critics, who see her as an antagonistic African woman writer who has been tainted by Western feminism. Ironically, Emecheta has not fully accepted the feminist label. She states in her essay "Feminism with a Small 'f!' " (1988: Uppsala) that

I see things through an African woman's eyes. I chronicle the little happenings in the lives of the African women I know. I did not know that by doing so, I was going to be called a feminist. But if I am now a feminist, then I am a feminist with a small "f."

Her comments not only suggest an attempt to renegotiate feminism, but also underscore the resistance of many African women writers to that label.

Clearly, it is the desire to give voice to African and other disempowered women that captivates Emecheta's readers. In fact, whereas many of the first generation of African women writers struggled for international recognition, Emecheta's work gained recognition rapidly. This success can be attributed to critics of African literature and feminist scholars who see an affinity between the themes in her works and feminist concerns and Emecheta's role as one of speaking out for black women. Indeed, for most of Emecheta's characters, the act of speaking out, claiming voice, becomes an initial step towards resistance against silencing. It is, therefore, that commitment to dismantling women's subjugation that has made Emecheta a force of transformation, particularly in the writing of black women's experiences.

Emecheta's works are dominated by two opposing yet historically linked geographic settings, Africa and Europe, and her works can be initially grouped in these categories. *In the Ditch*, *Second-Class Citizen*, and *Adah's Story* are set in London and are based on Adah's experiences as an émigré in London. The works focus particularly on the character's struggle to overcome her husband's sexism, antagonism from other Nigerians, poverty, and British racism. The works also expose oppressive cultural attitudes and tensions within the Nigerian emigrant community. Ironically, as Adah finds out, as does Kehinde in *Kehinde*, the emigrant Nigerian community of London has replicated the gender biases and cultural mores of its homeland (see **gender and sexuality**).

The second group of novels, *The Bride Price* (1976), *The Slave Girl* (1977), *The Joys of Motherhood* (1979), *Destination Biafra*, *Naira Power* (1982), and *Double Yoke* (1983), are set in Nigeria. Whereas the first three works address cultural practices, which subordinated women in traditional Igbo societies as well as in postcolonial Nigeria (see **colonialism, neocolonialism, and postcolonialism**), the latter group focuses on Nigeria after independence. These works examine themes such as nationalism and nationality (see **nationalism and post-nationalism**), neocolonialism, and the construction of a national identity (*Destination Biafra*), and the tensions between tradition and modernity in *Double Yoke* (see **modernity and modernism**). In

Destination Biafra, Emecheta also moves away briefly from the autobiographical to explore political and national concerns – specifically Biafra and the Nigerian civil war.

Despite the dominance of discrete settings in Africa (Nigeria) and Europe (London/England) in Emecheta's works, some of these stories shift between England and various sites in the African diaspora (see **diaspora and pan-Africanism**). This shifting location is indicative of the characters' identities as migratory subjects and of Emecheta's attempt to construct an African diaspora community for the characters. Such works include *Gwendolen* (1989) and *The Family* (1990), where events occur between Jamaica and London, London and Nigeria in *Kehinde* (1994), and "an imaginary country by the edge of the African Sahara" and England in *The Rape of Shavi* (1983). Although *Gwendolen* deals with the violence of incestuous rape and the psychological fragmentation stemming from that experience, it is also about power and gender marginalization. Moreover, like *Kehinde*, *Gwendolen* explores the possibilities of African diaspora communities in London, as well as the cultural tension stemming from those connections. Emecheta's later work, *The New Tribe* (2000) explores a similar exploration of a diaspora identity and community.

In *The Rape of Shavi*, however, Emecheta addresses global politics, specifically colonialism and its aftermath. In this novel, the invasion of Shavi by the "albino aliens" becomes a symbolic rape of culture, and perhaps, a metaphor for Africa's or any colonized group's experience. The resulting erosion of Shavi's identity by a more powerful and technologically advanced race who introduce "new forms of language, custom and exploitation" is akin to the fate of Africans and other colonized peoples who experienced Western colonization. The book can be read also as a commentary on new forms of colonization and cultural imperialism which have emerged today in the form of globalization.

Head Above Water is Emecheta's only autobiography. It explicitly explains many of the autobiographical aspects of *In the Ditch* and *Second-Class Citizen*. Whereas Adah's experience in *Second-Class Citizen* begins in Nigeria, much of the story is set in London and continues in *In the Ditch*, which was

published first. In explaining the autobiographical nature of these books, Emecheta states that she used the fictional name Adah because "the truths were too horrible and because I suspected that some cynics would not believe me." She adds that the fictitious name gave the book "a kind of distance," which "gave the book the impression of being written by an observer."

Emecheta's writing is informed by the story-telling traditions of women in her Ibuza community, women who commanded power as storytellers. In "A Conversation with Dr Buchi Emecheta" (1996: Trenton), she tells Oladipo Joseph Ogundele that, as a writer, her motive is to "tell the world our stories while using the voices of women." Critics also note an intertextual relationship between the late Flora **Nwapa** and Emecheta. Both Nwapa's *Efuru* (1966) and Emecheta's *The Joys of Motherhood* address the construction of female identity through motherhood. In fact, the title of Emecheta's novel is signaled in the closing paragraph of Nwapa's *Efuru* (1966: London), which states,

> Efuru slept soundly that night. She dreamt of the woman of the lake, her beauty, her long hair and her riches … She gave women beauty and wealth but she had no child. She had never experienced the joy of motherhood.

Like Nwapa, Emecheta established her own publishing company, although that was short-lived.

Increasingly, Emecheta, who continues to live in London, has turned her attention to the issue of diasporan identities defined by race and culture. In *The New Tribe*, she explores a man's attempt to understand his blackness and African heritage. Although Emecheta suggests that Chester does not experience virulent racism, the character is, nevertheless, displaced as the only black child in an all-white town and as an African who does not understand his own heritage. Indeed, the "new tribe" of the future, as Emecheta suggests, would be children of the African diaspora, those occupying the borderlands of culture, neither black nor white, neither European nor African, but inhabiting those spaces where identities continue to shift and to be contested.

Further reading

Emecheta, Buchi (1988) "Feminism with a Small 'f'," in Kirsten Holst Peterson (ed.) *Criticism and Ideology*, Uppsala: Scandinavian Institute of African Studies.

Ngcobo, Lauretta (1987) *Let It Be Told: Black Women in Britain*, London: Virago.

Nwapa, F. (1966) *Efuru*, London: Cox and Wyman.

Ogundele, Oladipo Joseph (1996) "A Conversation with Dr Buchi Emecheta," in Marie Umeh (ed.) *Emerging Perspectives on Buchi Emecheta*, Trenton, New Jersey: Africa World Press.

MAUREEN N. EKE

Emenanjo, 'Nolue

b. 1943, Katsina state, Nigeria

writer and scholar

'Nolue Emenanjo (Emmanuel Nwanolue Emenanjo), professor of linguistics and the foundation executive director of the National Institute for Nigerian Languages, Aba, in Abia state, Nigeria, is a most versatile and erudite scholar of Igbo language and linguistics (see **Igbo literature**). He has been at the forefront of the struggle for Igbo language development since the 1970s, and has contributed to the growth and worldwide recognition of Igbo language studies, perhaps more than any other living scholar today. No history of the development of Igbo language and literature in the twentieth century would be complete without his contribution. He has had a multifaceted career ranging through teaching, publishing, university administration, and public service, and in all of these capacities he has never ceased in his unalloyed dedication to the promotion of Igbo language studies at all levels of the Nigerian educational system. A renowned creative writer, Emenanjo combines his versatile skills and competences as a descriptive linguist, folklorist, poet, bilingual translator, lexicographer, literary critic, and educator to produce countless invaluable Igbo language and literature texts for young readers, high school and tertiary students, and the general reader. As sole and co-author, he has published nearly fifty textbooks and creative works for Igbo

language learners and teachers, and over sixty articles in learned journals all over the world. No author has matched him in productivity in the field of Igbo language and literature. His *Elements of Modern Igbo Grammar* (1978) is the most comprehensive and up-to-date descriptive grammar of the Igbo language today. In the development of Igbo language and literature, 'Nolue Emenanjo remains an incomparable pioneer, facilitator, visionary, and spokesperson.

ERNEST EMENYONU

Equiano, Olaudah

b. 1745, Nigeria; d. 1797

slave, abolitionist, and writer

One of the pioneers of African, Afro-British, and African-American literature, Equiano was born in the Igbo country of present-day Nigeria and was captured and enslaved at the age of 10. It was as a slave, and later as a free man, that Equiano was to travel in the West Indies, the southern United States, and Britain. His unique travels and experiences make him one of the most famous subjects of the African diaspora (see **diaspora and pan-Africanism**) in its early years and one consequence of this has been the fact that the narrative he wrote to represent these experiences has come to be considered a foundational text of black writing in African, the Americas, and Europe. Of the group of enslaved Africans who became writers in the late eighteenth century, Equiano was the most popular and influential, and his work, *The Interesting Narrative of the Life of Olaudah Equiano, or Gustavus Vassa, the African, Written by Himself*, was to provide a model for other slave narratives in several continents over two centuries. Equiano's remarkable life is narrated in his narrative: his idyllic childhood in West Africa, his capture as a boy, his horrendous journey in a slave ship, his life in the plantations of the Caribbean and North America, and his subsequent journey to freedom, the acquisition of an English identity, and his struggle against slavery. But more than the story it told, Equiano's narrative provided an enduring structure, ideology, and idiom for the narrative of slavery and emancipation. The *Interesting Narrative* was a black subject's movement from a utopian childhood through the horrors of slavery to a place of redemption as citizen and human being. In using this structure, Equiano was also using literature and literacy to question some of the most persistent eighteenth-century theories about Africans, not least the claim that they were incapable of originality in **art** and moral values. Because Equiano wrote his work to influence British debates on slavery and enslavement, he was keen to present himself as the kind of civil subject – a master of manners and capitalism – that the dominant culture privileged. At the same time, his work used the language of evangelicalism, not least the notion of Providence, to marshal his readers to the anti-slavery cause. On its publication in 1789, *The Interesting Narrative* became an instant bestseller; it went through at least eight editions in English and was translated into several European languages. During this time, Equiano became a prominent figure in English society, a friend of many writers of the period, and a strong advocate of Afro-British rights and interests.

Further reading

Edwards, Paul and Walvin, James (1983) *Black Personalities in the Era of the Slave Trade*, London: Macmillan.

Equiano, Olaudah (1995) *The Interesting Narrative and Other Writings*, ed. Vincent Carretta, New York: Penguin.

Gates, Henry Louis, Jr (1988) *The Signifying Monkey: A Theory of African-American Literary Criticism*, New York: Oxford.

Sandiford, Keith (1988) *Measuring the Moment: Strategies of Protest in Eighteenth-Century Afro-English Writing*, London: Associated Universities Press.

SIMON GIKANDI

Espirito Santos, Alda de

b. 1926, São Tomé

teacher, writer, and journalist

The São Tomé teacher, writer, and journalist Alda de Espirito Santos, who was born in a bi-racial family in the plantations of the then Portuguese colony, was one of the few women writers in Lusophone Africa during the period of colonialism (see **colonialism, neocolonialism, and post-colonialism**). Educated in Portugal in the 1950s, she was involved in nationalist politics and was jailed for a while in 1965–6. She became the minister of culture when São Tomé became independent. Santo's poems closely mirror the issues of nationalism and gender that were an important part of her political education (see **nationalism and post-nationalism**; **gender and sexuality**): it is primarily concerned with the lives of ordinary people, especially women, struggling with the demands of impoverished lives, but they also strive to present the beauty of life and the ability of people to overcome social and physical decay. Most of her poems have been collected in the 1978 text *E nosso o solo sagrado da terra: poesia de protesto e luta* (To Us Belongs the Sacred Soil: Poetry of Protest and Struggle).

SIMON GIKANDI

Essafi, Tahar

b. 1893, Tunisia; d. c.1960

writer

The Tunisian writer Tahar Essafi, like his compatriot Mahmoud **Aslan**, was extremely active in the literary life of the French Protectorate of Tunisia (1881–1956), writing for a variety of journals such as *Tunisie illustrée* and *La Kahéna*, directing the Society of North African Writers for several years, and founding in 1936 the newspapers *Tunis-Midi*, *La Phare de Tunis*, and *La Jeunesse littéraire*. Essafi's fictional work recounts tales from both folklore and his childhood. In *Le Collier d'émeraude* (The Emerald Necklace) (1937), his third book of short stories and folk tales from Tunisia and Morocco, Essafi presents stories at once humorous and moralistic that narrate lives as diverse as those of a desert trader and a man with an insatiable appetite. Essafi was as interested in sociology and politics as he was in literature. In 1934 he published *Au secours du fellah* (To the Help of the Peasant), an indictment of the miserable economic and health situation in rural Tunisia, and in 1935 he published *La Marocaine* (The Moroccan Woman) in which he decried the position of the Muslim woman in Islamic society and advocated the benefits of interracial marriages.

Further reading

Essafi, Tahar (1937) *Le Collier d'émeraude* (The Emerald Necklace), Paris: Malfère.

KATARZYNA PIEPRZAK

Ethiopian literature

Ethiopian literature began with inscriptions in stone over two thousand years ago. The language developed into Ethiopic (also called Geez), which later became a very important literary tool when Christianity was adopted in the region in the fourth century. But it was only in the nineteenth century that Ethiopia started to use Amharic for written purposes, and the twentieth century saw a flood of books in Amharic published in Ethiopia.

Ethiopic (or Geez) literature

This had its beginning when immigrants from the southern part of the Arabian peninsula (present-day Yemen) in the millennium before Christ left inscriptions in stone in northern Ethiopia. Several tribes from southern Arabia mixed to form a specific Ethiopian language and a characteristic script, Ethiopic or Geez, at first consisting only of consonants, later with vowel signs added to the consonantal stems. This development of a new language and a new script would prove to be of tremendous importance for Ethiopia.

When Ethiopia adopted Christianity in the fourth century (see **Christianity and Christian missions**), there began a fruitful work of translating the Bible, including apocrypha books. Some of these books, for example the book of Enoch, exist complete only in Ethiopic and in modern translations made from it. These works were soon followed by other religious and theological literature. Much of the latter has been collected in

Haymanote Abew (The Faith of the Fathers). Ethiopia also has a unique collection of liturgies, lives of saints (mostly foreign, but also a few Ethiopian), and prayer books, the use of which is a salient feature of Ethiopian Christianity. At the same time, the Church started schools to educate the laity as well as to train clergy, and this education system (see **education and schools**) has supplied Ethiopia with a great number of literate people over many centuries, from all classes of society. Education in church institutions made it possible for Ethiopians from almost any background to advance to the highest positions in society. Soon, the interest of writers widened to include other matters, including magical texts (for example scrolls and *kitab*) and the natural world (a "bestiary" or *fisalgos* is a book in which spiritual lessons are drawn from the description of various animals). Texts were also produced in fields such as philosophy, especially two books about which there has been some controversy. Genuine Ethiopian modern critical philosophy may have started in Ethiopia at the same time as in Europe. There were also texts in law: *Fitha Negest* (The Royal Law) was the basic Ethiopian law until well into the second half of the twentieth century. In history, a series of royal chronicles were produced. Finally, a typical (so-called classical) Ethiopian form of poetry (*qinê*), was composed both in Geez and Amharic.

Geez literature had a great flowering in the middle ages, when Amharic had largely replaced Geez as a spoken language. From the early fourteenth century until well into the twentieth century, there was an almost unbroken chain of histories of Ethiopia in the form of royal chronicles, many of immense importance for the understanding of Ethiopia's past and present, although they are often biased in favor of the rulers at the time.

A fictional work from the fourteenth century, *Kibre Negest* (The Glory of Kings), has had a special place in Ethiopian tradition, pretending to tell the true story of King Solomon of Israel and the Ethiopian Queen of Sheba and their son Minilik I, who is said to have founded the Solomonic dynasty which ruled Ethiopia from 1270 to 1974, but which according to this legend goes back to around 1000 BC. It was a royal charter that gave considerable stability to the royal line, and the story inspired a great amount of pictorial art.

Amharic literature

Geez remained practically the only literary language of Ethiopia until the middle of the nineteenth century, when the Emperor Téwodros II (1855–68) had chronicles from his reign recorded in Amharic, the present national language of Ethiopia. After that time, the volume of writing in Amharic increased steadily, especially from the early twentieth century, but it became a flood in the last quarter of that century. Although the country has over eighty languages, little is written in languages other than Amharic. However, Geez is still used in the Church and in some historical works, and so-called classical – that is, traditional, church-inspired – poetry, dealing with all kinds of topics (far from only religious ones) is still composed in Geez. As scholarship has largely been transmitted orally in Ethiopia, much is still being recorded from dictation by traditional scholars in Geez.

Amharic had its beginning as an important written language in historical works, apart from the oral literature, which is still being collected. But in 1908 came the first Amharic novel, written in Naples and published in Rome because Italian scholars wanted texts for the study of the language. The author was **Afewerq Gebre-Iyesus** (note that Ethiopians should be referred to by their first or both names, never by the second name only, which is the father's first name). This book did not reach Ethiopia until much later, and the real pioneer of Amharic literature in Ethiopia is **Hiruy Welde-Sillasé**, who wrote over twenty books. Newspapers in Amharic were started early in the twentieth century as well, and Hiruy was also active in this area. Playwriting began not long after.

We shall mention only the most important of early writers here. Welde-Giorgis Welde-Yohannis and **Mekonnin Indalkacchew** both belonged to the conservative school of writers. The former wrote much about the royal family; the latter had a wider spectrum, and had many readers due to his romantic stories and his entertaining style. Girmacchew Tekle-Hawariyat is best known for a rather progressive *Bildungsromanen* called *Araya*, and a play about the Emperor Téwodros II, who has become more and more of a national hero. **Kebbede Mikaél** started writing when the Italians ruled Ethiopia but wrote mostly, and reached his greatest fame, in postwar years. The Italian invasion and occupation of Ethiopia (1935–41) delayed further developments for some years, but soon after, new writers appeared, and prominent among these early postwar authors were modernizers like **Imru Hayle-Sillasé** and **Haddis Alemayyehu**, besides Kebbede Mikaél and others mentioned above who continued writing for many years.

Haddis Alemayyehu went on making important contributions until late in the twentieth century, but there came a new generation of writers in the second half of that century who became more and more involved with the cultural, social, economic, and political developments of Ethiopia. **Abbé Gubennya** was at one time Ethiopia's most popular writer, presenting ideas about the speedy development of Ethiopia that fired the imagination but were rather removed from reality. Negash Gebre-Mariyam took up the position of women in a poignant way in a well-written novel about a prostitute. Tesfayé Gessese revolutionized the theater in Ethiopia with his plays, acting, direction, and teaching. **Tseggayé Gebre-Medhin**, probably Ethiopia's greatest playwright and poet, was nominated for the Nobel Prize for Literature in the year 2000. **Mengistu Lemma** is best known for having introduced comedy to the Ethiopian theater as a means of social criticism, but he was also a significant poet. **Dannyacchew Werqu** is almost philosophical in his analysis of society, particularly in his major novel, *Adefris*. **Taddese Liben** has published little, but he pioneered the short story in Ethiopia, taking up many contemporary issues, particularly those relating to urban youth. **Birhanu Zerihun** wrote much about the situation and exploitation of the underdog, especially women and, late in life, the peasantry, and he wrote in a very accessible style. Perhaps more than anyone else, **Be'alu Girma** used literature to take up issues of his day in Ethiopia; he finally had to pay for this with his life, when in his social criticism he attacked the socialist rulers who had counted him as their man.

Among authors who made their mark in the last few decades of the twentieth century, one can note Taddele Gebre-Hiywet, who wrote *Mannew Ityopiyawiw* (Who is a True Ethiopian?); Aberra Lemma, experimental poet and short story writer;

the novelist Gebayyehu Ayyele (e.g. *Tamra Tor*, The Two-Pronged Spear); and the poet Debbebe Seyfu. During the same period, some writers such as **Sahle-Sillasé Birhane-Mariyam** and Dannyacchew Werqu also started writing novels in English in order to circumvent the censors in Ethiopia. The former also wrote the first book ever in Guragé, another Ethiopian language. But the Ethiopian literary scene continued to be dominated by authors writing in Amharic.

Ethiopian literature is eminently national and African in orientation, although the country was rather cut off from much of the rest of Africa for centuries due to its early adoption of Christianity, its isolating landscape, and its heroic resistance to colonial encroachment. **Swahili literature** has also developed a truly national African literature, but foreign influences are stronger in this tradition, and due to colonialism literature in English has had higher prestige in Swahili-speaking areas of East Africa. This has made Ethiopian literature unique, and in volume and quality it surpasses any other literature written in a purely African language. Its study is rewarding but not easy for foreigners because Amharic, unlike Geez, is extremely difficult (and mostly taught in antiquated ways).

The fall of imperial Ethiopia and the rise of socialism brought new hope to Ethiopia, and in spite of censorship and restrictions of many kinds the two decades after the 1974 revolution saw an unprecedented outpouring of fictional literature in Ethiopia. With low prices, books reached a wide audience for the first time. In the last years of the twentieth century, however, there was a reduction in literary output due to higher prices and other economic restrictions. As in other parts of Africa, Ethiopian literature has been geared toward utilitarian value, to influence people and shape a better society. But there have been exceptions to this rule: Yilma Habteyes writes detective stories with the sole aim of entertaining, and Mammo Widdineh has written and translated many spy stories. More and more young people read such books. Some superficial romantic love stories, mainly in translation, have also found readers. This seems to indicate that foreign tastes in literature are also influencing Ethiopian reading habits.

Since Amharic has gradually come to be used as the medium of instruction in Ethiopian schools, its literature has become easily accessible to people all over the country. Schoolbooks have also been written in Amharic in all school subjects, and this has led to the intense study of the language, with the publication of many excellent dictionaries. The development of the language has also led to the publication of other literary materials such as folklore and proverbs by award-winning writers like Mahteme-Sillasé Welde-Mesqel. History books and biographies by Tekle-Tsadiq Mekuriya have become an important part of Ethiopia's cultural heritage. Finally, an important phenomenon of the late twentieth century has been the emergence of a small émigré literature among Ethiopians who have chosen to live abroad due to the political turmoil after the fall of the last emperor. The literature of the Ethiopian diaspora is increasingly developing a life of its own.

Further reading for Ethiopic/Geez literature

Cerulli, E. (1968) *Storia della letteratura Etiopica* (History of Ethiopian Literature), 3rd edn, Milan: Nuova Accademia Editrice.

Further reading for Amharic literature

Kane, T.L. (1975) *Ethiopian Literature in Amharic*, Wiesbaden: Harrassowitz.

Molvaer, R.K. (1980) *Tradition and Change in Ethiopia*, Leiden: E.J. Brill.

——(1997) *Black Lions*, Lawrenceville, New Jersey: Red Sea Press.

Tadesse, Adera and Jimale, Ahmed (1995) *Silence is Not Golden. A Critical Anthology of Ethiopian Literature*, Lawrenceville, New Jersey: Red Sea Press.

REIDULF MOLVAER

Eybers, Elisabeth

b. 1915, South Africa; d. 2007, Amsterdam

poet

Eybers' debut, *Belydenis in die skemering* (Confession at Dawn) (1936) was the first volume of Afrikaans poetry published by a woman (see **Afrikaans literature**). She received the Hertzog Prize for *Belydenis* and *The Quiet Adventure* (*Die stil avontuur*) (1939) at the age of 28. Five more volumes were published, of which *Die helder halfjaar* (The Vivid Half-Year) (1956) was especially highly regarded. Her life in Johannesburg ended in 1961 when she divorced the father of her four children and went to Amsterdam. These events gave a metaphorical power and tension to her poetry which have led to her unique position at the crossroads of two literatures. Her Afrikaans poems are simultaneously published in Cape Town and in Amsterdam, receiving accolades in both countries, including the prestigious Dutch P.C. Hooft Prize. *Balans* (1962) was her first Amsterdam collection, followed by the impressive *Onderdak* (Shelter) in 1969 and another ten volumes, of which some, e.g. *Winter-surplus* (1999), include many English poems. She holds three honorary doctorates. In her late eighties she was still writing new poems and translations into English of poems from her twenty-one volumes.

Further reading

Jansen, Ena (1998) *Afstand en verbintenis: Elisabeth Eybers in Amsterdam* (Correspondence and Connections: Elisabeth Eybers in Amsterdam), Amsterdam: Amsterdam University Press.

ENA JANSEN

F

Faarax Maxamed Jaamac "Cawl"

b. 1937, Somalia; d. 1991, Somalia

novelist

Faarax published the first long novel in Somali, *Ignorance is the Enemy of Love (Aqoondarro waa u Nacab Jacayl)* in 1972. It is set during the time of the Dervish movement in the first two decades of the last century against which the central love story is played. Literacy has a central role in the plot in that the illiterate hero is unable to read a message from the woman he loves, with tragic consequences. Faarax went on to publish two other novels: *Garbaduubkii Gumeysiga* (The Shackles of Colonialism) (1989) looks back at the history of the Somali territories through the words of an old man dictating to his son, who completes its writing in his own blood when he runs out of ink. The third novel *Dhibbanaha aan Dhalan* (The Unborn Victim) is set during the war between Somalia and Ethiopia in the late 1970s and is the story of a young woman caught up in the turmoil. Faarax brought Somali poetry into his novels, and this, interplaying with the narratives, gave them a distinctive and powerful style, a key contribution to Somali literature.

Further reading

Faarax M.J. "Cawl" (1982) *Ignorance is the Enemy of Love*, trans. B.W. Andrzejewski, London: Zed.

MARTIN ORWIN

Fagunwa, Daniel Olorunfemi

b. 1903, Òkè-Igbó, Western Nigeria; d. 1963, Nigeria

novelist

The Nigerian writer D.O. Fagunwa is one of the best-known figures of the pioneering generation of African writers. This generation did much of their work in the first half of the twentieth century, during the formative stages of cultural nationalism (see **nationalism and post-nationalism**). Fagunwa used an indigenous African language to develop a narrative style that fits into a tradition of the picaresque novel but also contains inflections that are specific to a colonial African context. He wrote in Yoruba, one of the major languages spoken in Nigeria (see **Yoruba literature**). His first novel, entitled *The Forest of a Thousand Demons: A Hunter's Saga (Ògbójú Ode Nínú Igbó Irúnmalè)* was originally written for a competition organized in 1936 by the education ministry in Nigeria (see **education and schools**). The novel was published by the Church Missionary Society in 1938 and became an instant success. The success of the novel inspired Fagunwa, with the encouragement of the Nigerian educational system, to write more novels using a similar innovative style.

Fagunwa was born in Òkè-Igbó in Western Nigeria. His parents had been converted to Christianity (see **Christianity and Christian missions**) and he himself worked at various levels of the Christian missionary educational system in colonial Nigeria. In addition to *Ògbójú Ode Nínú Igbó Irúnmalè*, he published four other novels: *Igbó*

Olódùmarè (The Forest of God) (1946), *Ìrìnkèrindò Nínú Igbó Elégbèje* (Wanderings in the Forest of a Thousand and Four Hundred) (1961), *Ìrèké Oníbùdó* (The Sweet One with a Secure Homeground) (1961), and *Àdììtú Olódùmarè* (God's Conundrum) (1961). He also contributed and wrote the introduction to a collection of short stories entitled *Àsànyàn Ìtàn* (Selected Stories) (1959). With G.L. Lasebikan, he co-authored a short story published as a pamphlet for schoolchildren, *Òjó Asótán Iwe Kínni* (Ojo the Storyteller, Book 1) (n.d.). He spent 1948–50 in England on a British Council scholarship, and his experiences form the subject of a travel memoir in two parts: *Irinajo Apa Kinni* (*Journey, Part One*) (1949) and *Irinajo Apa Keji* (*Journey, Part Two*) (1951).

Although he wrote in a variety of modes, Fagunwa's reputation rests primarily on his work as a writer of fiction. His importance for African letters, and his legacy for other writers of Nigerian origin, is to be located in his achievement as a novelist. The novels that constitute his major work were influenced by classics of the European picaresque tradition like *Pilgrim's Progress* and *Robinson Crusoe*. Likewise, the landscape his texts evoke, and the way in which many of his characters are drawn, reveals the influence of texts like *Paradise Lost* or *Aesop's Fables*. The plot usually involves a protagonist who finds himself in an alien forest populated by supernatural forces. He undergoes many trials but triumphs over them through bravery and moral steadfastness. Along the way, the narrative voice interjects didactic themes, often in the form of direct address to the reader and specifically to schoolchildren.

Fagunwa's novels deploy two interrelated rhetorical modes. First, there is a moralistic and didactic rhetoric about human beings confronting adversity, of perseverance being repaid by spiritual and material prosperity. This rhetorical mode owes much to Fagunwa's investment in Christian doctrine, but it also derives from the fact that, as a schoolteacher, he sought to use his writings for the moral instruction of youth. At a second level, Fagunwa's rhetoric reveals a cultural–nationalist undertone. At this level, collective prosperity is presented as an ideal worth striving for, but it is understood in more mundane terms. Here, the impulse is not simply to propagate moral lessons

based on Christian doctrine, but also to contribute, through fictional narrative, to the material advancement of black people. Fagunwa's cultural nationalism is elaborated on behalf of black peoples everywhere, but he focuses that black collectivity in the figure of the discerning reader or the well-mannered schoolchild. Consequently, the heroes of his five novels represent the Nigerian and black African subject. They are fallible because they are human. But the strength of character they show in the course of their wanderings indicates Fagunwa's sense of what history demands of black peoples in the mid twentieth century.

An important testimony to Fagunwa's place in the literary history of Nigeria in particular, and the intellectual history of black Africa in general, is that three of his major works have been translated into English. This indicates that his work continues to be relevant to Africa's postcolonial situation. Fagunwa himself translated his last novel *Àdììtú Olódùmarè* (God's Conundrum) into English. The unpublished manuscript, which Fagunwa translates as "The Mysterious Plan of the Almighty," is located at the School of Oriental and African Studies (SOAS) in London. His writings have also offered a fertile ground for the development of the academic study of Yoruba in secondary and tertiary education. His novels have been reprinted numerous times, and in the 1980s were republished in revised editions that updated the texts' diacritical tone-marks. The impulse behind the revised editions was to make his texts more easily readable to the average reader of Yoruba. In this way, his texts retain their currency in contemporary, postcolonial Nigeria. Fagunwa's significance can also be seen in the influence he exerted on writers who use the English language, like the late Amos **Tutuola** and Wole **Soyinka**. The influence of Fagunwa can also be seen in the magical realism of Ben **Okri**'s *The Famished Road*. Okri's evocation of a universe of forest-dwelling demons and metaphysical entities shows a profound, if indirect, debt to Fagunwa's trail-blazing work.

The most important achievement of Fagunwa is the skill with which he deploys the Yoruba language to fashion a narrative idiom that was uniquely his, but that also gave expression to a crucial transitional period in Yoruba culture. As has often been remarked, the most influential

African writers have been committed to developing a narrative form that is adequate to the historical and cultural complexities of postcolonial black Africa. The success of these writers in fashioning creative ways of elucidating Africa's experience in the modern world serves to make the continent the *subject*, rather than the object, of literary representation and philosophical knowledge. This achievement is an ongoing one, and it is in this sense that Fagunwa's pioneering work stands as an inspiring model of intellectual and cultural work. Located at a historical juncture when traditional African cultures were (and still are) undergoing transformations as they confront Western literacy and secular-scientific values, Fagunwa's fiction rises to the occasion. He thereby makes a crucial part of Africa's cultural history available to us in compelling language.

Further reading

Bamgbose, Ayo (1974) *The Novels of D.O. Fagunwa*, Benin City, Nigeria: Ethiope.

Irele, Abiola (1981) "Tradition and the Yoruba Writer: D.O. Fagunwa, Amos Tutuola, and Wole Soyinka," in Abiola Irele, *The African Experience in Literature and Ideology*, Bloomington and Indianapolis: Indiana University Press.

Smith, Pamela J. (1991) "D.O. Fagunwa: The Art of Fabulation and Writing Orality," *The Literary Griot* 3, 2: 1–16.

OLAKUNLE GEORGE

Fall, Khadidjatou (Khadi)

b. 1948, Dakar, Senegal

poet

Khadidjatou Fall was born into a distinguished Muslim family in Senegal and spent most of her childhood in Dakar. After secondary education in Senegal she completed her undergraduate studies at the University of Toulouse in France and later attended the University of Strasbourg where she obtained a doctorate. In 1995, she attended the International Writing Program at the University of Iowa before returning to teach in Senegal. Many of her poems deal with what she calls "the mask of language." Her novel *Mademba*, which won the Prix du Roman in the Senegal-Culture Competition in 1985, chronicles a boy who writes his life story because he fears he will lose his voice. *Senteurs d'hivernage* (Scent of the Rains) (1993) describes a woman's return to South Africa, and to her native Sotho language.

MEREDITH MARTIN

Fall, Malick

b. 1920, Saint Louis, Senegal; d. 1978, Senegal

poet and novelist

Although Malick Fall published only two books, his contribution to African literature has been crucial. His collection of poems entitled *Reliefs* (1964), prefaced by **Senghor**, placed him among the most gifted of the post-**negritude** poets. To underscore his originality, Senghor called him "un poète nouveau" (an original poet). Distancing himself from facile exoticism, his descriptions of the African condition are rooted in precise evocations of personal experiences of pain and joy. With great economy of words and images, his poems convey a lasting universal appeal.

His novel *The Wound* (1973) (*La Plaie*) (1967) tells the story of Magamou Seck, the victim of an accident which leaves him with an incurable leg wound that becomes a stinking sore. This novel stands even today as one of the most original African novels. It announces the wave of postcolonial novels of disillusionment in the face of an aborted decolonization (see **colonialism, neocolonialism, and postcolonialism**), beginning in 1968 with such works as Ahmadou **Kourouma**'s *The Suns of Independence*, Yambo **Ouologuem**'s *Bound to Violence*, and Ayi Kwei **Armah**'s *The Beautyful Ones Are Not Yet Born*. In spite of its specific reference to the postcolonial condition in Africa, *The Wound* can also be read as a universal meditation on traumatic experience, a reflection on the conflict between the individual and society, and as quest narrative.

KANDIOURA DRAME

Fantouré, Alioum

b. 1938, Guinea

economist and novelist

The name Alioum Fantouré is the pseudonym of an eminent Guinean-born economist. Fantouré studied in France and Belgium, qualified as an economist, lived in Austria, and throughout his life worked with a variety of international organizations. Yet in spite of professional success he was deeply hurt by his condition of exile. Like many intellectuals of his generation, he had little choice but to flee Sekou Touré's reign of terror. Shaken by the spiral of violence that engulfed his country and destroyed traditional values, he became a strong advocate of justice and compassion for others. "Nothing vindicating division or intolerance can be found in my writings," he said. His novels explore the horrors of totalitarian regimes and argue that indifference to the plight of others, rather than injustices *per se*, have become the evil of our time. His major novels include *Tropical Circle* (*Le Cercle des tropiques*) (1972); *Le Récit du cirque ... de la vallée des morts* (The Tale of the Circus ... of the Valley of Death) (1975); *L'Homme du troupeau du Sahel* (The Man of the Herd of Sahel) (1979); *Le Voile ténébreux* (The Dark Shroud) (1985); and *Le Gouverneur du territoire* (The Governor of the Territory) (1995).

Further reading

Midiohouan, G.O. (1984) *L'Utopie négative d'Alioum Fantouré: essai sur Le cercle des tropiques* (The Negative Utopia of Alioum Fantouré's Essay on Tropical Circle), Paris: Silex.

JEAN-MARIE VOLET

al-Faqīh (Fagīh), Ahāmad Ibrāhīm

b. 1942, Mizda, Libya

writer and journalist

Born in Mizda in southern Libya, al-Faqīh is a fiction writer and journalist. He received his doctorate degree in Islamic and Middle East Studies from the University of Edinburgh in 1982. He lives in Egypt where he devotes his time to his fiction and essay writing and contributes a regular article to the Egyptian daily *al-Ahram*, having previously worked as general editor of various literary magazines. His trilogy, *Sa'ahibukī Madīnatan Ukhrā* (I Shall Offer You Another City), *Hādhihī Tukhūmū Mamlakatī* (These are the Borders of My Kingdom), and *Nafaqun Tuḍī'uhu Imra'atun Wāḥida* (A Tunnel Lit by One Woman) (1991), was translated into English and published in a single volume, *Gardens of the Night* (1995). It is a trilateral look at the past that shapes us, the present we experience in a semi-conscious state, and the unattainable future that we can consider only from a distance. Al-Faqīh is also concerned with the struggle between old traditions and modernity. Yet he considers himself a global writer and sees humanity united by common characteristics. He relies on Arab folk culture to convey some of his symbolism and his novel *Fī'rān bilā Juḥūr* (Homeless Rats) (2000) makes use of Libyan legends.

Further reading

Faqīh, Ahāmad (2000) *Charles, Diana and Me, and Other Stories*, London and New York: Kegan Paul International.

——(2000) *Gazelles and Other Plays*, London and New York: Kegan Paul International.

——(2000) *Valley of the Ashes*, London and New York: Kegan Paul International.

——(2000) *Who's Afraid of Agatha Christie and Other Stories*, London and New York: Kegan Paul International.

Sakkut, Hamdi (2000) *The Arabic Novel*, vol. I, Cairo: American University in Cairo Press.

AIDA A. BAMIA

Farag, Alfred

b. 1929, Egypt

playwright

Alfred Farag is one of Egypt's outstanding playwrights in the second half of the twentieth century. His first play was staged in Cairo in 1956. He has distinguished himself in the use of popular literature in the Arabic tradition, for example *The Thousand and One Nights*, as well as Egyptian and other Arab historical sources, as a resource from which to draw characters and stories, which are then recast in such dramatic moulds (sometimes tragic, sometimes comic) as to make a political or philosophical comment on the modern world. His best-known comedies include *The Barber of Baghdad* (1964), *Ali Janah al-Tabrizi and his Servant Quffa* (1968), and *The Good, the Bad and the Beautiful Woman* (1994), all of which draw mainly on *The Arabian Nights* to make a comment on Egypt's political realities of the day and the human condition beyond. Foremost among his tragedies is *Sulayman of Aleppo* (1965), which recreates Shakespeare's Hamlet as a Syrian political assassin offering resistance to Napoleon's army in early nineteenth-century Egypt. Farag also wrote social dramas, including *Marriage by Decree Nisi* (1973), dealing directly with contemporary reality in Egypt. All Farag's plays, regardless of mould and setting, are characterized by an ardent quest for justice (political, social, metaphysical, as the case may be), usually undertaken by the main character. Farag's plays are noted for his experimentation with language, always trying to convey a sense of period through style, and to bridge the traditional gap in Arabic between high literary style and the language of everyday speech. Several of his plays have been translated into English.

Further reading

Badawi, M.M. (1987) *Modern Arabic Drama in Egypt*, Cambridge: Cambridge University Press, pp. 171–82.

El-Enany, R. (2000) "The Quest for Justice in the Theatre of Alfred Farag," *Journal of Arabic Literature* 31, 2: 171–202.

RASHEED EL-ENANY

Farah, Nuruddin

b. 1945, Baidoa, Somalia

novelist

Nuruddin Farah, the Somali novelist who has won several literary awards, was born in Baidoa, Somalia, and was educated in Ethiopia, Somalia, India, and Britain. Before proceeding to the University of Chandigarh, where he studied philosophy and literature for the BA degree, Farah worked in the Ministry of Education in Mogadishu. After graduation, he taught at Dagaxtur and Wardhigley secondary schools and at the National University of Somalia. Farah's writing career began early in his life. His unpublished novel, "Why Dead So Soon," was serialized in Somali in 1965, and his unpublished play, "Doctor and Physician," was broadcast there when he was still at Chandigarh. His play, *The Offering*, was accepted in place of a thesis and he was subsequently awarded the MA degree in literature at the University of Essex, where he had transferred from the University of London. In 1998, Farah was awarded the Neustadt International Prize for Literature, one of the major literary awards in the United States. Equally importantly, his short story "The Affair" was shortlisted for the 2001 Michael Caine Prize in Literature. Because of the complexity and sophistication of his novels, Farah is difficult to categorize, but his work can be placed in three phases: the opposition to elements of Somali cultural norms; the critique of postcolonial dictatorship; and the concern with war, dependency, and the collapse of the state in Africa.

In 1968, while at Chandigarh, Farah wrote his first published novel, *From a Crooked Rib* (1970). The text bears a resemblance to, yet is radically different from, the aesthetics of cultural nationalism (see **nationalism and post-nationalism**) championed by Chinua **Achebe** in *Things Fall Apart* (1958) and **Ngugi wa Thiong'o** in *The River Between* (1965). Unlike these two pioneering works of African literature, Farah does not highlight the conflict between colonialism and precolonial African culture (see **colonialism, neocolonialism, and postcolonialism**). He instead deals with problems caused by and affecting Somali people in the late 1950s when echoes of independence were beginning to be heard. In this novel, Farah questions the preparedness of Somalia for independence. He examines the position of women in society from a cultural point of view and criticizes culture, tradition, and religion as the three norms that male members of society combine to oppress and humiliate women. Basing the title of his book on a Somali religious proverb, he shows that preparations for independence should have included redressing gender inequality. He illustrates the unreasonableness of the male-ordered society in using myths to justify the stifling and stigmatization of women, and criticizes the outdated Somali practice of female "circumcision," which he represents as barbaric, unhygienic, and dehumanizing. He also criticizes the practice of forced marriage and castigates society for sanctioning the material aspect that governs it. Through her two successful attempts to escape from the practice of forced marriage, the protagonist of the novel embarks on a search for individual freedom as a woman, and this quest is what structures Farah's novel. Through her personal choice of the man she marries, she grasps freedom. Through her tit-for-tat behavior when her husband cheats her while on a short course in Italy, she establishes her equality with her husband. With this equality, Somalia becomes, symbolically, ready for her independence.

It was while he was teaching at the National University of Somalia in the early 1970s that Farah wrote his second novel, *A Naked Needle* (1976). Two features of Somali politics form the focus of the text. First, the democratically elected government that took over the reins of power at independence became chaotically corrupt. Second, the military government that overthrew it became increasingly dictatorial. The focus of Farah's criticism is built around the recurrent theme of the urgent need for radical change and reform in social, cultural, and political matters. There is a sense in which the narrative directs the reader into the underlying philosophy at the heart of Farah's intellectual perception. He seems to suggest that morality and immorality crystallize in action and inaction. The will to fight against evil seems to be the mark of morality, while the unwillingness to do so, or the readiness to foment evil, is the mark of immorality. Thus in *A Naked Needle*, Siad Barre's 1969 *coup d'état*

and its revolutionary zeal seem at first to epitomize action and morality, while its subsequent degeneration into corruption and dictatorial practices epitomizes the immorality which in Farah's view emerges from inaction. The strongest criticism, however, is of the Somali intellectuals who fail – or refuse – to recognize the regime's development of dangerous political practices. The author criticizes Somali intellectuals for their lack of insight, their revolutionary pretension and total surrender to bourgeois ideas and practices. He also criticizes the few who realized the direction the regime was taking but failed to map out clear strategies and goals of opposition. Their naïve rattling renders them inconsequential and the regime totally sidelines them in the issues affecting the state.

During the second phase of his writing career, in the late 1970s continuing to the 1990s, Farah was disheartened by the gradual decay of postcolonial Somalia. Koschin, the dirty and disorganized protagonist of *A Naked Needle*, provides a vivid representation of the dirt and disorganization of Somali society. Koschin's disappearance into obscurity at the end of the novel functions as Farah's prophetic warning that Somalia is sliding into total obscurity and inconsequentiality in world affairs. In the two trilogies that follow *A Naked Needle*, Farah provides one of the most persistent representations on the theme of variations on an African dictatorship and the radical collapse of the African state into a world of blood and chaos. The first theme is treated in *Sweet and Sour Milk* (1977), *Sardines* (1981), and *Close Sesame* (1983); the second theme is taken up in *Maps* (1986), *Gifts* (1993), and *Secrets* (1998). In all these works, the faint echoes of the novels of cultural nationalism written in the critical realist tradition (see **realism and magical realism**) give way to the resounding voices of political nationalism and pan-Africanism. However, these are obscured by the preponderance of the writer's disenchantment with political leadership in post-independence Africa. In *Sweet and Sour Milk*, for instance, Farah examines the state of Somalia after the military dictatorship has firmly consolidated itself. The nation has assumed hideous proportions and the postcolonial state has become monstrous.

In 1984, in an attempt to understand the link between postcolonial and colonial dictatorship,

Farah traveled to Italy to research into the culture of the former colonizers, and he was able to discern the similarity between the Somali head of state's tactics and those of Italian officials in colonial Somalia. *Sweet and Sour Milk* is a culmination of this research. Tactics of repression in both eras include the use of illiterate sycophants to do the dirty work of the state. These torture, kill, and maim, harass and harm the innocent, encourage betrayal among family and friends, and sow seeds of disharmony and mistrust. Finally, they misuse Islam (see **Islam in African literature**), culture, and traditions to prop up a regime that is disgusting in all its manifestations. In *Sweet and Sour Milk*, Farah demonstrates how a repressive regime cordons itself in the comfort of the mystification it constructs for this purpose. His argument is that it is only through demystification of the edifice of such constructions that individuals can free themselves and their nations. Failure to do so, Farah seems to suggest, is a license to the success of dictatorial political expediency. Using the image of the family as a symbol of the state, Farah grapples with the issues of patriarchal oppression and matriarchal submission. The two notions function as metaphors in which the oppression of the ruling oligarchy is felt by the weak and defenseless.

However, in *Sardines*, which Farah wrote when he was a visiting professor at Bayreuth University in Germany, matriarchy shifts to symbolize both resistance (Medina) and tool of oppression (Idil), while patriarchy symbolizes weakness and political naïvety (Samatar) in the tin Somalia has become. The point Farah makes here is that both the male and the female categories are equally susceptible to good and to evil. They both have the capacity to be either the vanguards of opposition or outright collaborators in the destruction of the nation. Seen in the totality of its sadistic manifestations, *Sardines* articulates Farah's criticism of the impunity with which the postcolonial African state sponsors the culture of murder, revenge, mutilation of the sanctity of the human body, humiliation of individual citizens, and the general barbarity of despotic regimes.

As intimated earlier, Farah constantly demonstrates the continuity of colonial links to the criminality of the postcolonial African state. This explains succinctly the presence of Sandra in what he terms the "incestuous circle" in *Sardines*. Sandra, as the Queen in the circle, reaps the benefits that are conferred on those who enable the dictatorship to destroy those who oppose it. Her presence in Somalia and her biological and historical links to the colonial era make the significance and relevance of *Close Sesame* clear, because it is during her grandfather's reign as governor-general that colonial brutality is felt. It would seem that "Queen" Sandra (former colonial boss) collaborates with the general to run down Somalia because she fails to condemn his atrocities. In the trilogy's interplay on the theme of "guest" and "gift," Sandra is presented as the colonial "guest" to whom the dictatorship hands over the "gift" of journalistic monopoly and policy-shaping. In her new position, one reads an inversion of roles: the trodden-upon Somali are turned into guests in their own country. This trend can only be reversed by a revolution in which the young and the old, such as Deeriye, his son, and his son's colleagues, die. In *Close Sesame*, Farah revamps the history of the Somali people for the benefit of the young generation, on whom hope for a better Somalia is bestowed.

In the second trilogy, Farah shifts focus to highlight issues that foment interstate wars, wars that complicate the notion of identity itself. He also focuses on the issues that infringe on the honor, freedom, and respect of individuals, families, groups, and nations. *Maps*, *Gifts*, and *Secrets* reflect on the issue of identity in varied yet connected ways. In *Maps*, Farah examines the war between Somalia and Ethiopia, a war in which people shed their blood in an effort to determine their national and individual identity. Somali people view the war as legitimate and just, as its objective is to oppose and dismantle imposed colonial boundaries which robbed them of their territory and falsified the national identity of their people. Supported by the OAU charter, Ethiopians see it as a war of aggression to which they have a legitimate duty to respond in order to defend the sanctity of colonial demarcations. The war thus complicates further relations between Somali people and Ethiopian people in the Ogaden. This results in further shedding of innocent blood in the most disgusting manner.

In *Gifts*, Farah grapples with moral, psychological, and political implications of dependency. He examines the loss of honor of those individuals, families, and nations that survive on handouts in the form of gifts, presents, or any label they may have. While living in the Gambia, Farah witnessed how that country's dependency on rice from the USA made a mockery of the dignity of the Gambian people. In 1992, because of wars and famine in the Horn of Africa, it was the turn of Somalia to suffer the humiliation of the syndrome. In *Gifts*, therefore, Farah castigates the culture of the Third World's dependency on aid, a tendency he depicts as a way of losing national honor and political freedom. Seen from the episodes of dependency in the rest of his novels, especially in *A Naked Needle*, Farah's criticism is valid given the humiliating conditions for aid in Africa.

In the corpus of his works, Farah appears to wrestle with the need to retrieve truth from the mash of falsehood. This is profoundly so in *Secrets*, which concludes the second trilogy and in which he examines the implications of inter-clan conflict in Somalia. *Secrets* is a sophisticated novel whose style of suspense plays tricks on the reader. In it, too, Farah experiments with and succeeds in incorporating magical realism in the modern African novel (see **realism and magical realism**). With this new stylistic venture, Farah succeeds in narrating the bizarre nature of Somalia's descent into chaos and state decay towards the end of Siad Barre's regime. While in *Maps* he examines issues related to individual identity, national identity, and loyalty to the nation, in *Secrets* he examines issues related to individual identity and the individual's loyalty to his/her paternal bloodline. The central conflict in the discourse of *Secrets*, therefore, is that between loyalty to paternal clan and loyalty to the truth of one's biological paternity, and its relevance to one's convictions and feelings. It is necessary to note that, unlike Askar, who in *Maps* traces his existence from the moment of his birth, Kalaman of *Secrets* traces his from the moment of conception. As such, he questions the notion of father's blood and its significance to the political and social chaos in Somalia. This helps him to decide where his loyalty belongs. The conclusion is that Kalaman's loyalty belongs to society and not to the clan, which ultimately eludes him.

Finally, it is important to note the uniqueness of Farah's art. As we have already seen, while he appears to have been influenced by Achebe's and Ngugi's early novels, he does not deal with the conflict between colonialism and African traditions. Equally, despite the signs of political nationalism in his later novels, he does not address issues of decolonization. He is simply a disenchanted African writer whose concerns are the failings of the postcolonial state in Africa. He writes in exile, yet Somalia is always his setting and point of reference. He depicts the plight of women, but unlike the **negritude** writers before him, Farah castigates them for their many failings. He points a finger at colonialism for the ills of Africa but does not exonerate the colonized. He accuses the capitalist world of creating neocolonial robbers in the name of rulers, but also accuses Russians, emblems of Marxism, of training a squad of systematic murderers of the Somali people. When the Russians are expelled and replaced by Americans in Somalia, Farah is not fooled, because he knows that the ruling oligarchy will use whatever means and whichever agent to commit genocide in order to remain in power. This gloomy picture notwithstanding, Farah sees hope in the youth of Somalia, such as the baby Soyaan in *Sweet and Sour Milk*, Ubax in *Sardines*, Samawade in *Close Sesame*, Nasiiba in *Gifts*, and Kalaman in *Secrets*. In terms of cross-border clashes in search of identity, Farah proposes regional federations as a way of avoiding the bitterness of interstate wars resulting from colonial demarcation lines.

Further reading

Ewen, D.R. (1984) "Nuruddin Farah," in G.D. Killam (ed.) *The Writing of East and Central Africa*, Nairobi: Heinemann Educational.

Ntalindwa, R. (1997) "Nationalism and the East African Writer: The Position of Nuruddin Farah," *Ufahamu: Journal of the African Activist Association* 25, 3: 67–85.

RAYMOND NTALINDWA

Farès, Nabile

b. 1940, Algeria

novelist

Criticized by some critics for being difficult and shunned by others, the Algerian writer Nabile Farès has engaged in experimentation with novelistic forms by introducing disjointed narrative, delirious prose, verse, and typographical innovations into his novels. Published in the 1970s, his first five novels –*Yahia, pas de chance* (Luckless Yahia) (1970), *Un Passager de l'Occident* (Western Passenger) (1971), *Le Champ des oliviers* (Olive Field) (1972), *Mémoire de l'absent* (The Absent Man's Memory) (1974), *L'Exil et le désarroi* (Exile and Distress) (1976) – share a number of place names and characters and explore the alienation brought about by exile and migration. The first three are structured as itineraries (physical, imagined, or remembered) and subvert conventional notions of plot with seemingly unrelated sections. The last three are grouped under the heading "Discovery of the New World," which Farès has called a "frenzied autobiography." Farès was only 14 when the Algerian revolution began, and his work (which includes poetry and texts that defy conventional genres) is profoundly marked by it. He has also been a critic of the post-independence situation in Algeria and a defender of Berber cultures.

Further reading

Bensmaïa, Réda (1993) "The Exiles of Nabile Farès: or, How to Become a Minority," *Yale French Studies* 83: 44–70.

JARROD HAYES

Fassi Fihri, Nouzha

b. Fez, Morocco

writer

The Moroccan writer Nouzha Fassi Fihri's novels in French often explore the tensions between traditional and modern forces in postcolonial Moroccan society (see **colonialism, neocoloni-alism, and postcolonialism**). The nationalist movement for independence and the aftermath of the French protectorate form the background against which her characters assert the aspirations of the new generation of Moroccans. Violence and revolt provide the framework within which historical events and the characters' personal narratives intersect. Nouzha Fassi Fihri's main novels, *Le Ressac* (The Backwash) (1990) and *La Baroudeuse* (The Fighter) (1997), are set in the traditional city of Fez and have, as central characters, independent and self-reliant women who challenge conventional gender roles and assert their place within the new independent nation. In both novels, the main protagonist is a rebellious and determined woman who expresses her dream of a freer and more equal society. Nouzha Fassi Fihri's novels also offer anthropological and sociological studies of modern Moroccan society through the use of series of realistic tableaux. The author's descriptive and realist portrayal of local customs contains a certain degree of exoticism, which could suggest at times that her work is being directed mainly towards a Western audience.

Further reading

Fassi, N. (1990) *Le Ressac* (The Backwash), Paris: L'Harmattan.

ANISSA TALAHITE-MOODLEY

feminist criticism

African female and feminist intellectuals had written and published their writing as early as the late nineteenth century, as in the case of the Sierra Leonean poet and memoirist Adelaide Smith **Casely Hayford** and the noted South African activist and novelist, Olive **Schreiner**. And from the late twentieth century, there has been a tremendous increase in the publication of scholarly work on Africanist, postcolonial, and feminist theory that has contributed to the development of feminist criticism of African literature. It is important to note, nevertheless, that in Africa, as everywhere else, feminist criticism is a relatively youthful subdiscipline, having gotten off to a later start than did other varieties of literary criticism. In contrast to American New Critical, British Leavisite, biographical or sociological criticism, or even its most comparable ideological partners, Marxist and pan-Africanist criticism, the feminist criticism of African literature is in a relation of belatedness, due primarily to the later arrival of women's writing on to the African bellelettristic stage.

Sub-Saharan and black female-authored novels first emerged in print in 1966, which is when Heinemann published Nigerian Flora **Nwapa**'s *Efuru*, and the East African Publishing House *The Promised Land* by Kenyan Grace **Ogot**. (By contrast, Sol **Plaatje** published *Mhudi* in 1930 and Amos **Tutuola** *The Palm-Wine Drinkard* in 1952.) Ama Ata **Aidoo**'s play *Dilemma of a Ghost* was published in 1965, though first performed in 1964. In South Africa, Nadine **Gordimer** published her first novel, *The Lying Days*, in 1953 and the Algerian Assia **Djebar** her first, *La Soif*, in 1957. Of course, the novel, a written and somewhat lengthy narrative mode, is of recent development, in contrast to oral literature, both poetic and dramatic. The feminist scholarship on the oral form, however, is of even later development. (See *Research in African Literatures* special issue on "Women as Oral Artists.")

Feminist literary criticism and its awkward beginnings

A great deal of the literary criticism of African literature developed in some relation to cultural nationalism, especially any literary criticism that had an investment in ideology or politics. For while there were certainly many practitioners of Leavisite and sociological criticism in Africa, what have emerged to become the most powerful traditions of literary critique are those that were in direct engagement with decolonizing nationalism. In this tradition, there were many who suggested of feminism in general that it was too European in its influence, too individualistic in its interests, not enough committed to the struggles of the larger group, whether the group was understood to be racially, nationally, clan or class based. One of the most outspoken of these critics was Femi Ojo-Ade. Curiously, there has been no similar critique of Marxism as an imported ideology, inauthentic or

somehow inappropriate to the African context. In response to the critique of feminism, the Nigerian Marxist and feminist critic 'Molara Ogundipe-Leslie opines:

> For those who say that feminism is not relevant to Africa, can they truthfully say that the African woman is all right in all these areas of her being and therefore does not need an ideology that addresses her reality, hopefully and preferably, to ameliorate that reality? When they argue that feminism is foreign, are these opponents able to support the idea that African women or cultures did not have ideologies which propounded or theorized woman's being and provided avenues and channels for women's oppositions and resistance to injustice within their societies?
>
> (1994: Trenton)

Because African feminist theory was strongly determined by the politics of independence movements feminist literary criticism developed in diacritical relation to cultural nationalism. That is to say, although it has been in defensive engagement with cultural nationalism, African feminist literary criticism has always included within its self-understanding a strong component of the advocacy of cultural nationalism. One such manifestation of this tendency is the popularity among many feminist critics of the term "womanism." Originally coined in 1967 in the African-American literary and cultural context by Alice Walker, womanism has become a productive term for Africanist feminist theory. Walker includes as part of the term's secondary definition, "Committed to survival and wholeness of entire people, male and female. Not a separatist, except periodically, for health" (1984: San Diego).

The so-called radical strain of feminist criticism which flourished and continues to flourish in European and EuroAmerican contexts, which attributes gender oppression or inequality to straightforward masculine power, and which celebrates sexual as well as social bonds between women, simply did not constitute a major strain of thought in African feminist criticism. Neither men nor even patriarchy were, in literary feminism's initial articulation, understood to be the only agent of subjugation of African womanhood. For while homosociality was celebrated, if not quietly assumed, female homosexuality – indeed, female sexuality as a whole – was almost never mentioned in the texts of the first generation of women writers. The rare representations of lesbianism tended to be negative by virtue of its association with racial or colonial divisions, as in Aidoo's *Our Sister Killjoy* (1979) or with an anxiety about urban modernity, as in *Ripples in the Pool* (1975) by Kenyan Rebeka Njau. In the 1980s Francophone African women, in particular Calixthe **Beyala**, Angèle **Rawiri**, Tanella Boni from the Côte d'Ivoire, and Véronique **Tadjo**, began exploring sexuality in their writing and Rawiri and Beyala incorporated depictions of lesbian love that had mixed relation to heterosexual love.

Even the liberal feminist analysis, which holds that women's emancipation will result from their greater access to education, to financial success, and, of course, to equal treatment before the law, became modified in the African context – for historically, African feminist expression has not been able to ignore the epistemic as well as material violence of colonialism as a primary inhibitor of the aspirations of women. The desire for equality in even its most conventional liberal expression is always bound up, for Africans, with the understanding that the individual nation, and usually the continent as a whole, is part of a global system of power relations, a system which has usually functioned to the disadvantage of most if not all Africans. However, as greater numbers of women become educated, and as the rhetoric of socialism and class-transformation becomes increasingly sullied by its co-optation by corrupt dictatorships, liberal feminism appears increasingly appealing to many.

Feminist scholars of women's writing

One of the earliest pieces of literary criticism written for an explicitly feminist politics about African women writers was published in *Présence Africaine* in 1972 by Maryse **Condé**, the Guadeloupean critic and novelist. By drawing attention to the themes and the styles of writing of the very first Europhone African writers, Nwapa, Ogot, Aidoo, and Efua **Sutherland**, and by devoting serious scholarly attention to the writings of the first three for the kind of perspective they bring to a

postcolonial African politics, Condé became one of the inaugurators of African feminist literary criticism. Just as interesting is the fact that Condé, who has herself since gone on to achieve acclaim with her novels written in French, asserts that at the time while "Francophone Africa had produced a number of researchers and writers of sociological studies, one [was] at a loss to find any lasting names in the literary field" (1972: *Présence Africaine*). Condé suggested that Anglophone writers constituted the more dynamic of the two linguistic groups. For several years, certainly, the criticism tended to support her claim.

Carole Boyce Davies' manifesto introducing the 1985 landmark collection of African feminist essays on literature, *Ngambika* (which is in dialogue with Ogundipe-Leslie), offers in polemical form many of the points that characterize African feminist literary criticism, namely that it is decidedly pro-nationalist, especially when such nationalism involves decolonization, and pro-socialist, in that it affirms the value of women's status as mothers and even as polygynous co-wives, and that it looks to indigenous feminist practices for its models. Most of the seven points Davies makes have to do with the interrelation of feminism with anti-colonial critique. She also calls for the development of an African and female aesthetic, and speaks in particular to celebrating the act of mothering, which she understands to be an important thematic in the literature of African women. In 1990, Susan Andrade published an influential essay, "Rewriting History, Motherhood and Rebellion," which, beginning with the thematic of mothering, argued that African women writers had self-consciously begun to represent themselves in genealogical terms, and that attentive close reading of the texts offered the critic better clues than did a priori notions of success or failure. Florence Stratton offered a bold, insightful and wide-ranging contribution in *African Literature and the Politics of Gender* (1994) which, among other things, registers the sex- and gender-based tensions of cultural nationalism. She points out, for example, that many male authors of African literature, novelists in particular, represented women as either Mother Africa figures, symbols of a fecund and untainted tradition, or prostitutes, figures of a corrupted modernity, and through a set of close readings puts her finger on the pulse of masculine literary responses to colonization via the discourse of tradition. Chikwenye Ogunyemi's *African Wo/Man Palava* (1996) develops her influential 1985 essay in *Signs*, "Womanism: The Dynamics of the Contemporary Black Female Novel in English," to its logical and literary ends, by using the boundaries of the Nigerian nation as a way to imagine a vernacular criticism, a space for dialogue amongst women, between women and men, and across the bounds of ethnicity and region for a feminist politics celebratory of African values.

In the Francophone tradition, Irene Assiba d'Almeida has taken up the question of female writers' relation to writing via a movement from individual to family to larger sociality in *Destroying the Emptiness of Silence* (1996). Odile Cazenave's *Femmes Rebelles* (1996), translated as *Rebellious Women* (2000), focuses on the figure of feminine transgression, and, positioning itself to engage the second wave of Francophone literary production, writing from the 1980s and 1990s, offers a thematically oriented literary history.

Cultural nationalism, gender symbolism and "images of women" criticism

Gender has been a notable means by which nationalism has symbolically worked out its relation to colonialism, modernity, tradition, and the new nation-state – and in this respect Africa is no exception. Here, as elsewhere in decolonizing nationalism, gender and sexual politics are often represented via woman as allegory of the nation, one way by which male authors symbolically resolve anxiety about embracing modernity, the nation-state, and things non-African. A fecund Mother Africa figure might well be read as native riposte to imperial depictions of geographic and social space bereft of European fertilization and agency. While this sign of woman might have its origins in a certain progressive nationalist moment, the fact remains that its logic replaces an imported phallocracy with a native one (see McClintock 1995). Anti-colonial movements appear as racialized versions of the Oedipal complex, wherein the sons of the nation seek to affirm their manhood in the process of redeeming the mother country, and restoring her to youthful beauty. Instead of this

yearning for an idealized past, the figure of the prostitute represents its logical extreme, degradation in an uncertain future. It represents authorial grappling with the dislocations that accompany modernity and modernization, including migration, changes in familial relations and economic structures, industrialization and technological development. The prostitute, the most famous of which appears in Cyprian **Ekwensi**'s immensely popular Onitsha-market novel, *Jagua Nana* (1961), signifies African women run amok in modernity: earning money and having multiple sexual relations without the benefit of patriarchal control. An unsullied Mother Africa and the alienated or degraded prostitute constitute two sides of the same coin of gender anxiety. The former yearns for a fixed past, the latter openly worries about the consequences of engaging a modern future. Another, more optimistic figure of gender figuration, at least at the level of surface representation, is that of the New Woman who leads the nation into the future. She is the African woman who has been produced by nationalism's successes, namely education and participation in a public civil sphere. This idealized figure is visible in **Achebe**'s *Anthills of the Savannah* (1987), in Nuruddin **Farah**'s *Sardines* (1981); in female-authored novels, she is most classically visible in *Une si longue lettre* by Mariama **Bâ** (1979).

Works cited

d'Almeida, Irene Assiba (1996) *Francophone African Literature and the Politics of Silence*, Gainsville, Florida: University Press of Florida.

Andrade, Susan Z. (1990/1996) "Rewriting History, Motherhood and Rebellion: Naming an African Women's Literary Tradition," *Research in African Literatures* (1990) 21, 1: 91–110; revised as "The Joys of Daughterhood," in Deirdre Lynch and William B. Warner (eds) *Cultural Institutions of the Novel* (1996), Durham, North Carolina: Duke University Press.

Cazenave, Odile (1996/2000) *Femmes rebelles: naissance d'un nouveau roman africain au féminin* (1996), Paris: L'Harmattan; translated as *Rebellious Women: The New Generation of Female African Novelists* (2000), Boulder, Colorado: Lynne Rienner.

Condé, Maryse (1972) "Three Female Writers in Modern Africa: Flora Nwapa, Ama Ata Aidoo and Grace Okot," *Présence Africaine* 82: 132–43.

Davies, Carole Boyce (1985) Introduction to Davies and Anne Adams Graves (eds) *N'gambika*, Trenton, New Jersey: Africa World, pp. 1–23.

McClintock, Anne (1995) *Imperial Leather: Race, Gender and Sexuality in the Colonial Context*, New York: Routledge.

Ogundipe-Leslie, 'Molara (1994) *Recreating Ourselves: African Women and Critical Transformations*, Trenton, New Jersey: Africa World.

Ogunyomi, Chikwenye (1985) "Womanism: The Dynamics of the Contemporary Black Female Novel in English," *Signs* 11, 1: 63–80.

——(1996) *African Wo/Man Palava*, Chicago: University of Chicago.

Research in African Literatures (1994) special issue on "Women as Oral Artists," 25, 3.

Stratton, Florence (1994) *Contemporary African Literature and the Politics of Gender*, London: Routledge.

Walker, Alice (1967) *In Search of Our Mothers' Gardens*, San Diego, California: Harcourt Brace.

SUSAN Z. ANDRADE

Feraoun, Mouloud

b. 1913, Kabylia; d. 1962, El Biar, Algeria

novelist, essayist, and critic

The novelist, essayist, and critic Mouloud Feraoun holds a unique position among Algerian writers. A Berber with no knowledge of Arabic, he was a fervent nationalist. Moreover, he maintained strong friendships with French intellectuals such as Albert Camus, even though they disagreed over the issue of Algerian independence. Feraoun's fiction is largely rooted in his home territory of Kabylia. His novels offer testament to the impoverished condition of the inhabitants and their suffering during the French–Algerian war. His first novel, *The Poor Man's Son* (*Le Fils du pauvre*) (1950), draws extensively upon Feraoun's own childhood to trace the life of an impoverished boy who comes of age as he struggles to attain an education in the French colonial system. Several chapters offering a critique

of French colonial education were omitted in the 1954 printing of the text, but were later published as part of the posthumous *The Birthday* (*L'Anniversaire*) (1972). Prominent among Feraoun's nonfictional texts is his journal (*Journal 1955–1962*) (1962), which details the havoc that the French–Algerian war wrought upon Kabylia. Feraoun was assassinated in 1962 by the French Secret Service (OAS).

Further reading

Feraoun, Mouloud (2000) *Journal, 1955–1962: Reflections on the French–Algerian War*, trans. Mary Ellen Wolf and Claude Fouillade, Lincoln: University of Nebraska Press.

NEIL DOSHI

Finbert, Elian-Juda

b. 1899, Palestine; d. 1977, Paris, France

novelist and poet

A Francophone writer, Finbert was born in Palestine and was brought as an infant to Egypt where his family settled in a village in Lower Egypt in the Delta. He attended the local Koranic school and then the French missionary school. He became involved in literary matters while studying pharmacy. He wrote a number of novels as well as poetry, and received several literary prizes and awards. Among his popular works is *Hussein*, a 1930 fictional account of the 1882 Oraby revolt in Egypt; the novel was republished in 1947 under a new title *Tempête sur l'Orient* (Tempest in the Orient).

His first novel, *Sous le signe de la licorne et du lion* (Under the Sign of the Unicorn and the Lion) (1925), condemned the policy of Britain in the Middle East and was banned in Britain and its colonies. He co-founded in 1925 (with Carlo Saurès) *Les Messages d'Orient* (Messages of the Orient), a magazine to which many prominent Arab writers, such as Taha Hussein and al-Akkad, contributed. Finbert translated their submitted essays to French. In 1929 he co-founded with Robert **Blum** the Association of Francophone Writers of Egypt. Many of his works dealt with the

Nile: *Le Batelier du Nil* (The Boatman of the Nile) (1928) and *Le Nil, fleuve du paradis* (The Nile, River of Paradise) (1933). His collection of poetry, entitled *Les Roseaux du Nil* (The Reeds of the Nile), won the Hentsch Prize. He also received the Renaissance Prize for his novel *Le Fou de Dieu* (God's Fool) (1933). He wrote a work on the life of camels entitled *Le Vaisseau du désert* (The Ship of the Desert) (1938). From then on he devoted himself to writing about animals.

Further reading

Finbert, Elian-Juda (1933) *Le Fou de Dieu* (God's Fool), Paris: Fasquelles.

FERIAL J. GHAZOUL

Fodéba, Keïta

b. 1924; d. 1969, Guinea

poet and dancer

Keïta Fodéba belongs to the generation of African intellectuals marked by **negritude** and eager to stress the value of African music and oral tradition transmitted by the griots (story and praise tellers). He belongs also to the era that saw an end to French colonialism in Guinea, his native country (see **colonialism, neocolonialism, and post-colonialism**). Keïta started his career as a teacher, but he went on to found the company Le Théâtre Africain (African Theater) in 1949. His Ballets Africains (African Ballets) gained considerable renown in the mid 1950s and early 1960s, with numerous recordings of African popular music and traditional folk songs, sung in African languages in collaboration with artists of various African regions.

His literary contribution consists mainly of a collection of texts titled *Poèmes africains* (African Poems) (1950) that were republished fifteen years later, slightly modified, under the title *Aube africaine* (African Dawn) (1965). This later edition included the previously published "Le Maître d'école" (The Teacher) (1952), his famous short story "Minuit" (Midnight), which had been published earlier but had been censored by the French colonial admin-

istration, and "Aube Africaine" which gave its name to the collection.

Fodéba saw an end to French colonization in Guinea, his native country, and he became successively home secretary and minister of security, defense, and agriculture in Sekou Touré's government. However, he was executed by that same government on 27 May 1969 after a short imprisonment in the infamous Camp Boiro near Conakry.

JEAN-MARIE VOLET

Fugard, Athol

b. 1932, Middelburg, Cape Province, South Africa

playwright

Athol Fugard is undoubtedly one of the leading African theater artists; indeed, over the last forty years of the twentieth century he emerged as a dominant figure on the world stage. The author of over twenty major works, including such classics as *The Blood Knot* (1963), *Sizwe Bansi is Dead* (1974), *The Island* (1974), and *Master Harold ... and the Boys* (1982), he is today one of the most frequently performed playwrights in the English-speaking world and beyond. As well as this, a number of his plays, including *Boesman and Lena* (1969), *Marigolds in August* (1982), and *The Road to Mecca* (1985), have been successfully transformed into motion pictures. In addition to his remarkable achievements as writer, he is an accomplished director and actor who has notably been involved in some of the most memorable productions of his plays in South Africa, Britain, and the United States. As a founding member of the Serpent Players between the late 1950s and early 1970s, he was instrumental in the establishment of an interracial politically committed alternative theater in South Africa during the apartheid years. Fugard is also the author of the novel *Tsotsi* (1980) and of *Cousins: A Memoir* (1994). But it is as South Africa's pre-eminent playwright, director, and actor that he has won the highest critical and popular acclaim.

Fugard's career as a dramatist is closely tied to the history of South Africa in the last half of the twentieth century. In *The Dramatic Art of Athol Fugard* (2000: Bloomington) Albert Wertheim contends that "Fugard's plays have been milestones and signposts of apartheid's devastating progress, its demise, and the future that is unfolding in its wake." However, despite their highly localized origins and idioms, his plays command a global audience on account of their enactment of universal existential dilemmas. Set for the most part in or around Port Elizabeth, South Africa, the plays typically depict two or three marginalized characters linked by bonds of blood, friendship, or love, struggling to survive difficult life circumstances. In this sense, the South African context provides a highly specified given circumstance that enables Fugard to explore the general drama of ordinary human life in the late twentieth century.

From its outset with the production of *No Good Friday* in the late 1950s, Fugard's life in the theater has unfolded in the shadow of apartheid, a system of racial discrimination officially adopted as South African state policy in 1948 and formally dismantled by the establishment of a multiracial democracy in 1994 (see **apartheid and post-apartheid**). Along with such other white South African writers as André **Brink**, J.M. **Coetzee**, Nadine **Gordimer**, and Alan **Paton**, Fugard emerged as a voice of conscience in South Africa during the apartheid years. Casting aside the privilege bestowed by race, these writers variously documented and protested against the injustices of apartheid. In Fugard's case, the protests took the form of active collaboration with such black theater artists as Zakes Mokae, John Kani, and Winston Ntshona, in theatrical productions that by their very enactment contravened the segregationist strictures of apartheid. Fugard aspired to multiracial casts and audiences whether he was performing at the Space Theatre in Cape Town in the late 1950s (where he worked with Yvonne Bryceland and Brian Astbury), or at the Market Theatre in Johannesburg in the early 1970s (where he worked with Barney Simon).

In a rich variety of plays written between the late 1960s and the mid 1970s – such pieces as *Nongogo* (1977), *Hello and Goodbye* (1966), and *People Are Living There* (1969) – Fugard sought to portray the experiences (the suffering as well as the heroism) of ordinary black people in apartheid South Africa.

Devised in collaboration with Kani and Ntshona, *Sizwe Bansi is Dead* and *The Island* represent perhaps the most powerful enactments of Fugard's anti-apartheid dramatic aesthetic. The two plays represent the culmination of Fugard's collaboration with black theater artists; Kani and Ntshona played decisive roles in the conception, development, and production of the pieces. Unsurprisingly, after successful premiere productions in South Africa, both plays toured Britain and the United States in the early 1970s to high critical and popular acclaim.

In many respects, *Sizwe Bansi is Dead* neatly encapsulates the aesthetic of Fugard's early drama. The play dramatizes an attempt by a dispossessed black man to survive – and subvert – the restrictions of the Group Areas Act. That Act sought to regulate and restrict the movement and settlement of blacks in South Africa by consigning the vast majority of them to abject poverty in deprived rural communities. An ordinary illiterate factory worker, the title character in the play, successfully resists being deported from Port Elizabeth under the Group Areas Act by assuming the identity of a dead legal resident. The death of his true identity – his taking over the identity of a dead man – allegorizes the spiritual death of a nation built on fundamental injustice, hence the title *Sizwe Bansi is Dead*.

One of the other characters in the play, Styles, is an industrious self-employed photographer who devotes his life to recording the everyday triumphs and failures of ordinary blacks in apartheid South Africa. His mission is to bear photographic witness to the lives of the

> simple people who you never find mentioned in the history books, who never get statues erected to them or monuments commemorating their great deeds. People who would be forgotten and their dreams with them, if it was not for Styles.
> (1974: New York)

In the context of the play, these lines depict the everyday heroism of an ordinary black man, a simple photographer, in the defiance of a brutal system. However, at a metatheatrical level, this statement condenses the aesthetics of Fugard's early anti-apartheid drama. His plays collectively embody the story of black South Africans under the yoke of apartheid, a story told from the perspective of ordinary people, "the people the writers of the big books forget about."

In contrast to emphasis on the lives of ordinary blacks in most of his early plays, *The Island* focuses on the extraordinary courage and exceptional sacrifices of black political activists in apartheid South Africa. Set in the notorious Robben Island prison, the play pays tribute to and memorializes a triumphal staging of Sophocles' *Antigone* by South African political prisoners. The play records not simply the fundamental injustices of apartheid but also the terrible human toil of the imprisonment, isolation, and torture then rampant in South Africa for both real and imagined political offences. Drawing from the classic confrontation between Creon and Antigone in Sophocles' text, *The Island* hinges on the triumph of morality over brutality, of right over might. The two prisoners in the play draw inspiration from the example of Antigone's defiance of an unjust law. When confronted with the prospect of certain retribution, Antigone disobeys Creon's unjust edict. She triumphs even in death. A moving affirmation of life against all odds, *The Island* bears witness to the indefatigability of the human spirit in the face of radical evil.

Sizwe Bansi is Dead and *The Island* marked the culmination of Fugard's collaborative dramaturgy. Following the production of the two plays, Fugard stopped creating plays with actors in rehearsal rooms. This discussion resulted in an important thematic shift in his writing. Unlike his earlier plays, which addressed apartheid from the perspective of dispossessed blacks, Fugard's plays between the late 1970s and early 1980s – such texts as *A Lesson for Aloes* (1981), *Master Harold ... and the Boys* (1982), and *The Road to Mecca* (1984) – confront the difficult and contentious question of the effects of a system predicated on racial injustice on the privileged white community. Although written during a particularly tumultuous period in South Africa's political history, a period characterized by increased political violence culminating with the declaration of a state of emergency in 1984, these plays are self-consciously set at earlier historical periods, thereby eschewing direct engagement with the crisis of the present. It is as if, overwhelmed by the crises of the 1970s and 1980s, Fugard sought to understand the present from a certain critical distance. During this period Fugard seems keen to explore, from a relatively abstract standpoint, the psychology of white consciousness. As well, he is keen to explore existential questions on the nature of art and the role of the artist in society.

A subsequent transformation can be discerned in Fugard's writing in the early 1990s. By the late 1980s, it was readily apparent that apartheid was a failed ideology and that, accordingly, South Africa was on the verge of radical social and political change. Anticipating the demise of apartheid, Fugard dramatizes the conditions for and consequences of South Africa's transition from white minority rule to a multiracial democracy. In *Playland* (1992), for example, he explores the conditions under which mutual forgiveness and reconciliation could take place between whites and blacks in post-apartheid South Africa. In an uncanny sense, the play anticipates the work of the Truth and Reconciliation Commission, a body established by the South African government in 1994 in a partially successful attempt to provide a mechanism for transcending the trauma of apartheid. In *My Life* (1994), Fugard records the autobiographical narratives of a racially diverse set of young South African women. The piece represents an optimistic engagement, from the perspective of the lives, inspirations, and thoughts of five youths, with the notion of a "rainbow nation" that was being promoted by the new nationalism of post-apartheid South Africa. The text was conceived and produced in a manner reminiscent of Fugard's earlier collaboration with Kani and Ntshona and is, therefore, not Fugard's play as such but, rather, a reflective testimonial created by five young South Africa women. In *Valley Song* (1995) and *The Captain's Tiger* (1998), Fugard continues to explore the horizon of possibilities opened up for South African society after the fall of apartheid. He is interested in the human capacity to transcend old boundaries and forge new identities.

It is paradoxical that while he has produced works of undeniable universal appeal, Fugard insists that he is a "regional writer" concerned with the unfolding of life in a small corner of South Africa. Perhaps we can begin to understand this paradox by considering his theory regarding the role of art and of the artist. In his memoir *Cousins*, Fugard makes clear that all his playwriting is driven by an "infallible touchstone" – that is, the desire to arrive at "a moment of truth." This moment is at once local and universal: it depends on intimate understanding of highly specific local circumstances but is recognizably universal in its effects. Fugard narrates his encounters as a youngster with a cousin named Garth as an example of a moment of truth. On the surface of things, Garth was incorrigibly delinquent. Despite his extreme youth – or perhaps because of it – Fugard was able to recognize that Garth's unpleasant exterior masked an inner pain and a burdensome secret: the weight of being gay in a hostile culture. Garth turns to Fugard, sensing in him the capacity for human understanding that could not be relied on from others. In a voice that is shorn of all pretence, a voice that commands undivided attention, Garth reveals his secret to an empathetic Fugard. Fugard's entire dramaturgy can be read in terms of such moments of truth, moments when the secrets that have burdened the diverse characters that populate his dramatic universe are finally disclosed and a vision for human understanding is articulated, however fitfully. The quest for such moments helps explain why Fugard's plays are invariably driven by a minimalist aesthetic: a handful of characters, a virtually bare stage, very few props, and very elementary lighting. The quest for such moments may also help explain why Fugard is at once an intimately regional writer and the most universal of contemporary playwrights.

Further reading

Fugard, Athol (1974) *Sizwe Bansi is Dead*, New York: Viking.
——(1974) *Statements*, London: Oxford University Press.
——(1997) *Cousins: A Memoir*, New York: Theater Communications Group.
Vandenbroucke, Russell (1985) *Truth the Hand Can Touch: The Theater of Athol Fugard*, New York: Theater Communications Group.
Walder, Dennis (1984) *Athol Fugard*, London: Macmillan.
Wertheim, Albert (2000) *The Dramatic Art of Athol Fugard*, Bloomington: Indiana University Press.

APOLLO O. AMOKO

Fula, Arthur Nuthall

b. 1908, South Africa; d. 1966, South Africa

novelist and poet

Arthur Fula was an unusual writer in the field of South African literature – a black African who wrote in Afrikaans at a time when the language and culture was associated with the oppressor (see **Afrikaans literature**). A gifted linguist, Fula was fluent not only in Afrikaans but also in the major African languages of South Africa and in French, and for many years he worked as a court interpreter in Johannesburg. Although he published poems in journals and anthologies, Fula's major works are two novels, *Jôhannie giet die beeld* (Johannesburg Molds and Shapes) (1954) and *Met Erbarming, O Here* (With Pleasure, Dear Sir) (1956). The first work belongs to a familiar tradition in South African literature – what has come to be known as the "Jim Goes to Jo'burg" novel, the story of a young man who goes to the city in search of wealth and fulfillment only to be corrupted. The second novel uses realism (see **realism and magical realism**) to capture the lives of the poor of the city and the terrible social and spiritual conditions under which they live and toil.

SIMON GIKANDI

G

Galaal, Muuse Xaaji Ismaaciil

b. 1920, Somalia; d. 1980, Somalia

scholar and poet

Muuse Galaal was a very important figure in the study of Somali oral literature and culture (see **oral literature and performance**). He was an avid collector of oral poetry, proverbs and stories and worked to bring these to a wider audience through his writings, broadcasts and lectures. He also undertook important research on Somali indigenous knowledge and education which he wrote up in two as yet unpublished books, including "Stars, seasons and weather in Somali pastoral traditions" (1970), an important work which deserves much wider recognition. A keen advocate of the writing of Somali, he developed orthography for the language in a modified Arabic alphabet and later in life contributed greatly to the development of the present writing system using the Latin alphabet. He is known also for his collaborative work with B.W. Andrzejewski, which resulted in some important works on Somali literature and culture. A poet himself, he composed a number of plays, including *Qayb Libaax* (The Lion's Share) and some fifty poems including "Hengel" (Mourning Cloth) (1952). He is remembered by Somalis as one of the great scholars and poets and has been commemorated in great poetry of today including in a poem by Maxamed I.W. "Hadraawi."

MARTIN ORWIN

Gallaire, Fatima

b. 1944, Algeria

playwright

The Algerian playwright Fatima Gallaire was born in east Algeria and studied literature in Algiers and cinema at Vincennes in France, where she now lives. Her professional career has been divided between fiction writing, drama, and cinema. Although she has published short stories in magazines and literary journals, most of the few novels she has written so far have not yet been published. Gallaire is mainly known for her plays, which have earned her popularity in French and Francophone theater. Many of her plays have been translated into English. Her most popular play is perhaps *Princesses, ou Ah! Vous êtes venus*, which was translated as *You Have Come Back* and performed by the New York Urbu Repertory Theater in 1988. In her plays Gallaire deals with issues related to gender and patriarchy in the Maghreb (see **gender and sexuality**). She discusses polygamy and the ordeal of women in a polygamous marriage, the segregation between the sexes, and the place of women in patriarchal societies, where they are often conceived and represented as part of male property. In her plays, especially *Princesses*, Gallaire describes the wives in a polygamous family as furniture and the daughters as merchandise. Her plays are often dramatic attempts to question the subordination and objectification of women in patriarchal societies. In making the question of gender relations in the Maghreb central to her plays, Gallaire seeks to establish a vital link between her adopted French homeland and Algeria, the country of her birth.

Further reading

Gallaire, Fatima (1987) *Témoignage contre un homme stérile* (Witness against a Sterile Man), Paris: L'Avant-Scène Théatre 815.

——(1988) *Princesses, ou Ah! Vous êtes venus*, Paris: Quatre-Vents.

——(1990) *Les Co-épouses*, Paris: Quatre-Vents.

ZAHIA SMAIL SALHI

Garmadi, Salah

b. 1933, Halfaouine, Tunisia; d. 1982, Tunisia

linguist and poet

The Tunisian linguist and poet Salah Garmadi was born in Halfaouine, where he received a bilingual education in French and Arabic. He taught linguistics and phonetics in Tunis, and made the question of language and the crisis of identity central to his writing, working tirelessly on the situation of bilingual writers like himself as linguistic hybrids.

Despite the end of colonization, Garmadi writes works in which linguistic hybrids are represented as remnants of colonization, but he also endeavored to claim back some Francophone works by translating them into Arabic, namely those by the Algerian writers Malek **Haddad** and Rachid **Boudjedra**. Salah belongs to the tradition of **North African literature in French**, but he has published his literary works in both French and Arabic, demonstrating the necessity of this linguistic duality for Maghrebi writers. His first collection of poems, *Avec ou sans* (With or Without) was published in 1970, and it was followed by *Nos Ancêtres les bédouins* (Our Bedouin Ancestors) in 1975. In both collections Salah continued to highlight the problems and prospects of linguistic hybridity, sometimes with bitter irony. He wrote

several articles on Tunisian literature, which he published mainly in the *Revue tunisienne de science sociales*. Garmadi died prematurely in a car accident in 1982.

Further reading

Garmadi, Salah and Baccar, T. (1981) *Écrivains de Tunisie* (Writers of Tunisia), Paris: Sindbad.

ZAHIA SMAIL SALHI

Gasarabwe, Édouard

b. 1938, Maliba, Kibeho region, south-west Rwanda

novelist and folklorist

Born in Maliba in the region of Kibeho in southwest Rwanda, Gasarabwe attended local schools before going to France for his university studies. He wrote a doctoral thesis on the mystical aspect of ancient Rwanda, published as *Le Geste Rwanda* (The Rwanda Gesture) (1978). His fictional works, some of which are bilingual, written in French and Kinyarwanda, the national language of Rwanda, include mainly folk tales recounting narratives of older days in his country, and were written after he went into exile in the early 1960s. In 1998, he published *Contes du Rwanda: soirées au pays des mille collines* (Folk Tales from Rwanda: Evenings in the Country of One Thousand and One Hills), a collection of traditional tales. In *Soirées d'autrefois au Rwanda: la colline des femmes* (Old-Time Evenings in Rwanda: The Women's Hill) (1997), he focused on traditional stories in which the central characters are women. Gasarabwe, who has been working and living in France for many years, is one of an increasing number of African writers whose works, though written and published out of Africa, still draw their theme, inspiration, and aesthetics from the oral traditions, literature, and language of his country of origin (see **oral literature and performance**).

ANTHÈRE NZABATSINDA

Gatheru, Mugo

b. 1925, Kenya

writer

A Child of Two Worlds (1966), Mugo Gatheru's story of growing up under the yoke of colonialism in Kenya (see **colonialism, neocolonialism, and postcolonialism**) is one of the many examples of **autobiography** produced in Africa as part of the project of nationalism and its questioning of colonial culture (see **nationalism and post-nationalism**). In this book, Gatheru, who had been born in a settler farm in Kenya to impoverished African workers, narrates his struggle for education (see **education and schools**) in colonial Africa, the beginning of a journey that was to take him to India, the United States, and Britain. In the process of narrating his journey towards education and a proper sense of selfhood, Gatheru's work provides important social background on Gikuyu (see **Gikuyu literature**) life in the lands dominated by white settlers. Although the anthropological details in this text are derived from Jomo **Kenyatta**'s classic *Facing Mount Kenya* (1938), Gatheru's work has had resonance for the postcolonial generation because of his own personal accounts of disappearing cultural experiences, such as rites of passage, and his first-hand account of the violence generated by the colonial government in its response to the nationalist uprising, known as Mau Mau, in Kenya.

SIMON GIKANDI

Gbadamosi, Bakare A.

b. 1930, Nigeria

poet, anthropologist, and short story writer

Bakare Gbadamosi is a prominent Yoruba poet, anthropologist, and short story writer (see **Yoruba literature**). A close associate of Ulli Beier, the Austrian founder and patron of several organizations involved in the production and promotion of African **art** and culture in Western Nigeria in the 1950s and early 1960s, Gbadamosi was involved in the collection and publication of Yoruba oral literature, especially traditional poetry (*oriki*) and folklore (see **oral literature and performance**). Most of his work was published by Mbari, a club founded by Beier at the university town of Ibadan. He also published Yoruba poetry in translation.

SIMON GIKANDI

gender and sexuality

The question of gender has been the source of debate in African literature and culture for two main reasons. First, there have always been important women writers within the tradition, and the male writers who dominated the canon of African letters in its initial phase were aware of women's lives and struggles in their works (some more than others). Second, in the 1960s a whole series of women writers who were aware, and critical, of patriarchal structures such as polygamy, wife-battering, the effects of colonialism (see **colonialism, neocolonialism, and postcolonialism**) on women's lives, and home-spun sexism, came to occupy an important role in the tradition. Like gender, sexuality in African literature is a complex and multidimensional subject, but it has rarely been the subject of sole concern for many African writers. On the contrary, it has often been a subject of peripheral concern by many writers, treated not as an enduring subject in itself but connected to larger social and political questions, including the question of gender as an important and inescapable mode of social identity.

The question of gender

An important observation to be made in regard to gender issues in Africa is that, in most of sub-Saharan Africa, women have always played an important role in both the rural and urban economies. Markets are predominantly controlled by women, especially in western Africa. This sort of economic viability has created differently informed gender issues to the ones common in the West. However, in spite of the important roles performed by women in African societies and cultures, there are a large number of novels written by African writers that simply reinstate patriarchal values. Even when they have created strong women characters, many male writers have often tended to define these women in terms of the roles assigned to them by a patriarchal society. In Cyprian **Ekwensi**'s classic novel *Jagua Nana* (1961), the main character's strength comes from her role as a prostitute rather than her ability to challenge male domination. Most of the women in Chinua **Achebe**'s novels, except Beatrice in *Anthills of the Savannah* (1987), are ensconced in the traditional roles of wives, mothers, and market women.

This tendency tends to be challenged in the works of African women writers. Buchi **Emecheta** and Flora **Nwapa** write prolifically about the roles of women as mothers, as wives, as slaves, and even as single working women who support large families when their husbands abandon them for younger women. Many women writers have produced works about polygamy, its problems, and even sometimes its benefits. Mariama **Bâ**, Bessie **Head**, Ama Ata **Aidoo**, and Tsitsi **Dangarembga** have written about how women are forced to compete with one another in demeaning ways because of polygamy and sexism. Mariama Bâ in *Scarlet Song* (1981) and Myriam Warner-Vieyra in *Juletane* (2001) have been concerned with the problems faced by European women married to African men and how they are unable to negotiate African traditions.

Similar gender issues informed the madness that dominates the novels of Bessie Head, but with a significant difference: Head's works were not directly informed by the same gender consciousness or social abuse we see in the works of the authors mentioned above; rather, her fiction was driven by the need to understand the nature of good and evil in the larger human context. But Head furthered the debate on gender in African literature by linking madness in women to the humiliations that wives and mothers endure on a daily basis. More importantly, her criticism went beyond the horrendous problems women endured, since she also created models for harmony, both sexual and emotional, between men and women. Because she wanted to create a world that was kind to women, Head believed, like many feminists, that

gender issues in Africa could be dissipated if men were able to treat women with more understanding, exclusive love, and respect for their struggles. Head, like Dangarembga after her, sought to show how the apartheid/colonial system, which forbade black men to have families in the workforce or created false systems of values based on European modes of life, exacerbated gender problems.

In general, many African women writers have had to negotiate the conflicting demands of social and cultural systems in periods of political transformation. In southern Africa, black women's writing has been mainly part of their political struggles against apartheid and colonialism, but women writers like Lauretta **Ngcobo** have been particularly sensitive to the problem of raising their children under an unjust social and political system. In Dangarembga's *Nervous Conditions* (1989), Nyasha's nervous breakdown comes from an alienation from her own culture and her father, but it is also linked to the transformations taking place in the last days of colonial rule. On the other hand, women from the Maghreb have tended to walk the tightrope between Islam, colonialism, and nationalism (see **Islam in African literature**; **nationalism and post-nationalism**). The tensions between the demands of Islam, nationalism, and modernity (see **modernity and modernism**) are dramatized in key works by Assia **Djebar**, Nawal **el-Saadawi** and Alifa **Rifaat**. In the works of these novelists, one perceives how sexuality, stature, and social interaction are all moderated by their authors' status as Muslim women.

Finally, it is important to note that male writers such as Ousmane **Sembene** have exhibited a feminist consciousness in regard to gender by depicting women as leaders of political struggles, as we see in his novel *God's Bits of Wood* (1960). Sembene's film *Faat Kine* (2001) is about a woman who, after being constantly cheated and abandoned by men, finally achieves economic and sexual autonomy in which the men who abandoned her naturally want to participate. It is her son and the traditional head of household who takes these men to task and publicly denounces their actions. Nuruddin **Farah** has represented the plight of women in his major novels *From a Crooked*

Rib (1970) to *Secrets* (1998), and practically all his novels have an acute perspicaciousness about the plight of women in Africa.

On sexuality

Both African men and women writers have written about various aspects of sexuality, but they have almost never written from within that discourse. In other words, while writers like Nuruddin Farah tend to be fairly descriptive about sexuality, both heterosexual and homosexual (see **homosexuality**), they tend to do so from a distance, from the outside looking in, as it were. Farah, for example, tends to use sexual oddity in works such as *Maps* (1986) as the source of mythical ambiance or political ambivalence, but he is rarely interested in writing about sexuality in its own right. Ama Ata Aidoo talks frankly about both marital rape and desire, but she does so without re-creating the context in which these acts occur and without graphic details of what the people involved in sexual acts are actually feeling and doing. Bessie Head has talked about promiscuity without really too much illumination as to why or wherefore it takes place. In his voluminous works, Dambudzo **Marechera** often wrote about heterosexuality and its connection to violence, but rarely did he depict characters involved deeply in sexual acts. There is some explicit sexual suggestion in Aidoo's *Our Sister Killjoy* (1979), where a lonely German *hausfrau* befriends and tries to seduce a young Ghanaian student, but again all of the gradual building up of the "romance" is undermined by the fact that the German woman is feeding the black woman European delicacies which seem rather decadent in the face of what is actually raised as a problem in the novel: how "been tos" succumb to corruption. Thus, most African writers are comfortable describing sexuality within the context of love or romance or seduction or polygamy, but are unwilling to invite readers to experience the sexual encounter as it takes place between two lovers.

Nevertheless, sexuality does function as crucial in the structures of some major writers, especially in novels published after the 1970s. Quite often, gender and sexuality coincide in key texts in African literature. Aidoo refers to lesbianism, a taboo subject in many parts of Africa, in *Our Sister*

Killjoy, as does Rebeka **Njau** in *Ripples in the Pool* (1975), as a way of thinking through the sexual identity of modern African women. In Aidoo's *Changes* (1991), where polygamy seems to be the preferable alternative for the professional woman's need for romance and a minimal family life, social relations are mediated through sex. In *Changes* a wife loses her sexual zest for a husband who does not earn as much as she does and wants children more than she does, and prefers a polygamous husband who is financially well off and professionally successful. For Bessie Head, heterosexuality is represented both as a nightmare (especially when African male promiscuity is paraded in stark images) and as part of the beautiful love that might be a cure for social ills. In *A Question of Power* (1973), however, all that constitutes passion in a woman is finally negated because desire, the author concludes, is ugly and one must turn away from it. From all these examples, one can conclude that the representation and discussion of sexuality in African literature takes place within a larger human and sometimes political context.

HUMA IBRAHIM

Ghachem, Moncef

b. 1946, Mahdia, Tunisia

poet

Moncef Ghachem had already published limited editions of his poems in the early 1970s when his first major collection appeared, titled *Car vivre est un pays* (For Living is a Country) (1978). Most of the poems in this collection, significantly dedicated to the poet Ghassan Khanafani, one of the exemplars of free verse in contemporary Arabic literature, explore the political consciousness of artistically and culturally engaged students in the 1970s. In subsequent works, Ghachem undertook what he characterized as a return to his origins as the son of a fisherman in the Mediterranean village of Mahdia, the milieu which serves as background and inspiration for the short stories in *Cap Africa* (Cape Africa) (1978) and *L'Epervier: nouvelles de Mahdia* (The Hawk: Stories from Mahdia) (1994). Since then he has cultivated the image of a homegrown intellectual, avoiding hermetic literary complexities in his explorations of Tunisian seafaring myths and Mediterranean imagery.

Further reading

Ghachem, Moncef (1996) "Mart Cid" in James Gaash (ed.) *Anthologie de la nouvelle maghrébine: paroles d'auteurs* (Anthology of New Maghrebian Writing), Casablanca: EDDIF, pp. 95–9, with an interview with the author.

SETH GRAEBNER

Ghalem, Nadia

b. 1941, Oran, Algeria

novelist, journalist, and short story writer

The Algerian-born writer Nadia Ghalem has lived much of her life since the end of the Algerian war (1954–62) in Canada, where she works as a journalist. Her first publication, the poems of *Exil* (Exile) (1980), treated themes of longing and absence from the perspective of a politically conscious woman. These themes reappear in *Les Jardins de cristal* (Crystal Gardens) (1981), the internal monologue of a woman suffering the psychiatric aftermath of the Algerian war. Her other work has included short novels and collections of stories, such as *La Nuit bleue* (The Blue Night) (1991) and *La Villa Désir* (Villa Desire) (1988), as well as children's books, several of which have been adapted for use in the Quebécois school system. Her work shows a remarkable sensitivity to the traumas of political upheaval and its consequences in the lives of ordinary people, often years later and in distant countries. She serves as a guide to the bifurcated consciousness of North African immigrants haunted by a violent past.

Further reading

Ghalem, Nadia (1981) *Les Jardins de cristal* (Crystal Gardens), La Salle, Canada: Hurtubise HMH.

SETH GRAEBNER

Ghallab, Abd al-Karim

b. 1919, Morocco

political journalist, cultural commentator, and novelist

One of the most prominent members of the "generation of Mohammed V," the Moroccan activists who led their country's independence movement, Abdelkrim Ghallab made a career as a political journalist, cultural commentator, and novelist. Following Moroccan independence in 1956, Ghallab worked as a journalist at *al-ʿAlam* (The Scholar), the daily paper of the Istiqlal Party. As its editor he contributed several decades' worth of columns and editorials on almost every political or cultural question concerning North Africa and the Middle East. He has published book-length studies of constitutional history in Morocco, as well as histories of the independence movement. He is also the author of five novels and three collections of short stories, including *Dafannā al-mʾādī* (We Buried the Past; *Le Passé enterré*) (1966), a major historical novel set in the period leading up to independence. His Arabic style is known for its graceful and at times scholarly classicism, traits which, together with the extremely broad range of his commentaries, made him a highly respected figure in Moroccan culture.

Further reading

Ghallab, Abd al-Karim (1988) *Le Passé enterré* (We Have Buried the Past), trans. François Grouin, Rabat: Éditions Okad.

SETH GRAEBNER

Ghānim, Fathī

b. 1924, Egypt; d. 2000, Cairo, Egypt

novelist

The author of some seventeen novels, Fathī Ghānim is a member of a generation of Egyptian writers of fiction whose careers were lived in the shadow of the much more widely known Najīb **Maḥfūz**. Ghānim's focus in his works was always on the problems of Egypt and its people, and it is within that context that his primary readership lay. In addition to a career in creative writing he also held posts within the administration of the cultural sector and also served as editor of magazines such as *Ṣabāḥ al-Khayr* and *Rūz al-Yūsuf*.

His first novel, *al-Jabal* (The Mountain) (1959), was set in Upper Egypt and depicted the struggles of a village whose members are much involved in the illegal trade in antiquities. Efforts by the government to move them to a new model village are fiercely resisted. With a generous use of the colloquial dialect in dialogue and a resort to a fast-paced journalistic style (the narrator is himself a journalist, thus very much reflecting the author's own experiences), the novel successfully captures the atmosphere of tension that surrounded such governmental attempts at social engineering. How-ever, it was Ghānim's next novel, *al-Rajul al-ladhī Faqada Ẓillahu* (The Man Who Lost His Shadow) (1961) that emerged as his most successful work. The context of the novel's plot was the cinema industry, itself a primary focus of the finances and energy of the cultural sector during that particular decade, but Ghānim considerably enhanced the narrative possibilities of the emerging Arabic novel genre by resorting to a multi-narrator format, a device that was later used by novelists such as Najīb Maḥfūz and Jabrā Ibrāhīm Jabrā. This work was in fact one of the first Arabic novels to be translated into English (by Desmond Stewart, 1966).

As was the case with many Egyptian novelists in the period that followed the June war of 1967, Ghānim used his fiction to debate many of the important issues that were confronting his society and, more often than not, to express a critical attitude towards them. Thus the policy of *infitah* (economic opening-up) that was instigated by President Sādāt in the 1970s is the topic of *Qalīl min al-Hubb wa-Kathīr min al-'Unf* (A Bit of Love and a Lot of Violence) (1985), while *Aḥmad wa-Dā'ūd* (Ahmad and David) (1989) explores the controver-sial topic of relations between Arabs and Jews.

Further reading

Allen, Roger (1995) *The Arabic Novel: An Historical and Critical Introduction*, Syracuse: Syracuse Uni-versity Press.

Meisami, Julie Scott and Starkey, Paul (eds) (1998) *Encyclopedia of Arabic Literature*, 2 vols, London: Routledge.

ROGER ALLEN

al-Ghitani, Gamal

b. 1945, Sohag, Egypt

novelist, journalist, and short story writer

The Egyptian novelist, journalist, and short story writer Gamal al-Ghitani is one of the most prominent writers of Egypt's "generation of the sixties." This name was given to the group of writers who, growing up with the advent of the 1952 revolution in Egypt and feeding on its new ideology of social and political reform, started writing in the 1960s as advocates of the revolution, but were morally destroyed by Egypt's defeat in 1967. One of al-Ghitani's main concerns, there-fore, is to express his critical opinions of the political situation in Egypt and the Arab world. He does this, for example, by making Cairo an allegory for social and political discord through scrutinizing the changes that have overcome the city, be they demographic, architectural, or social. Like Najīb **Maḥfūz**, al-Ghitani's literary model, Cairo is a personal fascination and a literary motif. Another characteristic of al-Ghitani's writing is intertex-tuality. He employs classical Arabic works and events, not as passing references, but as cardinal components of his writing in order to reconstruct history and create a framework through which he can express his political ideologies. This is evident in his masterpiece *al-Zayni Barakat* (1971) in which the author's disappointment with Nasser's regime is symbolized by al-Zayni Barakat, a despotic tax-collector of Mamluk Egypt. Al-Ghitani is the editor of the literary journal, *Akhbar al-Adab*, published in Cairo.

Further reading

Mehrez, Samia (1994) *Egyptian Writers between History and Fiction*, Cairo: American University in Cairo Press.

RIHAM SHEBLE

Gikuyu literature

Literature in the Kenyan language Gikuyu speaks to contemporary concerns as well as to historical issues and is more available in translation than works composed in other African languages. Accessible works in Gikuyu include novels, plays, poetry, autobiographies and diaries, journalistic writing, and transcriptions of performed works. Many works in Gikuyu have addressed the topics of economic and social equality, political freedom, and human, linguistic and artistic rights. The best-known writer in Gikuyu is **Ngugi wa Thiong'o**.

The earliest literary forms in the Gikuyu language were those of **oral literature and performance**. The primary genre of oral literature and performance in Gikuyu are *ng'ano* (stories), *nyimbo* (songs), *marebeta* (poetry), *gicaandi* (competitive poetry), *ndai* (riddles), and *thimo* (proverbs). There are some *ng'ano* that are unique to the Gikuyu language, such as that of Wacu who changed Gikuyu customs so that women would be allowed to eat meat. There are also many legends about mythical creatures such as the *irimu* (ogre) that can change its form to become different animals and even appear as a human being with a mouth at the back of its neck. Other legends include those about historical figures such as Waiyaki wa Hinga, an early twentieth-century leader who resisted colonial rule. Children often learn to tell stories at an early age because participation in storytelling sessions is encouraged. Storytellers frequently use *nyimbo* to structure their performances and *thimo* to make their songs as appealing to adults as to children. Older people often enjoy exchanging *ndai*. *Gicaandi* is a performance genre in which poets compete with each other by composing sung verses that are based upon each poet's interpretation of ideographic symbols engraved on a calabash. *Nyimbo* are performed at events such as weddings and at political meetings, and many cassette tapes of *nyimbo* are available.

In 1926 the New Testament of the Bible was first published in Gikuyu. Some books of the Old Testament were published earlier, but the Old Testament as a whole was not published until 1951. Biblical language, imagery, and narratives have been widely used in works written in Gikuyu because the major writers in Gikuyu have all been educated in Christian schools.

Jomo **Kenyatta** began publishing the first newspaper in Gikuyu, *Muigwithania*, in 1928. The name of the paper means "one who causes people to listen to each other." The Kikuyu Central Association (KCA) sponsored this paper. Many newspapers were published in Gikuyu during the late 1940s and early 1950s.

During the 1930s a number of ethnographic works were published in Gikuyu. These works discussed cultural practices such as female circumcision and polygamy that were issues of dispute between the churches, the colonial government, and the KCA. The ethnographies published included Stanley Kiama Gathigira's *Miikarire ya Agikuyu* (1934) and Justin Itotia wa Kimacia's *Endwo ni Iri na Iriiri* (1937). Jomo Kenyatta's *Facing Mount Kenya* was published in English in 1938 while Kenyatta represented the KCA and studied anthropology in England. *Facing Mount Kenya* was important to pan-Africanism (see **diaspora and pan-Africanism**) because of its critiques of colonialism.

Gakaara wa **Wanjau** was the first prolific writer of fiction in Gikuyu. In 1946 he published *Uhoro wa Ugurani* (And What About Marriage). The story "Ngwenda Unjurage" (I Want You to Kill Me) was included in this work. It is about the suicide of a young woman whose father kept insisting that her fiancé pay additional amounts of bride-wealth. During the late 1940s and early 1950s, Gakaara was one of many politically active publishers and writers who produced political newspapers, booklets, and pamphlets in Gikuyu. These writers who wrote in opposition to colonial government policies and practices included Bildad Kaggia, John Kabogoro Cege, Isaac Gathanju, Kinuthia wa Mugiia, Stanley Mathenge, Victor Murage Wokabi, Muthee Cheche, Morris Mwai Koigi, Mathenge Wacira, and Henry Mwaniki Muoria. Many of these writers were active in the Kikuyu Central Association and the Kenya African Union. The best-known works of these authors are four booklets that contained the lyrics to political songs. These songs were sung at political meetings and are still remembered because of their condemnations of exploitation and racism. The political songs of this period and those sung during the armed struggle against colonialism are available in Maina wa Kinyatti's *Thunder from the Mountains: Mau Mau Patriotic Songs*.

Gakaara was detained from 1952 to 1960, and in 1983 his prison diary was published as *Mau Mau Writer in Detention* (*Mwandiki wa Mau Mau Ithaamirio-ini*). After his release from prison, Gakaara established a printing and publishing business and began publishing a series of forty stories about the character Kiwai wa-Nduuta, a former freedom fighter who confronts social issues of concern to ordinary Kenyans. The best-known work in this series is *Wa-Nduuta During the Coup Attempt* (*Hingo ya Paawa*) (1982/3), a compilation of three issues about the 1982 coup attempt in Kenya.

Ngugi wa Thiong'o is the best-known writer in Gikuyu. He began his major writing in Gikuyu in 1976, when he worked cooperatively with Ngugi wa Mirii and Limuru community residents at the Kamiriithu Cultural Center on the development of the play *I Will Marry When I Want* (*Ngaahika Ndeenda*). The play was popular with audiences, who recognized the contemporary political relevance of the *nyimbo* in the song. Ngugi's work on the play and with the community group led to his reflections on the **language question** and his decision to continue writing in Gikuyu. In December 1977 Ngugi was arrested because of the play and was detained for one year. He wrote the novel *Devil on the Cross* (*Caitaani Mutharaba-ini*) (1982) while he was in detention. The characters in this novel attend a feast of thieves and robbers that has been organized by the devil. At the feast the thieves and robbers compete to determine who is the greatest exploiter. The figure of the *gicaandi* player is of symbolic import to this novel.

In 1986 Ngugi published *Decolonizing the Mind*, in which he made his famous declaration to write subsequently in Gikuyu and Kiswahili, and in the novel *Matigari ma Njiruungi* (translated as *Matigari* in 1989). The novel is based on an oral narrative and is about how a survivor of the war against colonialism struggles against neocolonialism (see **colonialism, neocolonialism, and postcolonialism**). Ngugi is completing his third novel in Gikuyu, *Murogi wa Kagogo* (The Sorcerer of the Crow).

Ngugi began editing the journal *Mutiiri* in 1994. *Mutiiri* includes literary criticism, poetry, and memoirs. Other writers who have contributed to *Mutiiri* have included Cege Githiora, Gicingiri wa Ndigirigi, Gitahi Gititi, K.K. Gitiri, Kimani Njogu, Maina wa Kinyatti, Ngina wa Kiarii, Ngugi wa Mirii, and Waithira wa Mbuthia. The journal has also included translations of poems by Abdilatif Abdalla, Alamin Mazrui, Ariel Dorfman, and Otto Rene Castillo. Gitahi Gititi has published a volume of poetry, *Mboomu Iraatuthukire Nairobi na Marebeta Mangi* (Bombs Exploded in Nairobi and Other Poems). The title poem concerns the 7 August 1998 bombing in Nairobi. Newspapers that are currently being published in Gikuyu include: *Mwihoko, Muiguithania*, and *Kihooto*.

Further reading

Maina wa Kinyatti (1980) *Thunder from the Mountains: Mau Mau Patriotic Songs*, London: Zed Press.

Ngugi wa Thiong'o (1986) *Decolonizing the Mind*, Portsmouth, New Hampshire: Heinemann.

Wanjiku Mukabi Kabira and Karega Mutahi (1988) *Gikuyu Oral Literature*, Nairobi: East African Educational Publishers.

ANN BIERSTEKER

Gomez, Koffi

b. 1941, Togo

novelist and playwright

Koffi Gomez is a Togolese novelist and playwright. He was awarded the President of the Republic's (Eyadema) Literary Prize for his first published text, the 1982 **novel** *Opération Marigot* (Operation Delta), which valorizes peasant life and agriculture. Since then, however, he has focused on drama, gaining success with the 1983 *Gaglo, ou, l'argent, cette peste: drame social en 4 actes, 11 scènes* (Gaglo or This Plague, Money: A Social Drama in 4 Acts, 11 Scenes). Most recently, he has adapted Paul **Hazoumé**'s classic novel into *Doguicimi, ou, la femme qui défia le roi, le prince et le mort: drame historique en six tableaux* (Doguicimi, or the Woman who Defied the King, the Prince, and Death: A Historical Drama in Six Tableaux). Gomez has been the director of the Renaissance Troupe of actors in Lomé and several of his plays have been adapted for television.

Further reading

Gomez, Koffi (1983) *Gaglo, ou, L'Argent, cette peste: drame social en 4 actes, 11 scènes* (Gaglo or This Plague, Money: A Social Drama in 4 Acts, 11 Scenes), Lomé: EDITOGO.

RACHEL GABARA

Gordimer, Nadine

b. 1923, Springs, Transvaal, South Africa

novelist and Nobel Prize-winner

South Africa's only recipient of a Nobel Prize for Literature, which she was awarded in 1991, Nadine Gordimer is a prolific writer of novels, short stories, essays, and political commentary. Her literary career began very early, with her first story published in a Johannesburg newspaper when she was only 13 years old. She has published twelve novels, thirteen collections of short stories, four collections of essays (translated into thirty-one languages) and two other works in the form of extended essays to accompany the photographs of South African photographer David Goldblatt, *On the Mines* (1973) and *Lifetimes under Apartheid* (1986). Calling herself a "white African," Gordimer has been widely acclaimed as an astute observer and interpreter of South African society, particularly to a readership outside South Africa. In her 1973 work of literary criticism, *The Black Interpreters*, she indicates her own identification as an African writer, suggesting that African writing is defined by "the experience of having been shaped, mentally and spiritually, by Africa rather than anywhere else in the world" and not merely by skin color.

From her first collection of short stories, *Face to Face* (1949), and her first novel, *The Lying Days* (1953) onwards, Gordimer's fiction has explored the tension between the private and the public, and the complex effects of apartheid on white and black South Africans (see **apartheid and post-apartheid**). Her work examines the impact of political systems on people, most particularly the dehuma-

nizing effects of apartheid and the power relations it engendered. This sense of writerly responsibility that Gordimer has called "the essential gesture" is an integral part of her work, based on her belief that the white writer should raise the consciousness of people "who have not woken up" while simultaneously maintaining the freedom to write what and how one chooses. The long span of her writing career has been seen as charting the history of South Africa, from apartheid's inception through its dying throes to post-apartheid democracy and liberation, as "history from the inside," in Stephen Clingman's phrase. She remains active in her contribution to ongoing debates about political and intellectual freedom, expressing her views in essays and interviews. Even uncomfortable subjects like that of increasing violence in post-apartheid South Africa become the material of her fiction, despite her unwavering support for the ANC-led government. *The House Gun* (1998), for example, explores the notion that the violence sponsored by the apartheid state (a theme dealt with, too, in her earlier novel, *None To Accompany Me*, 1994) infected personal relationships in its aftermath, and that moral questions of retribution and punishment affect not just the body politic but individuals therein. Whereas her earlier novels explored the unequal relations between black and white characters, her later novels deal with the process of recovering from the "disease" of apartheid by coming to terms with forgiveness, guilt, and responsibility.

Gordimer's work has been the subject of a great deal of critical attention, from within and outside South Africa. At least ten book-length studies of Gordimer's work were published between 1974 and 1994, and three collections of essays on her work – Rowland Smith's *Critical Essays on Nadine Gordimer* (1990), Bruce King's *The Later Fiction of Nadine Gordimer* (1993), and *A Writing Life: Celebrating Nadine Gordimer*, edited by Andries Walter Oliphant (1998) and published on the occasion of Gordimer's seventy-fifth birthday. Additionally, the large number of interviews Gordimer has granted have been collected in *Conversations with Nadine Gordimer* (1990) edited by Nancy Topin Bazin and Marilyn Dallman Seymour. An *NELM Bibliography* published in 1993 and introduced by Dorothy Driver provides a comprehensive list of Gordimer's own work and of critical responses to it. While Stephen Clingman's study, *The Novels of Nadine Gordimer: History from the Inside* (1986, repr. 1993), emphasizes the historical and political aspects of Gordimer's fictional engagement with South African historical experiences, Dominic Head in his *Nadine Gordimer* (1994) focuses on the changing nature of Gordimer's use of literary form, with her more recent novels moving away from the earlier Lukácsian critical realism to a more postmodern and self-reflexive narrative mode. In its development from narrative realism to a more complex, ironic, and polyphonic form, Head suggests that her writing has adapted to developments in critical literary theory and to changing intellectual trends as well as to political and historical change. Other critics have commented on the paradoxical and ambivalent aspects of Gordimer's writing, underlined by her own position as a privileged white woman espousing black liberation. Kathrin Wagner, for example, in her book, *Rereading Nadine Gordimer* (1994), draws attention to the ways in which Gordimer's novels subtextually "reinscribe and valorise" some of the very patterns of oppression she is seeking to resist.

Gordimer herself has been a prolific commentator on literature, politics, and culture. Her essays have been collected in *The Essential Gesture: Writing, Politics and Places* (1988) edited by Stephen Clingman, *Writing and Being* (1995), and the end-of-millennium collection entitled *Living in Hope and History: Notes from our Century* (1999). These essays cover a wide range of topics but, as is evident from their titles, are concerned with writing and politics, both within a specific South African situation and within Africa as a whole. In them, Gordimer reflects on her own writing practice as well as on the work of other writers, outlining the links between politics and writing.

Questions of race and gender are central to Gordimer's fiction. While she herself has adapted her initially antagonistic attitude toward "liberal feminism", in which she suggested that issues of race take precedence over feminism, her more recent fiction and essays acknowledge their complex intersections. One of her often reworked themes, in the novels and short stories, is that of the white South African woman who, in Robin Visel's phrase, "ventures into blackness" to find herself

and her own part in the political struggle. This quest for subjectivity is often shown to end fruitlessly or ambiguously. Her often-ironic representations of such white characters echo the gap in perception between white and black South Africans, a gap that was enforced by the apartheid system and that prevented racial interaction and understanding. Such cross-cultural misreadings are an essential aspect of Gordimer's characters, resulting in their sometimes stereotypical and limited perceptions of others. While some critics have suggested that this reflects Gordimer's own limitations, it is more convincingly argued to be part of her ironic figuring of black–white relations under apartheid. Her white male characters, like Mehring in her joint Booker Prize-winning novel, *The Conservationist* (1974), can sometimes be seen to represent the links between colonial and sexist attitudes. However, while women and black South Africans could be seen as trapped in unequal and exploitative power relationships with white men, Gordimer is keen to emphasize the greater importance of "human rights" over "women's rights." Thus, while Gordimer is generally seen as moving, via her fiction and her essays, from a position of liberalism to radicalism in terms of racial and gender politics, she still resists being labeled a "feminist" writer.

Irony has been a marker of Gordimer's narrative style: indeed, she has herself suggested that her method has "so often been irony." This ironic detachment has sometimes been interpreted by critics as enacting a certain coldness and a formulaic approach to characters; others have seen it as part of her experimentation with narrative perspective that embodies, within her very fictional mode, the blindness of some characters to their own position and role, their "place," within South African society. Yet each novel adopts what Gordimer has described as "the right means to express what I'm discovering" so that she "enter[s] a new phase with every book." In her Nobel Prize acceptance speech, Gordimer claimed that "nothing factual I write or say will be as truthful as my fiction." This remark draws attention to the ways in which fiction can complicate and make paradoxical what might, in essays and interviews, be seen simply as statements of fact, drawing attention to the complex layering of narrative voice and perspective in Gordimer's fiction.

Most of Gordimer's critics discuss her work chronologically, starting with the early novels of the 1950s and 1960s; the "middle novels" of the 1970s and 1980s; and the more technically innovative novels since then. Many of the themes that are seen as characteristic of Gordimer's fiction are already present in her first novel, *The Lying Days* (1953). It is generally read as semi-autobiographical and as charting the concerns that Gordimer would return to in her fiction: the protagonist's physical and psychological journey from small mining-town to big-city Johannesburg; the awkwardness of black–white relationships, particularly illegal sexual relations, under an apartheid regime; the inevitable link between the private and the intimate, and the apartheid state's surveillance and legal control over individuals; the nature of white "guilt"; the displacement of European culture in Africa; and the exploration of a "South African consciousness." Many of these themes are taken up again in relation to the ownership of land and possession in subsequent short stories and novels, in particular "Six Feet of the Country" (1956), *The Conservationist* (1974), and *None to Accompany Me* (1994). Both *A World of Strangers* (1958) and *Occasion for Loving* (1963) explore the possibilities of black–white interaction, and the latter is usually read as thematizing the failure of liberal humanism in the wake of the Sharpeville massacre of 1960.

Many of the "middle novels" are concerned with the nature of individual duty and political responsibility, with *Burger's Daughter* (1979) her most notable fictional exploration of the ethical choices for political resistance via its protagonist, Rosa Burger, whose father, Lionel (based on the Afrikaner resistance figure Bram Fischer) died in prison for his political views. The novel includes references to the Sharpeville massacre and the Soweto uprising, and was banned by the South African Board of Censors for propagating Communist opinions and threatening the safety of the state. Gordimer herself has been a vocal opponent of censorship and in 1980 published *What Happened to Burger's Daughter, or, How South African Censorship Works*. *July's People* (1981) explores the identity crises encountered by the Smales family and their ex-servant, July, after an imagined anti-apartheid

revolution, revealing the distorted relationships engendered under apartheid.

Gordimer's later novels, while still examining the nature of freedom, restriction, and betrayal, are more experimental in form, as in *A Sport of Nature* (1987) in which Hillela's celebratory sense of identification with Africa, figured mainly through her sexuality, is undercut by irony which suggests that overcoming racial difference involves more complex negotiations, and *My Son's Story* (1990). The "post-apartheid" novels include *None to Accompany Me* published in 1994, the year of South Africa's first democratic elections, in which an exiled black couple return to a changing South Africa to take part in the drafting of its constitution, and in which Vera Stark, a white lawyer, attempts to right the wrongs of the past. *The House Gun* (1998) is concerned with the after-effects of apartheid, particularly the legacy of violence it bequeathed to both black and white, and which was so chillingly unearthed in the hearings of the Truth and Reconciliation Commission. *The Pickup* (2001) explores the relationship between a privileged white South African woman and an illegal Arab immigrant.

Gordimer's thirteen collections of short stories (some containing republished material) published between 1949 and 1992 reveal her mastery of this genre alongside her novels. While receiving less critical attention than her novels, the short stories show similar manipulation of point of view and irony.

Gordimer's strong belief that literature is created "inescapably *within* the destined context of politics" is the underlying motivation behind her own fiction and her essays, as is her endorsement of Salman Rushdie's notion of the writer's need to "say the unsayable, speak the unspeakable, and ask difficult questions."

Further reading

Ettin, Andrew Vogel (1993) *Betrayals of the Body Politic: The Literary Commitments of Nadine Gordimer*, Charlottesville: University Press of Virginia.

King, Bruce (ed.) (1993) *The Later Fiction of Nadine Gordimer*, New York: St Martin's Press.

Smith, Rowland (ed.) (1990) *Critical Essays on Nadine Gordimer*, Boston: G.K. Hall.

Temple-Thurston, Barbara (1999) *Nadine Gordimer Revisited*, Boston: Twayne.

SUE KOSSEW

el Goulli, Sophie

b. 1932, Sousse, Tunisia

novelist and art historian

The Tunisian writer and art historian Sophie el Goulli, who was born in Sousse, is very active in North African literary, artistic, and cinematic life. She has written four collections of poetry, including the 1973 publication *Signes* (Signs), in which songs and soliloquies are used to celebrate, mourn, and expound on being, death, destiny, and art. In 1993, she published *Les Mystères de Tunis* (The Mysteries of Tunis). Located historically at the beginning of the twentieth century, the novel tells the story of several Tunisian, French, and Turkish families during the French Protectorate of Tunisia (1881–1956). Narrating their lives and loves, el Goulli presents the image of a cosmopolitan Tunis, a society rich in multiple identities. A professor of art history, el Goulli has published a monograph on the Tunisian painter Ammar Farhat *Ammar Farhat* (1979), as well as an exploration of the origins and development of canvas painting in Tunisia, *Peinture en Tunisie* (Painting in Tunisia) (1994). El Goulli is an involved critic of the Tunisian cinema, and she regularly contributes to the journal of cinematic arts *SeptièmArt* (Seventh Art).

Further reading

El Goulli, Sophie (1993) *Les Mystères de Tunis* (The Mysteries of Tunis), Tunis: Éditions Annawras.

KATARZYNA PIEPRZAK

Goyémidé, Etienne

b. 1942, Ippy, Central African Republic; d. 1997, Central African Republic

novelist, poet, and short story writer

Etienne Goyémidé, a talented writer in various genres, held several positions in the education system in the Central African Republic, including minister of education. He was also involved in publishing and served as the head of the national press. His fiction draws mainly on the history and traditions of his country. In *Le Silence de la forêt* (The Silence of the Forest) (1984), he rehabilitates the pygmy culture of the southern forests; in *Le Dernier Survivant de la caravane* (The Last Survivor of the Caravan) (1985), he turns to the slave trade for his subject matter in a narrative enriched by proverbs, poetry, and songs borrowed from the oral tradition. Although Goyémidé also wrote poetry and short stories, he is best known for his work in the theater. During his lifetime he directed the national theater company and wrote prize-winning plays, including *Le Vertige* (Vertigo) (1981), a satirical work on the life of a government minister.

Further reading

Ugochukwu, Françoise (1988) "Le Silence de la forêt: un roman d'explorateur" (The Silence of the Forest: An Exploratory Novel), *Annales aequatoria* 9: 73–88.

JANICE SPLETH

Gray, Stephen

b. 1941, Cape Town, South Africa

editor, novelist, and literary critic

Born in Cape Town, Gray was educated at St Andrew's College, Grahamstown, the University of Cape Town and Cambridge University (1964). He received a DLitt et Phil in English at Rand Afrikaans University (1978). Gray has lectured at the University of Aix-Marseilles, the University of Iowa, and the University of Queensland. His anthologized multi-generic volumes on southern African literature (1978 to 1998) include the profound literary history and cross-cultural source book, *Southern African Literature: An Introduction*, (1979). Gray's voluminous editions cover notable figures in South Africa like H.C. **Bosman**, Stephen Black, and Athol **Fugard**. His creative contributions address common human struggles, underpinning the enigma of nationalism (see **nationalism and post-nationalism**) and nation-building. These works include poetry (*The Assassination of Shaka*, 1974; *Hottentot Venus and Other Poems*, 1979; *Apollo Café and Other Poems*, 1989), drama (*An Evening at the Vernes*, 1977; *Schreiner: A One-Woman Play*, 1983), and novels (*Visible People*, 1977; *Born of Man*, 1989; and *War Child*, 1991). Gray's novels explore class, gender, race, and sexuality in the political complexities of life, including the controversial theme of **homosexuality**. He is acclaimed as one of the best-known researchers and promoters of a real literary identity for southern Africa.

ZODWA MOTSA

Greki, Anna

b. 1931, Batna, Algeria; d. 1966, Algiers, Algeria

poet

Colette Anna Grégoire, who published her poetry under the name Anna Greki, was born into a European family living in Batna, Algeria. After abandoning her studies in Paris, she returned to Algiers to teach, and to work for the Partie Communiste Algérien during the early years of the revolution (1954–62). In 1957, she was arrested, tortured, interned, and finally deported. She returned following independence, finished her degree, and taught literature at the Algiers high school. Her two collections of poetry contain some of the most compelling work to come out of the Algerian war: *Algérie, capitale Alger* (Algeria, Capital Algiers) (1963) and *Temps forts* (Great Moments) (1966). Even her most topical verses show a concern for form underlying her political engagements, and her poems dispense with the conventional pieties of most revolutionary movements. Her work has descendants and affinities among the other major poets of independent Algeria, notably Tahar **Djaout** and Jean **Sénac**.

Further reading

Greki, Anna (1966) *Temps forts* (Great Moments), Paris: Présence Africaine.

SETH GRAEBNER

Guingané, D. Jean Pierre

b. 1947, Ganrango, Burkina Faso

playwright, actor, and director

Born at Ganrango (Boulgou) in Burkina Faso, D. Jean Pierre Guingané is renown mostly for his work in drama, but in addition to being a playwright he has also been an actor and director. He has occupied different positions both at the University of Ouagadougou, where he was dean of humanities, and within the government. He has also served as the chair of the National Drama Association and the regional coordinator of the project "Culture in the Neighborhood"; he succeeded Wole **Soyinka** as the African representative in the UNESCO Executive Commission for the International Institution of Drama. His major plays included *Le Fou* (The Madman) (1984), *Papa, oublie moi* (Daddy, Forget Me) (1990), *Le Cri de l'espoir* (The Cry of Hope) (1992), *La Savane en transe* (The Savannah in Trance) (1997), and *La Musaraigne* (The Shrew) (1997). Involved in the theater since secondary school, Guingané sees drama as an efficient, powerful, and expressive means to reach the mind and conscience of the masses with regard to the most pressing social, cultural, economic, and political issues. He has argued that drama enables the artist to communicate directly with ordinary people. For him, dramatic works can be used as effective tools for social, cultural, political, and economic development. For this reason, he has been heavily involved in the development of the concept of culture in neighborhoods, insisting on the active and creative participation of the local community in the promotion of sociocultural events.

MICHEL TINGUIRI

Gurnah, Abdulrazak

b. 1948, Tanzania

novelist and critic

The Tanzanian novelist and critic Abdulrazak Gurnah is one of the most prolific and refreshing figures in the field of East African writing in the 1990s. Born in Zanzibar, he has lived in England for much of his life. His six novels *Memory of Departure* (1987), *Pilgrim's Way* (1988), *Dottie* (1990), *Paradise* (1994), *Admiring Silence* (1996), and *By the Sea* (2001) have been widely acclaimed. He has also edited two volumes of literary criticism, *Essays on African Writing: A Re-evaluation* (1993) and *Essays on African Writing: Contemporary Literature* (1995).

At the center of *Memory of Departure* is a young protagonist growing up in an unidentified East African coastal town. As he matures, he comes to realize that his immediate community is too small to fulfil his desire for an urbane life. The central themes of this first novel set the tone for Gurnah's later works in which he is equally preoccupied with subjects like migration, travel, and diaspora (see **diaspora and pan-Africanism**). *Pilgrim's Way* amusingly deals with the consequences of wanderlust as a student from Tanzania struggles against the insular culture of a provincial English town. Since England, an icon for the worldliness he desires, rejects him, he remains shackled to the memories of his life back in Africa. *Paradise*, arguably Gurnah's most successful novel, was shortlisted for the Booker Prize in 1994. Set before the First World War, it tells the story of Yusuf, sold by his father to Uncle Aziz, whom he accompanies to dangerous trading missions in the interior of the continent. Critics have often drawn comparisons between the novel and Joseph Conrad's *Heart of Darkness*, seeing Gurnah's as a radical, postcolonial revision of this canonical text of English literature (see **colonialism, neocolonialism, and postcolonialism**).

The narrator of *Admiring Silence* is a Zanzibari man, exiled in Britain after a ruthless regime comes to power in Zanzibar, who woos his way into the heart of an Englishwoman by spinning romantic tales about his childhood in Africa. He also endears himself to her father by telling embellished stories about the British empire. Marginalized in many ways in his new abode, he is shielded by these tales

from the uncomfortable truth of his loss. When, after twenty years of life in England, he abandons his family and returns to Zanzibar, he comes to grapple with the harsh reality that he has been living a lie, that Africa is no longer "home." When the asylum-seeking protagonist in *By the Sea* arrives at London's Gatwick Airport, he is detained pending the processing of his application. The immigration official dealing with his case steals his mahogany box of rare incense, thus depriving him of his store of memories about Zanzibar. Left metaphorically rudderless upon his entry into England, he has to piece together a narrative of his life. Gurnah's use of the mahogany box as a mnemonic device in this novel bears faint echoes of Moyez **Vassanji**'s *The Gunny Sack* (1989). Gurnah's novels meditate sensitively, in the tradition of the best diasporic fiction, on questions of exile, memory, and cosmopolitanism.

DAN ODHIAMBO OJWANG

Gwala, Mafika Pascal

b. 1943, Verulam, Kwa-Zulu Natal, South Africa

poet

Born in Verulam, Kwa-Zulu Natal, and educated at Inkamana High School at Vryheid, Mafika Gwala came into prominence in the 1970s as one of the leading black poets associated with the black consciousness ideology, which was prominent in the struggle against apartheid (see **apartheid and post-apartheid**). This group of poets, commonly known as the New Black Poets or Soweto Poets, includes Mongane **Serote**, Oswald Mbuyiseni **Mtshali**, and Sipho **Sepamla**. He has published two volumes of poetry, *Jol'iinkomo* (1977) and *No More Lullabies* (1983), and co-edited, with Liz Gunner, a collection of praise poems (*izibongo*) entitled *Musho! Zulu Popular Praises* (1991). Gwala's poetry is largely underpinned by the philosophy of black consciousness and utilizes jazz rhythms and colloquial speech patterns. He has also published critical articles, poems, and short stories in various literary magazines in South Africa. His essay entitled "Writing as a Cultural Weapon" appeared in *Momentum : On Recent South African Writing* (1984). As part of the black consciousness movement's varied cultural program, Gwala edited the *Black Review* (1973), a collection of articles on black art and thought. Gwala's poetry features in most anthologies of South African English poetry.

Further reading

Ngwenya, Thengani H. (1992) "The Poetry of Mafika Gwala," *Staffrider* 10, 2: 43–51.

THENGANI H. NGWENYA

H

Haddad, Malek

b. 1927, Constantine, Algeria; d. 2003,
Addis Ababa

novelist and poet

Promoting the notion of an Algerian homeland
while concurrently expressing profound unease
over cultural identity, novelist and poet Malek
Haddad's writings describe the struggles of a
generation of writers to create a literature that
was truly Algerian. In *Sadness in Danger* (*Le Malheur
en Danger*) (1956), arguably his most prominent
collection of poetry, Haddad's work displays its
militancy in its revalorization of Algerian history
and celebration of human liberty. The themes
expressed in the collection reflect the author's
political efforts during the Algerian war and his
involvement in the Algerian National Liberation
Front (FLN). Concurrently, however, Haddad's
texts betray both a profound despair over the
violence of war and a pervasive sense of cultural
alienation, manifest at the level of language. For
Haddad, the French language could not adequately
represent thoughts and concepts that were Arab-
Berber in origin. As his fiction and his essay *Zeros
Turn Round* (*Les Zéros tournent en Rond*) (1961) describe
it, the French language became, for Haddad, an
emblem of the disjuncture between a nascent
Algerian national identity and a rich Arab-Berber
cultural history.

Further reading

Haddad, Malek (1956) *Le Malheur en danger* (Sadness
in Danger), Paris: La Nef.

NEIL DOSHI

Haddis Alemayyehu

b. 1909, Gojjam Province, Ethiopia

novelist

Haddis Alemayyehu is Ethiopia's most popular and
widely read author, first of all due to three
monumental novels published between 1965 and
1985 and set against a historical background: *Fiqr
iske meqabir* (Love unto the Grave), *Wenjelennyaw
dannya* (The Criminal Judge), and *Yelm-izyat* (Plenty
in a Dream, or Pie in the Sky). He went to church
and modern schools and trained as a teacher. For
his classes he wrote plays, thus becoming one of
Ethiopia's earliest playwrights. His anger at Italy's
aggression against Ethiopia in the 1930s was
expressed in his early writings, and he also joined
the patriotic war until captured and sent to Italy as
a POW; later he published his war memoirs. After
the war, he worked for the government in Addis
Ababa, holding important ministerial posts and
becoming a senator. He was ambassador to
Jerusalem, Washington (where he also studied
law), the United Nations in New York (where he
made efforts to ban the use of nuclear weapons),
and London. After the 1974 revolution, he
declined the offer to be president. He valued his

political work highly, but he is best known for his stories and novels.

Further reading

Molvaer, R.K. (1997) *Black Lions*, Lawrenceville, New Jersey: Red Sea Press.

REIDULF MOLVAER

al-Ḥakim, Tawfiq

b. 1898, Alexandria, Egypt; d. 1987, Cairo, Egypt

dramatist, novelist, short story writer, and essayist

The prominent Egyptian dramatist, novelist, short story writer, and essayist Tawfiq al-Ḥakim was born in Alexandria to a Turkish mother and an Egyptian father. Sent to the Cairo Law School, al-Ḥakim soon found himself inclined more towards the arts and the theater than he was to the study of law. He began writing his own plays and publishing them in the school literary magazines. Soon after, he was composing plays for the popular theater of the 'Ukasha Brothers under a pseudonym, "Hussein Tawfiq," to avoid calling the attention of his family to his artistic endeavors. However, al-Ḥakim's father was concerned for his son's future and, determined to see him well established, he insisted on him learning the French language and sent him to Paris soon after to acquire a doctorate degree in law. Al-Ḥakim, however, mastering the French language in a very short time, defied his father's intentions and used his new knowledge to acquaint himself with French literature. Once in Paris, al-Ḥakim was infatuated by the glamour of France. He spent the years from 1925 to 1928 in Paris attending theaters and the opera, visiting museums, reading, learning music, and meeting with other artists, and when he was finally summoned back to Egypt by his father, he went without having fulfilled the academic purpose for which he had been sent. He started working as a deputy public prosecutor in many villages in Egypt, a period in his life that had an extreme effect on his

outlook and his literature. He then served in the Ministry of Education and the Ministry of Social Affairs until he resigned in 1943 following a series of clashes with the government authorities. From then on the author committed himself to his writing.

Al-Ḥakim's years in Paris exposed him to Western cultural and social values. He began to feel the conflict between his Eastern upbringing and his Western experiences. Reconciling himself to both aspects of his identity, al-Ḥakim decided to live with the best both worlds had offered him. Discovering himself and strengthening his identity through travel, al-Ḥakim was quick to express this in his writing, as he does in his novel *Bird of the East* (1967) (*'Uṣfur min al-Sharq*) (1938). He went on to discuss the Egyptian identity in his writings. In the wake of the 1952 Egyptian revolution, al-Ḥakim attempted to define the origin of the Egyptian identity, whether Pharaonic or Arab. This question is addressed in his play *Isis* (1978) (*Izis*) (1955), narrating the Pharaonic myth of Isis and Osiris and their struggle to preserve the Egyptian identity. Isis represents the force of the Egyptian people, and is determined to protect and preserve the Egyptian nation. This symbolism characterizes al-Ḥakim's style of writing.

Al-Ḥakim never fails to include elements of his life in his writing. His novel *Maze of Justice: Diary of a Country Prosecutor* (1989) (*Yawmiyyāt Na'ib fi al-Aryāf*) (1937), refers to that part of his life when he worked as a prosecutor in Egypt's rural areas. This post gave al-Ḥakim another opportunity to study the Egyptian identity from the point of view of the Egyptian peasants. He found himself again tackling the issue of identity, since during his service he was constantly being treated as a stranger and a man not to be trusted because his values were unlike those of the village people; theirs was a closed society that did not welcome any interference in its law and order by any outsider. Writing became al-Ḥakim's only companion during this period in his life.

Another major element of al-Ḥakim's fiction was his cynical view of women. Believing women to be the culprits of all evil, the author supported the confinement of women to the private sphere of the home and approved of male dominance over female frailty and malice. This attitude was evident as early as 1923 when al-Ḥakim wrote *al-Mar'a al-Gadida* (The Modern Woman) a play in which he poked fun at the idea of the emancipation of women from male-dominated society, including their unveiling and entering the workforce. Also, his novel *al-Ribat al-Muqaddas* (The Sacred Bond) (1944) portrays women as callous, shallow, and obsessed with their own gain and their own satisfaction, be it sexual or otherwise. He went on to reassert this ideology in his short story collection *Arini Allah* (Show Me God) (1953) in which he used the grand narrative of Adam and Eve to expose Eve's intentional plot to ruin Adam and cause his fall and subsequent misery on earth.

In his play *Pygmalion* (1974) (*Pygmalyun*) (1942), the author also combined his attitude to women with the relationship of the artist to his art. Pygmalion, the artist, creates a statue of a female figure and, after falling in love with it, attempts to confine it, refusing to display it to the public and insisting on being its sole owner. His play reflects not only the subjugation of the female to the male will, but also the obsession of the artist with his artistic production in which he entraps himself and stifles any further creative expression he may have had.

The sources of al-Ḥakim's inspiration are numerous, and range from Pharaonic and Greek mythology to biblical narratives and Koranic stories. In *The People of the Cave* (1989) (*Ahl al-Kahf*) (1933) al-Ḥakim utilizes a story from the Koran to explore the question of time and change through his unnerving tragi-comic account of seven men who fall asleep in a cave and wake three hundred years later.

Although al-Ḥakim avoided political affiliation to a specific party, he nonetheless was affected by the 1952 revolution. His plays *al-Aydi al-Na'ima* (The Soft Hands) (1954) and *al-Sultan al-Ha'ir* (The Sultan's Dilemma) (1960) discuss the revolution as he saw it, in two different ways. The first play is written in staunch support of the revolution and its promise of social justice. The second play tackles political strategies, questioning which is the more justifiable measure to take to ensure social stability: force or democracy? In this debate, al-Ḥakim reveals his critical attitudes towards the violent

measures taken against the opposition by Nasser's regime.

It can be said of al-Ḥakim that he was a non-conventional man, believing in individuality and not in predetermined social values. Religion to al-Ḥakim was not a combination of rituals or set code of conduct, but a personal relationship between man and God, elevating both mind and spirit without the confinement of the individual. His theater also reflected this call for freedom from convention. Influenced by Brecht, al-Ḥakim sought not to preach at his audience, but to illuminate their understanding, to encourage them to think and act instead of obeying and trusting blindly. Although he was nominated several times for the Nobel Prize for Literature, it was more important for al-Ḥakim to be remembered, as he is, as the father of modern Arabic theater.

Further reading

Long, Richard (1979) *Tawfiq al-Hakim: Playwright of Egypt*, London: Ithaca Press.

Hamdi, Sakkut (2000) *The Arabic Novel*, vol. I, Cairo: American University in Cairo Press.

RIHAM SHEBLE

Halilou Sabbo, Mahamadou

b. 1937, Niger

novelist and playwright

Although the Nigerien writer Mahamadou Halilou Sabbo has written in various genres, his best-known works are two novels, *Abboki, ou l'appel de la côte* (Friend, or The Call of the Coast) (1978) and *Caprices du destin* (The Whims of Destiny) (1981). Having begun his career as an educator in Maradi, Niger, in 1979, Mahamadou Halilou Sabbo became secretary of state for national education. Interested in national languages, Halilou Sabbo created a Zarma experimental school and was the director of INDRAP (Institut National de Documentation, Récherches et Pedagogie). Both of his novels raise questions of the central character's relationship to the society around him. *Abboki* focuses on the story of the main character,

Amadou, and his exodus to the Côte d'Ivoire where he goes in search of work and remains for twenty years. Following political troubles in the Côte d'Ivoire, Amadou becomes wounded and returns home to Niger. *Caprices du destin* is concerned with the educational system of Niger and focuses on the people's distrust of education. *Gomma, Adorable Gomma*, a work of drama, was published in 1990; Halilou Sabbo has also collected stories and legends of Niger in *Gaton! Gatanko! Ta Zo! Ta Koma!* (Gaton! Gatanko! It Came! It Returned!). Given his interest in national languages, Halilou Sabbo's works are notable for their incorporation of numerous proverbs, many of them translated from Hausa into French.

SUSAN GORMAN

Hama, Boubou

b. 1906, Sadouré, Niger; d. 1982, Rabat, Morocco

politician and writer

In addition to having a prominent political career under the government of Hamani Diori, Boubou Hama was one of Niger's most prolific writers and was renowned for his work in such diverse genres as stories, theater, novels, essays, and history. Between 1958 and 1974, Hama, who studied at the École Normale William Ponty in Senegal and began his career as a teacher, held the position of president of the National Assembly of Niger. He first gained international literary prominence for his three-volume autobiography *Kotia-nima*, which won the Grand Prix Littéraire de l'Afrique Noire in 1971. In the same year, his essay entitled "Essai d'analyse de l'éducation africaine" (Essay of Analysis of African Education) won the Senghor Prize for the best work written in the French language by a foreigner. Greatly interested in Songhay and Nigerien history, Hama produced multiple works on different facets of the country's history, drawing upon legend, stories, and oral sources. He also composed a six-volume work of stories and legends from Niger. The importance Hama placed on oral sources (see **oral literature and performance**) marks all of his works and

accounts for the immense significance of his contribution to Francophone African literature.

Further reading

Hama, Boubou (1971) *Kotia-nima*, 3 vols, Niamey: République du Niger.

SUSAN GORMAN

Hamzaoui, Muhammad Rachad

b. 1934, Tunisia

playwright and novelist

The Tunisian author Dr Muhammad Rachad Hamzaoui is a short story writer, a playwright, and a novelist. His early works, such as his novel *Bū-Dūda māt!* (Bū-Dūda Has Died!) (1989), depict humanity's struggle against many hostile forces, most especially the encounter with a harsh natural environment, with scarce resources and numerous adversities. Despite the severity of these forces, be they natural, political, or social, the characters of Hamzaoui, albeit of modest social and intellectual background, are oftentimes optimistic and unyielding. On a political level, Hamzaoui does not concern himself so much with colonial themes (which have preoccupied a number of Tunisian writers of his generation) as he does with the postcolonial condition (see **colonialism, neocolonialism, and postcolonialism**). His three plays, which constitute the work *Zaman al-turrahāt* (The Time of Absurdity) (1988), focus on absolute regimes in which the responsibility for authoritarianism is blamed not only on the ruler but also on the ruled. In these plays, the actors who represent different political tendencies or parties seem to be preoccupied with great theories and ideologies and play no active role in changing the situation, while the intellectual elite remains isolated from the political reality, imposing self-censorship on itself.

Further reading

Hamzaoui, M.R. (1989) *Bū-Dūda māt* (Bū-Dūda Has Died!), Tunis: al-Dār al-tūnisiyya lī al-nashr.

SARRA TLILI

Hawad

b. 1950, Nigeria

poet

A Tuareg poet from the Air mountains of the central Sahara in what is now Niger, Hawad rejects national affiliation with the Republic of Niger, remaining a fierce champion of an independent Tuareg state in the Sahel across Mauritania, Mali, Burkina Faso, Niger, Algeria – Tuareg territories from time immemorial. His commitments to Tuareg independence have forced him into exile in Aix-en-Provence, France, though he often travels into the Sahara. His poetry, like his politics, militates against political affiliations of any sort, with the possible exception of Western anarchist traditions as well as militant movements like the Zapatistas in Mexico: "We peddle neither / the Quran of Mohammad / nor the Gospel of Mary's son, / nor the Torah of Moses," Hawad writes. "Don't look for us in these places" (2001: Boulder). Like many of his fellow non-black "blue-men" of the Sahel, Hawad insists upon the nomadic integrity of Tuareg life, and the importance of resisting neocolonization under the guise of tourism, which he identifies as a particularly lethal form of orientalism. Hawad has written more than ten books, including works of poetry, lyrical prose, and a novel-in-progress. His works are often embellished with Tifinagh calligraphy, an art form that Hawad calls "furigraphy," which is based upon a precolonial Tuareg alphabet. Hawad's writings are recited orally in Tamazight and then translated into French by Hawad and his wife Hélène Claudot-Hawad. In France and the United States, Hawad is perhaps best appreciated as a nomadic poet and (anti-) philosopher of the desert.

Further reading

Gugelberger, Georg M. (2001) "Tuareg (Tamazight) Literature and Resistance: The Case of Hawad," in Christopher Wise (ed.) *The Desert Shore: Literatures of the Sahel*, Boulder, Colorado: Lynne Rienner, pp. 101–12.

Hawad (2001) "Anarchy's Delirious Trek: A Tuareg Epic," trans. Georg M. Gugelberger and Christopher Wise, in Christopher Wise (ed.) *The Desert Shore: Literatures of the Sahel*, Boulder, Colorado: Lynne Rienner, pp. 113–25.

CHRISTOPHER WISE

Hazoumé, Flore

b. 1959, Congo-Brazzaville

novelist

Born in Brazzaville of a Congolese mother and a father from Benin, and resident since 1979 in the Côte d'Ivoire, Hazoumé eschews claiming a national affiliation. Like many of her fictional characters, she spent her adolescence in France and is unapologetic about her assimilation. In her 1984 collection of short stories, *Rencontres* (Encounters), a character who echoes the author's point of view declares her fatigue with the themes of colonialism, neocolonialism, and cultural alienation (see **colonialism, neocolonialism, and postcolonialism**). Hazoumé's subsequent works complicate this attitude by exploring the persistent memory of traditional culture, especially fetishism, as it creeps into the lives of assimilated characters. In the 1994 collection of stories, *Cauchemars* (Nightmares), Hazoumé focuses increasingly on the social guilt of an African bourgeois class that lives off the backs of a mostly invisible populace. Her major work to date, the novel *La Vengeance de l'albinos* (The Albino's Vengeance) (1996), narrates the adolescent protagonist's discovery that her father's wealth came as a consequence of his involvement in the ritual sacrifice of an albino child. Lydie also discovers her illegitimacy; she is the daughter of her father's mistress. Steeped in shame about her origins, she wreaks havoc on the other women in her comfortable Paris home.

ELENI COUNDOURIOTIS

Hazoumé, Paul

b. 1890, Dahomey (now Benin); d. 1980, Dahomey (Benin)

novelist

Paul Hazoumé was born in Dahomey (present-day

Benin) and educated by French Catholic missionaries. His work borrowed from history and ethnography and aimed at a nationalist restitution of Dahomean culture. Dahomey had been vilified in colonialist writing because of its practice of human sacrifice. Hazoumé's first work, published in 1937, was an ethnographic monograph, *Le Pacte de sang au Dahomey* (The Blood Oath in Dahomey). Hazoumé shows how the traditional blood oath survived colonial rule, although it was driven underground and criminalized by French authorities. His historical novel, *Doguicimi* (1938) is set during the reign of King Guézo of Dahomey (1818–58) and gives a detailed account of human sacrifices. Hazoumé places the sacrifices in the context of the slave trade and implicates the Europeans indirectly in the practice. The heroine, Doguicimi, articulates a critique of both her king and the European slave traders. Hazoumé contributed an important ethnographic essay to the journal *Présence Africaine* in 1957, where he argued that the ethnography of Africa must be informed by oral history and that the teaching of African languages must be encouraged.

Further reading

Hazoumé, Paul (1990) *Doguicimi: The First Dahomean Novel*, trans. Richard Bjornson, Washington, DC: Three Continents Press.

ELENI COUNDOURIOTIS

Head, Bessie

b. 1937, Pietermaritzburg, South Africa;
d. 1986, Serowe, Botswana

novelist

Bessie Head was born in a mental institution in South Africa, where her white mother had been incarcerated for having a sexual relationship with a black man (her father) at a time when interracial relations were considered illegal under the apartheid government's Immorality Act (see **apartheid and post-apartheid**). She attended schools in South Africa in the 1950s, became a teacher in Cape Town, and worked briefly for *Drum* maga-

zine. In 1964 she left South Africa on an exit visa and settled in Botswana, where she was to live and write for the next twenty years. Head wrote *When Rain Clouds Gather* (1968), *Maru* (1971), *A Question of Power* (1973), *The Collector of Treasures* (1977), *Serowe: Village of the Rain Wind* (1981), and *A Bewitched Crossroads* (1984); *The Cardinals* (1993) was published posthumously. There has been an enormous amount of interest in Bessie Head since her death; her short stories, letters, interviews, and talks have been collected in several volumes: *A Woman Alone* (1990), *Tales of Tenderness and Power* (1989) and *A Gesture of Belonging* (1991). A biography, *Thunder Behind Her Ears* was published in 1996, only ten years after her death.

If one were to characterize Head's work one would say that her fundamental engagements have been with equality, harmony, and a certain sense of human endeavor. When she went to Botswana she began writing in earnest, an activity that had been jeopardized, in her words, by a "culture of hate," which is how she saw South Africa under apartheid. *When Rain Clouds Gather*, her first work in exile in Botswana, was enormously euphoric – euphoric about the Old Africa she had imagined, a perfect country where people lived in harmony with one another and the land. Head represented her adopted country as a landscape defined by concord and love, a direct counterpoint to the strife she had left behind in her native South Africa. Indeed, the South African exile who is the protagonist of this novel seems to turn to the peace and accord of a small village in Botswana to escape from the disquiet of politics and life in his home country. Head's second novel, *Maru*, was a bit more complex than her first. *Maru* was written as a beautiful "fairy-tale" about racism but ended up being a very complex study of gender, nationalism, and minority discourses as they affect issues of race and class (see **gender and sexuality**; **nationalism and post-nationalism**). Although the novel is about a Khoisan woman's marriage to a Paramount Chief, it raises complex issues about human desire and the inequalities of gender and class, which it nevertheless leaves in abeyance.

Head's third novel, *A Question of Power*, which is her most important and mature work, was written out of, and within, her own experience of a mental breakdown. In this novel, Head negotiated questions of power, good and evil as well as how humanity, identity, and sexuality were affected by societies, such as apartheid South Africa, which was built on oppression. The main character, Elizabeth, seems in part to share Head's auto-biographical and psychological trauma, but the larger concerns of the novel are the forces that compel people to do good or evil. In the final analysis, Head uses the discourse between Eliza-beth, the heroine of her novel, and the three characters who are the products of her delirium to probe the inner recesses of the human soul. Through the discourse with her imaginary char-acters, and the rehabilitation provided by the process of exile, Elizabeth comes to an awareness of the essential goodness of humanity and the possibility of salvation. Through the exploration of the consciousness of exile, she reconciles the larger issues of good and evil to the questions of sexuality and human endeavor.

The Collector of Treasures, Head's third work, was a collection of tales drawn from her experiences as a woman living in rural Botswana, but she also used the tales to engaged with the life lived by a diversity of women in the village, women who seem to share the same experiences and struggles whether they are members of the nobility or simple poor village women. In the main stories of the collection, such as "The Collector of Treasures," the women tend to fight with courage to surmount adversity in the form of patriarchal social and cultural structures, and in the end they are able to turn their pain into a story of human triumph and love. In "The Collector of Treasures," the protagonist comes to self-consciousness when she meets other women who, like her, have vented their rage at patriarchal structures by killing their husbands. The rage these women experience emerges from the enormous insult they feel when their husbands assume they can have sex with them without any tenderness or consent.

Bessie Head also wrote two historical narratives about figures she admired in Botswana history such as members of the Khama family and Patrick van Rensberg. Serowe: Village of the Rain Wind was a gathering of individual testimonies from village elders who had lived through the country's momentous history under colonialism (see **coloni-alism, neocolonialism, and postcolonial-ism**). The second historical work, A Bewitched

Crossroads, was Head's attempt to fictionalize the history of British attempts to colonize Botswana and bring it under the wing of **Christianity and Christian missions**. Head's last work, The Cardinals, published posthumously, is about the strange effects that apartheid has on familial relations. The novella revolves around a father and daughter who unknowingly enter into an incestuous relationship. Since the apartheid gov-ernment's Immorality Act made relations between blacks and whites illegal and rendered the progeny of these unions invisible, what is represented as most horrifying in the story is not so much the incest itself but the system that makes it possible.

By the time of her death, Head had come to be acknowledged as one of the foremost African writers of the twentieth century. Her major works are now considered to be central to the canon of African letters and to have made questions of gender and sexuality important concerns in the criticism of this literature.

Further reading

Ibrahim, Huma (1996) Bessie Head: Subversive Identities in Exile, Charlottesville: University of Virginia Press.

HUMA IBRAHIM

Henein, Georges

b. 1914, Egypt; d. 1973, Paris, France

poet

A Francophone writer, Henein was born in an aristocratic family of an Egyptian land-owning father and an Italian mother. Since his father was a diplomat, Henien lived and studied in different European countries, and he grew up in a Francophone milieu and cosmopolitan social con-text. He discovered surrealism when he was studying in France in the mid 1930s and became its spokesperson in Egypt during the period 1936–48, publishing a manifesto in 1935 entitled "De l'irrealisme" (On Irrealism), in which he de-nounced the real and claimed the importance of inner creations. Despite his belonging to a privileged class, Henien was a powerful advocate of the rights of the dispossessed in Egyptian society, but he never joined a political party. In addition to writing poetry and short stories, Henien was an active promoter of literary culture in Egypt, founding a literary group, Art et Liberté (Art and Liberty), in the 1930s and a journal and a publishing house under the name of La Part du Sable (The Side of Sand) in 1947. His collected poetic works were published as *La Force de saluer* (The Power of Greeting) (1978). He also wrote short stories that were collected under the title of *Notes sur un pays inutile* (Notes on a Useless Country) (1982). In his poetry, the notion of freedom and self-expression as liberating force was pushed to its extreme, influenced by the anarchist inclination of French surrealists. However, Henein fused the surrealist's quest for freedom with a vision of socialism. Eroticism and love are recurrent themes in his poetry, which often engages in word-play and subverts clichés, leading to parody and humor. His poetry has been translated to Arabic, and it has influenced modern Egyptian Arabic poetry.

Further reading

Henein, Georges (1978) *La Force de saluer* (The Power of Greeting), Paris: La Différence.

FERIAL J. GHAZOUL

Henshaw, James Ene

b. 1924, Calabar region, Nigeria; d. 2007, Calabar, Nigeria

doctor and playwright

The Nigerian doctor and playwright James Ene Henshaw was born in a prominent family in the Calabar region and was educated in local schools before qualifying as a doctor at University College Dublin. In addition to having a distinguished medical career in Nigeria during both the colonial and the postcolonial periods (see **colonialism, neocolonialism, and postcolonialism**), Henshaw was one of the first playwrights in the English language in Africa. His first and perhaps most famous play, *This is Our Chance*, was first performed

in Dublin in 1948. In this play, as in the works that followed, Henshaw was mainly interested in social foibles and domestic conflict, often presenting dramatic encounters between generations separated by opposed traditions, beliefs, and mores. His one-act play *Jewels of the Shrine* won the first prize at the All Nigeria Festival of the Arts in 1952. During the 1950s, and later in the first decade of Nigerian independence, Henshaw wrote plays attacking corruption in his country; but the themes of his plays continued to be constantly focused on the clash of generations or traditions in an era of social transformation.. Henshaw's plays were usually comedies, and many of them were performed regularly in schools and in amateur theaters across Nigeria. These plays were perhaps more popular because of the topicality of their themes rather than their form, but Henshaw has been credited for popularizing drama in West Africa.

Further reading

Henshaw, James Ene (1956). *This is Our Chance*, London: University of London Press.
——(1964) *Children of the Goddess and Other Plays*, London: University of London Press.

SIMON GIKANDI

Hetata, Sharif

b. 1923, Egypt

physician, creative writer, and political activist

Sharif Hetata is an Egyptian physician, creative writer, and political activist. His revolt against the monarchy in Egypt saw him imprisoned in 1948 for fifteen years. This and his marriage to renowned feminist Nawal **el-Saadawi** are two major events that affect his life and writing. His imprisonment remains a recurring motif throughout his novels, giving rise to subsequent themes of social, political, and personal freedom. Hetata's personal relationship with el-Saadawi enabled him to break what he calls the "masculine" barrier within himself, that strict barrier of male self-composure. El-Saadawi released this bind by introducing him to creative writing. Allowing himself to voice the personal, he broke out of the reserved attitude expected by society. His wife's pioneering efforts for women's rights also acquainted Hetata with the feminist cause which he defends throughout his works. The women in Hetata's novels are not objects, but strong and active subjects. His writing is also distinctive because the characters in his fiction have vivid psychoanalytic dimensions. Since starting his career as a writer in the 1960s with the novel *al-Ayn Dhat al-Jufn al-Ma'daniyya* (The Eye with an Iron Lid) (1982), Hetata has published six other novels, along with two travelogues and an autobiography in three volumes entitled *al-Nawafidh al-Maftūha* (Open Windows). Hetata has worked for the United Nations as an expert on migration and as a visiting professor at Duke University.

Further reading

Hetata, Sherif (1999) "Tagrubati ma'a al-Dhukurā" (My Experience with Masculinity), *Alif: Journal of Comparative Poetics* 19: 16–22.

RIHAM SHEBLE

Hien, Ansomwin Ignace

b. 1952, Zinkoni, Burkina Faso

novelist, poet, and storywriter

The Burkina Faso writer Ignace Ansomwin Hien is a well-known novelist, poet, and storywriter at both the national and international levels. He tackles social, cultural, educational, and political themes in his writings to draw the attention of society to the evils that hinder its present and future development. He has published many books in different genres, including novels such as *L'Enfer au paradis* (Hell in Paradise) (1996), *Secrets d'Alcôve* (The Recess Secrets) (1988), *Au gré du destin* (The Dictates of Fate) (1988), and *La Queue de guenon* (The Tail of the Female Monkey) (1988). His other prominent works are *Au coin des petits* (Poems for Children) (1988); *Le Conte de la Volta Noire* (The Tale of the Black Volta River) (1995), *Les Trois Jumeaux* (The Three Twins) (1996), and *Les Larmes de tendresse* (The

Tears of Tenderness) (1996). Hien's style relies heavily on the techniques borrowed from the tradition of realism (see **realism and magical realism**). As a novelist, a poet, and a storywriter, he sees his duty as primarily one of educating his people by writing stories that enable them to reconsider some long-nurtured and, in his mind, negative precolonial values such as the victimization of the African woman and the power of the gerontocracy. He also deals with the drawbacks of modernity, including urbanization and the modernization of the African societies (see **modernity and modernism**). *Les Larmes de tendresse* is a striking instance of his critical view on postcolonial Africa, where he condemns the victimization of the African woman and advocates self-reexamination, reconciliation, peace, and love as conditions for the harmonious social, cultural, political, and economic development of society (see **colonialism, neocolonialism, and postcolonialism**).

MICHEL TINGUIRI

Himmich, Ben Salem

b. 1947, Morocco

novelist

The Moroccan writer Ben Salem Himmich is the author of a number of fictional and non-fictional works, within both the Arabic and French literatures of North Africa (see **North African literature in Arabic**; **North African literature in French**), but he is particularly renowned for his novels, all of which are in Arabic. His prize-winning novel, *Majnūn al-ḥukm* (The Deranged Ruler) (1998) is a well-documented biography of the mysterious and tyrannical Fātimid Caliph, al-Ḥākim bi-Amr Allah (r. 996–1021), who deified himself toward the end of his life, and whose reign was one of the darkest chapters in Egypt's history. *Al-'Allāma* (1997) is also a biographical novel in which he depicts the life of the fourteenth-century prominent historian and sociologist, 'Abd al-Raḥmān Ibn Khaldūn (d. 1406). Tyranny, despotism, and social turmoil are constant themes in Himmich's literary works, regardless of whether they are biographical, purely fictional, or set in the past, present, or future. In both *Samāsirat al-sarāb* (Peddlers of Illusion) (1996) and *Miḥan al-fatā Zīn Shāma* (The Afflictions of the Youth Zīn Shāma) (1993) the main characters are persecuted and tortured by the despotic regimes under which they live. Despite the chaotic and dark political and social conditions prevailing in his novels, Himmich's main characters are usually full of life, optimism, and determination, and hence quite captivating.

Further reading

Ben Salem, H. (1998) *Majnūn al-ḥukm* (The Deranged Ruler), 2nd edn, Rabat: Matba'at alma'ārif al-jadīda.

SARRA TLILI

Hiruy Welde-Sillasé

b. 1879, Ethiopia; d. 1938, UK

novelist

Hiruy Welde-Sillasé pioneered fictional writing in Ethiopia. He had illiterate parents who were eager to educate him. All his formal education was in church schools. He learned some English in evening classes, and although strongly attached to Ethiopian traditions he had many foreign contacts and held modern views. Many of his books have a religious content or flavor. For example, *Wedajé libbé* (I Am My Own Best Friend) (1922/3), considered to be Ethiopia's first play, was an imitation of Bunyan's *Pilgrim's Progress*. He also worked hard to modernize Ethiopia, and his novel *Addis alem* (New World) (1932/3) is intended to promote modernity (see **modernity and modernism**). Hiruy Welde-Sillasé also wrote history and travel narratives and reports, and he published materials drawn from traditional sources. He was early noticed by prominent people, and came close to the center of power, ending up as foreign minister. He served three rulers, and went into exile in Britain with the emperor in 1936 when Italy invaded Ethiopia, dying there in 1938. Hiruy Welde-Sillasé published more than twenty books on different subjects.

Further reading

Molvaer, R.K. (1997) *Black Lions*, Lawrenceville, New Jersey: Red Sea Press.

REIDULF MOLVAER

homosexuality

One of the most pervasive myths about homosexuality in Africa is that it is a foreign imposition and not an indigenous cultural practice. Vilified as a "white man's problem" or alternatively as something that owes itself to the Arab presence in Africa, homosexuality has often been subjected to hostile treatment in the larger African public imaginary. Yet rigorous scholarly research has shown the prevalence not only of homosexual behaviors in a variety of traditional African societies but also of patterns of identity formation and indigenous cosmologies that give the lie to the notion that such sexualities were only the result of foreign cultural contact. Indeed, the evidence suggests that in many cases homosexual behaviors, while not always explicitly discussed or identified as such in the larger public sphere, were often treated with more tolerance in precolonial Africa than in Africa after the colonial period. Ironically then, one might say that Africa's contact with the West, and its colonial contact in particular, saw the rise not of homosexuality but rather of homophobia.

In some respects the rise of homophobia in colonial and postcolonial Africa may be seen to be the direct result of the psychological and cultural wounds imposed by the colonial encounter. Often portrayed as "primitive," feeble-minded, sexually promiscuous, hypersexual, and sometimes as effeminate, Africans sought to counter these negative stereotypes by articulating expressions of heteronormativity and their allegiance to heterosexual modes of behavior. In the interests of establishing cultural autonomy, some chose to defend other indigenous practices such as polygamy that were looked upon with skepticism by the colonial authorities, but few, in the early period of nationalism and independence, came forward in defense of homosexuality. The cultural and literary production of this early period reflects much of the hostility towards homosexuals but, as we will note below, different ways of reading these texts, informed by a less homophobic orientation, may shed new light on a great variety of sexual practices in Africa.

Definitional issues

Much of the confusion and misunderstanding that surrounds the discourse of homosexuality in Africa results from a divergence in the terminology used by various commentators. Some of this has also to do with the associations and stereotypes that have been handed down in the global media, which are then circulated as the last word on a particular sexual identity. It is important to dissect these stereotypes with care and to then dissociate them from the larger cultural claims in which they get mobilized. Thus, for instance, when someone suggests that there are no "gays" or "queers" in Africa, it is well worth questioning whether or not the reading of "gay" or "queer" in that suggestion is based on very specific cultural practices that are, indeed, of Western descent. But the rejoinder to that observation must necessarily be that the question as to whether or not there are "gay" and "queer" identified people in Africa today (which increasingly there are) leaves untouched the historical and ethnographic observation that a great range of homosexual *practices* have indeed been recorded on the continent, and that such practices continue to articulate themselves, albeit in forms modulated according to the changing demands of African modernity. "Gay" and "queer," it must be remembered, are terms that specify a particular constellation of identities that are sexual as well as sociocultural. While they are predicated upon a set of same-sex object choices, they are not the necessary or inevitable result of such behaviors. Indeed, one of the most significant aspects of homosexuality in Africa is that in many cases the individuals who engage in homosexual acts do not necessarily identify themselves as homosexuals. Homosexual *acts* need not always translate into homosexual *identities*, and this makes discussions of African homosexuality all the more difficult.

While much more research needs to be done on the history of sexual practices in Africa as well as their current manifestations, the work done so far shows that homosexual practices in Africa have followed all three of the major types of homosexuality that have been observed by scholars worldwide. The first type of homosexuality is based on age-stratification and typically involves an older male penetrating a younger male, who often plays a social role that is gendered feminine. Such relations have been noted in institutionalized as well as informal settings, the most interesting being the case of the Zande, in which, traditionally, the older man was obliged to pay a "bride price" to the younger boy's family. In this kind of homosexual relationship, the younger boy would be expected to exit the arrangement and enter a heterosexual married life upon entering adulthood. A second type of homosexuality is that based more strictly on a gender as opposed to an age division. This kind of relationship involves both men and women who are to varying degrees cross-gendered, sometimes in the manner of their clothing, sometimes in their behavior and sometimes in the social roles they play. While not all cross-gendered individuals admit to same-sex relationships, many in Africa do. The third kind of relationship might be labeled "egalitarian." Here the partners are relatively similar in terms of both their social and age status, and their relationship is not necessarily coded in any given "gendered" manner. This type of relationship is arguably more recent, and in fact its detractors are right to point to its dependence on colonial and postcolonial conditions of modernity. But along with the other fruits of modernity – technology, industrialization, the growth of literacy, the expansion of the public sphere, and so on – the formulation of newer forms of sexual identities is a challenge that contemporary Africans must face. Claims that homosexual practices are not indigenous to the continent – which are false in any case – cannot be reasonably or humanely used to justify the continued repression of sexual minorities today. Regardless of whether they identify themselves with a larger international "gay and lesbian" movement or whether instead they read their practices along the more traditionally institutionalized forms of same-sex roles, or, indeed, whether they engage in homosexual acts without identifying themselves *as* homosexual, the sexual tendencies and activities of such individuals, many believe, should not be criminalized. Informed by an increasingly international public sphere which recognizes that sexual rights are an important aspect of human rights, South Africa, for instance, has codified an explicit constitutional provision protecting sexual minorities. But at the same time, the possibilities of severe backlash against Africans who mobilize in defense of homosexual rights are ever present and this demands increasing vigilance on the part of human rights advocates.

Representational issues

In an important article that surveys the treatment of homosexuality in African literature, Chris Dunton suggests that the great majority of African literary works that represent homosexuality do so in a monothematic way. By this he means that the function of the homosexual character is often one that is reducible to a political, economic or moral condition that is held in the larger context of the novel to be reprehensible. In some instances, such as Ayi Kwei **Armah**'s *Two Thousand Seasons* (1973) and J.P. **Clark-Bekederemo**'s play *The Raft* (1964), homosexual relations between Africans and foreigners (Arabs in Armah's case and Europeans in Clark-Bekederemo's) are seen to be exploitative and alienating to the African subjects. A similar characterization of homosexuality as exploitation is evident in novels like Camara **Laye**'s *A Dream of Africa* (*Dramouss*) (1966) that depict the life of African students in Europe. When indigenous, traditionally sanctioned practices of homosexuality are represented, as they are in Wole **Soyinka**'s *Season of Anomy* (1973), which represents a Zaki – the head of a traditional Muslim court who in this case has a liking for boys, or Mariama Bâ's *Scarlet Song* (*Un Chant ecarlate*) (1981) which depicts an effeminate young man destined in the eyes of his neighbors to be a *gor djiguene* (man–woman, used to refer to those regarded as effeminate as well as homosexuals), they too are represented negatively – in the former case as the expression of a politically repressive system and in the latter as social failure. In some cases, most noticeably in Bessie **Head**'s *A Question of Power* (1973) and Calixthe **Beyala**'s *It is the Sun that Burned Me* (*C'est le soleil qui m'a brulée*) (1987), male homosexuality and lesbian desire are associated

in a complex way with both a creative potential as well as with psychological and social disintegration.

While the great majority of African literary representations of same-sex desire – both male and female – have historically been negative, we must pay attention to two important developments. The first is that as consciousness of alternative sexualities on the continent begins to grow and particularly as sexual minorities begin to represent themselves, literary and cultural texts are beginning to be produced that are more sensitive to the representation of sexualities and to the stereotypes that have been circulated. The second is that, informed by this new critical consciousness and recognizing the power of alternative anti-homophobic readings, critics are beginning to re-read canonical texts that previously seemed entirely monothematic. These re-readings show that, when it comes to the ironies surrounding the issue of sexuality, even texts that have been traditionally read by critics as anti-homosexual display textual ambiguities. Thus, for instance, a case in point is the criticism surrounding Yambo **Ouologuem**'s *Bound to Violence* (*Le Devoir de violence*) (1968). In this novel, just about every sexual relationship except one is "bound to violence" – we are presented with incest, bestiality, voyeurism, and rape. Furthermore, none of these sexual encounters are ever presented as loving or tender ones. The one exception is the relationship between Raymond Kassoumi and the Frenchman Lambert, which while by no means perfect is nevertheless insistently portrayed by Ouologuem as a loving and tender one. Working within the existing stereotype of the desiring predatory homosexual white man (Lambert) and the unsuspecting young African subject (Kassoumi), the conventional criticism on the novel has ignored the tenderness of the relationship and seen it instead as continuous with the other violent relationships by virtue of its homosexual aspect alone. Newer readings of the novel force us to ask not only about the possible homoerotic tones that remain to be heard in this case and other such canonical African literary texts, but also about the legacy of our own critical complicity with a social agenda that remains unsympathetic to alternative sexualities.

If a more tolerant critical stance is beginning to develop among readers of African literature and culture this is surely also the result of the increasing emergence of literary and cultural production that is eager to portray positive images of alternative sexualities in Africa. The development of such a sympathetic portrayal of homosexuality has been particularly evident in the genre of African film. While their production and reception has been fraught with much protest and debate, films such as *Dakan* (Destiny) (1997) and *Woubi chéri* (Darling Woubi) (1998) show that cultural discourses on African homosexual desires are becoming increasingly urgent. Billed as the first feature film on homosexuality in sub-Saharan Africa, *Dakan* presents the story of two young schoolboys in Conakry, Guinea. Attracted towards each other, Manga and Sori find themselves reprimanded by their parents who wish to keep them separated. Under pressure, they do part ways, with Manga being sent by his mother to a traditional healer who she hopes will "cure" him of his homosexuality, and Sori being encouraged to join his father's successful business in the fisheries and later being married to a young woman in the village. While Sori's introduction to the heterosexual life does lead to marriage and a child, Manga's attempt at a heterosexual relationship fails. Towards the end of the film, Manga visits Sori's household and is introduced to his wife and child. The final scene, ambiguous in its tone, shows the reunited Sori and Manga driving off into the distance, leaving behind Sori's weeping wife.

If *Dakan* casts a sympathetic but finally uncertain note on the future of Manga and Sori and their homosexual relationship in a censuring world, *Woubi chéri* is a film that focuses on pride. Documentary in nature and intended to be an education into a world that others have refused to see, *Woubi chéri* literally begins with a vocabulary lesson. A *woubi* we are told, is a man who plays the role of a "wife" in a relationship; a *yossi* is a man who plays the "husband" and he may indeed also be married heterosexually. A *toussou bakari* is a lesbian and a *controus* is a homophobe. This film shot in the Côte d'Ivoire is unlike any other, in that it presents from an internal point of view the lifestyle and cultures of a variety of alternatively sexed and gendered individuals in Abidjan. Along with the emergent homosexual literature – essays, short stories, poems – published in limited circulation and oftentimes by underground presses, films

such as *Dakan* and *Woubi chéri* herald a new phase in the representation of African sexualities.

Further reading

Desai, Gaurav (1997) "Out in Africa," *Genders* 25: 120–43.

Dunton, Chris (1989) " 'Wheyting be Dat?' The Treatment of Homosexuality in African Literature," *Research in African Literatures* 20, 3: 422–48.

Gevisser, Mark and Cameron, Edwin (eds) (1994) *Defiant Desire: Gay and Lesbian Lives in South Africa*, New York: Routledge.

Krouse, Matthew (ed.) (1993) *The Invisible Ghetto: Lesbian and Gay Writing from South Africa*, Johannesburg: Congress of South African Writers.

Murray, Stephen and Roscoe, Will (eds) (1998) *Boy-Wives and Female Husbands: Studies in African Homosexualities*, New York: Palgrave.

GAURAV DESAI

Honwana, Luís Bernardo

b. 1942, Maputo, Mozambique

novelist and short story writer

The black Mozambican writer Luís Bernardo Honwana was born in Lourenço Marques (now Maputo). His father was an interpreter for the colonial administration. Luís Bernardo worked for a number of newspapers in the Portuguese colony. His collection of short stories, *We Killed Mangy-Dog* (1987) (*Nós Matámos o Cão-Tinhoso*) (1972), critiques the racist policies of the colonial regime, using vernacular language and marginalized narrative voices. He spent three years in prison in the 1960s for his opposition to the colonial regime, and became minister of culture in the post-independence government of Mozambique.

Further reading

Honwana, Luís Bernardo (1987) *We Killed Mangy-Dog*, trans. Dorothy Guedes, Harare: Zimbabwe Publishing House.

PHILLIP ROTHWELL

Hope, Christopher

b. 1944, Johannesburg, South Africa

novelist, short story writer, poet, reviewer, playwright, and travel writer

Christopher Hope, South African novelist, short story writer, poet, reviewer, playwright, travel writer, was born into a Catholic family in Johannesburg and educated at the universities of the Witwatersrand (BA, MA) and Natal (BA Hons). Though living in voluntary exile in London since 1975, he has paid frequent visits to South Africa. In scattered interviews in the 1980s, he describes writing as "a rather mischievous occupation." His carefully crafted satire is characterized by acerbic wit ridiculing the corruption, brutality, bizarre prejudices, and absurdities of politics and society. "Power," he says, "is obliged of its very nature to make itself ridiculous. I like to celebrate that ridiculousness." He admits to a "pessimistic" view of history: "Anger recalled in exile is my spur," he says. "I write not to change the world but to undermine it." He has published the poetry collections *Whitewashes* (with Mike Kirkwood, 1970), *Cape Drives* (1974), *In the Country of the Black Pig* (1981), and the long poem *Englishmen* (1985), which was dramatized by the BBC. He has won numerous South African and international literary awards, among them the Pringle and Cholmondeley awards for poetry.

His novels include *A Separate Development* (1980), which won the David Higham Prize and was briefly banned in South Africa, *Kruger's Alp* (1984), winner of the Whitbread Award, *The Hottentot Room* (1986), *My Chocolate Redeemer* (1989), *Serenity House* (1992), *Darkest England* (1996), and *Me, the Moon and Elvis Presley* (1997). For the semi-autobiographical *White Boy Running* (1988) about growing up in South Africa, he received the CNA Literary Award. Hope's other writings include two volumes of short stories: *Private Parts* (1981; revised and reissued as *Learning to Fly*, 1990) and *The Love Songs of Nathan J. Swirsky* (1993); a novella *Black Swan* (1987); a non-fictional account of a visit to Russia *Moscow, Moscow* (1990), and *Signs of the Heart* (1999), set in southern France, where he now lives. He has also written several successful plays for radio and television and two children's books.

MALCOLM HACKSLEY

Houari, Leila

b. 1958, Casablanca, Morocco

novelist

Leila Houari is a writer of Moroccan origin living in Brussels. Her first novel, *Zeida de nulle part* (Zeida from Nowhere) (1985), was published in Paris alongside novels by other emerging Beur writers (see **Beur literature in France**), many of whom started to make their voices heard in the early 1980s. Her first novel, which is largely based on autobiographical experiences, retraces the journey of self-discovery of a young girl of Moroccan immigrant parents who decides to "return" to her parents' homeland. Zeida's journey of initiation brings her face to face with the recognition that her future lies not in a return to an imagined homeland but in the synthesis between Europe and Africa. One of the main concerns of Houari's theater and poetry is the lives and worlds of individuals estranged from themselves and from society. Houari has also shown a particular interest in the plight of immigrant women, and has published an illustrated collection of portraits that record the history of women of North African background in France and Belgium. The writer is also known for her active involvement in community projects and writing workshops with young people of Moroccan origins living in Brussels.

Further reading

Houari, L. (1985) *Zeida de nulle part* (Zeida from Nowhere), Paris: L'Harmattan.

ANISSA TALAHITE-MOODLEY

Hove, Chenjerai

b. 1956, Zvishavane, Zimbabwe

novelist, poet, critic, and editor

The, novelist, poet, critic, and editor Chenjerai Hove was born in Zvishavane, Zimbabwe. His first published work of fiction was *Masimba Avahnu* (1986), a novel in the Shona language (see **Shona and Ndebele literature**) and he was also the editor of *Matende Mashava: Bumbiro reNyaya*, a collection of short stories (1982). Hove's international acclaim, however, derives from his works written in English. His early writings in English include *Up in Arms* (1982), a collection of poems protesting against colonialism in Rhodesia (see **colonialism, neocolonialism, and postcolonialism**) and reflecting, optimistically, on the war of liberation as the path to freedom for Africans. By contrast, in *Red Hills of Home* (1985), his second collection of poems in English, Hove revises his optimism and depicts the betrayal of the masses by their leadership in postcolonial Zimbabwe. Hove has penned *Shebeen Tales* (1997), *Shadows (1991)*, *Swimming in Floods of Tears: A Collection of Poetry* (with Lyamba wa Kabiba, 1983), *Guardians of the Soil: Meeting Zimbabwean's Elders* (with Ilija Trojanow, 1996), *Ancestors* (1996), and *Bones* (1988), which won the Noma Award for Publishing in Africa (see **publishing**). In *Bones*, Hove focuses on the historical role of African women in the liberation of Zimbabwe. The book also explores the theme of the betrayal of the masses by the nationalist leadership. What is most memorable about *Bones* is the author's use of Shona idioms and expressions to register the dislocation of African people's lives during and after the war of liberation.

M. VAMBE

Ḥūḥū, Aḥmad Reḍā

b. 1911, Sidi Uqba, Algeria; d. 1956, Constantine, Algeria

writer, playwright, journalist, and translator

Algerian short story writer, playwright, journalist,

and translator Ḥūḥū was born in Sidi Uqba and lived in Saudi Arabia between 1934 and 1945. He wrote a novella, *Ghādāt Umm al-Qurā* (Meccan Lady) (1947), two collections of short stories, *Namādhij bashariyya* (Human Types) (1955) and *Ṣāḥibat al-waḥy wa qisas ukhrā* (The Muse and Other Stories) (n.d.), and a series of dialogues, *Maʿa ḥimār al-Ḥakim* (With [Tawfiq] **al-Ḥakim**'s Donkey) (1953), all in Arabic. He also contributed to two Islamist newspapers, *al-Baṣāʾir* and *al-Shihāb* and wrote a number of plays. Ḥūḥū sharply criticized the condition of women and championed their education and emancipation. He also attacked social and moral ills and accused the Algerian politicians of hypocrisy and collaboration with the French. Ḥūḥū's writings, especially his plays, which were written and performed in Algerian spoken Arabic, reached a wide audience and were deemed so subversive that French colonial authorities had him assassinated.

Further reading

Bamia, Aida (1996) "Huhu, Reda," in Reeva Simon, Philip Mattar, and Richard Bulliet (eds) *Encyclopedia of the Modern Middle East*, New York: Macmillan.

WAÏL S. HASSAN

Ḥusayn, Ṭāhā

b. 1889, Maghaghah, Egypt; d. 1973, Cairo, Egypt

autobiographer and essayist

Born in a small village in Upper Egypt, Ṭāhā Ḥusayn lost his sight at the age of 2, through the erroneous use of popular medicine. Nevertheless, he went on to become one of Egypt's renowned authors and educators. Throughout his eighty-four years, Ḥusayn established himself as a prominent critic, historian, novelist, short story writer, and poet. He also worked as journalist, editor, translator, and professor of literature.

Early in life, Ḥusayn was affected deeply by his impairment. Growing up around many healthy brothers and sisters only made him feel more at a loss and more unable to enjoy the spontaneity of life as children his age do. He describes in his autobiography, *al Ayyām* (The Days) (1929), his reliance on his sister to accompany him wherever he needed to go. He developed a sense of suspicion towards others, always feeling watched and poked fun at. This outlook would stay with him and affect his life and writing. Husayn developed an aggressive attitude that helped him in surmounting life's other obstacles as well.

His model at a very early age was the controversial Abbassid poet and philosopher, Abū al-'Ala' al-Ma'arri. Al-Ma'arri was also blind his entire life, and yet, unlike his role model, Husayn fought against a life of seclusion, playing an important role in his country's cultural life.

Despite his modest means of living, Husayn's father insisted on having all his sons educated, including Husayn. After accomplishing the great task to which most children of that time were dedicated, the rote memorization of the whole Koran, in the village *kuttab* (a small informal school teaching religion), Husayn moved to Cairo in 1902 to join al-Azhar University. Being primarily an Islamic institution, al-Azhar offered Husayn religious teaching, in addition to a few lectures on Arabic literature. There, he had the opportunity to attend lectures given by Sheikh Muhammad Abdu, the renowned religious and literary scholar. Husayn attended Abdu's last two lectures before the sheikh was expelled from al-Azhar for his unconventional ideas, teaching methodology and reformist philosophy, a role that Husayn himself would assume later on.

Disappointed with the outdated knowledge and practices of the educational system of al-Azhar, Husayn did not hesitate to express his criticism openly, which antagonized his instructors and resulted in his dismissal from the university. Months later he was readmitted, but by this time he was already emotionally and mentally divorced from it, since he had experienced a more intellectual and liberal way of learning at the Egyptian University (the current Cairo University) and preferred it. Studying at both universities simultaneously, Husayn managed to pass his exams at the Egyptian University in 1914, writing a thesis on his role model al-Ma'arri. Despite having failed his exams at al-Azhar University in 1912, he was

the Egyptian University's most outstanding graduate and was granted a scholarship to study in France. Five years later, Husayn returned to Egypt, having earned his doctorate from the Sorbonne on the Arab sociologist Ibn Khaldun, and having married his French reader. Husayn began teaching at the Egyptian University and it was there that he began his prolific but nonetheless problematic career.

In 1926, Husayn's book *Fi al-Shi'r al-Jahili* (On Pre-Islamic Poetry) was met with much criticism and scorn. This book clearly pronounced his skeptical ideas on the sources to which we owe the preservation of classical literature, transmitted through the oral tradition. His views were seen as blasphemous, because by suspecting the authenticity of classical poetry he seemed to be questioning the authenticity of the Koran, as it was also preserved through the same oral tradition. His book managed to revive the hostility of al-Azhar sheikhs against him. Clarifying his ideas, however, Husayn managed to avoid being dismissed from his position as professor at the Egyptian University. The importance of this stage in Husayn's academic career lies in the shift he made towards outstanding scholarly research. Unlike the naïve use of sources he displayed in his graduate thesis in 1914, *Fi al-Shi'r al-Jahili* shows a deep analysis of the subject at hand and the great influence of the Orientalist approach that he was exposed to in France. From then on, Husayn managed to produce effective critical works on classical and modern Arabic literature. One of his greatest achievements was bringing classical texts close to the modern reader, despite the difficulty of classical language. Husayn emphasized the universal meaning and message of the texts, endearing the study of literature to his readers.

In addition to his fictionalized autobiography, which was published in three volumes in 1929, 1940, and 1967 respectively, Husayn's outstanding literary works include novels, *The Call of the Curlew* (1980) (*Du'a' al-Karawan*) (1941), *al-Hub al-Da'I'* (The Lost Love) (1942), *Ahlam Shahrazad* (Scheherazade's Dreams) (1943), *Shajarat al-Bu's* (The Tree of Misery) (1944), *Adīb* (Man of Letters) (1994) and *al-Qasr al-Mashur* (The Enchanted Palace) (1936) co-authored with Tawfiq **al-Hakim**. Husayn's formation as an educator explains his didactic tendency and the frequent inclusion of a social message in his writings. In *Du'a' al-Karawan*, for example, he heavy-handedly expresses his resentment towards patriarchal society. He preaches against honor killing of women for the preservation of male honor. He appeals to love as the means by which humans can transcend all vile emotions such as vengeance and pride. In his collection of short stories, *The Sufferers: Stories and Polemics* (1993) (*al-Mu'adhdhabun fi al-Ard*) (1949), he blames society for the poverty in which many of its citizens are immersed. In it he reaches out to readers as individuals in the community and to the government to fulfill their social duty towards the less fortunate. Another of Husayn's achievements is *Shajarat al-Bu's*, which is considered to be the first Arabic "novel of generation," the first story of its kind to span the life of at least three generations of its characters. It is recognized as paving the way for Najīb **Maḥfūz**'s masterpiece *Ath-thulathiyya* (The Trilogy) published in 1956.

Another major contribution of Husayn's is *Mustaqbal al-Thaqafa fi Misr* (The Future of Culture in Egypt) (1938). In his writings Husayn stresses the importance of primary education as the foundation of the individual. He sees that teachers should be well trained and calls for a development of school curricula to suit the needs of modernity. He also mentions that al-Azhar is an important educational institution that played a fundamental role in the renaissance of the nation, regardless of the merit and character of those in charge of it. He insists upon government support and encouragement for publishing and translation on a wide scale to enhance Egypt's role as the cultural leader of the Arab world. Husayn managed to implement many of his ideas when he was appointed minister of education (1959–62). He passed the decree to abolish school fees in order to provide school education to all Egyptians. He also helped in creating two new universities, and excelled as an editor and translator of texts from various cultures, such as Greek and Latin classics.

Husayn's principal concern was to protect the Arabic language, guarding it from being corrupted by the use of colloquial Arabic. He was instrumental in the study of the history of literature. He received many awards in Egypt and abroad, as well as honorary doctorates from many universities, among them Oxford University. For his efforts in enhancing the quality of education and defending the freedom of expression, he was awarded the United Nations Prize for Human Rights, and his reputation and dedication to literature earned him the prestigious title of Dean of Arabic Literature to this day.

Further reading

Cachia, Pierre (1956) *Ṭāhā Ḥusayn: His Place in the Egyptian Renaissance*, London: Luzac.
Fadwa-Malti, Douglas (1988) *Blindness and Autobiography: al-Ayyam of Ṭāhā Ḥusayn*, Princeton, New Jersey: Princeton University Press.

RIHAM SHEBLE

Hussein, Ebrahim

b. 1943, Tanzania

playwright, essayist, poet, and translator

Ebrahim Hussein, born in southeastern Tanzania, is the country's foremost playwright. He is also an essayist, poet, and translator, as well as an astute theorist of African drama. His plays are rooted in historical and political and social struggles and events in East Africa.

Kinjeketile (1969), his first major play, is based on a popular uprising in southern Tanzania between 1905 and 1907 against German colonialism. In that struggle, the Africans used a magical medicine, which they believed would turn the Germans' bullets into water. The medicine was called *maji* which means water, and the uprising itself was called Maji Maji. Though the medicine failed to stop the bullets and many people were killed, Kinjeketile, the spiritual leader of the uprising, never lost faith in the vision of liberation, thus sending a powerful enduring message. The subsequent struggle for independence was inspired to some degree by the Maji Maji uprising.

The history and the legacy of colonialism are central concerns in Hussein's work (see **colonialism, neocolonialism, and postcolonialism**). He also deals with the complex problems and issues of postcolonial Africa. In *Mashetani* (Devils) (1971), for example, he explores the enduring negative consequences of colonial education (see **education and schools**), while in *Wakati Ukuta* (The Wall of Time) (1970) he deals with the issue of the coexistence between people of different cultures and faiths. *Kwenye Ukingo wa Thim* (Around the Neck) (1988) presents a struggle between conflicting ethnic customs regarding inheritance and burial. Although he treats broad social issues and experiences, Hussein dwells on the impact of these issues on individuals. He explores the dilemmas of life and the impact of these dilemmas on the lives of individuals. His plays are thus reflective and philosophical, just like his poems and essays.

Hussein is conversant with European, African, and other artistic traditions. He draws from all these sources, seeking in certain cases to capture the universality of the problems and dilemmas that his characters confront. The struggle between old and new values, between local and foreign influences, between various faiths, between hope and despair, all these are part of the human condition, which Hussein tries to capture, even while remaining rooted in the African situation. Much like Bertolt Brecht, whom he studied for his PhD degree in the former German Democratic Republic, Hussein tends to problematize issues rather than seeking to offer simplistic solutions. However, Hussein's work is not confined to African issues. He has written, for example, a poem about the fall of the Berlin Wall, in which he criticizes bureaucratic socialism.

From his African roots Hussein derives the basic techniques of his drama. *Ngao ya Jadi* (The Ancestor's Shield) (1976) and *Jogoo Kijijini* (The Village Rooster) (1976), for example, imitate the technique of the folk narrative. His poems often resemble traditional songs, such as those of the praise singer. Some of his works are allegories. He writes Swahili with exemplary precision and discipline. The question of freedom is central in Hussein's works. However, he sees freedom as highly problematical, since it involves resolving the dialectic between the desires of the individual and the reality of social norms, expectations, and imperatives, which are external to the individual. Hussein's plays inspire much thought; they are not meant merely to entertain.

Further reading

Ricard, Alain (2000) *Ebrahim Hussein: Swahili Literature and Individualism*, Dar es Salaam: Mkuki na Nyota.

Topan, Farouk (1985) "Contemporary Issues in Swahili Poetry," in J. Maw and D. Parkin (eds) *Swahili Language and Society: Papers from the Workshop Held at the School of Oriental and African Studies in April 1982*, Vienna: Afro-Pub, pp. 127–38.

JOSEPH MBELE

I

Ibrāhīm, Ṣunᶜ Allah

b. 1937, Egypt

writer and essayist

A highly respected Egyptian fiction writer and essayist, Cairo native Ṣunᶜ Allah Ibrāhīm began his literary career in Egyptian newspapers while a law student at Cairo University. He was imprisoned from 1959 to 1964 for his leftist political views.

Shortly thereafter, Ibrāhīm worked as a journalist in East Germany, then moved to Moscow, where he studied film-directing. Some of his novels have been translated into English, French, German, Spanish, and Chinese. Ibrāhīm's fiction is extremely experimental, constantly incorporating "nonfictional" elements into his narrative: personal letters, newspaper clips, and governmental documents. His first novel, *The Smell of It* (1971) (*Tilka al-Rā'iha*) (1966) reveals, in an autobiographical mode, the dehumanization and destructiveness of incarceration, and how the intellectual is reduced to a meek victim upon his release from prison. The political message and the explicit sexual scenes in the novel led to its banning in 1966. *Najmat Aghusṭus* (The Star of August) (1974) is a complex work whose structure reflects the construction of the High Dam in Aswan, Egypt. In an inflexible language, the deeply alienated narrator questions the point of this technological enterprise in a sociopolitically awkward society. Written in a docufictional form, *Dhāt* (1992) is a condemnation of oppression and corruption in the 1980s in Egypt.

Further reading

Mehrez, Samia (1994) *Egyptian Writers Between History and Fiction: Essays on Naguib Mahfouz, Sonallah Ibrahim, and Gamal al-Ghitani*, Cairo: American University in Cairo Press.

KHALED AL MASRI

Idé, Oumarou

b. 1937, Niamey, Niger; d. 2002, Niamey, Niger

politician, diplomat, and writer

Born in 1937, Oumarou Idé has attained both political and literary prominence in Niger, but he is also known for his distinguished political and diplomatic career, having served as his government's cabinet director under Seyni Kountché, as Niger's representative to the United Nations, and as the secretary general of the Organization of African Unity. His two most widely known works are the novels *Gros Plan* (Close-Up), which won the Grand Prix Littéraire for Francophone Africa in 1978, and *Le Représentant* (The Representative) (1981). *Gros Plan* takes place over the course of a single day and the central plot focuses upon the wrongful arrest and detention of the main character, Tahirou, a chauffeur. Focusing on diverse scenes, including the homestead and the public, political, space, Idé uses his narrative to explore the everyday problems experienced by Nigerien society as it is forced to cope with the changes brought about by independence. *Le Représentant* hones in on the problems of the postcolonial political system (see **colonialism, neocolonialism, and postcolonialism**) as Idé focuses on the nomination of people without qualifications for important political posts. In order to depict the abuses and inequalities of post-independence Africa, the author is concerned with the lives and experiences of ordinary people who are excluded from the elite political structure but who are, however, manipulated by members of the ruling classes.

Further reading

Idé, Oumarou (1977) *Gros Plan: roman* (Close-Up: a novel), Dakar: Nouvelles Éditions Africaines.

SUSAN GORMAN

Idris, Yūsuf

b. 1927, Sharqiyya Province, Egypt;
 d. 1991, London, England

novelist

The instinctive genius of the modern short story genre in Arabic, Idris also made contributions to the drama and novel and was a prominent participant in the cultural life of his homeland until shortly before his death. An early childhood in the Delta countryside of Egypt, early separation from his parents (at the insistence of his mother), and long walks to school – these aspects of his younger years were all to have a profound effect on his later career as a writer. His move to Cairo to study medicine coincided with one of the most unsettled periods in modern Egyptian history, that immediately preceding the revolution of 1952. This period sees Idris arrested, along with many other protesting students, and it also marks the beginning of his writing career. Following his graduation from medical school, Idris served for a time as inspector in some of the poorest quarters of the city. However, he eventually abandoned his medical career in order to devote himself to creative writing and to journalism, alongside his continuing interest in vignettes of city and country life, and a growing

concern with the darker side of Egyptian society, expressed in often cryptic and symbolic terms (the consequence, as Idris noted with his customary candor, of both artistic and practical considerations). Collections of the 1960s, such as *Lughat al-Āy-Āy* (Language of Screams) (1965), *al-Naddāhah* (The Siren) (1969), and *Bayt min Lahm* (House of Flesh) (1971), are interesting medleys of the old portraits of individuals and situations and of more pessimistic visions of human society and especially its Egyptian subset.

It is perhaps because of Idris's genius for the shorter genre that his novels and most of his dramas are less successful. The most accomplished of his novels is certainly *al-Harām* (The Taboo) (1959), a tale set in his beloved countryside and involving one of his favorite topics, the fishbowl atmosphere created by class and gender tensions within a traditional village. His play, *Farāfīr* (Farfours) (1964), was performed with immense success for a considerable number of performances until it was realized that behind the attractive combination of *théâtre en ronde* and traditional slapstick farce lay an extremely nihilist message. Many of his other plays were also performed on stage (often accompanied by considerable controversy over production), but none achieved the success of *Farāfīr*.

Idris's status as one of the relatively few masters of the short story genre in Arabic is assured. While he often expressed resentment for the fame that his colleague Najīb **Maḥfūz** acquired, he was able to capture for readers of his inspired flashes of imagination segments of life and society that had rarely, if ever, been a focus of interest before he brought them to life.

Further reading

Allen, Roger (ed.) (1994) *Critical Perspectives on Yusuf Idris*, Colorado Springs: Three Continents Press.
Beyerl, Jan (1971) *The Style of the Modern Arabic Short Story*, Prague: Charles Publishing.
Kurpershoek, P.M. (1981) *The Short Stories of Yusuf Idris*, Leiden: E.J. Brill.

ROGER ALLEN

Igbo literature

Igbo literature is clearly defined as literature produced orally or in writing by Igbo people exclusively in the Igbo language. This is necessary in order not to confuse it with literary works in European or other languages produced by Igbo writers. The foundation of Igbo literature is the Igbo oral tradition (see **oral literature and performance**) which embodies oral performances such as folk tales, folk songs, riddles, proverbs, prayers (including incantations), histories, legends, myths, drama, oratory (forensic and otherwise), and festivals. The Igbo traditional narrator was, for his audience, an educator, entertainer, philosopher, counselor, visionary, and technician. He entertained as he instructed and strove to make the community values and beliefs enshrined in the tales come alive. The Igbo people in the precolonial era (see **colonialism, neocolonialism, and postcolonialism**) did not derive their entertainment from books or such modern media as the television, radio, movies, or the newspaper. Imagination was developed through oral narratives. Logic was inculcated through proverbs and riddles. Good speaking habits were learnt from experienced practitioners who embellished their language with appropriate imagery, folk idiom, anecdotes, and witticism. Through these the young learned to appreciate the basic ideas of life, the fundamental values, systems of personal relationships, and sense of humor of the community.

The Igbo traditional narrator (artist) had a clear conception of his or her immediate community, its problems and needs; and these were addressed in specific human terms in the course of the oral performances. The narrator was relevant to the community because he or she projected through the ethical formulas in the tales a direction for the community and specific individuals caught in the peculiar dilemmas apparent in the narratives. The Igbo society had a large stock of legends and fairy-tales, which were constantly exploited by the artist to add life and excitement to the performances. A skilled narrator would use many stylistic devices in the course of storytelling. These devices could take the form of proverbs, sayings, anecdotes, songs, or gestures incorporated in the narrative itself. When proverbs, aphorisms, or any other type of cryptic imagery appear in stories, they make the stories more challenging, and the process of understanding the full impact of the stories becomes a further exercise for the faculties of the young audience. The devices enlarged the entertainment and aesthetic pleasure of an oral performance. These attributes of the traditional artist became legacies for the writer at the stage of Igbo written literature.

The first writer to publish fiction in the Igbo language was the legendary Pita Nwana, whose only novel *Omenuko* is today the most outstanding of the three classic novels in Igbo literature. *Omenuko* was published in 1933 by Longmans, Green of London, after it had won an all-Africa literary contest organized by the International Institute of African Languages and Culture. Pita Nwana was followed by D.N. Achara, whose novel *Ala Bingo* (Bingo's Island) (the second classic Igbo novel) was published by Longmans, Green in 1937. It took thirty years before the third classic Igbo novel, Leopold Bell-Gam's *Ije Odumodu Jere* (Odumodu's Adventures) was published, again by Longmans, Green, in 1963. The three pioneer authors – Nwana, Achara, and Bell-Gam – are thus the founders of Igbo written literature, and their works, *Omenuko, Ala Bingo*, and *Ije Odumodu Jere*, constitute the origins and foundations of the modern Igbo novel. Any serious study of Igbo literature in the twenty-first century must invariably begin with them. Each of the three authors published only one known novel, but each was assured a lasting place in the annals of Igbo literature by that single output. Of the three, however, Pita Nwana is recognized as "the father of the Igbo novel." By accident or design, he defined the nature, form, and tone of the Igbo novel, and set the pace that is still followed today by subsequent Igbo writers. His novel *Omenuko*, therefore, deserves the close critical attention of a pace-setter and the mainspring of a literary tradition.

Omenuko is a biographical novel based on actual events in the life of the hero Omenuko, whose home (far more than the home of the author, Pita Nwana), remains a place of pilgrimage for Igbo people and a tourist attraction for visitors to Igboland. The novel has been reprinted many times in various Igbo orthographies. Generations of Igbo schoolchildren began their reading in the

Igbo language with *Omenuko*. Children who did not have the opportunity to go to school still read *Omenuko* at home or at adult education centers. Proverbs, sayings, and anecdotes in the novel, as well as peculiar expressions of the hero Omenuko, became part of the Igbo speech repertoire, which the young adult was expected to acquire and use.

Omenuko is set in Okigwe, a densely populated area in the present Imo state of Nigeria. The action takes place in the village squares and market centers of remote rural communities, where bargaining and haggling go on at one corner while palm-wine drinking and pouring of libations go on at another corner. Communities are joined to each other by a tight pattern of intersecting paths that converge at the marketplace where the clan meets to deliberate on matters of general interest as well as to adjudicate disputes.

This setting is relevant to the action in the novel because it portrays clearly the conflicts and dilemmas of the hero of the novel. To exist is to live with the group. Ostracism, whether voluntary or compulsory, is as a result of an individual alienating himself from the group or going consciously against the tenets of communal life. The theme of the novel, offence and expiation, emerges from this communal attitude to life. The protagonist openly commits a criminal act against his society. He is a merchant by profession. When the novel opens, he has lost all his goods on the way to a distant market following an accident at a rickety bridge. With amazing ruthlessness, he sells into slavery all his apprentices (his neighbors' children) just to recoup his loss. The consequences of this crime against a whole community occupy center stage in the novel. Its resolution at the end of the novel is the only thing that can restore harmony for the individual as well as the group.

Unfortunately, the bestseller image of Pita Nwana has not resulted in the blossoming of Igbo literary creativity, as one might tend to expect in the decades following the publication of *Omenuko*. If anything, Igbo literature since the second half of the twentieth century has suffered a stunted growth and checkered identity. This has been the subject of acrimonious controversy among scholars of Igbo studies for more than three decades. The root cause is the Igbo language itself.

The Igbo language has a multiplicity of dialects, some of which are mutually unintelligible. The first dilemma of the early European Christian missionaries who introduced writing among the Igbo people in the mid nineteenth century was to decide on a common orthography for all the competing dialects. That dilemma, far from being over at the turn of the twenty-first century, has instead acquired the mask of an intra-ethnic feud. Since 1841, three major solutions have been proffered but all failed woefully. The first was an experiment to forge a synthesis of selected representative dialects. The end product, a kind of Igbo Esperanto called the Isuama Igbo, lasted from 1841 to 1872 before it was swept aside. The second experiment, the Union Igbo, functioned from 1905 to 1939 owing largely to the determined efforts of the Christian missionaries who used it to produce the Bible and hymnbooks in the Igbo language. Eventually it too was swept aside by unrelenting sectional contentions. The third attempted solution, Central Igbo, was a kind of standard arrived at by a combination of a core of dialects. It lasted from 1939 to 1972, and although it appeared to have significantly reduced the thorniest issues in the controversy, it still did not receive the collective acceptance of all Igbo speakers. While the Igbo people (scholars mostly) quarreled over a common orthography and written standard, creativity in the Igbo language suffered greatly, to a point of sterility, and with it the development of Igbo literature in general.

The emergence in the mid twentieth century of Frederick Chidozie Ogbalu, a pan-Igbo nationalist educator and language enthusiast, provided the first strong hopes of a permanent solution. In 1972, Ogbalu, as Chairman of the Society for Promoting Igbo Language and Culture (SPILC) which he had founded in 1949, set up a committee to recommend a standard form of written Igbo that would be acceptable to all and thus stem the tide of further controversy. The result was the establishment of Standard Igbo in 1973. It was not perfect, but it gave practicing and aspiring Igbo writers a standard form for their creativity. Since then Igbo literature has witnessed increasing creative outputs. By the end of the twentieth century a significant number of works had been produced. Roughly estimated, there exist today about 70 novels, 42 plays, 15 collections of poetry, and over a dozen collections of short stories. However, this compares very poorly with the output by Yoruba writers (see **Yoruba litera-ture**), who have an estimated record of 185 novels and 80 plays for the same period. The first novel in the Yoruba language was published in 1928, not far from 1933 when the first Igbo novel was published. Writing was introduced to Yoruba speakers by Christian missionaries at about the same time as they introduced it to Igbo people. Although the Yoruba speak a multiplicity of dialects, like the Igbo, and experienced similar controversies over the establishment of a written standard, it is the attitude and approach of their scholars that has made all the difference. The result is that while creativity has flourished in the Yoruba language since Nigerian independence, the reverse has been the case with the Igbo language. Even now, at the turn of the twenty-first century, the Igbo controversy over a standard written form is far from resolved. In a lecture delivered to a pan-Igbo audience at Owerri, Imo State, on 4 September 1999, Africa's legendary novelist Chinua **Achebe** (himself an Igbo) called for the total abolition of the existing standard in which Igbo literature has been created since 1973. He condemned the way and manner the standard was devised, advocating instead that writers should write freely in their local dialects until such time as a more acceptable standard was evolved and agreed upon by all Igbo speakers. It is, however, unlikely that Igbo literature will be able to survive another prolonged "black-out" as a result of renewed intra-ethnic linguistic feuding.

Further reading

Emenyonu, Ernest N. (1973) "Early Fiction in Igbo," *Research in African Literatures* 4, 1: 5–20.

——(1978) *The Rise of the Igbo Novel*, Ibadan: Oxford University Press.

Emenyonu, Ernest N. and Narasimhaiah, C.D. (1988) *African Literature Comes of Age*, Mysore, India: Dhvanyaloka.

ERNEST EMENYONU

Ike, Vincent Chukwuemeka

b. 1931, Eastern Nigeria

novelist and educator

The Nigerian novelist and educator, V. Chukwue-meka Ike was, like his more famous contemporary Chinua **Achebe**, born in Eastern Nigeria and educated at Government College, Umuahia, and University College, Ibadan. Ike also spent some time as a graduate student in the United States. After a few years of teaching in local schools in Nigeria, he was appointed an administrator at the University of Nigeria, Nssuka, where he rose to be registrar of the university. He later served as the chief administrator of the West African Examina-tions Council, a regional body in charge of high school examinations. Ike's early novels were comic representations of the situations he had encoun-tered as a student and educator in Nigeria. *Toads for Supper* (1965) was set in the world of under-graduates at University College, Ibadan, trying to reconcile their regional and ethnic identities with the aggressive individualism promoted by the colonial university. In *The Naked Gods* (1970) and *The Potter's Wheel* (1973), Ike presented the corrupt world of the postcolonial landscape (see **colonial-ism, neocolonialism, and postcolonialism**) as it was played out in the common rooms of the university and other instructions of education, while *Sunset at Dawn* (1976) was an attempt to go beneath the ethnic rhetoric of the Nigerian civil war and expose its class and gender contradictions (see **gender and sexuality**). In the 1980s and 1990s, Ike published at least five novels, all dealing with aspects of Nigerian contemporary life, often within a comic mode. His novels have been popular with ordinary readers, but they have not been the subject of any comprehensive criticism.

Further reading

Griswold, Wendy (2000) *Bearing Witness: Readers, Writers, and the Novel in Nigeria*, Princeton, New Jersey: Princeton University Press.

SIMON GIKANDI

Ilboudo, Monique

b. 1931, Ouagadougou, Burkina Faso

novelist and academic

The first woman writer from Burkina Faso, Ilboudo is a law professor at the University of Ouagadougou and is a contributor to several local newspapers, including *L'Observateur paalga*, for which she writes a daily column. Her novel *Color Complex* (*Le Mal de peau*) (2001) tells the story of a mother and her daughter, two different generations marked by colonialism and struggling with its consequences. A French officer raped the mother, Sibila, a peasant. Her daughter Cathy leaves to attend university in France and falls in love with a young Parisian. In this relationship she experiences racism, which becomes the very negation of her being, a repetition of her mother's rape and hence a new kind of violation. This experience brings Cathy to the realization of the extent to which her life has been shaped by violence, the violence that has characterized the encounter between Africa and the West.

Further reading

Ilboudo, Monique (1987) *Adama, ou, la force des choses: roman* (Adama, or The Power of Things), Paris: Présence Africaine.

FRIEDA EKOTTO

Imam, Abubakar

b. 1911, Nigeria; d. 1981, Nigeria

writer, newspaper editor, and public servant

Abubakar Imam was a Hausa writer, newspaper editor and public servant whose reputation as the doyen of the first generation of writers of imaginative Hausa prose in Roman script was reinforced by his continued presence in the public eye as the first Hausa editor of the main Northern Nigerian Hausa-language newspaper *Gaskiya Ta Fi Kwabo* (Truth is Worth More Than a Penny),

founded in 1939 (see **literature in Hausa**). His first novella, *Ruwan Bagaja* (The Water of Cure) (1934), was a picaresque quest narrative of humorous encounters and fantastical adventures. His three-volume rendering of a wealth of Hausa and non-Hausa tales, *Magana Jari Ce* (Speech is a Capital Asset) (1960), came to be seen as one of the most vivid and witty deployments of the Hausa language in written form. Younger brother of Bello **Kagara**, author of another early Hausa novella, Imam was a product of Katsina College, and was a central participant, with Rupert East, in the establishment of the Gaskiya Corporation, a center of **publishing** and the production of books in Hausa and other northern Nigerian languages. Imam's public role extended to politics, as a founder member of the conservative Northern People's Congress, and into public service, as chairman of the Northern Region Public Service Commission.

Further reading

Furniss, Graham (1996) *Poetry, Prose and Popular Culture in Hausa*, Washington: Smithsonian Institution Press.

GRAHAM FURNISS

Imbuga, Francis Davies

b. 1947, Maragoli, Kenya

playwright

Francis Davies Imbuga was born in Maragoli, western Kenya, and educated at Alliance High School and the University of Nairobi, where he earned bachelor's and master's degrees. He taught at Kenya's Kenyatta University, and later earned a doctoral degree from the University of Iowa (USA) for a dissertation on the works of his fellow East African playwright, John **Ruganda**. In the late 1990s, Imbuga moved to Rwanda to help establish a faculty of arts at the Kigali Institute of Education. Imbuga is generally regarded as Kenya's leading playwright. His most important work is perhaps *Betrayal in the City* (1976), one of Kenya's two official entries to the second FESTAC (World Black and African Festival of Arts and Cultures), held in Lagos, Nigeria, in 1977. He is the author of other important plays such as *Man of Kafira* (1984), *The Successor* (1979), *Aminata* (1988) and *The Burning of Rags* (1989), and a novel, *Shrine of Tears* (1993). Imbuga's drama is founded on what John Ruganda has described as the telling of truth through laughter. According to Ruganda (1992: Nairobi), it is through comedy that Imbuga undertakes "transparent concealment," the strategic use of "serio-comedy" and "the distancing of context" that allows him to treat serious political topics without appearing to be a threat to established authority. It is this strategy that helped him stay clear of jail and detention at a time when the Kenyan state was systematically imprisoning the country's leading writers, including **Ngugi wa Thiong'o**.

Further reading

Ruganda, John (1992) *Telling the Truth Laughingly*, Nairobi: East African Educational Publishers.

GEORGE ODERA OUTA

Imru Hayle-Sillasé (Emeru Haile-Sillassie)

b. 1892, Gursum, eastern Ethiopia; d. 1980, Addis Ababa, Ethiopia

reformer and novelist

Imru Hayle-Sillasé grew up with his cousin, Ethiopian Emperor Hayle-Sillasé, with whom he collaborated until the emperor was deposed in 1974, but they often differed on many political and social issues since Imru, unlike the conservative emperor, was progressive. Imru held high office in the imperial government, serving as a provincial governor, and as ambassador to the United States and India. When the emperor went into exile after Italy had invaded Ethiopia in 1936, Imru continued the resistance until captured and sent as a POW to Italy. After the liberation, Imru was involved in the ongoing debates on reforms, especially land reform. When landowners resisted

reform, Imru gave land to the peasants; this upset the nobility and the emperor, who sent him abroad as ambassador to thwart his moves. During a coup attempt in 1960, rebels proclaimed Imru prime minister. After the revolution of 1974, he was revered for his acts on behalf of the poor. His literary production is small – three novels: *Alemawi tigil* (World Struggle) (1974), *Fitawrari Belay* (1955/6), and *Sewinna iwqet* (Man and Knowledge) (1959): his valuable memoirs have not been published – but influential, due to his stature. He always advocated the modernization of Ethiopia.

Further reading

Molvaer, R.K. (1997) *Black Lions*, Lawrenceville, New Jersey: Red Sea Press.

REIDULF MOLVAER

insiders and outsiders

Insiders and outsiders define themselves or are defined on the basis of criteria such as culture, class, race, gender, or mixtures of some or all of these criteria. Diverse perspectives on insiders and outsiders left traces not only in African cultures but also in academic questioning and reasoning. Here we will briefly discuss insiders and outsiders from three angles: from the perspective of African authors as a way of reacting or "writing back" to earlier representations of Africans and Africa in European literature; the representation of gender in oral and written literatures; and the perspective of research in African literatures in the academic context.

Africa versus Europe

In precolonial oral literature (see **oral literature and performance**), Westerners hardly, if at all, played a role. Later on, they became characters in stories and songs. Many stories about difference in skin color are unmistakably linked to the historical fact of colonialism and colonization (see **colonialism, neocolonialism, and postcolonialism**): Europeans came to colonize and Africans were colonized. The explanation for the inequality in material wealth and technical skill between black and white people was couched in a mythical story in which the European is the "other," the outsider coming from far away or sent far away at the dawn of time because, being too different, he no longer fitted in with the ordinary people. He is represented preferably as the stranger belonging to an unknown world, living underwater or in a country overseas, or he becomes a ghost from the kingdom of the dead. Numerous collected oral stories on the subject clearly show the idea of the white outsider to be firmly rooted in the collective imagination.

In order to explain the power and the apparent happiness of the Europeans, African stories tell how and why the white men came to have the first choice when resources were being distributed; how and why they received the paper and the books and the stationery, the guns, the machines, and the money. All sorts of qualities are attributed to them, from the supernatural to the strange. All in all, it is a remarkably gloomy and negative image Africans present of themselves in these stories of creation – a picture of victimization and material poverty.

The theme of the mystery of the white man's power has also repeatedly been dealt with in the continent's written literature. Here, however, conditions have been presented with much less resignation. On the contrary, the existing relations on an unequal footing became a subject of debate. "From the white men, we have to learn how you become the boss without being right," as one of the characters puts it in *Ambiguous Adventure* (*L'Aventure ambiguë*) (1961: London), a novel by the Senegalese author Cheik Hamidou **Kane**. Particularly in their novels about the colonial period, African novelists have tried to put an end to the myth that riches and power make the white man superior. African literature set in the colonial period shows what oppression and racism meant for those who were their victims. The novels written in European languages write back to European colonial novels about Africa and comment on the colonial myths of race and color.

Like Europe, Africa also developed myths about its outsiders. Up until the mid 1960s, white characters continued to play a significant role in African literature. In fact, various authors admitted they initially wrote more for a European than for an African reading audience: if one was to change

the colonial situation in any way, one had to address the colonizer and use their language.

Obviously an outsider can never look like us and is thus labeled as deviant or peculiar. Interestingly, the stereotyped picture of Africans developed by Europeans bears some striking similarities to the one Africans have of Europeans, as the literature clearly bears out. From the European point of view the African "other" looks different from a normal human being: he smells, he looks like an animal (monkey, gorilla), he is sexually dangerous (the "virile" black man who is a menace to "our" women), he steals, he is lazy and uncivilized – that, at least, is the prevalent Western myth.

The curious thing is that African literature bears witness to a very similar myth about white people as outsiders. In this case, though, the Europeans are the ones who look like apes (apes have straight rather than kinky hair) or pigs (they are just as pink); they are sexual perverts (in Africa the colonial men could often have their choice of the local women or children who pleased them). They are rude, they steal (emptying Africa of its riches); they are lazy (and have Africans do the work for them, paying them very little to do so). And what kind of "civilization" is it that counts two world wars among its achievements?

The image of the white man as an outsider, just like its counterpart, consists of numerous observations that are indicative of a world of deep mistrust and misunderstanding, dividing black from white. On both sides of the colonial fence, the myths served as obstacles to mutual understanding. Colonial Europeans were often totally unaware of what was being thought about them, while Africans were only too familiar with the stereotyped ideas about them. The Europeans, the masters, were never hesitant to speak freely in the presence of their servants; they could well afford to do so. But the Africans were wise to save their opinion for after hours. In their novels, African writers present characters who, in their own group, comment in great detail on all the peculiarities of the white man, without his ever suspecting that "white" did not necessarily mean "right."

The whites and the West are a main theme in the African literature of the 1950s and 1960s. The colonial situation illustrates how easily people tend to abuse their position of power; in present-day

Africa, this has once again proved to be more a question of human weakness than of skin color. In contemporary African literature, white people no longer play a role of any significance. Times have changed, as has literature: other power relations have created other insiders and outsiders in African literature, such as division of wealth, labor, language, gender, etc.

Gender matters

In most small-scale African societies, to be a girl means working hard, being patient and obedient to male relatives. Such subservience is compensated for by the importance attached to motherhood. In many stories, the suffering of the once-maligned wife is eventually transformed into successful motherhood, with children not only prettier than those of the jealous and malicious co-wife, but also incredibly successful otherwise. In African oral tales, but also elsewhere, the character of the mother is treated with great respect, whereas other women, especially wives, are often discussed in a critical or even contemptuous tone. In Africa (no less than in the rest of the world), proverbs also reveal a predominantly favorable evaluation of mothers as well as a negative stereotyping of wives. Such imposed collective norms, inspired by the interests of the ruling group, can be traced in the behavior of characters in stories, where rules are temporarily suspended, allowing for behavior socially unacceptable in the real world, until the existing order is triumphantly restored in the end. The dangers and consequences of female uncontrollability and lawlessness are expanded upon in numerous proverbs and stories. Sanctions follow at the end of the story: the transgressor is punished, whereby order and respect for the rules are restored.

Like the construction of racial differences, the construction of gender differences (see **gender and sexuality**) hides an ideological power struggle, in which one party benefits from the preservation of existing differences and the imposed norms for inclusion and exclusion, while the other party constantly seeks to reduce them. These conflicting interests are often reflected in the different ways male and female authors tell the same story from oral tradition. The difference

between male and female versions is often one of a different gendered perspective on inclusion or exclusion, on being represented as an insider or as an outsider. The variation between different versions of the same story is not without significance, as comparative research in East Africa has demonstrated. The male narrator would rather complain nostalgically about the loss of old values, whereas the woman narrator is critical of the way things used to be. Male storytellers stick to the dominant ideology, whereas their female counterparts are out to change traditions that oppress women.

Right up to the 1980s, African literature and literary criticism has mainly been the province of male authors. So, the question naturally arises of whether, and to what extent, this has affected the way images of men and women are constructed, since literature, by its very nature, contributes to this process of creating "insiders" and "outsiders."

Just like the orally transmitted stories, quite a few novels show that women who act independently eventually get punished. There is very little suggestion that breaking with the past can have any positive or liberating aspects. "Modern" women who behave in an emancipated fashion are reproached for losing their "femininity" and their African identity. Another frequent criticism is that women who seek more freedom are contaminated with Western feminism and feminist ideas, as if the idea that male authority is disadvantageous to women could not occur to them of their own accord. Often, African women avoid the term "feminism" because of its negative connotations and effects. There are women who actually associate the term with Western feminism; others avoid using it for strategic reasons. Still, in African novels by women writers, entrenched dominance is no less challenged in many ways.

African women writers have mainly made their way in the world outside Africa through black feminist criticism in the United States, in which African-American and African literature have often been regarded as inseparable. Sometimes this unity was expanded to include some universal school of female writing, supposedly unconnected to any specific culture. In this manner, African women writers have been linked to (and sometimes inextricably bound up in) traditions and patterns of thought originating outside Africa, with the danger of their work being submerged in white or black Western feminist issues and interests. For a long time this meant that there was little attention paid to internal African dialogues and experiences.

A similar thing had happened earlier to male African writers: because of the exaggerated international attention paid to the dominant Western postcolonial discussion, research into internal African local developments has been so neglected that once more the overall suggestion seems to be that nothing happens without Western culture. One of the issues mostly overlooked in the above-mentioned literary gender discussion is the way African women writers have entered into a literary dialogue with the texts and writing traditions of their male predecessors.

Africa and the academy

For both African insiders and foreign outsiders, the process of doing research needs self-criticism, humility, constant efforts, possible failure, and it cannot do without a free and open dialogue. Although growing up and living in a culture may be an advantage, one's perspective and research is not automatically more qualified for reasons of birth, or class or gender. It all depends on the seriousness of the resulting product. Different perspectives may throw different light on the same material, and thus lead to different interpretations, which is not negative *per se*. It can be very rewarding if some researchers stand, culturally speaking, close and others far from the object of research, thus complementing each other's readings.

New data, new insights, and new knowledge on Africa have led to new discussions and ideas. Research in Africa has indeed transformed the human sciences. There is not necessarily only one correct distance leading to only one correct view or interpretation. This does not mean, however, that the US, Europe, and Africa have profited equally from these new data and insights. In this respect, there is a point that needs careful attention in the context of research. Critical African scholars such as Biodun Jeyifo or Paulin Hountondji have observed that the shift has been away from the African continent and the African universities, and

that the agenda of Africanists in the West still does not seem to have in mind the bridging of the knowledge gap between Africa and the West in the academic field.

An enormous brain drain from Africa to the West has taken place, because the necessary academic infrastructure is mostly lacking in Africa. Totally different conditions pertain, depending on whether a researcher from the North goes to the South or the other way round. The European or American going to Africa is not in search of science but of scientific "raw materials"; in Africa he or she is not in search of paradigms, of theoretical and methodological models, but in search of new information and facts to enrich their own paradigms. The comparison with the proverbial colonial economic greed for African "material raw materials" may seem obvious.

Much of the contemporary knowledge went, so to speak, behind Africa's back, but it has been enriching indeed for Europe and America. In this system, Africa seems no more than a detour to be made on the scientific highway leading to the academic insiders' bulwark of knowledge. In the meantime, what is happening to traditional knowledge and skills? In the best case, these continue to exist next to the new knowledge; in the worst, they are wiped out from the collective memory.

Such observations do not give much cause for postcolonial celebration. African literature, for example, is mainly processed in Western-located academic discourse factories with Western-invented tools, and mostly meant for students' consumption in the West. The postcolonial center for African literary studies is situated in Western universities. In the desperately unequal exchange between powerful societies in the Western world and the impoverished societies in the Third World, Africa seems to have little or no say in the international discussion, not even as far as its own cultural products are concerned, except via the Africans who are part of the postcolonial intelligentsia in the West.

African academics, whose voices are hardly heard in Western academic circles, bring up for discussion the right of self-determination in cultural and scientific matters as far as their own continent is concerned. The problematic fact remains that a discourse from the center of the economic, technological, cultural, and scientific power has at its disposal most knowledge and research material from Africa without sharing it with researchers and universities *in* Africa. In spite of all the "self"– "other" discussions, power relations continue to determine the casting of roles of insiders and outsiders in all fields: the subjects and objects of knowledge and the perspectives on available materials in all disciplines.

In contemporary global relations, then, the inequality in access to data, information, and dialogue remains a neglected issue which has led to academically divide insiders and outsiders. First, it has created a divide along the lines of deprivation of or access to contemporary knowledge. As long as this problem remains unsolved, academic status will continue to hamper the much-lauded post-colonial diversity of perspectives and dialogues, due to the very geographic location from where this diversity is celebrated, as well as to its limited scope, globally speaking.

Second, an equally hampering view is the pretension that, outside the antagonistic relation with the economically dominant Western world, nothing of importance happens in cultures and societies elsewhere. Both points inevitably lead to questionable research results, including those in African literatures. Therefore a strong plea has to be made for globally more balanced exchange and distribution of cultural and scientific knowledge, and of research results between those studying African literature in Africa and those outside, in Western academia.

Further reading

Hountondji, Paulin (1990) "Scientific Dependence in Africa Today," *Research in African Literatures* 21, 3: 5–15.

Jeyifo, Biodun (1990) "The Nature of Things: Arrested Decolonization and Critical Theory," *Research in African Literatures* 21, 1: 33–46.

Kabira, Wanjiku Mukabi, Masinjila, Masheti, and Obote, Milton (eds) (1997) *Contesting Social Death. Essays on Gender and Culture* Nairobi: KOLA.

Kane, C.H. (1961) *Ambiguous Adventure*, trans. Katherine Woods, London: Heinemann.

Schipper, Mineke (1999) *Imagining Insiders. Africa and the Question of Belonging,* London: Cassell; New York: Continuum.

MINEKE SCHIPPER

Iroh, Eddie

b. 1945, Nigeria

novelist

Eddie Iroh is one of the many writers who came of age during the Nigerian civil war, and like many works connected with this traumatic event in postcolonial Africa, his novels are not concerned so much with the wider politics of the war but with its immediate effect on the people who lived through it. Because he was trained as a soldier and was an actual combatant in the war, Iroh's novels are memorable for their concern with its immediate effect on the people who lived through the conflict rather than the wider politics of the war. His novels are concerned with the drama of war rather than its politics or morality. In *Forty-Eight Guns for the General* (1976), the dramatic conflict is drawn from the competing interests of both soldiers and mercenaries with differing agendas and allegiances, while *Toads of War* (1976) traces the fortunes of former soldiers as they try to survive in the bleak last days of the secessionist Republic of Biafra. Iroh's civil war trilogy ends with *Sirens of the Night* (1982).

Further reading

Griswold, Wendy (2000) *Bearing Witness: Readers, Writers, and the Novel in Nigeria*, Princeton, New Jersey: Princeton University Press.

SIMON GIKANDI

Islam in African literature

The spread of Islam in North, West, Central, and East Africa has resulted in its expression in both the oral and written genres of African literature. The written genres are further divisible into categories of literature written in indigenous African languages and in languages such as English, French, and Arabic (though the latter belongs to both). Although the genres have developed within the cultural and sociopolitical structure of their own respective peoples, they display features that are a response to a historical engagement with Islam, its beliefs, thoughts, practices, and language.

The introduction of Islam into these areas brought with it the requirement of having to read the Koran in Arabic. Its teaching was done through Koran schools which varied in size and methods in different areas: from a small one-man class to a well-structured organization underlined by discipline, sometimes excessively so. The latter model is portrayed in Cheikh Hamidou **Kane**'s *Ambiguous Adventure (L'Aventure ambiguë)* (1961), whose royal student, Samba Diallo, later rebels and rejects its teaching when faced with the challenges of living in a foreign culture in Paris. However, a positive aspect of the schools was the introduction of the Arabic alphabet into the regions. After it was adapted to accommodate sounds absent in Arabic – most notably for *p*, *v*, and some consonant clusters – the alphabet was used as a vehicle for writing early poetry.

The themes of these early poems likewise drew from Arabic sources, mainly the Koran, and narratives transmitted from the formative period of Islam. A common theme is praise of the Prophet Muhammad, which has developed into its own genre, the *qasida* (spelt variously in different African languages). An Arabic *qasida* that has received attention in several African languages is the *Hamziyyah* of al-Bûsîrî (d. 1296); it was, for instance, rendered into Swahili verse (see **Swahili literature**) by Aidarus Othman in 1792 and represents one of the earliest poems in that language. (Some Swahili scholars date the translation of the *Hamziyyah* as 1652.) Other Islamic themes included the transient nature of human life in this world and the everlasting aspect of the hereafter; the rewards in heaven and punishment in hell; and narratives of the life of the prophets. Where Sufi brotherhoods flourished, drawing their teachings from the mystical dimensions of Islam, poems were composed extolling the lives of their founders (especially of the Qadiriyya and the Tijaniyya orders), and of local leaders revered by the people because of their charisma and power to bestow blessings.

The Arabic script was replaced by a standardized Latin script in the orthography of African languages from the 1930s onwards. Initially, the change was brought about by administrators during the colonial period – for example, for Swahili in 1930 – but the move continued even after African countries had become independent: the Fulani made the change in 1966 and the Somali in 1972. It has been argued that the change from the Arabic to the Latin script helped to widen readership, particularly after the introduction of the printing press. Schools established by the colonial regimes employed the Latin script, and it is through this medium that new genres were introduced into African literature – the novel, drama, and, with some controversy, the free verse in poetry.

Oral literature

Two parallel genres exist in the oral literature of African Muslim communities. One reflects notions and beliefs present in the pre-Islamic period, e.g. songs associated with spirit cults, ancestors, and some rites of passage, particularly funeral and burial ceremonies. But even here one sees the influence of Islam, especially in cases where the need is to address a supreme being in prayer. Swahili songs sung in a spirit cult of Mombasa, for example, exhibit a tripartite hierarchy in which God is at the top, Muhammad comes after him, and spirits occupy a position below the Prophet.

The second genre shows moral and ethical norms introduced through the teaching of Islam when Muslim motifs came to be reflected in some of its contents, especially in songs and stories. There are thus tales about various aspects of one's relationship with God; tales which comment on historical events from a Muslim perspective; animal fables; and tales illustrating the varied character of human nature, advocating a morality underpinned by Muslim ethics. There are also "sermon-songs" preached by peripatetic Muslim scholars among the Hausa (see **literature in Hausa**).

The interface between dimensions of oral literature and Islamic values is represented most strikingly in the works of Amadou Hampâté **Bâ**, who has analyzed in depth Fulani and Bambara oral literature and their religious traditions, as well as those of the Dogon and Malinke peoples. To Bâ, the relationship between Islam and traditional religions is one of fusion; he considers traditional religions to have provided the foundation for the growth of Islam in sub-Saharan Africa. Although this is a claim that may be open to debate, Bâ demonstrates the compatibility of the two in his poetic trilogy on Fulani initiation which reflects the esoteric dimension of Islam. The works are seen as a cycle: *Kaidïra* (Kaidïra) (1964) represents the quest for knowledge; *L'Eclat de la grande étoile* (The Brightness of the Great Star) (1974) the quest for wisdom; and *Njeddo Dewal, mère de la calamité* (Njeddo Dewal, Mother of Calamity) (1985) the quest of one who has attained both, and applies them to the resolution of the conflict between good and evil.

The esoteric dimension of Islam also features prominently in Somali oral poetry (see **Somali literature**) attributed to sheikhs and *wali* ("saints"), both Sufi – mainly of the Qadiriyya brotherhood – and non-Sufi. Among those well known are Sheikh Abdulrahman Seylici (d. 1882), Sheikh Abdulrahman Abdalla, also known as Sheikh Sufi (d. 1905), and Sheikh Uways Muhammad of Brava (d. 1910). Some of their compositions are regarded as prayers; their tombs are places of annual pilgrimage, when their poems are sung. Poems also derive from the oral narratives on the miracles performed by the sheikhs for the benefit of their followers; such tales are recited by teachers and preachers who move from place to place in the countryside.

As in the case of the Hausa, when the writings and poems of Usman dan Fodio (d. 1817) mobilized the people in *jihad* (holy war), religious poetry was used among the Somali by leaders of the Dervishes movement (especially Sayyid Muhammad Abdallah Hassan, d. 1921) to gain the support of the people against the British. The Somali struggle was also projected as a *jihad*. Unlike dan Fodio, however, the Dervishes did not enjoy total support among their fellow clerics; their critics attacked the Dervishi leaders through poetry as well.

Written literature

As already noted, poetry developed first as a vehicle of expressing Muslim values in indigenous African languages. Although at the beginning the content reflected themes from Arabia, these were then adapted to local contexts and settings. For example, the topic of the ephemeral nature of life on earth – and, conversely, the everlasting character of the hereafter – is treated in depth in the Swahili poem *al-Inkishafi* (The Soul's Awakening) composed by Abdallah Nasir (d. 1820). The poet draws lessons from the ruin and decay of the city of Pate in the Lamu archipelago, off the northern coast of Kenya. At its zenith, the wealthy patricians of Pate had demonstrated their grandeur in many lavish ways, not least in ornate buildings and extravagant social gatherings held in them. Now the silence of their ruins evokes thoughts on the higher spiritual aspects of life.

It has been noted that, among the Hausa, poets gave increasing attention to secular topics after World War II. For the Swahili, the change had come much earlier, mainly in the work of the Mombasa poet Muyaka (d. 1840); one critic has attributed to him the role of moving Swahili poetry from the mosque into the marketplace. Such a change in Muslim societies might have come about because poets now came from all walks of life, and not just from among the clerics. Radio, television, and newspapers have also aided the process by providing a wider forum for public participation.

The emergence of the novel during the colonial period provided fresher avenues for the expression of views on Muslim identity, exploring various situations and contexts of being Muslim. Not all views have been favorable. The critics include Ousmane **Sembene**, whose novels (and films) view Islam as an intrusion into African society with some of its practitioners using it as a mask for material gains. Another novelist, Driss **Chraïbi**, attacks Arab-Muslim traditional beliefs for hindering the development of the nation; however, he does not totally accept Western values and ways either. While the Muslim school system, with its over-emphasis on physical punishment, had incited rebellion and hatred, the French educational system was seen as repressive and served as a conduit for racial prejudice. Despite Chraïbi's criticisms of traditional beliefs, the character of the mother in *Mother Comes of Age!* (*La Civilisation, ma* *mère!*) (1972), represents Chraïbi's return to his Islamic heritage with a sense of belonging.

Issues related to gender in a Muslim society are another major topic reflected in literature. Mariama **Bâ**'s *So Long a Letter* (*Une si longue lettre*) (1980) treats the subject of polygamy, or, more specifically, being co-wife to a younger woman, with sensitivity and depth. The relationship is cast within a wider framework of colonial imposition in which the young are given an upper hand. Old values are seen as being outdated: the young (represented by the new wife) make new demands which the old (the husband) could only fulfil through wealth and through appearing and acting young. It is such interactions of values, played out within the tripartite boundaries of Islam, colonialism, and indigenous traditions, that interweave the works of other Muslim writers such as Nuruddin **Farah** and al-Tayyib **Salih**. In the latter's *Season of Migration to the North* (1966), for example, patriarchy as a norm prevalent in Muslim societies is challenged when a daughter refuses to accept in marriage the man chosen by her father. And when she is forced to marry him, she kills both the bridegroom and herself. An interesting syncretism is displayed in Aminata **Sow Fall**'s *The Beggars' Strike* (*La Grève des battus*) (1979): the basic premise of the plot is derived from the Islamic tenet of *zakat* and *sadaqa* which requires the faithful to give in charity so as to purify themselves and their wealth. But the need to give can only be fulfilled through people ready to receive; the process is institutionalized through the "beggars" whose role is to receive the money and goods of the faithful. In Sow Fall's novel, the beggars go on strike so as to protect their status and their rights. Injected in the plot is belief in spirits and their human mediums who are believed to possess powers of bringing good fortune to their clients.

Finally, mention must be made of the two volumes on Islam in African literature edited by Kenneth Harrow (listed below) which provide a rich reservoir of analysis and bibliography in this vast field. The papers offer insights into the issues that emerge from a Muslim's engagement with his faith, underlined and shaped by a consciousness of the interplay between doctrine and history. Harrow's introductions to the volumes also provide avenues for exploring and understanding the discourse inherent in Muslim writings. Not least among these is the rationale and process of negotiating meaning within the wider framework of Muslim values, affected both by contact with the colonial "other" and a reassessment of the ground realities within Muslim nation-states.

Further reading

Harrow, Kenneth W. (ed.) (1991) *Faces of Islam in African Literature*, London: Heinemann.

——(ed.) (1996) *The Marabout and the Muse*, London: James Currey.

Hay, Margaret Jean (ed.) (2000) *African Novels in the Classroom*, London: Lynn Rienner.

Sperl, Stefan and Shackle, Christopher (eds) (1996) *Qasida Poetry in Islamic Asia and Africa*, 2 vols, Leiden: Brill.

FAROUK TOPAN

Ivray, Jehan d'

b. 1861, Montpelier, France; d. 1940, Paris, France

novelist

This is the pen name of Jeanne Puech d'Allissac, who was born in France where she met and married an Egyptian medical doctor. She accompanied him back to Egypt, where she studied Arabic. She lived in Egypt for about forty years, often mixing with Egyptians and visitors from other countries. During this time she became a prolific writer, with a talent for observation and psychological penetration. She wrote articles in the Egyptian Arabic press and literary works in French. She espoused the cause of Egyptian women, and her novels are considered to be important sociological documents. She also wrote historical romances and novels of manners. There is a strong element of exoticism in her fiction, as she was attracted to modes of life that were on the wane in a modernizing Egypt, including the life of the harem and of eunuchs, as in *Coeur du harem* (In the Heart of the Harem) (1910) and *Les Mémoires de l'eunuque Béchir Agha* (The Memoirs of the Eunuch Bashir Agha) (1921).

Further reading

Ivray, Jehan d' (1921) *Les Mémoires de l'eunuque Béchir Agha* (The Memoirs of the Eunuch Bashir Agha), Paris: Albin Michel.

FERIAL J. GHAZOUL

Iyayi, Festus

b. 1947, Nigeria

novelist

When Festus Iyayi's first novel, *Violence*, was first published in 1979, it was considered to be a major development in Nigerian fiction both because of its uncompromising and radical political perspective and for its use of a harsh style in the tradition of social realism style (see **realism and magical realism**). Educated at the Kiev Institute of National Economy in the former Soviet Union and later in England, Iyayi started his career as a teacher of economics at several Nigerian universities where he was a key figure in the trade union movement among faculty and staff, a movement which for most of the 1980s was engaged in a protracted struggle against the military dictatorship. Iyayi was arrested on charges of treason for a brief period in 1986. After his release he was dismissed from his position as a lecturer at the University of Benin. The vision driving Iyayi's political activities was directly registered in his novels, which, like the later works of **Ngugi wa Thiong'o**, present the violence surrounding everyday life in the postcolonial state (see **colonialism, neocolonialism, and postcolonialism**), corruption among the members of the ruling elite, and the despair of the poor and dispossessed. The unifying structure in Iyayi's works, which also makes them distinctive within the Nigerian tradition, is the conflict between social classes. In *Violence*, this opposition is between a wealthy, politically connected couple and their laborers. In *Contract* (1982), Iyayi seeks to capture the chaos and corruption engendered by a selfish business elite and the consequences of social aggrandizement: more specifically, the disruption of ordinary social life and the degradation of the physical environment engendered by a relentless quest for wealth. Iyayi's work are explicitly political in their depiction of political corruption and economic failure. As an economist and unabashed Marxist, he is particularly sensitive to the relationship between economic relationships and social life in postcolonial Nigeria and the class war that results from the unequal distribution of wealth. For Iyayi, even the Nigerian civil war, which other writers of his generation saw as a failure of political will and moral gumption, is shown, in *Heroes* (1986), as the struggle between ordinary people and a privileged military elite. But the privileging of the class struggle in Iyayi's novel can be deceptive, for ultimately what makes his work memorable is not simply his use of a powerful language of social realism and the radical opposition between social classes, but his acute sense of the moral and cultural dilemmas that individuals are confronted with when political and economic institutions are plundered or destroyed. The stories collected in *Awaiting Court Martial* (1996) are exemplary in this regard. Here, the author is concerned with themes taken up in his earlier novels – political violence, social deprivation, and class struggle – but now the focus is on the inner turmoil of characters who are forced to make difficult political and moral choices to save themselves or their families from a political oligarchy that has lost any sense of human decency.

Further reading

Griswold, Wendy (2000) *Bearing Witness: Readers, Writers, and the Novel in Nigeria*, Princeton, New Jersey: Princeton University Press.

SIMON GIKANDI

J

Jabavu, Davidson Don Tengo

b. 1885, King William's Town, South
Africa; d. 1959, East London, South
Africa

autobiographer

The son of the distinguished South African
scholar, teacher, and editor, John Tengo **Jabavu**,
Davidson Jabavu was also the father of Noni
Jabavu. A gifted linguist, Davidson Jabavu was
educated in the Eastern Cape and at the
University of London, where he studied languages
and music. On his return to South Africa in 1916
he taught African languages at the University of
Fort Hare and also edited *Imvo Zabantsundu* (Black
Opinion), the famous Xhosa journal founded by
his father and one of the pillars of the **vernacular press** in Africa. Many of his poems
appeared in this journal and were later collected
in two collections *Izithuko* (Abuses) (1954) and
Izidungulwana (Twigs) (1959). Davidson Jabavu
traveled widely during his lifetime and his
experiences were represented in three travel books
in Xhosa: *E Jerusalem* (To Jerusalem) (1928), *E
Amerika* (To America) (1932), and *E-Indiya nase-East
Afrika* (To India and East Africa) (1951).

SIMON GIKANDI

Jabavu, John Tengo

b. 1859, Eastern Cape, South Africa; d.
1921, South Africa

writer and editor

John Tengo Jabavu is considered to be one of the
founders of African literature in South Africa.
Born into a Christian family in the Eastern Cape,
he taught himself Greek and Latin and became
involved in journalism, writing for both Xhosa
and English language newspapers in the Cape.
While he rarely wrote fiction, Jabavu was the
editor of some of the most important Xhosa
newspapers in which early African writers in the
language were published. One of the most
important of these newspapers was *Imvo Zabantsundu* (Black Opinion), which was to provide a
forum for debates about the most pressing issues
of the day, including racial politics, land, and
political representation. John Tengo Jabavu was a
tireless advocate of education for blacks in South
Africa (see **education and schools**) and a
relentless advocate for a college of higher education for Africans. It was largely through his efforts
that the historic University College of Fort Hare
was established in 1916.

SIMON GIKANDI

Jabavu, Noni

b. about 1920, Cape Province, South Africa;
 d. 2008

writer

Noni Jabavu was born into a highly educated and prominent Xhosa family. Her grandfather was John Tengo **Jabavu**, editor of *Imvo Zabantsundu* (African Opinion), a prominent newspaper in the **vernacular press** in South Africa. Her father, D.D.T. **Jabavu**, was a professor at Fort Hare University and a leading figure in early South African nationalism (see **nationalism and post-nationalism**). She went to England to study at the age of 13, met and married an English filmmaker and lived primarily in Britain and later in Zimbabwe in the 1980s. Jabavu wrote two works of **autobiography**, *Drawn in Color* (1960) and *The Ochre People* (1963), drawing on her own life to reflect on the lives and conditions of blacks in South African. *Drawn in Color* is primarily about her personal journey through Africa, a combination of a travelogue and documentary in which she records her horror at the way people live and interact socially in Uganda, the differences among Bantu peoples, and the nature of racism in colonial Rhodesia. In her second work, *The Ochre People*, Jabavu's goal is to document the social life of her Xhosa people, including her grandparents, who are often represented through the vantage point of her English education.

HUMA IBRAHIM

Jabès, Edmond

b. 1912, Cairo, Egypt; d. 1991, Paris,
 France

poet and novelist

A Francophone writer, Jabès was born in Cairo in a banking family and moved to France in 1957, where he lived until his death. His early poetry reflects the innovations of the surrealists. Jabès' first collection of poetry, bringing together poems written between 1943 and 1957, was published in 1959 under the title *Je bâtis ma demeure* (I Build My Dwelling). Since then, he has been writing works that defy genre classification, combining poetry, lyrical prose, rabbinical commentaries, aphorisms, puns, and philosophical meditation. His fiction dislocates narrative unity and at the same time allows for reflection. The desert and the concentration camp are master motifs and metaphors in his writing. He has written a seven-volume work published in 1963, often referred to by the title of the first volume, *The Book of Questions* (*Le Livre des questions*). Other prominent works include the three volumes entitled *Le Livre des ressemblances* (The Book of Resemblances) published in 1976. In 1978 and 1980 Jabès published *Le Soupçon, le désert* (The Suspicion, the Desert), and *L'Ineffaçable, l'inaperçu* (The Indelible, the Unnoticed) respectively.

All these works are characterized by Jabès' mixture of genres and his concern with unspeakable events. In *The Book of Questions*, for example, the love story between Sarah and Yukel is narrated in a fragmentary and allusive way. The lovers are separated by Nazi deportation; Sarah is deported to a concentration camp and when she returns she has lost her mind, while Yukel becomes the writer who has to function as a witness to her suffering. The story is expressed in passionate love letters, but nowhere is it fully told, since it is, like all terrible human suffering, unspeakable. This narrative core is commented on by a variety of imagined rabbis as they would the Word of God. The interpretations deal in some sense with an absence analogous to that of the hidden God in theology.

The root of the ambiguity of Jabès lies in his conviction that each word contains a multiplicity of words and that each sentence triggers a variety of readings and interpretations through questioning meaning. Consequently, behind each book there is a multiplicity of books. In this sense, Jabès' work, though hermetic on the surface, has an open core of meaning. The profundity of Jabès is complemented by his poetic working of the surface through alliteration and punning. The layout of his books makes use of brackets, italics, and blank spaces on the page. Jabès mixes innovative techniques with traditional material, poetics with Kabbalah. His themes are God, silence, absence, death, exile, and writing. Inasmuch as he perceived himself as an exile who had never felt perfectly at home in France – despite friends and critical reception – he viewed writing as the homeland of the writer, and inversely every writer lives in the diaspora. He has been acclaimed in France by critics including Blanchot and Derrida, and is considered a major figure in contemporary French literature: he has received major literary awards, including the Prix des Critiques in 1970, the Prix des Arts, des Lettres et des Sciences of the Foundation of French Judaism in 1982, and the Grand Prix National de Poésie in 1987.

By writing in a transgeneric mode, Jabès inaugurated a hybridity of forms and discourses. His speculative bent, sense of the tragic, fascination by the spiritual and questioning of the divine, intertwining of past and present, of the real and the fantastic, contribute to the correspondence of his oeuvre to the postmodern condition and its manifestation in literature.

Further reading

Gould, Eric (ed.) (1985) *The Sin of the Book: Edmond Jabès*, Lincoln: University of Nebraska Press.

Jabès, Edmond (1976) *The Book of Questions*, trans. Rosemarie Waldrop, Middletown: Wesleyan University Press.

——(1991) *Le Livre des ressemblances* (The Book of Resemblances), Paris: Gallimard.

FERIAL J. GHAZOUL

Jacinto, António

b. 1924, São Paulo de Luanda, Portuguese West Africa (now Luanda, Angola); d. 1991, Lisbon, Portugal

poet and political activist

The Angolan poet and political activist António Jacinto, who started writing in the 1940s, was one of the leading figures of the literary renaissance that took place in Lusophone Africa in the 1950s, a movement that was intimately connected to the struggle against Portuguese colonialism (see **colonialism, neocolonialism, and postcolonial-**

ism) and had a crucial effect on the emergence of a **Portuguese language literature** on the continent. Like many other young writers of the period, Jacinto was arrested for his political activities in 1961 and sentenced to fourteen years in the Cape Verde Islands. His first story, "Vóvó Batolomeu," was written in 1946, but like many of Jacinto's other works it remained unpublished until the end of Portuguese colonialism in the late 1970s. Given his political involvement in the nationalist movement in Angola, Jacinto wrote short stories and poems mostly directed at oppressive colonial social practices such as forced labor, but the political message of these poems is often represented through an intimate, personal, and lyrical voice. "Letter from a Contract Worker" (1961), for example, is a poem against forced labor, but it is written in the form of a love lyric.

Further reading

Dickinson, Margaret (1972) *When Bullets Begin to Flower*, Nairobi: East African Publishing House.

Jacinto, António (1961) *Colectánea de poemas* (Collected Poems), Lisbon: Edição da Casa dos Estudantes do Império.

SIMON GIKANDI

Jacobs, Steve

b. 1955, Port Elizabeth, South Africa

novelist and short story writer

Born in Port Elizabeth, Jacobs spent his student days at the University of Cape Town, graduating with a degree in law. He spent a year practicing as an advocate at the Johannesburg Bar, leaving to take a job in a bookstore and subsequently work in journalism. He used his writing as one way of dealing with the "inevitable despair" of living in South Africa under apartheid (see **apartheid and post-apartheid**), his legal background and the political situation providing ready-made plots for his novels, novellas, and short stories. A human and animal rights campaigner, in 1986 he joined "Jews for Justice," a group committed to helping blacks in trouble with the authorities. He emigrated to Australia in the mid 1990s, where he found a job as sub-editor of *The Straits Times*. His contribution to African literature includes two collections of short stories, *Light in a Stark Age* (1984) and *Cross Roads and Other Stories*, which was shortlisted in the 1990 Weekly Mail/Heinemann Literary Competition; his novellas include *Diary of a Exile* and *Crystal Night* (1986); he has also published two novels, *Under the Lion* (1993) and *The Enemy Within* (1995), which was shortlisted for the 1996 Commonwealth Prize (Africa section). Two of his short stories have been broadcast by the BBC.

JENNY MOSDELL

Jacobson, Dan

b. 1929, Kimberley, South Africa

novelist and short story writer

Born in Kimberley, South Africa, of Latvian/Lithuanian parents, Jacobson was educated at Kimberley Boys' High and obtained his BA in 1949 at the University of the Witwatersrand. He spent two years on a kibbutz in Israel and then worked for a while in South Africa in business and journalism, taking up visiting academic appointments in America before going into self-imposed exile in England in 1976. He was appointed a professor of English at the University of London in 1985 and became Professor Emeritus in 1995. He has written numerous novels, short stories, essays, poems, reviews, and a play, bringing to each a special understanding of human nature and the complexities of race relations. In 1958 he received the John Llewellyn Rhys Award for his short stories *A Long Way from London*, the W. Somerset Maugham Award in 1962 for his essays *Time of Arrival*, the H.H. Wingate Award in 1979 for *The Confessions of Josef Baisz*, the 1986 J.R. Ackerley Prize for Autobiography for his **autobiography** *Time and Time Again*, and, in 1992, the Mary Elinore Smith Poetry Prize for *A Month in the Country*. The University of Texas (Austin) holds a comprehensive archive of his works, which have been translated

into nine languages. In 1997 Jacobson served as a judge for the Booker Prize in London.

JENNY MOSDELL

Jannat, Muhammad al-Mukhtar

b. 1930, Gafsa, Tunisia

novelist and short story writer

The Tunisian author Muhammad al-Mukhtar Jannat started his writing career as a novelist mainly preoccupied with Tunisia's modern history from a political perspective, and his primary concerns have been with questions of colonialism and nationalism (see **colonialism, neocolonialism, and postcolonialism**; **nationalism and post-nationalism**). His longest work, *Urjuwān* (Purple) (1970) (which is constituted of seven parts, only three of which are published), records Tunisia's independence battle against the French colonizers. In his two-part novel *Nawāfidh al-zaman* (Windows of Time) (1974) he reconstructs, in a cinematographic and documentary style, the evacuation of the French soldiers from the city of Binzart, Tunisia, in the early 1960s. In the latter stage of his writing career Jannat turned to the short story genre, possibly in reaction against the limited circulation of his novels. In several of his later writings, he also moved away from the realistic style of his later works and started experimenting with surrealistic and fantastic forms. Throughout his work, Jannat is concerned with questions pertaining to postcolonial Tunisian society and its complex reality. As a result, some of the major themes in his works are political oppression, social injustice inflicted on the disadvantaged, and inferiority complexes Tunisians have developed *vis-à-vis* foreigners, in particular those from the West.

Further reading

Jannat, M.M. (1993) *Qindīl Bāb M'nāra* (Bāb M'nāra's Lamp), Tunis: Ceres līal-nashr.

SARRA TLILI

Johnson, Lemuel

b. 1940, Maiduguri, Northern Nigeria; d. 2002

poet and academic

The Sierra Leone poet and academic Lemuel Johnson was born in Nigeria of Sierra Leone parentage. He spent his childhood and youth in Freetown, Sierra Leone, before proceeding to the United States for his education. He attended Oberlin College and did graduate work at the University of Michigan, where he started writing short stories and poems. Johnson was one of the pioneer critics of African literature in the 1970s and 1980s and a distinguished scholar of comparative black literatures in Africa, Europe, and the Americas. But he has also been a prolific poet, with his poems, mostly about the black experience in the early modern period and the inscription of Africans in the discourses of Europe, appearing in major periodicals. These poems have been collected in the three volumes that constitute Johnson's Sierra Leone trilogy, *Highlife for Caliban*, *Hand on the Navel*, and *Carnival of the Old Coast*, all published in 1995.

Further reading

Wynter, Sylvia (1995) "The Politics and Poetics of *Highlife for Caliban*," Afterword to Lemuel Johnson, *Highlife for Caliban*, Trenton, New Jersey: Africa World Press.

SIMON GIKANDI

Jordan, Archibald Campbell

b. 1906, Mbokotwana, South Africa; d. 1968, Wisconsin, USA

novelist and critic

The South African writer and critic A.C. Jordan died in exile in the United States after leaving his home country illegally in 1961. He started his career teaching in high school before moving on to the first black university college in South Africa, Fort Hare, to become a lecturer. From there he went to the University of Cape Town, and after migrating to the United States he taught at the universities of California, Los Angeles, and Wisconsin. His first and last novel, *Ingqumbo Yeminyanya* (1940), written in IsiXhosa, was translated into English by the author Phyllis Ntantala, who was also his wife, and was published as *The Wrath of the Ancestors* (1980). The novel is based on a familiar conflict in African literature – the tension created by the meeting of Western and African culture. His contribution to IsiXhosa language is his doctoral thesis, "A Phonological Study of Literary Xhosa" (1964), submitted to the University of Cape Town. Jordan also wrote a series of articles on IsiXhosa literature in *Africa South*. Some of his poems were published in two newspapers, *Imvo Zabantsundu* (Black Opinion) and *Ikhwezi Lomso* (The Morning Star).

Further reading

Gerard, A.S. (1971) *Four African Literatures: Xhosa, Sotho, Zulu and Amharic*, Berkeley: University of California Press.

N.P. MAAKE

Joubert, Elsa

b. 1922, Paarl, South Africa

novelist and journalist

Afrikaans author Joubert was a journalist before setting out, since 1948, on journeys through Africa, Europe, and the Far East. Books on Africa include *Die staf van monomotapa* (Cane of Monomotapa) (1964), while *Gordel van smarag* (Belt of Emeralds) (1997) describes a journey to Indonesia. Her prose includes *To Die at Sunset* (*Ons wag op die kaptein*) (1963), situated in Angola, and the novels *Bonga* (1971), *Missionaris* (Missionary) (1988) and *Die Reise van Isobelle* (Travels of Isobelle) (1995). She received the prestigious Hertzog Prize for *Isobelle* in 1998. Joubert will be remembered for *The Long Journey of Poppie Nongena* (*Die swerfjare van Poppie Nongena*) (1978). The novel, related to the testimonial genre, is a structured transcription of the story of a displaced survivor of the apartheid regime (see **apartheid and post-apartheid**) who chose to remain anonymous. Many white South Africans were persuaded to think differently about apartheid after exposure to *Poppie* and the debate it provoked. It was widely translated and awarded many prizes, including by the Royal Society of Literature.

Further reading

Lenta, Margaret (1984) "A Break in the Silence," in M.J. Daymond (ed.) *Momentum: On Recent South African Writing*, Pietermaritzburg: University of Natal Press.

ENA JANSEN

Jumbam, Kenjo

b. near Bamenda, Cameroon; d. 2005, Kumbo, Cameroon

novelist

The Cameroonian Anglophone novelist Kenjo Jumbam wrote a very influential novel, *The White Man of God* (1980), from which he continues to garner praise and a place, alongside Mbella Sonne **Dipoko**, as one of the foremost writers of Anglophone Cameroonian literature. Upon initial consideration, *The White Man of God* appears to be another in a line of African novels criticizing the role of **Christianity and Christian missions** in Africa. While such an assessment is correct, in that the novel deals with the cultural conflict that arises when some missionaries attempt to install Christianity and eliminate indigenous religious practices in a remote village, there are two characteristics that distinguish the novel somewhat from others of its thematic genre. First, unlike similarly focused novels such as Mongo **Beti**'s *The Poor Christ of Bomba* (*Le Pauvre Christ de Bomba*) (1956) and **Ngugi wa Thiong'o**'s *The River Between* (1965), Jumbam's novel is less strident and opinionated, focusing on the incongruity of Christian and indigenous religious practices rather than on condemning the cultural intrusion. Second, the text is very "anthropological," describing in detail several indigenous cultural practices, primarily religious, of the Bamenda region.

Further reading

Jumbam, Kenjo (1980) *The White Man of God*, London: Heinemann.

STEPHEN BISHOP

K

Kachingwe, Aubrey

b. 1926, Malawi

novelist

Aubrey Kachingwe was the first Malawian to be published in the Heinemann African Writers Series when his novel *No Easy Task* came out in 1966. As such he was a great inspiration to aspiring young writers in the country. He had shown that Malawians could make it into the top literary league of African literature. Focusing on the life of a young journalist, his novel is a study of the gradual development of the consciousnesses of nationalism (see **nationalism and post-nationalism**) in a colonized subject, raising him to a level whereby he is able to resist rather than accept the colonial order as immutable (see **colonialism, neocolonialism, and postcolonialism**). Written around the time of the independence of Malawi, it also captures the euphoria that accompanies the attainment of the ultimate prize of the national liberation struggle. Through its graphic portrayal of the unpredictability of human behavior, we get a subtle warning that perhaps the struggle is never really over. Additionally, it covers issues of Christianity, missionary education and urban life in Malawi (see **Christianity and Christian missions**; **education and schools**).

Further reading

Msiska, Mpalive-Hangson (1999) "Malawian Literature" in *Encyclopedia of World Literature in the Twentieth Century*, Detroit: St James Press.

Roscoe, Adrian (1977) *Uhuru's Fire: African Literature East to South*, Cambridge: Cambridge University Press.

MPALIVE-HANGSON MSISKA

Kagame, Alexis (Abbé)

b. 1912, Kiyanza, Rwanda; d. 1981

priest, scholar, and writer

Born at Kiyanza in Rwanda, Kagame was a Catholic priest and one of his country's most distinguished scholars. Doctor of philosophy, eclectic humanist, and prolific writer, he also practiced journalism in the 1940s as chief editor of *Kinyamateka* (The Newspaper), the famous Catholic weekly newspaper in Kinyarwanda, the language of Rwanda. During his lifetime he was a member of several African as well as European academies and institutes of ethnohistorical research, and a member and president of the Rwandan Academy of Culture from its creation in 1971. On his death he left numerous manuscripts to the diocese of Butare in Rwanda, and his *Amazina y'inka* (Pastoral Poems) was edited and published in two volumes by the poet Cyprien (Sipiriyani) **Rugamba** in 1988.

Kagame wrote on African philosophy from what he termed a Bantu perspective, and his most prominent work in this tradition is *La Philosophie bantu-rwandaise de l'être* (The Rwandan-Bantu Philosophy of Being) (1956). He also produced works in linguistics, poetry, religion, ethnology, and oral literatures (see **oral literature and**

performance). His literary production in Kin-yarwanda includes works of poetry conceived by his own imagination or in other cases collected from oral sources and transposed into the written form. He translated some of his works into French, thus adding transformations to initial literary forms, images, aesthetics, rhythms, and languages. For example, *La Divine Pastorale* (The Divine Pastoral) (1952) and *La Naissance de l'univers* (Birth of the Universe) (1955), totaling over 2,500 verses, were translated into French from his *Umulirimbyi wa Nyili-ibiremwa* (In Praise of the Creator), first published in 1952. Kagame asserted that the purpose of his translations was to present "a Bantu text dressed in French."

An illustrative work of Kagame's fictional compositions is the masterpiece *Indyohesha-Birayi / Le relève-goût des pommes de terre* (The Flavor-Enhancer of Potatoes) first published in 1949. It is a satiric poem depicting and mocking, in some 1,100 verses, aristocratic chiefs and the king of Rwanda, who is represented eating pork. The panegyric songs composing the poem are praise poems for the pig, presented here as an animal endowed with the extraordinary values of a warrior. This poem is constructed as a parody of Rwandan pastoral poetry, which is built around the praise of cattle, and borrows many features of traditional warrior poetry from the physical form of noble cows, whose long horns are seen as symbols of power. Kagame's poetical practice was overall motivated by the project of nationalism underlying his oeuvre (see **nationalism and post-nationalism**); his goal was to represent Rwanda as one "nation" consolidated by political, historical, and ethnological elements, as well as by philosophical, religious, linguistic, and literary traditions. But his desire was also to open up the richly esoteric and naturally cloistered or land-locked literary territory of Rwandan literature, thus bringing original contributions to African literature.

Further reading

Ministère de l'enseignement supérieur et de la recherche scientifique (1988) *Alexis Kagame: l'homme et son oeuvre; actes du colloque international, Kigali, 26 novembre – 2 décembre 1987* (Alexis Kagame: The Man and His Work; Proceedings of the International Conference, Kigali, 26 November – 2 December 1987), Kigali: Ministère de l'enseignement supérieur et de la recherche scientifique.

ANTHÈRE NZABATSINDA

Kagara, Bello

b. 1890, Nigeria; d. 1971, Nigeria

novelist

Bello Kagara was one of the first generation of writers of Hausa creative prose (see **literature in Hausa**). Like his younger brother, Abubakar **Imam**, he entered his novella *Gandoki* in a competition organized in 1933 by Rupert East for new creative writing in Hausa. When he wrote *Gandoki* Kagara was a teacher of Islam (see **Islam in African literature**) and Arabic studies at the only secondary school in Northern Nigeria of the time, Katsina College (founded 1921), having been a product of the first Northern Nigerian primary school, founded by Hanns Vischer in Kano in 1908. He remained a teacher at Katsina College until his retirement in 1945, and was then chief Islamic judge (*alkali*) and Wali of Katsina. His early experience of flight with his parents from the advancing British around 1900 informed the structure and first part of his novel. *Gandoki* tells the story of the eponymous hero and his son, Garba Gagare, who are caught up in the military resistance to the British and who swear never to surrender. Repeated setbacks find them eventually with their backs to the wall in the real geography of Northern Nigeria, and consequently transported by jinns into a fantastical world of pagan realms where oft-repeated victorious battles lead to Gandoki converting kings and populations to the community of Islam.

GRAHAM FURNISS

Kahiga, Samuel

b. 1940, Kenya

novelist and short story writer

The Kenyan novelist and short story writer Samuel

Kahiga was part of a generation of Kenyan writers who came of age during the Mau Mau period in Kenya (1952–60), and most of his fiction reflects the impact of this violent period. His short stories collected in *Potent Ash* (1966), a project in which he collaborated with his brother, Leonard **Kibera**, are about the fear induced in individuals by the state of emergency and the rapid disintegration of social life, especially in colonial villages and detention camps. After a hiatus of almost ten years, Kahiga returned to fiction writing, publishing stories and novels on contemporary social problems aimed at a mass readership. These works, which include *The Girl from Abroad* (1974), *The Flight to Juba* (1979), and *When the Stars Are Scattered* (1979), are considered to be an important part of the tradition of **popular literature** in East Africa. His most popular work, however, was *Dedan Kimathi: The Real Story* (1990), a "documentary novel" on the life and times of one of the leaders of the Mau Mau uprising against British colonialism (see **colonialism, neocolonialism, and postcolonialism**). While the novel represented familiar events in Kimathi's life, many already represented in plays on Kimathi by **Ngugi wa Thiong'o**, Micere **Mugo**, and Kenneth **Watene**, Kahiga's novel is written in the style of a thriller with fast-moving action and many melodramatic scenes.

SIMON GIKANDI

Kalimugogo, Godfrey

b. 1943, Kigezi district, Uganda

novelist and short story writer

Godfrey Kalimugogo was born in the Kigezi district of Uganda. He was educated in local schools and at Makerere, where he earned an honors degree in literature. He later took a postgraduate degree in African and Caribbean literatures at the University of Dar es Salaam. After graduation he served in Uganda's foreign service in Congo-Zaire. Kalimugogo remained one of the most versatile and popular Ugandan writers in the 1970s. He is the author of at least five full-length works, four novels, and one collection of short

stories. His published works include *The Department* (1976), *Trials and Tribulations in Sandu's Home* (1976), *Dare to Die* (1972), *The Pulse of the Woods* (1974), *Pilgrim to Nowhere* (1974), and *The Prodigal* (1979). Kalimugogo's works have been described as traversing an old theme in African literature – the cultural conflict arising from the encounter between precolonial society and white Europe – and the general societal disintegration caused by increasing urbanization and modernity in general (see **modernity and modernism**). While these are familiar themes in African literature, Kalimugogo's work stands out because of its constant use of comic situations to comment on some of the most pressing issues in postcolonial society in East Africa (see **colonialism, neocolonialism, and postcolonialism**).

GEORGE ODERA OUTA

Kalitera, Aubrey

b. 1949, Malawi

novelist, publisher, and filmmaker

The Malawian writer, publisher, and filmmaker Aubrey Kalitera has the distinction of having been a full-time professional writer, at least for a while in the early 1980s. He subscribes fully to the notion that literature should both entertain and teach. His work is usually a variation on detective and romantic fiction. His publications include novels: *A Taste of Business* (1976), *A Prisoner's Letter* (1979), *Why, Mother, Why?* (1983), *Fate* (1984), *To Felix, With Love* (1984), a collection of short stories, *She Died in My Bed* (1984), and a film *To Ndirande, with Love* (1988). Kalitera's work transposes and transforms traditional proverbial wisdom into a modern language of morality: for example, his crime story, "She Died in My Bed," warns against taking easy opportunities in life, as they may not be what they appear to be. Kalitera's uniqueness lies in the way he has brought the African cautionary tale, an important aspect of the oral tradition (see **oral literature and performance**), into a happy and cheerful cohabitation with the received genres of crime and romance.

Further reading

Lindfors, Bernth (1989) *Kulankula*, Bayreuth: Bayreuth University.

Msiska, Mpalive-Hangson (1989) "Sexual Politics in Malawian Popular Fiction: The Case of Aubrey Kalitera's *Why Father, Why?*," *Kunapipi* 11, 3: 23–33.

MPALIVE-HANGSON MSISKA

Kane, Cheikh Hamidou

b. 1928, Matam, Senegal

novelist

With *Ambiguous Adventure* (*L'Aventure ambiguë*) (1961), winner of the Grand Prix de l'Afrique Noire, the Senegalese novelist Cheikh Hamidou Kane has made a lasting contribution to African literature by creating a narrative of rare intensity and beauty in Francophone African fiction. He has also brilliantly portrayed the central place of Islam in an African society (see **Islam in African literature**). The book goes far beyond the familiar tropes of conflicts of cultures, to probe, with great economy of words, an issue that lies at the heart of the human condition, namely the question of change. Through an interrogation of the relation between the particular and the universal, the spiritual and the material, the collective and the individual, the elite and the masses, the novel confronts the issue of the passing of a way of life, of a religious and cultural tradition, into the untested territory of a modernity imposed by colonial rule. How can one manage such a transformation without perishing in the process? This is the sad and agonizing question *Ambiguous Adventure* confronts directly and forcefully. While the philosophical issues it presents seem timeless, the mystical dimensions remain the vessel of its enduring universal power of evocation. Here Kane draws from his Muslim cultural background a wealth of intellectual and spiritual resources that constitute a major pole of the narrative.

Ambiguous Adventure is now considered to be one of the most important works in the African literary tradition. Indeed, few African novels have received more critical attention than Kane's first novel, and dozens of probing essays have been devoted to it in many languages. It has received the rare distinction of being translated into Puular, the mother tongue of the author. One of the reasons why the novel has received enormous critical interest is because it has achieved the almost impossible task of summing up, with astonishing concision and depth, a century of the intellectual effort by Africans to come to terms with their encounter with Europeans.

Les Gardiens du Temple (Guardians of the Temple) (1995), Kane's second work, turns to the problems of the postcolonial society and its fast-paced rhythm (see **colonialism, neocolonialism, and postcolonialism**). It is a thinly veiled fictional account of the turbulent events in the history of the Republic of Senegal. However, the story is applicable to the postcolonial state in Africa in general. In this novel the conflict of cultures opposes the traditional animist society of the Sessene people to the government's coercive attempt to modify their religious practices. Whether Islamic or animist, Kane maintains the urgent necessity to protect the cultural identities of African communities if Africa is to flower and flourish. This view is underscored in the novel by the union of the principal character Daba Mbaye, daughter of the Sessene chief, history professor, and leading political activist, with Farba Mari Seck, the griot of the Diallobe people. The narrator describes the couple as the "guardians of the temple" par excellence. Rather than succumb to the homogenizing onslaught of globalization, Cheikh Hamidou Kane stakes a claim for cultural difference.

Further reading

Little, J.P. (2000) *Cheikh Hamidou Kane: L'Aventure ambiguë*, London: Grants and Cutler.

KANDIOURA DRAME

Kariara, Jonathan

b. 1935, Kenya; d. 1993, Kenya

poet, short story writer, and editor

Although he is not well known outside East Africa, the Kenyan poet, short story writer, and editor Jonathan Kariara was one of the pioneers of literary culture in Anglophone Africa. He was among the first English honors graduates at Makerere University College, where he was editor of *Penpoint*, the university's student literary magazine. It was as editor of *Penpoint* that he published the first works of some of the early East African creative writers in English, most notably **Ngugi wa Thiong'o**. Some of Kariara's early poems and short stories were also published in the magazine. During the first two decades of independence, Kariara was associated with some important literary projects in East Africa, editing anthologies for schools even as he worked as a book production editor for major **publishing** companies in the region. In spite of his education at Makerere in the "great tradition" of English literature, a language that many African students considered alienating, Kariara used his poetry to try and reconcile the conventions of English verse and local traditions. His poetry represents one of the early attempts to adopt mythologies, images, and symbolisms from the Gikuyu oral tradition to modern prosody. Local circumstances were to shape Kariara's short stories more than his poetry. In thematic terms, Kariara's short stories fall into three categories: those that seek to recover the rhythms and romance of a precolonial Gikuyu culture; stories that vividly dramatize the period of Mau Mau and the state of emergency in Kenya (1952–60); and postcolonial stories concerned with the effects of the new power on social relationships (see **colonialism, neocolonialism, and postcolonialism**).

Further reading

Cook, David (ed.) (1965) *Origin East Africa: A Makerere Anthology*, London: Heinemann.
Kariara, Jonathan (1986) *The Coming of Power and Other Stories*, Nairobi: Oxford University Press.

SIMON GIKANDI

Kariuki, Joseph E.

b. 1931, Banana Hill, Kenya

poet, teacher, and administrator

After his secondary education at the prestigious Alliance High School, the Kenyan poet, teacher, and administrator Joseph Kariuki proceeded to Makerere University College where he was one of the first group of students to graduate with a BA degree. After teaching at local high schools in the late 1950s, he studied English at King's College, Cambridge. He later became an administrator with United Nations organizations in East and North Africa. His poems, mostly concerned with precolonial life, were first broadcast on the BBC. His most famous poem is "Ode for Mzee" (1965), a work written to commemorate the life and triumphs of Jomo **Kenyatta** on the occasion of his becoming president of Kenya.

SIMON GIKANDI

Kariuki, Josiah Mwangi

b. 1929, Kenya; d. 1975, Kenya

politician and writer

The radical Kenyan politician and writer J.M. Kariuki came to the reading public's attention when he published *Mau Mau Detainee*, a powerful eyewitness account of his experiences at a series of detention and prison camps set up by the colonial government to contain the activities of radical nationalists. The book was published in 1963, the year of Kenya's independence, a time when the new government, led by prime minister Jomo **Kenyatta** was trying to balance the interests and claims of nationalists and a powerful white settler establishment. Kariuki's book provided one of the first positive accounts of African nationalism in Kenyan from the perspective of one who had actively participated in the struggle against colonialism (see **nationalism and post-nationalism**; **colonialism, neocolonialism, and postcolonialism**). His book was considered to be a powerful testimonial, especially given the fact that the nationalist movement had been the subject of loathing and demonization in the local and international media. The book was also a celebration of the radical side of the nationalist movement, one which the new postcolonial order wanted to contain or even repress. His vivid account of political activities as the child of a squatter in the so-called "white highlands" and his representation of Mau Mau as the movement that had given his life meaning made Kariuki's **autobiography** a model for other writers, especially **Ngugi wa Thiong'o**, trying to liberate the nationalist movement from colonial history. Kariuki was the model for the lawyer in Ngugi's novel *Petals of Blood* (1977). His gruesome murder by agents of the Kenyan state generated a lot of protest in Kenya and abroad, and it led to the radicalization of the Kenyan intelligentsia in the 1970s and 1980s.

Further reading

Ngugi wa Thiong'o (1981) *Writers in Politics*, London: Heinemann.

SIMON GIKANDI

Karodia, Farida

b. 1942, South Africa

writer

The South African writer Farida Karodia started writing after she left the country of her birth and moved to Canada, but her fiction often revolves around the lives of the Asian communities in South Africa, the education of girls, and questions of social status among the colored people of the Cape. Her first novel, *Daughters of Twilight* (1986), is about a Muslim couple trying to survive in apartheid South Africa (see **apartheid and post-apartheid**) while maintaining the dignity of their family, especially of their daughters. Karodia's novel adopts a documentary style to record how people were forcibly moved from their homes and locations by the white government or had their identities changed through an arbitrary system of racial classification. In her second novel, *A Shattering of Silence* (1993), she records the life of a half-Portuguese girl in Mozambique whose parents are killed and who becomes deaf as a result. This novel, however, is only concerned peripherally with the suffering of children caught in war zones, for Karodia is more interested in the individual

problems of her main characters than in the larger political milieu in Mozambique, which she uses merely as a backdrop. In her books of short stories, *Coming Home* (1988) and *Against an African Sky* (1997), she again commemorates life as it is lived by Asian people in South Africa, with a specific interest in the cultural constraints imposed by apartheid.

HUMA IBRAHIM

Karone, Yodi

b. 1954, France

playwright and novelist

Yodi Karone, although born in France, is a writer of Cameroonian origin. One of the premier characteristics of his work is his concern with diversity of literary genres. Indeed, although he inaugurated his literary career through a play entitled *Palabres de nuit* (Discussions of Night) (1978), it was with his novels that he gained recognition. Thus *Le Bal des caïmans* (The Dance of the Caymans) (1983) revealed him to the general public and *Nègre de paille* (Negro of Straw) (1985) earned him the Grand Prix Littéraire de l'Afrique Noire. With *Esclave de l'aube* (Slave of the Dawn) (1988), he explored new literary terrain even as he celebrated his twenty years of writing. Yodi Karone draws his inspiration first from the history of Cameroon, of which he analyzes, among others, the events of the national struggle. Colonial and independent Africa, as well as France, is the site of his aborted dreams (see **colonialism, neocolonialism, and postcolonialism**). In his writings, Karone, who also defines himself also as a travel writer, prefers an intertextual approach which consists of taking up again, in a critical perspective, the diverse currents that have run through African literature in the twentieth century, all the way from the **negritude** of Léopold Sédar **Senghor** to the mythological world of Wole **Soyinka**.

ANDRÉ NTONFO

Kateb, Yacine

b. 1929, Constantine, Algeria; d. 1989, Grenoble, France

poet, playwright, and novelist

Yacine Kateb is most widely known for a body of poems, plays, and novels that comprise his Nedjma corpus, a complex national allegory in which desire for the sexually liberated Nedjma represents a longing for an independent Algeria. Part Arab, part Jewish (and therefore part French), Nedjma represents the heterogeneity of Algerian culture and identity. The characters' complicated and interconnected genealogies are associated with a deconstruction of national origins and their inextricable relation with the rest of the Mediterranean. Kateb intertwines his characters' stories with their childhood narratives, the life stories of their parents, and the history of their ancestors. These works' landscapes are haunted by the ghosts of history and littered with ruins left by the numerous invaders and multiple cultures that have pervaded throughout Algeria's lengthy and tumultuous history. Within each individual work, Kateb blurs the distinction between genres, and he often revised fragments of this corpus or moved passages to different works; the Nedjma corpus was thus eternally a work in progress.

Published in 1956, the novel *Nedjma* is at the center of this corpus. Described by the author as an autobiography in the plural, it tells the stories of Rachid, Mourad, Lakhdar, and Mustapha, who end up in Bône with their beloved Nedjma after the brutally repressed demonstrations in Sétif on 8 May 1945. The novel's narrative style, described by Abdelkebir **Khatibi** as exemplifying "a terrorist technique," scrambles the order of events even as it firmly roots them in fragments of Algerian history. Eschewing linear narrative, the novel begins and ends at the same point in its chronology, which Kateb leaves up to the reader to reconstitute. In the sequel, *Le Polygone étoilé* (The Starred Polygon) (1966), Lakhdar goes to France as an immigrant worker (as Kateb had done in the 1950s) after having served as a dock worker in Algiers. A number of events from *Nedjma* are explained in more detail as the plot (though harder to

reconstitute than *Nedjma*'s) returns to Algeria and includes references to independence.

Another major part of the Nedjma corpus is a series of plays published together in *Le Cercle des représailles* (The Circle of Retribution) (1959): *Le Cadavre encerclé* (The Surrounded Corpse) and its sequel, *Les Ancêtres redoublent de férocité* (The Ancestors' Ferocity Intensifies). These plays focus on Lakhdar (here a nationalist militant acknowledged to be Nedjma's lover and the father of her child), who begins the first play in prison with Mustapha and Hassan. Lakhdar is tortured and, after escaping execution, is finally stabbed by his stepfather, a colonial collaborator whom Mustapha kills in the sequel for revenge. Lakhdar has become the vulture, messenger of the ancestors, to whom Nedjma is sacrificed for the revolution. Both plays, displaying the influence of Greek theater, contain a chorus and a coryphaeus and explore the political potential of tragedy. Kateb once combined both plays with a number of other fragments into a single play, "La Femme sauvage" (The Wild Woman), which has never been published in its entirety. The Wild Woman first appears as a character in *Les Ancêtres*, during which she literally unveils herself to be Nedjma.

Nedjma's sacrifice in *Les Ancêtres* makes explicit what was implicit in *Nedjma*, in which Rachid and one of Nedjma's potential fathers set off on a pilgrimage that they never complete. They later kidnap Nedjma and take her to the land of their ancestors, where she is kidnapped in turn by descendants who still live there. The meaning of this double kidnapping and failed return to origins has been the topic of a lively debate within feminist criticism. When the ancestors abduct and veil Nedjma, does the text reproduce the patriarchal enclosure of women? Or, with this enclosure, does the text reveal the relation between a nationalist cult of origins and patriarchy? Some have argued that Nedjma abandons a false liberty (her sexual freedom) to join her people's struggle. Others point out that this view requires a male-centered vision of nationalism (see **nationalism and post-nationalism**). Still others argue that the episode foregrounds this very tension between feminism and nationalism by demonstrating how women's

interests are sacrificed to fundamentalist nationalism in an unquestioning attempt to retrieve a
precolonial past. Kateb has described the poet's
role of being eternally disruptive in the midst of
upheaval and questioning prevailing values even
within a revolutionary movement. As Algerian
nationalism has often attempted to stifle feminist
demands, Kateb's highlighting of these tensions
was one means of carrying out this disruption.

Though Kateb once declared that he was a one-
book writer, to neglect works outside the Nedjma
corpus would be to miss the humorous, satirical
aspects of his work. *L'Homme aux sandales de
caoutchouc* (The Man in Rubber Sandals) (1970) is
Kateb's play – mostly in free verse – on the
Vietnam war, which is presented as a carnivalesque
political farce. *La Poudre d'intelligence* (Intelligence
Powder) (1959), Kateb's first comedy, is both a
farce and a political and social satire that provides
the comic relief between *Le Cadavre* and *Les Ancêtres*.
In the late 1960s, he began to turn more and more
towards theater in dialectal Arabic (with parts in
Berber) as a means of reaching a wider popular
Algerian audience. "Mohammed, prends ta valise"
(Mohammed, Pack Your Bags) and "La Guerre de
2000 ans" (The Two-Thousand-Year War) were
two plays he created as part of this effort. Equally
critical of Francophonie and of writing in a classical
Arabic that the vast majority of Algerians could not
understand, through his practices Kateb articulated a unique position on the **language question**.

Further reading

Aresu, Bernard (ed.) (1992) *Translations of the Orient:
Writing the Maghreb*, special issue of *SubStance*, 69.
Arnaud, Jacqueline (1986) *Le Cas de Kateb Yacine*,
vol. 2 of *La Littérature maghrébine de langue française*,
Paris: Publisud.
Hayes, Jarrod (2000) "The Haunted House of the
Nation," in Jarrod Hayes, *Queer Nations: Marginal
Sexualities in the Maghreb*, Chicago: University of
Chicago Press.
Kateb, Y. (1959) *Le Cercle des représailles* (The Circle
of Retribution), Paris: Seuil.
——(1966) *Le Polygone étoilé* (The Starred Polygon),
Paris: Seuil.
——(1991) *Nedjma*, Charlottesville, Virginia: Uni-
versity of Virginia Press.

JARROD HAYES

Katiyo, Wilson

b. 1947, Zimbabwe

novelist

The Zimbabwean writer Wilson Katiyo belongs to
a generation whose lives were indelibly marked by
the oppressive policies of colonialism (see **colonialism, neocolonialism, and postcolonial-
ism**) and in particular Ian Smith's Rhodesian
government, which sent millions of them in exile.
Like that of many of his contemporaries, Katiyo's
work was inspired by the experience of exile and
the war of liberation. Katiyo has published two
novels, *Son of the Soil* (1976) and *Going to Heaven*
(1979). His work focuses on how the colonial
experience and travel shape personal and public
identity. In his first novel, for example, we are
shown how violent state apparatuses in Rhodesia
produced violent counter-identification with the
state among African subjects. He is also concerned with the conflict between tradition, precolonial society, and modernity (see **modernity
and modernism**), showing the need to preserve
some of the values embodied in the rural
experience. His novels fall within the *Bildungsromanen* genre, as they are principally concerned
with the development of young protagonists into
full maturity, a process that is often a truly rude
awakening.

Further reading

Msiska, Mpalive-Hangson and Hyland, Paul (eds)
(1997) *Writing and Africa*, London and New York:
Longman.
Zimunya, Musaemura (1982) *Those Years of Drought
and Hunger: The Birth of African Fiction in English in
Zimbabwe*, Gweru: Mambo Press.

MPALIVE-HANGSON MSISKA

Kaunda, Kenneth

b. 1924, Zambia

nationalist and writer

The Zambian nationalist and writer Kenneth. Kaunda was born at a Church of Scotland mission in the northern province of what is today Zambia, where his parents, who had migrated from Malawi, were missionaries. He grew up among the Bemba people. After education at local institutions he was trained as a teacher; he taught at schools in northern Zambia and Tanzania before becoming a welfare officer in colonial Southern Rhodesia. Returning to Zambia in 1949, Kaunda acted as interpreter for one of the region's most powerful politicians, Sir Stewart Gore-Brown, and became involved in nationalist politics, becoming the organizing secretary and later secretary general of the African National Congress. He was imprisoned several times in the 1950s for opposing the Central African Federation. On his release in 1960, Kaunda became president of the United National Independence Party (UNIP), the party that led Zambia to independence in 1964. Kaunda has written many essays on his doctrine of African humanism, but his major work is *Zambia Shall Be Free* (1962), his autobiographical account (see **autobiography**) of his life in colonial Northern Rhodesia, his education (see **education and schools**), and his coming of age within the tradition of African nationalism (see **nationalism and post-nationalism**).

SIMON GIKANDI

Kayira, Legson

b. 1940, Malawi

writer

The Malawian writer Legson Kayira is famous for his **autobiography**, *I Will Try* (1966), an account of the remarkable journey that he undertook on foot in search of higher education, walking from Malawi to the Sudan and eventually ending up in the United States. He has written the following novels: *The Looming Shadow* (1968), *Jingala* (1969),

The Civil Servant (1971), and *The Detainee* (1974). Kayira's early novels are a nostalgic return to his homeland, providing a rich description of the physical and cultural landscape of Malawi. He touches on issues of cultural conflict as well as of Malawian migrant labor to Southern Rhodesia and South Africa. However, in his last novel he comments directly on the dictatorship of Dr Hastings Kamuzu Banda, satirizing the haphazard nature of political surveillance in the country, as we are shown an old man who on his way to the hospital for a hernia operation is mistaken for a rebel simply because of his eccentricity and is detained by the over-enthusiastic Party youths.

Further reading

Msiska, Mpalive-Hangson (1999) "Malawian Literature" in *Encyclopedia of World Literature in the Twentieth Century*, Detroit: St James Press.

Roscoe, Adrian (1977) *Uhuru's Fire: African Literature East to South*, Cambridge: Cambridge University Press.

MPALIVE-HANGSON MSISKA

Kayo, Patrice

b. 1942, Bandjoun, Cameroon

poet, short story writer, and oral storyteller

A Cameroonian writer born in Bandjoun, Kayo started his writing career as a poet and gained prominence with the publication of two collections of poems, *Chansons populaires bamiléké* (Popular Bamileke Songs) (1968) and *Hymnes et sagesse* (Hymns and Wisdom) (1970). But he has also been a short story writer with collections such as *Tout au long des saisons* (Throughout the Seasons) (1985), an oral storyteller (see **oral literature and performance**) with *Fables et devinettes de mon enfance* (Fables and Riddles from my Childhood) (1978), and a pamphleteer whose works include *Lettre ouverte à un roi bamiléké* (Open Letter to a Bamiléké King) (1984). In all these works Kayo shows the recurrent pedagogical preoccupations that he has drawn from the Bamiléké culture of West Cameroon. The term "Bamiléké" recurs, indeed, in five of his seventeen titles. But if he exalts certain aspects of this culture, he critiques others and attacks numerous abuses of postcolonial power in Africa (see **colonialism, neocolonialism, and postcolonialism**).

Kayo has also taken an active role in the struggle for the promotion of Cameroonian literature. He was president of the Association of Cameroonian Poets and Writers as well as director of the magazine *Le Cameroun littéraire* (Literary Cameroon), founded by René **Philombe** (1983). As a teacher in the École Normale Supérieure in Yaoundé, he has been prominent in the development of Cameroonian literature and has edited important anthologies of this literature in *Anthologie de la poésie camerounaise* (Anthology of Cameroonian Poetry) (1978) and *Panorama de la littérature camerounaise* (Panorama of Cameroonian Literature) (1978). Finally, Kayo is also an anthropologist, interested particularly in Bamiléké traditional pharmacology.

ANDRÉ NTONFO

Kayper-Mensah, Albert William

b. 1923, Ghana

poet

After completing his education in England, Kayper-Mensah returned to Ghana in the late 1950s, before embarking on a diplomatic career. It was while on assignments in London and Bonn that he wrote and published his first poems. He won the Margaret Wrong Literary Prize for his collection *The Dark Wanderer* (1970), published by Horst Erdmann Verlag in Tubingen. His poetry is generally optimistic, reflecting the hopes of postcolonial Ghana and its potential for development (see **colonialism, neocolonialism, and postcolonialism**). He and Horst Wolff also edited *Ghanaian Writing: Ghana as Seen by Her Own Writers as well as German Authors* (1972). By the time he published *The Drummer in Our Time* (1975), Kayper-Mensah's vision had become more subdued but no less lyrical, with a focus on the complex and often contradictory relationship between Europe and Africa.

Further reading

Awoonor, Kofi and Adali-Mortty, G. (eds) (1977) *Messages: Poems from Ghana*, London, Heinemann.
Moore, Gerald and Beier, Ulli (eds) (1984) *The Penguin Book of Modem African Poetry*, Harmondsworth, England: Penguin.

VINCENT O. ODAMTTEN

Kebbede, Mikaél

b. 1914, Ethiopia; d. 1998, Ethiopia

playwright and poet

Mikaél Kebbede was a prominent Ethiopian playwright and poet, much admired for his elegant language. He first attended church school, then Catholic mission schools in Addis Ababa, receiving elementary and higher education in French. During the Italian occupation (1935/6–41), he learned and read Italian. His interest in literature was kindled in school and strengthened when he became tutor to a prince. He wrote his first books, including *Birhane-hillina* (Light for the Mind) during the occupation, and adapted folkloristic materials, published as *Tarikinna missalé* (Fables), for use in schools. He wrote both historical and contemporary plays as well as history books. His poems were loved and memorized, notably those reflecting racial pride in the face of colonial arrogance. He translated Shakespeare and Goethe, but adapted them to fit the needs of Ethiopian audiences. He was in government service and became vice minister, but was most proud for having established the Archaeological Museum in Addis Ababa. He suffered under the Marxist regime (1974–91), but before he died he was again honored, and he received an honorary doctorate from Addis Ababa University.

Further reading

Molvaer, R.K. (1997) *Black Lions*, Lawrenceville, New Jersey: Red Sea Press.

REIDULF MOLVAER

Keïta, Fatou

b. 1955, Soubré, Côte d'Ivoire

writer

Fatou Keïta was born in Soubré, Côte d'Ivoire, and was educated at local schools before going to France for her higher education. She also studied in Britain and the United States before returning to the Côte d'Ivoire to teach English literature at the University of Cocody. Fatou is primarily known as a writer of **children's literature** and many of her works in this genre have won prestigious literary awards. But she is also the author of major novels, including her most famous work, *Rebellé* (Rebelled), published in 1998. In this novel, as in her other works, she questions certain traditional practices, including clitoridectomy and arranged marriages, which she considers detrimental to the proper functioning of African society, and represents the experiences of a young woman who rebels against such practices and asserts her freedom to choose her destiny. Keïta's novels have been recognized with the award of the Prize of Excellence in Literature sponsored by the Ministry of Culture in the Côte d'Ivoire.

OUSMANE BA

Kente, Gibson

b. 1932, East London, South Africa

playwright

Born in East London, the nephew of Nelson Mandela, Kente (Bra Gib) is known as the godfather of black theater in South Africa. He has written over twenty-five plays portraying urban African life in township dance and song, with plots drawn from the South African black experience. Although only six or seven of his works have overtly political content, dealing with the politics of apartheid (see **apartheid and post-apartheid**), his melodramas *How Long*, *I Believe* and *Too Late*, written in the 1970s, led to his short detention, while his 1987 play *Sekunjalo* was banned for a while shortly after its Arts Festival premiere. Independent and creative, Kente has written several plays for

television, has engaged in producing, directing, choreography, and composing, and has written and arranged songs for Miriam Makeba and other performers. In addition, he has established a theater school, and trained and influenced many black actors. Believing that protest theater stifles what he considers to be real art, he now works constantly towards advancing the African renaissance, addressing social issues, taking the theater to the people, and finding sponsorship. His efforts have been recognized: he has garnered numerous South African awards and in 1997 he received acclaim in New York at the Woza Africa-After-Apartheid Festival for his contribution to South African theater.

JENNY MOSDELL

Kenyatta, Jomo

b. 1893, Kiambu, Kenya; d. 1978, Kenya

nationalist and anthropologist

The Kenyan nationalist and anthropologist Jomo Kenyatta was one of the major figures in the politics of culture and nationalism in East Africa for most of the twentieth century (see **nationalism and post-nationalism**). Born at the beginning of formal colonialism in Kenya at the end of the nineteenth century, he was to live long enough to witness the drama of politics in the colony, from early nationalism in the 1920s, through the Mau Mau rebellion in the 1950s to the achievement of independence in 1963. The narrative of Kenyatta's life is closely identified with the history of the Kenya under colonialism and the crisis of the postcolony (see **colonialism, neocolonialism, and postcolonialism**). Enchanted by the emerging culture of colonialism in Kenya, Kenyatta, then known as Kamau wa Ngengi, left home early to join the Church of Scotland mission at Kikuyu, outside the capital Nairobi. For most of the 1920s he was active in several nationalist movements, the most important being the Kikuyu Central Association. He served as the secretary general of this organization and the editor of its Gikuyu-language newspaper, *Muguigwithania* (The Reconciler). In the late 1920s, Kenyatta was sent to England by the

Kikuyu Central Association to represent the movement's case against white settlement in Kenya before the British government. He briefly returned to Kenya in the early 1930s, but he was to stay in England until 1946, during which time he studied anthropology at the University of London and served as a research assistant on major research projects in phonetics and the creation of a Gikuyu dictionary. It was while he was a student of Bronislaw Malinowski at the London School of Economics that Kenyatta wrote *Facing Mount Kenya* (1938), his most famous and influential work. Although the book was intended to be an anthropological narrative of Gikuyu customs and traditions, its impact in the field of African literature and politics was more apparent in its systematic articulation of a cultural nationalist counterpoint to colonialism than in its ethnographical method, which was largely in the functionalist tradition associated with Malinowski. What made Kenyatta's book central to the debate on culture in East Africa was its ability to make the case for precolonial African customs and traditions as systematic and rational, rather than preconscious primitivist cultural systems. In addition, *Facing Mount Kenya* was predicated on a vision of African society that was to dominate modern African literature after World War II. In this vision, African cultures were presented as custodians of stable traditions and customs, and enlightenment in fields as diverse as land tenure, social relations, religion, and education. Within this context, colonialism was represented as a form of violent intrusion, one that threw African cultures into perpetual crisis and alienated African subjects from their traditional anchors. Finally, Kenyatta argued that nationalism was not necessarily opposed to Western modernity (see **modernity and modernism**); rather, the imperative for nationalism was the modernization of African society outside European political control. Kenyatta wrote other minor anthropological texts, but his later life was devoted to politics. Arrested in 1952 for being the mastermind behind Mau Mau and confined to remote parts of Kenya for almost ten years, Kenyatta was to live long enough to be the president of an independent Kenya during a period that is the subject of Ngugi's novels.

Further reading

Desai, Gaurav (2000) *Subject to Colonialism: African Self-Fashioning and the Colonial Library*, Durham, North Carolina: Duke University Press.

SIMON GIKANDI

Kgositsile, William Keorapetse

b. 1938, Johannesburg, South Africa

poet and cultural activist

The South African poet and cultural activist Keorapetse Kgositsile was born in Johannesburg, but he left the country when he was about 22 and lived in exile, first in Tanzania, where he worked as a writer for a local magazine, and later in the United States, where he attended major as an undergraduate and graduate student. Kgositsile started writing poetry at the height of the civil rights movement in the United States, and, given the similarities between the racial situation in America and in his native South Africa, his work from this period was heavily influenced by ideologies of the black aesthetic associated with the black arts movement. Indeed, his major collections of poems, including *Spirits Unchained: Poems* (1969), *For Melba: Poems* (1970), and *My Name is Africa* (1971) were published by independent African-American presses. If his poetry from the 1960s was described as aggressive, driven by the poet's anger against institutions of power and oppression, it is perhaps because Kgositsile's goal was to write verse whose tones and rhythms would match the intensity of political feelings he shared with other South African poets in exile. He was also closely associated with the cultural wing of the African National Congress. Kgositsile has been a prolific writer; he has published five collections of poetry and his verse has been included in many anthologies of African literature. In the 1980s he returned to Africa and held positions at the universities of Dar es Salaam and Nairobi.

SIMON GIKANDI

Khaïr-Eddine, Mohammed

b. 1941, Tafraout, Morocco; d. 1995, Casablanca, Morocco

novelist

Mohammed Khaïr-Eddine, one of the most compelling writers of post-independent Morocco, was born in the southern Moroccan Berber village of Tafraout and died in Casablanca. In both his iconoclastic fiction and his incendiary poetry Khaïr-Eddine extols a poetics of violence carried out against all established orders and conventions – language, society, religion, and morality. His first novel *Agadir* (1967), a cataclysmic and iconoclastic attack on the monarchy inspired by the earthquake that leveled the city in 1960, set the tone for the rest of his fictional work. *Agadir* earned him a prize but also the reputation of the *enfant terrible* of Maghrebian letters. Whether in *Corps Négatif* (Negative Body) (1968), *Le Déterreur* (The Unearther) (1973) or *Moi l'aigre* (Me, the Bitter One) (1970), Khaïr-Eddine foregrounds the figure of the grandfather, the anti-father par excellence, as a symbol of the purity of the Berber race in the face of perennial calamities. Paramount in Khaïr-Eddine's highly autobiographical work is his use of psychoanalysis as a tool to probe both his individual and his collective psyche. Khaïr-Eddine was an inveterate dreamer, and some of his books are essentially transcriptions of his dreams and hallucinations. For example, the aesthetic vision in such books as *Une Odeur de mantèque* (1976) and *Une Vie, un rêve, un peuple, toujours errants* (A Life, a Dream, a People, Always Wandering) (1978) is explicitly identified with the dream state.

But Khaïr-Eddine is first and foremost a poet. To say that his poetry is haunted by the social and political predicament of his native Morocco is but an understatement. From his juvenile *Nausée noire* (Black Nausea) (1964) to his more elaborate *Faune détériorée* (Damaged Faun) (1966), to the incandescent *Soleil arachnide* (Sun Spider) (1968), and to the vehement *Ce Maroc!* (This Morocco) (1975), each volume is traversed by Khaïr-Eddine's singular preoccupation with the negative impact of monarchist politics in today's Morocco. His last and remarkable collection, *Mémorial* (Memorial) (1991), speaks in prophetic tones of the impending chaos

following the collapse of Communism, an ideology which held for Khaïr-Eddine a promise of universal friendship and brotherhood. What is so remarkable about Khaïr-Eddine, unlike so many of his predecessors, is that he never felt in "exile" in the colonizer's language. For him, French was a wondrous tool, the colonized's counter-hegemonic weapon, that he relentlessly had to revamp and reinvent in order to make it express his Moroccan ethos and aesthetics.

Further reading

Abdel-Jaouad, H. (1992) "Mohammed Khaïr-Eddine: The Poet as Iconoclast," *Research in African Literatures* 23, 2: 145–50.

HÉDI ABDEL-JAOUAD

Khaketla, Benett Makalo

b. 1913, Lesotho; d. 2000, Maseru, Lesotho

poet

B.M. Khaketla is perhaps one of the most important poets of Lesotho and his reputation as a serious contender to the title poet laureate of the country is perhaps equal to that of K.E. Ntsane. His plays, poetry, and novels are characterized by a melancholic tone. His first published play, *Moshoeshoe le Baruti* (Moshoeshoe and the Missionaries) (1947) concerned the meeting of King Moshoeshoe I, builder of the Basotho nation, with the first missionaries who entered Lesotho (Basutoland) in the nineteenth century. His other important plays are *Tholoana tsa Sethepu* (The Fruit of Polygamy) (1954) and its sequel, *Bulane* (1958). Both plays deal with problems that result from polygamy and primogeniture among the Basotho aristocracy. His first novel, *Meokho ea Thabo* (Tears of Joy) (1951) is based on the story of a young couple who are traditionally subjected to an arranged marriage, ending on a note of a happy coincidence. *Mosali a Nkhola* (The Woman Betrayed Me) (1960) is one of the most somber works ever written about Lesotho (Basutoland) in the latter half of the twentieth century, dealing with medicine murders. His only poetic work is an anthology entitled *Dipjamathe*

(Tidbits) (1954). He translated Haggard's *King Solomon's Mines* into Sesotho (*Merafo ea Morena Salemone*) (1963). Khaketla also published two Sesotho grammar books and a book on the politics of Lesotho after independence, *Lesotho 1970: An African Coup under the Microscope* (1970). In the mid 1950s he was editor of *Mohlabani* (The Warrior), a cultural journal.

Further reading

Maake, N.P. (1998) "'Murder They Cried': Revisiting Diretlo–Medicine Murders in Literature," *South African Journal of African Languages* 18, 4: 91–101.

N.P. MAAKE

al-Kharrāṭ, Idwār (Edwar al-Kharrat)

b. 1926, Alexandria, Egypt

writer

Al-Kharrāṭ was born into a Coptic family in Alexandria, Egypt, where he was raised and educated. He received a degree in law from the University of Alexandria in 1946. From 1948 to 1950 he was held in detention for involvement in revolutionary activities. He served in a variety of official capacities in both the Afro-Asian Peoples' Solidarity Organization and the Afro-Asian Writers' Association. In 1959, al-Kharrāṭ published his first collection of stories, *Ḥiṭān ʿĀliya* (High Walls), in Arabic. Following upon the publication of two additional collections of stories, his first novel, *Rāma wa at-Tinnīn* (Rama and the Dragon), appeared in 1979. His writing style is characterized by experimentation in language and form. His works frequently engage in flights of fancy and shifts in time. Two novels to receive international acclaim, *City of Saffron* (1989) (*Turābuhā Zaʿfarān*) (1986) and *Girls of Alexandria*) (1993) (*Yā Banāt Iskandarīyah*) (1990), are comprised of fragmentary meditations on sensuality and memory. His later novel *Sukhūr al-Samāʾ* (The Rocks of Heaven) (2001), highly autobiographical, is a tribute to the author's Coptic (Orthodox) faith.

In his roles as critic and editor, al-Kharrāṭ advocates literary innovation. From 1968 to 1971 he served on the editorial board of the influential avant-garde journal *Gālirī 68*. His critical essays of the 1990s promoted works by emerging experimental writers. Al-Kharrāṭ has also published several notable translations of literary works from English and French into Arabic.

Further reading

Al-Nowaihi, Magda (1994) "Memory and Imagination in Edwar al-Kharrat's *Turābuhā Zaʿfarān*," *Journal of Arabic Literature* 25: 34–57.

Starkey, Paul (2000) "Idwār (Edwar) al-Kharrāt 1926–, Egyptian novelist and short-story writer," in Olive Classe (ed.) *Encyclopedia of Literary Translation into English*, vol. I, London and Chicago: Fitzroy Dearborn.

DEBORAH A. STARR

Khatibi, Abdelkebir

b. 1938, Morocco

scholar

The Moroccan Abdelkebir Khatibi is one of the Maghreb's most adept theoreticians of decolonization, which, he argues, must involve a deconstruction of both Western metaphysics and Islamic theology. In many works he has sought to safeguard the Maghreb's heterogeneity. Mixing theory, fiction, autobiography, and genres, he has written poems, essays, novels, and a play. Recurring topics in his works include calligraphy, the Maghrebian tradition of tattooing, Orientalism, art history, translation, the importance of the proper name, narrative seduction, and the body as text. His key concept of a *pensée-autre* (thinking through/as the "other") eschews binary thought to defend an intractable difference, the "other" found within the self. *Love in Two Languages* (*Amour bilingue*) (1990) offers an original approach to the **language question** by going beyond linguistic duality to demonstrate how polyglossia is central to Maghrebian identity. His concept of the *bi-langue* (double tongue) – different from bilingualism – is the linguistic component of a *pensée-autre*. The figure of the Androgyn appears throughout Khatibi's work as a sign of his deconstruction of gender and of a notion of decolonization that encourages sexual diversity and polymorphous eroticism (see **gender and sexuality**).

Further reading

Khatibi, A. (1990) *Love in Two Languages*, Minneapolis: University of Minnesota Press.

JARROD HAYES

Khrayyef, Bashīr

b. 1917, Nefta, Tunisia; d. 1983, Tunis, Tunisia

writer and teacher

Khrayyef was born in Nefta, Tunisia. His road to fiction writing passed through trading in fabrics, an experience which provided him with a rare insight into Tunisian society and contributed to the realism of his writing. He later became a teacher and looked back fondly on those years as a merchant. His early works were published in the Tunisian journal *al-Fikr* (Reflection) (founded in 1955).

Khrayyef depicted Tunisian life with realism and a sense of humor, but shied away from philosophical themes. This is clear in his short story collection, *Mashmūm al-Full* (The Smell of Arabian Jasmine) (1971) which reveals his ability as a fiction writer but his failure to write thematic fiction. His works provide a rich panorama of life at a time when Tunisia was shifting from a traditional to a modern society, describing student life in the Zaytuna Mosque–University in *Iflās aw Hubbak Darbānī* (Penniless or Your Love Hit Me) (1959). He depicts desert life in *Al-Daqlāh fī 'arājīnihā* (Dates on Their Twigs) (1969). He wrote his first short stories in colloquial Tunisian and published them in *al-Dustūr* (The Constitution) in 1937. The negative response of the readers kept him from publishing for a period of twenty years.

Khrayyef's repertoire counts two historical novels which reflect his nationalist feelings, *Barq*

al-Layl (Night's Lightning) (1961) and a posthumous novel *Ballāra* (1992).

Further reading

Bamia, Aida A. (1996) *Encyclopedia of the Modern Middle East*, vol. 2, New York: Macmillan, p. 1023.

Fontaine, Jean (1997) "The Tunisian Literary Scene", *Research in African Literatures* 28, 3: 73–84.

——(1999) *Histoire de la Littérature Tunisienne* (History of Tunisian Literature), vol. II, Tunis: Éditions Cérès.

AIDA A. BAMIA

Khrayyif, Muhyi al-Din

b. 1932, Nafta, Tunisia

poet

The Tunisian poet Muhyi al-Din Khrayyif's works are mostly written in a symbolic and condensed language which, despite its beauty and originality, is not easily accessible to the reader. This choice of symbolism could partly be explained by the poet's views of the nature of poetry (as he says in his definition of poetry in the introduction to *Subā'iyyāt* (1996)), but also by the nature of his themes, which combine the mystical and the political. In its mystical aspect, his poetry reflects some of the significant relationships between Islam and literature (see **Islam in African literature**). His mystical poetry is reminiscent of the medieval Sufi (Islamic mystical) poetry, in both its figurative language and its suggestive imagery. On a political level, the intellectual's lack of freedom of speech in his country, which represents one of Khrayyif's main themes, also seems to be an incentive for his use of symbolism. Khrayyif's poetry manifests a preoccupation with social and ethical issues, such as moral decline, thus giving a romantic touch to his poems. On the formal level, Khrayyif has written works both in classical Arabic meters and in free verse, occasionally mixing the two forms in the same poem while maintaining a harmonious rhythm.

Further reading

Khrayyif, Muhyi al-Din (1990) *al-Sijn dākhil al-kalimāt* (A Prison of Words), Tunis: Manshūrāt dār al-ma'ārif lī al-ṭibā'a wa-al-nashr.

SARRA TLILI

Kibera, Leonard

b. 1940, Kenya; d. 1983, Nairobi, Kenya

novelist and short story writer

Like his brother, Samuel **Kahiga**, the Kenyan novelist and short story writer Leonard Kibera came of age during the Mau Mau period in Kenya (1952–60) and most of his fiction reflects the impact of this violent period. In *Potent Ash* (1966), the collection of short stories that he co-published with his brother, Kibera drew on his own experiences growing up under the shadow of Mau Mau to represent the effects of the landscape on individual relationships and social life and in colonial villages and detention camps. These stories were the earliest voices from the second generation of modern fiction writers in East Africa. But Kibera's major work was been *Voices in the Dark* (1966), a haunting novel on the crisis of decolonization in Kenya. The novel was one of the first attempts to combine the abstract language of modernism with social realism to capture the alienation of individuals in a stark and hostile postcolonial landscape (see **modernity and modernism**; **realism and magical realism**; **colonialism, neocolonialism, and postcolonialism**). Although this novel is not well known outside East Africa, its use of the techniques of modernism, such a fragmented story line, interior monologue, and impressionistic descriptions of scenes and situations makes it comparable to other great novels of disillusionment, including Wole **Soyinka**'s *The Interpreters* (1965) and Ayi Kwei **Armah**'s *The Beautyful Ones Are Not Yet Born* (1968).

Further reading

Gikandi, Simon (1984) "The Growth of the East African Novel," in G.D. Killam (ed.) *The Writing of East and Central Africa*, London: Heinemann.

SIMON GIKANDI

Konaté, Moussa

b. 1951, Kita, Mali

novelist, playwright, academic, and editor

A prolific novelist and playwright, the Malian author Moussa Konaté is also a professor and editor in Bamako. While his early novels, which were published in Paris, were not easily available to local readers, Konaté's later works have been published by his own publishing house, Le Figuier, and this has made them more accessible to people in Mali. In addition to directing Le Figuier, Konaté has served as the head of Édition Jamana, a publishing house founded by President Alpha Konaré. More importantly, he holds the distinction of being one of the few writers in the region who makes a living from a series of detective novels. Among his most notable works are *Le Prix de l'âme* (The Soul's Price) (1926), *Une Aube incertaine* (Uncertain Dawn) (1985), *L'Or du diable* (The Devil's Gold) (1985), *Le Cercle au féminin* (Women's Circle), and *Fils du chaos* (Son of Chaos) (1986). In both his fictional and non-fictional writings, Konaté's written works are intended to challenge the self-imposed culture of silence in Mali and to expose the problems of everyday life in the country. His works are concerned with the world of prisons, childhood trauma, the military dictatorship, and poverty. In such works as *Le Prix de l'âme* and *Une Aube incertaine*, both published in the 1980s, the author weaves through the conflict of generations, the exodus of villagers to the city, the education of youth, the conditions of women in both traditional and urban settings, and the culture of the new military and civilian elites. In later works such as *Goorgi* (1996), there is an apparent softening of the author's early political tone; here he draws heavily from his childhood encounters to write a comedy where the power of the imagination supersedes politics. When he wrote *Goorgi*, during what he considered to be the darkest moments of his life, Konaté had concluded that his novels could not change Malian society, and he was thus searching for a novel that would provide him with a sense of escape. Drawing on memories from his childhood, he seeks to capture Mali at the crossroads of cultures and peoples focusing on the world of the Goorgi, a shrewd sweet-talking Wolof tradesman, and the Mossi of Burkina Faso. In this novel, Malinké and Wolof are linked by a jesting tradition or *cousinage à plaisanterie*. In his later works, Konaté remains committed to educating the younger generation about the mistakes of their elders while providing some perspective to the social, economic, and political malaise of a postcolonial society (see **colonialism, neocolonialism, and postcolonialism**). His play *Un Appel de nuit* (A Call in the Night) (1995) poses the question of disorientation lived by African immigrants to the West. It tackles issues such as the problem of communication, language, and the inevitable loss of the mother tongue. In this work, the glorious history of the Malian people enters an unpleasant chapter brought about by the failed socialist policies of Modibo Keita, the treason of the military saviors and their civilian allies, and the many falsehoods and assassinations of the postcolonial period. While Konaté's attacks are directed at the repressive and intolerant regime in his native Mali, his works seek to expose the widespread crisis of governance in the whole of Africa.

JEAN OUÉDRAOGO

Koné, Amadou

b. 1953, Burkina Faso

novelist, playwright, and short story writer

Amadou Koné was born in Burkina Faso and raised in the Côte d'Ivoire, where he attended high school in the capital city of Abidjan. After earning his doctorate in France, he returned to teach African literature at the University of Abidjan. Koné began his first novel at the age of 17 and has to date published a total of six novels, three plays, and several short stories. Much of his work turns around clashes between modernization and traditional ways of life in Africa, as with, for example,

the construction of a dam in the 1980 play *Le Respect des morts* (Respect for the Dead). Also well known for his literary criticism, Koné co-edited a 1983 anthology of Ivorian literature and has written several works of literary history and criticism in which he examines the influence of the oral tradition (see **oral literature and performance**) on the modern African **novel**. Koné has lived in the United States since 1990, and in the late 1990s became professor of French and African studies at Georgetown University in Washington DC.

Further reading

Koné, Amadou (1976) *Jusqu'au seuil de l'irréel* (To the Threshold of the Unreal), Dakar-Abidjan: Nouvelles Éditions Africaines.

RACHEL GABARA

Kouame, Adjoua Flore

b. 1964, Abidjan, Côte d'Ivoire

novelist

Ivorian author Adjoua Flore Kouame was born in Abidjan. She graduated in law from the National School of Administration of the Côte d'Ivoire and became a civil administrator and deputy director at the Ministry of the Interior in the 1990s. In 2000 she was working in Abidjan's prefecture. Although her university courses did not allow her to study the arts, she always had a very keen interest in literature, poetry, and music. Her decision to write her first novel stemmed from the desire to share her religious beliefs and humanitarian ideals with her readers and to help them overcome the many difficulties in life. In fact, she described her first novel, *La Valse des tourments* (The Merry-Go-Round of Torments) (1998) as "an hymn to love"; and yet her portrait of modern African society (see **modernity and modernism**) is far from rosy, as the title of the novel indicates. She constantly returns to the problems people encounter as they move around and about the business of everyday life.

JEAN-MARIE VOLET

Kourouma, Ahmadou

b. 1927, Boundiali, Côte d'Ivoire; d. 2003, France

novelist

Born in 1927 in Boundiali, Côte d'Ivoire, Ahmadou Kourouma spent part of his early childhood in Togobala, Guinea, before returning to his birthplace at age 7 to live with his uncle and attend the local primary school. He was later sent to the regional school in Korhogo and then to Bingerville. In 1947 he was admitted to the École Primaire Supérieure in Bamako. Expelled from school in 1949, he was arrested, repatriated, and drafted into the French colonial expeditionary forces. From 1951 to 1954, Kourouma served in Saigon, where the French were involved in a war against Vietnamese nationalists. After the war he entered the École de Constructions Aéronautiques et Navales in Nantes. In 1959 Kourouma graduated from the Institut des Actuaires in Lyons having earned an actuary's diploma and a certificate of business administration. Besides his actuary studies, he conducted extensive researches on African ethnology and sociology. After returning home in 1960, Kourouma was appointed assistant director of the Caisse Nationale de Prévoyance Sociale, only to be arrested in 1963 as a suspected conspirator in a foiled coup against the regime of Houphouët-Boigny. He was subsequently exiled to Algeria where he worked on, and completed, his first novel, *The Suns of Independence* (*Les Soleils des Indépendances*) (1968), a novel written to bear witness to the falsehood of the accusations that sent many of his friends to prison.

After five years in Algeria, he moved to France where he worked for the Société Générale de Banques, a large Parisian bank, which later appointed him assistant director of its branch in Abidjan. Kourouma's response to his return from exile was the writing and production of *Tougnatigui ou le diseur de vérité* (The Truth Teller), a vehement denunciation of the postcolonial regime (see **colonialism, neocolonialism, and postcolonialism**). On its first production in late 1972, the play was immediately censured and banned by the political authorities, and it remained unpublished until the 1998 Acoria edition, which brought it

back from a quarter of a century of oblivion. In the meantime, Kourouma's much anticipated second novel *Monnew* (*Monnè, outrages et défis*) appeared in 1990 and proved as captivating as the first. His *Waiting for the Vote of the Wild Animals* (*En attendant le vote des bêtes sauvages*) (1998), a poignant and masterful rendition of Cold War politics as they were played out in Francophone West Africa, borrows from the decades spent in foreign countries as well as his exceptional talent as interpreter of postcolonial African governance.

Often pitted against the political establishment in Francophone West Africa, Kourouma defied all odds to write three novels that are now considered to be classics of African fiction. After its incredible debut in Montreal, where it received the Prix de la Francité sponsored by Études Françaises, *The Suns of Independence* was republished by Éditions du Seuil and awarded the Prix de la Fondation Maille–Latour–Laudry of the Académie Française, and the Prix de l'Académie Royale Belge. *Monnew* received the Prix des Nouveaux Droits de l'Homme, the Grand Prix du Roman de l'Afrique Noire, and the Prix de l'Association des Journalistes Francophones des Télévisions et Radios. *Waiting for the Vote of the Wild Animals*, Kourouma's third novel, collected three impressive prizes: the Grand Prix des Gens de Lettres de France, the Prix de France Inter, and the Prix des Tropiques. Kourouma's 2000 novel, *Allah n'est pas obligé* (Allah is Not Obligated), continued the winning tradition, garnering praise from both his most loyal local readers and the always critical French literary establishment. It received the much coveted Prix Renaudot (2000) and tied, in the preliminary rounds, for the Goncourt. In its treatment and display of the brutal and senseless reality of violence, *Allah n'est pas obligé* is reminiscent of Yambo **Ouologuem**'s 1968 novel, *Bound to Violence*, which also won the Renaudot on its publication. Centered on the tribal wars of Liberia and Sierra Leone, the novel exposes African and Western complicity in the perpetuation of violence in the region.

Throughout his career, Kourouma has written narratives that seek to capture the main historical and political voyages of the continent, particularly the encounters of West Africa with the West through slavery, colonization, the Cold War, and tribal wars. In his novels, there is a clear attempt to promote African internal dialogues and to provide a critique of bad governance both in the past and in the present. Kourouma's fiction is hence a literature of contestation, of testimony, denunciation, and disillusionment. His novels leave their readers with tough questions and unresolved issues; but his narrators are fashioned after traditional storytellers and in this sense they are bound to be humble enough not to proclaim any tailor-made solutions to the problems of Africa. In his narratives and play, Kourouma juxtaposes the protagonists' identity crisis/quest with the imperative for an ideological journey; yet the author does not advocate a backward-looking approach to history or to life. His heroes are not absolved for not understanding the new foe, nor for domesticating their old selves. The points of no return to which they ascend are as much proof of internal weakness as revelations of the disorientation caused by the turmoil all around.

The circular structure of Kourouma's last two novels testifies to the predicament faced by their main protagonists. In *The Truth Teller*, the law of return underlies the dramatic action. The playwright taps into the folk tale of Princess Lala to bring the play to the known territory of the tale. The only real return is that which brings the downtrodden of Seguedougou back to their dictatorial president–chief Diarra. Kourouma's realism reveals a certain pessimism but does not make a pessimist out of the writer, who enjoys pillorying ancient and modern African myths.

Beside the timeliness of his novels' subject matter, Kourouma captures the reader's attention through his use of innovative narrative techniques, his subjugation of the French language to the world, and the linguistic constructs of his native characters. Griots, *sèrè*, *donsomana*, *palabres*, and other kinds of comical interpreters fill the narrative voices and spaces of his works. But Kourouma is quick to dispute the notion that his subjugation of French to vernacular traditions is done for the sake of innovation. On the contrary, he says, this subjugation allows him to "translate the prevailing situation … each time there was a correlation to the protagonist. And given the protagonist, one has

to select the technique used in Africa," As a result, Kourouma's characters have almost instantaneous resonance with African readers who see in them easily recognizable figures or types drawn from their everyday experiences. There is hence a continuum in the main protagonists of Kourouma's writings: Fama, Diarra, Houphouët, Djigui, Koyaga are but different faces of African leaders separated by time and fortune, but all linked to the continent and its future.

Further reading

Borgomano, Madeleine (1998) *Ahmadou Kourouma: le "guerrier" griot* (Ahmadou Kourouma: The "Warrior" Griot), Paris: L'Harmattan.

——(2000) *Des Hommes ou des Bêtes? Lecture en attendant le vote des bêtes sauvages, d'Ahmadou Kourouma* (Men or Beasts? Reading Waiting for the Vote of the Wild Animals), Paris: L'Harmattan.

Gassama, Makhily (1995) *La Langue d'Ahmadou Kourouma ou le français sous le soleil d'Afrique* (The Language of Ahmadou Kourouma, or French under the African Sun), Paris: ACCT-Karthala.

Harrow, Kenneth W. (1994) *Threshold of Change in African Literature: The Emergence of a Tradition*, Portsmouth, New Hampshire: Heinemann.

Kourouma, Ahmadou (2001) *Waiting for the Vote of the Wild Animals*, trans. Carrol F. Coates, Charlottesville: University Press of Virginia.

Ngandu Nkashama, Pius (1985) *Kourouma et le mythe* (Kourouma and Myth), Paris: Silex.

Nicolas, Jean-Claude (1985) *Comprendre "Les Soleils des Indépendances" d'Ahmadou Kourouma* (Understanding Ahmadou Kourouma's *The Suns of Independence*), Issy-les-Moulineaux: Les Classiques Africains.

JEAN OUÉDRAOGO

Krog, Antjie

b. 1952, Orange Free State, South Africa

poet, political journalist, and translator

Based in Cape Town, Afrikaans poet, political journalist, and translator Antjie Krog grew up on a

Free State farm, started publishing at age 17 and was even then challenging traditional political beliefs and sexuality in evocative volumes of poetry: *Dogter van Jefta* (Daughter of Jephta) (1970), *Januarie-suite* (January Suite) (1972), *Mannin* ((Wo)man) (1974), *Beminde Antartika* (Beloved Antarctica) (1974), *Otters in bronslaai* (Otters in Watercress) (1981), *Jerusalemgangers* (Travelers to Jerusalem) (1985), *Lady Anne* (1989), *Gedigte 1989–1995* (Poems) (1995) and *Kleur kom nooit alleen nie* (The Color of My Skin) (2000). The English volume *Down to My Last Skin* appeared in 2001. Her poems are vivid, bold, and emotional, therapeutically charged, poetically controlled – reminding one of the work of Breyten **Breytenbach**. She has written verse for children and a play about South African women. Her confessional prose, which often relates directly to the landscape and realities of South Africa, includes such works as *Relaas van 'n moord* (Report of a Murder) (1995) and the internationally acclaimed *Country of My Skull* (1998). Krog has received numerous prizes for her poetry and journalistic and non-fiction work, the most prestigious being the award from the Hiroshima Foundation for Peace and Culture (2000).

Further reading

Conradie, Pieter (1996) *Geslagtelikheid in die Antjie Krog-teks*, Goodwood: Nasionale Handelsdrukkery.

ENA JANSEN

Kuimba, Giles

b. 1936, Zimbabwe

novelist

Giles Kuimba is one of the mostly widely read writers of the colonial period in Zimbabwe. His two fictional romances, *Gehena Harina Moto* (Hell Has No Fire) (1963) and *Tambaoga Mwanangu* (Tambaoga, My Son) (1965), are part of the library of Zimbabwean primary schools. The writer has suspense-driven plot lines with vivid scenes and conversations presented in fascinating

expression, and his dramatic style, which contains elements of oral storytelling (see **oral literature and performance**), makes his works easily adaptable to radio performances. While overtly set in precolonial Shona society, *Gehena Harina Moto* appears to be an adaptation of Shakespeare's play *Romeo and Juliet*, while *Tambaoga Mwanangu* echoes *Hamlet*, works to which Kuimba, like other early Shona writers, had been exposed through his education (see **Shona and Ndebele literature**; **education and schools**). *Rurimi Inyoka* (A Wagging Tongue is Destructive) (1994) marks the author's shift from romances towards the realism that typifies Shona literature in the 1970s (see **realism and magical realism**). The plot of the novel revolves around problems arising from gossip about the apparent barrenness in a young couple. The resolution of the problem comes with the intervention of Western medicine and prayer, an ending which expresses the author's bias towards Western medicine and Christianity (see **Christianity and Christian missions**).

EMMANUEL CHIWOME

Kulet, Henry Ole

b. 1946, Kenya

novelist

Born of a Maasai background, the Kenyan writer Henry Ole Kulet is the author of works that typically portray the experiences of life among the Maasai people of East Africa. His first work, *Is It Possible?* (1971), is the story of a young Maasai man's attempts to get an education (see **education and schools**), while the second novel, *To Become a Man* (1972), deals with experiences of cultural conflict that arise when the Maasai face up to the new influences that are generated by modernity (see **modernity and modernism**). Kulet's other works, including *Daughter of Maa* (1987) and *Moran No More* (1990), are concerned with the conflict between the values and institutions of precolonial culture and the forces of modernization (see colonialism, neocolonialism, and postcolonialism).

GEORGE ODERA OUTA

Kunene, Mazisi

b. 1930, Durban, South Africa; d. 2006, Durban, South Africa

poet

Mazisi Kunene is a great poet belonging to a vernacular tradition that includes, among its preeminent predecessors, the great Xhosa poet S.E.K. **Mqhayi** (1875–1945) and the outstanding Zulu poet, Benedict Wallet Vilakazi (1906–47). The vernacular literature(s) have been engaged in perpetual struggle in South African literary history against the English language literary tradition across the twentieth century. Mqhayi represents a transition from tradition to modernity. At least, that is how he was viewed by a particular generation of intellectuals, such Jordan K. **Ngubane** (1917–85) and H.I.E. **Dhlomo** (1903–56). Vilakazi's historic importance was in indicating that vernacular literature(s) had been as responsible as any other literary tradition in the making of literary modernism in South Africa (see **modernity and modernism**). Kunene derived his inspiration directly from Vilakazi. The singular contribution of Kunene in writing his two published epics, *Emperor Shaka the Great* (1979) and *Anthem of the Decades* (1981), has been an unparalleled and unequalled synthesis of the poetics of historical imagination, African nationalism (see **nationalism and post-nationalism**), and the idea of progress. This epical quality is developed in new directions in the three anthologies Mazisi Kunene has published in South Africa since his return in 1993 from a thirty-three-year political exile: *Isibusiso Sikamhawu* (1994), *Amalokotho Kanomkhubulwane* (1996) and *Umzwili Wama-Afrika* (1996). With these achievements, Mazisi Kunene is perhaps the culminating point of the making of South African literary modernity within the New African movement.

NTONGELA MASILELA

al-Kūnī, Ibrāhīm

b. 1947, al-Hamāda al-Hamrā', Libya

short story writer and novelist

Al-Kūnī is Libya's most prolific fiction writer with approximately seven collections of short stories and eighteen novels published to this day. His birth in a Tuareg family in al-Hamāda al-Hamrā' in Libya provided him with the deep knowledge of desert life that permeates his fiction work. He studied at the Gorki Institute in Moscow and worked for a few years at the Libyan Embassy in the Russian capital. He is at present an employee of the Libyan Embassy in Bern, Switzerland.

Al-Kūnī's fiction writings are a tribute to desert life and an appreciation of the spiritual and moral values attached to it. Those characteristics provide the inhabitants, in al-Kūnī's opinion, with the appropriate tools to survive in the harsh desert conditions. In his novel *At-Tibr* (Gold Dust) (1990) he warns against the intrusion of urban life and the threat it poses to desert society, which he sees as a lieu for Sufi contemplation and the absence of an attachment to materialism and the comfort of urban life. Few of al-Kūnī's works have been translated into English; among those which have are *The Bleeding of the Stone* (2002) (*Nazīf al-Hajar*) (1990).

Further reading

Ewa Machut-Mendecka (1997) "The Visionary Art of Ibrahim al-Kawni," *Research in African Literatures* 28, 3: 141–9.

AIDA A. BAMIA

Kuzwayo, Ellen

b. 1914, Thaba Patchoa, South Africa; d. 2006, Soweto, South Africa

autobiographer

The South African writer Ellen Kuzwayo came to prominence with the publication of her **autobiography** *Call Me Woman* in 1985. Born on a family farm that was later declared to be in a white area, Kuzwayo grew up in Soweto, outside Johannesburg, where she was a prominent social activist and was arrested and imprisoned for five months in 1978 for activities against apartheid (see **apartheid and post-apartheid**). Since Kuzwayo was born in 1914, her value as a historian and chronicler of events that shaped South African history are important and have been acknowledged by other writers in the country. As Nadine **Gordimer** wrote in the preface to *Call Me Woman*, "Ellen Kuzwayo is history in the person of one woman," a point echoed by Bessie Head in a foreword for the same book. Like several of the women from her generation, then, Kuzwayo's autobiographical work has become an important historical record of an actor in the political struggle against white minority rule in South Africa. Kuzwayo's work was particularly notable for its ability to highlight the role of women in the long struggle against apartheid. In 1960 she wrote a five-page pamphlet on "The Role of the African Woman in Towns" for the Institute of Race Relations. In *Sit Down and Listen* (1990), she provided a series of stories which sought to represent the folk wisdom of South African women and, in Gordimer's words express her "faith in the new and different South Africa." In the stories collected in *Sit Down and Listen*, she sought to present a post-apartheid way of looking at polygamy, housing, Christianity, and poverty among black South Africans. She also wrote a book of Tswana proverbs, *African Wisdom* (1998).

HUMA IBRAHIM

Kwantagora, Salihu

b. 1929, Niger

song-writer and poet

Highly involved in the production and promotion of literature in the Hausa language (see **literature in Hausa**), Salihu Kwantagora is most widely known in Northern Nigeria. Kwantagora began his literary career writing songs. Eager to disseminate his work to a larger audience, he also started singing on the radio. At the same time he was active in the Hausa Teachers' Union and even taught briefly in the United States in the mid 1960s. From 1963 to 1971 he taught at Barewa College in Nigeria, after which he worked at the Northern Nigerian Publishing Company as an editor of Hausa books. He collected stories about Hausa culture and customs, publishing them in a work entitled *Labaru Na Dâ Da Na Yanzu* (Stories of Before and of Now) (1978). He eventually became interested in writing textbooks in Hausa and published, among others, *Yula: rubutattun wakokin hausa: don kananan makarantum firamare na jihohin arewacin Nigeria* (Yula: Written Hausa Songs: for Elementary Schools of Northern Nigeria) (n.d.) and *Kimiyya da fasaha: wakokin Hausa* (Science and Art: Hausa Songs) (1972).

SUSAN GORMAN

L

la Guma, Alex

b. 1925, Cape Town, South Africa; d. 1985, Havana, Cuba

novelist, journalist, and political activist

The South African political activist, writer, journalist, and cartoonist Justin Alexander la Guma was born in Cape Town. His father, Jimmy la Guma, was a leading and sometimes controversial figure in progressive trade union and political circles who expressed uncompromising support for the Soviet Union – as did his son. From childhood la Guma was exposed to the debates and strategies that informed national liberation politics in South Africa, and to the idea that literature and politics were always closely linked.

La Guma grew up in District Six, a bustling and often violent slum on the edge of Cape Town's central business district inhabited predominantly by coloreds and later destroyed by the apartheid authorities (see **apartheid and post-apartheid**). It was the setting for much of his fiction. He displayed an interest in art from an early age, and attended drawing classes in the late 1930s. Around this time he provided illustrations for political journals and campaigns on which his father worked, and to which Peter **Abrahams** refers in *Tell Freedom* (1954). There is no evidence that Abrahams and la Guma met then or later when the former was in Jamaica and the latter in Cuba.

Influenced by romantic ideas about the Spanish civil war, la Guma tried to enlist in the International Brigade. Later he volunteered for World War II. In both cases he was unsuccessful. After leaving school in 1941 he held a succession of "dead-end" jobs before completing his education part time. By the late 1940s, la Guma's interest in writing, politics, and art had taken adult form. He joined the Young Communist League and the SACP (Communist Party of South Africa), attended life-drawing classes, completed a correspondence course on journalism, and wrote letters on Communism to the local press.

The election of the National Party, the dissolution of the SACP, and resistance to apartheid by the ANC (African National Congress) saw la Guma take a leading role in its colored ("mixed race") sister organization, the South African Colored People's Organization. Despite arguments that the term "colored" was an apartheid creation, la Guma saw no contradiction between his commitments to socialism, non-racialism, and the assertion of a colored identity. For la Guma the problems were not about being colored or whether coloreds existed, but how to disentangle colored identity from its origins in racial prejudice and apartheid legislation, and to ensure that coloreds identified with and participated in a liberation struggle led by the African majority.

La Guma's formal writing career began in the late 1950s as a reporter for *New Age*, a left-wing weekly with strong links to the ANC. His early short stories covered a range of themes common to the period, such as tough tales, passing for white, and interracial relationships. His journalism and the short stories published in South Africa were characterized by satire, code-switching, local "Cape" humor with its rich tradition of subversive word play, and an enjoyment of American popular culture that reappears in his more serious prose fiction (see **popular literature**). His serialized comic strip story, *Little Libby: The Adventures of Liberation Chabalala* (1993), is the most obvious indicator of this interest in popular culture. Published in *New Age* during 1959, it is his first piece of extended fiction. The comic deploys in graphic form the cinematic techniques and tropes found in his first novella. Due to its Johannesburg setting – unusual for la Guma – the comic focuses on urban African concerns. He returned to this topic relatively late in his writing. He had barely established himself as a short story writer and journalist when he and 155 other activists from around the country were arrested on charges of high treason. By 1961 all defendants had been acquitted, but not before he and many others had been detained without trial in the 1960 state of emergency.

A Walk in the Night (1962) was one of the first texts produced by the pioneering Nigerian publishing house Mbari in which Ulli Beier and la Guma's compatriot Es'kia **Mphahlele** played a leading role at that time. Praised by Chinua **Achebe** and Wole **Soyinka**, the latter commending la Guma's terse economic style, the novella received an enthusiastic reception at the 1962 African Litera-ture Conference in Kampala and established his international reputation. However, la Guma and the South African public were denied access to the work. In response to la Guma's opposition to apartheid, his writings were banned and he spent the rest of his time in South Africa under house arrest or in jail. Several times in the following years he was detained without trial for several months.

The novella is notable for its frank exploration of colored racism towards Africans, and skin color consciousness among coloreds. Set in District Six, *A Walk in the Night* tracks the moral degeneration of Michael Adonis. While in a drunken rage at losing his job, Adonis accidentally kills Uncle Doughty, an alcoholic white man with whom he is sharing a drink. Adonis escapes and is drawn into a life of crime. Willieboy, an acquaintance of Adonis, becomes the murder suspect and the police hunt him down and kill him. This stirs the anger of the District's inhabitants, whose emotions la Guma communicates through images of wild animals and the elements. This anger, the altruism of the homeless and unemployed Joe, Uncle Doughty's rejection of racial categories, and the glimmerings of political consciousness in the stevedore Charlie hold out hope for greater resistance to injustice and oppression, and express the first traces of socialist thought.

During his last four years in South Africa (1962–6), la Guma wrote several short stories – some of which appeared in the journal *Black Orpheus* – a biography of his father, *Jimmy la Guma* (1997), and two more novels. He also returned briefly to painting, but his output never survived the many moves between houses and continents that he and his family made. Prevented by house arrest from writing a history of colored politics, he partly fulfilled this wish through the biography. The biography also enabled him to experiment with narrative strategies and to explore aspects of naturalism and Hemingway's brand of modernism.

La Guma's second novel, *And a Threefold Cord* (1964), is set in a slum modeled on Windermere, a waterlogged informal settlement on the outskirts of Cape Town. Like District Six, it too had a multiracial population and faced destruction at the hands of apartheid regional planners. For this novel he drew on his wife's work as midwife among shanty dwellers, his own journalism, and Stein-beck's *The Grapes of Wrath*. This was his first novel that he knew a South African audience would be unable to read. In part he wrote it to expose the reality beneath tourist brochure publicity about "sunny South Africa" at a time when the country was recuperating its image after the Sharpeville killings, mass arrests, and the banning of the ANC and PAC.

His third novel, *The Stone Country* (1967), was the last to be completed wholly in South Africa. He wrote it while he was under house arrest and subjected to numerous unpredictable raids, in which the police would confiscate whatever work of his they could find. Whether or not these conditions contributed to its final form, the novel contains more narrative voices, subplots, and temporal shifts than its predecessors do. It is set in Roeland Street, a jail on the edge of District Six where he had been imprisoned. The work is autobiographical. It incorporates his own prison experiences and reworks his earlier journalism and fiction on a prison theme. Much of this articulated fears about the physical, moral, and political degeneration of those subjected to the jail's "law of the jungle." La Guma drew on descriptions from Sir Walter Scott's *The Talisman* to express these concerns and to establish hierarchies based on physical appearance and intellect exemplified in characters like Yusef the Turk and the Casbah Kid. Unlike his fellow prisoners and the guards, Adams, the main character of *The Stone Country*, has a global perspective. While he acts with conscious moral purpose, the majority of the prison's inhabitants act out of narrow self-interest or in the manner of animals. Despite his challenges to the formal and informal systems of control and power in the prison, he has no more power to change his environment than the other guards and inmates do. This novel shares with its predecessors an attention to physical detail through which he constructs the work's symbolic setting, in this case South Africa as a police state in which the minority controls the majority through a policy of divide and rule.

In 1966 la Guma and his family left South Africa. In exile he devoted most of his time and energy to full-time political work for the ANC. He was also an office bearer for the Afro Asian Writers' Association and the World Peace Council. He made several submissions on apartheid to the United Nations, and attended many cultural and literary conferences as a representative of the ANC. In South Africa, la Guma's reviews for *New Age* had supported the idea that literature and culture in general should stand in an unmediated relationship to society. In exile his view of culture modified into the demand that art should be entirely at the service of the struggle for freedom and that in South Africa there was no place, as he put it, for "art for art's sake."

La Guma edited *Apartheid* (1971), an anthology of writings on apartheid. This was followed by *In the Fog of the Season's End* (1972). Here the changes in the representation of time and memory are more obviously the product of a more conscious process. It too is set in Cape Town and follows the efforts of Beukes and Tekwane, two underground political activists, to fulfil their political mission under the difficult and dangerous conditions of the early 1960s. Here the main characters have embraced the need for armed resistance since the apartheid regime has refused to compromise with the peaceful expression of political demands. Beukes drops off batches of leaflets and then ensures that three activists leave the country for military training, while Tekwane, who has been captured by the security police, endures brutal torture and is killed by them. When viewed in sequence, la Guma's first four novels show a steady progression in the level of political consciousness, forms of resistance, and degree of multiracial political cooperation among their chief protagonists. Simultaneously, the limitations to la Guma's ability to represent Africans and their experiences of apartheid in comparison with his depiction of colored characters became clearer in this and his following novel.

A Soviet Journey (1978) is a travelogue of the Soviet Union. It provides la Guma scholarship with valuable autobiographical material and confirms his debt to Hemingway's *For Whom the Bell Tolls* – a source for *Time of the Butcherbird* (1979), la Guma's last published novel, and the only one not set in Cape Town. In it, dispossession, resistance to forced removals, and the desire for personal revenge are integrated into a story of South Africa. This story ranges from skirmishes between Khoisan and Boers to industrialization, urbanization, and a national liberation struggle reinvigorated by the success of anti-colonial campaigns to the north and a burgeoning domestic trade union movement.

In 1979 the ANC sent la Guma and his wife Blanche to Havana as the movement's chief representative for the Caribbean region. La Guma died in Cuba in October 1985 and was buried in the family plot belonging to the parents of José Marti – the founder of the Cuban nation.

Further reading

Balutansky, K. (1990) *The Novels of Alex la Guma: The Representation of a Political Conflict*, Washington, DC: Three Continents Press.

Chandramohan, B. (1992) *A Study in Trans-Ethnicity in Modern South Africa: The Writings of Alex la Guma*, Lampeter: Mellen Research University Press.

Field, R. (1998) "Kaaps, Colouredism and Comics: Alex la Guma's Early Writings," *Pretexts: Studies in Writing and Culture* 7, 1: 57–79.

Yousaf, N. (2001) *Alex la Guma: Politics and Resistance*, Portsmouth: Heinemann.

ROGER FIELD

Laâbi, Abdellatif

b. 1942, Fez, Morocco

poet, essayist, and editor

The Moroccan writer Abdellatif Laâbi is a prolific and inspired poet and essayist as well as founder and editor of *Souffles* (Breaths), the most influential literary and political journal in the Maghreb in the 1960s and early 1970s. This publication ceased to exist when Laâbi was imprisoned in 1972 for his political activities. His eight-year ordeal in prison is represented in *Le Règne de Barbarie* (The Reign of Cruelty) (1976), *Sous la bâillon la poème* (Under the Gag the Poem) (1981), and particularly his prose poem *Le Chemin des ordalies* (The Stations of Ordeals) (1982) based on his prison letters. Along with his prison-inspired writings, one needs also to mention his book-length interview, *La Brûlure des interrogations* (The Burn of Questioning) (1985), where Laâbi probes the question of political engagement and the role of the writer in society. Laâbi's prison output is both lyrical and sober, emotional and lucid, moralistic and engaging. It stands in stark contrast to the freewheeling and surrealistic bend that marks his early poetry (*L'Oeil et la nuit*) (The Eye and the Night) (1969). In his later works, Laâbi has again begun tapping this earlier lyrical strain. In *Poèmes périssables* (Perishable Poems) (2000), for example, he is concerned with the nature of poetry for its own sake, distancing himself from his earlier political and social concerns and thus heralding a new poetry premised upon language, the sheer pleasure of using words and images. Although called "perishable," unmistakably these last poems possess an enduring appeal.

Further reading

Alessandra, Jacques (1992) "Abdellatif Laâbi: A Writing of Dissidence," *Research in African Literatures* 23, 2: 151–66.

HÉDI ABDEL-JAOUAD

Ládiípò, Dúró

b. 1931, Nigeria; d. 1978, Nigeria

theater director

Dúró Ládiípò was one of the greatest experimental directors in the popular Yoruba traveling theater movement. His troupe introduced into modern Yoruba theater indigenous musical instruments such as talking drums and various traditional expressive movements and gestures such as ritual dances, acrobatics, mime, and magic. Gripping realization of the lives of legendary Yoruba heroes was the trademark performance of Ládiípò's theater. He was also an accomplished producer of musical drama and television sketches. His most famous play, *Ọba Kò So* (The King Did Not Die), which received the first prize at the Berlin Festival in 1964, is about the apotheosis of Ṣàngó, an old king of Ọ̀yọ́, after, in anger, he used his power to invoke thunderbolts at will against his people. The play is remarkable for its spectacular drumming, chants, poetry, and the pathos of Ṣàngó's despondency and suicide.

Further reading

Ogunbiyi, Yemi (ed.) (1981) *Drama and Theatre in Nigeria: A Critical Sourcebook*, Lagos: Nigeria Magazine.

ADÉLÉKÈ ADÉÈKÓ

Lahbabi, Mohammed Aziz

b. 1922, Fez, Morocco; d. 1993, Rabat, Morocco

poet and philosopher

Throughout his work, Moroccan poet and philosopher Mohammed Lahbabi shows a commitment to the development of Arab and Islamic humanism. His 1954 dissertation *De l'être à la personne*

(From the Being to the Human) was the first philosophy dissertation written by a Moroccan to be published by the French University Press and explores the idea of "being" and "man" in both Western philosophy and Islamic thought, attempting to articulate a position for the North African man that is beyond both traditions, located firmly in a new understanding of the term "human." His 1968 book of poetry, *Ma voix à la recherche de sa voix* (My Voice in Search of Its Voice), pushes these ideas further, questioning what it means to be a poet, a being and a god. In 1980, Lahbabi published the largely political work *Le Monde de demain* (The World of Tomorrow), a powerful indictment of neocolonialism and the politics of development in Africa. Through the philosophy of "tomorrowism," Lahbabi explores the place of technology, the question of identity, and the idea of the "Third World" human in a North African and African context.

Further reading

Lahbabi, Mohammed Aziz (1980) *Le Monde de demain* (The World of Tomorrow), Casablanca: Dar el-Kitab.

KATARZYNA PIEPRZAK

Laing, Bernard Kojo

b. 1946, Kumasi, Ghana

novelist and poet

Educated in Ghana and at the University of Glasgow in Scotland, Kojo Laing has worked in local government administration and been secretary to the Institute of African Studies at the University of Ghana. His novels *Search Sweet Country* (1986), *Woman of the Aeroplanes* (1988), *Major Gentl and Achimota Wars* (1992), and his poetry collection *Godhorse* (1989), are unique within contemporary Ghanaian fiction for problematizing the conventional distinctions between the real and the ultra-mundane worlds (see **realism and magical realism**). In all of Laing's work, there is an easy recourse to the supernatural, the mythical, and the fantastic, which for the novelist is a means of

representing life as a series of fragmented experiences that can be encased within different narrative genres. An immediate affinity is thereby established between Laing's eclectic fusion of seemingly incompatible narrative modes and his interrogation of a range of societal and cultural attitudes.

The characters from Laing's first novel *Search Sweet Country* are chosen from all walks of life. Although inhabiting a recognizable world, they live and act out their otherwise realistic dreams within an ethereal and often idealistic realm. A community of Western-educated elite, cultural and religious zealots, and local ne'er-do-wells, the majority of whom are under the spell of individuals with access to supernatural and spiritual power, are represented as seeking upliftment of one kind or another. For a poor man like Beni Baidoo who wants to found a village, it is material emancipation from poverty. For many others, it is liberation from certain social, psychological, sexual, and other needs that predominate. Laing stakes a claim to knowledge about his people; for, throughout *Search Sweet Country* and his other novels, his language derives from the everyday rhetoric and speech patterns of Ghanaians. Local popular culture and other modes of communication consequently sustain a form of social realism that gives voice to the people. In *Search Sweet Country*, the individuals in search of self-development are also quick to manipulate those with whom they associate and to whom they look for assistance. Thus, although the novel presents an unflattering image of the post-independent military government of 1970s Ghana, it is not merely an indictment of the specific attitudes, or even the particular ideologies of this ruling class and of its inability to provide exemplary leadership. The story also foregrounds the validity of local knowledge systems in relation to neocolonial culture. However, the examination of the domestic and public lives of intellectuals like university professor Kofi Sackey, the depiction of the malicious attitudes of certain less-privileged government functionaries, and the interrogation of African royal systems, all demonstrate that local philosophies and ways of life require equal scrutiny.

In *Woman of the Aeroplanes*, a select group from the Tukwan community, led by Pokuah, a spiritually powerful woman, flies to Levensvale in Scotland to negotiate business arrangements with their foreign counterparts. Ostensibly about trade, the journey also facilitates an examination of Ghanaian/ African and Scottish/European cultural attitudes, beliefs, and practices. Different aspects of past and contemporary life including such touchy issues as racism and slavery are highlighted. The characterization of Levensvale parson David Mackie is as central to the story as the portrait of Kwaku Babo as a communal guardian for Tukwan. In this respect, the novel is interesting, not only for exploring cultural and ideological differences and similarities between communities and nations, but also for focusing on love stories and romances, such as the rivalry between "evil" twin Kwame Atta and "good" twin Kwaku Babo for the affections of Pokuah. While focusing on certain individuals, rather than being the usual elite figures in Ghanaian nationalist fiction these include less privileged members of society. Particular African cultural norms are affirmed simultaneously as it is demonstrated that there are no easy choices between systems and ideologies. For this reason, the novel explores the effects of ritual, myth, sorcery, witchcraft, and magic as representative of the different but interrelated religious and cultural systems of the two communities of Tukwan and Levensvale. Friendships and rivalries between and among both the Africans and Europeans are thus set within a modern utopian society full of vast possibilities of self-fulfillment through an adoption of either of the different modes of existence.

Major Gentl and Achimota Wars evaluates Ghanaian life and politics against the background of contemporary problems within Africa such as war, civil strife, dictatorship, and corruption. The phantasmagoric and surrealist landscape of Achimota City is the setting for the epochal battle of good versus evil that rages between the self-assured and humanistic Major Gentl and the power-drunk and avaricious mercenary Torro the Terrible, who has political links with apartheid South Africa. The evaluation of African post-independence governance and military rule is located within a futuristic narrative, which is nevertheless tangible because it unfolds within an elaborate world of socio-economic, cultural, and political struggles of the kind that have bedeviled Africa for ages. Events are related through a variety of characters – partly pleasant, partly grotesque – who live in a make-

believe world of opposing ideological forces. Achimota City is fighting a war of survival and existence against the neocolonial invasion led by Torro. Major AMofa Gentl, leader of the forces of good, is ably aided in combating this threat by the dynamism of mighty spiritual forces like Nana Mai, a woman who contributes to the liberation of her community without seeking the spoils of power. Her portrait is reflective of Laing's portrait of other female protagonists, such as Adwoa Adde of *Search Sweet Country* and Pokuaa of *Woman of the Aeroplanes*, who are combinations of precolonial matriarchs and modern revolutionaries. Nana Mai, ironically nicknamed Grandmother Bomb, yearns for a return to a precolonial world devoid of the technologies of war and mass destruction. Given that Laing is himself is a noted ecologist, Nana Mai's stance seems to represent a progressive ideological viewpoint. There are other less ideologically clear-cut conflicts in the private world of the antagonists. For example, Major Gentl struggles to cope with family problems as his children take sides in his disagreements with his wife. Similarly, Torro the Terrible is upstaged by his own trusted guards and treated with contempt by his superiors and advisors.

KWADWO OSEI-NYAME, JNR

Langa, Mandla

b. 1950, Durban, South Africa

poet, short story writer, and novelist

Mandla Langa was born in KwaMashu in Durban, South Africa. His writing career began in the 1970s at the time when poetry in South Africa was seen as one of the most important weapons in the struggle against apartheid (see **apartheid and post-apartheid**). His early publications include, among others, poems such as "Pension Jives" and "They No Longer Speak to Us in Song," a long poem dedicated to Steve **Biko**, his comrade during the era of the black consciousness movement. He subsequently tried his hand at prose, an experiment that culminated in the publication of his first short story, "The Dead Men Who Lost Their Bones," which won a competition sponsored by *Drum* magazine in 1980. The story is told from the point of view of children who yearn for the love of parents that have been taken away from them. The success of this short story seems to have prompted Langa to devote more attention to the writing of extended prose. His first novel, *Tenderness of Blood* (1987), is an ambitious work that effectively uses flashback techniques to recreate the gradual involvement of its hero, Mkhonto, in the context of the wider political struggle against the oppressive apartheid of South Africans from around 1960 until after 1976. The novel ends when Mkhonto meets a character called the Old Man, who, like him, is involved in the underground work of the Movement (the African National Congress) and they discuss the possibility of training people inside the country to fight against the government. In its wider canvas and in its focus on the politics of the struggle against apartheid, the novel has some affinity to Mongane **Serote**'s first novel, *To Every Birth Its Blood*. The significance of both novels is that they provide a depiction of the South African struggle from the perspective of the anti-apartheid movement (more specifically the African National Congress) and from inside the liberation movement, as it were, since both authors are active members of the ANC.

An insider's perspective of the ANC is one of the distinguishing characteristics of Langa's fiction. In fact, Langa's avowed intention in his second novel, *A Rainbow on the Paper Sky* (1989) is to "show the human face of the ANC," and thereby counteract the apartheid version of the activities of the movement. *A Rainbow on the Paper Sky* also attempts to redress the marginalization of women in fiction. For this reason, the plot is presented from a female viewpoint and deals with how the children of a rural chief grapple with the problem of political involvement in the light of their father's position as the leader of resistance against balkanization. What is perhaps more remarkable about this novel is that it was collectively conceived: Langa tells how the plot is based on a real incident that a fellow comrade of his in the ANC shared with him, and how he consulted other fellow activists to make the final product a collective product.

After Langa's return to South Africa from exile in the early 1990s, he published a collection of stories, *The Naked Song and Other Stories* (1998), which includes a few of his post-apartheid narratives, stories dealing with how ordinary people contend with the "new" South Africa. The significance of Langa's short stories is that they clearly indicate a shift away from the literature of struggle to what might be considered to be a post-struggle or post-apartheid narrative, one that critically examines how the new dispensation has affected people's lives. His novel *The Memory of Stones* (2000) is a panoramic exploration of the nature of South African society after the end of apartheid, taking on such large themes as the struggle to reconcile conflicting interests over questions of land, the struggle between those who supported apartheid and those who opposed it, the role of memory in the rethinking of the nature of South African society, the role of women in the new order, and the challenge of truth and reconciliation against a social and historical canvas defined by violence.

JABULANI MKHIZE

language question

The issue of language is central in discussions of African literature since literature is inconceivable outside the context of language. Questions pertaining to language always arise in any discussion of the subject. They assume even greater importance with regard to African literature than in relation to other literatures, since in Africa the medium of literary expression is not only the writer's mother tongue but also the dominant foreign European language imposed over the indigenous African languages in the process of colonization and under the culture of colonialism (see **colonialism, neocolonialism, and postcolonialism**). Indeed, as Chantal Zabus (1991) points out, the multiplicity of languages and the concomitant language contact situation in Africa have always been not only a fertile soil for the germination of linguistic conjectures but also a source of challenge and discomfort.

It must be pointed out, however, that even before the imposition of European languages on the continent, many Africans were multilingual precisely because of the existence of several languages within the same community and the social contact that took place among people of differing linguistic backgrounds. However, these languages existed without any official hierarchy, and the question of which language to use in a given social situation was conditioned by the linguistic milieu in which speakers found themselves. The added imposition of European languages as a result of colonization changed the linguistic landscape in Africa. The African situation was still characterized by multilingualism, but there was a re-ordering of the language situation where the European languages assumed a position of power and therefore became the languages of official discourse. As official languages, the European languages were privileged and used in most areas of national endeavors. Henceforth, the African linguistic landscape was characterized by the situation of diglossia, one in which the linguistic functions of communications were distributed in a binary fashion between a culturally powerful language spoken by a minority on one hand, and on the other hand another language, generally widely spoken but devoid of power.

The question of what language to use as a literary medium in Africa has repeatedly cropped up in literary discussions. Since the 1960s, it has generated a large amount of scholarship and criticism testifying to the sociohistorical importance and the necessity of the debate. **Ngugi wa Thiong'o** argues that the only way to retain an African literary identity is to write in African languages, and critics such as Abiola Irele have argued that the European-language literatures in Africa have at best only an official acceptance, since they are neither indigenous to the societies and cultures on which they have been imposed, nor are they national in any real sense of the word. In the most quoted article in African literary criticism, "The Dead End of African Literature," Obiajunwa Wali claimed that no African literature could develop except in African languages. As he puts it, "until [African] writers and their Western midwives accept the fact that any true African literature must be written in African languages, they would be merely pursuing a dead end, which can only lead to sterility, uncreativity, and frustration" (1963).

The language question in African literature should therefore be seen in the wider context of what constitutes literature. Is language the determining feature in any literature? Should it be the main feature in African literature? Is it acceptable for African writers to write in foreign languages? Obi Wali's statements came as a bombshell at a time when most African intellectuals favored European languages, when even Ngugi wa Thiong'o, who now champions the cultivation of African literatures in indigenous languages, preferred English mainly because, he claimed, it has a large vocabulary.

Quite obviously the language question in African literature is not just a linguistic event but a political one as well. Ngugi's preoccupation with language, as indeed the preoccupations of others concerned with the very notion of African literature, represents an anxious interrogation of language as a function of literature. Many Africans continue to write in European languages because of the existence of what Abiola Irele (1981) terms "Euro-African intertextuality." Irele sees the development of African literature in European languages as being in a very close relationship with, and sometimes a continuation of, European literature. For him, African literature in the European languages can be said to have begun with European writing on Africa, for the Europeans not only initiated modern discourse on Africa but also established the terms in which that discourse has been carried on till the present day. Africa, seen as an exotic and primitive land, fascinated the European mind for several centuries. Shakespeare's *Othello* represents in part the fascination with Africa that filled the court of Elizabeth I. The theme of Rider Haggard's *King Solomon's Mines* (1885) was the mysterious heart of Africa. In Joseph Conrad's imagination, Africa came to acquire a mythological dimension. His *Heart of Darkness* (1903), set in Central Africa, explores a world of darkness of many kinds, among which is the reality of colonial exploitation. Indeed, there is a long tradition of Westerners or non-African writers who utilized the subject matter of Africa in their literature before Africans themselves took up the mantle to refute the negative image of Africa portrayed in most of these works. In other words, when Africans themselves began to produce literature in the languages of their colonizers they were continuing a long-established tradition of Europhone writing on Africa.

Even though the bedrock of African literature can be traced to African oral traditions (see **oral literature and performance**), its form and style are clearly modeled on the European conventions of literature. In other words, one could describe the modern African novel as a hybrid product that draws on African oral traditions and literature and yet is clothed in imported literary traditions. Thus, Africans borrowed European literary traditions and language precisely because of the incident in history that brought Africa into contact with Europe.

Evidently, there has been a broad range of responses to the legacy of colonialism in terms of its impact upon the use of language. Kofi **Anyidoho** (1992) has categorized the diversity of opinion and practice in African literature (and the literature of the diaspora) under four broadly defined tendencies: (1) an acceptance of the languages of enslavement and colonization as the only practical, albeit inadequate, tool of self-expression; (2) an Africanization of the colonizer's language and the attempt to transform it into a weapon of cultural liberation and identity; (3) a repudiation of the imposed language of enslavement/colonization and a return to the mother tongue; (4) a reinvention of the "mother tongue" as *nation language* in the African diaspora. These categorizations all seem to indicate the very fact that African and writers of African heritage have had to deal with the problem of language at a fundamental level. It is doubtful whether the language question will cease to be a central preoccupation in African literature. What is not in doubt is that European languages will come to be seen as one available register among others in specific contexts of cultural production.

Further reading

Anyidoho, Kofi (1992) "Language and Development Strategy in Pan-African Literary Experience," *Research in African Literatures* 23, 1: 45–63.

Irele, F. Abiola (1981) *The African Experience in Literature and Ideology*, London: Heinemann.

Ngugi wa Thiong'o (1986) *Decolonizing the Mind: The Politics of Language in African Literature*, London: Heinemann.

Wali, Obiajunwa (1963) "The Dead End of African Literature," *Transition* 3, 10: 13–15.

Zabus, Chantal (1991) *The African Palimpsest: Indigenization of Language in the West African Europhone Novel*, Amsterdam and Atlanta, Georgia: Rodopi.

KWAKU A. GYASI

Laye, Barnabé

b. 1941, Benin

poet

One of Benin's best-known poets, Barnabé Laye is nonetheless better known in France than in his native country. He left Dahomey after high school in order to attend medical school in France and has since lived and worked as a doctor in Paris. He has simultaneously flourished as a writer, publishing four collections of poetry (see **poetry and poetics**) and three **novel**s. His 1989 novel *Mangalor* describes the corruption, terror, sickness and death which was the aftermath of Benin's 1972 Marxist–Leninist revolution. Laye's poetry grows out of the African oral tradition (see **oral literature and performance**), which he considers to be intrinsically poetic, as well as the tradition of French resistance poets during World War II; he has said that poetry is the "literary expression of times of trouble" and that he is a modern griot. His 1999 collection, in fact, is entitled *Requiem pour un pays assassiné* (Requiem for an Assassinated Country). Laye has also published a cookbook and, together with Liliane Prévost, an annotated collection of African proverbs.

Further reading

Laye, Barnabé (1986) *Les Sentiers de la liberté* (Paths of Liberty), Paris: Éditions Saint-Germain-des-Près.

RACHEL GABARA

Laye, Camara

b. 1928, Kouroussa, French Guinea (now Guinea); d. 1980, Senegal

novelist, journalist, and diplomat

The Guinean novelist, journalist, and diplomat Camara Laye came into literary prominence with the publication in 1953 of one of the earliest and also most enduring statements of cultural nationalism (see **nationalism and post-nationalism**) in French prose fiction by an African, *The Dark Child* (*L'Enfant noir*). This was followed a year later in 1954 with a second novel, *The Radiance of the King* (*Le Regard du roi*), both written in Paris where the author had gone to study in 1947. Both novels, the first autobiographical and the second a richly textured symbolist narrative, can be read as the imaginative and critical exploration of colonial modernity, the civilizing claims of colonialism, and their limits (see **modernity and modernism**; **colonialism, neocolonialism, and postcolonialism**). *The Dark Child* is an account of Laye's growth and development from childhood to maturity. Shot through with nostalgia and written in intensely poetic prose, the work evokes a childhood world of innocence, suffused with spirituality and a sense of community. But beneath its sentimentality lies a strong statement of cultural assertion and resistance. This derives from the reversal in polarity effected by the author between the urban world of colonial modernity into which the narrator matures – a world presented in the romantic binaries of classical anti-colonial nationalism as a locus of spiritual impoverishment and alienation – and the traditional world of rural Guinea from which he emerges, as a kingdom of grace. In other words, the rationality of Westernized adulthood into which Laye develops, rather than fulfilling the promise of "progress" held out for it by his French education, leads to "disenchantment."

But it is in *The Radiance of the King*, through the chastening experiences of the novel's French hero Clarence, that Laye works out his cultural nationalism most fully, and exposes the problematic nature, as he sees it, of the emancipatory and civilizational project of colonial rule. The novel rewrites, in a polemical mode, the journey motif so prevalent in modern African literature. This time, however, the central character in, and the direction of, the journey are reversed. The hero is no longer a young African, like Laye himself in *The Dark Child* or Samba Diallo in the Senegalese novelist Cheikh Hamidou **Kane**'s *Ambiguous Adventure* (1971), launching out into the scientific and secular world of the modern West. He is a Frenchman traveling into the heart of Africa in search of understanding and fulfillment; an Africa, however, not of impenetrable Conradian mystery and darkness, but of spiritual enlightenment. It is an Africa whose threatening alterity (to a rationalist) – deriving, as Laye has it, in its cultivation of the emotions, the body and the senses – becomes luminous and intelligible as soon as it is apprehended on its own terms. This is the wisdom to which Clarence accedes in the end. For it is only when he is able to see his body, senses, and passions not as obstacles to knowledge, to be repressed or from which, in true rationalist style, to purify himself (his initial attitude), that he achieves complete understanding and thus redemption, and his long quest comes to an end.

To confer epistemological value on the passions and the senses is, whatever the problematic status of the conferral, to subvert the rationalist discourse of colonial modernity which associated those passions with the "native," or colonized "other" (in the same way that the Enlightenment from which that very discourse derives associated them with "woman" and "child" in Europe), and saw it as its "burden," or mission, to deliver him from their embrace. Seen in this way, *The Radiance of the King* becomes a pedagogical act, an act of ceremonial induction or initiation into a subjugated but, to Laye, superior path to certain knowledge. The novel is built on the tripartite rhythm of such a ceremony, with Clarence as the initiate going through a phase of separation (when he leaves the causally intelligible world of Adramé for the south), liminality (in the thick of the equatorial forest where he has the most harrowing and surreal of experiences), and finally reincorporation in Azania, where he achieves a higher consciousness and is touched by, and received into, the radiance of the king.

Laye's third novel, *A Dream of Africa* (*Dramouss*) (1966) was written in Guinea where he returned in

1958. He rapidly assumed important administrative and political positions in the newly independent nation. But by 1965 he had become profoundly disillusioned with his country's slide to autocratic rule, and so left for Senegal in self-imposed exile. The nightmare sequence in *A Dream of Africa*, in which a giant preys on a hapless community, is a thinly veiled allusion to the growing climate of tyranny of this period. But the novel is about more than just political repression in post-independence Guinea. It is a sequel to *The Dark Child* whose narrator, now called Fatoman, has just returned home from France. But unlike *The Dark Child* it is written using the techniques of realism (see **realism and magical realism**), and emphasizes social and political details. Its tone is factual and evokes nothing of the enchanted world of the former. An important dimension of the book and a sign of the author's future literary interests and endeavors is its attempt, in the tale about Imam Moussa, to write orality in the novel (see **oral literature and performance**). Where *The Dark Child*, on the author's admission, uses Flaubert's *Sentimental Education* (*L'Éducation sentimentale*) (1869) as a literary model, and *The Radiance of the King* derives its inspiration, as several critics have remarked, from Kafka, *A Dream of Africa* and Laye's last work especially, *The Guardian of the Word* (*Le Maître de la parole*) (1978), are anchored in the indigenous traditions of narrative whose performance dimension he tries to recapture. An adaptation of the Sunjata epic of his Mandingo people, this work is also notable for the way Laye weaves into an ancient tale some of his lifelong concerns: his relationship with his mother, the role of destiny, the theme of exile and the supernatural. But beyond his concern with pitting his creative talents against an ancient legend, Laye pays homage in *The Guardian of the Word* to those creative artists like Babou Condé who narrated the epic to him – workmen of metal, leather, and the word – of whom he sees himself and his father before him as the worthy embodiments.

While the significance of Laye's work lies in its reclamation of the marginalized forms of knowledge and narrative art of his people, his cultural nationalism, it must be pointed out, remains ironically mired in one of the most enduring dualisms by which colonial discourse both produced and marginalized the colonized: that of the *necessarily* rationalist European and the equally *necessarily* spiritualist African. For sure, as has been noted, Laye reverses the valency on the terms of the dualism – an audacious gesture for the period. He also undermines the teleological character of the discourse of colonial modernity by making the identity of the colonized absolute and irreducible, and not a mere phase in a linear progression (that could be hastened by colonial rule) towards a final goal of rationality. But what looks like transgression can also be read from a different perspective as entrapment. For Laye does not challenge the structure of dualisms by which the colonizer defines both himself *and* the colonized – either on the grounds of its ahistoricity, its factual incorrectness or its foreclosing on the (infinitely more liberating) possibilities of human self-definition. If anything, he reproduces it, works within it. In short, he performs, as the Cameroonian novelist Mongo **Beti** observed as early as 1954 in a review of *The Dark Child*, a certain European idea of being African.

To point to the pitfall in Laye's strategy of reverse discourse is emphatically not to dismiss it as ineffectual. As Jacques Derrida observes in the context of a discussion of the dismantling of the "violent hierarchy" of philosophical oppositions in *Positions*,

> to deconstruct the opposition, first of all, is to overturn the hierarchy at a given moment. To overlook this phase of overturning is to forget the conflictual and subordinating structure of opposition. We know what always have been the *practical* (particularly *political*) effects of immediately jumping *beyond* oppositions … in the simple form of neither this nor that.
>
> (1972: Chicago, p. 42; italics in original)

He does not spell out the effects, but one of them is to stay on the sidelines of a conflict that has been structured, and is waged, for better or for worse, precisely in terms of *either* this *or* that. It is, in the short term, to contract out of the world as it is with its ugly binaries, for the world as it should be. In the historical conjuncture of the moment, Laye may have had no choice but to take possession of, and inhabit the best way he could, an identity imposed on him, and to use it as a basis for solidarity and resistance. Viewed this way, his nationalism, as Sartre observed in connection with **negritude**, becomes a *necessary* negative moment in a dialectic that eventually transcends the antinomies of colonial identity and its discourses.

Further reading

Conteh-Morgan, J. (1997) "Camara Laye," in Brian Cox (ed.) *African Writers*, New York: Simon and Schuster.

Derrida, J. (1972) *Positions*, trans. A. Bass, Chicago: University of Chicago Press.

Lee, Sonia (1984) *Camara Laye*, Boston: Twayne.

JOHN CONTEH-MORGAN

Leipoldt, C. Louis

b. 1880, Worcester, South Africa; d. 1947, Cape Town, South Africa

poet, writer, and pediatrician

Leipoldt was the first important Afrikaans poet (see **Afrikaans literature**) before Louw and the "Thirties" group. He wrote plays such as *Die heks* (The Witch) (1923) and *Die laaste aand* (Last Evening) (1930), detective and ghost stories, novels, books on Cape wines and cookery, besides being an ardent botanist. He was educated at home in the Western Cape by his German-born missionary father and was a journalist for pro-Boer publications during the Anglo-Boer war (1899–1902). Deeply moved by the human suffering he witnessed during the war, he wrote the English novel *Stormwrack* (1980) and, besides shorter poems, impressive dramatic monologues in Afrikaans. He reached his zenith early in *Oom Gert vertel en ander gedigte* (Uncle Gert Narrates and Other Poems) (1911), *Dingaansdag* (Dingaan's Day) (1920) and *Uit drie wêrelddele* (From Three Continents) (1923). *Slampamperliedjies* (Good-For-Nothing Songs) (1933) is a collection of sentimental but playful verse. Leipoldt also produced works of **autobiography** which are now of interest to students of post-colonial culture (see **colonialism, neocolonialism, and postcolonialism**). These include *Uit my Oosterse dagboek* (From My Oriental Diary) (1932), an account of his visit to the Far East in 1911, and *Bushveld Doctor* (1937), based on his work as a doctor. Leipoldt, who had studied pediatrics at Guy's Hospital in London, lived in Cape Town for the greater part of his life.

Further reading

Kannemeyer, J.C. (1999) *Leipoldt*, Cape Town: Tafelberg.

ENA JANSEN

Lemsine, Aicha

b. 1942, Nemencha region, Algeria

novelist

Aicha Lemsine is the pseudonym of the author of two novels and a book-length essay on women in the Arab world. Her novels, *The Chrysalis* (*La Chrysalide: chroniques algériennes*) (1976) and *Beneath a Sky of Porphyry* (*Ciel de porphyre*) (1978), take place during and immediately after the Algerian war of independence (1954–62). The first tells the story of a Berber family's evolution as social changes follow the struggle for political liberation. Its heroine pursues her studies and avoids undesirable marriages in an optimistic account of liberation following the revolution. The second novel tells a similarly heroic tale, but then outlines the disillusionments and compromises of its aging actors during the years following independence. Lemsine's other work, *Ordalie des voix* (Trial by Voices) (1983) proves the author much less optimistic about the condition of Arab women than her novels would indicate. Drawing on interviews in the field across the Middle East, she presents a picture of failed reforms and struggling feminist movements.

Further reading

Lemsine, Aicha (1990) *Beneath a Sky of Porphyry*, trans. Dorothy S. Blair, London: Quartet.

SETH GRAEBNER

Leshoai, Bob

b. 1920, South Africa

short story writer and playwright

The South African short story writer and play-wright Bob Leshoai was a member of a group of South African writers who began writing in exile in the 1960s. Leshoai was educated at the University of Fort Hare and was a high school teacher in Johannesburg before he resigned in opposition to the apartheid government's educational programs for blacks (see **apartheid and post-apartheid**). He was actively involved in dramatic societies in South Africa before his exile. Once he left South Africa, Leshoai became a lecturer at colleges in Zambia, Tanzania, and later Lesotho. Leshoai had studied theater at the University of Illinois in the mid 1960s, and on his return to Africa he was actively involved in the development of drama at the universities of Dar es Salaam and Lesotho. *The Wrath of the Ancestors* was published in East Africa in 1971. But Leshoai's most important work was his collection of short stories, *Masilo's Adventures and Other Stories* (1968), a retelling of traditional tales drawn from Sotho culture and history. Although these stories were written in English, they are considered an important aspect of Sotho literature.

Further reading

Gérard, Albert S. (1971) *Four African Literatures*, Berkeley: University of California Press.

SIMON GIKANDI

Lessing, Doris

b. 1919, Khermanshah, Persia (now Iran)

writer

Considered to be one of the most distinguished British novelists of the post World War II period, Lessing has published many works in a variety of genres ranging from social criticism to science fiction, but readers of her work are rarely aware of her African background. Lessing was born in Persia (Iran) in an British expatriate family. The family moved to Rhodesia (Zimbabwe) when she was a young girl and her early life was marked by the culture of colonialism (see **colonialism, neocolonialism, and postcolonialism**) and of white settler farmers. She moved to London in 1949 and became involved in British left-wing politics and a key member of the angry generation of writers that emerged in Britain after World War II. After a visit to Rhodesia in 1956 she was declared a prohibited immigrant and banned from returning to the country because of her opposition to colonial rule in the region. Although Africa, its landscape and culture creep into almost all of Lessing's fiction, they are most prominent in her so-called African novels, especially *The Grass is Singing* (1950), a psychological exploration of the colonial settler class and the frustrations caused by imposed racial and sexual boundaries. This was one of the first novels to treat the theme of **gender and sexuality**, and especially sexuality across racial lines, in African fiction. Lessing's other stories, many of them dealing with themes of psychic violence in the white settler community in southern Africa and the effects of colonialism on African communities, were published in *Collected African Stories* (1973), in two volumes. After the independence of Zimbabwe, Lessing returned to the country for several visits in the 1980s, the result of which was *African Laughter: Four Visits to Zimbabwe* (1992).

Further reading

Lessing, Doris (1989) *The Doris Lessing Reader*, New York: Knopf.

SIMON GIKANDI

Likimani, Muthoni

b. 1926, Kahuhia, Kenya

novelist

Muthoni Likimani (Gachanja) was born and brought up at the Kahuhia mission, daughter of one of the first Anglican priests in Kenya. She was educated in Kenya and in the UK. She has worked in various capacities but notably as a teacher and a broadcaster for the national broadcasting station in Nairobi. She is the author of several fiction and non-fiction works that touch on the social history of women. In *Passbook F.47927* (1985), Likimani describes the impact of the Mau Mau revolt in Kenya on women's daily lives. In *They Shall Be Chastised* (1974), she tells the story of Kimori and the people of Shimoni whose lives were affected by the arrival of the missionaries, thus illustrating the confusion caused to young women by Christianity and the culture of colonialism (see **Christianity and Christian missions; colonialism, neo-colonialism, and postcolonialism**). In *What Does a Man Want?* (1974), her concern is the dilemma that women face as they try to understand men whom they find mysterious, difficult, and exasperating.

GEORGE ODERA OUTA

Liking, Werewere

b. 1950, Bondé, Cameroon

novelist

Born in Bondé, Cameroon, Werewere Liking was raised by her grandparents in a completely traditional environment. She has lived in the Côte d'Ivoire since 1978. Liking is self-taught in the arts of writing, painting, theater, cinema, and dancing. Her renowned theater group, Ki-Yi Mbock, has performed throughout the world. In general, her work is closely related to her experience of growing up in her grandparents' village, to the renaissance of African **art**s, to pan-Africanism and the fertile encounter among the range of arts in the black world or diaspora (see **diaspora and pan-Africanism**). Her work has clearly shown how writing, for a Cameroonian woman, can open up a space of power within such dichotomies as traditional society versus modernity (see **modernity and modernism**), West versus non-West, and theories of women versus "other" women. Although deconstruction of dichotomies is a familiar textual strategy in Liking's works, she is aware of how subjects who experience racial, class, or gender oppression still deal with such dichotomies on an everyday basis (see **gender and sexuality**). She is also aware of the power of dichotomization as an epistemological and practical weapon. In Liking's major works, readers are shown how, for a Cameroonian woman, the practice of writing is enforced and structured by dominant discourses. In *Orphée d'Afric* (African Orpheus) (1981), Liking questions the decentering of wisdom by the colonial text and its systems of knowledge. In this book, Liking argues that since the arrival of the colonial "civilizer," Africans have become alienated from their own culture, and that under colonialism it became impossible to learn without the support of material objects such as books, and necessary to recite those texts without understanding or questioning them. Interspersed throughout Liking's complex treatment of socio-logical discourse we find jewels of hope and subversion, not in cryptic or allegorical form but rather in a narrative flow in which Eurocentric gestures that tend to disguise their harshness are exposed. Her concern with social reality is accompanied by close attention to how language functions, not so much in the creation of formal beauty as in the concealment of ideology. She sees this form of vigilance as particularly crucial for a Cameroonian woman writer using the language of her oppressors.

Liking has presented her vision of African women and their future eloquently and persuasively in numerous articles and interviews, where she argues that the African woman must reinvent her body of writing and invent a new language in order to free herself. In her narratives, Liking uses a multiple structure built on a reservoir of images, stories, rhymes, and songs borrowed from her society. At the same time, however, her works are concerned with the lives and experiences of a self-conscious isolated artist in the process of transposing the act of storytelling into the act of writing. Thereby Liking's narratives question the possibility of survival of the very traditional forms. For Liking, transferring oral speech (see **oral literature and performance**) into the conventions of writing – what Derrida would call "the violence of the letter" – amounts, in a way, to the betrayal of orality; the process might lead, in the long run, to a concomitant modification of these traditional forms. Well-concealed under the elegiac surface of the last pages of Liking's novels lies the violent subtext of the death of a community, a culture, a meaning. The horizon of meaning, the dream of transcendence, has become a solution for all of us.

If Liking's writing expresses faith and hope in the future, it also expresses suffering and bitterness. There is a difference between the aspiration of the Cameroonian woman writer and the condition that society designs for her, between the tasks she assigns herself and the means she has available to her. Liking's work indicates the incredibly important role Cameroonian women may play at this historical moment. While women have always played a central role in Cameroonian history and culture, their contributions have usually been hidden, invisible, and silent. Liking's call to reinvent a new body of literature is beginning to reverse certain stereotypes and to encourage more and more Cameroonian women to write about their images, empowering others through this process.

Further reading

Liking, Werewere (1981) *Orphée-d'afric: roman* (African Orpheus), Paris: L'Harmattan.
——(1983) *Elle sera de jaspe et de corail* (She Will Be of Jasper and Coral), Paris: L'Harmattan.

FRIEDA EKOTTO

literary criticism

Introduction

Of the many issues that have been central to the history and study of African literature, the question of literary criticism and theory has been one of the most complicated and enduring. At the heart of this problem lies the question of the identity of African literature itself and the appropriateness of modes of interpretation developed in other, mainly European, traditions. Can African literature, especially the one written in European languages, claim a distinctive identity? And if this literature is to be considered distinctive from its European counterparts, does it demand alternative traditions of interpretation? These questions were at the center of some of the earliest discussions on the criticism of African literature in the 1950s and early 1960s,

and they were to dominate the consolidation of African literary studies as a field of scholarship in schools and universities in the 1970s and 1980s; the same questions were to return in debates on the efficacy of Western theories to African literature in the 1990s.

Each major period of African literature has presented this question with a different focus. In many of the debates about the possibilities of an African literature in the period after World War II, for example, the issue seemed essentially to focus on the relation between language, nationalism, and the African image (see **language question**; **nationalism and post-nationalism**). In 1949, the Ghanaian scholar K.A.B. Jones Quartey dismissed the notion that an African literature could emerge out of European languages, arguing that "the African genius" dwelt in African languages. But as African literature continued to be produced in European languages, especially English and French in the period leading to decolonization, it was not possible to ignore its claims to a distinct identity. Indeed, one of the most interesting aspects of the criticism of African literature in the early 1960s was the emergence of a series of influential studies that tended to take the authenticity and unity of African literature for granted.

This thread is apparent in influential literary histories such as Jahnheinz Jahn's *Neo-African Literature: A History of Black Writing* (*Geschichte der neoafrikanischen Literatur*) (1966), Lilyan Kesteloot's *Les Écrivains noirs de la langue française* (Black African Literature in French) (1963), and Claude Wauthier's *The Literature and Thought of Modern Africa* (*L'Afrique des Africains: inventaire de la négritude*) (1964), and pioneering works of criticism, most notably Ezekiel (Es'kia) **Mphahlele**'s *The African Image* (1962) and Gerald Moore's *Seven African Writers* (1962). But as D.S. Izevbaye was to argue in an influential review appropriately entitled "The State of Criticism in African Literature" (1975), the confidence these critics had in the idea of a unified African literature came from outside the literature itself, either in the ideologies of cultural nationalism or from an unquestioned metropolitan perspective. In the case of Moore's *Seven African Writers* (1962), considered to be the first work of criticism of African literature in

English, the confidence was drawn from what Izevbaye called "an accepted metropolitan tradition." Mphahlele's *The African Image*, like the sweeping histories written by Jahn, Keesteloot, and Wauthier, represented the goals and desires of cultural nationalism.

All these works were driven by a common assumption: that, irrespective of the languages in which they were produced, African literatures drew from a common history and tradition. But what was this history? What was this tradition? The early history of African literary criticism was obsessed by such questions, and as the criticism of African literature expanded to account for the new literatures in the late 1960s and 1970s, doubts were still being expressed about the ability of a critical enterprise whose tools had been borrowed from elsewhere to account for what were considered to be literatures whose goal had been to represent a unique cultural and historical experience.

A literature and its identity

Debates about the identity of African literature, its criticism and language, have taken place against a background in which the rhetoric of criticism seems to be at odds with its practice: even when critics of African literature were obsessed with the issues of critical traditions and standards mentioned above, they were busy applying all the theories available to them to African literature. In fact, as even the most cursory survey of the criticism of African literature will show, there is perhaps no school or tradition of literary criticism and theory in the world that has not been applied to African literature. Indeed, the criticism of African literature has tended to reflect the dominant critical and theoretical tendencies in Europe and the United States. In the late 1950s and 1960s, for example, critics of African literature in English tended to reflect the dominant thread in European and American criticism, namely the literary criticism associated with F.R. Leavis in Britain and its former colonies and American New Criticism. In its early volumes, the influential journal *African Literature Today*, edited by Eldred Jones, took these two traditions, as centers of the critical enterprise, for granted. The only difference

between the most influential contributors to the journal in its early years was that those who had been educated in the Leavis tradition in Britain or the African university colleges tended to focus on moral consciousness as the unifying principle of literature, while American-educated critics tended to favor the autonomy of the work of art and its informing metaphors or symbols.

When structuralism became the key paradigm in discussions of European literature in the late 1960s, especially in France, African critics educated in France, most notably Thomas Melone and Sunday Anozie, brought this highly technical and linguistic practice to bear on African literature. But because of the hegemony of the Leavis and New Critical traditions in African literary circles, structuralist criticism (see **structuralism and poststructuralism**) faced strong resistance in the institutions of interpretation and Anozie was forced to found his own journal, *The Conch*, in what turned out to be a short-lived attempt to sustain the structuralist project in Africa. During the same period, Marxist criticism, often mediated through the works of Frantz Fanon, was to become central in African universities associated with the radical tradition of literary studies, most notably Dar es Salaam in Tanzania and Ife in Nigeria.

In the 1980s and 1990s, the movements that emerged under the rubric of poststructuralism in the 1980s (feminism, deconstruction, postcolonial theory) met strong resistance in African institutions, but by the end of the century they had come to occupy the space that once used to be dominated by Leavis's literary criticism and American New Criticism. Evidence of this shift can be found in the pages of *Research in African Literatures* (*RAL*), the leading journal in the field, founded by Bernth Lindfors at the University of Texas. Like *African Literature Today*, the early issues of *RAL* reflected the influence of Leavis's literary criticism and American New Criticism. But as the winds of literary criticism and theory shifted in the 1980s and 1990s, the journal began to shift towards poststructuralist models. From 1990 onwards, critical work published in *RAL* has generally reflected the poststructuralist turn in the criticism of African literature, with occasional dissenters.

But in reviewing these shifts in the criticism of African literature, it would be a mistake to argue that these threads have been determined by the desire, among critics of African literature, to adopt and apply European or American models and techniques to African literature. Sometimes European modes of literary criticism have attracted critics of African literature because they seem to provide alternative models to counter what might appear to be the dominant discourses in the study of African literature. Among a younger generation of African critics, for example, poststructuralism, including deconstruction and feminism, was attractive because it provided instruments for questioning the Leavis model of criticism and New Criticism. **Feminist criticism** provides a powerful example of how critics of African literature have both adopted dominant ideas (in this case Western feminist discourse) and also transformed them to account for the circumstances and histories of African women's lives.

Two conclusions can be drawn from this brief account. First, the criticism of African literature has not developed in isolation from international movements, schools, and theories; rather, it has evolved in relation to them, in a variety of forms of appropriation, affiliation, and contestation. In this sense, this criticism reflects the institutional practices of its time. The critical practice of even African-born scholars reflects the interests and practices in which they were educated, and what sometimes appears to be a conflict of ideologies and methods is often one of different pedagogical traditions. Second, as V.Y. Mudimbe observed in the midst of debates about literary theory and the African text, African literary criticism has been the consequence of a larger intellectual enterprise – "the process of inventing and organising African literature" (1985: Washington, DC) The debates and counter-debates that have come to dominate African literary criticism are part of this process of invention and reinvention.

Debates and counter-debates

Although almost all schools of criticism are reflected in the study and explication of literature in Africa, there is a sense in which the critical tradition on the continent has revolved around a set of issues that are peculiar to this tradition of letters or ones that are considered central in its

interpretation. At the core of these issues, as we have already noted, is the problem of definition: what exactly is African literature and what makes it different in relation to other traditions? From its very beginning the criticism of African literature has been simultaneously shaped and haunted by this question. After all, what made the identity of African literature a problem was the fact that when it emerged in a critical mass in the period after World War II it was considered to be a new phenomenon. Produced within the culture of colonialism (see **colonialism, neocolonialism, and postcolonialism**) and its institutions of higher education, African literature tended to resonate with models drawn from the European tradition from John Bunyan to Shakespeare, from romanticism to surrealism. But did this mean that this literature was an extension of the European tradition or did it also draw on other sources?

If we were to read Amos Tutuola's first novel *The Palm-Wine Drinkard* as a rewriting of Bunyan, as Moore did in his pioneering study *Seven African Writers*, what were we to do with the equally important influences of Yoruba folklore (see **Yoruba literature**) and the works of Chief Daniel **Fagunwa**? L.S. **Senghor**'s poetry was cast in familiar European forms such as the elegy and the lyric, but its referents were studiously drawn from African traditions and experiences; indeed, his most important poems were attempts to bring together African music and European prosody. So, where did these works belong in terms of literary history and criticism?

Criticism of African literature, especially in the 1950s and early 1960s, was torn between the desire to account for the European character of its forms and its African referents and, ultimately, the very nature of its Africanness. But what exactly distinguished the literature itself? Almost without exception, African writers during this period had been trained in the European tradition, but what made their works distinctive, compared to an earlier generation of writers early in the century, was their attempt to incorporate elements borrowed from oral traditions, including figures of speech, into their works (see **oral literature and performance**). For many African writers in the twentieth century, the major claim to literary difference was embedded in the appeal to an

African world, especially one defined by precolonial cultures and traditions. Out of this claim arose the notion, articulated by Abiola Irele in *The African Experience in Literature and Ideology* (1981), that African letters had a specific character that distinguished it from other literatures and thus demanded at least an adjustment of Western critical formulations. Irele's powerful claim was that it was out of the oral tradition that Africans derived an image of themselves and their history as part of a collective consciousness.

Such claims of distinctiveness needed, however, to contend with the diversity of African cultures and traditions themselves. Indeed, one of the reasons why the identity of African literature became such a central issue in criticism was that it was not clear what the continent's writers, whose identities and backgrounds ranged from the Islamic (see **Islam in African literature**) and Arabic traditions of North Africa to the colored writers of the Cape Province, had in common, except perhaps the experience of being colonized by Europeans. Earlier literary histories of African literature like the ones by Jahn and Keesteloot had found a center of interests in the mythologies of black culture and negritude, but for the critics of the postcolonial period in the 1960s who were writing when these unifying mythologies were unraveling, criticism could not simply be founded on the myth of an African world promoted by the writers themselves. Still, the question of definition could not go away. It would reappear in different paradigms, especially in literary history. It would appear, for example, in attempts in the 1970s and 1990s to produce literary histories based on national or ethnic identities.

The question of the identity of African literature was, of course, overshadowed by the persistent and controversial question of language. The debate had started at the dawn of African independence with Obi Wali's essay (1963: *Transition*), "The Dead End of African Literature," in which the Nigerian critic argued that "the uncritical acceptance of English and French as the inevitable medium for educated African writing [was] misdirected, and [had] no chance of advancing African literature and culture." Wali was adamant in his claim that "any true African literature must be written in African languages." Wali's position was opposed by many

influential figures in African literary circles, including Mphahlele and Chinua **Achebe**, who pointed out that English had itself become a national language in Africa, or that its use was a pragmatic response to the African condition during and after colonialism. But whether one spoke against or in favor of European languages as vehicles of African literary expression, the persistence of the debate was itself a symptom of the crisis of identity that continued to plague the study of African literature even at what appeared to be its moment of triumph.

And the crisis was about much more than the choice of language. After all, the forum in which the issue of language was debated in the 1960s was one in which the most famous and distinguished writers in African languages were conspicuous for their absence. Much more important than the choice of language was the association between linguistic expression and structures of feeling. Wali made this association succinctly: "An African writer who thinks and feels in his own language *must* write in that language" (1963: *Transition*). Even critics like Irele who did not have a strong view on the issue of language in African literature were still concerned with what they saw as the gap between the African experience and the language used to represent it, the lack of a "natural correspondence denied to the African writer who wishes to express his African world in a European language." And when **Ngugi wa Thiong'o** decided to abandoned writing literature in English in the 1980s, he justified this by arguing, in *Decolonising the Mind* (1986), that writing in an African language restored harmony between the writer (and the reader) and their environment, while the colonial language was an agent of alienation.

Nevertheless, beneath the debates on the identity and language of African literature lay another set of ancillary issues which criticism had to grapple with. There was, for example, the problem of audience: whom did African writers write for – a foreign readership or an African elite? How did audience impact the formal aspects of literature? Added to the question of audience was the issue of **insiders and outsiders** in the criticism of African literature. At the heart of this issue, foregrounded in Christopher Miller's *Theories of Africans*, was whether it was imperative for

African literature to be studied within models and frameworks developed in Africa itself and how an inside knowledge of African culture could be acquired by outsiders. Miller's preference was for an anthropological approach that could give the critical a point of entry into African traditions and their literature, but critics such as V.Y. Mudimbe wondered whether anthropology was not itself too associated with dubious theories of Africa and Africans to provide any new knowledge about the continent.

Feminist criticism

But perhaps the most important development in African literary criticism in the 1980s was the emergence of feminist criticism. Feminist criticism was crucial in shifting the center of attention in the study of African literature from a male-centered approach. Its focus on the experiences and histories of African women and their representation in literature was to change the terms of debate of African literary criticism. Most importantly, feminist criticism problematized some dominant traditions of literary scholarship in Africa, including the nature of the canon of African letters and the place of women writers in the African imagination.

When feminist criticism started to appear in the study of African literature sometime in the 1980s, it did so against the background of the international feminist movement and its radical attempt to rethink the place of women in politics, society, and culture. At the same time, however, the critics who turned to feminism and feminist criticism in search of new models for the study of African literature did so with a keen sense of two problems. First, these critics were aware of the tension between some of the universal claims being made by the international feminist movement, especially in regard to the question of difference, and the specific experiences of African women under colonialism and postcolonialism. While international feminism was premised on the notion that women had been excluded from the public sphere, the earliest works on the experiences of African women such as *The Black Woman Cross-Culturally* (1981), edited by Filomina Chioma Steady, were actually attempts to show how black women in Africa and the diaspora had not been confined to a

private domestic space, but had been forced by colonialism and slavery to function as second-class citizens in spaces of economic production.

Second, the feminist turn in the study of African literature was taking place against what appeared to be an absence in literary and critical history: African literature as it was studied in the 1960s and 1970s had come to be defined as primarily male, and the few women who had been writing during this period, most notably Flora **Nwapa**, Grace **Ogot**, Assia **Djebar**, and Ama Ata **Aidoo** had been either willfully neglected or subjected to a critical apparatus that was incapable of accounting for their experiences and interests as women writers. These absences were aggravated by what had always been a tendency in African literature in the modern period: the simultaneous representation of women as symbols of African traditions and cultural values and as stereotypes. Faced with this situation, the pioneering work of African feminist criticism, including the essays collected in *Ngambika: Studies of Women in African Literature* (1986), edited by Carole Boyce Davies and Anne Adams Graves, tended to focus more on the absence of women in male texts or their stereotyped representation as agents of male ideologies or projects. In the few cases where feminist critics of African literature, like Marie Umeh, were able to find their way into the emergent tradition of African-American feminist criticism published in works such as *Sturdy Black Bridges* (1979), they tended to correct the existing situation by calling attention to the positive and different images of female characters in texts produced by women.

Whatever the approaches that critics were adopting towards feminist criticism in the 1980s, they were still dealing with a small corpus of writing. The project of feminist criticism, then, was primarily one of championing existing women writers and constructing or reconstructing a canon. The project of African feminist critics, as sketched out in Boyce Davies' introduction to *Ngambika*, was to develop the canon of African women writers, examine stereotypes and negative images in African literature, explore the role of African women writers in the development of an African female aesthetic, and examine the role of women in the field of oral literature. Early feminist criticism in Africa can hence be described as both an attempt to establish a canon of women's literature and the search for models for examining this literature.

This process was to be dramatically altered by the explosion of writing by African women writers in the late 1980s and 1990s. Whereas, before, the feminist tradition had revolved around images of women in male literature or where women writers such as Nwapa, Ogot, and Aidoo fitted in the literary tradition, the field was dramatically expanded with the emergence of new women writers, such as Mariama **Bâ**, Buchi **Emecheta**, Tsitsi **Dangarembga**, Calixthe **Beyala**, and Werewere **Liking**, and the rediscovery of existing but marginalized ones, such as Bessie **Head** and Djebar. By the end of the 1990s, there was no doubt that women writers were no longer marginal to the canon of African letters; the critical issue was no longer one of recovery or valorization; rather, the task of feminist criticism in the 1990s was to sharpen debates about the nature and appropriateness of its models to African women's writing.

The 1990s was hence the period of what Nana Wilson-Tagoe has aptly described as the retheorization of African women's writing. According to Wilson-Tagoe, this retheorization took several forms. For a start, there was a new desire to go beyond the claim that feminism and feminist criticism were models of thought and analysis borrowed from outside and were hence alien to African traditions. Rather, the challenge for criticism at the end of the twentieth century was to use the feminist framework to recognize what Wilson-Tagoe called new energies and contexts for the study of African women's writing.

Another issue that became central to feminist criticism in the 1990s was a rethinking of the question of difference – of **gender and sexuality** – and its impact on both the subject and form of African literature. The basic claim in most feminist writing was that a focus on women's experiences and differences in relationship to the themes that had come to dominate African literature, including colonialism, tradition, modernity (see **modernity and modernism**), and the crisis of the post-colonial state, was paramount in the reinterpretation of African literature. When women's lives were recognized as central to the African text, the result was a new way of reading older canonical texts and

the newer women's literature that had blossomed in the 1990s. Within this overall project, the feminist criticism of African literature has not been a monolithic enterprise. On the contrary, African feminist criticism reflects the same diversity of views and interests as feminist criticism elsewhere.

Conclusion

In its beginnings in the 1950s and 1960s, the criticism of African literature was obsessed with the identity of African literature and whether Western models of criticism were appropriate to its study. By the end of the twentieth century these questions no longer seemed as important as they had been in prior decades. There was general acknowledgement that African literature emerged out of diverse cultural and linguistic experiences, was produced in multiple localities, and did not hence demand a common identity or model of criticism. Still, one question remained: did critical models or theories emerge from African cultures and traditions themselves or was Africa the producer of literatures which had to be analyzed according to European or American models? This question was highlighted by scholars of African language literatures such as Karin Barber, who noted that in spite of the growth of literary criticism and theory in Africa, and the proliferation of debates about the study of African literature, African language literatures had been subjected to "a definitive theoretical lockout." African language literatures remain understudied, both on the continent and abroad. Yet it is to these literatures that criticism must turn if it is to rethink the relationship between theoretical models and literary works.

Further reading

Barber, Karin (1995) "African-Language Literature and Postcolonial Criticism," *Research in African Literatures* 26, 4: 3–30.

Bishop, Rand (1988) *African Literature, African Critics: The Forming of Critical Standards, 1947–1966*, New York: Greenwood Press.

Davies, Carole Boyce and Graves, Anne Adams (1986) *Ngambika: Studies of Women in African Literature*, Trenton, New Jersey: Africa World Press.

Harrow, Kenneth, Ngaté, Jonathan and Zimra, Clarisse (eds) (1991) *Crossing Boundaries in African Literatures*, Washington, DC: Three Continents Press.

Irele, Abiola (1981) *The African Experience in Literature and Ideology*, London: Heinemann.

Izevbaye, D.S. (1975) "The State of Criticism in African Literature," in *African Literature Today No. 7: Focus on Criticism*, London: Heinemann, pp. 1–19.

Mudimbe, V.Y. (1985) "African Literature: Myth or Reality," in Stephen Arnold (ed.) *African Literature Studies: The Present State/L'État Présent*, Washington, DC: Three Continents Press.

Wali, Obijunwa (1963) "The Dead End of African Literature?" *Transition* 10: 13–15.

Wilson-Tagoe, Nana (1997) "Reading Towards a Theorization of African Women's Writing: African Women Writers within Feminist Gynocriticism," in Stephanie Newell (ed.) *Writing African Women: Gender, Popular Culture and Literature in West Africa*, London: Zed Books.

SIMON GIKANDI

literature in Hausa

Oral narrative, poetry, praise singing, riddles, clichés, proverbs, and dramatic performance are the major forms of Hausa literature. The novel in Hausa and English is a late twentieth-century addition to Hausa literary culture. Although much of Hausa literature is available in translation into English, it cannot be fully appreciated without some knowledge of Hausa language and culture. Graham Furniss's *Poetry Prose, and Popular Culture in Hausa* (1996) offers a thorough and accessible introduction to this vast topic. Hausa culture is concentrated in what is now Northern Nigeria, though the Hausa cultural diaspora stretches from Senegal to Sudan. Since the establishment of Islam in the region in about the tenth century, Arabic poetic style has been a major influence on local literatures, with Fulani clerics and Islamic scholars writing a variety of tracts (religious, commercial, social) for their patrons (see **Islam in African literature**). Hausa always was the language of the masses, while Arabic and Fulfulde were the region's written languages until the nineteenth century, and these were both written in the Arabic script (*ajami*). When Hausa began be written, and until the end of the nineteenth century, it too was expressed in *ajami*.

Colonial influence

In the 1920s British colonial rule in Nigeria brought about the national promotion of literacy and book culture. A Hausa publishing company was established in Northern Nigeria, and literacy in Hausa and English, both written in roman script, was promoted through writing contests held throughout the region. The influence of colonialism in the nineteenth century in Nigeria and Niger meant that English and French respectively became these country's official languages. Therefore, many works of Hausa literature have been published in English and French as well as in Hausa since the mid nineteenth century.

Oral narrative

Oral narrative (*tatsunyoyi*, plural, *tatsuniya*, singular) is one of the oldest forms of **popular literature** in Hausa. In the nineteenth century travelers collected examples of these folk tales, and later a three-volume collection of tales by local Hausa scholars was set down in Hausa *ajami* by colonial officer Frank Edgar (1913). It was subsequently translated into English by Neil Skinner (1969). The stories, which are told by both women and men, run the gamut from secular to sacred. They include tales about animals, tricksters, heroes and villains, origin, morality, histories, warfare, the Sokoto *jihad*, and the Prophet Muhammad and his Companions. The *tatsuniya* is pertinent to Hausa culture and reflective of its foundations.

Poetry

In the twentieth century poetry was arguably the most popular mode of expression in Hausa culture. The Hausa word for poem (*waka*, singular) also means "song," reflecting the likelihood of poems being delivered in oral performance, regardless of their origins in written or extemporaneous modes (see **oral literature and performance**). Thus

Hausa poetry includes both oral and written forms, and in many cases these works are expressed in both modes, depending on the audience being served. Extemporaneous performers include both sedate and bawdy entertainers who chant their works alone or with an entourage. Their works often are recorded for and broadcast on radio and television stations. Extemporaneous poets also are hired for private celebrations such as weddings and naming ceremonies. While both male and female entertainers may perform for public events, only women may entertain in the secluded women's quarters of a private setting. Written poetry may be performed orally, but it originates in the written form, created by both men and women. Its topics range from sacred to secular. Nana Asma'u's nineteenth-century poems are representative of those grounded in Islamic values. Poems may appear only in print, but some occasionally are also recorded for dissemination on the radio. Poetry chapbooks are commonly used at the secondary school and adult education levels for exposition on political and current events. Mervyn Hiskett's research on Hausa poetry has been especially important to the field.

Praise singing

One of the most socially significant Hausa literary forms is praise singing. The late M.G. Smith studied the social functions of male Hausa praise singers (1957), finding that these performers maintained the status quo by declaiming their wealthy patrons' exemplary attributes, family connections, and political and social positions. Both male and female praise singers perform for formal occasions like political rallies or annual Eid el-Fitr celebrations following the month of Ramadan fasting, as well as for quotidian occasions like weddings and naming days. Praise singers may be attached to royalty or may be less well positioned, performing for families in town. These works are always delivered in public performance.

Riddles, clichés, proverbs, drama, novels

While poetry and praise singing are central to Hausa culture, riddles, clichés, and proverbs are integral parts of ordinary interchange. Drama and prose are relative newcomers to the culture. Riddles, clichés, and proverbs are integrated into Hausa daily life at all levels. Children incorporate word-play into games, and adults sprinkle casual conversation with proverbial allusions. Indeed, familiarity with Hausa proverbs is a sign of fluency in the language. Like praise singing, drama in Hausa functions primarily in public performance to promote specific social messages and advocate the maintenance of the status quo. Hausa drama is especially popular in Niger, where annual contests draw enthusiastic crowds. In both Nigeria and Niger, Hausa drama has been popular since the 1950s on radio, television, and in live performance. Romance novels comprise a new genre in Hausa culture, appearing in both English and Hausa roman script, and result from the establishment of printing presses and mass production, along with the rise of literacy in both languages.

Further reading

Boyd, Jean and Mack, Beverly (1997) *The Collected Works of Nana Asma'u. Daughter of Usman Dan Fodiyo (1793–1864)*, East Lansing, Michigan: Michigan State University Press.

Furniss, Graham (1996) *Poetry, Prose, and Popular Culture in Hausa*, London: International African Institute Press.

Hiskett, Mervyn (1975) *A History of Hausa Islamic Verse*, London: School for Oriental and African Studies.

Skinner, A. Neil (trans.) (1969, 1977) *Hausa Tales and Traditions: An English Translation of "Tatsunyoyi Na Hausa"*, originally compiled by Frank Edgar, vol. 1, London: Frank Cass; vols 2 and 3, Madison: University of Wisconsin Press.

BEVERLY B. MACK

Livingstone, Douglas

b. 1932, Kuala Lumpur; d. 1996, South Africa

poet

The South African poet Douglas Livingstone was born in Malaya but grew up and was educated in southern Africa. Like many other white South African poets writing in the shadow of apartheid (see **apartheid and post-apartheid**), Livingstone's poetry reflects his struggle to secure and preserve what he calls a common humanity founded on the unique experience of individuals within a highly politicized culture, and at the same time to reconcile his mastery of European traditions of poetry, especially romanticism and modernism (see **modernity and modernism**), with his complicated identity as a white African. Livingstone has been at once interested in Africa as a source of his poetic language but skeptical at what he considers political poetry; he has sought to use his work not only to hold on to what he considers to be appropriate poetic standards but also to escape the claims of political affiliations that might come between the poet and his goal to use language as a weapon against a chaotic world. Livingstone's poetry has been published in collections spanning a period of forty years. These range from *The Skull in the Mud* (1960) and *Sjambok and Other Poems from Africa* (1964) to *A Littoral Zone* (1991), published at the end of apartheid.

SIMON GIKANDI

Liyong, Taban Lo

b. 1938, southern Sudan

poet and critic

The northern Ugandan/southern Sudanese poet and critic Taban Lo Liyong was born in the southern Sudan and educated in local high schools in northern Uganda before attending Howard University in the United States. He was one of the first Africans to graduate with an MFA from the famous International Writers' Workshop at the University of Iowa. His academic career has been global in scale: he was a research fellow and later lecturer at the University of Nairobi, where he initiated a program to replace the existing English curriculum with one focused on African literatures; he was one of the founders of the programs in literary studies at the universities of Papua New Guinea in the Pacific and Juba in the southern Sudan; later he taught at the University of Venda

in South Africa. Liyong's major works can be placed in three categories. The first includes his highly polemical essays, which have been responsible for transforming the literary terrain in East Africa. In this category belong "Correcting Literary Barrenness in East Africa," an essay that Liyong wrote in 1964 decrying what he considered the emptiness of East African literature when compared to the literary landscapes in West and southern Africa. In 1968, Liyong was the co-author, with **Ngugi wa Thiong'o** and Owour Anyumba, of "On the Abolition of the English Department," the manifesto that initiated the transformation of English departments in East Africa. In this manifesto, Liyong and his colleagues argued that African experiences and African literature, especially oral literature (see **oral literature and performance**), should occupy a central role in institutions of education in the region (see **education and schools**). The second set of Liyong's works revolves around the projects he initiated to popularize the teaching of oral literature in African universities. His collection and adaptation of Lwo oral stories was published in *Eating Chiefs: Lwo Culture from Lolwe to Malkal* (1970). Finally, Liyong has published several collections of poems, the most prominent of which is *Frantz Fanon's Uneven Ribs* (1971). His poems are renowned for their acerbic and mocking tone and their dense allusions to other African writers and their works.

Further reading

Liyong, Taban Lo (1969) *The Last Word*, Nairobi: East African Publishing House.

SIMON GIKANDI

Loakira, Mohammed

b. 1945, Morocco

poet

The literary activity of Moroccan poet Mohammed Loakira can be roughly divided into two periods. His earlier work participates politically in the Moroccan intelligentsia's efforts to battle a culturally neocolonial relationship with France after

Moroccan independence in 1956. His poems appeared regularly in the Moroccan cultural journal *Integral*, directed by the famous Moroccan canvas painter Mohammed Melehi, and his first collection of poems *L'Horizon d'argile* (The Horizon of Clay), published in 1971, is introduced by the Moroccan poet, writer, and intellectual Abdellatif **Laâbi** who calls Loakira a voice of witness and accusation. Loakira's later work does not completely abandon politics; however, in collections such as the 1975 *Marrakech* and the 1986 *La Soif: semblable à la soif* (Thirst: Comparable to Thirst), the poet's focus shifts to the tactile qualities of language, building a Moroccan world that stimulates all the senses. Extremely sensitive to the auditory aspect of his poetry, in the late 1990s Loakira developed interdisciplinary projects that juxtaposed and combined poetry with music and painting.

Further reading

Loakira, Mohammed (1971) *L'Horizon d'argile* (The Horizon of Clay), Paris: Pierre Jean Oswald.

KATARZYNA PIEPRZAK

Loba, Ake

b. 1927, Côte d'Ivoire

novelist

The Ivorian novelist Ake Loba made his literary debut on the eve of the independence of most African countries with the publication of *Kokoumbo, l'étudiant noir* (Kokoumbo, Black Student) (1960). Two other novels, *Les Fils de Kouretcha* (The Sons of Kouretcha) (1970) and *Les Dépossédés* (The Dispossessed) (1973) followed a decade later. His writings are, therefore, set in a transitional moment for his country and most of Africa. Consequently, as with much of the literature of the time, its thematic matter is informed by questions of change. Like Camara **Laye**'s earlier work, *The Dark Child* (1953), and Hamidou **Kane**'s *Ambiguous Adventure* (1961), *Kokoumbo* depicts a young person's double rite of passage and the concomitant problems of such a coming of age under colonialism (see

colonialism, neocolonialism, and postcolonialism). Loba's second and third novels portray the dilemmas of modernity (see **modernity and modernism**) for an emerging nation, including issues of urbanization and its impact on tribal relations, modernization and its implications for marriage, traditional customs, and beliefs. In these works Loba appears to favor progress over tradition. However, his 1990 novel *Le Sas des parvenus* (Upstarts' Screen) reflects the possible complementarity between tradition and modernity.

WANGAR WA NYATETŪ-WAIGWA

Lomami-Tshibamba, Paul

b. 1914, Brazzaville, Congo; d. 1985, Kinshasa, Zaire

writer

Considered the father of the Congolese novel and the first truly Zairian writer, Paul Lomami Tshibamba was born in Brazzaville, but his family originated in the then Belgian Congo, where he resided after 1920. He studied in a seminary but did not enter the priesthood. He served on the editorial board for *La Voix du Congolais* (Voice of the Congolese) and published articles critical of the colonial administration that led to his imprisonment and eventual exile to Brazzaville where he directed the review *Liaison* (1950–9). In 1948 his novel *Ngando* (Crocodile) received first prize in a literary competition sponsored by the colonial fair in Brussels. The work, which in many ways marks the beginning of Congolese national literature in French, depicts traditional beliefs during the colonial period in a story set on the banks of the Congo River. Its themes of alienation and cultural conflict are further developed in his subsequent works. Lomami-Tshibamba returned to Congo-Zaire after independence and held several government posts. In 1962 he started a newspaper, *Le Progrès*, later known as *Salongo*.

JANICE SPLETH

Lopes, Henri

b. 1937, Leopoldville (now Kinshasa,
Democratic Republic of the Congo)

novelist and short story writer

Henri Lopes, born in Leopoldville (Kinshasa)
under Belgian colonialism (see **colonialism,
neocolonialism, and postcolonialism**), is
the author of numerous novels and collections of
short stories, among which are notably *Tribaliks:
Contemporary Congolese Stories* (1987) (*Tribaliques*)
(1971), *Sans tam-tam* (Without a Drum) (1977), *La
Nouvelle Romance* (The New Romance) (1976), *The
Laughing Cry: An African Cock and Bull Story* (*Le Pleurer-
rire*) (1982), *Le Chercheur d'Afrique* (The African
Researcher) (1990), *Sur l'autre rive* (On the Other
Bank) (1992), and *Le Lys et le flamboyant* (The Lily
and the Blazing) (1997). Lopes' writing takes place
on the margin of an intense political career that led
him from prime minister, to assistant director of
UNESCO, to the post of ambassador. The year of
his birth corresponds also with that of the
publication of *Pigments* by the Guyanese Léon-
Gontran Damas, the first collection of the
negritude movement. The birth of Lopes in the
world of writing will thus have, in addition to the
inevitable colonial library, another horizon of
reference, the counter-discourse of negritude.

Henri Lopes takes his first steps with *Sans tam-
tam*, a collection of short stories published by the
Éditions CLE of Yaoundé, where he also published
Tribaliques, another collection of short stories, and
Nouvelle Romance, a novel that explores the dramatic
condition of the postcolonial African woman, the
disasters of tribalism, and the ethnic weights that
hinder the full accomplishment of African modernity (see **modernity and modernism**). *Le
Pleurer-rire*, a novel of postcolonial derision, is a
reflection on a burlesque dictatorship in the
situation of neocolonial dependence in the context
of a multi-ethnic society. The novel reflects
innovations in language, narration, and structure,
but also introduces something that was rare in
Francophone African literature, namely a crude
eroticism. This novel also marks the passage of
Lopes from CLE to Présence Africaine, the highly
symbolic temple of African culture in the heart of
Paris. Lopes crosses the other bank of this romantic

pathway with a novel that transports the reader
from Brazzaville to the Antilles. *Sur l'autre rive* is the
tragedy of a couple who espouse the paradoxes of
Africa, confronted with the impasses of a tortured
modernity. The interior search of Marie-Eve, the
main character of the novel, who runs away to
Guadeloupe, is reminiscent of the identity crisis
that is at the center of *Le Chercheur d'Afrique*, a novel
that demonstrates how the heritage of colonialism
can have tragic consequences for individual
destinies.

The key to understanding Lopes' development
as a novelist is his relationship to negritude and its
counter-discourse. This relationship is important
because African literature in the French language
has a history that leads back to the first texts
written by those educated in the colonial school. In
their immense majority, these texts, often prefaced
by colonial administrators, constitute an apologia
of the civilizing mission. Then come negritude and
the anti-colonial literature, with authors such as
Senghor, David **Diop**, Mongo **Beti** and **Tchicaya UTam'Si**. Literature of protest gives way,
once independence comes, to a writing of disillusionment. After lamentations for the "suns of
independences," the African writing of Henri
Lopes is part of the third generation of African
writers. The literary production of Lopes is thus
totally focused on the problems of postcolonial
Africa.

CILAS KEMEDJIO

Lounes, Abderrahmane

b. 1952, Algiers, Algeria

novelist and poet

The Algerian novelist and poet Abderrahmane
Lounes was born in the Kasbah area of Algiers.
Largely self-educated, Lounes has called himself a
graduate of the street (*diplômé de l'école du trottoir*). In
his poetry as well as in his novels, he uses a style
that is acerbic and ironic, reflecting the kind of
violence that the author feeds into the words and
actions of the characters or speakers in his works.
This violence is easily detectable from the titles of
Lounes' books, such as his first collection of poetry,

which is *Poems with Punches and Kicks* (*Poèmes à coups de poings et à coups de pieds*) (1981). Lounes is known for his bitter criticism of prevailing political issues on both the national and the international scene. He tackles sensitive issues relating to the developing world, which he calls "le fier-monde" (the proud-world) instead of the "le tier-monde" (the Third World). Lounes' second collection of poetry, *Poèmes du fier-monde ou la marre-vie* (Poems of the Proud World), is concerned with the problems affecting postcolonial societies as they struggle with questions of development and the improvement of social life. In other works, including a novel and a regular strip cartoon, he discusses the social dilemmas confronted by Algerian youth, especially in the late 1970s and early 1980s. Some of Lounes' non-fictional works have been collected in *Histoires extra et ordinaires du cimetiers-monde*.

Further reading

Lounes, Abderrahmane (1981) *Poèmes à coups de poings et à coups de pieds* (Poems with Punches and Kicks), Algiers: SNED.
——(1982) *Chronique d'un couple ou la Birmandreissienne* (Chronicle of a Couple, or The Birmandreissian Woman), Algiers: SNED.
——(1984) *Le Draguerillero sur la place d'Alger* (The Sweeper of the Square in Algiers), Algiers: Laphomic.

ZAHIA SMAIL SALHI

Louw, N.P. van Wyk

b. 1906, Sutherland, South Africa; d. 1970, Johannesburg, South Africa

academic and writer

One of the most influential Afrikaans intellectuals, Louw was born in the Karoo town of Sutherland, studied at the University of Stellenbosch, and lectured at the University of Cape Town. He was professor of literature in Amsterdam and Johannesburg and the recipient of five honorary doctorates. Intellectual legitimization for the formation of an independent **Afrikaans literature** stems from his volumes of essays published in 1939: *Loyale verset*

(Loyal Resistance) and *Berigte te velde* (Messages from the Front), while *Vernuwing in die prosa* (Renewal in Prose Texts) (1961) paved the way for the avant-garde "Sestigers" ("Sixties") movement whose members included André **Brink** and Breyten **Breytenbach**. Louw's plays, including *Dias* (1952) and *Germanicus* (1956) are prophetically poetic, while his pioneering volumes *Alleenspraak* (Soliloquy) (1935) and *Die halwe kring* (The Half Circle) (1937) made him the spokesman for the "Dertiger" ("Thirties") poets. In the epic poem *Raka* (1941), Louw problematizes dichotomies between Western civilization and Africa, hero versus masses, while *Gestaltes en diere* (Shapes and Animals) (1942) contains impressive soliloquys, e.g. "Die hond van God" ("The Dog of God"). The revolutionary section "Klipwerk" ("Stonework") in *Nuwe verse* (New Verse) (1954) harks back to the language and landscape of Sutherland, while *Tristia* (Tristesse) (1962), his last volume, is staggering in its monumental complexity and diversity.

Further reading

Steyn, J.C. (1998) *Van Wyk Louw*, Cape Town: Human and Rousseau.

ENA JANSEN

Lubega, Bonnie

b. 1929, Uganda

novelist and children's writer

Like many other writers from East Africa, Bonnie Lubega, the Ugandan novelist and author of **children's literature**, was most prolific in the decade immediately after independence, but he has done little creative work since the 1970s. Trained at a teacher and a journalist, Lubega was also the editor of a pictorial magazine in Kampala, and a scriptwriter and a radio program producer for the Ugandan Broadcasting Corporation. Lubega's literary works include *The Burning Bush* (1970), *The Outcasts* (1971), and *The Pot of Honey* (1974), novels dealing with familiar themes such as cultural conflict, the crisis of society and politics, and the alienation of individuals in societies undergoing radical transformation after decolonization. His simultaneous interest in literature for children resulted in *Great Animal Land* (1971) and *Cry Jungle Children* (1974). Lubega's poetry has been anthologized in journals and anthologies, including *Poems from East Africa* edited by Cook and **Rubadiri** (1971), and he has also produced *Olulimi Oluganda Amakula*, a Luganda language dictionary (1995).

GEORGE ODERA OUTA

Ly, Ibrahima

b. 1936, Kayes, Mali; d. 1989, Dakar, Senegal

novelist and mathematician

Born in Kayes, Mali, Ibrahima Ly held a doctorate in mathematics. As a student in Paris, he served as president of the Fédération des Étudiants d'Afrique Noire en France (FEANF). When he returned to his home country, Ly opposed the dictatorial government of Moussa Traoré and was arrested for his political activities in 1974. This began a series of detentions that took him to the most notorious government jails in Mali. Eventually Ly was exiled to Senegal and taught mathematics at the Université Cheikh Anta Diop until his death in 1989. This mathematician gave a compelling testimony of the underworld of prison, exploitation, and lies created by the postcolonial regime in Mali by weaving his work around his personal experiences as well as those of his family and friends. His works gave voice to the traumatic pilgrimage of ordinary people through the labyrinth of police stations, military camps, prisons, and forced labor camps of the "Republic"; he saw his writings as a way of bearing witness to the sufferings of fellow prisoners and a way of exposing society's own corruption and failures. These are the kinds of experiences represented in Ly's 1982 novel, *Toiles d'araignées* (Spiders' Web), which was banned in Mali on its publication. In the novel, the main protagonist, a woman named Mariama, is sentenced to prison and thrown into the web of human cruelty for having refused to marry Bakary, a member of the local elite. As an admirer of Ousmane **Sembene** and Mongo **Beti**, Ly wrote novels which were meant to mobilize what he considered to be the few uncorrupted members of society to actively work for a better Mali, a task he considered imperative if the new generation of Africans was to meet its historical responsibility. In his 1988 *Les Noctuelles vivent de larmes* (The Nightlife of Tears), Ibrahima Ly decries the ills and evils of modern-day Africa, rich in rag-like flags and rogue leaders, but beset by corruption and ostracized from the community of modern nations.

JEAN OUÉDRAOGO

M

Maake, Nhlanhla P.

b. 1956, Eastwood, Pretoria, South Africa

novelist and academic

The South African writer Nhlanhla Maake is one of the most distinguished authors in the Sotho (Sesotho) language. Maake, who was born in Eastwood, Pretoria, started his literary career with three radio plays broadcast by Radio Sesotho between 1975 and 1980. A translation of H.C. Andersen's *Dipale le Ditshomo* (Stories and Tales) followed in 1987. Maake's development in both linguistic and literary studies was enhanced by his membership in various music, drama, and arts groups in the 1980s, and his later participation in editorial committees on African languages and cultures, as well as his extensive involvement in the study and teaching of literature, which culminated in the award of a doctorate from the University of South Africa (UNISA). Of the thirteen books he wrote between 1991 and 1999, five novels have won the Maskew Miller Longman's African Heritage Literary Award: *Sejamonna ha se mo Qete* (That Which Eats Man Does Not Destroy Him) (1993), *Ke Phethisitse Ditaelo tsa Hao* (I Have Fulfilled Your Commands) (1994), *Kweetsa ya Pelo ya Motho* (The Depth of the Heart of Man) (1994), *Mme* (Mother) (1995), and *Ya se nang Sekaja Mmae a Tele* (He Who Has No Strength His Mother Should Give Up) (1996). *Kweetsa ya Pelo ya Motho* (The Depth of the Heart of Man) also won the M-Net Book Prize in 1995. Maake is also the author of *Matshohlo a Dingolwa tsa Basotho* (The Best of Sesotho Literature) (1993), three monographs that critique selected Sesotho books, and *Hlwaya Tsebe* (Open Your Ears) (1993), a handbook on the study of radio drama.

ROSEMARY MOEKETSI

Mabanckou, Alain

b. 1966, Congo-Brazzaville

poet, novelist, and essayist

Born and raised in Congo-Brazzaville, the poet, novelist, and essayist Alain Mabanckou has spent most of his adult life in France. His poetry explores the pain of exile and the profound links between exile, loss, and the search for "another" country. Mabanckou has written five collections of poetry; one of these, *L'Usure des lendemains* (The Wearing Away of Tomorrow) (1995) was awarded the Prix de la Société des Poètes Français. His first novel, *Bleu-Blanc-Rouge* (Blue-White-Red) (1998), which was awarded the Grand Prix d'Afrique Noir, is an original and complex narrative of African migration to Europe. It tells the story of Massala-Massala, an African migrant who suffers a series of mishaps in Europe and ends up in prison before being forced to return to Brazzaville, his original place of departure. *L'Enterrement de ma mère* (My Mother's Funeral) (2000) is a powerful short narrative written for beginners studying the French language and Francophone culture.

FRIEDA EKOTTO

Mabasa, Ignatius Tirivangani

b. 1971, Zimbabwe

poet and novelist

One of the most innovative writers in Shona literature (see **Shona and Ndebele literature**), Mabasa holds a first degree in linguistics and Shona and a diploma and postgraduate degree in media and communication studies. Before joining the Reserve Bank of Zimbabwe, he was a senior sub-editor of *The Herald*, a Zimbabwean daily. Mabasa made his first appearance in modern Shona poetry in the anthology *Tipeiwo Dariro: Manzwi Matsva Munhetembo* (Please Give Us Some Space: New Voices in Poetry) (1994), to which he contributed eighteen poems. The collection is a notable attempt to depart from the entrenched thematic and stylistic trends set in the 1960s by the pioneers of modern Shona poetry such as Joseph Kumbirai, Mordekai Hamutyinei, and Wilson Chivaura. Mabasa's prize-winning novel *Mapenzi* (Fools) (1999) is a powerful satire on post-independence Zimbabwe. The sociopolitical satire blends a wide range of aspects of African oral literature (see **oral literature and performance**), such as folk tales, myths, songs, and proverbs, with urban Shona slang and other dynamic aspects of the language to capture various serious social situations convincingly. The success of Mabasa's works has been due to his ability to simultaneously capture the social, psychological, economic, and political problems of modern Zimbabwean society while demonstrating the resilience, breadth, and depth of Shona traditional and contemporary expressive terms.

EMMANUEL CHIWOME

Mabuza, Lindiwe

b. 1938, Newcastle, Natal, South Africa

poet, short story writer, and cultural activist

In 1977 Lindiwe Mabuza joined the African National Congress (ANC) in exile and started making her name as a poet, short story writer, and cultural activist. From her position as chief ANC representative in Stockholm, she pays tribute in her earliest volume of poetry, *From ANC to Sweden* (1987), to assassinated premier Olof Palme. In her second book, *Letter to Letta* (1991), she turns a critical gaze on global racism and US imperialism from her official vantage point in Washington, DC. Images of victimization and survival persist into *Voices that Lead* (1998), poetic homages to the ANC leadership that brought democracy to South Africa. Many of her poems use imagery of motherhood, fertility, birth, and abortion in an epic, heroic voice – Mabuza speaks of being strongly influenced by the *izithakazelo* (IsiZulu praise poems) of her youth. Among her few short stories, she is celebrated for the piece entitled "Wake ... ", technically more experimental than most other black South African fiction of the time, which addresses the political awakening of an 8-year-old girl at a funeral. This appears, inter alia, in *One Never Knows: An Anthology of Black South African Women Writers in Exile* (1989), which Mabuza edited.

DOROTHY DRIVER

Macgoye (Oludhe-Macgoye), Marjorie Oludhe

b. 1928, Southampton, England

novelist, essayist, and poet

The Kenyan novelist, essayist, and poet Marjorie Oludhe Macgoye is often lauded by critics as "the mother of Kenyan literature" for her work bears keen witness to the coming of age of Kenya as a nation. Born in Southampton, England, she went to Kenya in 1954 to work as a bookseller for a Christian mission. In 1960, she married a Kenyan man and became immersed into local society. As a transplanted Englishwoman, her ability to establish herself within the Kenyan literary scene has indeed been remarkable. One of her earlier poems, "A Freedom Song" – originally published in *Poems from East Africa* (1971), the anthology edited by David Cook and David **Rubadiri** – firmly established her reputation when it was popularly received as part of the literature curriculum for secondary school students. In the poem, a poor rural girl is employed by mean relatives. When she dies after complications in childbirth, the feasting at her funeral is in marked contrast to her earlier treatment. Macgoye's first volume of poetry, *Song of Nyarloka and Other Poems* (1977), featured the 1,200-line poem "Song of Nyarloka," which was to become a template for many of her later works. Sung by Nyarloka, who like Macgoye herself has crossed over to her husband's community – *nyarloka* is the Luo word for "woman from abroad" – the poem tells a story that is both personal and that of the country as a whole. Nyarloka, like most of Macgoye's women characters, tethers her own story to the important historical landmarks in Kenya's evolution.

Macgoye's presence as a novelist was registered outside East Africa for the first time in 1986 when she won the Sinclair Prize for her novel *Coming to Birth*, published in the same year. It juxtaposes the story of a young woman's growth into maturity with the history of a country emerging from colonialism. *The Present Moment* (1987) is perhaps Macgoye's most ambitious novel. Set in an old people's refuge, it tells the story of seven Kenyan women who hail from different parts of the country. Although they are divided by language, religion, and ethnicity, they come to realize their essential sisterhood as they reveal to each other their intimate life histories. *Homing In* (1994) deals with more or less the same theme by presenting the memories of two women: one the widow of a colonial settler, and the other her African maid. Macgoye's other novels include *Murder in Majengo* (1972), *Street Life* (1987), and *Chira* (1997), which deals with the AIDS pandemic. Her second volume of poetry, *Make It Sing and Other Poems*, appeared in 1998. She has also published two works of non-fiction: *The Story of Kenya* (1986) and *Moral Issues in Kenya* (1996).

Macgoye's legacy to African literature is her transformation of a partial "outsider" status into one from which she can speak with empathy, and with the advantage of perspective, about life in modern Kenya. It also lies in her recognition of the important link between the private lives of individuals and the larger national story.

DAN ODHIAMBO OJWANG

al-Madanī, 'Ez-Eddīn

b. 1938, Tunisia

novelist, short story writer and journalist

Tunisian novelist, short story writer, and journalist al-Madanī is primarily known as a playwright. He is a prolific writer with a modernist approach and an interest in experimental literature. His book *al-Adab al-Tajrībī* (Experimental Literature) (1972) expounds on his theory in the field.

Al-Madanī's two collections of short stories, *Khurāfāt* (Superstitions) (1968) and *Min hikāyāt hādhā az-zamān* (Of the Stories of This Time) (1982) provide examples of his innovative approach to fiction as he uses the structure of the folk tale in narrating stories about modern Tunisia. He also addresses the issue of the individual and authority in his writings. As for his concern with power and society's social structure, it is the subject of his quartet of plays where the events occur within the context of Arab–Islamic history, *Thawrat Ṣāḥib al-Ḥimār* (The Revolt of the Donkey Owner) (1972), *Diwān al-Zinj* (The Council of the Negroes) (1972), *al-Ḥallāj* (Hallaj) (1973), and *Mawlāy as-Sulṭān al-Ḥasan al-Ḥafṣī* (My Master Sultan Hasan al-Hafsi) (1977). One of al-Madani's major preoccupations is the issue of exploitation in developing countries.

Further reading

Fontaine, Jean (1990) *La Littérature Tunisienne contemporaine* (Contemporary Tunisian Literature), Paris: CNRS.

AIDA A. BAMIA

Maddy, Yulisa Amadu (Pat)

b. 1936, Freetown, Sierra Leone

playwright, novelist, and choreographer

The Sierra Leonean playwright, novelist, and choreographer Yulisa Maddy was born and grew up in Freetown, but he left for France and Britain in 1958. He started his career as a broadcaster in Denmark and Britain, writing and producing radio plays. He also worked for Radio Sierra Leone and was a choreographer for the Zambian National Dance Theater in 1970. Maddy's early plays, which were initially produced on the BBC African Service, were published in 1971 as *Obasai and Other Plays*. These plays are often an innovative combination of modern dramatic forms and traditional African, especially Sierra Leonean Creole, dances and songs. Maddy's novel, *No Past, No Present, No Future*, originally published in 1973, was, like many postcolonial fictions of the period, concerned with the failure of the dream of independence and decolonization; structuring the work in the form of a political novel of education (see **education and schools**), the author registers the reactions of his young protagonists to the uncertain drama of political life in a fictional African country and the tough choices they have to make as they come of age. While the themes of the novel are familiar ones in the literature of the late 1960s and 1970s, Maddy's novel is unique and unusual in its use of Creole phrases, idioms, and popular songs.

SIMON GIKANDI

Magagula, Salayedvwa Modison

b. 1958, Swaziland

playwright

Salayedvwa Modison Magagula was born in Swaziland and obtained his teacher's diploma at William Pitcher College in Manzini. Introduced to writing by the special workshop for writers in Mbabane in 1986, Magagula blossomed into a multifaceted dramatist, poet, narrator, and prose writer. Over a decade this versatile writer has produced short stories, poems, and plays in siSwati. He first contributed to siSwati literature in a co-authored work, *Ingcamu* (A Journey's Provision) (1987), and *Idubukele* (Dinner is Served!) (1988). His major works include an anthology of twenty short stories, *Indlanganye* (Our Gain) (1989), a one-act play, *Asingeni Lapho* (It is None of Our Business) (1989), a full length play, *Tentile* (Hoist with Your Own Petard) (1990), and *Kwesukesukela* (Once Upon a Time) (1990). Magagula addresses social themes like postcolonial life in Swaziland (see **colonialism, neocolonialism, and postcolonialism**),

juvenile delinquency, and sectarianism. In 1989, he conceived and founded the first traveling theater in Swaziland, the Siphila Nje Drama Society (Such is Our Way of Life Drama Society). Fashioned in the style of Brecht's Berliner Ensemble and Yoruba Apidan theater, Siphila Nje performs sketches in the streets and community halls. These sketches are sometimes performed in one-man shows, satirizing topical issues like religious sects, decaying morality, and political dishonesty.

ZODWA MOTSA

Magona, Sindiwe

b. 1943, South Africa

autobiographer and short story writer

Sindiwe Magona's life story of growing up and living in apartheid South Africa is detailed in her two-part **autobiography**, *To My Children's Children* (1990) and *Forced to Grow* (1992), which adopt the speaking voice of a Xhosa grandmother bequeathing her cultural heritage and history to the young. Her writing takes as its primary subject matter the destruction wrought upon African families and communities by various legislations enacted by the apartheid state (see **apartheid and post-apartheid**), and, more recently, the ravages of the rampant AIDS pandemic. Often garnered from first-hand experiences, the stories in *Living, Loving and Lying Awake at Night* (1991) expose the plight of domestic workers, while the historical novel *Mother to Mother* (1998) is based on the chain of events that led to the fatal stabbing of American Fulbright Scholar Amy Biehl in Cape Town in 1993. Biehl's death received extensive media coverage and became one of the most sensational stories of the late apartheid era; Magona's account is unique in its sensitive recreation of the seldom-glimpsed world of the killer and his family, with the killer's mother placed on center stage. Diagnosing the ills of her society with a keen eye, Magona searches for antidotes in the empowerment of women and a synthesis between community and individual.

MEG SAMUELSON

Magwa, Wiseman

b. 1962, Zimbabwe

playwright

The Zimbabwean writer Wiseman Magwa is one of the few Shona artists who has blended oral performance with written texts in order to intervene in issues related to social stability and nationalism and nation-building (see **nationalism and post-nationalism**). From the late 1980s through the 2000s, Magwa, a Shona lecturer at Gweru Teachers' College, together with colleague and fellow playwright Willie Chigidi, has steadily written scripts for local educational drama and community theater under the banner of the Midlands Drama Association for Schools and Colleges. They co-authored *Atsunzunya Rega Atsikwe* (One who Closes One's Eyes should be Left to be Trampled) (1991), a satire on false prophets in the post-independence era. Magwa's plays "Nhumbu Ndeyenyu" (You are Responsible for the Pregnancy) and "Tawanda Mwana'ngu" (Tawanda, My Son), published under the collective title *Mafaro* (Carnal Pleasure) (1990) were the result of work done in community theaters in Zimbabwe. The first play explores the problem of determining paternity in a promiscuous relationship, while the second urges the young to adhere to the ways of their people. Magwa's other play, *Njuzu* (Water Spirits) (1991), allegorically traces the now familiar plight of the former combatants in the war of liberation as they move from the war front, through the demobilization process, into destitution and political oblivion. Magwa has also published works on the AIDS epidemic as well as educational books on various aspects of Shona language teaching.

EMMANUEL CHIWOME

Maḥfūz, Najīb (Naguib Mahfouz)

b. 1911, Cairo, Egypt; d. 2006, Cairo, Egypt

novelist and Nobel Prize-winner

Najīb Maḥfūz is the Arab world's most famous littérateur, Egyptian novelist, and 1988 Nobel Laureate in Literature. Until his retirement in 1971 Maḥfūz spent his working life in the cultural sector of the civil service; during the 1950s and 1960s that involved work in the cinema, one of his great enthusiasms and a medium for which he wrote many scenarios. The writing of fiction was thus for many years an avocation, but it was one that he pursued with a relentless devotion, arranging his time with a typically methodical approach so that he could spend time each day writing.

Maḥfūz's writing career began in earnest while he was still a student, working on a degree in philosophy in the early 1930s. He penned a number of short stories, many of them concerned with the philosophical issues that were the subject of his own studies at the time. He was also interested in the current trend to study the ancient history of Egypt, and that led him not only to translate into Arabic a popular study of that period by James Baikie, but also to set some of his earliest works in ancient Egyptian contexts. The 1930s were a decade in which many Egyptian littérateurs were turning their attention to the newly emerging **novel** form. In another typical gesture, Maḥfūz's reaction to this trend involved reading John Drinkwater's manual, *An Outline of Literature*, followed by a systematic reading of many of the Western examples of the genre that were included in this survey work.

When Maḥfūz embarked upon his novel-writing project, these various strands came together in three novels that are set in ancient Egypt: *'Abath al-Aqdar* (Mockery of Fates) (1939), *Radubis* (Rhodopis) (1943), and *Kifah Tiba* (Conflict at Thebes) (1944). Maḥfūz tells us that he had made plans to write a whole series of such works, but a combination of factors – not least the impact of World War II and the disastrous state of Egyptian political and social life – led him to focus his attention on the representation of the present. Thus began the development of a writing career that made the novel genre a central player in the development of Arab societies in the period immediately before and after independence. His novels of the 1940s, the majority of them named after quarters in the older parts of Cairo, portrayed the daily lives, the loves, and the struggles of the urban middle and lower classes, with an authenticity and attention to detail that were entirely new, and with an ever-improving application of novelistic technique that was to provide future generations of novelists with a solid basis upon which to build and experiment. Outstanding among these novels is *Midaq Alley* (*Zuqaq al-Midaqq*) (1947), in which the tensions involved in the love affair between 'Abbas the barber and Hamidah the acknowledged beauty of the alley in question become emblematic of Egypt as it suffered under British army occupation and aspired to modernize itself.

This series of novels reached a culminating point in a single monumental contribution to modern Arabic fiction, Maḥfūẓ's renowned Trilogy, published in 1956 and 1957: *Bayn al-Qasrayn* (Between the Two Palaces; English translation: *Palace Walk*, 1990), *Qasr al-Shawq* (English translation: *Palace of Desire*, 1991), and *al-Sukkariyyah* (English translation: *Sugar Street*, 1992), a work on which the Nobel Committee lavished praise in its 1988 citation. Maḥfūẓ acknowledges spending five years on researching and writing this work; so complex were the narrative strands running through the work that he maintained separate files on each of the major characters. Here all the trials and aspirations of the Egyptian people, and by extension those of other nations deeply impacted by Western colonialism, were laid out on a huge canvas that portrayed the circumstances of a single family, that of Sayyid 'Abd al-Jawwad (Gawwad), as the members of its different generations confronted or resisted the inevitable forces of change. It is in the second volume that we encounter all the tensions involved in the struggle between the old and the new, as the younger son of the family, Kamal (closely modeled, it would appear, on the author himself), goes to teachers' college and is introduced to the methods of modern science – not least the theories of Darwin – and then has to face the fury of his tyrannical father, whose beliefs in traditional values and teachings do not prevent him from indulging to the full in the pleasures of life during his nocturnal excursions. This volume also reveals the ways in which change is having its impact upon class structures in Egypt. The availability of higher education to members of the middle class, and indeed the initial stages of coeducation, lead to some interesting encounters between classes and genders. Kamal himself is smitten with the sister of one of his student colleagues, and the novel is replete with his musings on his hopeless love, all expressed through a combination of dialogue and interior monologue which displays Maḥfūẓ's increasing sophistication in novelistic technique. In the third volume, a third generation is portrayed (once again through a different spatial environment). 'Abd al-Jawwad's grandsons typify the societal tensions that were to become evident in the early years of the Egyptian revolution and the era of President 'Abd al-Nasir (Nasser): one is a member of the Muslim Brethren, the other of the Communist Party. Both groups were united in their diehard opposition to British colonial occupation and the corruption of the *ancien régime*, and both found their members consigned to jail (or worse) once the new revolutionary regime was in place. Thus, when Maḥfūẓ's Trilogy appeared in 1956–7, it provided for a younger generation of newly independent Egyptians (and Arabs) a fictional history of the recent past, the period of struggle and sacrifice from which they had just emerged. The building of the Aswan High Dam, the Bandung Conference, and the Suez debacle of 1956, all indicated the beginnings of a new world order, and Maḥfūẓ's novelistic monument was read throughout the Arab world as not merely an entirely new level of fictional writing in Arabic but a totally realistic portrayal of the circumstances that had made the struggle so necessary.

The Trilogy had in fact been completed before the Egyptian revolution of 1952, but such was its size that it took four years to see publication. In those years Maḥfūẓ wrote no fiction. While many have suggested that he was waiting, like many others, to see what particular shape the new post-independence society would take, it can be observed on a more practical plane that he concentrated his attentions at this time on the writing of a number of film scenarios. When he did resume his fictional career, it was with his most controversial work, *Awlad Haratina* (1959, 1967; English translations: *Children of Gebelawi*, 1962, 1997; *Children of the Alley*, 1996). In a five-section work originally published in serial form in the Cairene newspaper *al-Ahram* (almost all Maḥfūẓ's works have initially appeared in Cairo dailies or weeklies), Maḥfūẓ traces the life of a "quarter" (one of his continuingly favorite symbols) monitored by an overseer named Gebelawi who lives in a big house outside the walls. Each of the five sections shows how a particular leader manages to direct the lives of the quarter's folk and also how to keep their proclivity of violence under control. In succession Adham (Adam), Jabal ("mountain" – Moses), Rifa'ah ("resurrection" – Jesus), and Qasim ("apportioner" – Muhammad) appear to serve as leaders and guides, but in the section devoted to the fifth figure, 'Arafah ("scientia"), we read of an encounter in the big house outside the walls, during the course of which Gebelawi is killed. Thus does Maḥfūẓ address himself in classic allegorical form to the dilemma of the encounter between religious belief and science (which, it will be recalled, had been an early concern of his). The literary value of the work was thrust aside as the religious establishment of Egypt, led by the sheikhs of al-Azhar in Cairo, protested at the allegedly blasphemous implications of the work. While *al-Ahram* continued to publish the work until its conclusion, an agreement was reached whereby it would not be published in book form (it eventually appeared in somewhat altered form in Beirut in 1967). During the course of the enormous controversy that surrounded Salman Rushdie's novel, *The Satanic Verses* (during Maḥfūẓ's "Nobel Year," 1988–9), this entire dispute was raised in Egypt once again and Maḥfūẓ was himself subjected to a death-threat, one that almost succeeded when he was stabbed in the neck in 1994 on the anniversary of the announcement of his Nobel award.

The year 1971 saw Maḥfūẓ's retirement from the civil service, and he was at last able to devote himself full-time to reading and writing. He became a regular contributor to the pages of *al-Ahram* (where he joined his literary colleagues, the playwright Tawfiq **al-Ḥakim** (d. 1987) and Yūsuf **Idris** (d. 1991), the acknowledged genius of the short story genre). Many of the novels that

Maḥfūẓ wrote during this period reflect his growing concern and often anger at the policies being adopted by the Sādāt regime, most particularly the social effects of the so-called *infitah* (economic "opening-up" of Egyptian markets) which served to financially cripple large segments of the middle class. Alongside these more local concerns, however, Maḥfūẓ was also joining the younger generation of novelists (most of whom acknowledged his status as the founder of the mature genre) in experimenting in varying ways with both theme and technique. Thus, while many of his novels of the 1980s and 1990s revisit earlier themes and techniques – *al-Baqi min al-Zaman Sa'ah* (Only an Hour Left) (1982), for example, as an updated kind of trilogy, and *Hadith al-Sabah wa-al-Masa'* (Morning and Evening Conversation) (1987) as a replication of the alphabetical organization of the earlier *al-Maraya* (Mirrors) (1972) (albeit concerned this time with a single family) – his most important contributions are those in which he points the genre in new and different directions. Within such a framework, *The Harafish* (1994) (*Malhamat al-Harafish*) (1977), *Arabian Nights and Days* (1995) (*Layali Alf Laylah*) (1982), and *Echoes of an Autobiography* (1997) (*Asda' al-Sirah al-Dhatiyyah*) (1995) stand out for their continuing participation in the process of expanding the world of Arabic fiction, not least through an invocation of the particularities of the earlier traditions of Arabic narrative.

Further reading

Beard, Michael and Haydar, Adnan (eds) (1993) *Naguib Mahfouz: From Regional Fame to Global Recognition*, Syracuse: Syracuse University Press.

El-Enany, Rasheed (1993) *Naguib Mahfouz: The Pursuit of Meaning*, London: Routledge.

Le Gassick, Trevor (ed.) (1991) *Critical Perspectives on Naguib Mahfouz*, Washington, DC: Three Continents Press.

Milson, Menahem (1998) *Naguib Mahfouz, Novelist–Philosopher of Cairo*, New York: St Martin's Press.

Moosa, Matti (1994) *The Early Novels of Naguib Mahfouz*, Gainesville: University of Florida Press.

Peled, Mattityahu (1983) *Religion My Own*, New Brunswick: Transaction Books.

Somekh, Sasson (1973) *The Changing Rhythm*, Leiden: E.J. Brill.

ROGER ALLEN

Mahjoub, Jamal

b. 1960, London, UK

novelist and short story writer

The Anglo-Sudanese novelist and short story writer Jamal Mahjoub was born in London to an English mother and a Sudanese father; he spent his childhood years in the English Midlands and later in Khartoum, returning to England in 1981 to study geology at the University of Sheffield. Mahjoub's novels belong to a new tradition of African writing that is concerned with the crisis of politics and culture on the continent from the perspective of hybrid, rather than simply monolithic, nationalist experiences. In his novels, especially *The Navigation of a Rainmaker* (1989), he experiments with fictional techniques to try and recover the contested history of the Sudan and to find an idiom for shifting experiences often told from competing points of view. In his second novel, *In the Hour of the Signs* (1996), he presents a panoramic history of the turbulent history of the Sudan in the nineteenth century, focusing on the events surrounding the confrontation between the Mahdist forces and the British at the Battle of Omdurman. Mahjoub's novels are often generated by historical events, but, like some of the postmodern writers who have influenced him, the novelist is not interested in the past for its own sake; rather, history is used as a mirror through which his readers can gaze at their postcolonial predicament (see **modernity and modernism**; **colonialism, neocolonialism, and postcolonialism**). In *Wings of Dust* (1999), Mahjoub turns his attention to the question of hybrid identities, using a fragmented postmodern style to negotiate the widening gap between identities secured by colonial modernity and resurgent Islamic traditions.

SIMON GIKANDI

Maïga Kâ, Aminata

b. 1940, St Louis, Senegal; d. 2005, Dakar, Senegal

novelist, essayist, teacher, and political activist

The Senegalese novelist, essayist, teacher, and political activist Aminata Maïga Kâ shares the social concerns of her peers, yet she takes a stronger stance in regard to feminism and women's rights. In her works, Kâ, a former secretary of state for women's status, addresses social problems such as marital infidelity, rape, single parenthood, and forced marriage, often denouncing injustice and calling for a return to humane values.

Kâ's most popular works of fiction, *La Voie du salut* (The Path of Salvation) and *Le Miroir de la vie* (The Mirror of Life), appeared in 1985. The first novella opens at the deathbed of Rokhaya and contains recollections of her life, including the difficulties she faced as a woman living in a traditional society and the subsequent marital problems faced by her daughter, Rabiatou. The story intimates that women should not abandon tradition but weigh its costs and benefits carefully. The second novella portrays the downfall of a bourgeois family and the pain that the competition for vain prestige can entail. In *En votre nom et au mien* (In Your Name and in Mine) (1989) and in *Brisures de vies* (Shards of Lives) (1998), Kâ focuses on poverty, but she also uses the novels to present her commitment to socialist values.

Further reading

D'Alméïda, Irène (1994) *Francophone African Women Writers: Destroying the Emptiness of Silence*, Gainesville: University Presses of Florida.

LISA McNEE

Maillu, David

b. 1939, Kenya

novelist

With more than forty titles to his name, David (Gian) Maillu is easily Kenya's most prolific author outside academic institutions and the country's major producer of **popular literature**. Born among the Akamba people of eastern Kenya, Maillu is a largely self-taught writer. From the beginning of his writing career in the early 1970s, Maillu caught the public imagination with his unprecedented frankness in the representation of sexual matters and his concern with the other seamy side of urban life in Kenya, including infidelity and drunkenness. In his most famous works, *Unfit for Human Consumption* (1973), *My Dear Bottle* (1973), and *After 4.30* (1974), Maillu surpassed Charles **Mang'ua** as the most explicit writer in Kenya, making him at once popular but equally shunned by those who felt his works went against the grain of common cultural decency. Nevertheless, in his later years Maillu has tried to refurbish his image, and in works such as *For Mbatha and Rabaka* (1980) and the more voluminous *The Broken Drum* (1991), he has tried to extricate his works from the notorious "bedroom scenes" of his early works as he seeks to be taken seriously as a novelist of contemporary Kenyan society. There has been much debate in Kenya on whether Maillu's writings deserve greater scholarly attention or even whether they can be taken seriously as works of popular literature and culture, but in the end his distinctiveness arises from the fact that he has, in Henry Indangasi's terms, been able to avoid the bigger ideological and political posturing of some of Africa's university-based authors.

Further reading

Indangasi, Henry (1996) "David G. Maillu," in Bernth Lindfors (ed.) *Dictionary of Literary Biography,* Detroit, Michigan: Gale Research, pp. 150–8.

GEORGE ODERA OUTA

Maimane, Arthur

b. 1932, South Africa; d. 2005, London, England

journalist and writer

The South African journalist and writer Arthur Maimane started working as a journalist soon after graduating from high school, working as a reporter, editor, and features writer for several South African news organization before he was forced into exile in 1958. He continued his journalist career in several African countries in the first decade of independence in the 1960s, working variously for the news agency Reuters as a correspondent in Ghana and Tanzania and for the British Broadcasting Corporation in London. During his distinguished career as a journalist, Maimane has also written stories dealing with township life and racial and sexual relations in South Africa under apartheid (see **apartheid and post-apartheid**). These stories were published in leading African journals such as *Transition* and *Drum*. Maimane's novel, *Victims* (1976), which belongs to the tradition of protest writing in South Africa, is a haunting portrait of a black man humiliated by the culture of racial segregation and forced into expressing himself through sexual rage. In this novel, as in his short stories, Maimane uses his reporter's skills to present both the surface and hidden rules that govern a racialized society, and their human consequences. Maimane has also written short plays.

SIMON GIKANDI

Makhalisa, Barbara

b. 1949, Zimbabwe

novelist

The Zimbabwean writer Barbara Makhalisa is one of the most prolific novelists in Ndebele (see **Shona and Ndebele literature**). She attended both rural and urban schools before training as a teacher. She is the second woman to be published in Ndebele after S. **Mlilo**. Makhalisa began her writing career in response to the Rhodesia Literature Bureau literature competitions, and her novel *Qilindini* (Crafty Person) (1974) was the first winner of the award in Ndebele. The novel focuses on a rural community during the period of colonialism (see **colonialism, neocolonialism, and postcolonialism**), which is duped by a charlatan who hides behind a decadent Ndebele chief. A young African police detective ultimately saves the community. The novel celebrates Western institutions of education and knowledge over African experiences (see **education and schools**). Makhalisa's works reflect common perceptions of Ndebele literature as a tool for spreading Christian values (see **Christianity and Christian missions**). At the same time, her writings reflect the interface between Africa and the West. In *Umendo* (Marriage) (1977), for example, she celebrates Christian marriage values in the face of African family instability. In the novel *Impilo Yinkinga* (Life is a Mystery) (1983), Makhalisa presents a condemnation of carnal pleasures, which are perceived, within Christianity, as the root cause of family instability in modern society. Her works and their central vision reinforce the common belief that Shona and Ndebele writers of the colonial period tended to see their works primarily as instruments of teaching, or preaching, Christian values to their newly literate African readers.

EMMANUEL CHIWOME

Makouta-Mboukou, Jean-Pierre

b. 1929, Congo-Brazzaville

novelist, poet, literary critic, and essayist

Jean-Pierre Makouta-Mboukou is a novelist, poet, literary critic, and essayist originally from Congo-Brazzaville. He has lived in exile for many years. His fiction and essays draw inspiration from the tragedies of his country, including: *coups d'état*, civil wars, and ethnic cleansings. These tragedies have an origin that writing does not often express – the curse of oil. But there is also, beyond the discourse on African peoples and the victimized workers in the capital, a veritable universalizing language in his works. His writings are committed to a humanist and religious tradition, and sacred, secular, and exile mix together with violence and the search for liberty. From *Les Initiés* (The Initiated) (1970) to *L'Homme-aux-Pataugas* (1992), continuing to *Les Exilés de la forêt vierge* (The Exiles from the Virgin Forest) (1981), the writer uses his works to create a space for reconciliation and peace. The executioner and the victim seem linked by the

same destiny, and often see their roles inverted by the unpredictability of history. In addition to a constant mysticism, Makouta-Mboukou creates a sort of theory of "return to the source," a return to what he considers to be supreme human values.

Further reading

Makouta-Mboukou, Jean-Pierre (1993) *Les Littératures de l'exil* (The Literature of Exile), Paris: L'Harmattan.
——(1996) *Enfers et paradis. Des littératures antiques aux littératures nègres* (Hell and Heaven. Ancient Literatures in Negro Literatures), Paris: Honoré Champion.

ALEXIE TCHEUYAP

El Maleh, Edmond Amran

b. 1917, Safi, Morocco

novelist

El Maleh was born into a Jewish family in the Moroccan port of Safi, a milieu he has used in several of his novels. In 1945, he became a founding member of the Moroccan Communist Party; from 1948 he served on its Central Committee. After Moroccan independence in 1956 he resigned from the party, and moved to France in 1965. He did not publish his first literary work, *Parcours immobile* (Motionless Journey) (1980), until the age of 63. Since then, however, he has produced five novels, including *Aïlen ou la Nuit du récit* (Aïlen or the Night of the Story) (1983), *Abner Abounour* (1995), and perhaps his most important work, *Mille ans, un jour* (A Thousand Years, One Day) (1986). *Mille ans, un jour* recreates the cosmopolitan cultural world of Moroccan Jews in the cities along the coast, before and after the colonial conquest. Its complex narrative structure, a hallmark of El Maleh's work, mixes voices and stories to produce a compelling overall picture of cultural mixity. El Maleh's novels lament the dispersal of the Moroccan Jewish community, and commemorate a period in which Arabs and Jews lived in an atmosphere of mutual tolerance.

Further reading

Scharfman, Ronnie (1993) "The Other's Other: The Moroccan–Jewish Trajectory of Edmond Amran el Maleh," *Yale French Studies* 82, 1: 135–45.

SETH GRAEBNER

Malindzisa, Gubudla Aaron

b. 1944, South Africa

playwright and translator

The South African writer Gubudla Aaron Malindzisa was educated at Ngwane primary and Emjindini secondary schools. He attained a Diploma Iuris from the University of the North (1981) and a DLitt from Marlborough University (2000). He is one of the pioneers of South African writers in siSwati. Notable among his contributions are a series of language grammar books for schools, five novels including *Sandla Semtsetfo* (The Arm of the Law) (1986), *Egaleni Lenyoni* (Deep in Trouble) (1987), and plays such as *Walutfota Lolumanti* (Touched a Hornets' Nest) (1997) and *Ngoneni Nkhosi Yami* (Why Me, Lord?) (1988). He has published collections of short stories including *Kahleni Phela* (Wait a Minute) (1988), and *Letiphuma Embiteni* (Fresh from the Pot) (1991); his works in translations include *Lifu Lelimnyama* (The Dark Cloud) (1988) and *Umhlaba Uyahlaba* (Life is Tough) (1986); he is also the author of two volumes of anthology entitled *Sekuhlwile* (Dusk has Come) (1988) and *Sekuhlonywe Tintsi* (It's Story Time) (1990). Malindzisa's major milestone in siSwati literature is his participation in the first translation of the Bible into siSwati, and his work as a member of the lexicography unit working on a siSwati–English dictionary, as well as in the co-founding of the Umhlahlandlela Writers' Guild in Mphumalanga Province. Malindzisa has also been involved in a project committed to the preservation of siSwati culture and literature in database and film.

ZODWA MOTSA

Mamani, Abdoulaye

b. 1932, Zinder, Niger; d. 1993, Niger

poet and novelist

From the start of his career as a trade unionist, the Nigerien writer Abdoulaye Mamani wrote poetry and prose that continuously sought to bring politics and aesthetics together. In 1972, he composed and published two volumes of poetry, *Poémérides* and *Eboniques* (Ebony Women). The first volume, *Poémérides*, focuses on African subjects and portrays the lives of African women, their relation to traditional life, and their quest for independence and equality. Some of the poems in this volume also deal with the aftermath of colonization and how that institution made its imprint on African society. The second volume, *Eboniques*, turns to the United States and presents poems on subjects such as Angela Davis and the "hippie" movement. This volume concludes with a longer poem dedicated to "Ebony," a generalized portrait of the black woman. Mamani also wrote many pieces for the theater, an introduction to *L'Anthologie de Poésie de Combat* (The Anthology of Poetry of Combat) (1972) and a novel, *Sarraounia* (Queen). His novel, published in 1980, was adapted into a film by Med Hondo and won first prize at the 1987 FESPACO film festival in Ouagadougou, Burkina Faso. Mamani was killed in a car crash in 1993 en route from Zinder to Niamey, where he was to accept the Boubou Hama Prize for Literature.

SUSAN GORMAN

Mammeri, Mouloud

b. 1917, Taourirt-Mimoun, Algeria; d.1989, Ain-Defla, Algeria

novelist and poet

Mouloud Mammeri was born in Kabylia, the mountainous Berber-speaking heartland of Algeria, and devoted his career to the study and promotion of Berber culture. He published four novels, two edited volumes of poetry collected and translated from the original Kabyle, a grammar and dictionary of the Kabyle language, and a large number of articles on Berber cultures across North Africa. Mammeri received his education in the French high schools of Morocco and Algeria before moving to Paris to prepare for entry into the prestigious École Normale Supérieure. The Second World War precipitated his return to Algeria; he was twice conscripted into the French army. After the war, he taught high school and began to write; he published his first novel, *La Colline oubliée* (The Forgotten Hill) in Paris in 1952. His second, *The Sleep of the Just* (*Le Sommeil des justes*) (1955), continued in the "ethnographic" vein of the first, while *L'Opium et le bâton* (The Opium and the Stick) (1965) moved toward broader novelistic portrayal, and also reached a broader audience with a film version by Ahmed Rachedi (1970). In the late 1960s and 1970s, Mammeri turned his attention to scholarly publications, and brought out his compilations of verse by the Kabyle poet Si Mohand ou Mhand, a Kabyle grammar and dictionary, and several Berber children's tales. He returned to fiction with *La Traversée* (The Crossing) (1986), a departure from his previous, more realistic work. Meanwhile, his scholarly production continued undiminished until his death in a car accident on 25 February 1989, returning from a conference in Oujda, Morocco.

The publication of *La Colline oubliée* placed Mammeri among the "Generation of '52," a group of Algerian novelists including Mohammed **Dib** and Mouloud **Feraoun** who also published their first books that year. Like the members of its cohort, it presents a wealth of ethnographic detail, documenting the young adulthood of a protagonist with a background similar to the author's. Like many first novels of Francophone African authors, it ends with the hero leaving his village for a problematic future, uncertain even of the possibility of return. Mammeri's novel is distinguished by its marked lyricism, together with a deep respect for oral traditions. When the novel won a French literary prize, certain Arab Algerians saw it as a deliberate attempt to separate the Arab and Kabyle peoples; this was only the first misunderstanding between the author and the proponents of Arab unity. Whereas the characters of Mammeri's first novel are relatively rooted in their village, Arezki, protagonist of *Le Sommeil des justes*, is a sort of Berber "angry young man" looking for an

elusive way out of the traps of colonial society and its impoverishments, both literal and figurative. These traps are still present for Dr Bachir Lazrak, the Westernized protagonist of *L'Opium et le bâton*, wrapped up in cultural contradictions and political impasses during the Algerian war.

In post-independence Algeria, writing about such tensions did not suit a government wishing to proclaim a national unity based on Islam, the Arabic language, and the collective experience of the war. Neither did Mammeri's wholehearted promotion of the Kabyle culture and language please the ruling class, and in the late 1960s the author found himself removed from his position as a professor of Berber anthropology at the University of Algiers. As if in answer, he turned in the 1970s from fiction to scholarship to preserve a disappearing cultural heritage. His collections of oral poetry, notably the works of the late nineteenth-century poet Si Mohand ou Mhand in *Les Isefra, poèmes de Si Mohand-Ou-Mhand* (1969), constitute one of his most important contributions to the field of Berber studies. In March of 1980, the authorities canceled a lecture Mammeri had scheduled at the University of Tizi Ouzou in Kabylia, and rumors spread of his arrest. This triggered the riots known as the "Berber Spring," a foreshadowing of the unrest that spread through the country beginning in 1988. Since then, the Algerian government has constantly rejected demands for cultural recognition from the Kabyles, despite Mammeri's optimism at the time of his death.

Mammeri had little patience for political activism himself, and readers may see his most direct response to the political crisis facing Algeria in the 1980s in his last novel, *La Traversée*, which is at once Mammeri's most lyrical and least realistic work. Mourad, the disenchanted main character, represents a grown-up Arezki; having worked for the FLN, he has returned in triumph to an independent Algiers, and then witnessed the steady degeneration of one-party politics. Early in the novel, Mourad publishes an article which uses the parable of a desert caravan cut off from its heroes and prey to the lies of its ideologues to criticize a collapsing social revolution. The chilly reception of this article forces Mourad to resign from his newspaper, and he plans his escape from the dead end of a silenced Kabyle journalist by fleeing to Paris. However, a trip to the Sahara Desert, where he meets Tuaregs ethnically related to his own Kabyle Berbers, makes him realize that flight is not an option, and he returns to his mountain village. There, amid general dilapidation and social collapse, the elders do not recognize him, and he dies, a victim of the physical and cultural suffocation inflicted on the Kabyles. Whether their sympathies lie with the pessimism of *La Traversée* or the optimism of Mammeri's scholarly works, Berber activists continue to recognize him as one of the founders and principal animators of their movement, a powerful presence in Algerian cultural affairs.

Further reading

CELFAN Review (1984) *Mouloud Mammeri: Special Issue* 3, 2.

Mammeri, Mouloud (1956) *The Sleep of the Just*, trans. Len Ortzen, London: Cresset Press.

Mortimer, Mildred (1982) "The *Isefra* of Si Mohand-ou-Mohand: The Song of a Berber Poet," in Lemuel A. Johnson (ed.) *Toward Defining the African Aesthetic*, Washington, DC: Three Continents Press.

SETH GRAEBNER

Mang'ua, Charles

b. 1939

novelist

Educated as an economist at Makerere University College, the Kenyan novelist Charles Mang'ua was one of the few authors of his generation who did not start their writing career at university. After graduating from Makerere he worked as a government social worker and international civil servant. The publication of *Son of Woman* in 1971 brought Mang'ua both fame and notoriety. Written in the tradition of the thriller, concerned with urban popular themes such as prostitution and promiscuity, drinking and nightlife, and written in racy language, Mang'ua's novel appealed to East African readers who saw it as a substitute for

Western entertainment. Its first print run of 10,000 copies was sold out in six months, an unprecedented record in East African publishing. While the novel replicated the familiar language of the American department store romance, its representation of local scenes and situations and the familiar drama of urban life in Africa were its most appealing qualities. Mang'ua tried to capitalize on the success of his first novel with *A Tail in the Mouth* (1972), a novel in which he used popular romantic language and a picaresque plot to deal with serious themes such as landlessness and the alienation of modern urban life. The novel was awarded the Jomo Kenyatta Prize for Literature, Kenya's major literary award. In 1986, after disappearing from the literary scene for almost fifteen years, Mang'ua published *Son of Woman in Mombasa*, the sequel to his first novel, and *Kanina and I* (1994). But by the time Mang'ua returned to the literary scene the kind of popular romantic fiction he had introduced in 1971 had become a staple of publishing in East Africa and the field of **popular literature** had become one of the most dynamic in the region.

SIMON GIKANDI

Mansour, Joyce

b. 1928, England; d. 1986, Paris, France

poet

A Francophone writer, Mansour was born Joyce Ades in England of Egyptian parents. After the death of her first husband when she was only 19, she married Samir Mansour and moved to Paris with him in the late 1940s, living there until her death. André Breton spoke enthusiastically of her first collection of poetry *Cri* (Cries) published in 1953. Known as a surrealist with multicultural strands, she nevertheless alluded to Egypt frequently, especially since her 1965 collection *Carré blanc* (Blank Square). Like that of her surrealist contemporaries, Mansour's poetry revolves around the eroticism of the body; she also depicts cruelty, violence, and ritual sacrifice in her poetry, in which some critics have seen echoes of ancient Egyptian mythology. Her style projects obsessive desires as well as bitter humor. Her imagery is powerful and stunning, sounding at times like hallucinatory phantasms. Her themes are love and death joined together, and she echoes occasionally and ironically the sacred in a carnal context. In the poems collected in *Phallus et momies* (Phallus and Mummies) and *Faire signe au machiniste* (Signal to the Mechanic), published in 1969 and 1977 respectively, Mansour is often graphic in her description of voluptuous encounters. Her poetry clearly constitutes an act of personal liberation, unhindered by the notion of sin or social control. Mansour also wrote narrative prose, which was no less in quantity and quality than her poetry; among her major works in this category are *Jules César* (Julius Caesar), a 1956 novel, and *Iles flottantes* (Floating Islands) published in 1973. Like her poetry, these novels are marked by their use of the language associated with the surreal imagination.

Further reading

Mansour, Joyce (1991) *Prose et poésie: oeuvres complètes* (Prose and Poetry: Complete Works), Arles: Actes Sud.

FERIAL J. GHAZOUL

Mapanje, Jack

b. 1944, Malawi

poet

One of the first significant writers to emerge from Malawi in the years of the Kamuzu Banda dictatorship, Jack Mapanje started writing poetry in order to express himself under very strict conditions of censorship and political repression. In the circumstances, his early poems, collected in *Of Chameleons and Gods* (1981) were very cryptic and coded representations of the political situation in postcolonial Malawi and the poet's relationship to a culture in crisis (see **colonialism, neocolonialism, and postcolonialism**). The political poems in this collection were highly allegorical. In order to find a voice in a situation in which writers and dissidents were under constant state pressure, Mapanje saw his poems as a means of securing the personal voice and overcoming the muffling engendered by the government. One way in which he could affirm the poet's voice was to provide sketches of places and situations outside Malawi, places Mapanje had lived in, such as London, or to assemble and reimagine the voices of people in familiar situations, such as the students in Soweto during the 1976 uprising against apartheid (see **apartheid and post-apartheid**). In spite of the coded nature of his political poems, Mapanje was arrested by the government of Malawi and imprisoned, without trial, at the Mikuyu maximum security prison for almost four years. The poems Mapanje wrote in prison and soon after were often attempts to find a voice that would turn his dehumanizing circumstances into objects of artistic reflection or angry responses to the people who had imprisoned him. The poems are collected in *The Chattering Wagtails of Mikuyu Prison* (1993). After his release from prison, Mapanje went into exile, living mostly in Britain. In the 1990s he wrote a series of new poems looking back on his imprisonment from the vantage point of exile, musing on his own displacement, his attachment and detachment from his roots, and the possibility of coming to terms with the people who had imprisoned and tortured him. These poems were collected in *From Skipping with Ropes* (1998). Critics were quick to note that, compared to the angry tone evident in the prison poems, Mapanje's third collection was much more mellow, full of irony and humor.

SIMON GIKANDI

Maphalla, Kgotso Pieter David

b. 1955, South Africa

poet and playwright

The South African writer K.P.D. Maphalla's illustrious career as a Sesotho author has been influenced by various factors, his upbringing in particular, which exposed him to the vicissitudes of life, compelled him to work at a very tender age as a waiter in a hotel, a gardener and handyman in people's homes, and also as a street vendor. This harsh life experience paid great dividends for literature in Sesotho, for Maphalla was only 16 years old when he wrote his first radio plays and poetry. He also wrote short stories and articles for Sesotho newspapers including *Tswelopele* (Progress), *Lehlaseli* (Sun-Ray) and *Lentswe la Basotho* (The Voice of the Basotho Nation) and the periodical *Bona* (See). In 1980 he won the first prize in a Radio Sesotho poetry competition. His first novel, *Tshepo le Metswalle* (Tshepo and Friends) was published by Educum in 1982. Between 1982 and 1985 Kgotso published an average of two books a year and for this prolific output he won the Roving Moiloa Trophy in 1985, a competition run by LESIBA, the Sesotho writers' association. This abundantly productive writer thrives on challenge and this is evident from his decision to write in several genres, on a variety of topics, and in both Sesotho and English. At the beginning of his career, he concentrated on radio dramas, for which effort he was recognized by Radio Sesotho in 1984 as the most proficient writer of short radio dramas. His literary corpus included novels, such as *Tshiu Tseo* (Those Days) (1982) and *Tefo* (Reward) (1984); collections of poetry, including *Mahohodi* (Debris) and *Fuba sa ka* (My Chest/Bosom) (both 1983); drama, *Tahleho* (Loss) (1983); and short stories, *Mohlomong Hosane* (Maybe Tomorrow) (1993). Maphalla has won the Thomas Mofolo Trophy for poetry (1991, 1992, 1993, and 1994), novels (1992 and 1994), and short stories in 1993. He has also won literary awards from De Jager-Haum (1993), Maskew Miller Longmans (1993), Sekila (1993), and M-Net (1996).

ROSEMARY MOEKETSI

Maran, René

b. 1887, Martinique; d. 1960, Paris, France

administrator and novelist

Maran was born in Martinique of Guyanese parents. He was educated in Bordeaux, and as a child traveled intermittently to Africa where his father was working. First he published two volumes of poetry and then he wrote his best-known work, *Batouala* (1921) (translated under the same title in 1987), while working for the French colonial

service in Equatorial Africa. *Batouala* won the Prix Goncourt. Maran was the first writer of African descent to be awarded the prestigious prize. Léopold **Senghor** considered Maran an important precursor of **negritude**, because Maran's aesthetic led to a positive revaluation of traditional African culture. *Batouala* and its sequel, *Djouma, chien de la brousse* (Djouma, Dog of the Bush) (1927), tell a story of cultural dissolution under colonial rule. Most important among his other works are the symbolic *Le Livre de la brousse* (The Book of the Bush) (1934), and *Bêtes de la brousse* (Animals of the Bush) (1942), which borrow from African oral literatures (see **oral literature and performance**) and extend Maran's preoccupation with traditional African culture, and the autobiographical *Un Homme pareil aux autres* (A Man Like Other Men) (1947), which explores the problems of assimilation. After returning from Africa in 1923, Maran lived in Paris until his death.

Further reading

Maran, René (1987) *Batouala*, trans. Barbara Beck and Alexander Mboukou, with an introduction by Donald E. Herdeck, London: Heinemann.

ELENI COUNDOURIOTIS

Marechera, Dambudzo Charles

b. 1952, Rusape, Vengere township, Zimbabwe; d. 1987, Harare, Zimbabwe

novelist

During his relatively short life, Dambudzo Charles Marechera was probably Zimbabwe's best-known and most controversial novelist in international circles. He was renowned as much for his controversial positions on questions of art and culture as for his distinguished work as a novelist, short story writer, poet, essayist, and playwright.

Dambudzo Marechera was born in Rusape, Vengere township, about 170 km from Harare, and received his early education in Rusape, St Augustine Penhalonga, and the University College of Rhodesia. While at the University College in 1972,

Marechera was expelled, along with other black Zimbabweans such as Hebert Simba Makoni, for agitating for racial equality at both the local university and in Rhodesia. Marechera soon received a scholarship that was to take him to New College, Oxford, where again he clashed with his lecturers over his poor performance and strong opinions. Marechera did not complete his degree at either the University College of Rhodesia or New College, Oxford.

The publication of *The House of Hunger* (1978), a collection of nine short stories, brought early fame to Marechera, winning the Guardian Prize for Fiction. The main story, "The House of Hunger," explores racial politics and colonialism in Rhodesia (see **colonialism, neocolonialism, and post-colonialism**), the poverty of Africans crammed on to unproductive communal land, and the urban ghettos such as Vengere township. But more than its social concerns, *The House of Hunger* signaled a new development in African literature because the short stories started to deconstruct nationalism (see **nationalism and post-nationalism**), and to pre-empt the crisis of postcolonialism, well before most countries in southern Africa had gained independence. Nationalist critics in Rhodesia, such as Musaemura **Zimunya**, could not understand why in 1978, at the height of the Zimbabwean liberation war, Marechera was already writing narratives focused on the contradictions of the ideology of nationalism.

In 1980, Marechera published his first novel, *Black Sunlight*. The latter did not have as much success and attention as *The House of Hunger* owing to what literary critics perceived as its turgid images and highly complex ideas, but in retrospect it is clear that the work marks a radical shift in the theme and style of African literature of the 1970s that was decidedly disillusioned with the consequences of independence. *Black Sunlight* shuns the realism (see **realism and magical realism**) of much of Africa's literature of independence and uses European notions of the carnivalesque and hybridity in order to destabilize official nationalist narratives of independence. At best, in *Black Sunlight* Marechera can be described as a "revolutionary anarchist," more concerned in revealing the endless paradox within new urban guerrilla movements of Africa. In the novel, Marechera also

rejects the linear model of representation common in realism in favor of a postmodern allegory that reveals a capacity to disrupt singular ways of seeing. *Black Sunlight* was banned in the newly independent state of Zimbabwe in 1980 largely because of its harsh critique of the discourse of cultural nationalism, which the author sees as an attempt to submerge Africa's cultural and ideological differences within the singular identity of an "African image." Although the ban on the novel was lifted the same year – 1980 – it was only in the late 1990s that it began to be reread as a prophecy on the senseless anarchy and paranoia of the Mugabe government and the state's hostility towards alternative voices. Marechera's love for fantasy, dream, surrealism, and allegory was further dramatized in his other novel, *The Black Insider* (1990), which was edited after his death by Flora Veit Wild.

Dambudzo Marechera returned to an independent Zimbabwe in 1982. He had come to help in the shooting of a film version of "The House of Hunger," but he soon fell out with the directors of the film and the project was never completed. In 1984, Marechera published *Mind Blast or The Definitive Buddy*. This book is made up of three plays, one narrative prose, and a collection of poems. The book, which denounces the material greed, intolerance, and corruption of the new postcolonial leadership, meant, according to Marechera (as recorded by Flora Veit Wild), to "blast" the minds of both the politicians and the masses. The mosaic structure of the book and its inclusion of different styles – novella, poetry, and plays – in one volume reflect the author's desire to reach out to a wider audience using a plurality of forms. The multiplicity of the genres used in *Mind Blast* also operates in a way that denies literary closure to the multiple narratives of the nation.

Dambudzo Marechera's poetry has been anthologized in many volumes since the 1970s. *Two Tone* (1973, 1976), a literary magazine in Rhodesia, contains some of Marechera's early poems. Other poems were published in Timothy McLoughlin's *New Writing in Rhodesia* (1976), Kizito Muchemwa's *Zimbabwean Poetry in English* (1978), and *Cemetery of Mind: Collected Poems of Dambudzo Marechera* (1992), edited by Flora Veit Wild. In his poetry, Marechera's primary concern was the contradictory nature of reality and the untenable posture of nationalist ideologies that claimed to represent the masses and yet were constantly obfuscating reality. As is demonstrated in one of his famous poems, "Oracle of the Povo" (1992), Marechera understood the predicament of the masses, but he was not willing to romanticize their everyday struggle for he felt that they too were often co-opted by the ruling class. His primary concern here, as in all his works, was the valorization of a language of hybridity that would help his readers deconstruct the dominant ideologies of both colonialism and nationalism. On his death in 1987, he left many unpublished works of poetry, short stories, and plays, some of which have been published posthumously under the editorship of Flora Veit Wild, Marechera's biographer.

Further reading

Wild, Flora Veit (compiler) (1992) *Dambudzo Marechera; A Source Book on His Life and Work*, Harare: University of Zimbabwe Publications.

Zimunya, M.B. (1982) *Those Years of Drought and Hunger: The Birth of African Fiction in English*, Gweru: Mambo Press.

M. VAMBE

Masiea, Rabotle Joshua Rawley

b. 1927, Alexander, South Africa; d. 1991, South Africa

poet and playwright

The South African writer, R.J.R. Masiea was born in Alexander outside Johannesburg but grew up in Senekal and Matwabeng in the Orange Free State. His love for the Sotho (Sesotho) language and literature was nurtured by his mother, an eloquent and perfect master of the language. Masiea acquired university degrees in African languages and wrote an MA dissertation on "The Traditional Games of Basotho Children." He taught at various schools and also lectured at the Cape Town University. Upon his return to the Free State he served the Qwaqwa government as a senior school inspector, language planner, secretary of education,

minister of education, and chairman of the Language Board. He belonged to various teachers' associations and sat on university councils. Masiea has translated two books into Sesotho (*Tahleho*, Loss, and *Kgabane ya Mokokotlofo*, The Gentleman of Mokokotlofo) and has written no fewer than twenty-five books of poetry, drama, and fiction. These include two collections of poems, *Dithothokiso tsa Disabonweng* (The Poetry of the Abstract) (1981) and *Boshwabotshwerwe* (Valuable Things) (1984), three works of drama (*Seyalemothati* (A Person Who Adjusts to Situations) (1981), *Boo Borena* (That Kind of Leadership) (1983), *Taelo ya Mofu* (Commands of the Dead) (1985)) and novels such as *Meriti ya Bosiu* (The Shadows of the Night) (1985) and *Ho se tsebe ke lebote* (It is Folly Not to be Wise) (1995).

ROSEMARY MOEKETSI

Masundire, Edmund

b. 1966, Zimbabwe

novelist

Edmund Masundire's works are inspired by his former career as Zimbabwe Republic police cadre. His three detective stories, *Mutikitivha Dumbuzenene* (Detective Dumbuzenene) (1991), *Mhandu Dzorusununguko* (Enemies of Freedom) (1991), and *Nyanga Yenzou* (The Elephant Tusk) (1992), and his only play, *Nyanga Yechipembere* (The Rhino Horn) (1996), are based on familiar postcolonial conflicts between the state's law-enforcing agents and law-breakers (see **colonialism, neocolonialism, and postcolonialism**). His themes include robbery, the national problem of dissidents in Matabeleland and the Midlands between 1982 and 1987, and the poaching of elephant tusks and rhino horns in Zimbabwe's national parks. In their themes, Masundire's novels are written in the tradition of the Shona detective story (see **Shona and Ndebele literature**), which was pioneered by Mordekai Hamutyinei. In the context of colonialism, detective stories teach the colonized that crime, as defined by colonial institutions, does not pay. But within the context of post-independence literary trends, the works are closely associated with the themes of development that are a very part of the rhetoric of nationalism (see **nationalism and post-nationalism**). In the postcolonial context, crime against state institutions is seen as a threat to national resources and thus as a cause of underdevelopment. In essence, Masundire's novels are concerned with the maintenance of law and order in the modern nation-state.

EMMANUEL CHIWOME

Maṭar, Muhammad 'Afīfī

b. 1935, Manūfiyya, Egypt

poet

Born in the Manūfiyya county in Egypt, Maṭar earned a degree in philosophy from Ain Shams University. From 1968 to 1972, he worked as a schoolteacher moonlighting as an editor-in-chief for the monthly *al-Sanābil* magazine. With his opposition to the Sādāt regime growing, Maṭar fled to Iraq where he served as one of the editors of the literary journal *al-Aqlām* from 1977 to 1983. Having encountered difficulties in publishing his poetry in Egypt, Maṭar was encouraged to publish in prominent literary journals such as *al-Adab* and *Shi'r* (Beirut) which assisted in establishing his recognition among academics and writers as one of the most provocative of Arab poets. Upon his return to Egypt in 1983, Maṭar enjoyed enormous critical success and eventually gained the State Prize for Literature in 1989. His poetry, known for its complex structure, is purposely vague and esoteric. His poems are directed to an hautecouture audience, thus mostly appealing to academics. In *Wa-al-Nahru Yalbasu al-Aqni'a* (And the River Wears Masks) (1976), Maṭar centers his energies on revealing the power of his imagination and the vivid freshness of his style. *Quartet of Joy* (*Rubā'iyyāt al-farah*) (1997) is a mystical contemplation of the creation, love, and beauty, exhibiting a thorough grounding in the stylistic peculiarities of the Koran, classical Arabic poetry, and the Sufi tradition.

Further reading

Ghazoul, Ferial J. "The Greek Component in the Poetry and Poetics of Muhammad 'Afifi Matar," *Journal of Arabic Literature* 25, 2: 135–51.

KHALED AL MASRI

Matsebula, James Shadrack Mkhulunyelwa

b. 1918, Maphalaleni, Swaziland; d. 1993

poet and historian

The Swazi writer and historian James Shadrack Mkhulunyelwa Matsebula was born in Maphalaleni, Swaziland, and was educated at Swazi National High School and St Chad's College in Mnambithi (1940) before obtaining a BA degree at the University of South Africa in the late 1940s. He taught at Ngwempisana in Mankayane, Holly Rood Mission in Piet Retief, Daggakral in Ermelo, and in Mjindini. Considered to be Swaziland's pioneer historian, biographer, and author, Matsebula wrote fluently in siSwati, SiZulu, and English. Matsebula was King Sobhuza II's *lisolenkhosi* (king's eye) or liaison officer between 1959 and 1962, the king's biographer (1967), and the first director of the Swaziland National Trust Commission (1974). He was honored with the doctor of letters degree by the University of Botswana and Swaziland (1978) for his outstanding contribution to siSwati literature and written history. His major works are *Izakhiwo ZamaSwazi* (The Origins of the Swazi) (1952; now translated into both Afrikaans and siSwati) and the unpublished "Somhlolo" (a Swazi king's name). Matsebula was also the editor of *Iqoqo Lezinkondlo* (A Collection of Poetry) (1957), the debut anthology of Zulu poetry, whose themes bewail the catastrophe of World War I on the African and protest against colonialism (see **colonialism, neocolonialism, and postcolonialism**). A fighter for language rights, Matsebula successfully petitioned the British colonial government to introduce siSwati as a school subject in Swaziland.

ZODWA MOTSA

Matsebula, Stanley Musa N

b. 1958, Makayane, Swaziland

economist and writer

The Swazi economist and writer Stanley Musa N Matsebula was born in Mankayane, Swaziland, and attended school in the same area before graduating with a bachelor's degree in economic administration from the University of Swaziland and a master's in economics in the US. His debut novella, *Mane Ungitfole Tsine* (Will You Please Adopt Me) (1986) takes up a familiar theme in African **popular literature** – that crime does not pay – telling the story of a hero who flees to the city where his character degenerates. Matsebula's major work is *Siyisike Yinye Nje* (We are in the Same Boat) (1989), a drama on women's rights within the home environment. Unfortunately, the theme is compromised by the mockery of the plea for equality, and the women's request for equal participation in home chores is trivialized. In Matsebula's novel, the character who advocates the liberation of women loses her home, employment, marriage, and dignity because of what she champions, and is accused of blindly adopting concepts that are not part of her Africanness. Matsebula's pioneer subject in siSwati literature has, however, opened up the debate of the woman's dignity in society and provoked debates on the question of gender (see **gender and sexuality**) and the status of the woman in siSwati society, introduced in the first siSwati novel, *Hamba Kahle Mdikileni* (Farewell, Mdikileni) (1975).

ZODWA MOTSA

Matsepe, Oliver Kgadime

b. 1932, Transvaal (now Limpopo province), South Africa; d. 1974, Transvaal, South Africa

novelist

The South African writer Oliver Kgadime Matsepe is generally regarded as the greatest Sepedi novelist to date. He wrote and had published eight Sepedi novels and six collections of poems.

Matsepe's novels mainly concern themselves with traditional life, especially with kingship and related concerns of power and land distribution, as well as with witchcraft and religion. Although his works were written during the apartheid years (see **apartheid and post-apartheid**), Matsepe did not deal directly with the politics of the time. Consequently, some observers have labeled him too conservative or politically irrelevant. However, in his discussion of cultural and religious matters, Matsepe critically engaged with issues that would have been indirectly critical of the apartheid system. It is this indirectness that possibly made him popular with the agents of the extremely repressive government of his time, as embodied in the language boards that consistently preferred his works above those of other novelists and poets as set texts for schools and universities anywhere in South Africa where Sepedi was taught. As one of the characters in his novel *Letšofalela* (*A Never-Ending Problem*) says, "A human being is a beast that when cornered throws away weapons and fights with the tongue" (1963: Pretoria). Many critics regard *Kgorong ya Mošate* (*The Kraal of the King*) (1962) as Matsepe's best novel, while *Megokgo ya Bjoko* (*A Harvest of Thought*) (1969) is perhaps the most popular.

Works cited

Matsepe, O.K. (1963) *Letšofalela*, Pretoria: Van Schaik.

PHASWANE MPE

Matshoba, Mthuthuzeli

b. 1950, Johannesburg, South Africa

short story writer and playwright

The South African writer Mthuthuzeli Matshoba is known primarily as a short story writer and a playwright, but he also writes scripts and reviews of films. He started writing in 1978 with the publication of a short story, "My Friend, the Outcast," and came to prominence with the publication of a collection of short stories *Call Me Not a Man* in 1979. An avowed exponent of the black consciousness philosophy associated with Steve **Biko**, Matshoba, like other South African writers in the late 1970s, saw himself as a social historian whose main responsibility was to reflect black experiences in his writing. Whether he is writing about the effects of the migratory labor system and hostel life or the absurdity of homeland politics, Matshoba's short story collection is marked by what one critic, Michael Vaughn, has referred to as popular realism (see **realism and magical realism**). In his 1981 play, *Seeds of War*, Matshoba tackles the issue of forced removals and the disastrous effect it has on the family of one man and his community. Like the Senegalese writer, Ousmane **Sembene**, Matshoba has turned to film in order to reach a wider audience. His first film, *The Mohole St Brothers*, a story of the murder of his own brothers, appeared in video form in Germany in 1989. Matshoba currently writes film reviews for the *Sunday Sun* newspaper.

JABULANI MKHIZE

Matthews, James

b. 1929, Cape Town, South Africa

short story writer and poet

The South African short story writer and poet James Matthews was part of a distinctive group of "colored" writers who came out of the impoverished culture of a Cape Town segregated by race and class in the 1950s and 1960s, the first two decades of apartheid (see **apartheid and post-apartheid**). Other members of this group who went on to distinguish themselves as writers in the fight against apartheid were Richard **Rive** and Alex **la Guma**. Like other members of this set, Matthews started writing short stories for South African journals and magazines, including *Drum*. Matthews' early stories drew on his experiences growing up in the violent world of the poor "coloreds" in Cape Town, focusing on the lives of people living in District Six, the center of "colored" Cape Town life, which was later destroyed because it happened to be in an area reserved for white people. Matthews' first collection of stories, *Azikwelwa*, was published in Sweden in 1963. Mat-

thews' poetry, most of it written in the 1970s, was influenced by the Black Consciousness Movement associated with Steve **Biko**; it was a poetry of both protest and affirmation, raging at the injustices of a segregated society but also affirming pride in histories and selves that the government had sought to control or repress. Indeed, Matthews' first collection of poetry, *Cry Rage* (1973) was the first book of poetry banned by the apartheid government under its draconian censorship acts. During the student uprisings of 1976, Matthew continued to produce poems of protest, but his poetry was considered so explosive that he had difficulties finding a publisher. During this tumultuous period in South Africa he was arrested and imprisoned, and he was forced into a brief period of exile in the late 1970s. In retrospect, Matthews' work can be seen as an important record of the long struggle for freedom in South Africa, beginning with his *Drum* stories, which served as testimonies of the lives of ordinary people in Cape Town tenements, through to his militant poems which were part of a collective moment that used poetry to defy the institutions of power and domination.

Further reading

Willemse, Hein (2000) *More than Brothers: Peter Clarke and James Matthews at 70*, Cape Town: Kwela Publishers.

SIMON GIKANDI

Maunick, Edourd J.

b. 1931, Flack, Mauritius

poet, writer, and diplomat

Well-known and well-respected poet, writer, entertainment mogul, and political ambassador Edourd J. Maunick was born in Flack, Mauritius, in 1931. His obsession with language has been described as an adventure in the ineffable, and his poems have been described as the incarnation of an idea of "metissage, exile, and the opening of the world." Not only a famous poet and writer, Maunick was a teacher and librarian, writer and producer for radio and television, collaborator for many years with ORTF (Office de Radiodiffusion-Télévision Française, the former French broadcasting service). In 1978 he became the chief writer for *Demain L'Afrique* (Africa Tomorrow). He was director of all publications at UNESCO, and was named ambassador of the island of Mauritius to South Africa. Personal friend of poet Léopold Sédar **Senghor** and Nelson Mandela, Maunick is the author of more than twenty collections of poems since 1954, including *Paroles pour solder la mer* (Poems to Seal the Sea) (1988) with Gallimard. He won the Apollinaire Prize for *Ensoleillé vif* (Living Sunlight) in 1976. He is a Chevalier (Knight) of Arts and Letters in the Legion of Honor.

MEREDITH MARTIN

Mazrui, Ali Al'Amin

b. 1933, Kenya

political scientist and novelist

Kenyan political scientist and novelist Ali Mazrui started his teaching career at Uganda's Makerere University during Milton Obote's rule in the 1960s, and it was then that he established his reputation as a social critic. For a brief period, he was an associate editor of *Transition* magazine, whose identity he helped shape by writing irreverent essays about revered African leaders such as Julius Nyerere and Kwame Nkrumah. His novel *The Trial of Christopher Okigbo* (1971) polemically deals with the question of the artist's commitment. In the imaginary landscape of the novel, the Nigerian poet Christopher **Okigbo** – killed in the Biafran war – is arraigned before a tribunal for having betrayed his poetic calling by taking up arms. In his TV series *The Africans*, Mazrui brings to audiences the stark history of Africa under colonialism and its aftermath (see **colonialism, neocolonialism, and postcolonialism**). Although he has several hostile critics, Mazrui is nonetheless important for popularizing African intellectual debates and bringing African issues before global audiences.

Further reading

Kokole, Omari H. (ed.) (1998) *The Global African: A Portrait of Ali A. Mazrui*, Trenton: Africa World Press.

DAN ODHIAMBO OJWANG

M'Baye d'Erneville, Annette

b. 1926, Sokone, Senegal

poet

Unlike many of her contemporaries, the Senegalese writer Annette M'Baye d'Erneville was educated primarily in local schools and institutions, receiving her teaching degree from the École Normale d'Institutrices (Teachers' College) in Rufisque in 1945. After a short tenure as the General Superintendent of the École Normale in Rufisque, M'baye left Senegal to study teaching and education in Paris. Upon her return to Senegal in 1959, M'baye became a reporter and (in 1960) the director of the Regional Information Bureau in Diourbel. In 1963 M'baye founded and became principal editor of the Senegalese women's magazine *Awa*, and shortly thereafter was appointed the program director of Radio Senegal. Throughout her various careers, M'baye continued writing poetry, but her work, while not entirely oblivious to the African struggle for independence, has rarely taken up the overtly political themes associated with her Senegalese colleagues, David **Diop** and Léopold **Senghor**. Her poems, which have been published in two volumes, are highly personal and stylized, exploring her love for humanity, the trials of human endeavor, and, especially, the power of women in African society.

MEREDITH MARTIN

Mbise, Ismael R.

b. 1944, Meru, Tanzania

novelist and academic

The Tanzanian novelist and academic Ismael Mbise was born among the Meru people who live on the slopes of Mount Kilimanjaro. After his education in local schools, Mbise went to the University of Dar es Salaam where he studied literature; he later undertook graduate studies in the United States. Mbise's major literary work is *Blood on Our Land* (1974), a historical novel dealing with a famous land case brought before the United Nations by the Meru people against the colonial government. Mbise's book was concerned with representing a historical account of the Meru resistance to colonial rule in the nineteenth century and the narrative of their forced eviction from their land. More significantly, Mbise's novel was written at a time when Tanzania itself was going through the significant political and social experiment known as Ujamaa, which, under the leadership of President Julius Nyerere, was intended to make the collective ownership of land the centerpiece of Tanzanian society. Mbise's novel is a significant fictional account of a historical event as it is seen within the context of postcolonial transformation. In addition, it is one of the few works of literature in English produced in Tanzania in the 1970s, a period when the country's major authors turned their attention to producing literature in Swahili, the national language (see **Swahili literature**).

SIMON GIKANDI

Mda, Zakes

b. 1948, Sterkspruit, Herschel district, South Africa

writer

Zanemvula Kizito Gatyeni Mda is an extraordinary South African writer, possessing a range of creative abilities, the most notable being his successes as a playwright, novelist, and painter. Mda was born in 1948 in Sterkspruit, Herschel district, and moved intermittently between Sterkspruit and Soweto before his family went into political exile and settled in Lesotho around 1963, after the arrest of Mda's father (Ashby Peter Solomzi) by the Nationalist Party government for his political activities in the Pan-Africanist Congress. Mda was educated in South Africa, Lesotho, Switzerland, and the United States.

Dead End (written in 1966 but not published until 1980), *A Hectic Weekend* (1967), and *Banned* (a radio play which was broadcast in 1982) represent Mda's early forays in playwriting and all three pieces were in the mold of township melodramas popularized by Gibson **Kente**. In 1978 Mda shot to national prominence with *We Shall Sing for the Fatherland* (1980), which marked his first substantial realized theatrical work that also includes the kernel of the aesthetic political vision that was to inform his later plays. Subsequent major dramas include *Dark Voices Ring* (1980), *The Hill* (1990), *Joys of War* (1993), *And the Girls in Their Sunday Dresses* (1993), "The Nun's Romantic Story" (unpublished play performed in 1995), and "You Fool, How Can the Sky Fall?" (unpublished play performed in 1995). Mda's plays are structured around strong, credible ordinary protagonists, "the wretched of the earth," who, faced with the machinations of colonialism and neocolonialism, have to challenge petty officialdom, discrimination, racial and gender oppression, and exploitation. The settings are always stark with minimal sets, props, and costumes, an aesthetic that is very much in line with the ideas of theater-for-development that Mda elaborated in *When People Play People: Development Communication through Theatre* (1993).

Mda returned to South Africa in 1994 after the end of apartheid (see **apartheid and post-apartheid**). In 1995 he published two novels, *She Plays with the Darkness*, set in Lesotho, and *Ways of Dying* (winner of the M-Net Book Prize in 1997), set in South Africa during the period of "transition" after the first democratic elections in 1994. Both novels revisit the issues of social and cultural inequalities, especially as manifest in poverty, the lack of democracy, and the pervasive presence of violence and death as social experiences. On the other hand, the exigencies of life are eased by the cultural resilience and creativity of Mda's main protagonists. *Melville 67* (1998) was followed by the important *Heart of Redness* (2000), where Mda explores the "cattle-killing episode" that occurred among the Xhosa in the Eastern Cape around the 1850s. Mda establishes links between the legend of Nongqawuse and contemporary struggles around questions of heritage, culture, the environment, and development.

Zakes Mda's elevated stature in South African theater is evident in the frequency with which professional groups are restaging his plays. In 1995, for instance, there were five Mda plays on stages around South Africa. Likewise, his novels are revered for their consummate and incisive delineations of the pleasures and pains of life in the region.

BHEKIZIZWE PETERSON

Meddeb, Abdelwahab

b. 1946, Tunis, Tunisia

novelist and poet

Unlike many of his contemporaries in North Africa, Tunisian writer Abdelwahab Meddeb has been less concerned with ideology and the voicing of a political identity than with explorations of the act of writing and the metaphysical. In his most famous work, *Talismano* (Talisman) (1979), Meddeb crosses wide geographical, mythological, and historical spaces painting a collection of scenes that call up the most fundamental questions of existence in a highly poetic style that has been both praised and criticized. In *Phantasia* (Fantasia) (1986), Meddeb takes formalist experimentation one step further, creating a work composed of only ten paragraphs, each spanning around twenty pages. The book is divided into four "circles" that encompass visions and dreams, the life of a woman named Aya, scenes of exile in Paris, and the nocturnal ascension of the Prophet Muhammad. After these two stylistically complex works, Meddeb abandoned experimentation of form for the unity of the novel, but he did not abandon his interest in mysticism and the Sufi tradition in particular, producing in 1987 *Le Tombeau d'Ibn Arabi* (The Tomb of Ibn Arabi). Meddeb is the founder of *Dédale*, a journal of postcolonial Francophone writing and theory.

Further reading

Meddeb, Abdelwahab (1979) *Talismano* (Talisman), Paris: Bourgeois.

KATARZYNA PIEPRZAK

Medou Mvomo, Rémy Sylvestre

b. 1938, Sangmélima, Cameroon

novelist and playwright

Rémy Sylvestre Medou Mvomo was born in Sangmélima, in southern Cameroon. In his novel, *Africa ba'a* (1969), as well as in his play *Les Enchaînés* (The Chained Ones) (1979), he is preoccupied with the future of Africa in contact with Europe. Connected to this idea, the journey of his characters recalls his personal development. Indeed, having left to finish his secondary studies in France, he returned to Cameroon to pursue studies of law and economics at the University of Yaoundé. He privileges, in his thematic concerns, the encounter of civilizations with the inevitable conflict between tradition and modernity (see **colonialism, neocolonialism, and postcolonialism**), as he deals with problems linked to colonization such as racism, exploitation, and oppression. In his work Medou Mvomo writes against ruthless ambition and other political problems of independent African nations. His tone, which is not too moralizing, allows for a certain linguistic freedom, but it sometimes appears slightly forced. In addition, he creates literary works that are committed to popular education. Concerned with the role of literature in the education of his people, Medou Mvomo has also been active in numerous cultural activities.

ANDRÉ NTONFO

Mekonnin Indalkacchew (Mäkonnen Endalkachew)

b. 1891, Ethiopia; d. 1963, Ethiopia

novelist

Mekonnin Indalkacchew was of noble family, married a princess, and held some of the highest political offices in Ethiopia. He cherished conservative values, which are reflected in his books, especially his novel about Emperor Téwodros II and Empress Tayitu, *Tayitu Bitul* (1957/8), for which he was much criticized. He often included autobiographical features in his books, for example

Yefiqir chorra (Rays of Love) (1956/7). He was educated in church schools and the royal palace, and was briefly sent to a government school to learn French. He fought against the invading Italians in 1935/6, and then went into exile in Israel until the liberation in 1941. He attached great importance to his books, which were often published in calligraphy. His fictional work, most notably *Tsehay Mesfin* (1956/7) and *Almotkum biyyé alwashim* (I Don't Deny that I Died) (1954/5), is largely romantic and sentimental in spite of much sadness in the lives of his characters. In his life of ease and affluence, he often expressed nostalgia for the simple, even ascetic life he wrote about, for example in the collection *Arrimuññ* (1954/5). He was also an enthusiastic amateur painter.

Further reading

Molvaer, R.K. (1997) *Black Lions*, Lawrenceville, New Jersey: Red Sea Press.

REIDULF MOLVAER

Mellah, Fawzi

b. 1946, Tunisia

playwright and novelist

Tunisian playwright and novelist Fawzi Mellah began his literary career with the publication of *Néron ou les oiseaux de passage* (Nero or the Birds of Passage) (1973). Dedicated to Albert **Memmi**, the play is a humorous and biting portrayal of life in colonial Tunisia (1881–1956) through the story of a petty French colonial, a radio salesman named after the Roman emperor Nero. While Nero is the principal character, Mellah writes that the true engine behind the play is rumor, specifically the rumor of impending independence. The force and dynamics of rumor are concepts that permeate Mellah's work, including both novels *La Conclave de pleureuses* (The Assembly of Crying Women) (1987) and *Elissa, la reine vagabonde* (Elissa, the Vagabond Queen) (1988). He has been praised as a writer who, while deeply engrained in his own culture, is not afraid to cross cultural borders. *Entre chien et loup* (Between Dog and Wolf) (1997) is the journal of a

man who travels to places as distant as Baghdad and New York, ultimately in a search for himself.

Further reading

Mellah, Fawzi (1973) *Néron ou les oiseaux de passage* (Nero or the Birds of Passage), Paris: Éditions Pierre Jean Oswald.

KATARZYNA PIEPRZAK

Memmi, Albert

b. 1920, Tunis, Tunisia

novelist and essayist

Albert Memmi is the most well-known and critically acclaimed Tunisian writer of the twentieth century. His famous 1957 work *The Colonizer and the Colonized* (*Le Portrait du colonisé*) remains one of the central texts on colonialism (see **colonialism, neocolonialism, and postcolonialism**), and the language of manifesto that it employs has been cited in nationalist movements against colonialism and imperialism around the world. Memmi's prolific non-fiction political and sociological works are complemented by novels that speak of identity and alienation, inspired by Memmi's own experiences, not only as a Tunisian but also as a Jew, with French colonialism in Tunisia (1881–1956) and its aftermaths.

The primary concern of Albert Memmi's literary production has been an exploration of identity and the categories in which a human is placed. In his 1953 autobiographical work *The Pillar of Salt* (*La Statue du sel*), Memmi questions his own position as a Jewish Tunisian during World War II through the character Alexandre Mordekhai Benillouche. The novel begins in the Jewish quarter of Tunis, the *hara*, with childhood and a sense of home, and follows Alexandre into exile as he discovers his sexuality, his intellect, and his personality, and seeks to reconcile this knowledge with the identity that is forced upon him from his family, from the Jewish community, from the young Arab nationalists, and from the French.

In the acclaimed 1969 novel, *The Scorpion or the*

Imaginary Confession (*Le Scorpion*) Memmi continues to explore themes of self-knowledge and alienation. Marcel, an ophthalmologist, attempts to make sense of the papers left in a drawer by his writer brother Emile. The novel opens with the central image of the book, Emile's account of a scorpion's suicide, that of a creature forced to turn upon itself. Through a narrative form that intertwines Marcel's narration and reaction to Emile's writing with texts from both Emile's journal and notes for a history of his family, Memmi plays with the slippage of text, the possibilities of language, and the limits of form. Through this structural experimentation, Memmi explores the idea of sight and knowledge, weaving together the memories and desperation of two men who see their lives, their country, and their history through different eyes.

The questions of image and knowledge present in Memmi's fiction take a radically political path in his non-fiction work. As Memmi explains in *The Colonizer and the Colonized*, there can be no understanding of social relations in Tunisia without an analysis of the violent principal force to which Tunisians were submitted and in which they functioned: colonialism. Like his contemporary Frantz Fanon, Memmi delves into the dynamics of colonial life, examining how defining categories such as "colonizer" and "colonized" are constructed and manipulated in order to produce and cultivate a world of dominance and subjection. However, when Memmi calls upon the "colonized" to break the psychological and political chains that hold him in a dehumanized position of subservience, he warns that this liberation cannot occur only through physical violence, but rather that the fundamental categories of colonial thought must be challenged. Both critics and Memmi himself have questioned the depth of his analysis; however, the fact remains that *The Colonizer and the Colonized* was one of the very first texts to explore the political, social, and mental violence of colonialism and continues to be extremely important to postcolonial theory.

Memmi's examination of categories of identity and structures of social relations extends throughout his opus. In both the 1962 *Portrait of a Jew* (*Portrait d'un Juif*) and the 1975 *Jews and Arabs* (*Juifs et Arabes*), Memmi uses his own position as an Arab Jew to destabilize preconceived notions of what it means to be Jewish, both in the diaspora and in the Arab world. With the Arab–Israeli conflict in mind, Memmi examines how the category "Arab Jew" has been manipulated in discourse to serve both Arab and European communities, and questions the myth of a historically peaceful coexistence between Arabs and Jews in the Middle East, arguing that the Arab Jew has always been the subject of a double domination and marginalization from both Arab and European powers.

Memmi's work on dependency and racism move him beyond questions of identity to an exploration of the structures of social relations. Both his 1979 work *Dependency: A Sketch for a Portrait of the Dependent* (*La Dépendance*) and 1998 *Le Buveur et l'amoureux: Le Prix de la dépendance* (The Drinker and the Lover: The Price of Dependency) examine the psychosocial structure of dependency and the uses and abuses of "need." In his 1992 study entitled *Racism* (*Le Racisme*), Memmi seeks to define racism as a social structure rather than merely a feeling or idea, arguing that racism cannot be understood through content because content is constantly shifting. Rather, racism is a hierarchical system that first establishes difference (whether real or imagined), then attaches values that place one human in a position of dominance over another. Indispensable to colonialism, according to Memmi, racism as a structure persistently allows the legitimization and justification of aggression and violence. He argues that, if understood properly, racism can be not only treated but also eradicated.

Throughout his entire body of work, Albert Memmi combines personal experience with theoretical and historical perspectives to produce insightful and detailed studies of human relations both during and after colonialism. Despite his forced exile from Tunisia in 1956, Memmi has remained engaged in North African politics and culture. He has edited several important anthologies of **North African literature in French**, including the 1985 *Écrivains francophones du Maghreb* (Francophone Writers of the Maghreb).

Further reading

Memmi, Albert (1955) *The Salt Pillar*, trans. Edouard Roditi, New York: Criterion Books.

——(1965) *The Colonizer and the Colonized*, trans. Howard Greenfield, New York: Orion Press.

——(2000) *Racism*, trans. Steve Martinot, Minneapolis: University of Minnesota Press.

KATARZYNA PIEPRZAK

Mendes, Orlando Marques de Almeida

b. 1916, Ilha de Moçambique, Mozambique; d. 1990, Maputo

novelist

Born in the Ilha de Moçambique, of Portuguese parents, Orlando Mendes was brought up in Lourenço Marques (now Maputo). He studied biology in Portugal for seven years before returning to the then Portuguese colony of Mozambique in 1951. His major works are *Trajectórias* (Trajectories) (1940) and *Clima* (Climate) (1959). In them, Mendes denounces the injustices of the colonial regime. A literary realist who sympathized with the Mozambican liberation movement, FRELIMO, he became the president of the Mozambican Writers' Association. His later work has been criticized as propaganda for the post-independence government of Mozambique. He died in Maputo. He is considered to be one of the first writers to inscribe a Mozambican national identity.

PHILLIP ROTHWELL

Menga, Guy (Gaston Guy Bikouta-Menga)

b. 1935, Congo

playwright and novelist

The literary career of Guy Menga closely matches that of his Congolese compatriot, Sylvain **Bemba**; both started as important playwrights before turning their interest to novels. When Menga's first play, *La Marmite de Koka-Mbala* (The Pot of Koka-Mbala), was first performed in 1966, its influence went beyond the Congolese borders; it was taken up and performed in many parts of central Africa. Another successful dramatic work, *L'Oracle* (The Oracle) followed in 1967, and was performed in the Champs Elysées in Paris. Menga's first novel, *La Palabre stérile* (A Sterile Dispute) (1968), won the Grand Prix Littéraire de l'Afrique Noire in 1969 and was a bestseller in Francophone Africa. Following the success of his first novel, Menga published other novels, including *Les Aventures de Mony-Mambou* (The Adventures of Mony-Mambou) (1971) and *Les Nouvelles Aventures de Mony-Mambou* (The New Adventures of Mony-Mambou) (1971), but none seemed to match the reputation of his early work. Menga, who has also published works that belong to the category of **children's literature**, has sought to create positive cultural heroes in his works, many of which have been deeply influenced by African traditional oral literature and culture (see **oral literature and performance**).

ANDRÉ DJIFFACK

Mengistu Lemma (Menghistu Lemma)

b. 1928, Ethiopia; d. 1988, Ethiopia

playwright and poet

Mengistu Lemma was among Ethiopia's foremost playwrights and poets. His father was a learned clergyman whose memoirs are a valuable part of Ethiopian culture. Mengistu first attended church school, then government schools until the end of secondary education, when he went to London to study sociology, political science, and economics, picking up some radical ideas. He then worked for the government, and for five years was based at the Ethiopian Embassy in India. After the 1974 revolution, he was attached to the Ministry of Culture as an expert on literary matters. His first collection of poetry, *Yegitim guba'e*, appeared in 1962/3, reflecting also his meeting with Western culture. His most famous plays were comedies, a new genre in Ethiopia: *Yalaccha gabiccha* (The Marriage of Unequals) (1964/5) and *Telfo bekisé* (Marriage by Abduction) (1968/9), reflecting the clash of old and new ideas. He also collected traditional stories, *Yabbatoch chewata* (Tales of the

Father), and wrote literary essays. In later years, he participated in a new translation of the Old Testament into modern Amharic.

Further reading

Molvaer, R.K. (1997) *Black Lions*, Lawrenceville, New Jersey: Red Sea Press.

REIDULF MOLVAER

Menkiti, Ifeanyi

b. 1940, Onithsa, Eastern Nigeria

philosopher and poet

The Nigerian philosopher and poet Ifeanyi Menkiti was born in Onitsha, Eastern Nigeria, and was educated in the United States where he has lived since the 1960s. Like many other African writers going to school in the 1960s, Menkiti started writing poetry under the influence of the black arts movement and the ideology of the black aesthetic. Although his poems from this period are concerned with potent political themes such as economic deprivation and social marginalization, and are often conceived as salvos directed at oppressive institutions, they are also memorable for their economy of expression. These poems were published both in mainstream journals such as *The Sewanee Review* and *Evergreen Review* and publications associated with the black aesthetic, most notably the *Journal of Black Poetry*. A collection of Menkiti's poems, titled *Affirmations*, was published by the Chicago-based Black Consciousness Press, Third World Press, in 1971.

SIMON GIKANDI

Mernissi, Fatima

b. 1940, Fez, Morocco

writer and sociologist

Moroccan writer and sociologist Fatima Mernissi, who was born in Fez, is known for her extensive and pioneering work on women and Islam, publishing over twenty books in French, Arabic, and English that record the lives, feats and challenges of women in the Islamic world (see **Islam in African literature**). Her critically acclaimed 1975 book *Beyond the Veil: Male–Female Dynamics in a Modern Muslim Country* challenges Western perceptions of the veil as a symbol of oppression by stepping behind and beyond it to examine gender relations in the Islamic world. Both *The Veil and the Male Elite: A Feminist Interpretation of Women's Rights in Islam* (*Le Harem politique: le Prophète et ses femmes*) (1987) and *The Forgotten Queens of Islam* (*Sultanes oubliées*) (1990) raise important questions about the role of Muslim women in politics, refuting the contention that women have never and should never play a political role in Islam. Mernissi's 1994 memoir of her life as a young girl in Fez, *Dreams of Trespass: Tales of a Harem Girlhood*, narrates her mental and physical escape from the harem, a world of seclusion and exclusion.

Further reading

Mernissi, Fatima (1991) *The Veil and the Male Elite: A Feminist Interpretation of Women's Rights in Islam*, Reading, Massachusetts: Addison-Wesley.

KATARZYNA PIEPRZAK

Metoui, Mohamed Moncef

b. 1943, Tunisia

playwright, director, and novelist

Playwright, film and theater director, Tunisian writer Moncef Metoui was one of the founders of the important Association of Young Tunisian Cinematographers. In his largely autobiographical novel *Racisme, je te hais!* (Racism, I Hate You!) (1973), Metoui describes his arrival to the stage and the cinema as a starving student in Paris. As the title indicates, Metoui's novel is in part an indictment of French attitudes towards North African immigrants and the treatment they receive. However, the novel is also a story of love and personal development, both through friendships he forms with teachers and actors and through the stage itself. During the 1960s, Metoui directed three films, *Le Silence ou la chatte blanche* (Silence or The White Cat) (1965), *Les Rues* (The Streets) (1968), and *Enquête* (The Investigation) (1969), which earned him the title of "the Moncef Phenomenon" from the Arabic press. His 1982 play *Messieurs! Je vous accuse!* (Sirs! I Accuse You!) is a reaction to the continued European influence in North Africa, urging Tunisians to break their neocolonial relationship with France.

Further reading

Metoui, Mohamed Moncef (1973) *Racisme, je te hais!* (Racism, I Hate You!), Paris: La Pensée Universelle.

KATARZYNA PIEPRZAK

Mezu, Sebastian Okechukwu

b. 1941, Nigeria

academic, poet, and novelist

The Nigerian academic, poet, and novelist S.M. Mezu was educated in Catholic schools in Eastern Nigeria and at University College, Ibadan, before proceeding to graduate studies in the United States, where he specialized in French with particular interest in the works of Léopold Sédar **Senghor** and wrote poetry, later collected in *The Tropical Dawn* (1966). During the Nigerian civil war Mezu was a senior official in the breakaway Republic of Biafra, and after the end of the war he published *Behind the Rising Sun* (1970), one of the first novels of the civil war. While many civil war novels were written well after the event and hence tended to be influenced by the postwar desire to affirm the principles of a united Nigerian federation, Mezu's novel was told from the Biafran perspective, and was a serious reflection on both the opportunism and cynicism of those involved in the secessionist cause and the commitment of those who believed in the goals of the Biafran Republic even when it seemed hopeless.

SIMON GIKANDI

Mgqwetto, Nontsizi

b. South Africa

poet

Not much in the matter of biography is known about this towering South African poet. Though slightly younger than the great Xhosa poet S.E.K. **Mqhayi** (1875–1945), she seems to have been contemporaneous with him. The credit for discovering this major talent in the pages of the newspaper *Umteteli wa Bantu* (The Mouthpiece of the People) belongs to Jeff Opland, the eminent scholar of Xhosa literature. The first poem "Imbongi U Chizama" (The Oral Poet of Chizama) was published in the issue of 23 October 1920, and the last poem "Zemk'Inkomo Zetafa – Vula Ndingene!" (1928) (1929) (The Cattle are Departing to Death – Open for My Entrance) appeared on 5 January 1929. Except for a prose piece that was written in the English language, all of her approximately ninety poems are in the Xhosa language. The example of Nontsizi Mgqwetto is a clear reminder of the fundamental role of women in the making of South African literary modernism (see **modernity and modernism**). Her predecessor in the literary representation of the new era or new age is Lydia **Umkasetemba**, who in all probability founded modern written Zulu prose in the middle of the nineteenth century.

A particular distinctiveness of Nontsizi Mgqwetto is that she seems to be a flare that lights up, in a spectacular way with a spectrum of colors, the whole topography on which South African literary modernism was enacted. In contrast to her contemporary, Mqhayi, who is profoundly philosophical and spiritual in a paradoxical way, Mgqwetto is deeply lyrical and sparkling. In all sorts of ways, she should be seen as Shelley's skylark, seemingly out of control but constructing an orderly pathway into modernity. It is doubtful whether either H.I.E. **Dhlomo** (1903–56) or Benedict Wallet Vilakazi (1906–47) has equaled the power of her lyricism: the affinities between Vilakazi and Mgqwetto are astonishing and fascinating, while the differences are intriguing. In her love of Africa and invocation of its ancestral spirits, Nontsizi Mgqwetto is on a par with the

Mazisi **Kunene** (1930–) of *Anthem of the Decades* (1981). This extraordinary woman may turn out to have been the true poetic voice of the New African movement.

NTONGELA MASILELA

Millin, Sarah Gertrude

b. 1888, Lithuania; d. 1968, Johannesburg, South Africa

novelist

The South African novelist Sarah Gertrude Millin was born in Lithuania but moved with her parents to the Kimberly diamond mines when she was only five months old. Like most writers at the turn of the twentieth century, Millin was influenced by theories of biological and social determinism, especially in regard to questions of race. She was particularly obsessed with the problem of miscegenation. For this reason, her works, including her most popular novel, *God's Stepchildren* (1924), represent the mixture of races as a manifestation of original sin, the source of tragedy and moral failure. In this and other novels, including *King of the Bastards* (1949), and *The Burning Man* (1952), Millin expressed her strong fears about miscegenation, which she perceived to be the greatest threat to white civilization in southern Africa. At a time when many white writers saw the racial situation in South Africa as a problem to be overcome if the country was to find its rightful place in the universe of liberal values, Millin was an unapologetic supporter of the government's racial policies, and she was praised by leading politicians, including General Smuts, for her insights into the so-called "native question."

Further reading

Chapman, Michael (1996) *Southern African Literatures*, London and New York: Longman.

SIMON GIKANDI

Mimouni, Rachid

b. 1945, Boudouaou, Algeria; d. 1995, Tangier, Morocco

novelist

Until his untimely death, Rachid Mimouni was one of Algeria's most outspoken authors writing in French. He was also one of its most productive, publishing seven novels, a collection of short stories, and a volume of political and cultural commentaries. His work is animated by lively but ironic sympathy for those forced to live with the consequences of an incompetent national administration, more concerned with self-enrichment than justice. Mimouni's novels furnish devastating indictments of the hollow ideologies and hypocritical relations of Algerian society. They also constitute an ironic artistic statement by an author who believed that brutal honesty and a sense of humor were the only ways to create literature in a one-party state.

Mimouni's first novel, *Le Printemps n'en sera que plus beau* (The Spring Will Only be More Beautiful) (1979) tells the hair-raising story of an FLN operative in the Algerian war ordered to murder his fiancée; the book did not receive the critical attention later accorded to *Le Fleuve détourné* (The Diverted River) (1982) or *Tombeza* (1984). In the latter two novels, Mimouni develops the full force of his kafkaesque vision of Algerian society. In the first, the protagonist returns to his village from the war to find his name on the local monument to the dead. As he attempts to rectify the error, he discovers the full extent of the political and social corruption which has taken hold since independence; the force of the revolution's "river" has been diverted. The realistic passages of the novel are interspersed with descriptions of a sort of penal colony which comes to stand in for the country as a whole. *Tombeza* tells a similar story of corruption, from the point of view of one of the most debased: a congenitally deformed orphan who learns to exploit the system. The reviled social outcast becomes an amoral and corrupt power broker. From this point on Mimouni's pessimism solidified, and his increasingly monstrous characters hesitated between amorality and nihilism in *The Honor of the*

Tribe (*L'Honneur de la tribu*) (1989) and *The Ogre's Embrace* (*La Ceinture de l'ogresse*) (1990).

The struggle against religious fundamentalism and the threat of terroristic executions of intellectuals dominated the last years of Mimouni's career, during which he published a closely argued essay, *De la barbarie en général et de l'intégrisme en particulier* (On Barbarism Generally and Fundamentalism in Particular) (1992), and a novel, *La Malédiction* (Malediction) (1993). In *La Malédiction*, a conscientious gynecologist refuses to hand over medical records to a committee of fundamentalists who wish to punish "fallen" women. His execution at the hands of his own brother is only the logical consequence of the civil war Mimouni saw destroying his country.

Further reading

Aresu, Bernard (1999) "Narrating the Tribe: Rachid Mimouni and Dystopia," *Research in African Literatures* 30, 3: 135–51.

Geesey, Patricia (1997) "Algerian Fiction and the Civil Crisis: Bodies under Siege," *World Literature Today* 71, 3: 484–94.

Mimouni, Rachid (1992) *The Honor of the Tribe*, trans. Joachim Neugroschel, New York: William Morrow.

——(1993) *The Ogre's Embrace*, trans. Shirley Eber, London: Quartet.

SETH GRAEBNER

al-Mis'adī, Mahmūd

b. 1911, Tunisia

novelist and playwright

The Tunisian author Mahmūd al-Mis'adī's fictional works are particularly arresting for their thematic concern with existential problems and linguistic innovation. The main theme shared by all his major works is the existential quest for absolute, divine truth, which often takes a Sufi (Islamic mystical) quality. In his novel *Ḥaddatha Abū Hurayra qāla* ... (Abu Hurayra Related, Saying ...) (1979) al-Mis'adī draws heavily from the classical Arabic and the heritage and mythology of Islam

and its literary traditions (see **Islam in African literature**). On a stylistic level, he uses this form of the novel to explore and remold the narrative form of *ḥadīth* (the sayings of the Prophet Muhammad and his companions) in an unprecedented way. His philosophical dramatic work, *al-Sudd* (The Dam) (1955), as well as his novel, *Mawlid al-nisyān* (The Genesis of Oblivion), deals with themes of rebellion, submission, movement, stillness, and time. Al-Mis'adī's fascination with the classical Arabic language is not only manifested in his fictional works, which are written in a language reminiscent of that of the Koran and the classical Arabic genre of *maqāma*: it is also evident in his analytical study *al-Īqā' fī al-saj' al-'arabī* (Rhythm in Arabic Rhymed Prose) in which, as the title indicates, he highlights the rhythmic rules governing Arabic rhymed prose.

Further reading

Al-Mis'adī, M. (1979) *Ḥaddatha Abū Hurayra qāl* ... (Abu Hurayra Related, Saying ...), Tunis: Dār al-janūb lī al-nashr.

SARRA TLILI

Mkhonta, Elias Adam Bateng

b. 1954, Hhohho, Swaziland; d. 2001, Manzini, Swaziland

novelist

The Swazi writer Elias Mkhonta attended school at Magodvonga, eNdzingeni Nazarene, Manzini Nazarene High School, and obtained a teacher's diploma from William Pitcher College. After a short stay in teaching, Mkhonta entered Parliament. He published his first novel, *Maphindisiganga* (Return to Motherland) in 1986. He is a winner of three prizes in a competition sponsored by Macmillan. Mkhonta's works include *Mhlupheki* (The Wretched) (1989), an autobiographical novel, and *Ubolibamba Lingashoni* (Stop the Clock of Time) (1990), a mild protest novel against Nazi Germany and the effects of World War II on the Swati people. Mkhonta is one of the "second generation" writers "schooled" in the 1986 special workshop for writers, and his short stories and plays, co-published with other notable writers like S.R. Mdluli-Dlamini, B.B. Malangwane, and J.N. Khumalo in the 1980s and 1990s, represent new developments in the literary tradition of siSwati. Using rural Swaziland and precolonial culture as his main points of reference, Mkhonta explores the themes of poverty, childrearing, fraud, and infidelity by often using very idiomatic and pristine language. A special quality of most of his narratives is their vivid and realistic representations of characters.

ZODWA MOTSA

Mkhonza, Sarah

b. 1957, Siphofaneni, Swaziland

sociolinguist and creative artist

The Swazi sociolinguist and creative artist Sarah Mkhonza was born in Siphofaneni, Swaziland, attended Manzini Nazarene High School, the universities of Botswana and Swaziland, and the University of Illinois, and obtained a PhD in English from Michigan State University. Her works include the 1988 Macmillan Boleswa Award-winning novel, *Pains of a Maid* (1988), *What the Future Holds* (1989), contributions in short story anthologies, *Ingcamu* (A Journey's Provision) (1987), *Idubukele* (Dinner is Served!) (1988), and *Khulumani Sive* (Speak Up) (2000). She also writes for the women's page in the *Weekend Observer*, Swaziland. In stories like "Nabondvukutihlala Kakhe" (The Beloved) (1987), "Buntfombi BaSontoyi" (Sontoyi's Youthful Escapades) (1988), "Liwashi LaMbekelwa" (Mbekelwa's Wristwatch) (2000), and "Indlovu Lengenamboko" (A Trunkless Elephant) (2000), Mkhonza expertly uses a unique narrative style and imagistic presentation of non-human figures to exploit mood variation and character depiction. Unlike her co-authors in the collections, she does not follow a stringent structuralist technique, but allows her tale to unfold naturally like the life of its progenitor, the siSwati oral narrative (see **oral literature and performance**). The woman character of varying ages features prominently in all her writing, creating a motif of resilience and strength.

ZODWA MOTSA

Mlilo, S.

b. 1924, Belingwe, Zimbabwe; d. 1995, Bulawayo, Zimbabwe

novelist

Born in Belingwe, southern Zimbabwe, S. Mlilo is the first woman novelist to be published in Ndebele (see **Shona and Ndebele literature**). Her two works, *Lifile* (Heroine) (1975) and *Bantu BeHadlana* (People of Hadlana) (1977), are popular works in educational institutions in Ndebele-speaking parts of Zimbabwe. In these works, Mlilo laments the erosion of Ndebele traditional values and customs through the encroachment of modernity, especially urbanization, on rural Ndebele society, and what she considers to be the subversion of the morals of single women by modernization (see **modernity and modernism**). In her novels, moral decay is, in turn, represented as resulting in the spread of disease and in social stress within families, as well as undermining the social foundation of African marriages. For Mlilo, the city of Bulawayo functions, in the culture of colonialism (see **colonialism, neocolonialism, and postcolonialism**), as the site of fatal attraction. She focuses on the politics of town planning and colonial labor policies of the 1940s and 1950s, which discouraged women from perceiving the city as an alternative home. From the point of view of Africans who are threatened by colonialism, her vision represents genuine attempts to protect girls, as the future mothers of the community, from the corrupting effects of urbanization.

EMMANUEL CHIWOME

modern drama

Problems of definition

The term "modern African drama" refers to a specific type of dramatic activity, an identifiable body of works, critical discourses, and theatrical institutions that emerged in Africa as a result of its encounter with Europe in the period of colonialism (see **colonialism, neocolonialism, and post-colonialism**). The works generally grouped under this label – by such playwrights as Wole **Soyinka**, Bernard **Dadié**, Athol **Fugard**, Ebrahim **Hus-sein**, Werewere **Liking**, **Ngugi wa Thiong'o** – by no means constitute a monolithic category. Not only do they have different thematic preoccupations, their form, performance styles, or even functions vary from one playwright to another depending on such factors as the latter's indigenous culture, the (colonial) history of their region or country of origin, or their cultural politics. Also there is no single set of aesthetic standards by which to judge modern African plays. What are notable are the manifestos and debates by critics and dramatists as to what constitutes or should constitute an "authentic" modern play.

In spite of its rather fluid character, modern African drama displays a number of core features that set it apart from the more ancient and so-called "traditional" or precolonial, but still lively, idioms of drama in Africa, some of which have given rise to new oral forms of popular theater (see **oral literature and performance**). The most important of these features are its scripted and text-based nature, even when some of it aspires, at its experimental best, to the improvisatory and participatory condition of the older idioms, and its medium of expression – predominantly Eur-opean languages, and the fact that it is deeply influenced by, often consciously modeled on, European stage conventions and dramatic proce-dures (the raised stage with its actor–audience divide, the emphasis on plot construction, spoken dialogue, and individualized characters), even when it is engaged in open rebellion against these conventions. Equally significant is modern drama's home: the urban areas, and more specifically within these, university and the state-run theaters like the Daniel Sorano in Senegal, the Kenya National Theatre, or the National Arts Theatre in Lagos, and European cultural centers like the British Council or the Alliance Française. Finally, unlike the more ancient traditions (and their many sub-varieties) whose producers and audience are essentially the semi- or non-literate majority,

"modern" drama is more socially exclusive. It is produced/written and watched/read by the Western-educated minority who alone can use and understand its languages and protocols and, not insignificantly, afford its gate-fee.

But its minority status and relative newness notwithstanding, modern drama has emerged as the hegemonic theatrical form in Africa. It not only represents and performs the nation and national-ism (see **nationalism and post-nationalism**) on radio and television at home or abroad, and at theater festivals and competitions, it also provides the canonical texts of the emergent national dramatic cultures. Widely studied and taught, it has also become synonymous, especially in Europe and America, with African drama as a whole. In short, modern drama, associated with literacy and the authority of modernity (see **modernity and modernism**), and in close proximity to the literary mainstream tradition in European theater, has come to represent not just "official," but also, on the cultural attitudinal scale, "high" theater culture. It has reduced in its development, in a classic example of cultural diglossia, the majority theater forms, to the status of "unofficial" and "low" theater. In this distribution of theatrical roles the latter forms cater to the needs of the subjects of ethnic communities (the private sphere), the former to the needs of the citizens of the nation (the public domain), in the same way that, in most African countries, indigenous languages are used in the domestic, affective, private realm, while European languages are reserved for the official or public domain. The division, in both the theatrical and language realms, is not merely functional – responding to different but complementary needs. It rests on a hierarchy of cultural values that is being contested by such modern playwrights as Ngugi Wa Thiong'o, Femi **Osofisan** or Werewere Liking.

To contrast "modern drama" with its so-called "traditional" counterpart, however, is not to suggest that each form (and its many sub-varieties) lives in splendid isolation from the other. That would be to distort reality. The fact is that both forms, like their respective practitioners and consumers, exist in a state of dynamic interaction. The members of the so-called elite do not constitute a group apart, certainly not in the same (cultural) sense as do, for example, Zimbabweans of European ancestry. For the most part, the elite share a language, kinship, religion, with the traditional folk, and are separated from them, sometimes only tenuously, by Western education (see **education and schools**). The result of the hybrid identity of Africa's modern elite is that its drama, for all its proximity to the Western model, sometimes deliberately cultivated, still betrays, and on occasion consciously draws on, the theatrical forms of its traditional backgrounds. Similarly, the older forms in varying degrees also react to the influence of, or borrow from, the modern theatrical culture of the elites, spawning in such neo-traditional, urban popular genres as the concert-party of Ghana and Togo, the Travelling Theatre of Nigeria or the *lifala* songs of Lesotho migrants to South Africa, new forms of theatrical expression.

It is clear, then, from the above that modern African drama is not a discrete category, but part of a continuum of dramatic forms on which it sits at the upper end, that closest to the mainstream European standard. On the conceptual model proposed here, then, modern African drama, in particular the literary or art variety of it, can be compared to what is described, in the theory of non-native Englishes, as "educated African English." While the spoken version of the latter contains Africanisms in the area of pronunciation, lexis, and discourse patterns, its syntax and semantics (especially among the well educated) remain very close to Standard British English. This makes it both marked and yet intelligible, particularly in its written form, to the global English-using community. Similarly, to pursue the analogy, for all its borrowings from the "traditional" and "urban popular" forms of theater, the "syntax" or under-lying structure of modern African drama remains close to the mainstream Western tradition of drama. This is particularly true of the most Westernized and thus, from an African point of view, not-so-original modern drama in which these theatrical "Africanisms" read and feel plated, even folkloristic in so far as they function as signs without referents, structures (of sound, color, movement) without meaning. It is true in the same way that the "modern" ingredients in traditional drama – the drama at the lower end of our continuum – perform a decorative or advertising function (for example advertising that drama's modern credentials), and do not affect its structural integrity or "syntax."

But not all African literary dramatists are satisfied with merely decorating their plays with the odd song or dance movement from the hearth. Although perhaps a necessary first step in the process of Africanizing the drama, this method is somewhat superficial. Some of Africa's most avant-garde dramatists, like Wole Soyinka, Femi Osofisan (Nigeria), Werewere Liking (Cameroon), Zadi Zaourou (Côte d'Ivoire), Efua **Sutherland** (Ghana), Credo Mutwa (South Africa), and Senouvo **Zinsou** (Togo), have taken the strategy a step further by appropriating entire indigenous performances such as masquerade theater, concert-party shows, *didiga*, *anansesem* storytelling, Zulu dance dramas, and building plays on their *structure* and format. In the process, they have broken away from the imported conventions of drama of their formal education, and created exciting new forms.

It should be noted, however, that the indigen-ization processes referred to above did not take place in all countries and regions at the same time, in part because of the colonial legacy. In Anglo-phone West Africa (especially Nigeria but also Ghana) where British policy did not seek to marginalize African languages and cultural tradi-tions with the single-mindedness of the French, experimentation with indigenous forms has basi-cally been the norm. It certainly goes back to the 1960s with Soyinka's *A Dance of the Forest* (1973), and arguably earlier, with the *Blinkards* of Kobina Sekyi (1915), which contains a mix of Fanti and English, and even earlier still with the so-called "native drama" genre that emerged among the Yoruba between 1890 and 1920, and which, like the then-emerging separatist churches, blended European and Yoruba performance conventions. In Franco-phone West Africa, on the other hand, where the French encouraged would-be dramatists to write "to European tastes," such experiments only started in the 1980s with the works of Werewere Liking, **Sony Labou Tansi** and Zadi Zaourou. In apartheid South Africa and pre-independence Zimbabwean guerilla camps, the struggle against minority rule witnessed the widespread use of indigenous performances. But because in South Africa any cultural nativization effort by blacks could be easily recuperated and used against them by a system intent on imposing "tribal" identities on them, black theater practitioners adopted a pragmatic approach to the use of these performances, borrowing specific devices from them for the equally specific purpose of communicating effectively with their audience, and not of formulating some metaphysics of blackness.

The origins of modern drama

But regardless of its varieties, the development of modern drama in Africa can be traced to colonial culture. First introduced by European administrators and settlers as a means of entertainment, and additionally (in countries like Kenya, then Northern and Southern Rhodesia) an instrument of racial and cultural cohesion and exclusiveness, the theater rapidly became, by the mid nineteenth century, an important component, in such places as Sierra Leone and Nigeria especially, of the cultural activities of an influential group of Africans known as returnees, products of the African diaspora (see **diaspora and pan-Africanism**). Made up of repatriated ex-slaves from the Americas and Britain, members of this group founded social and cultural clubs and staged concerts of Western music and variety shows modeled on the vaudeville tradition. Strictly imitative in the beginning, these concerts had, by the 1880s, taken to incorporating indigenous cultural elements in a gesture of nationalist assertion. While these clubs played an important role in the growth of modern drama in Africa, by far the most important part was played by the Church, whose proselytizing activities included the dramatization of scenes from the Bible, and the school (Achimota in Ghana and William Ponty in Senegal stand out in this regard), where the study of Molière or Shakespeare was integral to the curriculum. William Ponty went beyond merely studying or staging European plays to actually teaching play-making.

Other important factors in the growth of modern drama in Africa include the radio drama competitions of the African services of the British and French broadcasting corporations, the creation by colonial and African governments of drama schools and institutes, the administrative take-over and cultural nationalization, as it were, of "na-tional" theaters, inherited from the colonial era, such as the Kenyan and Ugandan national theaters, and the founding by nationalist theater activists of drama groups and associations like the University of Zambia theater group devoted to the promotion of an African-based modern theater.

Types of drama

Arguably the most significant impetus to the growth of modern drama in Africa was not any single institution but a political phenomenon: the struggle for independence. The theater's relative accessibility, even in its modern form, to largely non-literate audiences, made it a privileged medium of communication of the nationalist values associated with that struggle. Although because of overlapping concerns plays cannot be easily pigeonholed into neat categories, four broad types of modern drama can be distinguished. The earliest, and a preferred type, especially in Francophone Africa, is the history play, of which *The Death of Chaka* (1962) by the Malian Seydou **Badian**, *L'Exil d'Albouri* (The Exile of Albouri) (1967) by the Senegalese Cheik **Ndao**, *Ovonramwen Nogbaisi* (1974) by the Nigerian Ola **Rotimi**, *The Trials of Dedan Kimathi* (1974) by Ngugi Wa Thiong'o and Micere **Mugo**, *Kinjetikele* (1970) by the Tanzanian Ebrahim Hussein are notable examples. Through the heroic dramatization of the careers of the title characters of these plays, the dramatists sought to promote a sense of nationalist pride and consciousness in the audience, to reclaim a heroic past which is then pressed into the service of cultural resistance. But not all history plays are celebratory or escapist. Many, like Soyinka's *A Dance of the Forest* (1973), **Tchicaya UTam'Si**'s *Le Zulu* (The Zulu) (1979), Bernard Dadié's *Iles de tempête* (Islands of the Storm) (1973), or even *Kinjetikele* adopt a satirical attitude, when they are not deeply critical of the past, its leaders and traditions.

Another widely practiced type is the political play. The abuse of power by the postcolonial state and its politicians, the delusions of grandeur and ruthlessness of its corporals-turned-field-marshals-turned presidents, the growing pauperization of the mass of its people by an unproductive and alienated elite, have provided the inspiration for such plays as *Le Président* (The President) (1973) and *Le Maréchal Ninkon Ninku* (Field Marshall Ninkon Ninku) (1979), by the Congolese Maxime Ndébéka and Tchicaya UTam'Si respectively, *Opera Wonyosi* and *A Play of Giants* (1984) by Soyinka, *I Will Marry When I Want* (1980) by Ngugi Wa Thiong'o and Ngugi wa Mirii, *The Chattering and the Song* (1977) and *Once upon Four Robbers* (1980) by Femi Osofisan. In South Africa, political theater was at the forefront of the fight against apartheid with such plays as *The Rhythm of Violence* (1964) by Lewis **Nkosi**, *Sizwe Bansi is Dead* (1974) by Athol Fugard, John Kani, and Winston Ntshona, *Shanti* (1981) by Mthuli Shezi, and *A Hungry Earth* (1993) by Maisha Maponye, the last two inspired by the ideology and politics of the black consciousness movement. The non-literary, agitprop character of a lot of political theater, with its preference for direct address, didacticism, a presentational style, and allegorical characters, is a function of that theater's objective to heighten political consciousness among theater-goers and mobilize them around the cause of radical political change.

A third type is social drama. Plays in this category include Soyinka's *The Lion and the Jewel* (1963), and *The Trials of Brother Jero* (1964), Dadié's *Monsieur Thogo-Gnini* (1965), Guillaume **Oyônô-Mbia**'s *Three Suitors One Husband* (1964), Efua Sutherland's *The Marriage of Anansewa* (1967), Werewere Liking's *La Puissance d'Um* (The Power of Um) (1980), and Ngugi wa Thiong'o's *The Black Hermit* (1968). These works are based on their authors' keen and critical observation of society and its customs. They tend to be satirical, and explore through comedy, and on a realistic register, the various conflicts (generational, religious, gender) which the encounter with modernity has precipitated in African societies.

One more trend that can be distinguished is what could be called the drama of moral and philosophical reflection. Although the setting, characters, and situations are firmly African, plays in this group – for example Soyinka's *Death and the King's Horseman* (1975) and *The Strong Breed* (1969), John Pepper **Clark-Bekederemo**'s *Ozidi* (1966), Ola Rotimi's *The Gods are Not to Blame* (1971) – use such features as mere cultural authenticating mechanisms for the exploration of moral and metaphysical issues.

Modern theater in Africa is not restricted to the art theater examined above. In countries like Burkina Faso, Malawi, Botswana, Nigeria, and Zimbabwe, there are strong traditions of community or development theater that seek to promote development projects in the areas of health, agriculture, literacy, or in its more activist form (like the Kamiriithu theater in Kenya) to foster among rural populations, especially, a revolutionary consciousness of the sociopolitical roots of their plight. Much of this theater, however, is not born of the initiatives of the target populations, but of international development agencies or radical intellectuals working in association with those populations.

A final sub-class of modern theater worth mentioning, in conclusion, is commercial theater. A feature of Nigerian urban popular theater is the commercial performances such as the famous Yoruba Opera, associated with figures such as Herbert **Ogunde**, which after a successful traveling phase now seems to be settling into video- and filmmaking. Commercial theater is also particularly strong in South Africa. Here, the so-called townships musicals of Gibson **Kente**, or such spectacular productions as *King Kong, Ipi Tombi*, and *Serafina*, make it the most profitable theater concern in Africa, and arguably the best known by international audiences.

Further reading

Conteh-Morgan, John (1994) *Theatre and Drama in Francophone Africa: A Critical Introduction*, Cambridge: Cambridge University Press.
Etherton, Michael (1982) *The Development of African Drama*, New York: Africana Publishing.

JOHN CONTEH-MORGAN

modernity and modernism

Modernity is perhaps one of the most persistent themes in African literature, but modernism is one of its most elusive categories. The reason for this paradoxical situation is that while modernism emerged in the West as a reaction, or in relation, to the process and discourse of modernity, the history of the two movements in Africa has been neither linear nor causal. In Europe, modernism arose in reaction to the process of industrialization or to a discourse on the nature of modern society. As it developed at the end of the nineteenth century, European modernism was an aesthetic whose goal was to account for, or resist, modernity. In Europe, then, the relation between the two processes or movements has been clear: modernity came before modernism. In Africa, on the other hand, it is not easy to establish a clear-cut relation between the two categories. Modernity, which was largely associated with the process of colonialism (see **colonialism, neocolonialism, and postcolonialism**), developed almost at the same time as modernism was developing in Europe, and it is still not clear that an aesthetic of modernism was appropriated by African writers and arts to counter modernity. Indeed, it is possible to argue that modernism was valued by African writers only to the extent that it enabled them to represent their cultures and peoples as entities and subjects that were essentially modern. Given this complex relationship, it is important to first map out the character of modernity in African literature and then reflect on the nature of the modernism that emerged in relation, and later in opposition, to the idea of the modern.

Modernity and modernization

One of the reasons why modernity has been such a dominant theme in African literature is that the African condition in both colonialism and postcolonialism has been defined by ideas about modernity and the process of modernization. While these two categories – modernity and modernization – tend to be closely related in African literature, it is important to distinguish their meaning if not implication. Modernity can essentially be seen as a philosophical and conceptual term, which, in a European context, dates back to the eighteenth century. When European intellectuals argued for the idea of a modern culture during this period, they were striving to achieve three main objectives: to free the human subject from what the German philosopher Immanuel Kant called the tutelage of tradition,

so that individuals would be responsible for their own actions; to assert the power of reason or rationality, so that subjects would be independent thinkers; and to affirm the supremacy of the freedom of individuals and their rights against those of religious and secular authority.

At the same time, however, advocates of modernity in Europe were aware of the extent to which the ideals of modernity were being negated by the realities of the emerging industrial society. They were aware of how industrial society constantly led to disenchantment, largely because it was premised on ideas of progress and self-improvement that were, nevertheless, negated by the contradictions of the new modes of social and economic organization, including urbanization. In the middle of the nineteenth century, even the strongest proponents of modernity were aware that the process of secularization, while admirable because it led to the break with religious tradition, led to the spiritual impoverishment of the modern subject, who was left unmoored in a world defined by psychological alienation and social displacement. Finally, the emphasis on the identity and rights of the self-conscious individual in the discourse of modernity tended to create split subjects, torn between the desire to define themselves in terms of self-engendered values and the claims of rapidly changing societies.

Modernity, then, has come to acquire a positive and negative narrative: the first insists on the ideals of self-conscious subjectivity and the desire for freedom; the other is driven by an acute sense of disenchantment and the splitting of subjectivity. In Africa, these two narratives have been complicated by the experience of colonization, since it was colonialism that introduced what were considered to be the institutions of modern life in many African communities, while at the same time depriving people of the rights that were associated with the project of modernity itself. In these circumstances, the ideals of modernity were bound to run into conceptual problems, because if colonialism was to be the major agent for transforming traditional precolonial societies into modern polities, it was difficult to reconcile the notion of free self-conscious individuals with colonial domination.

From another perspective, however, it could be

said that Africans who were attracted to colonialism because of its association with modernity often became disillusioned with it precisely because the process of colonization was often premised on the destruction of precolonial society without providing a free autonomous modern culture in return. It is hence difficult to think about modernity in Africa outside the process of modernization. As a political and economic project, colonialism was posited as a project of modernizing the African; its goal was to transform African cultures from what were seen as their traditional foundations into cultures of modernity, ones defined by reason, notions of progress, and civilization. Colonialism was premised on the belief that the African was backward, unmodern, that they could become industrialized in time to cater to the needs of Africans who had become Europeanized. What Africans needed, it was argued, was modernization. But this notion of modernization was not simply one imposed on colonized Africans by European agents and institutions.

Modernization was appealing to many Africans. It was to become one of the cornerstones of the politics of nationalism on the continent, because, almost without exception, African nationalists opposed colonialism not simply as a system of domination and exploitation, but failing in what they considered to be the mandate of modernization. In the discourse of nationalism (see **nationalism and post-nationalism**), the critique of colonialism was necessitated by its failure to complete the project of modernity, as it were. As Jomo **Kenyatta** noted at the end of *Facing Mount Kenya* (1938: London),

> If Africans were left in peace on their own lands, Europeans would have to offer them the benefits of white civilization in real earnest before they could obtain the African labor which they want so much. They would have to offer the African a way of life which was really superior to the one his fathers lived before him, and a share in the prosperity given them by their command of science.

Some of the most prominent works in the African literary tradition, from Chinua **Achebe**'s *Things Fall Apart* (1956) to Tsitsi **Dangarembga**'s *Nervous Conditions* (1989), were written to negotiate

the conflicting desire for "the benefits of white civilization" and the desire for emancipation.

African literature and modernity

Within the culture of colonialism, modernity tends to be associated in African literature with the loss of autonomy and freedom. But this loss does not emerge directly from how modern institutions were instrumental in enforcing the violence associated with colonialism, nor were they necessarily imposed from outside on an unwilling populace. On the contrary, in order for disenchantment to become a major theme in African literature, there had to be enchantment in the first place, and this is often the source of irony. In other words, the key works dealing with the disenchantment of modernity (**Oyono**'s *Houseboy* (1958), Achebe's *Arrow of God* (1964), or Dangarembga's *Nervous Conditions*) start with subjects who are forced to enter the realm of colonial modernity because it is either an attractive illusion, a political strategy, or an inevitable process of social formation; but the education of these characters is usually a negative process, the discovery that the allure of the modern is deceptive, that it often leads to death, madness, or unhappiness. The gap between the mirage of modernity and its consequences is, of course, what generates ironic discourse in these novels. A larger irony in modern African literature is that in spite of their disillusionment with modernity and their craving for a postcolonial culture, often associated with the romance of the hearth and home, African writers and their narrators tell their stories from the vantage point of an incomplete modernity, one which comes with alienation even when it dangles the material privileges that make narrative possible. African novels such as Camara **Laye**'s *Dark Child* (*L'Enfant noir*) (1953) evoke the romance of a childhood untouched by the pain of the modern, but this craving for the past only calls attention to the overwhelming reality of the institutions of modern life, including the European language in which the novel is produced. In other works, most notably Flora **Nwapa**'s *Efuru* (1966), modernity appears to be absent, but beneath the veneer of a precolonial society that runs according to its old rules and norms is a deep sense of the power of modern notions such as individualism and acquisitiveness.

The existence of the grammar of modernity in these works does not, of course, suggest that African writers have written works to fulfil the mandate of European modernity. In significant cases, literature became an important site for questioning some central tenets of modernity even when endorsing others. This is especially the case in regard to the question of subjectivity. While European modernity has always privileged the self-conscious individual as its ideal subject, African literature has as a rule struggled to reconcile the need for subjectivity as a condition of the novel: for example, with the larger project of cultural nationalism that sought to recover and celebrate the communal values which, many writers argued, were threatened by the process of modernity itself.

The question of modernism

The relation of modernism to modernity in African literature has historically been complex and sometimes contradictory. Because of their commitment to recovering an African culture and imagining the new community of the nation, many African writers did not identify directly with the key tenets of modernism. In particular, they were suspicious of three central claims in the discourse of high modernism – the critique of history, the negation of realism, and the insistence on the autonomy of art. These three claims seemed to be at odds with the project of African literature as it was defined in the crucial period between the end of World War II and decolonization in the early 1960s. European modernism had attacked history as a nightmare and prisonhouse, repressing the desire for newness to inherited traditions and forms. African writers, however, lived under the shadow of Hegel and his claim that African had no history; for this reason, they sought to write novels that would recover and valorize the historical moment as palpable and logical. While European modernism asserted its newness by attacking nineteenth-century traditions of realism, African writers turned to realistic forms to counter the representation of the continent as an uncultured and irrational space. And because many African writers believed that art had a pedagogical function or was tied to a larger

nationalist project, many of them were suspicious of the claim, in the manifestos of modernism, that art had a transcendental value.

At the same time, however, there was no doubt that the most important period in the history of African literature had been triggered by modernism, albeit indirectly. This point becomes clearer if we recall that the most important and influential African writers were products of a colonial literary education (see **education and schools**) that celebrated European cultural forms and texts often at odds with the experiences of the colonized. By attacking this tradition, the discourse of modernism opened up a crucial space for African writing: it was through their association with modernist and avant-garde moments in the 1920s and 1930s that African writers such as the poets of **negritude** were freed from the strictures of their colonial education and the rigid forms of the colonial language itself. It was from reading the key texts of modernism at colonial universities in the 1940s and 1950s that another generation of African writers discovered an idiom for rerouting the African imagination from its previous attempts to imitate the high forms of European literature.

Nevertheless, it was not until the late 1960s and 1970s that another generation of African writers turned explicitly to techniques and ideas borrowed from European modernism to try and represent the crisis of postcolonialism. The imperative for this self-conscious turn to modernism was the feeling that realism as a form intended to imagine the nation and celebrate a usable African past had become so identified with the nationalist project that it was incapable of accounting for the crisis of decolonization. The imperative to break away from the national imaginary and its forms had already been hinted as early as 1960 in Chinua **Achebe**'s *No Longer at Ease* and Wole **Soyinka**'s *A Dance of the Forests*. Modernism, then, was to become prominent as a simultaneous critique of realism and nationalism. It was to become most pronounced in a cluster of novels in which the utopian claims that had driven nationalism were seen as empty signs, history become a nightmare, the narrative of decolonization itself a tyrannical totality that repressed the self-conscious individual and imprisoned language. In some of the prominent works from this period, including novels and plays by

Ama Ata **Aidoo**, Ayi Kwei **Armah**, Ahmadou **Kourouma**, **Ngugi wa Thiong'o**, and Wole Soyinka, what was at issue was not simply the neocolonial order but the narratives that had willed it into being. In these works, the imperative for writing was the urgent need to demythologize nationalism itself, and this could only be done by fracturing experience, providing multiple and dispersed perspectives, insisting on the primacy of the subjective experience over the objective, and even the parodying of the ethnographic mode.

Further reading

Cascardi, Anthony J. (1992), *The Subject of Modernity*, Cambridge: Cambridge University Press.
Kenyatta, J. (1938) *Facing Mount Kenya*, London: Secker and Warburg.

SIMON GIKANDI

Modisane, Bloke

b. 1923, Sophiatown, South Africa; d. 1986, Dortmund, Germany

short story writer, critic, and journalist

William Bloke Modisane was born in Sophiatown. He was employed as a music critic by the *Golden City Post*, and later worked as a reporter for *Drum* magazine. Modisane belongs to a group of black South African writers, critics, and journalists who at some stage in their careers lived in Sophiatown and worked as journalists for *Drum* magazine. This group, popularly known as the "*Drum* writers," includes such well-known writers as Es'kia **Mphahlele**, Lewis **Nkosi**, Nat **Nakasa**, and Can **Themba**, all of whom feature in Modisane's **autobiography**, *Blame Me on History* (1963), a book which is arguably Modisane's most significant contribution to African literature in general and to life-writing in particular. While working for *Drum*, Modisane had three of his **short stories** published in the magazine between 1951 and 1954: "The Dignity of Begging" (September 1951), "The Fighter Who Wore Skirts" (January 1952), and "The Respectable Pickpocket" (February 1954). Like his autobiography, Modisane's short fiction

examines the attempts of a self-taught writer/ intellectual to come to terms with feelings of powerlessness and alienation in the face of repressive government legislation.

Further reading

Ngwenya, Thengani H. (1989) "The Ontological Status of Self in Autobiography: The Case of Modisane's *Blame Me on History*," *Current Writing: Text and Reception in Southern Africa* 1, 1: 67–76.

THENGANI H. NGWENYA

Mofokeng, Sophonia Machabe

b. 1923, South Africa; d. 1957, South Africa

dramatist and essayist

Sophonia Mofokeng was a South African dramatist and essayist of great promise, but his life was interrupted by spells of ill health which resulted in his spending almost a whole year bedridden in hospital in the late 1940s. His first play, entitled after the protagonist, *Senkatana* (1952), was based on the legend of the swallowing monster referred to in Sesotho as *moshanyana wa Senkatana* (the boy Senkatana). He modeled it on a Sesotho legend but he also incorporated elements borrowed from Greek tragedy, especially the use of the Seer and the Chorus. He also published a collection of short stories, *Leetong* (On Pilgrimage) (1952) and essays, *Pelong ya Ka* (In My Heart) (published posthumously in 1962). Both works are poignant, using the journey as a metaphor for life. Mofokeng also collaborated with Professor C.M. Doke to produce one of the most seminal Sesotho grammar books to date, *Textbook of Southern Sotho Grammar* (1957). His contribution to literary criticism were his unpublished master's and doctoral theses, entitled "A Study of Folk Tales in Sotho" (1951) and "The Development of Leading Figures in Animal Tales in Africa" (1955) respectively, which were conferred by the University of the Witwatersrand.

N.P. MAAKE

Mofolo, Thomas Mokopu

b. 1876, Khojane, Basutoland (now Lesotho); d. 1948, Teyateyaneng, Basutoland

novelist

Although Thomas M. Mofolo published only three novels, he has left an indelible mark in African literary history. His first novel, *Moeti wa Bochabela* is considered to be the first novel by an African to appear in Africa. The novel first appeared as a series in the Sesotho journal *Lesedinyana* in 1906 and was published in book form in 1907. It was later translated into English by H. Ashton in 1934 as *Traveler to the East*. This novel, and perhaps Mofolo's authorship in general, was inspired, among other things, by his being employed as a proof-reader and editor at the famous Morija's Printing Works and Book Depot in Lesotho. Born to Christian parents, Mofolo grew up and went to school at Qomoqomong in the Quthing district. He proceeded to the Bible School in Morija Training College in 1896, whereupon he secured the editorial job at Morija Printing Works in 1899. When the South African war of 1899–1902 compelled the Morija Press to shut down, Mofolo returned to Quthing to learn carpentry at Leloaleng Technical School. He then taught at Bensonvale High School and later returned to teach in Maseru, Lesotho, until 1904 when he rejoined Morija Printing Works at its reopening.

Mofolo's second novel, *Pitseng* (In the Pot), was published in 1910, after being serialized in *Lesedinyana*. Following on the tradition of autobiographical fiction, this novel draws on Mofolo's days as a student and portrays his favorite teacher, Everitt Segoete, as the character Katse, and his classmate whom he later married, as Aria Sebaka. But it was Mofolo's third novel, *Chaka*, a literary epic based on the Zulu king Shaka, which transformed him into an author of international renown. Literary reviews speculate on why the manuscript, purportedly completed in 1910, was only published in 1925. However, one thing is certain, that *Chaka* is the only piece of literature of its time that inspired serious and innumerable critical debates. By 1948, six editions of the novel had been republished. Between 1926 and 1928 a number of letters depicting readers' mixed feelings about the novel were published in *Lesedinyana*. The novel has appeared in two English translations, by F.H. Dutton in 1931 and D.P. Kunene in 1981. A French translation by Ellenberger appeared in 1940, a German one by P. Sulzer in 1953, an Italian one by L.P. Berra in 1959 and another by J. Wilkinson and I. Vivan in 1988. An Afrikaans translation (see **Afrikaans literature**) by C.F. Swanepoel was published in 1974. *Chaka* stimulated creative writing in West African authors such as L.S. **Senghor**, K. Seydou, and A.A. Ka, which drew on the character of Chaka and his exploits as represented in Mofolo's novel. The novel has been the subject of many scholarly books and articles.

Despite his achievements as a writer, Mofolo was severely affected by the discriminatory land acts of the South African government, which dispossessed him of his acquired land and rendered him unemployed. He thus lived his last years in ill health and poverty. Nevertheless, he is considered to be a pioneer of African writing and a key figure in the history of the novel on the continent.

ROSEMARY MOEKETSI

Moiloa, James Jantjies

b. 1916, Wepenaar, Orange Free State, South Africa; d. 1994, Bloemfontain, South Africa

poet, novelist, and educator

The South African writer James Jantjies Moiloa was a pioneer and trendsetter in the field of education in the country and a major contributor to various areas of Sotho (Sesotho) literature. He was the first African principal of Lereko High School in Bloemfontein and the first African language assistant in the Department of African Languages at the University of the Free State. Born in Wepenaar in the Orange Free State, he attained a Teacher's Certificate in 1940 at Moroka Training School, and a BA degree from the University of South Africa in 1958. An active educationist and an ardent custodian of his native language, Moiloa helped to found the Sesotho Association of Language and Culture, was a member of the

African Library Association, and of LESIBA, the Sesotho writers' association to which he even contributed a trophy, which has since been the basis for the annual Roving Moila Trophy, a literary competition. His celebrated contribution to Sesotho literature includes eleven translations of grammar books and religious writings (*Bophelo bo botle* (Good Life), *Thutabodumedi* (Religious Studies), *O re rute ho rapela* (Teach Us to Pray), *Katekisima ya Wesele* (Catechism of the Wesleyan Church), *Boromuwa ba Bokreste* (Christian Missionary), all undated church publications), essays (*Sediba sa Meqoqo* (The Fountain of Essays), undated church publication), short stories (*Dipale le Metlae*, (Stories and Jokes) (1970)), poetry (*Mohahlaula Dithota, Ditswakotleng* (The Wanderer) (1970)), drama (*Jaa o siele Motswalle* (Eat and Leave Some for a Friend) (1970), *Molomo wa Badimo* (The Mouth of the Gods) (1977), *Mosadi a Ntlholla* (The Woman Who Distressed Me) (1981)), novels (*Paka Mahlomola* (Tragedy) (1965), *Mehla e a Fetoha* (Times Change) (1971)), and folk tales (*Ditshomo* (Tales) (1986)). Moiloa has co-authored two dictionaries and no fewer than ten grammar books.

ROSEMARY MOEKETSI

Monenembo, Tierno

b. 1947, Porédaka, Guinea

novelist

Tierno Monenembo (the pseudonym of Tierno Seydou Diallo) was born in Porédaka, Guinea, but he left the country in 1969 to escape the dictatorship of Sékou Touré. After living successively in Senegal, Côte d'Ivoire, Algeria, and Morocco, Monenembo moved to France in 1973 to pursue further studies, graduating with a doctorate in biochemistry. He currently lives in France. Since the 1970s, Monenembo has published over eight novels on subjects ranging from *Les Crapauds-brousse* (The Bush Toads) published in 1979 to *L'Aîné des orphelins* (The Eldest of the Orphans) (2000). In these works, Monenembo has found in the novel the ideal weapon to denounce the topical issues of tyranny and dictatorship in postcolonial Africa (see **colonialism, neocolonialism, and postcolonialism**). Concerned with what might be called

the writing of the nightmare or disaster of postcolonialism, he produces work that focuses on the language of the absurd, accentuating the sense of postcolonial collapse and representing a world dominated by decomposition and existential fear.

OUSMANE BA

Moore, Bai T.

b. 1916, Liberia; d. 1988, Monrovia, Liberia

writer

One of the few Liberian writers who have gained some recognition outside their country, Bai Moore was born into a Vai family. After local education in a mission school he went to study at the Virginia Union Seminary in the United States, where he studied biology. It was while he was in the United States, still learning English, that Moore published *Golah Boy in America* (1938), an autobiographical account comparing his life in Liberia with his experiences in the United States. Returning to Liberia in 1941, Moore held various positions in the Liberian civil service and with UNESCO. He continued to write poems, mostly in free verse, representing his African and American experiences or derived from scenes from his travels in Europe and Asia. These poems have been collected in *Ebony Dust* (1963). Moore's most famous work is a short story, "Murder in the Cassava Patch" (1968), which was later expanded into a novel of the same title. He has also published *Categories of Traditional Liberian Songs* (1969), a collection of Liberian oral literature (see **oral literature and performance**).

SIMON GIKANDI

Moyo, Aaron Chiwundura

b. 1959, Zimbabwe

novelist and playwright

Aaron Moyo entered the Shona literary creative scene (see **Shona and Ndebele literature**) with his didactic novels, *Uchandifungawo* (You Shall Miss Me) (1975) and *Ziva Kwawakabva* (Remember Your

Roots) (1977), which advocate the consolidation of African values in the face of colonialism and cultural imperialism (see **colonialism, neocolonialism, and postcolonialism**). These were succeeded by novels and plays on the African experience in the colonial and postcolonial periods. His works helped him secure a job with the Zimbabwe Broadcasting Corporation. In the mid 1980s, Moyo wrote novels dealing with the common themes related to the war of liberation in Zimbabwe. These include *Yaive Hondo* (That Was War) (1985) and *Nguo Dzouswa* (An Awkward Situation) (1985). In *Wakandicheka Nerakagomara* (You Gave Me a Raw Deal) (1982), *Wakandibaya Panyama Nhete* (You Hit Me on a Soft Spot) (1987), and the play *Chenga Ose* (Do Not Discriminate) (1983), he continued with the analysis of topical social issues. His play, *Kuridza Ngoma Nedemo* (Out of Bounds) (1985), satirizes the landlessness of peasants; *Ndabve Zera* (I Have Come of Age) (1990), one of the most widely studied plays in Zimbabwean schools, satirizes Western-oriented human rights education in Shona society. Moyo also uses radio programs to promote the Shona culture.

Further reading

Kahari, G.P. (1990) *The Rise of the Shona Novel*, Gweru: Mambo Press.

EMMANUEL CHIWOME

Mphahlele, Es'kia

b. 1919, Marabastad, South Africa;
   d. 2008, Lebo Wakgomo, Polokwane, South Africa

writer

Es'kia Mphahlele's most enduring legacy may be in **autobiography**. In all his prodigious output, which includes short fiction, literary essays, the novel, poetry, and social commentary, it is in the two autobiographies, *Down Second Avenue* (1959) and *Afrika My Musik* (1989), that we see the singularity of his career. The shape of that career can best be understood as a series of representative crises and encounters in the life of a black South African,

both in his own country and in the wider diaspora. Mphahlele's formative years coincided with the hardening of apartheid; subsequently, he found himself in exile as a participant in several major centers of cultural ferment in the black world; finally, he returned to "lay his shadow on ancestral soil" during the period of apartheid's demise (see **apartheid and post-apartheid**).

Down Second Avenue tells the story of a childhood lived between the crucible of an urban ghetto, Marabastad, the dormitory township near Pretoria where he was born, and the bewildering emptiness of rural Maupaneng, where he was a goatherder in his grandmother's homestead. It covers schooling and teacher-training in the mission ethos, and early professional years as a clerk, teacher, and journalist before his remove into exile in 1957. After being barred from teaching owing to his opposition to apartheid's Bantu Education system, he spent a brief period as a political reporter and fiction editor on *Drum* magazine before leaving to take up a position in a grammar school in Lagos. Soon afterwards, he taught English in the extension program of the University of Ibadan.

Afrika My Musik covers the next twenty years of exile and return. Having participated in one kind of renaissance, that associated with the *Drum* generation, he was precipitated into another, for in Nigeria he became associated with the Mbari club and collaborated with Ulli Beier on the journal *Black Orpheus*. In the early 1960s, publication by Faber in quick succession of *Down Second Avenue* and the essays collected in *The African Image* (1962) established Mphahlele as a public intellectual on the diasporic circuit. (The title of *The African Image* was extrapolated from an MA thesis, "The Non-European Character in South African English Fiction," written for the University of South Africa before his departure.) He was appointed and traveled extensively as director of the Africa program of the Congress for Cultural Freedom, based in Paris. In this period he became widely known for his opposition to the "cult" of **negritude**, largely on the grounds that it denied the urban, proletarian experience Mphahlele had known under apartheid.

After Paris, Mphahlele moved to Nairobi, where under the auspices of the Congress he became director of the Chemchemi Creative Centre, which tried with mixed results to repeat Mbari's successes in East Africa. A brief contract lectureship in English at University College, Nairobi, followed, then admission to the creative writing program at the University of Denver, Colorado. At Denver, he was awarded his PhD on completion of *The Wanderers* (1971), an autobiographical novel whose irresolution speaks of the awkwardly persistent rootlessness of the South African émigré elsewhere on the continent.

Despite the inauspicious implications of the novel, Mphahlele tried to settle in Lusaka following his PhD, but soon returned to Denver, then Philadelphia, where he became a full professor at the University of Pennsylvania. This period saw Mphahlele working closely with Houston Baker and Sonia Sanchez, reaching more deeply into African-American traditions, the results of which are partly recorded in essays collected in *Voices in the Whirlwind* (1972). The early 1970s saw a sea-change, reflected in the revised edition of *The African Image*. In the first edition (1962), Mphahlele had wanted to vindicate the cross-cultural, urban experience of the black South African in a diasporic culture dominated by negritude; the second edition (1974) represents a *volte face*, for it turns inward to reflect more deeply on racial identity. The factors at work here include the influence of black America and the echoes reaching him of the black consciousness movement of Steve Biko's generation at home.

It is in this period, too, that Mphahlele begins to think of abandoning the "glass-house" of exile, despite the obvious censure such a move would bring, given the prevailing cultural boycott of South Africa. Mphahlele had decided that one's right to confront mortality in community and on ancestral soil superseded one's political obligations. The phrase used most frequently in explanation of his return – which coincided with the suppression of the Soweto revolt – is "the tyranny of place," suggesting the uncomfortable but inescapable necessity of home. *Afrika My Musik* ends with the adjustment following this relocation.

Since his return, Mphahlele's larger theme has been African humanism, expressing principles of accommodation, continuity, and holism that are familiar in the black world, but in Mphahlele's

example incorporating both a return to racial self-affirmation and an embrace of secular modernity (see **modernity and modernism**), the two axes around which the collected essays turn. A mature statement of this position can be found in "Poetry and Humanism: Oral Beginnings," a lecture given at the University of the Witwatersrand, where he became the inaugural professor in the Division of African Literature, his last appointment before retirement. Throughout his career, Mphahlele has been eloquent on the subject of racial injury, but he has never adopted a position of isolationism.

Mphahlele's first appearance as a writer of note was in *Man Must Live and Other Stories* (1947). Apart from the autobiography, the short fiction continues to fuel critical and public interest. *Drum* carried several pieces under the pseudonym Bruno Esekie, and a particularly successful series known as the Lesane stories. Later collections were *The Living and the Dead* (n.d.), *In Corner B* (1967), and *The Unbroken Song* (1981) – the last of these containing a representative collection of the poetry. Several stories, like "Mrs Plum," "In Corner B," and "Grieg on a Stolen Piano," have been much anthologized, becoming classics in modern African short fiction. A second, less successful novel was *Chirundu* (1979), based on the Zambian experience. Mphahlele's early fiction is infused with cross-cultural humanism, but later stories move to protest. In all his writing, however, he gives equal weight to the political and the aesthetic. He must be seen, therefore, as a precursor in the line of critical interventions in South African black fiction, a line which includes Lewis **Nkosi** and Njabulo **Ndebele**, questioning the subordination of aesthetic self-awareness in the name of protest.

Mphahlele has attracted a good deal of academic criticism, including several monographs, ever since the appearance of Janheinz Jahn's *Muntu* (1961). One biography has appeared, *Exiles and Homecomings*, by Noel Chabani Manganyi (1983). Written in the first person, it should be read as a contribution to the establishment of a black consciousness psychology, stressing the integrity of the self. Manganyi also collected and published a volume of selected letters, *Bury Me at the Marketplace* (1984).

DAVID ATTWELL

Mqhayi, Samuel Edward Krune

b. 1875, South Africa; d. 1945, South
Africa

poet and novelist

The South African poet is one of the pioneers of
IsiXhosa literature. He worked first as a teacher
and later as editor of a newspaper called *Izwi
Labantu* (Voice of the People) and later *Imvo
Zabantsundu* (People's Opinions). His first novel,
Ityala Lamawele (The Case of the Twins) (1914) is
based on a case of primogeniture involving the
dispute of which of the two twins was the older.
The novel was serialized posthumously on TV by
the South African Broadcasting Corporation
(SABC) in the 1990s. His publications include a
biography of one of the first Xhosa ministers of the
Church, John Bokwe, entitled *U-Bombi Bomfundisi u
John Knox Bokwe* (The Life of Reverend John Knox
Bokwe). He also published a collection of poems,
Imihobe Nemibongo Yokufundwa Ezikolweni (Songs and
Poems for Reading at School) (1927) and *Inzuzo*
(Gain) (1943). Included in the former collection
was an eight-stanza poem entitled "Umhobe
kaNtu" (The Hymn of Ntu), which later, as *Nkosi
Sikele' I-Afrika* (God Bless Africa) was to become the
de facto national anthem of South Africa during
the years of the struggle against apartheid (see
apartheid and post-apartheid). He also published *U-Don Jadu* (1929), an idyllic portrayal of
Xhosa life, *U-Mhlekazi U-Hintsa* (The Great
Hintza), a poem on the Xhosa king of the title
name, and *U-Mqhayi wase Ntab'ozuko* (Mqhayi of the
Mountain of Glory) (1939), an autobiography
translated into Xhosa from the original German.
Mqhayi is regarded as one of the greatest Xhosa
poets.

Further reading

Opland, Jeff (1998) *Xhosa Poets and Poetry*, Cape
Town: David Philip.

N.P. MAAKE

Mrabet, Mohammed

b. 1940, Morocco

novelist and short story writer

Mohammed Mrabet recorded his short stories and
novels on cassette in Moroccan Arabic, to be
transcribed and translated into English by the
American expatriate author Paul Bowles. Mrabet,
an autodidact storyteller from northern Morocco,
met Bowles in Tangier in 1965; he became one of
the circle of Bowles' protegés which occasionally
included the writer Mohammed Choukri and the
painter and storyteller Ahmed Yacoubi. Mrabet's
work, from *Love with a Few Hairs* (1967) and *The
Lemon* (1969) to *Marriage with Papers* (1986),
demonstrates the continued vitality of a storytelling
tradition in Morocco, with a range of expression
and subject matter that surpasses purely "traditional" concerns. The stories reflect an intimate
knowledge of popular life in Morocco, as well as a
brilliant sense of humor and dramatic timing. His
short tales evoke the traditional Moroccan fantastic, while his longer works are more realistic
settings of emotional and social dilemmas. Notwithstanding Mrabet's evident concern for literary
effect, his work retains the oral character of its
original narration.

Further reading

Dawood, Ibrahim (1989) "Mohammed Mrabet
and the Significance of his Work," *International
Fiction Review* 16, 2: 119–22.

SETH GRAEBNER

Mtshali, Oswald Mbuyiseni

b. 1940, Vryheid, Natal, South Africa

poet

Oswald Mbuyiseni Mtshali's first collection of
poetry, *Sounds of a Cowhide Drum* was first published
to wide acclaim in 1971. It was the first collection
of poetry by a black South African published inside
the country in English. Most of the poems in the

collection deal with the devastating impact of the apartheid system (see **apartheid and post-apartheid**) on the lives of black South Africans, especially in urban areas. Mtshali's style is often one of graphic exposition rather than overt analysis, and while he in some ways celebrates the resilience of blacks under the draconian apartheid acts, rules, and policies, he never neglects to show that blacks were occasionally complicit with the oppressive government of their time. Mtshali's exposition generally works by providing a portrait of the urban landscape, and then links the landscape to an aspect of the human condition that he wishes to address. Mtshali's subsequent collection, *Fire Flames*, published in the late 1980s, never really found much favor with the general reading public and literary scholars, and some critics, like Stephen Watson, even declared it inferior to *Sounds of a Cowhide Drum*. Some poems from the earlier collection have been widely anthologized. Despite his subsequent setback, Mtshali remains popular and is regarded as one of the foremost black South African poets of English expression during apartheid.

PHASWANE MPE

Mudimbe, V.Y.

b. 1941, Zaire

philosopher, classicist, and novelist

The work of V.Y. Mudimbe, the Zairean philosopher, classicist, and novelist, takes form from its reflection on the moment of independence. In this sense it is, on an epistemological and institutional level, a reflection of the meaning of independence in relation to the established knowledge and institutions, especially the ones inherited from colonialism (see **colonialism, neocolonialism, and postcolonialism**). The question of the order of African discourse is at the heart of Mudimbe's preoccupations as they unfold in poetic, fictional, and analytic registers. The secession of Katanga, the assassination of Patrice Emery Lumumba, and the accession of Mobutu to power inform *Déchirures* (Tears) (1971), a veritable poetic anthology of the Congolese tragedy. The theme of tears returns in

Entre les eaux, un Dieu, un prêtre, la revolution (1973) (translated in 1991 as *Between Tides*), a novel whose action takes place in post-independence or post-colonial Zaire and asks, through the tortured consciousness of a Catholic priest, the question of the theology of liberation in Africa in the future. *Bel immonde* (1976) (translated in 1989 as *Before the Birth of the Moon*) continues the reflection on the consequences of independence by staging the misfortunes of power in a perspective as much political and social as ethical. The fictional work of Mudimbe, without conforming to aesthetic and formal research, presents itself as another compartment of philosophic reflection. *L'Ecart* (1979) (translated in 1993 as *The Rift*) articulates thus the necessity of a decolonization of established knowledge, contests the scientific nature of Western approaches, and denounces the mystification of African history, but also questions **negritude** and its obsession with the past.

In such texts as *The Invention of Africa: Gnosis, Philosophy and the Order of Knowledge* (1988), Mudimbe constantly asks the question of the gap of African knowledge in relation to the "colonial library." The colonial library, fundamental in the conceptualization of African intellectual and cultural practices, is part of the problematic conditions of possibilities that found this discourse. The interpellation of postcolonial counter-discourse and more particularly that of negritude, a literary and cultural movement that dominates the scene at the moment at which Mudimbe started out in the world of writing, is all the more necessary as the identifying search theorized by this movement is recuperated by post-independence governments with the intent to legitimate negative utopias such as the sadly famous "authenticity." The represented collection edited by Mudimbe at the time of the fortieth anniversary of Présence Africaine, *The Surreptitious Speech: Présence Africaine and the Politics of Otherness. 1947–1987* (1992), prolongs the reflection on the conditions of possibility of African knowledge. The reflection on the humanities continues with an exploration of the contribution of research on Africa to the humanities and social sciences (*Africa and the Disciplines: The Contribution of Research in Africa to the Social Sciences and Humanities*, 1993). *L'Odeur du Père: essai sur les limites de la science et de la vie en Afrique noire* (The Odour of the Father: An Essay on the

Limits of Social Science in Black Africa) (1982) analyzes the limits of Western science in the perception of the "other," interrogates that which a completely liberated African word signifies, and asks itself if it is possible to really escape the West.

Mudimbe's obsession with questioning the place of the West in the genesis and existence of an African discourse situates his work at the crossroads of cultures, that which provokes interrogations of the centrality of Africa in this reflection. Does Mudimbe simply record the dependence of the order of African discourse or is he able to reinforce it through a constant interpellation of its colonial origins? Does there exist a project, other than rhetorical, of emancipation (theoretical, institutional, or epistemological) in the reflection that Mudimbe leads, after almost four decades, on knowledge in Africa? Such are some of the questions the reasoning of Mudimbe raises, questions that demonstrate that this work espouses the paradoxes of what can be called, for lack of a better expression, African modernity (see **modernity and modernism**). The work of Mudimbe poses in a remarkable manner the questions that confront the production of knowledge in Africa, even if it is necessary to recognize that there are few answers. And it is perhaps in these contradictions that this work is representative of the postcolonial condition.

CILAS KEMEDJIO

Mugo, Micere Githae

b. 1942, Kirinyaga district, Kenya

poet and playwright

Born in the Kirinyaga district of Central Province, Micere Githae Mugo was educated at Makerere University, where she graduated with a BA degree in English, and the University of New Brunswick, Canada, where she completed her doctorate. She later taught literature at the University of Nairobi where she was also dean of the Faculty of Arts. She has lived in exile since 1982, first in Zimbabwe and later in the United States. In her two collections of poems, *Daughter of My People Sing* (1976) and *My Mother's Poem and Other Songs* (1994), Mugo's goal is to poeticize a wide range of issues in postcolonial society (see **colonialism, neocolonialism, and postcolonialism**), including social relationships, personal and communal experiences, alienation, and conflict. It is in these poems, perhaps more than her other works, that her prowess as a poet, feminist, and advocate of pan-Africanism finds voice (see **diaspora and pan-Africanism**). Through the poems we hear echoes from the "song school" made famous by the Ugandan poet, **Okot p'Bitek**. Mugo's political concerns are evident in her two plays, *The Long Illness of Ex-Chief Kiti* (1976) and *The Trial of Dedan Kimathi* (1976) (co-written with **Ngugi wa Thiong'o**), works that present powerful critiques of colonialism in Kenya and the culture of betrayal and oppression that characterizes the postcolonial state. In the 1990s, Mugo's work increasingly focused on the nature of oral literature and its relation to questions of development and human rights in Africa, arguing that oral traditions espouse a vision of human rights that is inherent in African cultural experiences (see **oral literature and performance**).

GEORGE ODERA OUTA

Mukasa, Ham

b. 1868, Uganda; d. 1956, Uganda

linguist and writer

Ham Mukasa was a Ugandan linguist and writer. He was employed as a page in the court of Mutesa, one of the most powerful Buganda kings of the nineteenth century. Mukasa converted to Christianity (see **Christianity and Christian missions**) at an early age and was involved in the war between various Christian factions and Muslims at the Buganda court at the end of the nineteenth century. He was a prominent member of the Anglican Church in Uganda, but his influence in the politics of the Ugandan colony depended on his fluency in English and Swahili, which enabled him to act as secretary to Sir Apolo Kagwa, the eminent Buganda statesman and prime minister of the kingdom during the period of British colonialism. Mukasa's work was mainly in language and linguistics and translation. He produced one of the first grammars and glossaries of the Luganda language and a commentary on the Gospel of St Matthew. In 1901, Mukasa accompanied Sir Apolo on a trip to England for the coronation of King Edward VII. Mukasa kept a journal on their travels and this was published as *Uganda's Katikiro in England* in 1904. The book, which has been issued in two editions since its initial production, is considered to be a significant example of African travel narratives in the colonial period, and an insider's view of the process of cultural contact and translation in the relationship between the colonizer and the colonized.

Further reading

Gikandi, Simon (1998) "African Subjects and the Colonial Project," Introduction to Ham Mukasa, *Uganda's Katikiro in England*, Manchester: Manchester University Press.

SIMON GIKANDI

Mulaisho, Dominic

b. 1933, Zambia

novelist

Dominic Mulaisho was born in Zambia. He received his education at the University Colleges of Nyasaland (Malawi) and Southern Rhodesia (Zimbabwe) and has had a distinguished career as a civil servant. His two novels are *The Tongue of the Dumb* (1971) and *The Smoke that Thunders* (1979). *The Tongue of the Dumb* brings to the surface the culture conflict between white Christian missionaries and the indigenous people of the fictional valley of Kaunga (see **Christianity and Christian missions**). The African people's response to the mockery of African polygamy and ancestor veneration by Christian converts is at best confused and at worst self-defeating, as Africans waste energy accusing each other of witchcraft and fighting among themselves. *The Smoke that Thunders*, set in Kandaha, a fictional country between Rhodesia and Zambia, focuses on the birth of African nationalism (see **nationalism and post-nationalism**). In the novel, white settlers are at

war with the governor, the queen's representative in Africa. Kawala and Katenga are African nationalists leading Africans to independence from both the British and white settlers. The process of interrogating African nationalism begins within the struggle with Kawala asking whether or not the African masses are prepared to face new challenges and contradictions of independence.

M. VAMBE

Mungoshi, Charles Lovemore

b. 1947, Zimbabwe

writer and editor

Charles Mungoshi is one of Zimbabwe's most acclaimed and prolific writers. Before going into full-time writing, he was an editor with the Literature Bureau and Zimbabwe Publishing House, and writer-in-residence at the University of Zimbabwe. Mungoshi has won several major literary awards including the PEN award, the Commonwealth Literary Prize for the Africa Region, and the Zimbabwe Book Publishers Association and the Literature Bureau awards. His English works have been translated into German and Dutch. His Shona works (see **Shona and Ndebele literature**) comprise three novels: *Makunun'unu Maodzamwoyo* (Brooding Afflicts the Heart) (1970), *Ndiko Kupindana Kwamazuva* (That's How Time Passes) (1976), and *Kunyarara Hakusi Kutaura?* (Is Silence Not a Form of Communication?) (1983). *Ndiko Kupindana Kwamazuva* represents a breakthrough in the psychological realism in Shona fiction (see **realism and magical realism**). Mungoshi's subsequent works attempt to introduce innovation in narrative techniques in modern fiction. His *Kunyarara Hakusi Kutaura?*, for example, employs the techniques of modernism to highlight the emotional stress that comes with modernity and modernization. His experimentation is also reflected in the play *Inongova Njakenjake* (Each One for Themselves) (1980), which focuses on domestic conflicts arising from the crisis triggered by high expectations in an urban family. In the context of Shona fiction, Mungoshi is outstanding for his relative psychological depth of characters, seriousness of tone, unique organic symbolism, and graphic depiction of subtle issues. Mungoshi has also published some outstanding works in English. His collection of **short stories** collected in *The Coming of the Dry Season* (1972) are considered to be some of the most engaging works of prose in this genre, while his novel, *Waiting for the Rain* (1975), which won the Rhodesia PEN award for 1976, has been admired for its penetrating psychological exploration of the turmoil that characterizes a family torn between conflicting desires.

EMMANUEL CHIWOME

Munonye, John

b. 1929, Akokwa, Eastern Nigeria

novelist and educator

Although he was part of the distinguished group of Africans educated at University College, Ibadan, in the early 1950s, the Nigerian novelist and educator John Munonye did not start writing until the mid 1960s. His first novel, *The Only Son* (1966), is the familiar story of a young African who struggles to acquire education (see **education and schools**) in order to rise beyond his family's poverty, but who discovers that his involvement with the culture of colonialism has instead led to extreme alienation from his mother and neighbors. In his second novel, *Obi* (1969), Munonye tells the story of a young couple struggling to fit into the rhythms of village after a sojourn in the city. These works, which were concerned with the disruption of Igbo life by the forces of modernity (see **modernity and modernism**), are heavily influenced by the early works of Chinua **Achebe**, Munonye's classmate and friend at Ibadan. In his later novels, *Oil Man of Obange* (1970), *A Wreath for the Maidens* (1973), *A Dancer of Fortune* (1975), and *Bridge to a Wedding* (1978), Munonye's interest is still with the intrusion of modernity and its harsh demands on individuals living in villages or small towns, but while there is a certain pessimism in these stories he still maintains faith in the ability of his characters to secure their identity and integrity through the process of education. While there is no doubt that

Munonye is one of the pioneers of African fiction, his works have existed under the shadow of Achebe and have hence not been given the recognition they deserve as original reflections on the process of education and social change in Africa.

Further reading

Griswold, Wendy (2000) *Bearing Witness: Readers, Writers, and the Novel in Nigeria*, Princeton, New Jersey: Princeton University Press.

SIMON GIKANDI

Mustaghānmi, Ahlām

b. 1953, Algeria

poet and novelist

The poet and novelist Ahlām Mustaghānmi is the first Algerian woman to have a novel written and published in Arabic. Her celebrated novel *Dhakirat al-Jasad* (1993) (Memory of the Flesh) (2000) won the Najīb **Maḥfūz** Prize for Literature in 1998. It is a reconstruction of Algeria's struggle for independence and its post-independence problems. Her novels speak particularly of Algeria's unfulfilled dreams, but also of Arab political and social hardships. Independence for Mustāghānmi is not simply a military goal but a cultural, social, and emotional aspiration which Algeria, as well as the developing countries, has yet to achieve. Adopting a male voice in her first novel and the voice of a female in the second, *Fawda al-Hawas* (Anarchy of the Senses) (1999), Mustāghānmi attempts to encompass all human concerns, wary that her writings should not be categorized as "womanist writing," written only to appeal to female masses. Though presently acclaimed as an outstanding novelist, Mustāghānmi's first contributions to literature were two collections of poetry, *ʿAla Marfaʾ al-Ayyam* (At Life's Harbor) (1972) and *al-Kitabah fi Lahdhat ʾUriyy* (Writing in a Moment of Nudity) (1976), where she revealed great freedom in expressing her emotions. The author's most significant contribution, however, is the way she resurrects the Algerian identity by using Arabic. She is one of a growing number of young Algerian writers who reinstated the use of Arabic language in literary texts. They use it poetically, with a postcolonial consciousness, thus giving hope to victims of all sorts of occupation to tell their own tale in their own tongue.

Further reading

Bamia, Aida A. (1997) "'Dhakirat al-Jasad' (The Body's Memory): A New Outlook on Old Themes," *Research in African Literatures* 28, 3: 83–93.

RIHAM SHEBLE

Mutswairo, Solomon Mangwiro

b. 1924, Zimbabwe

novelist and poet

The Zimbabwe novelist and poet Solomon Mutswairo published *Feso*, the first novel in Shona, in 1956 (see **Shona and Ndebele literature**). A romance of the past, love, and adventure, *Feso*'s adoption of the Nehanda legend led to its interpretation as an allegory of colonial oppression. Because of its apparent subversiveness, the novel did not find favor with the institutions of colonialism and it went out of circulation for the rest of the colonial period (see **colonialism, neocolonialism, and postcolonialism**). With other writers, Mutswairo pioneered the writing of poetry in Shona in the ground-breaking collection *Mutinhimira weDetembo* (The Rhythm of Poetry), published in 1965. His novel, *Murambiwa Goredema* (1959), represents the African's tragic encounter with colonialism. While he was living in the United States in the 1970s and 1980s, he published *Chaminuka: Prophet of Zimbabwe* (1978) and *Mapondera: Soldier of Zimbabwe* (1983), two novels belonging to the tradition of African nationalism in fiction. Back in Zimbabwe in the late 1980s, he published *Mweya WaNehanda* (The Spirit of Nehanda) (1988), based on the woman spirit medium who started the 1896 Shona war against British settlers. He also published *Hamandishe* (1988), a novel based on his experiences abroad. In addi-

tion, he contributed to *Nduri DzeZimbabwe* (Zimbabwean Poetry) (1983), an anthology of poems celebrating the independence of Zimbabwe, and also composed lyrics for Zimbabwe's national anthem. Most of Mutswairo's works are based on Zezuru oral traditions and history (see **oral literature and performance**).

Further reading

Chiwome, E.M. (1996) *A Social History of the Shona Novel*, Zimbabwe: Juta.

EMMANUEL CHIWOME

Mwangi, Meja

b. 1948, Nanyuki, Kenya

novelist and journalist

The Kenyan novelist and journalist Meja Mwangi burst on to the East African literary scene when *Kill Me Quick*, his first published novel, won the prestigious Jomo Kenyatta Prize for Literature in 1973. Since then Mwangi has published almost fifteen novels and collections of short stories, including works for children. He is certainly one of the most prolific and popular novelists in East Africa, producing works that are appealing because of the topicality of their themes and their fast-moving narrative style, often fashioned on American popular fiction and film. In spite of his popularity among the reading public, the critical reception of Mwangi's fiction has been mixed or ambivalent at best, and this reflects both his unusual literary career and the variety of genres he writes in, genres in which the line that separates so-called high and **popular literature** is not always clear. In terms of his literary education, Mwangi is unusual among African novelists: he did not go to university until much later in his life and he was hence not part of the community and culture that nurtured writing in Kenya in the postcolonial period; he was, indeed, considered to be an outsider in Nairobi's literary circles. The advantage to this unusual situation was that when it came to literary matters, Mwangi was self-educated, unfamiliar with the models promoted as good literature at the university, and hence open to a whole range of references, including memories of his own life as a child growing up in the military town of Nanyuki during the Mau Mau conflict, the popular films he watched when he moved to Nairobi in the 1960s, and his close observations of urban life. At one point in his career, in the late 1970s, Mwangi decided to give up his job as a sound engineer for French radio and television and become a professional writer. What this meant, among other things, is that he needed to write novels that would sell enough to support himself and his family. Many of his popular thrillers belong to this period.

In general, Mwangi's novels fall into four categories that reflect his own unusual experiences as a writer. The first set of novels, the ones that critics have tended to take more seriously, are the novels of the urban postcolonial experience (see **colonialism, neocolonialism, and postcolonialism**), most notably *Kill Me Quick* (1973) *Going Down River Road* (1976), and *The Cockroach Dance* (1979). In these novels, Mwangi presents vivid images of the world of the urban poor, using a descriptive language and idiom that tries to capture the hidden world of this class in the broadest way possible. Mwangi's second category of novels are concerned with the theme of Mau Mau. In these works, including *Carcass for the Hounds* (1974) and several children's stories, Mwangi's interest is not in the contested politics of Mau Mau, but the movement as the source of dramatic stories of war, love, and betrayal. A third category of Mwangi's works includes novels written when he was working as an assistant producer in the making of Western movies set and filmed in Africa. Novels such as *The Bushtrackers* (1979), *Bread of Sorrow* (1987), and *Weapon of Hunger* (1989) are notable for their fast-paced action, their grandiose plots, their use of American slang, and their cinematic techniques. Here, Mwangi's goal is nothing less than the production of African versions of Hollywood thrillers.

Mwangi was attracted to the thriller genre both because he was fascinated by the possibilities offered by cinematic techniques in the production

of fiction, and also because he wanted to write novels that would sell. In this sense he had an acute sense of the kind of fiction that was popular with the urban class in Kenya. At the same time, however, he seemed disappointed that he wasn't taken seriously enough as a writer, and he was determined to produce novels that would be serious in theme but also popular in terms of their style and idiom. The result is the fourth category in his oeuvre – works such as *The Return of Shaka* (1989) and *Striving with the Wind* (1989) – in which Mwangi takes on some of the most important issues in Africa in the 1980s – apartheid (see **apartheid and post-apartheid**) in South Africa and rural poverty in Kenya – and tries to make them appealing to readers of popular novels.

Further reading

Calder, Angus, "Meja Mwangi's Novels," in G.D. Killam (ed.) *The Writing of East and Central Africa*, London: Heinemann.

Kurtz, John Roger (1998) *Urban Obsessions, Urban Fears: The Postcolonial Kenyan Novel*, Trenton, New Jersey: Africa World Press.

SIMON GIKANDI

Mzamane, Mbulelo

b. 1948, Johannesburg, South Africa

academic and short story writer

Mbulelo Mzamane is a South African academic who also writes short stories. His first collection of short stories, *Mzala* (1980), breaks new ground in the way it examines a rural man's first encounter with an urban environment. Writing in a humorous vein, Mzamane inverts the usual so-called "Jim comes to Jo'burg" theme by inviting his readers to appreciate Mzala's resourcefulness despite his lack of "streetwise" ways. His first novel, *The Children of Soweto* (1982) recreates, in fictional form, the 1976 Soweto insurrection by schoolchildren against the system of apartheid (see **apartheid and post-apartheid**). Mzamane has also edited an anthology of southern African short stories by black writers, *Hungry Flames and Other Stories* (1982). In *The Children of the Diaspora and Other Stories of Exiles*, published in 1997, he brought together short narratives based on his recollection of life in exile during the struggle against apartheid. As an academic, Mzamane has published numerous critical essays on South African writing and culture and has held important positions in South African institutions of higher education, including serving as vice-chancellor of the University of Fort Hare.

JABULANI MKHIZE

N

Nadir, Chams

b. 1949, Tunisia

novelist and short story writer

The Tunisian writer Mohammed Aziza publishes his fiction under the name Chams Nadir, Arabic for "radiant sun." His best-known work is a widely translated collection of short stories entitled *The Astrolabe of the Sea* (*L'Astrolabe de la mer*) (1980) and prefaced by Léopold **Senghor**. It uses the framing device of an astrolabe, an ancient navigational instrument in this case endowed with speech, which tells a series of stories criticizing Western materialist values. Nadir is also the author of *Silence des sémaphores* (Silence of the Semaphores) (1979), *Le Livre des célébrations* (The Book of Celebrations) (1983), and *Les Portiques de la mer* (The Portals of the Sea) (1990). Under his given name, Aziza has also published a number of works on Arab theater and, in conjunction with his work in public affairs for the Organization of African Unity and Unesco, several books on African and Islamic art.

Further reading

Nadir, Chams (1996) *The Astrolabe of the Sea*, trans. C. Dickson, San Francisco: City Lights Books.

SETH GRAEBNER

Nagenda, John

b. 1938, Gahini, Rwanda

poet and critic

As one of the first group of students to study literature at Makerere University College in the early 1960s, the Ugandan poet and critic John Nagenda was one of the pioneers of writing in East Africa and was closely associated with the "Makerere school" of writing which was to produce important figures like David **Rubadiri** and **Ngugi wa Thiong'o**. At Makerere, Nagenda was editor of *Penpoint* and his early poems and stories appeared in this journal and other regional publications, including *Transition*. In his early poems and short stories, Nagenda's work is located at the transitional moment in East African literature in English, when writers educated in the British tradition were trying to adopt the forms of prose and poetry learnt in the colonial school and university to represent the African landscape, to find local substitutes for Wordsworth's Lake District, as it were, and to account for their own coming into being as subjects caught between old and modern ways. These two tendencies are pronounced in poems such as "Gahini Lake" and the short story "And This, At Last," both published in the pioneering Makerere anthology, *Origin East Africa*, edited by David Cook (1965). During Uganda's turbulent history in the 1970s and most of the 1980s, Nagenda lived in exile in Britain and did little writing during this period. He returned to the literary scene in 1986 with the publication of *The Seasons of Thomas Tebo*, a novel about an idealistic man who becomes involved in politics only to be caught in the horror and violence of a corrupt polity.

SIMON GIKANDI

Nakasa, Nathaniel ("Nat") Ndazana

b. 1937, Durban, South Africa; d. 1965, New York, USA

journalist, short story writer, and critic

The South African journalist, writer, and critic Nathaniel ("Nat") Ndazana Nakasa was born in Durban in 1937. Nakasa spent the major part of his adult life in Johannesburg where he worked as a reporter, critic, and columnist for the *Rand Daily Mail*, *Drum* magazine, and its sister publication the *Golden City Post*. Apart from his journalism, social commentary, and literary criticism, Nakasa will be remembered for his role as founder and editor, in 1963, of *The Classic*, a literary magazine devoted to promoting the work of aspirant black writers. Like other *Drum* writers, most of whom lived in Sophiatown, Nakasa wrote critical essays and short stories and thus made a significant contribution to what some critics have described as the "Sophiatown Renaissance" of the 1950s in South African literature. Like his colleague Lewis **Nkosi**, Nakasa was awarded the Nieman Journalism Fellowship to study journalism at Harvard University in 1964. He left the country on an exit permit as the apartheid regime (see **apartheid and post-apartheid**) wouldn't grant him a passport. Nakasa's promising career as a creative journalist and critic came to a tragic and unexpected end when he committed suicide on 14 July 1965 in New York.

Further reading

Patel, Essop (1975) *The World of Nat Nakasa*, Johannesburg: Ravan Press.

THENGANI H. NGWENYA

Nanga, Bernard

b. 1934, Bankomo, Cameroon; d. 1985, Yaoundé, Cameroon

novelist

A former professor of philosophy at the University of Yaoundé (Cameroon), Bernard Nanga is the author of two powerful novels which seek to provide an analysis of African politics and society in the postcolonial era (see **colonialism, neo-colonialism, and postcolonialism**). *La Trahison de Marianne* (Betrayed by Marianne) (1984) is a familiar story of disillusionment and enlightenment with a character struggling to come to terms with his acculturation. In the novel, the protagonist, who had married the beautiful Frenchwoman he idolized and embraced every bit of her culture as well, looks back on his life fifteen years later, focusing on the clichés firmly installed in the minds of colonized subjects. The novel, which parallels the author's own experience, echoes many African autobiographical fictions (see **autobiography**). *Les Chauves-souris* (The Bats) (1980) is a more straightforward address of postcolonial issues. It portrays Robert Bilanga, a high-ranking civil servant of an imaginary African country, the quintessence of individualism and detachment, the representative figure of a society that values money and power above almost everything else. The metaphor of the bats (*Chauves-souris*), renowned for their ambiguous nature and rapacious reputation, appears particularly accurate to represent postcolonial society, as does the character Bilanga, the very incarnation of its rampant corruption. In his critique of neocolonialism in Africa, Bernard Nanga belongs to a tradition of radical writing represented by writers such as **Ngugi wa Thiong'o** and Mongo **Beti**.

Further reading

Bjornson, Richard (1994) *African Quest for Freedom and Identity*, Bloomington, Indiana: Indiana University Press.

EMMANUEL TENÉ

nationalism and post-nationalism

In the epoch of globalization, or what has been called "the post-national constellation," and within the context of crippled institutions and the preponderance of failed states such as we have in Africa, the very idea of nationalism in literature appears quaint and contradictory. Indeed, in the face of a retreat from the nation by constituting nationalities in many parts of the continent, and the strident cries for a return to precolonial roots echoing from the radical intelligentsia, is it too far-fetched to locate an ethnic consciousness as the dominant logic of contemporary African literature which then renders nugatory the very idea of national literature on the continent? Yet matters have not always been like this, and literature and politics are not always what they appear to be. Nationalism and the national, whatever their contemporary fortunes, have been, and remain, crucial factors in African literature.

However that may be, that these questions have to be framed within a global and international framework shows how the fate and fortunes of African literature, in the main, are tied to developments outside the continent. In a sense, the very notions of nationalism and post-nationalism in African literature are critical responses to developments in the postcolonial metropole (see **colonialism, neocolonialism, and postcolonialism**). In order to grasp the full implications of these developments, an exploration of their colonial origins is in order, and it is to these that we must now turn.

Colonial origins

Contemporary African literature was born in a great crisis, the crisis of colonization and Western imperialism. It is a measure of the enormity of the crisis and its subsequent working out that the trajectory and parameters of a whole continental literature should be dominated and defined by the nature of that upheaval. There is a profound irony to all this. The impending crisis of colonization could be already glimpsed in the crisis of nationalism and the struggle for economic and political supremacy that convulsed Europe at the end of the nineteenth century and the beginning of the twentieth. This conflict reverberated through the colonial possessions, often leading to a brisk exchange of ownership and a change of linguistic masters. Eventually, it was to have an even greater political resonance for the literary development of the continent.

Between 1870 and 1915 the entire continent of Europe was rocked by a series of wars which in retrospect were the fall-out from the consolidation of the post-Westphalian paradigm of the nation-state. As the old empires dissolved in fiasco and confusion, the nations which mutated out of them also became embroiled in international wars. From 1870 when Prussia defeated France till 1916 when the unified German military machine was back at the gates of Paris, Europe seemed to have known little peace. As old boundaries collapsed and new nations emerged from the ruins of empires, so did ancestral feuds. The economic momentum generated by capitalism in its powerful prime also fueled raw aggression and naked expansionism among the emergent European powers. It was obvious that the first international war to draw world powers into its chaotic and unwieldy theater was inevitable.

If World War I then represented the ugly summit of European nationalism, it also began the process of its dramatic unraveling. Economic innovations had raced ahead of the old paradigm of warfare. As such the war revealed the bungling and sheer incompetence of the old military command. The horrific butchery and colossal wastage of human beings attendant to some of the pitched battles, particularly the infamous Battle of the Somme in France, led reasonable people to recoil in horror. Never in the history of modern warfare had so many been sacrificed for so minimal a strategic and tactical advantage. The war not only demystified soldiers, it also shattered the myth of a superior race ordained by God to direct the affairs of lesser human beings. As the soldiers from the overseas territories were to discover, fear and misery make no distinction among the enlisted. Death does not recognize any racial category. The end of colonization was at hand.

African nationalism was thus an ironic product of the ruins of European nationalism, delivered on its death bed. After World War I, it became very hard, if not impossible, to justify the civilizing trope of colonization or the notion of a superior race on a God-ordained mission to rescue savages from their historic cul-de-sac. Emboldened by the collapse of European values and the exposure to Western education of some of the natives, fertilized by the cross-continental stirrings of the American civil rights movement and the pilgrimage to Africa of some of its illustrious children, the cry of freedom rent the entire continent. The struggle for decolonization began in earnest. As a result of the dynamics that generated it and gave it its crushing momentum, it was a pan-African movement with little respect for inchoate and yet-to-be-formalized colonial borders. This was to have startling consequences for the emergent African literature with regards to its pan-continental nature. But it was not the inauguration of modern African literature. It was merely joining a tradition that had begun much earlier, albeit in a hazy and shadowy manner.

Nationalism and literature

Modern African literature began with active colonization and the efforts of early missionaries to "civilize" the continent. The most revolutionary contribution of colonization to the literary evolution of Africa was the transcription of many vernacular languages in their area of domain. This radical innovation, coupled with the introduction of the accommodating and relatively easy Western alphabet, was a major literary turning point for Africa as it leapfrogged the entire continent from one cultural epoch to another all within a generation. To be sure, before colonialism there had been some feeble indigenous attempts to produce certain embryonic scripts in several communities on the continent, particularly in West Africa. Among these ideographic scripts were the Aroko of the Yoruba, the ideographs of the Ewe of Ghana, and in fact the relatively more advanced Nsibidi of contemporary southeastern Nigeria. But these were used mainly for communication and exchanges of intelligence among cults and confraternities. Inevitably, their asocial and apopular tone and the restricted nature of their potential and

actual sharers led to arrested growth and speedy extinction.

Colonialism engendered first an internal mutation in African cultural production and then a new generic development: the African novel. Indeed, without the advent of literacy, the whole idea of African literature would have been a contradiction in terms. The coastal elite, made up of educated descendants of freed slaves, recaptives, and other ambitious indigenes together with the new hinterland elite made up of products of missionary education, began by aping the literary production of the colonizing metropolis, and as they grew in confidence and flair began turning this into a vehicle for launching increasingly defiant assaults on the racist assumptions of the colonial masters. As the struggle for independence intensified in many African countries, there was to be a fusion of these two groups to form an anti-colonial historic bloc. Traditional African poetry which was hitherto oral in expression (see **oral literature and performance**) as a result of the absence of a literate culture came to be set down in verse with new genetic hybrids imitating classical European poetry with an African sensibility.

At this point, the traditional African ritual and travelling theater, particularly the Alarinjo theater of the Yoruba, was complemented by morality plays and revues based on the Bible. In East Africa, Shakespeare's more popular plays were domesticated and adapted to the needs of a local audience. Throughout the continent, important dates in the Christian calendar such as Christmas, Easter, and Palm Sunday spawned traditional festivals replete with drama sketches based on the Bible. There was even a tradition based on Sheridan's comedy of manners which could be clearly seen in the work of the turn-of-the-century Gold Coast lawyer and anti-colonial hell-raiser, Kobina **Sekyi**. Sekyi, however, merely deployed the form of the theater to launch a violent ideological offensive against Western civilization and its arrogant pretensions.

By the end of World War I, several pan-Africanist movements had sprung up in the metropolitan capitals of Europe with the sole aim of decolonizing Africa and liberating the continent from the clutches of the imperialist masters (see **diaspora and pan-Africanism**). The leading figures of these movements were also destined to play stirring roles in the struggle for independence of their respective countries. Among those operating from the British theater were: Hastings Kamuzu Banda of the then Federation of Northern Rhodesia and Nyasaland; Julius Nyerere of the then Tanganyika; Jomo **Kenyatta** of Kenya; Kwame Nkrumah of the then Gold Coast; and Herbert Macauley and Dr Akinola Maja of Nigeria. In Paris, Léopold **Senghor** of Senegal, Félix Houphuet-Boigny of the Côte d'Ivoire, and Leon Mba of Gabon became rallying figures of resistance to French imperialism. In Lisbon, Eduardo Mondlane, the assassinated founding father of FRELIMO, the Mozambican liberation movement, Amilcar Cabral, the martyred president of Guinea Bissau, and Agostinho **Neto**, the founding president of Angola and leader of the MPLA, kept the Portuguese colonial masters permanently on their toes.

By some happy historical coincidence, virtually all of these African freedom fighters and fathers of nationalism on the continent also happened to have been artists and writers of considerable distinction. In the particular cases of Senghor and Neto, they not only went on to rule their respective countries, but they also become poets of international renown, with the former an exemplar of **negritude** poetry and the latter a master of fine and sensitive verse. Amilcar Cabral was justly celebrated for his rigor and profundity as a radical philosopher. These political intellectuals found the domesticated genres of drama, poetry, and the essay very handy in their polemical assaults on the ideological rationale of colonization and its intellectual assumptions. The legacies they left are indeed worthy of an African cultural and political renaissance.

It was, however, in prose genre that the most radical transformation of African cultural production could be seen. This is perhaps the most important literary heritage of colonialism, the genre being synonymous with a literary culture and therefore absent from traditional African artistic corpus. Products of missionary education began imitating and transforming moral tracts and biblical fables. Particularly popular were stories based on John Bunyan's *Pilgrim's Progress*. These early Christian soldiers of African origins invariably had proselytizing ambitions, their chief aim

being to re-educate and redeem their "savage" brethren and sisters. It was this missionary and evangelizing milieu that threw up pre-independence writers such as the trio of Thomas **Mofolo** from South Africa, Daniel **Fagunwa**, and the less formally educated Amos **Tutuola** of Nigeria. Well before them was Joseph Ephraim Casely Hayford of the then Gold Coast whose *Ethiopia Unbound*, published in the mid nineteenth century, was a barely disguised fictionalized polemic against colonization and a sustained literary philippic against the evils of slavery and inequality based on racist distinctions. But even before them all was the triumvirate of Olaudah **Equiano**, Ottabah **Cuguano**, and Ignatius **Sancho**, liberated slaves of African extraction who had seized literary London by the scruff of the neck by the late eighteenth century.

These titans were without doubt the founding figures of literary and political nationalism in Africa. To write at all, many of them had to triumph against unimaginable odds, and their creative labor was a tribute to indomitable will and exceptional perseverance. In the particular case of Mofolo, he had to work for the Morija Press, the sole outlet for the dissemination of literature in South Africa. The complex negotiations the great South African was forced into as far as this missionary leviathan was concerned are refracted for posterity in the tricky and tortured dissembling of his earlier narratives. Fagunwa was a missionary-educated tutor, and his burning nationalism often had to be couched in the guise of biblical morality based on the notion of sin and punishment.

The moment of independence

As has been noted in the foregoing, once the struggle to liberate the continent intensified, these isolated titans were joined by more educated Africans to become a critical mass in the struggle for the liberation of the continent. One curious and interesting fact about this emergent African elite was the fact that they took to heart the paradigm of the nation-state handed down to them by the colonial masters. While striving for the ultimate unity of the continent and the emancipation of the black race in general, they took their respective countries as they were "invented" by the imperialist overlords and never questioned the colonial map or the national boundaries externally imposed on them. Politically, this visionary policy enabled them to cut the ground from under traditional chieftains, who were also engaged in the anticolonial struggle but with a view to revalidating the old boundaries of lapsed empires and fiefdoms. The old order had changed in Africa for ever. If this strategy was to turn the new indigenous masters into ultra-nationalists and founding fathers of new nations, it was also to have unintended consequences as the dream of a new Africa began to fade in the postcolonial chaos that engulfed the continent. Forged by colonial will, the new nations were in the event an ironic tribute to the departing colonial masters and their power to deterritorialize and reterritorialize.

The eve of independence brought an explosion of literary talents to the African scene, the like of which had not been seen before and was unlikely to be seen again for a long time. Writers of different talents and temperament stormed the African literary stage. From Nigeria came several, including Wole **Soyinka**, the future Nobel laureate; Chinua **Achebe**, author of *Things Fall Apart* and arguably the most influential African writer of the period; Christopher **Okigbo**, a poet of exceptional promise; and John Pepper **Clark-Bekederemo**; from Kenya came the then James Ngugi (**Ngugi wa Thiong'o**); from Guinea came Camara **Laye**; from Senegal came Léopold Sédar Senghor and Ousmane **Sembene**; from Cameroon came Alexandre Biyidi, known as Mongo **Beti**, and Ferdinand **Oyono**; from Mali came Ousmane Kane; from Malawi came David **Rubadiri**; and from South Africa came Es'kia **Mphahlele** and Peter **Abrahams**.

It is to be noted that virtually all these writers were products of higher education, with the possible exception of the Senegalese Ousmane Sembene who came from the ranks as a trade unionist. Indeed, all the Nigerian writers mentioned were students and contemporaries at the then University College at Ibadan, which was affiliated to the University of London for degree-awarding purposes. It was in the throbbing and heady ambience of student experimentation and collaboration with many of their teachers that they

honed their literary skills and broadened their cultural awareness. Independence brought even greater liberalization of educational facilities and the devolution and democratization of the new literary culture. Many more universities and institutions of higher education were established to cater for students coming through the secondary education line. This had two immediate and profoundly salutary effects. First, it broadened the base of the reading culture as affordable books began to flood the homes of the emergent middle class, even though the vast majority of Africans still remained illiterate and ignorant of Western ways. Second, literary criticism became professionalized. It took up residence in the new universities and this complemented the efforts of the creative artists. Before this time, what passed for the criticism of the emergent African literature was, in the main, a function of sociological and anthropological trawling for offensive and "dangerous" materials by concerned patrons from other disciplines.

Writing and the crisis of nationalism

It was in this atmosphere of hope and great expectations that independence came to many African countries. It was a time of political and cultural ferment, of a literary renaissance, and the most optimistic might be excused for concluding that Africa was headed for paradise. Unfortunately, this turned out to be a great hoax. It was clear by the end of what has come to be known as the decade of independence – that is, by 1969 – that there has been a colossal failure of nerve. Rather than bring the solace and succor it had promised, independence brought deepening misery and misfortunes. Worse still, the political space which was opened up by the struggle for independence and the decolonization of the continent swiftly contracted as indigenous tyrants stepped into the shoes of the departing colonial masters. What made things more galling in one or two cases was the phenomenon of yesterday's freedom fighters who transformed overnight into civilian despots.

African writers who had not been co-opted into governance responded to this tragic development with varying degrees of outrage and injured sensibility. This was immediately reflected in the literature. The euphoria that accompanied independence quickly evaporated. Disillusionment, disappointment, and despair became the dominant markers of post-independence literature in Africa. It was no longer a question of how colonialism ruined Africa, but of how African leaders aborted the great hopes and expectations of indigenous rule.

This was literature bristling with indignation and dripping with venom and vitriol. Virtually every African country south of the Sahara produced its great representative figure of literary opposition and its native rebel. From Nigeria the distinguished troika of Soyinka, Achebe, and Okigbo laid siege to the postcolonial state with anti-authoritarian plays like *Kongi's Harvest* (Soyinka, 1967); scorching satires against "big man-ism" like *A Man of the People* (Achebe, 1967), and poems forewarning political disaster such as *The Path of Thunder* (Okigbo, 1971). They were joined from neighboring Ghana by Kofi **Awoonor** who wrote *This Earth, My Brother* (1971), an elegy of lost hopes; and Ayi Kwei **Armah** who penned the classic *The Beautyful Ones Are Not Yet Born* (1968), a bitter lamentation about corrupted genius and the miscarriage of expectations. In Cameroon, Mongo Beti became a scourge of the authorities with his satires and sharp indictment, notably in *The Poor Christ of Bomba* (1956) and *Remember Ruben* (1974). From Uganda and Kenya, the poet **Okot p'Bitek** and the novelist Ngugi wa Thiong'o were branded first-class enemies of the government as a result of the uncompromisingly critical nature of their work.

The rulers responded with startling ferocity, clamping some of the writers in jail and forcing many others into precipitate exile. A long trail of absconding literary refugees stretched across the continent and beyond its shores. Never had such a record of political collaboration ended in such bitter recrimination and mutual disenchantment. As political collapse was compounded by economic fiasco and under the gale of the phenomenon of globalization, the trickle mutated into an avalanche leading to the establishment of a diasporic community of African writers and migrant intellectual workers. Nevertheless, however, it is to be noted that this African diaspora is yet to produce a distinct literature which can be labeled "post-national." Indeed, the interventions of this diasporic intelligentsia often suggest an abiding romance with the colonial nation-state despite its concrete horrors. While a few of them in their essays and polemical sorties often call attention to the fiction and "imagined" nature of the nation-state in Africa, this is yet to extend to their creative canvas.

One can then summarize by noting that although the cultural nationalism of pioneering African writers was often framed and filtered through an ethnic consciousness which bypassed the national in order to reconnect with the continental project of decolonization, the literature of post-independence disillusionment is framed within a grim national canvas. Despite the arrival on the scene of postcolonial and global intellectuals of African extraction, it is not yet post-national for African literature. If this is an ironic compliment to the former colonial masters, it is also a salutary reminder that national identities and consciousness once assumed under whatever circumstances and historical provenance cannot be so easily discarded.

ADEBAYO WILLIAMS

Nayigiziki (Naigiziki), J. Savério

b. 1915, Mwulire, Save region, Rwanda; d. 1984, Rwanda

educator, translator, and writer

Born at Mwulire in the southern region of Save in Rwanda, Nayigiziki was educated at a Catholic seminary, where, after the completion of his high school studies, he became a schoolmaster. Later, he worked as a translator, the editor for a Congolese periodical, and a clerk for an import businessman. Nayigiziki was awarded the literature prize of the Brussels Colonial Fair in 1949 for a portion of his autobiographical novel, *Escapade ruandaise; journal d'un clerc en sa trentième année* (Rwandese Escapade). In 1955, the novel was published at Butare as *Mes transes à trente ans* (My Trances at Thirty Years of Age). Drawing on the tradition of **autobiography**, the story portrays the character of an adventurous and freshly "civilized" African intellectual, an "évolué" who goes through the turmoil of social and ethnic inequalities in modern

Rwanda. The writer also published a play entitled *L'Optimiste* (The Optimist) (1954).

ANTHÈRE NZABATSINDA

Nazareth, Peter

b. 1940, Uganda

literary critic, playwright, and novelist

The Ugandan literary critic, playwright, and novelist Peter Nazareth began his writing career by contributing to *Penpoint* magazine and to *Origin East Africa: A Makerere Anthology* (1965), edited by David Cook. Although he started his vocation as a critic by writing primarily on African literature, Nazareth later extended his scope to include writers from diverse parts of the world. He has, in his own words, become a "moving target": "When they try to block me as an African novelist, I am editing a Goan anthology. When they try to put me down as a Third World critic, I am teaching a class on Elvis" (1998: *Sunday Herald*). His first novel, *In a Brown Mantle* (1972), recounts the steps through which an African country degenerates from the ideals of nationalism (see **nationalism and post-nationalism**) to a state of violence and destruction. The novel predicted the coup that brought Uganda's Idi Amin into power as uncannily as Chinua **Achebe**'s *A Man of the People* anticipated Nigeria's first military coup in 1966. *The General is Up* (1991) is about the expulsion of Asian Ugandans by Amin. Nazareth is notable for his penetrating analysis of post-independence African politics and for his role in the development of the literature of the Asian diaspora (see **diaspora and pan-Africanism**).

Works cited

Shah, Rasik (2000) "Re: Introducing Peter Nazareth – 2," online posting 8 June, East African Asian Diaspora, Namaskar-Africana-LHome.Ease.Lsoft.com.
Torcato, Ronita (1998) "The Eyes of the Peacock," *Sunday Herald* (Bangalore, India), 12 April.

DAN ODHIAMBO OJWANG

Ncongwane, Jabulani Johan

b. 1961, Carolina, Mphumalanga, South Africa

novelist, dramatist, and short story writer

The South African novelist, dramatist, short story writer, poet, and folklore anthologist Jabulani Johan Ncongwane was born and raised in Carolina, Mphumalanga, and educated at Mgwenya College of Education (1985) and the University of South Africa (1996). A winner of five awards, including the prestigious 2000 M-Net Nguni Novel of the Year award (for *Naloyishayile* (Even He who has Won Her Heart), published the same year), Ncongwane has over thirty publications to his name. His popular short story anthology *Emahemuhemu* (Rumors) (1987) reflects a rich repertoire of subject matter. Presenting socioeconomic plight via the theme of unscrupulous self-advancement, Ncongwane shows the absurdity of modernity (see **modernity and modernism**) and modern living amid the crumbling structures of the old precolonial values that have been upholding society for centuries. Through themes like disrespect, subversion, and usurpation of authority, Ncongwane sets out to disturb the false sense of comfort where moral erosion permeates the rural environment with little regard for gender, age, and class. While his poems address the natural environment and love matters (in, for example, *Kuyophela Situnge* (Loneliness Will Subside) 1986), Ncongwane's prose assumes a loftier stance showing humans as threatened by disease and being a lost species in their own environment, especially where religion, education, and the marriage institution have lost their hold on society.

ZODWA MOTSA

Ndachi Tagne, David

b. 1958, Cameroon

novelist and journalist

The Cameroonian writer David Ndachi Tagne is primarily known as a penetrating literary critic and book reviewer for the national newspaper *Cameroon*

Tribune and he has also worked for many years as a correspondent for Radio-France International in Cameroon. The author's first publication *Roman et réalités camerounaises* (The Novel and Reality in Cameroon) (1986), a critical investigation of Cameroonian fiction, was theoretical. However, Ndachi Tagne's literary achievement covers a wide range of genres. He has published drama: *Mr Handlock* (1985); fiction: *La Reine captive* (Queen in Captivity) (1986), *La Vérité du sursis* (The Respite of Truth) (1987); poetry: *Sangs mêlés, sang péché* (Mixed Blood, Sinner Blood) (1992); essays and biographies with an emphasis on local musicians: *Anne Marie Nzié, voix d'or de la chanson camerounaise* (Anne Marie Nzié, Golden Voice of Cameroon Song) (1990), *Francis Bebey* (1993). In novels such as *La Reine captive*, Ndachi is concerned with the African experience under colonialism and the now familiar conflict between tradition, or the values of precolonial society versus modernity (see **colonialism, neocolonialism, and postcolonialism**; **modernity and modernism**); he is also concerned with the significance of communities as the centers of morality. Ndachi Tagne's multifaceted skills as a writer are represented in *Sangs mêlés, sang péché*, which blends a historical tale with a poetic narrative to address, in a dramatic form, contemporary issues of race, sex, and gender (see **gender and sexuality**).

EMMANUEL TENÉ

Ndao, Cheik Aliou

b. 1933, Senegal

writer

The Senegalese writer Cheik Aliou Ndao is one of the most accomplished Francophone writers and his work touches on all aspects of creative writing as well as on all genres, including the novel, drama, poetry, and short story. In all his writings, the author tries to encompass many aspects of the African mind, spirit, life, and civilization. A recurring theme in his novels – *Buur Tilleen* (1972), *Roi de la Médina* (King of the Medina) (1992), *Excellence, vos épouses* (Excellency, Your Wives) (1983), *Un Bouquet d'épines pour elle* (A

Bouquet of Thorns for Her) (1988), and *Mbaam dictateur* (Mbaam the Dictator) (1997) – is the sharp contrast between the city and the countryside, the experiences of country folk moving to the city in search of a better life and the difficulties they have in acquiring urban values. Ndao's novels also focus on the interface and clash between Islam (see **Islam in African literature**) and the remnants of precolonial religion and the maintenance and survival of rural values such as dignity and honor. In *Excellence, vos épouses*, for example, the author satirizes the postcolonial educated African elite and its corrupt nature as well as its inability to manage its countries well, thus assuring a harmonious economic development. Ndao also tackles many debated social problems, including polygamy and its survival in modern African society and the question of the caste system in Senegal, where people are considered and judged according to their lineage, birth, and blood line. In his collection of short stories entitled *Le Marabout de la sécheresse* (The Marabout of Dearth) (1979), the author describes in depth the ways in which Islam is lived and practiced but also abused by charlatans who take advantage of the gullibility, poverty, and lack of education of a big chunk of the Senegalese population.

In his plays *L'Exil d'Alboury* (The Exile of Alboury) (1967), *Le Fils de l'Almamy* (The Son of the Almamy) (1973), and *Du sang pour un trône* (Blood for a Throne) (1983), to cite just these three, Ndao seeks to relive the ancient kingdoms and empires of the West African savannah. Embedded in these plays is a historical flavor and epic realism (see **realism and magical realism**); in addition, the reader feels the presence and influence of African oral traditions and literatures in these plays (see **oral literature and performance**). In the plays dealing more specifically with the Wolof kingdoms, the playwright recreates, juxtaposes, and translates the Wolof speech code into French, thus highlighting an interesting paradigm that is prevalent among colonial and postcolonial African writers, namely the quest for identity and the clash between the innate African mother tongue (such as Wolof) and the acquired colonial language through schooling, in this case French. As a poet, Cheik Aliou Ndao is considered to be a spiritual heir to Léopold **Senghor** and the **negritude** school and its commitment to the celebration and rehabilitation of African culture. Thus, in *Mogariennes* (The Women from Mogar) (1970), the poet celebrates elements of nature such as the savannah and the Harmattan and evokes the West African landscapes, rivers, and towns, including Dakar, Kayes, Bamako, Djoliba, Segou, and Dahomey. Like the poets of the negritude school, Ndao is concerned with the beauty and power of African dance, singing, and the rhythm of musical instruments such as the tam-tam. The griot tradition also occupies a pre-eminent place in Ndao's poetry. In addition, Ndao echoes both pan-Africanism (see **diaspora and pan-Africanism**) and universal cultural themes in his poetry, emphasizing the kinship that links poets, countries, nations, and peoples.

SAMBA DIOP

Ndebele, Njabulo Simakahle

b. 1948, South Africa

short story writer and educator

Njabulo S. Ndebele is a hugely important figure in South Africa's cultural and literary scene and he also commands an equally respected presence in the tertiary education sector. Educated in Swaziland, the United Kingdom, and the United States of America between 1961 and 1983, Ndebele returned to South Africa in 1991 and has been vice rector of the University of the Western Cape, vice-chancellor of the University of the North and chancellor of the University of Cape Town. Ndebele's reputation rests largely on a collection of seminal essays and public addresses offered since 1984, collected in *Rediscovery of the Ordinary: Essays on South African Literature and Culture* (1991), as well as in his 1984 Noma Award-winning collection of short stories, *Fools and Other Stories* (1983).

Many of Ndebele's political and aesthetic provocations are detailed in two very influential essays, "Turkish Tales, and Some Thoughts on South African Fiction" (1991) and "Rediscovery of the Ordinary" (1991). Ndebele argues that the most serious limitation in most of black writing has been its superficial exploration of life under apartheid (see **apartheid and post-apartheid**), with writers comfortable with detailing "the interaction of surface symbols of the South African reality." Motivated by the political and thematic need to bear witness to and pass moral judgements on the horrors of apartheid, characters operated within the stark binaries of good and evil; they were either victims or perpetrators, heroes or villains, and black characters were seldom allowed any agency or moments of fear, doubt, or anxiety. Also, since the city and apartheid exercised a tyrannical hold on the imagination of writers, little attention was given to the experiences of peasants, women, and ordinary people and, in particular, their immense resilience, resourcefulness, creativity, and stubborn will to make, live, and narrate life even in the most dire circumstances.

The stories in *Fools and Other Stories* are, in some respects, an apt creative demonstration of Ndebele's ideas. In his desire to probe the complexities of township life, which is consummately delineated in a textured and detailed manner, and to critically engage readers in the unfolding narratives, Ndebele uses young protagonists whose narrations are marked by the preoccupations, strengths, and weaknesses of their youthful desires. *Fools*, on the other hand, retraces the life of a once-respected teacher who has disgraced himself in the eyes of the community. In all the stories, Ndebele's overwhelming focus is on the ambiguities that inform the intimate, private journeys of his protagonists, but their introspections and struggles are subtly linked to the larger public and historical developments in the society. In Ndebele's schema, agency and independence is restored to black life while whites are rendered peripheral and devoid of any major definitional presence and power except through the imprints that they have left on the country's socio-economic and political history. The import of Ndebele's theoretical and fictional writings in South Africa is in their recasting of the notion of "committed writing" as to allow for the emergence of new thematic directions and ways of representation.

BHEKIZIZWE PETERSON

Ndiaye, Marie

b. 1967, Pithiviers, France

novelist

Marie Ndiaye was born in Pithiviers (France) of a French mother and a Senegalese father. She published her first novel *Quant au riche avenir* (About a Hopeful Future) (1985) at only 17. Her second book *Comédie classique* (Classic Comedy) (1987), in which a single phrase stretched over 96 pages, was also an exceptional accomplishment for such a young writer. After her third novel, *La Femme changée en bûche* (The Woman Metamorphosed) (1989), Ndiaye's style matured significantly, and this is evident in the novels she published in the 1990s, including *En famille* (In the Family) (1991), *Un Temps de saison* (A Time of the Season) (1994), *La Sorcière* (The Sorceress) (1996), and *Hilda* (1999). Most of Ndiaye's novels explore intricate familial or social relations. In *Hilda* (1999), a subtle dialogue between a bourgeois French lady and her less privileged maid provides an opportunity for Ndiaye to revisit the "master and slave" relationship. In *Rosie Carpe* (2001), Ndiaye's favorite shifts the location of her novels from continental Europe to Guadeloupe.

What about Africa? So far, the land of Ndiaye's ancestors appears to be the missing part of her prolific achievement, a situation she once candidly acknowledged in the magazine *Lire* (1996–7) in these plain words: "I do not benefit from a double culture, nor do I suffer from its disadvantages."

Further reading

Payot, Marianne (1996–7) Interview with Marie Ndiaye, *Lire*, December 1996/January 1997.

EMMANUEL TENÉ

Ndongo-Bidyogo, Donato

b. 1950, Equatorial Guinea

journalist, critic, and novelist

Journalist, critic, and novelist Donato Ndongo-Bidyogo is a member of what Equatorial-Guinean

poet Juan Balboa Boneke describes as "la generación perdida" (the lost generation), a group of cultural creators whose first works were published while in exile during the authoritarian regime of Francisco Macias Nguema (1969–79). His early works include two short stories, "El sueño" (Sleep) and "La travesía" (The Crossing), collected in a small volume entitled *Nueva narrativa guineana* (New Guinean Stories) (1977). In "La travesía" he uses the nom de plume of Francisco Abeso Nguema. Ndongo-Bidyogo's *Antología de la literatura guineana* (Anthology of Guinean Literature) (1984) was the first attempt to establish a literary canon for Equatorial Guinea and to disseminate a little-known African literature in Spanish. It includes texts from the era of colonialism in the country to the early postcolonial period (see **colonialism, neocolonialism, and postcolonialism**). *Las tinieblas de tu memoria negra* (The Darkness of Black Memory) (1987), his first novel, is the first part of a trilogy whose second part, *Los poderes de la tempestad* (The Power of the Storm), was published in 1997. He has also co-edited *Literatura de Guinea Ecuatorial Antologia* (An Anthology of the Literature of Equatorial Guinea) (2000), which covers texts by Equatorial-Guinean writers from the colonial period through the year 2000. Donato Ndongo-Bidyogo is the director of Centro de Estudios Africanos at the University of Murcia, Spain.

Further reading

Ndongo-Bidyogo, Donato (1984) *Antología de la literatura guineana* (Anthology of Guinean Literature), Madrid: Ediciones Morandi.

——(1987) *Las tinieblas de tu memoria negra* (The Darkness of Black Memory), Madrid: Editorial Fundamentos.

M'BARE NGOM

Ndoye, Mariama

b. 1953, Rufisque, Senegal

novelist and short story writer

The Senegalese writer Mariama Ndoye, the author of several novels, short stories, and children's books, belongs to the second generation of African women writers, following in the footsteps of the pioneers of what is referred to as *l'écrit féminin sénégalais* (the feminist writers of Senegal), including such prominent writers as Mariama **Bâ** and Aminata **Sow Fall**. However, Mariama Ndoye deserves a special place not because she is the heir to any school or writer but rather because she has produced a consistent, rich, varied, and versatile body of works composed of powerful novels and short stories including *Soeurs dans le souvenir* (Sisters in Memory) (1985), *De vous à moi* (From You to Me) (1990), *Parfums d'enfance* (Perfumes of Childhood) (1993), *Sur des chemins pavoisés* (On Paved Roads) (1993), *La Légende de Rufisque* (The Legend of Rufisque) (1997), and *Soukey* (1999).

Like many writers of her generation, Mariama Ndoye grew up in a semi-traditional, semi-modern setting in which a French education and Islam, African traditions and Western urban lifestyle, African and French languages, all coexisted side by side, and occasionally coalesced (see **education and schools**; **Islam in African literature**). In her writings, the author attempts to present this cultural maelstrom and syncretism. Some of her novels, most prominently *Soukey*, express a certain nostalgia for rural village life where time seems to have suspended its course and the symbols of rural life – the hut, the well, cocks crowing at dawn, and a subsistence life – have a simple and rudimentary appeal. Added to these symbols is the power of magic, witchcraft, and sorcery, which Ndoye considers to be a major influence on contemporary African society. At the same time, however, Ndoye throws her characters into the travails of city life and the demanding nature of modernity (see **modernity and modernism**), transporting some of those characters all the way to France and the West.

Overall, Mariama Ndoye elaborates on and captures the transitory nature of life in Senegal and Africa during the periods of colonialism and postcolonialism (see **colonialism, neocolonialism, and postcolonialism**); her concern is with societies in which people are still grappling with a Manichean reality, caught between African and Western values. Thus, it is no surprise that Mariama Ndoye also attempts to translate and transpose Wolof oral traditions, lore, and folklore

into French (see **Wolof literature**; **oral literature and performance**). In addition, she is concerned with questions of gender and female solidarity (see **gender and sexuality**); the figure of the grandmother is ever-present in her writings, and between the grandmother and the daughter one finds, of course, the mother who constitutes the complementary link in the chain. Mariama Ndoye is a strong advocate of feminism in Senegal and an outspoken supporter of the emancipation and liberation of African women.

SAMBA DIOP

negritude

From the 1940s, the concept of negritude was a rallying term for peoples of the African diaspora, affirming black cultural values against Euro-American white ones, and an identity grounded in shared, if different, experiences of colonialism and African origins (see **diaspora and pan-Africanism**; **colonialism, neocolonialism, and postcolonialism**). The difference is between those whose ancestors suffered the Atlantic Middle Passage of the sixteenth to nineteenth centuries to the American colonies, and those whose people endured physical colonization in Africa from the early nineteenth century. These different dates and experiences of racial slavery suggest why negritude's roots may go back to Caribbean and American maroon communities and Haitian revolutionaries, who all felt the need to establish *new* societies and cultures *against* white plantation ones. The earliest African writers against slavery and for the humanity of Africans, **Equiano**, **Cuguano**, and **Sancho**, had experienced the Middle Passage. Edward Blyden was born and educated in St Thomas before going to Liberia. Early in the twentieth century, French Caribbean politicians urged participation as equals in the world community. In Cuba, *negrismo* was important in the struggle against US occupation.

At the same time, blacks in the US were voicing identity grounded in similar experiences. W.E.B. DuBois' *The Souls of Black Folk* (1903) was germinal, sparking intellectual life that led to the writers of the 1920s to 1930s Harlem Renaissance. In Haiti in 1928, Jean Price-Mars published *Ainsi parla l'oncle* (So Spoke Uncle), a manifesto of indigenous cultural and religious life and Africanist identity, the second emphasized in a 1929 book on the Harlem Renaissance. All asserted blackness as means of political and cultural opposition, as did the Martinican René **Maran** in his 1921 novel attacking French colonialism in central Africa, *Batouala* (*Batouala: Véritable roman nègre*). These writers stirred the French-speaking students who met around the Parisian journals *Légitime Défense* (1932: Legitimate Defense) and *L'Étudiant noir* (1934–6: The Black Student): Aimé Césaire of Martinique, Léon Gontran Damas of French Guiana, Birago **Diop** and Léopold Sédar **Senghor** of Senegal. They saw Price-Mars and the Harlem writers Langston Hughes and Claude McKay (from Jamaica) as vital precursors, the latter even as "the true inventor of negritude" (Nesbitt, 1999: New York, p. 1404).

The word's first printed use was probably in Césaire's 1939 *Cahier d'un retour au pays natal* (Notebook of a Return to a Native Land). In this great poem the notebook writer returns to a native land ravaged and tortured by its planter colonizers to reckon with their racism and his subjugation, his negritude. The last is his salvation:

> my negritude is not a stone, its deafness hurled against the clamor of the day
> my negritude is not a leukoma of dead liquid over the earth's dead eye
> my negritude is neither tower nor cathedral
> it takes root in the red flesh of the soil
> it takes root in the ardent flesh of the sky
> it breaks through the opaque prostration with its upright patience.
>
> (1971: Paris)

He answers Émile Zola's famous "J'accuse" (I accuse), against corruptions of official France, with "J'accepte" (I accept) for *not* having invented the powder and compass, the steam and electricity of empire and colony, crying spirit and presence of place as savior.

If this negritude expresses a certain embedding in the land (and in "our dances" and rhythms), its *historicization* of the poet's and land's identity and demand for the people's emancipation from oppression and poverty differ from others' essenti-

alism. Negritude poetry, said Senghor's *Shadow Songs* (*Chants d'ombre*) (1945), protested "against machines and cannons," but did so, he explained in "The African Road to Socialism," not by Western analytical reason, but with "sympathetic reason," a "loving dance," a "reasoning … intuitive by participation" that voiced Africans' collective being, unity with nature, rhythm and emotion. The idea gained currency among many African writers.

There was also fierce dissent. Wole **Soyinka**'s quip about tigers not promoting their tigritude is familiar. Es'kia **Mphahlele** noted that in apartheid South Africa, negritude hymned the Bantustan, not freedom. As "a march back to indigenous culture," he objected in "What Price Negritude?", it would aid "the Government to reconstruct ethnic groups and help work the repressive machinery." Although protest and "assertion of African cultural values," he agreed in "Remarks on Negritude," yet by urging a romanticized Africa "as a symbol of innocence, purity and artless primitiveness," of emotion, circularity, community, participation and harmony, it excised everything not tied to these values, detailing itself point by point the West's "other," reliant on its ideas. Frantz Fanon answered Jean-Paul Sartre's celebrated 1949 preface to Senghor's manifesto, *Anthologie de la nouvelle poésie nègre et malgache de langue française* (Anthology of the New French-Language Black and Malagasy Poetry) by accusing the philosopher of again trying to highjack blacks into Western history. Similarly, **Ngugi wa Thiong'o** urged the perils of judging African history by a European one: it was not true, says the protagonist of *The Trial of Dedan Kimathi* (1977) in reply to Césaire, that blacks had invented nothing. Their inventiveness involved different cultural modes and exigencies.

By the 1960s, revolutionary diasporic thinking focused on Cuba and Algeria. The Martinican Fanon in the second and Haitian René Depestre in the first protested against essentialist negritude, Depestre, too, arguing that it served Western ends. He had in mind Price-Mars but, above all, François "Papa Doc" Duvalier, who asserted that negritude underpinned and valorized his dictatorship. While contemporary US Afrocentrism often echoes essentialist negritude, elsewhere writers warn against its fetishizing of blackness. African and

Caribbean writers mostly argue today that negritude was necessary to African, pan-African, and diasporic intellectual decolonization, political liberation, and aesthetic and psychological awareness, but has now fulfilled its historical function (see **diaspora and pan-Africanism**). The debates it provoked, however, about identity and culture, language and political independence, freedom, and economic and social development remain essential.

At least in the US, the concept has entered popular culture. *The New York Times* of 10 September 2001 reported that after the sisters Venus and Serena Williams met in the 2001 final of the US Open tennis tournament, the film director Spike Lee explained their superstar status: "They can play. They got game. They got ball." For black America especially, he concluded, "They've got, you know the word? . . . negritude."

Further reading

Césaire, Aimé (1971) *Cahier d'un retour au pays natal* (Notebook of a Return to a Native Land), Paris: Présence Africaine.

Depestre, René (1980) *Bonjour et adieu à la négritude* (Hello and Goodbye to Negritude), Paris: Laffont.

Mphahlele, Es'kia (1962)"What Price Negritude?" in Es'kia Mphahlele, *The African Image*, London: Faber and Faber.

—— (1967) "Remarks on Negritude," in Es'kia Mphahlele (ed.) *African Writing Today*, Harmondsworth: Penguin.

——(1974) "Negritude Revisited," in Es'kia Mphahlele, *The African Image*, new and revised edn, London: Faber and Faber.

Nesbitt, Nick (1999) "Négritude," in Kwame Anthony Appiah and Henry Louis Gates, Jr (eds) *Africana: The Encyclopedia of the African and African American Experience*, New York: Basic *Civitas* Books.

Senghor, Léopold Sédar (1964) "The African Road to Socialism," in L.S. Senghor, *On African Socialism*, trans. and introd. Mercer Cook, New York: Praeger.

TIMOTHY J. REISS

Neogy, Rajat

b. 1938, Kampala, Uganda; d. 1995, San Francisco, USA

magazine editor and social critic

The Ugandan magazine editor and social critic Rajat Neogy was born to one of the few Bengali families in Kampala. Returning to Uganda in 1958 after studying at the University of London, Neogy found the intellectual atmosphere of Kampala too provincial for his liking, and sought to change this by setting up a magazine, partly modeled on Ulli Beier's *Black Orpheus*, that would promote lively intellectual exchange. Always an iconoclast, Neogy sought to cultivate a magazine that would embody his own self-professed status as an "outsider." The product, *Transition*, became one of the finest landmarks in the development of African letters while also providing an outlet for cosmopolitan interests worldwide. Avant-garde and bohemian, *Transition* was the forum for many upcoming writers such as Grace **Ogot**, Paul Theroux, **Okot p'Bitek**, Ali **Mazrui**, **Ngugi wa Thiong'o**, and for many more established ones. Driven into exile by an increasingly paranoid government, Neogy died in San Francisco, reportedly disappointed at the turn the resurrected *Transition* had taken. By then he had bequeathed to Africa one of its most important sites for cultural debate.

Further reading

Benson, Peter (1986) *Black Orpheus, Transition, and Modern Cultural Awakening in Africa*, Berkeley: University of California Press.

DAN ODHIAMBO OJWANG

Neto, (António) Agostinho

b. 1922, Bengo province, Angola; d. 1979, Moscow, Russia

politician, doctor, and poet

The first president of the Republic of Angola and a medical doctor, Agostinho Neto was also a poet. While studying in Lisbon, he belonged to the Casa dos Estudantes do Império, a venue where he met a range of anti-colonial Lusophone intellectuals including Amílcar Cabral. His opposition to the Portuguese colonial regime that ruled Angola until independence led to him being sent to prison on several occasions, where he wrote resistance poetry. He was closely involved with *Mensagem*, the journal of a group of writers influenced by **negritude**. Neto's poetry pioneered a sense of Angolan identity. His *Sacred Hope* (*Sagrada Esperança*) (1974) expresses the aspirations for freedom of a colonized nation. He founded the Angolan Writers' Association.

Further reading

Neto, Agostinho (1974) *Sacred Hope*, trans. Marga Holness, Dar es Salaam: Tanzania Publishing House.

PHILLIP ROTHWELL

Ngal Mbwil a Mpaang

b. 1933, Mayanda, Congo-Zaire

novelist

Ngal Mbwil a Mpaang (also known as Georges Ngal) is a founding figure in Congolese letters and one of his country's first major novelists. Following studies in philosophy and theology in Congo-Zaire, he earned a doctorate in literature from Fribourg, Switzerland. He is the author of numerous critical works, beginning with *Aimé Césaire, un homme à la recherche d'une patrie* (Aimé Césaire, a Man in Search of a Native Land) (1975). In 1994, he published a study of African literature entitled *Création et rupture en littérature africaine* (Creation and Division in African Literature). After teaching for a decade in Congo-Zaire, where he served as dean of the Faculty of Letters at the National University of Zaire in Lubumbashi, he held faculty positions at a number of institutions abroad, including Middlebury College, the University of Paris, Grenoble III, and Bayreuth. His early fictional works *Giambatista Viko (ou le viol du discours africain)* (Giambatista Viko, or The Rape of African Discourse) (1975) and its sequel *L'Errance* (Wandering) (1979) deal with an

African intellectual seeking to reconcile African traditions and Western narrative. The 1994 work *Une Saison de symphonie* (A Symphony Season) features erudite characters reflecting on contemporary aesthetic and philosophical issues.

JANICE SPLETH

Ngandu Nkashama, Pius

b. 1946, Mbujimayi (Congo-Kinshasa)

academic, poet, and playwright

Born in Mbujimayi (Congo-Kinshasa), Pius Ngandu Nkashama is first a brilliant academic, having taught in his country before going to various foreign universities in the course of his long exile. In Francophone literary circles, he is considered to be a legend in the institution of African literature. This pertains not only to the quality but also to the quantity of works produced: twenty-four texts covering literary criticism, linguistics, political science, and sociology of religion, two collections of poetry, four plays, and seventeen novels. He is one of the rare writers to have successfully found a way of allying theory and practice in fiction writing. This double identity is, moreover, perceptible in his works.

Ngandu probably reached literature through teaching it. Inspired by Césaire, his first work, *La Délivrance d'Ilunga* (The Deliverance of Ilunga) (1977), marks the cycle of a writing that can be divided into four stages. First the cycle of the curse, which is characterized by one particular set of concerns – the world of monsters, mischance, and reckless myths to deconstruct. This initial and unsuspecting form is the richness of the subsoil. *La Malédiction* (The Curse) (1983) and *Yakouta* (1994) are in fact marked by the "theory of the industrial diamond" that makes the mining of precious stones the easiest and quickest way of starving Africans. The earth is no longer a public possession, but the object of lust that has led to bloody wars and occupation such as in the case of Congo-Kinshasa. This concern with death and destruction is further elaborated in the defeatism of various characters who have succumbed to the so-called complex of

Cham: the impossibility of attaining well-being, hence the obsession with failure.

The other form of the curse is the proliferation of states infested with a general, a "guide," a "nuisance" or bloodthirsty king. When one considers *Le Pacte de sang* (The Pact of Blood) (1984), *La Mort faite homme* (Death Made a Man) (1986), *Un Jour de grand soleil sur les montagnes en Ethiopie* (A Day of Great Sun on the Mountains of Ethiopia) (1991), *L'Empire des ombres vivantes* (The Empire of Living Shade) (1991), *May Britt de Santa Cruz* (1993), *Le Doyen Marri* (1994) or *Mayiléna* (1999), one observes that Ngandu Nkashama's work is built around the unveiling of stupid despotisms. The generalization of the cannibal state and despair combine to break the psyche of subjects who, through an insidious form of contagion, become victims of the violent insanity that characterizes the height of vampire states in the aberrations in which they are tangled.

The second cycle of Ngandu Nkashama's writing is concerned with madness, to which the novels give a sustained literary and theoretical dimension. The lack of reason in the subjects of this fiction often takes clinical forms resulting from claustrophobia, acceleration of the imagination, and even association with spaces of concentration. In this concern with madness, the aesthetic is pushed aside, burst open, and sometimes becomes completely unintelligible. But there always exists another dementia whose distinctive form is revolution.

The last cycle in his writings is that of hope, evident in works such as *Citadelle d'espoir* (Citadel of Hope) (1995). In the works written during this phase of his career, Ngandu Nkashama anticipates the collapse of African dictatorships in the 1990s. But even in these works, life passes through madness and death, until love, as embodied in the figure of the poet, becomes strength.

Like a number of African writers of his generation, Ngandu Nkashama's writing is militant and overtly subversive. The journeys of many of his characters, which resemble his own journey, take them through internment camps, expose them to social torment, and subject them to the most sordid imprisonment. Indeed, before he was forced into exile in 1982, he was himself declared "insane" by the authorities and he was confined to the village of Mbujimayi. If much of his fiction takes place on a

campus or involves youth, it is because the author is keen to represent the meeting of national and personal trauma as he has experienced or observed them in the postcolonial state (see **colonialism, neocolonialism, and postcolonialism**). His novels are indeed full of the traumatic experiences of Congo under Mobutu: the martyrdom of Patrice Lumumba, the "pacified" rebellion of the Lovanium University, the killings of Katekelay or Lumumba, and the war in Katanga.

Ngandu is thus a political writer whose discourse of protest, sometimes polemical, is also visible in his theoretical works which, like his fiction, mark decisive moments in the critical discourse of his country and the whole of Africa. *Écritures et Discours littéraires* (Writings and Literary Discourse) (1991) reveals the parameters of creation, then expresses the pertinent paths for the interpreting of African poetics since its beginnings. *Littératures et écritures en langues africaines* (Literature and Writings in African Languages) (1991) definitively disqualifies the myth of an Africa without writing, reveals its sites, the modalities of circulation and the practice of a "science of texts" before the colonial venture. *Théâtres et scènes de spectacles* (Theaters and Scenes of Spectacle) (1993) offers pathways for a semiology of gestural arts. *Rupture et écritures de violence* (Rupture and Writings of Violence) (1997) brings elements for the understanding of recent literary and filmic texts. In these and other works, the critique of politics is coupled with a political criticism that disposes of certain reckless foundations of a triumphant hegemonic Western discourse.

Further reading

Bello, M. (1994) *L'Aliénation dans le pacte de sang de Pius Ngandu Nkashama* (Alienation in Pius Ngandu Nkashama's Pact of Blood), Paris: L'Harmattan.

Kalonji, Zezeze T. (1992) *Une Écriture de la passion chez Pius Ngandu Nkashama* (Writing on the Passion of Pius Ngandu Nkashama), Paris: L'Harmattan.

Tcheuyap, A. (1998) *Esthéthique et folie dans l'oeuvre romanesque de Pius Ngandu Nkashama* (Aesthetics and Folly in the Romanesque Work of Pius Ngandu Nkashama), Paris: L'Harmattan.

ALEXIE TCHEUYAP

Ngcobo, Lauretta

b. Ixopo, South Africa

novelist

Lauretta Ngcobo is one of the most politically conscious writers from South Africa, and her first two novels *Cross of Gold* (1981) and *And They Didn't Die* (1990) are stories about the necessity of political action in South Africa in the era of apartheid (see **apartheid and post-apartheid**). In these works and elsewhere, her main focus is on the nature of political action, its necessity in the struggle against injustice in South Africa, and its effects on children. In *Cross of Gold*, for example, a young black child, Mandla, is orphaned because of politics, and at the end of the novel he leaves his own child orphaned because of his involvement with the liberation struggle. In *And They Didn't Die*, Ngcobo is concerned with the ways in which apartheid cripples a black family through restrictive practices that make it difficult for a wife and husband to lead ordinary lives. In this novel, Zenzile, the main character, has to get a "pass" to visit her husband Siyalo in a workers' hostel in Durban in order to get pregnant. Her husband is caught stealing milk to keep his children alive and is thrown into jail. She herself is raped and has to raise the child of a white boss because she has to work after her husband's incarceration. Ngcobo, who has lived in Britain since the 1980s, has also edited *Let It Be Told* (1987), a collection of essays by black women in Britain.

HUMA IBRAHIM

Ngubane, Jordan Kush

b. 1917, Ladysmith, Kwa-Zulu Natal; d. 1985, Ulundi, South Africa

short story writer, scholar, and journalist

The Zulu novelist, short story writer, scholar and journalist Jordan Ngubane was born in Ladysmith, Kwa-Zulu Natal, and educated at Adams' College. During various periods in his eventful life Ngubane was assistant editor of *Ilanga lase Natal* (The Natal Sun), editor of *Inkundla ya Bantu* (Bantu Forum) and

Bantu World, and correspondent for *The Forum*, *Indian Opinion*, and the London *Observer*. Ngubane worked closely with Chief Albert Luthuli prior to the latter's confinement by the South African authorities to his farm in the 1950s. Ngubane published widely on Zulu literature, African literature, philosophy, and politics. His published creative works include an IsiZulu novel, *His Frown Struck Terror* (*Uvalo Lwezinhlozi*) (1957), and a historical novel, *Ushaba: The Hurtle of Blood River* (1974). Two of his non-fiction works are *An African Explains Apartheid* (1963) and "Conflict of Minds," an essay in *South Africa: Sociological Perspectives* (1971). Some of Ngubane's critical essays appeared in the *Native Teachers' Journal* while several of his short stories were published in *Drum* magazine in the 1950s.

Further reading

Rosenberg, Graeme (2000) "Auto/Biographical Narratives and the Lives of Jordan Ngubane," *Alternation* 7, 1: 62–9.

THENGANI H. NGWENYA

Ngugi wa Thiong'o

b. 1938, Kamiriithu, near Limuru, Kenya

novelist, dramatist and essayist

The Kenyan novelist, dramatist, and essayist Ngugi wa Thiong'o dominates the transitional period of modern African literature (1964–70), and his major works constitute an important link between the pioneers of African writing, such as Chinua **Achebe** and Camara **Laye**, and a younger generation of postcolonial African writers (see **colonialism, neocolonialism, and postcolonialism**), including Dambudzo **Marechera** and Tsitsi **Dangarembga**. In his later works, plays, and essays, primarily focused on the relationship between power and culture in the postcolonial state, Ngugi has been one of the most perceptive students of postcolonial cultural politics, and his writings on culture and politics in Africa have influenced many Third World writers. His decision to stop writing fiction in English and to use Gikuyu instead reignited the debate about language and the identity of African literature (see **Gikuyu literature**; **language question**).

Starting his career at a time when African literature was trying to free itself from the European tradition, Ngugi's early works were marked by the influence of his education at Makerere University College in Uganda, where he studied English in the early 1960s. The teaching of English at Makerere, where Ngugi was also the editor of *Penpoint*, one of the leading literary journals in East Africa at the time, followed the tenets of literary criticism enunciated by F.R. Leavis at Cambridge. At the heart of these tenets was the claim that the best English literature represented the essential humane values of English society and that language was most effective and creative when it reflected an intense moral interest. Following this desire to use language to represent moral conflict, Ngugi's early stories were focused on the struggle between alienated individuals and collective entities, but they were also engaged in the exploration of a problem that was central to African fiction in the late 1950s and early 1960s, namely how to translate what Leavis had called moral intensity to situations that were removed from English, Englishness, and its tradition of writing.

Ngugi's early project, then, was how to create a literature in English, an African literature, outside the values of English. In particular, Ngugi had been born in a colonial situation that reflected the radical opposition between Englishness, as it was presented in school culture, and the political and cultural aspirations of colonized Africans. His family was part of a large group of Kenyans who had been dispossessed when large chunks of fertile land in central Kenya and the Rift Valley were set aside for white settlement. Ngugi came of age during the Mau Mau revolt against British colonialism, a revolt driven by grievances over the lost lands. At Alliance High School and in Makerere, the institutions of education, and literary culture in general, were intended to shelter those lucky enough to be admitted from the vagaries and violence of the colonial situation. Literature was the site of a liberal sensibility and a transcendental aesthetic. It was about moral conflict, not that other ugly conflict out there in the real world. At the same time, however, Ngugi could not escape from this other conflict. It was part of the realities that determined his life. The school and the university might offer protection, literature might be the place of moral awakening, but this did not simply make the overwhelming realities of colonialism and the violent struggle against it disappear. Ngugi became a writer seeking to establish a compromise: the reconciliation of moral intensity (as it had been defined by Leavis) and his own memories and experiences of the colonial situation and its violence.

Influenced particularly by the works of British modernists like D.H. Lawrence and Joseph Conrad, Ngugi started his career producing novels that would use the African landscape of his childhood and youth to represent what he considered to be larger universal values such as the morality of action and the conflict between individual desires and collective yearnings. But as the drama of decolonization became more complicated, the older forms of representing individual consciousness seemed wanting; independence had undermined the paradigmatic opposition between the colonizer and colonized that had shaped African literature in the formative 1950s; new social relationships and oppositions were not clearly defined in the early 1960s when Ngugi started writing; in the 1970s and 1980s his novels and essays were to become important in elaborating the relationship between culture and the state and the role of the writer in a neocolonial society. Ngugi's writing career has thus developed in several phases closely identified with the nature of late colonialism in East Africa and postcolonial politics in Kenya; they are also part of a journey that has taken him from the liberal culture of Englishness, as promoted by the colonial school and university, to his later role as a writer sufficiently committed to radical social change to risk imprisonment and exile.

In his first two novels, *Weep Not, Child* (1964) and *The River Between* (1965), Ngugi was primarily concerned with the tension between a violent colonial past and the dream of cultural nationalism (see **nationalism and post-nationalism**). Focusing on some of the historical events that had shaped the history of modern Kenya – the female circumcision controversy of the late 1920s and early 1930s, and the Mau Mau conflict in the

1950s – Ngugi produced powerful narratives that examined a violent colonial past and provided a tentative critique of the culture of decolonization. In *The River Between*, which was his first written novel, Ngugi sought to dramatize a defining moment of cultural nationalism in central Kenya – the female circumcision conflict of the late 1920s/early 1930s, when an influential group of leaders sought to reconcile certain cultural practices, which the colonial government and the Church found repulsive, with their aspirations for modernity. The novel is one of the most powerful representations of the new African subject caught between the need to uphold tradition as the basis of national consciousness while promoting the modernizing institutions of colonialism. As in all of Ngugi's early works, the center of the conflict was not political; rather, the tragedy of the hero arose when he found himself unable to reconcile two opposing moral positions: the ideology of cultural purity and the claims of self-enlightenment. In contrast to the concern with landscape and the morality of action in *The River Between*, *Weep Not, Child* took the structure of an autobiographical novel (see **autobiography**): here, Ngugi's aim was to understand the Mau Mau conflict through the eyes of a child, growing up with dreams and aspirations for social upliftment, only to be caught in the powerful conflict between a white settler and Mau Mau nationalists. While what made this novel so striking was its ability to voice the fears and aspirations of those caught in the Mau Mau conflict, its more subtle goal was its concern with a process of negative education, which seemed to be at odds with the larger claims of colonialism itself. Colonialism had found a foothold in central Kenya by privileging the process of education as the point of entry into the modern world; Ngugi's novel was a reflection on the false premises on which this kind of social upliftment was predicated.

Another important phase in Ngugi's career was marked by his discovery of Marxism and the works of Frantz Fanon when he was a student at Leeds University. When he arrived at Leeds to undertake graduate studies, Ngugi was having serious doubts about the liberal politics he had espoused in his early works, a politics vividly represented in the early essays collected in *Homecoming* (1972). In those essays he had argued that the moment of

independence was not simply a time when African aspirations would be fulfilled, but also a point of reconciliation when the racial and class conflicts dramatized in his early works would be transcended. But in the very first few years of independence, Ngugi was discovering, as were many African writers of his generation, that both tenets were under threat: the new government seemed eager to embrace white settlers and to protect their economic interests at the expense of the peasants who had opposed them. In addition, the postcolonial regime was now dominated by those Africans who had actively fought Mau Mau, although Jomo **Kenyatta**, the great nationalist, was now president. Among the Marxist professors and students at Leeds, Ngugi seems to have discovered a more radical method of social and cultural analysis, one that would enable him to account for the persistence of neocolonialism in the new African state.

But it was from Fanon's *The Wretched of the Earth* (1963) that he was to discover the tropes that would enable him to narrate the crisis of decolonization. In his book, one of Fanon's key concerns was the failure of nationalism to live up to its mandate and the continued dominance of colonial institutions in the new African state. He provided a powerful and prophetic warning of a failed decolonization and its consequences on art, culture, and society:

> National consciousness, instead of being the all-embracing crystallization of the innermost hopes of the whole people, instead of being the immediate and most obvious result of the mobilization of the people, will be an empty shell, a crude and fragile travesty of what it might have been.
>
> (1963: New York)

Like most of the literature produced in Africa in the late 1960s and 1970s, Ngugi took up the powerful motif of expectation and betrayal in *A Grain of Wheat* (1966), one of his most popular novels. And he sought to represent a stillborn independence using the techniques of modernism, including interiorized consciousness, flashbacks, and divided perspectives which underscored the uncertainty involved in the task of making sense of the new politics of independence in which things rarely appeared to be what they were.

From 1965 to the end of the 1970s, then, Ngugi was concerned with questions of postcolonial failure and the disjuncture between the dream of independence and its betrayal. His goal was to psychoanalyze the narrative of nationalism and to capture the disenchantment that had replaced the euphoria of independence. In the newer essays published in *Homecoming* (1972), Ngugi sought to intervene in public debates on the role of culture in decolonization and the African writer's relation to the society, the state, and the historical past. These themes, first taken up in *A Grain of Wheat*, were to be repeated almost ten years later in *Petals of Blood* (1977), and in some of the stories collected in *Secret Lives* (1975). The key themes in these new works remained the same as they first appeared in *A Grain of Wheat*, although some critics have allowed the high modernism of the later to camouflage this thematic continuity. *Petals of Blood* was, of course, a much more radical novel, with a plot and rhetoric driven by powerful Marxist notions on the relation between culture and politics, underdevelopment, and revolution. But beneath this new grammar of politics, the central motif of the novel was still that of expectation and betrayal, of the dream of nationalism and its sacrifice at what Ngugi considered to be the altar of capitalism. What was perhaps different about *Petals of Blood* was its rejection of the form and rhetoric of high modernism Ngugi had flirted with in *A Grain of Wheat* for social realism, which Ngugi believed was a better mode of producing fiction that would both represent the neocolonial polity and provide a utopian resolution to the politics of everyday life.

A defining characteristic of Ngugi's career, especially in its middle period (the 1970s and 1980s) was his search for modes of fictional representation that would mediate the politics of everyday life better than traditional novelistic genres. While he had often privileged the role of the novel as the form most attuned to the process of social change, Ngugi was also aware of the extent to which his early novels had been co-opted into the educational system, where they were valued as outstanding examples of the nationalist imagination. He was compelled to rethink the relationship

between the novel and politics. This questioning took two forms. First, Ngugi began to probe the relation between genres and the kind of radical political intervention to which his work was committed. Second, he turned his attention to the language question as a symptom of the crisis in African writing. In *Decolonising the Mind* (1986), for example, he questioned the assumption that European languages were the natural vehicles for the African imagination, arguing that a literature produced in the language of the colonizer was inherently alienating.

Ironically, it was through his marginal dramatic works rather than his canonical novels that Ngugi was forced to confront his own identity as a radical writer in a conservative postcolonial state. As early as 1962, when the production of *The Black Hermit* (1968) was halted after a few runs at the National Theatre in Kampala, Ngugi's plays seemed to be politically more effective than his novels. This point was confirmed by the political problems surrounding the production of *The Trial of Dedan Kimathi* (1977), a play co-written with Micere **Mugo**, at the National Theatre in Nairobi in 1976. By the end of the 1970s, as is apparent in the essays collected in *Writers in Politics* (1981) and *Barrel of a Pen* (1983), Ngugi had become convinced that his novels were not accessible to the workers and peasants whom he thought to be agents of radical change and the real subjects of a committed literature. In *I Will Marry When I Want* (1982), a controversial play in Gikuyu co-written with Ngugi wa Miriie, he invited his peasant audience to become major players in the representation of their own lives and, as he later noted in *Penpoints, Gunpoints, and Dreams* (1999), to break down the boundary between the theatrical and social space.

Another turning point in Ngugi's career began with his arrest and imprisonment without trial, in 1978, for his involvement with the community theater in Kamiriithu. The circumstances surrounding this case were narrated in *Detained: A Writer's Prison Diary* (1981), simultaneously a scathing attack on the neocolonial state that had imprisoned him and a reflection on the culture of silence in Africa. It was in prison, however, that Ngugi wrote *Devil on the Cross* (1982), his first novel in Gikuyu, a work that was to provoke many debates about the role of language in the shaping of African literature, but one in which he began to open his works to elements, such as orality and popular culture, that had not been pronounced in his previous novels (see **oral literature and performance**). Forced into exile in 1982, Ngugi continued to insist that his decision to write in Gikuyu represented an epistemological break; it would accord the African novel its own genealogy and tradition. The publication of *Matigari* (1989), a work that was considered so dangerous by the Kenyan state that it was banned on publication, was intended to affirm this break with previous novelistic practices, and in particular to open the novel to new audiences. While there have been debates on whether *Matigari* marked the epistemological break it was intended to make, it is generally considered to have represented a crucial point of transition in Ngugi's career, taking up questions of orality and cultural transition in unprecedented ways.

Now, if Ngugi is considered to be one of the most influential voices on the relationship between literature, performance, and the politics of culture in Africa, it is because his works have provided readers with powerful stories about what it means to be an African subject under colonial and postcolonial conditions. With the attention he has focused on questions such as nation and narration, power and performance, language and identity, Ngugi has proven to be both a pioneer and innovator in the tradition of African letters.

Further reading

Fanon, F. (1963) *The Wretched of the Earth*, New York: Grove Press.

Gikandi, S. (2000) *Ngugi wa Thiong'o*, Cambridge: Cambridge University Press.

Ogude, James (1999) *Ngugi's Novels and African History: Narrating the Nation*, London: Pluto Press.

Sicherman, C. (1900) *Ngugi wa Thiong'o: The Making of a Rebel. A Source Book in Kenyan Literature and Resistance*, London: Hans Zell.

Williams, Patrick (1999) *Ngugi wa Thiong'o*, Manchester: Manchester University Press.

SIMON GIKANDI

Ngwenya, Mthandazo Ndema

b. 1949, Zimbabwe; d. 1992, Bulawayo–Harare highway, Zimbabwe

novelist, radio playwright, and poet

The Zimbabwean novelist, radio playwright, and poet Mthandazo Ngwenya belongs to the second generation of Ndebele writers (see **Shona and Ndebele literature**) whose works dominate the late 1970s and early independence period. His novel *Ngitshilo Ngitshilo* (I Have Made My Final Statement) (1978), focuses on the tension between Ndebele traditional values and the social changes engendered by colonialism (see **colonialism, neocolonialism, and postcolonialism**). In this novel, the father represents the patriarchal point of view founded on the belief that when there is a scarcity of financial resources in the family, daughters should drop out of school and seek material security in marriage to a member of an approved family. In Ngwenya's novel, however, the mother advocates the education of girls and in the process confronts gender inequality and its relation to colonial economic conditions (see **gender and sexuality**). His satire, *UNgcingci KaNdoyi* (UNgcingci, Child of Ndoi) (1982), analyzes the discrepancy between physical beauty and moral virtue. The plot extols the African adage that beauty is both extrinsic and intrinsic. *Ilifa Lidliwa Ngumninilo* (Inheritance Should Go to the Rightful Person) (1985), a novel on warfare and witchcraft, comprises a captivating narrative in which oral traditional devices are uniquely deployed (see **oral literature and performance**). His poetry is largely devoted to Ndebele cultural and historical issues.

EMMANUEL CHIWOME

Niane, Djibril Tamsir

b. 1932, Conakry, Guinea

novelist and historian

Born in Conakry, the Senegal-Guinean novelist and historian D.T. Niane completed his secondary education at the Collège de Conakry and the

Institut des hautes écoles de Dakar before studying literature and history in Bordeaux. Upon his return to Conakry in 1959, he taught history at the Lycée classique before occupying important administrative and research positions in Guinea. He was later imprisoned by Sékou Touré and eventually "exiled" to Senegal, where he assumed ministerial positions in Léopold S. **Senghor**'s government. Renown as a historian, researcher, novelist, playwright, and short story writer, D.T. Niane is one of the greatest scholars of Mandé history. His meticulous compilations of oral narratives (see **oral literature and performance**) pertaining to the medieval Mali empire are central to any real knowledge and appreciation of the region's history. As dean of the School of Social Sciences at Conakry, his work rehabilitated the oral sources of African history; he also applied the rigors and skepticism of Western historiography to the search of the West African past. An indefatigable listener of Mandé griots, and a transcriber and defender of the veracity of oral traditions, Niane was himself an initiate to the griot art and a fervent believer in its oath of secrecy. His most notable works include *Sundiata: An Epic of Old Mali* (*Soundjata ou l'épopée mandingue*) (1960), *Le Soudan occidental au temps des grands empires XI–XVI siècles* (Western Sudan in the Time of the Great Empires, XI–XVI centuries) (1971), *Mery: nouvelles* (Mery: Short Stories) (1965), *Recherches sur l'Empire du Mali au Moyen Age* (Research on the Mali Empire of the Middle Age) (1959), *Sikasso ou la dernière citadelle suivi de Chaka* (Sikasso or the Last Citadel Followed by Chaka) (1971), *Contes d'hier et d'aujourd'hui* (Tales of Yesterday and Today) (1985), *Histoire des Mandingues de l'Ouest* (History of the Western Mandingoes), and *La République de Guinée* (The Republic of Guinea). Niane's literary work, as well as his other scholarly publications, displays a predilection for history, and in his works characters such as Soundjata and Chaka are meant, through their heroic deeds, to be inspiring figures in the struggle for political emancipation. In essence, Niane's project is didactic since it provides readers and spectators with the trials, triumphs, and tribulations of the Africa past against the backdrop of colonialism and decolonization (see **colonialism, neocolonialism, and postcolonialism**). Maryse **Condé** and Ahmadou **Kourouma** could be said to have followed in D.T.

Niane's interrogative mode with their historical novels, *Segu* (1984) and *Monnew* (1990) respectively, whereas Camara Laye's *The Guardian of the Word* (*Maître de la parole*) (1978) complements it. The success of *Keita: The Heritage of the Griot* by Burkinabé filmmaker Dani Kouyaté speaks to the continued appeal of Niane's writings even in more recent genres such as film (see **cinema**).

JEAN OUÉDRAOGO

Niang, Mame Bassine

b. 1951, Senegal

writer and lawyer

The Senegalese writer Mame Bassine Niang is one of the most prominent lawyers in her country, and in 1975 she became the first woman member of the Senegalese Bar. She is a founder member of the Association of Senegalese Lawyers and vice-president of the International Foundation of Women Jurists (FIDA). In politics she has been active in the areas of human rights and especially the rights of women, and has served in high positions in the Senegalese government. In the 1980s she turned to creative writing and brought her concerns with issues of justice and gender rights to bear on her work. Her major literary work to date is *Mémoires pour mon pè* (Memoirs for My Father), an autobiographical novel (see **autobiography**) intended to commemorate her father's life as a leader of a canton in Senegal, but one which turns in the end to be an emotional invocation of her youth and adolescence in a time of political and cultural translation. In the process of evoking the mythic face of a dead father, Niang is able to reflect on the lives and experiences of Senegalese women before and after colonialism.

OUSMANE BA

Nicol, Abioseh (Davidson)

b. 1924, Sierra Leone; d. 1991, London

doctor and short story writer

The distinguished Sierra Leonean doctor wrote

mostly short stories dealing with everyday life under colonialism (see **colonialism, neocolonialism, and postcolonialism**), focusing on the ordinariness of life in a colonized society rather than the larger dramatic events favored by most African writers within the tradition of cultural nationalism (see **nationalism and post-nationalism**). In the stories collected in *The Truly Married Woman and Other Stories* (1965), Nicol focuses on such things as jobs and pensions, rituals of governance and social conduct, and, occasionally, racial relations in Sierra Leone. In *Two African Stories* (1965), however, he is much more interested in the political conflicts that arise out of racial misunderstandings. In "The Leopard Hunt," the lead story in this collection, Nicol tells the story of what happens when an African subordinate is forced to accompany a European on a hunt and gets killed in the process. The second story of the collection, "The Devil at Yolahun Bridge," is constructed around the misunderstanding that arises when a white colonial official discovers that the visiting residential engineer is an African. Nicol also wrote stories detailing life in the Creole community of Freetown.

SIMON GIKANDI

Nicol, Mike

b. 1951, South Africa

novelist

The South African writer Mike Nicol is noted for producing verse in sparse, unadorned language. The poetry collected in *Among the Souvenirs* (1979) and *This Sad Place* (1993) explores loss, displacement, and exile at home and abroad. His novels – particularly *The Powers That Be* (1989) and *This Day and Age* (1992) – offer powerful allegories of South Africa as colony and apartheid state (see **apartheid and post-apartheid**) and their style, which goes beyond traditional forms of realism, has led to Nicol's being hailed as a South African practitioner of magical realism (see **realism and magical realism**). In general, Nicol's writing is characterized by a sometimes effortless, sometimes contrived transgression of all textual boundaries. Characters

are lifted out of fairy-tales to share the stage with historical figures, Christopher Marlowe is harnessed to a parody of the cheap airport thriller, and the millenarian Xhosa Cattle-Killing of 1856–7 is grafted on to the Bullhoek Massacre of 1921. Alluding to a range of historical events and landscapes, Nicol's fiction is equally concerned with post-apartheid South Africa. *The Ibis Tapestry* (1998), whose title is a meditation on the texture of its own fabric, applies itself to the questions raised by the Truth and Reconciliation Commission. Nicol has also published a tribute to the *Drum* writers of the 1950s and a memoir of living in Cape Town, the city of his birth, in *Sea-Mountain, Fire City* (2001).

MEG SAMUELSON

Nirina, Esther

b. 1932, Madagascar

poet

The Madagascan poet Esther Nirina (pronounced "nerine") prefers not to use her family name in her published poetry so as not to be linked with her more famous countryman, Jacques **Rabemananjara**, to whom she is not related. She left her island of birth in 1959 and spent twenty-seven years in Orleans, France; here she started writing her poetry which, over a period of twenty years, was published privately. Her four volumes, *Silencieuse respiration* (Silent Respiration) (1975), *Simple voyelle* (Simple Vowel) (1980), *Lente spirale* (Slow Spiral) (1990), and *Multiple solitude* (Multiple Solitude) (1997) have been published collectively in *Rien que lune* (Just the Moon) (1998). In free verse which is strongly influenced by the Madagascan oral tradition genre *hain-teny* (see **oral literature and performance**), she addresses the difficulty of poetic creation, the symbiotic relationship with exists between poet and nature, and the fragility of human existence. Her deep and committed Christianity finds expression in her compassion for fellow human beings and their suffering. Multidimensional evocations, the use of periphrases, ellipses, and a succession of apparently incoherent, unrelated images make her poetry hermetic but, as she herself has stated, the key to understanding lies in a collaborative creation between poet and reader.

Futher reading

Nirina, Esther (1998) *Rien que lune* (Just the Moon), Saint-Denis, Réunion: Éditions Grand Océan.

CAROLE M. BECKETT

Njami, Simon

b. 1962, Lausanne, Switzerland

novelist

Born in Lausanne, Switzerland, of Cameroonian parents, Njami has written extensively on African artists since the late 1980s, and he has also been an active figure in the international African **art** scene as the editor of the literary and arts magazine *Revue Noir* (Black Review). His two novels, *African Gigolo* (1989) and *Coffin and Co.* (*Cercueil et Cie*) (1985) are concerned with the experiences of homosexuals in Europe and gay communities in the African diaspora in general (see **homosexuality**; **diaspora and pan-Africanism**). These novels are largely inspired by sites of African-American cultural tradition, such as the Parisian jazz club (in *African Gigolo*) or Chester Himes' detective novels (in *Coffin and Co.*). His biography of James Baldwin, *James Baldwin: ou, le devoir de la violence* (James Baldwin: or, The Duty of Violence) (1991) documents some of the many links among artists of the African diaspora in Europe, America, and Africa.

Further reading

Njami, Simon (1987) *Ethnicolor*, Paris: Éditions Autrement.
——(1989) *African gigolo: roman* (African Gigolo: a novel), Paris: Seghers.

FRIEDA EKOTTO

Njau, Rebeka (Rebecca)

b. 1932, Kenya

artist, playwright, and novelist

The Kenyan artist, playwright and novelist Rebeka Njau was educated at Alliance High School, Kikuyu, and Makerere University College, where she graduated as a teacher. It was during her career as a teacher that she started writing short stories and plays, most of which were published in *Transition*, one of the leading literary journals in East Africa in the 1960s. One of the plays published in transition was *The Scar*, which won an award at the National Theatre in Kampala in 1963. In 1975, Njau published her first novel *Ripples in the Pool*, a work exploring the struggle between the politics of modernity and the claims of old systems of belief (see **modernity and modernism**). Like many novels of postcolonial disillusionment in East Africa, Njau's fiction is concerned with the emergence of a new economic class that wants to exploit the landscape and its people to fulfil its illusions of wealth and social advancement (see **colonialism, neocolonialism, and postcolonialism**). The language of her novel is highly symbolic and she prefers the use of realism (see **realism and magical realism**) to the fragmented modernist style of other writers in this tradition, most prominently Leonard **Kibera** and Peter **Palangyo**. It is through the use of symbolism that she is able to capture the state of dissonance that exists between new postcolonial subjects and the spaces they want to claim for their own.

SIMON GIKANDI

Nkollo, Jean-Jacques

b. 1962, Douala, Cameroon

novelist

Jean-Jacques Nkollo is one of the Cameroonian writers associated with the "Generation of Independence" in the early 1960s. Indeed, he was born in Douala two years after Cameroon became independent. Like many other writers of his generation, Nkollo considers his literary works to be the site of a dialogue with both himself and others. This theme dominates his two first works, *Brouillard* (Fog) (1990) and *Le Joyeuse Déraison* (Joyous Unreason) (1992), whose heroes are in search of harmony and personal and collective stability. He is also preoccupied with inscribing his work in history and African political realities, drawing upon both mythic and present-day African experiences. Thus he not only recreates, in works such as *Le Paysan de Tombouctou* (The Peasant from Timbuktu) (1994), the ancient historical and mythical tradition suggested by the title, but includes, among the protagonists of the novel, the historian–storyteller Amadou Hampaté **Bâ**, a character who appears mythic. In this novel Nkollo also reflects on the possibility of the coexistence on African soil of the world of science and that of tutelary spirits, a concern that structures the journey of the main character, Koné, an engineer in nuclear physics who, in order to rediscover his origins, becomes a peasant. But however courageous may be the choice of this character, who resembles Samba Diallo of *L'Aventure ambiguë* of Cheikh Amidou **Kane**, he nevertheless remains implausible.

ANDRÉ NTONFO

Nkosi, Lewis

b. 1936, Durban, South Africa

novelist and literary critic

Lewis Nkosi's main achievement is that of being one of the most acute of commentators on South African literature. Known mostly as a literary critic, especially on South African writing and culture, Nkosi gained his apprenticeship as a writer and journalist working for such newspapers as *Ilanga lase Natal* (The Natal Sun) and later *Drum* magazine. In 1964 Nkosi published a play, *The Rhythm of Violence*, which explores the theme of racially motivated violence as it manifested itself in South Africa in the early 1960s. Subsequently, Nkosi seems to have devoted most of his attention to essay writing, starting first with the publication

of *The Transplanted Heart* in 1975, which looked mainly at the country's political situation, and thereafter a 1981 publication, *Tasks and Masks*, which provides a useful survey on themes and styles in African literature. Nkosi revisits politics and culture in his next collection of essays, *Home and Exile and Other Selections*, published in 1983, which could be regarded as autobiographical (see **autobiography**). In his 1987 novel, *Mating Birds*, Nkosi demonstrates his consummate skill in writing long fiction by using post-realist techniques to examine, in an innovative way, the puzzling nature of an interracial sexual relationship. His novel, *Underground People* (1993), is an ambitious work on **apartheid and post-apartheid**, exploring the complex history of South Africa from the turbulent and violent period in the early 1960s and ending with the release of Nelson Mandela from prison and the suspension of the armed struggle against apartheid in the early 1990s.

JABULANI MKHIZE

Nokan, Zégoua Gbessi Charles

b. 1936, Yamoussoukro, Côte d'Ivoire

poet and novelist

Charles Zègoua Gbessi Nokan – an anagram of his last name, Konan – was born in Yamoussoukro, in the Côte d'Ivoire. His first book, *Le Soleil noir point* (The Black Sun is Rising) (1977), mixes poetry and drama in sixty-three tableaux, alternating between lyrical, elegiac, and allegorical images. Openly didactic, the book focuses on such virtues as freedom, harmony, and happiness as the content of the sought political independence. Nokan's most acclaimed novel, *Violent était le vent* (So Violent was the Wind) (1966), is one of the first to cope with a theme that later became predominant in African Francophone writings in the 1970s: the disillusionment and bitterness that arose when the idealized narrative of decolonization and independence unfolded into an often brutal neocolonial or postcolonial economic and political system (see **colonialism, neocolonialism, and postcolonialism**). Nokan's commitment to Marxism, which was barely disguised in *Violent était le vent*, becomes more pronounced in his subsequent writings, *Les Petites Rivières* (Small Rivers) (1983), *Le Matin sera rouge* (Announcing the Red Morning) (1984), *Mon chemin débouche sur la grande route* (My Road Opens into the Great Highway) (1985), which all emphasize his adherence to Communism and his belief in that ideology as the fitting answer for African quest of identity, justice, and freedom.

EMMANUEL TENÉ

North African literature in Arabic

Introduction

Although Arabic literature throughout North Africa spans a wide range of definitions, histories, genres, and national specificities, the literary productions of Morocco, Algeria, and Tunisia share several features that bind them together into a cohesive literary culture that may be best termed as Maghrebian (pan-North African). These features include:

1 emergence from colonial rule and the nationalist struggle for independence (see **nationalism and post-nationalism**);
2 a constant tension between tradition and modernity (see **modernity and modernism**);
3 the "othering" of the Westerner;
4 intertextuality with Western literatures;
5 the perennial search for identity;
6 the quest for indigenous forms of literary expression;
7 intertextuality with Arabic literature;
8 social and political engagement;
9 the polymath nature of the artist and the literary product.

The political and social history of these three countries throughout the twentieth century, along with centuries of a shared Berber-Arab Islamic civilization, has cultivated a literary sensibility that often transcends the current tendency toward political and cultural differentiation.

The development of modern Arabic literature throughout North Africa is intricately connected to the colonial experience (see **colonialism, neo-colonialism, and postcolonialism**). The early stages of the national struggle for independence found strong expression in poetry and drama. This struggle continued into post-independence literature in all its forms as North Africans' colonial experience remained fresh in the collective memory and in the literary consciousness. Permeating North African Arabic literature is the tension between tradition and modernity. The challenges of modernity elicit opposing responses, often contrasting the rural and urban, the secular and the religious, Europeanism vs native authenticity (*al-aṣālah*), and the liberated and traditional role of women in society. This generates the third feature, which is the ongoing problematic relationship with the European (often French) "other." The intellectual, physical, cultural, and linguistic residue of French imperialism continues to haunt North African literature, providing texts with a richness and complexity of reading. Also, Europe's role as locus of exile for the intellectually or politically alienated and the economically disenfranchised has expanded the boundaries of "othering" in post-independence or postcolonial literature. Naturally, this coincides with the feature of a strong intertextuality with Western literatures. From its inception, modern Arabic literature drew heavily from Western imports via translation, imitation, adaptation, indigenization, and subversion of Western texts. In addition to drama, which was nonexistent in the premodern Arabic literary tradition, the short story and later the novel attracted the modern writer in North Africa. Poetry, although subjected to the influences of modernity, was the genre least affected by Western canons, given the long and powerful tradition of classical Arabic poetry.

The search for identity is a major theme common to North African literature, one that crisscrosses ethnic, religious, social, linguistic, and ideological boundaries. The North African Arabic literary text assumes the role of defining, negating, negotiating, and "othering" the self in the face of rapid change. In the post-independence era, Arabic writing emphasizes the complex self as reflected in the identity politics of national discourses. But the most compelling feature of North African literature is the quest for "indigenous" forms of literary expression. Aligned with the political movements for self-determination, North African writers eventually rejected the dictates of the Western canon and explored wider realms of literary expression by blurring formalistic boundaries and contesting conventional notions of genre. The experimentation with painting, sculpture, music, theater, poetry, and folklore led to a variety of narrative styles and techniques that defy precise categorization. The uses of surrealism, interior monologues, stream of consciousness, imaginary escapades, flashbacks, and fast forwards propelled North African literature into the modern and postmodern.

In contesting Western traditions and searching for indigenous forms, the North African writer interacts textually with Arabic literature, both with its classical literary heritage (*turāth*) and its eastern Arab (especially Egyptian, Lebanese, and Syrian) contemporaries. This feature, shared by all the Arabic literatures of North Africa, distinguishes it from its Francophone counterpart. The rediscovery of classical literature allowed modern literature to develop without a complete rupture from its precolonial history. The rewritings of the *maqāma*, a picaresque tale of a trickster, and the *rihla*, a journey of quest, have been effective in disseminating modern messages of hope and despair while remaining on familiar literary terrain. North African Arab writers have also been influenced by Egyptian and Syrian writers who share the same language, religion, and literary heritage, and who were also engaged in both the struggle against European imperialism and in national campaigns for social, political, and cultural reform. The expansion of the printing press and the proliferation of edited texts and literary journals reinforced links between the Arabic literature of the Arab east and the Arab west.

Another feature of North African Arabic literatures is the writers' social commitment, reflected in the symbiosis of modern creative writing and contemporary historical events. The Marxist notion of literary "engagement" resonated with a whole generation of North African writers in their literary and artistic projects. Concomitant with the idea of a socially committed literature was a proclivity towards existential themes that express the disorientation and alienation felt by North

African writers both during and after the colonial period. The bitterness of the anti-colonial struggle and the failure of postcolonialism to improve the political, social, and economic conditions of the newly independent states, not to mention the oppressive censorship on artists and intellectuals by the authoritative regimes, reinforced the absurdity of the human condition and provided a subtext to Arabic literature. What was once a hopeful mission for social progress became an existential angst and a new quest for self-liberation.

Lastly, there is the multifaceted profile of North African writers themselves. From the turn of the century, Arabic creative writing was often penned by the historian, political reformer, or journalist. As is very much the case today, especially in Morocco, it is the playwright, literary critic or historian, social scientist, anthropologist, artist, and musician who has turned to creative writing, particularly the novel and short story, as a means of self-expression. This contributes to the polymorphous and polyphonic nature of contemporary North African Arabic literature.

Tunisia

Arabic literature in the modern sense has an early start in Tunisia. Tunisia's inclusion within the Ottoman empire and its contacts with Egypt and other centers of the Arab East brought it much closer to the Arabic mainstream. The role of the Zaytūna Mosque and other Islamic institutions of learning produced literate Arabic-speaking intellectuals who formed a second literary tier to the rising Francophone intelligentsia during the colonial period. In addition, the Berber language, confined to remote areas of the south, left Arabic as the only indigenous language of opposition to French cultural imperialism.

Modern Arabic literature in Tunisia is intricately connected to the reformist movements of the nineteenth century. Poetry was the natural vehicle for anti-colonial and nationalistic sentiment. Abū al-Qāsim al-Shābbi (1909–34), Tunisia's first literary giant of international fame, advocated a complete break from the conventions of classical poetry and espoused a radical modernity. His impact was immediately felt by the generation of Tunisian writers who became the architects for modern literature during the 1930s. As journalists, poets, playwrights, historians, critics, and fiction writers, they all shared in the political mission of ending colonial rule and improving the lot of society's downtrodden, while committing themselves to creating a popular, national Arabic literature. They sought inspiration from a multiplicity of media, from ancient mythology to the latest trends in Western literature, as well as from classical Arabic prose and poetry. Their experimentation with theater, film, photography, and music brought both visual and polyphonic dimensions to their art, and their focus on the Tunisian landscape and the preoccupations of daily life represents the first stages of modern realism in Tunisian literature.

Ironically, the polymath nature of this group dissipated as its members went on to be identified with one genre. Mustafā Khrayyef (1909–67) is best known as a poet who composed verses on national and historical events. His brother Bashīr **Khrayyef** (1917–83) concentrated on novels, and his grand epic, *Al-Daqlāh fī 'arājīnhā* (Dates on Their Stalks, 1969) narrates the struggles of the oppressed and exploited workers of Tunisia's rural south. It breaks ground with its vivid detail of daily life and its bold use of the southern vernacular in the dialogue. 'Alī **al-Dū'ājī** (1909–49) emerged as "the father of the Tunisian short story," experimenting with different narrative forms and language registers, mixing humor and stoic realism (see **realism and magical realism**) to portray the daily life of ordinary people. His stories were posthumously collected into one volume, *Sleepless Nights* (1991) (*Sahirtu minhu al-layālī*) (1987).

Mahmūd **al-Mis'adī** (b. 1911) is one of Tunisia's most accomplished writers. His novelistic project extends beyond the borders of the Tunisian landscape and deals with the universal human condition. His novels, *al-Sudd* (The Dam) (1955), a romance written in the form of a play, and *Haddatha Abū Hurayra qāla* (Thus Abu Hurayra Narrated) (1973), a novel written in the form of the Muslim prophetic traditions, combine contemporary themes of existential angst and alienation from society and early Islamic legends, language, and narrative forms. Muúammad al-'Arūsī al-Matwī's (b. 1920) prose and poetry focus on the colonial experience, while Hasan Nasr (b. 1937), considered

by many to be Tunisia's most successful short story writer, mixes a variety of narrative styles, surrealism, and fantasy, combining tragedy and comedy to write about the search for the self in the struggle between tradition and modernity. 'Ez-Eddīn al-Madanī (b. 1938) reworks historical chronicles and Islamic themes in his theatrical writings, an example being *The Zanj Revolution* (1995) (*Dīwān al-Zanj*) (1973).

Since the early 1980s, Tunisian literature has gravitated toward the flexible form of the novel as the preferred vehicle for creativity and self-expression. With the disappointment of post-independence, the flight of the rural population to the city, widespread unemployment, emigration to Europe and the breakdown of the traditional family structure, the rise of the police state, and the emergence of Islamic movements as political opposition, the novel has evolved into the literary text that best expresses the interconnections of art and society. 'Arūsiyya al-Nālūtī (b. 1950), long identified with the short story, has shifted her literary project toward the novel. Muhammad al-Hādī Bin Sālih (b. 1945) deals with the problematic role of the intellectual and literary commitment in a developing nation in his seventh novel, *Min haqqihi an Yahlum* (The Right to Dream) (1991). Muhammad Ridāal-Kāfī/Kéfi (b. 1955), journalist, short story writer, and novelist, continues the tradition of the modern Tunisian writer as social critic and creative artist in his recent novel, *al-Qinā taht al-jild* (The Veil Beneath the Skin) (1990). Using the bread riots of 1984 as background, al-Kāfī narrates the withdrawal of the protagonist amidst a series of personal, financial, and social setbacks.

Algeria

Arabic literature in the modern sense of the term emerges relatively late in Algeria. Its early appearance in the popular press since the 1930s reveals a crude imitation of old forms: poetry is still subjected to the archaic conventions of the classical Arabic canons of panegyric and elegy, and prose narratives are composed in a gilded language with heavy-handed touches of didacticism and determinism. However, it does reflect the contemporary national mood, as themes of religious and social reform, the preservation of Islamic values, anti-colonialism, and the quest for independence rise to the surface. A generation later, a more sophisticated level of writing emerges, especially in the short stories of Ahmad Ridā **Ḥūḥū** and Ahmed Ben Ashūr, both of whom make a conscious attempt to bring Algerian literature to a higher level of artistry, delving into the psychological motives of the protagonists, experimenting with various narrative techniques, and mixing romanticism with social realism. Inspired by the increasingly sophisticated discourses of anti-colonial politics, nurtured by the rise in literacy and education, and taking example from both Western and contemporary Arabic modes of writing from the East, creative writing in Algeria, especially in the form of the short story, comes into its own by the time the struggle for independence erupts into war in 1954.

A truly modern Algerian Arabic novel emerges a decade after independence in 1962. French colonialism had a more powerful cultural, psychological, linguistic, and social impact on Algeria than other regions of the Maghreb, and this helps explain the late development of a modern Arabic literature. The cultural agenda of French imperialism imposed French as the national language of high culture and education, and to accomplish this goal established a comprehensive school system in French. It banned the teaching of classical Arabic, discouraged the promotion of Islam, which it considered hostile to modernity and secularism, and discouraged Algerians from maintaining contacts with the Arabs of the East. While French colonialism distanced the Algerian from his literary and cultural past, it did produce generations of literate and well-educated men and women immersed in French civilization.

Although Ridā Ḥūḥū is credited with producing the first Algerian Arabic novel, *Ghādat umm al-qurā* (The Maid of the City) in 1947, the first Arabic texts of the post-independence period follow an already well-developed modern Algerian novel written in French, often semi-autobiographical in tone, intending to address the French colonizer and call attention to the plight of the colonized. The first Arabic novels produced from the late 1960s and early 1970s naturally interact textually with these Francophone novels. They continue to narrate the bitter experiences of being colonized

and the national struggle for independence, but they differ in that they seek to reunite Algerians to their historical, linguistic, and cultural roots. The major features of the literature of this period include the reworking of Islamic themes and the re-creation of the premodern fictional world of the Arabic *turāth* literature, populated by mystics and dervishes, tyrants and bandits, swindlers and chivalrous gangsters. ʿAbd al-Hamīd Ben Hadūgah (1925–99), a pioneer of modern Arabic Algerian literature, taps into the rich vein of Algerian folklore in both his short stories and his novels. By drawing on historical events, usually those fraught with tensions, and popular lore, Algerian Arabic writers have succeeded in reconnecting Algerians to their literary past, while opening up new venues to express the search for a modern identity and opposition to the authoritative forces of contemporary Algerian society.

The most prolific of contemporary Algerian Arabic novelists is al-Tāher **Wāttir** (b. 1936). His literary trajectory, typical of modern North African literature, begins with theater, passes through short story writing, and matures with the novel. In all his works, the Algerian struggle for independence in both its historical and mythological modes figures prominently. His epic *al-Lāz* (The Ace) (1974) returns to the scenes of armed resistance and creates a fictional world that blends myth and history, imbued with the language and symbols of heroes and villains engaged in conflict. His second novel, *The Earthquake* (2000) (*al-Zilzāl*) (1974), is set in postcolonial Algeria and is a parody of a conservative religious instructor who sets out on a quest (*rihla*) to find lost relatives. In his wanderings through the city of Constantine and his mental escapes back to colonial times, the protagonist devolves into the rogue trickster of the *maqāma* tradition whose mission is to deceive the government and battle the forces of change. The novel is laced with Islamic apocalyptic motifs, enhancing the richly ironic and ambiguous meanings of the text. The plot of Wāttir's 1995 novel, *al-Shamʿa wa al-dahālīz* (The Candle and the Underground Tunnels), presents a fictional hypothesis of an Islamic revolution, whose every possible political and literary consequence rings true of the present horrific state of affairs. The poet-protagonist is caught between the battling forces of modernity and tradition as the war for independence loses much of its historical meaning. Struggling to find his role in society the poet/writer must redefine himself and examine his sense of commitment, a theme that has permeated Arabic literature since the late 1970s. The Algerian Arabic novel continues to flourish with Wasīnī al-'Araj (b. 1954), who draws upon the *Arabian Nights* in his two-volume *Fāji'at al-sābi'a Ba'da al-Alf* (The Tragedy of the 1007th Night) (1993–5). He narrates the uprootedness and angst of the post-independence generation betrayed by the revolution in *Dhākirat al-jasad* (The Memory of Water) (1997); and Ahlām Mustaghānmī, residing in Lebanon, infuses highly poetic language though a multiplicity of narrating voices to tell the story of modern Algeria and its people in her back-to-back novels, *Memory in the Flesh* (2000) (*Dhākirat al-jasad*) (1993) and *Fawdā al-Hawāss* (The Chaos of the Senses) (1998).

Morocco

A chronology for the development of modern Arabic literature in Morocco is not as easy to construct as those of Tunisia and Algeria. Literary historians debate the origins that span the decades from the 1920s to the 1950s, but many consider that Moroccan Arabic literature blossomed into modernity in the 1960s: that is, in the postcolonial period. As elsewhere in the Arab world, early twentieth-century Morocco produced a corpus of travel literature often taking the form of a "romance." Poetry in Morocco passes through several stages in the process of which the articulation of modern ideas and sensibilities within the classical poetic forms gives way to the development of free verse poetry, in great part inspired by the radical changes taking place in Arabic poetry elsewhere. Muhammad Bannīs (b. 1948) editor, critic, and poet, has published four anthologies of poetry that expand the formalistic and thematic boundaries of modern poetry. Although poetry and the short story flourished in the 1960s and 1970s, due in great part to their publication in cultural journals and newspapers, the explosion of novel-writing best exemplifies the development of modern Moroccan Arabic literature.

Two essential features of artistic writing in Morocco warrant mentioning: the first is the strong autobiographical voice; and the second is the documentary mode of narrating simultaneously the development of the collective national consciousness and the individual's quest for identity within society. Historical events and changing social structures and attitudes are the contexts for creative literature in all its genres, while ideology and a new political consciousness determine the form of the text, thus allowing it to remain in a perpetual development.

Tahāmī al-Wazzāni (1903–72) gives a strong autobiographical dimension to his mystical (Sufi) historical romance, *al-Zāwiya* (The Shrine) (1942). 'Abd al-Majīd Bin Jallūn (1919–81) structures his autobiography, *Fī al-Tufūlah* (On Childhood) (1956) in the form of a *Bildungsromanen* that begins in Manchester and follows a trajectory of return to the homeland in early adolescence, creating an inverted *rihla* that takes him from the familiar world of the "other" to the unknown "self." Muhammad Shukrī (Choukri, b. 1935), Morocco's best-known writer internationally due to the early translations of his work into French and English, bases his novelistic project on his life story. His first novel, *al-Khubz al-hāfī* (For Bread Alone) (1973) may be read in the tradition of the picaro whose journey is from the Rif mountains to the slums of Tangier, from utter poverty, domestic violence, crime, and illiteracy to education and self-respect. Its graphic language and vivid details of misery and deprivation give voice to the most disenfranchised of Arab society, and it continues to spark controversy throughout the Arab world.

Literary scholar and short story writer Muhammad Barrāda (b. 1938) brings sophistication to the autobiographical voice in his "novelistic text" *The Game of Forgetting* (1996) (*Lu'bat al-Nisyān*) (1987). The polyphony of narrating and narrated voices, the multiplicity of language registers, and the varied and often incongruent narrative modes and structures chronicle simultaneously the development of contemporary Moroccan society from colonialism to independence, the history of an extended family from its origins in the old quarter of Fez to the modern metropolis of Casablanca, the biography of the mother told from conflicting points of view, and the coming of age of the writer/narrator/self. The playful jostling between narrator(s) and implied author, time and space, life and death, and reality and fiction reflect the postmodern direction of contemporary Arabic literature.

Khanātha Banūna often transcends the boundaries of the Moroccan landscape in her short stories and novels, e.g. *al-Nār wa al-Ikhatiyār* (Fire and Choice) (1966) and uses the loss of Palestine to express the continual need to struggle for social and political justice throughout the Arab world.

'Abd al-Karīm **Ghallab** (b. 1917) is one of the most prolific Arabic writers in Morocco, and through his travel writings, essays, and novels, he espouses an Arab socialist view of literary commitment. In his prison memoirs, *Sab'at abwāb* (Seven Doors) (1965), and his epic novel of family life set in pre-independence Morocco, *Dafannā al-Mādī* (We Buried the Past) (1966), Ghallab draws attention to social inequities, such as slavery and the oppression of women. Although somewhat archaic in its language and linear plot line, not to mention frequent didactic asides, the novel succeeds in raising a voice against the traditional power structures of society. The revolt against the patriarchal system and the constrictions of an unhappy marriage are eloquently narrated in Layla Abū' Zayd's (b. 1950) *Year of the Elephant* (1989) (*'Ām al-Fīl*) (1983), a *Bildungsromanen* that recounts the journey of a young woman searching for independence.

The nexus of thought and literary creativity continues in the ongoing process of becoming so characteristic of the Moroccan novel. Muhammad Zifzāf (b. 1945) explores Moroccan identity particularly in its encounters with the West, while Ben Salem Himmich draws heavily upon the classical Arabic *turāth* to write historical novels that convey relevant political and philosophical messages. Ahmad al-Tawfiq (b. 1943) has embarked upon a novelistic project that mixes mystical themes with problems of contemporary Moroccan society.

Modern Arabic creative writing documents political events across a wide ideological spectrum. Pan-Arabism dominated the political scene in North Africa immediately following independence, in part a reaction against European cultural domination and in solidarity with Arab brethren who lived a similar history, language, religion, and culture. The national campaign for Arabization in education and government bureaucracy was an attempt to assert a non-European, Muslim identity. Self-determination, socialism, often expressed through support for the working class and an end to class distinctions, and the reaffirmation of Arabic as the national language and Islam as the national religion/culture have been hallmark themes in the development of Maghrebi literature of Arabic expression.

Further reading

Accad, Evelyne (1978) *Veil of Shame: The Role of Women in the Contemporary Fiction of North Africa and the Arab World*, Quebec: Éditions Naaman.

Allen, Roger (1982) *Arabic Literature in North Africa: Critical Essays and Annotated Bibliography. Mundus Arabicus vol. 2*, Cambridge, Massachusetts: Dar Mahjar.

——(1995) *The Arabic Novel: An Historical and Critical Introduction* 2nd edn, Syracuse: Syracuse University Press.

Bamia, Aida (1982) *The North African Novel: Achievements and Prospects. Mundus Arabicus vol. 5*, Cambridge, Massachusetts: Dar Mahjar.

Dejeux, Jean (1975) *La Littérature algérienne contemporaine* (Contemporary Algerian Literature), Paris: PUF.

Fontaine, Jean (1990) *La Littérature tunisienne contemporaine* (Contemporary Tunisian Literature), Paris: PUF.

Khatibi, Abdelkabir (1974) *Écrivains marocains du protectorat à 1965* (Moroccan Writers of the Protectorate up to 1965), Paris: Sindbad.

WILLIAM GRANARA

North African literature in French

Introduction

Initially the by-product of colonialism and the French "civilizing mission," North African or Maghrebian literature of French expression nevertheless continued to flourish after the independence of Algeria, Morocco, and Tunisia, even experiencing a revival in the 1980s and 1990s. Despite the

Arabization of the Maghreb since the 1960s, North African Francophone literature was not destined to die young as the Tunisian writer and sociologist Albert **Memmi** had mistakenly prophesied in the mid 1950s. Many Arab and Arabo-Berber authors residing in the Maghreb and abroad continue to produce outstanding literary works in French, even though French is not their mother tongue or national language. One could say that the French language has become an intercultural space allowing for linguistic experimentation, cultural innovation, dissident expression, refuge from fundamentalism, and access to modernity.

This article focuses on the literature of Arab and Arabo-Berber authors. However, this writing did not exist in isolation from authors of European descent (formerly considered colonial, today *pied-noir*) and Judaeo-Maghrebians, who resided for a millennium in North Africa before becoming a diaspora spread over several continents (see **diaspora and pan-Africanism**). Furthermore, like *pied-noir* writers, Maghrebians have implanted a new Beur literature on the other side of the Mediterranean (see **Beur literature in France**). Finally, since the 1990s, a number of Algerian writers have sought political asylum in France. This only goes to show that the postcolonial reality of the Maghreb is deeply intertwined with France and the French language. If Algeria has produced substantially more literature in French than Morocco and Tunisia, it is because it was considered part of France for over a century. As protectorates, Morocco (1912–56) and Tunisia (1881–1956) retained more cultural autonomy and therefore Arabic literature continued to flourish there.

Beginnings: the Generation of 52

Maghrebian literature of French expression came of age in the 1950s with the Generation of 52. These were autochthonous writers who began publishing in the early 1950s, shortly before or at the time of the outbreak of the Algerian revolution (1954–62) and the independence of Morocco and Tunisia (1956). One could argue that a literary revolution preceded a political one. With the Generation of 52, Francophone literature became an instrument of cultural and political subversion

in North Africa. Autochthonous writers used the colonizer's language, refashioning it in such a way as to express the new identity of emergent nations.

Prior to this time, there were only a few autochthonous writers of French expression, such as the **Amrouche**s, who began diffusing Berber (Amazigh) culture and writing about their hybrid (French–Berber) identity in the 1930s and 1940s. Lesser-known authors include Mohammed Ben Si Ahmed Bencherif, Abdelkader Hadj Hamou, Mohammed Ould Cheikh, Rabah Zenati, Salah Farhat, and Djamila Debêche. There was, however, a rich literary tradition of North African writers of European descent such as Louis Bertrand, Robert Randau, Gabriel Audisio, Albert Camus, Jules Roy, Emmanuel Roblès, Jean Pélégri, and Jean **Sénac**. A number of them, such as Roblès and Sénac, were instrumental in gaining recognition for autochthonous writers in the 1950s. Writers of the Generation of 52 include: Mouloud **Feraoun**, Mouloud **Mammeri**, Mohamed **Dib**, and Yacine **Kateb** from Algeria; Albert Memmi from Tunisia; and Ahmed **Sefrioui** and Driss **Chraïbi** from Morocco.

By writing in French and using a European genre (the novel), these writers managed to seize the colonizer's linguistic and cultural tools in order to transform themselves from absent or stereotyped figures in French writing on North Africa to writing subjects of Maghrebian literature. This is not to say that writing in French did not make them ill at ease, in so far as they were forced to testify against the injustices of colonialism in the oppressor's language. If Camus considered the French language his "homeland," the Generation of 52 felt exiled in it. Formed by the French colonial school, these writers comprised an elite group who felt cut off from the majority of their compatriots who were illiterate. Consequently, they wrote about being torn between two cultures, unable to assume a stable and legitimate identity. It is not surprising that they adopted an autobiographical mode in their novels, for the French language provided them with the necessary critical distance to regard the fragile site of selfhood. This is particularly evident in Feraoun's *Le Fils du pauvre* (The Poor Man's Son) (1950), where the dialectic between autobiography and fiction is bound up with the colonial school and acculturation. Ferouan wanted to provide an authentic translation of the Kabyle soul while tracing the trajectory of a poor child who managed to become a French schoolteacher.

Feraoun was not an assimilationist and regionalist writer as many of his contemporaries claimed. His nationalism is quite evident in his posthumous *Journal, 1955–62* (Journal, 1955–62), but it is mitigated by his revulsion towards violence. This diary of a pacifist and humanist, disheartened by the atrocities of the French and distressed by the terrorism of the Algerians, is an original and subtle analysis of a revolution that is also a civil war, where the beliefs and doubts of individuals conflict with the tenets of independence. Ferouan's visionary spirit allows us to better understand the violence underpinning post-independence Algeria.

Mammeri would also be criticized for emphasizing local Kabyle culture in his early novels *La Colline oubliée* (The Forgotten Hill) (1952) and *Le Sommeil du juste* (The Sleep of the Just) (1955). In so far as French colonizers and politicians had adopted a divide-and-rule strategy that opposed Arabs, Berbers, and Jews, Mammeri's "Berberism" was seen as running counter to Algerian nationalism. This dimension of his writing would take on different political connotations after independence, when he claimed that "Berberism was the true test of democracy in Algeria," meaning that the recognition of Tamazight as a national language and the defense of Berber culture were viewed as a threat to national unity by Algerian politicians interested only in an Arabo-Muslim identity dating from the Arab (Islamic) conquest of North Africa. Although its official enemy was French, Arabization was also directed against Tamazight, and even dialectal spoken Arabic.

The literature produced during the 1950s was always viewed through a political lens. This is even more apparent in the case of Chraïbi's controversial novel, *The Simple Past* (*Le Passé simple*) (1954), which was written at the height of the French–Moroccan conflict. Chraïbi had the audacity to attack both Moroccan patriarchal society and French colonial rule. Moroccans accused Chraïbi of having betrayed his country at a time when it was seeking independence from France, whereas French right-wing journalists referred to this novel to justify the preservation of the French protectorate in Morocco. Disturbed by the controversy

surrounding his novel, Chraïbi publicly disowned it in 1957, only to regret his action later.

Dib's "Algeria" trilogy comprised of *La Grande Maison* (The Large House) (1952), *L'Incendie* (The Fire) (1954), and *Le Métier à tisser* (The Weaving Loom) (1957) provides a naturalist tableau of the sociopolitical problems of the Algerian city and countryside from 1939 to 1942 as seen through the eyes of a young boy, who personifies the emergent nationalist aspirations of his country. A revolutionary and poetic work, Kateb's *Nedjma* (1956) is a unique text, characterized by multiple narrative voices, alternating narrative sequences, and overlapping individual and collective realities that take on mythical dimensions. The autobiographical, historical, and mythical dimensions of the novel comprise a multifaceted reality in which individual stories derive their meaning from collective history. *Nedjma* is often considered the masterpiece of Maghrebian Francophone literature. It is probably the only novel of the Generation of 52 to remain completely opaque to purely political interpretations.

The Algerian revolution and its aftermath

The testimonial quality of the writing of the Generation of 52 reached its climax during and shortly after the Algerian revolution. A nationalist poetry, often written in prison, gave rise to collaboration in the literary sphere as well as the political one, between autochthonous and European writers. Some of the most revolutionary and original texts were written by Europeans, such as Henri Kréa, Anna **Greki** and Jean Sénac, in addition to Algerians such as Jean Amrouche, Djamal **Amrani**, Noureddine **Aba**, Malek **Haddad**, and Nadia Guendouz. At its onset, the Algerian revolution sought the help of all communities in Algeria, and this multi-ethnic and cross-cultural collaboration is evident in both the writing and the politics of the time. Sénac played a major role in colonial and independent Algeria in disseminating the work of such writers as Kateb, Dib, Feraoun, Mammeri, Malek Haddad, and later Rachid **Boudjedra**, Tahar **Djaout**, and Youcef Sebti.

The revolution was also the central theme of such key novels as Mammeri's realist *L'Opium et le bâton* (The Opium and the Stick) (1965), Dib's allegorical *Who Remembers the Sea?* (*Qui se souvient de la mer?*) (1962), and Yamina Mechakra's poetic *La Grotte éclatée* (The Blown Up Cave). Criticized for writing a first novel *The Mischief* (*La Soif*) (1957) about the discovery of female sexuality when other Algerians were waging a revolution, Assia **Djebar** subsequently inscribed the question of female sexuality and liberation in war novels such as *Les Enfants du nouveau monde* (Children of the New World) (1962) and *Les Alouettes naïves* (The Innocent Larks) (1967), thereby insinuating that the liberation of Algeria, also fought for by Algerian women, would not necessarily lead to their liberation.

If the Algerian revolution continues to be a central theme of post-revolutionary writing of the 1960s and 1970s, in its best instances (not those supporting the status quo) it is a denunciation of a post-revolutionary society that has betrayed its ideals. Memory and amnesia, madness and repression, pain and healing are central to such subversive novels and texts as Mouloud Bourboune's *Le Muezzin*, Rachid Boudjedra's *The Repudiation* (*La Répudiation*) (1969), Rachid Mimouni's *Le Fleuve détourné* (The Diverted Current) (1982), Assia Djebar's *Women of Algiers in Their Apartment* (*Femmes d'Alger dans leur appartement*) (1980), and *Fantasia, an Algerian Cavalcade* (*L'Amour, la fantasia*) (1985), Tahar Djaout's *L'Exproprié* (The Expropriated) (1981/1984) and *Les Chercheurs d'os* (The Bone Seekers) (1984), and Myriam **Ben**'s collection of stories *Ainsi naquit un homme* (Thus a Man was Born) (1982). The critique of a revolution gone astray led to a literary revival in French during this period. Even writers of the Generation of 52 took on this critique; Dib in *La Danse du roi* (The Dance of the King) (1968) and *Dieu en Barbarie* (God in Barbary) (1970), and Mammeri in *La Traversée* (The Crossing) (1982). Many of the works of the 1970s and 1980s that decry the failed revolution point the way to the abuses of fundamentalism and the subsequent civil war of the 1990s, which are central to Mimouni's *La Malédiction* (The Curse) (1993), Boudjedra's *Timimoun* (1994) and *La Vie à l'endroit* (Life on the Right Side) (1997), Djaout's *Les Vigiles* (The Vigilanti) (1991), and Abdelkader Djemaï's *Un Été de cendres* (A Summer of Ashes) (1995).

In the 1990s, the name of Yasmina Khadra made headlines because no one knew who was hiding behind this mysterious pseudonym, the author who had brought the detective novel to bear on the civil war of the 1990s and its climate of terrorism, violence, paranoia, and fear. Contrary to expectations, a former Algerian military officer, Mohamed Moulessehoul, had published *Morituri* (1999), *In the Name of God* (2000) (*Les Agneux du Seigneur*)(1998), *À quoi rêvent les loups?* (What Do Wolves Dream About?) (1999), and *L'Automne des chimères* (The Autumn of Impossible Dreams) (1999). He chose a female pseudonym in order to pay homage to the courage of Algerian women during this period.

Algerian women's writing proliferated in the 1990s: new authors include Malika Mokeddem, Fériel Assima, Maissa Bey, Latifa Ben Mansour, Fatima **Gallaire**, Hawa **Djabali**, and Nina **Bouraoui**. Djebar also produced a number of key works such as *So Vast a Prison* (*Vaste est la prison*) (1999), *Algerian White* (*Le Blanc de l'Algérie*) (1996), *Oran, langue morte* (Oran, Dead Language) (1996), and *Les Nuits de Strasbourg* (The Nights of Strasbourg) (1997).

Moroccan literature

Like Algeria, Morocco experienced a literary renewal in French after independence. Chraïbi continued to produce outstanding works such as *Heirs to the Past* (*Succession ouverte*) (1962), *The Flutes of Death* (*Une Enquête au pays*) (1982) and *Mother Comes of Age* (*La Civilisation, ma Mère!*) (1972). He was considered the precursor of the avant-garde literary journal and group *Souffles* (1966–72) founded by Abdellatif **Laâbi**, who would subsequently be imprisoned from 1972 to 1980 and tortured for his opposition to the regime. Although highly experimental on a formal plane, the works of *Souffles* writers are also subversive at the level of ideas. Writers associated with the group include Mostafa Nissaboury, Mohamed **Khaïr-Eddine**, Abraham Serfaty, Abdelkebir **Khatibi**, and Tahar **Ben Jelloun**. They considered poetic language a form of dissident expression, worked beyond generic distinctions such as prose/poetry, fiction/autobiography/theory, and articulated cultural renewal to political activism. They advocated a progressive national culture willing to recognize its plural (Berber, Jewish, and Arab) identity and to dialogue with the West. Key works of this period and subsequent years include: Khatibi's *La Mémoire tatouée* (Tattooed Memory); Ben Jelloun's *Harrouda* and *The Sacred Night* (*La Nuit sacrée*) for which he received the coveted French Prix Goncourt in 1987; Khaïr-Eddine's *Agadir* and *le Déterreur* (The Unearther) (1967); Nissaboury's *The Thousand and Second Night* (*La Mille et Deuxieme Nuit*) (1975) Laâbi's *Le Chemin des ordalies* (The Path of Ordeals) (1982) and *Chroniques de la citadelle d'exil: lettres de prison, 1972–1980* (Chronicles from the Citadel of Exile: Prison Letters, 1972–80). More recent Moroccan writers include Edmond Amran **el Maleh**, Abdelhaq **Serhane**, Leïla **Houari**, and Mohammed **Loakira**.

Tunisian literature

Before independence, Memmi was the only well-known Tunisian writer of French expression. He described the plight of a Tunisian Jew in his autobiographical novel *The Pillar of Salt* (*La Statue de sel*) (1953) and went on to theorize the colonial relation in *The Colonizer and the Colonized* (*Portrait du colonisé, précédé de portrait du colonisateur*) (1957). Since the 1970s, a significant number of Tunisian authors, residing both in Tunisia and abroad (Europe, North America), have made a name for themselves. A growing body of French language literature has established itself parallel to Arabic writing. Many of the French language authors are bilingual and are also academics or intellectuals, so they bring an intercultural, critical, postmodern edge to their writing. This is evident in the writing of Mustapha **Tlili**, whose novels explore the delayed psychological impact of colonialism on exiled third-world intellectuals, at once attracted and repulsed by the West: *La Rage aux tripes* (Rage in the Guts) (1975), *La Montagne du lion* (The Mountain of the Lion) (1990). Abdelwahab **Meddeb**'s intertextual and intersubjective writing explores the mystical movement of Sufism in terms of modernity: *Talismano* (1979), *Phantasia* (1986), and *Le Tombeau d'Ibn Arabi* (The Tomb of Ibn Arabi) (1987).

There are many important Tunisian poets: Salah **Garmadi**, Moncef **Ghachem**, and Chems **Nadir** (a pseudonym for Mohamed Aziza), Amina **Saïd**, Hédi Bouraoui, Tahar **Békri**, and Majid El

Houssi, to name but a few. Arabic language and culture is often present in this poetry of French expression, either explicitly or more subtly as a palimpsest, making for an authentic and rich poetic expression willing to move beyond linguistic borders, geographical frontiers, cultural traditions, and such dichotomies as past and present, East and West. For these poets, the creative enterprise necessarily implies a social or historical critique.

The confrontation between tradition and modernity is subtly explored by women writers such as Hélé Béji in *L'Oeil du jour* (The Eye of the Day) and Emna Bel Haj Yahia in *Chronique frontalière* (Border Chronicle) and *L'Étage invisible* (The Invisible Floor). Both writers advocate cultural hybridity as a means of combating narrow-minded nationalism or reactionary fundamentalism.

The other shore

Many Tunisian – as well as Algerian and Moroccan – writers at the forefront of modernity reside abroad. This is not to say that they have abandoned the question of Africa or their Arab identity. Are we now dealing with African literatures in French or a new literature of French expression that acknowledges the "otherness" that has always unconsciously inhabited it? In bringing the Orient to bear on their writing in French, Maghrebian authors are responding to the Orientalism that once marked the exotic travel writing from France. They are decentering the French language, making place for their excentric concerns and pluralistic vision.

Even if they do not necessarily reside abroad, their writing crosses over continents and historical periods, as it brings the past to bear on the present, the Orient on the Occident. Examples include Djaout's *L'Invention du desert* (The Invention of the Desert); Chraïbi's Berber trilogy comprised of *The Flutes of Death* (Une enquête au pays), *Mother Spring* (*La Mère du printemps*) and *Birth at Dawn* (Naissance à l'aube); Nabile **Farès**' *Le Champ des oliviers* (The Olive Field) (1972), *Mémoire de l'absent* (The Absent Man's Memory) (1974), and *L'Exil et le désarroi* (Exile and Distress) (1976); Boudjedra's *La Prise de Gibraltar* (The Taking of Gibraltar); Habib Tengour's *Le Vieux de la montagne* (The Old Man from the Mountain) (1983). The return to the past becomes a means of bypassing a present blocked by monolithic political discourse: literature thus takes over where the official history of non-democratic regimes ends. The defense of Berber (Amazigh) cultural identity and the reclaiming of an Islam not corrupted by fundamentalism are also important themes in these works, as well as in Chraïbi's *Muhammed* (*L'Homme du Livre*) (1994), Djebar's *Far from Medina* (Loin de Médine) (1991).

The journey to France of *pieds-noirs* and Maghrebian immigrants has resulted in a new writing that will eventually be considered part of French literature. Since the mid 1950s, the term *pied-noir* has come to designate the French from North Africa (especially Algeria) who immigrated to France in the 1950s and 1960s. *Pied-noir* writers include Jules Roy, Anne Loesch, Emmanuel Roblès, Jean-Pierre Millecam, Janine Montupet, Marcel Moussy, Francine Dessaigne, Marie Elbe, Jean Pélégri, Marie Cardinal, Jeanne Terracini, Alain Vircondelet, and Albert **Bensoussan**. Their writing, often nostalgic in nature, is dominated by the themes of exile and uprooting, loss and memory.

While Beur and *pied-noir* writing are similar in that both deal with questions of split identity, Beur writing is directed more towards the future than the past. The term "Beur," which appeared in the Larousse dictionary of 1986, is backslang (*verlan*) for Arab and designates a young Maghrebian born or brought up in France of immigrant parents. Beur writing expresses the plight and aspirations of second-generation Maghrebian youth residing in France. The "Beur Generation" is torn between the cultural traditions of France and the Maghrebian one of its parents. Beur authors include: Mehdi Charef, Akli Tadjer, Farida Belghoul, Nacer Kettane, Azouz **Begag**, Sakinna Boukhedenna, Jean-Luc Yacine, Tassadit Imache, and Ferrudja Kessas. The work of Leïla **Sebbar** is often included with that of the Beurs. As catalysts for cultural and sociopolitical change, the Beurs represent a movement for equality and tolerance in the multiracial France of today.

Further reading

Aresu, Bernard (ed.) (1992) "Translations of the Orient: Writing the Maghreb," *SubStance*, 69.

Déjeux, Jean (1978) *Littérature maghrébine de langue française* (Maghrebian Literature in French), Sherbrooke, Quebec: Éditions Naaman.

Geesey, Patricia (ed.) (1992) guest editor, special edition, "North African Literature," *Research in African Literatures* 23, 2.

Marx-Scouras, Danielle (ed.) (1999) guest editor, special edition, "Dissident Algeria," *Research in African Literatures* 30, 3.

Mortimer, Mildred (ed.) (2001) *Maghrebian Mosaic*, Boulder/London: Lynne Rienner.

Woodhull, Winnie (1993) *Transfigurations of the Maghreb: Feminism, Decolonization, and Literatures*, Minneapolis: University of Minnesota Press.

DANIELLE MARX-SCOURAS

Nortje, Arthur

b. 1942, Oudtshoorn, Cape Province, South Africa; d. 1970, Oxford, UK

poet

The South African poet Arthur Kenneth Nortje was born in Oudtshoorn, Cape Province, the product of an illicit liaison between a young colored woman and an unidentified white Jewish student. He grew up poor with relatives in Port Elizabeth, where he received his schooling, first in Afrikaans, then in English. One of his teachers was Dennis **Brutus**. He studied English at the (then segregated) University of the Western Cape (BA, 1964) and at Oxford (BA, 1967). After teaching in Canada (1967–70), he returned to Oxford where he died of a barbiturate overdose in 1970. His poems – personal, lyrical, and intensely self-aware – are characterized by vivid imagery and taut, complex expression. While many appeared in numerous journals, his only two collections (*Dead Roots* and *Lonely Against the Light*) were published posthumously in 1973. In 2001 a scholarly edition of his collected poems, *Anatomy of Dark*, was edited and published by Dirk Klopper. His sense of personal displacement, his social and cultural marginalization – classification as "colored" under South Africa's apartheid legislation (see **apartheid and post-apartheid**) meant that he was officially neither black nor white – are central to

Nortje's poetry. His themes reflect an agonized awareness of his own multifaceted alienation and exile, a pervasive sense of loss, perpetual homelessness, the search of a damaged psyche for a tenable identity. They also reveal his resistance to the political repression, racism, and economic exploitation, which he experienced in South Africa, England, and Canada.

MALCOLM HACKSLEY

novel

Introduction

To raise the question of the novel as a genre in Africa is to be immediately confronted by a set of paradoxes: Africa did not have a tradition of long fiction or the novel in the modern sense of the word before the period of colonialism (see **colonialism, neocolonialism, and postcolonialism**), yet the novel has become the most influential literary genre on the continent. For many students of African culture, the novel is the genre that brought the continent to the attention of the world, and it is impossible to have a sustained discussion of African history, culture, or society without reference to its major novelists who have become an inescapable point of reference. The novel has hence become a major source of knowledge about Africa. And yet the irony persists: a genre introduced through colonization, one nurtured by colonial institutions, and one closely associated with Western modes of interpretation, has come to function as the gateway to African worlds ranging from the nature of precolonial society to the crisis of postcolonialism.

A second paradox revolves around the question of language (see **language question**), one of the most disputed issues in the study of African literature. Since the colonial period, novels have been produced in almost every language on the continent. Indeed, novels have been central to the emergence of a modern tradition of letters in African languages such as Amharic, Igbo, Yoruba, Hausa, Swahili, Xhosa, and Zulu (see **Ethiopian literature**; **Igbo literature**; **Yoruba literature**; **literature in Hausa**; **Swahili literature**; **South African literature in African languages**). And yet, the most influential form of long fiction on the continent, the one that has made Africa crucial to the study of modern literature, is novels written in the major European languages. Many African writers have always been uneasy with this production of African fiction in the language of the colonizer and some, like **Ngugi wa Thiong'o**, have decided to break with the European language in preference for their native tongues, while others, like Ousmane **Sembene**, have turned to film as a form of expression that is more accessible to a larger audience. But the form of the African novel has been intimately tied to its existence in European languages and hence its ambivalent identity.

Attempts to circumvent the European language in the African novel, or conversely to celebrate it as the God-given right of the colonized, call attention to a third paradox: that the novel is both the most popular genre in terms of its readership and prestige, yet, given the high rates of illiteracy in Africa, it is the least accessible to a majority of people on the continent. A final paradox concerns the enigmatic history of the novel in Africa: very little fiction was produced in Africa before the period after World War II. There were exceptions to this rule: Joseph Ephraim **Casely Hayford**, Thomas **Mofolo**, Sol **Plaatje**, and Chief Daniel **Fagunwa** produced novels before this period and their works are important for those who seek a long historical view of African literature. These early novelists were the first to call attention to the African search for a narrative form of protest against colonialism, a medium for asserting a nascent pan-Africanism (see **diaspora and pan-Africanism**) and the compromised conditions in which an African literature tried to emerge early in the twentieth century and found itself stifled by colonial institutions. Still, the novels that are now considered to have constituted a breakthrough in African literary history, Camara **Laye**'s *The Dark Child* (*L'Enfant noir*), first published in 1953, and Chinua **Achebe**'s *Things Fall Apart*, written in 1952 but not published until 1958 were produced in the last decades of colonial rule in Africa.

The story of the novel in Africa is a story about these paradoxes and the fiction that emerged in response to them or as an effect of them, as much as it is a product of the history of colonialism and postcolonialism on the continent.

The condition of an African fiction

In responding to the paradoxes discussed above, there has been the erroneous assumption among influential critics such as Janheinz Jahn (*Neo-African Literature: A History of Black Literature*) (1968) and Claude Wauthier (*The Literature and Thought of Modern Africa*) (1978) that the challenge of African literature has essentially been a search for authenticity. Ironically, however, major novelists on the continent have seen their task not so much as the establishment of forms of fiction that were essentially and purely African, but as one of adapting European forms to respond to specific and local experiences. Indeed, quite often the most influential African novels are those that have self-consciously adopted a European form to assert the identity of the African self or to recover a repressed part of the African experience. As almost every major study of the African novel has shown, African fiction has developed in constant conversation with the dominant European novelistic discourse, from the realism novel of the nineteenth century to high modernism, from autobiographical and historical fiction to the epistolary novel (see **realism and magical realism**; **modernity and modernism**; **autobiography**). At the same time, however, these appropriations of the European tradition reflect the dichotomy that has come to define African fiction: in its formal concerns most African fiction recalls dominant European tendencies, but its thematic concerns are fundamentally African.

It can hence be argued that one of the major conditions for an African fiction was how to Africanize the novel while retaining its modern generic identity. Perhaps this point can be made better if we compare the novel to poetry and drama. African writers who chose to write poetry or drama had a choice of traditions in front of them: they could draw from the forms of modernist poetry or drama, Arabic classical verse, Swahili *tendi*, medieval Malinke epics, or the Zulu or Xhosa *izibongi*. Writers of poetry and drama had a distinctly African formal repertoire available to them. For this reason, the major breakthroughs in African poetry (**Okot p'Bitek**'s songs, for example) took place when these African forms were made the source of a new prosody or performative

genre. Without such a tradition in the realm of fiction, novelists could not fall back on precolonial forms of writing; novelists in search of an epistemological or formal breakthrough had nowhere to turn except to the European novel itself, which now needed to be either subverted from within or transformed to account for African historical, social, and cultural experiences that were sometimes at odds with the interests of the values and politics associated with the colonial language. This adaptation could take various forms. Some novelists, such as Amos **Tutuola** in Nigeria, would (consciously or by accident) bring the European language into a tortuous confrontation with African fables. Conversely, other writers, notably Fagunwa, Mofolo, and Shabaan **Robert**, would bring an African language into a dialogical relationship with European forms and texts such as the Bible or Bunyan's *Pilgrim's Progress*. In both cases, however, it is important to note that irrespective of whether they were writing novels in African or European languages, what seemed to matter most to African writers was that they were producing novels in the European sense of the word, and it is fair to say that the African novel has not witnessed the kind of radical breakthroughs we have witnessed in other genres. Ngugi's novels in Gikuyu, for example, have opened his writing to new formal concerns, including a large repertoire of popular and oral literature (see **popular literature**; **oral literature and performance**), but there is no evidence that their identity as novels is considerably different from the works he produced in English early in his career.

What accounts for this lack of a radical break between African fiction and the European novel? Why has the African novel held on to modes of identity borrowed from elsewhere and not built on the oral tradition in ways that are apparent in other genres? The most obvious response to these questions concerns the generic structure of the novel itself: that it is a genre that travels across cultures, but because it is welded to certain characteristics (a concern with time, subjective experience, and psychological analysis) it does not adapt to change on a deeper level. Novels do change to the extent that they appropriate local material, everyday experiences, and, in the case of

Africa, elements borrowed from the oral tradition and everyday discourse. But more often than not these adaptations and appropriations have not seemed to affect the deep structure of the novel as a genre. There are, of course, exceptions to this rule, and some African novelists such as Ahmadou **Kourouma** have sought to transform the French language by contaminating it with Malinke speech forms. But even here, Korouma's experiment is notable because of its deviation from an established novelistic tradition rather than its abandonment of the novel as a genre.

A far more compelling reason why African writers have tended to hold on to the generic structure of the novel irrespective of the language in which it is produced or the specific local circumstances it has responded to is the close association between the genre and literacy. The question of literacy and the status of African fiction can be approached from two directions. From a sociological perspective, African fiction is seen as the direct result of the process of literacy associated with colonialism and its institutions of education, including the Church and the school (see **education and schools**). In his now classic study of the African novel, *Culture, Tradition and Society in the West African Novel* (1975), Emmanuel Obiechina has argued that the most important factor in the rise of the novel in West Africa was the introduction of literacy and literary education. Obiechina's major claim is that the introduction of literacy shifted the locus of African literary and cultural expression from the oral to the written tradition, and that this shift had tremendous social and psychological consequences. The shift from the oral to the written as the privileged site of literary expression transformed the relationship of artists and audiences, the subject of literature, and the authority of genres. Literary expression was no longer conceived as a transmission of practices from authors whose authority depended on traditional forms of power (the griots and *izibongi* oral artists, for example), but as the unique product of educated and Westernized Africans. Literature was no longer about the institutions of precolonial society, but the unique experiences of individuals making their way in the modern world. It would appear, then, that at one point in the colonial period, African culture came to be defined by an opposition between the

oral and the written. And the novel was the genre that seemed to serve the interests of the new class of writers and readers.

At the same time, however, as Christopher Miller has noted in *Theories of Africans*, the opposition between orality and writing was not as absolute as the sociological account may suggest. Indeed, from what one may call the anthropological perspective, the oral and the written were, in Miller's (1990: Chicago) words, mutually imbricated, and this situation continues to this day: "Orality and literacy are two worlds that coexist in a state of tension, enriching and contradicting each other in daily life." The important point to underscore, though, is that the relationship between the written and the oral was uneven and unequal, and the African novel started as a genre that celebrated the power and authority of the written over the oral. The didacticism of early African novels was not simply due to the need to teach readers about the political grievances of Africans; it was also an exhibition of literacy and its consequences; what appears to be the derivativeness of these novels, their reliance on other models of rhetoric such as the Bible, is part of a genuine desire to show off the author's mastery of writing.

Colonialism and nationalism

Colonialism is perhaps the most persistent theme in African fiction, but the impression created by this preponderance – the assumption that if the colonial encounter had not taken place, the African novel as we know it would not exist – has created a false center of gravity for this literature. In regard to the production of African fiction the legacy of colonialism is a divided one: the process of colonization created the conditions that enabled African writing including the school, the printing press, and a system of education that privileged literary culture. But if colonialism was such an overwhelming force in the production of African literature, why were there no important novels written in the nineteenth century, the great period of colonization? Foundational African novels are concerned with the colonial situation – they seek to diagnose the effects of colonialism of African societies and to represent the traumatic consequences of this encounter – but all these novels, considered to be the foundational texts of modern African literature, were produced in the last phase of colonial rule. There were actually no known novels written in the period of the painful first encounter with colonialism itself. African novels arose in the period of nationalism (see **nationalism and post-nationalism**) – of organized resistance to colonialism. Thus it is nationalism rather than colonialism that created a space for the genre. The rise of the African novel was the medium through which nationalists imagined a decolonized polity, and for this reason, among others, it arose at the same moment when the African elite decided that their destiny did not lie in the embrace of a European identity, but rather in the new community of the nation. It was during this period that the educated African elite also sought to rediscover traditions and cultural practices that their colonial education had foreclosed. In the moment of the nationalist awakening, nationalist writers sought to let Africa speak through their works. They assumed that part of the reason why the continent had such a poor image in the global imaginary was that Africa was primarily represented through the works of European writers, most notably Joseph Conrad, Joyce Carey, and even Albert Camus, who had either represented the continent as the heart of darkness or deprived the African or Arab of the ability to act and challenge the colonial order. It is hence not accidental that foundational African fiction by Achebe and Laye, to use the two most popular examples, was initially conceived as a reaction to the European novel on Africa.

Irrespective of their local circumstances, the novels of the 1950s and early 1960s are retrospective accounts of the trauma of the colonial encounter. They are also concerned with the effects on the production of African subjects initially seduced by the culture of colonialism and later destroyed by it. The most famous examples here are Mongo **Beti**'s *Mission to Kala* (*Mission terminée*) (1957), Ferdinand Oyono's *Houseboy* (*Une Vie de boy*) (1956) and *The Old Man and the Medal* (*Le Vieux nègre et la médaille* (1956), Achebe's *No Longer at Ease* (1960), and Cheikh Hamidou **Kane**'s *Ambiguous Adventure* (*L'Aventure ambiguè*) (1961) Some of the writers of this period saw their works as essentially ethnographic in function, accounts of the colonizing process and its transformation of the institutions of society, including the transformation of the value systems of African culture itself. But beneath their overt concern with colonialism and their search for a usable African past, works such as Achebe's *Things Fall Apart*, **Kateb**'s *Nedjma* (1956), and Driss **Chraïbi**'s *A Simple Past* (*Le Passé simple*) (1954) are collective accounts of both individuals and communities dealing with the trauma of colonialism but from the vantage point of the cause of decolonization. Other novels from this period, the great period of independence, are concerned with the material consequences of colonization, including the emergence of new urban centers that attract migrants from the rural areas. Novels such as Cyprian **Ekwensi**'s *People of the City* (1954) and *Jagua Nana* (1961) are celebrations of the city as the space of popular culture and the coming together of people from different classes and ethnicities in the nationalist spirit. Similarly in the Cairo novels of Najīb **Maḥfūz**, the city is the center of social life, the microcosm of Egyptian society, and the source of new energies and tensions. In contrast, in highly urbanized South African society, in novels such as Peter **Abrahams**' *Mine Boy* (1941) and Alan **Paton**'s *Cry the Beloved Country* (1948), the city had, as early as the 1940s, been defined as space in which the dehumanization of the African under new regimens of race and capitalist production would be found at its most extreme. In reaction against what were seen as the alienating effects of the city, novels were produced in Africa in both the 1950s and early 1960s celebrating rural life and promoting the village as the center of an alternative society. Flora **Nwapa**'s *Efuru*, Grace **Ogot**'s *The Promised Land*, and Elechi **Amadi**'s *The Concubine*, all published in 1966, are stories of human beings forced to face many of the problems and tragedies of everyday life, but the rhythms of this life and the claims it makes on those who transgress social rules take place outside the orbit of colonialism. Among the foundational texts of African literature during this period were autobiographical novels by Mouloud **Mammeri**, Mohammed **Dib**, and **Ngugi wa Thiong'o**.

Novels of disenchantment

The history of African fiction is marked by another remarkable enigma: in the mid 1960s the form and function of this novel changed almost overnight. Consider the titles of the novels published between 1965 and 1970: Ayi Kwei **Armah**'s *The Beautiful Ones Are Not Yet Born* (1968), Yambo **Ouologuem**'s, *Bound to Violence* (*Le Devoir de violence*) (1968), Ngugi's *A Grain of Wheat* (1967), Wole **Soyinka**'s *The Interpreters* (1965), and Kourouma's *The Suns of Independence* (*Les Soleils des indépendances*) (1968). What do these works have in common? For one they represent a different tone in African fiction, one that moves the reader away from the sometimes celebratory and utopian tone of earlier novels to a grim critique of the narrative of cultural national-ism, often through satire and parody. Then there is the subject of these novels. They are all concerned, some might say obsessed, with the failed logic of nationalism, in particular what is seen as the betrayal of its mandate by the new ruling class. If colonialism had been the target of earlier literature, the novels of disenchantment are almost without exception attempts by an angry generation of writers to distance themselves from the project of cultural nationalism. Indeed, the obvious prefer-ence for certain techniques of modernism in these works – the inward turn, the interior monologue, the rhetoric of failure – is intended to mark the distance between the narrators and heroes of these novels from the realistic and euphoric narratives and subjects of decolonization. The novels seemed to simultaneously mock their precursors and the national state they had presumably willed into being. Ouologuem's *Bound to Violence*, for example, subjects the novels of **negritude** (such as Laye's *The Dark Child*) to ridicule.

Now, given its close association with cultural nationalism, the African novel was bound to change its form and function after decolonization, but no one expected this change to be reaction against prior forms of novelistic expression. Indeed, few critics had noticed the close relationship between realism and the failed narrative of decolonization. In retrospect, however, this asso-ciation seems obvious, especially if we consider how nationalism had sought its form and legiti-macy in narrative form. The connection between narrative form and nationalism was made strongly in the works of Frantz Fanon, one of the masterminds of the narrative of decolonization in Africa. In his reflection on late colonialism, especially in a keynote address given at the Congress of Black Writers and Artists in Rome in 1959, Fanon had argued that the truths of the nation, which in his mind was the depository of freedom and human liberty, would take narrative form. Narrative form, Fanon was to argue in *The African Revolution* (1968) was an "illuminating and sacred communication." As a result, the triumph of nationalism would reveal the truths and realities that colonialism had sought to foreclose and to repress. In Rome in 1959, before an audience that included some of the people who were going to shape cultural policy in Africa, Fanon asserted that the native intellectual who wanted to "create an authentic work of art" had to realize that "the truths of the nation are in its first place its realities."

But what would happen if the realities of the nation did not take the form the artist had anticipated? Fanon was aware of this potential problem. As he noted in *The Wretched of the Earth* (1968: New York): "Each generation must out of relative obscurity discover its mission, fulfill it, or betray it." For the generation writing in the mid 1960s, it was quite apparent that the African elite that had come to power had betrayed the nationalist mandate. Against this background, the novelists of disenchantment produced works in-tended to achieve two things: first, to diagnose and represent the causes of what Fanon, who was their mentor just as he had been the advisor to the failed generation, had aptly called "the pitfalls of national consciousness"; second, to find a new narrative form for the strange and unexpected realities of the nation after decolonization. In this sense, we can say that the new novels of the late 1960s and early 1979s were reacting not simply against the polity but against novels that had been seen as legitimiz-ing the nationalist project.

The rise of women novelists

But perhaps one of the most significant reactions against the foundational narratives, the novels of cultural nationalism, was the slow emergence of the works of women writers, beginning in the mid

1960s with the early novels of Nwapa, Ogot, Assia **Djebar**, and Nadine **Gordimer**, and coming of age in the 1970s and 1980s with the publication of award-winning novels by Mariama **Bâ**, Tsitsi **Dangarembga**, and Yvonne **Vera**. In the 1990s, African women novelists came to redefine the terms of the African novel and its trajectory. Three points are salient in the emergence of fictions by women and their transformation of the novelistic tradition in Africa. The first point to note is one that has often been made by feminist critics of the tradition: that women writers were not actually a phenomenon that emerged in the 1980s, but a key part of the tradition, which nevertheless remained unrecognized for many years. After all, the early novels of Gordimer, Nwapa, Djebar, and Ogot were the first to problematize the very nature of the nationalist narrative by calling attention to the role of women in the precolonial and colonial order of things, challenging the assumptions of the major male novelists, and insisting on the centrality of women's lives in the reconstitution of society. A second point to note is the role of women novelists in redirecting the energies of African literature. This redirection could be thematic, where women novelists were still involved in the same larger questions as male writers but were operating under what Nana Wilson-Tagoe (1997: London) has aptly called "a different climate of imagination." Although women writers like Nwapa and Ogot wrote novels that were similar to the works of the dominant male novelists in their concern with questions of tradition, their focus was on the spaces that were occupied by women. Djebar's early novels were engaged with the same questions of nationalism and decolonization as her male counterparts, but they stood out because of their concern with the turbulent history of Algeria as it affected women's lives and from the perspective of her female protagonists. Similarly, Gordimer and Bessie **Head** were concerned with the politics of apartheid in their native South Africa, but their novels focused on a different terrain, the tension between the public and the private in the former's case and the interiorized world of the schizophrenic subject that was the product of the mad logic of apartheid itself in the latter's. In their early novels Djebar, Nwapa, and Ogot are still involved in understanding the essential nature of the African

world in the aftermath of colonialism, but their works foreground, rather than celebrate, the traditions that were already evident in the discourse of cultural nationalism. Modernity, a continuous preoccupation of African novelists in general, was the key theme in Buchi **Emecheta**'s *Joys of Motherhood* (1980) and Dangarembga's *Nervous Conditions* (1988), but in these works it was represented not as the opposite of tradition but as a process that was both liberating and injurious to women's lives. By the end of the 1990s, however, we see the emergence of a self-conscious feminist tradition in which women novelists adopted new forms of writing as the only way of deconstructing the dominant male novel. One of the most important works in this regard is perhaps Bâ's *So Long a Letter* (1980), which used an epistolary mode to provide a devastating critique of patriarchy in the postcolony.

The "new" novel

With the establishment of a strong body of novels by African women, it is possible to argue that by the end of the 1990s, there was a convergence of interest between male and female novelists so that the gender gap that had been so apparent in the tradition from the 1960s to the 1980s had almost disappeared. An important aspect of the African novel since the end of the 1980s is that canonical male novelists such as Achebe, Ngugi, and Ousmane Sembene have made women characters central to their projects. With a few exceptions, younger writers, both male and female, work in a world in which the question of gender has become embedded in novelistic discourse. Another source of convergence is the collapse of what had initially appeared to be a monolithic narrative of nationalism and traditional forms of representation, including realism and modernism, that have increasingly been replaced by more hybrid and pluralistic forms. One of the distinguishing characteristics of the novels published by Africans in the 1990s and after was their concern with formal experimentation and their admixture of forms ranging from the oral fable to magic realism. This is evident in the works of Ben **Okri**, Leïla **Sebbar**, and Vera.

A final source of transformation in the tradition of the novel in Africa concerns the very dislocation of the notion of tradition itself. Remember that African fiction came into being as an attempt to Africanize the tradition of the novel as it had been inherited from Europe through colonialism and its institutions. The search for a novelistic tradition in Africa paralleled the search for a political tradition. This is how the novel and cultural nationalism became allies. The modernist novels that emerged in the 1960s and 1970s sought to question this alliance by providing a powerful critique of the mask of nationalism (and, by implication, realism). Women novelists further undermined tradition (and its novels) by exposing their patriarchal assumptions. All these movements were, however, predicated on one thing – the authority and cartography of the nation. Even the critique of the state that is implicit in the last two movements was done in the name of reproducing a healthy national body. A good deal of the fiction produced in the 1990s and after was written outside the body of the nation by African writers who lived elsewhere. The number of African novelists who work outside the continent is too large to list here, but one point can be made without hesitation: the most important novels that have come out of Africa by writers as different and diverse as **Ben Jelloun**, Okri, Sebbar, **Liking**, and **Beyala** have been produced outside the continent. Africa continues to be an important point of reference for these novelists, but it is no longer the Africa dreamt of by early novelists, one in which the body of the nation would be the condition of possibility of a decolonized African self. Rather, the history of the African novel is now the story of the African subject at home in the world.

Further reading

Fanon, Frantz (1968) *The Wretched of the Earth*, trans. Constance Farrington, New York: Grove Press.

Julien, Eileen (1992) *African Novels and the Questions of Orality*, Bloomington: Indiana University Press.

Miller, Christopher (1990) *Theories of Africans: Francophone Literature and Anthropology*, Chicago: University of Chicago Press.

Mortimer, Mildred (1990) *Journeys through the French African Novel*, Portsmouth, New Hampshire: Heinemann.

Obiechina, Emmanuel (1975) *Culture, Tradition and Society in the West African Novel*, Cambridge: Cambridge University Press.

Wilson-Tagoe, Nana (1997) "Reading Towards a Theorization of African Women's Writing: African Women Writers within Feminist Gynocriticism," in Stephanie Newell (ed.) *Writing African Women: Gender, Popular Culture and Literature in West Africa*, London: Zed.

SIMON GIKANDI

Nsué Angüe, Maria

b. 1945, Ebebeyin, Continental Guinea

novelist

Maria Nsué Angüe is said to be the first Equatorial-Guinean novelist of the postcolonial era (see **colonialism, neocolonialism, and postcolonialism**). Born in 1945 in Ebebeyin, Continental Guinea, she is the daughter of a diplomat and has traveled extensively around the world following her father in his assignments. A journalist, a poet, and a novelist, she is also the first female novelist of Equatorial Guinea. *Elcorno* (1985), her first novel, examines, among other issues, the condition of women in Fang traditional society and the ongoing tension between African traditional or precolonial values and imposed European culture. Translated into French as *Ekomo au coeur de la forêt guinéenne* (Ekomo in the Heart of the Guinean Forest) (1995), Nsué Angüe's novel has now reached a much wider international audience in Africa as well as the rest of the world. Nsué Angüe has also published a collection of poems, *Delirios* (Delirious) (1991), in *Africa 2000*, a publication of the Centro Cultural Hispano-Guineano in Malabo, and a collection of short stories, *Relatos* (Relations), inspired by the literary corpus of Fang cultural traditions. Nsué Angüe lives in Madrid where she is very active in the cultural life of the city. In addition to giving lectures and directing seminars, she writes articles which appear regularly in the Spanish as well as the Guinean press.

Further reading

Nsué Angüe, Maria (1984) *Ekorno*, Madrid: Ediciones de la UNED.

——(n.d.) *Relatos*, Malabo: Ediciones del Centro Cultural Hispano-Guineano.

M'BARE NGOM

Ntiru, Richard

b. 1946, Uganda

poet

The Ugandan poet Richard Ntiru was, like many other prominent East African writers, a product of the undeniably vibrant period in the late 1960s and early 1970s when authors from the region were involved in a project whose goal was nothing less than the creation of a modern regional literature. Ntiru earned a first class honors degree in English from Makerere University, worked for a publishing house in Nairobi, and occasionally taught at the university there on a part-time basis. His most famous work is the poetic collection *Tensions* (1971), which was once recommended for the Commonwealth Poetry Prize. On its publication *Tensions* was praised by critics such as Chris Wanjala for its capacity to create tensions in its readers' minds and for functioning as "a handbook" for understanding East African society. In the late 1960s Ntiru was a regular contributor of poetry to the most important journals in the region, including *Zuka*, *Dhana*, and *Transition*. In these early poems he tried, like many other poets from the region in this period of transition from colonialism to national independence, to adopt poetic forms borrowed from the European tradition to represent local postcolonial subjects. Unlike some of his contemporaries, notably **Okot p'Bitek**, Ntiru did not seek to appropriate oral poetic forms to change the nature of his poetry. Indeed, his works can be read as subjective and lyrical responses to public issues such as corruption and urbanization, often using the dramatic monologue to represent experiences from the headlines of the late 1960s, from the miniskirt to the Nigerian civil war. For inexplicable reasons, Ntiru has not published much poetry since the publication of *Tensions* and his silence has been noted by many historians of East African literature. Nevertheless, his published poems are considered to be some of the finest examples of poetry to have been produced in East Africa during the literary renaissance of the 1960s and 1970s.

GEORGE ODERA OUTA

Ntsane, Kemuel Edward

b. 1920, Lesotho; d. 1983, Lesotho

novelist

The Lesotho writer Kemuel Ntsane is popularly renowned for his satirical poetry, compiled in two anthologies, *Mmusapelo I* (Heart Restorer I) (1946) and *Mmusapelo II* (1961). Although he was born and bred in Lesotho (Basutoland), the setting and themes of his poetry straddle the border into neighboring South Africa, and his sharp lampoons of apartheid society (see **apartheid and post-apartheid**), the migrant labor system, pass laws, and religious cant are famous in the region. His first novel, *Masoabi Ngoan'a Mosotho oa Kajeno* (Masoabi, the Modern Sotho Child) (1947), portrays the transformation of the Basotho into an industrialized people, and highlights the benefit of modernity (see **modernity and modernism**). This first novel was later followed by *Nna Sajene Kokobela CID* (I, Sergeant Kokobela CID) (1963), which is based on the exploits of a first-person narrator's hunting for a suspected murderer during the heydays of ritual murders in Basutoland. This novel also raises questions about legal justice for the poor and illiterate. Ntsane's other novels are *Bao Batho* (Such People!) (1968) and *Bana ba Roma* (Our Children) (1954). The latter was meant for young readers. He also wrote a collection of essays entitled *Makumane* (Crumbs) (1961), and left an as yet unpublished novel manuscript, "Bohloko ba Lerato" (The Pain of Love). Ntsane's attempt at playwriting resulted in a biblical drama, *Josefa le Maria* (Joseph and Mary), and *Mohwebi wa Venisi* (1961), a translation of Shakespeare's *The Merchant of Venice*.

Further reading

Lenake, J.M. (1984) *The Poetry of K.E. Ntsane*, Pretoria: Van Schaik.

N.P. MAAKE

Nwankwo, Nkem

b. 1936, Unofia, Anambra state, Nigeria; d. 2001, Nigeria

novelist

Although he was educated at University College, Ibadan, during the memorable decade before Nigerian independence, Nwankwo did not published his first novel, *Danda*, until 1963, which meant that by the time he started writing he could draw upon a tradition of African fiction associated with writers such as Chinua **Achebe**. In fact, Danda, the main character in Nwankwo's first novel, a village ne'er-do-well who prefers music and leisure to the Igbo culture's cherished values of hard work, is based on Unoka, the anti-hero in Achebe's *Things Fall Apart*. On its publication and for most of the 1960s, *Danda* was one of the most popular novels in Nigeria, enjoyed by readers for its picaresque structure, humorous language, and irreverence. Nwankwo has clearly been one of the masters of satire in African fiction. In his second novel, *My Mercedes is Bigger Than Yours* (1975), for example, he uses humor and irony to parody the values of the new ruling class and to provide cautionary tales about a culture in which acquisitiveness has become the idol of the rich and the powerful. Nwankwo has also published stores for children, collected in *Tales Out of School* (1963) and *More Tales from School* (1965).

SIMON GIKANDI

Nwapa, Flora

b. 1931, Oguta, Nigeria; d. 1993, Enugu, Nigeria

novelist

It was Flora Nwapa, Nigeria's premier female novelist and one of the leading women publishers in the Anglophone African world, who gave the enterprising and industrious women of Oguta in Eastern Nigeria a voice and a place in world literary history with the publication of her first novel, *Efuru*, in London in 1966 and the establishment of Tana Press in Enugu in 1977. Prior to Nwapa's entrance into a male-dominated and exclusionary Nigerian literary culture, African women in literature were largely marginal figures playing stereotypical roles with little or no authenticity. Women were variously represented as sacrificing and sweet mothers, sullen and silent wives, or rebel or wayward daughters, contrary to the experiences of the strong, complex, and vibrant women of Oguta whom Nwapa had observed growing up.

In responding to this quasi-fixed trajectory of distorted portraits of women as baby-machines, beasts of burden, and femme fatales, Nwapa – utilizing her Igbo foremothers and oral traditions as models (see **oral literature and performance**) – introduced fresh and innovative ways of thinking about African women in her two collections of short stories, novels, plays, poetry, and children's books. Besides initiating and promoting the womanization of Nigerian letters, Nwapa founded and directed a publishing enterprise, Tana Press (for the printing and distribution of adult fiction), and Flora Nwapa Books (for the printing and distribution of **children's literature**). The piracy of her books by Nwamife Publishers in Nigeria, as well as the poor distribution of them in London by Heinemann, forced her to strike out on her own. For approximately two decades, the twin presses published her postcolonial novels, *One is Enough* (1981) and *Women are Different* (1986), and her children's books, such as *Mammywater* (1979), *The Miracle Kittens* (1980), and *Journey to Space* (1980), not to mention her plays and poetry. Other writers published by Flora Nwapa Books were Ama Ata **Aidoo**, Ifeoma Okoye, and Patience Ifejika, to name only three.

With the Igbo female deity Ogbuide, the beautiful and rich goddess of the lake, as her matrix, Nwapa's (re)presentation of African women effectively evokes women of character, power, and action. In her female-centered novels *Efuru* (1966) and *Idu* (1970), Nwapa rewrites her story, dismantling the patriarchal myth of female inferiority and male superiority. In opposition to her husbands who are lazy and truant, Efuru, the main character in the novel of the same title and the typical Oguta woman, is good, intelligent, and industrious. So is Idu, who is also a prosperous trader. Ironically, both characters, despite their strengths and kind-heartedness, are oppressed by Igbo traditional attitudes about women. Efuru is deserted by both her husbands because she is barren. Idu commits suicide in retaliation against Igbo widowhood practices that dictate she becomes the second wife of her dead husband's feckless younger brother. In her quest for change, Nwapa uses her novels to initiate a sexual revolution that can give women control over their lives, and self-fulfillment outside marriage and children.

Similar to their rural sisters, Nwapa's urban women are unlucky in love and marriage. Amaka, the heroine in *One is Enough*, is a victim of domestic abuse. Her husband, Obiora, not only beats his faithful wife, but he also betrays her by having affairs with other women and begetting children outside their marriage. When Amaka leaves Obiora and meets Reverend Father Mclaid in Lagos, she is blessed with twin boys. However, she rejects the father of her sons, and his marriage proposal, rationalizing: "as a wife, I am never free. I am a shadow of myself … impotent. I am in prison, unable to advance in body and soul. Something gets hold of me as a wife and destroys me. I said farewell to husbands the first day I came to Lagos" (1981: Enuru). Agnes, Dora, and Rose, the "three musketeers" in *Women are Different*, are also sophisticated urban women, with lucrative professions, power, and privileges. Nevertheless, love and tenderness in marriage elude them. Agnes is the victim of an arranged marriage that does not work; Chris deserts Dora and their children, and Rose is jilted by her lovers.

In these novels, which contain trenchant analysis of the sociocultural realities of African women, Nwapa unashamedly dismantles the Law of the Fathers on marriage and redefines African woman-hood. She instead invokes the Law of the Mother, one premised on the belief that a woman can be happy and fulfilled without a husband, and children. Hence, the mantra for today's women, presented succinctly in *Women are Different*, that "there are different ways of living one's life fully and

fruitfully. Women have a choice to set up a business of their own, a choice to marry and have children, a choice to marry or divorce their husbands. Mar-riage is not the only way" (1986: Enuru).

What then is Flora Nwapa's sexual politics? Is she truly a womanist who, in the words of Chikwenye Okonjo Ogunyemi (1993: Lincoln), is "committed to the survival and wholeness of the entire people, both male and female"? When Nwapa ends her novels with the dissipation of male–female relationships, it is to voice African's women's agony, anger, and frustration over gender dominance and blatant sexism. For this reason, Nwapa is a womanist who pragmatically accepts the breakdown in marital relationships today as one direct result of women's quotidian experiences. Her writings are premised on the belief that to be complicit in the oppression of others is cowardly. On the other hand, to challenge patriarchal structures which are harmful to women is coura-geous. And if "survival" and "wholeness" for some women means that "marriage is not the only way" – so be it. For many of the women in Nwapa's novels, to remain in a bad marriage that does not bring "wholeness" and happiness is suicidal, regardless of what tradition demands. Thus in her dramatic work *Two Women in Conversation* (1993), Niki advises her friend Juma to divorce her husband, who has abandoned her and their three children for years, and thus be true to herself. For Nwapa, when equality, love, and respect are absent in marriage, the relationship has failed. It is to this dilemma that Nwapa speaks in her literature of resistance.

Works cited

Nwapa, F. (1981) *One Is Enough*, Enuru: Tana Press.
——(1986) *Women Are Different*, Enuru: Tana Press.

Further reading

Davies, Carole Boyce and Fido, Elaine Savory (1993) "African Women Writers: Toward a Literary History," in Oyekan Owomoyela (ed.) *A History of Twentieth-Century African Literatures*, Lincoln: University of Nebraska Press.
Ogunyemi, Chikwenye Okonjo (1993) "Woman-ism: The Dynamics of the Contemporary Black Female Novel in English," in VèVè A. Clark,

Ruth-Ellen B. Joeres and Madelon Sprengnether (eds) *Revising the Word and the World: Essays in Feminist Literary Criticism*, Chicago: University of Chicago Press.

Umeh, Marie (ed.) (1998) *Emerging Perspectives on Flora Nwapa: Critical and Theoretical Essays*, Trenton, New Jersey: Africa World Press.

MARIE L. UMEH

Nyamufukudza, Stanley

b. 1951, Wedza district, Zimbabwe

novelist and short story writer

The Zimbabwean novelist and short story writer Stanley Nyamufukudza was born in the district of Wedza and received his education in Zimbabwe and at Oxford University, where he graduated with a BA in 1977. Nyamufukudza shares with Dambudzo **Marechera** the anger, betrayal, and alienation of a generation of Africans that both welcomed but were skeptical of the potential of African nationalists to lead the masses towards total independence. His best-known novel, *The Non-Believer's Journey* (1980), is the story of Sam, a teacher in Highfield, a high-density suburb of Harare. Sam snubs the liberation war and is killed by armed guerillas fighting for majority rule. Through the questioning of the words and promises of the new political class, Nyamufukudza portrays the complications of the armed struggle and introduces the theme of disenchantment and skepticism into postcolonial Zimbabwean literature (see **colonialism, neocolonialism, and postcolonialism**). In *Aftermaths* (1983), a collection of short stories, he pursues the theme of the betrayal of the nationalist dream at independence by the new leadership. In the title story, "Aftermaths," African women emerge from the war a battered lot, reduced to prostitution. *If God Was a Woman* (1991), another collection of short stories, modifies the picture of cultural malaise among Africans after independence by depicting the ordinary Zimbabwean woman as socially disadvantaged but boldly fighting hard to be recognized in the new political order.

M. VAMBE

Nyembezi, Cyril L.S.

b. 1919, South Africa; d. 2000, Pietermaritzberg

novelist

Cyril Nyembezi's Zulu novel *Mntanami, Mnatanami* (My Child! My Child!) (1950) was usually the first novel read by Zulu readers in South Africa in the 1950s. Its intellectual power and critical realism (see **realism and magical realism**) has not diminished since its publication over half a century ago. This major Zulu writer has written two other novels: *Ubudoda abukhulelwa* (Age Does Not Mean Manhood) (1953) and *Inkinsela yase Mgungundlovu* (The Man from Mgungundlovu) (1962). He has also written some poetry: *Imikhemezolo* (Rain) (1963), *Amahlungu aluhlaza* (Green Grass) (1963), *Izimpophoma zomphefumulo* (Waterfalls of the Spirit) (1963). Besides being a creative writer, Nyembezi is also a serious scholar of Zulu culture, assembling three landmark anthologies: a collection of Zulu heroic poetry, *Izibongo zamakhosi* (Heroic Poems of the Chiefs) (1958); a collection of Zulu proverbs, called appropriately enough *Zulu Proverbs* (1954); and, written with O.E.H. Nxumalo, a volume of Zulu customs and traditions, *Inqolobane yesizwe* (Storehouse of the Nation) (1960). C.L.S. Nyembezi belongs to a group of Zulu intellectuals such as H.I.E. **Dhlomo**, Benedict Wallet Vilakazi, E.H.A. Made, and Jordan Kush **Ngubane** who revolutionized South African culture in the 1940s, comparable to what Xhosa intellectuals had achieved in the 1880s.

NTONGELA MASILELA

Nyonda, Vincent de Paul

b. 1918, Mandji, Gabon; d. 1995, Libreville, Gabon

playwright

The Gabonese writer Vincent Nyonda was born in 1918 in Mandji, Gabon, and became interested in politics at an early age. In the late 1950s he was appointed a delegate to the territorial assembly and later served as a minister in Gabon after independence. But Noynda's major interest has been in the theater and he has written plays whose goal is to present, in a simple and direct way, the historical and cultural traditions of Gabon and to resurrect legendary figures in the region, including the famous King Mounga. This desire to recover the historical past, its traditions and legends, is evident in works such as *Le Roi Mounga* (King Mounga) (1988). In other plays published in 1981, notably *La Mort de Guykafi: drame en cinq actes* (Guykafi's Death: A Play in Five Acts), *Suivi de deux albinos à la M'Passa* (With Two Albinos in M'Passa), and *Le Soûlard* (The Drinkard), Nyonda shifted his interest from the historical past to represent and criticize certain social customs in contemporary Gabon. In 2000, in recognition of his efforts toward the development of literature and culture in Gabon, a Paul Nyonda Literary Prize for young and new writers was established.

OUSMANE BA

Nzeako, Mazi J.U.T.

b. Nigeria

novelist

The Nigerian author Mazi J.U.T. Nzeako is a prolific Igbo novelist who has published to date seven novels: *Erimma* (1972), *Nkoli* (1973), *Okuko Agbasaa Okpesi* (1974), *Aka Ji Aku* (1974), *Emecheta* (1980), *Juochi* (1981), and *Chi Ewere Ehihie Jie* (Sunset at Noon) (1985). He is the author of a book on Igbo customs and traditions entitled *Omenala Ndi Igbo* (Igbo Customs) (1972). He has also contributed six poems in an anthology edited by R.M. Ekechukwu entitled *Akpa Uche: An Anthology of Modern Igbo Verse* (1975).

Very little is known about his early life except that he worked as a broadcaster in the former Eastern Nigerian Broadcasting Corporation. He is known today very much by his creative works. One remarkable thing about his fiction is its dominant influence by the Igbo oral tradition (see **oral literature and performance**). He draws freely and generously from Igbo narrative art, Igbo folk tales, festivals, and legends. He strives to recreate in some of his novels the Igbo traditional way of life, highlighting its successes and failures, triumphs and setbacks. Generally he emphasizes the rich values of Igbo communal life, extended family relationships,

the potency of rituals, ancestors, gods, diviners, and oracles. His commitment as a writer seems to lie in his conscious efforts at the preservation of Igbo customs and traditions through literature. Critics of **Igbo literature** have expressed reservations over some of his literary techniques in the articulation of the traditional and the modern in Igbo writing. He has been criticized for the superficial use of proverbs in modern settings and a faulty manipulation of the language *vis-à-vis* its syntax and metaphorical usage, especially in his early works, which seem to be largely experimental. These problems notwithstanding, J.U.T. Nzeako has contributed immensely to the development of the contemporary Igbo novel. His later novels are evidence of his increasing growth and maturity as a novelist. He is widely read in the Nigerian school system and his fiction is attracting increasing focus in research studies by graduate students of Igbo language and literature.

ERNEST EMENYONU

Nzekwu, Onuora

b. 1928, Kafanchan, Nigeria

novelist

The Nigerian novelist Onuora Nzekwu started his career as a teacher and later became a magazine editor, working primarily for *Nigeria Magazine*, an important journal for the arts and culture sponsored by the Nigerian government. His major novels, all published in the 1960s, belong to what may be considered the transitional period of African fiction, coming after the foundation works of writers such as Chinua **Achebe**, and hence drawing on some of the themes that had taken root in African writing, most notably the conflict between modernity and traditional or precolonial culture (see **modernity and modernism**; **colonialism, neocolonialism, and postcolonialism**), and the novels of disillusionment that dominated the literary scene in the late 1960s. Nzekwu's novels are often structured by the opposition they represent between a mythological past threatened by the forces of change; they are also haunted by the fear that modernization does not necessarily lead to fulfillment. In *Wand of Noble*

Wood (1961) a magazine editor discovers that his Western education cannot help him overcome the traditional curse that has been cast on his bride; in *High Life for the Lizards* (1965), the novelist uses comedy to explore the problems barrenness brings to a marriage; and in *Blade among the Boys* (1962), a young man's desires to join the priesthood are resisted by a mother who holds to the old Igbo dictum that a man's primary responsibility is to marry and procreate. Nwekwu's novels may appear old-fashioned in both their thematic and their stylistic concerns, but they represent an important phase in the literary history of Africa, a time when fiction was committed to representing the dilemmas of the new societies emerging out of colonialism.

SIMON GIKANDI

Nzuji, Clémentine Madiya

b. 1944, Kasaï

poet and linguist

Born in Kasaï, Clémentine Madiya Nzuji (Clémentine Falk-Nzuji) emerged in the 1960s as a leading member of the literary circle in Kinshasa known as the Pléiade du Congo. With the appearance of *Murmures* (Murmurings) in 1967, she became one of the first African women poets to publish in French. Her interest in oral forms soon became evident in *Kasala* (1969), a volume of poems containing original works in Ciluba with translations into French. In 1969, Nzuji was awarded the Prix Littéraire Senghor for her poetry. Critics have labeled much of her subsequent lyrical production *intimiste*. Nzuji has also written several tales in the oral tradition (see **oral literature and performance**) and well-crafted short stories, including "Frisson de la mémoire" (Shiver of Memory), winner of a competition sponsored by Radio-France International in 1990. Educated as a linguist, she received a doctorate in African studies in Paris, and her scholarly work has contributed significantly to the study of Ciluba language and literary forms, especially the heroic epic. She lives in Belgium and teaches at the Linguistic Institute of the Catholic University of Louvain, where she is the founder and director of the Center for African Languages, Literatures, and Traditions.

JANICE SPLETH

O

Oculi, Okello

b. 1942, Uganda

poet, novelist, and political scientist

The Ugandan poet, novelist, and political scientist Okello Oculi came to prominence with the publication of *Orphan* (1968), a long poem fashioned after **Okot p'Bitek**'s ground-breaking poem *Song of Lawino*, which had been published two years earlier. Oculi's poem was welcomed by critics of African literature who saw it as an important addition to what became known as the "song school" of poetry in East Africa. The poem explores the fate of an orphan boy named Okello and uses various characters in his village to comment on the fate of the orphan. The diverse views of the characters give the reader a graphic picture of what lies ahead for the orphan as he tries to survive in a hostile environment, caught between the worldviews of his stepmother, who holds him responsible for the death of his mother, and his grandfather, who is more positive about the fate of the orphan. The poem challenges the reader to take stock of his/her own attitude to the many orphans in our communities, the products of our modern postcolonial society (see **colonialism, neocolonialism, and postcolonialism**). Oculi's other long poem, *Malak* (1976), is also fashioned on the "song" tradition and dramatizes the conflicting positions of two speakers to present competing views of African society as it struggles to secure an identity between the claims of precolonial values and encroaching modernity (see **modernity and modernism**). Similar concerns

are taken up in Oculi's short novels, including *Prostitute* (1968) and *Kookolem* (1978).

CHARLES OKUMU

Odilora, Ude

b. Nigeria

teacher and novelist

Ude Odilora, a schoolteacher by profession, has published only one novel, *Okpa Aku Eri Eri* (The Miser) (1981), albeit a novel that is extremely popular with students, teachers, and the general reader in Eastern Nigeria. This is apparently because of its theme, which addresses the Igbo perennial love of material acquisitions and wealth to the point of worshipping material possessions. In his preface to the novel, Odilora points out that the pursuit of wealth and material possessions is in itself not bad, but when it becomes an obsession to the total disregard of the fine virtues and sane values of human existence it invariably leads to tragedy. Success through hard work is advocated, but success which negates pleasure and good neighborliness is the bane of human existence. These are the aspects of life portrayed in the story and symbolized by the hero, Akubuzo, from the checkered nature of whose experiences in life the author asks the reader to learn. *Okpa Aku Eri Eri* is a well-crafted novel which has been praised for the structural unity of its plot, a conscientious development of true-to-life characters, and a dexterous use of language. Critics draw attention to charming imagery, the absence of proverb clusters, exquisite narrative skills, and the blending of exciting action with well spaced-out moments of suspense. Although Ude Odilora has only one novel to date to his credit, he is regarded by readers, teachers, and critics of **Igbo literature** as a major contemporary Igbo novelist who has contributed immensely to the form and art of the modern Igbo novel.

ERNEST EMENYONU

Odinga, (Jaramogi Adonijah Ajuma) Oginga

b. 1912, Sakwa, central Nyanza, East African Protectorate (now in Kenya); d. 1994, Kisumu, Kenya

writer, sage, philosopher, and politician

The Kenyan writer, sage, philosopher, and politician Oginga Odinga was educated Maseno School and Makerere University, Uganda. For several years he worked as a schoolmaster before entering the world of business and anti-colonial politics in the 1940s. He became the first vice president of independent Kenya in 1963, but soon fell foul of Jomo **Kenyatta**'s government which, in his estimation, had strayed from the nation's founding principles. A year after his resignation from the ruling party and from the vice presidency, his **autobiography** *Not Yet Uhuru* (1967) was published, and its catchy title soon fell into popular usage as a term for expressing discontent with the aborted process of decolonization across the continent (see **colonialism, neocolonialism, and postcolonialism**). As was often the case with many political autobiographies of the time, *Not Yet Uhuru* was more about the progression of the country to independence than an intimate look into the author's life history. His last title, *Oginga Odinga: His Philosophy and Beliefs* (1992) in collaboration with the philosopher Odera Oruka, outlined his core ideas as a sage. Throughout his political career, much of it spent in opposition to colonialism and postcolonial governments, Odinga repre-

sented a tradition of radical populism that often set him against the status quo.

DAN ODHIAMBO OJWANG

Ogali, Agu Ogali

b. 1931, Nigeria

writer

Ogali Ogali is one of the most distinguished writers of what has come to be known as Nigerian market literature, an important genre in African **popular literature** and culture. Produced for mass entertainment and for educating the urban class in the ways of modernity (see **modernity and modernism**) and morality, this literature developed mostly in provincial towns and markets, one of the most important being Onitsha on the banks of the Niger. Trained as a journalist and teacher, Ogali started writing mostly novelettes and fictional pamphlets in the 1950s, and his most popular chapbooks, including *Veronica, My Daughter*, date to this period. Ogali has been a prolific writer of short novels and plays and collections of Igbo folk tales, and while his work was for a long time not considered central to the emergence of African literature, it is now clear that despite being written in a language that was accessible to a mass audience, the themes and concerns of his works – the conflict between traditional beliefs and the institutions of modernity, and the relation between morality and the new money economy – paralleled those of many established Nigerian writers. The key difference is that while the canonical writers were read primarily by a small elite, Ogali's work was bought and circulated across a cross-section of Nigerian society. *Veronica, My Daughter* might well be the best-selling Nigerian novel after Achebe's *Things Fall Apart*.

Further reading

Ogali, Agu Ogali (1980) *Veronica, My Daughter and Other Onitsha Plays and Stories*, Washington DC: Three Continents Press.

SIMON GIKANDI

Ogbalu, Frederick Chidozie

b. 1927, Nigeria; d. 1990, Abagana, Nigeria

writer and publisher

Chief (Dr) Frederick Chidozie Ogbalu, the Oba Odezulumba of Abagana in Anambra state, Nigeria, was the doyen of Igbo language studies. His vision, vitality, nurturing, and ceaseless mentoring took Igbo language studies to a pedestal unprecedented in the history of any indigenous language development in Nigeria. Ogbalu's death in a tragic motor accident in his home town of Abagana on 21 October 1990 was considered to be the greatest single setback suffered by Igbo language studies in the second half of the twentieth century.

As early as 1949, while colonialism was in full force in Nigeria (see **colonialism, neocolonialism, and postcolonialism**), Ogbalu had founded the Society for Promoting Igbo Language and Culture (SPILC) which for half a century remained the most effective proactive forum for the development and popularization of Igbo language, literature, and culture as authentic fields of study, nationally and internationally (see **Igbo literature**). He later became the chairman of SPILC and labored so hard and assiduously for the goals and objectives of the society that his name became synonymous or even coterminous with Igbo language studies. He established a publishing company, University Publishing, to facilitate and promote publications in Igbo language, literature, and culture.

Ogbalu was himself a prolific author. He wrote and published over seventy titles in the various genres of **Igbo literature**, writing works for children (see **children's literature**) and for adults. He produced works in a cross-section of genres, ranging from grammar books to books on Igbo customs and traditions, and pedagogy. He also published poetry, short stories, folklore, and novels as well as non-fiction, all geared towards making the Igbo language an accepted and vital major language in Nigeria. Wherever there was a gap in Igbo language development he moved to fill it. That was how, in the early stages of Igbo language studies, he came to write and publish two

major Igbo reference works – *Okowa–Okwu* (1962), and *Osua–Okowaa* (n.d.), both dictionaries. In 1972, he established a Standardization Committee, an arm of SPILC which produced meta-linguistic books that enhanced knowledge of words in Igbo and English.

Ogbalu's publications in Igbo literature and culture are too many to fully enumerate. They include *Omenala Igbo* (1966), *Nza na Obu* (1973), *Ebubedike* (1974), *Onuora* (1975), *Mbediogu* (1975), *Uwaezuoke* (1976), *Igbo Attitude to Sex* (1978), *Obiefuna* (1983), *Uyoko Mbem* (1984), *Abu Umuaka* (1979), *Nzamiriza* (n.d.), and *Uri Igbo* (Igbo Dance Songs) (n.d.). Perhaps no other Igbo scholar has achieved more in the development of Igbo language and culture as authentic fields of study. Frederick Ogbalu, a literary pioneer and creative genius, goes down in history as the most important scholar of Igbo language studies in the twentieth century.

ERNEST EMENYONU

Ogola, Margaret A.

b. 1958, Kenya

novelist

Kenyan novelist Margaret Ogola is a trained pediatrician and has worked as executive director of the Family Life Counselling Association of Kenya, and in several organizations that deal with youth, family, and health matters. She has often stated her belief in what she calls the complementarity of gender and antipathy to any form of feminism that advocates confrontation between the sexes (see **gender and sexuality**). She is the author of the novel *The River and the Source* (1994), winner of the Commonwealth Prize and the Jomo Kenyatta Prize for Literature, and *Cardinal Otunga: A Gift of Grace* (1999), a biography of the prominent Kenyan clergyman. *The River and the Source* narrates four generations of Kenyan women. It begins as the story of an insular, precolonial Luo ethnic community, but gradually transforms into a chronicle of the Kenyan multi-ethnic nation. In telling the story of Kenya, Ogola celebrates the family as the basic building block of society. Thus, she avoids the theme of public politics and focuses more on the personal lives of her women characters. Her novel is notable for the way in which it experiments with Luo oral traditions (see **oral literature and performance**) and for its attempts to reinsert women into Kenyan historiography.

DAN ODHIAMBO OJWANG

Ogot, Grace (Emily Akinyi)

b. 1930, central Nyanza district, Kenya

politician, short story writer, and novelist

The Kenyan politician, short story writer, and novelist Grace Ogot shares with Nigeria's Flora **Nwapa** the distinction of being the first woman novelist in Anglophone Africa. Her short stories first appeared in *Black Orpheus* and *Transition* in the early 1960s, and in 1966 she published *The Promised Land*, her first novel. Originally subtitled "A True Fantasy," it is about a young Kenyan Luo family that migrates to neighboring Tanganyika in pursuit of wealth but is thwarted when a jealous Tanganyikan neighbor casts a spell on them. This novel was notable for the way it examined the anxieties around modern materialism, and for the way it tried to place women at the forefront of a nationalism that questioned the fascination with the trappings of colonial modernity. If colonialism, in collusion with traditional male-dominated institutions, had contributed to the sidelining of women by denying them access to modern education and to the modern economy, Ogot sought to undo this by presenting women's marginal status as a source of moral authority. As such, the heroine in *The Promised Land* – depicted otherwise as an obedient, traditional wife – in the end prevails over a dictatorial and materialistic husband.

In her collection of short stories, *Land Without Thunder* (1968), Ogot was mainly concerned with the European colonial contact with African society and the many conflicts that this engendered. For example, in "The Green Leaves," she examined the contending colonial and traditional understandings of the concept "justice." In publishing the collection, Ogot also brought together for the

first time a number of stories that drew creatively on the Luo oral tradition (see **oral literature and performance**), and which could signal to native sources of meaning in the face of the amnesia wrought on Kenyan society by colonialism (see **colonialism, neocolonialism, and postcolonialism**). In the novella *The Graduate* (1980) Ogot was, for the first time, to deal explicitly with the problems of governance in postcolonial Kenya, this time reading Kenyan nationalism (see **nationalism and post-nationalism**) through its exclusion of women from positions of leadership. The woman graduate of the novella's title only secures a post in the country's cabinet after the male minister originally appointed to the position dies in a road accident.

Although she is not much celebrated in this regard, Ogot is one of the many East African writers, besides the more famous **Ngugi wa Thiong'o**, who have championed the cause of writing in African languages. She has published at least four titles in Luo, one of which has been translated into English under the title *The Strange Bride* (1989). Her other titles include *Island of Tears* (1980) and *The Other Woman* (1976). In spite of her prolific output and her seminal status as one of the "mothers" of contemporary African literature, Ogot has not been a favorite of many critics, with some dismissing her work as melodramatic and others considering her stance on gender questions to be rather resigned (see **gender and sexuality**). In the 1990s, however, she received more complimentary readings which recognize her standing as a pacesetter in African writing.

DAN ODHIAMBO OJWANG

Ogunde, Hubert Adédèji

b. 1916, Nigeria; d. 4 April 1990, London

entertainer and businessman

Hubert Ogunde was the Nigerian ex-policeman who became a pioneer entertainer – singer, actor, and musician – and a wealthy and successful businessman. In his book, *The Development of African Drama* (1982: London), Michael Etherton said that Ogunde is "frequently described as 'the father of

Nigerian theater,' " although he feels that he was more of "a father-figure, an embodiment of success and his art as a popular expression of Yoruba sensibility." Two of his first plays, *The Garden of Eden* and *Throne of God*, were folk operas without political overtones, performed while he was in the Nigerian police force. By 1945, his performances had become so politically charged that the performance of *Strike and Hunger* sparked off the general strike of 1945 and the play was subsequently banned. Ogunde's clash with the colonial authorities in the 1940s and 1950s caused him the denial of a passport to travel to England. After independence, the performance of his most famous song composition "Yorùbá Ronú" (Yoruba – think!) (1964), brought him into conflict with the politicians, and after April 1964 Ogunde and his company were banned.

Further reading

Ebun, Clark (1979) *Hubert Ogunde: The Making of the Nigerian Theatre*, London: Oxford University Press.

Etherton, Michael (1982) *The Development of African Drama*, London: Hutchinson.

B. AKIN OYÈTÁDÉ

Ogunyemi, Wale

b. 1939, Nigeria; d. 2001, Nigeria

playwright and actor

One of a leading group of Nigerian playwrights who draw heavily on Yoruba history and myth (see **Yoruba literature**), Wale Ogunyemi is also a distinguished actor and has featured prominently in productions of Wole **Soyinka**'s plays. In fact, Ogunyemi came under the influence of Soyinka when he attended the drama school at the University of Ibadan in 1966 and he started his theater career as an actor with the Nobel laureate's theater group, 1960 Masks. It was during this period that his first play, *Born with a Fire in His Head*, was first published. Many of Ogunyemi's plays concern the lives of Yoruba gods and deities and their cosmic struggle to control the elements with

which they are associated. Plays that fall under this category include *Be Mighty, Be Mine* (1968) and *Eshu Elegba* (1970). But some of Ogunyemi's plays can be considered historical to the extent that they deployed themes and events from specific events in the Yoruba past. In *Ijaye War* (1970), for example, he dramatizes the major political and military events from nineteenth-century wars among the Yoruba states. In *Kiriji* (1976), undoubtedly his most ambitious and popular historical play, Ogunyemi uses one specific episode from the Yoruba wars to create an epic drama. Before it was published in 1976, *Kiriji* was one of the key plays in the repertoire of the University of Ibadan's "Theater on Wheels" project, whose goal was to take drama to communities in Western Nigeria. In general, Ogunyemi's plays are concerned with the somber events of history and rely heavily on Yoruba ritual and oral tradition for their epic effect (see **oral literature and performance**). The exception is a few comedies, such as *The Divorce* (1977), which deal with domestic conflicts.

SIMON GIKANDI

Ojaide, Tanure

b. 1948, Nigeria

poet

Tanure Ojaide is one of the most prolific Nigerian poets in the English language. Apart from a long break between his first collection of poems *Children of Iroko* (1973) and his second *Labyrinths of the Delta* (1986), Ojaide published several volumes of poetry in quick succession and has continued to write and publish poetry since. He has also published *Great Boys: An African Childhood* (1998), a memoir in prose, and several works of criticism. The time break between his first collection and the second signifies a stylistic and epistemological break in Ojaide's vision of poetry and the role of the poet in the society. In *Children of Iroko*, the influence of Christopher **Okigbo** and the generation of modernism in Nigerian poetry is so palpable that the young poet appears to be struggling fruitlessly to find his own personal voice. Thereafter, in subsequent volumes of poetry, Ojaide acquires a new voice and vision stylistically rooted in oral poetry and its tradition of employing poetry as means of social commentary and criticism (see **oral literature and performance**).

Further reading

Sallah, T.M. (1995) "The Eagle's Vision: The Poetry of Tanure Ojaide," *Research in African Literatures* 26, 1: 20–9.

HARRY GARUBA

Okai, Atukwei

b. 1941, Accra, Ghana

poet

Born in Accra, Ghana, Okai had his tertiary education in the former Soviet Union between 1961 and 1967. After finally securing a position teaching Russian and literature at the University of Ghana at Legon, Accra, Okai was very active in the organization of the Ghana Association of Writers. Like a prophet in the wilderness, his style of declamatory performance-oriented poetry distinguished him among his fellow Ghanaian poets. Many of his public performances involved dancing, drumming, chants, and a certain degree of audience participation. His many collections of poems include *Flowerfall* (1969), *The Oath of the Fontomfrom and Other Poems* (1971) and *Lorgorligi Logarithms and Other Poems* (1974), all of which brilliantly use traditional techniques of **oral literature and performance** in a contemporary context. His innovative use and transformation of language, as well as his promotion of younger Ghanaian and African writers under the auspices of the Pan-African Writers' Association, has secured Atukwei Okai's reputation in Ghana's literary world.

Further reading

Fraser, Robert (1986) *West African Poetry: A Critical History*, Cambridge: Cambridge University Press.
Moore, Gerald and Beier, Ulli (eds) (1984) *The Penguin Book of Modern African Poetry*, Harmondsworth, England: Penguin.

VINCENT O. ODAMTTEN

Okara, Gabriel

b. 1921, Ijaw region, Niger Delta, Nigeria

poet and novelist

The Nigerian poet and novelist Gabriel Okara is one of those writers who have the uncanny ability to be both central and marginal at the same time. Though he began writing before the major figures of Nigerian literature – his short story "The Iconoclast" having won the first prize in the British Council short story competition in 1952 and his poem "The Call of the River Nun" adjudged the best entry at the Nigerian Festival of Arts in 1953 – his reputation has not matched that of the major Nigerian writers. His reputation as a writer has rested on his collection of poems *The Fisherman's Invocation* (1968) and his allegorical novel *The Voice* (1964). However, his ability to thematize the perennial issues of African literature has ensured that his poems are extensively anthologized and evoked in critical discussions of the themes of modern African literature. His novel, written in the form of a quest narrative with an enigmatic hero in search of an elusive "it," is also constantly cited in studies of the question of language (see **language question**) and linguistic representation in African literature in the European languages.

Further reading

Echeruo, M.J.C. (1992) "Gabriel Okara at Seventy: A Poet and His Seasons," *World Literature Today*, 66, 3: 452–7.

HARRY GARUBA

Okephwo, Isidore

b. 1942, Nigeria

scholar and novelist

Although he is perhaps better known as a classicist

and one of the leading scholars of African **oral literature and performance**, Isidore Okephwo is the author of three important novels, *The Victims* (1970), *The Last Duty* (1981), and *The Tides* (1993), penetrating psychological explorations of people caught up in what appear to be ordinary practices which are, nevertheless, made tragic by changing economic circumstances in which the values of precolonial society are often at odds with the claims of modernity (see **colonialism, neocolonialism, and postcolonialism: modernity and modernism**). In *The Victims*, for example, a polygamous family is torn apart by the failures of the father who discovers that he cannot support his family in a culture of acquisitiveness and mass poverty. A similar conflict between social practices and circumstances is dramatized in *The Last Duty* where a young woman, left alone without means of support, is forced into adultery. The larger causes and consequences of this act are explored through the stories of six narrators. In his later novel, *The Tides*, Okephwo, like many other Nigerian writers of the post civil war period, is concern with the destruction of characters by malevolent social forces, but unlike novelists such as Festus **Iyayi** who focus on the conflict of social classes, he tends to be interested in the crisis the social environment triggers in the internal world of his characters.

SIMON GIKANDI

Okigbo, Christopher

b. 1932, Ojoto, Nigeria; d. 1967, Nigeria

poet

Alongside his compatriots Wole **Soyinka** and J.P. **Clark-Bekederemo** with whom he is often grouped, Christopher Okigbo is recognized as the leading poet of the generation of Nigerian writers, influenced by modernism (see **modernity and modernism**), who came into prominence in the early 1960s. Okigbo's ten-year writing career (1957–67) coincided with the last few years of colonialism in Nigeria and the immediate post-independence period, which was brought to an abrupt end by the civil war (1967–70), in which he was killed. His poetry thus occupies a significant period in Nigerian history and captures the exhilarating times associated with independence and nationalism (see **nationalism and post-nationalism**) by mirroring the new horizons opened up by political freedom and the innovative and experimental cultural energies it unleashed. The distinctive mark of Okigbo's poetry is his ability to link personal experiences to public themes in a highly sophisticated manner, to achieve a creative synthesis of the inner, spiritual, and aesthetic realm and the outer, phenomenological, and social domain. His poems are characterized by the search for a poetic idiom flexible enough to contain the complex cultural forces that shaped those times and at the same time prove an adequate medium for plumbing the subtle depths of personal experience. By the time *Heavensgate* was published in 1962, it was clear that he had found the solution in the artistic form of ritual, which allowed him ample scope for the interlinking of diverse and fragmentary experiences and the objectification of subjective states and feelings.

Okigbo published his early poems in the University of Ibadan student publication *The Horn* and the literary journals *Black Orpheus* and *Transition*. Some of these early poems, later brought together as the "Four Canzones," are regarded as apprentice pieces which he was to exclude from his more mature poems collected in the volume *Labyrinths* (1971). Nevertheless, these poems set the style, tone, and direction of his later poetry. The predisposition to lyricism and lament, his endless ritualization of experience, his predilection for musical accompaniment, and his striving to capture the rhythms and cadences of specific musical instruments in his poems are all evident in these early poems. In his introduction to *Labyrinths* (1971: London), Okigbo insisted that though the "poems were written and published separately, they are, in fact, organically related." Indeed, the whole corpus of his poetry, beginning with the earlier canzones to the unfinished "Path of Thunder," sequence, can be read as one long poem in which the central character, a poet-protagonist, journeys through a series of discrete but inter-related experiences. This journey achieves episodic unity through the use of the quest motif and the recurrence of particular images and symbols that give the entire body of poems a mythic coherence.

Though his entire poetic output is limited to the poems collected in *Labyrinths* and a more inclusive edition *Collected Poems*, issued in 1986 by Heinemann, Christopher Okigbo is still regarded as Nigeria's foremost poet.

Works cited

Okigbo, Christopher (1971) *Labyrinths*, London: Heinemann.

Further reading

Achebe, C. and Okafor, Dubem (eds) (1978) *Don't Let Him Die*, Enugu: Fourth Dimension.

Anozie, S.O. (1972) *Christopher Okigbo: Creative Rhetoric*, New York: Africana.

Nwoga, D.I. (ed.) (1984) *Critical Perspectives on Christopher Okigbo*, Washington, DC: Three Continents Press.

HARRY GARUBA

Okot p'Bitek

b. 1931, Gulu, Uganda; d. 1982, Kampala, Uganda

poet and anthropologist

The Ugandan poet, folklorist, religious thinker, and cultural activist is best known for his "invention" or popularization of a tradition of long poems, known as songs, based on the oral and rhetorical practices of the Acholi people of northern Uganda (see **oral literature and performance**). Okot's poetic ability began as a student in his junior high school but matured during his senior years as a student at King's College, Budo, in the 1950s. His first composition was an opera called *Acan*, which was partly influenced by Mozart's *The Magic Flute*. However, this Western influence was not what made Okot the important poet he was to become in the 1960s. In an interview with Bernth Lindfors in 1980 he says his greatest influence came from his mother, who was a well-known composer–singer among the Acoli women. In his own right, he composed Acoli oral songs which, he claims, "were sung in Gulu where I grew up, at Budo where I

went to school and in the 1950s they were disseminated even wider … It was touching to hear them. I think it was my mother's influence that was important in making me a singer." He developed into a writer as a challenge to his mother, but as he confesses, his written poems were nowhere near his mother's oral composition, a fact he acknowledges in his famous *Song of Lawino* (1966).

Okot's first piece of creative writing was a novel in Acoli called *Lak Tar Miyo Kinyero Wi Lobo* (White Teeth Make Us Laugh on Earth) published in 1953. The novel was developed from the opera *Acan*. In the opera, the main aria is that of an orphan boy whose father dies while he is still young and he has no bride-wealth to pay for his marriage. In the novel, the central character is called Okeca Ladwong and the novel is about his search for bride-wealth since his father died while he was young. As a young man, he falls in love with a beautiful woman whose father demands a high bride-wealth. Okeca cannot raise the bride-wealth and his maternal uncles and clansmen break tradition by refusing to help him. In the novel, Okot is critical of the unreasonably high bride-wealth demanded by parents for their daughters. Thus, Okeca's suffering which he shares with other Acoli boys who cannot raise the bride-wealth is solely blamed on the greedy parents who try to make as much money as possible from the "sale" of their daughters. Okot was also critical of relatives who refused to help their kinsmen, as required by Acoli tradition, but he understood that the collapse of kinship ties was itself dictated by the economic hardships that a new generation of Africans faced in a modern urban economy where the cost of living was too high. In *Lak Tar*, Okot uses a loose plot and techniques borrowed from Acoli oral prose narratives to capture the tension between old values and the claims of modernity (see **modernity and modernism**), but he also uses humor to lighten the depressive situation represented in the novel.

But Okot came to prominence as the author of a series of long poems, known as songs, published in the late 1960s and early 1970s. In addition to *Song of Lawino*, works in the song genre include *Wer pa Lawino* (1969), the Acoli version of *Song of Lawino*; *Song of Ocol* (1970); *Two Songs (Song of Prisoner* and

Song of Malaya) (1971). In addition to his Acoli language novel, *Lak Tar*, he also published three collections of works from the Acoli oral tradition, containing both the original Acoli texts and his translation into English. These collections include *Horn of My Love* (1974) (a collection of Acoli oral songs including some composed by his mother, Cernia Lacwe), *Hare and Hornbill* (1979) (a collection of Acoli folk tales), and *Mere Words* (1985) (a collection of Acoli proverbs).

Okot was not only a creative writer but also a religious thinker, and some scholars would say he was a sage too. His two publications on religion, *African Religion in Western Scholarship* and *Religion of the Central Luo*, both published in 1971, support his claim to being an African religious thinker. As a cultural activist, Okot published significant essays expressing his stand in the debate on the place of culture in East Africa in particular and Africa in general in the postcolonial period (see **colonialism, neocolonialism, and postcolonialism**). His early interventions in the cultural debate in East Africa are collected in *Africa's Cultural Revolution* (1973). In these essays, Okot was convinced that the role of the artist in society was that of a ruler, and that whether this artist was a creative writer, composer–singer or painter, society needed to heed what he or she had to say. This perception dominates his collection of essays on **art**, culture, and values collected in *Artist the Ruler* (1986).

The recurrent theme in all four poems is that of cultural conflict. Okot examines this theme at two levels: cultural conflict caused by the colonial educational system and the Western values imposed on Ugandan in particular and Africans in general; and religious conflict caused by the confrontation between Christian missionaries (see **Christianity and Christian missions**) and the African religious leaders. The colonial system of education (see **education and schools**) created a middle class, which became increasingly aware of colonial subjugation and economic exploitation. They sought out ways to gain political freedom from the colonial power. Despite their involvement in nationalism (see **nationalism and postnationalism**) and the anti-colonial movement, the educated class become alienated from the masses after independence. In his poetry, then, Okot is critical both of the colonial power and the

African middle class. His primary targets in all his songs are the political leaders who have brought disunity in the decolonized society through the infighting of the two political parties formed to fight the colonial power. He is also critical of the middle class, which replaced the colonial power at "flag independence" in the early 1960s, for their failure to produce social and economic programs to eradicate ignorance, poverty, and disease.

In his analysis of cultural conflict, Okot identifies the educational system imposed on colonized people as the root cause of this conflict. The individual who goes through the school system eventually turns away from his cultural roots as he acquires more Western values. In *Africa's Cultural Revolution* (1973: Nairobi) Okot describes the process of cultural alienation that he himself went through: "The child that goes to school becomes an exile physically and culturally. This is the first step on the path that leads to power, money and the good life. A life better than that of those who stay behind (in the rural areas)." This is an apt summary of Ocol's progress from village boy to political minister in the newly independent Uganda. It is power, money, and the good life that lead to the conflict between him and his village wife Lawino in both *Song of Lawino* and *Song of Ocol*. Ocol (representative of the educated middle class and whose name translates as "black man") has no moral obligation and social responsibility toward the masses that elected him and his fellow politicians to a position of leadership with all its benefits. In *Song of Ocol*, Ocol laments his blackness, which his colonial mentors have taught him to associate with primitivism, sin, and backwardness. He wants to obliterate all that reminds him of his precolonial or traditional culture. In *Song of Lawino*, the pumpkin that Ocol wants to uproot symbolizes this culture. Not content with attempting to uproot himself from the Acoli culture, he wants to cut himself free from his ancestral spirits too. Thus, Lawino and his relatives are horrified when he threatens to cut down the okango tree and *abila*, which houses the family gods. Lawino blames the Catholic fathers for infusing this self-hatred in Ocol and his class towards their cultural and religious belief systems. In both *Songs*, Okot's criticism of the culturally rootless individuals borders on contempt. He is contemptuous of their degree of submissive dependency on their former colonial masters and the Western values that they aspire to achieve but cannot, as exemplified in Tina, Ocol's modern girlfriend who has displaced Lawino, the lawful wife. Thus, the personal conflict between Ocol and Lawino cannot be resolved, since they believe in differing cultural values.

Okot's criticism of the politicians includes their desperate attempt to shield themselves from the masses that elected them to power. Ocol, in his *Song* (1970: Nairobi), is adamant that the masses must be kept away from them since they are regarded as "trespassers" who "must be jailed/For life ... Disloyal elements/Must be detained without trial." This statement becomes the central theme in *Song of Prisoner*, where we find not one prisoner but a multiple of detained prisoners unified by their plea of not guilty to any of the charges brought against them, trumped-up charges brought by the ruling class to protect its political power and all its benefits. One of the prisoners in the poem is an ex-minister who might have fallen out with his head of state, while the other is a voter who has come to the city to demand a share of the "national cake" from the man whom he voted into power, money, and the good life.

In *Song of Malaya*, the central figure is Malaya (Swahili for prostitute), an honest woman who does not share the hypocrisy of modern society influenced by Western culture and governed by the outmoded moral dictum of "one man, one wife." She knows that a sexless life is incomplete and she therefore criticizes those who want to condemn her to a sexless life. Through Malaya, the poet voices his criticism of the double standards of the church, political, and civic leaders who publicly condemn Malaya and her lot and yet seek her out under the cover of darkness. Okot does not support prostitution as a profession, just as he argues that political assassination is not the answer to the social ills of any country. Nevertheless, he presents the Malaya and the assassin prisoner as rebels against an oppressive social and economic system and the middle class, which is responsible for the creation of this system.

Although Okot was one of the major figures in East African literature and the founder of an influential school of poetry, he remained unknown outside the region for many years largely because his works were available only to local audiences. But he is increasingly being recognized as one of the most innovative poets of the postcolonial era, as an astute student of African culture and religion, and as one of the first poets of his generation to have made rhetorical strategies borrowed from traditional culture to be the basis of a new poetics.

Further reading

Heron, George (1976) *The Poetry of Okot p'Bitek*, London: Heinemann.

Goodwin, Goodwin (1982) *Understanding of African Poetry*, London: Heinemann.

Lindfors, Bernth (1980) *Mazungumzo: Interviews with East African Writers, Publishers, Editors, and Scholars*, Athens, Ohio: Ohio University Press.

Lo Liyong, Taban (1969) *The Last Word*, Nairobi: East African Publishing House.

Okot p'Bitek (1970) *Song of Ocol*, Nairobi: East African Publishing House.

——(1973) *Africa's Cultural Revolution*, Nairobi: Macmillan Books for Africa.

CHARLES OKUMU

Okoumba-Nkoghe, Maurice

b. 1954, Alélé, near Okondja, Gabon

poet and teacher

The poet Okoumba-Nkoghe was born in Alélé, near Okondja, in the province of High Ogooé, Gabon. His secondary education was in Libreville, the capital of the country, and his university studies were completed in France where he obtained a "doctorate of 3rd cycle" in letters. He has been teaching at the University El Hadji Omar Bongo of Libreville since 1983, while also serving as the cultural advisor to the president of Gabon. In literary circles, Okoumba-Nkoghe is primarily known for his poetry, which expresses deep feelings and a phosphorescent sensibility. His poetic talents have been most apparent in his epic poems, such as *Rhône Ogooué* (The Ogooe River) (1980) and *Olende* (1989), but he has also written romantic poems, which have been collected in *Paroles vives écorchées*

(Lively and Sensitive Words) (1979). Okoumba-Nkoghe has also written several novels, the most prominent of which is *La Mouche et la glu* (The Fly and the Flypaper) (1984), treating, like his poems, a variety of subjects including economic deprivation, the conflict of generations, love and politics, using a style that mixes tragedy and satire to comment on contemporary Gabonese society.

OUSMANE BA

Okri, Ben

b. 1959, Minna, Nigeria

novelist and short story writer

The Nigerian novelist and short story writer Ben Okri was born in Minna, a small town in the Delta region of central Nigeria. He spent seven years of his early childhood in England, where his father studied law. The family returned to Lagos, where Okri's father practised among the poor. This provided Okri with first-hand material for his fiction. Ironically, he failed to get a place at a Nigerian university, so he took an unskilled job working in a shop and started publishing his writing in Nigerian women's journals and evening papers. By the time he turned 18, he had completed his first novel, *Flowers and Shadows*; he moved to England when he was 19, in 1978, and studied literature at the University of Essex. He continues to live, read, and write in London.

This early and then long-term relocation away from Africa is somewhat unusual among African writers. But the same time as being much more acculturated by the West than some of his fellow Nigerian writers, Okri's work remains steeped in indigenous images and West African oral forms (see **oral literature and performance**), especially those of Yoruba culture (see **Yoruba literature**), an influence which he has selected and transformed. All of this mixture of experience, culture, and travel contributed to Okri's production of his masterpiece, *The Famished Road*, which won the Booker Prize for 1991, the year of publication, and which remains his most significant achievement. It has been called the classic magical realist novel of

West Africa (see **realism and magical realism**), although that naming has also been contested and debated.

Okri's first novel, *Flowers and Shadows* (1980), is firmly within the tradition of the conventions of realism. It critiques the excesses of the corrupt rich classes governing and plundering newly independent Nigeria. It is obviously a still immature work. His second novel, *The Landscapes Within* (1982), revised and reissued as *Dangerous Love* (1996), covers similar ground. In this early phase of his fiction, Okri does not radically experiment with technique, but nonetheless begins to develop a powerful voice as part of a younger generation of writers, who are maturing and assessing the nation's wounds within a post civil war Nigeria.

It is in his collections of short stories, *Incidents at the Shrine* (1986) and *Stars of the New Curfew* (1988), however, inspired primarily by the horrors of the Nigerian civil war, that we see the beginning of a new phase of Okri's writing. The first collection won the Commonwealth Prize for Africa in 1987. It is in these stories that Okri searches for experimental narrative tools with which to express his social and political vision more forcefully. This technique relies on infringing the boundaries between old and new beliefs, styles, and tales in ways which will serve him well in *The Famished Road*.

The Famished Road is set in the historical reality of Nigeria at a very specific moment of its transformation. Independence from Britain is about to become a reality, along with the construction of modern communications, of roads and cars, photography and electricity. Azaro, the protagonist, lives with his poverty-stricken parents in the slums. Instead of optimism, there is foreboding, and their lives are touched destructively by the corrupt political parties who use dishonest, ruthless, and violent means to try to win support. The story is simultaneously situated in the world of the dream, of the nightmare, of the dead, of those waiting to be born, and crucially, linking up with the circularity of time, of those *abiku* babies, with their repeated deaths and rebirths. Azaro, through whose eyes the bulk of the novel unfolds, is himself an *abiku* baby.

The road of the novel's title refers to many things. It is the danger of curiosity and adventurousness that can kill the restless traveler. It is the degradation of colonialism (see **colonialism, neocolonialism, and postcolonialism**), the African past and the road of life of the universal human condition, and a way into the transformations of the future. What is clear, notwithstanding the labyrinth within which the road symbolism is constructed, is that in Okri's society edges blur between tradition and change, old and new, science and magic. There is no simple linear process of modernization or modernity (see **modernity and modernism**) as the road encroaches on the bush. The spirits dwell as much in the past as in the present, on the road as much as in dreams or the spirit world itself. All of this is in the mode of the magical realist's ironic inversion of reality, where the spirits are a routine part of the mundane everyday, and electric light, gramophones, and photography constitute the awesome and the unbelievable.

The Famished Road is profoundly influenced by Yoruba stories, which have been harnessed, manipulated, and transformed. It warns against the abandonment of ancient wisdoms, but through the eyes of a migrant, a diaspora writer (see **diaspora and pan-Africanism**) based in London, who views Nigeria ironically through the long lens of his magical telescope. The photographer in the novel is an enigmatic, autobiographical, migrant figure on the margins.

Okri has not yet managed to build on the extraordinary achievement of The Famished Road and appears to be stuck in a groove. His two sequels to The Famished Road, Songs of Enchantment (1993) and Infinite Riches (1998), seem to meander through much of the same landscape, without the force of innovation and energy of discovery of the first of the trilogy. The fiction becomes trapped in the labyrinth of its own formula when repeated in this way, or, as in the revised Astonishing the Gods (1995), the development of the narrative structure has been almost entirely abandoned.

In addition to his stories, novels, and fables, Okri has produced a volume of poetry, An African Elegy (1992), a long poem, Mental Fight (1999), and two collections of essays, Birds of Heaven (1995) and A Way of Being Free (1997).

Further reading

Cooper, B. (1998) Magical Realism in West African Fiction: Seeing with a Third Eye, London: Routledge.

Ogunsanwo, O. (1995) "Intertextuality and Post-Colonial Literature in Ben Okri's The Famished Road," Research in African Literatures 26, 1: 30–9.

Quayson, A. (1997) Strategic Transformations in Nigerian Writing, Oxford: James Currey.

BRENDA COOPER

Omotoso, Kole

b. 1943, Akure, Western Nigeria

novelist, short story writer, dramatist, and critic

Resident in South Africa since the 1990s, the Nigerian novelist, short story writer, dramatist, and critic was born in Akure in Western Nigeria and was educated in Nigeria and British universities where he specialized in Arabic and French. He has taught at the Obafemi Awolowo University in Nigeria and the University of Western Cape and Grahamstown University in South Africa. He is a prolific and acclaimed African writer, one of the most widely published of the "second generation" of Nigerian novelists. His earlier works include The Edifice (1971), a novel on interracial relations, The Combat (1972), a novel of the Nigerian civil war, and a series of novels and plays (Sacrifice, 1974, Memories of Our Recent Boom, 1982, and Just Before Dawn, 1988) dealing with the crisis of postcolonial society and politics (see **colonialism, neocolonialism, and postcolonialism**), especially the misadventure of a self-destructing Nigerian polity.

His more recent works have included essays on the crisis of modern African societies and cultures – Season of Migration to the South: Africa's Crises Reconsidered (1994) – and plays that are critical of the subjugation of marginalized groups by powerful capitalist interests: Open Space: Six Contemporary Plays from Africa (1995), Woza Africa (1997), and Yes and No to the Freedom Charter (2001).

ZODWA MOTSA

Onwuchekwa, Julie

b. Nigeria

writer and lecturer

Julie Onwuchekwa is a lecturer in the Department of Special Education at the University of Ibadan. She could best be described as an industrious enthusiast who, though not in the field of Igbo studies, has contributed immensely to the development and growth of **Igbo literature** through her works of fiction in the Igbo language. During her undergraduate studies, she took some courses in Igbo language and literature which spontaneously kindled her interest in Igbo studies, an interest she has continued to sustain. This early interest has metamorphosed into two major literary works, a novel entitled *Chinaagorom* (My God is My Defender) (1979) and a book of poems *Akpaala Okwu* (Book of Igbo Verse) (n.d.). They are both didactic and moral-oriented in nature, reflecting Onwuchekwa's moral preoccupations and social commitments as a writer.

Critics have described Onwuchekwa as a feminist Igbo writer. This is partly because of the subject matter of her works, but mainly because of her manner of handling the events and characters in her fictional works. She essentially strives to champion the cause of gender or womanhood in the Igbo culture through her writing (see **gender and sexuality**). In *Chinaagorom*, for example, she portrays the travails of the educated woman in the midst of uneducated people in a rural setting. But womanhood triumphs because of inner strength, intellectual prowess, and unfailing feminine intuition. In the poems in her collection, *Akpaala Okwu*, the qualities of feminine beauty, judgement, and resilience are portrayed in all of life's situations, including tragedies. Onwuchekwa draws from the rich oral heritage to add relevance and vitality to her creativity. *Chinaagorom* is very popular with readers and has helped to establish Onwuchekwa as a contemporary female Igbo writer of great promise.

ERNEST EMENYONU

Onwueme, Osonye Tess

b. 1955, Ogwashi-Ugwu, Delta state, Nigeria

dramatist

Nigerian-born dramatist Tess Onwueme has established herself as one of the leading African female playwrights in Africa, Europe and North America today. She has a BA and MA in drama from the University of Ife, Nigeria, and a PhD from the University of Benin, Nigeria. She has published nearly fifteen plays, several critical essays on African drama and women's writing, and a collection of short stories, *Why the Elephant Has No Butt* (2000). She has taught at Nigerian and American universities, and is currently the Distinguished Professor of Cultural Diversity and Professor of English at the University of Eau Claire, Wisconsin. In 2000, she received a Ford Foundation research grant for her project, "Who Can Silence the Drums? Delta Women Speak!" which examines the lives of rural women of the oil-producing regions of the Niger Delta in Nigeria. Her play, *Then She Said It* (2002) is a product of that project.

Her plays explore the experiences of Nigerians and people of African diasporic descent, addressing topics such as slavery and the connections between Africans and their descendants in the Caribbean and the United States. According to Onwueme, many Africans on the continent have forgotten or do not know about slavery and need to be re-educated to help them remember their stories. *The Missing Face* (2002) and *Riot in Heaven* (1997) are representative of her attempt to activate the repressed memory of slavery to uncover the silences over the experience.

Onwueme is also an advocate for women, particularly Nigeria's rural women, whom she describes as those "who have the 'power to make and unmake the land' " (*Tell It to Women*, 1997: Detroit). Several of her plays are women-centered and explore how certain cultural practices, class, gender, national and global politics disenfranchise women. To give women voice, she creates combatant female characters who fight their subordination. Examples are Wazobia in *The Reign* of *Wazobia* (1993), recently adapted into film as *Wazobia* (2002) and Oshun, Obida, Koko, Niger, and Benue in *Then She Said It*. Although Onwueme's plays are about women, she does not vilify men. She is equally critical of women like Ruth and Daisy in *Tell It to Women* who subordinate or help to oppress other women. Consequently, Onwueme insists that women must unite to empower themselves.

Clearly, Onwueme has established herself as one of Africa's most prolific and engaged playwrights. Each of her plays seduces the audience out of its complacency, asking it to probe and critique a variety of historical, social and political concerns at communal, national, international levels. These plays contribute to larger national, African and pan-African or international discussions of culture, gender, race, history, and politics.

Works cited

Onwueme, Osonye Tess (1997) *Tell It to Women*, Detroit: Wayne State University Press.
——(2002) *Then She Said It*, Detroit: Wayne State University Press.

MAUREEN N. EKE

Opperman, D.J.

b. 1914, District of Dundee, South Africa; d. 1985, Stellenbosch, South Africa

academic, poet, and writer

Opperman played an influential role in **Afrikaans literature** as professor at the universities of Cape Town and Stellenbosch for thirty years, a mentor of budding poets, and a reviewer for publishers. He received numerous prizes and four honorary doctorates. His anthologies, especially *Groot Verseboek* (Big Book of Poems) (1951) determined the Afrikaans poetry canon for decades. Opperman was born and bred in KwaZulu-Natal, but moved to the Cape in 1946. Zulu and Indian cultures were strong influences in his work, especially apparent in his debut *Heilige beeste* (Holy Cows) (1945). His other eight poetry volumes include *Negester oor*

Ninevé (Ninestar over Nineva) (1947), *Joernaal van Jorik* (Jorik's Journal) (1949), *Engel uit die klip* (Angel from the Rock) (1950), *Blom en baaierd* (Flowers and Chaos) (1956), *Dolosse* (Throwing the Bones) (1963) and *Komas uit 'n bamboesstok* (Comas from a Bamboo Cane) (1970), with Marco Polo's journey as intertext. His uncompleted *Sonklong oor Afrika* (Boy of the Sun in Africa) was published posthumously in 2000. Opperman engaged intertextually with world literature, often working from the concrete South African landscape to a metaphysical level. In his three verse dramas, historical figures such as W.A. van der Stel (*Vergelegen* (Faraway) 1956), the Voortrekkers (*Voëlvry* (Outlawed) 1968), and a Greek titan (*Periandros van Korinthe*, 1954) are the "vehicles" through which his metaphysical concerns are expressed.

Further reading

Kannemeyer, J.C. (1986) *D.J. Opperman*, Cape Town: Human and Rousseau.

ENA JANSEN

Oraka, Louis Nnamdi

b. 1945, Nigeria

historian and linguist

Louis Nnamdi Oraka, the Nigerian historian and linguist, is a senior lecturer at Ebonyi State University in Ebonyi state, Nigeria. His interest in Igbo language and culture started with his membership in the Society for Promoting Igbo Language and Culture (SPILC). This interest evolved into a commitment to and vocation in Igbo language studies. His *Foundations of Igbo Studies* is a major resource and reference book frequently cited by scholars and teachers in the field of Igbo studies. Oraka has written and collaborated in writing a number of Igbo language texts for the Nigerian school system. His *Igbo Ndi Oma* (Igbo Primer) is widely used in primary schools.

Oraka has published one highly successful novel, *Ahubara Eze Ama* (Kings Bear No Royal Marks at Birth) (1975). The novel is very popular with teachers and students at all levels of the school system. It is also popular with the general public. The theme of the novel is mainly responsible for its popularity. Exploiting the proverbial "from grass to grace" motif, Oraka tells the story of a poor man, Okonkwo, who rises from "ashes" to opulence through the dint of hard labor, courage in the face of devastating odds, and perseverance through life's harsh vicissitudes. These are virtues cultivated in traditional or precolonial Igbo society because they hold out the hope that hard work and patience are the raw materials for success and greatness. The reader reads such stories believing inwardly that he or she could achieve greatness by following the examples of those who have achieved greatness because they ventured. It becomes more attractive when the greatness is achieved after suffering and abject poverty.

In the preface to the novel, the author admonishes the reader to heed the truism that "no condition is permanent in life." No one knows what a child may grow up to become, nor can anyone rule out the possibility of a poor man today becoming a rich king tomorrow. There are no identity marks for future kings and queens. The author warns also that when a person is rich, countless friends cluster around him or her, but many of them sooner or later turn out simply to be no more than "fair-weather friends." This type of didactic and highly moralistic story was very popular in the Igbo oral tradition (see **oral literature and performance**). When recaptured in the pages of a modern novel or drama, the reception is no less effective. Thus, with his very first novel Oraka hit the right chords for the right ears.

ERNEST EMENYONU

oral literature and performance

Introduction

Despite the ravages of slavery and colonialism (see **colonialism, neocolonialism, and postcolonialism**) on Africa's political, economic and social systems, the continent's cultures and aesthetic sensibilities remain independent and vibrant, particularly in the orally based forms of cultural expression. Although African societies have developed writing traditions, Africans are primarily an oral people, and it is that tradition that has dominated the cultural forms created on the continent. Artistic expression plays an important role in the lives of African peoples, providing a forum for participation in the community and for exploring the mysteries of humanity. Orature means something passed on through the spoken word, and because it is based on the spoken language it comes to life only in a living community. Where community life fades away, orality loses its function and dies. It needs people in a living social setting; it needs life itself. Thus orature grows out of tradition, and keeps tradition alive.

African orature is a development of a complex literary genre that demands the establishment of its own aesthetics for its interpretation and evaluation. Orature is a strategic communal tool for non-literate societies in their consolidation and socialization processes, and its spoken nature guarantees its widest circulation. Unlike written literature, orature has unfixed boundaries, which gives it greater freedom in its execution and interpretation – it can thus be used to praise and criticize those in power. The principal execution of orature is by performance, which combines sound, action, and meaning. Performance brings to the fore and concretizes the interaction among the principals of text, medium, performer, and audience so that an utterance can most adequately be interpreted and evaluated within the context of the total performance. African oral forms include ritual, divining/healing, folk tales, myths, legends, and song and dance.

Genres of oral literature

Oral traditions can be divided stylistically into those transmitted in a stereotypical way and those transmitted freely, changing with differences of time, place, and individual speakers. The first category includes traditions that function in ritual and cult, such as invocations, incantations, funeral songs, praise songs, etc. Language in this category is highly stylized, and meter and rhythm are more important than conceptual coherence because in traditional society every word is charged with a particular force. The second category includes stories and legends of the origin of man's institutions, as well as stories told for didactic purposes and for entertainment. Myths and legends are concepts and beliefs about the early history of a race, or explanations of natural events, such as the seasons, handed down from olden times. They are a people's search for meaning: concepts of the human mind, creations of man invented to give meaning and purpose to the enigma that is called life on earth and to explain the phenomena of nature, events, and human behavior. Thus myths are burdened with all that cannot be explained except by divine intervention: they reconcile man to the human condition and reveal the conditions and problems, social and personal, that people face in life.

Epics, as an example of legends, are poetic accounts of the deeds of great heroes and heroines, or of a nation's past history orally transmitted as well as performed in a ceremonial context. The most frequently cited examples of African epics are Sunjata in West Africa, Shaka in South Africa, Mwindo in Central Africa, and Liongo in East Africa. The Sunjata epic is performed in the septennial Kamabolon ceremony in Kingaba, Mali. The ceremony is performed in the Kamanolon sanctuary – a traditional hut with colorful paintings on which a new roof has been restored the night before. The occasion determines the length of the performance, some allowing elaborate embellishment of the text, and others, more formal ones, being more restrictive under the assumption that the elaborations (stories) are already known to the audience. Sunjata and Mwindo ceremonies may last for several days, and may be regarded as a re-creation of society: they have the function of inaugurating a new generation since the young generation is responsible for most of the ritual labor, such as restoring the walls of the sanctuary.

Folk tales are popular stories ingrained in people's minds, memories which are centuries old and testify to a core of truth handed down orally from generation to generation. Themes of folk tales may range from the creation, people's relationship with the universe, the origin of disease, witchcraft, marriage and family, and human relationship with animals. Tales are important because they give useful insights into psychological understanding of the communities that produced them; they are a manifestation of the human condition (predicament) and human imagination, and much of modern literature (and thinking) is based on them. The art of storytelling is such an important aspect of African life that most societies have an animal character as the designated teller of tales. Among the Akan in West Africa the traditional storyteller is Anansi the Spider; among the Chewa in Central Africa it is Nadzikambe the Chameleon; and among the Zulu in South Africa it is Fudukazi the Tortoise.

By its very nature, orality tends to simplify the structure of leadership in society, and by doing so manages to present issues to the audience in a very powerful way. Since orature has a social and political function in society, oral texts can only be understood and interpreted within their wider political and social contexts. African oral forms seem to have fairly recurring common themes, such as sibling rivalry, exile and the prodigal son, corruption at court, return of exile, restoration of order, kindness and generosity, respect for the weak/elderly/parents, mysterious birth, orphanage, etc. The distinctive organizing motifs in African orature include journey, departure, moral decay, corruption of home, obstacle and triumph, return, restoration, etc. Genealogy or the mention of a list of ancestors from whom the hero descends is a very important part of oral histories. Specialized language is used to communicate experiences and concerns, life events, human struggles that orature articulates, and such language exhibits artistic beauty in content and draws its power from specific linguistic features, such as alliteration, repetition, rhyme, rhythm, mnemonic, ideophone, antithesis, parallelism, assonance, allegory, euphemism, and synecdoche. These devices not only make the expression unusual but also make it also appealing and therefore easily remembered. Where there is a combination of form and content, the artistic expression is born and literature is created. Women dominate the artistic mastering of language during courting, wedding, and the telling of folk tales and stories, when the grandmother becomes the immediate teacher in the use of carefully chosen language.

Apart from epics, folk tales, and legends, song and dance is also a distinctive feature of African orality, and African musical culture and its fusion with various modern forms such as jazz, choral, and gospel singing has produced a unique sound and a major export for the continent. The musical event provides a useful departure point for a discussion of other African art forms such as instrument design, masks, and costume that are part of dance performance. In African practice there is no divide between music and dance, since music and movement constitute an integrated form of expression. Music mirrors a culture's social and political arrangements and protocols, and it provides the accompaniment for an individual's rites of passage throughout life. Because histories are kept and recited by specialist performers, people throughout Africa maintain and transmit fundamentally similar values in their expressions of the oral-aesthetic. The size of the continent means that Africa is a land of diversity of cultures in many forms, sometimes related, sometimes diametrically opposed. Thus, in contrast to the highly rhythmic instrumental music from Central and West Africa, southern Africa has vocal music that, under the influence of missionary-taught hymns, has taken on the form of simple Western harmony. The social dynamics have resulted in both the flourishing of some music and the struggle of others to survive.

Performance as a genre

Performance is a contested concept with no agreed-upon definition and calls into question conventional understanding of tradition, repetition, mechanical reproduction, and ontological definitions of social order and reality. African oral performance forms include mimic, narrative, and music and dance. In narrative, the element of narration, of addressing an audience directly, interspersed with mime of significant episodes from the narrative, is a central element of this category of performance, particularly to a largely illiterate and rural audience where orality is the principal means of communication. Narrative is the representation of an event or sequence of events, real or fictitious, by means of language. But orality also bridges the divide between spirit and flesh, and even between the present and the eternal. Thus the funeral dirges and dances will often range from expressions of grief to joyous sounds and fertility

dances, so transforming the trauma of confronting death into a celebration of life for the benefit of those still living.

Performance is not only an enabling facilitator in the duality of communication to the body and soul, but also an important dimension of culture as well as an indicator of how knowledge about culture is produced and utilized. It is the primary site for the production of knowledge, and the place where multiple and often simultaneous discourses are employed. It is a means by which society reflects on its current condition, on the members' relationship with each other and their environment. It enables people to define and/or reinvent themselves and their society and either reinforce, resist, or subvert prevailing social orders. In performance, subversion and legitimization can emerge in the same utterance or act.

The earlier studies of performance in Africa have been from a structuralist paradigm pioneered by scholars like Gluckman and Victor Turner. Victor Turner's (1982) theory on performance is based on his social drama model that projects traditional ceremony as not only articulating and reasserting bonds between members of the community, but also simultaneously expressing underlying tensions within society. Social drama, according to Turner, is a process-based structured public action composed of four phases: (1) break of social relations; (2) crisis, when people position themselves as antagonists in relation to each other; (3) redress action to resolve the crisis; (4) either reintegration of contending parties or schism. Turner claims that the major genres of cultural performance (from ritual to theater and film) and narration (from myth to the novel) not only originate in the social drama but also continue to draw meaning and force from it (1986). But Turner's anthropological approach to the study of performance lacks political, contextual and resistance analysis since performance is necessarily a metaphor for social meaning.

Current studies approach performance as an agency for social/political action. This presupposes three things: (1) text; (2) the agency (i.e. space, medium); and (3) resistance or opposition (i.e. performance). A functional framework situates performance, like all forms of cultural work, in an embedded resistance mode, replacing aesthetics as the primary concern. Orality and performance have to be approached from a balanced perspective that avoids projecting orality as a fossilized artifact, or the performer and audience as passive, disengaged bystanders. Thus performance is viewed from process paradigm which is temporal, participatory, and interactive. By focusing on the specific performers, there is also a shift from the narrative timeless to the time-centered, particular, and historically situated – in other words, a shift from structure to process. Something that clearly emerges from the African creative process is the multidimensional nature of performance, founded on the interplay between the forces of narrative, rhythm, and dance. The African oral literary traditions reveal the great variety and depth of imaginative expression with which African languages sustain the creative activities of African societies. Performances of song lyrics, for example, are subtly variable in nuance and style, sensitive to content and occasion, and intimately dependent on the performer's rapport with his/her audience. In this sense, oral performance is a collective enterprise rather than an individualistic one.

In oral performances specific texts are recited, although only a few individuals may know the actual words in the text, and the style and manner of the recitation of the text may differ with individual performer and occasion. Because performance styles vary, no two oral performances and their narratives ever contain exactly the same material, and this may result in textual variation of the "ultimate version" of an oral text. For this reason, the manner of performance is often more important than the content. Although performance is inseparable from its context of use, verbal art can be treated as self-contained, bounded objects separable from their social and cultural contexts of production and reception, and decontextualized and recontextualized. Oral performance involves public rendition because the most memorable performances are done at large events before a substantial audience. The performer is usually given enough space at the performance site to allow movement and interaction with other participants, whether it is within a fireside circle or an open public arena where the performer may be required to walk up and down. The language is usually in a highly stylized poetic form, rendered in

chant rather than ordinary speaking voice and accompanied by rhythmic body movements. Thus words and action complement each other in oral performance.

Oral performance in society

In African societies cultural production and aesthetics become associated with specific oral performers, such as the griot as oral historian among the Mandika in West Africa, and the imbongi as praise poet among the Nguni in southern Africa. In all these cultural practices, initiates are trained, within their cultural environment, by more experienced performers who provide the model and supervise the rehearsals. A potential performer may be recognized as such from early childhood, and may then be entrusted to an experienced performer from whom he or she learns the traditional way of presenting the art form. The initiate and experienced performer may train and rehearse in relative seclusion before the trainee can perform in public. During training the trainee learns the appropriate voice qualities and movements for effective performance, learns how to posture, what language to use, and what costume to wear at what occasion. The careful training of the performers and the close supervision of the performance by elders of the culture ensure that variation in texts from different periods and by different performers is limited. The presence of and supervision by elders also gives the performance prestige and stability. Sex and age of the performer may determine the style of the performance; younger performers tend to be more vigorous than older ones. Thus the fact that the performer belongs to a particular sex, age, and social group influences his/her performance and its reception by the audience.

Performance is generated through, participated in, and shaped by the community and its needs. Apart from providing entertainment for the community, the performances of the various oral forms have also a social purpose. Weddings, for example, are performed to elaborate the continuation of the community, while epic and praise poetry are performed to record the history of the community and urge courage and endurance. Oral performance also plays a religious role, becoming a medium of communication between the living and the dead. Ceremonies can be held involving the whole family when oral performance is used as an appeal or prayer to the ancestors, sometimes with some offering and/or sacrifice. Thus, performance can become an intermediary between the ancestors and the people present. In healing, performance is not just a process to cure the invalid of his/her ailment, but an entertainment for the village audience. So although it is true that such performance is meant as a link to the absent ancestors and to symbolic time, it is also performed for the present village audience, with emphasis on its relevance to their current situation and experience, usually as indicated by the accompanying lyrics. Because the healer is also an entertainer, in interpreting the text the whole social context of the performance must be understood, since the actor is performing within the confines of space, time, and social context which determine the form of the performance and gives it its meaning.

The functional orientation of African orality is absent from most of modern Western theater. African performance can be a way of expressing public opinion, and as such provides an effective means of social control, for the recitations are in the public arena and are shouted out for all to hear. This function of oral performance in the legitimation of power in the constant power struggles involving forms of rule explains the logic of its organization, the material justification of each situation, and why some performances are peculiarly male or female. The structure and function of the oral performance institution is highly flexible and adaptable, and the performer's qualities include the ability to adapt to the immediate sociopolitical environment. Since performance can be used for social maintenance, social identity, and re-creation of society with the corroboration of the political content, it can easily be abused by those with money and power, creating tension for the performers and raising a serious question about their credibility. The performer's position in the community relies on his/her ability to gauge the political current in that community and the power structure, to extemporize and compose, and to use the aesthetics of persuasion to sway audiences with his/her performance.

Oral performance is also an important instrument in the educational system, for not only does it act as an incentive to and reward for socially approved actions, but also its recital is a reminder to all present of what qualities and conduct are praiseworthy. It re-establishes communal values and discourages individual tendencies by keeping the oral tradition not only a "secret" known to the few initiated, but also a group "heritage," communally owned. In orature and performance, focus is on the collective, on group action, and the performer is always surrounded, encouraged, prompted, and accompanied – the performer is never alone on the stage.

The most defining feature of African orature and performance is the close and intense interaction between performer and audience actualized in the traditional multi-part organization of voices: the call-and-response aesthetic relationship that is also manifested in clapping hands, snapping fingers, whistling, stomping feet, and other body movements. In song performance, for example, the chorus is divided into two voice parts, each of which recites a different text. The temporal relationship between these parts is governed by the principle of non-simultaneous entry, in such a way that the narrator's "calling" phrase is followed by the chorus "response," the two voices alternating throughout the performance. The voice of the lead singer who introduces the song is allowed to intermingle with the melody provided by the chorus, thus foregrounding the melodious nature of the lyric that dominates the rhythm of the song. The employment of melodious language enables listeners themselves to work through the words of the song to attain the meaning behind them.

Thus the African oral aesthetic event brings the principle of creation into play in a variety of forms: in the interplay between spirit and flesh, in the antiphonal patterns of sound between leader and chorus, and in the audio-visual integration of music and dance. Through call-and-response, the spontaneous interaction of the audio and the visual, the oral-aesthetic event becomes a creative transition that takes place within each person participating and among the group as a whole. Call-and-response also establishes and reinforces social and political order within the community since each member contributes a note or phrase at predetermined points in a performance, reflecting their decentralized system of consensus and the inter-dependence that is necessary for group success. Call-and-response is not just an opening and closing device, it is also meant to enlist audience participation in the performance.

Further reading

Hale, Thomas (1990) *Scribe, Griot, and Novelist*, Gainesville, Florida: University of Florida Press.

Okpewho, Isidore (1979) *The Epic in Africa*, New York: Columbia Press.

——(1992) *African Oral Literature*, Bloomington: Indiana University Press.

Turner, Victor W. (c.1982) *From Ritual to Theatre: The Human Seriousness of Play*, New York: Performing Arts Journal Publications.

——(1986) *The Anthropology of Performance*, New York: PAJ Publications.

LUPENGA MPHANDE

Osadebay, Dennis Chukude

b. 1911, Asaba, Nigeria; d. 1994, Nigeria

poet and politician

Dennis Osadebay was a pioneer of both African nationalism (see **nationalism and post-nationalism**) and poetry in English. He was one of the founders of the National Council of Nigeria and the Western Cameroon and served as premier of the Mid West region of Nigeria from 1963 until the first military coup in 1966. Osadebay started writing poetry when he went to study law in England in the 1930s, and his verse was collected in the 1952 collection entitled *Africa Sings*. Like most early African poetry in English, Osadebay's poetry relied heavily on English models while at the same time trying to capture his experiences as a colonized African trying to balance the claims of tradition and custom with the realities of modernity. One of Osadebay's most anthologized poems, "Young Africa's Plea," echoes the sentiments of cultural nationalism dominant in the 1930s and 1940s: it is a call to European

readers to recognize the humanity of Africans and their desire for freedom.

SIMON GIKANDI

Osofisan, Femi

b. 1946, Erunwon, Western Nigeria

playwright

Femi Osofisan is one of the most prominent and controversial playwrights to have emerged in Nigeria after the civil war. He has published over twenty plays and a similar number exist in unpublished scripts. In both their themes and form, his works represent a radical engagement with themes of postcolonial disillusionment and failure, but also a self-conscious engagement, rewriting, and deconstruction of the first generation of Nigerian playwrights. In fact, it is difficult to understand Osofisan's work outside the emergence of a postcolonial culture (see **colonialism, neocolonialism, and postcolonialism**) defined by the corruption of political institutions, the displacement of social and cultural life, and violence. In Nigeria, the moment that came to define this culture was the civil war, which broke out soon after Osofisan arrived at the University of Ibadan to study drama. As many commentators have argued, the aftermath of the war provided the themes that have come to be associated with Osofisan's work, themes such as the collapse of social institutions and the emergence of a polity driven by crude materialism and the negation of basic moral and social values.

In engaging with these themes, Osofisan was undoubtedly responding to the crisis that the postcolonial ruling class had imposed on his generation. At the same time, however, his response to the crisis of postcolonialism in Nigeria was driven by the feeling that the first generation of African writers had not adequately developed new forms of writing to respond to this crisis. Osofisan's works are unique in their intertextual relation to the works of the major Nigerian playwrights of the 1960s, most notably Wole **Soyinka**, J.P. **Clark-Bekederemo**, and Ola **Rotimi**. But in writing works that countered the tradition of Nigerian drama, Osofisan was also acknowledging his own debt to his predecessors.

But it would be an error to see Osofisan's works as simply emerging under the anxiety of influence of his powerful predecessors. His works echo the texts of an older generation of Nigerian playwrights, but he has brought to his drama his own unique background, which marks him as a different playwright even in regard to those writers, most notably Soyinka, who have influenced him most. For one, Osofisan was orphaned early in his life and he grew up destitute in the Yoruba countryside (see **Yoruba literature**). This background provided him with unique insight into the inequalities that were to trouble Nigerian society in the postcolonial period, and it perhaps explains his interest in class as a social structure. At the same time, this underprivileged rural background meant that Osofisan grew up in close contact with the beliefs and practices of traditional Yoruba social life. In spite of his underprivileged background, however, Osofisan's writing career was, like those of many African writers, determined by the institutions of education (see **education and schools**). Indeed, it was through his education that Osofisan encountered the world of other Nigerian writers. Like Soyinka, he was educated at Government School, Ibadan, and the University of Ibadan, where he studied in the school of drama. At Ibadan, Osofisan studied French, with particular interest in the works of the tradition of absurdist drama associated with writers such as Artaud, Sartre, and Beckett, the same writers who had influenced the young Soyinka at the same university a generation earlier. Soyinka was in jail or exile when Osofisan was an undergraduate at Ibadan, but his long shadow could still be felt at the school of drama. Indeed, Osofisan started his dramatic career acting with groups associated with Soyinka.

When Soyinka returned from exile in the early 1970s, Osofisan was already doing graduate work at Ibadan, but he was to work with Soyinka in the first production of the latter's first postwar play, *Madmen and Specialists* (1970). But the impact of Soyinka on Osofisan's work has not come solely from the direction of influence, but also from one of opposition and interrogation. As a lecturer at the University of Ife after the completion of a PhD on

West African drama, Osofisan was part of a group of young radical intellectuals associated with *Positive Review*, a Marxist journal of society and culture whose major target was Soyinka and what they considered to be the absence of social commitment in his plays and his use of mythology as a form of mystification. It was in a lively atmosphere of debate on the nature of literature and society and social responsibility that Osofisan wrote his major plays.

These plays can generally be classified into four categories. The first category includes those works that he has written as forms of intervention into the debate on the responsibilities of the intellectual in society. The earliest and most prominent example here is *The Oriki of a Grasshopper* (1995), a one-act play that explores the dilemma faced by a radical intellectual who is increasingly alienated from the political elite. In this play, the influence of minimalist and absurdist theater, especially Beckett's *Waiting for Godot*, is apparent. A second category includes plays that are both controversial and populist works, most notably *Esu and the Vagabond Minstrels* (1991) and *Once Upon a Robber* (1982), in which Osofisan tries to use the shock effects borrowed from the absurdist tradition to force his audience into an uncomfortable engagement with topical issues such as official corruption and armed robbery. A third category includes plays that can be characterized as historical because they are based on episodes from Yoruba history. In *The Chattering and the Song* (1977), Osofisan dramatizes an eighteenth-century revolt against the Yoruba King Abiodun; in *Moroundtodun* (1982), he retells the legend of Moremi, the legendary woman warrior who used her femininity to infiltrate the enemy of the Yoruba. While Osofisan uses legends or historical traditions from the Yoruba tradition, his concern is to question the popular and official views of historical figures and, in some cases, to revise the dominant views of Yoruba history and historiography. More significantly, Osofisan's historical plays echo other, earlier attempts to interrogate the representation of history in African literature. In its critique of the nation's aborted desire for a usable past and in his use of two timeframes, *The Chattering and the Song* almost seems to take off from Soyinka's *A Dance of the Forest*.

The fourth category in Osofisan's oeuvre is the

set of overtly intertextual plays in which he tries to subvert the central and celebrated themes in the works of his predecessors. *No More the Wasted Breed* (1982) takes on the theme of the scapegoat popularized by Soyinka's *The Strong Breed* (1969) and questions the latter's privileging of the heroic figure who embodies transcendental value; *Another Raft* (1988) parodies and reverses J.P. Clark-Bekederemo's classic play, *The Raft* (1964). Ultimately, it is in its intertextual relationship with other Nigerian texts that Osofisan's drama comes to represent the emergence of a new tradition of African theater, for while the playwright's textual references are to the whole field of African drama, from Shakespeare to the French absurdists, his works acknowledge an often forgotten aspect of what has come to be known as the postcolonial generations of African writers – that their works are not just reactions to the condition of political failure in Africa, but also attempts to locate a new kind of African writing in relation to a by now established canon of writing on the continent.

Further reading

Irele, Abiola (1995) "Introduction," to Femi Osofisan, *The Oriki of a Grasshopper and Other Plays*, Washington, DC: Howard University Press.

Osofisan, Femi (1995) *The Oriki of a Grasshopper and Other Plays*, Washington, DC: Howard University Press.

Richards, Sandra (1996) *Ancient Songs Set Ablaze: The Theater of Femi Osofisan*, Washington, DC: Howard University Press.

SIMON GIKANDI

Osuagwu, Bertram Iwunwa Nkemgemedi

b. 1937, Mbieri, near Owerri, Nigeria

teacher and writer

Dr Bertram Iwunwa Nkemgemedi Osuagwu, a teacher by profession, is associate professor (reader) in the Department of Nigerian Languages at the Alvan Ikoku College of Education, Owerri, in Imo state, Nigeria. He started very early to write and publish in the Igbo language. His first known published work was a piece, *Onyeije na Onyeakuko*, literally "A Traveler and a Storyteller," published in a student magazine, *Mbieri Chronicle*, at the University of Nigeria, Nsukka, in 1965. In 1974, Dr Osuagwu founded the Department of Igbo Language and Culture at the Alvan Ikoku College of Education, Owerri, making it the first ever full-fledged department of Igbo studies to be established in the Nigerian tertiary education system. Over the past three decades he has trained and produced countless students of Igbo language and literature for all levels of the Nigerian educational system.

Dr Osuagwu has written, edited, and co-authored over three dozen publications in the past three decades. His first book, a play, *Nwa Ngwii Puo Eze* (An Orphan Soon Grows Teeth to Bite His/Her Benefactor) (1977), was a set text for Igbo drama for the West African Examinations Council (WAEC). The play is an examination of the paradox of human philanthropy, where an orphan matures to bite the very fingers that fed him. It remains popular reading inside and outside formal classrooms in Nigeria. Osuagwu's other creative works include *Egwuruegwu Igbo Abuo* (Igbo Plays) (1977), *Ndi Igbo na Omenala ha* (The Igbo and Their Customs) (1978), *Akuuwa Na Uka Akpara Akpa* (Wealth versus Honor) (1977), *Soro M Chia* (Come and Laugh with Me) (1982), and *Nkem Ejee America* (Nkem Goes to America) (2001). He has also published Igbo language texts for the school system. These include *Asusu Igbo Na Koleji A Na-Azu Ndi Nkuzi* (Igbo for Schools and Colleges) (1979), *Igbo Ndi Koleji* (Igbo for Teacher Training Colleges) (1980), and a science book in Igbo, *Akwukwo Sayensi* (1985), *Fundamentals of Linguistics* (1997), and *Igbo Metalanguage* (2001). In 1999 he co-authored *Omeokachie Omenuko*, a biography of Pita Nwana, the legendary author of the Igbo pioneer novel, *Omenuko* (1933). Osuagwu's greatest contribution lies in his stringent efforts in the last three decades to raise the level of learning and teaching of Igbo language, literature, and culture in Nigerian tertiary institutions.

ERNEST EMENYONU

Osundare, Niyi

b. 1947, Nigeria

poet

Niyi Osundare is generally regarded as the leading poet of the generation of Nigerian poets which emerged after the civil war. His first volume of poems, *Songs of the Marketplace* (1983), signaled the new orientation of his poetry in its title. In "Poetry Is", the opening "manifesto" poem of this collection, Osundare enunciates the guiding principle of his poetry through a series of binary oppositions, which define what poetry is against what it should not be. Poetry, he says, is "not a learned quiz/ entombed in Grecoroman lore"; rather, poetry is "the hawker's ditty/the eloquence of the gong/the lyric of the marketplace" (1983: Ibadan). Having so clearly defined the objectives of his poetry early in his career, his subsequent volumes of poetry have, among other things, been devoted to realizing these goals. Beginning with *Village Voices* (1984) and then from *The Eye of the Earth* (1986) to his experimentation with newspaper poetry, Osundare's imaginative deployment of the oral tradition to serve his sociopolitical, ethical, and ecological purposes has been the hallmark of his poetry.

Works cited

Osundare, N. (1983) *Songs of the Marketplace*, Ibadan: New Horn Press.

Further reading

Ezenwa-Ohaeto (1998) "Patterns of Orality: Niyi Osundare," in Ezenwa-Ohaeto, *Contemporary Nigerian Poetry and the Poetics of Orality*, Bayreuth: Bayreuth African Studies Series, pp. 151–68.

HARRY GARUBA

Ouane, Ibrahim Mamadou

b. 1907, Mali

writer

Although he is primarily know for his earlier novel

L'Énigme du Macina (The Enigma of Macina)(1952), Ibrahim Mamadou Ouane is also an established poet, having published *Pérégrinations soudanaises* (Peregrinations in Old Mali) (1960) and *Les Filles de la reine Cléopâtre* (The Daughters of Queen Cleopatra)(1961). He is also an essayist concerned with law and religion in such works as *L'Islam et la civilisation française* (Islam and the French Civilization)(1957), *La Pratique du droit musulman* (Practice of Islamic Law), *Le Principe du droit musulman* (Principle of Islamic Law), and *Lettres d'un Africain* (Letters of an African). In his novella, *Fadimâtâ, la princesse du désert suivi de drame de Déguembéré* (Fadimâtâ, Princess of the Desert, Followed by the Drama of Déguembéré), Ouane tackles the very difficult question of succession by adopting a less than conventional approach. Having established the impotence of her husband, Fadimâtâ finds a lover to guarantee a heir to their rich plantation. Captured and humiliated by neighboring Arabs only to be freed by his wife's lover, the husband welcomes the fruit of this adulterous relationship. Ouane's novella raises some of the most difficult issues in the literature of the Sahel, including paternalistic attitudes *vis-à-vis* the Tuareg and lack of solidarity for the Arabs of North Africa in their struggle for independence. *Le Collier de coquillages* (The Shell Necklace) revisits the days of the Union Française (the French Union) to highlight the displeasure of Africans with their new status as colonial Frenchmen and women, an identity that serves to exacerbate the misunderstandings between colonial authorities and the indigenous populations.

JEAN OUÉDRAOGO

Ould Cheikh, Mohammed

b. 1905, Béchar, Algeria; d. 1938

poet and novelist

The Algerian poet and novelist Mohammed Ould Cheikh was one of the pioneers of Algerian fiction in French, a very small and disparate group of writers of the first third of the twentieth century which includes authors such as Mohammed Ben Cherif, Khodja Choukri, and Hamou Abdelkader.

His work includes a collection of poems titled *Chants pour Yasmina* (Songs for Yasmina) (1930), and a novel, *Myriem dans les palmes* (Myriem among the Palms) (1936). Ould Cheikh typified the Algerian authors of his generation in two ways: first, in his concern with cultural alienation, and second, in his apparently contradictory positions regarding the politics of colonialism and assimilation. Practical and political conditions made it impossible for Ould Cheikh to express overtly his opposition to cultural assimilation. However, *Myriem dans les palmes*, which recounts the melodramatic adventures of a liberated half-French, half-Algerian woman, demonstrates the author's resistance to the cultural policies of colonial Algeria. This resistance would become a characteristic trait of the Algerian writers to follow him in the 1950s.

Further reading

Djeghloul, Abdelkader (1984) *Elements d'histoire culturelle algérienne* (Elements of Algerian Cultural History), Algiers: ENAL.

SETH GRAEBNER

Ouologuem, Yambo

b. 1940, Bandiagara, Mali

poet and novelist

Born in 1940 in Bandiagara, Mali, Yambo Ouologuem is known as a poet and novelist. In 1968 he was awarded the prestigious Prix Renaudot for his controversial novel *Bound to Violence* (*Le Devoir de violence*). The book was criticized for its violence, the open criticism of African rulers as players in the enslavement of their populations, and its eroticism. The stance of the writer is a radical one and shows his willingness to do away with the myth of African innocence that had dominated the literature of **negritude**. Indeed, the novel is famous for its forceful attack of the romanticized precolonial Africa of the negritudists. In opposition to the image of an innocent Africa, Ouologuem presents the despotic and tyrannical rule of the Saïfs and its litany of horrors and slavery as part of African history. Rather than under-

mining its power and reputation, the accusations of plagiarism that followed the novel on its publication served to expand and explain Ouologuem's parodic intent. The parodic element is also pronounced in his other works: in 1969, he published *Lettre à la France nègre* (Letter to Black France) and, under the pseudonym Utto Rodolph, *Les Mille et une bibles de sexe* (The Thousand and One Bibles of Sex). *Lettre à la France nègre* decries French bigotry and racism by exposing its anti-racist institutions. He later published, in collaboration with Paul Pehiep, a school manual titled *Terres de soleil* (Lands of Sun). In recent years he has been leading a secluded life in the Sahel, devoting himself to religion while remaining a political activist outside the borders of his native Mali. His bitterness for the French, the literary establishment, and his seclusion have created a mystic aura around the figure of this important African novelist, but his reputation continues to depend on the power and quality of his first novel, which has become a classic in the tradition of modern African writing.

Further reading

Wise, Christopher (ed.) (1999) *Yambo Ouologuem: Postcolonial Writer, Islamic Militant*, Boulder, Colorado: Lynn Rienner.

JEAN OUÉDRAOGO

Oussou-Essui, Denis

b. 1934, Côte d'Ivoire

novelist

Ivorian author Denis Oussou-Essui is best known for three major **novel**s published between 1965 and 1975: *Vers de nouveaux horizons* (Toward New Horizons), *La Souche calcinée* (The Charred Stump), and *La Saison sèche* (The Dry Season). These works constitute a trilogy, even though their heroes have different names. The first was published one year before Oussou-Essui's return to Africa after fifteen years in Paris, spent studying for degrees in the social sciences, international studies, and journalism. The novel describes the struggle of its hero to improve life in his native village in the Côte d'Ivoire, despite his attraction to city life and desire for a formal French education. Oussou-Essui presents the conflicts between African traditions and modern Western culture, valorizing rural life without calling for a return to the past. In the second of the novels, a young Ivorian leaves his country to study in France but ends up penniless, dreaming only of his return home. In the third, an engineering student returns home from France only to be disappointed to find himself working for a corrupt and incompetent administration. Oussou-Essui has since published short stories, a book of poems, and a political novel.

Further reading

Oussou-Essui, Denis (1965, 1999) *Vers de nouveaux horizons* (Towards New Horizons), Paris: L'Harmattan.

RACHEL GABARA

Out-el-Kouloub

b. 1892, Cairo, Egypt; d. 1968, Austria

novelist and short story writer

The Francophone Egyptian writer Out-el-Kouloub was born in Cairo in an aristocratic and wealthy family who presided over a Sufi order known as *al-tariqa al-dimirdashiyya* (Dimirdashi Way). Religious and proficient in Arabic, she nevertheless chose to write her fiction in French and her novels were prefaced by well-known men of French letters including Jean Cocteau. Educated at home, she was captivated by books and read voraciously French literature, social science, philosophy, and works of contemporary Egyptians, including those espousing women's emancipation. After the Egyptian revolution and especially after the agrarian reform and the confiscation of property of large land-owners, Out-el-Kouloub left Egypt and lived abroad until her death.

She wrote five novels, using classical French and dominant French styles of writing while occasionally enriching her prose with Egyptian usage and expressions. In her works, Egypt is usually presented through the eyes of women protagonists of different social classes and of different eras starting with the nineteenth century. Her style is realistic, with elaborate details which indicate an ethnographic inclination, and many of her novels published in the 1940s and 1950s are concerned with various aspects of Egyptian society in a period of translation. In *Harem*, one of her earliest works published in 1937, Out-el-Kouloub provides rich ethnographic details, while her 1947 novel *Zanouba* depicts middle-class life in Egypt in the early twentieth century through the use of poems, songs, proverbs, and rituals as well as scenes revolving around family conflicts and manners from a particular social era. Other novels from the 1950s explore Egyptian society from a multiplicity of perspectives: *Ramza* explores the generation gap through the lives of women and is considered largely autobiographical. *Le Coffret hindou* (The Indian Safe) revolves around a woman journalist who writes using a masculine pen-name; *La Nuit de la destinée* (The Night of Destiny) depicts faith and religious memories. But perhaps her most popular work is *Trois contes de l'amour et de la mort* (*Three Tales of Love and Death*), a collection of tales published in 1940, which have been compared by some critics to Flaubert's *Trois contes* (*Three Tales*). These tales revolve around three woman protagonists whose lives are used to both depict and obliquely criticize the patriarchal order: Nazira, who is married sight unseen to an old merchant, betrays him with a lover and pays for it with her life; Zarifa, separated from her lover, also ends up tragically; and Zaheira, the daughter of a servant, is brought up with the children of the rich household and ends up falling in love with the son of the master, but is unable to marry him.

Further reading

Out-el-Kouloub (1994) *Ramza*, trans. Nayra Atiya, Syracuse, New York: Syracuse University Press.
——*Zanouba* (1996), trans. Nayra Atiya, Syracuse, New York: Syracuse University Press.
——(2000) *Three Tales of Love and Death*, trans. Nayra Atiya, Syracuse, New York: Syracuse University Press.

FERIAL J. GHAZOUL

Owondo, Laurent

b. 1948, Libreville, Gabon

playwright

The Gabonese writer Laurent Owondo was born in Libreville and was educated in local primary and secondary schools before going to France for higher education. After studying at Aix-en-Provence and the Sorbonne, he proceeded to the United States for his doctoral studies where he specialized in the African-American novel. Since his return to Senegal, he has taught English literature and civilization at the University Omar Bongo in Libreville. Owondo is the founder of the troupe Le Théâtre de la Rencontre (The Theater of Encounter) and he is also a director of the National Theater of the Gabon. In his play *La Folle du gouverneur* (The Lunacy of the Governor) (1990) he uses techniques from the theater of the absurd to comment on the culture of silence in the postcolonial state. A similar theme is taken up in *Au bout du silence* (At the End of Silence) (1985), where he also rejects the simplistic opposition between tradition and modernity and claims a dialectical position that brings the two into play.

OUSMANE BA

Oyono, Ferdinand

b. 1929, Ngoulemekon, near Ebolowa, Cameroon

novelist

The Cameroonian Francophone novelist Ferdinand Oyono enjoyed great success with his early works, especially *Houseboy* (*Une Vie de boy*) (1956), in the period just before Cameroonian independence, but has since abandoned his literary career. His works strongly criticize the colonial administration, the Catholic Church, and the general imbalance of African–European relations. Oppressive and discriminatory colonial institutions are not the sole targets of attack, however, as Oyono also critically writes of the need for Africans to reject buying into, respecting, and searching for an identity within such colonial institutions and practices. While

Oyono was certainly one of the pioneering writers to attack both colonial oppression and indigenous passivity, he is considered an important writer more for his use of ironic situations that reveal the underlying social tragedy in place. This irony touches the situation of both colonizer and colonized alike, and is a means to push the reader into active consideration and critique of the problems Oyono presents.

Although it is not considered to be part of the tradition of **children's literature** in Africa, *Houseboy* is a childhood narrative detailing the life of a young Cameroonian, Joseph Toundi Ondoua. Through the boy's journal, discovered after his death, the reader explores the world of a young boy who turns his back on his African heritage and seeks a better life in colonial society, literally fleeing his male initiation ceremony to seek refuge with a Catholic missionary. Although initially happy with his newfound station as a colonial insider and reverent towards his employers, Toundi slowly discovers his true status as an alienated and subaltern colonial subject as he becomes a scapegoat for his employers' internal problems and disagreements. He finds himself increasingly punished by and separated from the society in which he sought refuge and recognition, and finally realizes that he must run away once again in order to survive. He is thus a double outcast, dying as such after having fled the only two cultures he has known.

Unlike other contemporaneous novels of cross-cultural experience, notably Camara **Laye**'s *The Dark Child* (1954), Toundi is not so much a hybridized individual who looks wistfully back at an idealized pure past as he is a lost soul who has rejected one identity only to be rejected in turn by the identity he has sought as a replacement. The revelation that Toundi's place and identity is not to be found within the colonial paradigm is particularly successful due to the slow, detached, and objective manner with which Toundi, and Oyono, report it. While certainly anticipated by the reader, the critique of the colonial system is never at the forefront of the narrative. It is often the reader who must supply the analysis of Toundi's observations that leads to the demystification of European colonial superiority. In this sense, the novel is similar to many epistolary novels ostensibly written by "foreign" spectators, where the reader is asked to supply the critical reading of the observing narrator's naïve accounts of curious and mystifying behavior. This approach allows Oyono to reveal the extreme hypocrisy and cruelty of European colonization while at the same time refusing to grant Toundi the status of the wise and faultless hero of conscience.

Oyono's second novel, *The Old Man and the Medal* (*Le Vieux nègre et la médaille*) (1956), echoes many of the same themes, although through a different narrative lens. The novel details a few transformative days in the life of Meka, an elderly Cameroonian man. Meka is set to receive a prestigious honor, the titular medal, from the colonial administration for his years of dutiful service to France and the Catholic Church, including having donated his land to the Church and having lost his two sons in World War II. While Meka and his friends and family are initially excited and proud about the upcoming event, over the course of the novel the irony of this honor becomes increasingly apparent. The ceremony itself and the subsequent celebration both degenerate into a series of humiliating delimitations of Meka's true status in colonial society, in which Meka increasingly recognizes the hypocrisy of his European "friends." Unlike Toundi, Meka's naïvety is symbolically washed away following a torrential downpour, and he makes the choice to reject his "privileged" relationship with the colonizers and return to his previous cultural identity.

Road to Europe (*Chemin d'Europe*) (1960) is his least known work, perhaps due to its more ambiguous message concerning African–European relations. The protagonist, Aki Barnabas, follows a long path, from the Catholic seminary to a job convincing Africans to buy at the shop of a corrupt merchant (Mr "Kriminopolous") to tutoring a colonial couple's child, until finally realizing his dream to leave Africa to study in Europe. The series of positions he fills before attaining his ultimate goal are representative of the various roles Africans accept in an unending quest to be more European. This idea that assimilation is the key to success is reinforced by the means by which Barnabas finally achieves his goal of studying in Europe. He stumbles across a European religious group and immediately fakes a conversion in order to gain

their assistance. Whether Oyono means to indicate that Africans need to use the same "win at all costs" strategy employed by their colonizers in order to be successful, or is simply further satirizing the blind willingness to be assimilated, remains one of the more debated questions of this work and of his work in general.

Despite the tremendous success of his work and promises of further literary production, Oyono stopped writing and concentrated on a steady progression of governmental jobs in his newly independent Cameroon. Among these jobs, Oyono has occupied several high-level governmental positions, including multiple ambassador positions in the 1960s and 1970s, minister of housing and town planning (1988–91), minister of foreign affairs (1994–8), and the post he has held since 1999, minister of state in charge of culture.

Further reading

Bjornson, Richard (1991) *The African Quest for Freedom and Identity: Cameroonian Writing and the National Experience*, Bloomington: Indiana University Press.

STEPHEN BISHOP

Oyônô-Mbia, Guillaume

b. 1939, Mvoutessi, near Sangmelima, Cameroon

dramatist and short story writer

The Cameroonian dramatist and short story writer Guillaume Oyônô-Mbia is one of the best-known Cameroonian and even African dramatists due to his enormously popular play *Three Suitors, One Husband* (*Trois prétendants ... un mari*) (1964). The play is a satire and comedy that condemns the tradition of *dot* or dowry, the practice of a family demanding cash and other material goods in return for their daughter's hand in marriage, as well as a number of other individual and social characteristics (greed, excessive pride, materialism, sorcery, sexism, etc.). It has been produced in countries throughout Africa, Europe, and the

Americas, and remains one of the best-selling publications from Cameroon. Its success is largely due to two elements. First, its condemnation of the *dot* is popular in feminist criticism and frequently leads to the play being produced at festivals and conferences discussing the African woman. Additionally, for better or worse, this "feminist" critique of an aspect of African society with which many Westerners are unfamiliar allows comfortable access to an oft-exoticized practice. Second, the comedy of the play is fast and furious and generally accessible to all manner of audiences.

While known primarily for this work, he has written a number of other plays as well as some short stories, including the collection *Chroniques de Mvoutessi 1 et 2* (Chronicles of Mvoutessi 1 and 2) (1971). Another short story, "Culture and Camembert" ("Culture et Camembert") is frequently anthologized as an example of intercultural influences. Although most of these works are listed by the publisher under the rubric "Pour tous" ("For Everyone"), designating their applicability for readers young and old, they should not be considered **children's literature**. While his works employ an everyday language and contain a lot of overt, visual humor, they are highly critical satires of African society where no archetype escapes ridicule. Oyônô-Mbia equally attacks the traditional and modern, urban and rural, young and old, and wealthy and poor, among other binary oppositions.

There are, however, some consistent underlying currents to this seeming chaos. One is that Oyônô-Mbia mocks all those who are pretentious, as well as those who accommodate such pretension with attendant respect. Another is that he rarely condemns outright any particular tradition. Rather, by mocking the extremes of both sides to a conflict, he calls both into question. In this sense, he is one of the early African critics of **negritude**, often satirizing images of a pure, ancient African culture that stands in opposition to Western cultural influences. Another characteristic of his writing is a liberal use of regional expressions and indigenous language vocabulary, occasionally providing a glossary and suggestions as to how to "translate" such language so as to be appropriate to the production's locale. He is also known for writing and translating his works in English and French, the two official languages of his country.

Further reading

Oyônô-Mbia, Guillaume (1969) *His Excellency's Special Train*, Yaoundé: Éditions CLE.
——(1974) *Three Suitors, One Husband; and Until Further Notice*, London: Methuen.

STEPHEN BISHOP

P

Pacéré, Titinga Frédéric

b. 1943, Manéga, Burkina Faso

poet, philosopher, and lawyer

The Burkinabé poet, philosopher, and lawyer Maître Titinga Frédéric Pacéré is famous throughout Africa, not only for his French language poetry but also for his countless contributions to the preservation of Mossé and other traditional Sahelian cultures, including the founding of a popular museum in his native village of Manéga (near Ouagadougou, Burkina Faso). He is the author of more than forty books on diverse subjects such as law, sociology, literature, human rights, history, and Mossé religion. Pacéré has won numerous prizes for his poetry, most notably the Médaille d'Honneur de l'Association des Écrivains de Langue Française and the Grand Prix Littéraire de l'Afrique Noire. In Europe and the United States, Pacéré is perhaps best known for his revolutionary theory of talking drums, or "bendrology," asserting the priority of the aural word of the drum (or *bendré*, the More word for a drum made from a calabash) over both the spoken and the written word. Though controversial, Pacéré's theory lays the foundations for an authentically Afrocentric theory of human language, eschewing speaking–writing binaries of the West. Pacéré has also been a vocal critic of Western literacy paradigms that routinely stigmatize "illiterate" peoples and undervalue African cultural systems.

Further reading

Ouedraogo, Albert (2001) "Bendrology in Question," trans. Christopher Wise and Edgard Sankara, in Christopher Wise (ed.) *The Desert Shore: Literatures of the Sahel*, Boulder, Colorado: Lynne Rienner, pp. 73–85.

Pacéré, Titinga Frédéric (2001) "Saglego, or Drum Poem (for the Sahel)," trans. Christopher Wise, in Christopher Wise (ed.) *The Desert Shore: Literatures of the Sahel*, Boulder, Colorado: Lynne Rienner, pp. 45–72.

Wise, Christopher (2001) "The Word beyond the Word: Pacéré's Theory of Talking Drums," in Christopher Wise (ed.) *The Desert Shore: Literatures of the Sahel*, Boulder, Colorado: Lynne Rienner, pp. 27–43.

CHRISTOPHER WISE

Palangyo, Peter K.

b. 1939, Arusha, Tanzania; d. 1993, Tanzania

novelist

The Tanzanian novelist Peter Palangyo was educated at Makerere University, Uganda, and at the University of Minnesota, where he abandoned his studies in biology and began his literary career. He served as Tanzania's ambassador to Canada, before his death in a road accident. His novel *Dying in the Sun*, published in 1968, was the first Tanzanian novel in English, in a country in which

Swahili (Kiswahili) has predominated as the language for literary expression. *Dying in the Sun* is the story of Ntanya, a young man estranged from his family and village, who attempts to repair his life through industry and by seeking reconciliation with those from whom he has been alienated. Ntanya's questioning mind, and his life of misery, lead him to depths of loneliness, yet he realizes that not everyone shares his fate. For while he walks the dusty roads in search of work, there are others who have reaped the benefits of independence: "big black fat faces in shining cars that blow dust in your eyes so that you cannot see the signs all over the road" (1968: Tanzania). *Dying in the Sun* was one of the earliest East African novels to meditate upon the meaning of political independence and the crisis of decolonization (see **colonialism, neocolonialism, and postcolonialism**).

Works cited

Palangyo, P. (1968) *Dying in the Sun*, Tanzania: Heinemann.

DAN ODHIAMBO OJWANG

Parkes, Frank Kobina

b. 1932, Korle Bu, Gold Coast (now Ghana)

poet

Parkes' poetry has been widely published in magazines such as the pre-eminent Ghanaian periodical *Okyeame*. During the early 1960s Parkes was elected president of the newly formed Ghana Society of Writers, which was renamed the Ghana Association of Writers. His poetry reflects the vitality and optimism of the newly independent nation. At his best, his poetry speaks of the need for a usable past, an unshakeable vision of the future, and the strength to be undaunted by the naysayers of the present. Some of Parkes' work expresses the same spirit as the Senegalese poet David **Diop**. His quietly combative attitude is exemplified in his only published collection, *Songs*

from the Wilderness (1965), in which the poet, reaffirming his faith in the ability of African future leaders, calls on them to solve the myriad problems caused by the legacy of colonialism (see **colonialism, neocolonialism, and postcolonialism**) and the shortcomings "of the many weak of Africa." His poetry has been anthologized in volumes focused on Ghanaian as well as continental African poetry and literature.

Further reading

Awoonor, Kofi and Adali-Mortty, G. (eds) (1977) *Messages: Poems from Ghana*, London: Heinemann.

Kayper-Mensah, A.W. and Wolff, Horst (eds) (1972) *Ghanaian Writing*, Tubingen: Horst Erdmann Verlag.

VINCENT O. ODAMTTEN

Patel, Essop

b. 1943, Germiston, South Africa

lawyer and poet

Essop Patel was born into a Muslim family of Indian extraction in Germiston, South Africa, and grew up in Natal. After legal training at the University of the Witwatersrand and several years spent in London, he practiced as an advocate in Johannesburg and Botswana, eventually being appointed a State Counsel. Much of his legal work involved defending victims of the apartheid regime (see **apartheid and post-apartheid**). He has edited collections of the work of *Drum* writers Nat **Nakasa** and Can **Themba**, and co-edited a volume of black South African poetry, *The Return of the Amasi Bird* (1982). His own poetry – *They Came at Dawn* (1980), *Fragments in the Sun* (1985), and *The Bullet and the Bronze Lady* (1987) – reflects his passionate concern with the social and political conditions to which the oppressed were subject under apartheid. His early "protest poetry" succeeded without ranting in asserting the value of black culture and human rights. He insists that his poetic task is to "cultivate the colorful world of loving," but alongside tender poems of personal love he has written bitter, occasionally satirical, depictions of social tensions and political conflict in South Africa and elsewhere. While he has experimented with the visual structure of poems, his style is direct, forthright, and without pretension.

MALCOLM HACKSLEY

Pato, Gladys Lomafu

b. 1930, Hhohho, Swaziland

short story writer

Born in Hhohho, Swaziland, Pato attended William Pitcher College and the University of Botswana and Swaziland, where she attained a Bachelor of Education degree (1980). Pato's work *Umtsango* (The Hedge) (1977) was the first study of the SiSwati modern short story in postcolonial Swaziland (see **colonialism, neocolonialism, and postcolonialism**). Her other important publications are the historical drama *Ingati Yemlungu* (The White Man's Blood) (1989), which explores colonial encounters, and another short story collection, *Khala Mdumbadumbane!* (Tell the Tale!) (1987). Pato's short stories provide an almost natural development of the genre from the oral to the written form (see **oral literature and performance**), exhibiting the sociopolitical influences prevalent at the time of its birth through constant metaphorical allusion to biblical stories and techniques from Swati oral culture. Despite major missionary influence in Swaziland, Pato freely embellishes her tale with folk narrative techniques. The motley literary background against which her short story emerges is the Bible, IsiZulu short story and SiSwati folk tales. She favors topics on the erosion of social values, deeds of heroism, education (see **education and schools**), and the corrosive effects of Westernization.

ZODWA MOTSA

Paton, Alan Stewart

b. 1903, Pietermaritzburg, Natal, South Africa; d. 1988, Durban, Natal, South Africa

writer, educator, and politician

The South African novelist, poet, biographer, educator, and politician Alan Paton produced the best-known of South African novels in the second half of the twentieth century, *Cry the Beloved Country* (1948). The great critical and popular success of this book made him internationally prominent, and he used his fame to fight apartheid (see **apartheid and post-apartheid**) in South Africa and to spread politically liberal ideas in that country, both through his writings and through his skills as a politician. Through much of the second half of the twentieth century he was regarded as the voice of his country's conscience.

Born in Pietermaritzburg in Natal, he was much influenced by his upbringing by a tyrannical father whom he learned to resist in ways that he would later apply to his struggle against the apartheid government. He worked as a teacher before taking on the running of a dangerous and crowded borstal for young black men, and he had outstanding success in reducing the number of escapees by treating the inmates more humanely and giving them responsibility for their own lives. It was while he was on a study tour of similar borstals in Europe and the United States that he wrote his first novel.

The success of *Cry, the Beloved Country* always overshadowed Paton's other work and tempted some critics to label him a one-book man. He was not. Having achieved financial independence through his literary success, he became a full-time writer, turning out a stream of poems and a succession of biographies and novels, including the haunting *Too Late the Phalarope* (1953), which focused attention on the tragedy of the Afrikaner, imprisoned and consumed by the apartheid he had created. Late in life he produced a third novel, *Ah, but Your Land is Beautiful* (1981).

Though neither of these later novels had the enduring and almost universal appeal of *Cry, the Beloved Country*, Paton himself remarked that they were better-constructed books. They succeed, too, in showing the extraordinary breadth of his interests, and his sympathies with all the major ethnic groups in South Africa, not excluding the Afrikaners. But they, and all his books, show also the extent to which Paton saw his writing as fitting into the wider framework of his political and religious activities. He refused to live the life of the dedicated writer – dedicated, that is, to writing above all else. He believed firmly that a life not lived for others rather than for oneself is a life not worth living. All his writings, therefore, his three novels included, are not just works of art but acts of urgent communication, demanding from their readers not merely comprehension and appreciation, but action.

In addition to his fiction he produced two important political biographies, of his political mentor J.H. Hofmeyr (*Hofmeyr*) (1965) and of the Anglican bishop Geoffrey Clayton (*Apartheid and the Archbishop*) (1974). He saw these two very different men as representative of the roots of South African liberalism, and his biographies, like his novels, poems, and other writings, are part of a consistent moral and political concern that actuated him all his life. The same is true of his two volumes of **autobiography**, *Toward the Mountain* (1980) and *Journey Continued* (1988), in which there emerges clearly his view of human life as a moral and spiritual pilgrimage.

In summary, his talent was multifaceted, showing itself not just in novels but in fine poetry, in two pioneering biographies, in his autobiographies, in his devotional volume *Instrument of Thy Peace* (1968), and that remarkable book *Kontakion for You Departed* (1969), which is a combination of the biographical and the devotional, written about his first wife immediately after her death and shortly before he remarried. Whereas his first marriage, to the widow Dorrie Lusted, had had periods of tension and difficulty, his second, to his secretary Anne Hopkins, was a source of great happiness to them both.

In pursuit of his non-racial ideals, Paton helped to found the South Africa Liberal Party in 1953, becoming its national chairman in 1956 and its president in 1958. From then on his career became increasingly political and dedicated to helping all racial groups in South Africa. Accordingly he was harassed by the Nationalist government, and only his international eminence saved him from imprisonment. He refused to be cowed or silenced, producing a steady stream of polemical articles, which kept him in the public eye, and a constant flow of fine poems, many of them unpublished in his own lifetime, most of them having a political message and a satirical edge.

The sheer range of his achievements makes it likely that a mature assessment of his full value in the context of South African literature cannot yet be made. His was a profoundly humane and civilized vision, and the apparent triumph, in South Africa in the 1990s, of the values for which he strove and wrote throughout his life, would have given him deep satisfaction had he lived to see it. He maintained with all his powers Judaeo-Christianity's unique affirmation of the worth and dignity of the individual. Running through all the richly varied fabric of his life is the unbroken thread of his commitment to what he saw as the moral course: he sought out (and believed he had found) the right way to live, which was to live for others. That way he pursued to the end.

His Christian creed was probably best summed up in practical essentials: to uphold human rights and dignity; to lift the downtrodden; and to promote a common society in opposition to the polarization of apartheid. He hated the power-hungry, exercised intelligence and independence, and had faith in the decency, tolerance, and humanity of the common man. A large part of his influence on generations of readers unquestionably lies in their sense of being in contact, not just with a fine writer, but with a profoundly moral consciousness.

Further reading

Alexander, Peter F. (1995) *Alan Paton: A Biography*, London: Oxford University Press.

Callan, Edward (1968, revised 1982) *Alan Paton*, New York: Twayne Publishers.

——(1991) *Cry, The Beloved Country: A Novel of South Africa*, Boston, Massachusetts: Twayne Publishers.

Paton, Anne (1992) *Some Sort of a Job: My Life with Alan Paton*, London: Viking Penguin.

PETER F. ALEXANDER

Pepetela (Artur Maurício Carlos Pestena dos Santos)

b. 1941, Benguela, Angola

writer

Regarded as one of the most important writers from Angola, Pepetela has also been deeply involved in the country's turbulent history, especially in its violent transition from colonialism to postcolonialism (see **colonialism, neocolonialism, and postcolonialism**). Born in Benguela and educated in Portugal where he studied sociology, he became involved in nationalist politics at early age and fought as a guerilla against the Portuguese in the Cabinda Enclave. After independence he became a teacher at the Universidade Augostinho Neto in Luanda. Pepetela's early works, including *As Aventuras de Ngunga* (The Adventures of Ngunga) (1976), *Muana Puó* (1978), and *Mayombe* (1982), draw on the experiences of the struggle against colonialism and the desire to write a narrative that would bring together the different social and cultural groups constituting the new Angolan nation. In *Mayombe*, in particular, Pepetela uses social realism to represent the ideals of nationalism (see **nationalism and post-nationalism**), falling back on the romantic plot to imagine a national community that transcends differences of ethnicity, gender, race, and class. Even when his characters are guerillas involved in a violent struggle against colonialism, he focuses on romance and idealism as the conditions that make nationalism possible and desirable. In his postcolonial novels, most notably *Lueji* (1989), *A Geração da Utopia* (The Generation of Utopia) (1992), and *O Desejo de Kianda* (The Desire of Kianda) (1995), he uses narrative both to try to represent and understand Angola's precolonial past and to relate it to the politics of postcolonial failure and decline. These novels are hence characterized by a double temporal and narrative perspective: they are concerned with history and the question of establishing myths of origins while at the same time they question the idealism and utopian perspective that had characterized Pepetela's nationalist novels.

Further reading

Peres, Phyllis (1997) *Transculturation and Resistance in Lusophone African Narrative*, Gainesville: University of Florida Press.

SIMON GIKANDI

Peters, Lenrie

b. 1932, Bathurst (now Banjul), Gambia

poet

Lenrie Peters was born in the Gambia, but his parents were originally from Sierra Leone where he returned for his high school education before proceeding to Cambridge where he trained as a doctor. Peters started writing poems in the early 1960s and some of his earliest works were published in *Black Orpheus* and other journals of African literature and culture. As with other leading poets of the generation of the 1960s, Peters' poems are concerned with a wide range of contemporary issues, but they are also unusual for their focus on the everyday experience rather than specific moments or events. Compared to the work of highly symbolic poets such as Christopher **Okigbo** or Wole **Soyinka**, Peters' early poetry is considered more spontaneous or improvised. In his first collection of poems, *Satellites* (1967), Peters often uses techniques borrowed from the poetics of high modernism (see **modernity and modernism**) to reflect on nature and other ordinary events of everyday life such as the city or the street. Even the poems that allude to specific events – the death of Winston Churchill, for example – are notable for speaking about their subject in an impressionist style that seems to want to capture the larger movement of life rather than the particular incident that triggered the poem in the first place. In the later poems collected in *Katchikali* (1971), however, Peters' poetic strategy seems to change, so that the movement of the poems is no longer from specific to generalized events but the other way around; he tries to read universal meanings in myths, objects, and institutions that are threatened by colonialism and its aftermath (see **colonialism, neocolonialism, and postcolonialism**).

Peters' novel, *The Second Round* (1965), follows the experiences of a young English-trained doctor who returns home to Sierra Leone eager to serve his country only to be alienated from his family and community. It is in his poetry, rather than his novel, that Peters stands out as one of the most innovative poets of the postcolonial period in Africa, and his work from the 1960s has been compared to the poetry of some of the major poets from this era.

Further reading

Fraser, Robert (1986) *West African Poetry*, Cambridge: Cambridge University Press.

Goodwin, Ken (1982), *Understanding African Poetry: A Study of Ten Poets*, London: Heinemann.

Peters, Lenrie (1981) *Selected Poetry*, London: Heinemann.

SIMON GIKANDI

Philombe, René

b. 1930, Batchenga, Cameroon; d. 2001, Cameroon

novelist and editor

René, né Ombede Philippe-Louis Philombe, was born in Batchenga, Cameroon. He produced an abundant oeuvre – over fifteen titles – beginning in 1959 with *Lettres de ma cambuse* (Letters from My Store-Room), which earned him the Prix Mottart from the Academie Française in 1966. Between 1966 and the 1980s, he published, among many others, *Sola ma chérie* (Sola My Dear) (1966), and *Un Sorcier blanc à Zangali* (A White Sorcerer in Zangali) (1969), as well as a play entitled *Africapolis* (1979), a collection of poems called *Choc, anti-choc* (Shock, Anti-Shock) (1979), and short stories. In his work, Philombe was mainly preoccupied with the socio-cultural and political problems with which colonial and postcolonial Africa was confronted (see **colonialism, neocolonialism, and postcolonialism**). Because of his fighting disposition, he earned the wrath of Cameroonian authorities and he was often persecuted. A man of commitment, Philombe was also a man of action. Although

physically handicapped, he took part in all the struggles for the influence of Cameroonian literature. He was the creator of the journal *La Voix du citoyen* (The Citizen's Voice) in 1957; he was also a founding member of the Association of Cameroonian Poets and Writers (1960) and of the magazine *Le Cameroun Littéraire* (Literary Cameroon) (1983).

ANDRÉ NTONFO

Picard-Ravololonirina, Hajasoa Vololona

b. 1956, Madagascar

writer

Born in Madagascar, Vololona Picard grew up and was educated in France where she obtained her doctorate in linguistics from the Sorbonne Paris IV in 1981. From 1980 to 1986 she lectured at the University of Antananarive and then moved to Réunion where she obtained a lecturing post at the University of Réunion. Actively engaged in politics, she has held positions as secretary of the Socialist Party and minister of sport and culture and, in 2001, ran for the position of deputy mayor of Saint Denis. Emotionally and spiritually divided between her country of birth and her country of adoption, Picard has tried to resolve her double cultural identity through her writing. She sees poetry as an act of resistance as well as a genre which allows one to rediscover one's true self. Her collection of poems *De Jaspe et de sang* (Jasper and Blood) (1998) reflects her strong attachment to Madagascar as well as her emotions as a woman, a wife, and a mother dealing with problems in a troubled and unjust world.

Further reading

Picard, Vololona (1998) *De Jaspe et de sang* (Jasper and Blood), Réunion: Saint-Denis.

CAROLE M. BECKETT

Plaatje, Solomon Tshekisho

b. 1878, Boshof, Orange Free State,
   South Africa; d. 1932, Johannesburg,
   South Africa

novelist and politician

Solomon Tshekisho Plaatje – a co-founder and the
first secretary general of the South African Natives'
National Congress (now the African National
Congress) – has the distinction of being the first
black South African, and possibly the first black
African, to write and publish a novel, *Mhudi* (1930),
in English. Written from 1917 until 1920, *Mhudi*
has undergone several editions since its first
publication. As Stephen Gray and Tim Couzens
show, the first edition of *Mhudi* had its political and
artistic edge blunted by severe editing by its
publishers, Lovedale Press, who were concerned
that its analytical engagement with the politics and
dynamics of land distribution in South Africa in the
1910s, and its general treatment of race relations in
the country, would get them into trouble with the
Union government. This severe editing also had
the effect of removing certain passages in which
another of Plaatje's main concerns, namely mediations of oral literature and history, and the artistic
and political use to which they could be put, were
at their best.

Mhudi deals with the history of South Africa in
the 1820s and 1830s. It specifically examines the
social movements of sections of society in their
attempts to locate and appropriate for themselves
some of the best pieces of land in the country. Of
particular significance is the novel's suggestion that
the ethnic wars and social movements among
blacks, generally known as the *mfecane*, are similar
in both intention and devastating outcomes to the
Great Trek, a migration of Boers from the Cape
into the inner parts of the country. It further traces
some of the developments and processes that led to
the formation of the Union of South Africa in
1910, and the Union's subsequently passing of the
Natives' Land Act of 1913, according to Plaatje the
most devastating Act passed by the government of
the time. *Mhudi* further deals with questions around
mediations of oral history and literature. Plaatje
draws on aspects of oral histories and literature to
demonstrate the wisdom embedded in indigenous

African languages, and to apply aspects of this
wisdom to analyze, often in allegorical ways, the
political concerns of South Africa in the 1910s and
beyond.

Plaatje's concern with issues of indigenous South
African languages, especially Tswana (Setswana),
orthography, and oral literatures are further dealt
with in his essays – in which the question of
translations across languages is also debated – and
other publications like *Sechuana Proverbs with Literal
Translations and their European Equivalents* (1916). He
provided a most comprehensive and critical
discussion of the Natives' Land Act in the book,
Native Life in South Africa (1916). In his attempt to
facilitate a dialogue between Setswana and English
languages and literatures, Plaatje translated several
of Shakespeare's plays into Setswana, in addition to
his *Sechuana Proverbs* and, with Daniel Jones, *A
Sechuana Reader in International Phonetic Orthography
(with English Translations)* (1916). Plaatje's phenom-
enal novel is now available in Setswana, published
by Heinemann (1999), but his translations of
Shakespeare appear not to have gained much
favor with Batswana readers in the second half of
the twentieth century.

PHASWANE MPE

Pliya, Jean

b. 1931, Djougou, Dahomey

playwright

Jean Pliya, one of Benin's best-known literary
figures, was born in Djougou, Dahomey, attended
secondary school in the Côte d'Ivoire, and went on
to study in France. He taught in Dahomey and
Togo before becoming the rector of the National
University of Benin in Cotonou as well as serving
in the government as secretary of education and
culture and minister of information and tourism.
Pliya's first play *Kondo le requin* (Kondo the Shark),
written in French but also translated into Fon, was
awarded the Grand Prize for Black African
Literature in 1967. To prepare his retelling of the
war of resistance waged by the Dahomean King
Gbêhanzin against the French at the end of the
nineteenth century, Pliya consulted both written

histories and oral storytellers (see **oral literature and performance**). In another of his plays, *La Sécretaire particulière* (The Private Secretary) (1973), Pliya satirized and denounced the corruption of a post- and neocolonial African administration. Pliya published several collections of short stories in the 1970s, several **novel**s and a collection of traditional Beninese folk tales in the 1980s, and has also authored a history of Benin.

Further reading

Pliya, Jean (1966, 1981) *Kondo le requin* (Kondo the Shark), Yaoundé: Éditions Clé.

RACHEL GABARA

Plomer, William

b. 1903, Natal, South Africa; d. 1973, Lewes, UK

poet

The South African poet William Plomer was born in Natal and educated there and in England, and he was at one point a close associate of Roy Campbell. After living in Japan for a few years in the 1920s, Plomer returned to England where he lived for the rest of his life, working as an editorial director for the British publishing house Jonathan Cape. In the 1960s Plomer was a major figure in the British literary scene: he was awarded the Queen's Gold Medal for Poetry in 1963 and from 1968 to 1971 he was the president of the Poetry Society. Plomer was a prolific writer in many genres, including **autobiography**, poetry, and short fiction, but his most famous African work was his early novel *Turbott Wolfe* (1925), written when he was only 19. In this novel, as in some of his poetry, he highlighted the liberal dilemma in South African writing – how to secure ideals of human rights and freedom in a situation defined by racial oppression and exploitation. Plomer sought to find a language that would simultaneously reflect his interests in formal experimentation and his larger moral concerns. But as in the later works of liberal writers like Nadine Gordimer, his characters, faced with the difficulties of constructing a society free of racial division, would seek consolation in the realm of the aesthetic.

Further reading

Chapman, Michael (1996) *Southern African Literatures*, London and New York: Longman.

SIMON GIKANDI

poetry and poetics.

There is a critical consensus that, unlike the novel, for instance, poetry was not first introduced to Africa as a result of the colonial encounter. Of the three major genres of literature – drama, the novel, and poetry – it is only poetry that has always been universally accepted by scholars and critics as being indigenous to Africa. While the novel – as different from other forms of prose narratives – is considered an import from Europe and there have been debates about the appropriateness of "drama" as a critical term for describing traditional ritual and secular performances, the roots of poetry in Africa have never been subject to any such critical controversy. This is due, in large part, to the almost limitless elasticity of the forms of verbal expression that can be broadly classified or designated as poetry. From the earliest ritualized hunting cry or the simple rhymed or rhythmic work song to the most sophisticated, complex verbal forms, oral or scripted (see **oral literature and performance**), the scope of what can be subsumed under the label of poetry is bewilderingly large. Thus, the scope of the poetic practice in Africa is so vast as to defy easy summation. Added to this is the fact that in Africa the most ancient poetic forms and the most modern experiments can be found side by side, thriving in a coeval contemporaneity.

However, in spite of this acknowledgement of the indigenous origins of poetry in Africa and the vast field that its practice encompasses, the criticism of African poetry has not been able to avoid the discursive and conceptual binarisms which colonialism imposed upon the description of African realities. As in other areas of African life, culture, and society, criticism of African poetry has often been figured around the issues of tradition, or the nature of precolonial society and modernity, the traditional standing for the African and the modern seen as the European (see **colonialism, neocolonialism, and postcolonialism**; **modernity and modernism**). In the domain of poetry, these issues have been configured along the lines of the oral, traditional, communal, public as opposed to the written, modern, individualistic, private. These sets of oppositions are often further premised on notions of the authentically African as opposed to the Eurocentric and therefore inauthentic. So prevalent have these become that they appear not only to constitute and define the terrain of African poetry but also to provide the enabling vocabulary through which the search for an African poetics has been conducted.

Poetics and the question of orality, language, and authenticity

A poetics is generally seen as a conceptual framework of criteria, which helps to account for a literature and provide the analytical tools for the evaluation of artistic production within a literary tradition. It may be described as a system of concepts and criteria available to artist and audience as genres, techniques, artistic devices, etc., that confer aesthetic merit and cultural authority. Thus, a poetics often functions as an instrument of cultural legitimation and authority. A poetics may be explicit or implicit, in which latter case it is not formally or theoretically elaborated. In traditional societies, for example, it was usually assumed that the oral artist and the community both partake of an implicit internalized poetics expressed in terms of patronage and recognition. In the more differentiated societies of modern times, a poetics may be explicitly formulated in writing as a theory of art and artistic production.

The assumption that the relatively undifferentiated nature of traditional societies implied a universally shared poetics that bound artist and society together in one unconflicted whole was primarily propagated by anthropological lore. Under colonialism, anthropology and the various paradigms it employed in the study of the folklore of so-called primitive societies, beginning with the evolutionist through the functionalist to the structuralist, hardly reserved any credit for the individual performer or the individualized voice. The search for origins, functions, and structures was the dominant impulse and oral poems were intended to serve as indexes or series of items within the ambit of what were considered to be more significant concerns. Recent scholarship, however, has called into question this myth of universal, unmediated, and undifferentiated access by drawing attention to the critical competencies of various constituencies within the communities, relations of power and the role these played in determining the genres, styles, and aesthetics of performance. As more studies of specific genres of oral poetry were done, the role of the individual artist and the contexts of performance began to be given greater prominence, casting doubt on – if not completely laying to rest – more simplistic notions of anonymous authorship and imitative reproduction. Indeed, the principal conceptual and methodological gains of studies of orality in African poetry have been not only to question old assumptions about oral poetry but also to destabilize some of the basic ontological categories – author, text, originality, etc. – through which literary studies were conducted.

The scholarly rehabilitation of oral literature fitted well with the agenda of anti-colonial nationalism (see **nationalism and postnationalism**) and the general emphasis on cultural decolonization that followed the independence of many African nations. Beginning with Obi Wali's argument in "The Dead End of African Literature" (1963) that African literature could only be authentically African if it was written in an African language, issues of language (see **language question**), orality and authenticity became central to the criticism of African poetry. As the language debate gathered pace, its parameters moved from the advocacy of the use of indigenous languages in literary works to an insistence that if foreign (colonial) languages were used they had to be imprinted with the essential irreducible orality of Africa. In African literature in general, the Kenyan writer **Ngugi wa Thiong'o** became the most vocal advocate of this view, while in African poetry the Nigerian polemicist **Chinweizu** became its most strident proponent. The poetics of nationalism and decolonization thus focused vigorously on issues of orality, language, and authenticity.

Oral poetry in African languages

Oral poetry in Africa may be as old as the continent itself but the "oral texts" to which we now have access are those that are either still performed or those that have been transcribed or translated and therefore reduced to the written medium. The oral poems still in performance, so to speak, pose a number of important questions about the nature of orality itself and the manner in which performances are constituted. The transcribed texts available in print pose other equally vexing questions about their ontological status as texts, the ways in which critics should proceed when dealing with simulacra, the problems of translation and transcription, and so on.

Nevertheless, a lot of critical work has been done in identifying the specific genres of oral poetry in various African cultures and communities, the characteristic features of these genres, the aesthetic codes and conventions through which they generate meaning and the general social context of performance and interpretation. Among the Yoruba of the Nigerian southwest, for instance, the multiplicity of poetic genres and their structural and semiotic properties has been fairly well documented. And this has proceeded apace with more or less the same degree of success with those from several other African communities. What these studies have brought to light is the simultaneous flexibility and fixity of oral genres themselves, the presence of "writing" within oral performances and the impossibility of fully recovering a pure "orality." Beyond these evidences of the instability of the categories of the oral and written as essentially different, the idea that orality is an ontologically given, innate property of Africa has also been replaced by a more historical view of the circumstances in which orality flourishes

Poetry in non-indigenous languages: periods, movements, and regions

On the evidence of quantity alone, it is fairly safe to say that poetry in the non-indigenous languages bequeathed by colonialism is thriving, despite the many reservations expressed about the role played by these languages in Africa. These concerns, nevertheless, have been influential in determining the uses to which the poets who write in them put the languages. Uniformly, in the utterances of the poets themselves and in the criticism of African poetry, the issue of language is often highlighted. The emphasis has been on the "domestication" of these languages, to use them in such a way as to reflect the African perspective and experience. From a historical perspective, it is easy to distinguish the poetry of the early African poets whose works were largely imitative of European poetic idioms and styles from those of later poets who were more imaginative and innovative in their approach. To take two examples, the poems of Phyllis Wheatley and Olaudah **Equiano** were completely modeled on the prevailing neo-classical idiom of English poetry of the time, even though the themes they explored may have been different. This kind of poetry which was highly imitative in form and structure was practiced well into this century, as can be seen in poetry of the so-called pioneer poets of West Africa, such as Raphael Armattoe and Dennis **Osadebay**.

After this poetry of the freed slaves and their successors, the birth of the **negritude** movement between the war years was to change the entire complexion of African poetry. Negritude as a philosophical and cultural movement, aimed at affirming the values and virtues of Africa and African civilizations, laid the foundations for a new and truly innovative African poetry in a colonial language. Negritude poetry combined a sensuous lyricism with a powerful ideological celebration of black identity. Léopold Sédar **Senghor**, usually regarded as the chief apostle of negritude, combined in his poetry a forceful evocation of the glory of African empires and civilizations with a colorful portrayal of precolonial African culture, drawing freely from its material artifacts and social mores. These were often framed in idyllic terms using nature, the African body, rhythm, and emotion as indicators of a primordial world of innocence unspoiled by the decadence of European culture.

Negritude was largely propagated by Francophone writers and was criticized by writers from English-speaking African countries who attacked its essentialist view of Africa and its narcissism. These writers espoused a slightly different kind of cultural nationalism. The Nigerian poets Christopher **Okigbo**, Wole **Soyinka** and J.P. **Clark-Bekederemo**, for instance, adopted an approach which mobilized traditional African culture as resources for a worldview which privileged the importance of myth and ritual in exploring contemporary issues and examining the African predicament. While surrealism and its emphasis on emotion was an influence on negritude poetry, modernism and its techniques for representing the multi-layered nature of human experience was an important model for these other poets.

Other regional peculiarities such as apartheid (see **apartheid and post-apartheid**), settler colonialism, and belated decolonization in southern Africa have also been instrumental in determining not only the themes explored by poets from this region but also the forms adopted. Indeed, the last two decades of apartheid in South Africa were to see the emergence of some of the most important poets in the English language, including such important figures as Dennis **Brutus**, Arthur **Nortje**, Sipho Sempala, Oswald **Mtshali**, and Wally **Serote**. Critical commentaries reflect this regional difference in the cleavage between two kinds of poetry often identified as characteristic. On the one hand is the poetry said to be distinguished by an emphasis on suffering, anguish, and alienation focusing on the individual and individual sensibility, and on the other is the poetry of collective struggle which is more communal in orientation. While the former is poetry of protest that depends on acute observation and the "closed" forms of the scribal tradition, the latter is a performance-based poetry influenced by the more "open," popular forms derived from the oral tradition. Most southern African poetry is often identified within this broad – somewhat reductive – divide.

The poetry of the East African poet **Okot p'Bitek** provides a good point at which to conclude because it occupies that indeterminate space between languages, the oral and the written, and thus encapsulates the salient issues of an African poetics. His *Song of Lawino* (1966), first written in his native Acholi tongue and then translated into English by himself, and later retranslated into English by Taban Lo **Liyong**, highlights yet again, in its several journeys, the issues of orality, authenticity, language, the ontological status of poetic "texts," and the blurring of boundaries between original and simulacrum which have defined the search for an African poetics.

Further reading

Chapman, M. (1984) *South African English Poetry: A Modern Perspective*, Johannesburg: Ad Donker.

Fraser, R. (1986) *West African Poetry: A Critical History*, Cambridge: Cambridge University Press.

Okpewho, I. (1992) *African Oral Literature: Backgrounds, Character and Continuity*, Bloomington and Indianapolis: Indiana University Press.

HARRY GARUBA

popular literature

African popular literature is of immense cultural and historical interest, especially given its steady growth over the sixty-year period spanning decolonization and the emergence of postcolonial states (see **colonialism, neocolonialism, and postcolonialism**). The term "popular literature" cannot, however, be transposed easily from Western into African settings, and it does not signify the same commercial conditions as can be found in the West. Popular authors and their readers in Africa are excluded from definitions of popular literature which depend upon the idea of mass-production, for most local literature in Africa is produced in relatively small print-runs of 800 to 2,000 copies. In some cases, such as the popular theater of West Africa, immensely successful plays might never be printed at all in the form of books: rather, this literature will take the form of **video**, songs or further plays. The term "mass-consumption" is also inappropriate to describe most material, for books cost too much for literate people to buy on a regular basis. Novels are luxury items, which most people regard as scarce commodities. Low-income workers will buy religious pamphlets, self-help books, newspapers, cheap magazines, and second-hand European novels: this is the popular literature of Africa.

Exceptions to these rules include "Onitsha market literature" which commanded impressive sales figures in Nigeria in the 1950s and 1960s. The most famous Onitsha pamphlet, *Veronica My Daughter* by Ogali A. **Ogali**, was first published in 1956 and sold 60,000 copies within a few years of its release. The pamphlet revolves around the themes of marriage, education, and money, and it makes a clear argument for letting young people choose their own marriage partners over and against the dictates of their parents. The readership of this pamphlet was composed almost entirely of young unmarried men who had no savings to pay the high bride-prices demanded by Igbo parents in the 1950s.

Ogali's success illustrates the definitive feature of popular literature in Africa: the popular text contains character types, plots, and genres through which local readers can address social and economic questions of vital importance in their lives. While people do not have money to buy books, sales figures can soar when a text promises to counsel readers in the most intimate aspects of their daily lives. Focusing on personal and social issues of relevance to the readership, popular authors help to resolve many problems affecting urban readers, particularly in the areas of relationships and money.

Production and marketing

The bulk of African popular literature circulates in the local economy, reaching bookshops and markets in the vicinity of the publisher and rarely reaching the shelves of distant or international booksellers. Authors are often responsible for the publication costs and sales of their own work, and the success or failure of a title often depends upon the amount of time an author can dedicate to marketing a book. In the case of certain entrepreneurial individuals such as Aubrey **Kalitera** in Malawi, David **Maillu** in Kenya, and Asare Konadu in Ghana, popular novelists bought their own printing machinery and took responsibility for the production process from typesetting to book sales. Numerous African writers have embarked on similar self-publishing enterprises.

Not all popular publishing is confined to the locality of its production. East African publishing houses such as Heinemann Kenya's Spear Books have outlets in Nairobi and Kampala; in Malawi, the nationwide publishing house Popular Publications has produced several successful novelists, including Steve **Chimombo**. Since the 1990s Francophone African publishers have opened up markets in popular literature: women readers in the Côte d'Ivoire can buy romances set in Abidjan with African middle-class heroines. Several international publishers have also recognized the potential for expansion in this market: Heinemann's Heartbeats Series contains a long list of romances published since the 1980s, and since the mid-1970s Macmillan's Pacesetters Series has proved immensely successful with its thrillers and romances in African settings.

In order to maximize sales in countries with several national languages, most African popular literature is written in a European language, particularly English. There are, however, several significant exceptions to this rule in regions with sizeable numbers of people who are literate in African languages. Swahili popular literature (see **Swahili literature**) is a growth industry in East Africa. Unlike Swahili poetry, these low-cost novels are rarely translated into English or taught in schools, but they are widely consumed by local readers. South Africa boasts a booming industry in Afrikaans romances aimed at white women readers. In Northern Nigeria since the early 1990s there has been an enormous expansion in Hausa language pamphlets, called "Kano market literature": often written by women and set in Islamic households, this indigenous literature addresses issues such as polygyny, sexual rivalry, poverty, and love (see **literature in Hausa**).

Frederick Forsyth, James Hadley Chase, Jackie Collins, and Danielle Steel are especial bestsellers in the second-hand market, and local African authors have to compete with these authors to attract readers. The popularity of James Hadley Chase even generated one remarkable successor in 1990s Nigeria, who uses Chase's name on the cover of racy, sensational thrillers that are set in distinctively Nigerian locations. Other popular African authors from the 1970s and 1980s, including Charles **Mang'ua** and Don Mattera, employ racy American and African-American slang in their work, creating characters who exclaim "gee, champ" and address one another as "dude" and "baby." Such apparent mimicry of international models has generated local concern among journalists and academics about the "poor quality" and "imitativeness" of African popular literature.

Despite these concerns, most popular literature produced locally in Africa is intimately bound up with local, rather than international, concerns. It is not regulated by governments or by the style sheets of publishing houses: this allows local producers to innovate and experiment with global and local art forms. The thriller and romance are common genres, but local genres and themes emerge within this framework. Popular authors tend to innovate with their borrowed forms, localizing the international models and instilling them with new meanings.

Historical contexts

By the mid 1880s and the consolidation of colonialism in Africa, many printing presses were operational on the continent, producing increasing numbers of pamphlets and journals by local writers for local readerships. This literature was inextricable from the activities of Christian missionaries in Africa (see **Christianity and Christian missions**). The missionaries were far more involved than the colonialists in establishing local schools, setting up printing presses, and encouraging African authors to produce manuscripts for local distribution and consumption. For many decades the missionaries controlled the flows of literature in and around the continent. They placed particular emphasis upon self-help books and morally uplifting literature: the How To Do It Series published by the United Society for Christian Literature (USCL) in London included topics such as letter-writing in English and making a success of marriage. Mission schools such as Lovedale and Fourah Bay College helped to generate fundamental social and aesthetic values among readers, and books by early African authors such as Thomas **Mofolo**, J. Benibengor Blay, and Ogali A. Ogali can be traced back to the didactic literature imported into Africa by missionaries.

Popular British novelists were increasingly available after 1890, when African readers could purchase a wide array of non-Christian titles ranging from *Beyond Pardon* by Bertha M. Clay to *The Sorrows of Satan* by Marie Corelli. Charles Dickens and William Shakespeare were also favorites with colonial readerships. Popular romantic magazines and Hollywood movies were also imported into Africa from Britain and America in the 1930s, as were Indian pamphlets with romantic images on the front covers.

African-owned newspapers played a vital role in establishing a reading culture in colonial Africa and providing outlets for new authors of poetry and prose. Editors and journalists encouraged the development of local reading cultures in which written interventions were the norm. In the colonial period, as in the late twentieth century, the African-owned press often provided the first print medium for local authors. Many popular novelists in the colonial and postcolonial periods served as journalists on local newspapers or as contributors to columns.

Key debates

In East African universities since the 1980s, a vocal debate has been underway about the literary merit and value of popular novelists such as David Maillu and Charles Mang'ua. Similarly, in Northern Nigeria so great is the academic concern about literary quality that in the late 1990s university lecturers offered their services as proof-readers of popular manuscripts. In extreme cases of criticism, the romance, thriller, and detective story are regarded as neocolonial imports and African authors as poor imitators of degraded Western forms. This position fails to acknowledge that African popular authors innovate with the "borrowed" forms and incorporate a diversity of local discourses, including oral narratives and proverbs. Other critics, including the novelist Chinua **Achebe**, have suggested that the reading of popular literature helps to establish a reading habit among newly literate Africans who will then progress from popular texts to "superior quality" literature.

As in the debates about popular culture taking place in the West, critics on the left have accused

African popular novelists of ideological conservatism, particularly in the area of gender, and African popular literature has been the subject of extensive feminist criticism (see **gender and sexuality**). With the exception of Northern Nigeria, the majority of African popular authors are men who engage in the active creation of gender ideologies. These writers have developed literary styles, themes, and formulas that convey their opinions on the topic of women's roles within marriage and society, and the images of women in their work often reveal a stereotypical, unrealistic, and entrenched way of thinking about gender relations.

Sympathetic commentators emphasize that African popular literature need not be judged by the terms of literary realism (see **realism and magical realism**). Apparent stereotypes and formulaic plots are not necessarily intended to convey accurate information about African society, and texts do not reflect social realities in an unmediated form. Many popular texts are didactic, fabulous, and moralistic rather than realistic. Authors promise "entertainment and also education" and many stories take the form of dilemma tales that are filled with advice. Readers are not invited to lose themselves in the narrative, as in Western popular texts, but to stand apart from the story, judging the dilemmas and extracting morals and ideological positions that will be relevant to them.

Common themes

The authors of popular literature in Africa are not highly educated members of the professional elite. Often they are secondary school-leavers with few further qualifications. They are in a unique position to give voice to the aspirations, dreams, and anxieties of ordinary people in urban Africa. Shared thematic concerns surface in popular literature throughout the continent, and titles such as *My Life with a Criminal, Confessions of an AIDS Victim, The Pregnant Virgin, Victims of Love,* and *Blood for Money* illustrate many of the issues explored within books.

Complex social and historical differences separate the popular literatures of Africa, and each region's popular traditions are distinctive and diverse. Narrative themes and preoccupations shift in response to social and economic transformations, and it is necessary to contextualize popular literature in relation to its time and place of production. Thus, in the 1990s, recurrent themes in East African popular literature included AIDS, criminality, prostitution, and graduate unemployment, while in West Africa the 1990s spawned numerous narratives about the acquisition of illicit wealth, satanic possession, and single motherhood. Charismatic and Pentecostal Christianity have become increasingly central in popular publications throughout the continent. Taken together, African popular literature offers a window into the attitudes, values, and ideological conflicts shaping ordinary people's lives in urban Africa.

Further reading

Barber, Karin (ed.) (1997) *Readings in African Popular Culture,* London, Oxford, and Bloomington: International African Institute, James Currey and Indiana University Press.

Chapman, Michael (1996) *Southern African Literatures,* London and New York: Longman.

Lindfors, Bernth (1991) *Popular Literatures in Africa,* Trenton, New Jersey: Africa World Press.

Newell, Stephanie (ed.) (2001) *Readings in African Popular Fiction,* London, Oxford, and Bloomington: International African Institute, James Currey, and Indiana University Press.

Obiechina, Emmanuel (1973) *An African Popular Literature: A Study of Onitsha Market Literature,* Cambridge: Cambridge University Press.

STEPHANIE NEWELL

Portuguese language literature

Gerald Moser made a telling observation in the late 1960s (1969: University Park): "Literature in the Portuguese language was the earliest written in Black Africa, but it has remained the last to be discovered." Today, Portuguese, the official language of seven nations, remains obscure to most literary scholars. The awarding of the Nobel Prize to Portuguese writer José Saramago has quickened interest, though only towards a few widely translated writers. This critical marginalization relates to the political marginalization of the Portuguese-speaking nations of Angola, Cape Verde, Guinea-Bissau, Mozambique, and São Tomé-Príncipe, whose independence is relatively recent and whose liberation struggles became battlegrounds for Cold War politics. Ironically, their importance to world politics faded dramatically just as their emergent literatures began to be translated with more frequency.

The nations of Portuguese-speaking Africa share a colonial experience marked by violent confrontation, exploitation, enslavement, and attempted forced assimilation. Conversely, this colonial experience revitalized oral traditions (see **oral literature and performance**) and led to cultural resistance and transformation by writers, intellectuals, and artists who often formed the vanguard of liberation movements. Independence has not brought political stability, and those postcolonial struggles have furnished the template for new literary discourses. Beyond the common histories of Angola, Cape Verde, Guinea-Bissau, Mozambique, and São Tomé-Príncipe, important differences exist which can productively be analyzed separately.

Angola

Angolan literature had its roots in 1483 when Portuguese explorer Diogo Cão's expedition arrived at the Zaire estuary in the Kongo kingdom, in what is now Angola. That initial encounter led to the establishment of a Christian stronghold ruled by a Christianized Manikongo, Afonso I. The Manikongo's 1540 highly stylized letters to the king of Portugal were among the first African writings in Portuguese, requesting protection for his kingdom from the slave traders of São Tomé.

The first printing press arrived in Angola in 1845, some three hundred years after those letters were written. Portugal had only exploited its African colonies in favor of developing first Asia and then Brazil, whose independence in 1822 forced Portugal to reassess its African possessions. The first book published in Angola, in 1849, was *Espontaneidades da Minha Alma* (Eruptions of My Soul), a collection of acculturated verse by the mestizo writer José da Silva Maia Ferreira that romanticized the Angolan landscape. This literary

tension between Portuguese acculturated discourse and the cultivation of Angolan themes resonates throughout the nineteenth and early twentieth centuries. This tension appears starkly in nineteenth-century "colonial" literary texts produced by Portuguese colonists (including those born in Angola), the most noteworthy of whom are Cândido Furtado (1820–1905), Ernesto Marecos (1836–79), Alfredo Troni (1845–1904), and Pedro Félix Machado (1860–). At the same time, the Angolan poet, philologist, and journalist Joaquim Dias Cordeiro da Matta (1857–94), an important member of the "Generation of 1880," collected traditional Kimbundu orature in the path-breaking text *Philosophia Popular em Provérbios Angolenses* (Popular Philosophy in Angolan Proverbs), published in 1891 as a first attempt by an Angolan intellectual to identify an autochthonous literature and style.

The Generation of 1880 is associated with the turn-of-the-century free press era in which numerous journals and newspapers, some of which contained bilingual Kimbundu–Portuguese materials, were established in Angola, edited by assimilated blacks and mestizos and critical of Portuguese colonialism.

The period between the literary and journalistic proto-nationalism and the radical nationalist writing of the mid twentieth century is dominated by a diverse group of writers. António Assis Júnior's 1934 highly ambiguous work, *O Segredo da Morta* (The Dead Woman's Secret), employs Kimbundu phrases and oral culture in a novel that is overtly imitative of Victor Hugo. Oscar Bento Ribas' (b. 1909) folkloric writings record the oral traditions, while Geraldo Bessa Victor's (b. 1917) poetry and fiction exoticize the Angolan people and landscape. Of Portuguese descent, Mozambican-born and Angolan-raised Castro Soromenho (1910–68) acerbically criticized the dehumanizing colonial enterprise in an influential trilogy set in the interior of Angola.

These writers are important links to the "Generation of 1950," a group of writers and activists who sought to rediscover Angola. The Luanda-based journal *Mensagem* (Message) (1951–2) published works of this movement and was banned by the Portuguese government after two issues. These writers created new outlets for their creative works in journals such as *Cultura* (Culture) (1957–61), and in publications edited by the Center of Students of the Empire (CEI), an important meeting place and cultural organ of African students in Lisbon. These writers struggled to express Angolan culture and reality in poetry that is replete with images of Mother Africa and the African earth, as well as poetic depictions of colonial exploitation such as contract labor, alienation, and displacement of Africans by the mass influx of Portuguese settlers following World War II. These writers include Agostinho **Neto**, Mário António, Viriato da Cruz, Mário de Andrade, Costa Andrade, Henrique Abranches, Antero Abreu, Tomas Jorge, Alda Lara, António **Jacinto**, António Cardoso, Benúdia, Arnaldo Santos, Manuel dos Santos Lima, and José Luandino **Vieira**. Many were to become active militants within the Popular Movement for the Liberation of Angola (MPLA), and their works are often described as arms in the independence struggle itself.

The liberation struggle of 1961–74 provided a fertile ground for narrative and poetry, much of which was published only after 1974. José Luandino Vieira (b. 1935) wrote the majority of his *estórias* (tales) and novels, including the groundbreaking *Luuanda* (1964), while imprisoned for MPLA activities. His *estórias* incorporate the storytelling structures of the Kimbundu *mussosso*, and are written in a language that reinvents the polyglot possibilities of Luanda's hybrid community. This *estória* variant is uniquely Angolan and has been elaborated by other writers such as Jofré Rocha, Arnaldo Santos, and Boaventura Cardoso. **Pepetela**'s war classic, *Mayombe*, written in 1971–2 and published in 1980, links myth and the problematic founding of nation, whereas his postcolonial works cover the gamut from historical fiction to critique of nation. Writers such as Xuanhenga **Xitu** (b. 1924) and Manuel **Rui** (b. 1941) whose works, like those of Luandino Vieira and Pepetela, span the liberation and postcolonial periods, are oftentimes ironic depictions of the contradictions of cultural nationalism (see **nationalism and post-nationalism**) and the formation of the Angolan nation. Prolific postcolonial writer and journalist José Eduardo **Agualusa** also explores the links between history and fiction in such works as his

1989 novel *A Conjura* (The Conspiracy), while Sousa Jamba's *Patriots* (written in English and published in 1992) deconstructs the aftermath of independence and the ensuing civil war.

Following the openly nationalist poetry of the Generation of 1950, postcolonial Angolan poets such as David Mestre, Arlindo Barbeitos, and Ruy Duarte de Carvalho experimented with language, aesthetics, and form to produce polyvalent poetry. Those poets who emerged in the 1980s are a diverse group whose struggles to define Angolan poetry incorporate elements that are alternatively telluric, ideological, political, and erotic as they limn the limits and expressive potentials of modern Angolan verse. Poets such as Ana Paula Tavares, João Melo, E. Bonavena, João Maimona, Lopito Feijóo K., and others, are part of an emerging generation of Angolan writers.

Cape Verde

In the middle of the fifteenth century, the Portuguese settled in the uninhabited archipelago of Cape Verde where they initially set up a network of Atlantic island sugar plantations. Even after sugar and the center of Portuguese colonialism had moved to Brazil, the islands continued to serve as an entrepôt during the early Atlantic slave trade, giving rise to a culture in which Crioulo (Creole) became the mother tongue. The Crioulo expressive tradition is largely oral and includes well-known narratives and folk tales.

Cape Verdean literature begins in the early twentieth century with three important writers: Eugenio Tavares, best known for his Crioulo *mornas*, the melancholic songs of the islands; Jose Lopes, whose poetry evoked a pan-Lusitanian consciousness; and the poet Pedro Cardoso, who also produced Crioulo verse. A significant year for Cape Verdean literature was 1936, when the first issue of *Claridade* (Clarity) was published. More than a literary-cultural journal, *Claridade* (1936–60) defined a generation of Cape Verdean writers and intellectuals who explored the sociocultural realities of the then peripheral colony. Located less than 500 kilometers off the coast of Senegal, the archipelago suffers both periodic drought and inundation, and its economic development was long neglected by the metropolis, leading to massive emigration, largely but not exclusively to the United States. Literary themes of insularity, exile and alienation, emigration, and *saudosismo* (longing) are constants of *claridoso* texts that seek to define a Cape Verdean ethos. Major writers of the *Claridade* generation include Manuel Lopes, Baltasar Lopes da Silva, and the poet Jorge Barbosa. The latter's works range from social and melancholic escapism to poetic celebrations of humble Creolized subjects. Manuel Lopes' novels *Chula Brava* (Fierce Rain) (1956) and *Os Flagellates do Vent Lester* (The Scourged People of the East Wind) (1960) belong to the tradition of social realism (see **realism and magical realism**) and are concerned with Cape Verdean suffering and survival. Baltasar Lopes da Silva, also a poet using the pseudonym Oswaldo Alcântara, produced the classic novel *Chiquinho* (1947), a representative coming-of-age story that ends with the title character's inevitable emigration to New England. A second literary review, *Certeza* (Certainty), which published two issues in 1944, was more cosmopolitan and influenced by both Marxism and Portuguese neo-realism, owing, in part, to the collaboration of the Portuguese writer, critic, and scholar Manuel Ferreira who lived in Cape Verde in the 1940s and whose fiction includes Cape Verdean novels such as *Hora de Bai* (Time to Leave) (1962) and *Voz de Prisão* (Voice from Prison) (1971).

Other important writers who emerged from the generations of *Claridade* and *Certeza* include fiction writer António Aurélio Goncalves and later writers such as Orlanda Amarílis, Corsino Fortes, and Teixeira de Sousa, who began systematically publishing only after 1974. Amarílis' work in particular explores relations of gender and alienation in the colonial and postcolonial eras. The works of 1960s post-*Claridade* writers such as Ovídio Martins, Gabriel Mariano, and Onésimo Silveira move away from the often-criticized escapist tendencies of the previous generation to identify openly with African political and social realities, most clearly articulated in Silveira's seminal essay, *Consciencializacão na Literatura Caboverdiana* (The Process of Self-Awareness in Cape Verdean Literature) (1963).

Postcolonial literary debate has centered on several themes, including the relationship between art and politics, particularly in the poetry of

Arménio Vieira and Oswaldo Osório, and the use of Crioulo as a literary language. Writers such as Tomé Varela da Silva, Kaoberdiano Dambará, Luis Romano, and Manuel Veiga all published in Crioulo, culminating in 1967 with Veiga's *Oju d'Agu*, the first Crioulo novel. Prolific fiction-writer Germano Almeida represents the emergence of a new Cape Verdean narrative that employs humor, parody, and multiple storylines to narrate the complexities of contemporary Cape Verdean society.

Guinea-Bissau

The literature of Guinea-Bissau is largely postcolonial and devoted to poetry, with some notable exceptions. Two Guineans, Vasco Cabral and Amílcar Cabral, were among those African students in Lisbon at the Casa dos Estudantes do Império, many of whom, including the Angolan Agostinho **Neto**, were to play important roles in the political and cultural independence of their respective nations. Amilcar Cabral would later lead the African Party for the Independence of Guinea-Bissau and Cape Verde (PAIGC). His militant essays explore the relations between cultural production and the liberation struggle. Vasco Cabral, also a leader of the PAIGC, has produced a poetic opus beginning in 1951 that both celebrates national liberation and mourns the violence of the struggle. This line of poetry, referred to as *poesia de combate* (combat poetry) was highly cultivated in the mid 1970s and gave way to a postcolonial production that is laudatory of the revolution within an African context, while still depicting the horrors of colonialism and war. Poets such as Agnelo Regalla, Pascoal D'Artagnan Aurigemma, Tony Tcheka, and Félix Siga are among the new generation of postcolonial writers that also includes the more widely translated Hélder Proença, whose works cover the gamut from didactic *poesia de combate* to lyrical love poetry. José Carlos Schwartz was a poet, musician, and composer whose Crioulo songs are widely popular in Guinea-Bissau even long after his 1977 death.

Narrative in Guinea-Bissau is largely emergent and postcolonial, with the first Guinean novel, Abdulai Sila's *Eterna Paixão* (Eternal Passion) published in 1994; several other writers have produced short fiction in a now flourishing literary-cultural scene. Revolutionary theater-dance groups established in the zones liberated by the PAIGC during the protracted liberation struggle against the Portuguese played an essential role in socio-political life. These revolutionary groups, very much a part of combat culture, continued during the first decade of nationhood.

Mozambique

Critics of African Portuguese-language literatures, such as Russell Hamilton, emphasize the tripartite racial division of social-cultural organizations in early twentieth-century colonial Mozambique. Writers associated with these groups published their literary endeavors in the newspapers *O Brado Africano* (The African Roar, published in Portuguese and Ronga), and *A Voz de Mozambique* (The Voice of Mozambique), important outlets for an emergent literature.

Among Mozambique's early twentieth-century historically significant literary voices are the poet Rui de Noronha (1909–43), whose sonnets touch on African themes, and Joao Dias (1926–49), the author of *Godido e Outros Contos* (Godido and Other Stories) (1989). The status of native-born white writers as distinctly Mozambican raises some critical controversy. The poet Rui Knopfli produced a significant body of work, but left Mozambique just before independence. He represents a case in point, since his poetry influenced new Mozambican writers, although some critics argue that his verse is undeniably Portuguese in language and form. There have also been questions about whether the hermetic verse of post-independence poet Luis Carlos Patraquim (b. 1953) can be considered truly Mozambican. Other white writers are included unquestionably in the Mozambican canon and include such important figures as Orlando **Mendes**, Rui Nogar, and Mia **Couto**.

The dominant figure of twentieth-century Mozambican letters is José **Craveirinha** whose poetic production begins in the 1940s. In this long span of creativity, Craveirinha's poetry combines aspects of social realism, oral traditions, political militancy, intimacy, and pan-Africanism (see **diaspora and pan-Africanism**) with a distinct Mozambican transformation of Portuguese language. Other pre-independence writers include Noémia da Sousa, whose poetry exalts the African landscape and establishes solidarity with oppressed Africans worldwide. There is also an important current of militant verse among writers associated with the Mozambican Liberation Front (FRELIMO) that includes poetry by Marcelino dos Santos, Jorge Rebelo, Sérgio Vieira, and Rui Nogar, among others. Journalist and political figure Luis Bernardo **Honwana** published a significant and influential collection of short stories, *We Killed Mangy-Dog* (*Nós Matamos o Cão Tinhoso*) in 1964.

Postcolonial Mozambican literature reflects the cultural and ethnic diversity of the new nation and includes writers who are black, mestizo, white, and of Indian descent, all of whom engage in literary explorations of different aspects of *moçambicanidade* ("Mozambican-ness"). The complex lyrical and prose poetry of prolific poet Eduardo White (b. 1963) celebrates love, eroticism, passion, and flight. Other emergent and diverse poets include Armando Artur, Nelson Sauté, Hélder Muteia, Juvenal Bucuane, Jorge Viegas, and Mia **Couto**, Mozambique's pre-eminent post-independence fiction writer. Born in 1955, Mia Couto explores in his narratives the multiple levels of Mozambican reality, irony, and imagination of daily life in a nation torn apart by political conflict. The innovations of literary language and form through popular discourse and traditional oral culture have opened new avenues in an emergent Mozambican literature. Novelist Ungulani Ba Ka Khosa's (b. 1957) works explore the relationship between literature and historiography, particularly in his 1987 novel *Ualalapi*. Prose fiction, long marginalized in Mozambique in favor of poetry, is now a varied practice cultivated by such diverse writers as Suleiman Cassamo, Marcelo Panguana, Albino Magaia, Paulina Chiziane, and Lília Momplé.

São Tomé-Príncipe

The West African islands nation of São Tomé-Príncipe has a rich Crioulo oral narrative tradition along with a theatrical one in the *tchiloli*, particular to the island of São Tomé. This Creolized festival performance is based on a sixteenth-century play from Madeira that has been transformed over the years by African ritual, music, and dance. Literary discourse also has a relatively long history that began in the nineteenth-century Crioulo poetry of Francisco Stockler (1839–84), while the first Portuguese-language poet of the islands is Caetano da Costa Alegre (1864–90) who studied medicine in Lisbon and whose love poetry is imbued with disillusionment, irony, and racial alienation.

In twentieth-century pre-independence Santomense poetry, the dominant figure is Francisco José **Tenreiro** (1921–63), a geographer, teacher, and colonial official whose first volume of poetry, *Ilha do Nome Santo* (Island of the Saintly Name) (1942), is deeply influenced by Harlem Renaissance and negritude writers and expresses an African diasporic consciousness. Tenreiro's contemporaries, Maria Manuela Margarido (b. 1925) and Tomaz Medeiros (b. 1931), both use the *socopé* (a popular Santomense dance) rhythm in their works. Marcelo Veiga (1892–1976), who was also influenced by negritude, published most of his anti-colonial and Príncipe regionalist works following national independence. Alda do Espírito Santo's (b. 1926) best-known poem, "Onde estão os homens caçados neste vente de loucura?" (Where are the Men Hunted in This Wind of Madness?) (1958), reimagines the War of Bateba, a police massacre of Santomense laborers that took place in 1953.

Postcolonial poets have had their works disseminated in nationally produced anthologies, and include Carlos Espírito Santo (b. 1952) and Fernando de Macedo, both of whose poetry is highly anti-colonial and touches on historic themes. While some pre-independence narratives were produced both by Portuguese colonials on the islands, including Fernando Reis who also edited collections of oral narrative, and Santomense in Portugal, such as Mario Domingues's *Bildungsromanen O Menino Entre Gigantes* (The Boy Among Giants) (1960), Santomense fiction is largely postcolonial. Novelists such as Rufino do Espirito Santo, Manu Barreto, and Sacramento Neto are part of an emergent group of post-independence writers whose works are influenced by rural cultural traditions and languages.

Further reading

Afolabi, Niyi (ed.) (2001) *Season of Harvest: Essays on*

the Literatures of Lusophone Africa, Trenton, New Jersey: Africa World Press.

Burness, Don (ed.) (1989) *Horse of White Clouds: Poems from Lusophone Africa*, Athens, Ohio: Center for International Study, Ohio University.

Chabal, Patrick (ed.) (1996) *The Postcolonial Literature of Lusophone Africa*, Evanston: Northwestern University Press.

Ferreira, Manuel and Moser, Gerald (eds) (1993) *A New Bibliography of Lusophone African Literature*, London: Hans Zell.

Hamilton, Russell G. (1975) *Voices from an Empire*, Minneapolis: University of Minnesota Press.

Moser, Gerald (1969) *Essays in Portuguese–African Literature*, University Park: Pennsylvania State University Press.

Peres, Phyllis A. (1997) *Resistance and Transculturation in Lusophone African Literatures*, Gainesville: University Presses of Florida.

PHYLLIS PERES

Pringle, Thomas

b. 1789, Edinburgh, UK; d. 1834, London, UK

poet

The Scottish/South African poet was born in Edinburgh and worked in the Scottish Records Office before his family was forced to migrate to South Africa in search of economic opportunities in 1826. Pringle worked as a librarian and editor in South Africa, and he was the founder of some early literary journals in the Cape Colony. His prose works, including *Narrative of a Residence in South Africa* (1834) belong to a tradition of frontier literature, of travel and adventure, following nineteenth-century conventions of discovery and revelation. But perhaps Pringle is better known for his African poems, many of them rediscovered and republished in the 1980s in *The African Poems of Thomas Pringle*, edited by E. Pereira and M. Chapman. Pringle's verse does not deploy the mythology that was to make white poets like Roy **Campbell** famous, and many of his poems did not attract much attention until after the end of apartheid (see **apartheid and post-apartheid**). Nevertheless, these African poems are now considered to be some of the earliest attempts by a white writer to treat the African landscape as a place populated by human beings forced into new modes of alienation rather than merely a stage for enacting desires or rehearsing romantic myths about Africa.

Further reading

Chapman, Michael (1996) *Southern African Literatures*, London and New York: Longman.

SIMON GIKANDI

publishing

Despite some differences in culture and history, the publishing industry across Africa bears many similarities. Like many sectors of the economy the publishing industry has developed in a context defined by political and economic crisis. For this reason, among others, the salient features of this industry reflect the complicated politics and cultures surrounding the nature and role of the book on the continent, the gulf between local and foreign publishers, and levels of literacy. The impact of these factors is evident across the whole spectrum of publishing in Africa, including the publishing of literary texts. But in discussing the nature of publishing in Africa, we need to keep in mind Peter Anderson's observation that "South African literature ... is not the best guide to literary publishing in South Africa" (1996: Johannesburg). Anderson's point is that most of the well-established writers in South Africa – and, one would add, in Africa generally – either live outside their respective countries, and/or publish overseas, especially in Europe, where their publishers can pay them the sums of money their writing merits. One way of thinking about the condition of literary publishing in Africa is to consider the reasons and the features that account for this state of affairs.

The business of publishing

First consider the facts. Educational publishing accounts for 70–80 percent of the industry's contribution to the continent's economic activity,

yet Africa imports about 70 percent of its book needs from (mainly) Europe and the United States of America. At the same time, the continent exports only about 5 percent of its local publishing output, and in indigenous publishing the private sector accounts for only about 20 percent of Africa-published books. In short, about 80 percent of titles in Africa are produced by multinationals. This situation is further complicated by the fact that in Africa in general there are extremely low levels of literacy and low per capita incomes. These two factors have contributed substantially to a poor book-buying culture on the continent. For example, according to Ruth Makosti and others, South Africa, with its estimated population of 40 million, has a book-buying public estimated at about 5 percent of the population.

The implications of the above factors for the literary publishing industry on the continent are clear and can be represented as follows. Since the local industry relies so heavily on educational publishing, many large publishers will often accept literary titles if they are believed to have a significant potential to be prescribed in schools and/or tertiary institutions in their respective countries. The success or failure of books is thus dependent on the criteria that different departments of education put in place for approval of school textbooks. Often, in countries dominated by political censorship (in the apartheid South Africa or postcolonial Kenya and Nigeria, to cite just a few examples), works that are critical of their respective states often run the risk of being rendered unacceptable for schools and, sometimes, tertiary institutions. Educational publishers in Africa are often multinational companies (South Africa is an exception here, with some big local companies), who may consider risking on certain titles that may be deemed unacceptable educational material in Africa, but that seem to have potential to sell elsewhere. This has meant that many established writers who object to the repression or censorship of their ideas often try to get published overseas. Clearly, if their works cannot get into educational institutions, with such low literacy levels and low per capita income how else can such writers earn their keep if not by resorting to the support of the companies on other continents? Also, since there are so few – and under-resourced – indigenous publishing houses, writers who choose to publish locally still face the dilemma: of publishing in their own countries but with a non-indigenous publisher (Swaziland, for example, has only one main publisher, Macmillan), with profits being taken to countries outside of Africa. In this sense, what one might loosely call the canon of Africa literature – the works of Chinua **Achebe**, Wole **Soyinka**, Es'kia **Mphahlele**, J.M. **Coetzee**, **Ngugi wa Thiong'o**, Ayi Kwei **Armah**, and others – is not reflective of the literary output of the African publishing industry.

The packaging of African writers

Given the dominance of multinationals in African literary publishing, then, the question of how these institutions go about packaging African writers in their promotional materials is an important one. In her unpublished study of "the constructions of South Africa" by leading British publishers such as Penguin, Bloomsbury, The Women's Press, Abacus, Vintage, and Pandora from 1985 to 1995, Laura Chrisman found that the "devices used to package this material are strikingly consistent, and cut across different publishing houses." Her conclusion was that: "From the predominantly photographic book covers through to the style of cover blurb and on to the authorities selected to provide endorsement, what we receive in the metropolis is the promise of a 'documentary' glimpse into the real South Africa." She further observed that "[b]eyond this consistency of general presentation, however, the writers are packaged through gender- and race-specific codes" that tend to neglect challenging South African cultural and intellectual productions undermining "the construction of South Africa as a transparent racial allegory." Even the authorities called upon to endorse the literature tend to emphasize the typicality of the writers' identities. Chrisman notes that the emphasis on this kind of packaging "downplay[s] the fictionality and artistry of such creative writers." Interestingly, when white writers are packaged, she observes that the writers' achievements (artistic and intellectual) and other information about them is provided. She argues that such packaging is reflective of the perceived buyers of these titles, namely (mainly) white Europeans.

Chrisman admits, of course, that her paper excludes the discussion of specialist publishers like Longman (Longman African Writers) and Heinemann (African Writers Series). While the emphasis on race – and I would add colonialism (see **colonialism, neocolonialism, and postcolonialism**), post-independence, and its subsequent litany of censorship and tyranny – might seem a popular trend in the packaging of African literature by the mainstream publishing houses that Chrisman refers to, I have to emphasize that the specialist publishers have also indulged in the practice for a long time. The development and promotion of African literature by Heinemann through their African Writers Series (AWS) began with the publication of Chinua Achebe's *Things Fall Apart*, and most titles in the series in its early years came from Nigeria and West Africa generally. This focus on West Africa was perhaps explained by the fact that Alan Hill, the then managing director of Heinemann, had a special interest in West Africa and, to some extent, East Africa. In addition, there were hardly any publishers of note in these regions, although cultural and political nationalism (see **nationalism and post-nationalism**), especially as articulated by intellectuals from institutions like Makerere University, provided rich resources of potentially publishable and saleable materials. With its financial muscle, Heinemann was to develop and promote AWS so well that African literature is in fact very closely associated in many people's minds with the Series. Indeed, *Things Fall Apart* is arguably now a symbol of African literature itself, despite the fact that the Nigerian Amos **Tutuola**'s *The Palm-Wine Drinkard* was published six years before it, while the first novel in English by a black person in Africa was perhaps Sol Plaatje's *Mhudi* (1930). Plaatje's novel raised the same issues that were to make Achebe's novel popular and influential in African literary studies, but it was not published by a major publisher and hence remained obscure until it was reissued in the African Writers Series in 1978.

In terms of packaging itself, many African works have historically been promoted in terms of the race of their author. For example, Peter Abrahams' *Mine Boy* is said to be "the first modern novel of black South Africa"; *Mhudi* is promoted as "[t]he first novel written in English by a black South

African"; and perhaps an ultimate representation of this concern with race and Africa as a dark continent is reflected in some promotional reviews of *Anthills of the Savannah*, in which the novel is commended for "bringing humanity where we feared it did not exist." The focus on gender in the packaging of the AWS titles does exist, but not to the extent that race does. This culture of book promotion is, arguably, reflective of the publishing strategy that Heinemann adopted very early in setting up the AWS. As already indicated, Alan Hill had a particular interest in West and East Africa, with southern Africa initially excluded because he thought that the region, or South Africa more specifically, had a number of well-established publishing houses. Heinemann broadened its geographical net wider by including North Africa and southern Africa. Even then, black writers were preferred, presumably because of their political disadvantages. Later, Asian and colored writers, and eventually white ones, were included in the series.

But if race, colonialism, and post-independence seemed to be good commodities, it was because former colonial masters and, later, post-independence states, were perhaps equally brutal in their dealings with their respective subjects. The imprisonment and exile of Ngugi wa Thiong'o in Kenya, Es'kia Mphahlele in South Africa and Wole Soyinka in Nigeria are some of the more famous examples of the political conditions that have made it difficult for some of the continent's leading writers to continue publishing in their home countries. At the same time, however, it was precisely this situation of repression and censorship that made these writers attractive to foreign publishers. Thus was established the basis of promoting and packaging African literature in political terms.

Problems and prospects

In spite of the domination of foreign publishing houses in the production and promotion of African literature, it is important to note that some local, indigenous publishers have issued literature of remarkable quality in the face of economic difficulties, repression, and oppression. In Zimbabwe, for example, Baobab Books published award-winning works by Charles **Mungoshi**, Chenjerai **Hove**, and Yvonne **Vera**. J.M. Coetzee's famous novella *Dusk Lands* and Njabulo **Ndebele**'s ground-breaking collection *Fools and Other Stories* were initially published by Ravan Press, and David Philip Publishers' Paperback South Series saw the publication and reissuing of many works by South Africans, including many works that had been banned in the apartheid years. Indeed, through legal appeals David Philip Publishers have been instrumental in getting many of the titles banned in the 1960s and 1970s unbanned in the 1980s.

In spite of these successes, however, the publishing of African literature, both on the continent and abroad, did not continue to flourish in the 1980s and 1990s the way it did in the late 1950s, the 1960s, and 1970s. In general, publishers seem to have become weary of new writers. There may be many reasons for this. One of them is that many publishers rely on their sales of a tested group of writers, or writers already well received by the reading public but published elsewhere. Two, many publishing houses are now subsidiaries of media conglomerates, which perhaps have little understanding of the dynamics of book publishing, especially how the industry's finances work, or which simply seek quick profits from an industry that takes long to become profitable. Well-established writers are clearly less of a risk than new ones because they can use their history to sell their new products. Another important thing to observe is that because of inadequately developed film industries in most African countries, titles published locally seldom get adapted into films, or even radio and television dramas. In other words, both writers and their publishers lose incredibly large amounts of potential income from subsidiary rights. This situation is not improved by the fact that the intra-African book trade is in a poor state. Indeed, it is far easier to get African books, published in Africa, if one orders titles through a European agent or book store rather than making a direct order from the relevant publisher. Furthermore, publishers do not seem to actively license translation rights to their counterparts in other African countries. And while a few exploit opportunities to co-publish, the practice is in fact kept to a minimum.

What about the state of publishing literatures written in or translated into indigenous African languages? Generally speaking, the challenges in this area are similar to the ones discussed above, except that there is an added challenge here: most of these languages cannot travel across countries, and for this reason they hardly ever find opportunities to get published elsewhere. Indeed, even in their respective countries, the publishers of African-language literatures are usually educational publishers who rely heavily on the willingness and ability of schools and tertiary institutions to prescribe their titles for classroom use. In schools in particular, this reliance on endorsement creates a whole series of political problems, especially when states are uncomfortable with the political and economic issues represented in certain works. Since African-language literatures generally have a negligible market outside educational institutions controlled by the state, many writers in indigenous African languages have to be particularly careful in the ideas and styles that they employ in their writing, if they wish to avoid censorship. The state of publishing African-language literatures in South Africa under apartheid provides us with the most dramatic example of how the policies of the state could determine the form and subject of literature.

Similar situations can be found in many parts of Africa during the colonial and postcolonial period. All these do not augur well for African literature published on its continent.

Further reading

Anderson, Peter (1996) "Literary Publishing in South Africa," in Basil van Rooyen (ed.) *How to Get Published in South Africa*, 2nd edn, Johannesburg: Southern Book Publishers.

Chrisman, Laura (n.d.) "Short Circuits: British Metropolitan Representations of South African Culture" (unpublished ms).

Makotsi, Ruth *et al.* (2000) *Expanding the Book Trade across Africa (A Study of the Current Barriers and Future Potential)*, London and Harare: ADEA and APNET.

Mpe, Phaswane (1999) "The Role of the Heinemann African Writers Series in the Development and Promotion of African Literature," *African Studies* 58, 1: 105–22.

Van Rooyen, Basil (1996) *How to Get Published in South Africa: A Guide for Authors*, 2nd edn, Johannesburg: Southern Book Publishers.

PHASWANE MPE

R

Rabearivelo, Jean-Joseph

b. about 1901, Antananarive, Madagascar; d. 1937, Madagascar

writer, poet, playwright

Marginalized from even before his birth, the great Madagascan Jean-Joseph Rabearivelo was born out of wedlock to an impoverished young woman belonging to a noble family of the Hova people in Antananarive in either 1901, 1903 or 1904 – he himself variously used the different dates. He was baptized Joseph-Casimir but later changed his name to Jean-Joseph so that he had the same initials as the "great French writer" (Jean-Jacques Rousseau). Rabearivelo was taken in by a maternal uncle; his formal schooling was cut short when he was expelled from school. From 1915 to 1919 he worked as secretary and interpreter for a Madagascan nobleman before being employed in 1923 as a proof-reader for the Imprimerie de l'Imerina (Imerina Press), a position that he held until his death by suicide in 1937. In 1926 he married Mary Razafitrima, with whom he had five children, one of whom, his beloved daughter Voahangy, died in 1933, aged only 2. Rabearivelo never recovered from her death and when another daughter was born shortly after, he named her Velomboahangy, Voahangy reincarnated.

Throughout his life, Rabearivelo had to contend with material difficulties, frequent illnesses, and a morbid personality. He sought escape from these conditions through the use of alcohol, opium, gambling, and promiscuity. These abuses were the result of his personal, interior exile which stemmed from his desire to be, at the same time, both Madagascan and French. Colonial society barred him from administrative posts for which he applied but did admit him as an associate member of the Académie Malgache (Madagascan Academy) in 1931. However, they refused to include him in the delegation which they sent to the prestigious Paris Exhibition of 1937 (judging basket weavers to be more representative of Madagascar) despite the fact that a local newspaper had already proclaimed the fact that his play *Imaitsoanala, fille d'oiseau* (Imaitsoanala, the Bird's Daughter) would be performed.

From early on, Rabearivelo was involved in literature, collaborating in and contributing to two literary journals, *18° latitude sud* (18° Latitude South) (1923–7) and *Capricorne* (Capricorn) (1930–1). He is the first major Madagascan poet to write in French. Through his art, he aimed at creating a literature in French that would somehow escape being classified as French literature. His work, when not written directly in French, is translated into the language of the colonizer in an attempt to appease his dual affiliation and to reconcile the racial, ethnic, and cultural differences which exist between his Madagascan and French selves. He wrote specifically so that he would be acknowledged as a writer, and his deep-rooted existential dichotomy is illustrated in his reason for writing "dans cette langue que j'ai choisie/pour préserver mon nom de l'oubli (the language I have chosen/to keep my name from oblivion)" ("Lamba" in *Presque-songes*, 1990: Paris).

Unlike many black writers of the early 1920s, such as Aimé Césaire and Léopold **Senghor**,

Rabearivelo did not live in Paris but remained on the island of his birth and was thus excluded from the hub of French culture. It is not therefore surprising that his works are rooted in the culture that he knew best. Of his creative works, six collections of poetry – *La Coupe de cendres* (A Goblet of Ashes) (1924), *Sylves* (1927), *Volumes* (1928), *Presque-songes* (Almost dreams) (1934), and *Traduit de la nuit* (Translations from the Night) (1935) – and two plays, *Imaitsoanala, fille d'oiseau* (Imaitsoanala, the Bird's Daughter) (1935) and *Aux portes de la ville* (At the City Gates) (1936) were published during his lifetime.

Rabearivelo's poetry is permeated with a fascination for death: not death as it is conceived of by the Western world, where it is seen as an end and as decay, but rather as a symbol of new life. Objects in nature undergo continual metamorphosis, such as a tree growing among the tombstones of the ancestors which feeds on the dead and brings forth fruit in a foreign language. This veneration of the dead is a typical feature of Madagascan society which is commemorated in the ceremony of *famadihana*, or exhumation of the dead, whereby the ancestors are taken out of their tombs, washed, dressed in new clothes, and reburied. This renewal of nature in cyclical form, night giving way to day, death to rebirth, is a distinctive feature of Rabearivelo's poetry. So too is his use of the *hainteny*, the important oral tradition genre of Madagascar (see **oral literature and performance**). Rabearivelo claimed that many of his poems were translated from Malgache, like his posthumous collection *Vieilles chansons des pays d'Imerina* (Old Songs from Imerina) (1967), but where bilingual editions exist one is never certain which came first: the French or the Malgache version.

Such is also the case with his plays, which exist in both French and Malgache versions. The French version of *Imaitsoanala, fille d'oiseau* (1935) was only published in its Malgache form *Imaitsoanala, zanaborona* in 1988, along with *Eo ambavahadim-bohitra*, which had appeared in 1936 under the French title of *Aux portes de la ville*. Both these plays were dramatizations of Malagasy folk tales which deal with the mystery of the origin of the Malagasy people and the Merina monarchy.

Rabearivelo's novels *Aube Rouge* (Red Dawn) (written in 1925) and *L'Interférence* (written in 1928) are denunciations of colonial rule and attempts to tell Madagascan history from the point of view of a Madagascan – up till then, previous accounts had been written by Europeans from their perspective. In spite of his prolific output, this tragic yet great Madagascan writer is today known as the forgotten poet, mainly because of the fact that all his earlier works are out of print except for *Poèmes* (re-edited by Hatier in 1990) which contains three previously published volumes: *Presque-songes*, *Traduit de la nuit* (arguably his greatest work), and *Chants pour Abéone*.

Further reading

Adejunmobi, Moradewun (1996) *J.-J. Rabearivelo, Literature and Lingua Franca in Colonial Madagascar*, New York: Peter Lang.

Boudry, Robert (1958) *Jean-Joseph Rabearivelo et la mort* (Jean-Joseph Rabearivelo and Death), Paris: Présence Africaine.

Joubert, Jean-Louis (1991) *Littératures de l'Océan Indien* (Literatures of the Indian Ocean), Vanves, France: EDICEF.

Rabearivelo, Jean-Joseph (1990) *Poèmes* (Poems), Paris: Éditions Hatier.

CAROLE M. BECKETT

Rabemananjara, Jacques

b. 1913, Mangabe, Madagascar; d. 2005, France

poet, playwright, and politician

Born at Mangabe (or, to give it its Malgache name, Maroantsetra), Rabemananjara was from his earliest days associated with the east coast of Madagascar which was settled by people from Indonesia and Malaysia. This accident of birth, together with the time spent as a youth with his maternal grandfather who taught him about Malgache traditions and the importance of ancestors, were to have a profound effect on his later literary creations.

After studying at the local school he entered the seminary in Antananarive and later left to take up posts in the colonial administration. In 1939 he was sent to France, as part of the Madagascan delegation, to participate in the 150th anniversary of the French revolution. When the rest of the delegation returned, he stayed on and obtained a job in the Ministry of Colonies while at the same time enrolling at the Sorbonne, where he obtained a BA degree. It was then that he met Léopold **Senghor** and Alioune Diop, who were greatly to influence and encourage him in his career as a writer. In 1946 he returned to Madagascar where he became actively engaged in politics. In November of that year he was elected the Madagascan deputy to the French National Assembly. During the massive nationalist uprising in March 1947, Rabemananjara was arrested for allegedly being one of the instigators of the revolt against the colonial authorities and was given a life sentence with hard labor. He was to spend nine long years in prisons in Antananarive, Nosy-Lava on the east coast, and in Marseilles. When he was conditionally freed in 1956 (he was obliged to reside in France and was to be kept under surveillance) he returned to Paris and renewed his contacts with the Negro-African writers of the **negritude** movement, becoming closely involved in the publishing house and journal *Présence Africaine* and the organization of the First Congress of Black Writers and Artists held in Paris in 1956, as well as their Second Congress, held in Rome in 1959.

When Madagascar obtained its independence in 1960, he returned and was elected deputy for the Tamatave (Toamasina) region. He was alternately minister of the national economy, of agriculture and rural development and minister of foreign affairs before being designated as vice-president. President Philibert Tsiranana resigned because of public pressure in 1972, and once again Rabemananjara left his homeland, this time in self-imposed exile, and resettled in France.

Rabemananjara's first poems were included in Léopold Senghor's *Anthologie de la nouvelle poésie nègre et malgache de langue française* (Anthology of New Negro and Malgache Poetry Written in French), published in 1948. His first long poem, *Antsa* (Eulogy) (1948), was written in prison when he heard that he was to be put to death by firing squad two days later. It is a bitter and passionate cry of a man who is to lose his life, but also the protest of an entire nation against the evils and injustices of the colonial period. His second collection, *Lamba* (the traditional form of dress in Madagascar) (1956), is

an evocation of his homeland and contains many highly erotic poems, for Rabemananjara sees the shape of the island as being the same as the female sexual organ. Rural scenes, traditional lifestyles, ancient customs and beliefs, the comparison between the country and the beloved form the major themes of this collection. In his critical work *Littératures de l'Océan Indien* (Literatures of the Indian Ocean) (1991), Jean-Louis Joubert stresses the importance of the pilgrim which is a leitmotif throughout Rabemananjara's poetry: the poet sees himself as undertaking a journey to a sacred place as an act of religious devotion. For the poet, this represents a rediscovery of the past with its rich traditions and an affirmation of self and an entire population who have been deprived of their past. These nostalgic elements and the desire to return to the country of birth are easily understood when one remembers that Rabemananjara spent much of his life in exile.

Apart from poetry, Rabemananjara also wrote three plays. The first, *Les Dieux Malgaches* (Madagascan Gods) (1942) was written when one of his teachers of French literature at the seminary he attended stated that none of his pupils would ever be able to write a play which could rival the classical French tragedies. Rabemananjara rose to the challenge and wrote a five-act play in alexandrins, the typical 12-meter verse of seventeenth-century theater. Based on the historical events surrounding the death of King Radama II, who was pro-Christian and in favor of foreigners, and his conflict with his prime minister who was violently opposed to the Westernization of his country, *Les Dieux Malgaches* deals with progress and modernization of the island. His second play *Les Boutriers de l'aurore* (The Boatmen of Dawn) (1957) was written in the prison of Nosy-Lava. Set in times past, the story is largely pessimistic: for reasons unknown, the gods have cursed the boatmen who have settled on the eastern coast of the island. *Les Agapes des dieux* (The Gods' Banquet) (1962), his third play, is once again inspired by Malgache legend and deals with two star-crossed lovers who throw themselves into a lake, formed by a volcanic crater, near the town of Antsirabé. Although Rabemananjara's plays allowed him to give voice to his homesickness by dramatizing ancient legends and political maneuverings, they have never been popular and have rarely been produced.

Very much a writer who claims adherence to the negritude movement, Rabemananjara's work is both an expression of personal emotions and a militant literature which fights for the reinstatement and recognition of the value of his own people. He accepted both his own culture and that of the country that adopted him, and that he adopted by using its language, French, to fight for equality and sharing without ever having to be subjected to humiliation and insults. It is in this sense that he called himself "the hijacker of language."

Further reading

Joubert, Jean-Louis (1991) *Littératures de l'Océan Indian* (Literature of the Indian Ocean), Vanves, France: EDICEF

Rabemananjara, Jacques (1978) *Oeuvres complètes* (Complete Works), Paris: Présence Africaine.

CAROLE M. BECKETT

Rabemananjara, Raymond William

b. 1917, Madagascar

historian and writer

Active member of the Malagasy movement of national liberation which led to the insurrection of 1947, Raymond William Rabemananjara has maintained a literary career together with political activism and a vigilant defense of humanistic values. His non-fiction literary works pay tribute to the Malagasy nation through a probing investigation of its civilization. In *La Vérité sur l'affaire malgache* (The Truth about the Malagasy Affair) (1948) he shares a detailed account of the trial that came in the wake of the failed revolution of 1947. *Chronique d'une saison carcérale en Lémurie* (Chronicle of a Carceral Season in Lemurie) (1990) recalls a period of Rabemananjara's life in the late 1970s when, returning to Madagascar from France, he found himself falsely accused and incarcerated by the new Marxist regime. As a historian, Rabemananjara offers through the study of political, economic, and social conditions in Madagascar a better understanding of Madagascar's identity and place in the world.

Further reading

Rabemananjara, R.W. (1990) *Chronique d'une saison carcérale en Lémurie* (Chronical of a Carceral Season in Lemurie), Antananarivo: Revue de l'Océan Indien.

MAGALI COMPAN

Rafenomanjato, Charlotte Arrisoa

b. 1938, Madagascar; d. 2008, Antananarivo, Madagascar

writer and translator

A bilingual author who writes in both French and her mother tongue, Malgache (Malagasy), Rafenomanjato (pronounced "rafenmanzat") has experimented in many genres: poems, novels, short stories, and plays. The child of a doctor and a gifted musician, she became a midwife and later married a diplomat, which enabled her to travel widely. Most of her works remain unpublished but her plays, some fifteen in all, have been widely produced both on stage and for film and have received many prizes. *Le Prince de l'étang* (The Prince of the Pond) (1988) has been translated into Italian and *Le Troupeau* (The Herd) (1991) has been translated into English. Her themes are varied but deal mainly with Malgache issues: superstitions, changing society, foreign settlers on her island, the disappearance of human values in modern times, the potentialities of life, and the discovery of hidden values and human dignity. A highly gifted writer who extensively reworks her texts, Rafenomanjato is one of many unknown Madagascan writers.

Further reading

Rafenomanjato, Charlotte Arrisoa (1988) *Le Prince de l'étang* (The Prince of the Pond), Paris: Buzoni.

——(1990) *Le Pétale écarlate* (The Scarlet Petal), Antananarive: Société Malgache d'Édition.

——(1991) *Le Troupeau* (The Herd), Paris: Ubu Repertory Theatre.
——(1993) *Le Cinquième Sceau* (The Fifth Seal), Paris: L'Harmattan.

CAROLE M. BECKETT

Rajemisa-Raolison, Régis

b. 1913, Madagascar; d. 1990, Madagascar

poet and educator

Régis Rajemisa-Raolison contributed to Franco-Malagasy letters as both a poet and an educator. In his sole published volume of verses, *Les Fleurs de l'île rouge* (Flowers of the Red Island) (1948), his poetry maintains continuity with classical French poetic forms and portrays Madagascar as an island of exotic pastoral beauty. His tone is highly nostalgic and draws heavily upon Malagasy cultural traditions. Rajemisa-Raolison also worked with poet and political activist Jacques **Rabemananjara** publishing and co-editing the *Revue des jeunes de Madagascar* (The Young Malagasy Review) (1935–6), a polemical publication espousing humanistic ideals. He also founded the Malagasy Union of Poets and Writers, of which he was president in 1952. His most important contribution to the humanities in Madagascar, however, was his publication of numerous grammar books, school textbooks, dictionaries, and articles on Malagasy language and literature.

Further reading

Rajemisa-Raolison, R. (1948) *Les Fleurs de l'île rouge* (Flowers of the Red Island), Antananarivo: Impr. Cath. Antanimena.

MAGALI COMPAN

Rakotoson, Michèle

b. 1948, Antananarive, Madagascar

writer

Born in Antananarive, Rakotoson left Madagascar in 1983 for political reasons and settled in Paris, where she obtained a DEA (Diplôme d'études approfondies) in sociology and where she became actively involved in the publishing of literary journals and radio and television work, as well as being in charge of the contest for unpublished works organized by Radio France 1. She was writer in residence at Providence University (USA) in 1990. Rakotoson writes in both Malgache and French and has published plays, short stories, and novels. It is the latter genre which has particularly created her reputation of a writer of consequence. Her novels, mainly set in Madagascar (*Elle, au printemps* (She, in Springtime) is the exception, as it is set in France) are filled with traditional Malgache customs and legends. Their tone is mainly despairing as they contain striking and bitter images of a country which is ruined, poverty stricken, and desolate because of political oppression, both foreign and indigenous.

Further reading

Rakotoson, Michèle (1988) *Le Bain des reliques* (Washing of the Relics), Paris: Karthala.
——(1994) *Dadabé*, Paris: Karthala.
——(1996) *Elle, au printemps* (She, in Springtime), Saint-Maur, France: Sépia.
——(1998) *Henoy: Fragments en écorce* (Listen: Fragments in Bark), Avin, Belgium: Luce Wilquin.

CAROLE M. BECKETT

Ranaivo, Flavien

b. 1914, Madagascar

poet and writer

Poet, filmmaker, essayist, journalist, government official, Flavien Ranaivo made his most important contribution to Franco-Malagasy literature with his interpretative translations of the *hain-teny*, a traditional form of oral Malagasy poetry consisting of competitive exchanges usually centered around the subject of love. Responsible for introducing this form of Malagasy creative expression to a larger international audience, Ranaivo published three volumes of verse: *L'Ombre et le vent* (Shadow and Wind) (1947), *Mes Chansons de toujours* (My Songs of Always) (1955), and *Le Retour au bercail* (Return to the Fold) (1962). His poetry is considered a free translation, an adaptation of the *hain-teny* into the French language. Using the French language to translate an oral tradition and express Malagasy subjectivity, his style is densely metaphoric as it draws upon Malagasy symbols, proverbs, and rhythms. The result is often difficult poetic verse requiring specialized knowledge of Malagasy history and culture as well as sophisticated poetic interpretation. Ranaivo's poetry amounts to more than simple translation, and his personal perceptions together with his mastery of French poetic techniques have informed his oeuvre.

Further reading

Ranaivo, F. (1947) *L'Ombre et le vent* (Shadow and Wind), Antananarivo: Imprimerie Officielle.

MAGALI COMPAN

Rawiri, Angèle Ntyugwetondo

b. 1954, Port-Gentil, Gabon

novelist

Angèle Rawiri is considered to be the first female novelist of Gabon. In her works she mainly explores the social and cultural contradictions of postcolonial Africa through narratives full of social realism (see **colonialism, neocolonialism, and postcolonialism**; **realism and magical realism**). In her first two novels, *Elonga* (1980) and *G'amerakano: au carrefour* (G'amerakano: At the Crossroads) (1983), Rawiri presents women characters who are trapped in the web of the complexities of a society struggling through the tensions and contradictions of modernity (see **modernity and modernism**), caught between European and African cultural values, which she examines closely. But, as with Emilienne in *Fureurs et cris de femmes* (Furies and Cries of Women) (1989), her third novel, most of Rawiri's characters end up overcoming the many obstacles erected by both

modern and traditional society to take control of their lives.

Further reading

Rawiri, Angèle Ntyugwetondo (1980) *Elonga*, Paris: Silex.
——(1983) *G'amerakano: au carrefour* (G'amerakano: At the Crossroads), Paris: Silex.
——(1989) *Fureurs et cris de femmes* (Furies and Cries of Women), Paris: L'Harmattan.

M'BARE NGOM

realism and magical realism

Introduction

Realism and magical realism are both modes of narrative which can be associated with particular social and historical contexts and struggles. They can also be identified by the narrative conventions and devices which help to define them. These struggles and conventions become ever more difficult to unravel when they migrate between different parts of the world, where they engage in new struggles and encounter indigenous aesthetic and storytelling heritages. Out of this crucible genres emerge and old modes are transformed. It is worth considering realism and magical realism both separately and also in relation to one another, and to avoid assuming either an absolute divide between them or a linear progression along a scale leading from one to the other.

Realism

While one should be circumspect about linking the rise of genres to social and historical forces too mechanistically, it is the case that the realist novel arose in Europe as a mode of expression of the ascendant bourgeoisie. This happened at the time when feudalism was being defeated by the rise of capitalism. Ironically, this realist novel, which was to have such a profound influence on African literary culture, arose out of the same historical conditions that were to lead to the colonization of Africa. Furthermore, the export of European culture was a tool in the arsenal of colonialism, part of what the colonizers saw as their "civilizing mission" (see **colonialism, neocolonialism, and postcolonialism**).

For all its ironies, however, this process of cultural migration should be understood as an unstable one, which simultaneously succeeded and backfired in Africa in interesting ways. From the beginning, African writers used the novel in order to interrogate the power of Western versions of history and the fictional traditions bonded to those versions. In many ways, they domesticated European forms and manipulated them to their own political and aesthetic ends, transforming them in the process.

The first novelists in Africa were part of a small elite of Western-educated writers, schooled in the colonizer's language. They were passionate about history – about the recovery of Africa's past in the face of its denigration on the part of the colonizer. The conundrum confronting these writers was that they were writing for mainly foreign audiences in European languages on order to reverse the narratives of colonialism. To "set the record straight" lends itself to the conventions of realism, with their emphasis on particular historical moments and actors.

These conventions of realism have to be understood as constructs and should not be confused with the successful capture of reality. They include identifiable settings in time and space; linear plots, which build up to climaxes which clinch all loose ends; characters are fully developed as individuals and the narrative point of view and moral purpose of the realist novel is unambiguous.

Ian Watt's by now classic study, *The Rise of the Novel* (1957), emphasizes that the plots of realism are not taken from myth or legend but relate to particular people in particular circumstances. Thus we can see how the early African novels were both attracted to the models of realism and distanced themselves from them. In particular, colonialism, as it impinged on characters, was the obvious inspiration of the early plots. However, the writers, without exception, harnessed the oral stories of myth and legend (see **oral literature and performance**) in order to turn the tables on the

colonizers and attempt to tell their own stories in their own ways.

What does appear to be the case is that women writers have tended to experiment with technique somewhat less than male writers. This may be so because of the greater urgency to tell their stories unambiguously in more literal fashion, given their double burden of both race and gender oppression. What is certainly also true, however, is that European forms, the English language and literary tradition, as well as African cultural means of expression, were transformed. In this way, boundaries between realism and various non-realistic modes became quite blurred. For this reason, it is useful to look at realism and magical realism both simultaneously and also separately.

Realism and magical realism

The use of the oral tradition – the incorporation of its style of storytelling, its proverbs and wisdoms, and the reverberation of many stories – has from the outset mediated European conventions of realism. In addition, and paradoxically, not only the cultural past but also the drive for modernity resulted in cracks and contradictions in even the earliest examples of African realism. For example, realist classics like **Ngugi wa Thiong'o**'s *A Grain of Wheat* (1966) or Chinua **Achebe**'s *Things Fall Apart* (1958) are experimenting with narrative voice and are as much influenced by Conrad's modernity (see **modernity and modernism**) as enraged by his representation of Africa.

If realism, in varied fissured and transformed ways, tended to be dominant at the moment of independence, then the heart of the emergence of magical realism in Africa lies with postcolonialism and postmodernism. While postcolonial writing comes in many shapes, sizes, and modes, it is probably true to say that magical realism is a form of postcolonial writing that most aggressively harnesses some of the tools of postmodernism – parody, irony, pastiche, and syncretism.

I am not implying, however, that realism and magical realism should be positioned on some evolutionary scale and polarized; there is not some linear progression from realism to modernism to postmodernism and magical realism. It is interesting to remember that European epic and chivalric traditions predated realism and have organic links with magical realism. Equally, Amos **Tutuola**'s *The Palm-Wine Drinkard* (1952), with its fantastic tales garnered and fashioned from the Yoruba folk tradition (see **Yoruba literature**), is the forebear of magical realism in West Africa and it was published a few years prior to Chinua Achebe's *Things Fall Apart* (1958). In other words, the syncretism between the oral and the written in Africa cuts across the realism/magical realism divide. But what, precisely, is magical realism?

Magical realism

African writers tend to reject the label of magical realism. One reason for this is that it implies the slavish imitation of Latin American narrative traditions. It suggests a denial, in other words, of local knowledge and beliefs, language, and rhetoric; it seems to perpetuate imperialist notions that nothing new, intellectually or spiritually, originated in Africa. While magical realism thrived in Latin America, it is not restricted to it.

It is probably true, as a generalization, that African magical realism has been a mode emerging predominantly from West Africa in general, and influenced by Yoruba stories most specifically. This could be the result of the survival of much more precolonial traces in indirectly ruled West Africa than elsewhere, where, for example, settlers trampled indigenous ways of life more comprehensively. Writers, not necessarily Yoruba themselves, select and manipulate Yoruba and other stories – African, Western or Latin American – in the postmodern mode of intertexuality. This Yoruba influence is buttressed by the powerful tradition established by D.O. **Fagunwa** and Amos Tutuola, whose use of Yoruba tales, which they molded and modernized, has had a profound influence on magical realist writers in Africa. Fagunwa, between 1948 and 1951, wrote his *The Forest of a Thousand Daemons* in Yoruba as one among at least nine other books. It has been translated into English by Wole **Soyinka** and, along with Amos Tutuola's mutated folk tales, written in a kind of Yoruba English, has

provided the ancestry for African magical realism. However, the fables that they wrote have to undergo crucial mutations, in both their narrative strategies and their politics, before they emerge as contemporary magical realist novels. It is important to acknowledge this ancestry and to recognize its limitations. African magical realists have used oral stories selectively and have in the process transformed them.

Magical realism thrives in a postcolonial context, given the history, culture, and politics of countries like Nigeria, which encountered Western capitalism, technology, and education haphazardly. Cities grew rapidly from rural origins, and families were divided between members who were Western-educated and those who remained inserted in precolonial economies and ways of seeing the world, with any number of positions in between. This social patchwork, dizzying in its cacophony of design, is the cloth from which the magical realist carpet is cut, mapping not the limitless vistas of fantasy but rather the new historical realities of those patchwork societies.

If magical realism can be characterized as arising from particular socio-economic circumstances, and if it can be seen to be participating in the cultural politics of postcolonialism, then it also has to be understood as a set of devices. These include its language of rhetoric, riddle, and doublespeak, which enables the fictional medium to enact its message of opposition to the hegemony of Western scientific thought. Magical realist writers contest the obliteration of indigenous ways of seeing by the blinding light of so-called progress.

At the same time, there is a tension at the heart of magical realism, which has often been seen as steeped in the beliefs and the points of view of an indigenous peasant class. There is, however, a fundamental distinction between everyday reality, among ordinary people, and the writers and intellectuals, who have had a far more thoroughgoing Western experience and who look on the culture's uneven development with self-knowledge and some distance. There is, thus, a simultaneous genuine faith in, and respect for, the magical beliefs of the peasants, and also the inevitable skepticism of Western-educated writers who assume an ironic distance from the lack of a "scientific" understanding.

It is obvious that only a writer who has traveled away from indigenous ways of life and belief can develop this ironic distancing. Or as Ben **Okri** puts it so well in *Dangerous Love* (1996: London), at first the artist saw all the terrors and rituals simply as part of the everyday reality, but "It was only later that he would learn to see them with estranged eyes" (201). This estrangement sums up the authorial point of view in magical realist novels. By contrast, in their comprehensive retention of belief in magic and in the penalties inherent in disobeying its rules, writers and storytellers like Fagunwa and Tutuola cannot write within the magical realist mode. But they have inspired and influenced such writers who do write magical realist fictions.

Magical realist writers strive towards incorporating indigenous knowledge on new terms, and their irony is employed in order to rethink tradition and to herald change. Magical realist plots deal with issues of borders, change, mixing, and syncretizing. At the same time, the unevenness of the development of their societies is reflected in the positioning of the writers themselves. They are urban and migrant, often living in, and working from, Western cultural centers. Insiders and outsiders, these writers are cultural hybrids, who grapple with the demands created by national atrocity and with the attractions inherent in contributing to national pride, but from a postcolonial perch, distant from their countries of origin. If magical realism attempts to capture reality by way of a depiction of life's many dimensions, seen and unseen, visible and invisible, rational and mysterious, such writers walk a political tightrope between capturing this reality and providing the exotic escape from reality desired by some of their Western readership.

Finally, it is important to stress the necessity of being quite specific in these definitions, given that the destabilization of the hierarchy between "magic" and "science" occurs quite broadly in African fiction. For example, magical realists may be distinguished from more culturally nationalistic writers, who employ myth and legend, deities and spirits, rituals, proverbs and injunctions, within projects of nation-building. For this reason, Harry Garuba has coined the term "animist realism" in order to signify a tendency in African fiction that is broader than magical realism.

Examples of interesting African magical realist fictions, along the lines defined here, include Ben Okri's *The Famished Road* (1991), B. Kojo **Laing**'s *Woman of the Aeroplanes* (1988), and Syl Cheney-Coker's *The Last Harmattan of Alusine Dunbar* (1990).

Further reading

Cooper, B. (1998) *Magical Realism in West African Fiction: Seeing with a Third Eye*, London: Routledge.

Garuba, Harry (2001) "Explorations in Animist Materialism and a Reading of the Poetry of Niyi Osundare," in Abdul-Rasheed Na'Allah (ed.) *The People's Poet: Emerging Perspectives on Niyi Osundare*, Trenton, New Jersey: Africa World Press.

Okri, B. (1996) *Dangerous Love*, London: Phoenix House.

Quayson, A. (1997) *Strategic Transformations in Nigerian Writing*, Oxford: James Currey.

Zamora, L.P. and Faris, W.B. (eds) (1995) *Magical Realism*, Durham and London: Duke University Press.

BRENDA COOPER

Rezzoug, Leila

b. 1956, Algeria

novelist

Algerian by birth, Leila Rezzoug has lived in France since 1973, where she works as an insurance executive. She has published two novels, *Apprivoiser l'insolence* (Tame Insolence) (1988) and *Douces errances* (Sweet Wanderings) (1992). Her work appeared at the height of French interest for Beur literature, writing by descendants of North African immigrants to France, of which her publisher, L'Harmattan, has produced its share. However, her work bears little resemblance to that of other Beur writers. She often sets her scenes far from the gritty suburban milieus favored by writers such as Morsy and Mehdi Charef, and social consciousness often takes a back seat to psychological study. Her novels tell the stories of women, frequently of Algerian origin, aware of but not haunted by their origins. Her characters, living through moments of great emotion, recount their lives in internal monologues which serve the author to move her plots toward their open-ended denouements.

Further reading

Rezzoug, Leila (1988) *Apprivoiser l'insolence* (Tame Insolence), Paris: L'Harmattan.

SETH GRAEBNER

Rifaat, Alifa

b. 1930, Cairo, Egypt; d. 1996, Egypt

short story writer and novelist

Within a controversial context of gender issues ranging through female circumcision, sexual satisfaction, and emotional oppression, Egyptian short story writer and novelist Alifa Rifaat makes a passionate plea in support of women's rights. Having herself endured oppression as a daughter and, later, a wife, Rifaat transcended her condition through her belief in the liberating and ennobling impact of Islam on women. Using this as a main theme throughout her fiction, Rifaat counteracts the prevalent misunderstanding that Islam favors the suppression of women. Her writings characteristically contain elements of the folkloric and the supernatural. Her first volume of short stories, *Hawwa' Ta'ud bi Adam* (Eve Brings Adam Back) was published in 1975. Symbolizing in her stories the union of man and woman in sex to that of the human and the Creator in death, Rifaat asserts her Sufi belief in marriage as a fulfillment, not only of the flesh, but also of the soul. Another collection of her short stories, *Man Yakun al-Rajul?* (Who is the

Man?), appeared in 1981 and reflected her position on various issues that touch Egyptian women's lives. Denys Johnson-Davies, the renowned translator of Arabic literature, was the first to expose the Western audience to the writings of Alifa Rifaat through his translation of a selection from her short stories under the title *A Distant View of a Minaret* (1983).

Further reading

Badran, Margot and Cooke, Miriam (1990) *Opening the Gates*, Bloomington: Indiana University Press.

RIHAM SHEBLE

Rive, Richard Moore

b. 1931, Cape Town, South Africa; d. 1989, Cape Town, South Africa

short story writer, novelist, editor, and critic

An educationalist, short story writer, novelist, dramatist, editor, and critic, Rive was born in District Six, Cape Town. He was educated at the University of Cape Town (1962, 1968), Columbia University (1966), and Oxford University (1974) for doctoral research on Olive **Schreiner**. Rive is often associated with the *Drum* school of writing in South Africa. Best known for his short stories and criticism, Rive's major works include such classics as *African Songs* (1963), featuring "The Bench," one of the most powerful stories of protest against apartheid (see **apartheid and post-apartheid**), the once-banned novel *Emergency* (1964), and an **autobiography**, *Writing Black* (1981). His works deal with painful political and social events in South Africa, including the displacement of communities (*"Buckingham Palace," District Six*, 1986) and the state of emergency (*Emergency Continued*, 1990). As a pioneering editor of such landmark anthologies as *Modern African Prose* (1964), Rive was involved in establishing a canon of African letters. His criticism and social commentary simultaneously reflected a commitment to the politics of non-racialism and a fundamental belief that works of literature should be judged on their own merit. Rive's work is mainly concerned with racial discrimination in South Africa, yet he draws from a wide-ranging experience that includes pan-Africanism and the black American Harlem Renaissance. Rive's reputation has been mainly for his short stories and plays much more than his novels.

ZODWA MOTSA

Robert, Shaaban

b. 1909, Tanga, Tanganyika (now Tanzania); d. 1962, Dar es Salaam, Tanzania

novelist and poet

Shaaban Robert is arguably the most distinguished Swahili writer of the modern era (see **Swahili literature**). He was born in Tanganyika, of Yao parents from Malawi. His work spanned various genres: poetry, prose fiction, essays, and biographies. He is widely regarded as the father of the modern Swahili novel. His translation of Omar Khayyam's *Rubbaiyat* into Swahili is hailed as a stunning masterpiece.

His poetic works are classics, as he followed the classical Swahili tradition, but he also used new patterns and styles. His major poetic works include *Utenzi wa Vita Vya Uhuru* (The Epic of the Struggle for Independence) (1961) and *Pambo ya Lugha* (A Question of Language) (1966). He established the foundation for the contemporary novel in Swahili, developing new narrative styles, marked by density of description and reflective commentary on matters such as ethics and customs, which gave his novels a didactic orientation, very much like the folk tale tradition which he obviously understood well. However, Shaaban Robert developed a tradition of descriptive detail which is more in line with the novel as we know it than the folk tale. This is evident in works such as *Kusadikika* (Believing) (1951), *Adili na Nduguze* (Adili and His Brothers) (1952), *Kufikirika* (Understanding) (1967), and *Utubora Mkulima* (Utubola the Farmer) (1968).

Shaaban Robert displayed profound awareness of the human condition; he opposed injustice, championed freedom, and extolled the dignity of labor. He was sensitive to the condition of women. He wrote poems celebrating women, and a biography of Siti Binti Saad, the famous female taarab singer, recounting the meteoric rise to fame of this woman from a humble rural background in a male-dominated world which put incredible obstacles in her path. He was proud of his Swahili language and culture, which he understood very well, appropriated, and celebrated in and through his writings. However, he deeply respected other languages and cultures and appropriated whatever he could from them. If colonialism had not limited his educational opportunities, he would have explored this dimension to the fullest. He greatly admired world writers like Shakespeare, whose artistic mind he described as a great ocean whose waves touched the shores of the whole world.

Like many of his contemporaries, Shaaban Robert experienced colonial injustices and constraints; though gifted and hardworking, he was not able to advance in his career. He worked for many years as a clerk. He was aware that, even as an artist, he was vulnerable to exploitation by publishers. He expressed these sentiments not only in his prose works but also, indirectly, in some of his fictional works, which can be read as critiques of colonialism. But Robert's poetic sensibility was deep and intertwined with his moral and ethical principles. Sensitive to the condition and plight of all creatures, he held that all things moved with the rhythm of poetry: the birds, streams, the sea, the wind and the thunderstorms, the seasons. The popularity and influence of Shaaban Robert in Swahili literature is unsurpassed. His vision of a just society was part of the shaping of the dream for an egalitarian society, which became his country's policy. His pride in the Swahili language and cultural heritage was shared by his compatriots in the wake of national independence; it became part of national policy. To the end of his life, Shaaban Robert continued to present a vision of the future society, which was marked by harmony among people of different faiths.

Further reading

Harris, Lyndon (1975) *Shaaban Robert: Man of Letters*, London: Présence Africaine.

Nagy, Geza Fussy (1989) "The Rise of Swahili Literature and the Oeuvre of Shaaban Robert," *Neohelicon* 16, 2: 40–58.

JOSEPH MBELE

Romano, Luis Madeiro de Melo

b. 1935, Cape Verde

novelist, poet, and critic

The Cape Verdean novelist, poet, and critic Luis Romano was trained as an engineer but became involved in nationalist activities in college, a fact that forced him into exile to Brazil. His first novel, *Faminto: Romano de un povo* (The Famished, the Tale of a People), published in 1962, was an epic attempt to represent the difficult conditions of workers and peasants in Cape Verde under Portuguese colonialism (see **colonialism, neocolonialism, and postcolonialism**). His poems, short stories, and collections of folklore are primarily attempts to recover and represent the Creole cultures of Cape Verde.

Further reading

Roman, Luis Madeiro de Melo (1962) *Faminto: Romano de un povo* (The Famished, the Tale of a People), Rio de Janeiro: Editôrio Leitura.

——(1967) *Renascença de uma civilizaço no Atlântico médio (Renaissance of a Mid-Atlantic Civilization)*, Lisbon: Ocidente.

SIMON GIKANDI

Rotimi, Ola

b. 1940, Sapele, Nigeria; d. 2001, Nigeria

playwright

Of the many Nigerian playwrights who emerged in the 1960s, Ola Rotimi had perhaps the most heterogeneous background. He was born, of a Yoruba father and an Ijaw mother, in the then Mid Western state, one of the regions in Nigeria not dominated by any one linguistic or cultural group, and he grew up speaking Yoruba, Igbo, and Ijaw. Rotimi was one of the few major writers from this period who were educated in the United States: he attended Boston University and Yale Drama School, where he studied theater direction. It was while he was at university that Rotimi started writing plays drawing on the Yoruba, Igbo, and Ijaw traditions of his childhood, the historical traditions of Nigeria, and classical drama. Rotimi's major plays, which were written in the 1960s and early 1970s, can be divided into three categories, although there is some overlapping in both themes and dramatic forms. The first set of plays represent Rotimi's struggle to adopt theatrical models borrowed from classical Greek tragedy. The most famous play in this category is *The Gods Are Not to Blame* (1971), in which Rotimi tries to rewrite the myth of Oedipus, placing the Yoruba King Odewale in the role of the tragic hero. The play was first performed at the Ife Festival of Arts in Western Nigeria in 1968 where it won the first prize in drama. The second category of plays are those that draw specifically from a major event in Yoruba history. In *Kurunmi: An Historical Tragedy* (1971), considered by many critics to be the playwright's major work, Rotimi built his tragic action on the conflict over succession and tradition in the Yoruba kingdoms in the tumultuous nineteenth century. In *Ovonramwen Nogbasi* (1974), Rotimi drew his tragic event from the British conquest of the kingdom of Benin in 1895. The last category in Rotimi's oeuvre is his domestic comedies, which, as with the works of many other Nigerian playwrights, have had the most popular appeal. In this category belongs *Our Husband Has Gone Mad Again* (1974). This play revolves around the tribulations that arise when a Nigerian military officer decides to venture into politics, a move that is opposed by his wives and children. The play was first performed at Yale Drama School under the directorship of Jack Landau, the famous American director, but it has been performed in many African countries since the 1960s. Later in his career, Rotimi had increasingly moved beyond tragedy and comedy and was writing plays, most notably *Holding Talks* (1979) and *Hopes of the Living*

Dead (1988), that used techniques borrowed from the theater of the absurd to respond to what he saw as the follies of postcolonial Nigerian society (see **colonialism, neocolonialism, and postcolonialism**). Rotimi's plays and his work in the theater are considered to be some of the most consistent attempts by an African dramatist to match the inherited language of classical tragedy with local historical materials.

SIMON GIKANDI

Rubadiri, David

b. 1930, central Nyasaland (now Malawi)

teacher and poet

David Rubadiri was born of Malawian parents in southwest Tanzania, but he grew up and went to school in what was then Nyasaland before moving to Uganda, where he attended King's College, Budo, and Makerere University College, finally going on to Cambridge University. He was arrested and imprisoned during the political emergency in Malawi in 1959, but when his country became independent he was appointed as its permanent representative at the United Nations. After falling out with Malawi's president, Kamuzu Banda, in 1965, Rubadiri returned to Uganda, where he taught at Makerere. He later taught at the Universities of Nairobi and Botswana. After the fall of Banda in the 1990s, Rubadiri was again appointed as Malawi's ambassador to the United Nations and later the vice-chancellor of the University of Malawi. Although he is not well known outside Africa, Rubadiri is one of the pioneers of creative writing in East Africa. Three of his early poems, "An African Thunderstorm," "Stanley Meets Mutesa," and "A Negro Laborer in Liverpool," all published in *Origin East Africa* (1965), the Makerere anthology edited by David Cook, were some of the earliest attempts to fit African subjects into the metrical language of English poetry. Rubadiri's novel, *No Bride Price* (1967), drew on his diverse experiences as a diplomat and political activist to narrate the story of an idealist African who tries to fulfil the mandate of nationalism (see **nationalism and post-**nationalism) within a corrupt political establishment but ends up imprisoned and adrift in a world that has lost its moral compass.

Further reading

Cook, David, and Rubadiri, David (1971) *Poems from East Africa*, Nairobi: East African Publishing House.

SIMON GIKANDI

Rugamba, Cyprien (Sipiriyani)

b. 1935, Rwamiko, Rwanda; d. 1994, Rwanda

scholar, poet, and composer

Born at Rwamiko in the south of Rwanda, Rugamba devoted most of his life to scholarship in history and the arts. He was a student of philosophy, literature, and history and received a doctorate in history at the Catholic University of Louvain in Belgium. He was director of the National Institute of Scientific Research of Rwanda for over twenty years, and the founder of the Museum of Rwandan Arts at Butare and of the National Ballet named "Amasimbi n'Amakombe," whose aim was to maintain and promote traditional dances and songs drawn from the Rwandese cultural heritage.

A poet and composer, Rugamba was also the choreographer of such memorable works as *La Nativité* (The Nativity) (1980) and the transcriber and editor of oral texts (see **oral literature and performance**), including *Contes du Rwanda* (Rwandan Folk Tales) (1983) and *Indilimbo z'Amasimbi n'Amakombe* (Ballet Songs) (1991). His literary production included the collection and translation into French of Rwandan texts and songs in diverse genres, especially pastoral and dynastic poetry. His collected works include *Le Prélude* (The Prelude) (1980) and *La Poésie face à l'histoire: cas de la poésie dynastique du Rwanda* (The Poetic Face of History: The Case of the Dynastic Poetry of Rwanda) (1987). Rugamba worked and collaborated with Alexis **Kagame**, whose *Amazina y'inka* (Pastoral Poems) he edited and published in two volumes in 1988.

ANTHÈRE NZABATSINDA

Ruganda, John

b. 1941, Kabarole, Uganda; d. 2008, Kampala, Uganda

playwright

The Ugandan-born playwright John Ruganda was born at Kabarole near Fort Portal, western Uganda, to a deeply Catholic mother. He was educated at St Leo's College, Ntare, and at Makerere University College where he received an honors degree in English in 1967 and edited *The Makererean*, the student newspaper. It was as a student at Makerere in the 1960s that Ruganda became involved in the theater. In 1966 his first play, *End of the Endless*, won the Uganda Theatre Guild Competition; the following year *Pyrrhic Victory* won the inter-halls competition at Makerere. He later won the East African Creative Writing Competition for *Covenant with Death* (1973), while *The Burdens* (1973) won the Kenyatta Prize in 1972. After leaving Makerere, Ruganda was the Oxford University Press representative in Kampala, but he left Uganda in the early 1970s and spent a good part of his "exile" in Kenya, where he taught literature at the University of Nairobi, founding the university's Free Travelling Theatre in 1973. Many of his most important plays were written for the Kenyan National Theatre in Nairobi.

Ruganda's most famous play is perhaps *The Burdens* (1972), a typical postcolonial (see **colonialism, neocolonialism, and postcolonialism**) African play that utilizes the conflict within one family to examine some of the political and social problems that have continued to plague African countries after independence. There is little doubt, however, that his most important and intellectually charged dramatic work is *The Floods* (1980), a play that represents the tragic era of tyranny under the dictatorship of Idi Amin in Uganda, but also passionately explores the challenges facing individuals as they try to reorganize their private lives against the background of the crisis of postcolonial Africa. The intersection between politics and the lives of individuals struggling to come to terms with the social pressures of postcolonial society is the subject of Ruganda's other major plays written in the 1980s, including *Music Without Tears* (1982), which was widely seen as a sequel to *The Floods*, and *Echoes of Silence* (1986). John Ruganda has justifiably been described as the "Athol **Fugard** of East Africa drama," largely because of his frequent use of an "Economy Theater," one featuring two predominant characters. Fugard perfected this technique in the South African context. But his works are also dominated by the use of powerful symbolism and a sense of tragic action, usually emerging from his representation of the politics of everyday life in East Africa.

Further reading

Imbuga, Francis Davies (1991) "Thematic Trends and Circumstance in John Ruganda's Drama," unpublished PhD dissertation, University of Iowa.

GEORGE ODERA OUTA

Rugyendo, Mukotani

b. Uganda

playwright

The Ugandan-born playwright Mukotani Rugyendo was educated at the University of Dar es Salaam in Tanzania, where he studied theater arts in the late 1960s and early 1970s, and later worked for the Tanzanian Publishing House. Like most writers living and working in Tanzania in the 1960s and 1970s, he was influenced by Julius Nyerere's ideology of African socialism and worked with a radical vision of both postcolonial society and the role of drama in the transformation of African societies after independence. The result of this radical vision is a series of experimental plays published in *The Barbed Wire and Other Plays* (1977). The title play in the collection is concerned with questions of social class and is built around the dramatic confrontation between Ugandan peasants and an oppressive landowner. In *The Contest* the playwright draws on the oral traditions (see **oral literature and performance**) of the cultures of the Lakes region of East and Central Africa and skillfully deploys features drawn from the heroic poetry. *The Storm Gathers* is a more explicit reaction of the Idi Amin coup in Uganda and its effects on common people.

GEORGE ODERA OUTA

Ruhumbika, Gabriel

b. 1938, Tanzania

novelist, short story writer, and critic

Tanzanian novelist, short story writer, and critic, Gabriel Ruhumbika received his BA at Makerere University, Uganda, and wrote his doctoral thesis on African theater at the Sorbonne, Paris. His first novel, *Village in Uhuru* (1969), tells of the painful process of transition as an isolated and conservative village gradually moves from its precolonial roots into a new era of freedom, nationalism, and socialism (see **colonialism, neocolonialism, and postcolonialism**; **nationalism and post-nationalism**). Musilanga, the royalist village headman, is pitted against his son, Balinde, who represents the new Tanzanian state and its belief in the possibility of modernization and development. Ruhumbika's other novels, *Uwike Usiwike Kutakucha* (Whether the Cock Crows or Not, It Dawns) (1978) and *Miradi Bubu ya Wazalendo* (Invisible Enterprises of the Patriots) (1991), are written in Swahili (Kiswahili), and both examine the failures of political independence. He has also edited a collection of essays *Towards Ujamaa* (1974), which deals with several aspects of Tanzania's move towards socialism in the 1960s. Ruhumbika's writings stand as important witnesses to Tanzania's emergence into the age of independence, but he will also be remembered for the stance he has taken since the 1970s, that creative writing in Swahili has to be promoted because Tanzanian children need literature that is local in style, content, and atmosphere.

DAN ODHIAMBO OJWANG

Rui, Manuel

b. 1941, Huambo, Angola

writer

Manuel Rui is a significant voice in postcolonial Angolan literature (see **colonialism, neocolonialism, and postcolonialism**) and his works constitute an important bridge between the first generation of Angolan nationalist writers such as **Pepetela**, José Luandino **Vieira**, Xuanhenga **Xitu**, and younger writers like José Eduardo **Agualusa**. Born in Huambo in the south of Angola, Rui studied law at the University of Coimbra in Portugal but returned to Angola after the fall of the fascist Portuguese state in 1974. On independence he became minister of information in the MPLA government. Unlike other Angolan writers who started writing in opposition to Portuguese colonialism, Rui's first works, including the poems collected in *Cinco Vezes Onze* (Five Times Eleven) (1985), were written to celebrate the independence of Angola. In *Regresso Adiado* (Postponed Return) (1978) and *Yes, Comrade* (*Sim Camarada*) (1977) he was interested in exploring the possibilities of reconnecting with the native land and its traditions as a way of escaping the alienation engendered by colonialism. But in his poems, short stories, and novels published in the late 1980s, Rui uses an ironic tone that expresses skepticism about the process of decolonization celebrated in his works. In fact, in the later postcolonial works like *Crónica De Um Mujimbo* (Chronicle of a Rumor) (1989), this irony is directed at the postcolonial order itself and its sense of crisis and failure.

Further reading

Peres, Phyllis (1997) *Transculturation and Resistance in Lusophone African Narrative*, Gainesville: University of Florida Press.

SIMON GIKANDI

Ryvel

b. 1898, Tunis, Tunisia; d. 1972, Cannes, France

writer and journalist

Raphael Lévy, who used the pseudonym Ryvel, was a Tunisian Jewish writer and journalist active between the world wars. His work consists of short stories and verse fables based on the lived experience of the Mellah, the traditional Jewish neighborhood of Tunis. Most of his stories appeared in Tunisian periodicals, later collected in *L'Enfant de l'oukala* (Child of the Oukala) (1931) and *Le Bestiaire du ghétto* (The Ghetto Bestiary) (1934). Ryvel's works are notable for the liveliness of their portrayals of street characters, and for the author's ear for the Tunis patois, a mix of Arabic, French, Italian, and other languages. Ryvel participated in the efforts of the Société des Écrivains de l'Afrique du Nord to promote the literature of colonial North Africa as a new regionalist production, radically different from the literature of mainland France. Ultimately, however, the attempts at ethnic inclusiveness of groups like the Société des

Écrivains failed, as did their hopes to create a durable multicultural society under French rule. Nonetheless, Ryvel's stories still constitute a compelling literary record of Tunisian Jewish society.

Further reading

Ryvel (1980) *L'Enfant de l'ouakala et autres contes du ghétto* (Child of the Oukala and Other Tales of the Ghetto), Paris: J-C Lattès.

SETH GRAEBNER

S

el-Saadawi, Nawal

b. 1932, Kafir Tahla, Egypt

novelist, feminist, and activist

Nawal el-Saadawi, the best-known Arab feminist, activist, and author, was born in Egypt, one of nine siblings (six sisters and three brothers) to a middle-class family. Her father was an employee of the Ministry of Education. "My daughter will never be made to stay at home," her mother, who has had a lasting influence on her children, would often remind her husband. El-Saadawi's recent autobiography *A Daughter of Isis* (1999) (*Izis*) (1986), translated by her husband Sherif **Hetata** (a medical doctor and author in his own right and major translator of most of her works), gives us new insights to the life achievement of this remarkable Arab feminist author of more than thirty avant-garde books, and mother of a budding young woman writer, Mona Hilmy, and a promising film director, Atef Hetata. (Nawal has been married three times.) So, for instance, we learn that both her mother and her father championed the cause of the education of girls, hence all her sisters received higher education. Nawal went to medical school and graduated among a small number of women in 1955. She went on to work for the Ministry of Health, from which she was subsequently dismissed because of her radical writings.

Nawal el-Saadawi certainly became politically aware at a young age through her family's involvement in politics. Her father is known to have been active in the 1919 Egyptian revolution; he was wounded in one of the demonstrations, an incident that was a source of great pride to the family. Early on, Nawal is known to have often marched in demonstrations along with her classmates, protesting the British presence in Egypt.

Dr Saadawi earned her medical degree in 1955, with honors. She started her career as a country doctor and went on to work in the Ministry of Health as director of public health. But it is her interest in writing that eventually eased her out of her civil service career. Her first work, *al-Mar'a wal-Jins* (Woman and Sex) (1972) caused such a stir that she was fired from her job. This proved to be a most influential work, not only for Egyptians but throughout the Arab world. Generations of young women to this day admit that reading this work was a defining moment in their lives. The mere title of the work was then considered a radical move. In *The Hidden Face of Eve* (1980: London), another controversial book, Saadawi highlights the reason behind her choice: "All the established leadership in the area suffer from a pronounced allergy to the word 'sex' and any of its implications, especially if it happens to be linked to the word 'woman' " (p. 38).

Women and sexuality have become the main issues of debate that arise from her writings. She questions deep-seated customs and traditions within Arab Muslim societies such as female circumcision (FGM), and undoubtedly her medical training lends greater credibility to her stances. Herself a victim of this ancient custom, which seems to be more revered in African societies than necessarily Arab Muslim ones, Saadawi has vociferously clamored for decades against this cruel custom.

Woman at Point Zero (1983) (*Imra'a 'inda nuqtat*

al-sifr) (1977) is the work that has catapulted her into fame in the West, since it has generated great interest in academic circles, particularly in the US. The prostitute Firdaws (ironically, her name means "paradise") is the epitome of all the ills that beset women in general but particularly those in the Arab East. From an early age she is repeatedly molested by male relatives, and as an orphan she is forced to live with an uncle who perpetrates all the traditional patriarchal wrongdoings on her.

We witness all the societal ills that ultimately lead her to prostitution and murder, finally resulting in her execution. Poverty, ignorance, deeply entrenched customs (FGM), and the marrying of young girls to much older men seem to lead her to a sealed fate. Yet it is the presence of the psychiatrist who is her confidant in the narrative (presumably Saadawi herself) that functions as a counterpoint to the predetermined fate that seems to be destined for women like Firdaws. Firdaws suffers almost all the indignities at the hands of men, though the woman Sharifa (whose name, ironically, means "noble") is the one who leads her to prostitution and ultimately – since she ends up by killing her pimp – to her death.

In 1981 Anwar Sadat threw into prison a cross-section of Egyptian politicians, activists, and Christian clergy as well as Muslim leaders and, of course, intellectuals. Nawal el-Saadawi was foremost among those incarcerated, presumably for "crimes against the state." Soon after her release she founded the Arab Women's Solidarity Association (ASWA). The organization grew to have several thousand members throughout the Arab world, and published a magazine which dealt with major issues of social injustices and discrimination against women. ASWA was to be banned in 1991. However, Saadawi attempted to resuscitate it in the late 1990s. Soon after her release from prison she wrote her *Memoirs from the Women's Prison* (1983) (*Mudhakkarati fi Sijn al-Nisa'*) (1982). In many ways this work reiterates the basic tenet she has fundamentally stood for since she was thrown into prison for her writings: freedom of expression. She poignantly and rhetorically asks: "Is free opinion a crime? Then let prison be my only refuge and my final fate. Since my childhood I have abhorred rulers and authority" (*Memoirs from the Women's Prison*, 1983: Berkeley, p. 117).

Saadawi's militancy extended to some utterances about religion which caused much controversy in the Arab media. "God is justice, freedom and love," she has often declared. As for holy scriptures, she would quote what her grandmother had often repeated to her: "God is not a book" (meaning the Koran), clearly a defiant stance to the general wisdom of the sacrosanct beliefs of the masses.

In the summer of 2001 Nawal el-Saadawi was once more targeted for her revolutionary writings, this time by extreme-right fundamentalists who desperately tried a ploy of forcibly divorcing her from her husband of thirty-five years on the pretext that since she was an apostate (deeming her writings heretical to true Islam) her Muslim husband couldn't remain married to her. Saadawi appealed the first court ruling and won her case, but once more she made the headlines worldwide.

Her essays, papers, and many speeches which form the bulk of her non-fiction writings document her rise to prominence, especially on the international scene. Her style in writing covers a wide gamut from the expository to the analytical, from the introspective to the rhetorical. Nawal el-Saadawi believes strongly that the liberation of women requires the liberation of all members of society. Similarly, Nawal el-Saadawi, Arab feminist par excellence, is equally aware of women's plight worldwide. "The oppression of women, the exploitation and social pressures to which they are exposed, are not characteristic of Arab or Middle Eastern societies or countries of the 'Third World' alone," she asserts in her preface to the English edition of *The Hidden Face of Eve* (1980: London). "They constitute an integral part of the political, economic and cultural system, preponderant in most of the world."

Further reading

Badran, Margot and Cooke, Miriam (eds) (1990) *Opening the Gates*, Bloomington: Indiana University Press.

El-Saadawi, Nawal (1980) *The Hidden Face of Eve: Women in the Arab World*, trans. and ed. Sherif Hetata, London: Zed Press.

——(1983) *Memoirs from the Women's Prison*, Berkeley: University of California Press.

Fadwa-Malti, Douglas (1995) *Men, Women and God(s): Nawal el-Saadawi and Arab Feminist Poetics*, Berkeley: University of California Press.

Tarabishi, Georges (1988) *Woman against Her Sex: A Critique of Nawal Saadawi*, trans. Basil Hatem and Elisabeth Orsini, London: Saqi.

MONA N. MIKHAIL

Sadji, Abdoulaye

b. 1910, Rufisque, Senegal; d. 1961, Senegal

writer and teacher

Alienation and the conflict between tradition and modernity (see **modernity and modernism**) are the major themes of the Senegalese writer and teacher Abdoulaye Sadji's two novels *Maimouna, la petite fille noire* (Maimouna, The Little Black Girl) (1953) and *Nini, mulatresse du Sénégal* (Nini, Mulatto Woman of Senegal) (1965), are both set in Senegal during the period of colonialism (see **colonialism, neocolonialism, and postcolonialism**). Sadji is the first Francophone writer to choose women as the central characters of his novels, many of which portray the condition of women as second-class citizens. The title characters in Sadji's early novels, *Maimouna* and *Nini*, are both condemned to remain at the bottom of the social structure, regardless of their ambitions and personal efforts. Abdoulaye Sadji's talent as a storyteller can be seen again in the posthumously published legend of *Tounka* (1965) and other heroic stories collected in *Ce que dit la musique africaine* (What African Music Says) (1985). Above all, the teacher is greatly admired and fondly remembered as the author (in collaboration with Léopold Sédar **Senghor**) of the folk tale entitled *La Belle Histoire de Leuk le lièvre* (The Beautiful Story of Leuk the Hare) (1953). This book is still one of the most enchanting works of **children's literature** in Senegal. It was designed and richly illustrated to serve as a reader for African schoolchildren at a time when few such books existed.

KANDIOURA DRAME

Sahelian literatures in African languages

As in the rest of Africa, the Sahel boasts a prolific oral literature (see **oral literature and performance**) produced by anonymous authors. The oral literatures of ethnic groups in the Sahel bear a striking similarity, and the legends of Ségou, Soundiata, and Wagadu are as widely known in Burkina Faso and Niger as they are in Mali and Senegal. This literature, if no more than for its ancient status, demands to be revived. The diverse peoples of the Sahel and Savanna regions of West Africa share both a long tradition written in the rise and fall of great empires and a variety of common cultural features. The praise singers and storytellers, known as griots and griottes, have contributed for centuries both to the survival of that narrative and to the diffusion of values common to these peoples. These traditional artists are the bearers of a deep Sahelian culture.

The mass of publications in or about African-language literatures in the Sahel tends to focus on traditional oral genres: tales, legends, epics, proverbs, songs, riddles, and sayings. These publications are often generated by African, European, and American scholars who transcribe the oral narratives and translate them into a colonial language, attaching a critical assessment. The results are frequently in the form of bilingual texts that chronicle historical and contemporary events. Among these works are: *Scribe, Griot, Novelist* (1996), which contains "The Epic of Askia Mohamed" in Zarma and English, edited by Thomas Hale; *La Geste de Zabarkane* (Zabarkane's Gesture) (1989) in Zarma and French, edited by Fatoumata Mounkaila; *Zamu ou les poèmes sur les noms* (Zamu or The Poems about Names) (1972) and *L'Essence du verbe* (The Essence of the Verb) (1972), in Zarma and French, both edited by Boubou Hama; *La Poésie de Youssou Ndour* (The Poetry of Youssou Ndour) (1998) in Wolof and French, edited by Oumar Sankhare; and *Chants traditionnels soninké* (Traditional Soninke Songs) (1990) in Soninke, Peul, and French, edited by Ousmane Moussa Diagana.

There exists a large body of African language texts composed with religious intent and transcribed using Arabic characters. The women in the family of the grand marabout Ousmane Dan Fodio developed educational materials and wrote poems in Hausa. Cheikh Amadou Bamba Mbacké, the founder of the Mouride brotherhood in Senegal, produced several volumes of religious poetry in Wolof. Also, the Bible has been translated into almost all of the dominant African languages in the Sahel, including Wolof, Bamanan, Zarma, Hausa, Fulfulde, and Tamajek.

It is important also to cite the huge number of unpublished plays and film scenarios in African languages. This is particularly true in the Sahel, where theater is a daily ritual through radio and television and where one finds the cradle of African **cinema**. Several of the pioneering sub-Saharan filmmakers emanate from Sahelian countries. Among them are: Souleymane Cissé Idrissa Ouédraogo and Gaston Kaboré (Burkina Faso); Med Hondo (Mauritania); Ousmane **Sembene** and Djibril Diop Mambéty (Senegal); Oumarou Ganda and Moustapha Alassane (Niger). These cinéastes, some of whom are also writers, consider the screen to be a space for visual and aural texts and a way to promote and preserve African languages. There are countless unpublished screen-plays, scenarios, and scripts in Wolof, Dula, Bamanan, More, Hausa, Zarma, and other Sahelian languages.

Popular theater in African languages is one of the new forms of oral literature that has resulted in a vast number of unpublished plays. In theater productions staged for radio and television, the most frequent themes are taken from daily life. For example, "Koteba" in Mali is a popular form of Bamanan theater that manifests a message charged with social criticism through its lively and comical character.

There is a long and impressive literary legacy of women in the Sahel and, as we can tell from even the names of women in Zarma society, women wield considerable powers in what might appear to be patriarchal societies. More importantly, it is important to contrast the fecundity of oral and written texts by women in Hausa and Peul societies when compared to the absence of such texts by women in French. Women are not voiceless, but rather they are just not "heard" because their creations are in an oral rather than a written literature. Female oral texts are literatures gener-

ated by women for women and for this reason, among others, they are not given as much value in the neocolonial or postcolonial literary arena (see **colonialism, neocolonialism, and postcolonialism**) as male texts which tend to predominate. Yet women's oral poetry and performance (see **women's poetry and performance**) is central to the cultures of the region. In Zarma culture, for example, the word is the most powerful weapon a woman uses to speak out on discrimination and injustice, to express and convey her feelings, her aspirations, and her frustration. In other words, it is through verbal creativity that the woman conveys her experience and also teaches others. Verbal creativity is a powerful weapon because people are afraid of being the subject of women's poetry, which may be very blunt and direct in denouncing injustice or bad behavior in the community.

In some cases, however, as in Muslim-Arab society in general and in Mauritanian society, art and culture, like science and politics, are considered to be the prerogative of men. Mauritanian women are more or less free to express themselves but are not expected to compose poetry, especially romantic verse. The poetic expression of love is considered to be a male affair. In the last decade of the twentieth century, Mauritanian women poets began to produce works in Hassaniya (a Mauritanian language derived from Arabic). However, these women are pejoratively referred to as "the ones who recite poetry." Two examples are Batta Mint El Bara, author of *Psaumes pour un seul pays* (Psalms for a Lone Country) and Maalouma Mint El Meïdah, one of Mauritania's most celebrated vocalists, whose songs have been transcribed from Arabic into French but never formally published.

In the Sahel, as elsewhere in Africa, the transformation from oral to written forms has stirred up the fear that Africa might lose its soul if the African language oral tradition were to be brutally interrupted. When Amadou Hampâté **Bâ** popularized the saying that "In Africa every old person who dies is a library that burns," he stimulated and encouraged those eager to preserve the African language oral heritage which has since been collected, transcribed, translated, interpreted, and glossarized. In the Sahel, writing has allowed African communities to develop the literary archives of oral Africa. At the same time, producers of literatures in African languages have adapted to the need for transformation, and if certain ancient forms have more or less disappeared, new forms have appeared enabled by modern technological and audiovisual media. Still, the task of rehabilitating African language literatures is far from being complete.

DEBRA S. BOYD-BUGGS

Sahelian literatures in French

The Sahel as a geographical space

In Arabic the term *sahil* means border or shore. The derived French term *sahel* designates the shore of the Sahara Desert. This region of Francophone West and Central Africa includes large parts or the entire area of countries that lie south of the Sahara Desert. These include Burkina Faso, Chad, Mali Mauritania, Niger, and Senegal. It is territory noted for its desert and desert-like environment: hot, dry, barren, populated by rocks, grains of sand, and sand dunes, with the occasional surprise of an oasis. Cultural and political histories of the Sahel differ from those of eastern and southern Africa in ways other than geography. Although Francophone nations emphasize their participation in a world linguistic community, the region also shares historical and cultural connections found immediately in the ethnic, religious, and other cultural similarities among its peoples. The Peul (also known as Fulani or Pulaar), Tuareg, Bambara, Dogon, Senoufo, Hausa, and Songhai are ethnic groups which can be found in large populations throughout the countries of the Sahel. Most of the Sahelian countries are at the crossroads where Arab and Berber Africa meet their sub-Saharan brothers. It is an intersection of civilizations where black populations, white ethnic groups, Muslims, Christians, and disciples of traditional beliefs skirt each other. A long tradition of communal life and exchange between these peoples has resulted in a true cultural richness formed from ethnic diversity. This can be seen in the variety of cultural and artistic manifestations that one encounters in the Sahel zone today.

The Sahel as a literary space

The desert has a poetry, drama, and fiction different from that of mountainous or coastal African countries. Due to the artificial borders created during colonization, a number of the countries in the Sahel share not only the same ethnic groups but also inhabitants who live the realities of Sahelian environment. Sahelian literary artists recognize this distinctive trait as evidenced by the titles of fictional works which often include the term "sahel" or "sahelian": *Poèmes sahéliens en liberté* (Sahelian Poems in Liberation) by Kélétigui Mariko from Niger; *Le Sahélien de Lagos* (The Sahelian from Lagos) by Lamine Diakhâté from Senegal; *Fleurs du Sahel* (Flowers of the Sahel) by Fatou Ndiaye Sow, also from Senegal; *Sahel! Sanglante! Sécheresse!* (Sahel! Bloodstained! Drought!) by Mandé Alpha Diarra from Mali; *Ça tire sous le Sahel* (It Shoots from the Sahel) by Titinga Frédéric **Pacéré** from Burkina Faso); and *Sahéliennes, et À l'orée du Sahel* (Sahelians, and On the Edge of the Sahel) by Youssouf Guèye from Mauritania. Other titles suggest the nature of life in the Sahel and include references to desert, drought, hunger, thirst, death, sun, vultures, misery, bitterness and degradation, the search for water, nomadism, and exile.

Drought, a natural force that wars against man's survival, frequently provides the physical setting where characters lead their lives and pursue their quests for meaning and wholeness. It also serves as a metaphor for the lack of basic necessities and other forces that are hostile to spiritual and social development underscoring what is absent and what no longer functions in the society. In the fictional universe, as in the real world of the Sahel, drought is multifaceted, encompassing ecological, religious, and political dimensions. The lack of water is inextricably linked to misery and despair – captured succinctly in works like *Le Baiser amer de la faim* (The Bitter Kiss of Hunger) by Adé Boureima of Niger and *Quand s'envolent les grues couronnées* (When the Crowned Cranes Fly Away) by Titinga Frédéric Pacéré of Burkina Faso. It leads to the fracturing of families and other units of society. At the same time as writers from the region see drought as a source of misery to many, they also point out that it paradoxically becomes a source of wealth for marabouts, politicians, and religious leaders who abuse power to render the lives of the poor even more miserable. Authors seek to awaken the consciousness of the people to visionary insight into the nature of the struggle for spiritual, cultural, and economic development of the nations.

The Sahel is a space that resists closure, making the struggle of Sahelian literary artists an effort to capture and contain that space. One way to locate oneself in the vastness of the desert, particularly in the cultural prism/prison of the novel, is to employ the cinematic eye of the camera in the fictive text. Thus it is no accident that theater and **cinema**, two forms that allow for moving panorama, flourish in this region of Africa. The cinematic eye is a characteristic of the Sahel and is clearly seen in the creative genius of Ousmane **Sembene**, who infuses a visual dimension into his written texts, many of which he later converted into films.

It is always risky to define the specificity of a body of regional literature. One way to examine the human space of the Sahel is to employ a geo-critical approach. Sahelian literature is in harmony with postmodernism. The "nomadic word" that characterizes these texts reflects the lives of desert travelers who put up their tents in the evening and dismantle them in the morning when they march towards unknown and unplanned horizons. It is writing whose themes are absence and wandering, mutation and a new logos or word. Sahelian texts are less affected by the militancy of other African literatures that preceded them. Whereas traditional Western literary discourse is constructed by the presence of logic and objectivity, postmodern thought is developed through subjectivity and the absence of predestined order paving the way for emerging discourses that reflect the dynamic relationship between void and creation.

Sahelian literature is the heir of two systems: ancestral or precolonial tradition mixed with a new language and forms brought from outside through either colonialism (see **colonialism, neocolonialism, and postcolonialism**) or migration. However, the originality of this body of texts is not determined by its antecedents. This body of literatures transcends earlier works. When the African literary landscape progressively fractured into national literatures after independence, the legacy of pan-Africanism (see **diaspora and pan-Africanism**) and the **negritude** movement ceded its place to terrains where centripetal and centrifugal forces come face to face. The emergence of Negro-African literature had long been confirmed when national literatures formed a distinctive body of works in the first half of the twentieth century. The only Sahelian country included in this pioneering corpus was Senegal. Other Sahelian literatures manifested themselves much later and were inscribed into the wake of an African literature that was recognized on the international scene. Table 1 lists a chronological arrangement of first-published texts in French from the Sahel.

Sahelian literatures did not emerge until the latter half of the century. However, an emerging literature is not virgin terrain. What is new is the unedited configuration that comes to light and imposes itself upon the literary scene.

The Sahel, a religious space

The Sahel is a cosmological and spiritual space where the search for a literary/philosophical esthetic of "Sahelian-ness" is played out in the

Table 1   A chronological arrangement of first-published texts in French from the Sahel

1920	Senegal	Amadou Mapâté Diagne	*Les Trois Volontés de Malic* (Malic's Three Wishes)
1943	Mali	Amadou Hampâté **Bâ**	*Kaydara*
1954	Niger	Ibrahim Issa	*Grandes Eaux noires* (Wide Black Waters)
1962	Burkina Faso	Nazi **Boni**	*Crépuscule des temps anciens* (Dusk of Ancient Times)
1962	Chad	Joseph Brahim Seid	*Au Tchad sous les étoiles* (Chad under the Stars)
1975	Mauritania	Tene Youssouf Guèye	*À l'orée du Sahel* (On the Edge of the Sahel)

tension between Islam, Christianity, and traditional religious beliefs (see **Islam in African literature**; **Christianity and Christian missions**). There is a universe that is Sahelian, as there is a universe in the Yoruba and other religious paradigms of Africa. Sahelian literature is, however, powerfully marked by the presence of Muslim themes: the advent of Islam in West Africa was accompanied by an important literary production that was more extensive in Arabic than in local languages. Islam introduced new genres and Islam recuperated certain traditional literary and cultural practices, influencing pre-existing social-cultural structures.

Sahelian prose fiction is populated by the presence of protagonists who issue from the Islamic context, dealing with issues of marabouts, polygamy, and beggars. Examples of such works include Cheik Aliou **Ndao**'s *Le Marabout de la sécheresse* (The Marabout of the Drought) (1979), Mandé Alpha Diarra's *La Nièce de l'imam* (The Imam's Niece), and Aminata **Sow Fall**'s *The Beggar's Strike* (*La Grève des battùs*) (1982). An example of the *mise en question* of certain traditional religious practices can be found in *La Mort des fétiches de Sénédougou* (The Death of the Fetishes of Senedougou) (1999) by Bokar Ndiaye of Mali. It is the story of a colonial investigation of the deaths of three men who were married successively to the same woman. The novel reaches its shocking climax when one of the main characters, a devout adherent to traditional religious beliefs, converts to Islam and reveals a priestly secret. Also, Moussa Diagana of Mauritania demystifies the legend of the serpent Wagadu-Bida in his play *La Légende du Wagadu vue par Sia Yatabéré* (The Legend of Wagadu as Seen by Sia Yatabéré) (1989).

Women writers in the Sahel

A central problem in the literatures of the Sahelian countries is that of gender and feminism. Suffering from the same "double yoke" borne by their African sisters on other parts of the continent, women writers in the Sahel foreground the conflicts arising from the compilation of colonial and post/neocolonial hegemony and patriarchal power(s). They are also subjected to the geographical and meteorological realities of the region in their daily struggles to survive physically and psychically.

In the past, Sahelian women played a significant role in African literatures, both oral (see **oral literature and performance**) and written. The legendary Princess Yennega of the Mossi people in Burkina Faso is heralded in epic and song as the warrior-mother of the current ruling dynasty of the country. Other legendary women include Sarrounia, queen of the Azna peoples of Niger, who resisted colonial forces. Nana Asma'aa and other women of the family of the grand marabout Ousmane Dan Fodio are known for the their sizeable corpus of religious and educational texts written in Hausa (see **literature in Hausa**) and Peul using Arabic characters. Yet up until recently the written literatures of the countries of the Sahel have worn an exclusively masculine face.

Senegalese women writers ushered in the era of female literary production in the 1970s with the emergence of authors such as Annette **M'Baye d'Erneville**, Mariama **Bâ**, Nafissatou Niang **Diallo** and Aminata Sow Fall. However, it was not to be until the 1990s that land-locked Sahelian countries would produce novels in French by women. The most important works in the tradition of women's writing in the region include Nafissatou Niang Diallo of Senegal's 1975 **autobiography**, *De Tilène au plateau, une enfance dakaroise* (A Dakar Childhood), Monique Ilboudo of Burkina Faso's *Le Mal de peau* (Skin Trouble) (1995), Aicha Fofana of Mali's *Mariage on copie* (Copies of Marriage) (1994), and Marie-Christine Koundja of Chad's *Al Istifakh ou l'idylle de mes amis* (Romance of Friends) (2001). As of this writing, there has not been a novel in French published by a woman writer from Niger or Mauritania. Prior to Aicha Fofana, Aoua Keita published her 1975 diary, *Femme d'Afrique* (Woman of Africa), which chronicles her experiences as a midwife in Mali. With the publication of *Alternances pour le Sultan* (Alternances for the Sultan) in 1982, Shaïda Zarumey (Fatoumata Agnès Diaroumèye) became the first woman from Niger to publish a volume of poetry in French. In their works, Sahelian women writers tackle issues of marriage, polygamy, childlessness, rejection, religion, motherhood, deception, friendship, *métissage*, rape, prostitution, etc. They also address nation-building, political corruption, ethnic conflict, and the crisis of education (see **education and schools**).

Theater in the Sahel

Theater, a genre that dates back as far as the oldest African civilizations, constitutes a creative pedagogical and transformative force in the countries of the African Sahel, stimulating social transformation and development. Sahelian theater has been confined to obscurity despite its extraordinary vitality. One can cite many reasons, but primarily: (1) it is a descendant of classical African theater and is not authored in the Western sense; and (2) for the most part it is not in French, and Francophone dramatic works are still in the minority.

There are two types of theater in the Sahel: one is popular (theater in national languages), and the other remains the privilege of a minority, those who speak French and for the most part live in cities. Plays in national languages are by far the more numerous. In the Sahel theater manifests a power to transform the public. It still retains traces of its ritualistic origins in celebration of birth, marriage, puberty, planting, and harvesting; its epic storytelling tradition of praising heroic and communal achievement; its visual and auditory spectacle provided by dance and music. Although modern theater in Francophone West Africa emerged with the advent of radio and grew after independence, plays in French are often thematically inspired by the oral tradition, tales in particular. At other times it is history or actual events that furnish the material: the exaltation of great heroes from the past in works such as André Salifou's *Ousmane Dan Fodio Serviteur d'Allah* (Ousmane Dan Fodio, Servant of Allah) (1988), Boubou Hama's *Sonni Ali Ber* (1977), and Seydou Kouyaté **Badian**'s *The Death of Chaka* (*La Mort de Chaka*) (1968). But these plays also deal with questions of everyday life such as marriage, polygamy, religion, charlatanism, corruption, infidelity, politics, and AIDS. While theater in the Sahel is considered to be first and foremost entertainment, it also seen as an important part of the social and economic development of the region, and in many community plays characters are often presented not so much as individuals, but as ritual figures who invite the audience to be participants rather than spectators in what is considered to be a communal experience.

National literatures in the Sahel

In spite of the distinctive regional character of the Sahel, the literature of each country in the region displays some important national characteristics. Writers in Burkina Faso have produced works that seek to enhance a Burkinabé national consciousness and to promote a collective destiny and national identity. Nazi Boni, a militant pan-Africanist who wrote in the context of negritude and African literature, was also considered to be a native son, a pioneer who founded what was to become Burkinabé literature at a time when the country was still known as the Upper Volta. Titinga Frédéric **Pacéré** and other newer writers in the country operate in a space that is clearly Burkinabé, reflecting the Burkinabé way of being African and a citizen of the world.

Francophone literary production in Chad has been characterized by a sense of political oppression and historical discourse. As in other Sahelian countries, the natural, social, spiritual, political, and economic drought in Chad has affected creative activity and has forced its most celebrated writers into exile or the diaspora. One example is Baba Moustapha, a prolific playwright and poet who died while residing in France.

All Sahelian literature is marked by the strong influence of the oral tradition, but Malian literature in particular reflects the attempt to construct a bridge between orality and writing, between tradition or the values of a precolonial culture and modernity (see **modernity and modernism**) even while striving to preserve the originality of the texts. Indeed, writers like Amadou Hampâté Bâ, Fily Dabo Sissoko, and Massa Makan **Diabaté** can be viewed as writer–translators who preserved their personal tones within texts that draw heavily on the oral tradition. In his novel *L'Étrange Destin de Wangrin* (The Strange Destiny of Wangrin) (1973), for example, Amadou Hampâté Bâ invents a Sahelian literary type who is the product of the cultural *métissage* imposed by the colonization of the Sahel.

On the other hand, Mauritania is a multicultural country that has been progressively populated by people who place it between "Arabness" and "Africanity." Wolof and Soninke farmers, followed by nomadic and pastoral Fulfulde or

Pulaar speakers, Berbers, and later Arabs from the north, came to occupy the Sahelian and Saharan zone of Mauritania. The Maures speak an Arabic dialect, Hassaniya, and there is abundant cultural production in this language. Texts composed in French are new in Mauritanian literary space and poetry is the first genre to surmount the obstacles imposed by the multiplicity of languages and diversity of cultures.

Niger also boasts of centuries of oral tradition transmitted by male and female griots, intermediaries who are the depositories of genealogy, history, and ancient religion. Colonization imposed writing in the country as a vehicle of literary expression when French became the language of communication in Niger. The first texts by writers from Niger appeared in newspapers and magazines in 1939. Modern Nigerien fiction did not emerge until the 1950s.

In contrast, Senegal has been central to the history of African prose fiction in French. A Senegalese was the first to publish a novel in French, and a Senegalese woman author, Mariama Bâ, ushered in the era of the "female voice" in African literature with her landmark work *So Long a Letter* (*Une si longue lettre*) (1980). It is in classic Senegalese novels such as Cheikh Hamidou **Kane**'s *The Ambiguous Adventure* (*L'Aventure ambigüe*) (1961) that the geophysical and spiritual aspects of a Sahelian–Muslim universe confront Western materialist philosophy.

Writers from Sahelian countries, even if they are late bloomers in French, have no reason to envy the African writers who preceded them. Many of these newer authors have won national and international literary prizes. Given the problem that literary artists face in the Sahel – absence of publishing structures, limited distribution and reading public – it is clear that the collective regional body of works by writers from Burkina Faso, Chad, Mali, Mauritania, Niger, and Senegal merit further recognition, study, and research.

Further reading

Boyd-Buggs, Debra and Hope Scott, Joyce (eds) (2001) *Camel Tracks: Critical Perspectives on Sahelian Literatures*, Trenton, New Jersey: Africa World Press.

Notre Librairie (1986) *Littératures nationales 2: langues et frontières* (National Literatures 2: Languages and Frontiers), *Notre Librairie* no. 84, Paris: CLEF.

DEBRA S. BOYD-BUGGS

Sahle-Sillasé (Sellassie) Birhane-Mariyam

b. 1936, Ethiopia

novelist

Sahle-Sillasé Birhane-Mariyam is a versatile Ethiopian author. He wrote the first novel ever in the Guragé language, *Ye-Shinega qaya* (*Shinega's Village*) (1964). He has also written in Amharic and English. After secondary school, he studied arts in Addis Ababa. For some time he studied law in France, then went to California and obtained an MA in political science. In 1963 he returned to Ethiopia, where he worked as a translator for the British Embassy. He early discovered a close connection between philosophy, politics, and literature, and this has influenced his writing. He is something of a Stoic, constantly rereading Epictetus. In English, he wrote *The Afersata* (1969), *Warrior King* (1974), about Emperor Téwodros II, and *Firebrands* (1979), about the turmoil in Ethiopia soon after the revolution of 1974. In Amharic, his major work is *Bassha Qitaw* (1986), about the war with Italy (1935–41). He has translated *A Tale of Two Cities* by Charles Dickens (*Yehulett ketemoch weg*) (1983) and *The Mother* by Pearl S. Buck (*Immiyyu*) (1987).

Further reading

Molvaer, R.K. (1997) *Black Lions*, Lawrenceville, New Jersey: Red Sea Press.

REIDULF MOLVAER

Saïd, Amina

b. 1953, Tunis, Tunisia

poet

Born in Tunis, Amina Saïd began her writing

career in 1980 with the publication of her first collection of poetry, entitled *Paysage, nuit friable* (Landscape, Crumbly Night), which has been followed since by several other collections of poetry. Among them, in collaboration with Ghislain Ripault, is an anthology of poetry entitled *Pour Abdellatif **Laâbi*** (For Abdellatif Laâbi) (1982). Her collection *Feu d'oiseaux* (Bird Fire) (1989) received the prestigious Jean Malrieu Prize, and the Charles-Vildrac Prize for poetry was awarded to her 1994 collection *L'Une et l'autre nuit* (The One and the Other Night). In addition to her poetic work, she has also published collections of Tunisian fables and stories and has translated several works from English into French.

The central concern of most of Saïd's poetry is exile in its metaphysical sense. Poetry is the search for something unattainable, something that always escapes and yet calls the poet. A distance that belongs to language is marked in poetry, thus assigning the poet to perpetual wandering in the desert, in the night, in language.

Further reading

Sorrell, Martin (ed. and trans.) (1995) *Elles: A Bilingual Anthology of Modern French Poetry by Women*, Exeter: University of Exeter Press.

NASRIN QADER

Salih, al-Tayyib

b. 1929, Debba, northern Sudan; d. 2009, London

novelist

Sudan's most important novelist, al-Tayyib Salih was born in the village of Debba in northern Sudan. He was first educated in the Arabic language and in Islamic lore in a traditional *khalwa*, or religious school. Afterwards he received colonial education at an intermediate school in Port Sudan, then attended secondary school in Umm Durman before studying biology at Khartoum University. He taught at an intermediate school in Rafaʿa, a small town south of Khartoum, then at a teacher training college in Bakht al-Rida. In 1953, he went to London to work for the Arabic

section of the BBC, and later on for UNESCO. Since then, Salih has lived in London, except for the period of 1974–80 when he was a high-ranking official in Qatar's Ministry of Information.

Salih writes in Arabic and his enormous reputation rests on a relatively small number of texts, especially his 1966 novel *Season of Migration to the North* (*Mawsim al-hijra il al-shamal*). He has written two other novels, *The Wedding of Zein* (1962) (*'Urs al-Zayn*) (1964) and the two-part *Bandarshah* (Bandar Shah) (1971, 1976), in addition to a number of short stories collected in *Dawmat Wad Hamid: Sabʿ qisas* (The Doum Tree of Wad Hamid: Seven Short Stories) (1969). Since 1988, he has been writing a column in the London-based Arabic weekly *al-Majallah*.

The majority of Salih's narratives are set in the fictional village of Wad Hamid in northern Sudan and form a continuous narrative cycle spanning the period from the mid nineteenth century to the 1970s. The main narrator of the Wad Hamid cycle, Meheimeed, appears as a child in an early short story, "A Handful of Dates" (1957), then again in *Season of Migration to the North* as a young man returning from England with a PhD in English literature shortly after Sudanese independence in 1956. He subsequently reappears as a middle-aged man in Salih's 1976 short story, "The Cypriot Man," and as a disenchanted and nostalgic old man in *Bandarshah*.

Salih's fiction deals with the impact of colonialism and Western modernity on rural Sudanese society in particular and Arab culture and identity in general. In his highly acclaimed short story, "The Doum Tree of Wad Hamid," the attempts of both colonial and postcolonial governments to impose modernization programs threaten to sever the villagers' ties to their spiritual world. Set a few years after Sudanese independence and narrated by an elderly villager, the story registers the bitterness and resignation of the elders who find themselves unable to preserve their way of life as their children, educated in modern colonial schools, eagerly set the village on an irreversible course of modernization. This younger generation are the village leaders in *The Wedding of Zein*. They oversee the introduction of modern schools, hospitals, and irrigation schemes into the village, and manage most other affairs of the village. They present themselves as benign and responsible, though shrewd, politicians who are capable of harmoniously integrating traditional culture with "progress," as they conceive it. They befriend and protect the protagonist, Zein, a village idiot regarded as a saintly fool in the tradition of Sufi dervishes, who marries the most desirable girl in the village. Zein's wedding represents both the leaders' ability to bring together the sometimes contentious factions within the village community and its spiritual unification through the agency of Zein's creative mysticism. As such, the novel constructs a utopia in which the new nation succeeds in fulfilling its material and spiritual potential.

Such idealism is shattered in *Season of Migration to the North*, which depicts the violent history of colonialism and racism as shaping the reality of contemporary Arab and African societies. A naïvely optimistic, Westernized Meheimeed confronts his double, Mustafa Sa'eed, a Kurtz-like figure who reverses the trajectory of Joseph Conrad's characters by journeying to the heart of darkness in the north, London, where he commits heinous acts of (psychological and physical) sexual revenge that literalize the violence of colonial discourse. The story continues in *Wad Hamid*, where Sa'eed returns to marry a young Sudanese woman, then disappears after a few years and is presumed dead. As her father forces her into an arranged marriage to an aged womanizer, Sa'eed's widow kills her new husband when he tries to rape her, then kills herself. This murder–suicide, an indirect result of Sa'eed's influence on his young wife, shocks and enrages the villagers, but unveils the violence of traditional patriarchy, linking it in kind to sexualized colonial violence. In this way, the novel shows that the synthesis of traditional culture and modern ideas, envisioned by liberal Arab ideology and to which *The Wedding of Zein* gave such poetic expression, can never be successful in the shadow of colonialism.

The crisis of Arab consciousness, ideology, and leadership which crystallized in the Arab defeat in the 1967 war with Israel is the subtext in Salih's third novel, *Bandarshah*, which centers around the relationship between past, present, and future, or in the allegorical scheme of the novel, grandfathers, fathers, and grandsons. This problematic relation-

ship is depicted as a vicious cycle in which the past repeats itself: grandsons are ever in conspiracy with grandfathers (of whom they are the spit image and whose first name they always bear) against fathers. The novel ends by suggesting that the vicious cycle can be broken only when the rigid patriarchal order reflected in the novel's central allegory and governing traditional society is broken.

Bibliography

Salih, Tayeb (1996) *Bandarshah*, trans. Denys Johnson-Davies, London: Kegan Paul International.
——(1997) *Season of Migration to the North*, trans. Denys Johnson-Davies, Boulder, Colorado: Lynne Rienner.
——(1999) *The Wedding of Zein and Other Stories*, trans. Denys Johnson-Davies, Boulder, Colorado: Lynne Rienner.

Further reading

Amyuni, Mona (1985) *Tayeb Salih's Season of Migration to the North: A Casebook*, Beirut: American University of Beirut Press.
Hassan, Waïl S. (1998) "Tayeb Salih: Culture, History, Memory," dissertation, University of Illinois at Urbana-Champaign.

WAÏL S. HASSAN

Sall, Amadou Lamine

b. 1951, Senegal

poet

Amadou Lamine Sall is one of Senegal's most prolific poets. He is perhaps best known for his first long poem, *Mante des aurores* (Dawn Mantis) first published in 1979. His many collections of poetry include *Comme un iceberg en flammes* (Like an Iceberg in Flames) (1982), *Locataire du néant* (Tenant of Nothingness) (1989), *Kamandalu* (1990), and *Le Prophète ou le coeur aux mains de pain* (The Prophet or the Heart with Hands of Bread) (1997). He is also the author of three landmark anthologies of poetry: *Poètes du Sénégal* (Senegalese

Poets) (1990) (with a preface by L.S. **Senghor**), *Nouvelle anthologie de la poésie nègre et malgache de langue française* (New Anthology of Negro and Malagasy Poetry in French) (1990), and *Poèmes d'Afrique pour les enfants* (African Poetry for Children) (1991). Amadou Lamine Sall is also an essayist and a syndicated columnist. As a poet, Sall can be considered an heir to the negritude school and he has, in fact, claimed Senghor as his spiritual father. Like Senghor, Sall celebrates the beauty and glory of the black African woman; he also inscribes his poetry within the frame and mold of oral African traditions, especially song and dance (see **oral literature and performance**). For Sall, the theme of love is intimately linked to the theme of the African woman. Other important dimensions of Sall's poetry include ethnicity (the Peul origins of the poet), and Islam (see **Islam in African literature**). In regard to Islam, Sall has written a long poem, *Le Prophète ou le coeur aux mains de pain*, in which he projects himself into the realm of the Arab Sufi tradition, providing an apology for the religion and the Prophet. In an 1994 essay entitled "Problématique d'une nouvelle poésie africaine de langue française: le long sommeil des Epigones" (Problematic of a New African Poetry in French: The Long Sleep of the Epigoni), which is a postface to his collection of poems entitled *J'ai mangé tout le pays de la nuit* (I Have Eaten Up the Country of the Night), Sall claims that he cannot be a novelist but only a poet for, according to him, the novel is the product of peaceful times whereas violence, hardship, and challenges are conducive to writing poems. He regrets that African poets do not write in their native languages and have been confined to writing in European languages such as French or English. At the same time, however, Sall is aware of the danger of limiting his poetry solely within the bounds of African traditions, songs, and dance. In the circumstances, he seems to follow Senghor's policy of "enracinement et ouverture" – rooting oneself first (into Africa) and then opening up (to the world). Finally, it is important to note that Sall has been at the forefront of the controversial Gorée Memorial, a monument planned to be built in Dakar in order to honor and recognize transatlantic slavery.

Further reading

Sall, A.L. and Carrere, C. (1990) *Nouvelle anthologie de la poésie nègre et malgache de langue française*, Luxembourg: Éditions Simoncini.

SAMBA DIOP

Sall, Ibrahima

b. 1949, Louga, Senegal

novelist, poet, playwright, and short story writer

The Senegalese writer Ibrahima Sall, like his contemporary Cheik Aliou **Ndao**, works in different traditions and genres; he is at once a novelist, a poet, a playwright, and a short story writer. What, however, differentiates Sall from all other Senegalese writers is the strong poetic touch he gives to his work. He is so concerned (even obsessed) with the poetic word or expression that there is a strong poetic strain even in his plays and novels. The development of Sall's work reflects his concern with perfection and his work seems to develop into a crescendo. From his first collection of poems (*La Génération spontanée* (The Spontaneous Generation) 1975) and short stories (*Crépuscules invraisemblables* (Improbable Twilights) 1977) to his later works (*Le Choix de Madior* (Madior's Choice) 1981) and *Les Routiers de chimères* (The Dream Drivers) 1982), Ibrahima Sall's writing style and syntax gets more sophisticated, mature, dense, and even difficult at times. Another interesting aspect of Ibrahima Sall's work is the ordinariness of the themes on which he chooses to write: the daily life of the ordinary African, Islam (see **Islam in African literature**), polygamy, interracial marriages, family, and death. Sall is simultaneously concerned with human greatness and degeneration, the harshness of urban life in postcolonial Africa (see **colonialism, neocolonialism, and postcolonialism**), and the struggle for human dignity. What makes Sall's work unique is perhaps his ability to function on a double register, his ability to give a poetic flavor to his writings and, at the same time, treat themes pertaining to routine daily life. One of Ibrahima Sall's favorite themes is the legacy of colonialism in Africa and the many ways in which Africans have negotiated the rough waters of modernity (see **modernity and modernism**). He highlights the web of paradoxes in which postcolonial Africa is caught by creating fictional characters who claim to be rooted in authentic African traditions and, at the same time, exhibit their Frenchness or their excellent mastery of the French language, the very mark of their alienation. In both his novels and his short stories, Sall's work reflects his mastery and understanding of the art of oral storytelling (see **oral literature and performance**) which he tries to replicate in the French language.

SAMBA DIOP

Samkange, Stanlake

b. 1922, Zvimba district, Zimbabwe; d. 1988, Zimbabwe

historian and novelist

Stanlake Samkange, the well-known historian and novelist, was born in Zvimba district, Zimbabwe. Samkange, who came from a distinguished Methodist family, attended school at Adams College in Natal followed by the University College of Fort Hare in South Africa, and did graduate work at universities in the US. A turning point in Samkange's political life came in the 1950s when he abandoned his previously held liberal political position, one invested in the idea of multiculturalism in the culture of colonialism (see **colonialism, neocolonialism, and postcolonialism**), toward supporting the nationalist liberation struggle that was just beginning to take root in Zimbabwe. This transition, which is often depicted as a conflict of ideas within the author himself, is evident in his early works of fiction. *On Trial for My Country* (1966), which was banned in Rhodesia due to its promotion of the politics of nationalism politics (see **nationalism and post-nationalism**), traces the political conflict between Lobengula, chief of the Ndebele, and Cecil John Rhodes, the architect of Rhodesia in the 1890s. Samkange's subsequent works, both fictional and historical, confirmed his status as one of the founders of modern Zimbabwe. These include *The Year of the*

Uprising (1978), which depicts Africans taking up arms to fight British colonialism between 1896 and 1897, *The Mourned One* (1975), *Origins of Rhodesia* (1968), *Hunuism or Ubuntuism* (1980), *African Saga* (1971), *Among Them Yanks* (1985), and *On Trial for that U.D.I.* (1986).

M. VAMBE

Sancho, Ignatius

b. 1729, South America; d. 1780, UK

writer

Like his compatriots Olaudah **Equiano** and Ottobah Quabna **Cuguano**, the Afro-British writer Ignatius Sancho was one of a group of writers who in the eighteenth century sought to produce a literary culture to oppose the claim, prominent among proponents of slavery, that Africans were not human beings. Born on a slave ship off the coast of South America, Sancho was taken to England as a baby and given to three sisters in Greenwich. He caught the eye of their neighbor, the Duke of Montagu, who taught him how to read. After the duke died in 1749 Sancho ran away from the three Greenwich maidens and sought refuge in the Montagu household, where he became a valet to the new duke. Thus began a long association – and correspondence – with some of the leading literary and cultural figures in the eighteenth century, including Samuel Johnson, Laurence Sterne, and David Garrick. Sancho's letters to these figures and others were published after his death as *Letters of the Late Ignatius Sancho, An African* (1782). Written in the best epistolary tradition of the period, Sancho's letters provide important insights into the life of an African in England in the era of the slave trade.

Further reading

King, Reyahn *et al.* (1997) *Ignatius Sancho: An African Man of Letters*, London: National Portrait Gallery.

SIMON GIKANDI

Saro-Wiwa, Ken (also known as Kenule Beeson Tsaro-Wiwa)

b. 1941, Bori, Nigeria; d. 1995, Port Harcourt, Nigeria

writer

Until he was hanged by the Nigerian military regime for his political activities in support of the rights of the Ogoni people of the Niger Delta, Ken Saro-Wiwa was an enigmatic figure in African literature. Although he was educated at the premier institutions of the country, Government College, Umuahia, and University College, Ibadan, Saro-Wiwa's literary career was marked by an interest in popular culture and fiction at a time when other writers of his generation were struggling to develop a canon of African letters. As a student at Ibadan, Saro-Wiwa was involved in the theater, and it was almost natural that his first creative works were plays, but instead of writing for the stage he chose to produce work for radio and television. Indeed, his reputation in Nigeria rested on *Basi and Company*, a series of four plays that he wrote for television. Saro-Wiwa did not consider writing to be the center of his life. On the contrary, he was involved in many political and social aspects of life in Nigeria, including business and trade, and after the civil war he served as a commissioner in the regional government of his native Rivers state.

In retrospect, his most important work is a fictional one, *Soza Boy: A Novel in Rotten English* (1985), a work unique as much for its acute observation of the meaninglessness of the Nigerian civil war as for its rejection of so-called standard English. In this novel, Saro-Wiwa, who had not shown much interest in the **language question** in African literature, rejected the formal English favored by other Nigerian writers, preferring to use a mixture of pidgin, broken English, and what he called "occasional flashes of idiomatic" English. His other two novels, *Prisoners of Jebs* (1988) and *Pita Dumbrok's Prison* (1991) were developed from commentaries Saro-Wiwa wrote for the *Vanguard* newspaper in Lagos and were concerned with political and moral corruption in postcolonial Nigeria in the 1980s (see **colonialism, neocolonialism, and postcolonialism**). In addition to his novels, Saro-Wiwa published two collections of short stories and one collection of poems, mostly dealing with the crisis of politics and nationalism (see **nationalism and post-nationalism**) in Nigeria, often using the rotten English of his first novel, and providing a satirical vista on a political culture in which reality was increasingly becoming stranger than fiction.

In his later years, Saro-Wiwa was increasingly embroiled in a conflict with the Nigerian military government over the rights of the Ogoni people and the degradation of their environment by international oil companies. Arrested on a trumped-up charge of murder, he was sentenced to death in November 1995 and hanged hastily and clumsily in spite of international efforts to save his life. Since his death Saro-Wiwa's life and works have generated a lot of biographical and critical interest.

Further reading

McLukie, Craig W. (2000) *Ken Saro-Wiwa: Writer and Political Activist*, Boulder, Colorado, and London: Lynne Rienner.

Ojo-Ade, Femi (1999) *Ken Saro-Wiwa: A Bio-Critical Study*, New York and Lagos: Africana Legacy Press.

SIMON GIKANDI

Sassine, Williams

b. 1944, Kankan, Guinea; d. 1997, Conakry, Guinea

novelist

Williams Sassine was born in Kankan (Guinea) in 1944. His father was Lebanese and his mother of Peul origin, a circumstance that set him apart from other children in the neighborhood. But it was possibly the stuttering that afflicted him from an early age, rather than his mixed parentage, that led him to a life of marginality and solitude. These two characteristics dominated his life and his writing. In 1961, Sékou Touré's repression of a students' strike and Sassine's fear of Guinea's infamous detention centers, such as the notorious Alpha Yaya Dialo Camp, left him with few options other than to leave his country and to begin what would turn out to be thirty years of exile. He went first to France, where he studied mathematics, but he soon abandoned this discipline, realizing that it was not possible to reduce life and personal feelings to a mathematical formula. His literary career began with his sojourns in various African countries: Niger, Gabon, the Côte d'Ivoire, Senegal, and eventually Mauritania, a country where he stayed for more than twenty years until expelled at the time of the bloody 1989 inter-ethnic fighting.

Sassine's subsequent return to Guinea was painful, due in part to his long absence and also to his outspoken criticism of the regime. It is therefore not surprising that, after publishing a first novel telling the story of *Saint Monsieur Baly* (1973) and his success in achieving his goal against the odds, his second novel, *Wirriyamu* (1976), and the third, *Le Jeune Homme de sable* (The Young Man of Sand) (1979), emphasized a double failure – of the people and the country. For Sassine, little good emerged from colonialism (see **colonialism, neocolonialism, and postcolonialism**), simply a lot of existential anguish, and he often suggested that only a return to the kind of wisdom inspired by African traditions, a reconnecting with the mystery of the past, would provide guidance for postcolonial society. His last two novels, *Le Zéhéros n'est pas n'importe qui* (Zéhéros is Not Anyone) (1985) and *Mémoire d'une peau* (Memory of a Skin) (1998), suggest that Africa has been further shattered by her modern experiences (see **modernity and modernism**) with little hope of revival in sight. This idea is also conveyed by the title of his collection of short stories, *L'Afrique en morceaux* (Africa Broken) (1994), comprised of texts that reflect both the continent's loss of its bearings and Sassine's strong support for the underdog. The author once said that throughout his life he attempted to eschew reality by "belting it with laughter." His refusal to be bought by officialdom no doubt provided numerous instances of such laughter – invariably punished by multiple vexations – but for the reader and the narrator's characters the situation often looks grim.

Further reading

Chevrier, J. (1995) *William Sassine, écrivain de la marginalité*, Toronto: Éditions du GREF.

Sassine. W. (1982) *L'Alphabète* (The Alphabet), Paris: Présence Africaine.

——(1995) *Légende d'une verité suivi de Tu ... Laura* (Legend of a Truth Followed by You ... Laura), Solignac, France: Le Bruit des Autres.

JEAN-MARIE VOLET

Schoeman, Karel

b. 1939, South Africa

novelist and journalist

The South African author Karel Schoeman is best known for his many award-winning novels in Afrikaans (see **Afrikaans literature**), meticulously probing a theme described by J.M. **Coetzee** as: "What is the meaning of Africa and how can it be known? How is it possible to overcome the alienation which the European feels in Africa?" Schoeman's outsider characters simply observe, succumbing to passivity, loneliness, and ultimately death in a country from which there is no escape, only, sometimes, the blessing of a fleeting mystic closeness to another person, to landscape, even to an angel. *Na die geliefde land* (To the Beloved Country) (1972), *Ander land* (Another Country) (1984), *Afskeid en vertrek* (Farewell and Departure) (1990), and most notably *Hierdie lewe* (This Life) (1993), *Die uur van die engel* (Hour of the Angel) (1995), and *Verkenning* (Reconnaissance) (1996) are good examples. Schoeman converted to Catholicism as a young man and spent many years in Europe before working in the South African Library, Cape Town. His non-fiction about early Cape and Free State history, as well as biographies about, among others, Olive **Schreiner**, Susanna Smit, and his Dutch emigrant grandparents (1999) add to his impressive oeuvre.

Further reading

Burger, Willie and Van Vuuren, H. (eds) (2002) *Sluiswagter by die dam van stemme: Beskonings oor die werk van Schoeman* (Lockkeeper at the Dam of Voices: Essays on the work of Karel Schoeman), Pretoria: Protea.

ENA JANSEN

Schreiner, Olive Emilie Albertina

b. 1855, Wittebergen, South Africa; d. 1920, Cape Town, South Africa

novelist and essayist

Usually hailed as the first South African novelist, Olive Schreiner is remembered also for her polemical essays, allegories, and letters (to Havelock Ellis, Karl Pearson, Edward Carpenter, and others). Her writing was formative of both a South African literary tradition and international feminist thought, and took up the cause of the victims of injustice, whether of the Boer under Britain, of black South Africans refused the vote, of women under patriarchal rule (white or black), or of workers exploited in the name of profit. Her first two novels, *Undine* (published posthumously in 1928) and *The Story of an African Farm* (1883), address a youthful need to break free of the religious and psychological repression of colonial settler existence, including the subordination of women. *From Man to Man* (1926) continues this theme but turns also to adult life and a mother's revisionist storytelling. In her allegorical novel *Trooper Peter Halket of Mashonaland* (1897), Schreiner made a vigorous attack on British racist colonialism in the figure of Cecil John Rhodes and his Chartered Company (see **colonialism, neocolonialism, and postcolonialism**). Besides her anti-imperialist and feminist polemics – continued in *Thoughts on South Africa* (1923) and *Woman and Labour* (1911) respectively, among other publications – she is remembered for the energy of her prose and her evocations of the South African landscape.

DOROTHY DRIVER

Sebbar, Leïla

b. 1941, Aflou, Algeria

novelist and essayist

Leïla Sebbar was born in Algeria, where her father, an Algerian, and her mother, who is French, were both kindergarten teachers. Sebbar is one of a few Franco-Algerian women writers who live and write in France. Known best for her novels, Sebbar has also written many essays and contributes regularly to literary magazines as well as the radio program *France Culture*. To date, several of Sebbar's novels have been translated from their original French into English. These are *Shérazade, Missing: Aged 17, Dark Curly Hair, Green Eyes* (1984) (*Shérazade, 17 ans, brune, frisée, les yeux verts*) (1982), *Silence on the Shores* (2000) (*Le Silence des rives*) (1993), *My Mother's Eyes* (1997), and *The Green Chinese from Africa* (*Le Chinois vert d'Afrique*) (1984). *Shérazade, Missing* is part of a trilogy whose other titles include *Les Carnets de Shérazade* (Shérazade's Notebooks) (1985) and *Le Fou de Shérazade* (Shérazade's Madness) (1991).

Throughout her writing, Sebbar has tried to show how the postcolonial subject is always forced to negotiate between two worldviews, two cultures, and two sets of values that are often in competition and conflict. Many of Sebbar's characters live in exile, but they are obsessed with the desire to return home to Algeria. While in exile, they make strong connections among themselves and are rooted in the diasporic communities they create (see **diaspora and pan-Africanism**). Sebbar narrates the experiences of a generation of Beurs (North Africans born in France), exploring relations between different histories, memories, and modes of artistic creation. Despite the painful history of colonialism (see **colonialism, neocolonialism, and postcolonialism**), her works try to bring France and Algeria together, and in her novels the meeting of French and Algerian culture in France and the circular migrations back and forth between the two countries are seen as creating new social relationships. Her Shérazade trilogy, for example, can be considered to be a cultural map of the main character as she makes her way through the landscape of the dominant French culture against the background provided by Algeria's painful history. Given the history of Algeria, which was a French colony until 1962, the relationship between these two countries and the culture that emerges out of it is marked by violence. One of Sebbar's goals, then, is to reinscribe the history of Algeria, not only to understand its complex relation to France but also to show how Beurs are compelled to deal with their new cultural space.

Ultimately, the Shérazade trilogy is concerned with the role of education and knowledge in the recollection of lost memories and history (see **education and schools**). Shérazade's recollection of the past is apparent in her name, which links her to the legendary narrator of *A Thousand and One Nights*, and by her eyes, which are green, like the eyes of *L'Odalisque* painted by the French artist Delacroix. Shérazade thus initiates herself into French culture through the process of acquiring knowledge in a cultural hexagon, one which moves constantly within the physical and symbolic spaces of high culture, the museums, libraries, and concerts, the places and events where she works out questions about power relations and knowledge.

In her juxtaposition of paintings by Delacroix with North African writers, Sebbar reveals the liminal entry point that triggers a process of recollection in the Shérazade trilogy and other works. In *Les Carnets de Shérazade*, Shérazade records the names of the French painters of the nineteenth century in a little notebook and juxtaposes them to contemporary North African writers she is interested in reading, writers ranging from Albert **Memmi** to Assia **Djebar** and **Ben Jelloun**, The paintings that represent and construct what she calls the "foreign bodies of Oriental women" are thus reread from the perspective established by modern North African literature.

In her quest for knowledge and redefinition, Shérazade is driven by her intellectual curiosity and willingness to learn about, and to understand her position in, the intertwined cultures of France and Maghreb. *Une Enfance d'ailleurs, 17 écrivains racontent avec Nancy Huston* (A Childhood from Elsewhere, Narration by Seventeen Writers in Collaboration with Nancy Huston) (1993), an anthology Sebbar co-edited with Nancy Huston, a Canadian writer living in France, contains recollections of childhood memories of Algeria by prominent writers from that country living in France. This collection brings together writers from different backgrounds: the children of colonialists, Jewish children, Muslim children, and children raised in and between different cultures, but they all have one thing in common – an Algerian childhood. In *Une Enfance d'ailleurs*, Sebbar's goal is to remember her native land, Algeria, and its colonial past in collaboration with others, and this

desire to remember the past in relation to the lives of Maghrebian immigrants in France is perhaps one of the most persistent themes in her work.

FRIEDA EKOTTO

Seck, Alioune Badara

b. 1945, Senegal

novelist

Senegalese French-language writer Alioune Badara Seck is known for novels that delve into the world of the Senegalese elite, revealing the corruption, the intrigue, and the crime of the upper classes. His 1988 novel *Le Monde des grands* (The World of the Mighty) centers around a love story between Mati Njaay, the daughter of a wealthy Dakar businessman, and Lat Sukaabe, a university student from a modest rural background. Although their story ties together the different threads of Seck's narrative, ultimately Seck's primary concern is the vicious realm of the mighty that lies behind the gates and manicured green lawns of Dakar villas: adulterous parents, illegitimate children, questionable business dealings, exaggerated concerns of class, even murder. In his 1990 novel *La Mare aux grenouilles* (The Pool of Frogs), Seck goes even further in his indictment of the upper echelons of Senegalese society. The novel charts the corruption of a young graduate hired by the Administration of Public Works in Dakar and his costly entry into the universe of the wealthy and powerful.

Further reading

Seck, Alioune Badara (1988) *Le Monde des grands* (The World of the Mighty), Paris: L'Harmattan.

KATARZYNA PIEPRZAK

Sefatsa, Suzan Limakatso

b. 1952, Lebabalasi, Clocolan, South Africa

short story writer

The South African writer Suzan Limakatso Sefatsa

is one of a very few women who have ventured to write books in Sotho (Sesotho). Born an only child in the small village of Lebabalasi in Clocolan, in the Free State, she obtained a teacher's certificate from the Strydom Teachers' College in Bloemfontein and taught at several schools in the region before becoming the principal of Lejweleputswa primary school in Meadowlands, Soweto. Sefatsa has been actively involved with associations charged with the development of the Sotho language; she has served on the Sesotho Language Board and has been the secretary of LESIBA, a Sesotho writers' association. Her first book, a drama called *Pakiso* (Repentance), was published by Educum in 1979. One of the themes of this drama concerns the demerits of a polygamous marriage. Her other books are *Makomo* (Conversations) (1988), a collection of short stories, and *Phokojwe le Phiri* (Jackal and Hyena) (1984), a folk tale published by Varia in 1991. In 1992, Sefatsa produced *Sesiu*, a collection of folk tales. Sefatsa is the author of *Mphatlalatsane* (The Morning Star) (1986), a series of Sesotho grammar books for elementary schools.

ROSEMARY MOEKETSI

Sefrioui, Ahmed

b. 1915, Fez, Morocco; d. 2004, Rabat, Morocco

novelist

Moroccan novelist Ahmed Sefrioui is widely considered to be one of the fathers of French-language Moroccan literature. In 1949, seven years before Moroccan independence from France, Sefrioui became the first Moroccan to be awarded the Prix Littéraire du Maroc for his book *Le Chapelet d'ambre* (The Amber Prayer Beads). Narrated by a young man who has given himself the perpetual age of 15, the book contains stories about his family, the neighborhood in which he lives, and the act of storytelling itself. Through these scenes of daily life in the city of Fez, Sefrioui presents a rich ethnography of Moroccan social interactions, customs, and habits. This propensity for ethnographic detail extends throughout Sefrioui's opus, resulting in projects as diverse as the 1954 novel *La*

Boite à merveilles (The Box of Marvels) and several coffee-table books on Morocco, such as the 1975 *Lumières du Maroc* (The Lights of Morocco) and the 1970 *Rêver du Maroc* (Dreams of Morocco), in which Sefrioui provides poetic texts to accompany photographs of Morocco.

Further reading

Sefrioui, Ahmed (1949) *Le Chapelet d'ambre* (The Amber Prayer Beads), Paris: René Julliard.

KATARZYNA PIEPRZAK

Segoete, Everitt Lechesa

b. 1858, Lesotho; d. 1923, Lesotho

novelist

Everitt Segoete is one of the pioneers of Sesotho literature in Lesotho (Basutoland). After graduating as a teacher he went to the Cape Colony in the then Union of South Africa (South Africa) where he worked as a teacher before returning home to Lesotho. His picaresque and highly didactic novel, *Monono ke Moholi ke Mouoane* (Wealth is Mist, Vapor) (1910) was the first novel published in Sesotho. The plot follows the exploits of a picaroon who inadvertently becomes a fugitive, and after many trials and tribulations is converted to Christianity (see **Christianity and Christian missions**). Segoete also published a monograph on the traditional life of the Basotho. His next publication was *Phepheng* (1913), a first-person narrative named after the title character. He went to the seminary in Morija and was later ordained as a minister of the Church. During his ministry he wrote two religious treatises, *Moea oa Bolisa* (The Spirit of Shepherding) (1913) and the posthumously published *Mohlala oa Jesu Kriste* (The Example of Jesus Christ) (1924).

Further reading

Maake, N. (1997) "The Narrative Perspective in Segoete's *Monono ke Moholi ke Mouoane*," *South African Journal of African Languages* 16, 4: 127–31.

N.P. MAAKE

Sekyi, Kobina

b. 1892, Cape Coast, Gold Coast (now
  Ghana); d. 1956, Gold Coast

playwright

Born in Cape Coast and educated at the local
Mfantsipim school and then in London, Kobina
Sekyi knew enough about local and foreign
political institutions and sociocultural norms to
make him believe that the people of the Gold Coast
(present-day Ghana) had a lot to lose from
uncritical imitation of the foreign at the expense
of cultivating the local. Sekyi's major literary work
was *The Blinkards* (1974), a play originally written in
both English and Fanti, and first performed in
1915. This play highlights Sekyi's brand of cultural
nationalism (see **nationalism and post-nationalism**). Blind imitation afflicts the semi-literate,
like Mrs Brofusem; the truly literate, like the Barrister,
tend to be as comfortable speaking the local language
and wearing the "native garb" as they are speaking
English and wearing "work" clothes; and the
matriarch, Nana Katawirwa, has no use for the
"barbarous tales" of the Anglophile. Anglophilia,
as a specific instance of Eurocentrism, is thus
dramatized as the opiate of the misguided. In the
end, the Barrister and the matriarch win a court
case that upholds local custom and tradition. Sekyi
intended his 1915 play to be set in "the present."
The timelessness of "the present" is assured by Sekyi's
creative response to the **language question** and
his stance on decolonizing the African mind.

KOFI OWUSU

Selormey, Francis

b. 1927, Gold Coast (now Ghana); d.
  1988, Ghana

novelist, scriptwriter, and sports administrator

The Ghanaian novelist, scriptwriter, and sports
administrator Francis Selormey is best known for
his novel *The Narrow Path* (1967: London). In this
novel, the broad conflicts between the traditionally
African and the Western are crystallized in the

disagreements Nani, the teacher, has with his
siblings, who are fishermen: "he thought them
uneducated, they thought him proud; they were
pagans, he a Christian; they were polygamists, he a
firm and outspoken advocate of monogamy."
Education (see **education and schools**) and
Christianity (see **Christianity and Christian
missions**) are seen as agents of change that
impact negatively on families. With admirable
psychological insight and a touch of irony,
Selormey shows how Nani breaks up his own
family in his attempt to keep members of the family
together. In the course of the narrative, the narrow
path of obedience that Nani demands from his wife
and children gets narrower and narrower until "all
the pent-up feelings … burst out." The cathartic
moment does not lead to healing: Nani subsequently dies and the father–son relationship his
son, the narrator, has been craving is "never
achieved." Selormey uses education and Christianity as flash-points for cultural conflict; he does
better than other novelists in suggesting that the
human cost of such conflicts is incalculable.

Works cited

Selormey, F. (1967) *The Narrow Path*, London:
  Heinemann.

KOFI OWUSU

Sembene, Ousmane

b. 1923, Ziguinchor, Senegal; d. 2007,
  Dakar, Senegal

novelist and filmmaker

Born in Ziguinchor, Senegal, Sembene is one of
Africa's foremost writers and filmmakers, and he
has used his work to provide scathing critiques of
social injustices in colonial and postcolonial Senegal
(see **colonialism, neocolonialism, and postcolonialism**). Within Francophone Africa, Sembene's fiction provides a bridge between the
concerns of writers from the pre-independence
period and those of the post-independence generation (a role comparable to that of **Ngugi wa
Thiong'o**'s work in Anglophone Africa). While the

vast majority of African writers are members of an educated elite, Sembene is largely a self-educated man, whose interest in literature was born while working as a docker and trade union official in Marseilles in the 1950s. Since the early 1960s, he has led a dual career as writer and film director, directing eleven films and publishing ten books (all in French) in total. Sembene has made film adaptations of several of his texts and has also transformed two of his films into books.

His first novel, *Black Docker* (*Le Docker noir*) (1956), focuses on a marginalized and tragic black African hero confronted and defeated by the white establishment in France. Diaw Falla, the docker of the title, is an aspiring writer whose novel is stolen and published by a white French author. A rather unsuccessful debut in terms of style and plot, the novel is nonetheless important for a number of reasons: it signals Sembene's interest in the social and political boundaries on individuals while also revealing his concern with literary form through the *mise en abyme* of Diaw Falla's novel within the novel.

Both of Sembene's novels published immediately prior to French West African independence, *O Pays, mon beau peuple!* (O This Land, My Beautiful People!) and *God's Bits of Wood* (*Les Bouts de bois de Dieu*), in 1957 and 1960 respectively, are infused with the optimism of the independence movement, and they also address many of the issues facing an increasingly urbanized and modern Africa. In both works, Sembene criticizes injustice and hypocrisy within the African community alongside his broadsides against the French colonial regime. Sembene did not believe that independence would bring back the glories of a mythical African past, nor that the replacement of one elite (white) with another (black) would constitute anything but a cosmetic change. Independence, for Sembene, was the first step on the road to the creation of new egalitarian African societies. His Marxism thus sets him apart from many of those involved in Francophone African literature in the 1950s and 1960s, particularly those of the **negritude** school (particularly Léopold Sédar **Senghor**) who emphasized the racial and cultural divide between Africa and Europe, neglecting social and political concerns.

The second of these anti-colonial novels, *God's Bits of Wood*, is generally considered to be Sembene's masterpiece, and it marked a significant development in his writing. Whereas his first two novels had focused on the individual tragic hero, Sembene now decentered his work, casting the community, through multiple narratives, as the hero of his novel (a process he would continue in all his later works). *God's Bits of Wood* tells the story of an historical railway strike on the Dakar–Niger line that took place between October 1947 and March 1948, presenting a vision of a radical Africa engaging with the challenge of modernity (see **modernity and modernism**). The extraordinary power of *God's Bits of Wood* lies in Sembene's ability to conceive of a complete transformation in the structure of African society and the way in which Africans imagine their social relations. The romanticized notion of a pure African tradition is replaced by the more historical vision of an African society gripped by social changes with which tradition must find some sort of accommodation.

Sembene's disillusionment with the process of decolonization led him to abandon the sweeping epic narratives of these early novels in his later works, adopting a more self-aware, elliptical, and ironic style (the epic tale of the 1958 referendum on independence from France, related in his unsuccessful and rather didactic novel, *L'Harmattan* (The Harmattan), published in 1963, is the exception to this rule). The short stories of *Tribal Scars* (*Voltaïque*), published in 1962, two years after Senegalese independence, provide the best example of this new stage in Sembene's work, in which a stylistic self-awareness is accompanied by an irony-laden critique of the failures of independence. In the stories "In the Face of History," "The Promised Land," and "Tribal Scars or The Voltaique," Sembene questions the role of both fiction and history, setting up competing narratives between which the reader is forced to choose. Rather than enfranchising the dispossessed, independence is shown to have led to the repressive hegemony of the bourgeoisie and the social domination of a stifling patriarchal Islam (see **Islam in African literature**). Sembene's work thus paves the way for the pessimistic novels of the post-independence generation of writers which exploded on to the Francophone landscape in 1968 with the publication of Yambo **Ouologuem**'s *Bound to Violence* (*Le Devoir de violence*) and Ahmadou **Kourouma**'s *The*

Suns of Independence (*Les Soleils des indépendances*), although these younger writers were to prove far more experimental than Sembene in their use of French.

In the novellas, *White Genesis* (*Véhi-Ciosane*) and *The Money Order* (*Le Mandat*), which won the literature prize at the Festival Mondial des Arts Nègres in Dakar in 1966, Sembene explores the problems facing rural and urban Africa respectively in the post-independence era. The urban world presented to us in *The Money Order* can be seen as an illustration of what happens when a traditional, village-based society such as that in *White Genesis* is being torn apart by the destructive force of capitalism. As the bonds that had previously joined the community together are broken down, the sole remaining value is money.

In *White Genesis*, Sembene also questions the role of the griot (or storyteller), continuing the problematization of the process of storytelling begun in *Tribal Scars*. The central character of the story is the griot, Dethye Law, and, through this figure Sembene invites the reader to reflect on the very nature and purpose of storytelling. Effectively, he asks which stories and histories the modern griot – or, by analogy, the modern African writer – should be telling. For Sembene, the modern griot must be the voice of truth and justice, denouncing all hypocrisy and corruption.

Sembene concentrated on filmmaking throughout the next period of his career. From the mid 1960s to the mid 1970s, he made five films – *Black Girl* (*La Noire de . . .*), *The Money Order* (*Le Mandat*), *Taaw*, *Emitaï* and *Xala*, and his sole literary text for the same period was the novella *Xala*, published in 1973, which he wrote while trying to raise the finance to make the film of the same name. Sembene had turned to film in the early 1960s, attempting to reach the illiterate African masses who had no access to his books. Indeed, he did not wait for the peasantry to come to him, choosing to tour his films around rural areas and organizing debates after the screenings. He has described the filmmaker as the closest figure to the griot, as film combines music, gesture, and storytelling, in a communal gathering. Since the late 1960s, Sembene's films have made almost exclusive use of indigenous Senegalese languages. In the early 1970s, he was very active in the promotion of

African languages, launching a Wolof-language newspaper, *Kaddu*. A highly political journal (one issue featured Sembene's translation of the *Communist Manifesto*), *Kaddu* sought to promote Wolof, which is spoken by the vast majority of Senegalese, as the official national language, thus replacing French. However, unlike Ngugi, Sembene has not opted to write his fiction in an African language.

Sembene's films deal with similar issues to his books and, like his fiction, they have worked broadly within the framework of realism, although his films of the 1960s and 1970s contain many symbolic non-realistic elements. The contrast between his films and fiction of this period can best be seen in relation to the two versions of *Xala*, the story of a corrupt businessman, El Hadj Abdou Kader Beye, who is struck with the curse of impotence on his wedding night. symbolizing the impotence of the African bourgeoisie as a class. In the novel, Sembene works largely within the conventions of the naturalist novel in terms of characterization and plot, but the film is far more interested in the presentation of archetypes than in the exploration of character. In the novel, he seeks to win the reader over to his side through the reality and verisimilitude of his story, whereas the film forces the spectator to take sides in a visual and ideological tussle between the oppressed and their oppressors. This capacity for film to present powerful social, political, and historical issues to a wide audience led Sembene to make three major historical films in the 1970s and 1980s: *Emitaï* and *Camp de Thiaroye* deal with the colonial history of Senegal, while *Ceddo* examines slavery and the rise of Islam.

The position of women within Senegalese society has been a central feature of all Sembene's work. Indeed, it is often the female characters who are obliged to replace their "impotent" menfolk as providers for the family. Sembene has consistently attempted to open up the representation of African women to include more dynamic and assertive female characters. Delving back into history, he produces a record of female resistance in stories such as "The Mother" (*Tribal Scars*). Sembene has also tried to suggest possible future avenues for the development of male–female relationships within Africa. For example, the dynamic role of young women such as Ramatalouye and Ad'jibid'ji (*God's*

Bits of Wood) illustrates Sembene's conviction that the increased participation of women in decision-making within African society is one of the keys to change. Sembene has also addressed the status of women within polygamous societies. In the novella *Taaw* and the short stories "The Bilal's Fourth Wife" and "Her Three Days" (both in *Tribal Scars*) we are presented with a complete breakdown of the traditional polygamous marriage, and, in the cases of Yaye Dabo (*Taaw*) and Penda (*God's Bits of Wood*), we are presented with characters who choose to lead a life outside the institution of marriage altogether. Sembene argues that impotent male-dominated society must give way to a more egalitarian society produced by the overthrow of all sexual and social repression.

Since *Xala*, Sembene has published only three books in almost thirty years, two of which (*Niiwam/Taaw*, 1987, and *Guelwaar*, 1996) are adaptations of his films. In the sole full-length novel of his later period, *The Last of the Empire* (*Le Dernier de l'empire*), published in 1981, he launches his most sustained political attack on the Senegalese post-independence regime of the Socialist Party. His antipathy towards the regime was compounded by the fact that the president from 1960 to 1980 was Senghor, the poet of negritude, who elevated this concept to a national ideology. For Sembene, negritude was a deliberately misleading notion that spoke of black pride while continuing the politics of African subservience to Europe.

Sembene's most creative period was in the 1960s and 1970s, and his best works encapsulate the revolutionary fervor and subsequent frustration of the immediate post-independence era. His radical Marxist agenda inspired many young African artists of this period, but in post Cold War Africa his ideological certainties have been questioned by many. Often praised for the political commitment of his fiction, his best works, *God's Bits of Wood*, *Tribal Scars*, and *White Genesis/The Money Order*, have also been acclaimed as classics of modern African literature.

Further reading

Gadjigo, Samba *et al.* (eds) (1993) *Ousmane Sembene:* *Dialogues with Critics and Writers*, Amherst, Massachusetts: University of Massachusetts Press.

Murphy, David (2000) *Sembene: Imagining Alternatives in Film and Fiction*, Oxford: James Currey; Trenton, New Jersey: Africa World Press.

Tsabedze, Clara (1994) *African Independence from Francophone and Anglophone Voices: A Comparative Study of the Post-Independence Novels of Ngugi and Sembene*, Frankfurt: Peter Lang.

DAVID MURPHY

Sénac, Jean

b. 1926, Béni-Saf près d'Oran, Algeria; d. 1973, Algiers, Algeria

poet

Jean Sénac is an Algerian poet of *pied-noir* (French settler) origin. Sénac shares the same background and follows, to some extent, the tradition established by writers such as Robblès and Albert Camus, of whom he was a close friend. At the same time, he saw himself as truly "Algerian" and claimed allegiance to the Algerian anti-colonial movement by joining the FLN after 1954. His support for the work of Algerian writers and artists after independence as secretary of the Algerian Writers' Union, and his work in setting up literary journals and organizing cultural events in the postcolonial period demonstrate his active involvement with the new nation (see **colonialism, neocolonialism, and postcolonialism**). Sénac's poetry reflects the intensity and passion as well as the uncertainties characteristic of the years leading to the country's independence. Influenced by French surrealism, it challenges conventional use of metaphors and images. The presence of the body which permeates his poems – which he called "corpoèmes" – is particularly reflective of the writer's desire to create a new language which bridges the gap between ideas and experiences and articulates the aspirations of the emerging Algerian nation.

Sénac was murdered in mysterious circumstances at his home in 1973, leaving behind a prolific body of work.

Further reading

Sénac, J. (1999) *Oeuvres poétiques* (Poetic Works), Paris: Actes Sud.

ANISSA TALAHITE-MOODLEY

Senghor, Léopold Sédar

b. 1906, Joal, Senegal; d. 2001, Paris, France

poet, statesman and scholar

The Senegalese poet, statesman, and scholar L.S. Senghor was one of the founders and architects of the **negritude** movement. He was recognized as its most prolific theorist and eloquent spokesperson. His extensive concurrent careers in literature and politics from the 1930s on established him as a seminal figure in twentieth-century African history. The first president of Senegal, he was elected to the prestigious French Academy in 1983, three years after voluntarily leaving the presidency.

Senghor began writing poems and essays while he was a university student in Paris. But his first book of poems *Shadow Songs* (*Chants d'ombre*) was published only in 1945. In this collection of poems, the themes of exile and return, cultural estrangement and the quest for the kingdom of childhood, the affirmation and aesthetic recovery of the protagonist's racial self stand out. It highlights the major elements of a burgeoning poetics of negritude. Senghor's second collection of poems, *Black Hosts* (*Chants pour Naët*) (1948), was essentially concerned with World War II and its consequences on Africa and the diaspora (see **diaspora and pan-Africanism**). These poems "document" war as experienced by black soldiers, register and valorize their sacrifices, their bravery, and their sentiment of revolt. The volume presents a sharp criticism of Western civilization and a challenge to its pretension of superiority. The publication of *Anthologie de la nouvelle poésie nègre et malgache de langue française* (Anthology of New Black and Malagasy Poetry in French) in 1948, with the now famous preface by Jean-Paul Sartre, represented a major breakthrough for Senghor and the poets of negritude because it presented, for the first time, their works as a coherent body to the public.

Ethiopiques (Ethiopians) (1956), a transitional volume, continues to amplify the themes of exile and return, love and hate, and the racial tension between colonized and colonizer. While it firmly establishes Senghor's vision of a pan-African cultural unity, it also introduces a more reflexive, intimate poetry. The volume strives to strike a balance between the heroic/public voice and the intimate murmur and rumination of an anguished persona. *Nocturnes* (1961) seeks to develop this newly unveiled voice of intimacy. The poems in this collection are mainly concerned with the struggle between night and light, love and abandonment. But they also praise the courage of the lion, the public figure, and the freedom fighter as in the polyphonic dramatic poem "Elegy for Aynina Fall." Inspired by his wife, the *Letters in the Season of Hivernage* (*Lettres d'hivernage*) (1972) constitute a kind of renewal of Senghor's art since they allow the reader to enter into the intimacy of the poet's love life more directly and in its quotidian rhythm. As the poems sing of the rainy season called "hivernage," they also hint at the "hivernage" of the lovers, the approach of old age and contemplation.

Major Elegies (*Elégies majeures*) (1979) pulls together all the elements developed in the previous volumes in a uniquely brilliant collection. The elegiac form initially introduced in *Nocturnes* reaches here its highest level of sophistication. The poems speak of, and are dedicated to, people who have died; and as they stage the battle between life and death, these poems trace the ways in which the poet transcends and translates the loss into a gain and into a victory of life. Throughout the volume the reader is invited into the deeper intimacy of the poet to witness the despair of the father, the friend, the companion, and the lover. The reader is immersed into the strongest evocation of the cycle of death and rebirth of the natural seasons as the poet struggles in the mystical language to find meaning in the death of his beloved. "Poèmes perdus" (Lost Poems), the section that closes *The Collected Poetry* (1991) (*Oeuvre poétique*) (1984) traces Senghor's evolution as a young poet, learning his craft, leaning on other poets while seeking to find his own voice and rhythm.

The poetry of L.S. Senghor is characterized by a highly refined use of symbolism and imagery which bring to the fore his vital conception of negritude, an almost physical love of Africa, and the sacred and sacramental function of the poet. He has earned the mantle of "griot of negritude" for the evocative force of his poetry deeply resonant of the word-image cluster, the solemn apostrophe, and the power to will into being felt from and ascribed to the oral diction, the exhortatory, and the emotional intensity of the griot's chant. Replete with images of the African landscape, significant words from African languages, and the names of musical instruments, yet written in a skillfully controlled language, the long free verse of Senghor's poems appears to be remarkably supple. It manages to bend softly enough to carry surprising elliptical forms and express inflections that are unique in French poetry.

Senghor has published a dozen books of essays on various subjects ranging from negritude and German philosophy to socialism, including scholarly articles on the Wolof and Serer languages as well as literary and **art** criticism. It is possible to divide Senghor's prose writings into two groups. On the one hand are his cultural studies, and on the other his political writings. The cultural studies are mainly texts aimed at defining and illustrating his concept of negritude as the "sum total of cultural values of the black world" viewed from the angles of literature, the fine arts, anthropology, and philosophy. The political essays, increasingly and significantly more polemical in tone, are a search for the foundations of a specific African model of nationalism, nation-building and nationhood (see **nationalism and post-nationalism**). The two groups of essays are ultimately interrelated because they seek to facilitate the birth of what he called, after Alain Locke, "the New Negro." However, in both cases, Senghor maintains that Africa must borrow and integrate what it finds useful in other cultures according to his famous dictum: "To assimilate and not to be assimilated." Once African civilization has been recognized as a cultural force of equal value, Africa can participate more freely in the world cultural trade of give and take, since all great civilizations are the product of a dynamics of *métissage* or cross-cultural fertilization.

These essays are best described as circumstantial pieces which still testify today to the efforts of a political leader fighting for power in order, as he believed, to better serve his people. But Senghor's brand of negritude was increasingly criticized by younger African writers of the postcolonial era as essentialist, backward-looking, and disconnected with the issues facing contemporary Africa.

Further reading

Irele, A. (ed.) (1977) *Selected Poems of Léopold Sédar Senghor*, Cambridge: Cambridge University Press.

Nespoulous-Neville, J.A. (1999) *Listen to Africa: A Call from L.S. Senghor*, Pretoria: Unisa Press.

Senghor, L.S. (1991) *The Collected Poetry*, trans. M. Dixon, Charlottesville and London: University Press of Virginia, CARAF Books.

Vaillant, J.G. (1990) *Black, French, and African: A Life of Léopold Sédar Senghor*, Cambridge, Massachusetts: Harvard University Press.

KANDIOURA DRAME

Sepamla, Sipho

b. 1932, Krugersdorp, South Africa; d. 2007, Gauteng, South Africa

poet, short story writer and novelist

Born in Krugersdorp, a typical South African mining town, Sepamla has made a significant contribution to African literature as a poet, short story writer, and novelist. Before joining the Federated Union of Black Arts (FUBA) which he currently heads, Sepamla worked as a personnel officer and a teacher. In spite of his obvious versatility as evidenced by his involvement in a variety of literary forms, it is mainly as a poet that Sepamla has achieved international recognition. As a poet he belongs to the group of South African black poets known as the Soweto Poets or the New Black Poets, who came into prominence during the politically turbulent years of the 1970s. Sepamla's poetry is marked by his deft use of irony and satire and his ingenious combination of township patois and standard English. His published volumes of poetry include: *Hurry up to It* (1975), *The Blues is You in Me* (1976), *The Soweto I Love* (1977), *Children of the Earth* (1983), *Selected Poems* (1984), and *From Gore to Soweto* (1988). Sepamla's novels, written in the mode of social realism (see **realism and magical realism**), examine black urban life under apartheid from a variety of perspectives (see **apartheid and post-apartheid**). He has published the following novels: *The Root is One* (1979), *A Ride on the Whirlwind* (1981), *Third Generation* (1987), and *A Scattered Survival* (1989).

Further reading

Chapman, Michael (1981) *Soweto Poetry*, Johannes-burg: McGraw-Hill.

THENGANI H. NGWENYA

Serhane, Abdelhak

b. 1950, Sefrou, Morocco

novelist and academic

Moroccan writer and professor of psychology and French literature, Abdelhak Serhane has been primarily interested in narrating the lives of those history often leaves behind. In his first novel *Messaouda* (1983) and in subsequent works such as *Les Enfants des rues étroites* (The Children of Narrow Streets) (1986), Serhane explores the fate of the disenfranchised in Moroccan society and gives voice to subjects often silenced, such as corruption, sexual perversion, and poverty. In these works Serhane shows how women and children navigate sites of patriarchal power to endure daily violence and humiliation, whether during the French Protectorate of Morocco (1912–56) or in contem-porary times. Throughout his opus, Serhane has shown particular attention and tenderness to those children who live in the streets in Morocco, and through their lives he presents a vicious indictment of late twentieth-century Moroccan society. In 1996, he published a work of non-fiction entitled *L'Amour circoncis* (Circumcised Love) that in a mixture of sociology and psychology examines the conventions and practices of love and eroticism in Morocco. Serhane is the founder of the

Moroccan cultural journal *Horizons maghrébins* (North African Horizons).

Further reading

Serhane, Abdelhak (1983) *Messaouda*, Paris: Seuil.

KATARZYNA PIEPRZAK

Serote, Mongane Wally

b. 1944, Sophiatown, South Africa

poet

Mongane Serote is perhaps the most prolific of contemporary South African poets. Born in Sophiatown, Serote started writing poetry in the early 1970s, and the publication of his first collection, *Yakhal'inkomo* (1972), earned him the Ingrid Jonker Prize for Poetry. From then onwards Serote went on to produce a number of collections while he was in exile. The volumes of poetry he published during this period included *Tsetlo* (1974), *No Baby Must Weep* (1975), *Behold Mama, Flowers* (1978), *The Night Keeps Winking* (1982), and *A Tough Tale* (1987), most of which bear the imprints of his penchant for lyrical verse, and reflect not only the different phases of struggle that have shaped his poetry but also his ideological shift from a black consciousness position to his adoption of the non-racial politics of the ANC. *A Tough Tale*, for example, takes the form of a poetic journey, reflecting on the protracted struggle for freedom in South Africa seen from the perspective of the ANC, thereby confirming Serote's position as a poet of the liberation movement. Coming back from exile did not deter Serote from writing poetry, as can be seen from the publication of his subsequent two long poems, *Third World Express* (1992) and *Come and Hope With Me* (1994), which provide a series of probing questions as the poet tries to grapple with the meaning of freedom and reconciliation and to deal with the uncertainties of a period of political transition and the prospects for a post-apartheid South Africa (see **apartheid and post-apartheid**). The two long poems were later published together and given the collective title *Freedom Lament and Song* (1997).

Serote's writing has not, however, been confined to poetry. In 1990 he published a collection of essays, *On the Horizon*, which provides more insight on this writer's conception of the role of literary production and culture in society. In addition Serote has published two novels. The first one, *To Every Birth Its Blood* (1981), received international acclaim, not just for its depiction of the South African struggle against apartheid from the 1960s to around 1980 but also for its employment of poetic diction and, perhaps more significantly, its experimentation with form. This experimentation seems to have been abandoned in Serote's second novel, *Gods of Our Time* (1999), which nevertheless covers a wider canvas of the political struggle against apartheid, shifting the focus to the late 1980s. *Gods of Our Time* celebrates the role of women in the struggle, a project that seems to have begun in Serote's early poetry and that became more obvious in the second part of *To Every Birth Its Blood*. As a person who was himself involved in the struggle against apartheid as a high-ranking member of the ANC and the head of its cultural division, it could be argued that in his writing Serote provides his readers with the history of the struggle from the inside. Serote is presently a member of parliament and chairperson of the portfolio Committee of Arts, Culture, Science and Technology.

JABULANI MKHIZE

Seruma, Eneriko

b. 1944, Uganda

novelist and short story writer

Eneriko Seruma is the pen name of Henry S. Kimbugwe, a Ugandan writer who was active in East African literary circles in the 1960s and 1970s, when he also worked for the East African Publishing House. He is known for his novel *The Experience* (1970) and a collection of short stories entitled *The Heart Seller* (1971). Seruma once described *The Experience*, his partly autobiographical portrait of an African's struggle to cope with life in the white world, as "an expressionistic painting of contemporary Africa." *The Heart Seller*, on the other hand,

deals with a variety of African-American experiences, with the title story derived from the saga of a man who advertises his heart for sale in *Newsweek* magazine. The offer is taken up by a racist white man who needs to replace his heart so as to boost his energies for a sexual affair with his secretary. Seruma also wrote poems and short stories for the leading East African journals and magazines of the 1960s and 1970s, including *Ghala*, *Busara*, *Zuka* and *Transition*.

GEORGE ODERA OUTA

Serumaga, Robert

b. 1939, Buganda, Uganda; d. 1982, Uganda

playwright

Robert Serumaga was born among the Buganda people and was educated at Makerere University College and Trinity College, Dublin, where he trained as an economist. Serumaga was closely associated with the theater movement in Uganda where he ran a professional company. He led an active political life and served briefly as a minister in the government of Yusuf Lule following the eventful overthrow of dictator Idi Amin in 1979. Together with John **Ruganda**, Serumaga is considered to be one of the founders of modern drama in East Africa. Although he died after only a short career, his plays *Majangwa and a Play* (1974) and *The Elephants* (1971), and the novel *Return to the Shadows* (1969), have made him a major figure in African letters. In *The Elephants* and *Return to the Shadows*, Serumaga's concern is with the now familiar world of postcolonial disillusionment, political refugees, and social displacement. *Majangwa*, too, is a representation of the postcolonial state of disillusionment that gripped many African countries in the 1960s and early 1970s, but it is also a vivid example of Serumaga's use of techniques borrowed from the "theater of the absurd," an unusual example in East African drama of the period. *Majangwa* features a hitherto revered traditional artist who is forced to eke out an existence by having sex with his wife on the streets. The absurdist elements in the play are apparent in

Serumaga's construction of his drama around lonely, alienated heroes that have been dislocated by the pressures of both precolonial and postcolonial society (see **colonialism, neocolonialism, and postcolonialism**).

GEORGE ODERA OUTA

Shona and Ndebele literature

Zimbabwe's indigenous literature is published in the two national languages, Shona and Ndebele. The two literatures were born out of twin efforts by the colonial government and Western missionaries, who saw literacy in general, and literature in particular, as an effective way of subverting African traditional cultures in order to create room for the dissemination of their own ideas and values. In 1954 the Southern Rhodesia Literature Bureau was created under the auspices of the Department of Native Affairs in the Ministry of Information. Its aim was to promote the publication of literature in the two mentioned indigenous languages. Both the colonial government and the missionaries believed that there could be no literacy without literature. Predominantly mission-trained potential writers attended Literature Bureau new and aspiring writers' workshops, where they learned the "dos" and "don'ts" of writing literature in the political context of colonialism (see **colonialism, neocolonialism, and postcolonialism**). The rules established at these workshops led to the crystallization of a literary tradition that most Zimbabwean writers have had to reckon with. In addition, the resultant literature grew under the watchful eyes of publications officers whose job was to ensure that writers did not publish politically subversive works. The first works to be sponsored by the Bureau were Solomon **Mutswairo**'s *Feso*, Ndabaningi **Sithole**'s African nationalist novel *AmaNdebele KaMzilikazi* (The Ndebele of Mzilikazi), and Herbert Chitepo's epic poem, *Soko Risina Musoro* (A Tale Without a Head), all published by the Oxford University Press in 1956.

But because of the emerging censorship and the channeling of creative works through institutions dominated by the colonial state, much of the tradition of African nationalism (see **nationalism and post-nationalism**) that characterized these pioneer works of the mid 1950s was not reflected in subsequent writing. This kind of literature was deemed to be subversive. While works written in African languages in Zimbabwe in the 1960s were still preoccupied with the African encounter with colonialism, they were generally characterized by narrow moralization. The Bureau encouraged writers to write about their precolonial past as well as their customs, but to do so in a way that showed that modernization (see **modernity and modernism**) was equivalent to cultural enlightenment. Authors who chose to focus on contemporary issues tended to portray reality out of context because they could not accurately delineate the sociopolitical setting of their stories without subverting colonialism. The books that won prizes in the competitions sponsored by the Literature Bureau were those that were considered good for schoolchildren. Many authors who could not freely confront colonial reality chose to expend their creative energy on demonstrating their mastery of indigenous languages, an exercise that was perceived as an important cultural nationalist gesture. The colonial missionary educational background of the writers also led to the production of literature that was preoccupied with Christianity and the basic teachings of the various Christian missions (see **Christianity and Christian missions**) and, in cases where there was no conflict with African traditions, African moral precepts.

What had been the channeling of writers into politically safe terrain crystallized into open censorship in the period between Rhodesia's Unilateral Declaration of Independence in 1965 and the attainment of independence in 1980. During this period, when there was an intensification of the war of liberation, censorship further stifled creative writing. The sensitivity of the Rhodesian government to subversion turned the promotional role of the Bureau into a censorial one. Manuscripts had to pass through the Bureau before they were submitted to publishers. The creative constraints notwithstanding, some cultural nationalist writers saw literature as an opportunity to transmit African traditions to the young generation. This was facilitated by the fact that many early writers, such as **Tsodzo**, **Chakaipa**, **Sigogo**, **Mlilo**, **Mutswairo**, Runyowa, and **Ngwenya**, were schoolteachers. The cultural nationalist strain in these writers accounts for the apparent interface between celebrating colonialism and asserting the African worldview. This explains the ambivalence in the social vision of most writing of the time.

Independence liberated writers from the Bureau tradition by allowing manuscripts to be submitted directly to publishers. It also allowed authors to explore themes that had hitherto been regarded as sensitive. The liberation war (*Chimurenga*, in Shona) was one such theme. By 1985 a number of writers had published poetry, fiction, and plays on the struggle, most of which had a celebratory tone. In the vein of the sensibility of the new political dispensation, war heroes and their guns were eulogized for liberating the country. The romances of the war became part of the Zimbabwe writer's effort to create national symbols that would legitimize the first African government in the country. Poetry collections that celebrated the war included *Isidlodlo SikaMthwakazi* (Mthwakazi's Headring), edited by D.N. Ndoda (1984), and *Giya Mthwakazi* (Mthwakazi, Celebrate Your Heritage) (1990), both in Ndebele; and *Nduri DzeZimbabwe* (Zimbabwean Poetry) (1983) and *Chakarira Chindunduma* (Resonations of the War) (1985) in Shona. Some nationalist writers, most notably Mutswairo, Mutasa, Matsikiti, Ndlovu, and Khumalo, reverted to precolonial legends and epics to resuscitate their heroic traditional narratives which had been marginalized by colonialism.

A departure from nationalist triumphalism came with more critical accounts of the war by Shona satirists like **Choto** and Chimhundu, who, apart from celebrating the war of independence, also highlighted corruption in the emergent nationalist bourgeoisie. This effort is complemented by Ndebele fiction of the 1990s focusing on the 1982–7 political disturbances in Matabeleland and the Midlands, which led to the massacre of thousands of civilians. This sensitive theme is given cautious treatment by writers such as **Magagula**, Hleza and **Masundire**, but it reflects a one-sided perspective that results in simplistic accounts of that phase of history.

One outstanding trend in Ndebele and Shona literature from the mid 1990s onwards is the theme of development and underdevelopment. The theme arises from the fact that, by the end of the first decade of independence, it had become clear that most of the economic targets set during and after the war had been missed. In the face of ever-increasing poverty, there was much official discourse on development. Some writers wrote about the impediments of national development like poaching, corruption in high places, and political unrest. Others chronicled the impact of the Economic Structural Adjustment problem on urban African communities. Yet others focus on AIDS-related problems in the narrow moralistic perspective of the colonial period.

Notable differences from dominant literary trends come through Chirikure Chirikure, one of the most vibrant performing poets in Zimbabwe. He has published three collections of satirical political poetry, *Rukuvhute* (Roots) (1989), *Chamupupuri* (Whirlwind) (1996), and *Hakurarwi* (We Shall Not Sleep) (1999). He performs his poetry to the accompaniment of music by popular musicians like Oliver Mtukudzi, Dumi Maraire, Ephart Mujuru, Chiwoniso Maraire, and the Uya Moya Jazz Band. He has succeeded in bridging the gap between publishing and performance.

Further reading

Chiwome, E.M. (1996) *A Social History of the Shona Novel*, Zimbabwe: Juta.

Kahari, G.P. (1990) *The Rise of the Shona Novel*, Gweru: Mambo Press.

EMMANUEL CHIWOME

Shongwe, John Pempela

b. 1951, South Africa

poet and educator

The South African writer and educator John Shongwe was educated locally at the universities of Zululand and Durban-Westville before he attained a PhD in geography at the University of Pretoria in 1999. Shongwe's novels *Bangani*

(Friends) (1984) and *Ayinabudzala* (No Age Limit) (1987) present a worldview of a struggling populace whose reward comes from perseverance in one's lot. On the other hand, the poems in *Tinkondlo Tayitolo Netalamuhla* (Poetry of Yesterday and Today) (1990) and *Sihlenge Setinkondlo* (Island of Poetry) (1985) are concerned with a more sublime theme accentuating natural phenomena and metaphysical perceptions. Although his thematic concerns are often very religious, Shongwe always de-emphasizes the use of Christianity as a panacea for human problems; he often uses images drawn from nature as a vehicle for communicating his feelings. Some of Shongwe's most powerful poems, such as *iSahara* (The Sahara), a poem on the drought-stricken Sahara Desert, display his use of vivid imagery.

ZODWA MOTSA

short stories

A publication renaissance

The African short story in recent times has been experiencing what might guardedly be termed a renaissance in respect to the increased frequency in the publication of multiple- and single-author anthologies and individual short stories in journals and magazines. There has also been a significant improvement in the quality of the critical responses attracted by these publications, which have continued to show expanding thematic concerns and sustained artistic excellence. In contrast to the trickle that in the past characterized the publication of short story anthologies by prestigious international houses, the present time has witnessed what might comparatively be called a flood. Simon and Schuster in 1990, for instance, published *Looking for a Rain God* (ed. Nadezda Obradovic). In 1992, Heinemann released *Contemporary African Short Stories* as a follow-up to its 1985 anthology, *African Short Stories*, both of which were jointly edited by Chinua **Achebe** and C.L. Innes. Penguin in 1993 published the collection edited by Stephen Gray titled *Contemporary South African Short Stories*. The following year, Heinemann again appeared with *South African Short Stories: From 1945 to the Present*, co-edited by Denis Hirson and Martin Trump. In 1997, Charles R. Larson published *Under African Skies* with Farrar, Straus, and Giroux, while in 2000 Macmillan produced Stephen Gray's *African Stories*.

The laudable aspects of these publications are the high quality of the stories selected and the promotion of new talents. Larson's anthology in this regard is a disappointment in not advancing much, content-wise, from the two collections he edited in the 1970s. His emphasis remains on older writers. On the other hand, of all the anthologies of African stories ever published, Stephen Gray's has the distinction of being the most inclusive in respect to gender representation and geographical, linguistic, and cultural coverage.

The short story publication harvest is significant for a number of reasons, one of which is that it is far more bountiful than the partial picture painted here suggests. The picture, for instance, does not include the anthologies and individual collections distributed by African publishing houses and self-publishing authors, of which there are many. In face of a drastically shrinking publishing industry in Africa, self-publishing became the only option left. It is also significant that the renaissance has been taking place despite the continental economic hardships which have produced an acute shortage in the publication and distribution of books that has affected literary books more than any other category.

Critical response

Several reasons can be advanced to explain the African short story renaissance, but two are primary. One is that in the last decade, literary scholars finally began the needed but long-delayed critical dialogue with African short story writers which could not but have attracted the attention of publishers, particularly since the critical evaluations resulting from this dialogue showed that the genre was not only popular with a ready market, but practiced at a level of artistic excellence which can withstand comparison anywhere. Short story writers who have been suffering neglect welcomed the new attention; new writers were encouraged to produce; and publishers, who as business people wanted returns on their investments, recognized the prospects of a revitalized market.

Generic characteristics

But the most important explanation for the renaissance is connected to the nature of the African short story as a genre. The distinctions between the formal aspects of the short story, an imported genre, and the indigenous oral African folk tale (see **oral literature and performance**) are clear and indisputable; among other things, the former is predominantly realistic while the latter is fabulous, parabolic, even surrealistic. However, given the circumstances of its history, the environment of its reception, and the literary preconditioning of African writers, the short story in Africa could not but be deeply implicated in the African oral tradition. It is obvious, for instance, from stories like Amos **Tutuola**'s surrealistic "The Complete Gentleman" (1952) and Jomo **Kenyatta**'s parable "The Gentlemen of the Jungle" (1938), that the first practitioners of the short story in Africa apprehended the genre as a variant of the folk tale. Similarly, the first major responses to the introduction of the short story to Africa took the form of assembling and transcribing folk tales in collections like *Eating Chiefs* by Taban Lo **Liyong** (1970) and *Three Solid Stones* (1975) by Martha Mvungi. Even after the short story has fully come into its own and has become essentially realistic, as in numerous collections by the masters of the genre like Alex **la Guma** (*A Walk in the Night*) (1962), Achebe (*Girls at War and Other Stories*) (1972), Ama Ata **Aidoo** (*No Sweetness Here*) (1970), **Ngugi wa Thiong'o** (*Secret Lives*) (1975), and others, the African short story refused to sever its connection with the oral tradition. Numerous stories in the listed collections, for instance, combine the devices of verisimilitude that characterize the formal short story with the fabulous themes and formulaic stylistic devices that define the folk tale. As Achebe's classic story, "The Madman" (1971) demonstrates, some of the best stories produced in Africa belong to this category of fused styles.

The African short story not only continues to maintain its symbiotic connection with the folk tale, but also has progressively strengthened it as it developed, particularly whenever it wishes to rise to the level of the extraordinary, to the status of the avant-garde **art**, which disdains the limiting boundaries of canonized rules and traditions. The most impressive examples of this trend are Taban Lo Liyong's *Fixions and Other Stories* (1969) and *The Uniformed Man* (1971) whose stylistic accomplishments match those of any Western avant-garde modernist and postmodernist narratives. One of the aspects of the African short story that has attracted the most comments is this connection with oral tradition. In the introduction to his anthology, *Hungry Flames*, Mbulelo **Mzamane** boldly asserts: "The short story in South Africa is as old as the Xhosa intsomi, the Zulu inganekwane, the Sotho tsomo and other indigenous oral narrative forms" (1986: Essex).

The continuity of the oral tradition in the South African short story was similarly affirmed in Walter Oliphant's essay "Fictions of Anticipation" (1996). Furthermore, Oliphant insists that the direction of stylistic developments in post-apartheid South Africa is not that of creating a new school of writing, as Stephen Gray has suggested, but that of an artistic return to the folk origin as exemplified by Joel Matlou's stories, which he says draw on written as well as oral stylistics. It appears that Gray, who places some African short story writers in the tradition of great Western masters like Chekhov, Maupassant, Mansfield, and Hemingway, generally takes a purist view of the short story as a realistic genre. Hence, even though he acknowledges Chinweizu's 1988 anthology *Voices from Twentieth-Century Africa: Griots and Towncries* as a treasure-trove, he nonetheless studiously excluded folklore-informed narratives from his Macmillan anthology.

Most scholars, however, welcome the influence of oral tradition. Ada Azodo, for instance, in *Surviving the Present, Winning the Future* (1999), calls the short story writer a modern-day storyteller. C.D. Ntuli, in "The Art of D.B.Z. Ntuli in Short Story Writing" (1999), celebrates the oral influence as the dynamic element that liberates the African short story from the straitjacket of formal realism and endows it with the flexibility for experimentation. Craig MacKenzie devotes to the subject an entire book titled *The Oral-Style South African Short Story in English* (1999). And it is in recognition of the positive role of the oral tradition that K. Limakatso

Kendall conceived the 1995 collection, *Basali!* as "a hybrid: a bridge, perhaps, between orature and literature."

Gender

The other positive development in the African short story is the notable improvement in the representation of gender, and the inclusion of women writers, at both the levels of production and critical consumption. Initially, except for few female writers as Ama Ata Aidoo, Grace **Ogot**, Bessie **Head** and Nadine **Gordimer**, anthologies of African stories featured almost exclusively male writers. Today, the picture has significantly changed; all across the continent, women are actively involved in the creation and critical assessment of the short story in the pages of anthologies, magazines, academic books, and journals. In *Under African Skies*, Charles Larson notes the dramatic improvement that has occurred not only in the number of female writers, but more significantly in the quality of their short stories. Larson concludes, optimistically, that "women's increasing presence may soon alter the literary scene in a way that they or we have yet to imagine" (1997: New York). In this regard, it is noteworthy that the joint Africa regional winners of the 1999 Commonwealth Short Story Competition were all women: Ifeoma Okoye of Nigeria for "Waiting for a Son," and Esther Zondo and Peggy Verbaan of South Africa for "The Waiting." One of the reasons for the strong showing of women's short stories is the conscious promotion of women writers, and *Basali!: Stories by and about Women in Lesotho* is a case in point. As the editor shows in the introduction, the anthology was literally willed into being by the determination to give women a literary voice where none previously existed.

Regional variations

Another welcome development in the study of the African short story is the recent trend in examining it from a regional perspective. This approach not only reflects the growth of the genre, but also promotes the task of adequate critical scrutiny. But for this regionalization of critical focus, it is doubtful if the intense historical survey and reassessment currently dominating the study of the South African short story would have occurred so soon and so pervasively. This trend, which is typified by Michael Chapman's *The Drum Decade* (1999) and Stephen Gray's introduction to *African Stories* (2000), is a necessary instrument of self-renewal for the South African short story.

The thematic preoccupation of the African short story, as well as the character of its artistic style and development, varies according to the region of origin. The genre has been most dominant in South Africa and an explanation for its patronage was provided by the short story pioneer Ezekiel **Mphahlele**. The South African writer, living a destabilized life under apartheid (see **apartheid and post-apartheid**) and called upon at the same time to artistically respond to the immediacy of the apartheid reality, could perhaps not patronize the time-consuming narrative of the novel. The short story, with its brevity of form, readily became the alternative choice. The explanation that has been advanced by Oliphant in "Fictions of Anticipation" (1996) for the recent upsurge of the genre in the post-apartheid era when writers are groping for new themes and new ways of expression is that its brevity and flexibility make it a dynamic genre for capturing the essence of a historic transition.

By comparison, the short story developed in other regions of Africa under conditions of relative leisure, a factor that made it less restricted in thematic focus and artistic practice. Thus, while the South African story was predominantly a one-theme genre – apartheid in its various manifestations – in other parts of the continent the subjects of the short story were more diverse, embracing both the local sociopolitical, economic, and cultural realities as well as the so-called eternal, universal themes of literature. The tone of the short story was also differently affected. A tragic mood, relieved only occasionally by the irony of tragic humor, permanently pervaded the South African short story. On the other hand, even though the other regions have their share of tragic humor associated with colonial racism and postcolonial failures of African political leadership, the short story frequently delights in the sort of pure humor for its own sake, as is represented, for instance, in Abioseh **Nicol**'s "The Truly Married Woman" (1965). Also the necessity to unambiguously address the apartheid situation sometimes precluded the South African writer from patronizing the stylistic resources of the oral tradition (see **oral literature and performance**), often clouded in the complexities of fantasy, symbol, and parable, as frequently as their counterparts elsewhere in the continent.

Apart from these distinctions, however, writers in all the regions in Africa are equally devoted to the serious and continued efforts, often involving daring experimentation, to make the short story aesthetically equally appealing as a verbal entertainment and as an entertaining expression of the African humanity in its many diversities.

Works cited

Larson, Charles (1997) *Under African Skies*, New York: Farrar, Strauss and Giroux.

Mzamane, Mbulelo (1986) *Hungry Flames*, Essex: Longman.

Further reading

Balogun, F. Odun (1991) *Tradition and Modernity in the African Short Story*, Newport, Connecticut: Greenwood.

F. ODUN BALOGUN

Sigogo, Ndabezinhle S.

b. 1932, Zimbabwe; d. 2006, Bulawayo, Zimbabwe

novelist and editor

The Zimbabwe writer Ndabezinhle Sigogo worked as a teacher, clerk, and book editor before joining the Literature Bureau as an editor of Ndebele literature (see **Shona and Ndebele literature**). As an editor, he has been influential in shaping the growth of Ndebele literature, but he has also been a prolific writer with over a dozen novels and many poems and plays. The major themes of his works, such as *USethi Ebukhweni Bakhe* (Sethi's Marital Experiences) (1962) and *Akulazulu Emhlabeni* (There is No Heaven on Earth) (1971), is the conflict between precolonial African values and the culture of colonialism (see **colonialism, neocolonialism, and postcolonialism**). In *Iziga Zalintombi* (The Antics of a Certain Girl) (1977), he satirizes the expediency of single women in the rearing of children. In *Ngenziwa Ngumumo Welizwe* (I Was Under the Influence of Prevailing Political Conditions) (1986) the author focuses on the impact of the war of liberation on individuals, while *Umhlaba Umangele* (The World Trembles) (1984) revisits the virulent Land Apportionment Act of 1931. *Lapho Intsha Isivukile* (When the Youth Finally Awakens) (1999) advocates the creation of cooperatives as the answer to the unemployment of young people in postcolonial Zimbabwe. In general, Sigogo's works echo the dominant themes in Zimbabwean literature in the translation from colonialism to independence, and the plot of his novels typifies the literary canons of the Literature Bureau.

EMMANUEL CHIWOME

Sithole, Ndabaningi

b. 1922, Chipinge, Zimbabwe; d. 2000, Philadelphia, USA

historian, politician, and novelist

The Zimbabwean historian, politician, and novelist Ndabaningi Sithole was educated in colonial Rhodesia and the US, and he has written extensively on the challenges of African nationalism in the context of colonialism and its aftermath (see **nationalism and post-nationalism**; **colonialism, neocolonialism, and postcolonialism**). In *African Nationalism* (1968), his seminal political treatise, Sithole traces his involvement with nationalist politics in southern Africa and reveals the internal contradictions of African resistance to white rule in Rhodesia. *Obed Mutezo: The Mudzimu Christian Nationalist* (1970), a biography of the Zimbabwe nationalist Obed Mutezo, emphasizes the tension that Africans confront as they try to reconcile their belief in Christianity with ancestral worship. Sithole's book suggests that Mutezo appropriated Christian and African cultural symbols in order to forge a modern nationalist identity in Rhodesia. The question of the meeting of two cultures, one African, the other European, is pursued further in Sithole's novel *The Polygamist* (1972). Other works by Sithole are *Busi* (1959), *Amandebele Mzilikazi* (1956), *In Defence of a Birth Right* (1975), and *Roots of a Revolution: Scenes from Zimbabwe's Struggle* (1977).

M. VAMBE

Smith, Pauline Janet Urmson

b. 1882, Oudtshoorn, South Africa; d. 1959, Dorset, England

novelist and short story writer

South African novelist and short story writer Pauline Smith spent her first thirteen years in the Little Karoo region of the Cape Colony, and after moving to England paid several return visits. She wrote about rural life in the Little Karoo, drawing on childhood experience and on a trip documented in *Secret Fire: The 1913–14 South African Journal of Pauline Smith* (1997). Her short story collection *The Little Karoo* (1924) confronts the social problems of "poor-white" Afrikaans-speaking communities before the white government began to protect them economically. She often focuses on degraded wives or single women, as in "The Sisters," where a daughter is "sold" in marriage so that her father may secure water rights for his farm. In her sole novel, *The Beadle* (1926), she adopts a more elegiac stance towards Afrikaner patriarchy, although she remains critical of Afrikaner Calvinism. The hesitant turn made in her stories to black and "colored" South Africans becomes little more than a haunting silence. Her prose has been celebrated for its economy, limpidity, and balance, and has also been appreciated for its incorporation of Afrikaans speech patterns, but she remains controversial: her essentially nostalgic vision is, it is sometimes

claimed, too little troubled by the destructive potential of Calvinism and racism in a settler community.

DOROTHY DRIVER

Socé, Ousmane (also known as Ousmane Socé Diop)

b. 1911, Rufisque, Senegal; d. 1973, Senegal

novelist

Ousmane Socé is perhaps the first Senegalese novelist, indeed one of the first Francophone African novelists, to emerge in the 1930s. His novel, *Karim, roman Sénégalais* (Karim, a Senegalese Novel) was first published in 1935 and was quickly followed by *Mirages de Paris* (Mirage of Paris) (1937). Socé then translated and adapted African legends and folk tales in *Contes et légendes africaines* (African Tales and Legends) (1949) and published a collection of poems under the title *Rythmes du khalam* (Rhythms of the Khalam) in 1962.

Ousmane Socé's legacy has been the introduction in African fiction of the themes of conflict of cultures and *métissage*, or cultural cross-fertilization. His works were driven by the conviction that if Africans were to survive the enormous changes introduced by colonialism (see **colonialism, neocolonialism, and postcolonialism**) they would have to change themselves by giving up the inoperable modes of the past and being willing to assimilate into the fabric of their cultures some of the usable elements of modernity (see **modernity and modernism**). It is this difficult balancing act that his oeuvre strives to convey in his two novels and in his folk tales by portraying heroic stories of great African rulers of the past, including the leaders of resistance to colonial occupation. His conviction was that tradition and modernity were not mutually exclusive in his vision of Africa.

KANDIOURA DRAME

Sofola, Zulu

b. 1938, Bendel state, Nigeria; d. 2001,
Nigeria

playwright

One of the most distinguished Nigeria playwrights,
Zulu Sofala was known for her interest in different
forms of dramatic performances ranging from
comedy to historical tragedy, all geared toward
the education of her audience and what she
considered to be their psychological well-being.
Educated primarily in the United States, where she
studied English literature and drama, Sofola's
doctorate in theater was from the famous University of Ibadan School of Drama. While Sofola
was sometimes overshadowed by the country's
major playwrights, notably Wole **Soyinka** and J.P.
Clark-Bekederemo, her work was known for its
range of interests and style and originality. In her
early comedies, which include *The Wizard of Law*
(1975) and *The Sweet Trap* (1977), she satirized the
mores and foibles of the Nigerian middle class,
while her tragedies were either concerned with the
struggle between individuals and malevolent social
forces (*Wedlock of the Gods*, 1972) or focused on the
lives of historical figures rising or failing to confront
their destinies (*King Emene*, 1975). In all her plays,
Sofola's works exhibited a keen sense of her
intimate understanding of Igbo and Yoruba oral
cultures, but she also used figures of speech drawn
from the everyday speech of Western Nigeria,
where she lived most of her life. Sofola's plays were
regularly produced on stage and television.

SIMON GIKANDI

Somali literature

Somali is spoken in the eastern Horn of Africa in
Somalia, the self-declared Republic of Somaliland,
southeastern Djibouti, eastern Ethiopia and northeastern Kenya, as well as by Somalis in the
diaspora (see **diaspora and pan-Africanism**).
It comprises a number of dialects, one group of
which has become a standard used in broadcast
and other media. Prior to the introduction of an
official writing system in 1972, Somali literature
was, with some very few exceptions, oral literature
(see **oral literature and performance**), but
since that time written prose literature has developed and writing is used more in the composition
and dissemination of poetry.

Central to Somali culture and society, virtually
all Somali poetry displays two important stylistic
characteristics: quantitative meter and alliteration.
Each genre of poetry has its own meter based on
the number and pattern of long and short vowels in
a line. The alliteration works such that each line (or
half-line, depending on the genre) includes a word
which begins with the same consonant sound or
with a vowel sound (all vowels alliterate with each
other), that same sound being sustained throughout
the whole poem. There is a distinction between
two major types of poetry: *maanso* (pl. *maansooyin*)
and *hees* (pl. *heeso*) (see below for the special category
of modern *hees* which differs significantly from the
general *hees* type discussed here).

Hees genres are predominantly work songs and
dance songs and are considered of lesser prestige
than *maanso*. Having said that, *heeso* play an
important role in the fabric of society, particularly
in the countryside, providing a rhythmic background to the work itself and relief from the
monotony of some tasks. As well as this, work
songs may also be used by individuals to make
their voice heard in a way otherwise unavailable to
them. For example, a woman who may not be able
to address her husband directly on a particular
matter might compose a work song in allusive
language, which she could perform, in the course
of her daily life, within earshot of her husband. In
this way she can express her feelings, which will
then be heard and understood by her husband
indirectly, bypassing the direct communication not
necessarily available to her. Dance songs are
another type of *hees*, which tend to be performed
by young people at times when they come together
socially. *Heeso* can become well known over a large
area and people may embellish and modify them
in their own performance; the original composer
of a *hees*, however, is generally not known nor
acknowledged when it is performed. All of the
different *hees* genres are distinguished not just by
the context in which they are performed, but also
by their metrical structure and the tune to which
they are recited.

In contrast to *hees* poetry, the composer of any *maanso*-type poem must always be acknowledged, and furthermore whenever it is performed the poem must be recited verbatim. In other words, there is the notion of a "definitive" text of any *maanso* poem. Changes are inevitably found when different recitations and/or transliterations are compared, but in those which have been discussed by scholars the changes are generally slight. There is no formal way in which poems are preserved in the society, but good poems are remembered and continue to be recited, and because of this we know poems which were first composed some time in the middle of the nineteenth century and a few probably earlier.

One of the earliest known poets is Raage Ugaas Warfaa, whose poetry from, it is assumed, the middle of the nineteenth century is still remembered today and is highly praised; some of it has been translated into English in *An Anthology of Somali Poetry* by B.W. Andrzejewski with Sheila Andrzejewski (1993). Coming up to the first two decades of the twentieth century, we see these are rich in poetry which is remembered, due in part to the poetry which was an important part of the Dervish campaign of Sayyid Maxamed Cabdille Xasan and which has been remembered and subsequently transcribed by Jaamac Cumar Ciise in *Diiwaanka Gabayadii Sayid Maxamad Cabdulle Xasan* (Anthology of the Poems of Sayid Maxamad Cabdulle Xasan) (1974). Sayyid Maxamed was the spiritual and military leader of the Dervishes and was also one of the greatest Somali poets to have lived, a talent which he put to great effect in his campaign. Such use in this campaign reflects one of its roles in society: *maanso* poetry was and still is used in the context of inter-clan discussion and politics and in legal matters; a message presented in the form of a good poem is a message powerfully presented. If a lineage or an individual has such a poem directed at them, then a response is appropriate, of which there are many examples. In some cases the response elicits a further poem from the original poet which may prompt a further response, and at times such a series of poems draws in other poets and the whole becomes a chain of poems from different poets, called a *silsilad* (from the Arabic word for

"chain"), in which the poems most often all alliterate in the same letter.

During the 1940s there were some important developments in Somali poetry which had a profound effect on its development to the present day. These began with a poet called Cabdi Deeqsi "Sinimo," a truck driver who broke down one day away from any help and composed a short poem bemoaning his fate, which he sang to a tune. He sang this later to others, and this was the beginning of the *belwo* (pl. *belwooyin*) genre of poetry. The stylistic base of this was genres of dance *hees*, but the *belwo* quickly became established as an urban genre and soon men and women were performing *belwooyin* together, a fact frowned upon by the religious leaders and elders. It was at this time also that the use of musical instruments was beginning through the efforts of Cabdullaahi Qarshe, who began to play the lute in a style which he intended to be, and which was, peculiarly Somali. As the *belwo* developed, poets began to link them together into strings, and eventually the longer version became a genre in its own right, known as the *heello* (pl. *heellooyin*). This was all happening in the context of urbanization, the political developments in the Horn of Africa following World War II, and the increasing importance of radio, all of which led to the *heello* becoming a powerful political force in its commentary on what was occurring.

At this time also, theater was becoming increasingly popular. Based on poetic texts, including *heellooyin*, the plays became a popular form of entertainment and a powerful form of social commentary, which reached audiences through traveling theater troupes such as the Walaalo Hargeysa (The Hargeysa Brothers), founded in 1955, who were important commentators in the struggle for independence. Plays and songs from them were also performed on the radio.

The *heello* developed into what is now generally known as *hees* (that is, modern *hees*). Despite the name, these poems are of the *maanso* type, in that the poet is always known and the text of the poem must be performed verbatim. This modern *hees* is performed to a musical instrument accompaniment, and most poetry is appreciated in this mode today, very often through the medium of the cassette tape. Some of the greatest modern poets who have composed poetry of this type include Maxamed Ibraahim Warsame "Hadraawi" and Cabdi Aadan "Cabdi Qays," both of whom composed poems which during the 1970s were powerful allusive criticisms of the former regime in Somalia and for which both were jailed.

Although some people had written in Somali prior to 1972, it was in that year that an official orthography was introduced. Some important collections of oral literature were soon published and written prose literature also began to be published (there had been very little prior to 1972), the first published novel being *Ignorance is the Enemy of Love* (*Aqoondarro waa u Nacab Jacayl*) by **Faarax Maxamed Jaamac "Cawl"**. Following these initial publications younger writers began to publish, one of the major figures being Maxamed Daahir Afrax, whose novels include *Maana Faay* (1981). These writers dealt with themes of concern to the growing urban society, such as relations and marriage in the towns and the growing differences between the ways of the town and the countryside. Despite the great amount of destruction and violence since the late 1980s in Somalia, written literature has continued, with short stories and novels being published. In 1994 Xuseen Sheekh Biixi published *Waddadii Walbahaarka* (The Road of Grief), a powerful tale of love set against the terror of Mogadishu in 1991 which leads to the displacement of the two main protagonists, who only eventually meet again and marry in Canada after going through awful experiences before reaching there.

Further reading

Ahmed, Ali J. (1996) *Daybreak is Near* ..., Lawrenceville, New Jersey: Red Sea Press.

Andrzejewski, B.W. and Andrzejewski, Sheila (1993) *An Anthology of Somali Poetry*, Bloomington: Indiana University Press.

Jaamac Cumar Ciise (1974) *Diiwaanka Gabayadii Sayid Maxamad Cabdulle Xasan*, Mogadishu: Wasaaradda Hiddaha iyo Tacliinta Sare.

Johnson, J.W. (1996) *"Heelloy" Modern Poetry and Songs of the Somali*, London: Haan.

MARTIN ORWIN

Sondhi, Kuldip

b. 1924, Lahore, Pakistan

playwright

Kenyan playwright Kuldip Sondhi, regarded by his peers as a "Renaissance man," was born in Lahore in present-day Pakistan to a Hindu family. Although his family settled in Kenya in 1932, Sondhi went to the prestigious Bishop Cotton School and Punjab University in India. Subsequently he took postgraduate aeronautical engineering courses at the Massachusetts Institute of Technology (MIT) and at Brooklyn Polytechnic, where he finished a five-year course in three and a half years. Upon the completion of his studies, he was invited by independent India's first leader, Jawaharlal Nehru, to head the development of the Gnat fighter engine in Bangalore. Afterwards he returned to Kenya, where he developed a career as an hotelier and a prolific playwright. His most successful play, *Undesignated*, which was first published in David Cook and Miles Lee's anthology *Short East African Plays in English* (1968), depicts the adversarial relationship between an African and an Asian engineer for a top government post in a post-independence African country. In an urbane, liberal style, Sondhi interrogates the residual attitudes that attend social and political transitions in independent African countries trying to reinvent themselves.

Further reading

Sondhi, Kuldip (1973) *Undesignated and Other Plays*, New Delhi: Orient Longman.

DAN ODHIAMBO OJWANG

Sony Labou Tansi (also Labou Tansi, Sony)

b. 1947, Kimwanza, Belgian Congo (now Democratic Republic of the Congo); d. 1995, Foufoudou, Congo-Brazzaville

novelist, poet, and playwright

Congolese novelist, poet, and playwright Sony

Labou Tansi wrote in French, mainly on political themes related to and against the background of the repressive and dictatorial regimes of Central Africa. He was born as Marcel Ntsoni (Sony Labou Tansi was a pseudonym) at Kimwanza in the then Belgian Congo, later known successively as Congo Leopoldville (until the 1960s), Congo-Kinshasa (until the 1970s), and Zaire (1972–97) before being named République Démocratique du Congo in the late 1990s. Sony Labou Tansi's father was a Congolese from Congo-Kinshasa (the Belgian Congo) while his mother was a Congolese from the neighboring Congo-Brazzaville (formerly the French Congo). Sony Labou Tansi learned French under strict and harsh methods at Brazzaville in the French Congo where he had moved at the age of 12. After his education at the École Normale Supérieure d'Afrique Centrale (the Central African High School), he was appointed to teach French and English in Congo-Brazzaville. He then worked in Brazzaville as a government official in several ministries. He was elected député (member of parliament) in 1992, shortly before his untimely death at the age of 48 at Foufoudou, Congo-Brazzaville.

The setting for Sony Labou Tansi's novels and plays is generally within the context of violence as experienced in postcolonial African countries with repressive, dictatorial, and frequently military states. Some critics, however, have found echoes and analogies between Sony Labou Tansi's writing and many Latin-American modern novels, especially those that deal with the problem of dictatorship, and use the style of magic realism (see **realism and magical realism**). Sony Labou Tansi's first novel, *La Vie et demie* (Life and a Half) (1979), is set in an imagined African country, the Katamalanasie, which has 228 imposed national holidays and where reigns a dictator, the self-appointed "Providential Guide" Marc-François Matéla-Péné. The Guide devours human flesh, in particular that of his political opponents, sometimes in the form of a raw dish that he calls "the kampechianata." In the novel, the Guide has had the chief opposition leader, named Martial, killed and cut up into pieces, and yet the spirit of the deceased opponent does not actually die. It keeps speaking and harassing the dictator. The novel portrays characters as *loques* (rags), the surroundings as *mochetés* or ugliness, which correspond to the notion of "putridity," which J.A. Underwood uses in her English translation of *The Antipeople* (*L'Anté-peuple*), Sony Labou Tansi's famous 1983 novel.

Sony Labou Tansi's first novel, *La Vie et demie*, had indeed set the tone for the fantastic and carnivalesque characteristics of his later works. The writer resorts to the usage of the fantastic, gigantic, and horrible chaos and non-realistic dimensions to conjure up the morbid, cast out the putrid, exorcise said chaos and injustice in African political life, and finally, to attempt awakening the dormant peoples that are subjected to the fantasies of dictatorship. The concerns and forms are evident in his other novels, including *L'État honteux* (The Shameful State) (1981), *The AntiPeople* (*L'Anté-Peuple*) (1983), *The Seven Solitudes of Lorsa Lopez* (*Les Sept Solitudes de Lorsa Lopez*) (1985), *Les Yeux du volcan*, (The Volcano's Eyes) (1988), and *Le Commencement des douleurs* (The Beginning of Sufferings) (1995). All these novels take place in settings dominated by political violence, devious sexuality, human cowardice, ugliness, corruption, silence, and death. In the circumstances, his oeuvre endeavors to lend a voice to those who live in situations of enforced silence, to resist death, and to stand up to dictatorship and repression.

Another important aspect of Sony Labou Tansi's writing career was his passion for the theater. In 1979 he founded the Rocado Zulu Theatre Company in Brazzaville, and for most of the 1980s the group staged plays in Africa and Europe. Like the novels, these plays, the most famous being *Parenthesis of Blood* (*La Paranthèse de sang*) (1978) and *Antoine m'a vendu son destin* (Antoine Sold Me His Fate) (1986), were about themes of violence, repression, and political resistance. Fantastic themes in the plays echo the political representations found in the novels: *Parenthesis of Blood*, for example, shows a group of sergeants and soldiers sent to kill a rebel leader named Libertashio, who is already dead. They interrogate, torture, and massacre Libertashio's family members and associates, and then, after the gratuitous killing, are informed that the dictator is no longer interested in the deceased rebel. In *Antoine m'a vendu son destin*, a dictator orders two of his faithful army generals to fictively overthrow him in order for him to see how plots are played out so that he can outsmart any future conspiracy.

One of the remarkable contributions that Sony Labou Tansi made to African literature was the way he worked on, and within, the French language in order to Africanize – or, according to his terminology, "tropicalize" – it. Sony Labou Tansi's aesthetics of tropicality allows the construction of languages as well as of literary forms that draw on the African tale (*fable africaine*) with its sparkling or exploding "tropical" rhythms. The main traits of such compositions, evident in his plays, are the unrestrained use of fantasy, the deployment of a carnivalesque open stage in which the audience is exhorted to participate in the verbal struggle against the grotesque dictatorship, and the imposition of silence. In relation to the question of language (see **language question**), the issues raised in Sony Labou Tansi's texts go beyond the specific use of languages as such. They concern the act of speaking itself and the possibilities involved in speech acts. His novels are full of characters entangled in the politics of language. In *Les Yeux du volcan*, for example, we have a mayor who is forced to cry not only in his three vernaculars, but in all the languages of the country. Thus, words acquire the utmost importance in Sony Labou Tansi's oeuvre; they are the elements that torment dictators. In *La Vie et demie*, opponents to the Guide's monstrous dictatorship, where "power is in the blood," strive to overcome ominous signs and acts by resorting to the means of words written in an indelible black ink, called Martial's ink ("l'encre de Martial," 1979: Paris). The same Guide wants to slaughter all the words in the country, and thus orders the burning of all books and films. Words are even more powerful when uttered by female characters such as Chaïdana in *La Vie et demie*, Yavelde in *The Antipeople*, and Lydie Argandov in *Les Yeux du volcan*.

In the foreword to *The Seven Solitudes of Lorsa Lopez*, Sony Labou Tansi warned his readers that his fiction was more "screamed" or "shouted" (*écriture criée*) than simply written. He died too soon to fulfil this dream of a "screamed" form of writing in Africa (although he had already noted, in a poetic preface to *The AntiPeople*, that "to die is to dream a different dream"), but his legacy of "tropicalized" writing constitutes a landmark in

the history of African literature and its modernity (see **modernity and modernism**). His talents were recognized by the awarding of several literary prizes in Africa as well as in Europe.

Further reading

Clark, Phyllis and Ricard, Alain (eds) (2000) *Research in African Literatures*, special issue on Sony Labou Tansi, 31, 3: 37–146.

Davesa, Jean-Michel (1996) *Sony Labou Tansi. Écrivain de la honte et des rives magiques du Kongo*, Paris: L'Harmattan.

Mwisha Rwanika, Drocella and Nyunda ya Rubango (eds) (1999) *Francophonie littéraire africaine en procès. Le destin unique de Sony Labou Tansi* (African Francophone Literature in Process. The Unique Destiny of Sony Labou Tansi), Ivry-sur-Seine, France and Yaoundé: Silex/ Nouvelles du Sud.

Sony Labou Tansi (1979) *La Vie et demie* (Life and a Half), Paris: Seuil.

ANTHÈRE NZABATSINDA

South African literature in African languages

Introduction

The writing of African literature(s) in the African languages, rather than in the imperial and hegemonic English, was a historical project undertaken by the New African movement in the process of constructing modernity (see **modernity and modernism**) in South Africa. Although Xhosa intellectuals of the 1880s such as Elijah Makiwane (1850–1928), Walter B. Rubusana (1858–1936), Pambani Jeremiah Mzimba (1850–1911), John Tengo **Jabavu** (1859–1921), William Wellington Gqoba (1840–88), and Isaac Wauchope (1845–1917) were part of the movement's historical horizon, it was in approximately 1904 in the essay "The Regeneration of Africa" that Pixley ka Isaka Seme clearly delineated and articulated the conceptual vision of the project. In the essay Seme writes the following:

The giant is awakening! ... Ladies and gentle-men, the day of great exploring expeditions in Africa is over! ... Yes, the regeneration of Africa belongs to this new and powerful period! By this term, regeneration, I wish to be under-stood to mean the entrance into a new life, embracing the diverse phases of a higher, complex existence. The basic factor, which assures their regeneration, resides in the awa-kened race-consciousness.

With the unfurling of this banner of modernity over the African continent four years after the beginning of a new century, Seme (1880–1951) effected its political realization by being the principal founder of the African National Congress (ANC) in 1912. Two other New African intellec-tuals in this critical year of 1904 similarly also hoisted above the continent their particular articulations of modernity in their equally avant-garde essays: Solomon T. **Plaatje**'s "Negro Ques-tion" and John Langalibalele **Dube**'s "Are Negroes Better Off in Africa? Conditions and Opportunities of Negroes in America and Africa Compared." Plaatje (1878–1932) was the first secretary-general of the ANC, and Dube (1871–1946) was the first president-general of the ANC. In actual fact, the necessity of modernity had already been given cognizance in the 1860s by Tiyo Soga (1829–71), the first modern African intellectual in South Africa.

At the center of the New African movement were the metamorphoses and phenomenology of the historical consciousness of the New African. That the ideology of New Africanism necessitated the creation and making of the New African movement, which in turn gave expression to the philosophy of "New" African nationalism, is indicated by two journalistic pieces written by two important members of the New African intelligentsia. In "Leaders of African National Congress Must Reconcile Differences," Pixley ka Isaka Seme notes:

The African National Congress is a new move-ment which is being implanted in the heart and blood of the Abantu people. All nations have national congresses of their own which help mould together the spirit and the good will of those nations ... We want to be able clearly to express our free will as a nation like all other peoples of the world today.

Two years later, in "European Students and Race Problems," appearing in a different New African newspaper of which he was editor, R.V. Selope Thema (1886–1955) observed:

There is a movement among Africans not only for the betterment of their economic conditions but for political freedom as well. If this move-ment is barred from its natural road of advance and deprived of its liberty of thought, expression and action, it will become a menace to the security of the white race, and a brake in the wheels of the country's progress.

Although political and intellectual adversaries at the time of the writing of these statements, both Seme and Thema were in unison in theorizing that a New African movement had come into being forging a dialectical unity of agency and structure, thought and life, theory and practice in the making of New African modernity.

It was within the historical parameters defined by the New African movement during the historical period of modernity that African literature written in the African languages of South Africa realized its efflorescence. The brilliant journalism of Thema had an incalculable inspiration on some of the third or fourth generation of the major exponents of this literature: the Xhosa novelist, poet, and translator Guybon Bundlwana Sinxo (1902–62); the Zulu historical novelist R.R.R. **Dhlomo** (1901–71); the Zulu novelist, intellectual provoca-teur, and political maverick Jordan K. **Ngubane** (1917–85); and the southern Sotho short story writer Peter D. Segale (1901–37), who died relatively young. Thema published the extremely rare Zulu journalism of H.I.E. **Dhlomo** (1903–56), who viewed the language of Shakespeare as the "authentic" language of modernity. Thema's acolytes, who were apprenticed under his editor-ship on the newspaper *The Bantu World*, went on to exemplary journalistic careers as well as to writing major literary works in their "vernacular" lan-guages. H.I.E. Dhlomo was the exception in this, as he was in many other things. In his intransigent belief in modernity against tradition, Selope Thema imparted a peculiar sense of historicity concerning the relation between the past, the present, and the future, to this particular intellectual generation. It was Thema also who made *The Bantu World* an intellectual forum for the last flowering period of the great Xhosa poet and biographer S.E.K. **Mqhayi** (1875–1945), arguably the greatest exponent of African literature in the African languages in South Africa.

The search for a literary history

It was a sense of historicity that enabled these New African intellectuals as well as their contemporaries to write some of the earliest and most durable literary histories of African literature(s) in the African languages, though paradoxically all of them were written in English. To many of these intellectuals, Mqhayi was a transitional figure between tradition and modernity. They considered him to be the demarcating point in South African literary history. But before S.E.K. Mqhayi there was Thomas **Mofolo** (1876–1948), and after him there was Benedict Wallet Vilakazi (1906–47).

The following literary histories, in the form of pamphlets or essays, were written within the purview of this dialectical relation between tradition and modernity: D.D.T. Jabavu's (1880–1959) *Bantu Literature: Classification and Reviews* (1921) and *The Influence of English Literature on Bantu literature* (1943); Benedict Wallet Vilakazi's "Some Aspects of Zulu Literature" (1942); and C.L.S. Nyembezi's (1919–) *A Review of Zulu Literature* (1961). Besides these preliminary mappings out of the topography of African literature(s) in the African languages, there were other more detailed investigations of the complex relationships between literary generic forms by other members of the New African movement, two of which were written within the academic context: Benedict Vilakazi's doctoral dissertation "The Oral and Written Literature in Nguni" (1946), A.C. Jordan's (1906–68) "Towards an African Literature: The Emergence of Literary Form in Xhosa" (1973), which originally appeared as a series of essays in the 1950s in the journal *Africa South*, and Mazisi Kunene's (1930–) master's thesis, "An Analytical Survey of Zulu Poetry: Both Traditional and Modern" (n.d., probably 1959). The voluminous columns and various reflections on cultural and literary matters by H.I.E. Dhlomo,

which appeared in the newspaper *Ilanga lase Natal* from 1943 to 1954, were part of this New African literary and cultural historiography.

But the foundational text of these New African literary histories was Isaac Bud-M'Belle's (1870–1947) *Kafir Scholar's Companion* (1903), which emphasized the central importance of newspapers in making possible the emergence African literature(s) in the African languages.

The role of Christian missions

It was the Christian missionaries who gave benediction to the making of modern and written African literature(s) in the African languages in South Africa, but not necessarily with the results they intended and anticipated. The missionaries revolutionized African cultural history by introducing the written word in opposition to, and in a Manichean struggle against, the oral word (see **oral literature and performance**). Through the written word the missionaries were able to control the ideological persuasion of many of the first few generations of New African intellectuals and writers. Principally, the missionaries were able to achieve this hegemonic control by initiating the schools in which the New African intelligentsia was educated, by controlling the newspapers in which the preliminary forms of written African literature(s) in the African languages initially appeared, and by founding the publishing houses in which these literatures were assembled in a textual or book form. The missionaries altered African cultural history in a fundamental way by launching the Morija Press in Maseru, the Marianhill Press in Durban, and the Lovedale Press in Alice.

From the moment many of the Xhosa intellectuals of the 1880s mentioned above first emerged, to the rise of the Zulu intellectuals of the 1940s, such as E.H.A. Made, Ngubane, R.R.R. Dhlomo, H.I.E. Dhlomo, and others, the critical issue in literary and cultural circles was whether the written literary word would serve only Christianity or whether it would also be in the forefront of the struggle to invent African nationalism (see **nationalism and post-nationalism**). The great Sotho novel *Chaka* by Thomas Mofolo was an indication of the monumentality of this struggle. Mofolo unequivocally condemned premodern and precolonial African history as essentially barbaric and backward, and represented Christian modernity as the essence of enlightenment and progress. Without renouncing their Christian beliefs, the founding of "independent" New African newspapers, such as John Tengo Jabavu's *Imvo Zabantsundu* (African Opinion) (1884), Plaatje's *Tsala ea Batho* (The People's Friend, originally known as *Tsala ea Becoana*, The Friend of the Bechuana, when launched in 1910), and John Dube's *Ilanga lase Natal* (The Natal Sun) (1903), were part of the process of the secularization of the New African intellectual and literary imagination.

The matter of secularization was related to the contentious issue of origins: what was the founding moment of written African literature(s) in the African languages? Was the founding moment of these literatures signaled by missionaries when they translated the Bible into the many African languages, or was it indicated by Tiyo Soga, when he translated John Bunyan's *Pilgrim's Progress* (1678) into the Xhosa text *uHambo lomhambi* (1866)? Alternatively, was the direction of this literature to be found in Tiyo Soga's decision to reduce Xhosa oral forms of literary representation into written form in Christian newspapers? What was the relationship between oral forms of representation and their written "counterparts": was it one of continuity or rupture and discontinuity? Was there a symmetry between a form of literary representation and the nature of historical periodization? In other words, were oral forms of literary representation synonymous with tradition and the written forms with modernity?

A historic conference held under the auspices of the Christian Council of South Africa, known as "A Conference of African Authors," was convened on 15 October 1936 in the city of Florida, Transvaal, not necessarily to engage the aforementioned questions, but rather to examine the status and crisis of African literature(s) in the African languages. Reporting on the conference in *The Bantu World*, J.D. Rheinallt Jones (1884–1953) named the following participants: D.D.T. Jabavu, Rueben T. Caluza (1895–1969), Vilakazi, Z.D. Mangoaela (1883–1950), Thema, D.M. Ramoshoana, and S.S. Mafoyane. This was a stellar list of African intellectuals (including a composer) who wrote in the African languages. Only H.I.E.

Dhlomo participated as a representative of African literature in the English language. The invitees who could not make it to the conference were equally stellar: J.J.R. Jolobe, H.M. Ndawo, S.E.K. Mqhayi, Mofolo, H. Maimane, and R.R.R. Dhlomo. Among the Europeans who participated in the conference were the missionaries R.H.W. Shepherd, Margaret Wrong, and A. Sandilands. Also in attendance were the editors of the scholarly journal *Bantu Studies*, C.M. Doke and J.D. Rheinallt Jones.

It is important to note that this unprecedented conference, which in all probability has never been subsequently surpassed in the brilliance of the minds gathered together, was sponsored by missionaries. Several issues were at the center of the gathering: the obstacles to publication of the manuscripts in the African languages; the establishment of an endowment to assist in the publication of such manuscripts; the role of newspapers and magazines in facilitating such a literature; the instituting of literary criticism that would set the standards of excellence for this literature; and the contentious question of orthography which invariably resulted in bitter quarrels between the New African intelligentsia and the Christian missionaries. The missionary-turned-academic C.M. Doke proposed to the conference participants the establishing of an Academy of African Arts, a proposal that was to be discovered anew in the 1940s by Jordan Ngubane and Anton Lembede in the newspaper *Inkundla ya Bantu* (Bantu Forum), the intellectual forum of the African nationalism of the ANC Youth League.

This innovative idea of the academy was in all probability related to the extraordinary linguistic work Doke had undertaken in the study of African languages in southern Africa, which he anticipated could inspire African literature(s) in the African languages into creating a renaissance or renascences. His establishing of an imprint in 1935 called the Bantu Treasury Series, whose first volume was Benedict Vilakazi's book of poetry *Inkondlo kaZulu* (Zulu Poetry), the first of thirteen volumes that were to appear into the 1940s, was part of the hoped-for cultural revolution. The assembling of the great Zulu–English dictionary (1948) by Doke and Benedict Vilakazi, as well as the Sotho–English dictionary by Doke and S.M. Mofokeng (1923–57), was fundamental in cultivating the intellectual and cultural space of the New African movement.

Literature, language, and national culture

However, it would seem that the objectives and achievements of the conference were overshadowed by the controversial question that was posed by H.I.E. Dhlomo to the participants: would it not lead to the creation of "tribal" cultures rather than a national culture if African writers persisted in writing African literature in the "tribal" languages? It was this question that led to the bitter intellectual argument between two great friends, H.I.E. Dhlomo and Vilakazi, a quarrel that two years after the conference broke out on the pages of *Bantu Studies* (subsequently changed to *African Studies*) and *South African Outlook* in 1938 and in 1939. The ostensible reason for the argument concerned the nature of Zulu poetic form and its capacity to absorb and incorporate European rhymes and stanzas.

But the real issue in contention was the role of African languages, not only in creating a national literature but in facilitating the construction of a singular national culture: was it possible to constitute a unified national culture through the use of multiple languages? It is the complexity of the question posed and the vehemence of the response rendered that has made the Dhlomo/Vilakazi debate such a legendary event in South African intellectual history. H.I.E. Dhlomo's position was enigmatic, for while he had absolutely demurred in writing creative work in the Zulu language, he wrote many journalistic pieces in *Ilanga lase Natal* extolling the greatness of the Zulu language. On the other side of the debate, Vilakazi never felt the necessity to extol the virtues of Zulu, the language in which he wrote his three novels *Noma Nini* (No Matter How Long) (1935), *Udingiswayo ka Jobe* (Dingiswayo, Son of Jobe) (1939), *Nje Nempela* (Just So) (1944), and his two books of poetry, *Inkondlo kaZulu* (Zulu Poetry) (1935), and *Amal' Ezulu* (Zulu Horizons) (1945). The question posed by H.I.E. Dhlomo would continue to persist in debates on the identity of African literature and its relation to national culture.

The establishment of a literary tradition

All literary histories of the major literature(s) in the African languages in South Africa are generally in agreement about certain fundamental issues pertaining to them. First, they concur in establishing that the foundational texts of Xhosa literature were M'Belle's *Kafir Scholar's Companion* (1903) and Walter B. Rubusana's anthology *Zemk' Inkomo Magwalandini* (The Cattle are Departing, You Cowards) (1906); those of Sotho literature were Azariel M. Sekese's *Mekhoa le maele a Basotho* (Basotho Customs and Proverbs) (1907) and Thomas Mofolo's *Moeti oa Bochabela* (The Traveler to the World of Light, also translated as *The Traveler to the East*) (1907); and that of Zulu literature was Magema M. Fuze's *Abantu Abamnyama: Lapa Bavela Ngakona* (The Black People: And Whence They Came) (1922). Second, they are in synchrony in designating the canon of these literatures: in regard to Xhosa literature, in poetry it is S.E.K. Mqhayi, in the novel it is A.C. Jordan, in the short story form it is Guybon Bundlawa Sinxo, and in the essay form it is J.J.R. Jolobe (also a major poet). In the field of Zulu literature, the major figures are Wallet Vilakazi in poetry, R.R.R. Dhlomo and C.L.S. Nyembezi in the novel, Violet Dube in the short story, E.H.A. Made in the essay form, and Nimrod Ndebele in drama. In Sotho literature the leading figures are considered to be Z. Mangoaela and Ephraim Lesoro in poetry; Mofolo is considered to be the major novelist in this tradition, but there also other important novelists including A.M. Sekese and E. **Segoete**. Third, these literary histories imply that the historical conjuncture of tradition/modernity was a central preoccupation of African literature in the African languages. The last of the pioneering literary histories of African language literature(s) was Nyembezi's *A Review of Zulu Literature*, which appeared in 1961, an appearance that coincided with the end of the New African movement marked by the Sharpeville massacre of 1960.

The Sophiatown Renaissance was perhaps the cultural expression of the movement in the period just before Sharpeville. Since the early 1960s, many extraordinary things have happened to African language literature(s) in South Africa. Arguably the most important has been the emergence of the poetic voice of Mazisi **Kunene**, an achievement that can stand comparison with any African poetic achievement in the twentieth century. Also impressive has been the scholarly work devoted to African oral literature(s) in South Africa, from Daniel Kunene's *Heroic Poetry of the Basotho* (1971) to Jeff Opland's *Xhosa Poets and Poetry* (1998). In between these two publications, there have been the three remarkable essays on the three major streams of this literature by Harold Scheub that appeared in *Literatures in African Languages: Theoretical Issues and Sample Surveys* (1985). But the most exhilarating event of the last two decades of the twentieth century in regard to this literature has been the rediscovery of two major women writers: Lydia **Umkasetemba**, the Zulu prose writer who wrote in the 1850s and in the 1860s, and Nontsizi **Mgqwetto**, a Xhosa poet who published approximately ninety poems in the newspaper *Umteteli wa Bantu* between 1920 and 1929, and who seems to have been a younger contemporary of S.E.K. Mqhayi.

Their appearance has completely altered our understanding of the cultural and literary history of the New African movement: it is with Lydia Umkasetemba that modern Zulu literature begins, not with Magema M. Fuze, as had been presumed for decades by major literary scholars including H.I.E. Dhlomo, among others; it is Nontsizi Mgqwetto who brings literary modernism through poetry to South Africa, not Vilakazi or H.I.E. Dhlomo or S.E.K. Mqhayi, as we had all supposed.

Further reading

Dube, John L. (1904) "Are Negroes Better Off in Africa? Conditions and Opportunities of Negroes in America and Africa Compared," *The Missionary Review of the World*, August 1904.

Jabavu, D.D.T. (1921) *Bantu Literature: Classification and Reviews*, Lovedale: Lovedale Missionary Press.

——1943) *The Influence of English Literature On Bantu Literature*, Lovedale: Lovedale Missionary Press.

Jones, J.D. Rheinallt (1936) "African Writers to be Encouraged: African Authors' Conference," *The Bantu World*, 14 November: 21.

Jordan, A.C. (1973) *Towards an African Literature*, Berkeley: University of California Press.

Kunene, Mazisi (1959) "An Analytical Survey of Zulu Poetry," MA thesis, Durban: University of Natal.

Malcolm, D.McK. (1949) "Zulu Literature," *Africa* 19, 1: 33–9.

Nyembezi, C.L.S. (1961) *A Review of Zulu Literature*, Pietermaritzburg: University of Natal Press.

Plaatje, Solomon T. (1904) "Negro Question," *Koranta ea Becoana*, 7 September.

Seme, Pixley ka Isaka (1905–6) "The Regeneration of Africa," *Royal African Society*, 4: 75–81.

——(1933) "Leaders of African National Congress Must Reconcile Differences," *Umteteli wa Bantu*, 16 December.

Thema, R.V. Selope (1935) "European Students and Race Problems," *The Bantu World*, 10 August.

Vilakazi, B.W. (1942) "Some Aspects of Zulu Literature," *African Studies* 1, 4: 270–4.

——(1946) "The Oral and Written Literature in Nguni," DLitt dissertation, Johannesburg: University of the Witwatersrand.

NTONGELA MASILELA

South African literature in English

English-language literature in South Africa is one of the oldest on the continent. It shares many features with other literatures produced in former British colonies in the region, but it has historically developed against an unusual political, cultural, and economic background. While English-language literature in the rest of the continent was initiated by Africans who turned to writing in order to oppose colonialism, South African literature was initially associated with white writers of English descent trying to establish a literary culture in the region, one that would match the literature that was being produced in Britain in the nineteenth century. The production of an English literature by white settlers of British origin was important because the cultural geography of South Africa in the period was being formed in a context dominated by a three-way political competition between Africans, the British, and Afrikaners (settlers of Dutch descent in the region). While the struggle was primarily over questions of land, resources, and political control, it had an important cultural component: each of these groups conceived literature as a most important instrument in the struggle for South Africa.

In the circumstances, each of these groups sought to produce a literature in its own language – or, in the case of the Africans, languages – and to make literary culture itself the basis of a new cultural configuration. Africans who wrote in African languages turned to literature to mediate their place in the colonial order of things; Afrikaners wrote in literature to assert their distinctiveness; similarly, English settlers in the region turned to literary production to retain elements of their Englishness and later to adapt the English language to local conditions. Given the association between language, literature, and group identity, it was inevitable that the history of South African literature would be intimately tied to the political conflicts in the country in the nineteenth- and twentieth-century. In key moments of political conflict or crisis, such as the Anglo-Boer war (1899–1902), the establishment of the apartheid state in 1948 (see **apartheid and post-apartheid**), and the Soweto uprising of 1976, questions of language and literary production have been at the center of debate, dispute, and conflict.

Another reason why South African literature in English has had a different trajectory is that because of a comparatively large white settler population, the politics of race have been central to the development of a literary culture. The narrative of race, from colonial policies of segregation in the nineteenth century to the establishment of the apartheid state in the late 1940s (a policy that made the separation of races the basis of political, economic, and cultural policy), has been unavoidable in South African literature in English. The effect of racialism on the development of literature has been apparent in two areas: First, because of the segregation of the institutions of literary production such as schools and universities, English literature tended to develop along racial lines: even when they were concerned with specifically South African themes, white writers have traditionally been closely associated with literary developments in Europe. Olive **Schreiner**'s novels, for example, reflect her interest in late nineteenth-century ideas on determinism, and J.M. **Coetzee**'s novels echo late

twentieth-century theories of postmodernism. Secondly, a large number of white South African writers were educated in Britain or spent long periods of time in the country, and some of them (for example, William Plomer) became important figures in the English literary establishment. In contrast, black writers were forced by the politics of racialism to be more engaged with more specific and local themes and issues. As a result, the nature of black fiction in English was more often determined by the large questions of the day – discrimination, displacement from ancestral lands, and economic hardship – than by literary trends in Europe.

With the aggravation of the racial situation in the 1940s and the establishment of the apartheid state, writers in English tended to share a common project: the use of literature to protest against apartheid, using a diversity of literary strategies ranging from Peter **Abrahams**' stark realism in *Mine Boy* (1946) to Alan **Paton**'s lyrical and elegiac prose in *Cry the Beloved Country* (1948). The close association between the forms of writing and the resistance against apartheid was to change the character of South African literature in English. Even in the post-apartheid moment in the 1990s, most literary debates in the country tended to be haunted by its painful racial past and the desire to account for and transcend it.

Colonial fiction and the idea of South Africa

Except perhaps for the literature produced by African slaves in the diaspora, South African literature in English is one of the oldest on the continent, and this fact can be explained primarily by the existence of a large white-settler population in the country. Most of the literature produced in the country in the early and middle nineteenth century consisted primarily of narratives produced by European missionaries, ethnographies of the people of the region, and Christian magazines for use in mission stations. There was little fiction produced in the country until the end of the nineteenth century. In the 1880s, however, as the British empire consolidated its authority in the world, a colonialist literature, made up mostly of adventure stories and novels set in the imperial frontier, emerged and appealed to a large cross-section of readers in the English-speaking world. In the genre of the adventure and romantic story, the region functioned as background for narratives built on some of the most cherished notions and fantasies of empire. Indeed, the most famous novels in this tradition, most notably Rider Haggard's *King Solomon's Mines* and *She*, used the adventure motif to bring together some of the themes that were dear to the Victorian imperial imagination, namely the imperial frontier as the place in which British masculinity was asserted, the African landscape as the site of desire, and Africans as objects of fear and revulsion.

Underlying the adventure story that tantalized Victorian readers, however, was a political subtext in which existing theories on issues such as race and sexual violence were dramatized and popularized. While it is possible to argue that the adventure story was only interested in South Africa as the background against which Victorian issues were represented, it had a significant effect on the literature of the country, for two closely related reasons. First, it was through the adventure tale that South Africa entered the international imagination; images of the country and its people were determined by the stories read in novels by writers like Haggard. Second, given the predominance of the adventure story in the national and international imagination, South African writers at the turn of the century wrote against the pressures of this genre, producing works that either satirized its explicit racialism (as in Douglas Blackburn's *A Burger's Quixote*, 1903) or endorsed existing racial theories (for example, Sarah Gertrude **Millin**, *God's Stepchildren*, 1924).

But perhaps the most significant development in South African literature in this period was the emergence of a kind of fiction, represented in the novels of Olive **Schreiner** (*Story of an African Farm*, 1883, and *Trooper Peter Halket*, 1897), which used realism (see **realism and magical realism**) or even literary naturalism to subvert the adventure romance. Schreiner occupies an important place in the literary history of South African literature in English for another reason: she was a writer influenced by the dominant European ideas of the time (social Darwinism, emerging feminism, and sexuality) who nevertheless sought to make the local landscape an integral part of her overall narrative scheme. It is even possible to argue that

what Schreiner did in her novels is bring European ideas about human nature and the landscape into a direct confrontation with the South African landscape. Certainly, it was through her intimate engagement with this landscape, especially the karoo, that she was able to promulgate a form of realism that was not simply the direct opposite of the colonial romance in its form, but that foregrounded the determinative nature of the land, especially its capacity to thwart the will and desire of people, to question the racial and imperial politics driving the imperial romance. From the beginning of the twentieth century until the establishment of the apartheid state, white writers in English produced works whose most explicit concern was the negotiation of colonial Englishness (and metropolitan ideas about literature) and the demands of the local, especially the politics of race. This concern is particularly pronounced in the poetry of Roy **Campbell**, which sought to domesticate South African themes to the dominant European poetic genres.

Literature and racialism

If the landscape seemed to be intertwined with the forms of South African fiction in the early parts of the twentieth century, this was largely because the whole identity of South Africa, and its conflicts, tended to revolve around the ownership of the land. In 1913, the colonial government passed the Native Lands Act. The first immediate impact was the displacement of thousands of blacks from their ancestral land: almost overnight, families and communities found themselves living vicariously in their native land transformed into a new proletariat, a pool of cheap labor for the mines and farms of the dominant capitalist class. The second impact of the act was the galvanization of political protest among the black population, giving new life to the then nascent African Native National Congress, the forerunner of the African National Congress, under the leadership of John **Dube** and Sol **Plaatje**. It is important to underscore the fact that the leaders of the new protest movements were also writers, and that their prose was animated by the urgent desire to account for the loss of the land and the nationalism it had generated. But the third consequence of the Native

Lands Act and the protest against it was the emergence of texts by black writers responding directly or indirectly to this crisis both in African languages and in English.

The most famous of the texts triggered by the Native Lands Act was Plaatje's *Native Life in South Africa* (1916), a book that provided an eyewitness account of the lives of the displaced Africans, a sharp analysis of the political and economic consequences of their displacement, and an allegorical account of black lives in the new racial order. In 1930 Plaatje published *Mhudi*, considered to be the first novel by a black South African in English. *Mhudi* was conceived as a historical romance, a historical account of the life of a woman against the background of the turbulent wars that followed the death of Shaka, the emperor of the Zulu. But beneath the romance and the evocation of a historic past, Plaatje's novel was very much an intervention in the debates surrounding the place of blacks in colonial South Africa. The novel's conception as both a historical narrative and a romance bore witness to this fact. For what motivated Plaatje's poetical evocation of the past through the trope of love (a process that was also evident in the epics that were to be produced by African language writers during the same period) was the need to insist on the black Africans' presence in the landscape from which the Native Lands Act had tried to evict them. This is the presence Plaatje asserted in the very first sentence of his novel: "Two centuries ago the Bechuana tribes inhabited the extensive areas between Central Transvaal and the Kalahari Desert" (1930: Lovedale). In order to understand the impact of what might appear to be the statement of a self-evident assertion in the opening lines of a historical romance, one must remember that at the center of the Native Lands Act was the audacious claim, systematically enforced throughout the rest of the twentieth century, that blacks were entitled to only 10 percent of the land in the Union of South Africa.

In the late 1930s and 1940s, some of the most important consequences of the Native Lands Act, and subsequent legislation intended to consolidate the union between English-speaking whites and Afrikaners, were becoming apparent. These included the massive migration of landless and poor blacks into the gold-mining towns of the Rand and the diamond fields of Kimberley. This experience found its way into literature through what has come to be known as the "Jim comes to Jo'burg" motif: the narrative of a naïve country boy who goes to Johannesburg, the gold capital of the world, expecting a better life, but instead becomes caught up in a vicious cycle of violence and crime. Two novels are exemplary in this genre: Peter Abrahams' *Mine Boy*, first published in 1946, and Paton's *Cry the Beloved Country*, published two years later. Both novels feature a protagonist who goes to Johannesburg in search of the good life and ends up lost in the city, consumed by a life of crime and its consequences. But what makes these novels paradigmatic texts of how literature was shaping up in the years leading to apartheid was the competing visions that informed them and the modes of representation associated with them. Abrahams had turned to literature to affirm his identity in the racial order; literature had opened a new world of social opportunities foreclosed to him by racist culture, including the radical politics of pan-Africanism (see **diaspora and pan-Africanism**). In *Mine Boy*, he turned to social realism to represent the disintegration of the African self in the new urban milieu and to contrast the alienation of modern life with the romance of a village life. Abrahams' critique of the city was undertaken in the name of radical politics. Paton, too, turned to the language of romance and pastoral to portray the devastation of African lives under the racial order, but his commitments were to a liberal sensibility that might survive the divisive politics of racism. Abrahams sought to come to terms with race consciousness and to deploy it toward a pan-African sensibility; Paton sought to transcend race in the name of Christian virtue. Both sought to find the center of their visions in the romance of the country – of the premodern, as it were.

Apartheid and the forms of literature

The hope that South African literature might be able to transcend a polarized racial situation diminished when the Nationalist Party came to power in 1948 and established the apartheid state, in which racial differences were to be policed stringently through legislative and policing methods. Within two decades of coming to power, the Nationalist government had passed laws that were to constitute the bedrock of the apartheid state and which were to have long-term implications for cultural production in the country. These included: the Group Areas Act, which restricted where people lived in terms of their race; the Immorality Act, which forbade sexual relations and marriage across racial lines; the Population Registration Act, which mandated the classification of people into racial categories; the Suppression of Communism Act, directed at all forms of radical opposition to the state; and, later, the Bantu Education Act, which mandated the teaching of texts that reinforced the government's stereotyped notions of the races. It can be said that South African literature after 1948 was determined, one way or the other, by the doctrine of apartheid as enforced by the state through these Acts. Indeed, the history of this literature is primarily a story of how different writers or groups of writers reacted to apartheid, its doctrines and discourses.

The effect of apartheid on the writing was most obviously manifested in how racial separation affected the institutions of literary production, such as universities. Since different races were by and large confined to separate universities, the possibility that literature might be the basis of a common culture was negated. In addition, specific policies aimed at controlling education or Communism (such as the banning of authors and writers) were to have a direct consequence on literary production. After the passing of the Bantu Education Act in 1959, writers such as Es'kia (Ezekiel) **Mphahlele**, Dennis **Brutus**, Alex **la Guma**, and Dan **Jacobson** were forced into exile or were imprisoned. The situation was aggravated by the almost wholesale banning of writers in the 1960s.

Ironically, these adverse circumstances did sometimes have a direct bearing on the nature of the literature. Certain genres became important precisely because of the conditions in which literature was produced. In the 1950s and early 1960s, for example, autobiographies (see **autobiography**) such as Abrahams's *Tell Freedom*, Mphalele's *Down Second Avenue*, and Bloke **Modisane**'s *Blame Me on History* were powerful testimonies to apartheid's deracination of the self and the will to power against it. The short stories of the *Drum* writers, including Lewis **Nkosi**, Can **Themba**, and Mphahlele testified to the lives of ordinary people in the streets of the reordered cities, while banned poets like Brutus sought ways of camouflaging their verse in works such as *Letters to Martha* (1968) to circumvent their silencing by the state. But if the nature of literature was determined by the imperative to react to the situation created by official doctrines of racial segregation, the response was more complicated than the label of protest literature that has rather casually been applied to the literature of the 1960s and 1970s. Draconian laws made the choices stark for black writers – one either wrote against apartheid or died – the only question was where you wrote and where you died. Sometimes, as in the case of Themba and **Nortje**, one wrote against apartheid and then died.

For white liberal writers, however, apartheid had triggered a series of uncomfortable questions. How could the liberal values espoused by many of them be reconciled to their genuine fear of black power? How could the registers of Englishness that were so crucial to white English writing be reconciled to a contested African landscape? Different writers responded to these questions in different ways. Some, like Guy **Butler**, chose to detach themselves from politics and try and espouse a hermetic aesthetic. Others, like R.N. Curry and Jacobson, preferred exile, from which they could look back on the land left behind and produce a fiction of testimony and longing.

But perhaps the most influential group of white writers were those who, like Nadine **Gordimer** and Douglas **Livingstone**, decided to turn the dilemma of being white and liberal in a divided society into the basis of writing itself. Gordimer's early novels are structured by what has come to be known as the liberal dilemma: they reflect the conflicting demands of subjective reflection and interiorization, often represented through interior monologue, and of public commitment to social justice. In fact, the exemplary work of the liberal dilemma is perhaps Gordimer's *The Late Bourgeois World* (1966), in which the techniques of modernism (see **modernity and modernism**), especially its rhetoric of failure, are deployed to expose the failure of the liberal project that the novel, nevertheless, espouses. The characters in these novels seek to establish fundamental relationships across the racial divide in the belief that personal relationships can provide salvation from the social engineering of the state; but these novels are ultimately about the failure of the intersubjective and private world recovered in language as a bulwark against the overwhelming power of the public sphere.

If white liberals writing in the 1960s turned inward to escape the threat of the public sphere, black and colored writing was driven by an overwhelming sense that since the apartheid state sought to control the private sphere itself, it was precisely through invocations of community that an overwhelming repressive and alienating environment could be transcended. The failure to find a community often accounts for the haunting language of the works of la Guma who, in stories such as a "A Walk in the Night," combines social realism with existentialism to depict the lives of apartheid's walking dead. The overwhelming sense of death that dominates la Guma's stories is not merely the expression of a certain aesthetic, one in which death yields images, allegories, and symbols. In many cases, death itself has become a central trope in both life and literature for, as we have already noted, by the end of the 1960s the repressive measures taken by the state against writers and intellectuals had sent many of them to prison, to death, or to exile. The nightmarish world of subjects produced by apartheid is the subject of Bessie **Head**'s groundbreaking work *A Question of Power* (1973). Inevitably, the verse of the most important non-white poets of the 1960s is either an attempt to measure language to account for incarceration of silencing (Brutus) or a post-mortem on a lost world (Nortje).

If the story of South African literature in English in the 1960s was a tense stand-off between the state and the writers it sought to silence, the 1970s witnessed a renewed period of political struggle with important implications for the nature and form of literature. During this period, the state sought to evict the black subject from the South African polity entirely through the establishment of Bantustans (independent homelands). In reaction, black intellectuals galvanized themselves around an ideology called black consciousness, heralded by Steve **Biko** and the South African Students'

Organization (SASO), and later the Black People's Convention (BPC). In order to understand the significance of this movement in the reshaping of South African literature in the 1970s, it is important to recall that up until this period, the struggle against apartheid had been spearheaded by white liberals on one hand, and on the other, African nationalists, including members of the banned African National Congress, who though holding different ideological positions were committed to the ideal of a non-racial society. The morality of political action, most of it reflected in the literature of the 1950s and 1960s, was that the ideology of racial division would be overcome and a new social body would emerge; the task of literature was to will this new body into being. But younger black activists were becoming impatient with this ideal and black consciousness was posited as an alternative to non-racialism; black identity and pride were promoted as the key to self-awareness and the basis of political struggle against apartheid. Art was considered crucial to the promotion of black consciousness, and numerous cultural organizations were formed as a result. It was out of the ideology of black consciousness and these forums that a group of new black poets, including Oswald **Mtshali**, Mongane Wally **Serote**, and Sipho **Sepamla**, emerged in the 1970s. Poetry became the most dominant form of writing, capturing the angry young voices of this new generation. Another major phenomenon of the 1970s was the Soweto uprising of 1976, in which schoolchildren rose in revolt against the introduction of Afrikaans as the language of instruction in African schools. The immediate consequence of the Soweto uprising was the continued development of a militant tone in poetry, the forcing into exile of a new generation of black South Africans, including Serote, Mbulelo **Mzamane**, and Mandla **Langa**. Miriam **Tlali**'s semi-autobiographical novel, *Muriel at Metropolitan* (1975), was one of the few examples to use fiction to represent everyday life in the apartheid city.

The state of emergency and the interregnum

Facing continued resistance at home and international isolation, including a cultural boycott, the apartheid state seemed determined to uphold on to its guiding doctrines by any means necessary. Continued state attempts to control writers and artists included the strengthening of censorship laws through the South African Publications Act of 1974, the imprisonment of writers such as the poet Breyten **Breytenbach** (in 1975), and the killing of cultural activists, including Biko (in 1977). These measures did not deter resistance against apartheid. In 1978, Prime Minister, later President, Botha launched what he called a total onslaught on the opponents of apartheid, but none of his efforts seemed to contain the tide and in 1985 he declared a state of emergency in the country, giving the government absolute powers to contain its perceived enemies at home and abroad. As has often been the case in the cultural history of South Africa, increased repression invigorated the literary tradition. Indeed, it was in the 1980s, writing in and against the state of emergency, that the most important and distinctive literature emerged in South Africa.

It could be said that the state of emergency liberated white writers from the liberal dilemma and the mimicry of colonial Englishness and black and colored ones from the prisonhouse of protest. Whether one accepts this assessment or not, it is fair to say that the form of South African literature in the 1980s was a reaction to the state of emergency. The key point is the different forms this literature took. Some writers fell back on the narrative of personal testimony to account for the long history of apartheid and its devastating effects on both communities and the psyche (for example Ellen **Kuzwayo**'s autobiography, *Call Me Woman*, 1985) or represented subjective experiences of everyday life under apartheid. For liberal white writers like Gordimer, the state of emergency forced a questioning of previous attempts to balance the needs of individual freedom and the ethical needs of the time, and in her novels published in the late 1970s and early 1980s (*Burgher's Daughter*, 1979, and *July's People*, 1981) she sought to deploy a new realism in which the interiorized life of her characters was determined by the political and radical choices they were forced to make, often against their own inner desires.

The same tendency – the attempt to understand how the inner life of the individual was trans-formed by an ethical imperative – was dramatized vividly in André **Brink**'s novels, especially *A Dry White Season*, the story of an Afrikaans schoolteacher who is forced into politics against his judgement when one of his friends dies mysteriously in prison. An alternative approach to the question of the ethical in a highly politicized environment was proposed by the works of J.M. Coetzee, one of the major novelists to emerge from South Africa during this period. Instead of engaging directly with history, which he considered to be a threat to the aesthetic ideal, Coetzee turned to allegory as the mode best suited to what he considered to be the inner life of literature. Coetzee's major works from this period (*Waiting for the Barbarians*, 1980, and *Life and Times of Michael K*, 1983) were certainly about South Africa and the state of emergency, but their engagement with such issues was indirect and highly allegorized, concerned with experiences that had been abstracted from the ordinary. Most importantly, while other writers of the period sought to use the South African experience as the source of their narrative energies, Coetzee, influenced by postmodern debates, wrote metafictions: works that referred to other works within the Western tradition. This focus on the self-referential nature of literature, Coetzee suggested, was perhaps one way in which art could retain its energies against the historical imperative.

Although not apparent at first, a similar realignment of the inner world of the self and the outer world of an inescapable politics was at work in black literature, too, but from a different direction. In an essay entitled "The Rediscovery of the Ordinary," published in the late 1980s, Njabulo **Ndebele** argued that the literature of protest in South African had been built around stereotypes and slogans that repressed the essential humanity of black life, a life whose essence was to be found in acts of ordinary or everyday life. Ndebele's goal, apparent in his collection of stories published as *Fools and Other Stories* (1983), was that a more productive and imaginative use of literature against apartheid was to privilege the ordinary itself.

It would, however, be a mistake to see South African literature in the period leading to the end of apartheid as contained within the genre of the novel and the debates it was provoking. In fact, one could argue that such debates were not uniquely South African, that the history of the novel has been a struggle between its pedagogical imperative and the performative, a struggle that becomes much more visible in moments of political crisis. It is hence interesting to see how questions about art and its political function were handled in poetry and drama. Developments in drama were apparent in popular black musicals by Gibson **Kente** and Percy Mtwa, some of which became international hits as the campaign against apartheid entered its final phase. At the same time, Zakes **Mda** was experimenting with theater for development across the border in Lesotho.

But perhaps the most important dramatist in South Africa to engage international attention during this period was Athol **Fugard**. Fugard became involved in the theater in the Eastern Cape in the 1950s, focusing mostly on regional issues with plays such as *No Good Friday* (1958) and *Nongogo* (1959), works in which the focus was everyday life under apartheid. Although Fugard's plays rarely elevated apartheid to the high political or allegorical level it had reached in the works of the novelists discussed above, his concern with the local and ordinary made them key touchstones in South Africa's social history. In *Sizwe Bansi is Dead* (1974), a collaboration with the actors John Kani and Winston Ntshona, Fugard brought a satirical edge to bear on serious issues such as mandatory pass laws for blacks and the façade of the Bantustans, while the semi-autobiographical *Master Harold ... and the Boys* (1993) was internationally recognized as a subtle and introspective commentary on the effects of apartheid on personal relationships.

In the field of poetry, in the works of Jeremy **Cronin** and Wally Serote on one hand and Douglas Livingstone and Lionel Abrahams on the other hand, we see two contrasting examples of the changing relationship between verse and politics in the interregnum. In the late 1980s and 1990s, Cronin and Serote, both political and cultural activists, in the ANC and the South African Communist Party respectively, wrote poems that sought to turn their own experiences of imprisonment (Cronin) and exile (Serote) into an allegory of the apartheid state while exploring the larger possibilities of a post-apartheid democratic culture. Abrahams and Livingston, on the other hand, saw poetry itself as a solitary mode that would protect them from the crisis of politics. These two tendencies were to dominate the search for a post-apartheid aesthetic in South Africa at the beginning of the twenty-first century.

Works cited

Plaatje, Solomon T. (1930) *Mhudi*, Lovedale: Lovedale Press.

Further reading

Attridge, Derek and Jolly, Rosemary (1998) *Writing South Africa: Literature, Apartheid, and Democracy, 1970–1995*, Cambridge and New York: Cambridge University Press.
Chapman, Michael (1996) *South African Literatures*, London and New York: Longman.

SIMON GIKANDI

Sow Fall, Aminata

b. 1941, Saint-Louis, Senegal

novelist

Aminata Sow Fall is arguably the most important woman writer in Senegal today. This is true not only because she has produced more works of fiction than most women writing in Senegal today, but also because she is a cultural and social activist as well as a writer. Her work as director and founder of the International Center for Studies, Research, and Reactivation of Literature, the Arts and Culture (CIRLAC) and of Khoudia Editions are extensions of her literary career. Both serve as important forums for presenting her social views, her critique of society, the furtherance of her vision for a better society.

Sow Fall has long criticized the aridity and vanity of the urban bourgeoisie and petite bourgeoisie in Senegal, but she emerged on the literary scene with the publication of a novel, *Le Revenant* (The Specter) (1976), in which the protagonist, Bakar, discovers that he is dearer to his family dead than alive when he fakes his own death and attends the funeral. It was, however, her second novel, *The Beggars' Strike* (*La Grève des battus*) (1979) that gained Sow Fall accolades and awards. In this work, Sow Fall was again concerned with the vanity of the bourgeoisie and its social consequences. In the novel, a civil servant receives the task of clearing the city of all beggars who bother foreign guests; when he does so with success, he is rewarded with a promotion to the rank of minister. Paradoxically, according to his system of religious beliefs, he must offer charity to beggars or risk losing his promotion.

L'Appel des arènes (The Call of the Arena), which appeared in 1982, affirms Sow Fall's pride in her African heritage. An assimilated couple find to their consternation that their son adores traditional wrestling and is being initiated into the world they sought to leave behind. This pride in an African heritage expresses itself clearly in *Douceurs du bercail* (The Comforts of Home) (1998) where the protagonist, a woman who resembles the author, is strip-searched and deported when she attempts to attend a conference in Paris. She renounces all plans to travel to the West, seeking happiness in her own garden, as Voltaire suggested. The novel is an explicit criticism of many young Africans' dream of finding wealth in the West.

Although Sow Fall takes great pride in her Senegalese heritage, she does not believe in taking a non-critical attitude toward her culture. In *Le Jujubier du patriarche* (The Patriarch's Jujube Tree) (1993), she intertwines modern narrative and traditional epic to create a synthesis that represents the social fabric that weaves slave and noble families together, in spite of the fact that the nobles reject their slaves' claims to a shared heritage. In the 1987 political novel *L'Ex-père de la nation* (The Ex-Father of the Nation), she offers the diary of an imaginary dictator very similar to **Senghor**. Idealistic as a young man, he shares his regrets that his dreams had turned to dictatorship.

Further reading

D'Alméïda, Irène. (1994) *Francophone African Women*

Writers: Destroying the Emptiness of Silence, Gainesville: University Presses of Florida.

Gadjigo, Samba (1989) "Social Vision in Aminata Sow Fall's Literary Work," *World Literature Today*: 411–15.

Stringer, Susan (1996) *The Senegalese Novel by Women: Through Their Own Eyes*, New York: Peter Lang.

LISA McNEE

Sowande, Bode

b. 1948, Nigeria

playwright

Although he has not garnered much critical attention compared to his more famous compatriots Wole **Soyinka**, J.P. **Clark-Bekederemo**, and Femi **Osofisan**, Bode Sowande is considered to be one of the important literary figures to have emerged in Nigeria since the 1970s, especially in the field of drama. Like those of Osofisan, Sowande's plays are intended to break with the theatrical tradition associated with the first generation of modern Nigerian playwrights, most notably Soyinka and Clark-Bekederemo, and to use drama as an agent of direct social intervention. In his Babylon trilogy, comprised of *The Night Before* (1972) *A Farewell to Babylon* (1978), and *Flamingo* (1982), Sowande's drama revolves around young students and intellectuals trying to master their destiny in an environment dominated by tyranny and fear. In *Tornadoes Full of Dreams* (1990), he takes on an unusual theme in African drama, the tragedy of Atlantic slavery and the French revolution as it affected the lives of slaves in the Caribbean. His novel, *Our Man the President* (1981), probes the crisis of leadership in Nigeria after the civil war, focusing on the conflict between youthful ideals and the draconian practices of a militarized political order. As a playwright and novelist, Sowande seems to be caught between his desires to break new aesthetic ground while at the same time being accessible to his readers. The result has been works caught between their need to be popular and at the same time to tackle serious themes.

Further reading

Dunton, Chris (1970) *Man Make Talk True: Nigerian Drama in English since 1970*, London: Hans Zell.

SIMON GIKANDI

Soyinka, Wole

b. 1934, Abeokuta, southwestern Nigeria

playwright, poet, novelist, and Nobel Prize-winner

In 1986, Wole Soyinka became the first black writer to win the Nobel Prize for Literature. He has published major works in practically every genre of contemporary writing: drama, poetry, fiction, **autobiography**, and the critical essay. Soyinka has an elaborately developed perspective on **art**, history, and the place of the artist in society. In his works, he seeks to synthesize his dual heritage as an African and as someone who has not only been exposed to European civilization, but also appreciates many aspects of that culture and its values. He seeks to make the worldview of his native Yoruba culture relevant to his work as an artist who uses Western forms. His success in doing this is testified to by the fact that the citation that accompanied the award of the Nobel Prize to him remarked the creativity with which his work explores traditional Yoruba culture to fashion a "universal drama of existence."

Soyinka was born in Abeokuta, southwestern Nigeria, to parents who were practicing Christians and closely associated with Christian missions and institutions of education (see **Christianity and Christian missions**; **education and schools**). His father was a schoolteacher, and as his autobiography *Aké* (1981) shows, his upbringing in that environment has had a crucial impact on his career as a writer. He attended Government College and later, University College, both in Ibadan. His training at these institutions made him part of an elite class within his generation, and prepared him to play an important role in the Nigerian nation-state that was then in the process of attaining its independence from Britain. Soyinka subsequently attended the University of Leeds, where he acquired a BA honors degree in English.

After his degree, he stayed on in the United Kingdom, working as playreader at the Royal Court Theatre. He had started writing in his days at University College in Nigeria, but it was during his time in the United Kingdom that he began writing dramatic pieces that revealed his dedication to being a serious writer. He returned to Nigeria in 1960, the year that Nigeria became independent from Britain. He formed a theater group that performed many of his plays. This period can be said to mark the first major phase in Soyinka's artistic career. Although they probably date from his days in the United Kingdom, *The Swamp Dwellers* (1964) and *The Lion and the Jewel* (1963), a comedy, can be identified with this period. Other plays like *A Dance of the Forests* (1963), a poetic drama written for Nigeria's independence celebrations, *Camwood on the Leaves* (1973), a radio play, and *The Trials of Brother Jero* (1964), a satire, can also be identified with this period.

From about the mid 1960s, the freshly independent Nigeria became mired in a series of political upheavals and violence. Soyinka's readiness to voice or act on his convictions made him a prominent participant in the political controversies and developments of the period. In October 1965, he was arrested and charged with holding up a radio station at gunpoint and replacing the tape of a speech by the premier of Western Nigeria, Chief Samuel Ladoke Akintola, with a different one accusing the premier of election malpractice. Soyinka was acquitted of the charges, but the very fact that he was thus charged speaks to his actively visible role in the affairs of his country. As a consequence of the controversies of the period, a brutal civil war broke out in 1967 in the country. The war (1967–70) pitted the federal government against the southeastern region which had seceded and declared itself as the independent nation of Biafra. Soyinka was arrested and incarcerated by the federal military government, allegedly for activities sympathetic to the Biafran secessionists. He spent a substantial part of his imprisonment in solitary confinement. Many writers from the West condemned the incarceration and called for his release, but it was not until 1969 that he was released. He addresses this experience in his prison memoir, entitled *The Man Died* (1972). As one might expect, Soyinka uses the opportunity of this prison memoir not simply to criticize his jailers, but also to reflect on the role of the artist in society.

The role Soyinka ascribes to vocational writers in the midst of political unrest accounts for the form and substance of his major works from this period. To this phase belong *Kongi's Harvest* (1967), a critique of authoritarian rule; *The Road* (1965), an exploration of a hubristic character's search for the meaning of death amid the corruption and cultural complexities of urban Nigeria; "Idanre" (1967), a long poem in which Soyinka first presents a sustained literary treatment of Ogun, the Yoruba god of iron, as metaphor for societal collapse and regeneration; and *A Shuttle in the Crypt* (1972), a collection of poetry that deals with his imprisonment. He also wrote *Jero's Metamorphosis* (1973) as a sequel to *The Trials of Brother Jero*. In this sequel, the main character, a fraudulent, self-proclaimed "prophet" named Brother Jero, adopts symbolic features like the military uniform and the marching band for his church. A thorough scoundrel and opportunist, Brother Jero transforms the image of his church so as to blend in with the prevailing militarized dispensation of the day. In this way, Soyinka makes fun of the hypocrisy and shallowness of the military rulers of the period, just as *The Trials of Brother Jero* had satirized the opportunistic politicians of the previous era in Nigerian politics. His brooding play *Madmen and Specialists* (1970) and his novels *The Interpreters* (1965), and *Season of Anomy* (1973) should also be interpreted in light of the moral demands and intellectual pressures that Soyinka must have felt as he contemplated his society's degeneration into sectarian violence, crass materialism, and collective disorientation.

In 1973 Soyinka accepted a position as Fellow at Churchill College in Cambridge University. During his stint at Cambridge, he wrote *Death and the King's Horseman* (1975), seen by many as his greatest achievement in the genre of poetic drama. He also wrote *The Bacchae of Euripides* (1973), a commissioned adaptation and rewriting of Euripides' play. A series of lectures on drama that he delivered at Cambridge became the book *Myth, Literature and the African World* (1976). This book includes as appendix an essay that Soyinka had written earlier, entitled "The Fourth Stage: Through the Mysteries of Ogun to the Origins of Yoruba Tragedy." The book encapsulates Soyinka's central ideas and constitutes a watershed in the writer's career. In it, he surveys modern African literature by setting out the diverse philosophical sensibilities of a number of prominent African writers. He also links what was going in African literature to artistic trends and productions in the African diaspora. And characteristically, he sought to account for these trends within an overarching framework that is based on traditional Yoruba mythology and ritual.

From the late 1970s on, Soyinka has continued to address black Africa's problems as the last vestiges of colonialism were being contested and defeated, even as independent African countries floundered or came under the mismanagement of politicians and tyrants. For instance, Soyinka turned to avenues other than the printed word by releasing a record album, *Unlimited Liability Company* (1983), and a film, *Blues for a Prodigal* (1984), to criticize the depredations of the civilian government that ruled Nigeria between 1979 and 1983. In the long poem *Ogun Abibiman* (1976), and the lead poems of the collection *Mandela's Earth and Other Poems* (1989), he addresses the apartheid situation in South Africa, then still under the racist regime of the Afrikaner Nationalist Party. The plays *Opera Wonyosi* (1984), *Requiem for a Futurologist* (1985), *From Zia with Love* (1992), and *The Beatification of Area Boy* (1995) offer biting critiques of the social and political contradictions of Nigeria under both civilian and military rule. *A Play of Giants* (1984) satirizes the murderous lust for power of African despots in general.

Myth, Literature and the African World constitutes Soyinka's most sustained elaboration of his theory of art, culture, and the individual in society. Consequently, a full apprehension of Soyinka's work to date requires proper understanding of the vision set out in this book. For Soyinka, the lessons of history and individual or collective struggle are often encoded in mythology. He set out to demonstrate that African peoples have rich cultural traditions and systems of knowledge that should be seen as alternatives to Euro-American traditions. As in his use of Western literary forms to explore the particularity of Africa's problems, Soyinka's theory shows his debt to two cultures – traditional Yoruba and Western European. From Yoruba mythology, he chooses the god of iron and metallurgy, Ogun, as the metaphor for artistic and technological creativity. By this choice, he makes Ogun a symbol of the kind of spirit that black Africa, like all other cultures in the modern world, requires to ensure spiritual health and social prosperity.

Soyinka identifies a commonality between Ogun and such classical archetypes as Orpheus and Prometheus, who stand for unwavering resolve and the capacity to act in the service of one's vision. Soyinka believes that the inevitable fate of the visionary archetype is punishment and suffering. But the suffering is not altogether bad, because it often accompanies a socially redemptive act of will. In this way, Ogun symbolizes visionary creativity and leadership. In the Yoruba mythological narrative that Soyinka adapts, all the spheres of existence, all of humanity's potentiality, were once concentrated in the figure of the deity Obatala, or Orisha-nla (arch divinity). According to Soyinka, Obatala embodies social order as well as what humankind is capable of within that conventional order. Obatala reigns over an inherited, precon-stituted cosmic/social situation and human destiny. To serve him in this dispensation is a slave, another mythic figure named Atunda or Atooda. This slave initiated a transformative rupture by rolling a huge boulder over Obatala, shattering the god into a thousand and one fragments. These fragments stand for the one thousand and one gods in the Yoruba pantheon, as well as the sphere of life with which each god is associated. Because of Atunda's action, the gods were separated from human beings and yearned to be reunited with us, even as we desire to get closer to them.

Ogun's sphere – his specialty, so to speak – is iron and metallurgy. His attribute as worker of iron makes him the one who among the gods undertook the original journey to reunite the realm of the gods with the world of mortals. He forged the first weapon, cleared the path separating gods from humankind, and led the way as the gods journeyed to be reunited with humans. For Soyinka, Ogun's journey symbolically promises a reunion of "self" with "essence," what we are in reality with what we can be. Ogun is able to achieve this restoration in Yoruba mythology, thereby offering symbolic en-actment of its possibility in the secular world, because he embodies a fusion of artistic and technological creativity. Thus, the artist and the scientist become for Soyinka members of society who should combine their creative gifts to ensure social progress.

The years 1995 through 1998 witnessed the consolidation of a particularly repressive military regime in Nigerian politics. Once again, Soyinka denounced the authoritarian and divisive tendencies of the nation's rulers, tendencies that brought the nation to the brink of another civil war. He was at the forefront of an international movement that agitated for a return to a democratically elected government. He published *The Open Sore of a Continent* (1996), in which he retraced the country's history and analyzed the roots of its political crisis. Soyinka's creative and political writings clearly put him in the company of the more explicitly politicized writers in African letters. It is perhaps to be expected that his work has sometimes generated intense critical debate. But there is no doubt as to the value of his work for various kinds of critical methodology or sociopolitical vision. In prose, poetry, or drama, Soyinka's contribution to African literature has been intensive and permanent. Alongside any other purposes it may serve, his writing holds our attention because of the combination, within it, of philoso-phical depth and stylistic grace.

Further reading

Gibbs, James (ed.) (1980) *Critical Perspectives on Wole Soyinka*, Washington, DC: Three Continents Press.

Jones, Eldred D. (1973) *The Writing of Wole Soyinka*, London: Heinemann.

Katrak, Ketu H. (1986) *Wole Soyinka and Modern Tragedy*, New York: Greenwood Press.

Wright, Derek (1993) *Wole Soyinka Revisited*, New York: Twayne Publishers.

OLAKUNLE GEORGE

Stein, (Roman) Sylvester

b. 1920, South Africa

journalist and novelist

After serving in the navy, the South African writer

Sylvester Stein became a reporter and then political editor on the *Rand Daily Mail*, one of the country's leading newspapers. In 1955 he took over editorship of *Drum* magazine, one of the most popular magazines in South Africa, where he spent three years working with and training a staff of black writers and photographers. These journalists, who included Can **Themba**, Nat **Nakasa**, Arthur **Maimane**, Bloke **Modisane** and Es'kia **Mphahlele**, faced police and political persecution yet worked tirelessly to expose the wrongs of the white regime. In the 1950s, when censorship under the apartheid state (see **apartheid and post-apartheid**) became impossible to dodge, Stein left for exile in London, carrying with him the manuscript of *Second-Class Taxi* (1957) – a carica-ture of South Africa in the 1950s as seen by a vagrant involved in resistance politics. It became a bestseller in Britain although within a week it was banned in South Africa. In London, Stein worked on Fleet Street, writing novels in his spare time. In 1999 he published *Who Killed Mr Drum?*, a memoir that reads more like a thriller than the history of a magazine, but one in which he sought to expose the horrors of apartheid using black farce.

ELAINE M. PEARSON

Stockenström, Wilma

b. 1933, Napier, South Africa

actress, playwright, poet, and novelist

This multi-talented South African actress and playwright is a renowned Afrikaans poet and novelist (see **Afrikaans literature**). She studied drama at the University of Stellenbosch and lived in Pretoria before retiring to Cape Town. Her 1970 debut novel, *Vir die bysiende leser* (For the Short-Sighted Reader), set the tone for other highly acclaimed and original volumes, including *Spieël van water* (Mirror of Water) (1973), *Van vergetelheid en van glans* (Of Oblivion and of Luminosity) (1976), *Monsterverse* (Monster Verse, 1984), the epic *Heengaanrefrein* (Farewell Refrain) (1988), *Aan die Kaap geskryf* (Written at the Cape) (1994), and *Spesmase* (Hunches) (2000). She has received many major and prestigious South African literary prizes and

she has provided gripping readings of her work at numerous poetry festivals. Her volume titles are ironically humble, her images strongly visual, and her vocabulary sparse and dry. Her poems, for example "By L'Agulhas 'n wandeling" (A Stroll at L'Agulhas) and "Die eland" (The Eland), are firmly based in Africa, exploring links between Afrikaans and other indigenous languages, forever problematizing her relationship to the landscape, coastline, fauna, and flora. The most famous of her five novels, *Die kremetartekspedisie* (1981), was trans-lated into English by J.M. **Coetzee** as *The Baobab Tree*. It hauntingly evokes a woman's exploration of Africa and of language.

ENA JANSEN

structuralism and poststructuralism

Although structuralism and poststructuralism have been some of the most influential theoretical movements during the period of the 1960s and after, when African literature emerged as a discipline of study, they have often been the source of controversy and even resistance on the con-tinent. More often than not this resistance has come from writers and critics who object to the central doctrines and methodologies promoted by structuralism and poststructuralism, either as a wholesale resistance to critical theories that seem to have been developed elsewhere and to have been imposed on the literature of the continent, or from scholars who object to specific claims in the ideologies of these movements on issues such as the nature of language and meaning and the political commitment of the writer. In the circum-stances, the resistance to structuralism and post-structuralism is based on a set of issues that have haunted the criticism (see **literary criticism**) of African literature since the late 1950s – what kind of criticism is most appropriate to the study of this literature and what is the role of extraneous theoretical models to the African text? In spite of the resistance to these theories, however, there is no doubt, as Robert Young has argued in *White Mythologies* (1990), that structuralism and poststruc-turalism are connected, both directly and indirectly, to African debates and experiences. Structuralism, for example, emerged as a critique of the philosophy of Jean-Paul Sartre, more specifically his ideas on history, consciousness, and existence. And while Sartre's philosophical work was conducted within specific French debates, one of its often-negated aspects was its concern with the colonial experience and Africa in general. Sartre's attempt to establish a philosophical basis for agency and subjectivity and to provide a phenomenological account of being was constantly conducted against the pressures of "otherness" as it had emerged in the colonial situation. In addition, in significant essays such as "Orphée noir" (Black Orpheus), his introduction to L.S. **Senghor**'s *Anthologie de la nouvelle poésie nègre et malgache de langue française* (Anthology of New Black and Malagasy Poetry in French) (1948) and the preface to Fanon's *The Wretched of the Earth* (1968), Sartre was a key figure in setting the terms of debate for African literature. If structuralism is premised on a critique of Sartre's claims for history and being, it must also be considered, indirectly perhaps, as a deconstruction of some of the central doctrines in African literary movements, most particularly **negritude**. There is, however, a more direct connection between poststructuralism and Africa, and this is to be found in the often-ignored fact that some of the major figures in this movement in France – Louis Althusser, Jacques Derrida, and Hélène Cixous – were born in Algeria and that it was the colonial war in the country in the 1950s that triggered the political and cultural crisis that demanded a rethinking of previous systems of thought, including Marxism and phenomenology.

The resistance to structuralism

It is fair to say that the history of structuralism in Africa was a short and controversial one. In the late 1960s and early 1970s there were variant attempts to introduce the methods of structuralism to the study of Africa society, culture, and history. Arguably, structuralism still dominates the works of leading African philosophers such as V.Y. **Mudimbe** and Paulin Hountoudji. But in literary studies, the area where it should have mattered most, structuralism did not take ground. In Anglophone Africa, for example, the Nigerian scholar Sunday Anozie wrote several books on the

sociology of African literature, including *Sociologie du roman africain* (Sociology of the African Novel) (1970), *Structural Models and African Poetics* (1981), and several structuralist studies of leading African poets, most notably Senghor and Okigbo, but the reaction to these quite innovative works was often negative. Indeed, well into the 1980s when the movement was considered to be over, structuralism was still generating hostile essays from leading African scholars and writers such as Anthony Appiah and Wole **Soyinka**.

One way of thinking about the short history of structuralism in Africa, then, is to pose a simple question: why did it meet such resistance? To answer this question, it is perhaps useful to consider how the central theoretical and methodological claims of structuralism seemed to go against the established doctrines of African literature. In regard to method, for example, structuralism was premised on a highly technical language with key terms borrowed from linguistics. It sought to develop a poetics based on what Anozie described in "Negritude, Structuralism, and Deconstruction" (1984: New York/London) as isolated aspects of language functioning on different levels of linguistic analysis including phonology, phonetics, syntactic and semantic elements. As an offshoot of generative grammar, structuralism sought to account for these elements by dealing with what Anozie aptly called "the internal coherence of the given work of art." What this meant, among other things, was that structuralism was not interested in the work of art as a diachronic phenomenon, one with a changing history, but in the text as a synchronic – that is, self-contained – object, explainable only in the terms it presented to the reader.

Underlying this interest in the work of art as a synchronic event was the belief that the nature of a linguistic sign was arbitrary. Drawing on the work of the Swiss linguist Ferdinand de Saussure, structuralists insisted that there was no logical relationship between a sign and the thing it represented, that language was a form, not a substance. And once language and criticism had been focused on form and language, some of the larger questions that had preoccupied students of African literature – questions of meaning, history, and subjectivity – were considered irrelevant. In short, structuralism sought to establish a symbolic order in language itself, not by appealing to what were considered to be extra-linguistic categories such as history, morality, and culture. This is why Anozie insisted, in his famous reading of Senghor's "Le Totem," that the poem did not have a history of its own and existed as a synchronic event. What he meant by this, and his reading proved the point, was that the cultural symbols denoted by the poem could only be explained by its language, not through an appeal to meanings located in, let us say, African cultural systems, or even to Senghor's ideology of negritude. Totemism had meaning only as it developed within the syntactic structures of the poem.

Now we can see why there was so much resistance to structuralism in the criticism of African literature: the notion of art as a synchronic event and of language as an arbitrary system of signification went against some of the most established doctrines in the production and study of African literature. For one, this literature had always tended to see itself as a diachronic event, as a system of meanings connected to developments and transformations in African history and culture and hence inevitably connected to such extraneous movements as colonialism and nationalism (see **colonialism, neocolonialism, and postcolonialism**; **nationalism and post-nationalism**). Indeed, in its early days modern African literature claimed to be different from other literatures precisely because of its diachronic nature and function. In addition, the criticism of African literature had tended to privilege its semantic character. It had sought to explain the central texts in this tradition in terms of the meanings it yielded about African histories, experiences, and traditions. The structuralists' insistence on the arbitrary nature of the linguistic sign undermined the semantic function or the text, not to mention its connection to transcendental systems of meaning.

On poststructuralism

While poststructuralism has presented itself as a break from structuralism, it is best seen as pushing the central claims of structuralism to their limits while allowing for the return of the diachronic. In its deconstructive mode, represented in the volu-

minous and influential work of Jacques Derrida, for example, poststructuralism has systematically undermined the claims of history and subjectivity, called into question the privileging of writing over speech in the Western tradition, underscored the arbitrary nature of signification, and debunked the ideology of the unified subject. Indeed, poststructuralism has gone further than structuralism: it has called the notion of a unified structure into question and insisted that meanings are themselves indeterminate. Given what might appear to be the extreme position in regard to questions of history, reference, and meaning that have been central to the project of African literature, it is ironic that poststructuralism has not generated much controversy in Africa. Indeed, poststructuralism in the guise of some its ancillary movements, such as postcolonialism, feminism, and cultural studies, has made some inroads into the criticism of African literature. There has been some serious questioning of the efficacy of terms such as "postcolonialism" in relation to African literature, but by and large this movement does not seem to be doomed to the same fate as structuralism.

There are several possible explanation for the relative success of poststructuralism in Africa. The first and most obvious one is that poststructuralism does not rely on a highly technical linguistic grammar and has no scientific pretensions. On the contrary, the deconstructive methodologies of poststructuralism are predicated on a kind of improvisation in which the target object is much more important than any alternative explanatory system. Second, in spite of its disclaimer of determinate meanings, poststructuralism has a cultural politics that critics of colonialism and postcoloniality in African have found particularly attractive: the central claim that poststructuralism is directed at Eurocentrism and the figures of white mythology, or the assumption that it seeks to deconstruct the discourse of power and systems of domination, has a special appeal to feminists and students of popular culture. The third reason why poststructuralism has appealed to a wide range of critics of African literature arises from historical contingency: the movement became popular at a time in the 1980s and 1990s when African literature itself was being transformed by the forces of globalization and the realities of migration and exile breaking out of the nationalist ideologies that had enabled it in the first place.

Poststructuralist critiques of identity, which emphasized difference and hybridity over the homogeneity promoted by the nation-state, were appealing to African writers located outside the continent or those trying to escape the prisonhouse represented by state power. It is not surprising, then, that poststructuralist and postmodern ideas have filtered into the works of writers against apartheid (J.M. **Coetzee**) or those crossing national boundaries (Ben **Okri**, **Ben Jelloun**, Leïla **Sebbar**). Indeed, some of the most prominent advocates of poststructuralism are African intellectuals, such as the Moroccan-born scholar Abdelkebir Khatibi, whose lives and works are divided between continents, countries, languages, and traditions.

Further reading

Anozie, Sunday O. (1970) *Sociologie du roman Africain* (Sociology of the African Novel), Paris: Aubier-Montaigne.

——(1984) "Negritude, Structuralism, Deconstruction," in Henry Louis Gates (ed.) *Black Literature and Theory*, New York/London: Methuen, pp. 105–26.

Appiah, Anthony (1984) "Strictures on Structures: The Prospects for a Structuralist Poetics of African Fiction," in Henry Louis Gates (ed.) *Black Literature and Theory*, New York/London: Methuen, pp. 127–50.

Khatibi, Abdelkebir (1983) *Magreb Pluriel*, Paris: Denoël.

SIMON GIKANDI

Sutherland, Efua Theodora

b. 1924, Cape Coast, Gold Coast (now in Ghana); d. 1996, Ghana

playwright, educator, and artist

Known as "the mother of the Ghanaian theater movement," Efua T. Sutherland became a leading member of those educators, writers, and artists whose vision and works were to shape and mould Ghana's creative and literary landscape during the latter half of the twentieth century. Along with other writers like Michael **Dei-Anang** and Joe **De Graft**, Sutherland provided inspiration for the development of the literary and dramatic arts in Ghana. She helped in the establishment of the Ghana Association of Writers, the Ghana Drama Studio, and the Ghana National Commission on Children. Also, Efua Sutherland has been noted for her **children's literature**, dramas, and innovative theatrical productions.

Sutherland began writing in 1951 and in 1953 published her first short story, "New Life in Kyerefaso," which was quickly recognized as a classic. It was not, however, until the late 1950s that she resumed a more active role on the Ghanaian literary scene when she, Michael Dei-Anang, and Dr R.E.G. Armattoe formed the Ghana Society of Writers, later renamed the Ghana Association of Writers. At the end of 1957, Sutherland helped launch *Okyeame*, Ghana's pre-eminent journal for established and aspiring writers. Then she started the Ghana Experimental Theatre Project as a means of reaching out to a larger audience. With support from the Rockefeller Foundation and a Danish architectural concern, Geelack and Gilles, her dream of an appropriate physical space for the new experimental theater was realized. The Ghana Drama Studio, opened in 1961 by President Kwame Nkrumah, was a significant achievement in Sutherland's career. The studio became part of the Institute of African Studies at the University of Ghana, Legon.

Among the initial dramas performed at the studio was a very successful adaptation of her critically acclaimed short story, "New Life at Kyerefaso," as well as the inaugural performance of a drama called "Odansani," which, after significant changes, was published as *Edufa* in 1967. Her view of drama as a communal activity led her to create Ghana's first community theater, the Kodzidan (House of Stories) at Atwia in Ghana's central region, and develop the uniquely Ghanaian genre of *Anansegoro*, both based on traditional oral storytelling techniques (see **oral literature and performance**). In 1975 Sutherland published *The Marriage of Anansewa*, which many critics see as exemplary of the directions in which she was taking Ghanaian drama. After the

1970s, she launched the Kusum Agoromba, which bridged the gap between the literary and popular "concert party" theaters while promoting excellent drama in the vernacular languages. Before leaving the Institute of African Studies, Sutherland had begun the Children's Drama Development Project, which became an avenue for the works of new writers like Kofi **Anyidoho**. Through the 1980s until her death, she was very active in the development of the Ghana National Children's Commission, as well as promoting the work of the W.E.B. Dubois Memorial Center and other pan-African activities.

Further reading

Lindfors, Bernth and Sanders, Reinhard (eds) (1992) *Twentieth Century Caribbean and Black African Writers*, Detroit: Gale.

Vieta, Kojo T. (1999) *The Flagbearers of Ghana: Profiles of One Hundred Distinguished Ghanaians*, Accra: Ghana Ena Publications.

VINCENT O. ODAMTTEN

Swahili literature

Swahili, an African Bantu language, evolved on the northern coast of East Africa before the tenth century AD. The Swahili were part of the cultural world around the Indian Ocean which included the Arabian peninsula, Persia, India, and other countries. As it evolved, the Swahili language and culture acquired influences from these countries. The Greeks sailed into the East African coast from at least the early years of the first millennium AD. However, real and durable European influence on Swahili can be dated to the coming of the Portuguese, at the end of the fifteenth century. Swahili literature evolved along the same axis. Originally an indigenous African oral tradition (see **oral literature and performance**) consisting of various genres, it later incorporated Arab, Persian, Indian, and other influences. With the introduction of literacy, whose first form was Arabic script, Swahili literature acquired new characteristics. The Swahili-Arabic script served initially to spread Islamic writings. With time, it was used for textualizing the oral tradition, the writing of chronicles, and the creation of written literature in Swahili.

The written Swahili literary tradition appears to have been well established by the seventeenth century. For several centuries, poetry was the main form of Swahili written literature. Most of the poems that are known to us deal with Islamic themes (see **Islam in African literature**), including stories of the Prophet Muhammad and his followers, and the spread of Islam in the Arabian peninsula and beyond. There was, however, always a strong secular tradition in Swahili poetry. The earliest known epic of the Swahili, *Liongo Fumo*, deals with secular themes, such as the struggle for kingship. The religious poems themselves were often not projecting true Islamic doctrine and values; they often embellished, parodied or subverted Islamic concepts. This fact has not been much acknowledged. Written Swahili poetry always had a symbiotic relationship with the oral tradition. Swahili poetry is written essentially for oral delivery in the form of recitation in front of an immediate audience or over the radio.

Towards the end of the nineteenth century, prose writing took root in the form of autobiographical (see **autobiography**) and travel narratives. It was during this time that Tippu Tip, the ivory trader, wrote his famous autobiography, *Maisha ya Hamed bin Muhammed el Murjebi* (The Life of Hamed bin Muhammed el Murjebi). This trend was enhanced with the establishment of newspapers and the rise of the **vernacular press** in the first two decades of the twentieth century, which provided a forum for writers in various genres. During this period, European colonialists and missionaries greatly influenced the development of Swahili literature. Out of the many dialects of Swahili, for example, they chose the Zanzibar one as the standard form of the language. This enhanced the status of this dialect and helped establish the canon of modern Swahili literature, as evidenced by the works of writers like Shaaban **Robert**. European literary works were introduced, in English or in Swahili translation, which contributed to the evolution of Swahili literature. The Swahili novel, the detective novel, the short story, drama, and poetry, all bear the influence of the European and American traditions.

Swahili literature has always been a dynamic tradition which has gone through major shifts and movements. From the northern East African coast, the centers of poetic creativity shifted gradually southwards through Kenya and Tanzania, which includes the islands of Pemba and Zanzibar. In the prose tradition, the shift has been from travelers' tales, autobiographies, and romances to realistic writing. During the struggle for independence in the 1950s, overtly political themes became prominent, and after independence these included themes on the reality of, and struggle against, neocolonialism and the search for social justice. In Tanzania this latter trend included visions of socialist society. Today, critical realism (see **realism and magical realism**) continues to be dominant, as writers in the language seek to represent the people's struggle against various forms of inequality and injustice from within their countries and from external forces of imperialism.

In more recent years, especially after the 1960s, upcountry writers, particularly in Tanzania, became major contributors to fiction, drama, and poetry in Swahili. Women have always been a major force in the history of Swahili literature, both oral and written, as creators, performers, and keepers of the tradition. The first half of the nineteenth century, for example, witnessed the emergence of the famous poetess Mwana Kupona Binti Mahamu, whose *Utendi wa Mwana Kupona* (The Epic of Mwana Kupona) is one of the classics of Swahili literature. In the early newspapers, women made signal contributions, often engaging in poetic debates with men on various issues.

Swahili literature continues to evolve in the context of, and in response to, internal and external forces and influences. Swahili writers adopt and experiment with new forms and techniques in the writing of fiction, drama, and poetry. In the writings of Ebrahim **Hussein**, for example, critics note the influence of such writers as Bertholt Brecht. They also see the influence of the European existentialists in the writings of Euphrase Kezilahabi. Films are another source of influence on contemporary Swahili literature.

Translations from European, American, Asian, and African works continue to enrich the environment of the Swahili writers. Through translations, certain Swahili works are being made available to the rest of the world. However, there is a great amount of Swahili literature which has not yet been translated, such as the epics.

The development of Swahili literature has been greatly aided by the growth of indigenous publishing houses, literary clubs, book fairs, and the promotion of Swahili as the official language of the East African countries. The adoption of Swahili as the medium of instruction in schools, universal literacy among children and adults, and government support for the publishing and distribution of books would ensure a brighter future for Swahili literature.

It is regrettable that the adoption and consolidation of the Roman script as the medium for publishing in Swahili has led to the virtual neglect of the Swahili-Arabic script. This has deprived many writers of the opportunity to be published. The fact remains that over the entire East African coast, people continue to write in Swahili-Arabic script, and hundreds of manuscripts exist, in private hands or in the archives and libraries of institutions, which may never be published. Many of the best works of Swahili literature, especially poetry, are still not published, since they are not in the Roman script. Some effort has been made, for example by the Institute of Swahili Research of the University of Dar es Salaam in Tanzania, to transliterate and publish these manuscripts in Roman script. This work needs to continue, to present the hidden treasures of Swahili literature to the world.

Further reading

Bertoncini, Elena Zbkov (1989) *Outline of Swahili Literature: Prose Fiction and Drama*, Leiden: E.J. Brill.

Knappert, Jan (1979) *Four Centuries of Swahili Verse: A Literary History and Anthology*, London: Heinemann.

JOSEPH MBELE

T

Taddese Liben

b. 1930, Ethiopia

short story writer

Taddese Liben is Ethiopia's greatest short story writer. Although he has published only two volumes, *Meskerem* (the name of the first Ethiopian month) (1956/7) and *Lélaw menged* (The Other Way, or The Alternative) (1959/60) his style and mode of storytelling have popularized the short story in Ethiopia. In his collections, he surveys and characterizes the best short story writers in the world (perhaps mostly Maupassant and Maugham), from whom he has learnt much; but he maintains that it was the Ethiopian oral tradition (see **oral literature and performance**) that made him an author. He deals with moral issues confronting urban youth, but also humorously treats traditional beliefs. He was educated in mission and government schools. After some teaching, he started a banking career which continued well to the end of the twentieth century, but he maintains that stories constantly live in his mind and he has been waiting for a chance to get them down on paper.

Further reading

Molvaer, R.K. (1997) *Black Lions*, Lawrenceville, New Jersey: Red Sea Press.

REIDULF MOLVAER

Tadjo, Véronique

b. 1955, Paris, France

author and illustrator

Véronique Tadjo, the Ivorian author and illustrator, claims the whole of African culture as her main source of inspiration. She sees the retrieval of elements of the African precolonial past as necessary to redeveloping a social consciousness and helping the individual rediscover her/his place in space and time. In an interview with Jean-Marie Volet, she states that her writing represents a quest for an understanding of the world and human beings and for "order, logic, and meaning in the world." The theme of love of life, of country, of the earth, and between man and woman serves as a unifying thread running through her work, from her first book, *Latérite* (Red Clay) (1984), to *Champs de bataille et d'amour* (Fields of Battle and Love) (1999).

In *Latérite*, a work of poetry, the theme of love and communication between man and woman parallels that of retrieving the past to help understand the present and influence the future. Much of the imagery in the book derives from nature. The theme of love recurs in Tadjo's other works, but in some of her later works she explores the theme through the intricate web of human relationships, relation to self and to the world. As in other works written in the 1980s, Tadjo considers women to be central to the issue of change. Issues of war and social justice are also important themes in Tadjo's writing, and the Rwanda genocide of 1994 is the subject of *L'Ombre d'Imana* (The Shadow of the Imana) (2000). However, Tadjo expands the concept of conflict to encompass the external and internal battles people wage in day-to-day living, focusing on people who, in Volet's words, are faced with the injustices of the world and dominated by their environment.

The metaphor of crossing cultures, genres, art forms, and styles, best exemplified by *As the Crow Flies* (2001) and in her works of **children's literature**, is a good descriptor of Tadjo's life and work. For instance, while the title of *Lord of the Dance* (*Le Seigneur de la dance*) (1993) was borrowed from an English hymn, the story itself owes its inspiration to African masks. Tadjo's illustrations for this and her other children's books are drawn from Sanufo art for style, but the colors are made brighter in order to appeal to a young audience. To date Tadjo has authored five self-illustrated books for children.

Further reading

Rice-Maximin, Micheline (1996) " 'Nouvelle écriture' from the Ivory Coast: A Reading of Véronique Tadjo's *À vol d'oiseau*," in Mary Jean Green, Karen Gould, Micheline Rice-Maximin, Keith L. Walker, and Jack A. Yeagers (eds) *Postcolonial Subjects: Francophone Women Writers*, Minneapolis and London: University of Minnesota Press.

Volet, Jean-Marie (1999) "Véronique Tadjo: champs de bataille et d'amour" (Véronique Tadjo: Fields of Battle and Love) *Mots Pluriels* 11 (September).

WANGAR WA NYATETŪ-WAIGWA

Tafawa Balewa, Abubakar

b. 1912, Nigeria; d. 1966, Nigeria

politician and writer

Abubakar Tafawa Balewa was the first prime minister of independent Nigeria. His career as first teacher, then conservative politician, came to an abrupt end through his assassination during the first military coup of January 1966. A modest man from Tafawa Balewa ("Black Rock") near Bauchi, he was a product of Bauchi Middle School and then Katsina College, where Islam and a combination of Islamic and Western education combined to create a new Northern Nigerian elite (see **education and schools**). Along with other Katsina College associates Bello **Kagara** and Abubakar **Imam**, he submitted a first novella to a literary competition in 1933. Published as *Shaihu Umar*, the novella (later produced by others as a play and as a television film) relates the story of a boy captured by slavers and transported across the Sahara, and his passage to adulthood, freedom, and eventual return to Northern Nigeria. The story presents a vision of a "good man" with all his qualities; however, the emotional core of the narrative is the search by his mother for the lost child. Written when he was a teacher at Bauchi Middle School, *Shaihu Umar* was Tafawa Balewa's only excursion into the world of creative writing and represented a set of values to which he would adhere for the remainder of his life.

GRAHAM FURNISS

Ṭāhir, Bahā'

b. 1935, Cairo, Egypt

novelist

The Egyptian novelist and short story writer Bahā' Ṭāhir has achieved significant critical acclaim and popularity across the Arab world. Born and educated in Cairo, Ṭāhir witnessed severe social, political, and economic upheavals that influenced his writings. In *Qālat Ḍuha* (Duha Said) (1985), the characters suffer from the disappointment of the 1952 revolution. Because of his political views, Ṭāhir was fired from his job in radio broadcasting and eventually forced to leave Cairo. From 1981 to 1995 he lived in Geneva, where he served as a translator for the United Nations. Exile served as a central source of his concerns. Set in a European city, *Bi al-amsi Ḥalumtu Bik* (Yesterday I Dreamt of You) (1984) explores the narrator's solitude against the monotony of daily life and the sense of false salvation that the past can offer. *Aunt Ṣafiyya and the Monastery* (1996) (*Khālatī Ṣafiyyah wa-al-Dayr*) (1991) tackles the relations between the Muslim and the Coptic communities of Upper Egypt with some allusions to the 1967 Arab–Israeli war. Its political theme stresses the importance of tolerance between religious communities. The helplessness and the alienation of intellectuals, love, human rights, and racism are embodied in Ṭāhir's novel *al-Hub fī al-Manfā* (Love in Exile) (1995). *Nuqṭat al-Nūr* (The Spot of Light) (2001) takes a turn and focuses on the inner world of its characters in their daily preoccupations rather than the political events of the 1970s.

Further reading

Sakkut, Hamdi (2000) *The Arabic Novel: Bibliography and Critical Introduction 1865–1995*, vol. 1, Cairo: American University in Cairo Press.

KHALED AL MASRI

Tati-Loutard, Jean-Baptiste

b. 1938, Ngoyo, Congo-Brazzaville

poet

The most famous of the Congolese contemporary poets, Jean-Baptiste Tati-Loutard was born at Ngoyo in the region of Pointe Noire in the west of Congo-Brazzaville. After graduating from the University of Bordeaux in France, he taught at the Congolese Centre d'Enseignement Supérieur (Center of Higher Schooling) for some years before embarking on an academic career at the University of Brazzaville, where he taught literature for many years. In addition to his academic career, Tati-Loutard has been a major advocate and promoter of Congolese cultural awareness and revival. He has held different government posts in Congo, including the position of minister of culture and arts for two decades in the 1980s and 1990s.

As a writer, Tati-Loutard has published mostly poetry. His poetic oeuvre, concerned with the exaltation of the Congolese people, their values and culture, marked a significant distance from the writing and underlying ideology of the prior generation of mainstream Francophone poets inspired by the works of the Senegalese poet

Léopold Sédar **Senghor** and the **negritude** movement. Tati-Loutard's poems place a strong emphasis on a national Congolese identity, which takes precedence over black identity. In collections such as *Poems of the Sea* (1990), originally published as *Poèmes de la mer* in 1968, and *Racines congolaises* (Congolese Roots) (1968), metaphors and references to the Congo are a recurrent motif in Tati-Loutard's poetry.

As in his poems, Tati-Loutard's short stories and novels, most notably *Chroniques congolaises* (Congolese Chronicles) (1974), *Nouvelles Chroniques congolaises* (New Congolese Chronicles) (1980), and *Le Récit de la mort* (The Story of Death) (1987), are concerned with the torments of everyday life, which culminate in death. In works such as *Les Normes du temps* (The Standards of Time) (1974), he is interested in the life and death of an artist against the background of the passing of time, African and Congolese traditions facing modernity (see **modernity and modernism**), intellectual life in Africa, and the notion of identity and roots. Tati-Loutard has also compiled *Anthologie de la littérature congolaise d'expression française* (Anthology of Congolese Literature in the French Language) (1976). But it is as a poet that he has contributed immensely to the renewal of poetic forms in contemporary African literature in French, and his work has been awarded several honors and prizes in Africa as well as in Europe, including one from the French Academy in 1992.

ANTHÈRE NZABATSINDA

Tchicaya UTam'Si

b. 1931, Mpili, Congo-Brazzaville; d. 1988, Bazancourt, France

poet, novelist, and playwright

Tchicaya UTam'Si, also known as Gérald-Félix Tchicaya, was born in Mpili in Congo-Brazzaville. In 1946, he moved to France with his father, who had been elected a deputy in the French National Assembly. After abandoning his studies, he supported himself in a variety of ways in order to write. He published his first set of poems, *Le Mauvais Sang* (Bad Blood) in 1955. His next volume *Feu de brousse*

(Bush Fire) won the Grand Prix littéraire de l'Afrique équatoriale française in 1957, beginning the first milestone in the career of an internationally celebrated writer. For a time, Tchicaya UTam'Si was involved in radio broadcasting, but when the Belgian Congo won its independence in the early 1960s he went to Léopoldville as a journalist and edited *Congo*, the newspaper of Patrice Lumumba's party. The poems in *Epitome* (1962) reflect the poet's reaction to Lumumba's assassination. Returning to France shortly after the death of Lumumba, Tchicaya UTam'Si embarked on a twenty-year career with UNESCO. In addition to his poetry, his literary production includes novels: *Les Méduses* (The Medusas) (1982), *Les Cancrelats* (The Cockroaches) (1980), and *Les Phalènes* (The Moths) (1984). He is the author of short stories and plays, including *Le Destin glorieux du maréchal Nnikon Nniku prince qu'on sort* (The Glorious Destiny of Marshall Nnikon Nniku) (1979).

JANICE SPLETH

Tejani, Bahadur

b. 1942, Kenya

poet, novelist, short story writer, and critic

The Ugandan poet, novelist, short story writer, and critic Bahadur Tejani was born in Kenya to Gujarati parents. He was educated at Makerere University College, Cambridge University, and the University of Nairobi, where he taught for a period in the 1970s. Among the writers of the Indian diaspora from Africa (see **diaspora and pan-Africanism**) he is a pioneer who has inspired others like Moyez **Vassanji** and Peter **Nazareth**. His novel *Day After Tomorrow* (1971) was the first by an Indian from East Africa. It is the story of Samsher, who breaks from the traditions of his Indian community by marrying an African nurse and forsaking a lucrative trading career to become a teacher. The novel meditates upon the possibility of inventing a viable postcolonial culture that negates the insularity of the preceding colonial period. Tejani's poetry has appeared in several anthologies, including *Pulsations* (1968) edited by Arthur Kemoli, *Poems from East Africa* (1971) edited

by David Cook and David **Rubadiri**, and *Poems of Black Africa* (1975) edited by Wole **Soyinka**. His volume *The Rape of Literature and Other Poems* (1989) is about life in India. His essays are an important contribution to the study of Africa's intellectual history, while his poetry and prose fiction offer valuable insights into the condition of exile.

DAN ODHIAMBO OJWANG

Tenreiro, Francisco José de Vasques

b. 1921, São Tomé; d. 1963, Portugal

poet and short story writer

The São Tomé poet and short story writer Francisco Tenreiro was one of a few writers in Portuguese involved in the **negritude** movement. A geographer by training, Tenreiro spent most of his life in Portugal, where he started writing poetry and studying African literature. The influence of negritude is evident in the rhetorical language of his poems, which are committed to black self-assertion as an antidote to colonial denigration. In his major poems, including *Ilha de nome santo* (The Island of the Holy Name) (1942), he simultaneously presented powerful critiques of the harsh conditions under which Africans lived in the Portuguese empire and celebrated their blackness as a source of moral authority. The critique of colonialism (see **colonialism, neocolonialism, and postcolonialism**) that preoccupied Tenreiro's life and work was continued in his short story, "Romance de seu Silva Costa" (The Ballad of One Silver Costa) (1962), the pseudo-biography of a white planter in São Tomé. In this story, Tenreiro used social realism to contrast the pampered lives of the Portuguese settler class and the extreme poverty of their African laborers. While São Tomé provided Tenreiro with his most pressing subjects, some critics felt that he had lived out of the islands for so long that his representation of them was distant and sometimes romanticized.

SIMON GIKANDI

Themba, Can

b. 1924, Marabastad, South Africa; d. 1968, Manzini, Swaziland

short story writer and journalist

Born in Marabastad, Pretoria, and educated at the University of Fort Hare, Can Themba has been described as having been at the center of the Sophiatown Renaissance of the 1950s. Having taught English at Madibane High School in Western Township and Johannesburg Indian High School, Themba joined *Drum* magazine and the *Golden City Post* as a journalist. Themba's creativity and flair for language are evident in his creative journalism and his short stories. A posthumously published collection of short stories entitled *The Will to Die* (1972) offers imaginative and fascinating vignettes of the vibrant and multifaceted culture of Sophiatown during the apartheid years (see **apartheid and post-apartheid**). A comprehensive collection of his stories and other writings, *The World of Can Themba* (1985), exemplifies the depth of Themba's creative talent.

Further reading

Patel, Essop (1985) *The World of Can Themba*, Johannesburg: Ravan Press.

THENGANI H. NGWENYA

Titenga, Pacéré

b. 1943, Manéga, Burkina Faso

lawyer and poet

Pacéré Titenga was born in Manéga (Oubritenga) in Burkina Faso and studied law at university. He is considered to be one of the brightest and most prominent Burkinabé lawyers, but he has also been involved in different cultural, social, and political activities as well as in professional associations. Titenga is also a prominent poet, and in 1982 he was awarded the literary Grand Prize for Black Africa for his innovative poetry. Titenga's major poems include *Ça tire sous le Sahel* (It Shoots in the Sahel) (1976), *Refrain sous le Sahel* (A Chorus in the Sahel) (1976), *Quand s'envolent les grues couronnées* (When the Crowned Cranes Fly Away) (1976), *La Poésie pour l'Angola* (Poems for Angola) (1982), *La Poésie des griots* (Poems of the Griots) (1982), *Du lait pour une tombe* (Some Milk for a Tomb) (1987), and *Poèmes pour Koryo* (Poems for Koryo) (1987). In the poems collected in these works, as in his essays, Titenga is interested in the preservation and perpetuation of precolonial values, but his works also represent a practical and dynamic range of vision, taking up themes of cultural and economic development and probing the ways in which old values can be revived and harmonized in the cause of modernity (see **modernity and modernism**) and development.

MICHEL TINGUIRI

Tlali, Miriam

b. 1933, Johannesburg, South Africa

novelist

The South African writer Miriam Tlali gained international attention with the publication of her first and most popular novel, *Muriel at Metropolitan* (1975), the chronicle of what it meant to be a young black woman, with some education, working as a secretary in an appliance store in apartheid South Africa (see **apartheid and post-apartheid**). Born in Johannesburg, Tlali started her education at the University of the Witwatersrand before it was declared off-limits to black students and she had to continue her studies at the University of Lesotho. She was active in the struggle against apartheid and was arrested and detained several times in the 1970s. Her works were powerful narrative responses to the social conditions she encountered both in her everyday life and in her political activities. *Muriel at Metropolitan*, for example, documents the daily racist humiliation faced by a black woman working in a white-run business. At the end of the novel, Muriel, who faces an unknown future, decides to leave her job because she cannot stand being part of a system which first exploits black people and then punishes them for their poverty. In her second novel, *Amandla* (1980), Tlali focuses her attention on a black family in Soweto during the 1976 uprising.

Like many South African writers of her generation, Tlali had a keen sense of the cultural politics of apartheid and it was perhaps her strong documentation of black lives under white domination that led to the banning of both of her novels on publication. In *Mihloti* (1984), which was published with an introduction by Richard **Rive**, she turned to **autobiography**, drawing on her record of arrests, travels, and celebrations to provide a powerful documentation of what it meant to be black in South Africa under apartheid. *Soweto Stories* (1989), her fourth book, published with an introduction by Lauretta **Ngcobo**, contains snapshots of life lived under apartheid. Although Tlali's later work is autobiographical in nature, its value resides in the documentation she gave to lives that were led, under great odds, during apartheid. Like most writers of her generation, Tlali, in "writing herself," was also writing about her society in flux from full-blown apartheid to comparative emancipation.

HUMA IBRAHIM

Tlili, Mustapha

b. 1937, Tunisia

novelist and academic

Tunisian novelist Mustapha Tlili has spent his adult life divided between two careers: writing fiction and working for the United Nations in New York. The literary consequences are novels that take his characters outside the geography of much North African literature: that is, outside North Africa and France. In placing his characters in international cities like New York, Tlili complicates questions of North African postcolonial identity (see **colonialism, neocolonialism, and postcolonialism**) and explores the concept of a double exile in which characters are distanced not only from their home country but also from the country of the colonizer and its cultural traditions. This is most clearly illustrated in Tlili's first novel *La Rage aux tripes* (Rage in the Guts) (1975) in which the main character, a journalist named Jalal Ben Cherif, lives

and works in New York City but is psychically torn between his childhood homeland Algeria, his young adult life in France, and his professional life in the United States. Tlili takes the reader into Jalal's mind, the site of an unstable identity, and as Jalal considers his place in the Western world he produces lengthy interior monologues about place, allegiance, vengeance, and justice. While *La Rage aux tripes* addresses exile through the prism of anger and outrage, Tlili's second novel *Le Bruit dort* (The Noise is Sleeping) (1978) explores exile through love and the sense of loss. Albert Nelli, an older French writer living in New York abandoned by his third wife and young daughter, delves into his isolation by devoting himself to writing the story of his closest friend, a young Tunisian named Adel Safi, Tara Matheson, Safi's Irish-American girlfriend who is mysteriously assassinated in New York, and Dr Hussein, a Third-World representative to the United Nations who escapes into his own world, writing a book on the passion of the Islamic mystic Hallaj. In writing their intertwined stories of exile, loss, and cultural allegiance, both Nelli and Tlili explore the lives and psyches of people broken by the burdens of identity. *Gloire des sables* (Sand Glory) (1982), named after a desert flower that blossoms only after rain, also presents a world of complex identities. The protagonist is abandoned by his Algerian father, raised by French teachers who are then assassinated, and sent to school in France. He becomes an active member of the Algerian resistance and eventually seeks refuge in the United States, where he marries the daughter of a psychiatrist who treats Saudi Arabian princesses. The novel takes the form of a detective story whose principal quest is the search for roots and origins. In keeping with his literary preoccupations of exile and justice, in 1987 Tlili co-edited *For Nelson Mandela* with French philosopher Jacques Derrida. In the novel *Lion Mountain* (*La Montagne du lion*) (1990), Tlili makes a literary return to his place of birth, narrating the lives of villagers in the Tunisian mountains.

Further reading

Tlili, Mustapha (1975) *La Rage aux tripes* (Rage in the Guts), Paris: Gallimard.

——(1982) *Gloire des sables* (Sand Glory), Paris: Collection Jean-Jacques Pauvert.

KATARZYNA PIEPRZAK

Toihiri, Mohamed A.

b. 1955, Mitsoudjé, Grande Comore

novelist

Born in the village of Mitsoudjé on the island of Grande Comore, Toihiri finished his secondary studies on the island before completing an MA and then a PhD in modern literature at the University of Bordeaux III in France. He returned to the Comores where he was a teacher before accepting a post as lecturer at the School of Higher Education at N'Vouni, just outside the capital of Moroni. He subsequently became director of education in the Comores and then lectured in Paris. He returned to his country of birth in 1995. Toihiri is important in the literary history of the Comores as being its first published novelist. Toihiri's first novel, *La République des imberbes* (The Republic of the Beardless) (1985), is a scathingly satirical novel based on the three-year despotism of the socialist president Ali Soilih, whom Toihiri names Guigoz, the brand name of a popular baby food in France. His second novel, *Le Kafir du Karthala* (The Kaffir of Karthala) (1992) deals with the battle to break out of the vice of stifling Comoran traditions and attempt to assert personal and group freedom.

Further reading

Toihiri, Mohamed A (1985) *La République des Imberbes* (The Republic of the Beardless), Paris: L'Harmattan.

——(1992) *Le Kafir du Karthala* (The Kafir of Karthala), Paris: L'Harmattan.

CAROLE M. BECKETT

translation

In a way all writing is translation, an attempt to interpret the meaning of life. But translation is not only a literary task but a historical one as well. It includes an interpretation of internal history and of the changing proceedings of consciousness in a civilization. In addition to translation, assimilation and exoticism are among some of the strategies Western scholars and critics use to accommodate or come to terms with alterity. Such representational strategies establish the perceived relationship between the West and the "other" as they illustrate the politics of power that are operative in those relationships. To this end, the "other" is sufficiently defined and explained within the Western matrix of understanding. Although translation used to be defined solely as the linguistic process that consisted of the transfer of meaning from one language to another, it has come to represent, in the wake of postcolonial studies (see **colonialism, neocolonialism, and postcolonialism**), the vehicle through which so-called "Third-World" cultures are transported or "borne across" to and recuperated by audiences in the West. In these circumstances, texts originating in or about non-Western cultures written in English, French, and other metropolitan languages come to be considered acts, or effects, of translation.

To "translate" means, literally, to "carry across," and this implies all other forms that carry the prefix "trans." It means not only transportation or transmission or transposition but also transformation and transmutation. Since all these activities come together in the specific context of African literature written in European languages, this literature can be considered as a form of creative or cultural translation. Translation therefore functions both as a critical and a creative activity in African literature. Even a cursory analysis of the creative use of European languages in African literature will clearly demonstrate the importance of translation.

Translation is significant in African literature in two ways. In the first place, translation makes it possible to explore the practice whereby texts are transferred from one language to another. The translator of an African literary text struggles to create communication and to find meaning in an otherwise impenetrable world of the "other." Second, cultural translation as practiced by African writers enables the landscape of the African experience and imagination to be transposed and transformed into an alien and often-dominant culture.

The first sense of translation has come to play an important role in the criticism and interpretation of African literature since more and more African work (in African or European languages) is being translated into other languages. Translators who translate African literary texts enable many people of different cultural backgrounds to know, understand, and appreciate African culture. However, the translation of African literary texts involves more than the possession of a certain linguistic competence. In addition to their linguistic competence, translators must be able to show proof of certain extra-linguistic abilities that consist in analyzing and interpreting the context in which the African literary text is embedded. The translator of Europhone African literature has to go beyond the European expression to the other culture, the other psychology that lies beneath it: that is, to reach the African context which is its focus. In other words, the translator has to make evident the African aesthetic which informs the work of the author and which is its driving force.

The second sense of translation manifests itself in African writing in various forms but especially in the author's transposition of African oral and traditional literary techniques of storytelling (see **oral literature and performance**) into the European written genre. For stylistic and ideological reasons, African writers tend to have been inspired by oral literature and traditions; this is evident in their use of oral elements such as imagery, proverbs, wise sayings, myths, folk tales, dramatic factors, and lyrical language.

African writers who translate their African languages to occupy the position that informs the European language, and who force the latter to refer back to the former for understanding and signification, also use translation as a strategy of literary decolonization. Obviously, the success of the effort to translate one's native language and to re-appropriate the foreign language in a meaningful way depends on the writer's ability to master both his/her mother tongue and the language of writing. It depends also on the writer's ability to construct a system in which context, culture, and language are harmonized.

According to Bassnett-McGuire, just as literary study has changed its nature and methodology since its development outside Europe, so notions of translation have begun to lose their overly European focus. Indeed, as literary studies have sought to shake off their Eurocentric inheritance, so translation thinking is branching out in new ways, because the emphasis on the ideological as well as the linguistic makes it possible for the subject to be discussed in the wider terms of postcolonial discourse. Oswald de Andrade, a Brazilian writer, has introduced a new metaphor, one that may be applicable to the African situation – this is the image of the writer as cannibal, devouring the colonial language in a ritual that results in the creation of something completely new. It is not difficult to find the creation of this new language in works by such African writers as Chinua **Achebe**, Gabriel **Okara**, Henri **Lopes**, and Ahmadou **Kourouma**, to name just a few.

Indeed, the emergence and continuing growth of postcolonial African literatures is bound to challenge and redefine many accepted notions in translation theory that has been debated and elaborated within the traditions of so-called Western humanism and universalism. As several critics have pointed out, postcolonial texts, frequently referred to as "hybrid" or "métissés" because of the cultural and linguistic layering within them, have succeeded in forging a new language that defies the very notion of a foreign text that can be readily translatable into another language. However, whatever definition one gives to translation, it is one of the primary means by which texts are made available in other cultures and languages. It should also be borne in mind that translation is not so much a discipline as an interdisciplinary practice that occurs in diverse contexts.

Further reading

Andrade, Oswald de (1970) "Manifeste anthropophage: le modernisme brésilien" (Anthropophagal Manifesto: Brazilian Modernism) *Europe*, March: 43–49.
Bassnett-McGuire, S. (1991) *Translation Studies*, London and New York: Routledge.

KWAKU A. GYASI

Tseggayé Gebre-Medhin (Tsegaye Gabre-Medhin)

b. 1936, Ethiopia

playwright and poet

Tseggayé Gebre-Medhin is probably Ethiopia's foremost playwright and poet. He attended church and government schools, where he wrote his first plays, *Harvest of Blood, I Am Also a Man*, and *The Sacrifice of Growth*. After commercial training, he wrote the plays *Belg* (Autumn) (1965/6) and *Yeshoh aklil* (The Crown of Thorns) (1959/60), and later *Yekermo sew* (The Seasoned One) (1965/6). He was very productive both in Amharic and in English (*Oda Oak Oracle*, 1965, and *Collision of Atlas*, 1977), and he translated canonical European works. His best poems are collected in *Isat wey abeba* (Fire or Flower) (1973/4). He obtained an LLB, and got a UNESCO scholarship to study experimental theater in London and Paris. He received many prizes, and became involved in research on African origins of theater arts, etc. After the 1974 revolution in Ethiopia, he assumed a more advisory role but continued writing. Since the end of the 1990s, he has been living in the US. In the year 2000, he was proposed as a candidate for the Nobel Prize for Literature.

Further reading

Molvaer, R.K. (1997) *Black Lions*, Lawrenceville, New Jersey: Red Sea Press.

REIDULF MOLVAER

Tsibinda, Marie-Léontine

b. 1953, Mayombe, Republic of the Congo

poet, writer, and editor

Marie-Léontine Tsibinda was born in Mayombe in the Republic of the Congo. Known primarily for her lyrical poetry, she published her first collection of poems, *Poèmes de la terre and Mayombé* (Poems of the Earth and Mayombé) in 1980. In 1981, she was awarded the Prix National de Poésie du Congo.

She has also received recognition for her short stories, many of which deal with women's issues. Her story "L'Irrésistible Dekha danse" (The Irresistible Dekha Dances) was a finalist in the eighth annual international competition for the best short story in French in 1996, and "Les Pagnes mouillés" (The Wet Loincloths) was accorded the Prix UNESCO–Aschberg. She is one of the editors of an anthology of Congolese literature published in 2000 and entitled *Moi, Congo ou les rêveurs de la souveraineté* (Me, Congo or the Dreamers of Sovereignty). Her university studies were in English, and she worked as a librarian for the American Cultural Center in Brazzaville before fleeing the political turbulence in the Congo in 1999 and eventually taking up residence in Benin. From 1979 to 1987 she acted in the Rocado Zulu theatrical company directed by **Sony Labou Tansi**. She is both contributor and editor for the woman's magazine *Aminata*.

JANICE SPLETH

Tsodzo, Thompson, K.

b. 1947, Buhera, Zimbabwe

novelist

Thompson Tsodzo's works derive from topical aspects of the social history of Zimbabwe before and after independence. It was as a student at the University of Zimbabwe that he published his first novel *Pafunge* (Imagine) (1972), a satirical novel on the experience of colonialism in the country (see **colonialism, neocolonialism, and postcolonialism**). The work was an attempt to move towards serious fiction in the Shona language (see **Shona and Ndebele literature**). After independence he also published satirical plays on social conditions in Zimbabwe, including *Babamunini Francis* (Uncle Francis) (1977), *Tsano* (Brother-in-Law) (1982), and *Rugare* (The Good Life) (1982), which decry moral decay, social stress, and the betrayal of the goals of the war of liberation in postcolonial society. *Shanduko* (Social Transformation) (1983) lampoons the discrepancy between the rhetoric of nationalism (see **nationalism and post-nationalism**), especially the discourse of economic transformation, and the corruption of the emergent nationalist bourgeoisie. Tsodzo's political satire is derived from his experiences as youth director in the Ministry of Youth, Sport, and Culture in the early 1980s. In other novels, such as *Mudhuri Murefurefu* (The High Wall) (1993), however, he is interested in the nature of precolonial African values, with a cultural nationalist stance reinforced by the author's experiences in the United States where he was a student in the 1970s. Tsodzo is also an accomplished Shona textbook writer and a senior government official in the government of Zimbabwe, where he has served in various positions including being the permanent secretary in the Ministry of Youth, Gender, and Employment Creation.

Further reading

Chiwome, E.M. (1996) *A Social History of the Shona Novel*, Zimbabwe: Juta.

EMMANUEL CHIWOME

Ṭūbyā, Majīd

b. 1938, Upper Egypt

novelist

A leading and prolific contemporary Egyptian novelist and short story writer, Majīd Ṭūbyā is known for his deeply portrayed characters and deliberately experimental style. Born in Upper Egypt to a Coptic family, Ṭūbyā moved to Cairo and served as a schoolteacher prior to studying cinematography at the Film Institute in Cairo. Ṭūbyā depicts intellectuals' sufferings, despair, and alienation in his novel *al-Hā'ulā'* (Oh, Them) (1976) through historical documents, black humor, and the fantastic. His fiction, set in the Nile villages, is concerned with the effect of folk tradition and superstitions on peasants as they struggle against illusionary forces as seen in his story collection *al-Walīf* (The Companion) (1978), which won him the State Prize for Literature in 1979. Ṭūbyā's fiction is usually interrupted by the intrusion of the unfamiliar into the normal order of events, while his characters are occasionally metamorphosed, as is

apparent in *al-Jāḥiẓūn* (The Bulge-Eyed) (1970). In his novels *Ḥanān* (1981) and *Rīm Taṣbugh Sha'raha* (Reem Dyes Her Hair) (1983), Ṭūbyā focuses considerably on women's melancholy as they endeavor to express their sexual desires. He has published eleven novels, five collections of short stories, two books of literature for children, one comic book, one book on the Suez Canal, and one book on the Egyptian fiction writer Yaḥya Ḥaqqī.

Further reading

Draz, Céza K. (1981) "In Quest of New Narrative Forms: Irony in the Works of Four Egyptian Writers (1969–1979)," *Journal of Arabic Literature* 12: 137–59.

KHALED AL MASRI

Tutuola, Amos

b. 1920, Abeokuta, Nigeria; d. 1997, Nigeria

novelist and short story writer

For most of his life, Amos Tutuola was perhaps the most controversial and underrated African writer in the English language. When his most important novel, *The Palm-Wine Drinkard* was published by Faber and Faber in 1952, it was welcomed and celebrated by European reviewers as an example of the primitive genius that the poets of modernism had been advocating since the 1920s (see **modernity and modernism**). When prominent British writers such as Dylan Thomas and V.S. Pritchett reviewed the book for prominent newspapers and magazines, including the *Observer*, the *New Statesman* and *Nation*, they were effusive in their praise of Tutuola's novel, its language, and imagination. They hailed what they considered to be Tutuola's untutored genius, his extravagant use of mythologies and fantasies, and his manipulation of the English language. But the response from African critics was generally hostile. In a review that was carried in the *West African*, one African reviewer noted that what Western critics considered to be Tutuola's genius and originality was nothing less than a translation of Yoruba ideas into English. For this critic, the novel should not have been published at all. After the initial controversy in the 1950s, Tutuola's work was treated with indifference and he was virtually excluded from African literary history. Although *The Palm-Wine Drinkard* had been published at a time when there were few African novels in the English language, it was quickly supplanted by newer works, most notably Chinua **Achebe**'s *Things Fall Apart*, as a foundational text of Anglophone African literature.

One of the reasons why Tutuola seemed to be an oddity in the history of the African novel was that his general and literary education was radically different from those of most of his contemporaries. The archetypal African writer, especially in the English language, was a product of the mission school and colonial university, often a student of English literature, or at least well read in the canon of European letters and a member of the colonial and postcolonial elite (see **colonialism, neocolonialism, and postcolonialism**). In contrast, Tutuola had a limited education, had trained as a blacksmith in the Royal Air Force during World War II, and was not a member of the Nigerian elite. It was precisely because he seemed to be indifferent to the world of other writers, especially their tense engagement with the culture of colonialism, that Tutuola appeared either untutored or extraordinarily imaginative. For early readers and reviewers, *The Palm-Wine Drinkard*, like the novels that followed, was located in a world of ghosts well beyond the concerns of everyday life in colonial and postcolonial Nigeria. For this reason, among others, his novels did not seem to fit into the dominant paradigm of African literature in its early period. More significantly, the structure and language of *The Palm-Wine Drinkard* and its very nature seemed at odds with what were then considered to be the major themes of African literature. At a time when most African writers were concerned with issues such as colonialism and its impact on traditional African society, the compelling forces of modernity and moderniza-tion, and the promise of decolonization, Tutuola's novel was a fantastic adventure of a hapless hero traveling in the world of the dead in search of his dead palm-wine taper. In addition, Tutuola's language was at odds with the patterns of language use at work in African literature during this period.

The novel was written neither in the proper English that more educated African writers were trying to emulate nor in the pidgin English common along the West African coast. Tutuola's language was his own creation. It was made up of broken-up rules of grammar, a limited vocabulary, unusual sentence structures, and neologisms.

The distinguished Welsh poet Dylan Thomas celebrated Tutuola's language as the example of a new English that would move the genre of the novel in new directions, but this view was not shared at home; for most of the 1950s and 1960s, Tutuola found himself and his work celebrated abroad and ignored or derided in Nigeria. But during this period he continued to produce novels closely fashioned after *The Palm-Wine Drinkard* and its now familiar quest motif. In *My Life in the Bush of Ghosts* (1954), he traced the journey of a boy traveling in the town of ghosts and the dead. *Simbi and the Satyr of the Black Jungle* (1955) and *The Brave African Huntress* (1958) repeated the quest motif perfected in the previous two novels, with the important exception that the main characters were now women forced by either compulsion or circumstances to undertake the journey into the underworld. In *Simbi and the Satyr*, the heroine enters the underworld because of the strange impulse that her life has been too comfortable and she needs to experience hardship and poverty in order to prove herself. The heroine of *Brave African Huntress* travels in a jungle of pygmies to rescue her four brothers.

In the novels published in the 1960s, Tutuola was drawing more and more from the books he had been reading since the publication of *The Palm-Wine Drinkard*. *Feather Woman of the Jungle* (1962) was fashioned after the *Tales of the Arabian Nights* and *Ajaiyi and His Inherited Poverty* (1968) reminded readers of Dante's *Divine Comedy*. Since these ghost novels seemed to repeat the structure of *The Palm-Wine Drinkard* they did not generate as much controversy as the first novel; indeed they were considered less successful in relation to it. For critics, then, Tutuola's reputation depended on his first novel with later works being dismissed as mere copies of a powerful original. But Tutuola remained undaunted by, or oblivious to, this critical neglect. His last novels *The Witch-Herbalist of the Remote Town* (1981), *The Wild Hunter in the Bush of*

Ghosts (1982), and *Pauper, Bawler, and Slander* (1987), were replays on the themes that had brought him international attention in the first place.

As critics continued to pay closer attention to Tutuola's works, especially in a period of reappraisal that began in the 1970s and continued in the 1980s, there was a significant rethinking of the sources of Tutuola's fiction, and this was crucial in the re-evaluation of his place in African literary history. Critics began to recognize the extent to which Tutuola had drawn from Yoruba oral culture and literature (see **oral literature and performance**), Christianity (see **Christianity and Christian missions**), and even the works of D.O. **Fagunwa**, one of the most important and influential writers in the Yoruba language. One could not discuss the originality of Tutuola's *Palm-Wine Drinkard* without considering the impact of Fagunwa's *Ògbójú Ode Nínú Igbó Irúnmalè* (1938), translated by Wole **Soyinka** as *The Forest of a Thousand Demons: A Hunter's Saga* (1968). In addition,

critics started paying closer attention to how the world of everyday life had been reinscribed into what appeared to be ghostly stories. Finally, the myth of an untutored Tutuola was undermined by recognition of the multiple literary sources that had gone into his writing, including the Bible and John Bunyan's *Pilgrim's Progress*. Unfortunately, Tutuola's reputation came too late to make any difference to his life and he died in poverty at the very time that his works were being celebrated as part of the African canon.

Further reading

Lindfors, B. (ed.) (1975) *Critical Perspectives on Amos Tutuola*, Washington, DC: Three Continents Press.

Owomoyela, O. (1999) *Amos Tutuola Revisited*, New York: Twayne.

SIMON GIKANDI

U

Ubesie, Tony Uchenna

b. 1949, Eastern Nigeria; d. 1993

novelist

Whereas Pita Nwana is given credit as the founder and "father" of the Igbo novel, and Frederick Chidozie **Ogbalu** is given credit for nurturing it through the development of Igbo language, Tony Uchenna Ubesie is indeed its creative genius. The most gifted Igbo novelist of the twentieth century, Ubesie's novels include *Ukwa Ruo Oge Ya Oda* (When the Fruit is Ripe, It Falls) (1973), *Isi Akwu Dara N'ala* (The Prime Palm Fruit that Falls on the Ground) (1973), *Mmiri Oku Eji Egbu Mbe* (Boiling Water to Kill the Tortoise) (1974), *Ukpana Okpoko Buru* (The Insect that is Caught by Okpoko Must Be Deaf: Okpoko is a ferocious bird that leaves a loud noise in its trail) (1975), and *Juo Obinna* (Ask Obinna) (1975). Ubesie's distinction as a novelist lies essentially in his stylistic innovations and thematic realism (see **realism and magical realism**). He brings a fresh awareness to familiar themes and discusses contemporary social and cultural issues in ways that show in the author a perfect understanding and acute perception of the varying alternatives that come with time. Ubesie's legacies in the art of the Igbo novel are in the four areas of language, humor, irony, and characterization.

Ubesie has an excellent mastery of the Igbo language usage, which makes his writing easy and fascinating to read. His sense of humor totally captivates the reader. His use of sophisticated irony leaves the reader musing about the motives of human behavior in complex situations. His authentic characterization plants the image of the protagonist so indelibly in the consciousness of the reader's mind that the reader continues to see the face long after finishing the story. His patterns for resolving human conflicts are neither forced nor melodramatic. The total effect of these in each of his novels is one of suspense, wonderment, curiosity, and aesthetic delight, all of which make the reader want to reach out for Ubesie's next novel. Some writers make us laugh once in a while by their amusing anecdotes, but Ubesie has a seemingly endless abundance of anecdotes that keep the reader laughing till the end of the novel. Ubesie's brand of humor is so effusive that it fills the reader with nothing but a feeling of recurring delight. These qualities are present in all of Ubesie's novels but he seems to have surpassed himself in his novel about the Nigerian civil war, *Juo Obinna*.

Juo Obinna, probably the best Igbo novel on the Nigerian civil war, is a skillfully crafted commentary on the phenomenon of the Biafran *straggler*, the loud-mouthed "we must fight to the last man" advocate who shows his bravery and commitment to the war effort by the unequalled dexterity with which he dodges conscription into the army. He is adept in military tactics without ever reaching any war zone. Ubesie creates him as a simple yet complex and pathetic character. He has a fantastic imagination and can effortlessly weave endless stories about his gallantry, fitting every minute detail of military maneuvers so that his audience cannot help but admire him as the incomparable war hero. His audience is always the womenfolk who adore him for his dare-devil adventures and his indefatigable commitment to the cause. "Biafrans" who survived the war will find in this character a revelation of sorts. He is the alarming ironic symbol of the people's delusion.

Whatever his theme, Tony Uchenna Ubesie is always consistent in his sensitivity to language and his geometric control of the subject matter. He is in the true Igbo narrative tradition, the story vendor and the owner of words. After nearly half a century of struggling to survive, Tony Ubesie seems to have restored to the Igbo novel what it lost in the era after *Omenuko* (1933) when it was eclipsed by the rifts and controversies over how to write or how not to write fiction in the Igbo language (see **Igbo literature**).

ERNEST EMENYONU

Ugochukwu, Sam

b. Nigeria

scholar and poet

Sam Ugochukwu is a professor in the Department of African and Asian Studies at the University of Lagos, Nigeria. A philologist and specialist in Igbo elegiac poetry, Ugochukwu has served on several government panels to design policies on literature and language teaching in the Nigerian school system. Generally respected by his peers as an erudite and brilliant scholar, Ugochukwu advocates and is committed to the promotion and use of African languages in literary creativity. Accordingly, he has published a substantial number of creative works, mostly poetry, in the Igbo language. His major works include *Mbem Akwamozu* (Funeral Dirges) (1985), *Abu Akwamozu* (Songs of Mourning) (1992), and *Akanka Na Nnyocha Agumagu Igbo* (Criticism of Igbo Poetry) (1990). *Mbem Akwamozu* and *Abu Akwamozu* are funeral dirges. Dirges (elegies) are a very important type of poetry in the Igbo culture. They exist mostly in oral forms (see **oral literature and performance**). Ugochukwu has devoted a lot of research and energy to the collection and documentation of Igbo elegiac poetry. He continues to identify the gifted oral performers (dirge singers) in rural parts of Igboland for data collection and preservation. The two

publications are part of the data he collected in the course of his research for a forthcoming book on *Elegiac Poetry of the Igbo: The Study of the Major Types*.

In focusing on dirges, Ugochukwu has played a very significant role in the development of modern **Igbo literature**. The collection of Igbo oral poetry, particularly elegiac poetry, has suffered great neglect over the years. Because elegies are about death and mourning the dead, they do not seem to draw much excitement and interest from researchers. Yet it is from them that much of Igbo praise poetry is harnessed. It is Ugochukwu's love for philosophy that has led him into conscientious collection, documentation, and preservation in written forms of the recitations and songs of rural chief mourners. *Abu Akwamozu* (Songs of Mourning) and *Mbem Akwamozu* (Funeral Dirges) now exist as important resources for scholars and teachers of Igbo poetry. In addition, he has subsequently published *Akanka Na Nnyocha Agumagu Igbo* so that literary critics, teachers, and students can have critical standards and models for assessing creative works, especially poetry, in the Igbo language. His devotion has paid off. Many students and young scholars have been inspired by both his creative and his critical works to engage in active collection and documentation of Igbo oral performances.

ERNEST EMENYONU

Ulasi, Adaora Lily

b. 1932, Nigeria

novelist

The Nigerian novelist Adaora Ulasi is primarily known as the pioneer of the detective novel in Nigeria. Educated in the United States, Ulasi has lived in Britain since 1976, but before then she was a journalist for prominent Nigerian newspapers and editor of *Woman's World* in Lagos. While Ulasi's novels reflect the influence of the detective genre as it has evolved in the United States, one of the most remarkable aspects of her novels is their setting in a colonial milieu rather than the urban world of postcolonial Africa. Her most popular novels, *Many Thing You No Understand* (1970) and *Many Thing Begin for Change* (1975), *The Man from Sagamu* (1978) and

Who is Jonah? (1978), involve the activities of Igbo rulers or prominent personalities and colonial agents such as district officers and traders.

SIMON GIKANDI

Umkasetemba, Lydia

b. c.1840, South Africa; d. c.1915, South Africa

prose writer

The disappearance of Lydia Umkasetemba from South African literary history cannot be better conveyed than by indicating her absence from three of the most important histories of vernacular literature(s): Benedict Wallet Vilakazi's University of Witwatersrand doctoral dissertation "The Oral and Written Literature in Nguni" (1946), Mazisi **Kunene's** University of Natal master's thesis "An Analytical Survey of Zulu Poetry: Both Traditional and Modern" (1958), and A.C. Jordan's *Towards an African Literature: The Emergence of Literary Form in Xhosa* (1959, 1973). The origins of written Zulu literature are usually ascribed to Magema M. Fuze's *Abantu Abamnyama: Lapa Bavela Ngakona* (1922) (translated as *The Black People: And Whence They Came*) (1979).

Even a literary and cultural historian of the caliber of H.I.E. **Dhlomo**, who was usually fastidious about historical facts, was also mistaken in tracing his literary origins in Fuze. The first person to indicate the importance of Lydia Umkasetemba was Harold Scheub, the American scholar of Xhosa literature. Umkasetemba's prose pieces, which read like folk tales and historical narratives, are to be found in Henry Callaway's *Nursery Tales, Traditions, and Histories of the Zulus* (1868). Her prose work is uncommon in its originality, its psychological complexity, and its cultural density. Given the development of the Zulu novel in the twentieth century by such serious practitioners as R.R.R. **Dhlomo**, Benedict Wallet Vilakazi, and Jordan Kush **Ngubane**, it would seem more likely that its origins are to be found in Lydia Umkasetemba rather than in Magema M. Fuze.

NTONGELA MASILELA

V

van Niekerk, Marlene

b. 1954, Caledon, South Africa

poet and writer

This Afrikaans author (see **Afrikaans litera-ture**) grew up in the Caledon district of the Western Cape. Her literary and philosophical interests led to theses on Nietzsche (at the University of Stellenbosch), and Lévi-Strauss and Ricoeur (at the University of Amsterdam), and she has taught at the universities of Zululand, Unisa, the Witwatersrand, and Stellenbosch. She made her debut with award-winning lyrical poetry in *Sprokkelster* (Gleaned Star) (1977) and the more satiric *Groenstaar* (Glaucoma) (1983), then changed to prose writing. The ten stories in *Die vrou wat haar verkyker vergeet het* (The Woman who Forgot Her Binoculars) (1992) were the preamble to her forceful multi-layered, often crude but hilariously funny novel *Triomf* (1994), named after the white Johannesburg suburb which arose from the debris left after the forced removal of the previously multiracial settlement of Sophiatown under apartheid (see **apartheid and post-apartheid**). *Triomf* is the story of an incestuous poor white family that plans survival strategies while awaiting the apocalypse they expect as a result of the 1994 democratic elections. The novel has won several prestigious prizes, including the Noma Prize for Publishing in Africa, and has been translated into various languages.

Further reading

Gräbe, I. (1996) "Brutalization of Cultural and Universal Values in Marlene van Niekerk's *Triomf,*" in H. Hendrix (ed.) *The Search for a New Alphabet*, Amsterdam and Philadelphia: John Benjamin.

ENA JANSEN

van Wyk, Chris

b. 1957, Soweto, South Africa

poet and writer

This South African author was born in Soweto and began writing while still at school. His first collection of poems, *It is Time to Go Home*, was published in 1979 and was awarded the Olive Schreiner Prize in 1981. He also writes short stories, novels, children's books, and easy-to-read booklets for adults who are learning to read English. A teenage novel, *A Message in the Wind*, was published in 1982 and in the same year was awarded the Adventure Africa Award. His short story, "Relatives," published in 1995, won the Sanlam Award for that year. His novel *The Year of the Tapeworm* was published in 1996. His short stories and poems have been published in the USA, Canada, Turkey, Denmark, Sweden, France, Germany, Italy, and Holland. A few of his poems have been anthologized, e.g. "Beware of White Ladies when Spring is Here" and "The Border" in Michael Chapman's *The Paperbook of South African*

English Poetry (1986). From 1981 to 1986 he edited the South African literary magazine, Staffrider, published by Ravan Press. He now works as a freelance literary editor and a fulltime writer. He has translated the Afrikaans novel, Vatmaar, into English (see **Afrikaans literature**).

ENA JANSEN

Vassanji, Moyez G.

b. 1950, Kenya

novelist and short story writer

The novelist and short story writer Moyez Vassanji was born in Kenya and raised in Tanzania. He relocated to Canada in 1978 and for ten years pursued the career for which he had been formally trained – that of a nuclear physicist. In 1980, he moved to Toronto and began writing his first novel, The Gunny Sack, which was eventually published in 1989. In 1982 he and his wife founded The Toronto South Asian Review, the Canadian multicultural journal. The Gunny Sack, winner of the Commonwealth Prize for the Africa Region, tells the story of a young Afro-Asian's quest for his identity and for the history of his community. The novel reflects powerfully on the burdens and benefits of memory, the problem of writing history, and the inevitable ambiguities of identity. His other works, No New Land (1991), Uhuru Street (1991), The Book of Secrets (1994), and Amriika (1999), take on more or less the same themes by telling stories about the Asian diaspora in Africa and North America (see **diaspora and pan-Africanism**). Vassanji's importance lies in his intimate probing of the idea of multiculturalism, his acute sense of history and narration, and his experiments with the novel form.

DAN ODHIAMBO OJWANG

Vaucher-Zananiri, Nelly

b. 1900, Alexandria, Egypt; d. Switzerland

poet

A Francophone Egyptian writer, Vaucher-Zananiri was born in Alexandria into an aristocratic family that had migrated several centuries before from Syria to Egypt. She studied in French schools in Egypt and became interested in theater; she later went to France to study drama. She also started working in journalism and married a Swiss journalist and economist. She returned with her husband, Georges Vaucher, to Alexandria, where she held a literary salon and headed an international club that welcomed literati passing through Egypt; she also ran an art gallery after the Second World War. Soon afterwards, she moved to Switzerland where she continued her interest in art and literature, writing mostly poetry. Her poetic output includes two collections published in the 1920s, Le Jardin matinal (The Morning Garden), Vierges d'Orient (Virgins of the Orient), and L'Oasis sentimentale (The Sentimental Oasis). À Midi sous le soleil torride (In Southern France under the Scorching Sun) was published in 1936, while Soleil absent (Absent Sun) was not published until 1972. Most of Vaucher-Zananiri's verse, including the poems that were published after she had left Egypt, carries the topography of her native country and has a romantic tinge to it. Besides poetry, she also published Voix d'Amérique: étude sur la littérature américaine d'aujourd'hui (The Voice of America: A Study of American Literature Today) (1945).

Further reading

Vaucher-Zananiri, Nelly (1974) Soleil absent (Absent Sun), Paris: Éditions St Germain des Prés.

FERIAL J. GHAZOUL

Vera, Yvonne

b. 1964, Bulawayo, Zimbabwe; d. 2005, Toronto

novelist, short story writer, and editor

Yvonne Vera is probably Zimbabwe's most prolific and leading female novelist, short story writer, and editor. She was born in Bulawayo and educated at Luveve and Mzilikazi secondary schools before proceeding to higher studies abroad. She acquired a doctorate, with a dissertation on prison literature, at York University in Canada, before returning to

Zimbabwe where she has worked as the director of the National Gallery in Bulawayo while writing fiction.

Vera's first published work is a collection of short stories entitled *Why Don't You Carve Other Animals?* (1992). In the collection, the writer displays a fascination with the role of African peasants during Zimbabwe's second Chimurenga (independence) war of the 1970s. As a creative writer, Vera's voice is particularly visible when she focuses on the tensions between Africans and Europeans, black men and black women during the war. Some of the stories in the collection, such as "It is Hard to Live Alone" and "The Shoemaker," bemoan the fact that after the liberation war not much has changed in the life of women, as most of them are forced into prostitution by hard economic circumstances. But other stories, such as "Why Don't You Carve Other Animals?", reject this pessimistic vision and insist that the imagination provides some space to experience potential identities other than those imposed on individuals by their suffering.

In *Nehanda* (1993) the reader is thrown back to the period of the first Chimurenga of the 1890s, when Africans in Rhodesia rebelled against the imposition of colonialism (see **colonialism, neo-colonialism, and postcolonialism**). In *Nehanda*, the author re-appropriates the male-dominated institution of spirit possession in order to project the heroic qualities of Nehanda, the great female figure in the revolt against white rule. *Nehanda* also reveals the author's desire to experiment with orality: through dreams, fantasy, and the folk tale mode, female characters are able to retell their stories of courage against the colonial system and, ironically, against the African patriarchal system. Vera's concern with questions of gender (see **gender and sexuality**), and with African women's desire for total freedom, is further manifested in *Without a Name* (1995). In the novel, a black woman named Mazviita is raped during the war of liberation only to emerge in post-independence Zimbabwe as a forceful voice demanding justice and accountability from the new government dominated by African men. Mazviita reveals the fractures inherent in the ideologies of nationalism (see **nationalism and post-nationalism**) and the liberation struggle by pointing out that black women were fighting to

recover their lost lands as well as their own freedom. By killing her own son, whom she carries on her back right into the town as an act of defiance, Mazviita (a name that can literally be translated into "You have done it") reveals the uncompromising nature of the postcolonial African woman. In symbolic terms, there is no guarantee that Mazviita's anger will in the future not be directed towards the nationalist government, which, in the words of Irene Staunton, has abandoned the "mothers of the revolution."

Yvonne Vera's third novel, *Under the Tongue* (1996), also foregrounds the national liberation war in order to deconstruct its deployment of women. *Under the Tongue* recognizes the paradoxical reality of the image of black womanhood that underlies nationalist constructions. Black women are depicted as "mothers" whose role is to beget nationalist sons. When black women fail to fit this stereotype, they are demonized as prostitutes. The image of the black woman as the depository of African culture, or its negative "other" (identified as the prostitute), is shown to be a form of authoritarian control of men over woman. *Under the Tongue* is a novel that is determined to "talk," and in doing so it reveals the bitterness, anger, and, ultimately, the truth that lies under the tongue of many black women in the novel. The novel reveals the harrowing experience of Zhizha, a girl whose life has been destroyed when her own father raped her. In the novel, the rape of African women becomes a metonym for the physical, mental, and spiritual abuse that black women have had to go through, not only under colonialism but also even after black majority rule. The reconstruction of the memory of rape and its subsequent vocalization by Zhizha suggests that black women can no longer accept being silenced by African men.

In her highly regarded novel *Butterfly Burning* (1998), Vera turns back to the culture of the 1940s in colonial Rhodesia, focusing on the life of Phephelaphi, a girl orphaned in clouded circumstances. Phephelaphi is attracted to Fumbatha, a man considerably older than herself. With Fumbatha, the heroine experiences freedom and independence even when this is not eventually fulfilled. *Butterfly Burning* covers a broad historical canvas and attempts to link the quest for freedom by the 1940s generation of women to their counterparts in the 1990s. In *Butterfly Burning*, women learn to speak out with a courage that disarms African patriarchy.

Vera has also edited a volume of short stories entitled *Opening Spaces: An Anthology of Contemporary African Women's Writing* (1999). The collection features stories of African women from southern Africa, East, West, and North Africa. In the preface to the anthology, Vera writes that African writing by male authors has "erred in its memory" for portraying African woman as passive onlookers in the drama of democratizing of African societies. The collection is meant to contain voices of African women who are prepared to stand up and be counted as heroic nation-builders. It is precisely because of the feminist dimension in her works that Yvonne Vera has evolved to be the most well-known Zimbabwean writer. Vera's works build upon the female literacy tradition started by such African female writers as Buchi **Emecheta** of Nigeria and Ama Ata **Aidoo** of Ghana. Vera's fiction reveals a desire to dismantle the ideological pretensions of nationalism (see **nationalism and post-nationalism**), revealing how, within nationalist iconography, women are considered second-class citizens. In her artistic works, Yvonne Vera revitalizes oral language (see **oral literature and performance**) within a written medium in ways reminiscent of Chinua **Achebe**'s success in *Things Fall Apart* (1958).

Further reading

Staunton, Irene (1990) *Mothers of the Revolution*, Harare: Baobab.

M. VAMBE

vernacular press

Introduction

To consider the importance of the vernacular press in the making of African literature is simultaneously to encounter the paradoxical role of Christian missionaries in both enabling and equally disabling the emergence of modern African literary sensibilities (see **Christianity and Christian missions**). It is vitally important at this post-colonial moment (see **colonialism, neocolonialism, and postcolonialism**) to formulate a proper and correct reconstruction of the African intellectual and cultural history in the making of modern Africa. The importance of intellectual integrity in reconstructing African cultural history cannot be possibly be over-emphasized in the context of the present profound crisis of Africa in relation to modernity (see **modernity and modernism**). The role of missionaries with the support of European imperialism and colonialism in initiating Africa into modernity cannot be denied. It is easier to criticize the imperial adventures and misadventures of missionaries in Africa than to specify their extraordinary contribution to the making of a "New" Africa. As Frantz Fanon has amply taught us, African cultural history is too complicated and too painful for quick and unreflective Manichean separations and judgements. For example, the missionary-turned-academic Clement Martyn Doke (1893–1980) is arguably the foremost South African intellectual in the twentieth century, partly because of his active participation in the construction of New African modernity (Jordan Kush Ngubane characterizes it as a "New Africanism") through the New African movement.

A recent crop of books by Michael Echeruo and Tiyo Falola and Philip S. Zachernuk on the intellectual history in the making of modern Nigeria (Nigerian modernity) gives prominence to the role of the vernacular press. Likewise too in South Africa in the late nineteenth century and across the first half of the twentieth century, the press played a similarly critical role. There is no reason for doubting that this was not also true in many other colonial territories or African countries. The vernacular press was instrumental in facilitating the historical transition from tradition to modernity. Three fundamental themes were at the center of this progressive movement from the "Old Africa" to the "New Africa": acquisition of an education propagated by missionaries, conversion into Christianity, and negotiation of European civilization.

The African vernacular press was also instrumental in forging the new articulations of resistance to European imperialism and colonialism, the very historical forces making modernities possible in particular African national contexts. It is because of the integrated nature of African experience at particular phases of the continent's history that the instance of South Africa concerning the relationship between the vernacular press and African literature can be seen as representative of what happened in other parts of Africa. While historical and cultural circumstances may have been different, there is no reason to believe that the relationship between the vernacular press and African literature in South Africa was not paralleled in many other African countries in the first half of the twentieth century.

Christian missions and the vernacular press

It was the missionaries of the Glasgow Missionary Society and the Wesleyan Methodist Missionary Society who founded the *Ikwezi* (Morning Star) newspaper in Chumi mission station near Lovedale in the Eastern Cape as an instrument for proselytizing the Xhosa nation into Christianity. Four issues appeared irregularly in English and Xhosa between August 1844 and December 1845. It was in this newspaper that the writings in Xhosa by the Xhosa themselves first appeared. These writings, written by the children of the first Xhosa converts, were unsurprisingly stories about their and their parents' conversion into Christianity. These authors were William Kobe Ntsikana (son of the prophet), Zaze Soga, and Makhaphela Noyi Balfour. It was the founding of the *Indaba* (The News) monthly by the Glasgow Missionary Society for African teachers and students that made a lasting impact on the evolution of Xhosa intellectual culture. It was through the monthly, published in Xhosa and English between August 1862 and February 1865, that the first incipient forms of Xhosa literary modernity emerged. Tiyo Soga (1929–1871), the first major modern Xhosa intellectual, published in its pages African fables, legends, proverbs, ancient habits, and customs of the Xhosa people, as well as the genealogy of Xhosa chiefs.

With these literary preoccupations, Tiyo Soga was forging an intellectual bridgehead from tradition to modernity for his students who were to become his intellectual descendants. Among these students were Elijah Makiwane (1850–1928), John Tengo **Jabavu** (1859–1921), John Knox Bokwe (1855–1922), William Wellington Gqoba (1840–88), Gwayi Tyamzashe (1844–1926), Pambani Jeremiah Mzimba (1850–1911), Isaac Wauchope (1852–1917), and Walter Rubusana (1858–1930), who two decades later were to make a cultural renascence of some sort in the newspaper *Imvo Zabantsundu* (Black Opinion). Like Soga, all these men were ordained African ministers of the Church.

Soga was anxious to impart to the students not only Xhosa customs and traditions but also a sense of African history as a counter-narrative to the European history that they were receiving in the form of the history of the Christian Church. It should be recalled that these students were learning classics (Greek and Latin literatures) from the Christian missionaries. Later on a remarkable debate occurred between the European missionary teachers and the African students as to the relevance of classics in the forging of modern consciousness and modern sensibility among the emergent Xhosa intelligentsia. This is among the reasons that made Lovedale such an important center of high intellectual culture in the nineteenth century.

The other importance of Soga beyond his launching of historical narrations of representation is that he appropriated the European essay form to interrogate the historical relationship between Christianity, racism, oppression, capitalism, and modernity. He was deeply engaged with the question of whether Christianity, European civilization, and modernity could have been imparted to the Xhosa people without the oppression and exploitation so endemic to capitalism. In these notations, which took the form of both essays and also letters to various newspapers, Soga was unrelenting in claiming that modernity was an unavoidable historical experience of the present.

In his writings, written in both Xhosa and English, Tiyo Soga left a rich cultural legacy to future generations of Xhosa intellectuals as to what their historical vision should be in their preoccupation with the making of African modernities. Soga was perhaps one of the first Africans to postulate the idea that the making of African modernities needed to be linked to the making of black modernities in the African diaspora. It should also be remembered that this political position was formulated by Tiyo Soga at the very moment Edward Blyden and Alexander Crummell were arriving in Africa. Crummell was to have an astonishing influence on Tiyo Soga's intellectual descendants. It was, however, left to William Wellington Gqoba, Soga's intellectual descendant and the first modern Xhosa poet, and later a newspaper editor, to negotiate the cultural space between the European and African forms of representations.

With the collapse of the aforementioned vernacular newspapers, the European missionaries founded yet another outlet, *Isigidimi SamaXosa* (The Xhosa Messenger), which appeared between October 1870 and December 1888. Initially editing it himself, James Stewart, the principal of Lovedale and publisher of Lovedale Mission Press, later had the foresight of giving the editorial responsibilities to the new African Christian intelligentsia. Many of Tiyo Soga's intellectual descendants, such as Makiwane, Bokwe, Jabavu, and Gqoba, at one time or another edited the newspaper. With the assumption of the editorship by Africans, the newspaper acquired a critical voice on the matter of the violent entrance of European modernity into African history. It also began a process that can be characterized as the secularization of the theologically shackled African imagination or imaginary.

With his translation of Bunyan's *Pilgrim's Progress* into Xhosa approximately two decades earlier and its serialization in the previous missionary newspapers, Soga had made the emergent modern Xhosa literary imagination largely preoccupy itself with theological matters, which were the fundamental and central aim of the missionaries. Within a decade of Tiyo Soga's death, the process of secularization of the modern Xhosa literary imagination produced significant critical essays, which are literary and philosophical, concerned with ontological matters rather than purely with things theological. There also began to appear extraordinary poetry about matters of existence, as well as protest poetry. Concerning the essay form, Elijah Makiwane ("Livingstone's Last Journals," 1 June 1875, and "Native Churches and Self Support," 1 August 1881), Gwayi Tyamzashe ("A Native Society at Kimberley," 1 April 1884), and

William Wellington Gqoba ("Notes from the Transkei upon Witchcraft," 6 January, 7 February, 7 March 1874, "Notes of Cases, from Fingoland Dispensary," 1 April 1880, and "The Native Tribes: Their Laws, Customs and Beliefs," 1 June, 1 July, 1 September 1885), are the major voices. Gqoba also started to write serious major poetry ("A Winter Scene in Fingoland," 1 August 1879). Other intellectuals like Pambani Jeremiah Mzimba concerned themselves with orthographic issues of the Xhosa language. With the death of William Wellington Gqoba in 1888, the *Isigidimi SamaXosa* newspaper collapsed. One of the reasons for the demise of the newspaper is that despite its achievements, the missionaries still sought to stifle its critical and secular literary voice in order to return it to theological matters.

The making of a literary tradition

When A.C. **Jordan**, author of the great Xhosa novel *Ingqumbo Yeminyanya* (The Wrath of the Ancestors) (1940), in the 1950s wrote a series of essays on the history of Xhosa literature in the journal *Africa South*, he praised William Wellington Gqoba as the dominant literary figure of the late nineteenth century. Discontented with the intervention of the missionaries concerning the content of *Isigidimi SamaXosa*, John Tengo **Jabavu** founded the *Imvo Zabantsundu* newspaper. Although the newspaper focused on political matters, it could not avoid the literary legacy initiated by Soga and expanded upon by Gqoba. In order to consolidate their thinking on cultural and political issues, the intellectual descendants of Tiyo Soga founded the Lovedale Literary Society and, in 1879, the Native Educational Association. Both organizations sought to facilitate the passageway of African people from tradition into modernity. As president of the Association, Elijah Makiwane made presentations, some of which were published as essays in *Imvo Zabantsundu*.

One of the cultural issues Makiwane grappled with was to what extent Africans would retain their "Africanness" when modernity demanded that they master English literary culture from William Shakespeare and Francis Bacon to John Keats and Alfred Tennyson. Would not this acquisition confirm the superiority of European cultures over

African cultures, something the missionaries considered self-evident fact? What should be the role of African languages and of traditional forms of literary representation in the context of emergent modernity? The consensus among these intellectuals of the Xhosa cultural renascence was that the English language had to predominate in South Africa in order for the African people to make a transition from "barbarism" and "heathenism" to "progress" and "civilization." In the process of grappling with these issues, Makiwane expanded the essay form beyond the attainments that Soga and Gqoba had achieved. These cultural and literary debates were spectacular in many ways. In the context of these debates, Isaac Wauchope in the pages of *Imvo Zabantsundu* published his biting poetry in Xhosa protesting the hegemony of European modernity in South Africa.

The Xhosa intellectuals were caught in the maelstrom of paradoxes and ironies so singularly characteristic of modernity. One other achievement of Makiwane is that he was the first African intellectual to write essays on the role modern cities in making modernity possible. It should be emphasized that despite these debates on the "necessity" of the hegemony of English literary culture as a facilitator of modernity, the monthly continued to publish literary contributions in both English and Xhosa languages, as it had always done. While these debates were occurring in the English language, the actual poetry and prose published in its pages in the Xhosa language were far superior to those published in the English language.

In *The Kafir Scholar's Companion* (1903), Isaac Bud-M'Belle (1870–1947), another member of the third generation of Xhosa intellectuals since Soga, observed the shifting literary practices and debates and recognized the role of African newspapers in facilitating the literary culture of modernity. Bud-M'Belle's book was a short history of vernacular newspapers in South Africa, from early missionary newspapers such as *Indaba* in the middle of the nineteenth century to those owned by the "New Africans" in the late nineteenth century, including C.N. Umhalla and Allan Kirkland Soga's *Izwi Labantu* (The Voice of the People; November 1897–April 1909) and Solomon T. **Plaatje**'s *Koranta ea*

Becoana (The Bechuana Gazette; April 1901–February 1908).

The person who made this dramatic shift in the late nineteenth century possible, despite the debates of the 1880s, was S.E.K. **Mqhayi** (1875–1945). Mqhayi made two incomparable contributions to the pages of *Imvo Zabantsundu*: he wrote modern Xhosa poetry in the traditional form of Izibongo that had no precedence in South African culture; and he wrote prose works whose complexity had not been attained before (autobiographies, novellas, short stories, biographies, articles, and essays). Mqhayi in effect completely transformed Xhosa literary culture. The serialization of his novella *Ityala lama Wele* (The Case of the Twins) (1914) marked a new beginning in Xhosa literature which was consolidated by the fourth generation of Xhosa intellectuals: Guybon Bundiwana Sinxo (1902–62), James J.R. Jolobe (1902–76), and A.C. Jordan (1906–68). With this novella and other prose writings, Mqhayi was in effect the founding moment of literary modernity, if not modernism itself, within the context of the New African modernity. It is because of this epoch-making event that later intellectuals like H.I.E. **Dhlomo** (1903–56) and Jordan K. **Ngubane** (1917–85) were to celebrate his contribution to South African literary history as marking a fundamental break between tradition and modernity. The year 1914 also saw the publication of John Knox Bokwe Ntsikana's *The Story of an African Convert* (1914), portions of which had been published in Xhosa monthly publications earlier.

A testament to the role the vernacular press had played in the emergence of a modern literary culture in South Africa was the 1906 publication of *Zemk' iinkomo maGwalandini* (The Cattle are Departing, You Cowards), a collection of the writings of Xhosa intellectuals and writers such as Bokwe, Ntsikana, and Gqoba collated from various newspapers. Another important anthology was *ImiBengo* (1936), put together by W.G. Bennie from writings in Xhosa newspapers and journals. What these collections show is that perhaps one of the reasons that the vernacular press played such a critical role in facilitating the emergence of modern South African literature is that intellectuals from Tiyo Soga to S.E.K. Mqhayi were from time to time editors of newspapers and journals. During his tenure for approximately two years as editor of *Imvo Zabantsundii* in the 1920s, Mqhayi used the newspaper to launch the literary careers of Jolobe and Sinxo, two major figures who were to dominate Xhosa literature in the twentieth century.

At least two of the three novels by Thomas **Mofolo** (1876–1948) were partly serialized in the *Leselinyana* newspaper (The Little Light, founded November 1863 and owned by the Paris Evangelical Missionary Society in Maseru), before they were published in book form. *Moeti oa Bochabella* (Traveler to the East) (1907) and *Pitseng* (n. d., but written in 1910) were read by well-educated Christian Africans as well as by those who were struggling with issues of illiteracy. There is no doubt that the works of Mofolo had profound influence on the development of modern literary consciousness in the Sotho nation. Although a novel like *Moeti oa Bochabella* was an allegory closely based on John Bunyan's *Pilgrim's Progress*, Mofolo's works attempted to open a secular cultural space for the nation relative to the religious space of the Sotho-translated Bible. This was one of the factors that caused the strained relations between Mofolo and the French missionaries who owned *Leselinyana* and the Morija Mission Press. All the novels of Thomas Mofolo were vetted for their religious correctness before they were published by the Press. This is the reason that although his classic novel *Chaka* was already written by 1910, it was only published in 1926 after many delays. Thomas Mofolo's biographer Daniel P. Kunene mentions that this is the reason he never subsequently engaged himself with literary matters after this traumatizing experience.

The French missionaries played both a negative and a positive role in the emergence of modern Sotho literature in the early part of the twentieth century, and this influence is evident in the problematic representation of the relation between tradition and modernity in Mofolo's *Chaka*. The ideological framework of Thomas Mofolo's fiction is constructed on Manichean terms as the unending struggle between African "barbarism" and European "civilization." It postulates the absolute necessity of the triumph of "enlightenment" over "darkness." In effect, Thomas Mofolo harnessed African literature to the civilizing mission of Christianity. It is not surprising that the next major

Sotho writer who followed a few decades later, although finding much inspiration in Mofolo, projected African literature in the direction of the then emergent African nationalism. B.M. **Khaketla** (1913–2000), novelist, poet, and playwright, founded his own monthly, *Mohlabani* (The Warrior; September 1954–April 1968) on whose pages politics were not displaced by literature.

The entanglement with colonialism

It was partly because of these entanglements with the forces of colonialism that Solomon T. Plaatje (1876–1932) founded his own newspaper, *Koranta ea Becoana*, as did John Langalibalele **Dube** (1871–1946) who launched his own newspaper *Ilanga lase Natal* (The Natal Sun) in April 1903. As H.I.E. Dhlomo noted in an obituary in 1932, there has been a general consensus that Plaatje is the most important New African intellectual in the twentieth century, especially with regard to the question of modernity. Although an earlier generation of intellectuals and writers such as Gwayi Tyamzashe and John Knox Bokwe were concerned with the orthography of African languages, Plaatje was the first one within the New African movement to examine this issue from a linguistic perspective. He was conscious that, without a correct resolution as to the proper orthography for the African languages, the makings of a great modern African literature he anticipated would be hindered. In *Koranta ea Becoana* he bitterly criticized the missionaries for proposing what he felt was incorrect orthography for the African languages.

It is in the context of these interminable linguistic battles that he published two books: *A Sechuana Reader in International Phonetic Orthography* (written with Daniel Jones) (1916) and *Sechuana Proverbs with Literal Translations and their European Equivalents* (1916). It is also in relation to these matters that he translated four of Shakespeare's plays into Tswana, including *A Comedy of Errors* (*Diphosho-Phosho*) and *Julius Caesar* (*Dintshontsho tsa bo Juliuse Kesara*). The last volume was published in the Bantu Treasury Series edited by Clement Martyn Doke.

When Solomon T. Plaatje moved from Mafeking to Kimberley in 1910, he founded a new newspaper, *Tsala ea Batho* (The People's Friend), also known as *Tsala ea Bechuana* (The Friend of the Bechuana). *Tsala ea Batho* would sometimes appear in three or four African languages within a single issue of the newspaper. With many of his writings in the new newspaper there began the prefigurations of the idea of a national literature. With *Mhudi* (1930) it is possible to argue that Plaatje sought to indicate how a "national" novel would be different from "regional" novels such as Enoch S. Guma's *Nomalizo* (1918), R.R.R. **Dhlomo**'s *An African Tragedy* (1928), and John Langalibalele Dube's *uJeqe insila kaShaka* (Jeqe the Bodyservant of King Tshaka) (1933; 1951). In contrast to these writers, Plaatje attempted to infuse a national consciousness into South African literary imagination. One other innovative contribution of Plaatje is that in *Tsala ea Batho* politics and literary culture engaged each other as well as history across its pages.

Although Plaatje never actually edited *Umteteli wa Bantu* (The Mouthpiece of the People; May 1920–) his name appeared on the paper's masthead with that of John Dube as co-editor in the first few months of its appearance Although it did not concern itself with literary matters directly, since it was preoccupied with political, social, and cultural issues, *Umteteli wa Bantu* had an inestimable impact on South African literary history. It was this newspaper that proclaimed in unambiguous terms that the fundamental national project that all African intellectuals had to confront was the construction of modernity. Previous to *Umteteli wa Bantu*, modernity had been theorized as merely the product of history, a historical process in which the African intelligentsia could intervene. The newspaper grappled with the nature of modernity in the 1920s in ways that have yet to be surpassed: it analyzed the industrial transformation of the country; it traced the emergent historical consciousness that transformed the "Old African" into the "New African"; it traced the genealogy of the New African; it established the connection between New Negro modernity and New African modernity; it theorized the role of cities in enabling the New African to emerge; it articulated the politics of African nationalism beyond tribal identifications; and it formulated the lines of intersection between politics and culture.

The contingent of "journalists" who worked for *Umteteli wa Bantu* was one of the most formidable cluster of African writers and intellectuals ever to work together: R.V. Selope Thema (1886–1955), H.I.E. Dhlomo, Allan Kirkland Soga (1862–1938), Abner Mapanya (c.1880–?), S.M. Bennett Ncwana (dates not known), H. Selby Msimang (1886–1982), Mark S. Radebe (dates not known), Richard Msimang (1884–1933), and Marshall Maxeke (1874–1928). *Umteteli wa Bantu* was a demarcating line in South African cultural history by arguing that literary modernism should be as much about national consciousness as about the literary devices of representation. The central figures on the newspaper were R.V. Selope Thema and H.I.E. Dhlomo.

Founded seventeen years earlier, John Langalibalele Dube's *Ilanga lase Natal*, in contrast with *Umteteli wa Bantu*, in its early years sought to establish the lines of continuity between the past and the present that had been ruptured by the entrance of European modernity into South African history. Given that it saw itself as descending from the heroic deeds of Shaka, it is not surprising that in its early years the newspaper emphasized matters of historical recovery, but it gave a forum to young unknown Zulu novices who later became major South African intellectuals in the twentieth century: the essayist and cultural historian H.I.E. Dhlomo; the journalist and political maverick Jordan K. Ngubane; and the scholar and poet Benedict Wallet Vilakazi. The essays, prose poems, satires, articles, and poems they published in the newspaper in the 1930s and in the 1940s made the newspaper one of the outstanding enlighteners of modernity in the twentieth century.

Concerning literary matters, *Ilanga lase Natal* by far surpassed *Umteteli wa Bantu*. From its inception Dube's newspaper announced itself as a forum for literary matters. Within eighteen months of its appearance, *Ilanga lase Natal* published Robert Grendon's epic *Pro Aliis Damnati* (For Others Doomed) which consists of 4,412 lines divided into twenty parts. It also published voluminously his other excellent poems. Generally, Grendon has unjustifiably disappeared from South African literary history. Another epoch-making event in its early years was the publication of excerpts from the writings of Magema M. Fuze (1845–1922) which were to be assembled together in a book called *The Black People and Whence They Came (Abantu Abamnyama)* (1922). A genealogy of the founding of the Zulu nation, though not wholly original, the book was the work of modern prose written in the Zulu language by a New African intellectual. H.I.E. Dhlomo was to celebrate it in his cultural history of the making of modern South Africa.

The third intellectual who featured prominently on the early pages of *Ilanga lase Natal* was Josiah Mapumulo. He has also unfortunately disappeared from South African cultural history. For approximately forty years, Mapumulo wrote columns in the form of short essays on the history of the Catholic Church and its philosophy, on the incomparable nature of Christian civilization, and on the importance of written culture. As though this embarrassment of riches were not enough, the newspaper published for decades the satires of R.R.R. Dhlomo. Though written in English, these satires were the training ground for the Zulu historical novels R.R.R. Dhlomo wrote in the 1930s. Lastly, the newspaper made available to the public over many years the short pungent miniature essays of A.H.M. Ngidi (1869–1951).

There is a fascinating symmetry of mutual admiration between the *Ilanga lase Natal* intellectuals in over a decade, and several acknowledge the influenced of their predecessors. Among his earliest writings for the weekly in 1932, Vilakazi pointed out that the newspaper had been instrumental in his intellectual formation, especially the meditations of Josiah Mapumulo. H.I.E. Dhlomo himself selected A.H.M. Ngidi as having been instrumental in the formation of Vilakazi's literary imagination. In 1946 in *Inkundla ya Bantu* (Bantu Forum; April 1939–November 1951) which he was then editing, Jordan Ngubane marked for praise Ngazana Luthuli (1874–?) who replaced John Dube as editor of *Ilanga lase Natal* from 1917 to 1943.

Also in the same newspaper in the same year of 1946, H.I.E. Dhlomo singled out his brother R.R.R. Dhlomo, who from 1943 to 1962 was the editor of *Ilanga lase Natal*, for praise. Ngubane wrote the first serious literary criticism to appear in a New African newspaper. In a 1941 critical appreciation of H.I.E. Dhlomo's *Valley of a Thousand Hills* (1941), Ngubane praised the poem as representing a new national spirit of modernity as well as giving expression to a New Africa. An appraisal of such serious intellectual content had not appeared on the pages of any New African newspaper before. Intellectual portraits of political and religious leaders had been appearing for decades, but not in the form of a penetrative literary appraisal of a brilliant literary work.

H.I.E. Dhlomo's achievements on the pages of *Ilanga lase Natal*, of which he was then an assistant editor to his brother, reflected his wide and amazing range of interests: he wrote a major theorization of literature, specifically the poetics of dramatic form; he contributed a cultural history of New African literature; he constructed an intellectual portrait of the most important New African intellectuals and political leaders; he appraised the possibilities of the Zulu language in creating a new modern national literature; and he formulated a cultural history of the New African writer and intellectual. In 1947, moving from theoretical preoccupations, he wrote a series of great prose poems, and then for over a decade before his death in 1956 he published a new series of essays. In one of his last important essays, written on the occasion of the golden anniversary of *Ilanga lase Natal* in 1953, H.I.E. Dhlomo made a retrospective evaluation of the contribution of the New African newspaper to the literary imagination of South Africa.

Conclusion

The short story form was to find its ideal representation in the 1950s in *Drum* magazine (March 1951–April 1965, original series). The monthly held numerous short story writing competitions, some of which were adjudicated by prominent writers like Langston Hughes and H.I.E. Dhlomo. It is not far-fetched to argue that Richard **Rive** was "discovered" by Hughes through one such competition. In dedicating his book of short stories, *African Songs* (1963), to the African American poet, Rive was taking cognizance of this fact. It was Langston Hughes who enabled Richard Rive and Ezekiel (Es'kia) **Mphahlele** to be aware of each other. This is one of the concrete manifestations of the unity between New Negro modernity and New African modernity.

The immediate effect of *Drum* magazine on South African literary history was in giving rise to a group of brilliant journalists and short story writers: Can **Themba** (1924–68), Henry Nxumalo (1918–57), Lewis **Nkosi** (1936–), Bloke **Modisane** (1923–86), Ezekiel (Es'kia) Mphahlele (1919–), and Arthur **Maimane** (1932–). Some of these intellectuals attempted to write novels during their exile period, although these were largely unsuccessful. The only member of the *Drum* writers who was successful at being both a novelist and a short story writer was Bessie **Head** (1937–86), who strangely enough during this historical moment of the hegemony of the *Drum* writers was marginalized from this intellectual constellation. This constellation of writers, including the brilliant photographers and outstanding musicians of the decade, has been retrospectively designated the "Sophiatown Renaissance." Another important contribution of *Drum* magazine as far literary matters is concerned was the brilliant intellectual portraits of New African intellectuals, writers, and leaders (religious and political), which graced its early years of publication. Both H.I.E. Dhlomo and Jordan K. Ngubane contributed portraits, respectively, of Benedict Vilakazi and A.W.G. Champion (1893–1975).

Although *Drum* magazine commissioned first-rate intellectual portraits, including those of African political leaders in other parts of Africa as well as those of African-American intellectuals and artists, as a forum of creative writing and intellectual thought it never reached the productivity and cogency attained by the publications whose genealogy has been traced here. In addition, it was the only publication that was monolingual, while most of the publications discussed above were trilingual. It is hence ironic that today *Drum* occupies a legendary status in South African cultural history. A new intellectual history needs to be written with the intent of repositioning the decade of the 1950s in its proper dimensions in relation to the intellectually and culturally stronger decades preceding it.

Further reading

Echeruo, Michael J.C. (1978) *Victorian Lagos*, London: Macmillan.

Falola, Toyin (2001) *Nationalism and African Intellectuals*, Rochester: University of Rochester Press.
Jordan, Archibald C. (1973) *Towards an African Literature: The Emergence of Literary Form in Xhosa*, Berkeley and Los Angeles: University of California Press.
Kunene, Daniel (1989) *Thomas Mofolo and the Emergence of Written Sesotho Prose*, Johannesburg: Ravan Press.
Masilela, Ntongela (2000) "Foreword. Foreshadowings in the Making of an 'African Renaissance'," in Bernard Makhosezwe Magubane, *African Sociology: Towards A Critical Perspective*, Trenton, New Jersey: Africa World Press.
Zachernuk, Philip S. (2000) *Colonial Subjects*, Charlottesville and London: University of Virginia Press.

NTONGELA MASILELA

video

In the 1980s, a video revolution dramatically altered the cultural landscape of most of Africa. The dumping of foreign films into the market, the deterioration of celluloid equipment, and the scarcity of the foreign currency needed to purchase film stock and absorb escalating production and processing costs made the production of local celluloid films financially untenable in most African countries. Film production, however, did not cease. A new generation of video filmmakers, with no prior film training or experience, exploited the availability of inexpensive and easy-to-operate video technology and began making feature films with video cameras. Almost overnight, in many African countries, especially in sub-Saharan Africa, Hollywood, Bollywood, or kung-fu films from Hong Kong were no longer the only options available to film audiences. Video films written, produced, exhibited, and distributed by local artists were suddenly being broadcast on television and projected in theaters and numerous small video centers scattered throughout many regions of the continent. By the end of the twentieth century, video stores and distribution centers were selling videocassettes of local productions and street vendors peddled them throughout major urban areas. To understand how video production developed in Africa and its impact on local cultures, we need to look at Ghana and Nigeria, two of the countries in which the video phenomenon was most dramatic.

Historical overview

The British brought film exhibition to the then Gold Coast as a mechanism for the promotion of colonialism (see **colonialism, neocolonialism, and postcolonialism**). The Colonial Film Unit, established by the British in 1939, distributed war propaganda and educational films in the British colony. After World War II, in an effort to create a larger, African market, the Unit turned toward the production of films in the colonies. To this end, Sean Graham established the Gold Coast Film Unit in 1946. Two years later, Ghanaians Sam Aryeetey, R.O. Fenuku, and Bob Okanta and Nigerians Awuni Haruna, R.F. Otigba, and F. Fajemism joined the Unit, and, under Graham's direction, made forty-four films.

In Ghana, after independence in 1957, Kwame Nkrumah nationalized film production and distribution and funded the construction of the Ghana Film Industry Corporation (GFIC), one of the most modern and complete film companies in all of Africa. Yet, despite Nkrumah's investment in the film industry, until the late 1980s more than 95 percent of all films shown in Ghana were foreign films. GFIC channeled its resources toward documentary filmmaking, producing during the forty-eight years of its existence over 200 documentaries and approximately 385 newsreels, but few feature films. After Nkrumah's initial efforts, no money has been allocated for either film production or exhibition by subsequent governments. Without investment, the state-owned celluloid film industry folded, and the exhibition and distribution of films increasingly became organized through private companies that imported and exhibited foreign films.

In the late 1970s and for most of the 1980s, the importation of video cameras and videocassette recorders enabled the development of a private amateur video film industry. Unlike celluloid films, videocassettes were easily imported into the country and duplicated privately, circumventing censorship boards and import regulations. Video recorders and decks, smaller, more readily available and far less expensive than celluloid film projectors and cameras, could be purchased in local shops or carried into the country. During this period, Ghanaian entrepreneurs exhibited pirated video copies of foreign films on 24-inch television screens and charged patrons nominal fees to huddle around privately owned sets. In 1979, Nii Atua opened Coconut Grove Video Center, the first video center in Ghana where video films were projected on to a screen. Others quickly followed. In 1987, the minister of information estimated that there were over 300 video centers in Accra alone.

In 1987, William Akuffo, an importer and distributor of celluloid films, premiered the first locally produced video film, *Zinabu*, to large and enthusiastic crowds at the Globe Cinema in Accra. Prior to Akuffo's *Zinabu*, Alan Jima, operator of Video City, had made a video film in Twi called *Abyssinia*, but the video was screened only in his theater. *Zinabu*, on the other hand, was widely available and so successful that the Globe ran showings three times a day for over a week and the film played at local theaters for months after its initial release. Socrate Safo is credited with producing the second Ghanaian video film, *Phobia Girl*, and in subsequent years, many others entered the industry. Video film production peaked in 1993, when censorship records indicate that fifty-two films were presented to the board for approval. Most of the video films were produced in English. Indeed, since Jima's video film, only one other film producer, Kofi Owusu, has sponsored two attempts to make films in Twi. The films, *Sika Sunsum* and *Kananna*, were successful but not as profitable as English-language films, which have the potential to reach a wider audience in and outside of Ghana. Most video productions are private endeavors. GFIC refused to use video to make films until 1992, and three years later the Ghanaian government sold 70 percent of its holdings in GFIC to a Malaysian investor, and the state film company became GAMA (Ghana and Malaysia) Film Company. GAMA owns and operates TV3, the first independent television station in Ghana, and television continues to be its top priority.

The history of film production in Nigeria is similar to that of Ghana. After Nigeria gained its independence in 1960, the Federal Film Unit assumed control over film production and, like its colonial predecessor, focused primarily on the production of documentaries and newsreels. In 1979, the Nigerian Film Corporation was founded with the intention of sparking film production in the country, but to no avail. Although television production was managed by the state, celluloid film production remained a private enterprise, organized by the filmmakers themselves. The 1972 Indigenization Act gave Nigerians exclusive rights for the distribution and exhibition of feature films to Nigerians and enabled the production of several feature films per year in Nigeria in English and Yoruba. The future of film production in Nigeria appeared promising in the 1970s as the country enjoyed the economic prosperity of the oil boom. But the declining price of oil in international markets and the implementation of a structural adjustment program in the 1980s brought celluloid film production to a halt in Nigeria.

Nigeria produced its first video film in 1988, one year after the release of *Zinabu* in Ghana. The first Nigerian films made on video were produced by Yoruba traveling theater artists who turned to video as a way of projecting their performances cheaply. In 1992, Igbo video production was launched by Kenneth Nnebue with the film *Living in Bondage*, and soon after other Igbo-owned production companies followed him. Two years later, Nnebue made the first English language film, *Glamour Girls*, and this trend continued among Yoruba and Igbo filmmakers who sought wider audiences for their films. A video film tradition in Hausa has also been developing in Northern Nigeria, but these films are rarely exhibited or sold in other parts of the country.

Production, distribution, and exhibition

Video features are shot with one camera, usually a Sony Betacam, although in the early years of the industry the first video filmmakers used VHS, Super VHS and U-Matic cameras to shoot their films. The film crew usually consists of a director, camera operator, sound technician, lighting technician, and one or two production assistants, and most films are shot in an average of ten to fifteen days. The equipment, camera, lights, and micro-

phones are rented on a daily schedule. Actors negotiate with the producer for their fees and the cast is comprised of between eight and fifteen members. In addition to all expenses incurred in the production and editing of the film, the producer assumes the costs of printing the cassette sleeves and advertising. No independent exhibition or distribution networks exist. Independently owned duplication facilities copy and market cassettes after they have been released in theaters. The film producer, who is sometimes also the film director, arranges for the screening of his/her films in the major theaters and small video centers. Without a regulated system, the pirating of cassettes and illegal exhibition create serious problems for producers.

Although Ghanaian filmmakers might have been the first to produce films on video, Nigerian video filmmakers have created an industry that produces more films, with far larger budgets, than their West African counterparts. Nigeria's population of over 120 million inhabitants guarantees a film audience far larger than that presented by Ghana's population of 24 million. Nigerian directors pay their actors and technical people more and can afford elaborate sets and the technical expertise needed to create special effects. Nigerians export their films to Benin, Togo, Ghana, Zambia, and South Africa, while not even Nigeria imports Ghanaian films.

Style and content

The video films adopt a melodramatic style and aesthetic. The video films of Socrate Safo are among the most popular video films in Ghana and representative of their content and style. Safo's film *Ghost Tears* (1992), one of the six highest grossing features, describes the devastating consequences of a husband's infidelity. Kwesi cannot resist the advances of his wife's niece, Esi, who lives with the family as a maidservant to Kwesi's wife, Dee. Esi, riddled with jealousy of and hatred for Dee, drowns her in the bathroom sink, and Dee's daughter is left to be raised by her new stepmother, who treats her like a servant. Dee comes back from the dead to avenge her death and protect her daughter from her evil stepmother. The conflicts among husband, wife, mistress, and daughter erupt when Esi overhears Kwesi apologize to his daughter for allowing her mistreatment and admits to her that Esi in fact killed her real mother. Esi is horrified that her crime has been revealed, and she hits Kwesi over the head and kills him. The daughter watches the murder of her father in horror, when suddenly the ghost of Dee enters the room and inhabits her daughter's body, driving her daughter to kill Esi.

In *Lover's Blues* (1994), Safo delivers a message to young women: beware of beautiful strangers. Sarwa is a young girl with a promising future. Her uneducated mother has struggled to save money to put her daughter through school, but when Sarwa returns home from school pregnant, her hopes are dashed. A rich and handsome man, Adu, has seduced Sarwa, but when he discovers she is pregnant refuses to marry her because his father has promised to send him to America if he vows to stay away from women. He insists that she must have an abortion, and when she refuses he promises to send her money when he can. Predictably, Adu never sends money, and so the film chronicles Sarwa's plight as a single parent. Her mother is hit by a car on an errand to the doctor for her pregnant daughter, who needs medicine. All alone, Sarwa cannot pay the rent and is evicted from her home. She struggles to pay her small daughter's school fees by working long hard days as an orange seller on the street. This harrowing tale is interrupted by scenes from Adu's life of wealth and prosperity, and the juxtaposition between what befalls a woman who bears an illegitimate child and what rewards the man who abandons his child receives presents a compelling case for abstinence. The stories converge when Adu befriends the young girl, not knowing that she is his daughter, and invites her to bring her mother to the house. When Sarwa and Adu recognize each other and Sarwa sees the luxury in which her lover lives, she is furious. She orders her daughter to leave; the young girl, confused and afraid, runs into the street, and, like Sarwa's mother, is hit and killed by a car. The film ends as Sarwa sobs over the body of her dead daughter.

As these plot summaries make plain, video films, like most of African **popular literature**, climax in didactic endings that offer lessons to their urban viewers. The video films tend to focus on family conflict, and despite the fact that they feature formulaic plots driven by high emotionality, the videos are extremely popular. It is estimated that between two and four video features are released in Ghana each month, and in Nigeria video films are produced at the rate of about one a day.

Further reading

Balogun, Françoise (1987) *The Cinema in Nigeria*, Enugu, Nigeria: Delta Publications.

Dadson, Nanabanyin (1995) "A Lookback on Ghanaian Cinema," *The Mirror*, 29 July–26 August: 11.

Diawara, Manthia (1992) *African Cinema: Politics and Culture*, Bloomington: Indiana University Press.

Haynes, Jonathan (ed.) (2000) *Nigerian Video Films: Revised and Expanded*, Athens, Ohio: Center for International Studies, Ohio University.

Meyer, Birgit (1999) "A Popular Ghanaian Cinema and 'African Heritage'," *Africa Today* 46, 2: 92–114.

Sakyi, Kwamina (1996) "The Problems and Achievements of the Ghana Film Industry Corporation in the Growth and Development of the Film Industry," MA thesis, University of Ghana.

CARMELA GARRITANO

Vieira, José Luandino (José Vieira Mateus da Graça)

b. 1935, Lisbon, Portugal

novelist and short story writer

José Luandino Vieira is one of the most distinguished Angolan writers and his life and works have closely mirrored that country's painful history of colonialism and decolonization. Born in Lisbon, Vieira moved to Angola as a baby and grew up on the outskirts of Luanda, the city that constitutes an important character in his works and the setting of most of his novels. Disillusioned with the settler and racist values and beliefs of his parents, Vieira became involved in nationalist politics (see **nationalism and post-nationalism**) early in his life and in the 1960s he was arrested by the Portuguese authorities and imprisoned for his activities against colonialism (see **colonialism, neocolonialism, and postcolonialism**). He was to spend eleven years at the infamous Tarrafal camp for political prisoners in Cape Verde. Most of his early works were written in prison and many of them, especially his collection of short stories *Luuanda* (1964) were repressed by the Portuguese state. It was not until after Angola became independent in 1975 that these works became available. In spite of the harsh conditions in which his works were produced, Vieira was recognized as an important writer early in his career. He was closely associated with important literary journals such as *Cultura* in colonial Angola in the 1950s. But it was the initial publication of *Luuanda* in the 1960s that gained Vieira a well-deserved literary reputation. The novel won the Angolan Literary Prize and the Portuguese Writers' Society Prize. Vieira is largely known as the novelist of the colonial and postcolonial city, and in novels such as *Luuanda* and *A Cidade e a Infância* (The City of Infants) (1978) he captures the hybrid experiences and speech rhythms of the cityscape. But Vieira's works are also memorable for their experimentation with language and narrative patterns. As early as *The Real Life of Domingos Xavier* (*A Vida Verdadeira de Domingos Xavier*) and *Nós, os do Makulusu* (We, Those of Makulusu), both written in the early 1960s but only published in 1977, he experiments with multiple narratives in order to capture the disparate and yet connected lives of individuals involved in the nationalist struggle in Angola. More importantly, these novels celebrate the hybrid language of Luanda with its mixture of various dialects of Portuguese and Kimbundu.

Further reading

Peres, Phyllis (1997) *Transculturation and Resistance in Lusophone African Narrative*, Gainesville: University of Florida Press.

SIMON GIKANDI

Vieyra, Myriam Warner

b. 1939, Guadeloupe

novelist

Myriam Warner Vieyra was born in Guadeloupe, but has lived in Senegal since 1958 when she married Paulin Vieyra, a cinematographer. Her fiction explores the lives of women whose assimilation into French culture comes into crisis because of their exploitation by black men. Her characters are adrift, in between cultures and places. Her first novel, published in 1980, *As the Sorcerer Said* (*Le Quimboiseur l'avait dit*) is narrated from the perspective of an adolescent girl from Guadeloupe who is abandoned in a mental institution in Paris. *Juletane* (1982) further develops the themes of madness and cultural identity. It tells the story of a West Indian woman who grows up in Paris and then follows her husband back to his home in Africa only to discover that he is already married. The betrayal unsettles her identity and leads to a progressive breakdown. Vieyra presents Juletane's first-person narrative as a manuscript read by another West Indian woman, Hélène, who is about to be married. Hélène examines her own life through Juletane's story. The double narrative structure has drawn a lot of attention from feminist critics. Vieyra is also author of a collection of short stories, *Femmes échouées* (Women Failures) (1988).

Further reading

Vieyra, Myriam Warner (1987) *Juletane*, trans. Betty Wilson, London: Heinemann.

ELENI COUNDOURIOTIS

Vincedon, Mirielle

b. 1910, Cairo, Egypt

poet

A Francophone Egyptian writer, Vincedon was born in Cairo of a Russian father and an Egyptian mother. She studied in French schools and did not show any interest in literature until the late 1940s.

She published in the local press before she left Egypt and settled in Paris in 1956. She is the author of two collections of poetry, short stories, and a novel. Her poetry attests to poetic economy and reflective depth. It revolves around existential concerns and the limits of language. Her first collection of poetry, published in 1953, is entitled *Le Dialogue des ombres* (The Dialogue of Shades); it contains poems in which the poetic persona is involved in a continuous search for its intimate self. Vincedon's 1957 novel, *Les Cahiers d'Annabelle* (The Notebooks of Annabelle) is set in Egypt and relates the fantasies and experiences of a boarding-school girl whose life closely matches that of the author. The novel is notable both for its mixture of fantasy and reality and for its use of the French that is spoken in Egypt.

Further reading

Vincedon, Mirielle (1955) *Le Nombre du silence* (The Number of Silence), Paris: P. Seghers.

FERIAL J. GHAZOUL

Vladislavic, Ivan

b. 1957, Pretoria, South Africa

short story writer and novelist

Born in Pretoria, South Africa, Ivan Vladislavic

lives and writes in Johannesburg. His volumes of short stories and novels – *Missing Persons* (1989), *The Folly* (1993), *Propaganda by Monuments* (1996), and *The Restless Supermarket* (2001) – have been met with critical acclaim and awarded prestigious local literary prizes. Among the themes that engage Vladislavic are those of public memory and space – the "monuments" of his short story cycle – during the collapse of the Communist bloc and apartheid South Africa (see **apartheid and post-apartheid**). Hallucinatory, surreal, and bizarre, his fiction breaks from realist (see **realism and magical realism**) conventions and is characterized by metafictional interrogation and self-reflexivity. This postmodernist (see **modernity and modernism**) aesthetic enacts a playful dismantling of the edifice of apartheid through deconstructing the material of language itself. Dismayed by what he perceives as slipping standards in the age of political transition, the hero of *The Restless Supermarket*, a retired proof-reader, fights a losing battle to impose order on linguistic experience, which becomes an extended metaphor of the fear of change as apartheid crumbles around him. Satirical and self-mocking by turns, it promises to become one of the classic novels of the South African transition. Vladislavic has also co-edited *Ten Years of Staffrider* (1988) and *Blank–Architecture, Apartheid and After* (1998).

MEG SAMUELSON

Waberi, Abdouraham A.

b. 1965, Djibouti

academic and writer

Born in Djibouti, Waberi is professor of English in Normandy, France. One of the few Francophone writers of Djibouti, Waberi's literary output includes: *Le Pays sans ombre* (The Country Without Shade) (1994); *Cahier nomade* (Nomad Book) (1996); *Balbala* (Balbala) (1997); and *Rift routes rails* (Rift Routes Rails) (2000). Like the Somali novelist, Nuruddin **Farah**, whom he considers to be a major influence, Waberi has constructed an oeuvre that closely scrutinizes his country Djibouti, and indeed the whole of northeast Africa, in narratives sprinkled with Arabaphone, Francophone, and Anglophone cultural references. Waberi has also published *Moisson de cranes* (Harvest of Skulls) (2000), a collection of texts written in response to the Rwanda genocide.

Further reading

Waberi, Abdouraham A. (2000) *Les Nomades, mes frères, vont boire à la Grande Ourse: poèmes* (The Nomads, My Brothers, Are Going to Drink at the Great Oasis), Paris: Serpent à Plumes.

FRIEDA EKOTTO

Wanjau, Gakaara wa

b. 1921, Gakanduini village, near Tumu Tumu, Kenya; d. 2001, Karatina, Kenya

writer and publisher

Gakaara wa Wanjau wrote and published works in Gikuyu for fifty-five years. His publications included short stories, a prison diary, a novel, songs and poetry, historical works, and political position papers. He promoted writing in African languages and began a series of books in twenty Kenyan languages for primary school teachers. During the last forty years of his life Gakaara ran a printing and publishing business in Karatina, Kenya. From 1947 to 1952 Gakaara wrote and published a newspaper, political statements, and political songs. He was arrested for these publications in 1952 and detained until 1959. In detention he secretly kept a diary that later was published: *Mau Mau Writer in Detention* (1986) (*Mwandiki wa Mau Mau Ithaamirio-ini*) (1983). The diary was awarded the NOMA Prize in 1984. Gakaara was again falsely charged, detained, and tortured in 1986. Human Rights Watch later awarded him a persecuted writer's grant. His novel about the 1982 coup attempt in Kenya, *Wa-Nduuta: Hingo ya Paawa*, was translated into English in 2002.

Further reading

Wanjau, Gakaara wa (1983, 1986) *Mwandiki wa Mau Mau Ithaamirio-ini* (*Mau Mau Writer in Detention*), Nairobi: Heinemann.

——(1984) *Wa-Nduuta: Hingo ya Paawa*, Karatina: Gakaara Press.

——(2002) *Hingo ya Paawa: Wa-Nduuta at the Time of the Coup*, transl. Ann Biersteker, Binghamton: Global Publications.

ANN BIERSTEKER

Watene, Kenneth

b. 1944, Kenya

playwright

Kenneth Watene was born in central Kenya and educated at Thika High School. In the 1970s, Watene was a student at the drama school of the Kenyan National Theater, where a number of significant Kenyan artists were nurtured during this period. It was during his tenure and training at the drama school that Watene wrote and produced *My Son for My Freedom and Other Plays* (1974), *Sunset on the Manyatta* (1974), and *Dedan Kimathi* (1974), the play that momentarily brought him fame and notoriety in the late 1970s. In *Dedan Kimathi*, Watene set out to provide an alternative portrait of Dedan Kimathi, the Kenyan freedom hero of the same name, but his representation of Kimathi as a weak subject obsessed with his own individual desires at the expense of the larger cause of freedom created a political storm in Kenyan artistic and academic circles. More significantly, it was in reaction that **Ngugi wa Thiong'o** and Micere **Mugo** wrote *The Trial of Dedan Kimathi* (1976), a play intended to present a "better" and more heroic portrait of Kimathi. On the whole, Watene's career seems to have been closely connected to the fate of the first and only production of this play at the Kenya National Theater.

GEORGE ODERA OUTA

Wāttar, al-Tāhir

b. 1936, Sedrata, east Algeria

novelist

al-Tāhir Wāttar was born in Sedrata in east Algeria, where he received a religious education before pursuing his studies in Constantine and the al-Zaytuna University in Tunisia. Known as a pioneer of the Arabic novel in Algeria, Wattar started his career as a short story writer. His first collection of short stories, *Dukhan min Qalbi* (Smoke from My Heart), was published in 1961. This was followed by two plays, two collections of short stories, and nine novels. In his novels, *al-Lāz* (The Ace), published in 1974, and its sequel, *al-Lāz: al-'Ishq wa al-Mawt fi al-Zaman al-Harrashi* (*The Ace: Love and Death in Terrible Times*), published in 1982, Wattar speaks of the heroic Algerian revolution against French colonialism and its major events (see **colonialism, neocolonialism, and postcolonialism**). He is mostly known, however, for his novel *al-Zilzāl* (1974), translated into French by Marcel Bois in 1977, and into English by William Granara in 1998, and his provocative short story, "The Martyrs Are Returning This Week" ("al-Shuhada' Ya'uduna hadha al-Usbu") (1980).

In his writings, Wāttar follows the social-realist tradition, believing that postcolonial Algerian authors have to play a positive and active role by committing themselves to the promotion of the values of socialism, as a means to contribute to the welfare of the Algerian people. His novels speak of such important social themes as agrarian reform and corruption, and provide vivid descriptions of urban poverty and suffering. Wāttar has served as the president of the Algerian Writers' Association, al-Jahidhiya, and editor of its literary journal *al-Tabyyin*.

Further reading

Wāttar, al-Tāhir (1980) *'Urs Baghl* (A Mule's Wedding), Algiers: SNED.

ZAHIA SMAIL SALHI

West African literature in English

The development of West African literature in English is a by-product of British colonization and the interplay of cultures and ideas. Colonialism may have destabilized cultural life in the region but it succeeded in transforming literary cultures in diverse ways. The introduction of English as an official language in the region diminished the importance of local vernaculars, yet literacy in English inspired new forms of literature that coexisted with the dominant cultural traditions of the spoken arts. West African literature in English has been greatly enriched by the intersection of these different literatures. Its trajectory dates as far back as the eighteenth century when literate West Africans in Europe used the English language to argue against slavery and invent their personal lives as literature. To link this diasporic literature to the literature on the continent is to uncover the roots of some of the common assumptions about literary production that have become part of our conception of literature in the twentieth century. The prevailing perception of African literature as a production of knowledge began almost from the moment Africans began to write.

Eighteenth-century forerunners

Early West African writers in Europe wrote about their lives and against slavery while at the same time revealing perceptions shaped by the Enlightenment ideas of their time. Ottobah **Cuguano**'s treatise on slavery and Olaudah **Equiano**'s autobiography inaugurated a double vision and consciousness in literature that exists in various shades in modern West African literature. Equiano's narrative in particular began a tradition of lively autobiographical writing, part literary and historical, that still continues in African-American and West African literature. Written from the actual experience of slavery, the two texts stand in a similar but different relation to the letters of Philip Quaque and the diaries of Antera Duke, both written in West Africa around the same time but from different contexts. Though Quaque was never a transported slave, he was the product of a particular Afro-European education in the era of the slave trade and suffered similar alienations. As the first African missionary to be educated in England, Quaque's letters represent the first narrative of alienation in West African literature. On the other hand, the diaries of Antera Duke, an eighteenth-century slave-trading chief in Southern Nigeria, reveal different relations between European merchants and African traders. Duke's appropriation of the English language for chronicling trading transactions and everyday coastal life reveals a domestication of the language that anticipates the development of West African pidgin and the various creative manipulations of English in twentieth-century African literature. Though these trends in literary production resurfaced in the flowering of creative literature in the twentieth century, it was a different Afro-European literary discourse that dominated literary culture in the nineteenth century.

Political, historical, and fictional writing in the nineteenth century

The emergence of political and historical writing during the nineteenth century is the direct result of two major historical events of the time. The resettlements of European-oriented Africans in Sierra Leone (1787) and Liberia (1822) helped to shape intellectual and literary life in the region. The combined talents and energies of a varied and mixed population produced the most significant body of writing in the nineteenth century. Excluded and alienated from their Euro-American worlds, diasporic intellectuals in West Africa worked to produce new knowledge about Africa through their ethnographic, historical, and political writing. Africanus Horton (1835–83), Alexander Crummel (1821–98), and Edward Blyden (1832–1912) explored questions of race, culture, identity, and nationalism in very influential texts. Though their writing sometimes revealed an ambivalence towards Africa, it projected a larger concept of Africa that still remains a vision.

Indigenous West African writers moved these diasporic ideas in other directions. They validated their cultures through their writing but were equally keen to access the fruits of British education. J.E. **Casely Hayford**, the most indebted to Blyden's idea of racial and cultural uniqueness, combined fiction and cultural theory as he explored Ghana's culture and modernity in the nineteenth century. His novel *Ethiopia Unbound* (1911) wrestles more with making Western knowledge native to Africa than with negating the ongoing modernity of the period. Other writers of the period cut similar paths, negotiating the new context and satirizing the pretensions of the educated elite. Kobina **Sekyi**'s *The Blinkards* (1974) actually moves beyond satire to incorporate the local vernacular, dramatizing a dual linguistic reality in Ghana and showing its creative possibilities. Thus in spite of Blyden's influence in the region, his negritude perspectives did not take solid roots and had to wait until the 1930s to resurface in a different context among French colonial students in Paris. In English-speaking West Africa, literature in the 1930s was preoccupied with the nature and quality of colonial modernity. Two poetry collections, R.E.G. Armattoe's *Between the Forest and the Sea* (1950) and *Deep Down in the Black Man's Mind* (1954), were the most significant works, though Gladys **Casely Hayford**'s experimentation with krio poetry was a new and fresh development.

Within the region, different political and social configurations were creating conditions that would marginalize these poets and bring other literary forms to prominence. The return of Nnamdi Azikwei and Kwame Nkrumah from the United States and their impact on politics widened the scope and style of nationalist agitation in the region. Azikwei's founding of *The West African Pilot* in 1937 and his book *Renascent Africa* (1937) added a vigorous and competitive edge to journalism and nationalist thought in the region. It was the proliferation of newspapers and journals in the popular press and in the universities that prompted the link between nationalist thinking and literary production. *The West African Review, The Africa Guardian, The Nigerian Magazine, The Gold Coast Leader, The Horn*, and *Black Orpheus* all saw the development of African literature as part of the ongoing nationalist agenda. The link produced a heterogeneous crop of literary works that can all be linked, however remotely, to the nationalist agitation of the period. Amos Tutuola's first novel, *The Palm-Wine Drinkard* (1952), with themes, motifs, and literary resources from Yoruba folkloric material, may be seen as part of the cultural nationalism of the time in spite of its essentially apolitical content.

The growth of popular literature in Nigeria and Ghana during this time was more a phenomenon of the growth of urban populations and a rising literate and commercial class than a direct offshoot of nationalist agitation. The producers of this literature shared similar social contexts and vocabulary with their audience, and their focus on themes of love, marriage, and religion mirrored the confusions and upheavals of the new modern contexts. Their attempts to bend the accents and registers of English to generate new local meanings have precedents in the earlier works of Antera Duke and Sekyi and anticipate later mediations in the fiction and plays of most West African writers of the 1950s and 1960s. The nationalist thrust of literature during this period also coexisted with the rise of women's voices even at this early period. R.T. Obeng's 1941 novel, *Eighteen Pence*, broaches the subject uneasily when it locates the emergence of the new modern woman in the general disruption of traditional values. But Mabel Dove **Danquah**'s short stories published in newspapers from 1947 to 1962 reverse Obeng's perspectives by linking the oppression of traditional systems and the superficially embraced modern order to women's subjugation. Her stories attack both traditional and modern worlds as they explore the phenomenon of the new woman of the times. Adelaide **Casely Hayford**'s short story "Mista Courifa" and her memoirs, published in the *Africa Guardian* of 1954, cast a similar critical eye on the new society from the perspective of the woman and raise issues about gender and modernity that are still pertinent in the writing of contemporary women.

All these literary and perceptual trends aided the flowering of the novel genre in the 1950s. The novel's rise and development transformed literary production in the entire region. Its ability to expose social conditions and at the same time invent new realities made it suitable not just for providing new knowledge about Africa but also for imagining the modern community of the nation. **Achebe**'s historical novels, *Things Fall Apart* (1958) and *Arrow of God* (1964), imagined the colonial encounter from the perspective of a precolonial Igbo world. In an unprecedented re-creation of the English language he constructed a fictional world whose physical and cosmic space, rhythms and accents made it a credible community for the struggles he explored. Though he was sympathetic to these communities he was also alert to the weaknesses that made them susceptible to conquest. His novels thus present the dynamic nature of acculturation and the modern conditions they generate. His writing is in this sense different from his contemporaries: Onuora **Nzekwu**, whose novels remain trapped in ethnographic explanations, and William **Conton**, whose only novel, *The African* (1960), focuses merely on the political intrigues of the new elite.

Achebe's fiction inaugurated a tradition of writing in which the English language was bent in various creative ways to evoke indigenous worlds and their vocabulary, registers, and rhythms of speech. The 1960s were in this sense revolutionary in inspiring the confidence to wrest the English language from its power base in Standard English. The new creative release generated a proliferation of novels, plays, and short stories during this period. T.M. **Aluko**'s three novels attempted to recreate a precolonial Yoruba society, though without the political thrust and the linguistic virtuosity of Achebe's fictions. In Sierra Leone Abioseh **Nicol**'s *The Truly Married Women and Other Stories* (1965) portrayed Creole society in insightful ways, and in Nigeria Elechi **Amadi**'s novels examined relations between gods and men in simple but elegant prose. Gabriel **Okara**'s novel, *The Voice* (1964), was the only text to have moved beyond this style of writing to reproduce a vernacular syntax in English prose, but the novel's language does not quite cohere with its subject and has thus not been influential in the region. The only woman novelist to use the novel form during this period found a style for representing a woman-centered world and its forms of communication and bonding. **Nwapa**'s *Efuru* (1966) also inaugurated a feminist appropriation of the sea goddess as myth, generating a counter-metaphor, which has been extended in women's writing in the region.

More than their linguistic impact, Achebe's novels created a context of critical commentary which has influenced the reception of novels in the region and authorized a regional canon. His constant linking of African writing with the emergence of the nation created a political focus for the novel around the allegory of the nation. Yet the subject of national emergence was explored in different, ambivalent, and contradictory ways throughout the 1960s. **Soyinka**'s play, *A Dance of the Forests* (1983) was the first to warn against the illusion that freedom and nationhood came inevitably with decolonization. Its highly symbolic action pits the moment of independence against a past historical cycle and reveals that freedom would be a perilous and moral choice in the face of division, confusion of values, and corruption. Achebe's *No Longer at Ease* (1960) and *A Man of the People* (1967) almost in fulfillment of this vision flay the modern nation with devastating satire, revealing its political, moral, and cultural corruption. In the late 1960s, civil war in Nigeria and chaotic destabilization of national governments in the region spawned only an intense masochistic flaying of the modern nation. The novels of this period are distinguished by their different artistic transgressions of the nation and representations of its corruption. While novels like **Okephwo**'s *The Victims* (1970) and *The Last Duty* (1981) focused on the civil war and dismemberment in Nigeria, **Armah**'s *The Beautyful Ones Are Not Yet Born* (1968) focused on the perversion of the national idea itself. In all the other novels of the period the pollution that engulfs politics, culture, and morality is characterized in repulsive images of decay, filth, and shit, deliberately presented to assault the senses. Though these images often exist in tension with a visionary ideal, the pollution appears also to overwhelm the potential of vision. Thus *A Man of the People* hints at a repetitive cycle when the young narrator begins to sound and act like the older corrupt politician. The frustration of Soyinka's interpreters is only slightly less deadening than the pathological withdrawal of **Armah**'s Teacher, and there is little to choose between the madness of Kofi **Awoonor**'s Amamu in *This Earth My Brother* (1971) and the total disorientation of Baako in Armah's *Fragments* (1970). Against these privileged male interpreters, **Aidoo**'s *Anowa* (1970) presents a different configuration of the nation that challenges the fundamental constructions of Achebe's precolonial worlds. In its emphasis on women and slaves and its revision of gender relations it introduces feminist perspectives that challenge Achebe's reconstruction of precolonial society. Aidoo's play should indeed be seen in historical terms as expanding the perspectives of Mabel Dove Danquah and Adelaide Casely Hayford, who had both sought to place women in a changing world. Danquah's view of the new woman of the 1940s as powerful and masculine is reinterpreted within a national context as power within a shared creativity between man and woman. This is a perspective which Aidoo herself explores in several dimensions in later works as she struggles with modernity, postcoloniality, and gender.

While the novel lent itself to the invention of the nation, the poetry of the time explored a diversity of themes, often linking in a single anthology poems celebrating a rich culture and poems castigating an emerging political elite. Most of the poetry of this period reveals paradoxical moods in which the perverted present is seen through a visionary ideal. Poets still looked to the past for a visionary perspective on the present, even though myths of the nation dominated the 1960s. For Ghanaian poets Kwesi **Brew** and Kofi Awoonor, myths of the past are what mediate a chaotic present. Brew's *Shadows of Laughter* (1968) and Awoonor's *Rediscovery* (1964) and *Night of My Blood* (1971) all project contrasting moods of the present and past. What distinguishes Awoonor's poetry, even in its early stage, is its ability to exploit the tones, rhythms, and music of the traditional oral poetry of his Ewe community. **Okigbo**'s *Labyrinths* (1971) similarly holds invocations for spiritual renewal and critiques of power simultaneously, and though Soyinka reconstructs the myth of Ogun in *Idanre and Other Poems* (1967) as a visionary paradigm for examining postcolonial society, the collection still hints at the violence and chaos of the civil war and foreshadows the prison poems of *A Shuttle in the Crypt* (1972). In the 1970s and 1980s, new and younger poets emerged with diverse and revolutionary visions of poetry and the function of the poet. Atukwei **Okai**'s *Lorgorigi Logarithms and Other Poems* (1974), Niyi **Osundare**'s *The Eye of the Earth* (1986) and *Waiting Laughters* (1991), Kofi **Anyidoho**'s *A Harvest of Dreams* (1985) and *Earth Child* (1985), and Tanure **Ojaide**'s *The Blood of Peace* (1991) harnessed various resources of oral poetry to express their disillusion and reinvent new ways of exploring the contemporary scene.

The early drama of the period derived a great many of its themes from the domestic worlds of family, marriage, and relationships and was much more confident in borrowing from popular and oral traditions of the region. Soyinka's plays *The Trials of Brother Jero* (1964) and *The Lion and the Jewel* (1963) owed a lot of their vitality and popular

appeal to the music and drama of the new Africanized churches and the theater traditions of Hubert Ogunde, which combined varieties of song, dance, and mime with European and African music. Soyinka's plays of the 1960s are equally dominated by themes of politics and cultural nationalism and by a search for a visionary construct of the nation. The myth of Ogun still functions in social criticism, though in the later drama rituals (associated with Ogun) become the main action. *The Strong Breed* (1969), *The Road* (1965), and *Death and the King's Horseman* (1975) all exploit rituals of mediation to explore the idea of the artist as a visionary and mediator. Soyinka's contemporary J.P. **Clark-Bekederemo** presented contrasting perspectives in his poetry and prose. While his poems project the modern subject as suspended between European and African values, his plays focus almost entirely on the collective beliefs of his Ijaw community and their rupture as a result of individual opposition and tension The plays produced in Ghana during this period focus less on ritual and tradition and more on relationships and communication within the family. The major playwrights, J.C. **De Graft**, Efua **Sutherland**, and Ama Ata Aidoo, were all influential in the development of theater traditions in Ghana. Sutherland's *Edufa* (1967) and *Foriwa* (1967) explore familiar subjects in novel ways, combining both European and traditional forms, and Aidoo's *Dilemma of a Ghost* (1965) was the first work to probe the impact of the Atlantic slavery on the psyche. In their different ways these playwrights exploited aspects of the oral tradition in their drama, though Sutherland's *The Marriage of Anansewa* (1975) was the most experimental in its transposition of an Ananse tale into a dramatic form. The drama of the 1970s and 1980s, represented mostly by the work of Femi **Osofisan**, Bode **Sowande**, and Tess **Onwueme**, provided dynamic political perspectives and innovative theater that both dialogued with and challenged the work of the older dramatists.

Because the novel and the nation were continually linked in both creative and critical literature, the failure of nation-building throughout the region occasioned a reorienting of theme, mood, and forms of narrative in the novel. Writers were forced to examine both the concept of the nation and the function of art in times of political turmoil. A number of them had been actively involved in the politics of the Nigerian civil war. Okigbo fought and died fighting for Biafra. Achebe was an ambassador for Biafra. Soyinka was detained by the federal government, and Armah was already living outside Ghana. Soyinka's prison notes in *The Man Died* (1972) signaled a new vision of the artist as a force for social change, and *Season of Anomy* (1973) enacts such a possibility and at the same time reveals the creative and destructive possibilities of such a force. In Armah's novels of the period, disenchantment led rather to a broader concept of community and a search for core values of precolonial Africa in both *Two Thousand Seasons* (1973) and *The Healers* (1979). From a different perspective, Achebe's *Anthills of the Savannah* (1987) enacts the failure of the nation but creates a parallel narrative that interrogates its assumptions in different contending voices. Though the novel still looks to the past of legend and mythology for illumination, it eschews those certainties which would conflate nationhood inevitably with freedom.

As older writers re-examined earlier perspectives and forms, other new and often competing ways of inventing the national story were emerging, challenging existing paradigms and reinventing new narrative forms. **Okri**'s *The Famished Road* (1991) situates itself within existing discourses of the nation yet charts a unique narrative. Rather than dramatize the nation's emergence from its past history, Okri focuses on its presentness as alone the nucleus of its future possibility. His discursive use of a protagonist who straddles real and fantastic worlds as well as conscious and unconscious states allows him to explore this dual possibility. Almost in an opposite direction to Okri yet harnessing a similar conflation of the real and the fantastic, Syl **Cheney-Coker**'s *The Last Harmattan of Alusine Dunbar* (1990) charts the evolution of Sierra Leone from ex-slave colony to the chaos of a modern nation. Its combination of historical writing, indigenous narrative, and the supernatural present alternative historical perspectives that link it to the tradition of historical writing begun by the Reverend Samuel Johnson in the nineteenth century.

The most spectacular challenge to existing national narratives has been the proliferation of writing by women. Aidoo's *Our Sister Killjoy* (1979) continues a tradition of female self-construction begun in Buchi **Emecheta**'s *Second-Class Citizen* (1974) but extends the context of definition to include the entire modern world. Emecheta's *The Joys of Motherhood* (1979) and Zaynab Akali's *The Stillborn* (1988) both tackle unequal gender constructions that still determine women's lives in the modern nation. West African women's writing, particularly in the 1980s and 1990s, has focused more specifically on women's negotiation of changing social and cultural contexts. Writers have been forthright in tackling intimate issues of sexuality, conjugal violence, marriage, divorce, and polygamy. Aidoo's *Changes* (1991) validates these areas of women's lives as equally pertinent in the discourse of the nation. In the 1980s and 1990s a number of women turned to poetry (a genre dominated by male writers) as they explored themes in politics, exile, personal relationships, and modernity. Aidoo brought out two volumes of poetry, Molara Ogundipe-Leslie published *Sew the Old Days and Other Poems* (1985), and Abena Busia produced *Testimonies of Exile* (1990). If the contemporary scene is any indication of future direction in literature, then women's voices will be heard even more in the next decades.

Further reading

Curtin, P. (1967) "Philip Quaque," in P. Curtin (ed.) *Africa Remembered*, Madison: University of Wisconsin Press.

Forde, D. (ed.) (1957) "The Diaries of Antera Duke," in D. Forde (ed.) *Efik Traders of Old Calabar*, London: Oxford University Press.

Griffiths, G. (2000) *African Literatures in English. East and West*, London: Pearson Education.

Lindfors, B. (1982) *Early Nigerian Literature*, New York: Holmes and Meier.

Owomoyela, O. (ed.) (1993) *A History of Twentieth-Century African Literatures*, Lincoln and London: University of Nebraska Press.

NANA WILSON-TAGOE

West African literatures in French

Introduction

With the Maghreb and Central Africa, West Africa is one of the three main regions where, as a result of colonization, French was not only imposed as the official language but also used by African writers as a vehicle to provide a counterpoint to European representations, claim the validity of ancestral African values, articulate political discourses, or express their conditions as modern subjects. The first Africans who wrote fiction in French were members of the elite formed within the institutions of French colonialism (see **colonialism, neocolonialism, and postcolonialism**) in Dakar, Senegal, in the 1920s and 1930s. Among them was Senegalese poet and future president Léopold Sédar **Senghor**, one of the leaders of the **negritude** movement which contributed to the visibility and legitimacy of black voices in the 1940s. Paradoxically, while it was the poetry of negritude which allowed the expression of a black aesthetics, the novel imposed itself as the dominant genre after the Second World War.

The increasing number and diversity of novels, and occasional plays, led to the recognition of African literature as an academic field in the 1950s and 1960s. West African novelists were among the first to inaugurate this early canon. The reshaping of West Africa into nine distinct nations during the period of independence called for reconfiguration of the field in order to account for the literary production of each separate country. As a result, the work of one particular author can today fall under several non-exclusive categories, defined among others according to national, regional and/or linguistic affiliation.

In the 1990s, Francophone West African literature evolved towards an ever more diverse production, adding new genres (such as the romance novel and the crime novel), and a growing body of women's literature. These writers ultimately confirmed the existence of a fully constituted West African canon with its own archetypes and topoi to which each generation has significantly contributed, by adding its own interpretations, appropriations, and rewriting of West African experiences.

Colonization and literature

The existence of a significant body of literature written in French by West African authors is a direct result of French colonization in this region of sub-Saharan Africa. France was one of the four European colonial powers, which, after a phase of discovery and conquest, officially partitioned the African continent at the end of the nineteenth century. France then regrouped its sub-Saharan possessions in two political federations: Equatorial French Africa (AEF) and Oriental French Africa (AOF). While frontiers shifted and the new nations sometimes changed names after the "independences" of the 1960s, the region we know today as Francophone West Africa corresponds to nineteenth-century French colonial holdings in AOF. In addition, while in other contexts Cameroon might be considered a Central African nation, it is included here as part of the West African block.

The field of West African Francophone fiction refers to literary production from the modern nations of Senegal, Guinea and Côte d'Ivoire, Togo, Benin, Burkina Faso, Mali, Niger, Mauritania, and Cameroon – all of which have French as their official language in addition to their own national languages. For historical reasons the literary evolution and production of each of these countries varies greatly. Two factors have proven especially significant: the extent of French institutional involvement in each sub-region during and after the colonial era, and governmental literacy policies in the decades following independence. Former hubs of colonial elite formation and education (see **education and schools**) like Senegal and the Côte d'Ivoire, for example, had the earliest and still the largest literary activity, while others like Burkina Faso (formerly Upper Volta) or Niger are considerably less represented in the corpus.

It is therefore no coincidence that the first acknowledged texts in Francophone African literature, Ahmadou Mapate Diagne's *Les Trois Volontés de Malic* (Malic's Three Wills) in 1920 and Bakary Diallo's *Force-Bonté* (Good Will) (1925), came from Senegal, where the famous École William Ponty was created at the beginning of the twentieth century in an attempt to form an African elite. Indeed, the first generation of Francophone African writers came from the elite actively produced by French schooling in West Africa. Among them are some of the writers who are significant figures in the sub-Saharan African literary canon, alongside authors from Central Africa.

The "birth" of a literature in French

The history of Francophone West African literature cannot be isolated, at least in its early stages, from the movement that helped give black writing subjects visibility on the French and international literary scene: the negritude movement. Although the novels of Senegalese Bakary Diallo and Ousmane **Socé**, and of Dahomeans (now Benin) Félix **Couchoro** and Paul **Hazoumé**, had been published before World War II, it is not until the 1940s, when Léopold Sédar **Senghor**, Aimé Césaire, and Leon Damas used poetry to let out "the great negro cry" of negritude whose purpose was to reclaim the specificity and positivity of the black subject, that voices by colonized people began to be heard.

The two decades of the 1940s and 1950s have been crucial to the constitution of African literature as a discipline, not only because of the primary creative texts it produced, but also because it initiated a number of scholarly works which would assert its legitimacy. Most notable are the two ground-breaking anthologies, the 1948 volume *Anthologie de la poésie nègre et malgache* (Anthology of Black and Malagasy Poetry) (1948) edited by Léopold Senghor with Jean-Paul Sartre's famous preface "Black Orpheus," and the 1947 collection *Poètes d'expression française* (Poets of French Expression), edited by Guyanese poet Leon Damas. In addition, 1946 saw the creation of the journal *Présence Africaine* by Senegalese intellectual Alioune Diop, which, as the title implies, served as a manifesto for, and established the reality of, a pan-African cultural presence. The support of a number of French intellectuals, such as Michel Leiris, André Breton, Jean-Paul Sartre, and André Gide, tremendously bolstered the visibility of early African poets. It should be noted that the "Africa"

which contributed to the negritude movement was mostly West Africa. Authors from Central Africa either did not affiliate themselves with the negritude movement or emerged on the French literary scene decades later.

While the poetry of negritude had eclipsed novelistic activity on the African continent, the 1950s saw the rise of what has been called "the era of the novel," with a sustained production by authors from the former AOF. In the following decades, this production was acknowledged by scholars like Lylian Kesteloot, Thomas Melone, Albert Gérard, Jahn Janzhein, Mohamadou Kane, and Jacques Chevrier, who furthered Negro-African literature's official status as an academic discipline.

Before acquiring the relative autonomy it has today, West African literature was subsumed under the common label of "Negro-African literature," which included the production of Martinique, Guadeloupe, Guyana, Madagascar, the island of Réunion, Haiti, sub-Saharan Africa, and, to some extent, the Maghreb. As decolonization in the 1960s stressed the geographic and politico-cultural particularities of each area, four main regions of Francophone literature began to be distinguished among the colonies: the Caribbean, the Maghreb, Central Africa, and West Africa.

Faced with the growing number of texts coming out of each region at decolonization, some scholars and publishers began to consider the production of single countries separately. Along with anthologies of national literatures, special issues of literary journals flourished, covering, over the decades, each country's specific corpus and canonical authors.

The question of whether to adopt a nationalistic approach to African literature has been the subject of much debate. While some argue that African production should not be an exception to the universal, nation-based categorization of cultural heritage, and that literature is crucial to the consolidation of national identity, others justify a linguistic-based and/or comparative approach, by pointing both to common preoccupations inherent to writing in a postcolonial context and to the necessity of maintaining a unified front against Western cultural hegemony. Although it seems that academic circles traditionally opt for the regional approach, both still prevail today in Africa and abroad. Since the purpose of this overview is to give a general picture of the literary production of the region, a diachronic exposition of thematic and generic recurrences across national boundaries appears more relevant.

Major trends

According to the central focus of the texts, which is often determined by sociopolitical changes affecting the region, four main concerns stand out in West African literature in French: (1) the quest for individual identity; (2) the reclaiming of the African past; (3) the questioning of political systems; (4) the exploration of private spheres.

From the 1930s on, a significant number of narratives presented the quest of a single protagonist who problematizes the difficult negotiation of identity between African heritage and European assimilation. One of the most famous illustrations of this trend was provided by Guinean author Camara **Laye**, whose 1953 *The Dark Child* (*L'Enfant noir*) is still one of the best-known *Bildungsromanen* in African literature. Subsequent novels of formation, more or less autobiographical, will bear on the dualities played out in Laye's novel. Orality (see **oral literature and performance**) and writing, black and white, authenticity and alienation, past and present, for example, are central to the narratives of Ake **Loba**, Ferdinand **Oyono**'s *Houseboy* (*Une Vie de boy*) (1956), Ousmane **Sembene**'s *Black Docker* (*Le Docker noir*) (1956), Bernard **Dadié**'s *Climbié* (1953), and Ken **Bugul**'s *Under the Baobab* (*Le Baobab fou*) (1982). But it is Cheikh Hamidou **Kane**'s *Ambiguous Adventure* (*L'Aventure ambiguë*) (1961) which remains the masterpiece of the genre, as it pushes the black subject's negotiation of identity to its highest level of sophistication. In these narratives and many more, travel to the colonial *métropole* constitutes a determining moment in the evolution of the protagonist, to the point that it has now become a topos in African literature. In the 1980s, the tradition of autobiographical narratives has been revived by writers such as Calixthe **Beyala** and Simon **Njami** in what has been called a new "literature of migration."

While many narratives of formation do include references to oral tradition in the form of proverbs, songs, and tales, other literary projects explicitly set out to reclaim ancestral memory as a way to struggle against collective acculturation. The recuperation of the African past has taken different forms throughout the decades. Similar to what is happening all over Africa, writers like Senegalese Birago **Diop** and the Malian Hampâté **Bâ**, among others, make it their mission to transcribe oral tales into French. More specific, perhaps, to West Africa because it was the site of several vast precolonial kingdoms, the epic tradition has inspired a number of writers, such as Boubou **Hama** from Niger, Nazi **Boni** from Burkina Faso, Djibril Tamsir **Niane** from Guinea, and Massa Makan **Diabaté** from Mali. The rich epic tradition of the region has also inspired dramas such as those of Seydou **Badian**, Cheik Alioune **Ndao**, Charles **Nokan**, and Jean **Pliya**. Later instances of this reclaiming of the precolonial African past can be found in the creative work of Ivorian Jean-Marie **Adiaffi**, whose 1980 *Carte d'identité* (The Identity Card) relies on non-Western chronology to narrate a modern identity quest, or in that of Senegalese Boubacar Boris **Diop**, who since 1980 has designated himself the writer of African memory.

In parallel, texts more closely related to the sociopolitical changes, which affect the evolution of the region or country, constitute the third great trend in Francophone West Africa. While this does not suggest that other categories did not convey, in one form or another, some kind of political discourse, the works in this category focus almost exclusively on interrogating the relation of individuals and communities to a given political system, especially in the postcolonial period. As a rule, in the years around independence, focus shifts away from relations to the colonizer to issues surrounding the process of decolonization. Exemplary of this shift is Ousmane Sembene's second novel *God's Bits of Wood* (*Les Bouts de bois de Dieu*), published in 1960, which marks the beginning of his own prolific career as one of the leading novelists in the tradition of realism in Africa (see **realism and magical realism**). More pessimistic accounts of African political life emerge around 1968 to denounce the failures of the African elite in the wake of independence. Ahmadou **Kourouma**'s 1968 *Suns of Independences* (*Les Soleils des indépendances*) remains the best illustration of what Jacques

Chevrier has called "novels of disenchantment" which later proliferate throughout sub-Saharan Africa.

Scholars like George Ngal see 1968 as a moment of double rupture. This was a paradigmatic rupture, triggered by the historical event of independence, and a stylistic rupture, brought on by Kourouma's insertion of Malinke syntactic structures into the French language and Yambo **Ouologuem**'s iconoclastic *Bound to Violence* (*Le Devoir de violence*), both published in 1968. Compared to the production of the early decades, the end of the 1960s therefore marks the beginning of a new, less "respectful" relationship to the French language, as writers detach themselves from French classical language and nineteenth-century models in their efforts to represent the absurd, fragmented reality of the postcolonial systems.

A noteworthy later development of the political novels centers on the resistance to the abusive power of the autocratic ruler. As is the case for central African literature, the dictator becomes a recognizable trope, especially in theater, where the brusque figure of the despot also comes under attack in the dramas of Williams **Sassine**, Senouvo **Zinsou**, and Cheik Aliou Ndao. But the most powerful and accomplished writer of this trend remained Mongo **Beti**, the Cameroonian writer who, during his career of almost half a century, consistently confirmed his image as militant author while always experimenting with new narrative forms. Other works in this tradition seek to explore the daily lives of less grandiose local characters, like shop owners in Massa Diabaté's Kouta trilogy, teenagers in Ivorian Tanella Boni's *Une Vie de crabe* (A Crab's Life) (1990), beggars in Senegalese Aminata **Sow Fall**'s *The Beggars' Strike* (*La Grève des battùs*) (1979), street children in Aicha Diouri's *La Mauvaise Passe* (In a Bad Way) (1990), or prostitutes and sportsmen in Togolese Florent Couao-Zotti's *Notre pain de chaque nuit* (Our Nightly Bread).

Within this category of texts focusing on more private spheres, though also occupying a position of its own, is the striking addition of women writers to the canon. The 1980s saw the appearance of women writers on the African scene spurred by the immense success of Senegalese Mariama **Bâ**'s *So Long a Letter* (*Une si longue lettre*) in 1979. In fact, Bâ's novel opened the way for what Odile Cazenave calls "a new generation of women writers" whose texts deal with the specificity of the female condition in the context of often-rigid patriarchal laws. As was the case with Bâ, women writers have been concerned not only with providing a literary counterpoint to the male heroes who have dominated the first five decades of West African literature, but also with articulating ways to negotiate the relation between tradition, modernity, and gender (see **modernity and modernism**; **gender and sexuality**). Issues such as genital mutilation in Fatou Keita's *Rebelle* (Rebellious) (1998), polygamy in Ken Bugul's second and third novels or arranged marriages in Anne-Marie **Adiaffi**'s *Une Vie hypothéquée* (A Mortgaged Life) (1984). While some of the autobiographical narratives lack stylistic complexity, authors like Véronique **Tadjo**, Anne-Marie Adiaffi and Tanella Boni, all three from the Côte d'Ivoire, have distinguished themselves both as sophisticated poets and as creative novelists. The work of Werewere **Liking** from Cameroon also stands out for its originality. Although Cameroonian Calixthe Beyala is the most visible and prolific, a majority of women authors come from Senegal and the Côte d'Ivoire, and the creation of the Nouvelles Éditions Africaines publishing house in both countries, where most of these new writers are published, has been crucial to the development of women's writing.

Publishing

Until 1972, with the exception of Éditions CLE based in Cameroon, the only place where West African authors could publish their work was in France. In the 1990s opportunities existed both in Europe and in Africa. The creation of Nouvelles Éditions Africaines in 1972 in Dakar, a project initiated by President Senghor, marks the beginning of active editorial policies designed to give voice to African authors. The creation of NEA has had significant repercussions on the visibility of Francophone literature in Africa in general and West Africa in particular. Significantly, the NEA was created as an editorial instrument aimed at promoting an inter-African cultural life and directed primarily towards the African market.

Later split up between Dakar, Abidjan, and Lomé, the Nouvelles Éditions Africaines today carries out the bulk of literary production in West Africa. Smaller publishing houses such as Khoudia in Dakar, Le Figuier in Bamako, and Arpakgnon in Lomé, also strive to provide writers with publishing opportunities at a more local level. In addition, publication venues in France include three types of houses: first, places that have, historically, specialized in Africa, like Présence Africaine, L'Harmattan, and, though they are not limited to fiction, Karthala and Silex; second, houses that promote the visibility of foreign and non-metropolitan literature in general, like Serpent à Plumes or Dapper; and third, general publishing houses who regularly include African authors in their catalogs, such as Seuil, Albin Michel, Stock, and Gallimard.

Conclusion

West African literature has flourished to the point where a real canon has formed. While poetry gave it visibility on the African and French literary scenes, the acceleration of novelistic production starting in the 1950s has made the novel the privileged genre in a diversity of literary expressions, from first-person narratives to political novels, transcription of oral patrimony, historical narratives and more intimate explorations of the quotidian. Since the late 1970s, women have added their own gendered perspectives to issues of collective and individual self-definition which run through this whole corpus, itself borne of a determination to counter, in the language of the colonizer, European constructions of African subjects.

Of the generations of writers who form this canon, some are deceased (Sassine, Mariama Bâ, Beti, Senghor) and some have stopped writing. But some of the pioneers have confirmed their status as the most prominent authors in the region (Kourouma, Kane, Sembene, Hampâté Bâ, and Ndao), and the generation of West Africans who wrote in the 1970s and 1980s have proved quite productive (Monenembo, Boubacar Boris Diop, Adiaffi, Ken Bugul, Aminata Sow Fall). A new generation, most of them women, assures that the field keeps expanding. It is also worth noting that the 1980s and 1990s saw the increased importance of popular literature, in the form of detective novels, **children's literature**, and sentimental novels.

Further reading

Cazenave, Odile (2000) *Rebellious Women: The New Generation of Female African Novelists*, Boulder, Colorado: Lynne Rienner.

Harrow, Kenneth (1993) *Thresholds of Change in African Literature. The Emergence of a Literary Tradition*, Portsmouth, New Hampshire: Heinemann.

Irele, Abiola (1981) *The African Experience in Literature and Ideology*, London: Heinemann.

Miller, Christopher (1998) *Nationalists and Nomads: Essays on Francophone African Literature and Culture*, Chicago: Chicago University Press.

Ngate, Jonathan (1988) *Francophone African Literature: Reading a Literary Tradition*, Trenton, New Jersey: Africa World Press.

LYDIE MOUDILENO

Wicomb, Zoe

b. 1948, Namaqualand, South Africa

novelist and short story writer

Although Zoe Wicomb is not the most prolific of writers, she is one of the most acclaimed South African prose writers, especially among the generation that came to prominence in the last days of apartheid (see **apartheid and post-apartheid**). Her first collection of short stories, *You Can't Get Lost in Cape Town* (1987), was welcomed, by Toni Morrison, among others, as a work full of seduction and brilliance, with a poetic language that seemed to be at odds with the harsh work represented in the stories. Her first novel, *David's Story* (2001), is considered to be a major work in the post-apartheid era, with the novelist J.M. Coetzee praising not only its witty tone and sophisticated technique but also its self-conscious attempt to remake the South African novel. In addition to taking up the paradoxes and contradictions of the narrative of decolonization and liberation, Wicomb's novel seeks to narrate the lives of the

Griqua, the original people of the Cape Region, and to wrestle with the paradoxes of their presence and erasure in both apartheid and post-apartheid South Africa.

HUMA IBRAHIM

Wolof literature

Wolof literature presents an interesting paradox. On the one hand, it is relatively old: many texts have been written in the Wolof language for more than two hundred years. On the other, there is an abundant production of Wolof literature that has been translated into French. In turn, these two categories – of "pure" Wolof literature and Wolof literature in French translation – can be split into sub-categories. The literature that is written in Wolof by Muslim clerics finds its inspiration from and has its *raison d'être* in religion, namely in Islam (see **Islam in African literature**). In contrast, the texts that draw from a Wolof corpus but are published in French tend to have a secular bent. In effect, Wolof literature is defined by a series of divisions and dichotomies, and particularly the tension between the temporal and the secular.

The two most prominent writers in the Wolof language are Cheikh Moussa Camara (c. 1864–1963) and Moussa Ka (1890–1965). Camara is the author of an **autobiography** of El Hadj Omar Tall which was translated into French by Amar Samb, whereas Ka's poems were translated into French by Bassirou Cisse and Amar Samb. Both sets of translations were published in the *Bulletin de l'IFAN*. There is also a Wolof literature that is written in Arabic but renders Wolof thought. In other words, since there is no Wolof alphabet, Senegalese authors use the Arabic alphabet; this trend of writings is referred to as *wolofal*. Authors in this tradition write mostly, if not entirely, panegyrics: that is, poems in which they sing and glorify the Prophet Muhammad and Islam. The most prominent writers in this school are Madiakhate Kala (1835–1902), El Hadj Malick Sy (1855–1922), and Amadou Bamba Mbacke (1850–1927). The latter two respectively founded the Muslim brotherhoods of Tijaaniya and Mouride. Today their followers still chant the poems and panegyrics

bequeathed to them by the founders of the brotherhoods.

If Wolof literature in Arabic is entirely produced by Senegalese men of letters, the literature available in French translation was spearheaded by French authors, priests, and colonial administrators. The most important works in this tradition include Jacques François Roger's *Fables sénégalaises recueillies de l'Oulof et mises en vers français avec des notes destinées à faire connaître la Sénégambie* (Senegalese Stories Collected from the Wolof and Presented in French with Notes Aspiring to Make the Senegambia Known) (1828), André Demaison's *Diéli le livre de la sagesse noire* (Dieli, the Book of Black Wisdom) (1931), Abbé Boilat's *Grammaire wolloffe* (Wolof Grammar) (1858), Laurent Berenger-Feraud's *Recueil de contes populaires de la Sénégambie* (Collection of Popular Senegambian Tales) (1885), Roland Colin's *Les Contes noirs de l'Ouest Africain* (Black West African Tales) (1957), and Victor François Equilbecq's *Contes populaires d'Afrique occidentale* (Popular Tales of West Africa) (reprinted in 1972). Another well-known author, actually the first to translate Wolof tales and folklore into French, was Birago **Diop**, the author of the popular *Les Contes d'Amadou Koumba* (The Tales of Amadou Koumba) (1947), *Les Nouveaux Contes d'Amadou Koumba* (New Tales of Amadou Koumba) (1958), and *Contes et lavanes* (Tales and Stories) (1963). Although Birago Diop produced no text in the Wolof language, his most influential works drew on this existing Wolof corpus. The translation of works of Wolof into French has been a marked feature of Senegalese writing. In his influential *Nations nègres et culture* (Black Nations and Culture) (1954), for example, Cheikh Anta Diop includes translations of poems performed by Wolof poets. L. Kesteloot's and B. Dieng's *Du Tieddo au Talib, contes et mythes wolof* (From Tieddo to Talib, Wolof Tales and Myths) (1989) contains a direct translation of Wolof tales into French. One also finds many critical studies bearing on the various linguistic and cultural aspects of Wolof society by authors such as Assane Sylla, Pathé Diagne, and Saxir Thiam.

The next important step in Wolof literature occurred in the 1990s when scholars embarked on the collection, transcription, translation (in French and English), and publication of Wolof epics by two Senegalese scholars: Bassirou Dieng, whose work bears on the Wolof kingdom of Kayor (*L'Épopée du Kayor*) (The Epic of Kayor), (1993), and Samba Diop, who focuses on the Wolof kingdom of Waalo (*The Oral History and Literature of the Wolof People of Waalo, Northern Senegal*, 1995, and *The Epic of El Hadj Umar Taal of Fuuta*, 2000). These collections and translations have been important in reviving the ancient Wolof epic traditions and, even more significantly, they have sought to make the original Wolof text available to the reader. In addition, the tradition of Senegalese literature in French that developed after independence, represented by famous writers like Ousmane **Sembene**, Mariama **Bâ**, Ousmane **Socé** Diop, Abdoulaye **Sadji**, and Aminata **Sow Fall**, to mention just a few, has been heavily influenced by Wolof culture and language. The fact, however, remains that the works of these writers do not belong to the category of Wolof literature, properly speaking, but rather to the Euro-African literary tradition or, to be more precise, to African literature in French.

A question that is often asked is the following: why don't Senegalese creative writers write in Wolof and other African languages? In the heyday of French colonialism (see **colonialism, neocolonialism, and postcolonialism**), the colonizer did not encourage education in African languages but, on the contrary, imposed his language on his colonial subjects. With the advent of political independence in the 1960s and in the postcolonial era when Africans were at the helm of the major political and cultural institutions of their countries, little or no effort was made toward making education universal and to encourage writing in African languages such as Wolof. Thus, there has always been a political undercurrent that easily explains the lack of will toward giving a greater visibility to African languages as well as to promoting them as literary and scientific languages. The result of this situation is that Wolof literature exists primarily in two other languages, namely Arabic and French. Nevertheless, a new trend of creative writing in the Wolof language has been developing and is bound to grow, for the simple reason that the Wolof language is spoken by the majority of the Senegalese population (over 50 percent). Furthermore, by reviving the ancient Wolof epics and by writing them in the Wolof language, Senegalese writers are providing models

for younger and aspiring authors who seek to explore fully writing in Wolof, thus giving it the place it deserves. As an example, Boubacar Boris Diop has just published his first novel in Wolof (*Doomi golo* (The She-Monkey and Her Little Ones) 2002). Until now, the author has been publishing only in French. However, this process of fully and creatively writing in Wolof is accompanied by a full recovery of the African personality, sense of worth and purpose, dignity, freedom, and liberty, all of which were overshadowed by the colonial experience and heritage. It is, however, discouraging to find out that there is a prevailing negative attitude *vis-à-vis* a politics of developing the national and local languages in postcolonial Africa.

Further reading

Samb, Amar (1972) *Essai sur la contribution du Sénégal à la littérature d'expression arabe* (Essay on Senegal's Contribution to Literature in Arabic), Dakar: IFAN.

SAMBA DIOP

women's poetry and performance

African women's poetry and performance have long been integral parts of their cultures, yet women's poetry has been conspicuously absent from twentieth-century collections of poetry. Common to most cultures is the extemporaneous expression of poetics, conveyed in oral performance (see **oral literature and performance**) that includes non-verbal expression, dance, and instrumental accompaniment. In regions with the enduring influence of Islam such as North, West, and East Africa, women have been active as scholars trained in the Islamic canon based on poetic influences of the Koran, with specific patterns of rhyme and meter. Long experience in religious pursuits has created a foundation in literacy, which is key to the pursuit of spirituality in Islam. Many cultures enjoy a combination of such written and oral forms of poetic performance, most of which is communicated in indigenous languages.

All of these works, both oral and written, often are broadcast on radio and television programs, and are thus available to wide audiences within their own cultures. And yet, these works have been lost to the West by virtue of Western scholars' ignorance of indigenous languages, and are thus absent from printed texts. These conditions lead to the expectation of the absence of African women's poetic performance, when in fact such works are central to the communication of current events, political concerns, and common interests within many African cultures. Women's poetry and performance often are not widely known outside their cultures for a multiplicity of reasons, primary of which is the patriarchal bias of the institutions of colonialism in the twentieth century (see **colonialism, neocolonialism, and postcolonialism**). These accomplishments of women performers are conspicuously absent from Western scholarship grounded in colonial languages.

For political and cultural reasons women artists have been little published and rarely recognized alongside men. With the advent of both the publication of African authors outside Africa and the establishment of African publishing houses in the early and mid twentieth century, African poetry began to be preserved in widely available printed form. It was in nearly every case male poets whose works were published both in and beyond Africa. In areas of strong colonial influence in the early twentieth century, poetic works most readily preserved in printed form were those that mimicked the European sense of poetry conveyed through colonial influence on African cultures. In addition to influencing style, colonialism also determined attitudes about which individuals were likely candidates for study abroad, and which ones were legitimate authors of both prose and poetry. The African men who received post-secondary education (see **education and schools**) in France and England constituted the elite of newly independent African nations, and appear in print as the novelists and poets of their countries. Indeed, until the late twentieth century it was almost universally the case that one was hard pressed – whether in Africa or outside Africa – to find literary works by African women at all.

Several anthologies that have stood for decades as representative of poetry produced in Africa have included the works of men alone. Many of these are published outside Africa, and some are from African publishing houses. For example, *The Penguin Book of Modern African Poetry*, edited by Gerald Moore and Ulli Beier (1984), has maintained its catalogue of male poets throughout the four decades of its existence, and through multiple revisions. In addition, works considered important sources for the student new to African poetry, such as *A Selection of African Poetry*, edited by K.E. Senanu and Theo Vincent (1973) and *Poems of Black Africa*, edited by Wole Soyinka (1975), are overwhelmingly if not exclusively male-focused. Even in significant literary histories such as *A History of Twentieth-Century African Literatures*, edited by O. Owomoyela (1993), the two chapters on African poetry mention only one woman (Sierra Leonean Gladys **Casely Hayford**) and address only works written in colonial, not indigenous, languages. Clearly, the existing anthologies of African poetry indicate only male-focused trends in publishing; these anthologies are not representative of the degree to which African women have created both written and oral poetry at any time in the history of Africa.

Poetic entertainments: singers and performers

Like oral cultures everywhere, African cultures have rich histories of poetic performance produced by both men and women. Indeed, poetry has long been an integral part of performance and communication in Africa, and for as long as poetry has been part of African cultures, women have been important to its production and expression. The poem is also the song, attesting to the oral nature of poetic traditions in Africa. In Hausa the word for song and poem is the same (*waka*). The oral performance includes a range of styles, from secular to sacred content, formal to informal tone, and with planned or extemporaneous delivery. Zimbabweans Stella Chiweshe and the late Susan Mapfurno, and South African Dorothy Masuka are performers whose poems are delivered in song. Similarly, Nigerians Maimuma Coge, Hajiya Paji, and Binta Katsina are women whose performances of chanted and sung verse are accompanied by non-verbal gesture which ranges from innocuous to bawdy, depending on audience, venue, and topic.

These women performers entertain crowds for political rallies, cultural events, and private celebrations. They perform alone, or accompanied by a chorus, and perhaps musicians, either male or female. These performers sing in indigenous languages – Shona, Zulu, Hausa – and very often deliver their performances extemporaneously. Their poems are not confessional or self-defining, but instead offer cultural definition, preserving traditional attitudes or criticizing social conditions. Like female entertainers everywhere, they suffer social marginality, labeled as pariahs, their economic and professional success notwithstanding. These women poets are perhaps the best gauges of the pulse of their cultures, yet their works are almost completely inaccessible to those outside the cultures, unfamiliar with the languages and cultural settings in which they are performed.

Secular praise singers

Women poets include praise singers whose chanted verse declamations underline publicly the status of wealthy, powerful individuals of whom they speak. Whether an emir or a wealthy merchant (male or female), these subjects of the song are the patrons whose generosity depends upon their satisfaction with the description of their positive characteristics. Thus women praise singers extemporize orally delivered verse that functions to preserve the status quo. In West Africa these performers are known as *griottes* (Wolof) in countries with a Francophone heritage, and as *zabiyoyi* (Hausa) among the Hausa. The *izibongos* of South Africa present social critique. Such performers are usually trained in the craft, and may accompany themselves, or be accompanied by other musicians.

Poets of the sacred

In West and East Africa, Islam is a primary cultural influence. Women poets in these areas express their faith in works that range from orature to orally performed written poems based on Arabic Koranic rhyme and meter (see **Islam in African literature**). In West Africa women have long pursued literacy as a means of spiritual expression. Nana Asma'u (b. 1793) was a scholar, teacher, and poet, whose sixty-four long poetic works range in focus from medicines of the Prophet, description of Sufi women saints, and remembrance of the Prophet, to descriptions of *jihad* battles, history of the Shehu, and elegies. Many of Asma'u's poetic works functioned as mnemonic teaching devices in the process of the resocialization of war refugees. Asma'u's works were originally in Arabic, Fulfulde, and Hausa, all written in Arabic script. They have been translated into English recently by Jean Boyd and Beverly Mack. In Somalia, *sittaat* performances involve women singing praise poems focused on the Prophet Muhammad, his daughter Fatima, and other Muslim saints. These works, *mawlid an-Nabi*, are performed in venues exclusive to women, and for celebrations such as the birthday of the Prophet Muhammad. The performances constitute an opportunity for women to express their spirituality and faith. Some have been translated from their Somali originals (see **Somali literature**) by Lidwien Kapteijns.

Poetic repositories of culture and resistance poets

Both North and South African poets have produced rich bodies of resistance poetry, finding the poetic voice to be an ideal means of resocialization and the forum for the establishment of a collective consciousness against colonial rule. Resistance poetry has been integral to South African culture since the advent of apartheid, a cryptic form of communication that allowed for freer uncensored communication than prose. In southern Africa the poetic works of Zimbabwean and South African women were some of the first to find their way to Western classrooms, while many others, published in small runs of ephemera during the apartheid era, will never be known in the West. Women have been active as resistance poets in primarily four areas: poetry in situations of armed resistance, prison poetry, resistance poems by and about domestic workers, and women's *izibongo*, Zulu praise poems. The two chapters on South African women resistance poets in Mary DeShazer's work provide a rich discussion of authors, poetic styles, and social functions of women's poetry in the region. In addition, grass-roots groups like the Zimbabwean Women Writers collective have given voice to women artists in the postcolonial period. Donald Burness's study of Lusophone resistance poetry includes examples of women poets from Cape Verde and Mozambique. The works of Yolanda Morazzo, Ana Julia, and Gloria de Sant'Anna deal with emigration, disenfranchisement, and remembrances of home. In South Africa, a formidable representative of southern African women poets is the Xhosa woman performer, Nongenile Masithathu Zenani, whose epic performed over the course of several days preserves the history of her culture. As an epic poet and teller of *ntsomi* traditions, Zenani is richly expressive of her culture and time, as well as a consummate intellect and performer. Her performances are in Xhosa, and many have been translated in several volumes by scholar Harold Scheub.

Conclusion

Despite the high demands on African women's time, and limitations on their access to Western modes of education, their poetry is representative of major cultural concerns, significant as commentary on social conditions, and reflective of the status quo. African women poets are writing in their own languages, and focusing on the predominant sociopolitical issues of their times. Oral poetic works combine traditional modes of communication in patterns of repeated images, expressed in consummate rhythm patterns. Written works convey literary conventions common in the culture, as in the Koranic poetic convention common in Islamic cultures. In some cases styles overlap. Investigating these complex canons of poetic works can lead to greater cultural insight, but knowledge of indigenous languages is the key for investigation of African women's poetry, whether oral or written.

Further reading

Boyd, Jean and Mack, Beverly (1997) *The Collected Works of Nana Asma'u. Daughter of Usman Dan Fodiyo 1793–1864*, East Lansing: Michigan State University Press.

Burness, Donald (ed. and trans.) (1989) *A Horse of White Clouds: Poems from Lusophone Africa*, Center for International Studies Monograph 55, Ohio: Ohio University.

Chipasula, Stella and Chipasula, Frank (eds) (1995) *The Heinemann Book of African Women's Poetry*, Portsmouth, New Hampshire: Heinemann Educational.

Chitauro, Moreblessings, Dube, Caleb, and Gunner, Liz (1994) "Song, Story and Nation: Women as Singers and Actresses in Zimbabwe," in Liz Gunner (ed.) *Politics and Performance: Theatre, Poetry, and Song in Southern Africa*, Johannesburg: Witwatersrand University Press.

Davies, Carole Boyce and Fido, Elaine (1993) "African Women Writers: Toward a Literary History," in Oyekan Owomoyela (ed.) *A History of Twentieth-Century African Literatures*, Lincoln: University of Nebraska Press.

DeShazer, Mary K. (1994) *A Poetics of Resistance: Women Writing in El Salvador, South Africa, and the United States*, Ann Arbor: University of Michigan Press.

Finnegan, Ruth (1977) *Oral Poetry*, Cambridge: Cambridge University Press.

Kitson, Norma (ed.) (1994) *Zimbabwe Women Writers Anthology No. 1 – English – 1994*, Harare: Jongwe Publishing.

Mack, Beverly and Boyd, Jean (2000) *One Woman's Jihad: Nana Asma'u. Scholar and Scribe*, Bloomington, Indiana: Indiana University Press.

Scheub, Harold (1977) *African Oral Narrative, Proverbs, Riddles, Poetry, and Song*, Boston: G.K. Hall.

BEVERLY B. MACK

Xitu, Xuanhenga (Agostino Mendes de Carvalho)

b. 1924, Kimbundu, Angola

novelist and short story writer

Like most other Angolan writers of his generation, Xuanhenga Xitu's career as a writer is interwoven with his involvement in his country's struggle for independence against Portuguese colonialism (see **colonialism, neocolonialism, and postcolonialism**). Born in a Kimbundu rural family, Xitu was one of the founders of the MPLA, the leading nationalist movement in Angola, and for his political activities he was arrested by the Portuguese colonial authorities and imprisoned in the infamous Tarrafal camp for political prisoners in Cape Verde from 1959 to 1970. It was while in prison that Xitu started writing fiction, but his works were not published until after Angola's independence in 1975. Xitu has served the Angolan postcolonial government in various capacities, as a minister and ambassador. Within the tradition of Angolan fiction, Xitu's work stands out for its use of farce, parody, and mimicry to subvert colonial culture and its conventions. This is evident in two works, *"Mestre" Tamoda e Outros Contos* ("Master" Tamoda and Other Stories) (1977) and *Os Discursos do "Mestre" Tamoda* (The Discourse of "Master" Tamoda) (1984), both published in English translation as *The World of "Mestre" Tamoda* (1988). Xitu is the master of satire and his ironic sense of life in the postcolonial landscape is reflected in his later works such as *O Ministro* (The Minister) (1990).

Further reading

Peres, Phyllis (1997) *Transculturation and Resistance in Lusophone African Narrative*, Gainesville: University of Florida Press.

SIMON GIKANDI

Y

Yaou, Regina

b. 1955, Côte d'Ivoire

novelist, poet, and short story writer

A contemporary of Véronique **Tadjo**, the Ivorian writer Regina Yaou prefers the novel, although poetry was her initial attempt at writing, and her name first caught public attention with the publication of a short story, *La Citadine* (The Urban Woman), which won the first prize in a competition sponsored by Nouvelles Éditions Africaines in 1977. Her work deals with modern-day concerns, especially the status of traditional customs, family, and marriage in a modern-day setting, and often revolves around the lives of female protagonists. However, Yaou's treatment of these themes is unusual when compared with other Ivorian writers who are interested in the same issues. For instance, Yaou's countryman Amon d'Aby has treated the theme of sorcery in some of his writing, as Yaou also does. However, whereas he denounces sorcery as fraudulent, Yaou takes it seriously, as is evident in her novel *Aihui Anka* (Aihui Anka) (1988). Regarding polygyny and men's extra-marital relationships, Yaou's stance seems, to an extent, to echo Mariama **Bâ**'s claim in *So Long a Letter* that there is a "polygamous instinct" in the male of the species. However, while Bâ's novel proceeds to demonstrate women's collusion in the oppressive institutions that mar male/female relationships, Yaou seems to allow for no such problematizing of marital relations or men's abandonment of women. For example, in her first novel, *Lézou Marie, ou les écueils de la vie* (Lezou Marie or the Vicissitudes of Life) (1982), all the villains seem to be men and all the angels are women.

One of the strengths of Yaou's writing is her gift for creating sympathetic characters plagued with a fatal flaw. In *Lézou Marie*, for example, Marie's penchant for luxury contributes to her final downfall, while Anka's intransigence in *Aihui Anka* leads to a similar end. In her novels, Yaou also offers an interesting study of the difficulties of adjusting to different milieus, whether her characters are moving from a rural to an urban setting or vice versa. In addition, her novels offer fascinating depictions of culture and customs – burial customs among the Alladians of the Côte d'Ivoire, matrilineal inheritance practice, and African foods, to mention only a few.

Early accused of neglecting the larger themes in African literature, Yaou responded that since literature is a means of communication, it can fairly be used to communicate any subject, and that her work appeals to the young and older generations because they recognize themselves in her characters. The themes that Yaou's work treats are not trivial; rather, she is interested in simple social acts with enormous consequences. For example, in *La Révolte d'Affiba* (Affiba's Revolt) (1985) the practice of depriving a widow of the couple's possessions at the husband's death contributes to the impoverishment of women and children. In this sense, the focus of Yaou's work on the problems of everyday life complements the larger political and social concerns of leading African writers.

WANGAR WA NYATETŪ-WAIGWA

Yavoucko, Cyriaque Robert

b. 1953, Central African Republic

novelist

The Central African writer Cyriaque Robert Yavoucko studied at institutions in Bangui, Abidjan, and Aix-en-Provence before getting a doctorate in English at the Sorbonne, after which he returned to the University of Bangui where he became a teacher. In his most prominent work, *Crépuscule et défi* (Dusk and Defiance), Yavoucko interrogates his nation's colonial history by offering variations on the theme of political and cultural resistance in a Mongbandi community in the eastern part of the country. Published in Paris by Harmattan in 1979 as the initial volume in the series Encres Noires (Black Inks), the work is subtitled in Sangho, the national language of the Central African Republic.

JANICE SPLETH

Yoka Lye Mudaba

b. 1947, Kinshasa

playwright and short story writer

Born in Kinshasa, Yoka Lye Mudaba is the author of numerous plays and short stories inspired by contemporary themes. His award-winning story "Le Fossoyeur" (The Gravedigger) has been successfully dramatized. Three of the stories published in 1991 in the collection *Destins Broyés* (Broken Destinies) were accorded international literary prizes. Yoka received a doctorate in literature from the University of Paris III with a dissertation on the relationship between oral tradition and contemporary African theater. He served as artistic director of the National Theater of Zaire and was professor of theater at the National Institute for the Arts. The ORTF edited his play *Kimpuanza* in 1974, prior to his work in the area of ritual theater where one of his best-known plays is *Tshira, ou la danse des ombres et des masques* (Tshira or the Dance of Shadows and Masks) (1978). He is also famous for *Lettres d'un Kinois à l'oncle du village* (Letters from an Inhabitant of

Kinshasa to the Village Uncle) (1975), a collection of satirical chronicles detailing life in the city, originally published in the biweekly magazine *Le Soft*, where Yoka serves on the editorial board, and in *Le Monde Diplomatique*.

JANICE SPLETH

Yoruba literature

If one were to make an overarching statement about modern Yoruba literature, it is that the most important writers self-consciously link their work to oral traditions (see **oral literature and performance**) that both predate the arrival of literacy and remain significant parts of cultural experiences in contemporary Yoruba society. In poetry and in drama, notions of rhythm, imagery, spectacle, and scenery retain clear connections to traditional forms. The best-known novelists neither simply domesticate "alien" methods and genres, nor simply produce their native equivalents, but rework, through tendencies in language use, characterization methods, and plotting, the "new" forms to fit Yoruba ontology.

Early history

European missionaries and early Yoruba Christians created, as tools of rapid evangelization, the first script and printed texts in the language in the mid nineteenth century. The creation of printing houses, grammar books, readers, primers, and translations of parts of the Bible between 1843 and 1849 led to a quick standardization of an alphabet and an orthography. In the following decade, these infrastructural investments became the foundation of a literary culture that goes with the publication of hymnals, a newspaper, and a translation of John Bunyan's *Pilgrim's Progress*. Studies designed to show the "falsehood" of pre-Christian Yoruba beliefs sprouted before the end of the nineteenth century. Ironically, these collections, gathered, edited, and annotated by indigenous Christian workers, soon became the first set of Yoruba writing to focus mainly on indigenous worldviews.

As soon as the missionary engagements stabilized and the means of material literary production came within reach of other interest groups like educated slave returnees from the Americas, a stream of secular writing culture started to grow early in the twentieth century. J.S.Ṣówándé, alias Ṣọ̀bọ̀ Aróbíodu Aláṣàrò Ọ̀rọ̀ ("the thoughtful one who resonates like a xylophone"), published poems on diverse topics. Several expository books about Yoruba culture also came out, on fashion, proverbs, and even dream interpretation. During the first two decades of the twentieth century, when focus further shifted to more explicitly literary endeavors, newspapers came to play significant roles: *Akede Eko* (The Lagos Herald) and *Eleti Ofe* (The Express) serialized the first two Yoruba novels and printed the earliest Yoruba play.

Yoruba poetry

Between 1902 and 1921 J.S. Ṣówándé, A.K. Ajíṣafẹ́, and D.A. Ọbasá produced a body of "secular" verse that did not promote exclusively religious and cosmic viewpoints. Ṣówándé, the most prolific of the three, structured his works after the well-established patterns of an easily recognizable chanting mode that was very popular in his Abẹ́òkúta home province. However, because this style required a very good control of a regional performance mode which was not reflected in the standard writing forms that were then developing, Ṣówándé's influence on subsequent poetry was less significant than that of his contemporaries who wrote less moving lines in standard Yoruba. Ṣówándé's poetry addressed excesses of the local colonial administration, criticized the immoralities of young Christian converts, and praised many local dignitaries both for their civic duties and for their generosity and kindness towards him. Ṣówándé, who several times reflects on his own private foibles, remains, perhaps even today, the most introspective Yoruba writer.

To praise the value of Christian education, Ṣówándé used his own ignorance and that of his friends as a negative example:

Àsèkò yí mbá lọ sùkúrù 're, mo fi ńrè 'gbàlè:
Nkì wọ́n l'ígbórò àt'igbó Agẹmọ;
Tèmi Déwùsì ọmọ Pesewu, a kì yé la jó bàtá igi lọ́nà 'Jàyè

(The time I should have gone schooling, I went roaming the groves:
Always at the Orò and Agẹmọ shrines;
I and Déwùsì Pesewu, dancing to *bàtá* drums all the time
along 'Jàyè road.)

(my translation)

Ṣówándé wrote moving lines about his poverty, his extramarital sexual exploits, and even the painful stomach problems he suffered after eating a serving of pounded yam. As early as 1906, Ṣówándé predicted that social atrocities related to colonialism would definitely pass:

Sùgbọ̀n pípẹ́ rèé má a pẹ́,
Agbọ̀ n kà ṣài dẹ́ adìe,
Kò níí pẹ́ títí kÓyìnbó máa
Wọkun lọ síyà ẹ̀hìn ọ̀ sà.

(It may take a while,
The coop will still cage the rooster,
Soon whites will leave
And disappear into the horizon.)

(my translation)

Yoruba poets that came after Ṣówándé can be grouped into three classes: neo-traditional writers, modern "artistes," and occasional poets who blend the practices of the other two. Neo-traditionalists follow the clearly defined chanting modes of oral traditions and "imitate" their genre structures and "techniques of recitation" as they relate to vocalization, tone pitch, and accompanying musical instrument. Àlàbí Ògúndépò and Ògúndáre Fọ́nyánmu are known for their inflections of the chant of the Hunters' Guild, or *ìjálá*, Yẹmí Ẹlẹ́bu-Ìbọn for his divination chant voice modulation, and Fóyèkẹ́ Àlàkẹ́ for her northern Yoruba *egúngún* masque entertainment pitch. Except for a few like Láwuyì Ògúnníran and Ọládiípọ̀ Yémiítàn, two well-known authors of books based on Hunters' Guild poems, and Yẹmí Ẹlẹ́bu-Ìbọn, the form of whose written poems derives from divination chants, neo-traditionalists distribute their works on the numerous early morning poetry-reading radio programs and audio cassettes.

The work of the typically well-educated writers of the "artistes" class is defined by their very self-conscious translation and modification of the "verbal" – as opposed to musical – characteristics of traditional poetry. Unlike neo-traditionalist chants, print media like books and newspapers do not alter in any fundamental way the realization of texts produced by the artistes because they do not depend as much on strict tonal and pitch formulations. As a result, the "stylistic" distinctions that separate each of the early literate poets and the neo-traditionalists from one another in the consumer's "ear" is lacking in the works of the artistes. An Adébáyò Fálétí line, for non-professional literary critics, is hard to distinguish from that of other "schooled" poets like Ayò Òpádòtun or Olánipèkun Olúránkinsé.

Occasional poets perform mainly "praise poetry," not infrequently from written scripts, with widely varying degrees of accomplishment, at wedding ceremonies, funerals, house-warmings, naming ceremonies, and other rites of passage. Rhythm in Yoruba poetry is determined not by meter, stress, or even melody, but by recurring or parallel syntactic structures, and the overall quality of a work is measured by how well the writer can manipulate the tonal features of the language. Commentators on Yoruba poetry have been unreceptive to innovations that might force the "free flowing" character of Yoruba poetic rhythm into a rigid prosody. Afolabi Johnson (1900–43) who tried strictly measured couplets and triplets was vilified as an inventor of *àda ewì* (counterfeit poetry).

Yoruba drama

The foremost Yoruba playwrights work outside of the well-known Yoruba popular traveling theater. Their works are distributed largely as "trade" books, as set texts in formal literary studies in schools and colleges, and as adaptations by professional troupes. History and satire are the main types in Yoruba literary drama. The former re-enacts episodes in Yoruba history and the lives of legendary Yoruba men and women, and the latter is typically a critique of official graft, marital infidelity, religious hypocrisy, and the machinations of jealous women and witches. Theatrically, histories celebrate elements of Yoruba high culture and performance arts in poetic rituals, court intrigues, and formal grandeur in both peace and war, and consummate traditional medicine-making, including efficacious uses of "magical" words,

incantations, and chants. For example, in Akínwùmí Ìsòlá's play about the life of Madam Efúnsetán Aníwúrà, a work that once played to a packed soccer stadium of almost 50,000 spectators, actions come to a head at the grand confrontation between the major antagonists in the form of a verbal duel in which great spells and potent words are the main weapons.

In the same vein, Dúró **Ládiípò**'s work about the apotheosis of King Sàngó climaxes around a spectacular invocation of thunderbolts, and the formal pomp of the Òyó palace animates action in the removal of the regicidal Gáà in Adébáyò Fálétí's play about the reign of King Abíódún. In satires, language and action can be either profane or very serious depending on the weightiness of the subject matter. A play that deals with the precipitous decline of the mind of a labor leader whose union has been ruined by state agencies uses the tragic hero's misappropriations of well-known proverbs to denote his confused thoughts. Solemn and measured language use matches the gravity of the moral conundrums of a Catholic priest who has to convince a confessor to turn himself over to civil authorities in a social dilemma play. Some plays mock in highly irreverent terms the misbehavior of social groups being criticized. In a play that is very critical of religious chicanery, for instance, the priest who carries the burden of the criticism is nicknamed "Toromóyàn," "one-who-hangs-on-women's breasts," in a clear mockery of his real name, Jeremáyà (Jeremiah). The nickname, which plays upon the last two syllables of the prophet's proper name, *àyà*, "chest," derives from a very clever manipulation of Yoruba morpho-tonemic structures. The play's self-conscious playfulness is further remarked when one characters says, "*Yèyé ni a ó fi lé e lọ* (We will drive him away with ridicule)." As promised, hilarious turns of words and events become the prophet's undoing when at the end of the play he is caught undressing a female congregant in the church sanctuary at a moment when he is supposed to be praying for her. When Jeremáyà is apprehended, his laughable deception is revealed when he responds not by calling on the Lord Jesus Christ but by pulling out from under his cassock a "pagan" leather amulet to scare off his moral assailants.

Yoruba fiction

The novels of D.O. **Fagunwa**, the most famous Yoruba fiction writer, hold a special place in the hearts of most literate Yoruba people because his vivid description of fantastic places, characters, and events tends to be unforgettable. As Wole Soyinka says in his translator's preface to *The Forest of a Thousand Demons* (*Ògbójú Ọdẹ Nínú Igbó Irúnmalẹ̀*) Fagunwa "is both the enthusiastic raconteur and pious moralist, and the battle of inventive imagination with the morally guided is a constant process in much of his work" (1968: London). These features of Fagunwa's tales of ghosts, mountains, dense forests, challenging tasks, conquests, and single-minded pursuits characterize the "majestic" pole of Yoruba fiction. The "profane" end is well represented by Ọládèjọ Òkédìjí whose major novels detail the exploits of an ex-policeman turned "peasant" detective who works on the farm and lives in the city. Between the Fagunwa pole that deals with archetypal conflicts and the other end where crime thrillers contrast the problems of everyday living in the peaceful village and the crime-infested city, there exists a very wide range of prose styles. Many writers, like Afọlábí Ọlábímtán, a professor of Yoruba literature, work in the realist mode to cover more explicitly contemporary political and topics. Kọ́lá Akínlàdé has successfully created a "franchise" style with his detective novels.

Each writer's inducement of what, in Yoruba, is called *àkàgbádùn* (pleasant reading) and *àkàtúnká* (pleasant rereading) in their works revolves around memorable characters who embody or betray what could be termed Yoruba attributes of good citizenship in whatever circumstances they happen to find themselves, be it in Fagunwa's forests, Ọlábímtán's corridors of power, Òkédìjí's villages, or Akínlàdé's cities. The characters are always extraordinary regardless of the narrative mode or overall thematic goal: hunters in stories set in forests usually combine bravery and wisdom; witches and kindred spirits can be very beautiful in spite of their wicked ways; unrefined detectives may be masterful users of proverbs and idiosyncratic lovers of certain foods; the grand thief may be a very passionate lover; the crafty and corrupt national politician may be a devoted husband and genuine lover of his local community. Most importantly, these characters are able to draw attention, sympathetic or otherwise, to their situations mainly on the quality of their creative use of language. Òkédìjí's very thoughtful peasant detective is also full of verbal *ẹ̀tàn* (deception/subterfuge). And both attributes often come out in his almost compulsive use of proverbs which many times come to his aid when he wants to encircle either incompetent police detectives or bumbling criminals.

At the beginning of the twenty-first century, it is very difficult to make definite statements on what directions Yoruba literature will follow in the near future. Many major writing talents have flocked to video production, a great portion of which is still in the Yoruba language. The schooling segment of the book and culture market is not expanding in favor of indigenous languages like Yoruba.

Further reading

Abimbola, Wande (ed.) (1975) *Yoruba Oral Tradition: Poetry in Music, Dance and Drama*, Ile-Ife: Department of African Languages and Literatures, University of Ife.

Ogunsina, Bisi (1992) *The Development of the Yoruba Novel*, Ibadan: Gospel Faith Mission Press.

Olatunji, Olatunde (1984) *Features of Yoruba Oral Poetry*, Ibadan: University Press

Soyinka, W. (1968) "Translator's Preface," in D.O.Fagunwa, *Forest of a Thousand Demons*, London: Nelson.

ADÉLÉKÈ ADÉẸ̀KÓ

Z

Zamenga, Batukezanga

b. 1933, Kolo-Luozi, Congo-Zaire; d.
2000, Congo-Zaire

novelist and essayist

During his lifetime, Zamenga was the most widely
read writer in Congo-Zaire. His simply constructed, often melodramatic tales taken chiefly
from real-life situations appealed to an audience of
readers who could relate to them and who found
inspiration in the author's moral perspective.
Publishing exclusively in local presses, such as
Éditions Saint-Paul-Afrique, Éditions Basenzi, and
Éditions Zabat, he produced around two dozen
titles, many of which have become classics of a sort
in the nation's literary canon. In *Carte postale*
(Postcard), which has sold over 55,000 copies since
its publication in 1974, Zamenga uses the experiences of an African student who goes to Europe to
attend university to satirize both the colonizer's
claims of cultural superiority and the alienation of
the been-to from his society. Zamenga was
educated in Belgium, where he studied applied
social sciences. He was a contributor to the review
L'Étoile du Congo on sociological subjects and served
as director of SONECA, the national society of
editors, composers, and authors.

Further reading

MacGaffey, Wyatt (1982) "Zamenga of Zaire:
Novelist, Historian, Sociologist, Philosopher

and Moralist," *Research in African Literatures* 13,
2: 208–15.

JANICE SPLETH

Zanga Tsogo, Delphine

b. 1935, Cameroon

feminist and writer

The Cameroon writer Delphine Zanga Tsogo was
trained as a nurse in France and came to literature
late in life with the publication of *Vie de femmes* (Life
of Women) in 1983. She creates in this work, which
has a very autobiographical flavor (see **autobiography**), a society where a woman, whatever her
status, is reduced to marginalization, caught in a
trap of numerous contradictions owing to the
encounter of an omnipresent tradition and a poorly
domesticated modernity (see **modernity and
modernism**). The feeling of an existence led
under the high surveillance of patriarchal society is
what inspired *L'Oiseau en cage* (Caged Bird) (1984). If
Zanga Tsogo shows her commitment to questions
of gender (see **gender and sexuality**), she
nevertheless retains a moderate tone in her works.
Beyond literature, Zanga Tsogo has been an active
participant in the struggle for women both in
Cameroon and in the rest of African, serving in
leading organizations committed to gender equality. She has served in the leadership of, among
others, the Conseil Nationale des Femmes Camerounaises (National Council of Cameroonian

Women) (1964) and at the Institut International de Recherches et de Formation des Nations Unies pour la Promotion de la Femme (International Research and Training Institute of the United Nations for the Promotion of Women).

ANDRÉ NTONFO

al-Zayyat, Latifa

b. 1923, Damietta, Egypt; d. 1996, Cairo, Egypt

novelist

An Egyptian writer who wrote literary works and critical studies in Arabic, al-Zayyat was born in Damietta, Egypt. In her childhood, she moved around Egypt as her father, a civil servant, was transferred from one city to another. She studied English literature at university, and after obtaining her doctorate she taught in, and chaired, the Department of English at 'Ain Shams University. She also headed the Egyptian Academy of Fine Arts. Al-Zayyat was involved in militant politics from her undergraduate days at Cairo University and continued to be a political activist preoccupied with the dispossessed in her country and in the world. For her political activities, she was imprisoned twice in two different periods of Egyptian history, first in the late 1940s under King Farouk and later in the early 1980s under President Sadat. In 1979 she founded and presided over the Committee for the Defense of National Culture. She wrote on New Criticism and Marxist aesthetics. Al-Zayyat considered women central to her work and in her essays she often sought to establish a vital link between the liberation of women and national liberation. Her work and thought has influenced many younger woman writers in Egypt, including Radwa Ashour and Salwa Bakr.

In 1960, al-Zayyat published *The Open Door (al-Bab al-maftuh)* considered a modern classic of feminist writing. It is a *Bildungsromanen*, a novel about the education and coming of age of a middle-class young Egyptian woman who has internalized the patriarchal values of her family and society. In al-Zayyat's novel, the young woman's true liberation from patriarchal authority is achieved at the same time as Egypt's liberation from neocolonialism in the battle with the British and the French over the nationalization of the Suez Canal in 1956. Another impressive work of al-Zayyat is her autobiography, *The Search: Personal Papers (Hamlat taftish: awaraq shakhsiyya)*, which was published in 1992. In 1994 and 1995, al-Zayyat published two novellas *Sahib al-bayt* (The Owner of the House) and *al-Rajul allathi 'rifa tuhmatahu* (The Man Who Knew his Charge) as well as a play, *Bay' wa-shira'* (Selling and Buying). She has also written a collection of short stories, *al-Shaykhukha wa-qisas ukhra* (Old Age and Other Stories) (1986) dealing with motifs of aging. Her style in *The Open Door* is characterized by a grand linear structure using a literary idiom marked by transparency and precision. Her later work has a labyrinth-like narrative structure and the language is dense and symbolic. Irony and humor also mark her later works. Al-Zayyat has also written a book on the narrative art of Najīb **Maḥfūz**, and another on the image of women in the Arabic novel. She has received several awards, including the Egyptian Merit Award and the Najīb Maḥfūz Medal for Literature.

Further reading

al-Zayyat, Latifa (1992) *The Search: Personal Papers*, trans. Sophie Bennett, London: Quartet.
——(1994) "On Political Commitment and Feminist Writing," in Ferial J. Ghazoul and Barbara Harlow (eds) *The View from Within: Writers and Critics on Contemporary Arabic Literature*, Cairo: American University in Cairo Press.
——(2000) *The Open Door*, trans. Marilyn Booth, Cairo: American University in Cairo Press.

FERIAL J. GHAZOUL

Zefzaf, Mohammad

b. 1945, Kénitra, Morocco; d. 2001, Casablanca, Morocco

novelist, short story writer, translator, and poet

Mohammad Zefzaf is a novelist, short story writer, translator, and poet. He was born and raised in the poor area of Kénitra, Morocco, and his career was influenced by the poverty in which he grew up. Zefzaf started publishing his short stories and poems in the mid 1960s in Moroccan newspapers and in Lebanese literary journals, namely *al-Adab, Shi'r* and *Mawaqif*. In 1970, he published his first collection of short stories, *Hiwar fi Layl Muta'akhir* (Dialogue in the Late Night), and in 1972 he published his first novel, *al Mar'a wa al-Warda* (The Woman and the Rose). He has published nine collections of short stories and nine novels. Zefzaf's literary work is not only a scream against poverty and deprivation but an act of commitment to the plea of the poor people of Morocco, who despite decolonization are still not free. "Independence gave us back the land but not food," says a character in *Sardines and Oranges*, first published in Rabat in 1993. In his work, Zefzaf speaks of two distinct "Moroccos," one of those who have never known hunger and the other of those who are constantly hungry. As a result, hunger becomes an important and recurring motif in his fictional work and poetry; it is often presented as a means of depriving people of their pride and dignity.

Further reading

Zefzaf, Mohammad (1999) *Complete Works*, Rabat: Moroccan Ministry of Culture.

ZAHIA SMAIL SALHI

Zéhar, Hacène Farouk

b. 1939, Boghari, Algeria

novelist

Though Hacène Zéhar was born in Boghari, Algeria, the setting for his work is primarily France where he has studied and spent much of his life. He came upon the literary scene with the publication of his collection of short stories, *Peleton de tête* (Leader) (1966), followed by his novel *Miroir d'un fou* (The Mirror of a Madman) (1979). Though the central character in this novel is an Algerian immigrant, Zéhar's preoccupation in this work as well in his short stories is the problem of strangeness in the larger existential sense. Rather than focusing on the outsider in terms of geography, nationality, or political status, Zéhar turns his attention towards the individual and the strangeness that abides therein. The remarkable characteristic of his work is this attentiveness to the human condition and the profound malaise that often marks existence.

NASRIN QADER

Ziani, Rabia

b. 1953, Dra' al-Mizan, Algeria

novelist

Born in 1953 in the Beni Smail village of Dra' al-Mizan, Algeria, Ziani left for France at the age of 15 and survived by doing odd jobs while trying to become a writer. Between 1970 and 1971, Ziani completed a long novel of 600 pages, of which only half was retained by the Algerian publishing company SNED; this was to appear in 1981 under the title *Le Déshérité* (The Underprivileged). The main theme of this novel is the postcolonial (see **colonialism, neocolonialism, and postcolonialism**) experiences of a war hero named Rais, whose story is told through many flashbacks that shuttle the reader between the years of the Algerian war of independence and independent Algeria. The novel is overloaded with many events and stories from the war for independence, and some critics have argued that so many details are packed in the scope of one novel that this makes it monotonous. *Le Déshérité* was followed by *Letters from My Garden* (*Lettres de mon jardin*) (1983) and *Ma montagne* (My Mountain) (1984), which the author calls "a relief from my inner suffering."

Further reading

Ziani, Rabia (1986) *La Main mutilée* (The Mutilated Hand), Algiers: ENAL.

——(1986) *L'Impossible Bonheur* (Impossible Good Fortune) Algiers: ENAL.

——(1992) *Et mourir à Ighil!* (And to Die at Ighil!), Algiers: ENAL.

——(1996) *Le Secret de Marie* (Marie's Secret), Paris: L'Harmattan.

ZAHIA SMAIL SALHI

Zimunya, Bonus Musaemura

b. 1949, Mutare, Zimbabwe

poet, critic, and short story writer

The Zimbabwean poet, critic, and short story writer Bonus Musaemura Zimunya was born in Mutare and educated at Goromonzi and the universities of Rhodesia and Kent, UK. Some of Zimunya's early poetry is published in Kizito Muchemwa's anthology, *Zimbabwean Poetry in English* (1978). Zimunya's poetic works include *Thought Tracks* (1982), *Kingfisher, Jikinya and Other Poems* (1982), and *Country Dawns and City Lights* (1985). *Thought Tracks* balances the happy mood of independence with sadness over the possibility of its betrayal by the new leaders. *Kingfisher, Jikinya and Other Poems* recaptures the beauty of nature. *Country Dawns and City Lights* bemoans the violent rupture of the "tranquil" African life by colonialism. Zimunya has also penned *Perfect Poise* (1993) and *Selected Poems* (1995). In *Night Shift* (1993) Zimunya revisits the theme of city life and the stresses it causes on the urban poor in contrast to the obscene acquisitive culture of the "old" guard of nationalist leaders. Zimunya has co-edited *And Now the Poets Speak* (1981) with Mudereri Khadhani and *The Fate of Vultures* (1988) with Kofi Anyidoho and Peter Porter. Zimunya is also the author of a critical work titled *Those Years of Drought and Hunger: The Birth of African Fiction in English in Zimbabwe* (1982).

M. VAMBE

Zinsou, Senouvo Agbota

b. 1946, Lomé, Togo

playwright and short story writer

Senouvo Agbota Zinsou, Togo's most prominent playwright and a writer of prize-winning short stories, was born and educated in Lomé. His first and best-known play, *On joue la comédie* (We Put On an Act), a caricature of South African apartheid (see **apartheid and post-apartheid**), was published in 1972, during his last year of college, and won Zinsou the Inter-African Radio Drama Competition Prize and a scholarship to do graduate work in Paris. Upon his return, he was appointed to Togo's Ministry of Culture and founded the National Company for the Performing Arts. Zinsou's company participated in festivals across Africa and Europe, bringing Togolese theater to an international audience. He has created a truly popular modern (see **modernity and modernism**) African drama in Ewe-inflected French and drawing on traditional Ewe theatrical forms, particularly the concert party and the cantata, in addition to the work of European modernists such as Samuel Beckett and Bertholt Brecht. Many of Zinsou's more than fifteen plays, including *La Tortue qui chante* (The Singing Tortoise) (1991), are adaptations of traditional folk tales. Zinsou left Togo for Germany in 1993 as a political refugee.

Further reading

Zinsou, S.A. (1991) *The Singing Tortoise* (*La Tortue qui chante*), in *New Plays: Madagascar, Mauritania, Togo*, New York: Ubu Repertory Theater.

RACHEL GABARA

Zirimu, Elvania Namukwaya

b. 1938, Uganda; d. 1979

short story writer and playwright

The Ugandan short story writer and playwright Elvania Namukwaya Zirimu was one of the few women members of what has come to be known as the Makerere school of writing, and her early works, published in *Origin East Africa*, the famous anthology edited by David Cook and David **Rubadiri**, represent one of the first concerted attempts to incorporate oral traditions in writing. In her dramatic works, as well as her short stories, Zirimu was interested in using Baganda notions of oral performance (see **oral literature and performance**) to comment on the urban scene in East Africa. Her two-act play, *When the Hunchback*

Made Rain, which was first performed in Kampala in 1970, was memorable for its representation of questions of modern moral decline using the framework of a Baganda folk tale.

SIMON GIKANDI

Zitouni, Ahmed

b. 1949, Saïda, Algeria

novelist

Born in Saïda, Algeria, Ahmed Zitouni has lived in France since 1973 where he launched his career as a novelist in 1983 with the publication of *Avec du sang déshonoré d'encre à leurs mains* (With Blood Dishonored by Ink on Their Hands). While he borrows the title from a poem by the French poet Paul Verlaine, Zitouni's story finds its playground among the crime stories in the *faits divers* ("in brief") sections of the newspapers. In 1998, Zitouni again found his inspiration in this same section and published *Amour, sévices et morgue* (Love, Cruelty, and Morgue). His third novel, *Attilah Fakir* (Fakir Attilah) (1987) was awarded the Prix de l'Evénement du Jeudi.

Ahmed Zitouni is among the most creative writers of Beur literature, loosely defined as literature written by Maghrebian immigrants in France. Though Zitouni was born in Algeria, his work is consistently turned towards the immigrant experience. The precariousness of this experience and this position not only manifests itself in the subject matter of his novels, but also in Zitouni's manner of writing, which challenges all traditional forms of narration and storytelling.

Further reading

Laronde, Michel (1993) *Autour du roman beur: immigration et identité* (On the Beur Novel: Immigration and Identity), Paris: L'Harmattan.

NASRIN QADER

Zongo, Norbert

b. 1949, Koudougou, Burkino Faso; d. 1998, Ouagadougou, Burkina Faso

journalist and novelist

Norbert Zongo was Burkina Faso's best-known journalist before his political assassination in 1998. As editor of the weekly journal *L'Indépendent*, Zongo was widely admired throughout West Africa as a fierce advocate of free speech, a tireless defender of the poor and disinherited, and a fearless critic of Blaise Compaoré's efforts to "mobutuize" Burkina Faso. Zongo also wrote two popular novels, both exposés of corrupt African leadership. His novel *The Parachute Drop* (1988) offers a psychologically complex portrait of a contemporary African president in the aftermath of a *coup d'état*. His later novel *Rougebêinga* (1990) explores the historical roots of governmental corruption during the colonial era. Following Zongo's murder at the hands of Compaoré's presidential guard, Burkina Faso has undergone a period of extreme civil unrest as citizens from nearly every sector have demanded justice – with little success – for Zongo and his three murdered travelling companions (including Yembi Ernest Zongo, Norbert's younger brother). Zongo's commitments to "truth-telling," whatever the personal costs, earned him the respect of millions of West Africans, including the reggae singer Alpha Blondy who wrote a popular song in his honor.

Further reading

Tinguri, Michel (2001) "Norbert Zongo: The Committed Writer," in Christopher Wise (ed.) *The Desert Shore: Literatures of the Sahel*, Boulder, Colorado: Lynne Rienner, pp. 151–6.

Zongo, Norbert (2001) "The Mobutuization of Burkina Faso," trans. Christopher Wise, in Christopher Wise (ed.) *The Desert Shore: Literatures of the Sahel*, Boulder, Colorado: Lynne Rienner, pp. 157–71.

——(forthcoming) *The Parachute Drop*, trans. Christopher Wise.

CHRISTOPHER WISE

Index